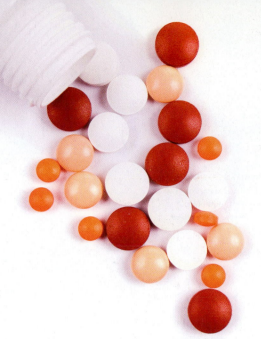

Pharmacology
An Introduction

6th
edition

Henry Hitner, Ph.D.

Professor Emeritus
Department of Neuroscience, Physiology,
Pharmacology
Philadelphia College of Osteopathic Medicine
Philadelphia, Pennsylvania

Adjunct Professor, Pharmacology
Physician Assistant Program
Drexel University
Philadelphia, Pennsylvania

Barbara Nagle, Ph.D.

President
Clinical Research Development and Education
III Associates
Bryn Mawr, Pennsylvania

McGraw Hill

Connect
Learn
Succeed™

PHARMACOLOGY: AN INTRODUCTION

Published by McGraw-Hill, a business unit of The McGraw-Hill Companies, Inc., 1221 Avenue of the Americas, New York, NY, 10020.

Some ancillaries, including electronic and print components, may not be available to customers outside the United States.

This book is printed on acid-free paper.

2 3 4 5 6 7 8 9 0 DOW/DOW 1 0 9 8 7 6 5 4 3 2 1

ISBN 978-0-07-352086-5
MHID 0-07-352086-1

Vice president/Editor in chief: *Elizabeth Haefele*
Vice president/Director of marketing: *John E. Biernat*
Publisher: *Kenneth S. Kasee Jr.*
Director of development: *Sarah Wood*
Managing Developmental Editor: *Christine Scheid*
Senior developmental editor: *Patricia Hesse*
Editorial coordinator: *Parissa DJangi*
Marketing manager: *Mary B. Haran*
Lead digital product manager: *Damian Moshak*
Director, Editing/Design/Production: *Jess Ann Kosic*
Project manager: *Marlena Pechan*
Buyer II: *Debra R. Sylvester*
Senior designer: *Marianna Kinigakis*
Senior photo research coordinator: *John C. Leland*
Photo researcher: *Danny Meldung*
Digital production coordinator: *Brent dela Cruz*
Outside development house: *Andrea Edwards, Triple SSS Press*
Cover design: *Alexa R. Viscius & Anna Kinigakis*
Interior design: *Jessica M. Lazar*
Typeface: *11/13 Perpetua Regular*
Compositor: *Laserwords Private Limited*
Printer: *R. R. Donnelley*
Cover credit: Image Copyright © 2010, Nucleus Medical Media, Inc. All Rights Reserved.
Credits: The credits section for this book begins on page 855 and is considered an extension of the copyright page.

Library of Congress Cataloging-in-Publication Data

Hitner, Henry.
    Pharmacology: an introduction/Henry Hitner, Barbara Nagle. —6th ed.
      p.; cm.
    Includes bibliographical references and index.
    ISBN-13: 978-0-07-352086-5 (alk. paper)
    ISBN-10: 0-07-352086-1 (alk. paper)
    1. Pharmacology. I. Nagle, Barbara T. II. Title.
    [DNLM: 1. Pharmacological Phenomena. 2. Drug Therapy. QV 4]
RM300.H57   2012
615'.1—dc22
                            2010043213

The Internet addresses listed in the text were accurate at the time of publication. The inclusion of a Web site does not indicate an endorsement by the authors or McGraw-Hill, and McGraw-Hill does not guarantee the accuracy of the information presented at these sites.

WARNING NOTICE: The clinical procedures, medicines, dosages, and other matters described in this publication are based upon research of current literature and consultation with knowledgeable persons in the field. The procedures and matters described in this text reflect currently accepted clinical practice. However, this information cannot and should not be relied upon as necessarily applicable to a given individual's case. Accordingly, each person must be separately diagnosed to discern the patient's unique circumstances. Likewise, the manufacturer's package insert for current drug product information should be consulted before administering any drug. Publisher disclaims all liability for any inaccuracies, omissions, misuse, or misunderstanding of the information contained in this publication. Publisher cautions that this publication is not intended as a substitute for the professional judgment of trained medical personnel.

Brief Contents

Table of Contents

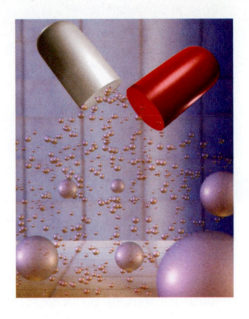

PART 2

Pharmacology of the Peripheral Nervous System   59

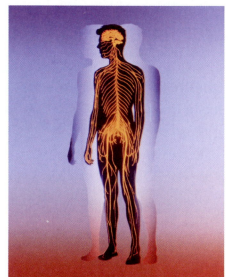

PART 3

Pharmacology of the Central Nervous System   147

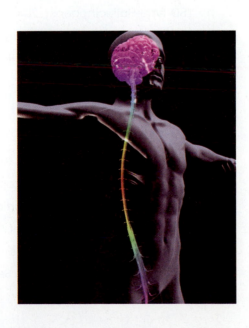

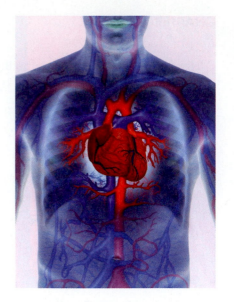

PART 5

Pharmacology of the Vascular and Renal Systems   375

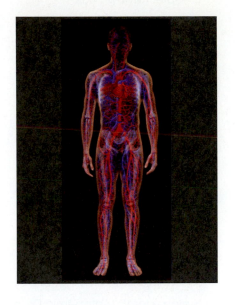

PART 6

Drugs That Affect the Respiratory System 499

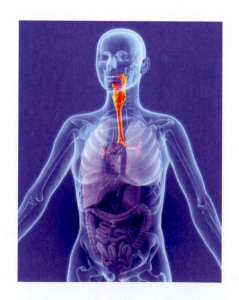

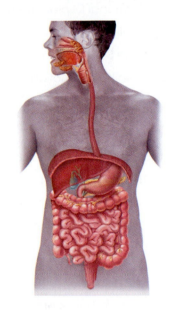
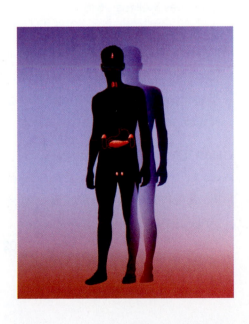

PART 9

Pharmacology of Infectious Diseases   711

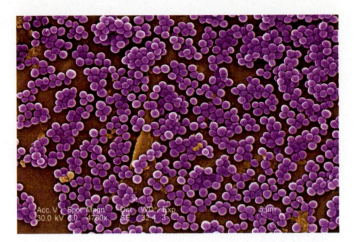

PART 10
Antineoplastics and Drugs Affecting the Immune System   801

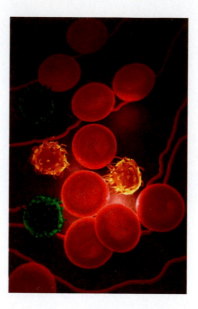

Henry Hitner earned a Bachelor of Science degree in biology from Moravian College in Bethlehem, Pennsylvania, and spent several years working in the pharmaceutical industry, first as a research assistant in toxicology for Wyeth Laboratories and then as a research pharmacologist for National Drug Company, both in Philadelphia. During this time he earned a Master of Education degree in biology from West Chester University. He attended graduate school at Hahnemann Medical College in Philadelphia, where he earned a Ph.D. in pharmacology. Dr. Hitner then went into academia, where he held numerous faculty positions, first as an instructor of biology and allied health sciences at Montgomery County Community College, followed by 30 years of teaching and research at the Philadelphia College of Osteopathic Medicine (PCOM). At PCOM he served as professor and vice chair of the neuroscience, physiology, and pharmacology department. Other positions included director of the animal facility and chair of the institutional animal care and utilization committee. Professional memberships included the Sigma Xi Scientific Research Society and the American Society for Pharmacology and Experimental Therapeutics. He was the recipient of the Lindback Foundation Award for Distinguished Teaching and a Mentor Award from the National Student Association. Henry and his wife Carlotta enjoy traveling, the beach, and time spent with family and their seven grandchildren.

Barbara Nagle earned a Master of Science and doctorate at Hahnemann Medical College and University in the department of pharmacology. Following postdoctoral training in ocular pharmacology at Will's Eye Hospital, Philadelphia, she taught pharmacology and physiology to medical students at the Philadelphia College of Osteopathic Medicine (PCOM) and to nursing students at Widener University. After several years in academia, she moved into the pharmaceutical industry as Director of Clinical Information and later Vice President of Clinical Research, Training and Quality Assurance. She has been part of the research effort to bring products through clinical development to FDA approval such as gastric acid suppressants (antihistamines), beta-blockers, anti-infectives, muscle relaxants, and oral contraceptives. The most recent affiliation was with Endo Pharmaceuticals in pain management research prior to her current activities as consultant and educator. She has served as International Director of Drug Development Training and Medical Education for BioPharm. Professional memberships include the Sigma Xi Scientific Research and American Medical Writers Association. Barbara is a freelance photographer, traveler, and silk painter.

Preface

The sixth edition of *Pharmacology: An Introduction* has been completely updated and redesigned, but the aim of this textbook remains what it has always been: to present a clear understanding of the basic concepts of pharmacology to the beginning student. Pharmacology is a complex subject that requires basic knowledge in many different scientific disciplines, particularly anatomy, physiology, and pathology. Health professions students often have limited exposure to these subjects and one of the objectives of our text is to provide the necessary background information and to refresh the student's memory of previously learned material through which the therapeutic action of drugs can be clearly understood.

The goal of this text is to explain the **mechanisms of action of drugs.** Understanding how drugs produce their effects allows the student to better understand the different pharmacologic actions and adverse effects that drugs produce. *Pharmacology: An Introduction* is designed for a variety of health professions programs requiring an understanding of pharmacology. The book presents a basic rationale for understanding current drug therapy. The drug information and chapter features are designed to be applicable and adaptable to many different educational programs. Personnel in the health and nursing professions spend much of their working time in direct contact with patients—observing, treating, and administering to the countless requirements and demands that constitute effective and responsible patient care. Therefore, it is important that students in health professions acquire a sound basic understanding of pharmacology as it relates to their particular needs.

New scientific discoveries and advances in the understanding of disease provide a continual introduction and approval of new drugs. At the same time, older drug therapies and drugs that cause serious adverse effects or other problems are eliminated. New advances in genetics and molecular biology have allowed the development of monoclonal antibodies and drugs with more selective mechanisms of action. These new agents can target specific receptors and physiologic functions that more accurately focus in on the pathology of a particular disease process. Thus pharmacology is an ever-changing, growing body of knowledge that continually demands greater amounts of time and education from those in the health professions.

Organization

The textbook is organized into **10 sections.** The introductory section, *General Concepts,* presents the basic concepts and pharmacologic principles that apply to all drugs. Subsequent sections present the drug classes that pertain to a specific body organ system (nervous, cardiovascular, respiratory, etc.) or therapeutic indication (antihypertensives, infectious diseases, antineoplastics, etc.). The discussion of each drug classification concentrates on the mechanisms of action, main therapeutic effects, clinical indications, adverse reactions, and drug interactions.

Features

Pharmacology: An Introduction hallmark features include:

- Readability: Short readable chapters that link theory to practice.
- Need-to-know Information: The content is focused on need-to-know information, so not to overload the learner.
- Patient Administration and Monitoring Boxes provide the student with critical patient information and patient instructions regarding the drugs discussed in the chapter.

Other key features:

- **Learning Outcomes**(LOs) The learning outcomes are correlated to the Revised Bloom's Taxonomy and are numbered at the beginning of each chapter. Learning Outcomes are linked to the main chapter topic headings and the end-of-chapter review questions. This allows the student to more quickly associate the LOs with the location of that information in the text and with the answers to the review questions.
- *Notes to the Health Care Professional* emphasizes important points and information for medical personnel involved in drug administration.
- **Drug tables** organize and summarize the main pharmacologic features of the different drug classes, so students can review the key drugs at-a-glance.
- **New design** with over 445 enhanced line art and photos that provide exciting and modern images showing the action of drugs and drug products.
- **Chapter reviews** at the end of each chapter progress from simple to complex and provide immediate reinforcement of terminology and pharmacological concepts important for acquiring knowledge. Review exercises include: Multiple choice, labeling, sequencing, matching, classification, and documentation questions. These have been added to test the student's ability to apply information presented in the chapter. The clinically relevant on-the-job questions allow students more opportunity to practice critical thinking skills.

What's New?

- New brilliant 4-color design that will draw the student's attention to key features of the chapter.
- 445 enhanced and new line art and photos bring content to life and engage the student to read further.
- Revision and numbering of all learning outcomes to reflect the Revised Bloom's Taxonomy guide the student on a clear path to mastering chapter content.
- Correlation of learning outcomes to all major chapter headings and end-of-chapter review questions will help the student and instructor focus on key chapter content.
- Addition of over 500 new end-of-chapter review questions and activities have been added to provide students with additional review opportunities that include multiple choice, multiple answer, labeling, sequencing, matching, classification, and documentation will challenge the student to test their knowledge of chapter concepts.
- *Drug Class at a Glance* image, appearing at the beginning of each drug chapter, has been redesigned to represent a PDA (Personal Digital Assistant), commonly used by health professionals to verify drug information and dosages, summarizes the over-the-counter and prescription status, schedule of controlled drug status, FDA (Federal Drug Administration) pregnancy categories, and the main clinical indications for the drugs contained within that chapter. It provides a quick reference to the chapter drug information.
- Over 140 revised tables organize and summarize the main pharmacologic features of the different drug classes. **The tables list the generic drug name first followed by the trade name(s) which are italicized and put within parentheses.**

Updated drug information has been found by using several key sources:

- US Federal Drug Administration (FDA) provides daily updates on drug approvals, drug safety issues, medication guides, and drug industry information.
- FDA database on drug approvals and discontinuations is used to check status of market availability of branded and generic drugs.
- HYPERLINK "http://www.centerwatch.com" www.centerwatch.com by Jobson Medical Information, LLC is a leading source of information about the clinical trials (pharmaceutical drugs and devices) industry.
- HYPERLINK "http://www.factsandcomparisons.com" www.factsandcomparisons.com by Wolters Kluwer Health is a searchable database by drug name or therapeutic category for all FDA approved drugs.
- National Library of Medicine and National Institutes of Health Medical provide information on conditions, diseases, wellness, over-the-counter (OTC) and prescription medication at different levels to facilitate understanding by professionals, students, patients, and consumers.
- WebMD Health Professional Network provides evidence-based content, updated regularly by more than 8,000 attributed physician or health care provider authors and editors, and the latest practice guidelines in 38 clinical areas. It is reviewed by physicians at Harvard University Medical School.
- Aetna InteliHealth provides credible information from trusted sources, including Harvard Medical School and Columbia University College of Dental Medicine.
- Professional Organizations are dedicated to providing accurate information to patients and health care providers on a specific disease or condition.

- **McGraw-Hill Connect Plus+** is a Web-based assignment and assessment platform that gives students the means to better connect with their coursework, with their instructors, and with the important concepts that they will need to know for success now and in the future. With Connect Plus+, instructors can deliver assignments, quizzes, and tests easily online. Students can practice important skills at their own pace and on their own schedule. With Connect Plus+, students also get 24/7 online access to an eBook—an online edition of the text—to aid them in successfully completing their work, wherever and whenever they choose.

Pharmacology: An Introduction, contains:

- 230 RMA and CMA style review questions correlated to CAAHEP and ABHES competencies
- 140 dosage calculation problems
- 230 NCLEX style review questions
- 460 chapter quizzes
- 23 animations with activities

- EZTest Test Bank containing over 900 multiple choice questions correlated to CAAHEP and ABHES competencies and tagged to chapter learning outcomes.

LearnSmart

- **McGraw-Hill LearnSmart: Pharmacology** is a diagnostic learning system that determines the level of student knowledge, then feeds the student appropriate content. Students learn faster and study more efficiently. As a student works within the system, LearnSmart develops a personal learning path adapted to what the student has learned and retained. LearnSmart is also able to recommend additional study resources to help the student master topics. In addition to being an innovative, outstanding study tool, LearnSmart has features for instructors. There is a Course Gauge where the instructor can see exactly what students have accomplished as well as a built-in assessment tool for graded assignments. Students and instructors will be able to access LearnSmart anywhere via a web browser. And for students on the go, it will also be available through any iPhone or iPod Touch.

Teaching and Learning Supplements

You will find many useful teaching and learning supplements with Pharmacology: An Introduction. These supplements create a complete package for today's learners whether they are learning through distance education or in the typical classroom setting.

- **Online Learning Center (OLC),** www.mhhe.com/hitner6e, includes the following instructor resources:
- **Instructor's Manual** featuring
  - lesson plans
  - lecture notes
  - discussion activities
  - answer keys
  - Internet connections that provide Web sites, directions, and suggestions that can be used to access additional information on diseases and the drugs used to treat them
  - additional readings from the literature that have been updated and provide clinically useful information regarding the use of drugs
- **McGraw-Hill's EZTest Test Generator,** a flexible electronic testing program with over 900 test questions correlated to CAAHEP and ABHES standards that allows instructors to create tests from book-specific items. It accommodates a wide range of question types, and instructors may add their own questions. Multiple versions of the test can be created and any test can be exported for use with course management systems such as WebCT, BlackBoard, or PageOut. EZTest Online gives instructors a chance to easily administer EZTest-created exams and quizzes online. EZTest Online is available for Windows and Macintosh environments.
- **PowerPoint® presentations** include notes and key images
- **Image bank** featuring selected textbook images that can be utilized in classroom presentations, handouts, or questions

Acknowledgments

A sincere thanks to our reviewers who helped shape the direction of this book.

Accuracy Reviewers

Dorene Adams RN, MSN
Solano Community College

Hooshiyar Ahmadi, MD, DC
Remington College

Laura G. Barrow, BS Pharm., MS Pharm., J.D.
Southwest Florida College

Suzanne H. Carpenter, Ph.D., RN., C.N.E.
Our Lady of The Lake College

Pamela deCalesta, O.D.
Linn-Benton Community College

Linda Haider, RN, MSN, Assistant Professor, Nursing
Minot State University

Lynda T. Harkins, Ph.D., RRT
McLennan Community College

Michael T. Mockler, R.Ph., MBA
Heald College

Marilyn M. Turner, RN, CMA (AAMA)
Ogeechee Technical College

Damandeep S. Walia, MD
The University of Kansas Medical Center

Supplement Contributors

Troy Andrew Cenac, MS, CPhT
Brookhaven College

Paula Lambert B.S., M.Ed., CPhT
North Idaho College

Pilar Perez-Jackson, CPhT
Sanford Brown Institute

Content Reviewers

Diana Alagna, RN
Branford Hall Career Institute

John Albrecht
Olympia College

Glenn D. Appelt, Ph.D., R.Ph.
Columbia Southern University

Jane Barker, MS, RHIA, CMA
Marshall University

Mary Barko, CMA, MAEd/AEDL
Ohio Institute of Health Careers

Kevin D. Barnard, MS, CDEMTP, NREMTP, EMSI
Cuyahoga Community College

Tim Bloom
Campbell University School of Pharmacy

Ilene Borze MS, RN
Gateway Community College

Deborah Briones, MSN
Medical Careers Academy

Jerry L. Bulen, D.O.
Keiser University, Hillsborough Community College

Dr. Beth Canfield-Simbro
Mount Union College

Troy Andrew Cenac, MS, CPhT
Brookhaven College

Kristin S. Coffman, RN, MSN
Connors State College School of Nursing

Leslie Z. Collier, RN, MSN/NE
Brunswick Community College

Roberta Connelley RN, BSN, MA
Louisiana Technical College

Laurie B. Cook, Ph.D.
The College at Brockport, State University of New York

Irene Coons MSN, RN, CNE
College of Southern Nevada

Carmen V. Cruz, MBA/HCM
Anamarc College

Brian Dickens MBA, RMA, CHI
Keiser Career College

James R. Dickerson
Remington College

Terry D. Edwards
Remington College

Richard Ray Espinosa, R.Ph., Pharm. D.
Austin Community College

Carla Lee Evans, RN
Yorktown Business Institute

Janet A. Evans, RN, MBA, MS, CCS, CPC-I
Burlington County College

Kimberly L. Fields, AAS RMA, CMA-AAMA, AHI
Davis College

Brenda Frerichs
Colorado Technical University

Paige S. Gebhardt, BA, RMT
Sussex County Community College

Sue K. Goebel, RN, MS, NP, SANE
Mesa State College

Stefanie Goodman MSN, RN, CMA (AAMA)
Ivy Tech Community College

Denise Gordon
Solano Community College

Margie Hair, RN, MSN
Minot State University

Lori Rae Hamilton RN, MSN
Otero Junior College

Catherine Harris RN, MSN
Cape Cod Community College

Julie Hart, RN, MSN
Northern Kentucky University

Robert M. Hawkes, MS, PA, NREMT-P
Southern Maine Community College

Terasa L. Hodges
Independence Community College

Charla K. Hollin, RN, BSN
Rich Mountain Community College

Jo Anne C. Jackson, EdD, RN
Middle Georgia College

Shelley Johnson, BBA, CPhT
Griffin Technical College

Patricia A. Kennedy, HM1USNR-RMA
Centura College

Joseph J. Krzanoski, Ph.D.
University of South Florida College of Medicine

Naomi Kupfer, CMA, CMBS
Heritage College

Richelle S. Laipply, Ph. D., MT(ASCP), CMA (AAMA)
The University of Akron

Paula Lambert BS, M.Ed., CPhT
North Idaho College

Anne P. LaVance, BS, CPhT
Delgado Community College

L.M. Liggan, M.Ed./PA/RMA/AHI-C
National College

Sarah M. Martin, Pharm.D., MBA
Rogers State University

Michelle C. McCranie
Ogeechee Technical College

D. P. Martinez, MD, MPH
School of Allied Health, Florida Career College

Michael Meir, MD
HIT TCI College

Laura Melendez, AA, BS, MA
Keiser Career College

Michael C. Melvin, R.Ph.
Griffin Technical College

Dr. William R Millington
Albany College of Pharmacy, Union University

Teresa Moore
Albany Technical College

Margaret L. Newton, MSN, RN
St. Catharine College

Frances Nicholson, CPhT
National College

June Petillo, MBA, RMC
Capital Community College

Pilar Perez-Jackson, CPhT
Sanford Brown Institute

Stephen J. Poling, BAEd, CPhT
Pima Medical Institute

Mary M. Prorok, RN, MSN
South Hills School of Business & Technology

Cathy L. Pederson, Ph.D.
Wittenberg University

Mary M. Prorok, RN, MSN
South Hills School of Business & Technology

Kellie Rigdon Lockwood, RN, MSN
East Central Technical College

Shelly Schoonover RN, MS
Connors State College School of Nursing

Nena Scott, MDEd, RHIA, CCS, CCS-P
Itawamba Community College

Patricia Sell, MSEd
National College

Cathy Shallenberger, MS, PA-C
Seton Hill University

Betsy W. Skaggs, RN, BSN
Ashland Community and Technical College

Lynn-Dee Spencer, CPhT
Hawaii Medical Institute

Laura Spinelli RN BSN MSNEd
Keiser Career College

Laura Southard Durham, BS, CMA (AAMA)
Forsyth Technical Community College

Ron Swisher, Ph.D.
Oregon Institute of Technology

Irene May G. Tabay, BS. CPhT
Heald College

Sandi Tschritter, BA, CPhT
Spokane Community College

Jana W. Tucker, CMA/LRPT
Salt Lake Community College

Denise Way Lagueux
Southeast Community College

Georgann Weissman, DNP
Keiser University

Barbareta A. Welch McGill, RN, MSN, DRS
North Carolina Central University

Carolyn Sue Wright Coleman, LPN, AS
National College

What Every Student Needs to Know

Many tools to help you learn have been integrated into your text.

Chapter Features

Learning Outcomes

present the key points you should focus on when reading the chapter. Consider this your road map to the knowledge and skills you will acquire upon studying this content.

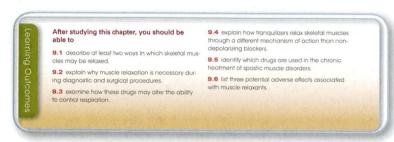

Learning Outcomes

After studying this chapter, you should be able to

9.1 describe at least two ways in which skeletal muscles may be relaxed.

9.2 explain why muscle relaxation is necessary during diagnostic and surgical procedures.

9.3 examine how these drugs may alter the ability to control respiration.

9.4 explain how tranquilizers relax skeletal muscles through a different mechanism of action than nondepolarizing blockers.

9.5 identify which drugs are used in the chronic treatment of spastic muscle disorders.

9.6 list three potential adverse effects associated with muscle relaxants.

Patient Administration and Monitoring

When skeletal muscle relaxants are used in surgical settings, the potential for adverse effects may be minimized through close observation of the patient during recovery. Following diagnostic procedures or intubations under outpatient conditions, or chronic therapy for spastic muscle conditions, there is a greater likelihood that patients may experience adverse effects that could put them at risk for injury. For this reason patients should receive clear instructions about which adverse effects are worthy of physician notification. The centrally acting skeletal muscle relaxants may cause persistent drowsiness that interferes with mental alertness and concentration. For chronic spastic conditions, this effect is usually tolerable so the treatment schedule does not need to be interrupted. It should be noted that dose adjustment does not always mitigate the drowsy effect. Therefore, with short-term therapy of muscle strain, the patient may need to incorporate other solutions to circumvent the difficulties associated with drowsiness.

Patient Instructions

The patient should be asked whether he or she performs tasks that require special equipment or machinery (sewing machines, motor vehicles) or coordination, focus, or physical dexterity (drill press, motor tools, assembly tools).

Skin rash, nasal congestion, persistent fever, or yellowish discoloration of the skin or eyes should be reported to the physician or clinic immediately for further evaluation.

Dantrolene causes photosensitivity so prolonged exposure to sunlight should be avoided.

Baclofen may cause nausea, headache, insomnia, and frequent or painful urination that should be reported to the physician for further evaluation.

Tizanidine is available in capsules and tablets, but they are not interchangeable during the course of treatment. Patients should be reminded to continue the same formulation to avoid fluctuations in absorption. Capsules can be opened and sprinkled on applesauce to improve patient compliance when necessary; however, food does impact the bioavailability of tizanidine.

Use in Pregnancy

Drugs in this class have been designated Food and Drug Administration (FDA) Pregnancy Category C or D. Safety for use during pregnancy has not been established through adequate and well-controlled studies in humans. All of these drugs, except diazepam, are category C because animal reproduction studies have shown an adverse effect on the fetus. Diazepam is category D because there is positive

Patient Administration and Monitoring

summarizes important patient information and patient instructions about the drugs discussed in that chapter. It will expand your knowledge of medications and conditions.

Notes to the Health Care Professional

emphasizes important points and information for medical personnel involved in drug administration.

Note to the Health Care Professional

Quitting the smoking habit is difficult for most individuals. Frequently, smokers will use nicotine replacement therapy (NRT) products but continue to smoke or chew tobacco. This can lead to nicotine toxicity. Warn smokers of the danger of using NRT products while continuing to indulge in tobacco use.

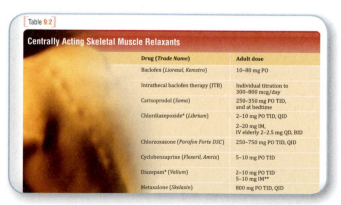

Table 9:2

Centrally Acting Skeletal Muscle Relaxants

Drug (Trade Name)	Adult dose
Baclofen (Lioresal, Kemstro)	10–80 mg PO
Intrathecal baclofen therapy (ITB)	Individual titration to 300–800 mcg/day
Carisoprodol (Soma)	250–350 mg PO TID, and at bedtime
Chlordiazepoxide* (Librium)	2–10 mg PO TID, QID
	2–20 mg IM, IV elderly 2–2.5 mg QD, BID
Chlorzoxazone (Parafon Forte DSC)	250–750 mg PO TID, QID
Cyclobenzaprine (Flexeril, Amrix)	5–10 mg PO TID
Diazepam* (Valium)	2–10 mg PO TID 5–10 mg IM**
Metaxalone (Skelaxin)	800 mg PO TID, QID

Drug Tables

organize and summarize the main pharmacologic features of the different drug classes. **The tables list the generic drug name first followed by the trade name(s) which are italicized and put within parentheses.**

Line Art and Photos

provide a dynamic visual picture of the action of drugs and drug products to help you understand pharmacological processes that are discussed in the text.

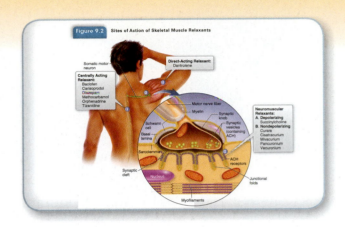

Figure 9.2 Sites of Action of Skeletal Muscle Relaxants

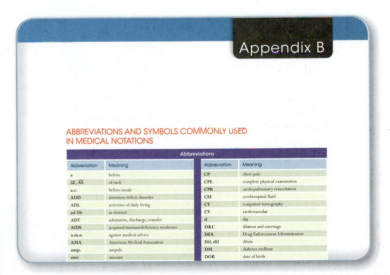

Chapter Reviews

provide immediate reinforcement of terminology and pharmacological concepts important for acquiring knowledge. Multiple-choice, matching, labeling, sequencing, and documentation questions have been added that challenge you to apply information presented in the chapter. The clinically relevant on-the-job questions allow you more opportunity to practice critical-thinking skills.

Appendices

provide additional information pertinent to the study of pharmacology. You will find lists of abbreviations and symbols used in medical notations, weights and measures, and mathematical functions and terms.

General Concepts

CHAPTER 1

Pharmacology: An Introduction   4

CHAPTER 2

Pharmacokinetics and Factors of Individual Variation   17

CHAPTER 3

Geriatric Pharmacology   36

CHAPTER 4

Math Review and Dosage Calculations   45

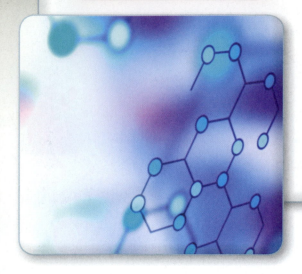

Pharmacology: An Introduction

KEY TERMS

adverse effect: general term for undesirable and potentially harmful drug effect.

agonist: drug that binds to a receptor and activates a physiologic response or drug action.

antagonist: drug that binds to a receptor and interferes with other drugs or substances from producing a drug effect.

chemical name: name that defines the chemical composition of a drug.

contraindications: situations or conditions when a certain drug should not be administered.

controlled substance: drug that has the potential for abuse and thus is regulated by law.

dose: a measurement of the amount of drug that is administered.

drug: chemical substance that produces a change in body function.

drug indications: intended or indicated uses for any drug.

ED50: effective dose 50, or dose that will produce an effect that is half of the maximal response.

generic name: nonproprietary name of a drug.

LD50: lethal dose 50, or dose that will kill 50 percent of the laboratory animals tested.

mechanism of action: explanation of how a drug produces its effects.

nonprescription, over-the-counter (OTC) drug: drug that can be purchased without the services of a physician.

pharmacology: study of drugs.

potency: measure of the strength, or concentration, of a drug required to produce a specific effect.

prescription drug: drug for which dispensing requires a written or phone order that can only be issued by or under the direction of a licensed physician.

receptor: specific cellular structure that a drug binds to and that produces a physiologic effect.

side effect: drug effect other than the therapeutic effect that is usually undesirable but not harmful.

site of action: location within the body where a drug exerts its therapeutic effect, often a specific drug receptor.

therapeutic effect: desired drug effect to alleviate some condition or symptom of disease.

therapeutic index (TI): ratio of the LD50 to the ED50 in animal studies.

toxic effect: undesirable drug effect that implies drug poisoning; can be very harmful or life-threatening.

trade name: patented proprietary name of a drug sold by a specific drug manufacturer; also referred to as the brand name.

After studying this chapter, you should be able to

1.1 define pharmacology and its major subdivisions.

1.2 describe what a drug is and explain the differences between a therapeutic effect, side effect, and toxic effect.

1.3 explain the terms *site of action, mechanism of action, receptor site, agonist,* and *antagonist.*

1.4 explain the relationship between drug dosage and drug response, and the relationship between drug response and time.

1.5 recall the guidelines for drug safety and drug approval by the FDA.

1.6 identify drug nomenclature and the different terminology used in naming drugs.

1.7 recognize the drug references and understand the information they provide.

Introduction

Pharmacology is the study of drugs. A drug can be any substance that, when administered to living organisms, produces a change in function. Thus, substances such as water, metals (iron), or insecticides can be classified as drugs. However, the term *drug* commonly means any medication that is used for diagnosing, curing, or treating disease.

Pharmacology is a subject that requires some background knowledge of anatomy, physiology, pathology, and related medical sciences. In that sense pharmacology is an integrative course of study that applies the relevant information of all medical sciences to the treatment of disease. Throughout this textbook the essential background information of anatomy, physiology, and pathology required for an understanding of drug action will be reviewed. Pharmacology is a large discipline that can be subdivided into different areas of study (Table 1:1). The major focus of *Pharmacology: An Introduction* is to provide an understanding of the mechanisms of action, main therapeutic effects, clinical uses, and adverse reactions of drugs. Completion of an introductory pharmacology course is only the beginning step in understanding this complex subject.

[Table **1:1**]

Major Areas of Pharmacology

Area	Description
Pharmacodynamics	Study of the action of drugs on living tissue
Pharmacokinetics	Study of the processes of drug absorption, distribution, metabolism, and excretion
Pharmacotherapeutics	Study of the use of drugs in treating disease
Pharmacy	Science of preparing and dispensing medicines
Posology	Study of the amount of drug that is required to produce therapeutic effects
Toxicology	Study of the harmful effects of drugs on living tissue

LO 1.1

DRUG SOURCES

A logical question to ask about pharmacology is "Where do drugs come from?" There are several sources of drugs. In the early days of medicine, most drugs were obtained from plant or animal sources. Plants and living organisms contain active substances that can be isolated, purified, and formulated into effective drug preparations. Examples of drugs derived from plants that are still widely used today include the analgesics morphine and codeine, which were obtained from the poppy plant (*Papver somniferum*); the heart drug digitalis, which was obtained from the purple foxglove (*Digitalis purpurea*); and the antimalarial drug quinine, which was obtained from the bark of the cinchona tree. Paclitaxel, an anticancer drug, is obtained from the yew tree. The search for new plant drugs is still very active. It is also interesting that many of the drugs of abuse such as cocaine, marijuana, mescaline, heroin, and others are derived from plants. Most of these drugs were used for hundreds of years by many different cultures in their religious and ritual ceremonies. Drugs obtained from living organisms include hormones such as insulin (from the pig) and growth hormone from pituitary glands. In addition, antibiotics such as cephalosporins and aminoglycosides have been derived from bacteria. The early history of pharmacology is filled with many interesting stories of discovery and medical experimentation. Textbooks devoted to the history of medicine and pharmacology are the best sources for additional information. Despite the many examples of drugs obtained from plants and living organisms, the main source of new drugs today is from chemical synthesis. Also, many of the drugs that once were obtained from plants and animals are now chemically synthesized in pharmaceutical laboratories. Advances in molecular biology and gene therapy have generated new types of drugs such as monoclonal antibodies.

LO 1.2

TERMINOLOGY RELATED TO DRUG EFFECTS

Another basic question that should be answered is "What actually is a **drug?**" Every pure drug is a chemical compound with a specific chemical structure. Because of its structure, a drug has certain properties that are usually divided into chemical properties and biological properties. The properties of any drug determine what effects will be produced when the drug is administered. An important fact to remember is that, structurally, the human body is composed mostly of cells, even though these cells are highly organized into tissues, organs, and systems. Consequently, drugs produce effects by influencing the function of cells.

Pharmacologists know that all drugs produce more than one effect. Every drug produces its intended effect, or **therapeutic effect,** along with other effects. The therapeutic use(s) of any drug is referred to as the **drug indication,** meaning indications for use. The term **contraindication** refers to the situation or circumstance when a particular drug should *not* be used. Some drug effects, other than therapeutic effects, are described as undesirable. Undesired drug effects are categorized as side effects, adverse effects, and toxic effects.

Side Effects

Many **side effects** are more of a nuisance than they are harmful. The dry mouth and sedation caused by some antihistamine drugs is an example. In many cases drug side effects must be tolerated in order to benefit from the therapeutic actions of the drug.

Adverse Effects

Adverse effects are also undesired effects, but these are effects that may be harmful (persistent diarrhea, vomiting, or central nervous system [CNS] disturbances such as confusion) or that with prolonged treatment may cause conditions that affect the function of vital organs such as the liver or kidney. Reduction of dosage or switching to an alternative drug often will avoid or minimize these harmful consequences.

Toxic Effects

Toxic effects, or toxicity, implies drug poisoning, the consequences of which can be extremely harmful and may be life-threatening. In these situations, the drug must be stopped and supportive treatment and the administration of antidotes may be required.

The term most frequently used to describe the undesirable effects of drugs is *adverse effects*. However, you should be familiar with the other terms because they are used and, if used correctly, describe the nature and potential severity of undesired drug effects.

Most drugs will cause all three types of undesired effects, depending on the dose administered. At low doses, side effects are common and often expected. At higher doses, additional adverse effects may appear. At very high doses, toxic effects may occur that can be fatal. Consequently, the undesired effects produced by most drugs are often a function of dosage, which is why a well-known physician from the Middle Ages, Paracelsus (1493–1541), made the famous statement, "only the dose separates a drug from a poison"—and we could add, "a therapeutic effect from a toxic effect." Allied health personnel spend the majority of their time in patient contact. Therefore, they have an important responsibility to observe the undesired effects of drugs, to recognize the side effects that are often expected, and to identify and report the adverse and toxic effects that are potentially harmful and that often require medical attention.

LO 1.3

BASIC CONCEPTS IN PHARMACOLOGY

As in any subject, fundamental principles and concepts form the basis upon which additional information can be added. Pharmacology is no exception, and the following basic concepts apply to any drug.

Site of Action

The **site of action** of a drug is the location within the body where the drug exerts its therapeutic effect. The site of action of some drugs is not known; however, the site of action for most drugs has been determined. For example, the site of action of aspirin to reduce fever is in an area of the brain known as the hypothalamus. Within the hypothalamus the temperature-regulating center controls and maintains body temperature. Aspirin alters the activity of the hypothalamus so that body temperature is reduced. Throughout this book, when the site of drug action is known or suspected, it will be presented.

Mechanism of Action

Mechanism of action explains how a drug produces its effects. For example, local anesthetic agents produce a loss of pain sensation by interrupting nerve conduction in sensory nerves. In order for nerve impulses to be conducted, sodium ions must pass through the nerve membrane. Local anesthetic agents attach to the nerve membrane and prevent the passage of sodium ions. Consequently, sensory nerve impulses for pain are not conducted to the pain centers in the brain. Knowledge of the mechanism of action of drugs is essential to understanding why drugs produce the effects that they do.

Receptor Site

Drug action is usually thought to begin after a drug has attached itself to some chemical structure located on the outer cell membrane or within the cell itself. For a few drugs and for some normal body substances, there seems to be a specific location on certain cells. This area is referred to as the **receptor** site. The attachment, or binding, of a drug to its receptors begins a series of cell changes referred to as the drug action.

When a specific receptor site for a drug is known, that receptor site becomes the site of action for that particular drug. Morphine, an analgesic drug, is an example of a drug that binds to a specific receptor. The receptors for morphine are located in the brain and are known as the morphine, or opioid, receptors. When morphine binds to its receptors, it produces cell changes that reduce the perception of pain. There are many different pharmacological receptors, and they will be described in the appropriate chapters.

Agonists and Antagonists

Drugs that bind to specific receptors and produce a drug action are called **agonists.** Morphine is an example of an agonist. Drugs that bind to specific receptors and inhibit agonist drug action or cellular functions are called **antagonists.**

Antagonists are also known as blocking drugs. Usually, antagonists bind to the receptors and prevent other drugs or body substances from producing an effect. Naloxone, a morphine antagonist, is administered to prevent, or antagonize, the effects of morphine in cases of morphine overdose. There are many examples in pharmacology where drug antagonists are used to prevent other substances from exerting an effect.

When both agonist and antagonist drugs bind to the same receptor and are administered together, they compete with each other for the same receptor site. This effect is known as *competitive antagonism*. The amount of drug action produced depends on which drug (agonist or antagonist) occupies the greatest number of receptors. The actions of a drug agonist and antagonist are illustrated in Figure 1.1. There is also uncompetitive antagonism, which occurs when the antagonist drug interferes with the agonist drug action but not by binding to the same receptor.

Figure 1.1

Competitive Antagonism at Work

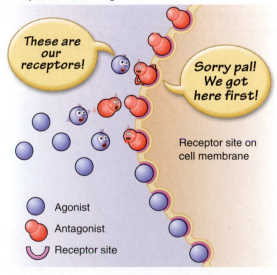

LO 1.4

DOSE-RESPONSE CURVE

A fundamental principle of pharmacology is that the response to any drug depends on the amount of drug given. This principle is known as the dose-response relationship. A **dose** is the exact amount of a drug that is administered in order to produce a specific effect. The effect is referred to as the response. When the relationship between the dose and the response is plotted as a graph, it is referred to as a dose-response curve.

Figure 1.2 illustrates the appearance of a typical dose-response curve for two similar drugs. The main feature of the dose-response relationship is that a drug response is proportional to the dose. As the dose increases, so does the magnitude of the response. Eventually, a *maximal response* is usually attained (100 percent response); further increases in dose do not produce any greater effect. This point on the graph is known as the ceiling effect. The *ceiling effect* reflects the limit of some drug classes to produce a particular effect. Above a certain dosage no further increase in effect is observed. Doses above those needed to produce the ceiling effect usually cause other undesired, often toxic, drug effects. Drugs within a drug class that are more potent than other drugs in the same class will produce the ceiling effect at a lower dosage, but they will not "raise the ceiling." Drugs that continue to cause an increased effect as long as the dose is increased do not have a ceiling effect.

A graded dose-response curve can be used to evaluate drug response among different drugs. In a graded dose-response curve, the increases in drug dosage are plotted against the increases in drug response. For example, dose-response curves are used to compare the potency of similar drugs. **Potency** is a measure of the strength, or concentration, of a drug required to produce a specific effect. The dose that will produce an effect that is half of the maximal response is referred to as the effective dose 50, or **ED50.**

The ED50 can be used to compare the potency of drugs that produce the same response. In Figure 1.2, the ED50 of drug A is 10 mg while the ED50 of drug B is 20 mg. Therefore, drug A is twice as potent as drug B. Twice the concentration of drug B is needed to produce the same response as drug A.

Quantal (referred to as all-or-none) dose-response curves are used to show the percentage of a human or animal population that responds to a specific drug dosage. This information is important for determining the dosages that are recommended for various treatments. Quantal dose-response curves require an understanding of mathematical statistics that is beyond the scope of this textbook.

Time-Plasma Drug Concentration Curve

The relationship of time and the plasma drug concentration is known as the time-plasma drug concentration curve. *Duration of action* is the length of time that a drug continues to produce its effect. Most individual drugs produce effects over a relatively constant period of time. Figure 1.3 illustrates the appearance of a typical time-plasma drug concentration curve. In this example, the

Figure 1.2

A Typical Dose-Response Curve

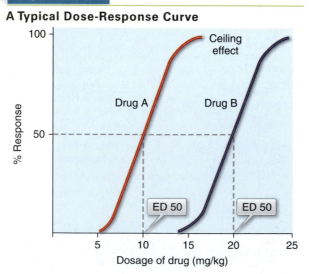

Figure 1.3

A Typical Time-Plasma Drug Concentration Curve

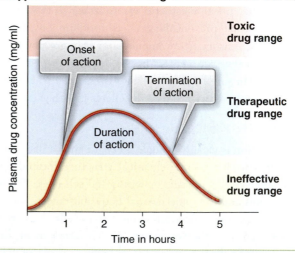

This curve shows the change in plasma drug concentration over time in relation to onset, duration, and termination of drug action. Plasma drug concentrations that exceed the therapeutic range produce drug toxicity.

plasma drug concentration is correlated with the onset, duration, and termination of drug action. After drug administration, a certain amount of time is required before a drug will produce an observable effect. The time from drug administration to the first observable effect is known as the *onset of action*. The drug response will continue as long as there is an effective concentration of the drug at the site of action. As the drug is metabolized and excreted, the response gradually decreases because the drug level is decreasing. When the plasma drug concentration falls below the therapeutic range, there is *termination of drug action*. Time-plasma drug concentration curves are used for predicting the frequency with which a drug must be administered in order to maintain an effective drug response.

LO 1.5

DRUG SAFETY

The federal Food and Drug Administration (FDA) has established guidelines that govern the approval and use of all drugs. Every drug must fulfill two major requirements before it can be approved for use in humans: efficacy (proof of effectiveness) and safety. The drug must be effective in the disease state for which it has been approved. Approved drugs must satisfy specific safety criteria as determined by extensive animal testing and controlled human testing. As discussed previously, the dose separates therapeutic effects from toxic effects.

Note to the Health Care Professional

All drugs will act as poisons if taken in excess. Only the dose separates a therapeutic effect from a toxic effect. The goal of drug therapy is to select a dose that is in the therapeutic range and avoid doses that produce toxicity. This task is not easy because many factors influence the amount of drug that reaches its site of action. These factors—such as route of administration, absorption, and drug metabolism—will be discussed in Chapter 2, Pharmacokinetics and Factors of Individual Variation.

Drug safety receives much attention today. It is a constant source of concern and debate because the public is more aware of the dangers of drugs. In order to receive approval for use in humans, a drug must undergo several years of both animal and human testing and evaluation.

Several animal species must be used in order to evaluate the effectiveness and toxicity of a drug. One of the first tests that is performed is the lethal dose 50, or **LD50.** The LD50 is the dose that will kill 50 percent of the animals tested. The results of the LD50 and other tests are used to predict the safety of a drug.

Therapeutic Index

The **therapeutic index (TI)** is a ratio of the LD50 to the ED50 of a drug. It gives an estimate of the relative safety of a drug. The equation is expressed as:

$$TI = LD50/ED50 = 1000 \text{ mg}/100 \text{ mg} = 10$$

In this example, the therapeutic index is 10. This index indicates that ten times as much drug is needed to produce a lethal effect in 50 percent of the animals as is needed to produce the therapeutic effect in 50 percent of the animals. The therapeutic index is used only in animal studies to establish dosage levels for other testing procedures. The goal of drug therapy is to achieve therapeutic effects in all individuals without producing any harmful effects.

Adverse Drug Effects

All drugs produce adverse and toxic effects if taken in excess. Most adverse effects are dose dependent, which means the higher the dose, the greater the chances for producing an adverse effect. Certain tissues are more frequently affected than others. Oral drugs often cause nausea, vomiting, and diarrhea because of gastrointestinal (GI) irritation. The liver, kidneys, brain, and cardiovascular system may be adversely affected because these organs are exposed to the highest concentrations of the drug. Drugs that produce birth defects, such as thalidomide, are known as *teratogens*. Drugs that promote the growth of cancerous tumors are called *carcinogens*.

A few adverse effects are not dose dependent. These effects, such as drug idiosyncrasy and drug allergy, are determined by individual variation. Although all human beings are basically similar, there may be minor variations in certain enzymes or other body proteins. These variations may produce changes in drug metabolism that lead to unusual responses to a particular drug. An individual reaction to a drug with an unusual or unexpected response is known as an *idiosyncrasy*.

Drug allergy occurs when an individual becomes sensitized to a particular drug (drug acts as an antigen) and produces antibodies against the drug. Subsequent administration of the drug leads to an antigen-antibody reaction. Antigen-antibody reactions involving drugs usually cause the release of histamine and other inflammatory mediators from cells known as mast cells. These inflammatory mediators produce the characteristic symptoms of allergy, which include rashes, hives, itching, nasal secretion, hypotension, and bronchoconstriction.

In serious allergic reactions, the symptoms may be so severe that death may occur. The term *anaphylaxis* is used to describe these serious allergic reactions, which include severe hypotension, respiratory difficulties, and cardiovascular collapse.

LO 1.6
DRUG NOMENCLATURE

All drugs are chemicals, and many have long **chemical-names.** As a result, all drugs are given a shorter name, known as the nonproprietary name, which is usually a contraction of the chemical name. The nonproprietary name is more commonly referred to as the **generic name.**

When the drug is marketed by a pharmaceutical company, it is given a third name, known as the proprietary name, or **trade name** or brand name. Since several different pharmaceutical companies may market the same generic drug, there may be several different trade names for any one drug. Figure 1.4 gives three names of a commonly prescribed drug.

Drugs are also divided into prescription and non-prescription drugs. **Prescription drugs** require a written or phone order (the prescription), which can only be issued by or under the direction of a licensed physician, dentist, or veterinarian. The prescription is a legal document that contains instructions for the pharmacist, who is licensed to dispense prescription medications. **Nonprescription drugs,** usually referred to as **"over-the-counter" (OTC) drugs** (such as aspirin, antacids, cold remedies), can be purchased anywhere and do not require the services of a physician or pharmacist.

Figure 1.4

Drug Nomenclature

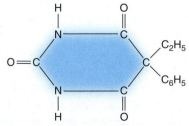

Chemical name: 5,5,-Phenylethylbarbituric acid
Nonproprietary name: Phenobarbital (generic name)
Proprietary name: *Luminal* (trade or brand name)

LO 1.7
DRUG REFERENCES

Medical libraries, hospital libraries, and educational institutions that provide medical education generally stock one or more drug reference books that provide drug information.

The United States Pharmacopeia/National Formulary (USP/NF) is the official drug list recognized by the U.S. government. It provides information concerning the physical and chemical properties of drugs. The *USP/NF* is revised every five years and is used primarily by drug manufacturers to ensure drug production according to official government standards.

The Physicians' Desk Reference (PDR®) is the reference most widely used by physicians, pharmacists, and nurses for information relating to the use of drugs in the practice of medicine. It is updated yearly and provides information on indications for use, dosage and administration, contraindications, and adverse reactions. You should learn how to look up drugs in the *PDR®*.

The *PDR®* is divided into sections, which are color-coded. However, the section colors change from year to year so it is best to have a general understanding of the major sections. The main sections and their descriptions are listed below.

Section 1: Manufacturers Index—Lists the pharmaceutical manufacturers, addresses, phone numbers, and emergency contacts as listed in the *PDR®*.

Section 2: Brand and Generic Name Index—Gives the page number of each product by trade (brand) name and generic name.

Section 3: Product Category Index—Lists all fully described products by prescribing category. Also includes information concerning controlled substances and FDA pregnancy categories.

Section 4: Product Identification Guide—Presents full-color, actual-size photos of tablets, capsules, and dosage forms. Arranged alphabetically by company.

Section 5: Product Information—Main section of book; describes pharmacology and clinical information concerning the use of these drugs. Arranged alphabetically by drug manufacturer.

Drug Facts and Comparisons (F&C) is a loose-leaf index and drug information service subscribed to by most medical libraries. Drug information and new drug additions are updated monthly. This index provides the most current drug information on a regular basis.

The United States Pharmacopeial Convention, Inc., publishes a series of volumes under the general title of

United States Pharmacopeia Dispensing Information (USP DI) that are updated yearly. Volume I—*Drug Information for the Health Care Professional*—provides in-depth information about prescription and over-the-counter medications, and nutritional supplements. Volume II—*Advice for the Patient*—provides drug information for the patient.

Drug Information—American Hospital Formulary Service provides detailed drug information. Drugs are organized according to therapeutic use and classification. It is updated yearly.

Drug Legislation Acts

During the last century there was an increase in the discovery and introduction of new drugs. Correspondingly there was an increase in the reports of adverse drug effects and toxicities. Consequently, the government began to enact legislation aimed at ensuring the safety and effectiveness of drugs. The following is a brief summary of the major legislative acts.

1906: Federal Pure Food and Drug Act. This was the first real drug law that required drugs to have minimal standards of drug strength and purity. This law did not address the issue of drug efficacy or effectiveness. In 1912 the law was amended to include regulations for labeling and false claims of effectiveness.

1938: Federal Food Drug and Cosmetic Act. This act set standards for drug safety and was enacted after 40 patients died from taking an antibiotic that contained diethylene glycol as a solvent. Drug manufacturers now had to show proof of drug safety.

1962: Amendment to 1938 Federal Food Drug and Cosmetic Act. In 1960 thalidomide, a hypnotic drug, was discovered to produce phocomelia, a rare birth defect that caused abnormal limb development.

This act required pharmacological and toxicological research testing in several animal species before a drug could be tested in humans. The act also established the clinical requirements for human drug testing and, in addition, established the standards for both drug safety and effectiveness. This act is enforced by the Food and Drug Administration (FDA).

1970: Federal Comprehensive Drug Abuse Prevention and Control Act. This act, commonly referred to as the Controlled Substance Act, was amended in 1990. This act is designed to regulate the dispensing of drugs, called **controlled substances,** that have the potential for abuse. The controlled drugs are assigned to one of five schedules, depending on their medical usefulness and potential for abuse. This act is enforced by the Drug Enforcement Administration (DEA). Table 1:2 describes the schedules and provides examples of some controlled substances.

Chapter Openers

In the chapters that deal with therapeutic drugs, a diagram will appear on the chapter opener page. The purpose of the diagram is to provide important information in a quick visual reference about the drugs included in that chapter. The information displayed informs the reader whether the drugs are available over-the-counter (OTC), by prescription, or a combination of both. In addition, it identifies which FDA Pregnancy Category (see Chapter 2) has been designated for the use of these drugs during pregnancy. Finally, the general clinical indications for the chapter drugs are presented. In the event individual drugs differ from the main representative drugs, the exceptions will be identified on the diagram.

Drug Schedules Defined in the Federal Comprehensive Drug Abuse Prevention and Control Act

Schedule	Definition	Controlled drugs
Schedule I	Drugs with high abuse potential and no accepted medical use	Heroin, hallucinogens, marijuana; these drugs are not to be prescribed
Schedule II	Drugs with high abuse potential and accepted medical use	Narcotics (morphine and pure codeine), cocaine, amphetamines, short-acting barbiturates (*Amobarbital, Secobarbital*), nabilone; no refills without a new written prescription from the physician
Schedule III	Drugs with moderate abuse potential and accepted medical use	Moderate- and intermediate-acting barbiturates, dronabinol, anabolic steroids, preparations containing codeine plus another drug; prescription required, may be refilled five times in 6 months when authorized by the physician
Schedule IV	Drugs with low abuse potential and accepted medical use	Phenobarbital, chloral hydrate, zolpidem (*Ambien*), antianxiety drugs (*Librium, Valium*); prescription required, may be refilled five times in 6 months when authorized by the physician
Schedule V	Drugs with limited abuse potential and accepted medical use	Narcotic drugs used in limited quantities for antitussive (codeine) and antidiarrheal purposes (diphenoxylate, *Lomotil*); drugs can be sold only by a registered pharmacist; buyer must be 18 years old and show identification. Some states require a prescription for schedule V drugs

Chapter Review

Understanding Terminology

Match the definition in the left column with the appropriate term in the right column. **(LO 1.1)**

___ 1. The study of the amount of drug that is required to produce therapeutic effects.

___ 2. The study of the harmful effects of drugs on living tissue.

___ 3. The study of the action of drugs on living tissue.

___ 4. The study of drugs.

___ 5. The science of preparing and dispensing medicines.

___ 6. The study of the processes of drug absorption, distribution, metabolism, and excretion.

___ 7. The study of the use of drugs in treating disease.

a. pharmacodynamics
b. pharmacokinetics
c. pharmacology
d. pharmacotherapeutics
e. posology
f. pharmacy
g. toxicology

Answer the following questions.

8. Define a drug. **(LO 1.2)**

9. Differentiate between therapeutic effect, side effect, and toxic effect. **(LO 1.2)**

10. What is the difference between site of action and mechanism of action? **(LO 1.3)**

11. What is the relationship between ED50, LD50, and therapeutic index? **(LO 1.5)**

12. Explain the difference between a prescription drug, OTC drug, and a controlled substance. **(LO 1.6)**

13. Explain the difference between idiosyncrasy and drug allergy. **(LO 1.5)**

14. Write a short paragraph describing the terms *receptor site, binding, drug action, agonist, antagonist,* and *competitive antagonism.* **(LO 1.3)**

Acquiring Knowledge

Answer the following questions.

1. Examine a copy of the *Physicians' Desk Reference (PDR®)*. Briefly describe the information found in Sections 1 through 5. **(LO 1.7)**

2. Look up the popular decongestant pseudoephedrine in Section 2 of the *PDR®*. What is your conclusion based on the available trade names? **(LO 1.7)**

3. What is a dose-response curve and what information is given by a dose-response curve? **(LO 1.4)**

4. What is the importance of a time-plasma drug concentration curve? How often would you estimate that a drug should be administered per day if the drug is eliminated in 4 hours? In 24 hours? **(LO 1.4)**

5. It is interesting that a drug can produce a therapeutic effect and an undesired side effect in one situation, and that the same side effect may be considered a therapeutic effect in another situation. Explain this phenomenon using the drug promethazine (*Phenergan*) as an example. **(LO 1.2)**

6. Obtain a copy of *Drug Facts and Comparisons* (F&C) from your school or library. It is divided into many sections. There are five sections that are frequently used. Examine each section and briefly explain how it might be useful in your field. **(LO 1.7)**
   a. Table of Contents
   b. Color Locator
   c. Color Locator Index
   d. Chapters; broken down by sections on drug classifications
   e. Index

Applying Knowledge on the Job

Use your critical-thinking skills to answer the following questions.

1. Obtain a copy of the *PDR*® from your school, nursing unit, or clinic and use it to do some sleuthing. Find the drugs that solve the following "medical mysteries." **(LO 1.7)**
   a. Dan is currently taking the drugs *Mephyton, Biaxin,* and *Entex LA* for his chronic celiac disease and acute sinusitis. He was just prescribed *Coumadin* for thrombosis, and it had no therapeutic effect. Dan's doctor suspects it's a case of drug antagonism. Which drug is Dan taking that is antagonistic with *Coumadin*?
   b. Mary's grandfather just came home from the doctor with a prescription for *Vaseretic* and he has already forgotten why he is supposed to take it. Explain what this drug is, its indications, and the most common adverse effects.
   c. Bill's young wife was just prescribed *Vibra-Tabs* for a respiratory infection. Bill asks you what this drug is and is it safe for his wife to take, since she may be pregnant. Is it safe?

2. Assume that your employer has asked you to help screen patients for potential prescription drug problems. Look up the following frequently prescribed prescription drugs in the *PDR*® and provide the information requested. **(LO 1.7)**
   a. *Indocin:* What would tip you off that a patient was showing adverse effects to the drug?
   b. *Bicillin:* Describe symptoms of a patient who is allergic to this drug.
   c. *Depakote:* For whom is this drug contraindicated?

Use the F&C or the *PDR*® to answer the following questions.

3. a. A patient calls you and states that he has found a single loose tablet on the carpet. He needs you to identify it for him. He describes it as a small blue tablet with a heart cut out of the middle. There is writing on the tablet, but it is too small to read. What is this medication? **(LO 1.7)**
   b. A patient calls with a minor problem. While traveling, she got her medications mixed together. She needs to take her *Cordarone* tablet but isn't sure which one it is. Could you please describe it to her? **(LO 1.7)**

4. a. A physician wants to know what glucose-elevating products are available and whether they require a prescription. Look under the hormone section and find these products. List the available products, strengths, forms, and status. **(LO 1.7)**
   b. A physician wants to know the available forms and strength of *Imitrex*. Using the index, look up the medication and list the available forms, strengths, and package sizes. **(LO 1.7)**

5. Sarah Roberts has liver damage due to a past history of alcohol abuse. She is also taking carbamazepine 400 mg TID. Can she safely take acetaminophen for her chronic headaches? **(LO 1.7)**

Multiple Choice

Use your critical-thinking skills to answer the following questions.

1. The study of drug absorption, distribution, metabolism, and excretion is known as **(LO 1.1)**
   A. pharmacotherapeutics
   B. pharmacodynamics
   C. pharmacokinetics
   D. pharmacy

2. The medical situation when a particular drug should not be administered is referred to as **(LO 1.2)**
   A. side effect
   B. adverse effect
   C. drug allergy
   D. contraindication

3. An unusual or unexpected drug reaction by an individual is known as **(LO 1.5)**
   A. toxic effect
   B. antagonism
   C. idiosyncrasy
   D. side effect

4. The proprietary drug name supplied by a pharmaceutical company is also referred to as the **(LO 1.6)**
   A. generic name
   B. over-the-counter name
   C. trade name
   D. chemical name

5. The time from drug administration to the first observable drug effect is known as the **(LO 1.4)**
   A. duration of action
   B. onset of action
   C. ceiling effect
   D. maximal response

6. A drug that has the potential for abuse and is regulated by the Drug Enforcement Agency is classified as a **(LO 1.7)**
   A. poison
   B. OTC drug
   C. prescription drug
   D. controlled substance

Multiple Choice (Multiple Answer)

Select the correct choices for each statement. The choices may be all correct, all incorrect, or any combination.

1. Select the terms below that relate to drugs having a dangerous result on the body. **(LO 1.2)**
   A. posology
   B. toxicology
   C. adverse effects
   D. antagonism

2. A medication that does not require a physician's service to obtain. **(LO 1.6)**
   A. trade
   B. nonproprietary
   C. nonprescription
   D. brand

3. Which of the following could be categorized as adverse reactions? **(LO 1.5)**
   A. idiosyncrasy
   B. allergy
   C. teratogenicity
   D. carcinogenicity

4. Which term(s) could be associated with an agonist? **(LO 1.3)**
   A. receptor site
   B. toxicology
   C. blocking drug
   D. site of action

5. The time a drug continues to produce its effect. **(LO 1.4)**
   A. ED50
   B. maximal response
   C. ceiling effect
   D. onset of action

Sequencing

1. Place the following in order of most beneficial to most harmful. **(LO 1.2)**

_____   _____   _____   _____

Beneficial   **Harmful**
adverse effect
therapeutic effect
side effect
toxic effect

Classification

1. Place the following drugs into the correct controlled substance classification. **(LO 1.5)**

Amphetamines	Narcotic antidiarrheals	Hallucinogens
Narcotic antitussives	Heroin	Anabolic steroids
Phenobarbital	Valium	Dronabinol
Short-acting barbiturates	Chloral hydrate	Lomotil
Marijuana	Morphine	Intermediate-acting barbiturates

Schedule I	Schedule II	Schedule III	Schedule IV	Schedule V

Labeling

Fill in the missing labels. **(LO 1.4)**

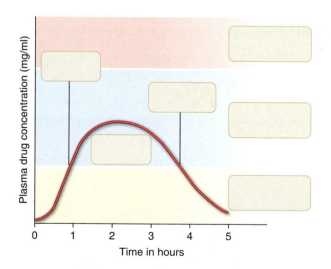

For interactive animations, videos, and assessment, visit:
www.mcgrawhillconnect.com

Chapter 2

Pharmacokinetics and Factors of Individual Variation

KEY TERMS

bioavailability: percentage of the drug dosage that is absorbed.

drug absorption: entrance of a drug into the bloodstream from its site of administration.

drug addiction: condition of drug abuse and drug dependence that is characterized by compulsive drug behavior.

drug dependence: condition of reliance on the use of a particular drug, characterized as physical and/or psychological dependence.

drug distribution: passage of a drug from the blood to the tissues and organs of the body.

drug excretion: elimination of the drug from the body.

drug metabolism: the enzymatic biotransformation of a drug into metabolites.

drug microsomal metabolizing system (DMMS): group of enzymes located primarily in the liver that function to metabolize (biotransformation) drugs.

drug tolerance: decreased drug effect occurring after repeated drug administration.

enzyme induction: increase in the amount of drug-metabolizing enzymes after repeated administration of certain drugs.

enzyme inhibition: inhibition of drug-metabolizing enzymes by certain drugs.

first-pass metabolism: drug metabolism that occurs in the intestines and liver during oral absorption of drugs into the systemic circulation.

half-life: time required for the body to reduce the amount of drug in the plasma by one-half.

individual variation: difference in the effects of drugs and drug dosages from one person to another.

intramuscular (IM) injection: route of drug administration; drug is injected into gluteal or deltoid muscles.

intravenous (IV) injection: route of drug administration; drug is injected directly into a vein.

loading dose: initial drug dose administered to rapidly achieve therapeutic drug concentrations.

maintenance dose: dose administered to maintain drug blood levels in the therapeutic range.

oral administration: route of drug administration by way of the mouth through swallowing.

parenteral administration: route of drug administration that does not involve the gastrointestinal (GI) tract.

pharmacokinetics: describes the processes of drug absorption, drug distribution, drug metabolism, and drug excretion.

After studying this chapter, you should be able to

LO 2.1 list different forms of drug products and the routes by which they are administered.

LO 2.2 understand the pharmacokinetic factors that determine the absorption, distribution, metabolism, and excretion of drugs.

LO 2.3 identify how half-life, blood drug level, and bioavailability relate to drug response.

LO 2.4 list several factors of individual variation that can alter drug response.

LO 2.5 understand the drug factors that relate to pediatric drug administration.

LO 2.6 define the different types of drug interaction.

LO 2.7 explain the basic terminology of chronic drug administration and drug dependence.

Introduction

The familiar saying "No two people are exactly alike" applies well to the effects produced by drugs. An identical drug and dose may produce an intense response in one individual and no observable effect in another. The major reasons for this are differences in **pharmacokinetics** and various factors of **individual variation** that exist among the patient population. Pharmacokinetics is a study of the factors that determine **drug absorption, drug distribution, drug metabolism**, and **drug excretion.**

Individual variation is caused by a number of physical and psychological factors, including differences in age, sex, weight, genetic variation, emotional state, patient expectations (placebo effect), and the presence of other disease conditions (pathology) or other drugs. The remainder of this chapter will describe what happens to a drug between its administration and its elimination from the body. The interplay among the various biological factors determines the actual drug response.

LO 2.1

DRUG FORMS

Drugs are prepared in various forms for administration. The physical and chemical properties of a drug usually determine which form will be most effective. In addition to the drug, most drug products contain other ingredients that facilitate the administration and absorption of the drug. Drug preparations should always be taken exactly as prescribed. Some of the more common drug forms and preparations follow.

Aqueous Preparations

Syrups are commonly used aqueous preparations. A syrup is a solution of water and sugar to which a drug is added. Addition of flavoring agents eliminates the bitter taste of many drugs.

Alcoholic Preparations

Elixirs, spirits, tinctures, and fluid extracts are drugs dissolved in various concentrations of alcohol, usually in the range of 5 to 20 percent.

Solid and Semisolid Preparations

The solid type of preparation is most common. A number of different kinds for different purposes are available.

Powders

Powders are drugs or drug extracts that are dried and ground into fine particles.

Tablets

Tablets are drug powders that have been compressed into a convenient form for swallowing. They usually disintegrate in the stomach more rapidly than most other solid preparations.

Troches and Lozenges

These flattened tablets are allowed to dissolve in the mouth. They are commonly used for colds and sore throats.

Capsules

Gelatin capsules are used to administer drug powders or liquids. Gelatin capsules dissolve in the stomach, thereby releasing the drug.

Delayed-Release Products

These are usually tablets or capsules that are treated with special coatings so that various portions of the drug will dissolve at different rates. Delayed-release products usually contain the equivalent of two or three single-dose units. They are designed to produce drug effects over an extended time.

Enteric-Coated Products

Some drugs are very irritating to the stomach. Also, the gastric juices of the stomach can inactivate certain drugs. In these cases, the drug tablet or capsule is coated with an acid-resistant substance that will dissolve only in the less acidic portions of the intestines. Enteric-coated products should be taken on an empty stomach with water, either 1 hour before or 2 hours after meals.

Suppositories

These are drugs mixed with a substance (cacao butter) that will melt at body temperature. Suppositories are intended for insertion into the rectum, urethra, or vagina.

Ointments

Ointments or salves are soft, oily substances (petrolatum or lanolin) containing a drug that is applied to the skin or, in the case of ophthalmic ointments, to the eye.

Transdermal Products

Transdermal products are administered through a bandage or patch system. The drug is released from the bandage or patch and is then absorbed through the skin into the systemic circulation. This method provides a continuous source of the drug over 24 hours or more. Nitroglycerin, estrogen, and clonidine are drugs available in this form.

Parenteral Injection

Parenteral injection involves the administration of drugs by needle and syringe. Different injection sites such as subcutaneous (SC), intramuscular (IM), intravenous (IV), and others provide different rates of drug absorption and onset of action. Parenteral injection requires the practice of sterile technique and various safety precautions.

ROUTES OF ADMINISTRATION
Oral Administration

The most common routes of drug administration are oral (PO) and parenteral. **Parenteral administration** is any route that does not involve the GI tract, including inhalation, hypodermic injection, and topical application. However, when the term *parenteral* is used, most individuals think of administration by injection with a needle and syringe. The **oral administration** route is the safest and the most convenient method. Oral administration usually requires 30 to 60 minutes before significant absorption from the GI tract occurs; therefore, the onset of drug action is delayed.

Although some drugs are irritating to the stomach and may cause nausea, heartburn, and vomiting, administration of such drugs with sufficient amounts of water or with meals minimizes gastric irritation. However, food also delays drug absorption and therefore delays the onset of drug action.

Besides convenience, another advantage of oral administration is that drugs given orally can be removed (within the first few hours) by gastric lavage or induced vomiting. This procedure is often employed in drug overdose (sleeping pills) or accidental poisoning.

Parenteral Administration

The most common routes of parenteral administration include intramuscular (IM) injection, intravenous (IV) injection, inhalation, and topical application. **IM injections** are usually delivered into the gluteal or deltoid muscles. Extreme caution should be observed with gluteal injections to avoid injury to the sciatic nerve. The onset of action with IM administration is relatively short, usually within several minutes. **Intravenous (IV) injection** is usually restricted to use in the hospital. IV injection offers the fastest means of drug absorption because the drug is delivered directly into the circulation; therefore, the onset of drug action is almost immediate. However, there is some degree of risk because the drug cannot be withdrawn once it has been injected. Dosage miscalculations resulting in overdose can produce serious, even fatal, consequences. Inhalation involves administration of drug through the nose or mouth and into the lungs during respiratory inspiration. This route is especially useful for the local administration of drugs into the respiratory tract. Topical application of creams and ointments is used for local effects in the skin and in certain conditions for systemic effects, as with nitroglycerin ointment for the treatment of angina pectoris.

Several other routes of administration are used in specific situations. The most commonly used routes are listed in Table 2:1 with examples of their indications for use. Other routes will be presented in the appropriate chapters.

LO 2.2

DRUG ABSORPTION

Drug absorption refers to the entrance of a drug into the bloodstream. In order for absorption to occur, the drug must be dissolved in body fluids. With the exception of IV or intraarterial administration, drugs must pass through membranes of the GI lining and blood vessels before they gain access to the blood. Cell membranes are composed of lipids and proteins, which form a semipermeable barrier.

Cells have special transport mechanisms that allow various substances (including drugs) to pass through the cell membrane. These mechanisms include filtration, passive transport, and active transport. Most drugs pass through membranes by passive transport. An important principle in passive transport is that the concentration of drug on each side of the membrane differs. In

[Table 2:1]

Routes of Drug Administration

Route	Approximate onset of action	Indications	Examples
Oral (PO)	30 to 60 minutes	Whenever possible, the safest and most convenient route	Most medications—aspirin, sedatives, hypnotics, antibiotics
Sublingual	Several minutes	When rapid effects are needed	Nitroglycerin in angina pectoris
Buccal	Several minutes	Convenient dosage form for certain drugs	Androgenic drugs
Rectal	15 to 30 minutes	When patient cannot take oral medications and parenteral is not indicated, also for local effects	Analgesics, laxatives
Transdermal	30 to 60 minutes	Convenient dosage form that provides continuous absorption and systemic effects over many hours	Nitroglycerin, estrogen
Subcutaneous (SC)	Several minutes	For drugs that are inactivated by the GI tract	Insulin
Intramuscular (IM)	Several minutes	For drugs that have poor oral absorption, when high blood levels are required, and when rapid effects are desired	Narcotic analgesics, antibiotics
Intravenous (IV)	Within 1 minute	In emergency situations, where immediate effects are required, also when medications are administered by infusion	IV fluids (dextrose), nutrient supplementation, antibiotics
Intraarterial	Within 1 minute	For local effects within an internal organ	Cancer drugs
Intrathecal	Several minutes	For local effects within the spinal cord	Spinal anesthesia with lidocaine
Inhalation	Within 1 minute	For local effects within the respiratory tract	Antiasthmatic medications such as epinephrine
Topical	Within 1 hour	For local effects on the skin, eye, or ear	Creams and ointments
Vaginal	15 to 30 minutes	For local effects	Creams, foams, and suppositories

passive transport, drug molecules diffuse from an area of high concentration to an area of low concentration (law of diffusion).

For example, following oral administration, there is a large amount of drug in the GI tract and no drug in the blood. Consequently, the drug molecules have a natural tendency to diffuse from the GI tract into the blood. The speed or rate of drug absorption also depends on the chemical properties of the drug and other factors such as the presence of food or other drugs. The properties of the drug that most determine absorption are lipid (fat) solubility of the drug and the degree of drug ionization.

Lipid Solubility

Cell membranes are composed of a significant amount of lipid material. In general, the more lipid soluble a drug is, the faster it will pass through a lipid substance like the cell membrane. With the exception of general anesthetics (highly lipid soluble), most drugs are primarily water soluble and only partially lipid soluble. Many water-soluble drugs are weak acids or bases that can form charged particles or ions (ionization) when dissolved in body fluids. The absorption of water-soluble drugs is mainly influenced by the degree of drug ionization.

Drug Ionization

Most drugs exist in two forms, ionized and un-ionized. Like electrolytes (Na^+ and Cl^-), ionized drugs are charged molecules because their atomic structure has lost or gained electrons. The molecules then become either positively or negatively charged. In general, ionized drug molecules do not readily cross cell membranes. The un-ionized (uncharged) form of the drug is required in order for absorption to occur.

The first generalization is that acid drugs (aspirin) are mostly un-ionized when they are in an acidic fluid (gastric juice). Consequently, drug absorption is favored. Conversely, acid drugs are mostly ionized when they are in an alkaline fluid; therefore, absorption is not favored and occurs at a slower rate and to a lesser extent.

The second generalization is that basic drugs (streptomycin, morphine) are mostly un-ionized when they are in an alkaline fluid (lower GI tract after rectal administration). Conversely, these drugs are mostly ionized when they are dissolved in an acidic fluid like the upper GI tract. This is the reason why morphine is usually administered parenterally. In the stomach (pH 1 to 3) and upper intestinal tract (pH 5 to 6), basic drugs like morphine are absorbed more slowly and to a lesser extent than acidic drugs because they are primarily in an ionized form.

The acid and base nature of drugs may be useful in treating drug toxicity (overdose). Drugs are generally excreted by the kidneys in an ionized form. To increase drug excretion, the pH of the urine can be altered. For example, to increase the renal excretion of an acid drug (aspirin), the urine is alkalinized (pH > 7). In an alkaline urine, acidic drugs are mostly ionized and more rapidly excreted. In the same manner basic drugs are more rapidly excreted by acidifying the urine (pH < 7).

Drug Formulation

Drugs must be in solution before being absorbed. Tablets and capsules require time for the dissolution to occur. For this reason, liquid medications are generally absorbed faster than the solid forms. Drug particles can be formulated into different sizes, such as crystals, micronized particles, or ultramicronized particles. The smaller the size of the drug particle, the faster the rate of dissolution and absorption.

LO 2.2
DRUG DISTRIBUTION

After a drug gains access to the blood, it is distributed to the various tissues and organs of the body. Several factors determine how much drug reaches any one organ or area of the body. The main factors are plasma protein binding, blood flow, and the presence of specific tissue barriers.

Plasma Protein Binding

Several different proteins (albumin and globulins) are in the plasma and form a circulating protein pool. These plasma proteins help regulate osmotic pressure (oncotic pressure) in the blood and transport many hormones and vitamins. In addition, many drugs are attracted to the plasma proteins, especially albumin. The result is that some drug molecules are bound to plasma proteins while some drug molecules are unbound (free in the circulation). Only the unbound or free drug molecules can exert a pharmacological effect. The ratio of the bound to unbound drug molecules varies with the drug used. Some drugs are highly bound (99 percent), while other drugs are not bound to any significant degree.

Occasionally, there is competition between drugs or other plasma substances for the same plasma protein binding site. In this situation, one drug may displace another. The result is that the concentration of free drug of one of the drugs increases, and this concentration can lead to increased pharmacological and adverse effects similar to overdosage.

Blood Flow

The various organs of the body receive different amounts of blood. Organs such as the liver, kidneys, and brain have the largest blood supply. Consequently, these organs are usually exposed to the largest amount of drug. Some tissues, such as adipose tissue, receive a relatively poor blood supply and, as a result, do not accumulate large amounts of drug. However, highly lipid-soluble drugs can enter adipose tissue easily, where they can accumulate and remain for an extended period of time.

Blood-Brain Barrier

In the case of the brain, an additional consideration is the blood-brain barrier. This barrier is an additional lipid barrier that protects the brain by restricting the passage of electrolytes and other water-soluble substances. Since the brain is composed of a large amount of lipid (nerve membranes and myelin), lipid-soluble drugs pass readily into the brain. As a general rule, then, a drug must have a certain degree of lipid solubility if it is to penetrate this barrier and gain access to the brain.

LO 2.2

DRUG METABOLISM

Whenever a drug or other foreign substance is taken into the body, the body attempts to eliminate it. This usually involves excretion by one of the normal excretory routes (renal, intestinal, or respiratory). Some drugs can be excreted in the same chemical form in which they were administered. Other drugs, however, must be chemically altered before they can be excreted by the kidneys. Drug metabolism, also referred to as biotransformation, is the chemical alteration of drugs and foreign compounds in the body.

The liver is the main organ involved in drug metabolism. Within the cells of the liver are a group of enzymes that specifically function to metabolize foreign (drug) substances. These enzymes are referred to as the **drug microsomal metabolizing system (DMMS).** The DMMS utilizes cytochrome P450 enzymes that are important in oxidation and reduction reactions that convert drugs into their metabolites. The main function of this system is to take lipid-soluble drugs and chemically alter them so that they become water-soluble compounds. Water-soluble compounds can be excreted by the kidneys. Lipid-soluble compounds are repeatedly reabsorbed into the blood. Although most drugs are inactivated by metabolism, a few are initially converted into pharmacologically active metabolites.

An interesting phenomenon occurs with some drugs, especially the barbiturates and other sedative-hypnotic drugs. When these drugs are taken repeatedly, they stimulate the drug microsomal metabolizing system. By stimulating this system, the drugs actually increase the amount of enzymes (cytochrome P450's) in the system; this process is referred to as **enzyme induction.** With an increase in the amount of enzymes, there is a faster rate of drug metabolism. Consequently, the duration of drug action is decreased for all drugs metabolized by the microsomal enzymes. In addition, other drugs can inhibit the drug microsomal-metabolizing enzymes to cause **enzyme inhibition.** This action slows the metabolism of all other drugs metabolized by these enzymes. This will increase the duration and intensity of the drugs inhibited. Enzyme induction and enzyme inhibition are common causes of adverse drug interactions.

After oral administration, all drugs are absorbed into the portal circulation, which transports the drugs to the liver before they are distributed throughout the body. Some drugs are metabolized significantly as they pass through the liver this first time. This effect is referred to as **first-pass metabolism.** It can significantly reduce bioavailability and the amount of active drug that reaches the general circulation.

LO 2.2

DRUG EXCRETION

The common pathways of drug excretion are renal (urine), GI (feces), and respiratory (exhaled gases). Although the liver is the most important organ for drug metabolism, the kidneys are the most important organs for drug excretion.

Renal Excretion

After the blood is filtered through the glomerulus of the kidneys, most of the filtered substances are eventually reabsorbed into the blood. The exceptions to this are the urinary waste products and anything else that is in a nonabsorbable form. In order for drug excretion to occur, the drug or drug metabolite must be water soluble and preferably in an ionized form. As mentioned, acid drugs are mostly ionized in alkaline urine and basic drugs are mostly ionized in an acid urine. In the case of barbiturate or aspirin overdose (acid drugs), alkalinization of the urine with sodium bicarbonate will hasten elimination of either drug in the urine.

GI Excretion

After oral administration, a certain portion of drug (unabsorbed) passes through the GI tract and is excreted in the feces. The amount varies with the particular drug used.

In addition, there is another pathway involving the intestinal tract, the enterohepatic pathway. Certain drugs (fat-soluble drugs) can enter the intestines by way of the biliary tract. After the drug is released into the intestines (in the bile), it may be absorbed from the intestines back into the blood again. This is referred to as the enterohepatic cycle. The duration of action of a few drugs is greatly prolonged because of this repeated cycling of the drug (liver → bile → intestines → blood → liver).

Respiratory Excretion

The respiratory system does not usually play a significant role in drug excretion. However, some drugs are metabolized to products that can be exchanged from the blood into the respiratory tract. General anesthetic gases are not totally metabolized. These drugs are excreted primarily by the lungs.

Miscellaneous

Some drugs and drug metabolites also can be detected in sweat, saliva, and milk (lactation). Infants can be exposed to significant amounts of certain drugs after nursing (see the Drug Exposure During Infant Nursing section).

In summary, following drug administration, the processes of drug absorption and distribution predominate as the drug is absorbed into the bloodstream and distributed to the various tissues. Later, drug metabolism and excretion predominate as the drug is eliminated from the body. However, once some drug reaches the

Figure 2.1

Movement of Drug in the Body

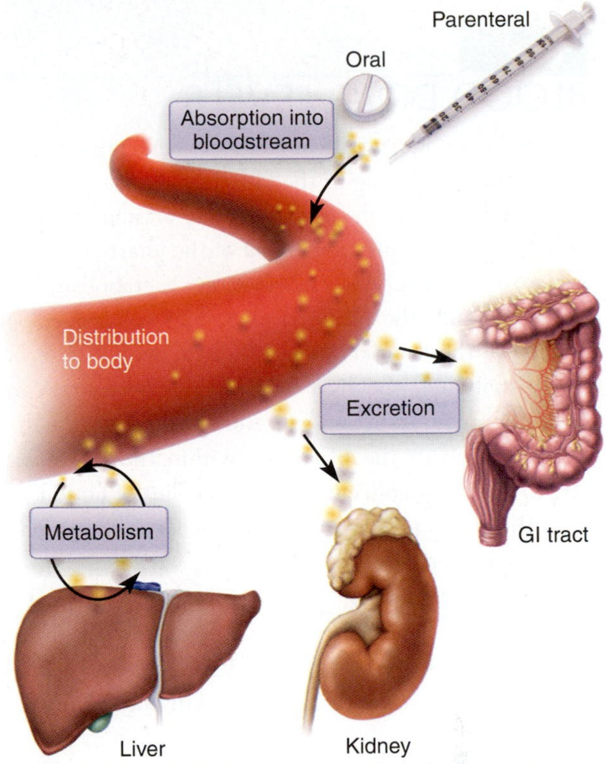

Following absorption the drug is distributed to all the tissues of the body. The liver metabolizes the drug so that the metabolites can be excreted by the kidneys and GI tract.

bloodstream, it is distributed to the liver and kidneys, which then begin metabolism and excretion. Consequently, all of the pharmacokinetic processes occur simultaneously to varying degrees depending on the time since administration. Figure 2.1 illustrates the interrelationship of the pharmacokinetic processes.

LO 2.3

HALF-LIFE

The **half-life** of a drug is the time required for the blood or plasma concentration of the drug to fall to half of its original level. For example, after two half-lives only 25 percent of the drug that was absorbed remains in the blood. Half-life is important in determining the frequency of drug administration. In order to maintain a continuous drug effect, the drug must be given at intervals that keep the plasma concentration above the minimal effective concentration. The major factors that determine half-life are the rates of drug metabolism and excretion. The half-life of any drug is relatively constant if the individual has normal rates of drug metabolism and excretion. It can be prolonged when liver or kidney disease is present. In these situations, the dose or the frequency of administration can be reduced.

LO 2.3

BLOOD DRUG LEVELS

The intensity of drug effect is mainly determined by the concentration of drug in the blood or plasma. The drug effect and the amount of drug in the plasma are determined by an interplay among all of the pharmacokinetic processes (absorption, distribution, metabolism, and excretion) and the pharmacodynamics (pharmacologic effects) of the drug (Figure 2.2). As a drug is absorbed and distributed, the liver and kidneys begin the processes of metabolism and excretion. As long as the drug concentration in the plasma is within the therapeutic range, the drug concentration at the site of action will be sufficient to produce the pharmacodynamic or pharmacologic effect.

Drug monitoring, the periodic measurement of blood drug levels, is performed to ensure that the level of drug in the blood is within the therapeutic range. Drug levels below the therapeutic range will not produce the desired drug effect, while levels above the therapeutic range cause increased side effects and toxicity. This concept is illustrated in Figure 2.3.

There are some drugs that require several dosages or several days or weeks to reach the desired drug effect. In some clinical situations, it may be necessary to reach therapeutic drug levels as rapidly as possible. In these cases, a loading dose may be administered. A **loading dose** is usually an initial higher dose of drug, often administered IV, to rapidly attain the therapeutic drug level and drug effects. Loading doses are usually followed by **maintenance doses** that are smaller and calculated to maintain the drug level within the therapeutic range.

LO 2.3

BIOAVAILABILITY

Bioavailability is the percentage of the dose of a drug that is actually absorbed into the bloodstream. Differences in drug formulation, route of administration, and factors that affect GI absorption can influence bioavailability. A particular drug may be manufactured by many different drug companies and sold under different trade

---

Figure 2.2 Illustration of the Relationship between the Pharmacokinetic and Pharmacodynamic Processes That Determine the Pharmacologic and Clinical Drug Response

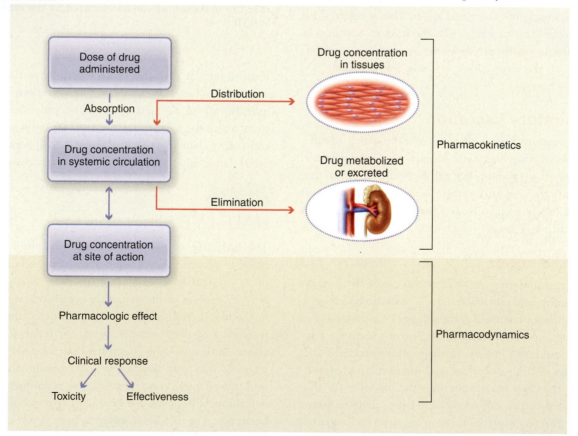

Figure 2.3

Illustration of the Therapeutic Drug Range

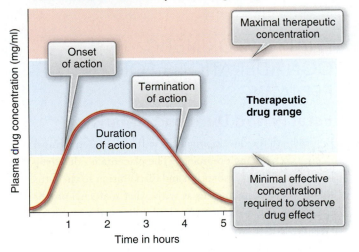

individuals (200 to 300 pounds), the dose may have to be increased. However, this approach does not always hold true, since many other factors are involved.

Sex and Percent Body Fat

Females possess a higher percentage of body fat and a lower percentage of body water than do males of equal weight. Consequently, females may experience a greater drug effect than do males because the drug is dissolved in a smaller volume of body fluid. Lipid-soluble drugs are more widely distributed and may produce longer durations of action in females than in males. This same concept also applies to the differences in body fat composition between members of the same sex.

Genetic Variation

Individuals tend to inherit the proteins and enzyme patterns of their parents. There is significant genetic variation in some of the drug-metabolizing enzymes, so individual differences can occur. If the difference affects the rate of drug metabolism, there may be a difference in the effects produced by the drug. An enzyme may be missing, in which case drug metabolism is extremely slow. A slowed metabolic rate may result in increased and prolonged drug effects that can lead to serious consequences. Examples of genetic variation will be discussed in specific chapters.

Emotional State

Differences in drug effects can be caused by the emotional state of the individual. For example, an individual who is excited or extremely anxious may require a larger dose of hypnotic or tranquilizer than an individual who is not emotionally stimulated but who still has difficulty sleeping.

Placebo Effect

Patients come to physicians and hospitals with varying expectations. It has been observed that if patients have a positive attitude and think that the drug or treatment will help, chances are the patients claim an improvement whether there actually is one or not.

In some studies, patients have been unknowingly given sugar pills or placebos instead of an actual drug. A large percentage of these patients claim an improved condition even though they received no real drug. Likewise, patients with hostile or negative attitudes, who feel that nothing will help their condition, usually say that they feel no difference or even worse after a specific treatment or medication. The influence of one's mind on the course of treatment is referred to as the placebo

names. In these situations, the amount of drug may be the same in each product, but the product may be different because of particle size, binders, fillers, and tablet coating. These differences may alter bioavailability. There have been examples of this in the past. Now, however, the Food and Drug Administration (FDA) regulates and requires bioavailability testing.

LO 2.4

FACTORS OF INDIVIDUAL VARIATION

Many factors affect individual variation. These factors include age, weight, sex, genetic variation, emotional state, placebo effect, the presence of disease, and patient compliance.

Age

The effects of drugs in different age groups is of particular importance. Infants, children, and the elderly are generally more sensitive to the actions of drugs than are younger adults. Drug considerations during pregnancy on fetal development, during the infant nursing period, and in infants and children are discussed in the section Pharmacokinetic Considerations for Pediatrics. Drug considerations for the elderly are presented in Chapter 3, Geriatric Pharmacology.

Weight

Most adult dosages are calculated for the average adult weight, 150 pounds between the ages of 16 and 65. Obviously, all adults are not 150 pounds. In small individuals (100 pounds), the dose may have to be reduced. In larger

effect. This phenomenon can be used by the medical and nursing staff to enhance the positive attitude of patients. Thus, the patients stand a better chance of responding successfully to therapy.

Presence of Disease

The presence of other diseases that are debilitating or that decrease the function of some vital organ usually makes an individual more susceptible to the effects and adverse reactions of drug therapy. As mentioned, the liver and kidneys are especially important, since these two organs are exposed to the highest drug levels. For this reason, liver and kidney function are often adversely affected by drugs. Patients with hepatic or renal disease suffer a greater incidence of adverse drug effects because they are unable to eliminate the drug and its metabolites effectively. Consequently, plasma drug levels are much higher in these patients due to accumulation of the drug in the plasma.

Patient Compliance

Drug compliance refers to taking a drug exactly as prescribed. If dosages are forgotten or skipped, the drug effects will be reduced or absent. This is referred to as noncompliance. Noncompliance is often a problem in geriatric patients who may have memory difficulties and who are easily confused by complicated dosing schedules, especially when several different drugs are involved. Particular care and sufficient patient instructions and training must be given to ensure that all patients understand dosing instructions.

PHARMACOKINETIC CONSIDERATIONS FOR PEDIATRICS

Fetal Period During Pregnancy

Before birth the developing fetus will be exposed to most drugs taken during pregnancy. The placenta is not a drug barrier, and drug absorption and distribution to the fetus follow the same principles as with other maternal organs (passive diffusion based on lipid solubility and ionization). Although there are relatively few drugs that have been proven to be teratogenic (cause birth defects), it is recommended that drug exposure during pregnancy should be avoided if possible. This is especially true during the first trimester when organogenesis, the formation of body organs, is occurring. Drugs that are teratogens may cause spontaneous abortion, growth retardation, birth defects, or carcinogenesis (development of cancer). The Food and Drug Administration has established guidelines, the FDA Pregnancy Categories (see Table 2:2), that classify drugs based on fetal risk. Table 2:3 lists some drugs that have been associated with teratogenicity in humans. Consult Section 6 in the *PDR*® for an expanded list of drugs assigned to the FDA Pregnancy Categories.

[Table 2:2]

Description of FDA Pregnancy Categories

Category	Description
Pregnancy category A	Drug studies in pregnant women have not yet demonstrated risk to the fetus
Pregnancy category B	Drug studies have not been performed in pregnant women; animal studies have not demonstrated fetal risk
Pregnancy category C	Drug studies have not been performed in pregnant women or in animals, or animal studies have revealed some teratogenic potential but the risk to the fetus is unknown
Pregnancy category D	Drug studies have revealed adverse risk to the fetus. The benefit-to-risk ratio of the drug must be established before use during pregnancy
Pregnancy category X	Drug studies have revealed teratogenic effects in women and/or animals. Fetal risk clearly outweighs benefit. Drug is contraindicated in pregnancy
Pregnancy category NR	Drug has not yet been rated by FDA

Examples of Drugs with Demonstrated Teratogenic Risk in Humans

Drug	Teratogenic effect
Androgens (male hormone)	Masculinization of female fetus
Carbamazepine	Craniofacial and fingernail deformities
Diethylstilbestrol	Vaginal tumors and genital malformations in offspring
Estrogen (female hormone)	Feminization of male fetus
Lithium	Cardiac defects
Phenytoin	Craniofacial and limb deformities, growth retardation
Retinoic acid	Craniofacial, cardiac, and *CNS defects
Thalidomide	Phocomelia (limb deformities)
Warfarin	Facial, cartilage, and CNS defects

*Abbreviations: *CNS, central nervous system*

Drug Exposure During Infant Nursing

Drugs administered to nursing mothers appear in breast milk to varying degrees. Unfortunately there is a lack of controlled studies and reliable information in this area. The major concern is that the drug concentration in the milk will be high enough to produce undesired or harmful effects in the infant. Generally, the recommendation is to avoid unnecessary drug administration. Usually the infant experiences the same pharmacological effects as in the mother. For example, laxatives may cause infant diarrhea, while sedatives and hypnotics will cause drowsiness and lethargy. Other drugs such as anticancer agents or drugs with increased toxicities are contraindicated unless the benefit to the mother clearly outweighs the risk to the infant. Table 2:4 lists some of the drugs that appear in breast milk.

Pediatric Considerations

There are a number of pharmacokinetic and pharmacodynamic differences between pediatric and adult patients. Neonates (0 to 1 month), infants (1 to 12 months), and children of increasing age are not simply "small adults." There are a number of factors that must be considered that generally require reduction in dosage beyond the obvious difference in body weight. These differences tend to decrease with advancing age, especially after the first year of life.

Drug Administration and Absorption

Neonates and infants have a small skeletal muscle mass. In addition, limited physical activity results in a lower blood flow to muscle. Therefore, absorption after IM injections is slower and more variable. There is also increased risk of muscle and nerve damage with IM injections. In serious situations the IV route is more reliable and generally preferred. The skin of neonates and infants is thinner and topically applied drugs are more rapidly and completely absorbed into the systemic circulation. With regard to oral administration, the gastric pH of premature babies and neonates is less acidic. This could result in decreased bioavailability and lower blood levels of orally administered drugs that are acidic in nature.

Drug Distribution

Pediatric patients possess a higher percentage of body water and a lower percentage of body fat. These differences decrease the distribution of lipid-soluble drugs to body tissues and organs. This tends to cause higher drug blood levels. Water-soluble drug distribution is increased (greater peripheral drug distribution), which

Examples of Drugs That Cross into Breast Milk Following Maternal Use

Drug class	Examples
Antibiotics	Ampicillin, erythromycin, penicillin, streptomycin, sulfa drugs, tetracyclines
Antiepileptic agents	Phenytoin, primidone
Antithyroid agents	Thiouracil
CNS stimulants	Nicotine
Laxatives	Cascara, danthron
Narcotic analgesics	Codeine, heroin, methadone, morphine
Nonnarcotic antiinflammatory agents	Phenylbutazone
Sedative-hypnotic agents	Barbiturates, chloral hydrate
Tranquilizers (antipsychotic agents)	Chlorpromazine, lithium

tends to lower drug blood levels. These effects are all in comparison to the adult effects. While pediatric patients have higher percentages of water, they are more easily dehydrated by vomiting and diarrhea. The resulting reduction of body fluids will increase drug concentrations and drug effects.

Plasma protein levels are also lower, especially in neonates. This results in lower plasma protein binding of drugs and, therefore, greater amounts of unbound or "free" drug. Since only the unbound drug exerts an effect, there will be a greater intensity of drug effect.

Drug Metabolism and Excretion

There is a reduced capacity for drug metabolism and drug excretion during the first several years of life. Consequently, drug elimination occurs more slowly and the duration of drug action is prolonged. The decreases in drug metabolism and excretion are most evident in the neonate and infant. After the first year, drug metabolism and excretion gradually become proportional to those of the adult.

Dosage Adjustment

Dosage calculations in pediatrics are based mainly on age, body surface area, and body weight. The rules and formulas used for these calculations are presented in Chapter 4, Math Review and Dosage Calculations.

LO 2.6

DRUG INTERACTIONS

Drug interaction refers to the effects that occur when the actions of one drug are affected by another drug. There are many different types of drug interactions. Some drugs interfere with each other during GI absorption and therefore should not be administered at the same time. Other drugs may interfere with plasma protein binding, drug metabolism, or drug excretion. Throughout this book, the common drug interactions will be given. Table 2:5 explains the general terms that are associated with drug interactions.

LO 2.7

TERMINOLOGY ASSOCIATED WITH CHRONIC DRUG USE AND ABUSE

The chronic use of certain drugs results in a number of physiologic and pharmacologic changes in drug response. Drug tolerance and drug dependence are two important phenomena involved in chronic drug use.

Tolerance

Drug tolerance is defined as a decreased drug effect that occurs after repeated administration. In order

Terminology of Common Drug Interactions

Term	Explanation
Incompatibility	Usually refers to physical alterations of drugs that occur before administration when different drugs are mixed in the same syringe or other container
Additive effects	When the combined effect of two drugs, each producing the same biological response by the same mechanism of action, is equal to the sum of their individual effects
Summation	When the combined effect of two drugs, each producing the same biological response but by a different mechanism of action, is equal to the sum of their individual effects
Synergism	When the combined effect of two drugs is greater than the sum of their individual effects
Antagonism	When the combined effect of two drugs is less than the sum of their individual effects

to attain the previous drug effect, the dosage must be increased. This is a common occurrence in individuals who abuse drugs such as cocaine, barbiturates, morphine, and heroin. There is also the phenomenon of cross-tolerance, which is the tolerance that exists between drugs of the same class. Tolerance is caused by changes or adaptations that occur in response to repeated drug exposure. The main types of tolerance are referred to as metabolic tolerance and pharmacodynamic tolerance. Metabolic tolerance is caused by enzyme induction—the drug increases the drug-metabolizing enzymes (DMMS) and the dose must be increased in order to attain the same previous effect. Pharmacodynamic tolerance is caused by the ability of some drugs to decrease the number of drug receptors. This usually takes several weeks or months and is referred to as "down-regulation." With the reduction in drug receptors there is a reduction in intensity of drug effect.

Drug Dependence

Drug dependence is a condition wherein reliance on the administration of a particular drug becomes extremely important to the well-being of an individual. Drug dependence is usually characterized as psychological and/or physical. When the drug is used repeatedly for nonmedical purposes, the term *drug abuse* is applied. Any activity that is repeated and that provides pleasure involves a psychological component of behavior. The smoking of tobacco, for example, is an activity associated with psychological dependence. Deprivation of smoking causes some unpleasant feelings, but does not result in serious medical consequences. All drugs that are abused have varying degrees of psychological dependence associated with them. Many abused drugs also produce physical dependence when taken for prolonged periods of time and usually at increasing dosages. Deprivation of these drugs leads to a physical withdrawal syndrome that is very unpleasant, characterized by measurable changes in many bodily functions, and that may cause serious medical consequences. The withdrawal reactions from alcohol, barbiturates, and opiate drugs are examples of this type of reaction. When drug dependence is particularly severe and compulsive drug behavior dominates all other activities, the term **drug addiction** is used. Information concerning tolerance and dependence of specific drug classes can be found in Chapters 12 (Sedative-Hypnotic Drugs and Alcohol), 13 (Antipsychotic and Antianxiety Drugs), 15 (Psychotomimetic Drugs of Abuse), and 19 (Opioid Analgesics).

Chapter Review

Understanding Terminology

Match the description in the left column with the appropriate term in the right column. **(LO 2.6, LO 2.7)**

____ 1. When the combined effect of two drugs, each producing the same biological response by the same mechanism of action, is equal to the sum of their individual effects.

____ 2. When the combined effect of two drugs, each producing the same biological response but by a different mechanism of action, is equal to the sum of their individual effects.

____ 3. When the combined effect of two drugs is greater than the sum of their individual effects.

____ 4. When the combined effect of two drugs is less than the sum of their individual effects.

____ 5. Usually refers to physical alterations of drugs that occur before administration when different drugs are mixed in the same syringe or other container.

____ 6. Decreased drug effects after chronic administration.

a. additive effects
b. antagonism
c. incompatibility
d. summation
e. synergism
f. tolerance

Answer the following questions in the spaces provided.

7. Differentiate between the following terms: *parenteral administration, oral administration, intramuscular injection,* and *intravenous injection.* **(LO 2.1)**

8. What is the main disadvantage to the IV method of drug administration? **(LO 2.1)**

9. By what method of cell transport are most drugs absorbed? What are the main requirements for drug absorption? **(LO 2.2)**

10. Explain why alkalinization of the urine increases the rate of excretion of drugs such as aspirin or phenobarbital. **(LO 2.2)**

11. Briefly describe the main factors that determine drug distribution. **(LO 2.2)**

12. What is the major requirement for a drug if it is to gain access to the brain? **(LO 2.2)**

13. What is the drug microsomal metabolizing system, and what is its main function? **(LO 2.2)**

14. List the major pathways of drug excretion. **(LO 2.2)**

15. Why is the plasma drug concentration important? What are the main factors that determine plasma concentration? **(LO 2.3)**

16. List the factors that can contribute to individual variation in drug response. **(LO 2.4)**

Acquiring Knowledge

Answer the following questions.

1. A single IV injection of 100 mg of a drug with a half-life of 4 hours is administered to a young adult. Approximately how many hours will it take to totally eliminate this dosage from the body? **(LO 2.3)**

2. A drug has a bioavailability of 70 percent after oral administration. How many milligrams of drug will be absorbed following a dosage of 200 mg? What would be the expected effect on bioavailability if a large meal was ingested just before administration? **(LO 2.3)**

3. Your grandmother has just been prescribed a very lipid-soluble drug. Would you expect her dosage to be larger or smaller than that for a younger adult? Explain. **(LO 2.5)**

4. Rifampin is a drug that causes enzyme induction. Would you have to increase or decrease the dosage of another drug taken concurrently if it required drug metabolism for elimination? What change in dosage would a very water-soluble drug require? (LO 2.2)

5. Individuals who become dependent on drugs such as alcohol or narcotics require a steady supply of drug for administration or they will experience unpleasant and potentially harmful effects. Individuals with diabetes require insulin injections on a daily basis or they will experience potentially harmful effects. Are the individuals taking insulin dependent on the drug? Is there a difference between the dependence on insulin versus alcohol? Explain. (LO 2.7)

Applying Knowledge on the Job

Use your critical-thinking skills to answer the following questions.

1. Assume that your new job in a neighborhood health clinic is to identify individual patient factors that might affect the bioavailability of drugs prescribed for the patients. Following are descriptions of five of the clinic's patients whom you dealt with this morning. For each patient, identify one factor that could affect drug bioavailability and explain how drug dosage could be changed to compensate for it.

   a. Jonathan is a 35-year-old male with a medical history of stomach complaints but no evidence of ulcer. When Jonathan visited the clinic this morning he weighed in at 324 pounds. He presented with upper respiratory symptoms attributable to allergy and was prescribed a decongestant and an antihistamine. (LO 2.3)

      Factor

      Dosage change

   b. Lisa is a 25-year-old female weighing 103 pounds. She is in good health. At her clinic visit this morning, she complained of muscle pain caused by moving furniture into her new apartment. She was prescribed a muscle relaxant and a pain reliever. (LO 2.3)

      Factor

      Dosage change

   c. Al is a 50-year-old male alcoholic weighing 150 pounds. His history reveals long-term alcohol abuse. Liver function tests run last month showed some enzyme abnormalities. Al's visit to the clinic this morning was for a sinus infection. He was prescribed an antibiotic and a decongestant. (LO 2.3)

      Factor

      Dosage change

   d. Janet is a 49-year-old weighing 130 pounds. Her visit to the clinic this morning was for insomnia, which she has suffered since her husband's death 2 weeks ago. It was clear from her behavior at the clinic today that she's emotionally distraught. She was prescribed a mild sedative. (LO 2.3)

      Factor

      Dosage change

   e. Jessie is a 5-year-old girl weighing 43 pounds. She presented at the clinic this morning with an upper respiratory virus and strep throat. She was prescribed an antibiotic for the strep throat and pediatric ibuprofen for fever and discomfort. (LO 2.3)

      Factor

      Dosage change

2. Assume that you have volunteered to work a nonprescription drug hotline. Your job is to give people who call assistance with over-the-counter drugs. How would you react—and why—to the following anonymous callers?

   a. Caller A is worried about taking too much aspirin. She didn't realize until after she took the capsules that they were double the dose of the product she usually takes. She wants to know if there's something she might have on hand at home that she could take to counter the effects of the extra aspirin in her system. (LO 2.2)

   b. Caller B wants to know if it's all right to take a laxative while she is breast-feeding her baby. (LO 2.5)

Multiple Choice Questions

Use your critical-thinking skills to answer the following questions.

1. The drug administration route demonstrating the slowest onset of action is **(LO 2.1)**
   A. inhalation
   B. transdermal
   C. intramuscular
   D. sublingual

2. In order for drugs to cross the blood-brain barrier, they must be **(LO 2.2)**
   A. ionized
   B. positively charged
   C. water soluble
   D. lipid soluble

3. First-pass metabolism refers to the metabolism of drugs in the **(LO 2.2)**
   A. kidney
   B. blood vessels
   C. liver
   D. heart

4. Drug X has a half-life of 6 hours. How much drug is left in the body 18 hours after an IV injection of 1200 milligrams (mg) **(LO 2.3)**
   A. 75 mg
   B. 150 mg
   C. 300 mg
   D. 600 mg

5. Drugs that have demonstrated teratogenic effects in women are classified as Pregnancy Category **(LO 2.5)**
   A. B
   B. C
   C. D
   D. X

6. When a drug increases the rate of drug metabolism of other drugs, the process is termed **(LO 2.2)**
   A. first-pass metabolism
   B. enzyme induction
   C. enzyme inhibition
   D. enterohepatic cycling

Multiple Choice (Multiple Answer)

Select the correct choices for each statement. The choices may be all correct, all incorrect, or any combination.

1. Drug absorption is affected by which of the following? **(LO 2.2)**
   A. drug ionization
   B. blood flow
   C. formulation
   D. half-life

2. Which factors of individual variation are dependent upon the patient's attitude toward treatment? **(LO 2.4)**
   A. weight
   B. age
   C. genetic variation
   D. placebo effect

3. Harm to a fetus has been demonstrated in which pregnancy categories? **(LO 2.5)**
   A. Category A
   B. Category B
   C. Category C
   D. Category D

4. Which types of drug interactions show a combined effect equal to the sum of the individual effects of two drugs? **(LO 2.6)**
   A. summation
   B. synergism
   C. antagonism
   D. incompatibility

5. Factors that affect bioavailability include which of the following? **(LO 2.3)**
   A. drug formulation
   B. route of administration
   C. GI absorption
   D. half-life

Sequencing

1. Place the following in order of quickest onset of action to slowest onset of action. **(LO 2.1)**

   _____   _____   _____   _____

   Quickest   **Slowest**
   Oral
   Sublingual
   Rectal
   Intravenous

Classification

1. Put the following drug forms into their appropriate type of preparation. **(LO 2.1)**

   Spirits   Capsules   Tinctures
   Syrups   Fluid extracts   Injectable
   Ointments   Powders

Alcoholic Preparations	Solid or Semisolid Preparations	Aqueous Preparations

Document Exercise

Based on the following drug labels, indicate the route of administration for each. **(LO 2.1)**

1. _____

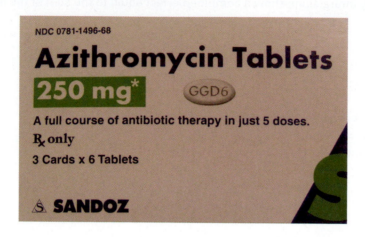

2. _____

3. _____

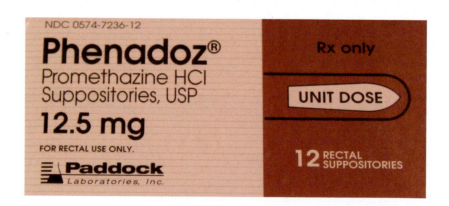

4. _____

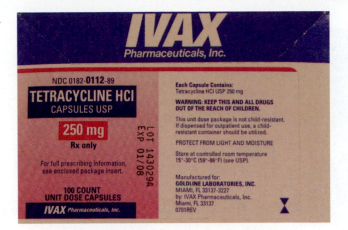

5. _____

Labeling

1. Fill in the missing labels. **(LO 2.2)**

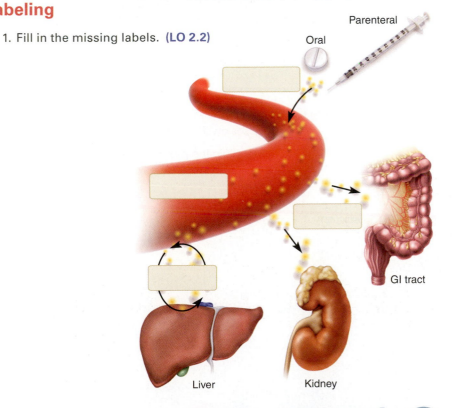

For interactive animations, videos, and assessment visit:

www.mcgrawhillconnect.com

Chapter 3

Geriatric Pharmacology

KEY TERMS

creatinine: a metabolite of muscle metabolism that is excreted in the urine in proportion to renal function.

creatinine clearance: a measure of renal creatinine excretion that is used to evaluate renal function.

drug compliance: following drug prescription directions exactly as written.

enterohepatic recycling: the process whereby drug is eliminated from the liver/biliary tract into the GI tract and then reabsorbed from the GI tract back to the liver.

geriatrics: medical specialty that deals with individuals over 65 years of age.

mixed-function oxidase system: drug microsomal metabolizing enzymes (DMMS) that decrease with age and slow the rate of drug oxidation and metabolism.

polypharmacy: the situation in patients whose treatment involves multiple drug prescriptions.

After studying this chapter you should be able to

3.1 describe the main physiological changes that occur with aging.

3.2 list several factors that affect the absorption and distribution of drugs in the elderly.

3.3 list several factors that affect the metabolism and excretion of drugs in the elderly.

3.4 recognize the effects of nutrition and age-related diseases on drug response.

3.5 explain the problems associated with drug compliance in the elderly.

Introduction

The process of aging begins slowly in the young adult and proceeds at varying individual rates throughout life. The effects of genetics, nutrition, exercise, injury, disease, environment, and many other factors affect the rate of aging. Regardless of the factors that can influence the aging process, there are predictable changes that occur in every individual with the passing of time. This chapter will focus on the age-related changes that influence drug response. The term **geriatric** refers to individuals over 65 years of age. Geriatric medicine, the medical treatment of the elderly, has developed into a medical specialty.

LO 3.1   **LO 3.3**

DRUG USE IN THE ELDERLY

The number of older individuals in the population is increasing and will continue to increase in the future. The dramatic increase in life expectancy over the past few decades has been a significant factor in the growth of this population. The progress of medical technology, including the discovery and development of many new and more effective drugs, has played an important role in improving health and quality of life, in addition to increasing the number of years a person can live. The cost and social impact of new and often expensive treatments also have raised a number of moral and ethical issues concerning the prolongation of life at any cost.

Compared to other age groups, the geriatric population accounts for the highest percentage of drug prescriptions per year. Drug use increases with increasing age, and the number of drugs consumed in the geriatric population averages between three and four drugs per individual. Both the nature and frequency of adverse drug reactions increase with age. It is not uncommon for elderly patients with multiple diseases such as hypertension, arthritis, chronic obstructive pulmonary disease, and heart failure to have prescriptions for 10 or more drugs. The number of possible adverse reactions and drug-drug interactions with this number of drugs is almost beyond calculation.

Physiological Effects of Aging on Pharmacokinetic Processes

Aging is a continuous process that begins when life is conceived. However, most healthy individuals do not begin, or will not admit to, feeling the effects of age until the third or fourth decade. It has been estimated that after 25 or 30 years of age, the cardiac output, the amount of blood pumped by the heart per minute, decreases by approximately 1 percent per year. This means that by the age of 65, the liver and kidneys, for example, are receiving significantly less blood per minute than they did 40 years ago at age 25. This, in particular, can have important consequences for drug action and the ability of the body to eliminate drugs. In addition, the size of most body organs decreases with age and, therefore, there are fewer cells to carry out organ functions. Each of the pharmacokinetic processes—drug absorption, drug distribution, drug metabolism, and drug excretion—is affected to some degree by the aging process.

LO 3.2

DRUG ABSORPTION

With age there is a decrease in blood flow to the intestinal tract, reduced intestinal absorptive surface area, a decrease in gastric acid secretion, and a decrease in intestinal motility. These changes tend to slow the rate of drug absorption and the onset of drug action. In addition, the peak drug blood level (highest drug concentration attained after administration) may be lower than it would be in a younger adult. While the peak drug level may be lower, the total amount of drug absorbed is usually not significantly affected. Consequently, the main effect of aging is to slow drug absorption and delay the onset of drug action.

Drug Distribution

There are significant alterations in body composition that occur with age. The percentage of lean body mass (muscle) and the percentage of total body water decrease. If one thinks of the body as a big beaker filled with 35 liters (l) of fluid and a drug dose dumped into the beaker, there will be a certain concentration of drug per liter. As the percentage of water decreases, the same dose will produce a higher concentration of drug in the beaker. The same thing occurs in the body. As one becomes older, the same dosage of drug given to a younger adult will produce a higher drug concentration in the elderly.

The percentage of body fat (adipose tissue) increases with age. This causes lipid-soluble drugs to be more widely distributed to the body organs that have a high fat content, such as adipose tissue and muscle (modest fat content, but large mass), and away from the liver and kidneys. Since the liver and kidneys are responsible for drug metabolism and excretion, any diversion from them will slow elimination of the drug from the body. The drug will then have a longer half-life and duration of action.

Water-soluble drugs will have less body fluid in which to dissolve and are less widely distributed out to the organs with high fat content. This produces higher plasma drug levels and greater pharmacological effects when compared to the same dosage of drug administered to a younger adult.

The concentration of plasma proteins, mainly albumin, decreases with age. Since most drugs are bound to some extent to plasma proteins and it is only the concentration of "free drug" that produces the pharmacological effect, any decrease in plasma proteins and plasma protein drug binding will increase the amount of free drug (unbound) and, therefore, the intensity of drug effect.

In summary, the overall effect of aging on drug distribution is to generally make any adult drug dosage produce greater pharmacological effects in the elderly if the drug is given in the same dosage. Drugs that are affected by the changes in drug distribution with age usually require a reduction in dosage.

LO 3.3
DRUG METABOLISM AND EXCRETION

In general, the rate of drug metabolism decreases with age, although there is much variability. The age-related decreases in liver blood flow and production of some drug microsomal metabolizing enzymes (DMMS) reduce the rate of drug metabolism. The enzymes that are most affected appear to be the enzymes that oxidize drugs, referred to as the **mixed-function oxidase system.** The pharmacological effects of drugs requiring oxidation, the benzodiazepines (diazepam, *Valium*) for example, are usually prolonged. In addition, drugs that normally undergo first-pass metabolism are not as extensively metabolized during the first pass through the liver. This allows a greater amount of drug to be absorbed, an example of increased bioavailability. Other factors such as smoking, alcohol consumption, and the administration

of certain drugs, all of which may cause microsomal enzyme induction, will increase the rate of drug metabolism. Consequently, it is difficult to accurately predict the effects of aging on specific drug metabolism, but the expected effect is a reduction in the rate of metabolism and an increase in the duration of drug action.

Drug Excretion

Drugs are eliminated from the body mainly by renal excretion and gastrointestinal elimination. Some drugs and drug metabolites pass from the liver through the biliary tract and into the intestinal tract for elimination. A few drugs are able to be reabsorbed from the intestinal tract back through the portal system to the liver. This pathway may be repeated and is referred to as **enterohepatic recycling.** Enterohepatic recycling can increase the drug half-life and the duration of drug action.

The reduction of renal blood flow with age has a significant effect on the renal elimination of drugs. Renal excretion is probably the most important pharmacokinetic process that is affected by age. Almost all measures of renal function, such as glomerular filtration rate and creatinine clearance, are significantly reduced with age. The duration of drug action, plasma drug concentration, and pharmacological effects will all be increased for drugs that are eliminated primarily by renal excretion. Drugs that are primarily excreted by the urinary tract usually require dosage reduction. The reduction in dosage is usually based on the urinary excretion of **creatinine.** Creatinine is a product of muscle metabolism that is excreted by the kidneys in proportion to glomerular filtration rate. The lab test to evaluate the ability of the kidneys to excrete creatinine is known as **creatinine clearance.** The test involves measuring the concentration of creatinine in the blood and using a mathematical formula to determine the creatinine clearance rate. This value is then compared to the expected normal value found in healthy younger adults. Dosage adjustments can then be calculated based on the level of individual renal function. The plasma concentration of creatinine increases with age and renal disease, and reflects the effects of age and disease to decreased renal function. Table 3:1 summarizes the major effects and consequences of aging on the pharmacokinetic processes.

LO 3.4
EFFECTS OF AGE ON DRUG RESPONSE

The effects of age on drug response are difficult to evaluate. Most of the information comes from observations that a specific drug or drug class appears to produce

Age-Related Changes in Pharmacokinetic Processes

Pharmacokinetic process	Age-related change
Drug absorption	Decreased intestinal blood flow, surface area, and motility delay drug absorption and slow onset of drug action
Drug distribution	Decreased body water, lean body mass, and plasma proteins along with increased fat content increase plasma drug concentrations and pharmacologic effects
Drug metabolism	Decreased liver blood flow, liver organ size, and enzyme concentrations decrease the rate of drug metabolism and increase the duration and intensity of drug action
Drug excretion	Age-related decreases in renal function and blood flow slow the rate of drug excretion and increase the duration and intensity of drug action

either increased or decreased pharmacological effects in geriatric patients when compared to the effects produced in younger adults. Increased pharmacological effects are more common and usually observed as an increase in adverse or toxic effects. The changes in drug sensitivity may be caused by a number of factors: general state of health, nutritional status, presence of chronic disease, and alteration in the pharmacodynamic response to specific drugs.

Nutritional Status

Nutrition is extremely important to the state of health. Many of the elderly live alone or in unfamiliar surroundings such as nursing homes. The desire, ability, and affordability to prepare well-balanced meals are often lacking. An adequate diet is important in relation to liver function and the ability to metabolize drugs. Lack of adequate protein intake lowers the concentration of plasma proteins, especially albumin, necessary for plasma protein drug binding. Protein intake is also important for synthesis of drug-metabolizing enzymes. Protein deficiencies may increase the concentrations of "free drug" (unbound) and reduce the rate of drug metabolism, both of which can increase the duration and intensity of drug action.

General health and the ability of the body to maintain homeostatic mechanisms such as regulation of body temperature, blood pressure, cardiac output, and many other physiological processes are dependent in part on proper nutrition. Nutritional deficiencies also increase susceptibility to infection, disease, and the adverse effects of drug treatment.

Presence of Disease

The major chronic diseases of aging—hypertension, coronary artery disease, diabetes, cancer, and many others—all have effects that reduce vital organ function, especially of the heart, liver, and kidneys. Reduction of organ function decreases the ability of these organs to metabolize and eliminate drugs. Consequently, the actions and adverse effects of most drugs are increased. The consequences of disease on drug action increase as the number of diseases in any one individual increase. Table 3:2 lists the main effect of some of the more common disease-drug interactions.

Alteration of Pharmacodynamic Response

It is very difficult to evaluate changes in drug response that are not related to changes in the pharmacokinetic processes. While there may be some decreases in the number of drug receptors or drug receptor sensitivity with age, there are very few examples that have been well documented. One example that is often mentioned is a decrease in sensitivity of the elderly to beta-adrenergic drugs. It appears that actually more of a drug, such as isoproterenol, is required to increase the heart rate of elderly individuals. However, in most cases the elderly are more sensitive to the actions of drugs and experience greater pharmacological effects and higher incidences of adverse effects.

The elderly are often more sensitive to drugs that depress the central nervous system. Sedatives, hypnotics, antianxiety agents, antipsychotics, and antidepressant drugs

Common Disease-Drug Interactions in the Elderly

Disease	Drugs	Consequence
Congestive heart failure	Cardiac depressants: beta-blockers, some calcium blockers (verapamil, diltiazam)	Excessive cardiac depression, hypotension, cardiac arrest
Diabetes mellitus	Thiazide and loop diuretics, beta-blockers	Alteration of blood glucose
Hypertension	Nonsteroidal antiinflammatory drugs	Interfere with antihypertensive actions of diuretics and *ACE inhibitors
Hypokalemia	Thiazide and loop diuretics, cardiac glycosides (digoxin)	Increase loss of potassium and may cause cardiac arrhythmias
Mental depression	**CNS depressants, propranolol, antihypertensives causing CNS depression (clonidine)	Increase mental depression, precipitate depressive episodes
Prostatic hypertrophy	Anticholinergic drugs	Increase difficulty of urination, urinary retention
Renal disease	Nonsteroidal antiinflammatory drugs, aminoglycosides, amphotericin B	Decrease renal function, may cause renal failure
Respiratory diseases, bronchitis, emphysema	Nonselective beta-blockers	Bronchoconstriction, respiratory distress

*Abbreviations: *ACE, angiotensin–converting enzyme; **CNS, central nervous system.*

often cause excessive pharmacological and adverse effects in the elderly. This is often in the form of mental confusion, disorientation, and other neurological disturbances. Some of the antipsychotic, antidepressant, and antihistamine drugs possess anticholinergic activity (Chapter 7). Excessive anticholinergic effects frequently cause urinary retention, constipation, and a variety of neurological disturbances. There are many examples of drugs that require special consideration when prescribed for the elderly. Additional geriatric considerations with specific drugs will be presented in the appropriate chapters.

LO 3.5

DRUG COMPLIANCE IN THE ELDERLY

Drug compliance is extremely important in the elderly. The elderly are frequently confused by their dosing regimens. They often have difficulty understanding and remembering what the drug is and exactly why it was prescribed. The confusion is increased in those who already have problems with memory, who live alone, and who are not provided with sufficient time for instruction and training on the proper procedures for drug administration. The confusion increases in direct proportion to the number of different drugs and administration devices with which the individual is confronted. The term **polypharmacy** is used to describe the situation that involves multiple drug prescriptions. Forgetting to take the drug or not remembering whether or not the drug was already taken is the cause of many missed doses. The presence of unpleasant drug side effects also encourages noncompliance. Since physicians are often too busy to take the time to instruct patients, this is one of the important functions of allied health personnel. Time and patience are of extreme importance in these instructions. The attitude and demeanor of the person providing drug prescribing instructions are sometimes the key ingredients to successful drug compliance (Figure 3.1).

Another important consideration for compliance is the dosage form; for example, liquid, capsule, or tablet. Many elderly patients have difficulty swallowing large capsules. In addition, they often cannot get the lid off the drug container. There are easy-to-open lids for the elderly, available upon request. The elderly often have trouble reading the small print on drug labels or identifying the different drugs. Sometimes describing the different drugs (the small white one, the large green one, etc.) may help them know which drugs to take at the proper times. Organizing a schedule of specific times for drug dosing, such as before a specific meal or just before bedtime, is also important for establishing a routine that is less likely to be forgotten.

Figure 3.1

Home care nurse explaining medication to patient and spouse.

Chapter Review

Understanding Terminology

Match the appropriate answer, a or b, with the numbered statement in relationship to drug use in the elderly. **(LO 3.1, LO 3.2, LO 3.3, LO 3.4, LO 3.5)**

a. Increased duration and/or intensity of drug action
b. Decreased duration and/or intensity of drug action

___ 1. Cirrhosis of the liver

___ 2. Drug noncompliance

___ 3. An increase in creatinine levels in the blood

___ 4. Drugs that cause microsomal enzyme induction

___ 5. Renal disease

___ 6. Malnutrition

___ 7. Drugs that increase liver blood flow

___ 8. Enterohepatic recycling of drugs

___ 9. Decrease in plasma proteins

___ 10. Lipid-soluble drugs

Acquiring Knowledge

Answer the following questions.

11. Describe three changes in body composition that occur with aging. **(LO 3.1)**

12. What are the major age-related changes that occur in the liver? **(LO 3.3)**

13. Briefly explain the importance of creatinine in relation to renal function. **(LO 3.3)**

14. Describe three factors of drug compliance that are relative to geriatric patients. **LO 3.5)**

15. What are adverse effects of excessive anticholinergic drug action in the elderly? **(LO 3.4)**

16. Explain how lower concentrations of plasma proteins can increase drug response. **(LO 3.2)**

Applying Knowledge on the Job

Use your critical-thinking skills to answer the following questions.

1. Mr. Green is 75 years old and in the doctor's office for his first checkup after being prescribed digoxin (*Lanoxin*) once daily and chlorothiazide (*Diuril*) two times a day (BID) for congestive heart failure. He still has some signs of heart failure and has admitted that he sometimes forgets to take his pills. He also has trouble reading the labels and isn't sure which pill he is supposed to take again at night. Can you give some instructions that might help Mr. Green become more compliant? **(LO 3.5)**

2. Mrs. Jones is 68 years old and has a history of diabetes and hypertension for which she takes medication. Over the years the diabetes seems to be decreasing her kidney function, and lately her urine samples show the presence of protein. She has recently experienced episodes of dizziness and her blood pressure recording during her checkup today was quite low. Could Mrs. Jones's blood pressure medication dosage be too high? What might be occurring here that may need some adjustment? **(LO 3.4)**

3. Mr. Smith has a cancer tumor that has become resistant to chemotherapy. He has experienced dramatic weight loss and his appetite is poor. Medications for his heart condition that were well tolerated in the past have now begun to cause toxicity. List the factors that may be responsible for this recent increase in drug toxicity. **(LO 3.3)**

4. Explain how the development of congestive heart failure could lead to a decrease in the rate of drug metabolism and drug excretion. **(LO 3.4)**

Multiple Choice

Use your critical-thinking skills to answer the following questions.

1. The main effect of aging on drug absorption is **(LO 3.2)**
   A. increased intestinal surface area
   B. increased onset of action
   C. slowing of drug absorption
   D. increased blood flow to intestines

2. Drug distribution is affected with aging due to **(LO 3.2)**
   A. increased lean body mass
   B. decreased total body water
   C. decreased percentage of body fat
   D. increased concentration of plasma proteins

3. The measurement of creatinine can be used to evaluate **(LO 3.3)**
   A. liver function
   B. renal function
   C. cardiac function
   D. intestinal function

4. Select the factor that **would not** cause a decrease in drug metabolism in the elderly. **(LO 3.4)**
   A. increased liver blood flow
   B. decreased drug microsomal enzymes
   C. reduced liver organ size
   D. decreased cardiac output

5. Nutritional deficiencies, particularly decreased protein intake, can **(LO 3.4)**
   A. increase plasma protein concentration
   B. decrease concentration of unbound free drug
   C. decrease drug metabolizing enzymes
   D. decrease duration and intensity of drug action

Multiple Choice (Multiple Answer)

Select the correct choices for each statement. The choices may be all correct, all incorrect, or any combination.

1. Select the factors of aging that affect the distribution of drugs. **(LO 3.2)**
   A. increased renal function
   B. decreased intestinal blood flow
   C. increased fat content
   D. decreased lean body mass

2. Which of the following drugs interact with renal disease to decrease renal function? **(LO 3.4)**
   A. aminoglycosides
   B. nonselective beta-blockers
   C. cardiac glycosides
   D. nonsteroidal antiinflammatories

3. Age-related physiological changes that occur in humans include **(LO 3.1)**
   A. decreased cardiac output
   B. decrease in organ size
   C. decreased blood flow to the liver
   D. fewer cells to carry out organ functions

4. Changes to which pharmacokinetic processes lead to longer duration of action of drugs? **(LO 3.3)**
   A. excretion
   B. distribution
   C. metabolism
   D. absorption

5. Factors that affect patient compliance include which of the following? **(LO 3.5)**
   A. creatinine clearance
   B. polypharmacy
   C. dosage form
   D. enterohepatic recycling

Sequencing

Place the following in order, first to last, of the processes that occur in the body. **(LO 3.4)**

_____ _____ _____ _____

First   **Last**

Reduced rate of drug metabolism

Increased duration of drug action

Inadequate protein intake

Decreased plasma protein concentration

Classification

Place the following age-related changes under the pharmacokinetic phase they affect. **(LO 3.2, LO 3.3)**

Decreased intestinal motility   Decrease in liver size

Decreased body water   Decreased blood flow to kidneys

Decreased plasma proteins   Decreased enzyme production

Decreased glomerular filtration   Decreased gastric acid secretion

Absorption	Distribution	Metabolism	Excretion

For interactive animations, videos, and assessment visit:

www.mcgrawhillconnect.com

Chapter 4

Math Review and Dosage Calculations

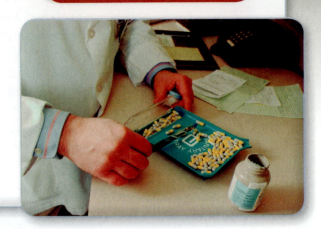

KEY TERMS

decimal: another way to write a fraction when the denominator is 10, 100, 1000, and so on.

denominator: bottom number of a fraction; shows the number of parts in a whole.

fraction: part of a whole.

improper fraction: fraction that has a value equal to or greater than 1.

mixed number: number written with both a whole number and a fraction.

numerator: top number of a fraction; shows the part.

percent: decimal fraction with a denominator of 100.

proper fraction: fraction that has a value less than 1.

proportion: a mathematical equation that expresses the equality between two ratios.

ratio: the relationship of one number to another expressed by whole numbers (1:5) or as a fraction ($\frac{1}{5}$).

solute: substance dissolved in a solvent; usually present in a lesser amount.

solution: homogeneous mixture of two or more substances.

solvent: liquid portion of a solution that is capable of dissolving another substance.

Learning Outcomes

After studying this chapter, you should be able to

4.1 solve basic arithmetical problems involving fractions, decimals, and percents.

4.2 write ratio and proportion equations and solve for the unknown term.

4.3 illustrate conversions from one metric unit of measure to another.

4.4 solve drug problems involving solutions and solid dosage forms.

4.5 solve problems involving pediatric dosing.

4.6 understand the monitoring of IV infusion rates.

Introduction

Because the intensity of drug response is directly related to dosage (dose-response relationship), administration of the proper drug dosage is essential to the practice of medicine. Drugs whose names look alike or sound alike (for example, *Demerol*/dicumarol, *Isordil*/isuprel) can cause improper drug selection. Mistakes in dosage calculation can cause insufficient drug response or excessive and potentially harmful drug effects. Consequently, it is essential for anyone responsible for administering medication to understand the proper procedures for dosage calculation. This chapter provides a brief review of math and dosage calculations in order to demonstrate the basic principles involved in these calculations. Programs requiring an extensive background in pharmacy and dosage calculations should consult textbooks devoted to this subject.

LO 4.1

FRACTIONS, DECIMALS, AND PERCENTS

A brief review of fractions, decimals, and percents is presented to refresh the memory for the basic arithmetical procedures used in dosage calculation.

Fractions

When something is divided into equal parts, one of the parts is referred to as a **fraction** (part of the whole). A fraction is composed of two numbers, a numerator and a denominator. The **numerator** is the top number of a fraction. It indicates how many parts are being referred to. The **denominator** is the bottom number of a fraction. It indicates how many parts something has been divided into.

Proper Fractions

Fractions whose values are less than 1 (the numerator is smaller than the denominator) are called **proper fractions.** The following are examples of proper fractions:

$$\frac{1}{4} \quad \frac{2}{3} \quad \frac{7}{8} \quad \frac{9}{10}$$

Improper Fractions

Fractions whose values are equal to or greater than 1 (the numerator is equal to or greater than the denominator) are called **improper fractions.** The following fractions are improper:

$$\frac{5}{5} \quad \frac{7}{5} \quad \frac{11}{6} \quad \frac{15}{8}$$

An improper fraction can be written as a **mixed number,** which is a whole number plus the fractional remainder. This is calculated by dividing the denominator of the improper fraction into the numerator and placing any remainder over the original denominator. If there is no remainder, the improper fraction is a whole number:

$$\frac{5}{5} = 1 \qquad \frac{7}{5} = 1\frac{2}{5}$$

$$\frac{11}{6} = 1\frac{5}{6} \qquad \frac{24}{8} = 3$$

The terms of a fraction can be changed without changing its value. Multiplying or dividing the numerator and the denominator of a fraction by the same number does not change the value of the fraction, as shown in the following examples:

$$\frac{2 \div 2}{4 \div 2} = \frac{1}{2} \qquad \frac{2 \times 3}{4 \times 3} = \frac{6}{12}$$

Fractions are generally written in their reduced, or lowest, terms. For example:

$$\frac{6}{12} \text{ reduces to } \frac{1}{2}$$

Reducing Fractions to Their Lowest Terms

Reduce a fraction to its lowest terms by dividing the numerator and denominator by the largest number that will divide into both of them evenly. For example:

$$\frac{15}{20} \div \frac{5}{5} = \frac{3}{4} \qquad \frac{35}{49} \div \frac{7}{7} = \frac{5}{7}$$

Multiplying Fractions

Multiply fractions by multiplying the numerators together and the denominators together and reducing to lowest terms. For example:

$$\frac{2}{3} \times \frac{3}{4} = \frac{6}{12} = \frac{1}{2}$$

If the fractions involve large numbers, reduce the numbers by dividing any numerator and any denominator by the same number. Repeat this cancellation process as often as possible. For example:

$$\frac{\overset{1}{\cancel{9}}}{\underset{2}{\cancel{18}}} \times \frac{\overset{1}{\cancel{27}}}{\underset{2}{\cancel{54}}} = \frac{1}{4}$$

$$\frac{\overset{1}{\cancel{4}}}{\underset{1}{\cancel{6}}} \times \frac{\overset{\overset{1}{\cancel{2}}}{\cancel{12}}}{\underset{\underset{2}{\cancel{4}}}{16}} = \frac{1}{2}$$

To multiply a whole number by a fraction, place the whole number over a denominator of 1 and then multiply numerators and denominators. For example:

$$10 \times \frac{1}{2} = \frac{10}{1} \times \frac{1}{2} = \frac{10}{2} = 5$$

Dividing Fractions

Dividing one fraction by another is similar to multiplying fractions. However, first you must invert the divisor before multiplying the numerators together and the denominators together. For example:

$$\frac{2}{3} \div \frac{3}{4}$$

$$\frac{2}{3} \times \frac{4}{3} = \frac{8}{9}$$

If the divisor is a whole number, place it over 1, invert it, and then multiply as before. For example:

$$\frac{3}{4} \div 4 = \frac{3}{4} \div \frac{4}{1} = \frac{3}{4} \times \frac{1}{4} = \frac{3}{16}$$

Decimals

Any whole number may be divided into tenths (0.1), hundredths (0.01), thousandths (0.001), and so on. These divisions of a number by orders of 10 (10, 100, 1000 etc.) are known as decimal fractions, or **decimals.** Decimals are another way of expressing fractions. For example:

$$\frac{1}{10} = 0.1 \qquad \frac{1}{100} = 0.01 \qquad \frac{1}{1000} = 0.001$$

To change a fraction to a decimal, simply divide the numerator by the denominator. Note that you may need to add zeros after the decimal point in the dividend. For example:

$$\frac{1}{4} = 4\overline{)1.00} = 0.25 \qquad (0.25)$$

To change a decimal to a fraction, place the decimal number over the order of 10 (10, 100, 1000, etc.) that corresponds to the last place of the decimal and reduce to lowest terms. For example:

$$0.5 \overset{\downarrow}{=} \frac{5}{10} = \frac{1}{2} \qquad 0.25 \overset{\downarrow}{=} \frac{25}{100} = \frac{1}{4}$$

tenths   hundredths

$$0.005 \overset{\downarrow}{=} \frac{5}{1000} = \frac{1}{200}$$

thousandths

Multiplying Decimals

Multiplying decimals is similar to multiplying whole numbers except for the placement of the decimal point. After multiplying the two decimal numbers, add the total number of decimal places (places to the right of each decimal point) and count off the total number of decimal places in the answer (product). Count from right to left, and put the decimal point in front of the last number you count. For example:

$$\begin{array}{r} 1.25 \quad \text{(2 decimal places)} \\ \times\, 0.25 \quad \text{(2 decimal places)} \\ \hline 625 \\ 250 \\ \hline 0.3125 \quad \text{(4 decimal places)} \end{array}$$

When an answer has fewer numbers than total decimal places, add zeros as placeholders to make up the difference.

$$\begin{array}{r} 0.5 \quad \text{(1 decimal place)} \\ \times\, 0.1 \quad \text{(1 decimal place)} \\ \hline 0.05 \quad \text{(2 decimal places)} \end{array}$$

Dividing Decimals

When dividing decimals, move the decimal place in the divisor to the far right and then move the decimal place in the number being divided by the same number of places. For example:

$$25 \div 0.05 = 0.05\overline{)25.000} \quad \overset{500.0}{}$$
(2 places)   (2 places)

$$0.010 \div 0.5 = .5\overline{)0.010} \quad \overset{0.02}{}$$
(1 place)   (1 place)

Percents

Percent means per hundred. So, **percents** are decimal fractions with denominators of 100. See the following examples:

$$10\% = \frac{10}{100} = 0.10$$

$$25\% = \frac{25}{100} = \frac{1}{4} = 0.25$$

Multiplying Percents

Change the percent to a decimal (in hundredths) and multiply. For example:

15 percent of 75   0.2 percent of 50

$$
\begin{array}{r}
75 \\
\times 0.15 \quad \text{(2 decimal} \\
\hline
375 \qquad \text{places)} \\
75 \\
\hline
11.25 \quad \text{(2 decimal places)}
\end{array}
$$

$$
\begin{array}{r}
50 \\
\times 0.002 \quad \text{(3 decimal places)} \\
\hline
0.100 \quad \text{(3 decimal places)}
\end{array}
$$

LO 4.2
DOSAGE CALCULATIONS

Health professionals today are very fortunate because pharmaceutical manufacturers prepare and market most drugs in convenient dosage forms. The metric system has essentially replaced the apothecary system, so mathematical conversions are rarely necessary. Also, the concept of unit dose packaging eliminates much of the time that was previously required for drug calculation and preparation. However, in certain situations, drug calculations are still required. These situations primarily involve the preparation of a drug dosage from a stock solution, vial, scored tablet, or calculation of dosage based on body weight or other body measurement.

Basic Calculations

Ratio is the relationship of one number to another expressed by whole numbers (1:5) or as a fraction ($\frac{1}{5}$). The lowest form of the ratio is determined by dividing the smaller number into the larger number. In this example, the ratio would be 5:1.

Proportion is a mathematical equation that expresses the equality between two ratios.

EXAMPLE   25:5 = 50:10
The first (25) and last terms (10) are called the extremes. The second (5) and third terms (50) are called the means. The product (multiplication) of the extremes must equal the product of the means.

$$
\begin{array}{c}
\text{means} \\
\downarrow \quad \downarrow \\
25{:}5 = 50{:}10 \\
\uparrow \qquad \uparrow \\
\text{extremes} \\
25 \times 10 = 5 \times 50 \\
250 = 250
\end{array}
$$

When one of the numbers in the proportion is not known, the proportion equation can be solved for the unknown (referred to as X).

EXAMPLE   There are 10 milligrams (mg) of drug per milliliter (ml) of solution. How many milliliters must be administered in order to provide 65 mg of drug?

10 mg:1 ml (what you know) = 65 mg:X ml (what you need to know)

$$
10X = 65
$$
$$
X = 6.5 \text{ ml}
$$

Remember, the smaller known ratio is put to the left of the equal sign and the unknown ratio is put to the right of the equal sign. Solve for X by multiplying the means and the extremes.

LO 4.3
SYSTEMS OF MEASUREMENT

Metric System

The metric system is the preferred system for scientific measurement. The units of measure for the metric system are meter (length), gram (weight), and liter (volume). A convenient feature of the metric system is that measurements are in decimal progression, so that 10 units of one size equal 1 unit of the next-higher size.

The names of the metric system are formed by joining Greek and Latin prefixes with the terms *meter, gram,* and *liter:*

milli— $\frac{1}{1000}$ (0.001)	deka—10
centi— $\frac{1}{100}$ (0.01)	hecto—100
deci— $\frac{1}{10}$ (0.1)	kilo—1000

Apothecary System

The apothecary system is an older system of measurement that is being phased out and rarely used today. The basic unit of measurement is the grain (gr). Only a few conversion values are included in this chapter to show the relationship to the metric system.

Household System

The household system is a less accurate system of measurement. It is mainly used in the home where dosages can be expressed in terms of common household measurements: teaspoon (tsp), tablespoon (tbsp), and liquid ounces (oz).

Conversion Tables
Weights

1 kilogram (kg) = 1000 grams (g)

1 gram (g) = 1000 milligrams (mg)

1 milligram (mg) = 1000 micrograms (mcg)

1 grain (gr, apothecary system) = 60.0 mg

$\frac{1}{2}$ grain (gr, apothecary system) = 30.0 mg

Volumes

1 liter (l) = 1000 milliliters (ml), 1000 cubic centimeters (cc), or approximately 1 quart

500 ml = approximately 1 pint

250 ml = approximately 8 fluid ounces = 1 cup

30.0 ml = approximately 1 fluid ounce

1.0 ml = 1.0 cc (cubic centimeters)

Approximate Household Measures

60 drops (gtt) = 1 teaspoon (tsp)

1 teaspoonful (tsp) = approximately 5.0 ml

1 tablespoonful (tbsp) = approximately 15.0 ml

2 tablespoons (tbsp) = approximately 1 fluid ounce (oz)

1 measuring cup = approximately 8 fluid ounces (oz)

Conversions

It is frequently necessary to make conversions of solution concentrations from liters (l) to milliliters (ml) and drug weights from grams (g) to milligrams (mg) or micrograms (mcg). Knowledge of metric system equivalents is essential to performing these simple conversions. Conversion problems can be set up as a proportion and solved for X.

EXAMPLE   Convert 1.5 liters (l) to ml.

$$1\,l{:}1000\ ml = 1.5\ l{:}X$$
$$1\,X = 1500\ ml$$
$$X = 1500\ ml$$

Alternate setup of proportion equation as a fraction:

EXAMPLE   Convert 1.5 liters to ml.

$$\frac{1\,l}{1000\ ml} = \frac{1.5\,l}{X\ ml}$$
$$X = 1000 \times 1.5$$
$$X = 1500\ ml$$

EXAMPLE   Convert 750 ml to liters (l).

$$\frac{1000\ ml}{1\,l} = \frac{750\ ml}{X\,l}$$
$$1000\,X = 750$$
$$X = \frac{750}{1000}$$
$$X = 0.75\,l$$

EXAMPLE   Convert 0.25 g to milligrams (mg).

$$\frac{1\,g}{1000\ mg} = \frac{0.25}{X\ mg}$$
$$X = 1000 \times 0.25$$
$$X = 250\ mg$$

EXAMPLE   Convert 350 mg to grams (g).

$$\frac{1000\ mg}{1\,g} = \frac{350\ mg}{X\,g}$$
$$1000\,X = 350$$
$$X = \frac{350}{1000}$$
$$X = 0.35\,g$$

Sometimes it is necessary to convert from one system of measurement to another.

EXAMPLE   Convert 500 ml to ounces (oz).

$$\frac{250\ ml}{8\ oz} = \frac{500\ ml}{X\ oz}$$
$$250\,X = 500 \times 8$$
$$250\,X = 4000$$
$$X = 16\ oz$$

PRACTICE PROBLEMS

Convert the following:

1. 500 mg = _____ g

2. 0.45 g = _____ mg

3. 0.03 l = _____ ml

4. 4 tbsp = _____ ml

5. 60 ml = _____ oz

Solve the following conversions by setting up a proportion equation:

6. 6 teaspoons (tsp) to tablespoons (tbsp)

7. 1.5 pints to ml

8. 5 grains (gr) to mg

9. 500 micrograms (mcg) to mg

10. 2500 grams (g) to kg

Solutions

A **solution** is a homogeneous mixture of two or more substances. The liquid portion of the solution is known as the **solvent** and the substance dissolved within the solvent is the **solute**. Solutions are commonly expressed as percentages (based on 100). There are three types of percentage solutions:

Weight in Weight (W/W)

Weight in weight solutions contain a given weight of drug (or other solute) in a definite weight of solvent so that the final solution is 100 parts by weight.

EXAMPLE   A 10 percent (W/W) solution of sodium chloride would contain 10 g of sodium chloride in 90 g of water.

Weight in Volume (W/V)

Weight in volume solutions contain a given weight of solute (drugs, salts) in enough solvent so that the final solution contains 100 parts by volume.

EXAMPLE   A 10 percent (W/V) solution of sodium chloride would contain 10 g of sodium chloride in enough water to make 100 ml of final solution.

Volume in Volume (V/V)

Volume in volume solutions contain a definite volume of solute added to enough water so that the final solution would be 100 parts by volume.

EXAMPLE   A 10 percent (V/V) solution of sodium chloride would contain 10 ml of sodium chloride (100 percent solution) in enough water to make 100 ml of final solution.

LO 4.4

CALCULATING DOSAGES

The proportion equation is useful for calculating dosages. Whenever three of the terms of a proportion are known, the unknown term can be determined if the equation is properly constructed.

EXAMPLE   Morphine sulfate injection for intravenous use is available in a concentration of 8 mg/ml of solution.

Calculate the number of ml required to administer a dosage of 20 mg of morphine sulfate.

$$\frac{8 \text{ mg}}{1 \text{ ml}} = \frac{20 \text{ mg}}{X \text{ ml}}$$
$$8X = 20$$
$$X = 2.5 \text{ ml}$$

EXAMPLE   There is a drug order for 50 mg of secobarbital (elixir). The stock bottle contains 22 mg of secobarbital in 5 ml of solution. How many milliliters should the patient receive?

$$\frac{22 \text{ mg}}{5 \text{ ml}} = \frac{50 \text{ mg}}{X \text{ ml}}$$
$$22X = 50 \times 5$$
$$22X = 250$$
$$X = 11.3636, \text{ or } 11.4 \text{ ml}$$

EXAMPLE   There is a drug order for 75 mg of meperidine (*Demerol*) to be administered intramuscularly (IM). *Demerol* is supplied in a 5 percent solution (W/V). A 5 percent solution (W/V) would be 5 g of *Demerol* in 100 cc or 50 mg/1 ml as it is written on the vial label. How many ml of *Demerol* should be administered to the patient?

$$\frac{50 \text{ mg}}{1 \text{ ml}} = \frac{75 \text{ mg}}{X \text{ ml}}$$
$$50X = 75$$
$$X = \frac{75}{50}$$
$$X = 1.5 \text{ ml}$$

EXAMPLE   Insulin is usually administered in a syringe (U-50 or U-100) that corresponds to the concentration of the insulin stock solution of 100 units per ml (U-100). If an insulin syringe is not available, a tuberculin syringe may be used (Figure 4.1). However, the unit dosage must be converted to ml using the proportion method. What would be the dose in milliliters for an order of 20 units of insulin U-100?

$$\frac{100 \text{ units}}{1 \text{ ml}} = \frac{20 \text{ units}}{X \text{ ml}}$$
$$100X = 20$$
$$X = \frac{20}{100}$$
$$X = 0.2 \text{ ml}$$

EXAMPLE   There is a drug order for 60 mg of drug. The drug is available in 20-mg tablets. How many tablets

Figure 4.1

Standard Insulin (U-100, U-50) and Tuberculin Syringes Used for Subcutaneous Injection of Insulin

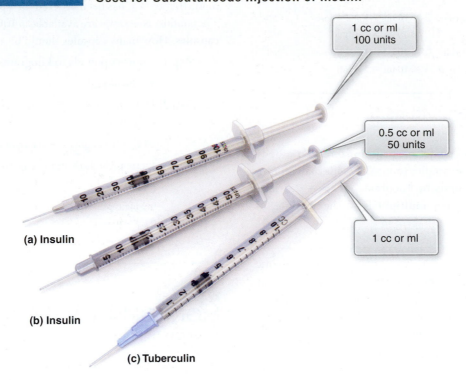

1 cc or ml
100 units

0.5 cc or ml
50 units

1 cc or ml

(a) Insulin

(b) Insulin

(c) Tuberculin

are required? The problem requires setting up a fraction based on the formula:

$$\frac{\text{desired dosage}}{\text{available dosage}} = \frac{\overset{3}{\cancel{60}}\text{ mg}}{\underset{1}{\cancel{20}}\text{ mg}}\,(1\text{ tablet}) = 3\text{ tablets}$$

A variation on this problem could be that 10 mg of a drug are desired:

$$\frac{\text{desired dosage}}{\text{available dosage}} = \frac{\overset{1}{\cancel{10}}\text{ mg}}{\underset{2}{\cancel{20}}\text{ mg}}\,(1\text{ tablet}) = \frac{1}{2}\text{ tablet}$$

(tablet must be scored for breakage)

EXAMPLE   An injection of 1000 units of tetanus antitoxin is ordered. The tetanus antitoxin is available in an ampule labeled 1500 units/ml. How many milliliters should be injected?

$$\frac{\text{desired dosage}}{\text{available dosage}} = \frac{\overset{2}{\cancel{1000}}\text{ units}}{\underset{3}{\cancel{1500}}\text{ units}}\,(\text{per milliliter})$$

$$= \frac{2}{3}\text{ ml} = 3\overline{)2.00}\;\;^{0.66\text{ ml}}$$

PEDIATRIC DOSAGE CALCULATIONS

Dosage calculations in pediatrics are based on age, body surface area (BSA), and body weight. BSA and body weight are the methods most frequently used to calculate pediatric dosages. Following are the formulas used for these calculations.

Clark's rule:

$$\frac{\text{weight of child}}{150\text{ lb}} \times \text{adult dose} = \text{child's dose}$$

Fried's rule:

$$\frac{\text{age in months}}{150} \times \frac{\text{average}}{\text{adult dose}} = \text{child's dose}$$

Body surface area (BSA) rule:

$$\frac{\text{body surface area of child (square meters)}}{1.7} \times \text{adult dose} = \text{child's dose}$$

EXAMPLE   Katie has just turned 3 years old and weighs 30 pounds. Her mother wants to know how much cough syrup to give Katie. The directions have worn off the bottle and she can only make out the dosage for adults—2 teaspoons every 4 hours. How much should Katie receive?

$$\text{Clark's rule: } \frac{30}{150} \times 10 \text{ ml} = \text{Katie's dose}$$
$$\frac{1}{5} \times 10 \text{ ml} = 2 \text{ ml}$$
$$\text{Fried's rule: } \frac{36}{150} \times 10 \text{ ml} = \text{Katie's dose}$$
$$0.24 \times 10 \text{ ml} = 2.4 \text{ ml}$$

Dosage Calculations Based on Body Weight

Drug dosages are sometimes administered on a body weight basis, for example, in mg/kg. This may require conversion of pounds to kilograms (1 kg = 2.2 lbs). The dose/kg is then multiplied by the number of kilograms.

EXAMPLE   There is a drug order for the antibiotic amikacin 7.5mg/kg administered intravenously (IV) for a patient weighing 110 pounds. Amikacin is available as 100 mg per 2-ml vial. How many milligrams of drug are required and in what volume?

Step 1: Convert pounds to kilograms.

110 lbs divided by 2.2 lb/kg = 50 kg

Step 2: Determine how many mg of drug are required.

7.5 mg/kg × 50 kg = 375 mg

Step 3: Determine how many ml of stock solution contains 375 mg, using the proportion equation method.

100 mg:2 ml = 375 mg:X ml
100 X = (375)(2) or 750
X = 750/100 = 7.5 ml of vial solution
($3\frac{3}{4}$ vials)

EXAMPLE   If the patient in the previous problem was an infant weighing 20 lbs with a body surface area of 0.44 square meter, what would be the dose according to the BSA rule?

BSA rule: BSA of child (square meters)/1.7 × adult dose

$$\frac{0.44}{1.7} \times 375 \text{ mg}$$
$$= 0.258 \times 375 = 96.75 \text{ mg or } 97 \text{ mg}$$

Since vials contain $\frac{100 \text{ mg}}{2 \text{ ml}}$, calculate volume

$$\frac{100 \text{ mg}}{2 \text{ ml}} = \frac{97 \text{ mg}}{X \text{ ml}}$$

100 X = (2)(97) or 194
X = 1.94 ml of vial solution

EXAMPLE   A loading dose of digoxin capsules (*Lanoxicaps*), 10 mcg/kg, has been ordered for a patient weighing 132 pounds. *Lanoxicaps* are available as 100- and 200-mcg capsules. How many capsules should be administered?

Step 1: Convert pounds to kilograms.

132 lbs divided by 2.2 lb/kg = 60 kg

Step 2: Determine how many micrograms are required.

60 kg × 10 mcg/kg = 600 mcg or 0.6 mg

Step 3: Determine how many capsules are required.

0.2 mg:capsule = 0.6 mg:X
0.2 X = 0.6
X = 3 capsules of 200 mcg

LO 4.6

MONITORING IV INFUSION RATES

Hospitalized patients often receive drug administration by slow IV infusion. Drugs are added to various sterile IV solutions such as sodium chloride injection, United States Pharmacopeia (USP), or dextrose (5%) injection, USP. Drug concentrations and solutions are prepared by the hospital pharmacy. The IV drug infusion solutions must be prepared under aseptic conditions, the drugs and solutions mixed must be chemically compatible, and often the infusion solution must be adjusted to a specific pH value. Preparation of these solutions should always follow established hospital procedures and be reviewed by a pharmacist.

After establishment of an open IV line, the drug solution is administered according to a specific infusion rate, in drops per minute (Figure 4.2). Usually there are 12–15 drops/ml of solution, but this number can vary with the viscosity of different solutions. Since allied health personnel are sometimes called upon to monitor IV infusion rates, the following example is presented to illustrate the principles involved.

Formula for adjusting IV infusion rate:

$$\frac{\text{ml of IV solution} \times \text{number of drops/ml}}{\text{hours of administration} \times 60 \text{ minutes}} = \text{drops per minute}$$

EXAMPLE   An IV infusion of furosemide (*Lasix*) 2 mg/min for 4 hours was ordered for a patient with severe edema. The hospital pharmacy prepared the infusion solution by adding 480 mg (2 mg/min × 60 × 4) in 500 ml

Figure 4.2

Adjusting the Drip Rate for Intravenous infusion

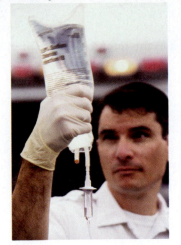

of sodium chloride injection, USP. How many drops per minute should be administered?

$$\frac{500 \text{ ml} \times 15 \text{ drops/ml}}{4 \text{ hours} \times 60 \text{ minutes}} = \frac{7500}{240} = 31.25 \text{ drops/min}$$

Regulate the IV flow by counting the drops (to nearest whole number) for 15 seconds and multiplying by 4 (for 1 min). Adjust the IV tube clamp until the correct rate is attained.

Chapter Review

Understanding Terminology

Match the term in the left column with the appropriate set of examples to the right. Use each set of examples only once. **(LO 4.1)**

___ 1.   Mixed numbers

___ 2.   Decimals

___ 3.   Proper fractions

___ 4.   Denominator

___ 5.   Fractions

___ 6.   Numerator

___ 7.   Improper fractions

a. $\dfrac{8}{16}, \dfrac{13}{27}, \dfrac{3}{4}$

b. $\dfrac{15}{12}, \dfrac{4}{3}, \dfrac{39}{18}$

c. $1\dfrac{1}{2}, 15\dfrac{4}{5}, 5\dfrac{17}{18}$

d. 1.5, 0.75, 12.3333

e. the 3 in $\dfrac{3}{4}$

f. the 4 in $\dfrac{3}{4}$

g. $\dfrac{1}{2}, \dfrac{7}{10}, \dfrac{5}{12}$

Answer the following question.

   8. Define *solution, solute,* and *solvent.* **(LO 4.4)**

Acquiring Knowledge

Answer the following questions and solve the following problems. **(LO 4.2, LO 4.3, LO 4.4)**

   1. Convert 0.125 g to milligrams.

   2. Convert 1200 ml to liters.

   3. Two teaspoons of cough syrup equal how many milliliters?

   4. One-quarter grain equals how many milligrams?

   5. Four fluid ounces equal how many milliliters?

   6. There is a drug order for 2.5 mg of glipizide (*Glucotrol*). Scored tablets are available in 5- and 10-mg strengths. Calculate the dosage. Why is the drug being given? (Refer to the *PDR*®.)

   7. After several days, the dosage of glipizide for the patient in Problem 6 has been increased to 7.5 mg. Calculate the dosage.

   8. There is an order for 75 mg of *Demerol Hydrochloride* syrup (USP). The syrup contains 50 mg of *Demerol Hydrochloride* per 5 ml. Calculate the dosage. What is the generic name of this drug? (Refer to the *PDR*®.)

   9. Several hours later, the patient in Problem 8 complained of severe pain. The order was changed to 100 mg administered by intramuscular (IM) injection. *Demerol Hydrochloride* is supplied as a solution in vials labeled 50 mg/ml. Calculate the parenteral dosage.

   10. A drug vial for parenteral injection is labeled "1 ml contains 50 mg." Calculate the amount required to administer a 30-mg dose.

Applying Knowledge on the Job

Use your critical-thinking skills to answer the following questions.

1. Assume that you're spending your summer as an intern in a university hospital pharmacy. One of your duties is to prepare desired dosages from available dosages to arrive at the correct weight or number of units of drug for each order the pharmacist fills. Show the calculations for the correct amount of drug for each of the following orders that were filled on your first day of work. **(LO 4.3, LO 4.4)**
   a. The first order called for 90 mg of drug. The drug is available in 30-mg tablets. How many tablets are required?
   b. The second order called for 2000 units of tetanus antitoxin. The tetanus antitoxin is available in an ampule of 1500 units/ml. How many milliliters should be injected?
   c. The third order called for 70 mg of secobarbital. The stock bottle contains 22 mg of secobarbital in 5 ml of solution. How many milliliters should the patient receive?

2. Bert just finished his training as a pharmacist assistant and started working in a nursing home dispensary last week. One of his job duties is to calculate the number of milliliters of drug-for-drug orders given in milligrams. Show how you would deal with the following patient orders if you had Bert's job. **(LO 4.3, LO 4.4)**
   a. There's a drug order for 100 mg of *Demerol* to be administered IM. The label on the stock bottle of *Demerol* says it's in a 5 percent solution, or 50 mg per ml.
   b. There's an order for a diabetic patient of 30 units of insulin. The stock bottle is labeled U-100, or 100 units per ml.

3. There is a drug order for diazepam (*Valium*), 0.5 mg/kg, administered orally. The patient weighs 110 pounds. *Valium* is available in 2-, 5-, and 10-mg tablets. How many milligrams and what combination of tablets will you administer? **(LO 4.3, LO 4.4)**

4. Ampicillin (*Omnipen*) oral suspension is available as 125 mg/5 ml. There is a drug order for 500 mg four times a day (QID). How many milliliters will you administer with each dose? How often will you administer the dose? **(LO 4.3, LO 4.4)**

5. The usual oral dose of ampicillin is 500 mg. How much should a 15-month-old baby receive according to Fried's rule? How much should a 50-pound child receive according to Clark's rule? **(LO 4.5)**

6. There is an order for 1000 ml of normal saline (0.9%) to be administered by IV infusion in 8 hours. The IV tubing delivers 15 drops per ml. How many drops should be administered per minute? **(LO 4.6)**

Multiple Choice Questions

Use your critical-thinking skills to answer the following questions.

1. The correct conversion from metric system to household system is **(LO 4.3)**
   A. 5 ml equals 1 tablespoon
   B. 15 ml equals 1 teaspoon
   C. 30 ml equals 1 fluid ounce
   D. 500 ml equals 1 measuring cup

2. Twenty percent (20%) of 90 equals **(LO 4.1)**
   A. 12
   B. 15
   C. 18
   D. 21

3. Drug X is to be administered intravenously at a dosage of 20 mg/kg. A patient weighing 60 kg should receive **(LO 4.1, LO 4.2)**
   A. 60 mg
   B. 120 mg
   C. 600 mg
   D. 1200 mg

4. There is a drug order for 75 mg of drug. The drug is available in 30-mg scored tablets. How many tablets should be administered? **(LO 4.2)**

A. 2   C. 3

B. 2½   D. 3½

5. An analgesic is ordered for intramuscular injection. If the concentration of analgesic available is 8 mg/ml, how many ml should be administered for a dosage of 20 mg? **(LO 4.4)**

A. 2.0   C. 3.0

B. 2.5   D. 3.5

Multiple Choice (Multiple Answer)

Select the correct choices for each statement. The choices may be all correct, all incorrect, or any combination.

1. Select all terms that define a denominator. **(LO 4.1)**

A. part of a whole

B. shows the part

C. parts in a whole

D. decimal fraction

2. Which of the following is the proper way to write the improper fraction $^{14}/_4$? **(LO 4.1)**

A. $^{14}/_4$

B. 1¾

C. 2½

D. 3¼

3. The correct way to divide one-half by five would be which of the following? **(LO 4.1)**

A. multiply ½ by ⅕

B. divide ½ by 5

C. divide 1 by ⅖

D. divide 1 by 10

4. Select the following terms that are equal. **(LO 4.2)**

A. 25000 mcg

B. 25 kg

C. 0.025 g

D. 0.0025 mg

5. Select the information needed to use Fried's rule. **(LO 4.5)**

A. height of child

B. body surface area

C. weight of child

D. age in months

Sequencing

Organize the following from largest to smallest. **(LO 4.3)**

_____ _____ _____ _____

Largest   **Smallest**

milliliter

kiloliter

deciliter

hectoliter

Classification

Place the following examples under the equal term. (LO 4.1)

0.5 $2^1/_5$ $^{66}/_{99}$

$^2/_3$ 0.75 $^{12}/_{24}$

$^{15}/_{20}$ ½   ¾

1½   0.66   2.2

$^{11}/_5$ $^6/_4$ 1.5

One-half	One and one-half	Three-quarters	Two-thirds	Two and one-fifth

Document Exercise

Using the prescription below, answer the following questions. (LO 4.3)

**Raven Clinic
Practice RX**

1000 Hospital Avenue
Anytown, USA   12345
360-555-1000

NAME: Jane Doe _____   DATE: _____

ADDRESS: _____

RX   Amoxicillin

Sig: 200mg twice daily for 10 days

Dr. Max Sanders _____ M.D.   _____ M.D.

Substitution Permitted   Dispense as written

DEA #: _____   REFILL: NR   1   2   3   4

Stock on hand available:

Amoxicillin 250 mg/5 ml in 150-ml and 75-ml bottles

   a. Calculate the amount needed for one dose.
   b. What would the total daily dose be?
   c. Calculate the total needed for the full prescription order.
   d. Which size of bottle would be most appropriate to dispense and why?

For interactive animations, videos, and assessment visit:
www.mcgrawhillconnect.com

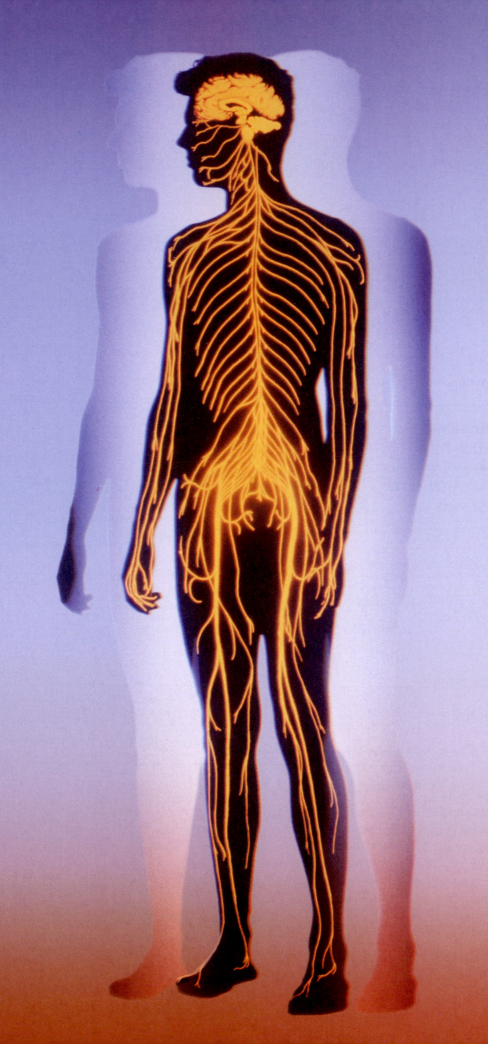

Pharmacology of the Peripheral Nervous System

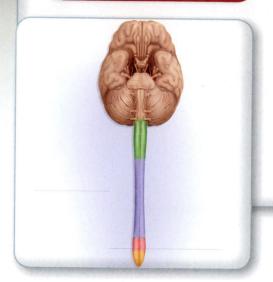

Chapter 5

Introduction to the Autonomic Nervous System

KEY TERMS

acetylcholine (ACH): neurotransmitter of parasympathetic (cholinergic) nerves; stimulates the cholinergic receptor.

adrenergic receptor: receptor located on internal organs that responds to norepinephrine and epinephrine.

afferent nerve: transmits sensory information from peripheral organs to the brain and spinal cord (central nervous system).

autonomic nervous system (ANS): system of nerves that innervate smooth and cardiac muscle (involuntary) of the internal organs and glands.

cholinergic (muscarinic) receptor: receptor located on internal organs and glands that responds to acetylcholine.

efferent nerve: carries the appropriate motor response from the brain and spinal cord to the peripheral organs.

epinephrine (EPI): hormone from adrenal medulla that stimulates adrenergic receptors, especially during stress.

fight or flight reaction: response of the body to intense stress; caused by activation of the sympathetic division of the ANS.

homeostasis: normal state of balance among the body's internal organs.

neurotransmitter: substance that stimulates internal organs to produce characteristic changes associated with sympathetic and parasympathetic divisions.

norepinephrine (NE): neurotransmitter of sympathetic (adrenergic) nerves that stimulates the adrenergic receptors.

parasympathetic: refers to nerves of the ANS that originate in the brain and sacral portion of the spinal cord; they are active when the body is at rest or trying to restore body energy and function.

sympathetic: refers to nerves of the ANS that originate from the thoracolumbar portion of the spinal cord; they are active when the body is under stress or when it is exerting energy.

After studying this chapter, you should be able to

5.1 describe the two divisions of the ANS and the main functions of each division.

5.2 explain how sympathetic and parasympathetic nerves interact with each other to regulate organ function (maintain homeostasis).

5.3 describe the fight or flight reaction and explain how sympathetic activation affects the activities of the different organs.

5.4 list the main organ effects caused by parasympathetic stimulation.

5.5 describe the different autonomic receptors that are stimulated by acetylcholine, norepinephrine, and epinephrine.

The primary function of the central nervous system is to control and coordinate the activity of all the systems in the body. The overall activity of the nervous system at any moment depends on neural communication (via nerve impulses) among many areas of the body. The autonomic nervous system is a subdivision of the central nervous system that regulates the activities of the internal organs and glands. The internal organs and glands are under involuntary or unconscious control. Before discussing the pharmacology of the autonomic nervous system, it is helpful to briefly review the general organization of the nervous system and the major anatomic and physiologic features of the autonomic nervous system.

LO 5.1

NERVOUS SYSTEM ORGANIZATION

The nervous system is an elaborate system that functions at both conscious (under control of the will, or voluntary) and unconscious (not under control of the will, or involuntary) levels.

Central Nervous System (CNS)

The central nervous system (CNS) consists of the brain and spinal cord. The CNS receives and interprets sensory information (via peripheral **afferent nerves**) and then initiates appropriate motor responses (via peripheral **efferent nerves**). The structural and functional features of the brain and spinal cord are presented in Chapter 11.

Peripheral Nervous System (PNS)

The peripheral nervous system is composed of 12 pairs of cranial nerves and 31 pairs of spinal nerves. It is separated into two divisions—the somatic and the visceral—based on the type of muscle to which these nerves travel (innervate).

Somatic Division

The somatic nerves are the branches of the cranial and spinal motor nerves that innervate skeletal muscle (voluntary). These nerves are under conscious, or voluntary, control of the cerebral cortex.

Visceral Division (Autonomic Nervous System)

The visceral nerves are the branches of the cranial and spinal motor nerves that innervate cardiac and smooth muscle (involuntary) of the internal organs and glands. The visceral nerves, which are not under conscious control, are regulated by the hypothalamus and the medulla oblongata. The visceral nerves are commonly referred to as the **autonomic nervous system (ANS).**

OVERVIEW OF THE ANS

It is important to emphasize that understanding the physiology and pharmacology of the ANS can be challenging to beginning students. However, understanding the ANS is essential to understanding the actions of many drugs.

The ANS is composed of the nerves that innervate (or travel to) smooth and cardiac muscle. These two types of involuntary muscle are found in the walls of the internal organs and glands and possess a special property, autorhythmicity, which allows them to initiate their own contractions. This process can be demonstrated by removing the heart or a piece of intestine from a frog, placing the organ in oxygenated Ringer's solution, and observing the contractions that occur without any stimulation.

If the internal organs can initiate their own contractions, why is the autonomic nervous system needed? The answer is the key to the purpose of the ANS: the ANS functions to regulate the rate at which these organs work, either increasing or decreasing their activity. In this way, **homeostasis,** the normal balance among the body's internal organs, can be maintained.

Whether the activity of the organ increases or decreases depends upon body activity. But the question arises, "How can an autonomic nerve going to any visceral organ both increase *and* decrease the activity of the organ?" The answer is that it cannot. There are two divisions of the autonomic nervous system, the parasympathetic and sympathetic. Generally, each visceral organ receives a nerve from each division. One division usually increases the activity of a particular organ while the other decreases the activity. This is referred to as *dual autonomic innervation.*

PARASYMPATHETIC AND SYMPATHETIC DIVISIONS

The ANS is composed of the parasympathetic and sympathetic divisions. The nerves of the **parasympathetic** division (also known as the craniosacral division) originate from the brain (cranial nerves 3, 7, 9, and 10) and spinal cord (sacral nerves S2 to S4). The cranial nerves supply the internal organs and glands of the head, thoracic cavity, and upper portion of the abdominal cavity. The sacral nerves supply the lower portion of the abdominal cavity and the pelvic cavity. The origin and distribution of parasympathetic nerves are shown in Figure 5.1. The nerves of the **sympathetic** division (known as the thoracolumbar division) originate from the thoracic and lumbar spinal nerves (T1 to L3). The thoracic nerves supply the internal organs and glands of the head, thoracic cavity, and upper abdominal cavity. The lumbar nerves supply the lower portion of the abdominal cavity and the pelvic cavity. The origin and distribution of sympathetic nerves are shown in Figure 5.2.

As a result, most of the major body organs and glands receive a nerve from each division. There are exceptions; for example, most blood vessels do not receive parasympathetic innervation. In this situation, blood pressure is controlled by either increasing sympathetic activity to cause vasoconstriction or decreasing sympathetic activity to cause vasodilation (Figure 5.3). However, the general plan is that one division is responsible for increasing the activity of a particular organ, while the other division decreases the activity of that organ. Unfortunately, one division does not *always* increase activity and the other division *always* decrease activity in each of the organs. How is the effect of each division predicted? The answer is that sympathetic stimulation produces changes in the body that are similar to changes observed during frightening or emergency situations. These changes are collectively referred to as **fight or flight reaction.** During the fight or flight reaction, the adrenal medulla releases epinephrine (also known as adrenaline) and some norepinephrine into the blood. These neurotransmitters then act as hormones and travel to all sympathetic receptor sites producing intense sympathetic stimulation.

During the fight or flight reaction, the sympathetic division increases the activity of certain organs to allow a greater expenditure of energy for both physical and mental exertion. For example, sympathetic stimulation increases heart rate and the force of myocardial contraction; also bronchodilation allows for more air exchange in the lungs. At the same time, there is a decrease in the activity of the organs whose functions are not required for the fight or flight reaction. For example, activity of the gastrointestinal and urinary tracts is inhibited.

The parasympathetic division is more active during periods of rest and restoration of body energy stores. The parasympathetic nerves increase body functions such as digestion and elimination of waste products (urination, defecation).

Normally, we do not experience situations in which we need the fight or flight reaction to enable us to fight or run. However, the daily stresses, anxieties, and illnesses we do experience are sufficient to activate the sympathetic system to produce changes that are similar

Figure 5.1

Schematic of the Parasympathetic Nervous System Showing the Origin and Distribution of Parasympathetic Nerves

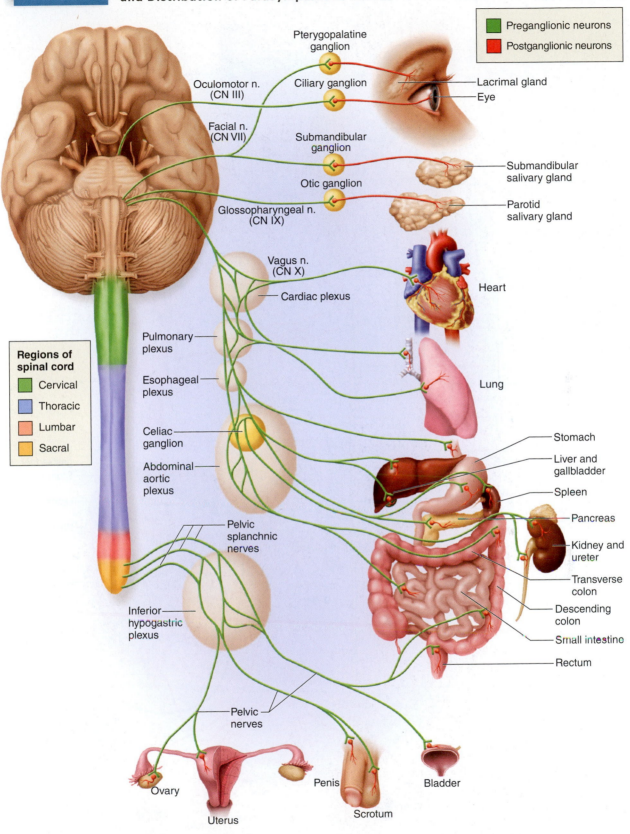

Pterygopalatine ganglion

Oculomotor n. (CN III)

Ciliary ganglion

Facial n. (CN VII)

Submandibular ganglion

Otic ganglion

Glossopharyngeal n. (CN IX)

Vagus n. (CN X)

Cardiac plexus

Pulmonary plexus

Esophageal plexus

Celiac ganglion

Abdominal aortic plexus

Pelvic splanchnic nerves

Inferior hypogastric plexus

Pelvic nerves

Lacrimal gland

Eye

Submandibular salivary gland

Parotid salivary gland

Heart

Lung

Stomach

Liver and gallbladder

Spleen

Pancreas

Kidney and ureter

Transverse colon

Descending colon

Small intestine

Rectum

Ovary

Uterus

Penis

Scrotum

Bladder

Preganglionic neurons
Postganglionic neurons

Regions of spinal cord
- Cervical
- Thoracic
- Lumbar
- Sacral

Figure 5.2 Schematic of the Sympathetic Nervous System Showing the Origin and Distribution of Sympathetic Nerves

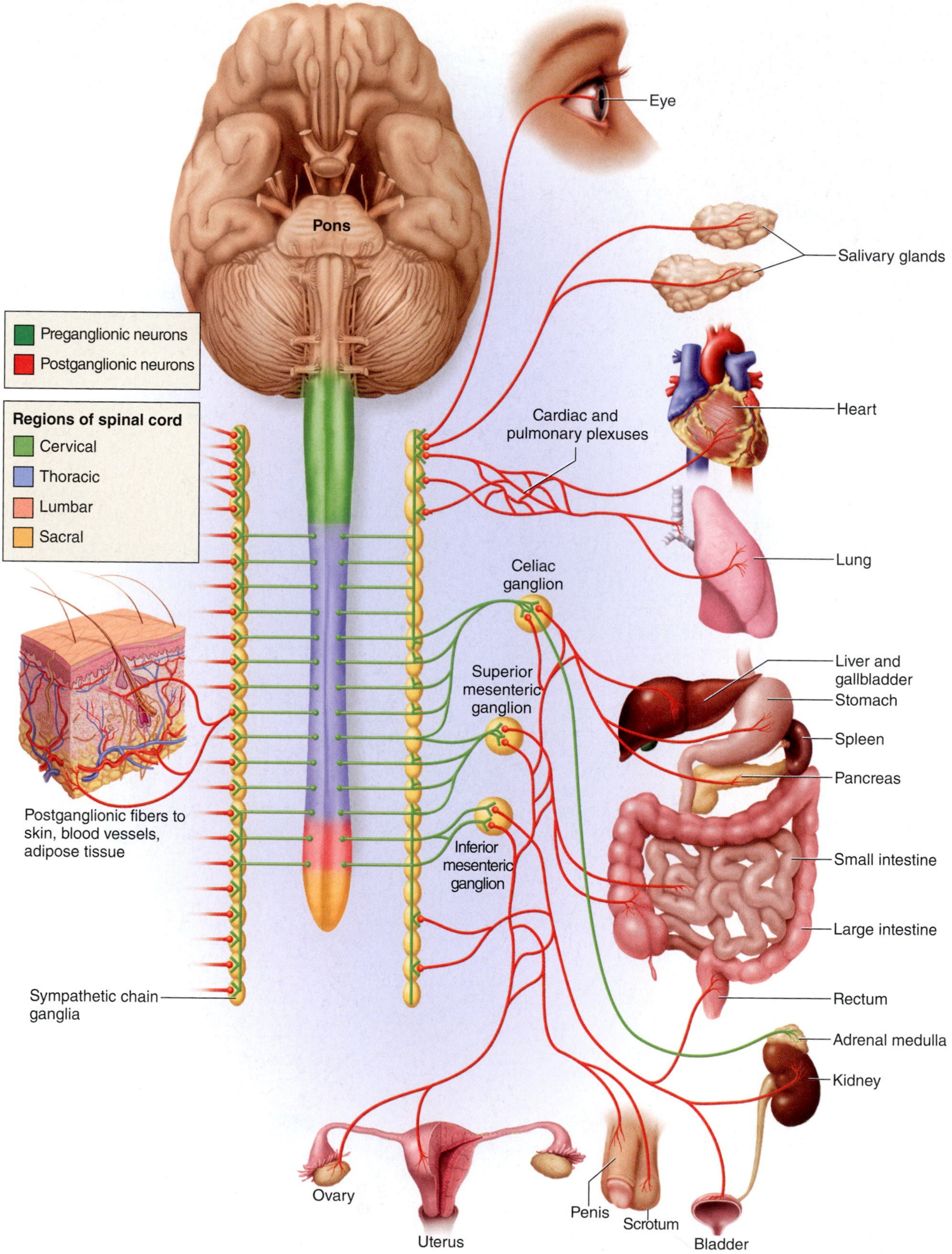

Pons

Preganglionic neurons
Postganglionic neurons

Regions of spinal cord
Cervical
Thoracic
Lumbar
Sacral

Postganglionic fibers to skin, blood vessels, adipose tissue

Sympathetic chain ganglia

Celiac ganglion

Superior mesenteric ganglion

Inferior mesenteric ganglion

Cardiac and pulmonary plexuses

Eye

Salivary glands

Heart

Lung

Liver and gallbladder

Stomach

Spleen

Pancreas

Small intestine

Large intestine

Rectum

Adrenal medulla

Kidney

Ovary

Uterus

Penis

Scrotum

Bladder

to the fight or flight reaction. When the sympathetic division is stimulated, all sympathetic nerves are activated at the same time. Therefore, the whole body is stimulated. With the parasympathetic division, only selected nerves can be stimulated, and the stimulation can be confined to a particular body system, for example, contraction of the urinary bladder during urination. The overall effects of sympathetic and parasympathetic stimulation are summarized in Table 5:1.

Usually in a beginning discussion of the ANS, only the peripheral motor (efferent) nerves are discussed. Peripheral autonomic nerves are the branches of the cranial and spinal nerves that travel to the cardiac muscle and smooth muscle of the internal organs. A typical peripheral nerve is composed of many neurons traveling together to the same destination. In an autonomic nerve, two groups of neurons are linked together by synapses as the nerve travels from the spinal cord to the internal organ. In the peripheral nervous system, a collection of synapses is referred to as a ganglion.

In the ANS, neurons that emerge from the spinal cord form the preganglionic nerve fiber. Neurons that travel from the ganglion to the internal organ form the postganglionic nerve fiber. The autonomic ganglion is the collection of synapses between the preganglionic and postganglionic nerve fibers, as illustrated in Figure 5.4.

The main pharmacological difference between the sympathetic nerves and the parasympathetic nerves is the **neurotransmitter** released from the postganglionic nerve ending of each division. The neurotransmitters bind to and stimulate various autonomic receptor sites (discussed below) that are located on the cell membranes of the internal organs and glands. This produces the characteristic effects that are associated with each division of the ANS (Table 5:1).

In the parasympathetic nervous system, the neurotransmitter released at the ganglia and the postganglionic nerve endings is **acetylcholine (ACH).** In sympathetic nerves, the neurotransmitter released at the

Figure 5.3 Vasoconstriction and Vasodilation

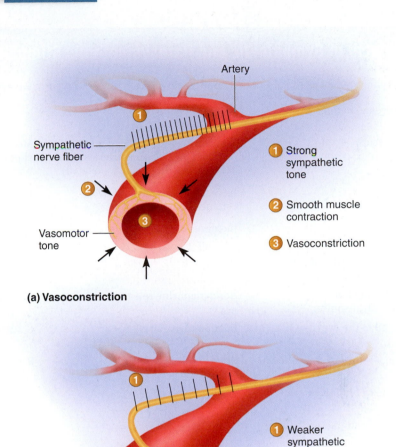

(a) Vasoconstriction

1. Strong sympathetic tone
2. Smooth muscle contraction
3. Vasoconstriction

(b) Vasodilation

1. Weaker sympathetic tone
2. Smooth muscle relaxation
3. Vasodilation

(a) Vasoconstriction in response to a high rate of sympathetic nerve firing. Vasoconstriction increases blood pressure but reduces blood flow. (b) Vasodilation in response to a low rate of sympathetic nerve firing. Vasodilation decreases blood pressure but increases blood flow. Black lines across each nerve fiber represent the firing frequency of action potentials.

ganglia is also ACH, but at the postganglionic nerve endings, it is **norepinephrine (NE).** Nerves that release acetylcholine are referred to as cholinergic, while nerves that release norepinephrine are referred to as adrenergic. The cardiac and smooth muscle membrane sites where these neurotransmitters act are known as the **cholinergic** (also known as **muscarinic**) **receptors** (ACH) and the **adrenergic receptors** (NE) as shown in Figure 5.5.

[Table **5:1**]

Effects of Sympathetic and Parasympathetic Stimulation

Organ	Sympathetic effect	Parasympathetic effect
Adrenal medulla	Release of epinephrine	—
Arteries	Vasoconstriction (exceptions are the coronary arteries and arteries to skeletal muscle, which are dilated)	Most arteries are not supplied by parasympathetic nerves
Heart	Increases heart rate and AV conduction	Decreases heart rate and AV conduction
	Increases contractility	Slight decrease in contractility
Intestines, GI motility, and secretions	Decreased	Increased
Postganglionic neurotransmitter	Norepinephrine released	Acetylcholine released
Pupil of the eye	Dilation (mydriasis)	Constriction (miosis)
Respiratory passages, lower	Bronchodilation	Bronchoconstriction
Urinary bladder	Relaxation	Contraction
Urinary sphincter	Contraction	Relaxation

Figure 5.4 **Diagrammatic Representation of an Autonomic Preganglionic Nerve Fiber**

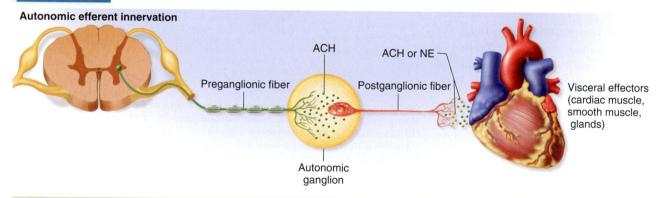

Autonomic efferent innervation

ACH

ACH or NE

Preganglionic fiber

Postganglionic fiber

Visceral effectors (cardiac muscle, smooth muscle, glands)

Autonomic ganglion

The nerve fiber (emerging from the spinal cord) synapses at an autonomic ganglion with a postganglionic nerve fiber that terminates on an internal organ (heart). In the parasympathetic division, the postganglionic nerve fiber is cholinergic and releases ACH. In the sympathetic division, the postganglionic nerve fiber is adrenergic and releases NE. The neurotransmitter released from preganglionic nerve fibers at the autonomic ganglion of both divisions is ACH.

In summary, the effects of parasympathetic stimulation are produced by the release of acetylcholine, which binds to the cholinergic receptors. The effects of sympathetic stimulation are produced by the release of norepinephrine from adrenergic nerve endings and also by **epinephrine** (EPI) released from the adrenal medulla. Both norepinephrine and epinephrine bind to and stimulate adrenergic receptors.

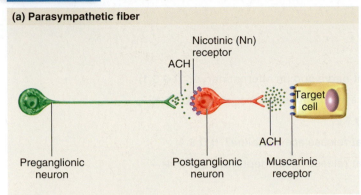

(a) Parasympathetic fiber

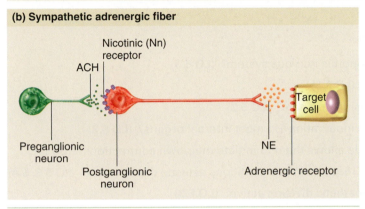

(b) Sympathetic adrenergic fiber

(a) Parasympathetic pre- and postganglionic neurons releasing ACH on both the ganglionic nicotinic (Nn) and muscarinic (cholinergic) receptors. (b) Sympathetic pre- and postganglionic neurons releasing ACH at the ganglionic nicotinic (Nn) receptor and NE at the adrenergic receptor.

LO 5.5

CHOLINERGIC AND ADRENERGIC RECEPTORS

The most confusing aspect of autonomic pharmacology is gaining an understanding of the different cholinergic and adrenergic receptors. What follows is a brief description and overview of these receptors that will be further discussed in the following chapters.

In the parasympathetic division there are two main types of cholinergic receptors: muscarinic and nicotinic. These names originate from early pharmacologic studies with substances (drugs) obtained from mushrooms (muscarine) and tobacco (nicotine). This terminology was established before the discovery of ACH. Muscarine and nicotine were found to stimulate the activity of different parasympathetic receptors. Following the discovery of ACH, it was determined that ACH stimulated both the muscarinic and nicotinic receptors and was the neurotransmitter of the parasympathetic division. The

term *cholinergic receptor* was introduced to refer to the receptor binding of ACH. The older terms, *muscarinic* and *nicotinic,* are still used because they differentiate the different cholinergic sites. Muscarinic receptors are located on the cell membranes of the visceral organs and glands and are stimulated by ACH released from parasympathetic postganglionic nerve endings. The resulting effects depend on the individual organ; some organ actions are increased (GI tract), while others are decreased (heart). There are two types of nicotinic receptors: nicotinic-nerve (Nn) and nicotinic-muscle (Nm). Nn receptors are located at both the parasympathetic and sympathetic ganglia and are stimulated by ACH released from preganglionic nerve endings to conduct impulses across the autonomic ganglia to the postganglionic fibers of both autonomic divisions. Nm receptors are located on cell membranes of skeletal muscle and are stimulated by ACH from somatic nerve endings to contract skeletal muscle. These Nm receptors are somatic, not autonomic, and will be discussed separately in Chapter 9 with the skeletal muscle relaxant drugs.

In the sympathetic division, the postganglionic neurons release NE, which stimulates the adrenergic receptors. The adrenergic receptors are divided into alpha and beta receptors. There are several subtypes of each. The most important with regard to drug actions are the alpha-1, beta-1, and beta-2 receptors. Individual organs usually possess one type of receptor, but there are a few exceptions. The definition or action of alpha-1 receptor stimulation is the contraction of smooth muscle; for example, vasoconstriction of blood vessels. Beta-1 receptors are located mainly on the heart and mediate cardiac stimulation, an increase in heart rate and force of contraction. Beta-2 receptors are located on smooth muscle and produce relaxation of smooth muscle; for example, relaxation of respiratory smooth muscle (bronchodilation).

There are specific drugs that can selectively bind to and stimulate or block the individual cholinergic and adrenergic receptors. For example, there are alpha-1 agonist and alpha-1 antagonist drugs, and a variety of beta-1 and beta-2 agonist and antagonist drugs. The effects produced by the agonist drugs are opposite to those of the antagonist drugs. Depending on the clinical situation being treated, it is possible to selectively increase or decrease the function of a particular organ or system. The following chapters will discuss the individual drug classes and major pharmacologic features.

Chapter Review

Understanding Terminology

Answer the following questions.

___ 1. What is the difference between an afferent nerve and an efferent nerve? **(LO 5.1)**

___ 2. Differentiate between adrenergic receptors and cholinergic receptors. **(LO 5.4)**

___ 3. What is the meaning of homeostasis? **(LO 5.2)**

___ 4. What terminology is applied to nerves that release acetylcholine? **(LO 5.4)**

___ 5. What terminology is applied to nerves that release norepinephrine? **(LO 5.4)**

Acquiring Knowledge

Answer the following questions.

1. What are the two main divisions of the autonomic nervous system? **(LO 5.3)**

2. What is the main function of each division? **(LO 5.3)**

3. From what areas of the CNS does each division originate? **(LO 5.3)**

4. What is the significance of "dual autonomic innervation" to most internal organs? **(LO 5.2)**

5. What property of smooth and cardiac muscle allows them to initiate their own contractions? **(LO 5.2)**

6. Describe what is meant by the fight or flight reaction. What conditions activate this reaction? **(LO 5.3, 5.4)**

7. During what body activities is the parasympathetic division active? **(LO 5.3)**

8. Think of an emergency situation requiring immediate and intense physical exertion. List as many body organs as you can and predict the desired level of activity (increased or decreased). Which neurotransmitter would produce this effect? Do your predictions correctly correspond to the fight or flight reaction? **(LO 5.3, 5.4)**

Applying Knowledge on the Job

Use your critical thinking skills to answer the following questions.

1. Use the *PDR*® product category index to look up drugs that mimic (parasympathomimetics) and drugs that inhibit (parasympatholytics) cholinergic activity. List one or two drugs from each category, the main drug effect, and clinical indications. Do your findings correspond to the expected effects of cholinergic stimulation and inhibition? **(LO 5.3, 5.4, 5.5)**

2. Use the *PDR*® product category index to find drugs that mimic (sympathomimetics) and drugs that inhibit (sympatholytics) adrenergic activity. List one or two drugs, the main drug effect, and clinical indications. Do your findings correspond to the expected effects of adrenergic stimulation and inhibition? **(LO 5.3, 5.4, 5.5)**

Multiple Choice Questions

Use your critical-thinking skills to answer the following questions.

1. Select the nerve–function combination that is correctly matched. **(LO 5.1)**
    A. afferent nerve—conducts nerve impulses to peripheral organs
    B. efferent nerve—conducts sensory nerve impulses
    C. autonomic nerve—conducts nerve impulses to visceral organs
    D. adrenergic nerve—conducts nerve impulses to skeletal muscle

2. Sympathetic activation produces all of the following effects *except* **(LO 5.3)**
   A. relaxation of urinary bladder
   B. increased heart rate
   C. pupillary dilation
   D. bronchoconstriction

3. The sympathetic postganglionic nerve ending releases **(LO 5.4)**
   A. epinephrine
   B. norepinephrine
   C. acetylcholine
   D. dopamine

4. The neurotransmitter released at both sympathetic and parasympathetic ganglia is **(LO 5.4)**
   A. acetylcholine
   B. dopamine
   C. epinephrine
   D. norepinephrine

5. Somatic nerves send nerve impulses to **(LO 5.1)**
   A. smooth muscle
   B. skeletal muscle
   C. cardiac muscle
   D. visceral organs

6. During the fight or flight reaction, the adrenal medulla predominately releases **(LO 5.4)**
   A. acetylcholine
   B. norepinephrine
   C. epinephrine
   D. dopamine

Multiple Choice (Multiple Answer)

Select the correct choices for each statement. The choices may be all correct, all incorrect, or any combination.

1. Which of the following belong in the CNS? **(LO 5.1)**
   A. spinal cord
   B. cranial nerves
   C. spinal nerves
   D. brain

2. Choose the body functions that occur during the fight or flight reaction. **(LO 5.3)**
   A. digestion
   B. urination
   C. elimination
   D. bronchoconstriction

3. Which of the following neurotransmitters work on the cholinergic nerves? **(LO 5.5)**
   A. norepinephrine
   B. epinephrine
   C. catecholamine
   D. acetylcholine

4. Select the nerves that are part of the parasympathetic division of the nervous system. **(LO 5.1)**
   A. thoracic
   B. lumbar
   C. cranial
   D. sacral

5. What happens when the parasympathetic nervous system is activated? **(LO 5.2)**
   A. All nerves are activated.
   B. Specific nerves are stimulated.
   C. The whole body is stimulated.
   D. No nerves are activated.

Sequencing

Place the following in order from first process to last process in vasoconstriction. **(LO 5.2)**

_____   _____   _____   _____

First   **Last**

vasoconstriction

smooth muscle contraction

strong sympathetic nerve firing

increased blood pressure

Classification

Classify the following as cranial or sacral parasympathetic nerves. **(LO 5.2)**

oculomotor nerve   vagus nerve

pelvic nerves   glossopharyngeal nerves

hypogastric nerves

Cranial	Sacral

Matching

Match the following effects of nervous system activation with the correct division. **(LO 5.4)**
   a. parasympathetic
   b. sympathetic

1. ____ increased GI motility
2. ____ urinary bladder relaxation
3. ____ increased heart rate
4. ____ pupil constriction
5. ____ urinary sphincter relaxation
6. ____ acetylcholine released
7. ____ vasoconstriction
8. ____ increased heart contractility

Labeling

Fill in the missing labels. **(LO 5.2)**

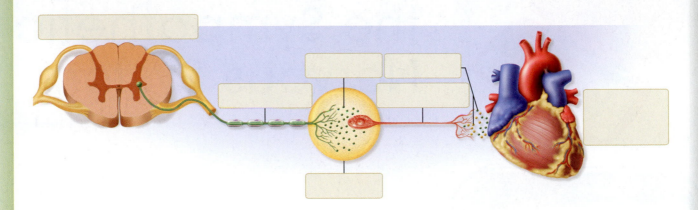

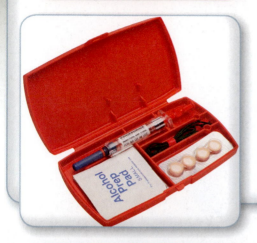

Chapter 6

Drugs Affecting the Sympathetic Nervous System

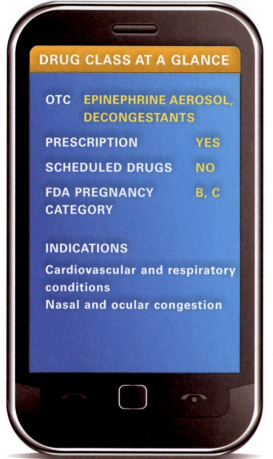

DRUG CLASS AT A GLANCE

OTC	EPINEPHRINE AEROSOL, DECONGESTANTS
PRESCRIPTION	YES
SCHEDULED DRUGS	NO
FDA PREGNANCY CATEGORY	B, C

INDICATIONS
Cardiovascular and respiratory conditions
Nasal and ocular congestion

KEY TERMS

adrenergic neuronal blocker: drug that acts at the neuronal nerve endings to reduce the formation or release of NE.

alpha-adrenergic drug: drug that stimulates the alpha adrenergic receptors.

alpha-1 adrenergic blocker: drug that blocks the alpha-1 effects of NE and EPI.

alpha-1 adrenergic receptor: receptor located on smooth muscle that mediates smooth muscle contraction.

alpha-2 adrenergic receptor: receptor located on adrenergic nerve endings that reduces the release of NE.

beta-1 adrenergic receptor: receptor located on the heart that increases heart rate and force of contraction.

beta-2 adrenergic receptor: receptor located on smooth muscle that relaxes smooth muscle when stimulated.

catecholamine: refers to norepinephrine, epinephrine, and other sympathomimetic compounds that possess the catechol structure.

false transmitter: substance formed in nerve endings that mimics and interferes with the action of the normal neurotransmitter.

nonselective beta-adrenergic blocker: drug that blocks both beta-1 and beta-2 adrenergic receptors.

nonselective beta-adrenergic drug: drug that stimulates both beta-1 and beta-2 receptors.

selective beta-1 adrenergic blocker: drug that blocks only beta-1 receptors.

selective beta-2 adrenergic drug: drug that stimulates only beta-2 receptors at therapeutic doses.

sympatholytic: refers to the action of an adrenergic blocking drug or an action that decreases sympathetic activity.

sympathomimetic: refers to the action of an adrenergic drug or an action that increases sympathetic activity.

After studying this chapter, you should be able to

6.1 explain how the adrenergic nerve endings function both to release and inactivate norepinephrine.

6.2 list the different adrenergic receptors and describe the actions they mediate.

6.3 explain the effects of norepinephrine (NE) and epinephrine (EPI) on alpha and beta receptors.

6.4 describe the main pharmacological effects and uses of alpha-adrenergic drugs.

6.5 describe the main pharmacological effects and uses of beta-adrenergic drugs.

6.6 describe the clinical indications and adverse effects associated with alpha-blocking drugs.

6.7 recognize the clinical indications and adverse effects associated with beta-blocking drugs.

6.8 describe the mechanism of action of the adrenergic neuronal blocking drugs.

Introduction

The sympathetic nervous system regulates the activity of the internal organs and glands when the body is expending energy during physical exertion and situations that are stressful or threatening to the body. Mental anguish, anxiety, physical trauma, and the discovery that one has developed a serious disease are examples of stressful conditions that activate the sympathetic nervous system. Peripheral sympathetic nerves, referred to as adrenergic nerves, release the neurotransmitter norepinephrine (NE). Norepinephrine binds to its adrenergic receptors and produces the effects that are associated with sympathetic stimulation.

The adrenal medulla releases the hormone epinephrine (EPI), which travels in the blood and also stimulates the adrenergic receptors. EPI (adrenaline) is released from the adrenal medulla in larger amounts during stress and emergency situations (fight or flight reaction). Norepinephrine and epinephrine are chemically similar and are generally referred to as the **catecholamines**.

The drugs used to affect sympathetic activity are classified as adrenergic drugs (agonists) that increase sympathetic activity and adrenergic blockers (antagonists) that decrease sympathetic activity. Adrenergic drugs are used to increase blood pressure, stimulate the heart, and produce bronchodilation. Adrenergic blockers are primarily used to lower blood pressure and reduce cardiac stimulation in conditions where there is excessive sympathetic activity.

LO 6.1
ADRENERGIC NERVE ENDINGS

It is important to have an understanding of how the adrenergic nerve endings function. The nerve endings are mainly concerned with the formation of NE. The adrenergic nerve ending takes up the amino acid tyrosine and through a series of enzymatic steps forms dihydroxyphenylalanine (DOPA) and then dopamine (DA), which is converted into NE. Norepinephrine is then stored within vesicles inside the nerve endings. When the adrenergic nerves are stimulated, NE is released. Norepinephrine then travels across the synaptic cleft to the smooth or cardiac muscle membrane, attaches to adrenergic receptors, and produces the sympathetic response. Most of the NE then passes back into the nerve endings (reuptake).

Inside the nerve endings, the NE may be reused or may be destroyed by the enzyme monoamine oxidase (MAO). These actions are illustrated in Figure 6.1.

Norepinephrine versus Epinephrine

Although NE and EPI are both adrenergic neurotransmitters, there are some important differences in the effects that each produces. Both NE and EPI stimulate many of the internal organs to increase sympathetic activity. EPI is only produced in the adrenal medulla. It is released into the bloodstream, where it acts as a hormone to stimulate all adrenergic receptors. One of the actions of EPI is to relax smooth muscle; NE does not relax smooth muscle. Relaxation of respiratory smooth

Figure 6.1

Schematic Representation of Neurohumoral Transmission at Adrenergic Nerve Endings

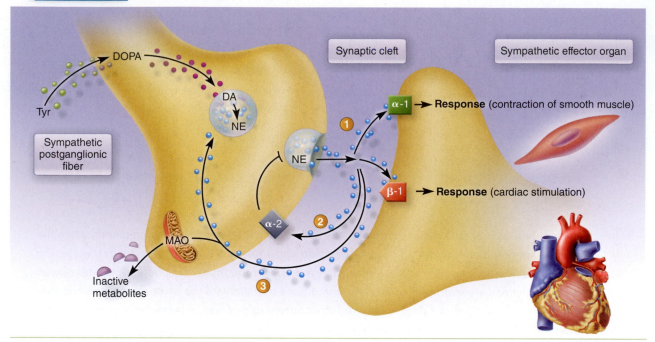

Tyrosine (Tyr) is taken up into the nerve ending and enzymatically converted to dihydoxyphenylalanine (DOPA). DOPA is converted to dopamine (DA), which enters storage vesicles where it is synthesized and stored as norepinephrine (NE). Upon adrenergic stimulation, NE is released from the adrenergic nerve ending into the synaptic cleft. NE then can (1) stimulate adrenergic receptors on internal organs and glands, (2) stimulate alpha-2 receptors on the postganglionic nerve ending to inhibit further release of NE, and (3) undergo reuptake back into the nerve ending for restorage in vesicles or metabolism to inactive metabolites by MAO.

muscle by EPI promotes bronchodilation. This effect fits into the fight or flight reaction because more oxygen passes into the lungs when the respiratory tract is dilated. Because of the differences in the responses produced by NE and EPI, several different adrenergic receptor types have been identified.

LO 6.2

ADRENERGIC RECEPTORS

The two main adrenergic receptor types are classified as alpha- and beta-adrenergic receptors. Alpha receptors are divided into alpha-1 and alpha-2 receptor subtypes. The beta receptors are divided into beta-1 and beta-2 subtypes. Although some organs contain more than one type of receptor, one receptor type usually predominates and determines the overall response of the organ. **Alpha-1 adrenergic receptors** are found predominantly on smooth muscle membranes of arteries, veins, and sphincters of the urinary and gastrointestinal tract. When stimulated by NE or EPI, they produce contraction; for example, vasoconstriction of most blood vessels. **Alpha-2 adrenergic receptors** are located on adrenergic nerve endings; they are activated by NE and EPI to activate a negative feedback mechanism that reduces and

regulates the release of additional NE. Drugs that affect this receptor are used in the treatment of hypertension and are discussed in Chapter 26.

Beta-adrenergic receptors are found on both cardiac and some smooth muscle membranes. In the heart, the predominant beta receptors are classified as **beta-1 receptors,** and when stimulated by NE or EPI, they increase heart rate and force of contraction. The predominant beta receptor in the smooth muscle of some organs and tissues is the **beta-2 receptor.** When these beta-2 receptors are stimulated by EPI, they produce vasodilation (mainly skeletal muscle blood vessels and coronary arteries) and bronchodilation (relaxation of bronchiolar smooth muscle). Note that alpha-receptor stimulation causes smooth muscle contraction at some organ sites while beta-2 receptor stimulation causes smooth muscle relaxation at other organ sites. Table 6:1 compares the effects of NE and EPI on the adrenergic receptors of several organs.

Although the classification system for the adrenergic receptors seems confusing, it is useful for classifying drugs. There are two general terms used to categorize drugs that affect the sympathetic nervous system. **Sympathomimetics** are adrenergic drugs (alpha and beta agonists) that produce effects that are similar to stimulating or mimicking the sympathetic nervous system.

Table 6:1

Effects of Norepinephrine and Epinephrine on Alpha and Beta Receptors

Receptor	Organ	Epinephrine effect	Norepinephrine effect
Alpha-1 (contraction of smooth muscle)	Most arteries and veins	Vasoconstriction	Vasoconstriction
	Iris muscle (eye)	Contraction—pupillary dilation	Contraction—pupillary dilation
Alpha-2	Adrenergic nerve ending	Decrease release NE	Decrease release NE
Beta-1 (stimulation of cardiac muscle)	Heart	Greater increase in heart rate, force of contraction, and atrioventricular conduction	Moderate increase in heart rate, force of contraction, and atrioventricular conduction
Beta-2 (relaxation of smooth muscle)	Bronchiolar smooth muscle	Bronchodilation	Norepinephrine does not stimulate beta-2 receptors
	Uterus	Relaxation	
	Skeletal muscle vessels and coronary artery vessels	Vasodilation	

Sympatholytics refer to adrenergic blocking drugs (alpha, beta, and neuronal blockers) that antagonize or decrease sympathetic activity.

Sympathomimetic drugs, including NE and EPI, that produce contraction of smooth muscle by stimulating the alpha-1 adrenergic receptors are referred to as **alpha-adrenergic drugs.** Drugs, including EPI, that both stimulate the heart (stimulate beta-1 receptors) and cause relaxation of smooth muscle (stimulate beta-2 receptors) are referred to as nonselective **beta-adrenergic drugs.** EPI is one of the few substances that stimulates all alpha and beta receptors. There are also beta-adrenergic drugs that selectively stimulate only the beta-2 receptors at therapeutic doses. These drugs are referred to as the **selective beta-2 adrenergic drugs** and are used primarily as bronchodilators.

Sympatholytic drugs that block the alpha effects of NE and EPI are known as the **alpha-adrenergic blockers.** Most alpha blockers available today only block the alpha-1 receptor (relaxation of smooth muscle). Drugs that block both the beta-1 and beta-2 effects of EPI are known as the **nonselective beta-adrenergic blockers.** Drugs that block only beta-1 receptors are known as **selective beta-1 adrenergic blockers.** The effect of these alpha- and beta-blockers is to decrease sympathetic activity, especially in the cardiovascular system. The blocking drug competes with NE or EPI for the receptor sites. When the blocking drug occupies the receptor, it prevents NE and EPI from producing an effect. Another method to inhibit the sympathetic system is to decrease the formation or the release of NE from the adrenergic nerve ending. Drugs that act at the adrenergic nerve endings to reduce the formation or release of NE are known as the **adrenergic neuronal blockers.** Table 6:2 summarizes the adrenergic drug classes, receptor sites, and main drug effects.

ALPHA-ADRENERGIC DRUGS

Norepinephrine is considered to be the parent or prototype drug for the alpha drug class. The alpha-adrenergic drugs have chemical structures and produce effects that are almost identical to those of NE. The most important clinical effect produced by the alpha-adrenergic drugs is stimulation of the alpha-1 receptors to cause contraction of smooth muscle. This includes vasoconstriction of most blood vessels, contraction of sphincter muscles in the gastrointestinal (inhibits movement of intestinal contents) and urinary (restricts passage of urine) tracts, and contraction of ocular muscles that causes dilation of the pupil of the eye (mydriasis). The actions on the sphincters of the GI and urinary tracts are not therapeutic and are usually side effects to the use of alpha drugs.

Clinical Indications

Alpha drugs are administered intravenously in hypotensive states; for example, after surgery, to increase

Summary of Major Adrenergic Drug Classes and Receptor Sites Acted Upon

Adrenergic drug class	Receptor site	Main drug effect
Sympathomimetics (Agonists)		
Alpha drugs	Alpha-1	Alpha-1 effect, contraction of alpha-1 mediated smooth muscle (vasoconstriction)
	Alpha-2	Alpha-2 effect, negative feedback effect to decrease release of NE
Nonselective beta drugs	Beta-1	Beta-1 effect, cardiac stimulation; increased heart rate and force of contraction
	Beta-2	Beta-2 effect, relaxation of beta-2 mediated smooth muscle (bronchodilation)
Selective beta-2 drugs	Beta-2	Beta-2 effect, relaxation of beta-2 mediated smooth muscle (bronchodilation)
Sympatholytics (Antagonists)		
Selective alpha-1 blockers	Alpha-1	Alpha-1 blockade, relaxation of alpha-1 mediated smooth muscle (vasodilation)
Nonselective beta-blockers	Beta-1	Beta-1 blockade, decrease cardiac function; decrease heart rate, contraction
	Beta-2	Beta-2 blockade, beta-2 mediated smooth muscle contraction (nontherapeutic)
Selective beta-1 blockers	Beta-1	Selective beta-1 blockade, decreases cardiac function (decrease heart rate, force of myocardial contraction)
Neuronal blockers	Adrenergic nerve ending	Interferes with synthesis and/or release of NE from nerve ending, decreases all sympathetic activity, lowers blood pressure and cardiac function

Note to the Health Care Professional

CAUTION

During intravenous infusion of alpha-adrenergic drugs, the IV needle should be checked frequently to make certain that the drug is not infiltrating the skin. Infiltration by alpha drugs causes intense vasoconstriction of skin blood vessels, which can lead to death of skin cells and gangrene.

blood pressure and maintain circulation. Vasoconstriction of blood vessels in mucous membranes of the nasal sinuses produces a decongestant effect. Consequently, some of these drugs are included in over-the-counter (OTC) cold and allergy preparations for relief of nasal congestion. A few of the alpha drugs also are used in ophthalmology to dilate the pupils (mydriatic drugs) and as ocular decongestants. Table 6:3 lists the alpha drugs and their main uses.

Adverse Effects

The major adverse effect of the alpha-adrenergic drugs administered by IV infusion is due to excessive vasoconstriction of blood vessels. This may result in increased blood pressure and hypertensive crisis. In some patients, this can lead to either hemorrhage (usually cerebral) or cardiac arrhythmias. Consequently, extreme caution must be observed with hypertensive or cardiac patients. Patients receiving parenteral administration of these drugs should have blood pressure recordings taken at frequent intervals. The most common side effect of decongestant use is irritation of the nasal sinuses or eyes due to excessive dryness caused by the vasoconstrictive decrease in blood flow.

Representative Alpha-Adrenergic Drugs

Drug (*Trade Name*)	Main use	Dosage forms
Drugs used to treat hypotension		
Metaraminol (*Aramine*)	Increase blood pressure	Parenteral injection
Midodrine (*ProAmatine*)	Increase blood pressure	Tablets
Norepinephrine (*Levophed*)	Increase blood pressure	Parenteral injection
Phenylephrine (*Neo-Synephrine*)	Increase blood pressure	Parenteral injection
Drugs used for nasal and ocular decongestion		
Naphazoline (*Privine*) (*Naphcon*)	Nasal decongestant Ocular decongestant	Nasal solution, spray Ophthalmic solution, drops
Phenylephrine (*Neo-Synephrine*)	Nasal decongestant	Nasal solution, spray
Pseudoephedrine (*Sudafed*)	Nasal decongestant	Tablets, capsules
Tetrahydrozoline (*Tyzine*) (*Visine*)	Nasal decongestant Ocular decongestant	Nasal solution, drops Ophthalmic solution, drops
Xylometazoline (*Otrivin*)	Nasal decongestant	Nasal solution, spray

LO 6.5

BETA-ADRENERGIC DRUGS

The beta-adrenergic drugs have a selective action to stimulate beta receptors. With the exception of NE and EPI, most beta drugs produce very few alpha effects.

Beta Drug Effects

The most important actions of the beta drugs are stimulation of the heart (beta-1) and bronchodilation (beta-2). Isoproterenol is the most potent beta-adrenergic drug that produces both of these effects. This dual action (heart and respiratory passages) is the main disadvantage of isoproterenol in treating bronchoconstriction caused by asthma or allergy. With isoproterenol, there is often overstimulation of the heart along with the bronchodilator effect. For this reason, a search was conducted to discover beta drugs that would selectively stimulate only the beta-2 receptors without causing excessive stimulation of beta-1 receptors in the heart. Several of these selective beta-2 drugs were discovered and are now widely used as bronchodilators. The use of beta-adrenergic drugs is discussed in Chapter 32 with the treatment of asthma.

Beta-2 receptors are also found in uterine smooth muscle. Stimulation of beta-2 receptors within the uterus relaxes smooth muscle and inhibits uterine contractions, which can occur during premature labor. Selective beta-2 drugs such as terbutaline may be used to arrest premature labor. Table 6:4 lists the various beta drugs and their main clinical uses.

Clinical Indications for Epinephrine

Epinephrine is the drug of choice for the immediate treatment of acute allergic reactions, such as anaphylaxis. Anaphylaxis can be caused by insect stings, drugs, or other allergens in sensitized individuals. There is difficulty in breathing, decreased blood pressure, and other symptoms of shock. In these situations, EPI (stimulates both alpha and beta receptors) administered by subcutaneous injection is the preferred treatment. For individuals who are susceptible to immediate-type (anaphylactic) allergic reactions, a preparation of epinephrine is available for immediate self-injection. *EpiPen* is designed as an auto-injector (*EpiPen Auto-Injector*) that delivers a

Beta-Adrenergic Drugs

Drug (*Trade Name*)	Receptors	Main use	Dosage form
Nonselective drugs			
Dopamine (*Intropin*)	Alpha, beta-1	Circulatory shock	IV infusion
Ephedrine (generic)	Alpha, beta-1, beta-2	Bronchodilator	Capsules, parenteral
Epinephrine (*Adrenaline*) (*EpiPen*) (*Primatene mist*)	Alpha, beta-1, beta-2 Same as above Same as above	Acute allergy/asthma Acute allergy Bronchodilator	Parenteral SC injection Parenteral IM injection Aerosol inhalant
Isoproterenol (*Isuprel*)	Beta-1, beta-2	Bronchodilator	Nebulization
Selective drugs			
Albuterol (*Proventil*)	Beta-2	Bronchodilator	Aerosol inhalant, tablets, syrup
Dobutamine (*Dobutrex*)	Beta-1	Acute heart failure	IV infusion
Isoetharine (*Bronkometer*)	Beta-2	Bronchodilator	Nebulization
Levalbuterol (*Xopenex*)	Beta-2	Bronchodilator	Nebulization
Metaproterenol (*Alupent*)	Beta-2	Bronchodilator	Aerosol inhalant
Salmeterol (*Serevent*)	Beta-2	Bronchodilator	Aerosol inhalant
Terbutaline (*Brethine*)	Beta-2	Bronchodilator Preterm labor	Parenteral injection, tablets

fixed amount of epinephrine by intramuscular injection (Figure 6.2). *EpiPen* must be carried by the individual and administered immediately following the onset of an anaphylactic-type allergic reaction. The alpha actions of EPI also are used during surgical procedures or in combination with local anesthetics to produce vasoconstriction. The alpha effect decreases blood flow and bleeding, and prolongs the action of local anesthetics at the site of injection. The beta effects of EPI are useful for cardiac stimulation (beta-1) in emergencies (such as cardiac arrest) and for bronchodilation (beta-2) in the treatment of asthma. Epinephrine is available OTC for inhalation as an aerosol for the relief of acute bronchospasm, but it is not recommended for the chronic control of asthma because of cardiac stimulation. The routes of administration and durations of action of the bronchodilators are presented in Chapter 32.

Dopamine

Dopamine functions as a neurotransmitter in the brain and also is formed as a precursor in the synthesis of NE in peripheral adrenergic nerve endings. When prepared as a drug and administered intravenously, dopamine produces several cardiovascular effects that are useful in the treatment of circulatory shock.

At low doses (0.5 to 2.0 mcg/kg/minute), dopamine stimulates dopaminergic receptors in renal and mesenteric blood vessels, resulting in vasodilation and increased renal blood flow. At moderate doses (2 to 10 mcg/kg/minute), dopamine also stimulates beta-1 receptors, which increases myocardial contractility and increases cardiac output. Increasing cardiac output and increasing renal blood flow are important actions during shock, when blood pressure and cardiac function are drastically reduced. At higher dosages, dopamine stimulates alpha receptors to produce vasoconstriction.

Dopamine is administered by continuous IV infusion, and the effects disappear shortly after the infusion is stopped. Adverse effects from overdosage usually involve excessive stimulation of the heart and increased blood pressure (alpha effect).

Dobutamine (*Dobutrex*) is a drug, similar to dopamine, that possesses greater beta-1 effects to increase myocardial contractility. The main use of dobutamine is in acute heart failure, where it is administered by IV infusion.

Adverse Effects

The beta drugs may produce central nervous system (CNS) stimulation resulting in restlessness, tremors, or

Figure 6.2

EpiPen Auto-Injector

The *EpiPen Auto-Injector* is used for self intramuscular injection of epinephrine immediately after the beginning of an anaphylactic-type allergic reaction.

anxiety. The main adverse effect of the older beta drugs (EPI or isoproterenol) is overstimulation of the heart, which may result in palpitations or other cardiac arrhythmias. These drugs are used with extreme caution in patients with existing heart disease. Drugs that produce beta-2 effects dilate the blood vessels of skeletal muscle. This dilation may lower blood pressure but rarely results in hypotension. At higher than therapeutic doses, the selective beta-2 drugs also can begin to stimulate cardiac beta-1 receptors, which may cause overstimulation of the heart. Use of beta-2 drugs to arrest preterm labor can cause a variety of cardiovascular effects and complications. Fetal heart rate and maternal pulse rate and blood pressure should be closely monitored.

LO 6.6

ALPHA-ADRENERGIC BLOCKING DRUGS

The alpha-blockers compete with NE and EPI for binding to the alpha-adrenergic receptors. When the alpha-blocker binds to the receptors, it prevents NE and EPI from producing the alpha sympathetic responses. Consequently, normal sympathetic activity is decreased in organs that have alpha receptors. The main pharmacologic effect of alpha-blockers is to cause relaxation of smooth muscle.

Clinical Indications

The alpha-blockers are used in the treatment of hypertension, especially when excessive vasoconstriction is present. The treatment of hypertension is discussed in Chapter 26. The alpha-blockers are also used in peripheral vascular conditions (poor blood flow to

skin and extremities) such as Raynaud's disease, where the vasodilation increases blood flow to the skin and extremities. Alpha-blockers are used in the treatment of pheochromocytoma, a tumor of the adrenal medulla where excessive catecholamine levels cause severe hypertension. Phenoxybenzamine, which has a long duration of action, is used to lower and control blood pressure until surgery to remove the tumor can be performed. In benign prostatic hyperplasia (males), there is enlargement of the prostate gland, which interferes with urine flow through the ureter. Alpha-blocking drugs relax the smooth muscle of the ureter, which improves urinary flow. Table 6:5 lists the alpha-blockers and their main uses.

Adverse Effects

Whenever the activity of one division of the autonomic nervous system is blocked (sympathetic), activity in the other division (parasympathetic) appears to increase. After alpha blockade, when sympathetic activity is blocked, the side effects are similar to an increase in parasympathetic activity in the organs that are blocked. You should note this generalization, that blocking one division of the ANS usually produces some effects that are similar to stimulating the other division. Constriction of the pupils (miosis), nasal congestion, and increased GI activity may be experienced after alpha blockade. Compensatory reflex tachycardia also occurs if the blood pressure is significantly lowered. In addition, the alpha-blockers interfere with normal cardiovascular reflexes that control blood pressure. Consequently, some patients experience orthostatic hypotension and fainting, especially when first starting therapy. Patients should be advised to exercise caution when changing positions from lying or sitting to standing.

Alpha-Adrenergic Blocking Drugs

Drug (*Trade Name*)	Main use	Common daily dosage range
Alfuzosin (*Uroxatral*)	Treatment of benign prostatic hyperplasia	10 mg PO
Doxazosin (*Cardura*)	Treatment of hypertension Treatment of benign prostatic hyperplasia	1–16 mg PO 1–8 mg PO
Phenoxybenzamine (*Dibenzyline*)	Treatment of pheochromocytoma	50–300 mg PO
Prazosin (*Minipress*)	Treatment of hypertension	1–20 mg PO
Tamsulosin (*Flomax*)	Treatment of benign prostatic hyperplasia	0.4–0.8 mg PO
Terazosin (*Hytrin*)	Treatment of hypertension Treatment of benign prostatic hyperplasia	1–5 mg PO 1–10 mg PO

LO 6.7

BETA-ADRENERGIC BLOCKING DRUGS

Beta-blocking drugs bind to beta-adrenergic receptors and antagonize the beta effects of EPI and NE. Patients with hypertension, angina pectoris, and cardiac arrhythmias often have increased sympathetic activity, with excessive amounts of EPI and NE being released. By occupying beta receptors, the beta-blockers antagonize and reduce the effects of EPI and NE on beta receptors. The heart (beta-1) is one of the most important beta organs and the main clinical use of beta-blockers is to decrease the activity of the heart. Blockade of the beta-1 receptors produces a decrease in heart rate, force of contraction, and impulse conduction through the conduction system of the heart. These effects are useful in patients with fast heart rates (tachycardia), cardiac arrhythmias, and other cardiac conditions where excessive sympathetic activity is present. Decreasing cardiac function also decreases blood pressure and beta-blockers are used in the treatment of hypertension. There are no specific therapeutic indications for blocking the beta-2 receptors.

Types of Beta-Blockers

The beta-blockers are divided into the nonselective beta-blockers (block both beta-1 and beta-2 receptors) and the selective beta-1 blockers. At therapeutic doses, the selective beta-blockers block only beta-1 receptors. At higher doses, the selective beta-blockers also may begin to block beta-2 receptors. Propranolol was the first beta-blocker used clinically; it blocks both beta-1 and beta-2

receptors. The other nonselective beta-blockers produce similar effects, except for labetalol, which also blocks alpha-1 receptors. The major pharmacokinetic differences among these drugs are the duration of action and the extent of drug metabolism. Table 6:6 lists the beta-blockers and their main indications.

Pharmacologic Effects

The main effects produced by propranolol are a decrease in rate, force of contraction, and conduction velocity of the heart. In addition, there is usually a lowering of blood pressure. Reducing the effort and work of the heart causes a decrease in oxygen consumption. This effect is beneficial in the treatment of various cardiovascular conditions such as angina pectoris, especially when there is hyperactivity of the sympathetic nervous system.

Propranolol is administered either orally or intravenously. After oral administration, the drug is carried directly to the liver by the portal system. With propranolol, there is significant metabolism on the first passage through the liver (first-pass metabolism), which reduces the amount of drug that eventually reaches the systemic circulation.

Beta-blockers also affect carbohydrate and lipid metabolism. Interference with carbohydrate metabolism is usually insignificant; however, diabetic patients may experience hypoglycemia. Serum lipid levels (triglycerides) may be increased by continuous therapy with these drugs.

Propranolol is the most lipid-soluble beta-blocker and passes into the brain, where it can exert pharmacological effects. These effects include CNS sedation, depression, and decreased central sympathetic activity,

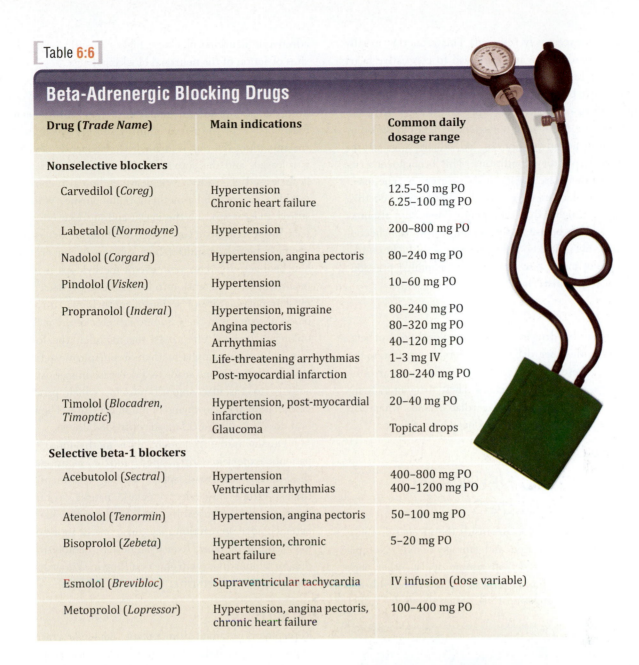

Table 6:6

Beta-Adrenergic Blocking Drugs

Drug (*Trade Name*)	Main indications	Common daily dosage range
Nonselective blockers		
Carvedilol (*Coreg*)	Hypertension Chronic heart failure	12.5–50 mg PO 6.25–100 mg PO
Labetalol (*Normodyne*)	Hypertension	200–800 mg PO
Nadolol (*Corgard*)	Hypertension, angina pectoris	80–240 mg PO
Pindolol (*Visken*)	Hypertension	10–60 mg PO
Propranolol (*Inderal*)	Hypertension, migraine Angina pectoris Arrhythmias Life-threatening arrhythmias Post-myocardial infarction	80–240 mg PO 80–320 mg PO 40–120 mg PO 1–3 mg IV 180–240 mg PO
Timolol (*Blocadren, Timoptic*)	Hypertension, post-myocardial infarction Glaucoma	20–40 mg PO Topical drops
Selective beta-1 blockers		
Acebutolol (*Sectral*)	Hypertension Ventricular arrhythmias	400–800 mg PO 400–1200 mg PO
Atenolol (*Tenormin*)	Hypertension, angina pectoris	50–100 mg PO
Bisoprolol (*Zebeta*)	Hypertension, chronic heart failure	5–20 mg PO
Esmolol (*Brevibloc*)	Supraventricular tachycardia	IV infusion (dose variable)
Metoprolol (*Lopressor*)	Hypertension, angina pectoris, chronic heart failure	100–400 mg PO

which may contribute to the lowering of blood pressure in the treatment of hypertension. Nadolol and atenolol are lipid-insoluble (water-soluble) beta-blockers, which do not pass into the brain and are excreted mostly unmetabolized in the urine.

Clinical Indications

Propranolol and other beta-blockers are used in the treatment of angina pectoris (Chapter 24), hypertension (Chapter 26), and various cardiac arrhythmias (Chapter 23). Beta-blockers also are one of the drug classes used in the treatment of chronic heart failure (Chapter 22), where decreasing excessive sympathetic activity slows the heart rate and appears to decrease the risk of sudden death. Other uses include the treatment of glaucoma, where beta-blockers decrease intraocular pressure; treatment of migraine headaches, where they often reduce the number of migraine attacks; and after myocardial infarction, where with chronic therapy beta-blockers appear to decrease the incidence of additional myocardial infarction and sudden cardiac death.

Esmolol is a short-acting drug that is administered intravenously in emergency situations. It has a quick onset of action to lower ventricular heart rate in cases of supraventricular tachycardia. The half-life of esmolol is about 10 minutes.

Adverse Effects

Common side effects of beta-blockers include nausea and diarrhea. More serious adverse effects occur when heart function is excessively reduced. This reduction usually produces bradycardia and may lead to congestive heart failure or cardiac arrest. In general, propranolol and nonselective beta-blockers should not be used in patients with asthma or other respiratory conditions. By blocking beta-2 receptor sites, nonselective beta-blockers may cause bronchoconstriction in individuals with asthma or other respiratory conditions. This bronchoconstriction may precipitate a respiratory emergency. The selective beta-1 blockers have less of a tendency to do this. However, at higher than therapeutic doses, they also may begin to block beta-2 receptors and cause bronchoconstriction. Beta-blockers that gain access to the brain like propranolol may cause drowsiness, mental depression, and other CNS disturbances.

Drug Interactions

The most serious drug interactions involve therapy of beta-blockers with other drugs that decrease cardiovascular function. These include cardiac glycosides, antiarrhythmic drugs, and calcium blockers. These drug interactions usually lower heart rate and cardiac output, which can lead to hypotension and drug-induced heart failure.

LO 6.8

ADRENERGIC NEURONAL BLOCKING DRUGS

The main activity that occurs inside the adrenergic nerve endings is the formation and storage of NE. Norepinephrine is synthesized from amino acids, either phenylalanine or tyrosine. Several drugs interfere with the formation or the storage of NE. Such drugs are called

Patient Administration and Monitoring

Check vital signs frequently with parenteral drug administration.

Observe patient frequently for signs of cardiac depression (beta-blockers) and hypotension (alpha- and beta-blockers).

Explain to patient the common drug side effects: weakness, fatigue, dizziness, and sedation.

Instruct patient to report slow pulse rate, chest pain, respiratory difficulties, mental confusion, nightmares, or impotency.

Diabetic patients should be warned that beta-blockers may affect insulin and blood glucose levels, and that they should report any changes.

adrenergic neuronal blockers. Figure 6.3 illustrates the sites of action of the neuronal blocking drugs.

Methyldopa (*Aldomet*)

Methyldopa (alpha-methyldopa) interferes with the synthesis of NE in the nerve endings and greatly reduces the amount of NE that is formed. Consequently, less NE is released, and the activity of the sympathetic system is decreased. The adrenergic nerve ending also converts methyldopa into alpha-methylnorepinephrine, which is stored and released by the nerve endings like NE. The term **false transmitter** is used to describe drugs that produce neurotransmitter-like substances but reduce neuronal activity. The main use of methyldopa is in the treatment of hypertension to lower blood pressure. The most important site of action of methyldopa to reduce blood pressure is in the vasomotor center of the medulla oblongata (central effect). In the medulla, the formation and release of alpha-methylnorepinephrine activates alpha-2 receptors and leads to a decrease in sympathetic activity to vascular smooth muscle, which produces vasodilation and a lowering of blood pressure. The usual oral dose is 250 to 2000 mg/day (divided doses).

During initial treatment with methyldopa, many patients experience drowsiness and/or sedation, but these effects tend to disappear as drug treatment continues. Other side effects include nausea, vomiting, diarrhea, nasal congestion, and bradycardia. In some patients, adverse reaction may cause one or more of the following: drug fever, liver dysfunction, hemolytic anemia, or a lupus-like syndrome resulting in skin eruptions and symptoms of arthritis.

Reserpine

Reserpine is obtained from a plant, *Rauwolfia serpentina*, found mainly in India. The site of action of reserpine is the adrenergic nerve endings. Within the nerve endings, reserpine prevents the storage of NE inside the storage granules. Consequently, the adrenergic nerve endings are depleted of NE. When this occurs, the level of sympathetic activity is greatly reduced. By reducing sympathetic activity, reserpine produces vasodilation and a lowering of blood pressure. Reserpine is rarely used today because of its numerous adverse effects.

In addition to its antihypertensive effect, reserpine produces CNS sedation and tranquilization. Before the introduction of the modern antipsychotic drugs, reserpine was widely used to treat psychoses.

Most of the side effects of reserpine are caused by the decreased sympathetic activity. Side effects are similar to parasympathetic stimulation and include increased salivation, diarrhea, nasal congestion, bradycardia, and

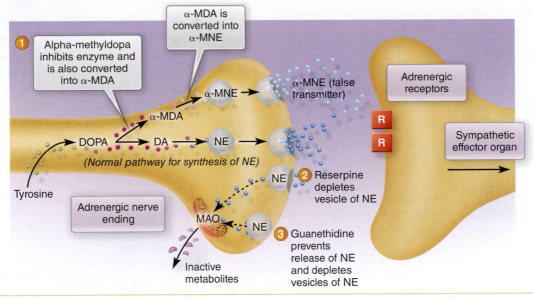

(1) Alpha-methyldopa inhibits the enzyme that normally converts DOPA to DA. In the process, DOPA is converted into alpha-methyldopamine (alpha-MDA) and then into the false transmitter alpha-methylnorepinephrine (alpha-MNE). (2) Reserpine depletes the nerve ending vesicles of NE, which is then metabolized by MAO to inactive metabolites. (3) Guanethidine acts on the nerve ending to block the release of NE and also depletes vesicles of NE, which is metabolized by MAO.

excessive hypotension. In the CNS, reserpine may produce excessive sedation, psychic disturbances such as confusion and hallucinations, or mental depression.

Guanethidine *(Ismelin)*

Guanethidine is a potent adrenergic neuronal blocker. There are two main actions that guanethidine exerts on the nerve endings. First, guanethidine prevents the release of NE from the nerve endings, and, second, guanethidine depletes the NE storage granules similarly to reserpine. These two effects produce a significant reduction of sympathetic activity.

The main clinical use of guanethidine is to treat severe hypertension; the usual oral dose is 25 to 300 mg/day. The half-life of guanethidine is relatively long. Therefore, the effects of guanethidine continue for several days after drug treatment is terminated.

The main adverse effects of guanethidine are caused by the decreased sympathetic activity and include diarrhea, nasal congestion, bradycardia, orthostatic hypotension, and impotency in males.

Guanadrel *(Hylorel)*

Guanadrel produces effects similar to those produced by guanethidine. It is used in the treatment of hypertension and generally produces a lower incidence of adverse effects than does guanethidine.

Preferred Treatment for Selected Conditions
Acute Allergic Reactions/Anaphylaxis

The drug of choice for treating acute allergic reactions caused by insect stings, drugs, or other allergies is epinephrine, administered by subcutaneous injection. Self-injectable preparations (*EpiPen*) are available and must be carried and administered as soon as possible. In addition, corticosteroids (Chapter 36) and antihistamines (Chapter 31) also can be administered but require time before the onset of action. Other supportive measures such as oxygen and IV fluids also may be required.

Benign Prostatic Hyperplasia

Alpha-blockers such as tamsulosin (*Flomax*) and alfuzosin (*Uroxatral*) are generally preferred to increase urine flow. In addition, finasteride (*Proscar*) and dutasteride (*Avodart*) are steroid inhibitors that block conversion of male testosterone to its active form and cause some reduction in the size of the prostate gland.

Bronchodilation

The selective beta-2 drugs such as albuterol (*Proventil*) or terbutaline (*Brethine*) with durations of action of 4–6 hours are usually the preferred drugs used to treat mild to moderate asthma. If longer-acting drugs are required, formoterol (*Foradil*) and salmeterol (*Serevent*) may be indicated. Preparations that combine either formoterol or salmeterol with antiinflammatory corticosteroids are available and indicated for moderate to severe asthma. Bronchodilators and the treatment of asthma are more extensively discussed in Chapter 32.

Hypertension

Alpha-blocking, beta-blocking, and adrenergic neuronal blocking drugs are all used in the treatment of hypertension. In addition, there are several other drug classes effective for hypertension; a discussion of hypertension and the antihypertensive drugs is presented in Chapter 26.

Summary of Sites of Action for Adrenergic Drugs

Figure 6.4 provides a diagrammatic summary of typical adrenergic nerve fibers, adrenergic receptors, and representative drugs that act on each receptor site. In addition, Table 6:7 summarizes the major sympathetic drug classifications and receptor site terminology with drug examples. It is hoped that the summary figure and table will help clear up some of the confusion that always occurs when first encountering the autonomic nervous system.

Figure 6.4 Diagrammatic Summary of Adrenergic Receptor Sites and Sites of Action of Adrenergic Drugs and Adrenergic Blocking Drugs.

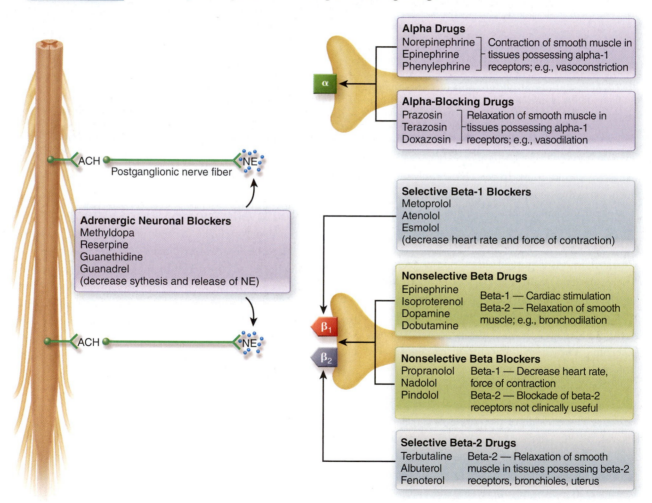

Alpha Drugs
Norepinephrine Contraction of smooth muscle in
Epinephrine   tissues possessing alpha-1
Phenylephrine receptors; e.g., vasoconstriction

Alpha-Blocking Drugs
Prazosin   Relaxation of smooth muscle in
Terazosin tissues possessing alpha-1
Doxazosin receptors; e.g., vasodilation

Selective Beta-1 Blockers
Metoprolol
Atenolol
Esmolol
(decrease heart rate and force of contraction)

Nonselective Beta Drugs
Epinephrine   Beta-1 — Cardiac stimulation
Isoproterenol Beta-2 — Relaxation of smooth
Dopamine   muscle; e.g., bronchodilation
Dobutamine

Nonselective Beta Blockers
Propranolol Beta-1 — Decrease heart rate,
Nadolol   force of contraction
Pindolol   Beta-2 — Blockade of beta-2
             receptors not clinically useful

Selective Beta-2 Drugs
Terbutaline Beta-2 — Relaxation of smooth
Albuterol   muscle in tissues possessing beta-2
Fenoterol   receptors, bronchioles, uterus

ACH
Postganglionic nerve fiber
NE

Adrenergic Neuronal Blockers
Methyldopa
Reserpine
Guanethidine
Guanadrel
(decrease sythesis and release of NE)

ACH
NE

Summary of Sympathetic Drug Classification and Receptor Site Terminology

Drug classification	Site of action	/	Main effect	Drugs
Sympathomimetics (Agonists)				
Alpha-adrenergic drugs	Alpha-1 receptor	/	Smooth muscle contraction, vasoconstriction	NE, EPI, metaraminol, phenylephrine
Nonselective beta-1 & -2 adrenergic drugs	Beta-1 and beta-2 receptors	/	Cardiac stimulation, smooth muscle relaxation, bronchodilation	EPI, isoproterenol
Selective beta-2 adrenergic drugs	Beta-2 receptors	/	Smooth muscle relaxation, bronchodilation	Albuterol, formoterol, salmeterol, terbutaline
Sympatholytics (Antagonists)				
Alpha-1 adrenergic blockers	Alpha-1 receptor	/	Smooth muscle relaxation, vasodilation	Doxazosin, prazosin, tamsulosin, terazosin
Nonselective beta-1 & -2 adrenergic blockers	Beta-1 and beta-2 receptors	/	Cardiac depression, smooth muscle contraction (beta-2 organs)	Nadolol, pindolol, propranolol, timolol
Selective beta-1 adrenergic blockers	Beta-1 receptors	/	Cardiac depression (decrease HR/force of contraction)	Atenolol, acebutolol, esmolol, metoprolol
Adrenergic neuronal blockers	Adrenergic nerve ending	/	Decrease sympathetic activity	Guanadrel, guanethidine, methyldopa, reserpine

Chapter Review

Understanding Terminology

Match the definition or description in the left column with the appropriate terms in the right column.
(LO 6.1, 6.2, 6.3)

___ 1. Drug that blocks or decreases sympathetic nervous system activity.

___ 2. Drug that acts at the neuronal endings to reduce the formation or release of NE.

___ 3. Receptor that mediates smooth muscle contraction.

___ 4. Adrenergic receptor located on either the heart or smooth muscle.

___ 5. Drug that blocks both beta-1 and beta-2 effects of EPI.

___ 6. Drug that blocks the alpha effects of NE and EPI.

___ 7. Chemical classification of norepinephrine and epinephrine.

___ 8. Adrenergic drug or effect that increases sympathetic nervous system activity.

___ 9. Hormone released from the adrenal medulla that stimulates the sympathetic nervous system.

a. adrenergic neuronal blocker

b. alpha-blocker

c. alpha receptor

d. beta receptor

e. catecholamine

f. epinephrine

g. nonselective beta-blocker

h. sympatholytic

i. sympathomimetic

Acquiring Knowledge

Answer the following questions.

1. What is the main function of the sympathetic nervous system? **(LO 6.1)**

2. List the different types of adrenergic receptors and relate them to specific organ functions. **(LO 6.2)**

3. What two neurotransmitter substances are associated with the sympathetic nervous system? Describe the effects of each. **(LO 6.1)**

4. A patient brought into the emergency room is experiencing severe hypotension. Blood pressure reads 90/50. What class of drugs is indicated for treatment? What precautions should be observed when these drugs are administered? What would be the first indication that too much drug has been administered? **(LO 6.4)**

5. Following cardiac surgery, a patient suddenly experiences a drop in cardiac function and blood pressure. The patient may be developing heart failure. What drugs would most likely be indicated in this situation? What autonomic receptor, in particular, needs to be acted upon? Should it be stimulated or blocked? **(LO 6.5)**

6. Alpha- and beta-blockers are both indicated for the treatment of hypertension. Explain the difference in the mechanism of action of these two drug classes to lower blood pressure. **(LO 6.6, 6.7)**

Applying Knowledge on the Job

Use your critical-thinking skills to answer the following questions.

1. Following emergency administration of epinephrine subcutaneously (SQ) for an acute asthmatic attack, the physician prescribes terbutalin (*Brethine*) tablets three times daily. How is this drug classified? What is it supposed to do? What are its advantages over epinephrine in the treatment of chronic asthma? **(LO 6.5)**

2. One of your coworkers has been taking propranolol (*Inderal*) regularly for a fast heart rate (tachycardia). Recently she has been complaining of tiredness and a feeling that she might faint. Is this effect drug related and if so, what is occurring? What advice might you give her? **(LO 6.7)**

3. Assume that your employer, a busy physician, has asked you to help screen patients for potential prescription drug problems. Patient X visited the doctor's office today complaining of "sinus"—sinus congestion, pressure, and headache. The doctor diagnosed an upper respiratory virus and prescribed phenylephrine for the sinus congestion and discomfort. You study Patient X's chart and note that he has a history of hypertension. What should you advise the doctor about the drug she has prescribed for Patient X? **(LO 6.4)**

4. Betty has asthma and diabetes. She also has developed high blood pressure, for which her doctor just prescribed the drug propranolol. One of your duties as physician's assistant is to make sure patients are not prescribed drugs that are contraindicated because of other health problems. What should you tell the doctor about Betty's prescription for propranolol? **(LO 6.7)**

5. Linda is a 24-year-old with bronchial asthma that is well controlled. She is in her 26th week of pregnancy and is experiencing preterm labor. Using the *PDR®* or *F&C,* determine whether ritodrine or terbutaline would be indicated to arrest her preterm labor. **(LO 6.5)**

6. Bill is a 38-year-old with a history of duodenal ulcers. He is currently maintained on cimetidine 800 mg HS. Today he was diagnosed with hypertension and his physician wants to initiate treatment with *Lopressor.* What dosing considerations should be made, if any? **(LO 6.7)**

Multiple Choice

Use your critical-thinking skills to answer the following questions.

1. The main pharmacologic effect of norepinephrine on alpha-1 receptors is **(LO 6.2)**
   A. increased heart rate
   B. bronchodilation
   C. vasocontriction
   D. contraction of urinary bladder

2. The pharmacologic effect of IV metaraminol is **(LO 6.4)**
   A. vasodilation
   B. vasoconstriction
   C. cardiac stimulation
   D. cardiac depression

3. Epinephrine stimulates **(LO 6.2)**
   A. alpha receptors
   B. beta-1 receptors
   C. beta-2 receptors
   D. all of the above

4. At therapeutic doses, albuterol stimulates **(LO 6.5)**
   A. alpha receptors
   B. beta-1 receptors
   C. beta-2 receptors
   D. all of the above

5. Tamsulosin is indicated for treatment of **(LO 6.6)**
   A. hypertension
   B. benign prostatic hyperplasia
   C. slow heart rate
   D. cardiac arrhythmias

6. Metoprolol is classified as a(n) **(LO 6.7)**
   A. alpha-blocker
   B. nonselective beta-blocker
   C. selective beta-1 blocker
   D. adrenergic neuronal blocker

7. The mechanism of action of guanethidine is **(LO 6.8)**
   A. increased release of NE from adrenergic nerve ending
   B. decreased release of NE from adrenergic nerve ending
   C. blockade of all adrenergic receptors
   D. formation of a false transmitter in adrenergic nerve ending

8. The drug of choice to treat acute allergic reactions is **(LO 6.4, 6.5)**
   A. norepinephrine
   B. phenylephrine
   C. pseudoephedrine
   D. epinephrine

Multiple Choice (Multiple Answer)

Select the correct choices for each statement. The choices may be all correct, all incorrect, or any combination.

1. Select all of the processes that occur with stimulation of a beta receptor. **(LO 6.2)**
   A. decreases artery constriction
   B. increases heart rate
   C. relaxes smooth muscle
   D. dilation of pupils

2. Norepinephrine works on the following receptors. **(LO 6.3)**
   A. Alpha-1
   B. Alpha-2
   C. Beta-1
   D. Beta-2

3. Which of the following are actions of beta-adrenergic blocking drugs? **(LO 6.7)**
   A. decreasing heart activity
   B. preventing NE from working
   C. vasodilation
   D. lowering of blood pressure

4. Select the mechanisms by which reserpine works. **(LO 6.8)**
   A. blocks the NE receptor
   B. produces neurotransmitter-like substances
   C. interferes with synthesis of NE
   D. prevents storage of NE

5. Select the effects of EPI on the body. **(LO 6.3)**
   A. bronchodilation
   B. vasoconstriction
   C. relaxation of uterus
   D. increased heart conduction

Sequencing

Place the following in reverse order of occurrence in the nerve ending. **(LO 6.1)**

_____   _____   _____   _____

Last   **First**

NE reuptake

NE released

NE stored in nerve endings

NE travels to smooth muscle

Documentation

Using the prescription below, answer the following questions. **(LO 6.6)**

    a. What is the brand name of the drug prescribed?

    b. What is the drug classification for this particular drug?

    c. In this dose, what is most likely being treated?

    d. List all applicable routes of administration.

Falls Clinic
Practice RX

1000 River Avenue

Anytown, USA   12345

931-555-1000

NAME: Bob Cross _____   DATE: _____

ADDRESS: _____

RX   terazosin   #30

Sig: 10mg once daily

Dr. G. Scott _____ M.D.   _____M.D.

   Substitution Permitted   Dispense as written

DEA #: _____   REFILL: NR 1 2 3 4

Labeling

Fill in the missing labels. (LO 6.4, 6.5, 6.6, 6.7)

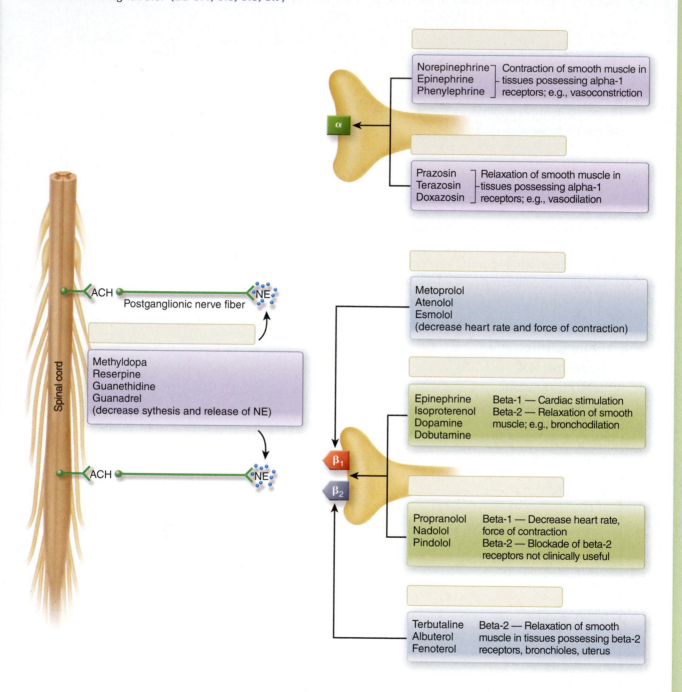

Norepinephrine Epinephrine Phenylephrine	Contraction of smooth muscle in tissues possessing alpha-1 receptors; e.g., vasoconstriction

Prazosin Terazosin Doxazosin	Relaxation of smooth muscle in tissues possessing alpha-1 receptors; e.g., vasodilation

ACH — Postganglionic nerve fiber — NE

Methyldopa Reserpine Guanethidine Guanadrel (decrease sythesis and release of NE)

Spinal cord

ACH — NE

Metoprolol Atenolol Esmolol (decrease heart rate and force of contraction)	

Epinephrine Isoproterenol Dopamine Dobutamine	Beta-1 — Cardiac stimulation Beta-2 — Relaxation of smooth muscle; e.g., bronchodilation

Propranolol Nadolol Pindolol	Beta-1 — Decrease heart rate, force of contraction Beta-2 — Blockade of beta-2 receptors not clinically useful

Terbutaline Albuterol Fenoterol	Beta-2 — Relaxation of smooth muscle in tissues possessing beta-2 receptors, bronchioles, uterus

McGraw Hill connect™ plus+

For interactive animations, videos, and assessment visit:

www.mcgrawhillconnect.com

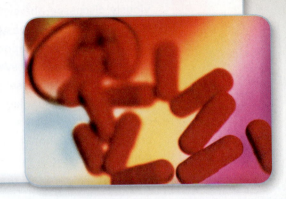

Drugs Affecting the Parasympathetic Nervous System

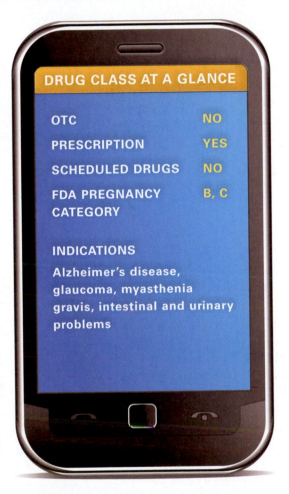

Chapter 7

DRUG CLASS AT A GLANCE

OTC	NO
PRESCRIPTION	YES
SCHEDULED DRUGS	NO
FDA PREGNANCY CATEGORY	B, C

INDICATIONS

Alzheimer's disease, glaucoma, myasthenia gravis, intestinal and urinary problems

KEY TERMS

acetylcholinesterase: an enzyme that inactivates acetylcholine.

anticholinergic: refers to drugs or effects that reduce the activity of the parasympathetic nervous system.

cholinergic: refers to the nerves and receptors of the parasympathetic nervous system; also refers to the drugs that stimulate this system.

muscarinic receptor: an older but more specific term for the cholinergic receptor on smooth and cardiac muscle.

nicotinic-muscle (Nm) receptor: cholinergic receptor located at the neuromuscular junction of skeletal muscle.

nicotinic-neural (Nn) receptor: cholinergic receptor located on both sympathetic and parasympathetic ganglia.

parasympatholytic: refers to drugs (anticholinergic) that decrease activity of the parasympathetic nervous system.

parasympathomimetic: refers to drugs (cholinergic) that mimic stimulation of the parasympathetic nervous system.

Learning Outcomes

After studying this chapter, you should be able to

7.1 describe the neuronal release and inactivation of acetylcholine.

7.2 list the three types of cholinergic receptors and the tissues where they are located.

7.3 compare the pharmacologic actions and uses of the direct-acting and indirect-acting cholinergic drugs.

7.4 list and briefly describe the clinical indications for the indirect-acting anticholinesterase drugs.

7.5 describe the pharmacologic actions, uses, and adverse effects of anticholinergic drugs.

7.6 list the preferred drug treatment for the most common conditions affected by parasympathetic activity.

The autonomic nervous system regulates the functions of the internal organs and glands. As previously discussed, the sympathetic division controls activity during physical exertion and stress (fight or flight). The parasympathetic division regulates body functions mainly during rest, digestion, and waste elimination. Parasympathetic stimulation increases the activity of the gastrointestinal and genitourinary systems and decreases the activity of the cardiovascular system.

Drugs that increase parasympathetic activity (cholinergic) are used in the treatment of Alzheimer's disease, glaucoma, myasthenia gravis, and urinary and intestinal stasis. Drugs that decrease parasympathetic activity (anticholinergics) are indicated for the treatment of overactive urinary and intestinal conditions, asthma and COPD, motion sickness, and during various ophthalmic procedures.

LO 7.1

CHOLINERGIC NERVE ACTIVITY

The neurotransmitter of the parasympathetic system is acetylcholine (ACH). Nerves that release ACH are called cholinergic nerves; receptors that respond to cholinergic stimulation are called cholinergic receptors. However, as previously discussed (Chapter 5), cholinergic receptors are more specifically classified as either muscarinic or nicotinic depending on their location (see below). Drugs that stimulate muscarinic receptors located on smooth and cardiac muscle that produce effects similar to those of ACH are more commonly referred to as cholinergic. Drugs that block muscarinic receptors are referred to as **anticholinergic.** The anticholinergic drugs prevent ACH from acting upon its receptors. Drugs that affect the other cholinergic receptors, nicotinic-neural (Nn) and nicotinic-muscle (Nm), have different terminology and are presented in Chapters 8 and 9, respectively.

Within the cholinergic nerve ending, acetylcholine is synthesized from a dietary substance, choline, and acetyl coenzyme A. ACH is then stored in vesicles until released by nerve stimulation. When a nerve is stimulated, ACH is released from its storage vesicles, travels across the synapse to the smooth or cardiac muscle membrane, and binds to the cholinergic receptors. The binding of ACH to the receptors initiates the changes that result in parasympathetic stimulation. In the area of the cholinergic receptors is an enzyme, acetylcholinesterase. **Acetylcholinesterase** inactivates ACH only when it is outside a nerve ending and not on the receptor. There is also an acetylcholinesterase enzyme, referred to as pseudocholinesterase, located in the liver and plasma that also can hydrolyze ACH and related drugs. Inactivation of ACH occurs quickly so that the effects of ACH last for only a few seconds.

The toxins of certain bacteria can cause food poisoning, referred to as botulism. Some of these toxins can inhibit the release of ACH from the cholinergic nerve ending to produce a flaccid type of skeletal muscle paralysis. In recent years, preparations of these toxins (*Botox*) have been injected into skeletal muscle to produce temporary paralysis in a variety of conditions (see below). Figure 7.1 illustrates the synthesis, storage, release, and inactivation of ACH that occurs at the cholinergic nerve ending.

LO 7.2

CHOLINERGIC RECEPTORS

Three types of cholinergic receptors are in the peripheral nervous system. Acetylcholine is the neurotransmitter for each receptor site. However, each of the cholinergic receptor types—muscarinic, nicotinic-neural (Nn), and nicotinic-muscle (Nm)—is blocked by a different drug class. There are three distinct classes of cholinergic blocking drugs, one for each type of receptor. Although the terminology used for the cholinergic receptors is confusing to beginning students, learning the terminology is essential for understanding the mechanism of drug action.

Muscarinic Receptors

The cholinergic receptors at the parasympathetic post-ganglionic nerve endings (as shown in Figure 7.2(a)) are known as **muscarinic receptors.** The term *muscarinic* is derived from the drug muscarine, which is an alkaloid obtained from a particular type of mushroom. One of the first drugs used to establish the function of the autonomic nervous system (ANS), muscarine produces effects that are similar to those of ACH, but only at these particular receptor sites. Consequently, early pharmacologists referred to these receptors as muscarinic, and the terminology is still in use. Drugs that act like ACH

Figure 7.1

Schematic Representation of Neurohumoral Transmission at Cholinergic Nerve Endings

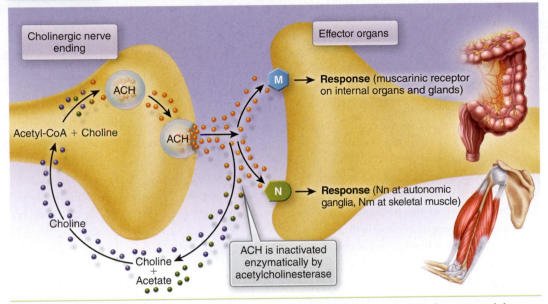

Choline is taken up into the nerve ending and combined with acetyl-CoA to form acetylcholine (ACH). ACH is stored in vesicles and upon stimulation is released into the synaptic cleft to stimulate muscarinic receptors (M) on internal organs and glands, nicotinic receptors (Nn) on autonomic ganglia, and nicotinic receptors (Nm) on skeletal muscle. ACH is inactivated enzymatically by acetylcholinesterase.

Figure 7.2   **The Cholinergic Sites of Drug Action and Their Associated Receptors**

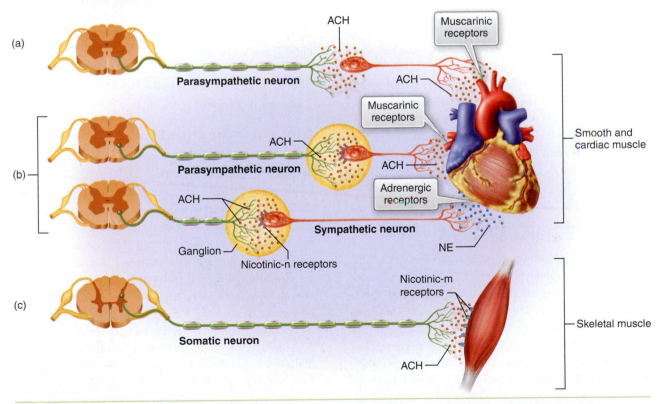

(a) Illustrates a parasympathetic neuron with pre- and postganglionic nerve fibers innervating smooth or cardiac muscle via the muscarinic receptor. (b) Illustrates the nicotinic-n receptor located on the ganglia of both parasympathetic and sympathetic neurons. (c) Illustrates a somatic neuron that innervates skeletal muscle via nicotinic-m receptors.

or muscarine at these receptors are referred to as either cholinergic or muscarinic. Drugs that block ACH at the muscarinic receptors are referred to as anticholinergic or antimuscarinic. Presently, the terms *cholinergic* and *anticholinergic* are preferred.

Nicotinic-Neural (Nn) Receptors

The cholinergic receptors at the ganglionic sites of both sympathetic and parasympathetic nerves (as seen in Figure 7.2(b)) are known as **nicotinic-neural (Nn) receptors.** Acetylcholine is the neurotransmitter for these receptors. The term *nicotinic* is derived from the drug nicotine, which is an alkaloid obtained from the tobacco plant. Early pharmacologists also used nicotine to study the pharmacology of the ANS, since nicotine stimulates the autonomic ganglia (sympathetic and parasympathetic) in low doses and blocks the autonomic ganglia in high doses. Drugs that act like ACH or low doses of nicotine at these receptors are known as ganglionic stimulants. Drugs that block ACH at these receptors or act like high doses of nicotine are referred to as ganglionic blockers. The ganglionic drugs will be discussed in Chapter 8.

Nicotinic-Muscle (Nm) Receptors

The cholinergic receptors at the neuromuscular junction (NMJ) of skeletal muscle (seen in Figure 7.2(c)) are known as **nicotinic-muscle (Nm) receptors.** Nicotine also stimulates or acts like ACH at the skeletal neuromuscular junction. Drugs that block the effects of ACH at the NMJ are referred to as neuromuscular blockers or skeletal muscle relaxants. The nerves and receptors associated with skeletal muscle are not part of the autonomic nervous system. Skeletal muscle is under voluntary control and belongs with the somatic division of the nervous system. The skeletal muscle relaxant drugs will be discussed in Chapter 9.

LO 7.3
CHOLINERGIC DRUGS

Cholinergic drugs mimic the actions of ACH at the cholinergic (muscarinic) receptors. Another term with essentially the same meaning is **parasympathomimetic.** Cholinergic drugs are subdivided into two groups: the direct-acting and the indirect-acting drugs (Table 7:1). The direct-acting drugs bind to the cholinergic (muscarinic) receptors and produce effects similar to those of ACH. The indirect-acting drugs inhibit the enzyme acetylcholinesterase. The indirect-acting drugs that inhibit acetylcholinesterase increase the concentration and actions of ACH at all muscarinic and nicotinic

receptor sites. The direct-acting drugs only increase activity at the cholinergic (muscarinic) sites. Figure 7.3 compares the receptor sites of action of the direct-acting and indirect-acting cholinergic drugs.

Direct-Acting Cholinergic Drugs

Direct-acting cholinergic drugs bind to the cholinergic (muscarinic) receptors. Acetylcholine is not useful as a drug because of its extremely short duration of action. Therefore, several derivatives of ACH were synthesized (bethanechol and carbachol) that produce effects like those of ACH, but they are more slowly inactivated by acetylcholinesterase. Consequently, the durations of action of these drugs are considerably longer than is the duration of action for ACH. In all other respects, the derivatives of ACH stimulate cholinergic receptors similarly to ACH.

Pharmacological Effects

The direct-acting cholinergic drugs primarily increase GI secretions and motility, increase urinary tract function (urination), and cause pupillary constriction (miosis). The effects of these drugs on the heart (decrease heart rate) and respiratory smooth muscle (bronchoconstriction) are usually clinically insignificant (review Table 5:1).

In addition to the derivatives of ACH, there are a few alkaloids, such as muscarine and pilocarpine, that have parasympathomimetic effects. Muscarine has no clinical importance except in cases of accidental mushroom poisoning. Pilocarpine is another alkaloid that acts like ACH and is used only in the form of eyedrops for the treatment of glaucoma.

Clinical Indications

Because of the short duration of ACH and some of its derivatives, the direct-acting cholinergic drugs are rarely used systemically. Bethanechol is the exception; this drug is administered orally to stimulate the urinary and intestinal tracts. Certain drugs (general anesthetics) and conditions, especially in the elderly, cause urinary retention and intestinal stasis (ileus). Bethanechol may be administered several times a day to stimulate urination and GI activity. The main adverse effects are due to overstimulation of the bladder and intestines, resulting in increased urinary frequency and diarrhea.

Cholinergic drugs are used locally during ophthalmic examinations as miotics to constrict the pupils and in the treatment of glaucoma. In glaucoma there is increased intraocular pressure. Increased intraocular pressure will gradually destroy the retina of the eye and cause blindness. Topical application (eyedrops) of

Cholinergic Drugs and Their Major Clinical Indications

Drug (*Trade Name*)	Clinical indications
Direct-acting drugs	
Acetylcholine (*Miochol-E*)	Miotic in ophthalmology
Bethanechol (*Urecholine*)	Urinary retention, postoperative ileus
Carbachol (*Isopto carbachol*)	Treatment of glaucoma
Pilocarpine (*Isopto carpine*)	Treatment of glaucoma
Indirect-acting drugs (anticholinesterases)	
Ambenonium (*Mytelase*)	Treatment of myasthenia gravis
Demecarium (*Humorsol*)	Treatment of glaucoma
Echothiophate (*Phospholine*)	Treatment of glaucoma
Edrophonium (*Tensilon*)	Diagnosis of myasthenia gravis
Neostigmine (*Prostigmin*)	Treatment of myasthenia gravis, postoperative ileus, and urinary retention; antidote to excessive cholinergic blockade with anticholinergic and skeletal muscle blockers
Physostigmine (generic)	Treatment of glaucoma, antidote to excessive cholinergic blockade with anticholinergics and skeletal muscle blockers
Pyridostigmine (*Mestinon*)	Treatment of myasthenia gravis
Donepezil (*Aricept*)	Treatment of Alzheimer's disease
Galantamine (*Reminyl*)	Treatment of Alzheimer's disease
Rivastigmine (*Exelon*)	Treatment of Alzheimer's disease
Tacrine (*Cognex*)	Treatment of Alzheimer's disease

cholinergic drugs produces miosis (pupillary constriction), which promotes better drainage of intraocular fluid from the eye. This lowers pressure and helps prevent retinal damage.

Indirect-Acting Cholinergic Drugs

The indirect-acting drugs are known as the anticholinesterases. These drugs inhibit the enzyme acetylcholinesterase and allow the accumulation of ACH at all cholinergic receptor sites. The anticholinesterase drugs are subdivided into the reversible inhibitors and the irreversible inhibitors of acetylcholinesterase.

Reversible Inhibitors

The reversible inhibitors are used in the diagnosis and treatment of myasthenia gravis and Alzheimer's disease, and as antidotes to reverse the effects of drugs that block cholinergic and nicotinic receptors. Myasthenia

Figure 7.3

The Receptor Sites of Action for Cholinergic Drugs

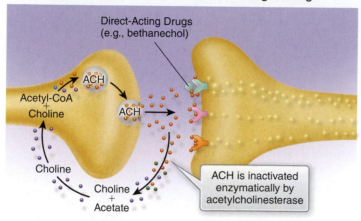

(a) Direct-Acting Drugs

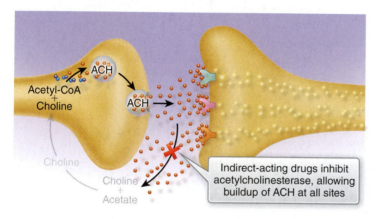

(b) Indirect-Acting Drugs

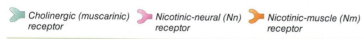

Cholinergic (muscarinic) receptor **Nicotinic-neural (Nn) receptor** **Nicotinic-muscle (Nm) receptor**

The neurotransmitter ACH normally stimulates all cholinergic receptor sites: cholinergic (muscarinic), nicotinic-neural (Nn), and nicotinic-muscle (Nm). (a) Direct-acting cholinergic drugs, like bethanechol (B), only stimulate the cholinergic (muscarinic) receptors. (b) Indirect-acting cholinergic drugs inhibit acetylcholinesterase and the metabolism of ACH. This allows the concentration of ACH to significantly increase in the synaptic cleft of all cholinergic nerve endings. Consequently, the indirect-acting drugs increase cholinergic activity at all receptor sites.

gravis is an autoimmune disease that causes skeletal muscle weakness and paralysis. By inhibiting acetylcholinesterase, the anticholinesterase drugs increase the concentrations of ACH at the Nm receptors, which increases the strength of muscular contraction. Edrophonium has the shortest duration of action, about 30 minutes. Myasthenia gravis is diagnosed by intravenous injection of a low dose of edrophonium. An increase in muscle strength that occurs within a minute or so is usually positive for myasthenia gravis. The durations of

neostigmine (2 to 4 hours), pyridostigmine (3 to 6 hours), and ambenonium (4 to 8 hours) are longer. These drugs are administered orally for the treatment of myasthenia gravis and intravenously to reverse the effects of excessive cholinergic blockade. The previously mentioned drugs are all quarternary amines (charged compounds) that do not cross the blood-brain barrier and produce effects only at peripheral receptor sites. Physostigmine is not a charged compound and does produce effects in the brain. It is used parenterally to reverse the central nervous system (CNS) effects of excessive anticholinergic blockade and as eyedrops in the treatment of glaucoma.

Additional anticholinesterase drugs that primarily increase the actions of ACH in the brain are used in the treatment of Alzheimer's disease (see below).

Irreversible Inhibitors

The irreversible inhibitors of acetylcholinesterase are derivatives of organophosphate compounds widely used as insecticides, pesticides, and chemical warfare agents. These compounds have extremely long durations of action because they form irreversible bonds with the acetylcholinesterase enzyme. Echothiophate (*Phospholine*) is the only drug used clinically; it is administered as eyedrops in the treatment of glaucoma. In larger doses these drugs produce severe toxicity, referred to as cholinergic crisis, that can quickly cause respiratory paralysis and death.

All of the anticholinesterase drugs, reversible and irreversible, produce effects that are similar to those of ACH and parasympathetic stimulation (parasympathomimetic).

Adverse and Toxic Effects of Cholinergic Drugs

The most common adverse effects of these drugs are caused by excessive stimulation of the parasympathetic nervous system. The symptoms include nausea, vomiting, diarrhea, blurred vision, excessive sweating, muscular tremors, bronchoconstriction, bradycardia, and hypotension. In toxic overdosage, muscular paralysis and respiratory depression may cause death. The main antidote is the administration of anticholinergic drugs such as atropine that compete with ACH for the cholinergic (muscarinic) receptor and reverse the effects of excessive cholinergic stimulation.

Figure 7.4

Auto-injectors Containing Antidotes Atropine and Pralidoxime

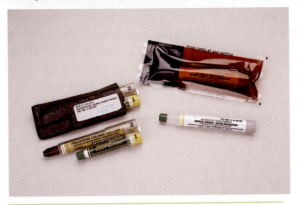

Atropine and pralidoxime can be self-injected following excessive exposure to irreversible anticholinesterase drugs (organophosphates) found in insecticides, pesticides, and chemical warfare agents.

Cholinergic Crisis

Cholinergic crisis is the term usually used to describe the effects of excessive drug dosage in patients with myasthenia gravis, farmers overexposed to insecticides or pesticides, or individuals exposed to chemical warfare agents. At high concentrations ACH causes excessive stimulation of cholinergic (muscarinic) receptors, but blockade (paralysis) of nicotinic receptors. This may result in respiratory paralysis because respiratory muscles are skeletal (voluntary) in nature. In these situations, anticholinesterase drug administration must be stopped until the levels of ACH return to normal. Atropine can be administered to block the effects of excessive cholinergic (muscarinic) stimulation.

Farmers who spray their fields with derivatives of the irreversible anticholinesterases (organophosphates) also may experience a cholinergic crisis. Unless protective masks or enclosed tractor cabs are used, the farmer may inhale too much of the insecticide or pesticide and develop signs of cholinergic crisis. With the irreversible drugs, the antidote is atropine to reverse the effects of excessive ACH and also an additional drug, pralidoxime (*Protopam*, Figure 7.4). Pralidoxime is a drug that can reactivate the acetylcholinesterase enzyme after it has been inhibited by an irreversible inhibitor. Pralidoxime is most effective immediately after organophosphate exposure. A process know as "aging," where the enzyme becomes resistant to reactivation, can occur within minutes. Pralidoxime is also the antidote to organophosphate chemical warfare agents.

CLINICAL INDICATIONS FOR ANTICHOLINESTERASE DRUGS

The reversible anticholinesterase drugs are more widely used than the direct-acting cholinergic drugs. They are used in the treatment of glaucoma, myasthenia gravis, urinary retention, intestinal paralysis, Alzheimer's disease and as antidotes to the curare-type skeletal muscle blockers and the anticholinergic drugs.

Topical Use in Glaucoma

Several of these drugs are used topically as eyedrops to lower intraocular pressure in glaucoma. By inhibiting the metabolism of ACH, they increase ACH levels in the eye to produce miosis, improved drainage of intraocular fluid, and lower intraocular pressure.

Treatment of Myasthenia Gravis

Myasthenia gravis is a disease of the skeletal muscle endplate where ACH functions to stimulate muscle tone and contraction. The condition is believed to be due to an autoimmune reaction where the body produces antibodies that attack the Nm receptor. The result is loss of skeletal muscle tone and strength. The eyelids droop and, as the disease progresses, there is difficulty in physical movement. Eventually patients may become bedridden and have difficulty breathing. The longer-acting reversible anticholinesterase drugs, pyridostigmine and ambenonium, are preferred and used orally to increase ACH levels and increase skeletal muscle tone and strength.

Patient Administration and Monitoring

Check and observe for signs of cholinergic overdosage, especially after parenteral administration: visual disturbances, salivation, nausea, increased frequency of urination, diarrhea, slow heart rate, respiratory difficulties, seizures (physostigmine).

Explain to patient the common drug side effects: visual disturbances (especially after eyedrops), sweating, increased frequency of urination, and defecation.

Instruct patient to report eye irritation or inflammation, excessive salivation, sweating, urination, diarrhea, slow pulse rate, muscle weakness, and respiratory difficulties.

Treatment of Urinary Retention and Intestinal Stasis

Urinary retention (also referred to as atony of the bladder) and intestinal stasis or paralysis (also referred to as paralytic ileus) are usually treated with neostigmine. The increased levels of ACH stimulate bladder contraction and intestinal peristalsis.

Treatment of Alzheimer's Disease

Alzheimer's disease is a degenerative brain condition that occurs in some individuals with aging. There appears to be a loss of neuronal synapses and, in particular, a reduction of ACH levels in the brain. These changes cause memory loss, dementia, and general deterioration of mental function. Currently there are four reversible anticholinesterase inhibitors available that have demonstrated modest effects to delay the progression of mental deterioration. Tacrine (*Cognex*) was the first drug introduced; it is associated with more side effects than the others, particularly hepatic toxicity. Donepezil (*Aricept*) is approved for treatment of all stages of Alzheimer's disease. Galantamine (*Reminyl*) and rivastigmine (*Exelon*) are the newest drugs approved for treatment of mild to moderate disease. These drugs are all centrally acting, reversible anticholinesterase inhibitors that increase ACH levels in the brain. Beneficial effects of the drugs are most notable in the early stages of the disease and lessen as the disease progresses. The most common side effects are nausea, vomiting, diarrhea, and other effects related to excessive cholinergic activity. A newer drug, memantine (*Namenda*) blocks excitatory glutamate receptors in the brain and appears to offer some protection against excessive excitation and nerve damage. Memantine is claimed to be better tolerated than the anticholinesterase inhibitors. Common side effects include headache, dizziness, confusion, coughing, and minor respiratory difficulties.

Antidotes to Skeletal Muscle Blockers

Skeletal muscle blockers (see Chapter 9) are used in surgery to produce paralysis of skeletal muscles (Nm receptor). At high doses they may cause respiratory paralysis. In these situations, administration of neostigmine will increase ACH levels and antagonize the actions of the skeletal muscle blockers.

Antidotes to Anticholinergic Drug Poisoning

Anticholinergic drugs, such as atropine and scopolamine (see Anticholinergic Drugs section that follows) block the cholinergic receptors (muscarinic) and produce effects similar to decreasing the activity of the parasympathetic system (parasympatholytic). This includes urinary and intestinal inhibition, cardiac stimulation (tachycardia), and central effects in the brain that can cause a variety of stimulant (seizures) and depressant (coma) effects. The antidote is usually to administer physostigmine because this drug can pass the blood-brain barrier. The increased levels of ACH produced by physostigmine compete with the anticholinergic drug for the receptor. As the levels of ACH increase, the central effects of excessive anticholinergic blockade are reversed.

Clinical Use of Botulinum Toxin

Botulinum toxin is derived from the toxin produced by the bacterium *Clostridium botulinum*. The toxin inhibits the release of ACH from cholinergic nerve endings. In skeletal muscle this action results in muscle paralysis. Local intradermal injections of the toxin (*Botox Cosmetic*) are used to temporarily decrease the wrinkling around the eyes, forehead, and face that occurs with aging (Figure 7.5). Other preparations of the toxin (Botulinum toxin type A, *Botox*, and Botulinum toxin type B, *Myobloc*) are injected intramuscularly in muscle disorders such as strabismus, blepharospasm, cerebral palsy, and other spastic conditions to provide muscle relaxation. Injections usually last 1–3 months.

Figure 7.5

Woman Receiving Botox Injection to Lessen Skin Wrinkling for Cosmetic Purposes

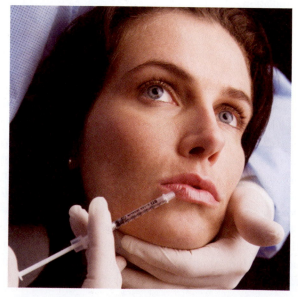

ANTICHOLINERGIC DRUGS

The cholinergic blocking drugs that bind to the muscarinic receptors are referred to as the **anticholinergic,** or **parasympatholytic,** drugs. They act by competitive antagonism of ACH. In the presence of anticholinergic drugs, sufficient amounts of ACH are unable to bind to the cholinergic receptors to produce an effect. The oldest anticholinergic drugs, such as atropine and scopolamine, were obtained from the belladonna plant (deadly nightshade) and are commonly referred to as the belladonna alkaloids. Atropine, scopolamine, and the newer synthetic drugs are listed in Table 7:2.

Pharmacological Actions and Clinical Indications

Cardiovascular System

By blocking the effects of ACH, anticholinergic drugs decrease the activity of the vagus nerve (parasympathetic nerve) on the heart. Consequently, there is an increase in heart rate. In patients with excessively slow heart rates (bradycardia), atropine may be used to increase heart rate and atrioventricular conduction. Isoproterenol (beta drug) that stimulates beta-1 receptors also can be used to increase heart rate. However, for the chronic treatment of bradycardia, nonpharmacologic therapy with a cardiac pacemaker is usually preferred.

Respiratory System

ACH increases the secretions of the respiratory tract and may cause bronchoconstriction. Anticholinergic drugs are administered preoperatively to inhibit secretions that can interfere with the administration of general anesthetics. In addition, ipratropium and tiotropium are anticholinergic drugs administered as aerosols that produce bronchodilation and are used in the treatment of asthma and chronic obstructive pulmonary disease (COPD) (see Chapter 32).

GI System

Anticholinergic drugs reduce salivary and GI secretions. In addition, they decrease the motility of the GI tract and therefore they should not be administered when there is intestinal obstruction. The anticholinergic drugs are used as antispasmodics in GI disorders such as irritable bowel syndrome. In the treatment of peptic ulcers, the anticholinergic drugs, which decrease gastric acid secretion, have been replaced by newer and more effective drugs (see Chapter 33).

Genitourinary System

Anticholinergic drugs inhibit urinary peristalsis and the voiding of urine. These drugs may be used in individuals suffering from enuresis (urinary incontinence) to promote urinary retention and in the treatment of overactive bladder that involves spasm and increased urinary urgency. However, anticholinergic drugs are contraindicated in males with hypertrophy of the prostate gland. These drugs increase urinary retention and further increase the difficulty of urination associated with this condition.

Central Nervous System

Most anticholinergic drugs that gain access to the brain produce a depressant effect, which generally results in drowsiness and sedation. Some over-the-counter preparations contain limited amounts of scopolamine and are used as sleep aids. At higher doses, there can be a mixture of both CNS stimulant and depressant effects. At toxic doses, both atropine and scopolamine may produce excitation, delirium, hallucinations, and a profound CNS depression that can lead to respiratory arrest and death. Anticholinergic actions are useful in the treatment of Parkinson's disease (see Chapter 17) and as antiemetics (see Chapter 33) in the treatment of motion sickness.

Ocular Effects

The anticholinergic drugs produce mydriasis (pupillary dilation) and cycloplegia (loss of accommodation). They are used in ophthalmology to facilitate examination of the retina and lens. Anticholinergic drugs increase intraocular pressure and should never be administered to patients with glaucoma. In glaucoma, there is a blockage of the drainage pathway for intraocular fluid. The anticholinergic effect causes pupillary dilation, which in glaucoma increases closure of the drainage pathway. The result can be a sudden increase in intraocular pressure and damage to the eye.

Adverse and Toxic Effects

The most frequently occurring adverse effects of the anticholinergic drugs are caused by excessive blockade of the parasympathetic nervous system. The symptoms include dry mouth, visual disturbances, urinary retention, constipation, flushing (redness) and dryness of the skin, fever (hyperpyrexia), tachycardia, and symptoms of both CNS stimulation and depression. The effects on the skin are due to anticholinergic effects that inhibit the sweating mechanism and that vasodilate certain blood vessels to cause a flushing reaction. In toxic doses, hyperpyrexia and CNS depression can be severe and may be accompanied by depression of the vital centers in the brain. If untreated this may result in respiratory paralysis and death.

The belladonna alkaloids are present in some over-the-counter preparations and in many common plant

Representative Anticholinergic Drugs and Their Main Clinical Uses

Drug (*Trade Name*)	Preparations	Main clinical uses
Atropine (generic)	Tablets, parenteral injection	Antidote for cholinesterase inhibitor poisoning, anticholinergic effects
Atropine (*Isopto atropine*)	Ophthalmic drops, ointment	Ophthalmic examinations
Darifenacin (*Enablex*)	Tablets	Relief of urinary spasms, urgency, incontinence
Dicyclomine (*Bentyl*)	Tablets, syrup, parenteral injection	Intestinal disorders, diarrhea, irritable bowel syndrome
Flavoxate (*Urispas*)	Tablets	Relief of urinary spasms, urgency, incontinence
Glycopyrrolate (*Robinul*)	Tablets	Intestinal disorders, diarrhea
Hyoscyamine (*Anaspaz*)	Oral tablets, capsules, parenteral injection	Intestinal disorders, diarrhea, irritable bowel syndrome
Ipratropium (*Atrovent*)	Aerosol, metered-dose inhaler	Bronchodilation, asthma, COPD
Methscopolamine (*Pamine*)	Tablets	Intestinal disorders, spasms
Oxybutynin (*Ditropan, Detropan XL*)	Tablets, syrup, transdermal patch	Relief of urinary spasms, urgency, incontinence
Propantheline (*Pro-Banthine*)	Tablets	Intestinal disorders, diarrhea, irritable bowel syndrome
Scopolamine (generic) (*Transderm scop*)	Tablets, parenteral injection Skin patch	Intestinal disorders Motion sickness
Solifenacin (*Vesicare*)	Tablets	Relief of urinary spasms, urgency, incontinence
Tiotropium (*Spiriva*)	Aerosol, metered-dose inhaler	Bronchodilation, asthma, COPD
Tolterodine (*Detrol, Detrol LA*)	Tablets, capsules	Relief of urinary spasms, urgency, incontinence
Trospium (*Sanctura*)	Tablets, capsules	Relief of urinary spasms, urgency, incontinence

Observe patient for signs of excessive anticholinergic effects, especially after parenteral administration: tachycardia, flushing of skin (redness), decreased urination, CNS stimulation or depression, respiratory difficulties.

Explain to patient the common anticholinergic side effects: dry mouth, blurred vision (pupillary dilation), sedation, or mental confusion.

Instruct patient to report excessive blurred vision, fast pulse rate, difficulty with urination, constipation, mental confusion, or hallucinations.

Geriatric patients are particularly susceptible to anticholinergic effects and should be observed more closely, especially for mental confusion and disorientation.

Anticholinergic drugs are contraindicated in patients with narrow-angle glaucoma, males with prostate hypertrophy, and patients with urinary or intestinal obstruction.

The antidote to anticholinergic overdose is administration of anticholinesterase drugs, especially physostigmine when there are CNS symptoms.

---

substances and noneatable plant berries. Poisoning usually occurs in children who have mistakenly eaten the berries. Such children usually develop fever, tachycardia, dryness and flushing of the skin, and mydriasis. Emergency treatment is essential. If sufficient quantities have been ingested, respiratory paralysis, coma, and death may occur within a few hours.

Treatment involves inducing emesis or performing gastric lavage to limit absorption. Activated charcoal and saline cathartics are administered to inactivate the drug and accelerate its elimination. Physostigmine, given intravenously, antagonizes the actions of the anticholinergic drugs and is useful when CNS symptoms such as delirium and coma are present.

LO 7.6

PREFERRED TREATMENT FOR SELECTED CONDITIONS

Urinary Retention/Difficulty in Urination

After prolonged urinary catheterization, surgery with general anesthetics, or other conditions, there is often difficulty in urination. Cholinergic drugs such as bethanechol (*Urecholine*) or cholinesterase inhibitors such as neostigmine (*Prostigmine*) are preferred to increase urinary tone and motility in these situations. In males with benign prostatic hyperplasia, the preferred drugs to increase urinary flow are alpha-blockers such as tamsulosin (*Flomax*) or alfuzosin (*Uroxatral*); these drugs were discussed in Chapter 6.

Overactive Bladder/Urge Incontinence

Anticholinergic drugs such as oxybutynin (*Ditropan, Ditropan XL*), tolterodine (*Detrol, Detrol LA*), darifenacin (*Enablex*), and solifenacin (*Vesicare*) are administered to relax the urinary bladder and reduce urinary urgency. The latter two drugs have longer half-lives and allow once-daily dosing.

Intestinal Stasis/Postoperative Ileus

Cholinergic drugs such as bethanechol (*Urecholine*) or the anticholinesterases such as neostigmine (*Prostigmine*) are administered to increase intestinal tone and motility.

Irritable Bowel Syndrome

Anticholinergic drugs such as dicyclomine (*Bentyl*), glycopyrrolate (*Robinul*), or hyoscyamine (*Anaspaz*) are administered to decrease intestinal secretions and motility.

Myasthenia Gravis

The preferred drug to increase ACH levels at the skeletal neuromuscular junction is pyridostigmine (*Mestinon*). Alternatives include ambenonium (*Mytelase*) or neostigmine (*Prostigmine*).

Alzheimer's Disease

The preferred drugs are the cholinesterase inhibitors. Galantamine (*Reminyl*) and rivastigmine (*Exelon*) are currently indicated for mild to moderate disease while donepezil (*Aricept*) is indicated for all stages of Alzheimer's disease. Memantine (*Namenda*) is a newer drug that also may be considered.

Chapter Review

Understanding Terminology

Match the drug effect or drug use in the left column with the appropriate drug in the right column. Each answer can be used more than once. **(LO 7.3, 7.4, 7.5)**

___ 1. Reactivates acetylcholinesterase.

___ 2. Directly stimulates cholinergic (muscarinic) receptor.

___ 3. Increases ACH levels in the CNS.

___ 4. Used to reverse CNS anticholinergic toxicity.

___ 5. Used to treat myasthenia gravis.

___ 6. Used to prevent motion sickness.

___ 7. Used before surgery to dry respiratory secretions.

___ 8. Indicated for treatment of Alzheimer's disease.

___ 9. Irreversibly inhibits acetylcholinesterase.

___ 10. Used to treat nonobstructive urinary retention.

a. bethanechol (*Urecholine*)

b. ambenonium (*Mytelase*)

c. scopolamine (*Transderm Scop*)

d. echothiophate (*Phospholine*)

e. atropine

f. physostigmine

g. pralidoxime (*Protopam*)

h. tacrine (*Cognex*)

11. Differentiate between parasympatholytic and parasympathomimetic. **(LO 7.3, 7.5)**

12. Explain the terms *cholinergic* and *anticholinergic.* **(LO 7.1)**

Acquiring Knowledge

Answer the following questions.

1. What is the function of the parasympathetic nervous system? **(LO 7.3)**

2. What is the function of acetylcholinesterase? Where is it found? **(LO 7.1)**

3. Where are the three different cholinergic receptors located? What class of drug is needed to block each receptor? **(LO 7.2)**

4. How do the direct-acting and the indirect-acting cholinergic drugs produce their parasympathetic effects? **(LO 7.3)**

5. List the potential adverse effects of the cholinergic drugs. **(LO 7.3)**

6. List the potential adverse effects of the anticholinergic drugs. **(LO 7.5)**

7. What is the preferred drug treatment for myasthenia gravis? **(LO 7.6)**

Applying Knowledge on the Job

Use your critical-thinking skills to answer the following questions.

1. As a nurse working for a team of doctors in a busy practice, you are sometimes given the task of screening patients for potential prescription drug problems. Patient X has just been diagnosed as having colitis, for which his doctor has prescribed dicyclomine. You note that in his first visit last year, Patient X mentioned he takes the drug timolol. You decide you'd better check the *PDR*® to see what timolol is used to treat before Patient X starts taking the dicyclomine. What should you report to the doctor? **(LO 7.5)**

2. Your next-door neighbor knows you are studying pharmacology so she sometimes comes to you when she has questions about health problems. A few minutes ago, she came to your door in a state of panic. She said her 3-year-old had just swallowed some scopolamine tablets, which your neighbor takes for her irritable bowel syndrome. What should you do? **(LO 7.5)**

3. Your elderly patient who was prescribed an antispasmotic drug for GI hyperactivity is complaining of increased sensitivity to light and notices that she has difficulty urinating. What do you think is happening to this patient? What class of drugs do you think she was most likely prescribed? What drug class would be indicated if her condition worsened and treatment was required? **(LO 7.5)**

4. Mr. Jones is being treated for myasthenia gravis. During his regular checkup you notice that he is sweating and his heart rate is below normal. You ask him how he's feeling and he says he's had diarrhea for the past few days and that he feels very weak. Can you explain what may be happening to Mr. Jones? Explain why some of his symptoms appear to be due to excessive cholinergic stimulation, yet he has skeletal muscle weakness. **(LO 7.3, 7.4)**

5. An elderly woman in a nursing facility is being treated with bethanechol for urinary retention. She is complaining of abdominal discomfort, excessive salivation, and feeling hot and sweaty. Could these symptoms be due to the medication? If so, what do they indicate? **(LO 7.3)**

6. A 28-year-old male has been diagnosed with irritable bowel syndrome. His health care provider has prescribed dicyclomine 20 mg TID. What side effects should be included in the patient counseling? **(LO 7.5)**

Multiple Choice

Use your critical-thinking skills to answer the following questions.

1. Parasympathetic receptors located on the membranes of the internal organs are classified as **(LO 7.2)**
   A. alpha-1
   B. nicotinic-neural (Nn)
   C. nicotinic-muscle (Nm)
   D. muscarinic

2. Select the pharmacologic effect produced by cholinergic drugs. **(LO 7.3)**
   A. increased heart rate
   B. increased gastrointestinal motility
   C. decreased urination
   D. pupillary dilation

3. Physostigmine (*Eserine*) is classified as a(n) **(LO 7.3)**
   A. direct-acting cholinergic drug
   B. reversible anticholinesterase inhibitor
   C. irreversible anticholinesterase inhibitor
   D. anticholinergic drug

4. Symptoms of cholinergic drug overdosage include **(LO 7.3)**
   A. slow pulse rate
   B. increased urination
   C. diarrhea
   D. all of the above

5. Anticholinergic actions include all of the following *except* **(LO 7.5)**
   A. bronchodilation
   B. increased heart rate
   C. increased gastrointestinal activity
   D. decreased respiratory secretions

6. The antidote for atropine poisoning is **(LO 7.3)**
   A. scopolamine
   B. bethanechol
   C. neostigmine
   D. physostigmine

7. Tolterodine (*Detrol*) is indicated for treatment of **(LO 7.5)**
   A. motion sickness
   B. relief of urinary incontinence
   C. ophthalmic examinations
   D. glaucoma

Multiple Choice (Multiple Answer)

Select the correct choices for each statement. The choices may be all correct, all incorrect, or any combination.

1. Which of the following are used for the treatment of myasthenia gravis? **(LO 7.4)**
   A. *Tensilon*
   B. *Mytelase*
   C. *Prostigmin*
   D. *Mestinon*

2. Select the conditions produced by anticholinergic drugs. **(LO 7.5)**
   A. mydriasis
   B. glaucoma
   C. cyclopegia
   D. sedation

3. Which of the following are not cholinergic receptors? **(LO 7.2)**
   A. muscarinic
   B. nicotinic-neural
   C. nicotinic-muscle
   D. sympathomimetic

4. Pick the correct pharmacological effects of direct-acting cholinergic drugs. **(LO 7.3)**
   A. respiratory paralysis
   B. urinary retention
   C. increased heart rate
   D. bronchodilation

5. Which of the following would be a preferred treatment for overactive bladder? **(LO 7.6)**
   A. *Cognex*
   B. *Detrol*
   C. *Pilocar*
   D. *Bentyl*

Sequencing

Place the processes in order from first to last as they happen in the body. **(LO 7.1)**

_____	_____	_____	_____
First			**Last**

Acetylcholinesterase deactivates ACH
ACH released from storage vesicles
Presynaptic nerve is stimulated
ACH is stored in cholinergic nerve endings

Classification

Place the correct drug under the condition it is most commonly used to treat. **(LO 7.6)**

darifenacin	_Exelon_
galantamine	_Detrol LA_
carbachol	_Mytelase_
neostigmine	solifenacin
pyridostigmine	_Cognex_
Humorsol	pilocarpine

Glaucoma	Alzheimer's disease	Urinary spasms	Myasthenia gravis

Documentation

Based on the symptoms listed upon admission to the hospital, answer the following questions. **(LO 7.5)**

Symptoms:
flushed skin
tachycardia
difficulty breathing
blurred vision

a. What type of drug overdose is the patient likely suffering from?
b. What is happening at the muscarinic receptors in this patient?
c. What medications would be given to treat this overdose?

Labeling

Fill in the missing labels. **(LO 7.2)**

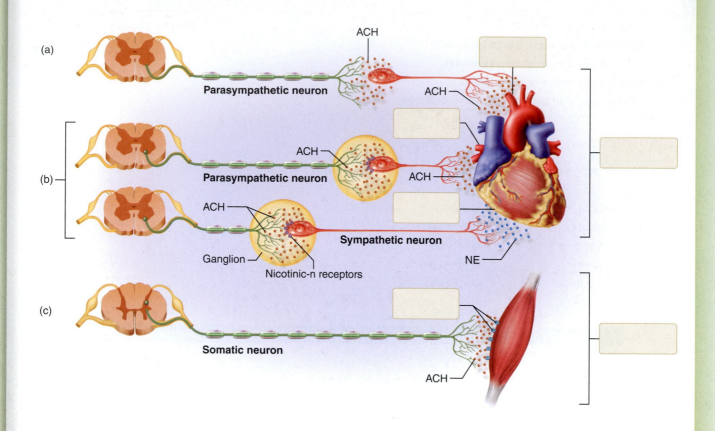

(a) Parasympathetic neuron

ACH

ACH

(b) Parasympathetic neuron

ACH

ACH

ACH

Sympathetic neuron

Ganglion

Nicotinic-n receptors

NE

(c) Somatic neuron

ACH

For interactive animations, videos, and assessment visit

www.mcgrawhillconnect.com

Chapter 8

Drugs Affecting the Autonomic Ganglia

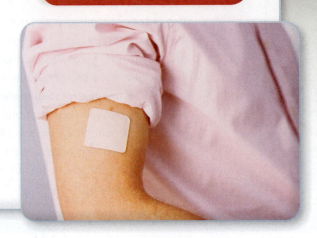

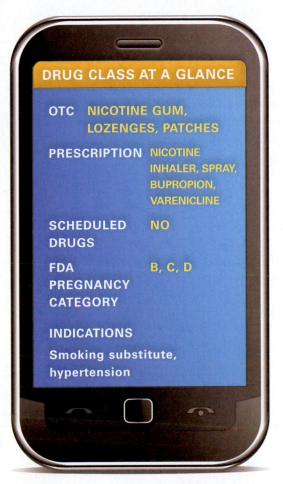

DRUG CLASS AT A GLANCE

OTC	NICOTINE GUM, LOZENGES, PATCHES
PRESCRIPTION	NICOTINE INHALER, SPRAY, BUPROPION, VARENICLINE
SCHEDULED DRUGS	NO
FDA PREGNANCY CATEGORY	B, C, D

INDICATIONS

Smoking substitute, hypertension

KEY TERMS

ganglionic blocker: drug that blocks the nicotinic-neural (Nn) receptors and reduces the activity of the autonomic nervous system.

ganglionic stimulant: drug that stimulates the nicotinic-neural (Nn) receptors to increase autonomic nervous system activity.

nicotine: alkaloid drug in tobacco that stimulates ganglionic receptors.

nicotinic-neural (Nn) receptor: cholinergic receptor at the autonomic ganglia.

Learning Outcomes

After studying this chapter, you should be able to

8.1 describe the pharmacological effects of ganglionic stimulation.

8.2 list the different drug preparations used in nicotine replacement therapy and the adverse effects associated with them.

8.3 describe the main pharmacologic effects and uses of ganglionic blockers.

8.4 discuss the adverse effects associated with the use of ganglionic blocking drugs.

The autonomic ganglia of both sympathetic and parasympathetic nerves are pharmacologically identical. Acetylcholine (ACH) is the neurotransmitter at both autonomic ganglia. Before the discovery of ACH, nicotine was found to stimulate the autonomic ganglia, and so the receptors at the ganglia were known as the nicotinic receptors. Currently they are more specifically classified as the **nicotinic-neural (Nn) receptors.** Drugs that stimulate the Nn receptors are called **ganglionic stimulants,** while drugs that block these receptors are called **ganglionic blockers.** There are very few clinical conditions where ganglionic stimulation or blockade is of significant clinical value. Nicotine-containing products that help smokers quit the tobacco habit and medications used in the treatment of severe hypertension are essentially the only drugs used clinically that act on autonomic ganglia.

LO 8.1

GANGLIONIC STIMULANTS

Acetylcholine is the neurotransmitter at the autonomic ganglia that normally stimulates the nicotinic-neural (Nn) receptors (Figure 8.1). Individuals who use tobacco absorb **nicotine,** which produces ganglionic stimulation that increases both sympathetic and parasympathetic activity. Theoretically, if both autonomic divisions are stimulated at the same time, the physiological effects should cancel out. However, sympathetic stimulation usually predominates in the cardiovascular system while parasympathetic stimulation predominates in the gastrointestinal tract. Consequently, after smoking, there is usually an increase in heart rate, blood pressure, and GI activity. More importantly, nicotine stimulates nicotinic receptors in the brain that provide the central nervous system effects of tobacco use. The actions in the brain are also the cause of the dependency and habitual use of tobacco products.

As a drug class, drugs that stimulate autonomic ganglia have little clinical use. However, for individuals who want to quit the tobacco habit, there are nicotine-containing preparations that substitute for tobacco. A number of nicotine-containing preparations are used in nicotine-replacement therapy (NRT). The purpose of NRT is to provide nicotine while the use of tobacco and the habit of smoking are discontinued. Preparations include chewing gum, lozenges, transdermal patches, oral inhalers, and nasal sprays. The intention of these products is to lessen the symptoms and withdrawal reactions caused by quitting the tobacco habit. Over time the use of these products can be reduced and then eliminated.

There are also drugs that act in the brain to reduce the cravings for tobacco products. These drugs do not contain nicotine but are used to affect behavior and the cravings for nicotine and cigarette smoking. Bupropion

---

Figure 8.1   **Illustration of an Autonomic Ganglion**

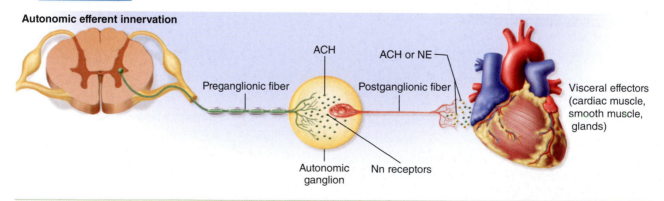

Acetylcholine (ACH) is the neurotransmitter at the ganglion that stimulates nicotinic-neural (Nn) receptors on the cell membrane of the postganglionic nerve fiber.

[Table **8:1**]

Drugs Used in the Treatment of Smoking Cessation

Drug preparation	Trade Name	Dosage
Nicotine gum	Nicorette	2 mg (limit 30 pieces/day) 4 mg (limit 20 pieces/day)
Nicotine lozenges	Commit	2 and 4 mg (limit 20/day)
Nicotine patch	Nicoderm CQ Nicotrol	7, 14, 21 mg (16–24 hours/day) 15 mg (16 hours/day)
Nicotine inhaler	Nicotrol Inhaler	Inhaled by mouthpiece and cartridges (10 mg/supplies 4 mg), dosage varies with individual
Nicotine nasal spray	Nicotrol NS	0.5 mg/spray/nostril 1–2 sprays/hour, dosage varies with individual
Bupropion		Antidepressant drug used to reduce nicotine cravings
	Wellbutrin, Zyban	25-, 50-, 75-, 150-mg tablets 150 mg, sustained release
Varenicline	Chantix	0.5- and 1-mg tablets, blocks effect of nicotine on CNS receptors

is an antidepressant (Chapter 14) that affects mood and is claimed to reduce the CNS effects of nicotine withdrawal. Varenicline is a drug that is claimed to block nicotine receptors in the brain to prevent nicotine from exerting its full effects. Behavioral counseling is also an important component in the effort to quit smoking. Table 8:1 lists the different drug preparations available for quitting the tobacco habit.

Cautions and Contraindications

Pregnancy

Nicotine has been shown to be harmful to the fetus. Consequently, tobacco and the use of nicotine substitutes should be avoided during pregnancy (Figure 8.2). These drugs are classified as Pregnancy Category D by the FDA.

Adverse Effects

Common adverse effects of nicotine gum and lozenges include taste disturbances, mouth and jaw soreness, and GI disturbances such as nausea and heartburn. Transdermal patches can cause soreness at the patch site, changes in taste, GI disturbances, and nervousness. Oral inhalers and nasal sprays may cause local mouth and throat irritation, minor breathing difficulties, and GI disturbances.

Figure 8.2

Pregnant Woman Drinking and Smoking a Cigarette

At toxic doses, ACH and nicotine desensitize both Nn and Nm (skeletal muscle) receptors and can act like ganglionic blockers and block both ganglionic and skeletal neuromuscular transmission. This blockade can result in respiratory paralysis and death.

Bupropion is capable of causing a large number of adverse effects that include dry mouth, insomnia, and a variety of GI disturbances. Also numerous neurological and neuropsychiatric effects such as confusion, hostility, and agitation are possible. The most common adverse effects of varenicline are nausea, vomiting, constipation, and headaches. In addition, psychiatric disturbances, mental depression, and suicidal ideation have been reported. In addition, after the first week of treatment, nicotine-containing products should not be taken during therapy with varenicline.

LO 8.3

GANGLIONIC BLOCKERS

Ganglionic blockers bind to and block Nn receptors. Since the sympathetic division has greater control over regulation of blood pressure, the ganglionic blockers cause a reduction in blood pressure and are primarily used in the treatment of severe hypertension. By blocking Nn receptors at the ganglia, the ganglionic blockers decrease the activity of the cardiovascular, gastrointestinal (GI), and genitourinary systems. The major effects are hypotension, bradycardia, decreased intestinal secretions and motility, and reduced urination. In males, impotence may occur. In addition, there are usually varying degrees of visual disturbances such as mydriasis and cycloplegia. The ganglionic blockers are potent drugs that are associated with numerous autonomic adverse effects. Clinical use of these drugs is limited and mainly indicated for treatment of severe hypertension.

Pharmacokinetics

The first ganglionic blockers that were discovered (hexamethonium, pentolinium, and trimethaphan) possessed a quaternary ammonium ion. Quaternary ammonium ions are permanently charged molecules and are poorly absorbed from the GI tract. Trimethaphan (*Arfonad*) is the only one currently available and it is administered by IV injection when blood pressure needs to be rapidly reduced. Mecamylamine, another ganglionic blocker, is not a quaternary ion and is almost completely absorbed after oral administration.

Clinical Indications

The only ganglionic blocker currently available for chronic use is mecamylamine (*Inversine*). The main indication for mecamylamine is for the treatment of severe hypertension when other drugs have not been effective. The pharmacologic action of mecamylamine is mainly due to ganglionic blockade of sympathetic ganglia, which causes profound vasodilation. Although mecamylamine is a very potent antihypertensive drug, it produces numerous adverse effects that many patients cannot tolerate. Mecamylamine usually is used in combination with other antihypertensive drugs, which allows reduction of the mecamylamine dosage and the frequency and severity of adverse effects.

LO 8.4

ADVERSE EFFECTS OF GANGLIONIC BLOCKERS

Almost all of the adverse effects of the ganglionic blockers are caused by excessive blockade of the autonomic ganglia. The result is a combination of anticholinergic and antiadrenergic effects, which usually include decreased GI activity (dry mouth and constipation), visual disturbances (mydriasis and cycloplegia), decreased cardiovascular function (hypotension and decreased cardiac output), and decreased genitourinary function (urinary retention and impotency). The ganglionic blockers are contraindicated in patients with glaucoma because the mydriatic effect increases intraocular pressure.

Drug Interactions with Ganglionic Blocking Drugs

Drug class	Result
Adrenergic drugs	Antagonism of antiadrenergic effect of ganglionic blockade, especially on cardiovascular system
Adrenergic blocking drugs	Additive antiadrenergic effect to produce hypotension and possible cardiovascular collapse
Cholinergic drugs	Antagonism of anticholinergic effect of ganglionic blockade, especially on GI and urinary tracts
Anticholinergic drugs	Additive anticholinergic effect
Vasodilator drugs	Additive vasodilating effect to produce hypotension and possible cardiovascular collapse

Drug Interactions

Many drugs act on autonomic receptors, and the possibility of a drug interaction with ganglionic blockers is significant. Table 8:2 lists the potential drug interactions with ganglionic blockers.

Chapter Review

Understanding Terminology

Answer the following questions.

1. Differentiate between a ganglionic stimulant and a ganglionic blocker. **(LO 8.1, 8.3)**
2. What is the name of the cholinergic receptors at the ganglia? **(LO 8.1)**

Acquiring Knowledge

Answer the following questions.

1. What neurotransmitter regulates ganglionic transmission? **(LO 8.1)**
2. List the main effects of ganglionic stimulation. **(LO 8.1)**
3. List the main effects of ganglionic blockade. **(LO 8.3)**
4. What are the main therapeutic uses of the ganglionic blocking drugs? **(LO 8.3)**
5. List the adverse effects of the ganglionic stimulants used in nicotine replacement therapy. **(LO 8.2)**
6. List the adverse effects of the ganglionic blocking drugs. **(LO 8.4)**
7. What other drugs might interact with the ganglionic blockers? **(LO 8.4)**

Applying Knowledge on the Job

Use your critical-thinking skills to answer the following questions.

1. Assume that you work in a health maintenance organization (HMO), where you act as patient liaison. Patients are encouraged to talk over problems with you if they feel that the problems have not been resolved by a doctor or if they feel uncomfortable discussing the problems with a doctor. One of the patients wants to talk to you about an "embarrassing problem." He says that ever since he started taking that "strong medicine" for his high blood pressure, he hasn't been able to make love to his wife. He also has a dry mouth, and he's constipated all of the time. What drug is the patient most likely taking? **(LO 8.3, 8.4)**

2. A patient has been brought by ambulance to the emergency room where you work. He's suffering from hypotension, and he's on the verge of cardiovascular collapse. The patient's wife, who accompanied him in the ambulance, says he was fine until he took some new medication for his high blood pressure. She has the bottle with her—the medication is mecamylamine. You ask her if he's taking any other medicine, and she replies that he takes propranolol for his angina. What is producing these effects in this patient? **(LO 8.3, 8.4)**

3. A young man brought into the emergency room could hardly walk, had difficulty breathing, and had very low blood pressure. Upon questioning he said he had been chewing some type of gum to help him quit smoking. He admitted that he was still smoking a pack a day. What is going on with this patient? **(LO 8.2)**

Multiple Choice

Use your critical-thinking skills to answer the following questions.

1. The receptors located on the ganglia of both autonomic nerve divisions are **(LO 8.1)**
   A. nicotinic-neural (Nn)
   B. nicotinic-muscle (Nm)
   C. muscarinic
   D. anticholinergic

2. The effects produced by ganglionic stimulation include **(LO 8.1)**
   A. increased heart rate
   B. increased intestinal activity
   C. increased blood pressure
   D. all of the above

3. Pharmacologic effects produced by mecamylamine (*Inversine*) include **(LO 8.3)**
   A. increased urination
   B. decreased blood pressure
   C. diarrhea
   D. all of the above

4. At high or toxic doses, nicotine may cause **(LO 8.2)**
   A. ganglionic stimulation
   B. ganglionic blockade
   C. skeletal muscle contraction
   D. increased respiration function

5. The drug that blocks nicotinic receptors in the brain is **(LO 8.2)**
   A. trimethaphan
   B. atropine
   C. varenicline
   D. mecamylamine

Multiple Choice (Multiple Answer)

Select the correct choices for each statement. The choices may be all correct, all incorrect, or any combination.

1. Which of the following is an effect of ganglionic blockade? **(LO 8.3)**
   A. hypotension
   B. reduced urination
   C. bradycardia
   D. impotence

2. Drugs used in smoking cessation come in what dosage forms? **(LO 8.2)**
   A. lozenges
   B. inhalers
   C. injectables
   D. patches

3. Ganglionic blocking drugs interact with which types of drugs? **(LO 8.4)**
   A. cholinergic
   B. anticholinergic
   C. adrenergic
   D. antiadrenergic

4. Ganglionic blocking drugs have which of the following adverse effects? **(LO 8.4)**
   A. hypertension
   B. dry mouth
   C. decreased ocular pressure
   D. diarrhea

5. The adverse effects of varenicline are **(LO 8.2)**
   A. constipation
   B. suicidal thoughts
   C. headaches
   D. hostility

Classification

Place the following in the proper drug classification.

Inversine	trimethaphan
Commit	*Wellbutrin*
Nicorette	*Pentolinium*

Smoking cessation	Ganglionic blockers

Matching

Match the following effects with ganglionic stimulant or blocker. **(LO 8.1)**
   a. stimulant
   b. blocker

1. _____ increased GI motility
2. _____ increased heart rate
3. _____ mydriasis
4. _____ reduced urination
5. _____ hypotension
6. _____ increased blood pressure

For interactive animations, videos, and assessment visit:

www.mcgrawhillconnect.com

Chapter 9

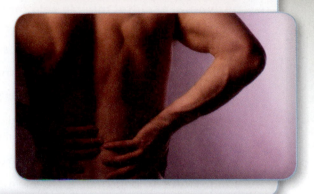

Skeletal Muscle Relaxants

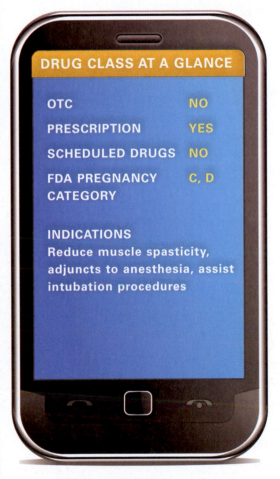

DRUG CLASS AT A GLANCE

OTC	NO
PRESCRIPTION	YES
SCHEDULED DRUGS	NO
FDA PREGNANCY CATEGORY	C, D

INDICATIONS
Reduce muscle spasticity, adjuncts to anesthesia, assist intubation procedures

KEY TERMS

black box warning (boxed warning): a warning that appears in the instructions for use surrounded by a thick black box to alert medical professionals to serious or life-threatening adverse effects associated with the drug usage.

centrally acting skeletal muscle relaxant: drug that inhibits skeletal muscle contraction by blocking conduction within the spinal cord.

depolarizing blocker: produces paralysis by first causing nerve transmission, followed by inhibition of nerve transmission.

fasciculation: twitchings of muscle fiber groups.

hyperthermia: abnormally high body temperature.

incompatibility: undesirable interaction of drugs not suitable for combination or administration together.

intrathecal: space around the brain and spinal cord that contains the cerebrospinal fluid.

malignant hyperthermia: condition in susceptible individuals resulting in a life-threatening elevation in body temperature.

microfilaments: minute fibers located throughout the cytoplasm of cells, composed of the protein actin, that maintain the structural integrity of a cell.

mitochondria: normal structures responsible for energy production in cells.

myelin: the fatty substance that covers and protects nerves and allows efficient conduction of action potentials down the axon.

neuromuscular junction (NMJ): space (synapse) between a motor nerve ending and a skeletal muscle membrane that contains acetylcholine (ACH) receptors.

nicotinic-muscle (Nm) receptor: cholinergic receptor located at the neuromuscular junction of skeletal muscle.

nondepolarizing blocker: produces paralysis by inhibiting nerve transmission.

peripheral skeletal muscle relaxant: drug that inhibits muscle contraction at the neuromuscular junction or within the contractile process.

potentiates: produces an action that is greater than either of the components can produce alone; synergy.

sarcolemma: a thin membrane enclosing a striated (skeletal) muscle fiber.

sarcoplasm: the cytoplasm of a striated (skeletal) muscle fiber

sarcoplasmic reticulum: specialized organelle in the muscle cell that releases calcium ions during muscle contraction and absorbs calcium ions during relaxation.

Schwann cell: any cell that covers the axons in the peripheral nervous system and forms the myelin sheath.

spasmolytics: drugs that relieve, interrupt, or prevent muscle spasms (intermittent muscle contractions often associated with pain).

synaptic knob: contains vesicles that store and release neurotransmitters.

synaptic vesicles: a small membrane-bound structure in the axon terminals of nerve cells that contains neuro-transmitters and releases them when an action potential reaches the terminal.

vagolytic action: inhibition of the vagus nerve to the heart, causing the heart rate to increase (counteraction to vagal tone that causes bradycardia).

vasodilator: substance that relaxes the muscles (sphincters) controlling blood vessels, leading to increased blood flow.

Learning Outcomes

After studying this chapter, you should be able to

9.1 describe at least two ways in which skeletal muscles may be relaxed.

9.2 explain why muscle relaxation is necessary during diagnostic and surgical procedures.

9.3 examine how these drugs may alter the ability to control respiration.

9.4 explain how tranquilizers relax skeletal muscles through a different mechanism of action than non-depolarizing blockers.

9.5 identify which drugs are used in the chronic treatment of spastic muscle disorders.

9.6 list three potential adverse effects associated with muscle relaxants.

Introduction

Contraction of skeletal muscles is voluntarily controlled by impulses that originate in the central nervous system (CNS). Impulses from the brain are conducted through the spinal cord to the somatic motor neurons (Figure 9.1). Somatic motor neurons eventually connect with skeletal muscle fibers forming a **neuromuscular junction (NMJ).** The neuronal endings of the somatic motor fibers contain the neurotransmitter acetylcholine (ACH). When ACH is released into the neuromuscular synapses, it combines with cholinergic receptors known as **nicotinic-muscle (Nm) receptors.** Although these receptors are cholinergic, they are not identical to the muscarinic (para-sympathetic) and ganglionic receptors previously discussed in Chapter 5. Review the terminology for the different cholinergic receptor sites presented in Chapter 7.

Depolarization of the muscle fibers occurs when ACH combines with the Nm receptors. Following depolarization, the contractile elements of the muscle fibers (actin and myosin) produce muscle contraction. Muscle relaxation occurs after ACH is hydrolyzed by acetylcholinesterase; this terminates the action of ACH. Skeletal muscle function is essential to life, since respiration depends upon the rhythmic contraction of the diaphragm and chest muscles. In addition, skeletal muscle tone permits coordinated movement of the entire body to maintain posture. This muscle activity occurs continually without our conscious awareness.

LO 9.1
SKELETAL MUSCLE RELAXANTS

Many drugs inhibit skeletal muscle contraction by interfering with neuromuscular function. Drugs that inhibit skeletal muscle contraction by blocking conduction within the spinal cord are known as **centrally acting skeletal muscle relaxants** (Figure 9.2, site 1). In contrast, **peripheral skeletal muscle relaxants** inhibit muscle contraction at the NMJ (Figure 9.2, site 2) or within the contractile process (Figure 9.2, site 3).

Motor neuron axons from the spinal cord enter the muscle fibers. The unmyelinated nerve fibers end in the NMJ (Figure 9.2, site 2). Presynaptic ends contain vesicles of acetylcholine. When triggered, acetylcholine is released into the synapse to bind with the nicotinic-muscle (Nm) receptors on the other side of the junction/synapse. This receptor binding with acetylcholine enables sodium ions to move into the cells and potassium ions to move out of the muscle cells (depolarization). As depolarization spreads across the surface of the muscle fiber, calcium ions are released and muscle contraction occurs.

Regardless of the site of action, drugs classified as skeletal muscle relaxants are clinically valuable because they selectively inhibit neuromuscular function. This inhibition then results in skeletal muscle relaxation.

LO 9.2
CLINICAL INDICATIONS

Skeletal muscle relaxation is desirable in spastic diseases (multiple sclerosis and cerebral palsy), conditions in which the spinal cord has been damaged (trauma, paraplegia), and injuries in which pain accompanies overexertion of the muscles. In addition, surgical and orthopedic procedures and intubation (for example, bronchoscopy) are often facilitated by the use of skeletal muscle relaxants. Without administering these agents prior to invasive diagnostic procedures, there is a greater possibility for the reacting muscles to tear or become strained.

LO 9.3   LO 9.4
PERIPHERALLY ACTING SKELETAL MUSCLE RELAXANTS

Mechanism of Action

Neuromuscular blockers inhibit skeletal muscle contraction by interfering with the nicotinic-muscle receptors. There are two types of neuromuscular blockers: nondepolarizing (curare and pancuronium) and depolarizing (succinylcholine).

| Figure 9.1 | **Somatic Efferent Pathway** |

Somatic efferent innervation

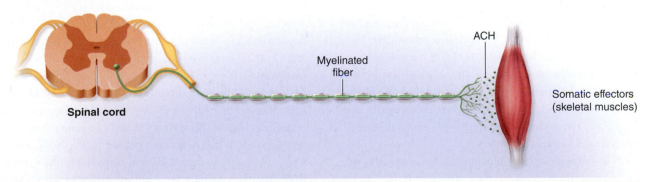

The entire distance from the CNS to the skeletal muscle fiber (effector) is one neuron. Acetylcholine (ACH) is the only neurotransmitter.

Figure 9.2 Sites of Action of Skeletal Muscle Relaxants

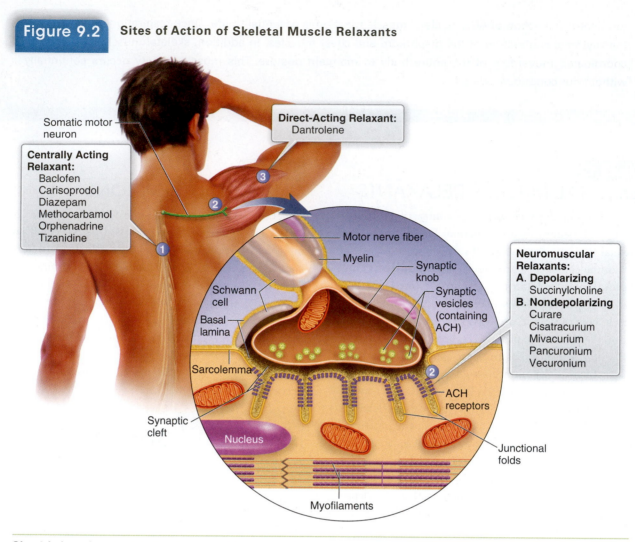

Direct-Acting Relaxant:
Dantrolene

Somatic motor neuron

Centrally Acting Relaxant:
Baclofen
Carisoprodol
Diazepam
Methocarbamol
Orphenadrine
Tizanidine

Motor nerve fiber
Myelin
Synaptic knob
Synaptic vesicles (containing ACH)
Schwann cell
Basal lamina
Sarcolemma
ACH receptors
Synaptic cleft
Nucleus
Junctional folds
Myofilaments

Neuromuscular Relaxants:
A. **Depolarizing**
   Succinylcholine
B. **Nondepolarizing**
   Curare
   Cisatracurium
   Mivacurium
   Pancuronium
   Vecuronium

Site 1 is impulse conduction from the CNS through the spinal cord, where the centrally acting muscle relaxants work. Site 2 is the neuromuscular junction (NMJ), where the depolarizing and nondepolarizing muscle relaxants work. The insert shows an individual NMJ. Site 3 is the skeletal muscle, where direct-acting drugs inhibit calcium ion release from the cell body. A complete list of skeletal muscle relaxants is presented in Tables 9:1 and 9:2.

The **nondepolarizing blockers** combine with the nicotinic-muscle receptors but do not stimulate the receptors. These agents occupy the nicotinic-muscle sites so that ACH cannot combine with the receptors and depolarization cannot occur (nondepolarizing, *no depolarization*). Curare, the original blow-dart poison you've seen in the movies, is the prototype of these drugs. Although curare use in the medical setting has been replaced by newer synthetic nondepolarizing blockers, the term *curare-like effect* is still used to identify side effects or symptoms associated with skeletal muscle paralysis and respiratory arrest.

The nondepolarizing blocking drugs used today are easily recognized because their name ends in *-curium* or *-curonium*. Table 9:1 shows examples of available

nondepolarizing blocking drugs such as atra*curium*, miva*curium*, pan*curonium*, ro*curonium*, and ve*curonium*.

The **depolarizing blockers** inhibit muscle contraction by a two-step process: (1) succinylcholine attaches to the nicotinic-muscle receptors and induces depolarization, observed as muscle **fasciculations;** and (2) then succinylcholine alters the nicotinic-muscle receptors so that they cannot respond to endogenous ACH stimulation. This phase is the neuromuscular blockade. Succinylcholine is the only available depolarizing neuromuscular blocking drug. If you can remember that acetylcholine is the neurotransmitter in the NMJ, then it should be easy to remember succinyl*choline* is the drug that stimulates (depolarizes) before it blocks the receptor. A small fact that might account for this action is that

Peripheral Skeletal Muscle Relaxant Doses and Routes of Administration

Drug (*Trade Name*)	Type	Adult dose
Atracurium besylate*	Nondepolarizing	0.4–0.5 mg/kg IV bolus
Cisatracurium besylate (*Nimbex*)	Nondepolarizing	0.15 or 0.2 mg/kg IV
Dantrolene (*Dantrium*)**	Direct-acting	25 mg PO BID, QID
Mivacurium	Nondepolarizing	0.15 or 0.2 mg/kg IV
Pancuronium bromide***	Nondepolarizing	0.06–0.1 mg/kg IV
Rocuronium bromide (*Zemuron*)***	Nondepolarizing	0.6–1.2 mg/kg IV
Succinylcholine chloride (*Anectine, Quelicin*)***	Depolarizing	0.3–1.1 mg/kg IV, 1–2 mg/ml at 2.5 mg/min continuous IV infusion
Tubocurarine (curare; presented for historic reference)	Nondepolarizing	—
Vecuronium bromide (*Norcuron*)	Nondepolarizing	0.08–0.10 mg/kg IV

*Indications * preparation for surgery, ** muscle spasticity, *** during surgery.*

succinylcholine is actually two acetylcholine molecules back-to-back.

Route of Administration

The nondepolarizing neuromuscular blockers are administered intravenously (IV). Examples of the IV doses of the peripheral neuromuscular blockers are presented in Table 9:1. The warning box that appears in the pancuronium FDA-approved instructions for use says, "This drug should be administered by adequately trained individuals familiar with its actions, characteristics, and hazards." This certainly applies to all parenterally administered NMJ blocking drugs, both nondepolarizing and depolarizing.

Following a single injection of a nondepolarizing blocker, neuromuscular blockade occurs within 3 to 5 minutes and lasts from 20 to 30 minutes. The muscles of the eyes and face are the first to become relaxed, followed by the limbs, trunk, and diaphragm. Recovery of muscle function occurs as the drug is metabolized and excreted.

As a class, these drugs are not similar in where and how they are metabolized before being excreted. Mivacurium is metabolized by plasma cholinesterases, while rocuronium is metabolized in the liver and cisatracurium

is spontaneously degraded in the plasma. The duration of action, therefore, varies with the type of metabolism the drug undergoes. Curare, mentioned for historical reference, has a duration of action up to 60 minutes, while mivacurium is the shortest-acting nondepolarizing blocker, lasting 10 to 20 minutes. Pancuronium has a duration of action more than 30 minutes, but the remaining nondepolarizing blockers cited in Table 9:1 have an intermediate duration of action up to 30 minutes.

The indication for use (i.e., tracheal intubation), duration of drug action, and condition of the patient will determine whether multiple administration or continuous IV infusion is required.

The depolarizing blocker succinylcholine is metabolized so rapidly that it is often administered by intravenous infusion to maintain skeletal muscle relaxation. Succinylcholine is rapidly hydrolyzed by the enzyme plasma cholinesterase, specifically butyrylcholinesterase, which is present in the blood. Some individuals do not have enough of these general plasma cholinesterases, or because of a genetic abnormality, they produce an abnormal (atypical) enzyme. These people metabolize succinylcholine very slowly, so its duration of action and potential for toxicity to occur increase.

As you can see in Table 9:1, there are many more nondepolarizing blockers (six) available for use today than depolarizing blockers (one). A goal of drug development in this class has been to find a drug that has a quick onset and duration of action with minimal adverse effects, primarily to replace succinylcholine. Well, succinylcholine is still with us and every new drug has some nontherapeutic effect(s) because of its site and mechanism of action. Nevertheless, the search for a new drug continues.

Effects on Cardiopulmonary Systems

Although the primary site of action is the NMJ, neuromuscular blockers also produce cardiovascular changes at therapeutic doses through a different mechanism of action. Pancuronium has no effect on the autonomic ganglia or histamine release; however, it may cause tachycardia by blocking the vagal tone on the sino-atrial (SA) node of the heart (**vagolytic action**).

Succinylcholine has been reported to produce ventricular arrhythmias and changes in blood pressure, which vary with the amount of drug administered. This depolarizing blocker does not have a direct effect on cardiac muscle (myocardium), but it does act at the ganglionic and muscarinic sites. Stimulation of these other cholinergic receptor sites can result in changes in heart rhythm, including cardiac arrest. Since the depolarization action of succinylcholine causes potassium leakage from the muscle cells, patients with electrolyte imbalances (burns or trauma) may develop arrhythmias more easily. Vecuronium has been reported to have little or no effect on the heart or blood pressure. Even when used in patients with pheochromocytoma (a tumor on the adrenal gland that secretes adrenaline), there were no remarkable changes in cardiovascular monitoring.

Some of the blockers (atracurium, mivacurium, succinylcholine) cause a release of histamine from mast cells, which can lead to the production of bronchospasms and increased bronchial secretions in sensitive patients. Asthmatic patients are especially sensitive to the respiratory complications induced by histamine. Therefore, in asthmatic patients, the neuromuscular blocking drug will be selected that minimizes bronchial (respiratory) complications. Clinical signs and symptoms of histamine release also may include hypotension (most common) and tachycardia (see Chapter 31, Antihistaminic Drugs and Mast Cell Release Inhibitors). It is not unusual for an H1-antihistamine to be given as a premedication to block potential classic histamine effects of the neuromuscular blocking drugs.

ADVERSE AND TOXIC EFFECTS

The major toxicity associated with all neuromuscular blockers is paralysis of the respiratory muscles. This is life-threatening because the patient can no longer control breathing, consciously or unconsciously. Skeletal muscle paralysis caused by the nondepolarizing blockers may be reversed by the use of neostigmine or edrophonium. Neostigmine and edrophonium inhibit acetylcholinesterase so that ACH accumulates within the junctions. The ACH displaces the blocker from the nicotinic-muscle receptors and, since their receptors are not damaged or changed, initiates depolarization and muscle contraction. An added benefit of neostigmine and edrophonium is their ability to directly stimulate the nicotinic-muscle receptors so that skeletal muscle paralysis is reversed.

A new drug with a relatively unique mechanism of action, sugammadex, was submitted for U.S. FDA review recently. Sugammadex is the first in a new class of drugs, known as selective relaxant binding agents (SRBA). This drug reverses the neuromuscular blockade of nondepolarizing blockers by selectively encapsulating and chelating the blocker. It has a special affinity for rocuronium. Although it hasn't yet been approved for use in the United States, it does speak to the continued interest in finding new drugs that affect the neuromuscular blockade.

Succinylcholine overdose presents a special problem because this drug alters the ability of nicotinic-muscle receptors to become stimulated. There is no known antidote that reverses the neuromuscular blockade produced by succinylcholine. Administration of the anticholinesterase drugs may worsen the respiratory paralysis. Respiration must be supported artificially until the drug is metabolized and receptor responsiveness returns to normal. Skeletal muscle paralysis may be dangerously prolonged when succinylcholine is used in a patient who has atypical plasma cholinesterase.

Succinylcholine produces an unusual acute toxicity that is probably due to an existing genetic abnormality in 1 out of 20,000 individuals. Occasionally, a normal dose of succinylcholine in combination with an inhalation anesthetic produces a condition known as **malignant hyperthermia.** This condition is associated with a drastic increase in body temperature, acidosis, electrolyte imbalance, and shock. The mechanism by which **hyperthermia** occurs is believed to be related to the anesthetic-induced potentiation of calcium hyperreactivity in susceptible individuals. The hyperactive biochemical reactions progress so quickly that treatment must be started immediately to reduce the risk of death. Treatment of hyperthermia includes reducing body temperature with ice packs and controlling arrhythmias and acidosis with appropriate drugs. Unfortunately, the incidence of fatality in malignant hyperthermia is high. Prevention is primarily directed at obtaining a good family history about other episodes of difficulty during operative procedures. Muscle biopsy and elevated muscle enzyme levels may identify potentially sensitive patients. Such a workup prior to an operation allows the surgical team to avoid the use of sensitizing agents.

Succinylcholine has a **black box warning** in its FDA-approved instructions for use that states: *"Succinylcholine has been associated with rapid muscle breakdown resulting in life-threatening heart rhythms, cardiac arrest, and death in children. Male children younger than 8 years of age seem to be at a higher risk, but cases have also been reported in adolescents. Because it is hard to determine which children may be at risk, Succinylcholine should only be used in an emergency situation."* This risk is identified for use in children. There still are situations where succinylcholine may be used to facilitate skeletal muscle relaxation (electroconvulsive therapy) or rapid tracheal intubation (emergency airway management). Its use is dependent on patient age, concomitant medical conditions in the patient, and training and experience of the anesthesiologist, surgical team, or emergency medical team.

Cautions and Drug Interactions

Neuromuscular blocking drugs should be used with extreme caution in patients with impaired neuromuscular function (myasthenia gravis and spinal cord lesions). Any medication that inhibits skeletal muscle function **potentiates** the action of neuromuscular blockers. Antibiotics (neomycin, streptomycin), antiarrhythmic drugs, and some general anesthetics (halogenated gases like isoflurane, halothane) directly inhibit neuromuscular function, causing skeletal muscle relaxation. Succinylcholine-induced neuromuscular blockade is potentiated by drugs that promote a loss of potassium, such as diuretics and digitalis. In contrast, drugs that stimulate the nicotinic-muscle receptors or inhibit acetylcholinesterase antagonize nondepolarizing blockers. Drug interactions associated with skeletal muscle relaxants can potentiate or eliminate the pharmacologic action of muscle relaxants. Drugs that decrease the effect of any neuromuscular blocker include corticosteroids, carbamazepine, insecticides, acetylcholinesterase inhibitors, and theophylline. Drugs that increase the effect of muscle relaxants include alcohol, antiarrhythmics (lidocaine, procainamide, quinidine), antibiotics (clindamycin, kanamycin, lincomycin, neomycin, pipericilllin, streptomycin, tetracyclines), general anesthetics, narcotic analgesics, tranquilizers, and sedatives. Succinylcholine is potentiated by digitalis and diuretics because these drugs induce a shift in potassium ions that enhances the action of succinylcholine. The only contraindication is the use in patients with a known hypersensitivity to any of these drugs.

The nondepolarizing and depolarizing neuromuscular blockers are prepared as solutions for parenteral administration. Mixing some solutions can result in drug **incompatibility** and should be avoided. Drug incompatibility may result in discoloration of the solution, precipitation of drug, or, most important, alteration of drug potency. Succinylcholine has been reported to be unstable when mixed in alkaline solution (pH > 7.0). Admixture to solutions of barbiturates should be avoided because the combination results in hydrolyzation (breakdown) of succinylcholine.

Clinical Indications

The peripheral neuromuscular blockers are used primarily before (premedication) and during surgical procedures (surgical relaxation) to relax abdominal or intrathoracic skeletal muscles. These agents are also used during electroconvulsive shock therapy and tetanus therapy to reduce muscle spasms. Airway management in emergency situations requires the use of these drugs to facilitate tracheal intubation. Airway management is the most important skill for an emergency physician to master because failure to secure an adequate airway can quickly lead to death or disability. Similarly, for diagnostic procedures such as laryngoscopy, the trachea must be relaxed to avoid muscle strain against the endoscope. Because of its short action, succinylcholine may be used to aid intubations for surgical procedures. Cisatracurium may be preferred in nonemergency situations because it has an intermediate duration of action and is not associated with histamine release. This permits control of the muscle relaxation without the hypotension or bronchospasm associated with histamine. Neuromuscular blockers are used in an ICU setting with critically ill patients who are compromised by their existing conditions of bronchospasm or chronic obstructive pulmonary disease (COPD), making it difficult for them to be properly externally ventilated. Peripheral neuromuscular blockers can reduce chest wall resistance (muscle relaxation), thereby increasing compliance and ventilation (oxygen/carbon dioxide exchange).

DIRECT-ACTING SKELETAL MUSCLE RELAXANTS

Dantrolene is considered a direct-acting peripheral skeletal muscle relaxant because it inhibits skeletal muscle fiber contraction by interfering with calcium ion release within the muscle fiber (Figure 9.2, site 3).

Mechanism of Action

Dantrolene prevents actin and myosin from interacting, thus preventing muscle contraction. By interacting with specialized receptors (*ryanodine receptor channel*) in the **sarcoplasmic reticulum,** dantrolene blocks the release of calcium ions. Calcium ions are critical for muscle contraction because they interact with the contractile filaments. The skeletal muscle contractile process cannot respond to stimulation even though conduction of impulses through the spinal cord and transmission across the neuromuscular junction are not affected. Dantrolene does not affect the nicotinic-muscle receptors or the NMJ. It is a direct-acting muscle relaxant because it acts within the muscle cell at calcium storage centers. Dantrolene dosing information is presented in Table 9:1 because it acts peripherally (outside the CNS) to produce skeletal muscle relaxation.

Clinical Indications

Dantrolene is used in the treatment of malignant hyperthermia and spastic conditions. Muscle spasms associated with multiple sclerosis, cerebral palsy, and spinal cord injuries may reduce patients' ability to function or perform activities required for daily living. Dantrolene, taken orally, relaxes spastic skeletal muscle and allows these individuals to make use of their residual motor function. In the prevention and treatment of malignant hyperthermia, dantrolene, given intravenously, interferes with the release of calcium in the sensitized muscles, reversing the biochemical crisis.

Adverse Effects

The most frequent adverse effects include dizziness, vomiting, fatigue, and weakness. Dantrolene has a potential for hepatotoxicity, which is indicated in a box warning in its instructions for use. As deaths have occurred due to hepatotoxicity, serum enzymes indicative of changes in liver function, aspartate amino transferase (AST/SGOT) and alanine amino transferase (ALT/SGPT), should be monitored frequently during dantrolene therapy. Contraindication to the use of dantrolene includes hepatitis and cirrhosis, as well as other active hepatic diseases. The long-term safety of dantrolene is being evaluated through its continued use. Any drug that decreases muscle strength or depresses the CNS may potentiate the muscle weakness produced by dantrolene. Drugs that increase the effect of dantrolene on skeletal muscle include alcohol, antiarrhythmics (lidocaine, procainamide, quinidine), antibiotics (clindamycin, kanamycin, lincomycin, neomycin, pipericilllin, streptomycin, tetracyclines), general anesthetics, narcotic analgesics, tranquilizers, and sedatives.

CENTRALLY ACTING SKELETAL MUSCLE RELAXANTS (SPASMOLYTICS)

Spastic contraction of skeletal muscles may occur in response to overexertion, trauma, or nervous tension. Usually, the muscles undergoing spasm are limited to the area of trauma (neck, back, or calf). Reflexes within the spinal cord repeatedly stimulate the motor neurons so that localized muscle fibers contract intermittently. This perpetuates a cycle of irritation or inflammation within localized muscle areas. Drugs that inhibit or interrupt painful intermittent muscle contractions are called **spasmolytics.**

Mechanism of Action

Drugs that relax skeletal muscle by a central mechanism depress reflex impulse conduction within the spinal cord. This change in conduction reduces the number of impulses available to produce muscle contraction. Centrally acting skeletal muscle relaxants do not alter the function of the nicotinic-muscle receptors or the skeletal muscle fibers. Some of these muscle relaxants interfere with select areas of the brain to interrupt the spasticity (reduce intraneuronal activity). Although all of the drugs listed in Table 9:2 relieve muscle spasticity, the benzodiazepines chlordiazepoxide (*Librium*) and diazepam (*Valium*) are primarily used as tranquilizers (antianxiety). These agents, which interact with GABA (gamma-aminobutyric acid), a neurotransmitter in the CNS, will be discussed in Chapter 12. See Figure 9.3 for sites of receptor interaction for centrally acting skeletal muscle relaxants.

Many people encounter muscle relaxants as outpatient therapy for muscle strain and overexertion during leisure activities. Baclofen and tizanidine reduce the spasms that interfere with daily activities in patients with multiple sclerosis. Baclofen (*Lioresal*) is chemically related to a substance that naturally occurs in the brain (gamma-aminobutyric acid [GABA]). Like other centrally acting muscle relaxants, it inhibits reflexes at the spinal level. GABA is

Centrally Acting Skeletal Muscle Relaxants

Drug (*Trade Name*)	Adult dose
Baclofen (*Lioresal, Kemstro*)	10–80 mg PO
Intrathecal baclofen therapy (ITB)	Individual titration to 300–800 mcg/day
Carisoprodol (*Soma*)	250–350 mg PO TID, and at bedtime
Chlordiazepoxide* (*Librium*)	2–10 mg PO TID, QID
	2–20 mg IM, IV elderly 2–2.5 mg QD, BID
Chlorzoxazone (*Parafon Forte DSC*)	250–750 mg PO TID, QID
Cyclobenzaprine (*Flexeril, Amrix*)	5–10 mg PO TID
Diazepam* (*Valium*)	2–10 mg PO TID 5–10 mg IM**
Metaxalone (*Skelaxin*)	800 mg PO TID, QID
Methocarbamol (*Robaxin*)	1.0–1.5 g PO QID
Methocarbamol injection	1 or 2 vials (1000 mg/vial) IM, IV
Orphenadrine citrate	100 mg PO BID
Orphenadrine citrate (*Banflex, Flexon, Norflex*)	60 mg (1 ampule) IV, IM (every 12 hours as needed)**
Tizanidine (*Zanaflex*)	4–12 mg PO every 6–8 hours

*Although these drugs are used primarily as antianxiety agents, they are also skeletal muscle relaxants.
**Should be changed to tablets as soon as the symptoms are relieved.*

the principal inhibitory neurotransmitter within the brain. The GABA receptors are a superfamily of membrane-bound proteins (see Figure 9.3). When GABA binds to its $GABA_A$ and $GABA_B$ receptors, pores (ion channels) open through the lipid membrane, allowing passive movement of small ions. This ion movement changes the potential across the membrane, affecting conductivity of the cell.

Benzodiazepines and baclofen bind with the $GABA_A$ and the $GABA_B$ receptors, respectively, and cause chloride ions (Cl^-, negative ion) to move across the membrane into the cells, making the membrane *hyperpolarized* (can't respond to stimulation). This decreases neuronal membrane "excitability." $GABA_A$ receptors are continually active, so anything that interacts with them has continual response.

Baclofen is primarily used to relieve the symptoms of spasticity (flexor spasms, clonus, muscle rigidity) in patients with multiple sclerosis but also may be of value in patients with spinal cord injury resulting in severe spasticity. Through a different mechanism of action, tizanidine (*Zanaflex*) reduces spasticity by interacting with alpha-2-adrenergic receptors in the CNS. Neither of these drugs reverses the pathology of multiple sclerosis. Both are adjunct medications that improve the quality of life for many patients with spastic muscle conditions.

Route of Administration and Adverse Effects

The centrally acting skeletal muscle relaxants may be administered orally or parenterally.

Figure 9.3   Sites of Action of Centrally Acting Muscle Relaxants

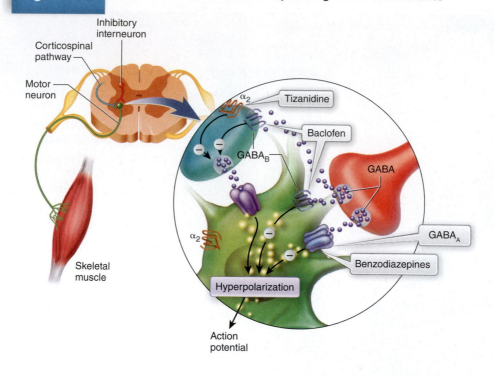

Proposed sites of action of tizanidine (alpha-2), benzodiazepines (GABA$_A$), and baclofen (GABA$_B$) in the spinal cord. Neuronal endings in the inset are color coded to match the motor neuron, corticospinal pathway and inhibitory interneuron.

While most of the drugs in this group are taken as oral tablet or capsule formulations, certain drugs are available for parenteral administration for severe chronic conditions. Methocarbamol (*Robaxin*) is given intravenously for the treatment of tetanus. Baclofen (*Lioresal*) is available for **intrathecal** injection. It is administered by a pump implanted under the skin in the area of the waistline. Candidates are thoroughly screened for compatibility to adapt to use of an implanted pump, but when selected, the drug delivery system is usually an alternative to otherwise destructive (ablative) neurosurgical procedures. To some degree, these drugs are metabolized in the liver and excreted in the urine. The most frequently reported adverse effects include blurred vision, dizziness, lethargy, and decreased mental alertness. The intensity of these effects may require patients to avoid driving or operating mechanical equipment. With large doses, skeletal muscle tone decreases, resulting in ataxia and hypotension. Tizanidine has the potential to decrease blood pressure because of its action on the sympathetic alpha-2 receptors. This may result in orthostatic hypotension in patients with multiple sclerosis. Prolonged use of diazepam and chlordiazepoxide may lead to dependency. Discontinuation of therapy in patients who have received any of these drugs for long periods (chronically) must be gradual to avoid precipitating withdrawal symptoms. Usually, the dose is decreased over a 4- to 8-week period.

Any of the muscle relaxants should be discontinued under medical supervision if a hypersensitivity reaction develops. However, this may require a gradual process of drug discontinuation to avoid the development of life-threatening events. Special precautions must be taken when reducing the dose of baclofen during chronic therapy. If an adverse reaction occurs that prompts termination of baclofen therapy, the dose must be reduced gradually. Although not associated with dependence, hallucinations and/or seizures have been reported to occur when the drug was abruptly stopped. Abrupt discontinuation of intrathecal baclofen infusion has resulted in muscle rigidity, rebound spasticity, and, in some cases, organ failure and death. This is a black box warning for intrathecal baclofen use.

Overdose of centrally acting skeletal muscle relaxants will produce symptoms of confusion, somnolence, and depression of vital functions including respiration, heart, and pulse rates. Coma may precede death if the patient does not receive adequate evaluation and treatment in time. There is no specific antidote for overdose associated with centrally acting muscle relaxants. The patient must be monitored for respiratory and cardiovascular activity while a clear airway is maintained and ventilation supported. In the event that hypotension develops, an IV infusion should be available for parenteral fluid therapy. There is a specific benzodiazepine antagonist, flumazenil (*Romazicon*), that can be used to reverse the depressive effects of chlordiazepoxide (*Librium*) or diazepam (*Valium*) overdose. This antagonist has no ability to reverse the depression associated with other centrally acting muscle relaxants.

Drug Interactions

Drugs that depress the CNS (alcohol, sedatives, and tranquilizers) or impair neuromuscular function potentiate the actions and adverse effects of all skeletal muscle relaxants.

Preferred Treatment for Selected Conditions

Surgical Relaxation

The selection of a neuromuscular blocking drug for surgery depends on the time of onset and the duration, adverse effects, and reversibility (ability to remove the NMJ blockade) of the drug; the duration of the surgery; and the specific condition (weight, medical history, current conditions) of the patient.

Intubation

None of the nondepolarizing blocking drugs equals the rapid onset and short duration of action of succinylcholine (*Anectine*). With a single 1-mg/kg dose of succinylcholine, tracheal relaxation occurs within 30 seconds and lasts up to 10 minutes. The nondepolarizing blocking drugs have an onset between 1.5 and 3 minutes and duration up to 90 minutes.

Relief of Back or Neck Pain

There are many over-the-counter (nonsteroidal anti-inflammatory drugs, Chapter 20) and prescription drugs available for the relief of pain from muscle strain or overexertion, but these drugs do not act to inhibit or interrupt the muscle spasms. Muscle spasms may occur in individual muscle groups (leg, neck) producing feelings of pain or tightness in and around joints but also can cause generalized low-back pain. For the short-term treatment of muscle spasm or strain, carisoprodol (*Soma*) and cyclobenzaprine (*Flexeril*) are often the drugs of choice. Cyclobenzaprine also can be given before bedtime to aid with sleeping. Diazepam (*Valium*) is a drug well known by patients and physicians and may be selected to relieve low-back pain associated with muscle spasm. Diazepam is usually limited to one to two weeks because of its habit-forming potential.

Disorders Associated with Chronic Spasticity

Chronic spasticity may be as mild as the feeling of stiffness or tightness of muscles, or it may be severe with painful uncontrollable spasms of the extremities, usually of the legs. Baclofen (*Lioresal*) has been widely used for spasticity of any etiology (cause). Most studies indicate that it improves clonus, spasm frequency, and joint range of motion resulting in improved functional status for the patient. Patients with cerebral palsy and traumatic brain injury respond to dantrolene sodium (*Dantrium*), while tizanidine (*Zanaflex*) is used for the treatment of spasticity caused by multiple sclerosis and spinal cord injury.

Treatment of Malignant Hyperthermia

Dantrolene (*Dantrium*) is the drug of choice for the treatment of malignant hyperthermia. Continuous parenteral administration of dantrolene proceeds until symptoms subside or the maximum cumulative dose of 10 mg/kg has been reached. If the physiologic and metabolic abnormalities reappear, the regimen may be repeated.

When skeletal muscle relaxants are used in surgical settings, the potential for adverse effects may be minimized through close observation of the patient during recovery. Following diagnostic procedures or intubations under outpatient conditions, or chronic therapy for spastic muscle conditions, there is a greater likelihood that patients may experience adverse effects that could put them at risk for injury. For this reason patients should receive clear instructions about which adverse effects are worthy of physician notification. The centrally acting skeletal muscle relaxants may cause persistent drowsiness that interferes with mental alertness and concentration. For chronic spastic conditions, this effect is usually tolerable so the treatment schedule does not need to be interrupted. It should be noted that dose adjustment does not always mitigate the drowsy effect. Therefore, with short-term therapy of muscle strain, the patient may need to incorporate other solutions to circumvent the difficulties associated with drowsiness.

Patient Instructions

The patient should be asked whether he or she performs tasks that require special equipment or machinery (sewing machines, motor vehicles) or coordination, focus, or physical dexterity (drill press, motor tools, assembly tools). Extra caution is needed, including identifying a coworker, on-site medical personnel, or a relative who is aware of the patient's medication schedule. If necessary, alternate transportation when driving is required may be necessary until treatment is completed.

Alcohol and other CNS depressant drugs should be avoided. This includes over-the-counter (OTC) medications that contain alcohol as a significant active ingredient. These drugs may potentiate poor coordination, drowsiness, and dizziness (postural hypotension).

Skin rash, nasal congestion, persistent fever, or yellowish discoloration of the skin or eyes should be reported to the physician or clinic immediately for further evaluation.

Dantrolene causes photosensitivity so prolonged exposure to sunlight should be avoided.

Baclofen may cause nausea, headache, insomnia, and frequent or painful urination that should be reported to the physician for further evaluation.

Tizanidine is available in capsules and tablets, but they are not interchangeable during the course of treatment. Patients should be reminded to continue the same formulation to avoid fluctuations in absorption. Capsules can be opened and sprinkled on applesauce to improve patient compliance when necessary; however, food does impact the bioavailability of tizanidine.

Use in Pregnancy

Drugs in this class have been designated Food and Drug Administration (FDA) Pregnancy Category C or D. Safety for use during pregnancy has not been established through adequate and well-controlled studies in humans. All of these drugs, except diazepam, are category C because animal reproduction studies have shown an adverse effect on the fetus. Diazepam is category D because there is positive evidence of human fetal risk based on adverse reaction data from investigational or marketing experience or studies in humans. It is recommended that no drug should be administered during pregnancy unless it is clearly needed and the potential benefits to the patient outweigh the potential risks to the fetus.

Patients who become pregnant or who expect to become pregnant during therapy should discuss with the physician the potential risks of therapy to the fetus.

Understanding Terminology

Answer the following questions.

___ 1. Differentiate between depolarizing blockers and nondepolarizing blockers. **(LO 9.1)**

___ 2. Explain the difference between peripheral skeletal muscle relaxants and centrally acting skeletal muscle relaxants. **(LO 9.1, 9.4)**

___ 3. Use the following terms in a short paragraph: *fasciculation, hyperthermia, vagolytic,* and *vasodilator.* **(LO 9.6)**

Acquiring Knowledge

Answer the following questions.

1. What are the physiological events that precede skeletal muscle contraction? **(LO 9.1)**

2. What is a neuromuscular junction (NMJ)? **(LO 9.1)**

3. What sites are involved in the production of skeletal muscle relaxation? **(LO 9.1, 9.4, 9.5)**

4. What are the two types of neuromuscular blockers? How do they differ in their mechanism of action? **(LO 9.1)**

5. Why are neuromuscular blockers administered IV? **(LO 9.2)**

6. What adverse effects are produced by the neuromuscular blockers as a result of histamine release? **(LO 9.6)**

7. Describe the major toxicity associated with neuromuscular blockers and the antidote used. **(LO 9.6)**

8. How does dantrolene differ from neuromuscular blockers? **(LO 9.1, 9.5)**

9. What is the mechanism of action of centrally acting skeletal muscle relaxants? **(LO 9.4)**

10. When are centrally acting skeletal muscle relaxants used? **(LO 9.2)**

Applying Knowledge on the Job

Use your critical-thinking skills to answer the following questions.

1. As a health care worker in a busy health maintenance organization (HMO), you work with dozens of patients each day. You've noticed that each of the following three patients who were treated today has been prescribed a drug that could cause problems. For each patient, identify and explain the potential drug problem.

   a. Patient A came to the HMO this morning complaining of muscle pain following a back injury. He was prescribed the muscle relaxant cyclobenzaprine. Patient A is always joking with the nurses about how much he drinks. It's clear that he takes several drinks of whiskey every day. **(LO 9.6)**

   b. Patient B came into the HMO last week with strep throat, for which he was prescribed streptomycin. Today, he's complaining of neck and shoulder pain, which he attributes to driving his car for a total of 20 hours over the past 2 days. Patient B was prescribed metaxalone for the muscle pain. **(LO 9.6)**

   c. Patient C takes lidocaine for a heart arrhythmia. Yesterday, she injured herself doing calisthenics and spent a sleepless night in pain. Today, she visited the doctor and was prescribed methocarbamol to relax her sore muscles. **(LO 9.6)**

2. Assume that you work in a surgical unit where you coordinate patient medications. For each of the following patients, identify a potential drug problem and how it might be avoided.

   a. Jeri is about to have a type of orthopedic surgery that requires a muscle relaxant for best results. Jeri's medical history indicates that she has asthma but is otherwise in good health. **(LO 9.6)**

b. Linda is scheduled for surgery on her back. Her surgeon is planning to give her succinylcholine to relax her muscles during the procedure. As far as the surgeon is aware, Linda is in great health other than the vertebrae that require surgery. Linda has confided in you, however, that she has bulimia, which you know can lead to electrolyte imbalance. **(LO 9.6)**

c. Susan has knee surgery scheduled. A note on her chart indicates that she will be given succinylcholine during the operation to relax the muscles in her leg. Her chart also indicates that she takes digitalis for a heart problem. **(LO 9.6)**

Multiple Choice

Use your critical-thinking skills to answer the following questions.

1. Which of the following is correct about skeletal muscle relaxants? **(LO 9.1, 9.2, 9.6)**
   A. intubation for emergency airway management may be accomplished quickly
   B. the clinical indication for these drugs is to prolong surgical procedures
   C. centrally acting skeletal muscle relaxants must inhibit nicotinic receptors
   D. their use is limited by the amount of histamine released from mast cells

2. Which of the following is correct about neuromuscular blocking drugs? **(LO 9.1)**
   A. the mechanism of action is the same as represented by dantrolene
   B. all of these drugs depolarize the muscle fiber before blockade occurs
   C. calcium ions are released from the storage sites
   D. there are two groups in this class: either depolarizing agents or nondepolarizing agents

3. Mivacurium and rocuronium are used to **(LO 9.1, 9.2)**
   A. relax muscle spasms from "week-end warrior" back strain
   B. block acetylcholine at the nicotinic-muscle (Nm) receptor
   C. stimulate the nicotinic-muscle (Nm) receptors
   D. produce muscle fasciculations in surgery

4. Succinylcholine is associated with which of the following actions? **(LO 9.1)**
   A. stimulation of the actin and myosin muscle fibrils directly
   B. liver damage because the drug is metabolized only by the liver
   C. peripheral neuromuscular receptor blockade after stimulating the Nm receptors
   D. longer duration of action than vecuronium

5. Centrally acting skeletal muscle relaxants **(LO 9.1, 9.4, 9.5, 9.6)**
   A. include dantrolene and cisatracurium
   B. inhibit or reduce activity within the spinal cord (intraneuronal), interrupting the central stimulus to muscle contraction
   C. can only be given parenterally
   D. cause systemic release of histamine, leading to hypotension

6. Which of the drugs is correctly paired with its effect? **(LO 9.6)**
   A. succinylcholine: life-threatening cardiac arrest in children
   B. tizanidine: hypertension and increased salivation
   C. cyclobenzaprine/metaxolol: antagonized by alcohol and sedatives
   D. vecuronium: increased blood pressure and heart rate

7. Skeletal muscle relaxants may alter control of respiration because **(LO 9.3)**
   A. the diaphragm is a skeletal muscle
   B. succinylcholine stimulates the respiratory centers in the brain

C. like dantrolene, all muscle relaxants inhibit the action of norepinephrine at the neuromuscular junction

D. relaxation of the muscles in the lower extremities pulls blood away from the lungs

Multiple Choice (Multiple Answer)

Select the correct choices for each statement. The choices may be all correct, all incorrect, or any combination.

1. Select the drugs that decrease the effects of neuromuscular blockers. **(LO 9.6)**
   A. neomycin
   B. corticosteroids
   C. theophylline
   D. carbamazepine

2. Which of the following are ways in which skeletal muscles may be relaxed? **(LO 9.1)**
   A. blockage of conduction in the spinal cord
   B. inhibiting nerve transmission
   C. blockage of the NI receptors
   D. increasing ACH in the neuromuscular junction

3. Which of the following drugs are used in chronic spastic muscle disorders? **(LO 9.5)**
   A. metaxolone
   B. cyclobenzaprine
   C. baclofen
   D. methocarbamol

4. Select reasons for using muscle relaxers during surgical or diagnostic procedures. **(LO 9.2)**
   A. reduce muscle tear
   B. decrease body temperature
   C. potentiate vasodilators
   D. reduce muscle strain

5. What are the adverse effects of peripherally acting skeletal muscle relaxants? **(LO 9.6)**
   A. acidosis
   B. electrolyte imbalance
   C. decreased respiration
   D. shock

Sequencing

Place the following steps of muscle contraction in the proper sequence. **(LO 9.1)**

_____   _____   _____   _____

First   **Last**

ACH combines with Nm receptor

ACH released in the neuromuscular synapse

depolarization of muscle fibers

impulse from CNS

Classification

Put the drugs in their correct classification. **(LO 9.5)**

Norflex   Robaxin

Soma   Zemuron

Nimbex   Flexeril

Centrally acting	Peripherally acting

Matching

Match the following terms with their correct definitions. **(LO 9)**

   a. fasciculation
   b. hyperthermia
   c. incompatibility
   d. myelin
   e. potentiates
   f. sarcolemma
   g. spasmolytics
   h. vagolytic

1. _____ produces an action greater than the individual components produce alone
2. _____ fatty substance that covers and protects nerves
3. _____ increased body temperature
4. _____ thin membrane enclosing a striated, skeletal muscle fiber
5. _____ undesirable interaction between two drugs
6. _____ drugs that relieve, interrupt, or prevent muscle spasms
7. _____ inhibition of the vagus nerve
8. _____ twitching of muscle fibers

For interactive animations, videos, and assessment, visit:

www.mcgrawhillconnect.com

Chapter 10

Local Anesthetics

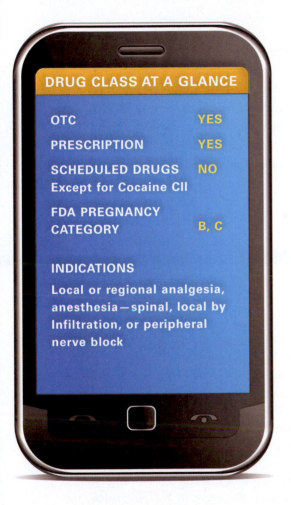

DRUG CLASS AT A GLANCE

OTC	YES
PRESCRIPTION	YES
SCHEDULED DRUGS	NO
Except for Cocaine CII	
FDA PREGNANCY CATEGORY	B, C

INDICATIONS

Local or regional analgesia, anesthesia—spinal, local by Infiltration, or peripheral nerve block

KEY TERMS

amide local anesthetic: anesthetic class that includes lidocaine, bupivicaine, and mepivicaine and has a moderate to long duration of action because metabolism occurs in the liver.

cardiac arrhythmia: variation in the normal rhythm (motion) of the heart.

caudal anesthesia: injection of a local anesthetic into the caudal or subcaudal spinal canal.

cryoanesthesia: removing the sensation of touch or pain by applying extreme cold to the nerve endings.

epidural anesthesia: injection of a local anesthetic into the extra-dural (the outermost part of the spinal canal) space.

ester local anesthetic: anesthetic class that includes procaine, cocaine, benzocaine, and tetracaine; metabolism is primarily by plasma cholinesterases.

general anesthetic drug that abolishes the response to pain by depressing the central nervous system (CNS) and producing loss of consciousness.

hypersensitivity: exaggerated response such as rash, edema, or anaphylaxis that develops following exposure to certain drugs or chemicals.

infiltration anesthesia: injection of a local anesthetic directly into the tissue.

intradermal anesthesia: injection of a local anesthetic into the part of the skin called the dermis.

local anesthetic: drug that reduces response to pain by affecting nerve conduction. The action can be limited to an area of the body according to the site of administration.

nerve conduction: transfer of impulses along a nerve by the movement of sodium and potassium ions.

regional nerve block: also called nerve block; the injection of a local anesthetic near the nerve root.

spinal anesthesia: injection of a local anesthetic into the subarachnoid space.

topical application: placing a drug on the surface of the skin or a mucous membrane (for example, mouth, rectum).

vasoconstriction: tightening or contraction of muscles (sphincters) in the blood vessels, which decreases blood flow through the vessels.

vasodilation: relaxation of the muscles (sphincters) controlling blood vessel tone, which increases blood flow through the vessels.

10.1 describe how a local anesthetic works (mechanism of action).

10.2 explain how a local anesthetic can reduce pain without affecting the muscles that control posture.

10.3 identify which local anesthetics must be administered by injection.

10.4 describe the adverse effects associated with local anesthetic use.

10.5 identify two local anesthetic drugs that are important in the treatment of cardiac dysfunction because of their action on the heart (antiarrhythmic).

Introduction

Drugs may be used in many different ways to control pain. **General anesthetics,** to be discussed in Chapter 18, abolish the response to pain by depressing the CNS and producing loss of consciousness. However, it may be desirable to relieve pain without altering the alertness or mental function of the patient. To accomplish this, analgesics (opioid and nonopioid, Chapters 19 and 20) or local anesthetics may be used. The source and intensity of the pain determine which of these pharmacological agents is most useful to decrease the response to the painful stimuli. **Local anesthetics,** as their name suggests, produce a temporary loss of sensation or feeling in a confined area of the body.

LO 10.1 **LO 10.2**

MECHANISM OF ACTION

The most common clinical use of local anesthetics is to abolish painful stimulation prior to surgical, dental (tooth extraction), or obstetric (delivery) procedures. In addition, local anesthetics are ingredients in many over-the-counter (OTC) products for sunburn, insect bites, and hemorrhoids because these topical applications get local anesthetics to injured (pain-producing) nerve endings quickly.

Local anesthetics abolish the response to pain because they inhibit sensory nerves that carry painful stimuli to the CNS. In particular, local anesthetics block nerve fiber conduction by acting directly on nerve membranes. Local anesthetics interact with nerve membranes to inhibit sodium ions from crossing the membranes. Neurons have sodium and potassium channels in their membranes. The sodium channel is actually a large protein (α subunit) in the membrane. Local anesthetics bind to this protein (α subunit) and effectively block the flow of sodium ions through the channel. This decreases sodium permeability across the membrane. If

sodium ion movement is inhibited, nerves cannot depolarize, and conduction of impulses along the nerves is blocked (Figure 10.1). Sodium influx (movement to the intracellular space) through these channels is necessary for the depolarization of nerve cell membranes and subsequent propagation of impulses along the nerve. When a nerve loses depolarization and the capacity to propagate an impulse, the individual loses sensation in the area supplied by the nerve. This blockade of **nerve conduction** is reversible, which means that when the local anesthetic is carried away from the nerve by the circulation, the action of the local anesthetic ends. The local anesthetic is then metabolized.

Local anesthetics are valuable because they block sensory nerves at doses that do not inhibit motor nerve function. Peripheral nerve fibers and their neurons are classified as A, B, or C according to the diameter of the axon, amount of myelin covering the nerve, and conduction velocity (fast or slow). Sensory nerves carry impulses for pain, touch, warmth, and cold to the brain. The sensory and autonomic nerves (C fibers) are the first fibers to become blocked by local anesthetics because

Figure 10.1	Action of Local Anesthetics on Nerve Conduction

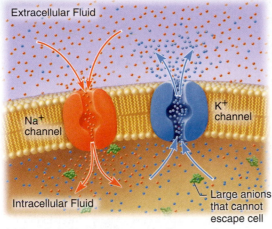

(a) Depolarization impulse conduction

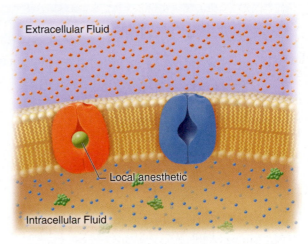

(b) Local anesthetic blockade of sodium ion channel. No impulse conduction.

(a) Depolarization—sodium ions (Na⁺) move in and potassium ions (K⁺) move out of the cells.
(b) Local anesthetics enter the sodium channel and prevent sodium ion flow and depolarization.

these fibers are relatively small in diameter and unprotected by myelin sheaths (unmyelinated). Therefore, local anesthetics can easily penetrate the membranes and inhibit nerve conduction. In contrast, the motor nerves that supply skeletal muscle (A fibers) are the last fibers to be inhibited because motor nerves are large fibers with thick myelin coverings. The degree of nerve depression by local anesthetics is presented in Table 10:1. The importance of this is that pain fibers can be blocked without altering skeletal muscle function (for example, diaphragm, posture). In addition, the pain fibers surrounded by local anesthetic are the last to recover from local anesthetic blockade (good duration of action).

LO 10.1   LO 10.3   LO 10.5

PHARMACOLOGY

The most commonly used local anesthetics are listed in Table 10:2 on page 135. All of these agents produce adequate, controlled nerve block by inhibiting nerve conduction. Local anesthetics are weak bases that travel in the body as either uncharged or positively (+) charged molecules. Both forms are critical to local anesthetic activity. Which form is present depends on the environment (pH, lipid matrix, water solubility) surrounding the molecule. One form allows the drug to cross membranes and the other form allows the drug to interact with charged proteins in the plasma or at receptor sites. The uncharged local anesthetic (the more lipid-soluble form) allows the molecule to cross into the neuronal membrane (lipid matrix) and gain access to the sodium ion channel receptor

that lies inside the membrane. As it migrates to the area of the sodium ion channel, a more water-soluble area, the local anesthetic returns to its charged (+) form and binds with the sodium ion channel receptor. The intensity of receptor binding (affinity) influences the duration of local anesthetic nerve block. Local anesthetics differ in their duration of action, site of metabolism, and potency.

There are two classes of local anesthetics: ester local anesthetics and amide local anesthetics. The **ester local anesthetics** have a short or moderate duration of action because they are metabolized by enzymes (cholinesterases) that are present in the blood and skin. Examples of ester local anesthetics are benzocaine, cocaine, cyclomethycaine, procaine, and tetracaine. Cocaine is the only naturally occurring drug among the local anesthetics. It is obtained from a plant in South and Central America. Cocaine, and the coca plant leaf, is classified as a Schedule II stimulant drug. It has a recognized medicinal use, but prescribing protocol and documentation must be followed (restricted drug). (See www.usdoj.gov/dea/pubs/scheduling.html for details.) Today all of the local anesthetics, even the recreational ones, are synthetically produced. Tetracaine is the only ester derivative that has a very long duration of action. Even though it is metabolized by plasma cholinesterases, tetracaine has a strong affinity for the sodium channel receptor that contributes to its significant duration of action, up to 3 to 5 hours.

The **amide local anesthetics** are usually the longer-acting drugs because these agents must be metabolized in the liver. The amide group includes dibucaine, lidocaine, mepivacaine, ropivacaine, and prilocaine.

Nerve Fiber Characteristics and Order of Depression by Local Anesthetics

Fiber type	Function	Diameter (μm)	Myelination	Conduction velocity (m/s)	Anesthetic block Sensitivity	Onset
Type C						
Sympathetic	Postganglionic	0.3–1.3	None	0.7–2.3	++++(most)	Early
Dorsal root	Pain	0.4–0.12	None	0.5–2.3	++++	
Type B						
	Preganglionic autonomic	<3	Light	3–15	++++	
Type A						
Delta (A$_\delta$)	Pain, temperature	2–5	Heavy	5–25	+++	
Gamma (A$_\gamma$)	Muscle spindles	3–6	Heavy	15–30	++	Intermediate
Beta (A$_\beta$)	Touch, pressure	5–12	Heavy	30–70	++	
Alpha(A$_\alpha$)	Proprioception, motor	12–20	Heavy	70–120	+ (least)	Last

Procainamide is not routinely used as a local anesthetic. Its local anesthetic attribute acting on the conduction system within the heart makes it valuable as an antiarrhythmic drug. (See Chapter 23.)

Potency is the ability of the anesthetic to produce a nerve block at a relatively low dose compared to other local anesthetics. The lipid solubility of the drug (uncharged form) directly contributes to its potency because it allows the molecules to gain quick access through the membrane and then on to the sodium ion channel. Tetracaine, bupivacaine, and ropivacaine are reported to be more than 15 times more potent than procaine. Other anesthetics like mepivacaine and lidocaine are 2 to 4 times more potent than procaine.

If the site of administration is highly vascularized, the blood supply will pull anesthetic away from the site of action, reducing its effective duration of action. Often epinephrine is injected with the local anesthetic because epinephrine will constrict blood vessels and keep the local anesthetic at the site of action longer.

LO 10.3
ROUTES OF ADMINISTRATION

The duration of action and potency of local anesthetics determine which route of administration to employ. Local anesthetics are administered topically or by injection. Local anesthetics are poorly absorbed through an intact epidermis, but they are well absorbed from breaks or abrasions in the skin and from highly vascularized sites

such as mucous membranes. Ester anesthetics, particularly those found in OTC preparations, readily are applied topically to the skin or mucous membranes. **Topical application** of local anesthetics also is known as surface anesthesia. Topical preparations are available as creams, lotions, ointments, sprays, suppositories, eyedrops, and lozenges. The most recent development in topical anesthesia includes combination local anesthetics applied to open and intact skin to reduce pain prior to suturing. The first available combination was TAC (tetracaine, adrenaline, cocaine). This preparation, although extremely effective, is being phased out by combinations that do not contain cocaine. LET (lidocaine, epinephrine, tetracaine) is not available commercially in this combination; it must be compounded as a liquid or gel by the pharmacist. EMLA (a eutectic mixture of local anesthetics) represents a major breakthrough in dermal anesthesia. Lidocaine and prilocaine are combined with a thickener and an emulsifier, applied as a thick layer to intact skin, and covered with clear plastic wrap to promote

Characteristics of Commonly Employed Local Anesthetics

Drug (*Trade Name*)	Duration	Route	Preparations
Esters			
Benzocaine (*Dermoplast, Lanacane, Solarcaine, Sting-kill swabs*)*	0.5–0.75 hr	Topical	5% cream, ointment 2–20% spray
Cocaine**	0.25–0.75 hr	Topical	1–4% solution
Chloroprocaine (*Nesacaine*)	0.25–0.50 hr	Injection	1–3% solution
Procaine (*Novocaine*) infiltration	0.25–1.0 hr	Injection	1–2% and 10% solutions
Tetracaine (*Pontocaine*)	2–3 hr	Injection	0.2, 0.3, and 1% solutions
Tetracaine (*Pontocaine Viractin*)*	—	Topical	1% cream, 5% ointment
Amides			
Bupivacaine (*Marcaine*)	2–4 hr	Injection	0.25–0.75% solution
Dibucaine (*Nupercainal*)*	0.5 hr	Topical	1% ointment
Lidocaine (*Xylocaine*)	0.5–1 hr	Injection	2 and 4% solution
Lidocaine (*Lidoderm*)	3 hr	Topical	5% lidocaine patch
Lidocaine (*Bactine spray*)** (*Solarcaine, Aloe extra burn relief*)	0.5 hr	Topical	2% jelly, 2.5 and 5% ointment
Mepivacaine (*Carbocaine*)	0.75–1.5 hr	Injection	1 and 2% solutions
Prilocaine (*Citanest*)	0.5–1.5 hr	Injection	1–4% solutions
Ropivacaine (*Naropin*)	2–6 hr	Injection	0.5–2% solution
Combinations			
EMLA (lidocaine, prilocaine)	0.5–2 hr	Topical	2.5% of each anesthetic in thick layer
LET (lidocaine, epinephrine, tetracaine)	Not established	Topical	4% lidocaine, 0.5% tetracaine, 1:2000 epinephrine
Septocaine (articaine and epinephrine)	Varies with dose	Injection	4% articaine, 1:100,000 epinephrine
TAC (tetracaine, adrenaline, cocaine)	Not established	Topical	0.5% tetracaine, 11.8% cocaine, 1:2000 epinephrine
Other surface cooling agents ***			
Ethyl chloride	Minutes	Topical	Spray
Benzyl alcohol, phenol, camphor, menthol	Minutes	Topical	Spray, lotions, creams
GumEase®	Minutes	Topical	Dental mouthpiece

*Over-the-counter preparations. **Federally restricted drug, Schedule II. ***Decreases surface temperature.*

penetration through the skin. The breakthrough is that this preparation permits much higher concentrations of local anesthetic to be absorbed topically than possible by individual surface preparations. EMLA also can be used to anesthetize skin before intramuscular injections, venipuncture, and procedures such as biopsies.

Parenteral administration of local anesthetics (injection) may involve several different sites, including under the skin (**intradermal anesthesia**) and into the spaces around the spinal cord (**spinal, epidural,** or **caudal anesthesia**). Figure 10.2 illustrates where local anesthetics are administered along the spinal cord to produce different levels of anesthesia. When local anesthetics are administered extradurally, it is called an epidural or caudal blockade. Injections around peripheral nerves are called perineural or paravertebral blockade. Injection into the subarachnoid space (cerebrospinal fluid) is a spinal blockade. The choice of anesthetic is usually based on the duration of action required. The long-acting, potent amide anesthetics are administered primarily by injection. Intravenous injection of a local anesthetic into a specific region, usually an arm or leg isolated by a tourniquet, for short surgical procedures is referred to as a Bier block. There are combination preparations containing the amide lidocaine that are applied topically to facilitate suturing or injection of additional anesthetic.

Note to the Health Care Professional

Local anesthetic solutions occasionally contain epinephrine to counteract the vasodilation that occurs with local anesthetics. Always read the contents of the bottle before administering a local anesthetic. Anesthetic agents come in a variety of containers and packaging. It is crucial to confirm the correct anesthetic and concentration and whether additional active agents are being delivered with the local anesthetic. Preparations containing epinephrine generally have *epinephrine* printed in red ink for easy visibility and a red top on multiple-use vials, as shown in Figure 10.3. Local anesthetic preparations that contain epinephrine should not be used for nerve block in the areas of the fingers, toes, ears, nose, or penis. In such areas, epinephrine may produce intense vasoconstriction, leading to ischemia and gangrene. Epinephrine also is contraindicated in conjunction with general anesthetics that increase cardiac excitability (arrhythmogenic).

Infiltration anesthesia is the most commonly used local anesthetic technique. Infiltrative anesthesia is achieved by injecting a local anesthetic directly into the tissue. The extent of anesthesia is determined by the depth of tissue penetrated—that is, the tissue infiltrated. The duration of action following infiltration anesthesia for several injectable local anesthetics is presented in Table 10:2. Lidocaine, in a 1% concentration, is most commonly used for this type of infiltration. However, when increased procedure times are expected, anesthetics with a longer duration of action are substituted. When these local anesthetics are administered in combination with epinephrine (usually 1:200,000 dilution), the duration of anesthesia may be doubled. For example, prilocaine (0.5–1.5 hr), mepivacaine (0.75–1.5 hr), dibucaine (3–4 hr), and bupivacaine (2–4 hr) administered with epinephrine may have their duration of action extended up to 6 hours. The addition of epinephrine retards transport of the local anesthetic away from the site of injection and the neuron continues to be bathed in local anesthetic.

A **regional nerve block** is achieved by injecting an anesthetic solution around a nerve root so that the whole area the nerve goes to becomes anesthetized. Regional blocks allow a smaller amount of anesthetic to be used, while anesthetizing larger surface areas and reducing the risk of systemic toxicity. Amide-type anesthetics, usually 2% lidocaine, are used most often for regional blocks. Regional nerve blocks are used in the management of pain associated with the lower back, neck, sciatica (from a herniated disc), reflex sympathetic dystrophy (a complex regional pain syndrome), shingles, cancer, and painful peripheral vascular disease. It also can be used in the treatment of migraine headaches.

Local anesthesia can be produced without the use of local anesthetic drugs. **Cryoanesthesia** refers to the external application of cold to the skin to produce numbness. Ice or ethyl chloride, a refrigerant spray, applied directly to the site for 30–60 seconds, provides superficial short-duration anesthesia that may be adequate for removing superficial lesions. This application is particularly useful in children or adults who have a fear of needles. Cryoanesthesia also is used with several skin laser machines that quickly spray a little coolant before each laser pulse to take away the sting of the laser.

GumEase® is a new easy-to-use disposable device for oral cavity pain management. A regional pain block is achieved by the local application of extreme cold to the maxillofacial nerves. The chilled nerve fibers can no longer transmit pain impulses to the brain. GumEase® resembles a teething ring containing a cryoanesthetic compound that sits comfortably within the patient's mouth. Patients can apply the device postoperatively as needed.

Figure 10.2 **Spinal Cord and Nerve Roots**

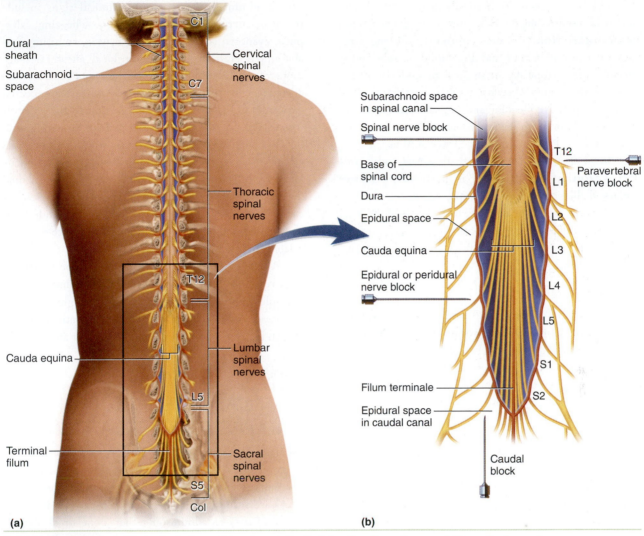

(a)

(b)

Schematic diagram with typical sites of local anesthetic injection in and around the spinal canal.

Figure 10.3

Safety Alert: Identification

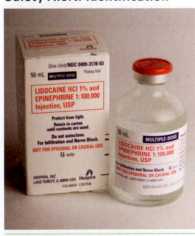

Red cap and red label for lido-caine containing epinephrine.

LO 10.4   LO 10.5

ADVERSE EFFECTS

Local anesthetics are administered to produce a pharmacological response in a well-defined area of the body. However, a local anesthetic occasionally is absorbed into the blood from the site of administration and, passing through the circulation, it affects tissues and organs along the way. The most frequent and serious side effects from systemic absorption of a local anesthetic involve the blood vessels, heart, and brain. When combination products are being used, additional adverse effects may occur from the adjunct medication, usually epinephrine (vasoconstriction, hypertension).

Vascular Effects

Cocaine was the first local anesthetic to be discovered. Although it has potent local anesthetic activity, cocaine cannot be used by injection because it produces intense **vasoconstriction.** Cocaine interferes with the sympathetic nervous system and the blood vessels. Today, cocaine is used topically in surgical procedures on the eyes and nasal mucosa because its vasoconstrictor action decreases operative bleeding and improves surgical visualization. Additional information on cocaine is presented in Chapter 15, Psychotomimetic Drugs of Abuse.

All of the other local anesthetics used today produce **vasodilation;** procaine, in particular, produces a marked dilation of blood vessels, which may lead to hypotension. Except for cocaine, toxic levels of the local anesthetics relax vascular smooth muscle and produce significant hypotension. These effects may lead to cardiovascular collapse.

Cardiac Effects

Local anesthetics depress the function of the cardiac conduction system and the myocardium. Usually, these drugs produce a negative chronotropic (bradycardia) and a negative ionotropic response on the heart. In toxic doses, local anesthetics produce **cardiac arrhythmias.** It must be pointed out that in therapeutic (subtoxic) doses, two of the local anesthetics can be administered intravenously to correct certain cardiac arrhythmias. Lidocaine and procainamide are unique drugs because at very low doses they can protect cardiac function, while at toxic doses they inhibit normal cardiac function. The role of lidocaine and procainamide in the therapy of cardiac arrhythmias is discussed further in Chapter 23.

Central Nervous System Effects

All of the local anesthetics can affect the CNS. In large or toxic doses, the local anesthetics can cross the blood-brain barrier and initially stimulate the cerebral cortex. The symptoms of cortical stimulation are nervousness, excitation, tremors, and convulsions. In general, the more potent the anesthetic, the more readily convulsions occur. As the concentration of local anesthetic increases in the brain, all areas of the CNS become depressed. Finally, at toxic levels, local anesthetics produce coma and death due to total depression of the CNS.

Treatment of a local anesthetic overdose when CNS excitation is present includes barbiturates and diazepam (*Valium*). Once total CNS depression has occurred, the only available treatment is supportive restoration of breathing and blood pressure. In particular, artificial respiration is the essential feature of treatment in the late phase of anesthetic intoxication.

Hypersentivity and Allergic Effects

Allergic contact dermatitis and delayed swelling at the site of administration are rare. Clinical signs include pruritus, urticaria, facial swelling, wheezing, dyspnea, cyanosis, laryngeal edema, nausea, vomiting, and abdominal cramping. The ester local anesthetics are more often identified when an individual develops an allergic or **hypersensitivity** reaction after repeated exposure to the drug. Allergic reaction to the esters is usually due to sensitivity to the metabolite para-amino benzoic acid (PABA). While cross-reactivity exists among ester anesthetics, it does not appear to occur between ester and amide anesthetics. If an individual develops an allergic reaction to ester anesthetics, all ester anesthetics should be avoided and an amide local anesthetic selected for use. These reactions are not dose related; they are idiosyncratic.

A patient who is allergic to an ester-type anesthetic may react to preservatives (sodium metabisulfate) in multiple-dose vials of amide anesthetics. Single-dose vials are preservative-free and may be used in patients with a known hypersensitivity reaction to the ester anesthetics.

LO 10.4

CLINICAL APPLICATIONS AND PREFERRED TREATMENT

Local anesthetics are vital to cutaneous surgery and dental procedures. They are used by medical personnel and nonmedical consumers for a variety of indications. These drugs are readily available, effective, relatively inexpensive, and easy to administer either alone or as adjunct medications to other procedures. Topical application of local anesthetics relieves pain and itching associated with sunburn, skin abrasions, insect bites and other allergic reactions, and skin eruptions from chicken pox. Rectal suppositories relieve the pain produced by hemorrhoids. Introduction of a patch containing local anesthetic has use in dental procedures to reduce the pain associated with anesthetic injection and to alleviate painful discomfort following *Herpes zoster* neuralgia. Especially to facilitate procedures in children, a lidocaine/tetracaine patch can be applied 20 to 30 minutes prior to venipuncture or IV cannulation. A patch containing 5% lidocaine (*Lidoderm*) is the first FDA-approved medication indicated to relieve the pain of postherpetic neuralgia. Injection of local anesthetics, especially the long-acting amides, is used for surgical, suturing, and obstetrical procedures (epidural, caudal, spinal anesthesia) where the patients remain conscious. Bupivacaine, chloroprocaine, etidodaine, lidocaine, mepivacaine, and ropivacaine, with or without epinephrine, are the most frequently used local anesthetics for infiltration, peripheral nerve block, or caudal and lumbar block. Procaine can be used for infiltration and nerve block of short duration. Dentistry is one of the most frequent clinical applications of local anesthetics. Articaine, bupivacaine, chloroprocaine, lidocaine, and prilocaine are most frequently used in dental procedures. Unless otherwise indicated, a vasoconstrictor such as epinephrine is usually preferred to minimize the need for reinjection.

Cautions and Contraindications

Local anesthetics are used in pregnant women as needed (see Patient Administration and Monitoring for more information). The physiology of pregnancy does alter the dynamics of the local anesthetic. During pregnancy, hepatic blood is increased and plasma protein binding is decreased, making the amide local anesthetics more available for metabolism and excretion. This results in an increased amide local anesthetic clearance from the body.

In the presence of kidney failure, the amide anesthetic clearance is decreased. In hepatic failure, amide metabolites may accumulate. These patients require special attention during a monitored recovery period.

Local anesthetics may release histamine from mast cells located at the site of injection, producing a rash and local itching typical of a histaminic response of Lewis (see Chapter 31). Occasionally, a patient is hypersensitive to local anesthetics. If a rash or edema occurs, the drug should be stopped immediately. **Hypersensitivity** may develop to ester local anesthetics when they are used frequently. When a complete medical history is available, the anesthesia team can avoid use of the offending drugs. Unfortunately, local anesthetics abound in OTC preparations and the hypersensitivity may result from prolonged use or abuse of topical preparations. For this reason, topical preparations (creams, ointments, and sprays) should never be used continually for prolonged periods. If hypersensitivity develops and a local anesthetic is required, amide derivatives may be substituted usually without fear of enhancing the allergic response.

Topical application of local anesthetics for sunburn, skin abrasions, and corneal wounds may result in systemic drug levels and toxic responses. When the skin is damaged or opened, local anesthetics can easily reach the blood vessels, and when the pain is intense, patients usually apply local anesthetics several times a day. It is not unusual for a patient to develop hypotension, tremors, and convulsions due to overdose of a local anesthetic.

Special Considerations

When administering a local anesthetic parenterally, monitor cardiovascular and respiratory vital signs after each injection. Restlessness, dizziness, blurred vision, and slurred speech may be early signs of CNS toxicity. Always inject an anesthetic slowly to avoid systemic reactions. Debilitated patients, as well as elderly and pediatric patients, may require reduced doses because these patients are often more susceptible to the actions of local anesthetics. Local anesthetic solutions that contain a vasoconstrictor must be used with extreme caution in patients who have a medical history of hypertension, cerebral vascular insufficiency, heart block, thyrotoxicosis, or diabetes. (Review the effects of sympathomimetic drugs on the cardiovascular and metabolic systems.)

Black Box Warning

As a class of drugs, the local anesthetics are closely monitored when administered parenterally by physicians and dentists. Among all the available local anesthetics, only one is associated with a significant warning for use above 0.5% concentration.

> Obstetrical anesthesia: The 0.75% concentration of bupivacaine is not recommended for obstetrical anesthesia because cardiac arrest with difficult resuscitation or death has occurred following rapid intravenous injection to pregnant women. The concentration is indicated only for lengthy nonobstetrical surgery requiring profound muscle relaxation.

Overdose of topical anesthetics may result in the same life-threatening response as from parentally administered drugs. If convulsions occur, it is an acute emergency. There is no specific antidote. Supportive treatment includes maintaining a clear airway and assisting ventilation with oxygen. If convulsions persist, an ultrashort-acting barbiturate or benzodiazepine may be given parenterally. Intravenous fluids and vasopressors are used when the circulation and organ perfusion are compromised.

Drug Interactions

Local anesthetics are not involved in many drug interactions. However, they may enhance hypotension that occurs with antihypertensive drugs and muscle relaxants. Drugs that directly relax skeletal muscle are enhanced by the use of local anesthetics introduced into the spinal canal. Local anesthetics may increase the release of histamine even when they are being used to relieve an allergic reaction, and this histamine release will only worsen the clinical condition.

Procaine has been shown to inhibit the action of sulfonamide antibiotics. Procaine is metabolized to *p*-aminobenzoic acid, which competes with the sulfonamide for the bacterial site of action.

Patients who have experienced a hypersensitivity reaction to an ester local anesthetic are more likely to experience a similar reaction if exposed to other ester local anesthetics. Generally, it is advisable to use an amide local anesthetic as an alternative; rarely, cross-sensitivity with lidocaine has been reported.

Sedatives may interact with spinal local anesthetics to potentiate CNS depression. Combination anesthetics that contain epinephrine may produce an increased sympathetic response and sustained hypertension when a patient is taking tricyclic antidepressants or MAO inhibitors.

Patient Administration and Monitoring

Assuming the patient is closely monitored during the procedure, adverse effects may be minimized when local anesthetics are used in operating and emergency rooms. The use of anesthetics in dental procedures as well as available products for self-medication exposes the general population to greater risk of experiencing certain adverse effects. Patients should be instructed about predictable local anesthetic action that could cause problems—namely, loss of sensory perception and motor function.

Patient Instructions

The patient should be advised that loss of sensory perception and motor function may persist for a short time. This means the anesthetized region cannot respond to hot or cold stimuli or to deep scratching. Avoid exposing the skin or mucous membranes (gums) to extreme temperature foods for at least 1 hour or until full pain sensation has returned.

Following topical application to relieve sore throat, the patient should not eat for 1 hour. Since sensation is impaired, there is always the danger that the patient may aspirate food particles.

Dental anesthesia will more than likely leave the patient with numbness of the tongue, lip, and/or oral mucosa for up to 1 hour after the procedure. The patient should be alerted to the possible annoying effect of accidentally biting the lips or cheeks during this time. Since pressure perception is impaired, the patient may unconsciously bite extremely hard and find terrific pain and blisters after the anesthetic has subsided. It is advisable that while the tissue is still anesthetized, the patient should not eat or chew gum because of the potential for aspiration to occur.

Notify the Physician

Patients routinely use OTC products containing local anesthetics for a multitude of conditions from sore throat to vaginal and/or rectal itch. While the patient may have 10 preparations for use on different body parts, they all probably contain a local anesthetic. Moreover, these are the type of products used by the more sensitive patients such as the elderly and children. The patient should be reminded that any time the skin or mucous membrane is broken, as in sunburn, minor scratches, or irritated mucosa, the local anesthetic may be more well absorbed. Development of mental confusion and changes in pulse or respiration should be reported to the physician for further evaluation.

A small percentage of people are allergic (hypersensitive) to the para-aminobenzoic acid metabolites of procaine and tetracaine. Local swelling, edema, itching, difficulty in breathing, and bronchospasm may indicate hypersensitivity to the anesthetic. If such symptoms occur while using any local anesthetic, the patient should notify the doctor immediately and discontinue the anesthetic.

Use in Pregnancy

Drugs in this class have been designated Food and Drug Administration (FDA) Pregnancy Category B and C. The safety of local anesthetic use in pregnancy has not been established through research in humans; however, the short-term exposure to these drugs during labor and delivery limits the potential risk to the patient and newborn. Adverse effects observed in the newborn, primarily depression of the CNS and cardiovascular tone, quickly reverse once exposure is terminated. The degree of depression is related to the type and amount of local anesthetic administered to the mother.

Chapter Review

Understanding Terminology

Answer the following questions.

1. Differentiate between local and general anesthetics. **(LO 10.1, 10.2)**
2. Explain the difference between vasodilation and vasoconstriction. **(LO 10.1, 10.2)**

Match the definition in the left column with the appropriate term in the right column.

___ 3. An exaggerated response (such as rash or edema) to a local anesthetic. **(LO 10.4)**

___ 4. Placing a drug on the surface of the skin or a mucous membrane. **(LO 10.4)**

___ 5. Injection of a local anesthetic into the subarachnoid space. **(LO 10.4)**

___ 6. Injection of a local anesthetic into the extradural space. **(LO 10.4)**

___ 7. Injection of a local anesthetic into the caudal or subcaudal canal. **(LO 10.4)**

___ 8. Injection of a local anesthetic directly into the tissue. **(LO 10.4)**

___ 9. Injection of a local anesthetic under the skin. **(LO 10.4)**

a. caudal anesthesia
b. epidural anesthesia
c. hypersensitivity
d. infiltration anesthesia
e. intradermal anesthesia
f. spinal anesthesia
g. topical application

Acquiring Knowledge

Answer the following questions.

1. Explain how local anesthetics block the response to pain. **(LO 10.1)**
2. Which nerves are first affected when a local anesthetic is applied? What is the order of depression? **(LO 10.1, 10.2)**
3. What are two classes of local anesthetics? How do they differ? **(LO 10.1, 10.4)**
4. What body systems are mainly affected by systemic absorption of local anesthetics? **(LO 10.4)**
5. What are the adverse effects of local anesthetics on the heart? **(LO 10.4)**
6. What are the adverse effects of local anesthetics on the CNS? **(LO 10.4)**
7. Compare the effects of cocaine and procaine on blood pressure. **(LO 10.4)**
8. Why is epinephrine added to some local anesthetic preparations? **(LO 10.1, 10.4)**
9. What precautions are associated with the use of local anesthetics and vasoconstrictors? **(LO 10.4)**
10. What drugs may interact with local anesthetics to produce undesirable effects? **(LO 10.4)**

Applying Knowledge on the Job

Use your critical-thinking skills to answer the following questions.

1. Mrs. Brown was rushed to the emergency room by ambulance after her husband found her lying on the kitchen floor having convulsions. She has no previous history of convulsions and appeared to be in good health earlier in the day. You notice that Mrs. Brown has abrasions on her lower right arm, which

her husband says she received when she fell to the pavement when bicycling yesterday. He says that she has been self-medicating with an over-the-counter ointment for pain ever since. What do you think caused Mrs. Brown's convulsions? **(LO 10.4)**

Use the *PDR*® or *F&C* to answer the following questions.

2. Lidocaine is available in a topical viscous solution preparation. List the strength, peak effect and duration times, and the indications. **(LO 10.1)**

3. Bupivacaine is available in the following strengths; 0.25%, 0.5%, and 0.75%. This is commonly used for obstetrical lumbar epidural. One strength is contraindicated for this procedure. Which strength is contraindicated and why? **(LO 10.4)**

Use *F&C* to answer the following question.

4. You are reviewing the medication orders for the cataract extraction procedures scheduled for the next day. The anesthetic that will be used is proparacaine (*Opthetic*). What dosing would you expect to find? **(LO 10.1, 10.4)**

Multiple Choice Questions

Use your critical-thinking skills to answer the following questions.

1. Which of the following is a significant therapeutic effect of the *ester* local anesthetics? **(LO 10.1, 10.4)**
   A. increase in diastolic blood pressure
   B. itching at the site of application
   C. loss of sensation to touch and warmth
   D. depression of motor neuron function

2. The duration of action of a single administration of *amide* local anesthetic dibucaine or bupivacaine **(LO 10.1)**
   A. is shorter than the duration of action of procaine
   B. is longer than 30 minutes
   C. is decreased by adding epinephrine to the local anesthetic
   D. depends on the amount of cholinesterase in the blood

3. Any local anesthetic decreases the response to pain (mechanism of action) **(LO10.1)**
   A. by binding and inactivating membrane ion channels that affect sodium movement
   B. after the drug reacts with receptors in the brain
   C. by removing sodium and potassium ions from the cells
   D. by increasing nerve conduction of painful stimuli

4. Local anesthetic therapeutic effect to block nerve conduction **(LO 10.1)**
   A. only happens if the local anesthetic is injected
   B. causes irritation and redness at the site of application
   C. reversibly binds chloride and magnesium ions in the skin
   D. can be achieved with topical creams, sprays, and ointments.

5. Local anesthetics other than cocaine **(LO 10.4)**
   A. are weak acids
   B. are Schedule restricted drugs because of their similarity to cocaine
   C. can only be metabolized by the liver to remove their effect
   D. produce vasodilation

6. Which of the following is a local anesthetic? **(LO 10.1)**
    A. ropivacaine
    B. norepinephrine
    C. succcinylcholine
    D. adrenaline

7. Which of the following local anesthetics is used to treat cardiac arrhythmias? **(LO 10.5)**
    A. prilocaine
    B. lidocaine
    C. tetracaine
    D. cocaine

8. Which of the following statements is correct about the local anesthetic? **(LO 10.3)**
    A. topical application of procaine establishes a caudal nerve block
    B. tetracaine can only be administered by injection
    C. injection of bupivacaine at the spinal nerve root such as at T4 establishes a regional nerve block
    D. articaine is administered with epinephrine to enhance vasodilation

Multiple Choice (Multiple Answer)

Select the correct choices for each statement. The choices may be all correct, all incorrect, or any combination.

1. Which of the following anesthetics are given by injection? **(LO 10.3)**
    A. dibucaine
    B. ropivacaine
    C. *Pontocaine*
    D. benzocaine

2. Lidocaine can be given to treat which conditions? **(LO 10.5)**
    A. sunburns
    B. cardiac arrhythmias
    C. vasoconstriction
    D. insect bites

3. The mechanism of action for local anesthetics includes **(LO 10.1)**
    A. altering skeletal muscle function
    B. blocking sensory nerve conduction
    C. inhibiting sodium ion movement
    D. depolarizing nerves

4. Select the adverse effects of local anesthetics. **(LO 10.4)**
    A. anesthetization of the skin
    B. inhibition of sensory nerves
    C. convulsions
    D. bradycardia

5. What are the early signs of CNS toxicity from injected local anesthetics? **(LO 10.4)**
    A. restlessness
    B. blurred vision
    C. slurred speech
    D. dizziness

Sequencing

Place the following in order from longest duration of action to shortest duration of action. **(LO 10.1)**

_____   _____   _____   _____

Longest   **Shortest**

Pontocaine

Nesacaine

Duranest

EMLA

Classification

Place each drug under the appropriate route of administration. **(LO 10.3)**

| Septocaine | *Nupercainal* | *Dermoplast* | *Novocain* |
| TAC | *Carbocaine* | *Naropin* | Ropivacaine |

Injectable	Topical

Documentation

Using the prescription below, answer the following questions. **(LO 10.3)**

   a. What is the route of administration for this drug?
   b. Has the doctor provided enough information for you to determine a route of administration?
   c. If the prescription was to be injected, what dosage strengths are available?
   d. What is the duration of action for the injectable form of this drug?

Day Surgery
Practice RX

12345 Main Avenue

Anytown, USA 12345

931-555-1000

NAME:: ___Holly Fields_____   DATE: _____

ADDRESS: _____

RX   Pontocaine

Sig: Use as directed

Dr. Warren Fisk _____ M.D. _____M.D.

   Substitution Permitted   **Dispense as written**

DEA #: _____   REFILL: NR   1   2   3   4

Labeling

Fill in the missing labels. (LO 10.3)

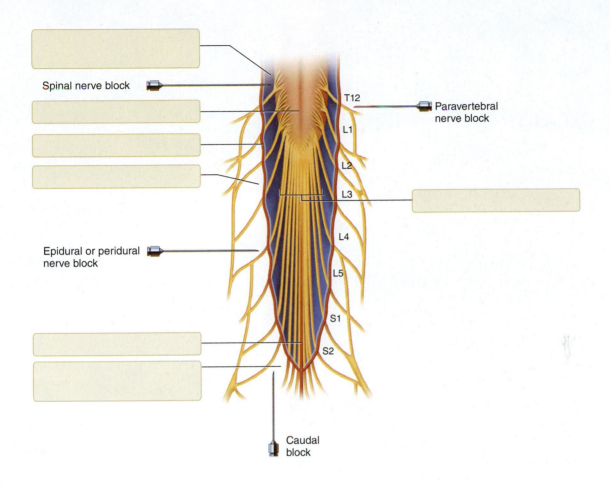

Spinal nerve block

Epidural or peridural
nerve block

T12

L1

L2

L3

L4

L5

S1

S2

Paravertebral
nerve block

Caudal
block

For interactive animations, videos, and assessment, visit:

www.mcgrawhillconnect.com

Pharmacology of the Central Nervous System

Chapter 11

Introduction to the Central Nervous System

KEY TERMS

basal ganglia: a group of cell bodies (gray matter) within the white matter of the cerebrum that helps control body movement.

cerebellum: part of the brain that coordinates body movements and posture and helps maintain body equilibrium.

cerebral cortex: uppermost layers of the cerebrum involved in sensory perception, voluntary motor control, and all higher intellectual abilities.

cerebrum: largest and uppermost part of the brain that is divided into right and left cerebral hemispheres.

electroencephalogram (EEG): a surface recording of the electrical brain.

hypothalamus: part of the diencephalon that regulates functions such as body temperature, water balance, appetite, and the pituitary gland.

limbic system: neural pathway connecting different brain areas involved in regulation of behavior and emotion.

medulla oblongata: lower part of the brainstem that controls cardiac, vasomotor, and respiratory functions.

pons: part of the brainstem that serves as a relay station for nerve fibers traveling to other brain areas; also involved in sensory and motor functions.

reticular formation: network of nerve fibers that travel throughout the central nervous system that regulates the level of wakefulness.

thalamus: uppermost part of the diencephalon that regulates sensory and motor impulses traveling to and from the cerebral cortex.

Learning Outcomes

After studying this chapter, you should be able to

11.1 describe the main anatomic structures of the brain, the difference between gray and white matter, and the functions of the cerebral cortical lobes and basal ganglia.

11.2 list the main parts of the brainstem and discuss the functions associated with each part.

11.3 explain the major function of the cerebellum.

11.4 explain the basic structure and function of the spinal cord.

11.5 describe the reticular formation and the limbic system and discuss the importance of each.

The central nervous system (CNS) is composed of the brain and spinal cord. The primary functions of the CNS are to coordinate and control the activity of other body systems. Distinct nerve pathways in the CNS interconnect different areas of the brain that serve the same function. Neurons in these pathways are linked together by synapses. These neurons release neurotransmitters, which regulate transmission across the synapses. In this way, nerve impulses are conducted to different areas of the brain to influence the levels of activity.

There are a significant number of neurotransmitters—including acetylcholine (ACH), norepinephrine (NE), dopamine, and serotonin—that have been identified in the brain. Some mental illnesses and pathological conditions are associated with abnormal changes in the amount or activity of a specific neurotransmitter. Many of the drugs that act on the CNS do so by affecting neurotransmitter concentrations and activity. While there are a large number of different neurotransmitters in the brain, the function and activities of each are similar to the functions of the neurons and nerve endings (adrenergic, cholinergic) previously discussed with the autonomic nervous system.

Generally, a neuron releases one specific type of neurotransmitter that crosses the synapse and binds to its receptor located on the dendrites of the next adjoining neuron. Neurotransmitters can be either excitatory or inhibitory. Excitatory receptor stimulation generates action potentials that flow along the nerve axon to stimulate release of the neurotransmitter from the nerve endings of that neuron . . . and so on. Inhibitory neurotransmitters produce actions on the next adjoining neuron that inhibit the generation of action potentials. In this manner, neurotransmitters function to either generate nerve impulses that transmit information among the different brain centers or inhibit the flow of action potentials, which reduces neural activity. The released neurotransmitters are inactivated by metabolism or reuptake into their respective nerve endings. Figure 11.1 illustrates the synaptic connections of a typical brain neuron.

In the CNS, neurons having the same functions are generally grouped together. The cell bodies of these neurons form control centers for the various body functions. Consequently, the CNS is anatomically divided into different structural and functional components. In order to understand how drugs affect the CNS, the main structures and functions of the CNS will be reviewed.

LO 11.1

STRUCTURAL AND FUNCTIONAL FEATURES OF THE BRAIN

The brain may be divided into the cerebrum, diencephalon, brainstem, and cerebellum. The basic anatomy and physiology of these structures will be briefly reviewed in order to provide background for the site and action of drugs acting on the central nervous system.

Cerebrum

The **cerebrum** is the largest and uppermost part of the brain. All of the higher intellectual abilities of human beings are controlled by the cerebrum. Anatomically, the cerebrum is divided into right and left cerebral hemispheres. Each hemisphere is composed of an outer layer of gray matter, the cerebral cortex, composed of nerve cell bodies, and an inner layer of white matter composed of nerve cell axons.

Cerebral Cortex

The **cerebral cortex** contains the cell bodies of neurons (gray matter) that perceive and are actively involved with all conscious activities of the mind and intellect. All sensory sensations are perceived and all voluntary muscle movements of the body are initiated from the cortex. The cortex is subdivided into four main lobes. The cortical lobes are named after the skull bones under which they are located and include the frontal,

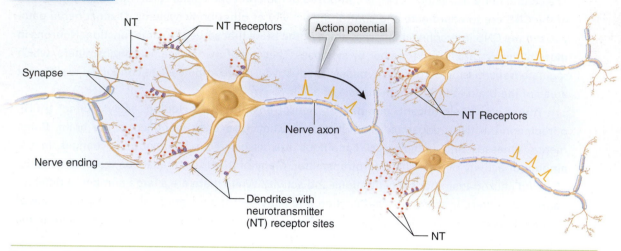

Nerve endings from one neuron release neurotransmitter (NT), which crosses synapse to bind to NT receptor (R) on dendrites of next neuron. Receptor stimulation generates an action potential that travels down the nerve axon to stimulate the release of NT from nerve endings.

parietal, temporal, and occipital lobes (Figure 11.2). The frontal lobe is responsible for control of muscle movement, the motor components of speech, abstract thinking, and problem-solving activity. The parietal lobe is responsible for the sensory sensations of touch, pressure, pain, temperature, and vibration. The temporal lobes are involved in hearing, learning, memory, and language functions. The occipital lobes function in vision. There are neural connections between the lobes and each area of the brain that allow communication, coordination, and integration of neural function. The lobes of the cerebral cortex are shown in Figure 11.2. An **electroencephalogram (EEG)** is a recording of the electrical activity of the brain. The EEG is useful in diagnosing various brain disorders and in evaluating the stages of sleep.

Figure 11.2

Lobes of the Cerebral Cortex

![Frontal lobe, Parietal lobe, Occipital lobe, Temporal lobe]

Each lobe is named according to the skull bone under which it is located.

The white matter of the cerebrum is composed of the myelinated axons of neurons. The axons conduct nerve impulses to and from the cerebral cortex to different areas of the nervous system. Within the white matter of the cerebrum is a group of cell bodies (gray matter) known as the basal ganglia.

Basal Ganglia

The **basal ganglia** receive nerve input from the cerebral cortex, cerebellum, and other areas of the brain involved in body movement. The main function of the basal ganglia is to help coordinate and regulate muscular activity. The basal ganglia are also referred to as the extrapyramidal system (EPS). The pyramidal system consists of all the descending motor nerves that come from the frontal lobes and travel to all the skeletal muscles. The pyramidal system controls the activity of skeletal muscle while the extrapyramidal system helps regulate skeletal muscle activity. Degeneration of neurons within the basal ganglia that produce dopamine are the cause of Parkinson's disease. Deficiencies of dopamine cause the tremors, muscular rigidity, and problems with posture and movement that are the major symptoms of this condition. The antiparkinson drugs are discussed in Chapter 17.

LO 11.2

DIENCEPHALON AND BRAINSTEM

The diencephalon includes the thalamus and hypothalamus which are located directly below the cerebral hemispheres. The brainstem includes the midbrain, pons, and medulla oblongata which are located below the diencephalons and that is continuous with the spinal cord. These structures are illustrated in Figure 11.3

Thalamus

The **thalamus** receives and evaluates almost all of the sensory nerve impulses from peripheral sensory receptors before passing this information to the parietal lobe of the cerebral cortex. These include nerve impulses for pain, touch, temperature, and other sensory information. The thalamus also is involved in motor control by integrating motor information from the basal ganglia and cerebellum.

Hypothalamus

Located below the thalamus, is the **hypothalamus.** The hypothalamus controls many body functions including temperature, water balance, appetite, sleep, the autonomic nervous system, and certain emotional or behavioral responses. The pituitary gland is attached to the hypothalamus. Referred to as the master gland of the body, the pituitary gland regulates the function of many other endocrine glands. The pituitary gland and the pharmacology of the endocrine system will be considered in Chapter 35.

Pons

Located below the hypothalamus, the **pons** is involved in both sensory and motor functions. It receives input from the reticular formation and has a role in the regulation of respiration and sleep. The pons also serves as a relay station for nerve fibers traveling to other brain areas.

Medulla Oblongata

The **medulla oblongata** lies just above the spinal cord. Within the medulla oblongata are the three vital centers: cardiac (heart), vasomotor (blood pressure), and respiratory (breathing). Normal functioning of the vital centers is essential for life support. Injury to the medulla oblongata frequently results in death. Overdose with drugs, such as alcohol or barbiturates, causes death by depressing the function of the vital centers. Several important reflexes also are regulated by the medulla oblongata, including swallowing, coughing, vomiting, and gagging.

LO 11.3
CEREBELLUM

The **cerebellum** lies behind the brainstem and below the cerebrum. The cerebellum is attached to the pons, medulla oblongata, and other areas of the brainstem. The major functions of the cerebellum, which is divided into right and left cerebellar hemispheres, are to coordinate body movements and posture and to help maintain body equilibrium. Disorders of the cerebellum can cause disturbances of posture and movement, tremors, muscle weakness, and decreased tendon reflexes. Drugs that depress the cerebellum, such as alcohol, usually decrease body coordination and reaction time.

LO 11.4
SPINAL CORD

The spinal cord is a collection of nerve axons that travel to and from the brain. Nerve axons traveling from the peripheral parts of the body (skin, muscle, visceral organs) to the brain (afferent neurons) carry sensory information (touch, pain, hot and cold sensations, etc.). Nerve axons traveling from the brain to the peripheral organs and skeletal muscle (efferent neurons) carry motor impulses that direct organ activity and muscle movement. Drugs that act on the spinal cord, mainly anesthetics, analgesics, and muscle relaxants, are primarily used to alter pain sensation and reduce the tone and activity of skeletal muscle.

LO 11.5
FUNCTIONAL COMPONENTS

In addition to the main anatomical parts of the brain just described, several other functional neuronal pathways are located within the brain. These components form diffuse nerve networks that connect many different areas of the brain together; the reticular formation and the limbic system are two such components.

Figure 11.3

Brain Section Showing the Structures of the Diencephalon and Brainstem from the Thalamus to the Medulla

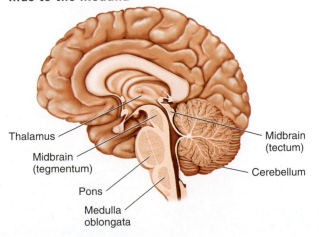

Thalamus

Midbrain
(tegmentum)

Pons

Medulla
oblongata

Midbrain
(tectum)

Cerebellum

Reticular Formation

The **reticular formation** is a network of nerve fibers that travel throughout the brain and spinal cord. The reticular formation has synaptic connections with many different brain areas that are involved, for example, in motor control, cardiovascular control, sleep, and wakefulness. It is composed of two types of fibers: excitatory and inhibitory.

When the excitatory fibers are stimulated by various external stimuli (noise, bright light, or danger), the degree of alertness increases, preparing the body for a situation that requires action. The excitatory fibers are usually referred to as the *reticular activating system* (RAS).

When there is a lack of external stimuli, the inhibitory fibers become more active, decreasing the activity of this system and, consequently, the degree of arousal or alertness. This decrease normally occurs during periods of rest or sleep. Consequently, the reticular formation helps regulate the degree of alertness or wakefulness of the nervous system.

The reticular formation is sensitive to the effects of many drugs. Alcohol, barbiturates, and other depressant drugs decrease its activity and may induce sleep or unconsciousness. Stimulants, such as amphetamines and caffeine, increase the activity of the reticular formation and are usually used or abused to stimulate the CNS and maintain wakefulness.

Limbic System

The **limbic system** refers to a collection of neurons and brain areas that form a specific interconnecting neural pathway. Major components of the limbic system include the amygdala, hippocampus, and cingulate gyrus (Figure 11.4). These structures are located around the hypothalamus and lower portions of the cerebrum. The limbic system is involved with the emotional and behavioral responses of the body associated with reward and punishment, sexual behavior, anger or rage, fear, and anxiety; therefore, the limbic system is important to mental health. Certain areas of the limbic system are referred to as pleasure or reward centers. Activities that activate these areas provide gratification and these activities are likely to be repeated. Certain addictions such as smoking and drug abuse affect these centers. Other areas of the limbic system are associated with unpleasant sensations or feelings and activities that affect these areas are likely to be avoided. Specific drug classes, such as the antianxiety agents and some antidepressant drugs, exert a selective inhibitory effect on the limbic system and are useful for the treatment of certain behavioral and emotional disorders.

The area of pharmacology that deals with drugs affecting the CNS is known as neuropharmacology. In the following chapters, the major classes of drugs that affect the CNS will be considered.

Figure 11.4

Major Anatomic Structures Forming the Limbic System

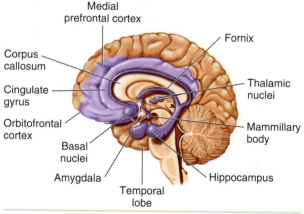

The structures of the limbic system are shown in violet.

Understanding Terminology

Match the description in the left column with the appropriate part of the brain in the right column. **(LO 11.1, 11.2)**

___ 1. Coordinates body movements and posture, helps maintain equilibrium.

___ 2. Group of cell bodies within the cerebrum.

___ 3. Composed of myelinated axons that conduct nerve impulses to and from the cerebral cortex.

___ 4. Largest and uppermost part of the brain.

___ 5. Regulates sensory impulses traveling to the cortex.

___ 6. Controls cardiac, vasomotor, and respiratory functions.

___ 7. Controls the body's higher intellectual and voluntary activities.

a. basal ganglia
b. cerebellum
c. cerebral cortex
d. cerebral white matter
e. cerebrum
f. medulla oblongata
g. thalamus

Acquiring Knowledge

Answer the following questions.

1. What are the main functions of the central nervous system? **(LO 11.1)**
2. List some of the neurotransmitters found in the brain. What is the function of a neurotransmitter? **(LO 11.1)**
3. Where are the basal ganglia located and what function is associated with them? **(LO 11.1)**
4. List the main structures in the brainstem. **(LO 11.2)**
5. List the main functions of the hypothalamus and the medulla oblongata. **(LO 11.2)**
6. What are the main functions of the cerebellum and spinal cord? **(LO 11.3, 11.4)**
7. What is the reticular formation? How does it function to regulate the level of wakefulness or arousal? **(LO 11.5)**
8. What is the limbic system? What functions are associated with this system? **(LO 11.5)**

Applying Knowledge on the Job

Use your critical-thinking skills to answer the following questions.

1. As patient liaison in a large metropolitan hospital, one of your duties is to educate patients and their families about their illnesses and treatments. For the following cases, explain why the patients present with the signs and symptoms that they do. **(LO 11.2)**
   a. Patient A, a 16-year-old female, took an overdose of one of the barbiturate drugs and was brought to the emergency room (ER) by her parents. She presents in the ER with a heart rate of 45, blood pressure of 85 over 55, and slow, irregular breathing.
   b. Patient B took an accidental overdose of an amphetamine and presents at the ER in a state of excitability, with rapid breathing, heart palpitations, excessive perspiration, anxiety, and irritability.
   c. Patient C is an 18-year-old male who has had a few beers once or twice a month since he turned 18. He has never consumed hard liquor until tonight, when he attended a party where he participated in a drinking contest. At that time, he drank several ounces of whiskey in a few minutes. He passed out and could not be awakened. A sober friend brought him to the ER, still unconscious. His heart rate is slow, his blood pressure down, and his breathing is irregular.

2. Assume a patient of the doctor you assist has Parkinson's disease. He and his wife think his problem is in his muscles. Explain to them what is really affected and why he has the symptoms he does. **(LO 11.1)**

Multiple Choice

Use your critical-thinking skills to answer the following questions.

1. Select the structure located within the brainstem **(LO 11.1)**
   A. hypothalamus
   B. cerebral cortex
   C. cerebral white matter
   D. medulla oblongata

2. Body temperature, appetite, and water balance are regulated by the **(LO 11.2)**
   A. pons
   B. cerebellum
   C. medulla oblongata
   D. hypothalamus

3. Sensory sensations such as touch, pressure, and pain are perceived in the **(LO 11.1)**
   A. frontal lobe
   B. temporal lobe
   C. parietal lobe
   D. occipital lobe

4. The "vital centers" are regulated by the **(LO 11.2)**
   A. hypothalamus
   B. reticular formation
   C. cerebral cortex
   D. medulla oblongata

5. The area of the brain that is involved with emotional and behavioral responses is the **(LO 11.5)**
   A. reticular formation
   B. limbic system
   C. basal ganglia
   D. occipital lobe

Multiple Choice (Multiple Answer)

Select the correct choices for each statement. The choices may be all correct, all incorrect, or any combination.

1. Select the main parts of the brainstem. **(LO 11.2)**
   A. spinal cord
   B. thalamus
   C. cerebral medulla
   D. medulla oblongata

2. Choose the main functions of the cerebellum. **(LO 11.3)**
   A. equilibrium
   B. body posture
   C. temperature control
   D. water balance

3. Which of the following is not a function of the spinal cord? **(LO 11.4)**
   A. sensation of hot
   B. recognition of pain
   C. direct organ activity
   D. regulation of breathing

4. Select the area or areas of the central nervous system involved with emotional and behavioral responses.
   (LO 11.2, 11.5)
   A. hypothalamus
   B. reticular formation
   C. limbic system
   D. pons

5. The basal ganglia control which of the following body functions? **(LO 11.1)**
   A. regulating the vomiting reflex
   B. regulating body temperature
   C. regulating muscular activity
   D. regulating sensory impulses

Sequencing

Place the following in order from the uppermost section of the central nervous system to the lowermost.
(LO 11.1, 11.2, 11.4)

_____   _____   _____   _____

Upper   **Lower**

cerebrum
cerebellum
medulla oblongata
spinal cord

Classification

Place the following body functions under the part of the brain that controls them. **(LO 11.1, 11.2)**

breathing   water balance
memory   appetite
sleep   blood pressure
regulation of swallowing reflex   language
abstract thought

Cerebrum	Hypothalamus	Medulla oblongata

Labeling

Fill in the missing labels. **(LO 11.5)**

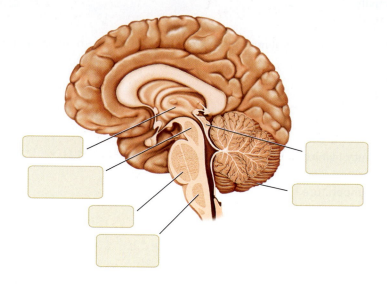

For interactive animations, videos, and assessment, visit:

www.mcgrawhillconnect.com

Chapter 12

Sedative-Hypnotic Drugs and Alcohol

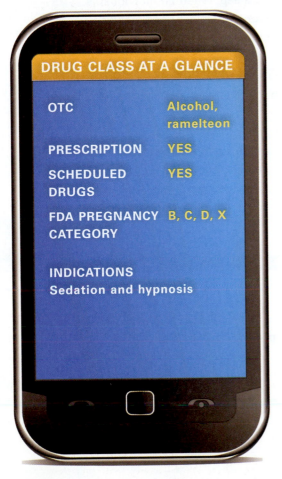

DRUG CLASS AT A GLANCE

OTC	Alcohol, ramelteon
PRESCRIPTION	YES
SCHEDULED DRUGS	YES
FDA PREGNANCY CATEGORY	B, C, D, X
INDICATIONS	

INDICATIONS
Sedation and hypnosis

KEY TERMS

automatism: drug-induced confusion that can cause increased drug consumption.

barbiturate: CNS depressant drug possessing the barbituric acid ring structure.

benzodiazepine: class of drugs used to treat anxiety and sleep disorders.

GABA: gamma-aminobutyric acid, an inhibitory neurotransmitter in the CNS.

hypnotic: drug used to induce and maintain sleep.

nonbarbiturate: refers to sedative-hypnotic drugs that do not possess the barbituric acid structure, such as benzodiazepines and related drugs.

NREM sleep: stages of sleep characterized by nonrapid eye movement (NREM).

REM sleep: stage of sleep characterized by rapid eye movement (REM) and dreaming.

sedative: drug used to produce mental relaxation and to reduce the desire for physical activity.

Learning Outcomes

After studying this chapter, you should be able to

12.1 describe the stages of the sleep cycle and the main characteristics of each stage.

12.2 explain the mechanism of action of the sedative-hypnotic drugs in relationship to their actions with GABA and the chloride ion channel.

12.3 describe the adverse effects of barbiturates, the addiction liability, and treatment of barbiturate overdose.

12.4 explain the mechanism of action of the benzodiazepine hypnotics and the pharmacokinetic differences between the short-acting and longer-acting drugs.

12.5 explain the mechanism of action of eszopiclone, zaleplon, and zolpidem and the advantages of these drugs over barbiturates and benzodiazepines.

12.6 describe the major pharmacologic effects and adverse reactions of ethyl alcohol.

The central nervous system coordinates and controls the activity of all other body systems. As a result, anything that directly affects the CNS ultimately influences the overall function of the body. With increased CNS stimulation, a person responds by becoming more alert, anxious, and occasionally more irritable. Excessive CNS stimulation can cause convulsions or various forms of abnormal behavior. Abuse of amphetamines or cocaine can cause these effects. In contrast, depression of the CNS reduces both physical and mental activity. Excessive CNS depression can produce unconsciousness, coma, and death. CNS depression is frequently related to abuse of barbiturates and alcohol.

Sedatives and hypnotics are used therapeutically to decrease CNS activity. The same drugs are used for both sedation and hypnosis; the difference is that the sedative dosage is lower. **Sedatives** are used to reduce the desire for physical activity. Usually a sedative will be prescribed after a heart attack or some other condition when overexertion may be harmful. Various emotional or medical situations can cause anxiety and tension to interfere with sleep. When an individual is unable to sleep (insomnia), excessive tiredness can contribute to greater anxiety and make any situation worse. In this instance, **hypnotic** drugs may be prescribed to induce and maintain sleep (Figure 12.1).

Use of hypnotics should be intermittent and only when really needed. Regular use should be limited to 2 to 4 weeks at any one time. Tolerance develops to the hypnotics and effectiveness usually decreases with prolonged and continuous use.

Several different drug classes are used as sedatives and hypnotics. These drugs are chemically classified as the barbiturates and the nonbarbiturates. The barbiturates are rarely used today as sedatives or hypnotics because of their high abuse potential and addiction liability. The **nonbarbiturates** include the benzodiazepines and several chemically unrelated hypnotics classified as miscellaneous drugs. Before discussing the pharmacology of the sedatives and hypnotics, a brief review of the sleep cycle will be presented.

Figure 12.1 **The Emotional Reaction to the Gradual Depression of the Central Nervous System**

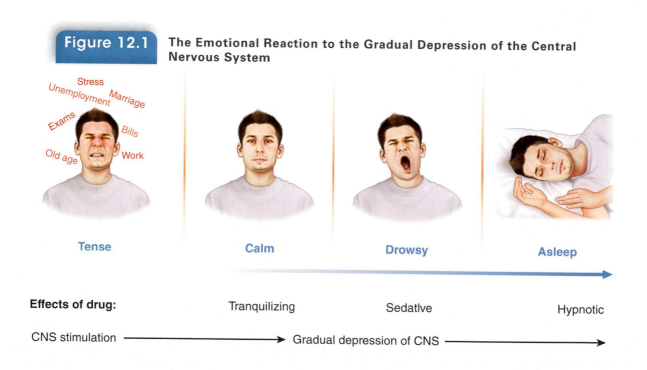

| Tense | Calm | Drowsy | Asleep |

Effects of drug: Tranquilizing   Sedative   Hypnotic

CNS stimulation ⟶ Gradual depression of CNS ⟶

Figure 12.2   Brain Waves Recorded from an Electroencephalogram

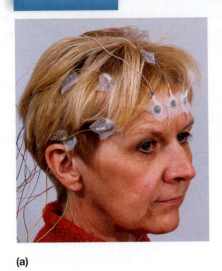

(a)

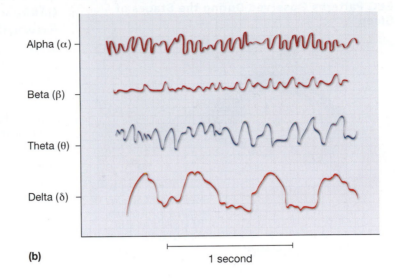

Alpha (α)

Beta (β)

Theta (θ)

Delta (δ)

(b)

1 second

LO 12.1

SLEEP CYCLE

Although sedative-hypnotic drugs are primarily used to induce and maintain sleep, many of these drugs alter the normal sleep cycle. The normal sleep cycle is divided into two different states: nonrapid eye movement (**NREM**) and rapid eye movement (**REM**) sleep.

NREM has been divided into four stages. Progression from stage 1 to stage 4 is characterized by a deeper level of sleep and usually takes 60 to 90 minutes. After stage 4, individuals normally enter REM sleep for approximately 20 minutes. Dreaming usually occurs during REM sleep. After a period of REM sleep, individuals return to NREM sleep and repeat the cycle. Depending on the length of sleep, most individuals usually go through four to six sleep cycles per night. The different stages of sleep produce brain waves that can be identified from an electroencephalogram (EEG) and are useful in evaluating sleep disorders. Examples of brain waves recorded from an EEG are shown in Figure 12.2.

Stage 1 NREM

Individuals are somewhat aware of surroundings but relaxed; the eyes are usually closed. Alpha waves predominate in this stage. Stage 1 normally lasts a few minutes and occupies 4 to 5 percent of total sleep time.

Stage 2 NREM

Individuals become unaware of surroundings but can be easily awakened. Brain waves in stage 2 are increased in

amplitude compared to alpha waves in stage 1 but occur at a lower frequency. Stage 2 occupies about 50 percent of total sleep time.

Stages 3 and 4 NREM

Stages 3 and 4 are referred to as "slow-wave sleep" because of the high-amplitude, low-frequency delta waves observed on the electroencephalogram (EEG). These are deeper stages of sleep and are particularly important for physical rest and restoration. They occupy approximately 20 to 25 percent of total sleep time. One of the effects that occurs with aging is a reduction in the amount of time spent in slow-wave sleep. This is one of the factors that can contribute to insomnia and problems with sleeping as individuals age.

REM

The REM stage is characterized by bursts of rapid eye movement (REM), increased autonomic activity, and dreaming. It is believed to be essential for mental restoration. During REM sleep, daily events are reviewed and information is integrated into memory. REM sleep appears to be an active state of sleep; the EEG records beta-type waves that are similar to those of the waking state. However, individuals are harder to awaken from REM sleep than other sleep stages. For this reason REM sleep is also referred to as "paradoxical sleep." REM sleep occupies about 20 to 25 percent of total sleep time. The sequence of brain waves during a normal sleep cycle is shown in Figure 12.3.

Figure 12.3

EEG Patterns Observed During the Stages of Sleep

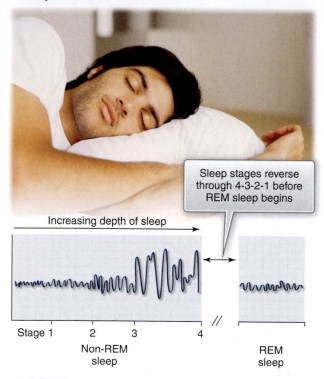

Increasing depth of sleep

Sleep stages reverse through 4-3-2-1 before REM sleep begins

Stage 1	2	3	4	REM

Non-REM sleep　　　REM sleep

MECHANISM OF ACTION OF SEDATIVE-HYPNOTIC DRUGS

The activity of the brain is in large part dependent upon the action of various neurotransmitters. Each neurotransmitter is released from a specific nerve ending and functions to either stimulate or inhibit neuronal activity. One of the most important inhibitory neurotransmitters is gamma-aminobutyric acid **(GABA).** GABA accounts for approximately 50 percent of the inhibitory activity of the brain and spinal cord.

Neuronal function is in large part also dependent upon the action of various ions such as sodium (Na^+), potassium (K^+), and chloride (CL^-). Each of these ions moves in through (influx) or out of (efflux) the neuronal membrane through specific ion channels. Nerve action potentials are generated when Na^+ ions influx through sodium channels to depolarize (inside more positive) the nerve membrane. Nerve action potentials are inhibited when Cl^- ions influx through chloride channels to hyperpolarize (inside more negative) the nerve membrane. The neurotransmitter that regulates the chloride channel is GABA.

The chloride channel is composed of five subunits: two alpha, two beta, and one gamma. These form a circular channel that when open allows the Cl^- ions to pass

through the nerve membrane into the neuron. GABA binds to a specific site on the channel referred to as the $GABA_A$ receptor. When GABA binds to the $GABA_A$ receptor, the channel opens and Cl^- ions influx into the nerve, causing hyperpolarization. This reduces generation of action potentials and inhibits neuronal activity. The chloride channel also contains additional receptor sites for barbiturates, benzodiazepines, and other hypnotic drugs. These hypnotic drugs increase $GABA_A$ receptor-mediated chloride influx by binding to their specific drug receptor sites on the chloride channel. Barbiturates prolong the duration of channel opening and increase Cl^- ion influx. Barbiturates also are believed to have additional inhibitory actions both related and unrelated to the chloride channel. The benzodiazepines bind to their receptors, named the benzodiazepine receptors (BZD receptors), and increase the activity of GABA by increasing the frequency of chloride channel opening. Drugs such as zaleplon, zolpidem, and eszopiclone demonstrate a more selective binding to a subunit of the benzodiazepine receptor (referred to as the BZD_1 receptor). This selective binding offers certain hypnotic advantages over barbiturate and benzodiazepine drugs. Each of these drug classes acts to facilitate the inhibitory actions of GABA to increase chloride ion influx. A diagram of the chloride ion channel with its binding sites for GABA and related drugs is illustrated in Figure 12.4.

BARBITURATE SEDATIVES AND HYPNOTICS

The barbiturates are among the oldest of drugs in the sedative-hypnotic class. These drugs have a number of disadvantages and their use as hypnotics has been mostly replaced by newer and more effective drugs. All of the **barbiturates** are structurally similar to the parent compound, barbituric acid. The barbiturates produce a dose-dependent depression of the CNS. At higher doses, all barbiturates can produce general anesthesia. Because these drugs are still available and indicated for conditions other than hypnosis, they will be briefly discussed. However, emphasis in this chapter will be to present the general pharmacology of the barbiturate drug class. Barbiturates that are used as anticonvulsants and general anesthetics will be discussed in Chapters 16 and 18, respectively.

Mechanism of Action

At lower doses, the barbiturates bind to their drug receptors on the GABA receptor-mediated chloride ion channel. This increases the influx of chloride ions and results in hyperpolarization of nerve membranes, as

Figure 12.4

Diagrammatic Representation of the Chloride Ion Channel

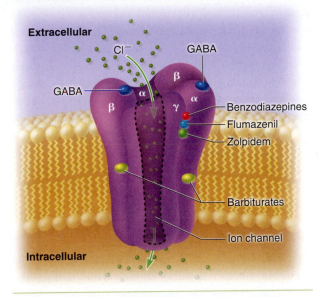

This diagram shows the location of receptor sites for GABA and the various hypnotic drugs. The hypnotic drugs enhance the inhibitory actions of GABA to increase the influx of chloride ions and inhibit neuronal activity.

previously discussed. In the reticular formation, these inhibitory actions decrease the activity of the reticular activating system (RAS) and promote either sedation or sleep, depending on the dosage.

At higher doses, barbiturates also cause a general depression of the entire CNS that is similar to the actions of the general anesthetics (Chapter 18). This action of the barbiturates is not well understood but may be related to the ability of the barbiturates to dissolve in neuronal membranes, where they interfere with the normal function and movement of ions that regulate neuronal excitability and the release of excitatory neurotransmitters.

When used as hypnotics the barbiturates usually increase stage 2 sleep but decrease slow-wave sleep (stages 3 and 4). In addition, barbiturates suppress REM sleep. When barbiturates are discontinued, patients often spend excess time in REM sleep during the next night or two so as to make up for the lost REM sleep (REM rebound). During the rebound period, there is increased dreaming that may cause restlessness, anxiety, and nightmares. The disruption of the normal sleep cycle caused by barbiturates is another reason why they are no longer recommended as hypnotics.

Pharmacokinetics

The barbiturates are well absorbed following oral administration. Once in the circulation, these drugs are readily distributed to all tissues. Symptoms of CNS depression occur within 30 to 60 minutes following oral administration. The drug microsomal metabolizing system (DMMS) in the liver is responsible for inactivation of the barbiturates.

When taken regularly for more than several days, barbiturates begin to induce the microsomal enzymes. Enzyme induction refers to an increase in the amount of drug-metabolizing enzymes in the liver. Enzyme induction results in faster metabolism of the barbiturate. Consequently, the duration of action is decreased, and patients must take larger doses of the drug to attain the same pharmacological effect as before. When this occurs, patients are said to have developed drug tolerance.

When enzyme induction of the metabolizing enzymes occurs, all of the drug-metabolizing enzymes are increased. Therefore, any other drugs taken at the same time also are metabolized faster. This effect is responsible for a number of drug interactions. Barbiturates are eliminated mostly by the urinary system.

Barbiturate Drugs

Phenobarbital (*Luminal*)

Phenobarbital is classified as a long-acting barbiturate, with a duration of 6 to 12 hours. When used as a hypnotic, phenobarbital may produce a "hangover effect," where individuals feel drugged the next morning because of the prolonged duration of action. Phenobarbital also is used as an anticonvulsant drug in the treatment of epilepsy (Chapter 16).

Pentobarbital (*Nembutal*)

Pentobarbital is classified as an intermediate-acting sedative-hypnotic, with a duration of 4 to 6 hours.

Amobarbital (*Amytal*)

Amobarbital is similar to pentobarbital. In addition, both of these barbiturates can be used parenterally to stop convulsions.

Secobarbital (*Seconal*)

Secobarbital is a short-acting hypnotic, with a duration of 2 to 4 hours. The hypnotic indication is for individuals who have difficulty falling asleep but not staying asleep.

Adverse Effects

The adverse effects associated with the barbiturates are an extension of their therapeutic action (CNS depression). Drowsiness, dry mouth, lethargy, and incoordination occur most frequently. These adverse effects are more annoying than harmful. However, depressed reflexes and impaired judgment may contribute to serious accidents if patients operate motor vehicles or heavy machinery while taking these drugs.

Elderly patients are particularly sensitive to CNS side effects, especially mental confusion and memory difficulties. When memory is impaired due to CNS depression, patients may not remember if the drug was taken. As a result, they may retake the drug repeatedly and experience an overdose. This phenomenon, known as **automatism,** may lead to drug intoxication and death. Mild overdosage of the sedative-hypnotic drugs resembles alcohol intoxication (inebriation). Slurred speech, ataxia, impaired judgment, irritability, and psychological disturbances are characteristic of intoxication.

Addiction Liability

Prolonged and excessive use of barbiturates results in tolerance and physical dependence. In addition, cross-tolerance (resistance) develops to the depressant effects of other CNS depressants, such as alcohol and benzodiazepines. This occurs because the mechanism of action of all these drugs involves the interaction with GABA and the chloride ion channel.

The mechanism for the production of tolerance and dependency has not yet been clearly determined. Physical dependency usually develops when greater therapeutic dosages are taken on a regular basis for more than 1 to 2 months. Once physical dependence develops, the drug must be used continuously to avoid the onset of withdrawal symptoms. Withdrawal symptoms include anxiety, insomnia, cramping, tremors, paranoid behavior, delirium, and convulsions. The abstinence syndrome (withdrawal) associated with barbiturates is especially dangerous. If withdrawal is not conducted within an adequately supervised medical center, convulsive seizures and death may occur.

Barbiturate Poisoning

Overdose with the barbiturates results in extensive cardiovascular and CNS depression. In large doses, these drugs depress all brain activity, including that of the vital centers in the medulla oblongata. Inhibition of vasomotor centers in the medulla oblongata removes sympathetic control of the blood vessels, and dilation of the blood vessels contributes to the production of hypotension and shock.

In the presence of hypotension, kidney function decreases. There is little or no production of urine (oliguria or anuria) to remove the toxic products from the body. Medullary respiratory centers also are depressed,

leading to irregular breathing and hypoxia (cyanosis). Severe intoxication with the barbiturates usually leads to coma, respiratory depression, and death.

There is no antidote for barbiturate overdose. Treatment of comatose patients includes supportive therapy to maintain respiration and blood pressure. Endotracheal intubation and artificial respiration may be employed. Also, sympathomimetic (alpha-adrenergic) drugs and intravenous (IV) fluids may be administered to elevate blood pressure. Osmotic diuretics administered intravenously may stimulate urine production so that renal excretion of the drug can occur. In addition, alkalinization of the urine (pH 7.0 or above) will increase the excretion of the more acidic barbiturates, like phenobarbital. Hemodialysis or peritoneal dialysis may be required when kidney function is depressed.

Cautions and Contraindications

The barbiturates are the drugs frequently used for attempted suicide. Because of their rapid action, the short-acting drugs are particularly dangerous. Many patients die before medical treatment can be administered. To prevent hospitalized patients from hoarding medication, always make sure they have swallowed the sedative-hypnotic at the scheduled time. Never leave pills lying on the nightstand to be taken at discretion.

The barbiturates are contraindicated in patients who have acute intermittent porphyria. In this condition, an overproduction of hemoglobin (porphyrin) precursors accumulate in the liver. Sedative-hypnotics like the barbiturates stimulate and increase the production of porphyrins that can precipitate an attack (may cause nerve damage, pain, paralysis) in patients prone to this condition.

Pregnancy

The barbiturates are designated as Food and Drug Administration (FDA) Pregnancy Category D, which indicates that they can cause harmful effects to the fetus. Consequently, these drugs should be avoided during pregnancy.

Drug Interactions

Sedative-hypnotic drugs undergo extensive interactions with other drugs. Sedative-hypnotic agents will potentiate the actions of other CNS depressant drugs, leading to greater CNS and respiratory depression. Sedative-hypnotics and alcohol can be a deadly combination and should never be taken together.

Because barbiturates cause enzyme induction, other drugs may be metabolized more rapidly in their presence. This rapid metabolism results in a decreased pharmacological effect of drugs such as the oral anticoagulants and oral contraceptives. Most of the sedative-hypnotic drugs are bound to plasma proteins; therefore, they compete with other drugs for protein-binding sites. Protein-binding displacement usually leads to a potentiation of the pharmacological effect of the drug displaced.

LO 12.4

BENZODIAZEPINES

The **benzodiazepines** are a class of drugs widely used in the treatment of anxiety. They are commonly referred to as the antianxiety drugs. The general pharmacology of the benzodiazepines is presented more fully in Chapter 13. However, in addition to producing antianxiety effects, all benzodiazepines exert sedative, hypnotic, muscle relaxant, and anticonvulsant effects. These pharmacologic actions are useful in a variety of clinical conditions. Several benzodiazepines are marketed specifically as hypnotics, and these drugs are included in this chapter (Table 12:1). The benzodiazepines are also the drugs preferred for producing sedation. However, the preferred benzodiazepines for sedation—diazepam, alprazolam, and lorazepam—are more frequently used to treat anxiety and are discussed in Chapter 13.

Mechanism of Action

The benzodiazepines produce sedative and hypnotic effects by increasing the inhibitory activity of gamma-aminobutyric acid (GABA). As previously discussed, the benzodiazepines bind to their drug receptor sites (BZD receptors) that are in close relationship to the GABA receptors. The combined action of GABA and the benzodiazepine drug increases the frequency of chloride ion channel opening, resulting in hyperpolarization of the nerve membrane and reduced neuronal activity. In the reticular activating system, this depression produces sedation or hypnosis, depending upon the dose of drug administered.

Pharmacokinetics

Benzodiazepines are lipid-soluble drugs that readily enter the CNS. They are well absorbed after oral administration. The benzodiazepines are metabolized by the drug microsomal enzymes. Some of the benzodiazepines are metabolized to active metabolites, which also produce sedation and hypnosis and prolong the duration of action. Unlike the barbiturates, the benzodiazepines do not cause enzyme induction of the microsomal metabolizing enzymes at therapeutic doses. Elimination is mainly by way of the urinary tract.

Flurazepam (*Dalmane*)

Flurazepam is classified as a long-acting benzodiazepine. It forms several active metabolites, some of which have long half-lives. For this reason, the sedative and antianxiety effects of flurazepam are usually evident the day following a hypnotic dose. This prolonged action can be

[Table **12:1**]

Frequently Prescribed Hypnotic Drugs

Drug (*Trade Name*)	Duration	t 1/2 life (hours)	Comment
Eszopiclone (*Lunesta*)	Intermediate	6	Rapid onset
Zaleplon (*Sonata*)	Short	1	Rapid onset
Zolpidem (*Ambien, Ambien-CR*)	Short	1.5–4	*Ambien-CR* extends duration of action
Benzodiazepines			
Estazolam (*ProSom*)	Intermediate	10–24	No active metabolites
Flurazepam (*Dalmane*)	Long	45–100	Several active metabolites
Quazepam (*Doral*)	Long	39–100	Several active metabolites
Temazepam (*Restoril*)	Intermediate	10–40	No active metabolites
Triazolam (*Halcion*)	Short	1.5–3	Rapid onset

useful in anxious patients when sedating drug effects are desired during the following day. On the other hand, daytime sedation and drowsiness may interfere with employment or other activities.

Temazepam (*Restoril*)

Temazepam is an intermediate-acting hypnotic that does not form any important active metabolites. The duration of hypnotic action is 8 to 10 hours, and there are usually little or no drug effects evident the following day. One preparation of temazepam is marketed in a hard gelatin capsule that gives a delayed onset of action. This drug dosage form should be taken 1 to 2 hours before sleep is desired.

Triazolam (*Halcion*)

Triazolam is a short-acting hypnotic with no active metabolites. This hypnotic does not usually cause residual effects the day following a hypnotic dose. However, the short duration of action may cause early morning awakenings.

Effects on Sleep Cycle

All benzodiazepines produce similar effects on the sleep cycle. NREM stage 2 is increased while NREM stage 4 is usually decreased. The benzodiazepines do not significantly suppress REM sleep and therefore do not usually cause REM rebound when discontinued.

Advantages of Benzodiazepine Hypnotics over Barbiturates

The benzodiazepines generally do not interfere with REM sleep. They produce less tolerance and therefore are effective for a few weeks longer than are the barbiturates when taken on a nightly basis. They also do not induce microsomal metabolizing enzymes significantly. When abused, the benzodiazepines generally cause less physical dependence than do barbiturates. These factors,

along with the low incidence of adverse effects, give the benzodiazepines a number of advantages over the barbiturates for both sedation and hypnosis.

Adverse Effects

The benzodiazepine hypnotics are well tolerated and produce few adverse effects when used properly. Flurazepam, because of its longer half-life, may cause sedation or a "hangover effect" the following day. Triazolam, which has a very short duration of action, has been associated with rebound insomnia. This involves insomnia occurring over several days following abrupt discontinuance of the drug. In addition, triazolam has been associated with increased daytime anxiety. The adverse effects of the benzodiazepines are further discussed in Chapter 13.

Use of Flumazenil (*Romazicon*)

Flumazenil is a benzodiazepine receptor antagonist that may be administered intravenously to reverse the depressant effects of the benzodiazepine drugs. It can be used in the management of benzodiazepine overdose to antagonize the effects of excessive CNS and respiratory depression. Flumazenil has a half-life of approximately one hour and may require repeated administration. The sedative effects of eszopiclone, zaleplon, and zolpidem also are antagonized by flumazenil.

Cautions and Contraindications
Pregnancy

Benzodiazepine hypnotic drugs have been shown to cause harmful effects during pregnancy. They are designated as FDA Pregnancy Categories D and X and, therefore, should not be used during pregnancy.

Drug Interactions

The benzodiazepines potentiate the actions of other CNS depressant drugs, such as alcohol and barbiturates. Such drugs should never be taken together unless specifically ordered by a physician.

The metabolism of the benzodiazepines has been shown to be inhibited by cimetidine (*Tagamet*), a drug used in the treatment of intestinal ulcers. Cimetidine and other drugs that cause enzyme inhibition can increase the duration of action of the benzodiazepines.

LO 12.5
MISCELLANEOUS HYPNOTIC DRUGS

The miscellaneous drugs are a diverse group of drugs with differing chemical structures and pharmacologic characteristics. These hypnotics include eszopiclone, zaleplon, and zolpidem. These drugs bind selectively to a subunit of the benzodiazepine receptor to increase the inhibitory effects of GABA. Because of this selectivity, these drugs lack other pharmacologic actions such as the anticonvulsant, muscle relaxing, and antianxiety effects produced by benzodiazepines and barbiturates. They also do not disrupt the normal stages of sleep like barbiturates and benzodiazepines. These drugs are summarized in Table 12:1. In addition, these drugs appear to be at low risk for the development of drug tolerance, dependency, and withdrawal reactions. Other miscellaneous drugs include ramelteon and chloral hydrate.

Eszopiclone (*Lunesta*)

Eszopiclone is rapidly absorbed after oral administration, with a half-life of approximately 6 hours. Studies have demonstrated that eszopiclone sustained its ability to induce and maintain sleep when taken daily for 6 months. There is little evidence for the development of drug tolerance or dependency. However, abrupt cessation of drug following prolonged use may result in some withdrawal reactions. Common adverse effects include dizziness, headache, dry mouth, and mild impairment of memory.

Zaleplon (*Sonata*)

Zaleplon is rapidly absorbed and provides a short duration of action. It is useful for individuals having difficulty falling asleep; it has not been shown to increase total sleep time. Adverse effects include dizziness, headache, and minor GI disturbances. The elderly may experience mental confusion and memory disturbances. The development of tolerance and dependency does not appear to be a significant problem and any withdrawal reactions are usually associated with abrupt cessation of drug following prolonged use.

Zolpidem (*Ambien, Ambien-CR*)

Zolpidem is currently the most widely prescribed hypnotic drug on the market. The drug is rapidly absorbed and has a rapid onset of action. Zolpidem decreases awakenings during the night and increases total sleep time. The extended release tablets supplied by *Ambien-CR* (controlled release) further prolong the duration of action. As with eszopiclone and zaleplon, the development of drug tolerance, dependency, and withdrawal reactions are usually associated with abrupt cessation of drug following prolonged use. Common adverse effects include headache, dizziness, and nausea. The elderly may experience some confusion and memory disturbances.

Ramelteon (*Rozerem*)

Ramelteon is classified as a melatonin agonist. Melatonin is produced by the pineal gland, released mainly at night, and involved with regulation of the sleep–wake cycle. The main effect of the drug is to promote sleep onset and it should be taken 30 minutes before bedtime. Adverse effects include headache, dizziness, and minor GI disturbances such as nausea and diarrhea. Ramelteon is not a controlled substance and is not associated with drug dependency.

Chloral Hydrate

Chloral hydrate is an old drug and is related in a general way to alcohol. In the liver, it is metabolized by alcohol dehydrogenase to trichloroethanol, which also produces hypnotic effects (active metabolite). The main use of chloral hydrate is as a hypnotic, particularly in the elderly. The usual dosage is 500–1000 mg administered as capsules or syrup; rectal suppositories are also available. Chloral hydrate produces less suppression of REM sleep than do the barbiturates. Side effects usually involve excessive CNS depression and gastric irritation. Although capable of producing tolerance and addiction, chloral hydrate is not particularly popular with drug abusers.

Preferred Therapy for Insomnia and Sedation

The preferred hypnotics for individuals having problems falling asleep and staying asleep are usually one of the miscellaneous drugs such as zolpidem (*Ambien, Ambien-CR*) or eszopiclone (*Lunesta*). These drugs cause minimal drug tolerance and dependency. In addition, when taken nightly they are effective for longer periods of time than barbiturates or benzodiazepines. For individuals whose insomnia is complicated with anxiety or stressful situations, one of the benzodiazepines can be considered. Either temazepam (*Restoril*) or estazolam (*ProSom*) provides an intermediate duration of action with little or no residual effects the following day. Flurazepam (*Dalmane*) or quazepam (*Doral*) may be considered when residual sedative and antianxiety actions are desired the following day. For individuals whose main problem is falling asleep, the shorter-acting drug zaleplon (*Sonata*) or the OTC drug ramelteon (*Rozerem*) may be helpful.

The preferred drugs for sedation are usually one of the benzodiazepine drugs. There are a variety of choices depending on the duration of action that is desired. The sedative dosage varies depending on the desired degree of sedation but generally is one-third to one-half of the hypnotic dose. The drugs preferred for sedation are the

Monitor vital signs and patient response when barbiturates and benzodiazepines are administered parenterally.

Explain the potential drug side effects: excessive drowsiness, mental confusion, and a drug hangover effect the following day.

Explain to patients the dangers of activities such as driving while under the influence of sedative and hypnotic drugs.

Explain to patients the dangers of combining alcohol and other CNS depressant drugs with sedatives and hypnotics.

Remind patients that these drugs should not be used for more than 2 weeks at a time unless otherwise instructed.

Warn patients of the potential for drug dependency when barbiturate and benzodiazepine hypnotics are used continuously for prolonged periods.

---

benzodiazepines more commonly prescribed for their antianxiety effects (see Chapter 13). These drugs usually include diazepam (*Valium*), alprazolam (*Xanax*), and lorazepam (*Ativan*).

LO 12.6
ALCOHOL

Alcohol (ethanol, whiskey, ethyl alcohol, or grain alcohol) is probably the most widely used (self-prescribed) nonprescription sedative-hypnotic and antianxiety agent.

Pharmacological Effects

Alcohol has many pharmacological effects that are seen throughout the body, including the CNS, heart, gastrointestinal tract, and kidneys.

CNS Effects

The CNS is extremely sensitive to the depressant action of alcohol. As with other sedative-hypnotic drugs, alcohol produces a dose-dependent depression of the CNS. After drinking alcoholic beverages, people usually feel "stimulated," uninhibited, and less self-conscious. However, this stimulation is actually due to an initial depression of inhibitory areas within the brain. As the level of alcohol in the brain increases, excitatory and inhibitory fibers are progressively depressed, leading to sedation, hypnosis, and possibly coma. Unlike the other sedative-hypnotic drugs, alcohol produces some analgesia and antipyresis (reduces fever). The mechanisms of alcohol's action in the CNS have not been fully established, but alcohol also appears to increase the inhibitory effects of GABA.

Vascular Effects

In low to moderate amounts, alcohol does not produce any direct deleterious effects on the heart. However, alcohol may induce dilation of the blood vessels in the skin (cutaneous), producing a warm, flushed

sensation. The dilation of blood vessels may lead to a rapid loss of body heat, so that body temperature begins to fall. Depression of vasomotor centers in the CNS is most likely responsible for producing the peripheral vasodilation.

Gastrointestinal Effects

Alcohol stimulates the secretion of saliva and gastric juices (acid and pepsin). Overall, this action usually results in an increased appetite. However, ingestion of strong concentrations of alcohol may irritate the gastric mucosa, causing a local inflammation (gastritis). Increased acid secretion coupled with gastritis may lead to gastrointestinal (GI) ulceration in sensitive patients.

Renal Effects

Alcohol promotes an increased excretion of urine (diuresis), which is partly due to the increased fluid intake that accompanies the ingestion of alcoholic beverages. In addition, alcohol blocks the pituitary secretion of anti-diuretic hormone (ADH), which decreases the renal reabsorption of water. Therefore, the water is excreted into the urine. Alcohol inhibits the renal secretion of uric acid by an unknown mechanism that allows uric acid to build up in the blood. In susceptible patients (with gout or gouty arthritis), this elevation in uric acid levels may lead to attacks of joint inflammation.

Nutritional Effects

Besides its direct effects on the various organs, alcohol exerts a profound influence on the nutritional state of individuals. Alcohol is a natural product that possesses calories. For this reason, many people often substitute alcohol for nutritionally rich foods, such as protein. Over a period of time, individuals who consume moderate to large amounts of alcohol in conjunction with a poorly balanced diet may suffer from vitamin and amino acid deficiencies. In particular, deficiency of the B vitamins leads to abnormal growth and function of nervous tissue.

Therefore, multiple nutritional deficiencies associated with alcohol consumption produce various conditions such as neuropathies, dermatitis (pellagra), anemia, and psychosis.

Metabolism of Alcohol

Alcohol is readily absorbed throughout the entire GI tract following ingestion. Subsequently, alcohol is distributed to all tissues. However, the CNS receives a significant concentration of alcohol because of its rich blood supply. The concentration of alcohol in the brain is proportional to the concentration of alcohol in the blood.

Unlike other drugs, alcohol is metabolized at a constant rate in the liver. No matter how much alcohol is consumed, only 10 to 15 ml of pure alcohol per hour is metabolized, which is the amount of alcohol in one beer, a glass of wine, or an average-size cocktail. This limits the amount of alcohol that can be consumed without producing intoxication. Alcohol is metabolized primarily to acetaldehyde, which the body can use in the synthesis of cholesterol and fatty acids. Overall, alcohol is efficiently metabolized (about 95 percent) to useful biochemical products and water.

Enzyme induction develops during chronic use of alcohol. Therefore, habitual drinkers often experience shorter durations of action of other drugs metabolized by the microsomal system of the liver (oral anticoagulants and many others).

Adverse Effects

The adverse effects associated with the use of alcohol are separated into acute and chronic effects. Acute intoxication (inebriation) produces extensive CNS depression. Individuals may exhibit ataxia, impaired speech, blurred vision, and loss of memory, similar to the symptoms of intoxication caused by other sedative-hypnotic drugs.

When CNS depression is severe, stupor and coma may result. The skin is cold and clammy, the body temperature falls, and the heart rate may increase. Treatment is usually directed at supporting respiration, so that the brain remains well oxygenated.

Chronic consumption of alcohol is associated with progressive changes in cell function. Elevated blood alcohol levels for long periods result ultimately in drug tolerance and physical dependence. The abstinence syndrome associated with alcohol addiction is similar to that described for the barbiturates and benzodiazepines. In addition, chronic use of alcohol produces alterations in body metabolism, some of which may be due to the development of malnutrition. Alcohol-induced malnutrition and vitamin deficiency can cause a number of neurological disorders such as Wernicke's encephalopathy and Korsakoff's psychosis. In addition, malnutrition and alcohol contribute to the production of fatty liver and cirrhosis of the liver.

Cautions and Contraindications

The symptoms of alcohol intoxication often resemble those associated with diabetic coma, head injuries, and drug overdose (other sedative-hypnotics). Patients who appear intoxicated should always be kept for observation until an accurate diagnosis is made. If possible, the blood alcohol level should be determined to confirm the suspected diagnosis.

Alcohol should never be combined with other CNS depressant medications. Potentiation occurs with any central-acting depressants, including muscle relaxants, anesthetics, analgesics, and antianxiety drugs. Alcohol is absolutely contraindicated in patients who have hepatic or renal disease, ulcers, hyperacidity, or epilepsy.

Pregnancy

The consumption of alcohol has been associated with harmful fetal effects and should be avoided during pregnancy. Alcohol readily crosses the placenta and distributes to all tissues of the fetus. Infants who were exposed to circulating levels of alcohol *in utero* have shown depressed respiration and reflexes at birth. Babies born to alcoholic mothers are unusually small, are frequently premature, and may be mentally retarded. It is not unusual for a newborn of an alcoholic mother to undergo withdrawal symptoms after birth. *Fetal alcohol syndrome* is the term used to describe the fetal abnormalities that may include low IQ, microcephaly, and a variety of facial abnormalities.

Clinical Indications

When applied to the skin, alcohol produces a cooling effect, due to rapid evaporation from the skin surface. For this reason, it is used as a sponge bath to reduce elevated body temperature. Also, 70 percent alcohol applied to the skin acts as a bactericidal agent (disinfectant). There is very little medicinal value associated with the consumption of alcohol. However, many over-the-counter (nonprescription) cold remedies and cough syrups contain a significant amount of alcohol; the alcohol present in these preparations is sufficient to produce sedation and hypnosis. Therefore, exposure of patients to alcohol may occur without their knowledge.

Disulfiram (*Antabuse*)

Disulfiram is a drug used to treat chronic alcoholism. It interferes with the metabolism of alcohol. Alcohol is metabolized through a series of steps to acetaldehyde, which is then converted into acetyl coenzyme A (CoA).

alcohol
↓
acetaldehyde
↓
acetyl coenzyme A

Disulfiram slows the conversion of acetaldehyde to acetyl coenzyme A. Therefore, acetaldehyde accumulates in the blood, producing nausea, vomiting, headache, and hypotension. This is known as a disulfiram reaction. Patients taking disulfiram are instructed not to ingest any alcoholic beverages, including cough syrups, special wine sauces, and fermented beverages (cider). As long as a patient is taking disulfiram, even a small amount of alcohol (1 ounce) will produce the unpleasant effects. In this manner, the disulfiram therapy acts as a reinforcing deterrent to alcohol consumption as long as the individual is willing to take the drug.

Chapter Review

Understanding Terminology

Answer the following questions.

1. Differentiate between REM sleep and NREM sleep. **(LO 12.1)**
2. What is the difference between a sedative and a hypnotic? **(LO 12.3)**
3. Explain the meaning of *automatism.* **(LO 12.3)**
4. Differentiate between barbiturates and nonbarbiturates. **(LO 12.5)**
5. What is GABA an abbreviation for? **(LO 12.2)**

Acquiring Knowledge

Answer the following questions.

1. What is the major indication for the use of sedatives and hypnotics? **(LO 12.1)**
2. Explain the mechanism of action of benzodiazepine hypnotics. What is the main site of action to produce this effect? **(LO 12.4)**
3. List the different stages of sleep and the characteristics of each. **(LO 12.1)**
4. How do barbiturates alter the normal sleep cycle? **(LO 12.3)**
5. What is the importance of enzyme induction caused by barbiturate drugs? **(LO 12.3)**
6. What adverse effects are caused by barbiturates? **(LO 12.3)**
7. How does GABA normally function? **(LO 12.2)**
8. Explain the mechanism of action of zolpidem and zaleplon. **(LO 12.5)**
9. How do benzodiazepine hypnotics alter the sleep cycle? **(LO 12.4)**
10. What is the main difference between flurazepam (*Dalmane*) and triazolam (*Halcion*)? **(LO 12.4)**
11. What are the advantages of the benzodiazepines over the barbiturate hypnotics? **(LO 12.3, 12.4)**
12. List some of the effects that alcohol produces on the different body systems. **(LO 12.6)**
13. Explain how disulfiram (*Antabuse*) is used in the treatment of alcoholism and describe the disulfiram reaction. **(LO 12.6)**

Applying Knowledge on the Job

Use your critical-thinking skills to answer the following questions.

1. An 82-year-old woman has been taking a sleeping pill for the past 6 months to help her fall asleep. What can you tell her about the use of hypnotic drugs? **(LO 12.3)**
2. Mary's husband John occasionally takes *Dalmane* when he has trouble sleeping. He came home late last night after a banquet and a few too many drinks; he took a *Dalmane* capsule because he wasn't tired and he had to get up early for an important meeting. At 8 a.m., John was sound asleep and Mary couldn't seem to wake him up. What do you think may have happened? **(LO 12.4)**
3. You receive a phone call at the doctor's office from Mr. Smith, who has a prescription for *Antabuse.* He complains that he feels terrible and has been vomiting. He claims to have just developed a chest cold and has taken a spoonful of *Vicks* cough syrup. Mr. Smith doesn't think the vomiting has anything to do with the cold. What do you think? **(LO 12.6)**
4. A young man with a history of occasional drug abuse is in the doctor's office complaining of difficulty sleeping. The physician is writing a prescription for a hypnotic with no refills. Which hypnotic agent might be the best choice for this patient? **(LO 12.5)**

Use the appropriate reference books if needed for the following questions.

5. June is a 36-year-old alcoholic. She has unsuccessfully attempted to quit drinking multiple times. Her physician has decided to initiate disulfiram therapy. What should June be told before taking this medication? **(LO 12.6)**

6. John is a healthy 29-year-old who has recently had trouble sleeping. His physician has prescribed *Dalmane* 30 mg. While talking with John, he tells you how happy he is to know that he is going to get a good night's sleep. He works in a high-energy office and was concerned that he might be in danger of losing his job due to his recent lack of energy. Do you think this should be brought to the physician's attention? Why? Would you expect the drug therapy to change? If so, which medication do you think it might be changed to? **(LO 12.4)**

7. Julie has never had trouble sleeping until the past month. She is going through a stressful period and is having difficulty falling asleep. Once asleep, she usually sleeps through the night. Her care provider had prescribed *Ambien* 5 mg in a quantity to last 2 weeks. Do you feel this is appropriate? Why? **(LO 12.5)**

Multiple Choice

Use your critical-thinking skills to answer the following questions.

1. Barbiturate and benzodiazepine hypnotics both **(LO 12.3, 12.4)**
   A. increase NREM stage 2 sleep
   B. decrease REM sleep
   C. decrease NREM stage 4 sleep
   D. only A and C are true

2. Disadvantages to the use of barbiturate hypnotics include **(LO 12.3)**
   A. development of drug tolerance
   B. risk of drug dependency
   C. disruption of normal stages of sleep
   D. all statements are true

3. The correct statement concerning the use of hypnotic drugs is **(LO 12.3, 12.4, 12.5)**
   A. zolpidem binds to the GABA receptor
   B. benzodiazepines increase chloride channel opening
   C. barbiturates block the GABA receptor
   D. ramelteon is a melatonin antagonist

4. Flurazepam **(LO 12.4)**
   A. is classified as long-acting
   B. forms active metabolites
   C. may cause next-day residual effects
   D. all statements are true

5. Triazolam **(LO 12.4)**
   A. forms active metabolites
   B. may cause next-day residual effects
   C. may cause early morning awakenings
   D. is classified as long-acting

6. Eszopiclone **(LO 12.5)**
   A. is classified as a benzodiazepine
   B. has a half-life of 1–2 hours
   C. increases total sleep time
   D. is used as an antianxiety agent

7. Zolpidem **(LO 12.5)**
   A. binds to the benzodiazepine-1 (BZD$_1$) receptor
   B. is useful as a muscle relaxant
   C. has a slow onset of action
   D. is useful as an anticonvulsant

Multiple Choice (Multiple Answer)

Select the correct choices for each statement. The choices may be all correct, all incorrect, or any combination.

1. Which stages of the sleep cycle are important for restoration? **(LO 12.1)**
   A. stage 1 NREM
   B. stage 2 NREM
   C. stages 3 and 4 NREM
   D. REM

2. Barbiturate sedatives work by **(LO 12.2)**
   A. binding to GABA receptors
   B. increasing the influx of chloride
   C. depolarizing nerves
   D. decreasing the activity of RAS

3. Select all of the adverse effects of barbiturates. **(LO 12.3)**
   A. slurred speech
   B. ataxia
   C. irritability
   D. automatism

4. The differences between long-acting and short-acting benzodiazepines include **(LO 12.4)**
   A. the shorter the duration of action, the more active the metabolites
   B. the shorter the duration of action, the more drug effect the next day
   C. the longer the duration of action, the more active the metabolites
   D. the longer the duration of action, the less daytime sedation

5. Alcohol has pharmacological effects on which body systems? **(LO 12.6)**
   A. central nervous system
   B. gastrointestinal system
   C. renal system
   D. vascular system

Sequencing

Place the following in order of longest half-life to shortest half-life. **(LO 12.4)**

_____   _____   _____   _____

Last   **First**

Halcion

Restoril

ProSom

Dalmane

Classification

Place each drug under the appropriate use. **(LO 12.3, 12.4, 12.5)**

ProSom	Lunesta
Restoril	Xanax
Rozerem	Ambien
Valium	Sonata

Falling & staying asleep	Insomnia due to stress	Falling asleep	Sedation

Matching

Match the following effects with the appropriate class of drugs. **(LO 12.2, 12.4, 12.5)**

    a. barbiturates
    b. benzodiazepines
    c. *ramelteon*
    d. zolpidem
    e. zaleplon

    1. _____ melatonin antagonist
    2. _____ used primarily for those who have difficulty falling asleep
    3. _____ referred to as antianxiety drugs
    4. _____ increases stage 2 NREM
    5. _____ decreases awakening during the night

Labeling

Fill in the missing labels. **(LO 12.1)**

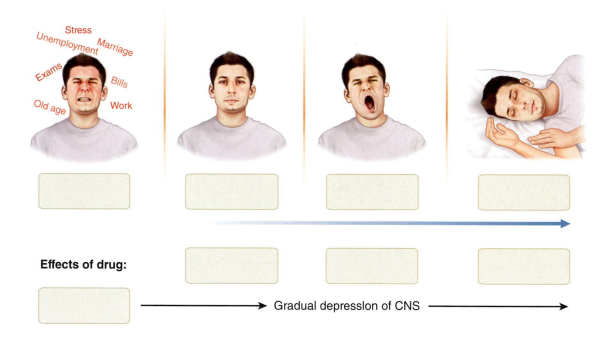

Effects of drug:

Gradual depression of CNS

For interactive animations, videos, and assessment, visit:
www.mcgrawhillconnect.com

Chapter 13

Antipsychotic and Antianxiety Drugs

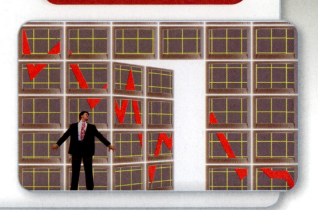

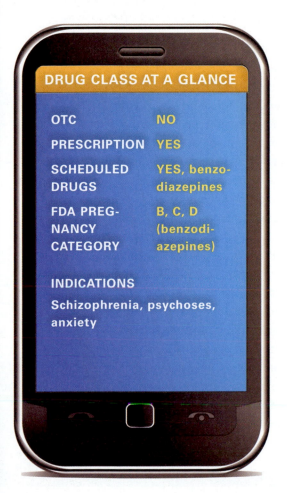

DRUG CLASS AT A GLANCE

OTC	NO
PRESCRIPTION	YES
SCHEDULED DRUGS	YES, benzodiazepines
FDA PREGNANCY CATEGORY	B, C, D (benzodiazepines)
INDICATIONS	Schizophrenia, psychoses, anxiety

KEY TERMS

akathisia: continuous body movement in which an individual is restless or constantly paces about.

antianxiety drug: drug used to treat anxiety; these drugs are also referred to as anxiolytics.

antipsychotic drug: drug used to treat schizophrenia and other psychotic conditions.

anxiety: a state of anxiousness and hyperemotionalism that occurs with uncertainty, stress, and fearful situations.

dystonic reaction: reaction characterized by muscle spasms, twitching, facial grimacing, or torticollis.

extrapyramidal syndrome (EPS): movement disorders such as akathisia, dystonia, and parkinsonism caused by antipsychotic drug therapy.

neuroleptic malignant syndrome (NMS): toxic syndrome associated with the use of antipsychotic drugs.

parkinsonism: disease or drug-induced condition characterized by muscular rigidity, tremors, and disturbances of movement.

psychosis: form of mental illness that produces bizarre behavior and deterioration of the personality.

schizophrenia: major form of psychosis; behavior is inappropriate.

tardive dyskinesia: drug-induced involuntary movements of the lips, jaw, tongue, and extremities.

After studying this chapter, you should be able to

13.1 explain the importance of dopamine and serotonin in relationship to psychosis and antipsychotic drug therapy.

13.2 list the different pharmacologic actions of the phenothiazine drugs and describe the adverse neurological effects associated with these drugs.

13.3 compare the pharmacologic actions and adverse effects of the butyrophenones with the phenothiazines.

13.4 describe the actions and adverse effects of the thioxanthine antipsychotic drugs.

13.5 explain the actions and advantages of the atypical antipsychotic drugs when compared to the typical antipsychotic drugs.

13.6 compare the mechanism of action and pharmacologic effects of the antianxiety benzodiazepines with buspirone.

The term *mental illness* refers to a number of emotional and mental disturbances that involve abnormal changes in personality and behavior. These changes may affect the ability of individuals to communicate with other people or to function in normal activities.

Psychosis is a mental condition characterized by disturbed thought processes, delusions, and hallucinations. While psychotic behavior can be caused by a variety of conditions, one of the main causes is **schizophrenia**. Symptoms of schizophrenia include bizarre behavior, auditory and visual hallucinations, lack of motivation and emotional expression, and diminished speech and thought processes. The cause of schizophrenia involves genetic defects that cause abnormal neural development. Excessive activity of certain brain neurotransmitters, especially dopamine and serotonin, in the cerebral cortex and limbic system appear to be responsible for the psychotic behavior. Drugs referred to as **antipsychotics** are used to treat these conditions

Anxiety is a very common emotion and increases whenever there is uncertainty or fear about some event or life circumstance. Certain types of anxiety have been classified and include general anxiety disorder (GAD), panic disorder, obsessive-compulsive disorder (OCD), and posttraumatic stress disorder (PTSD). The limbic system plays a major role in the regulation and control of emotions. In stressful and uncertain situations, the activity of the limbic system dramatically increases. Anxiety also activates the sympathetic nervous system and the reticular activating system, which in turn cause hyperarousal of the cerebral cortex. The result is a highly emotional state accompanied by many physical symptoms that can interfere with normal function and daily activities. Drugs used to treat anxiety, the benzodiazepines and buspirone, are referred to as the **antianxiety drugs** or anxiolytics. In addition, some of the antidepressant drugs (Chapter 14) are also effective for the treatment of anxiety.

LO 13.1 LO 13.2
LO 13.3 LO 13.4 LO 13.5

ANTIPSYCHOTIC DRUGS

Antipsychotic drugs are used to suppress the symptoms of schizophrenia and other psychotic conditions. The main site of action of antipsychotic drugs is on neural pathways involving the cerebral cortex and limbic system. The cause of psychosis is not completely understood. However, excessive activity of neurotransmitters in the cortical and limbic pathways is involved in the development of schizophrenia and other psychoses. Dopamine (DA) appears to be particularly important, and drugs that block or reduce the effects of dopamine are effective in treating psychosis, especially schizophrenia. There are at least five different types of DA receptors, identified as D_1 through D_5. However, the mechanism of action of antipsychotic drugs involves the ability of these drugs to block a specific DA receptor, the D_2 receptor. This reduces dopaminergic activity by preventing dopamine from binding to and activating its receptors. Excessive blockade of dopamine receptors is the main cause of the **extrapyramidal syndrome (EPS).**

Serotonin (5HT) is another brain neurotransmitter that is involved in psychotic behavior. There are a number of different 5HT receptors but the receptor identified as $5HT_{2A}$ is the one most important for antipsychotic effects. Antipsychotic drugs primarily antagonize both D_2 and $5HT_{2A}$ receptors. The main difference among the various antipsychotic drug classes is the degree to which they block each of these two neurotransmitter receptors. Antipsychotic drugs also affect other neurotransmitter receptors, but these actions are associated with adverse effects.

There are four classes of antipsychotic drugs. The phenothiazine, butyrophenone, and thioxanthine drugs are referred to as "typical" because they all primarily block D_2 receptors. They also produce a higher incidence of EPS because of the D_2 blockade. The remaining drug class is referred to as the "atypical" antipsychotic drugs. Unlike the other three antipsychotic drug classes, the atypical drugs reduce serotonin activity more than they reduce the activity of dopamine, and for that reason they cause a significantly lower incidence of EPS. Several classes of drugs are used for their antipsychotic effects.

In addition to blocking dopamine and serotonin, most antipsychotic drugs produce varying degrees of anticholinergic, alpha-adrenergic-blocking, and antihistaminic effects. Figure 13.1 provides an overview of the neurotransmitter receptors blocked by antipsychotic drugs and the resulting drug effects.

Phenothiazines

The term *phenothiazine* refers to the basic chemical structure of a large number of drugs similar in structure and pharmacological action. Although some of these drugs are more effective than others, all produce the same pharmacological effects. These drugs block D_2 receptors to a greater degree than they block $5HT_{2A}$ receptors. The first phenothiazine, chlorpromazine, was discovered in the early 1950s. Within a few years, chlorpromazine had revolutionized the treatment of mental illness. Many patients who were previously institutionalized were able to return home and assume more active roles in society. Within a few years, the number of patients in mental institutions was cut almost in half.

The phenothiazines are a very active group of drugs. In addition to an antipsychotic effect, they possess anticholinergic, antihistaminic, alpha-adrenergic-blocking,

and antiemetic effects. These additional effects allow the phenothiazines to be used for treating nausea, vomiting, pruritus, and certain allergic reactions; however, these actions also increase adverse drug reactions. The phenothiazines are administered orally (PO) and parenterally (IM and IV). Table 13:1 lists the most frequently used phenothiazines and their main pharmacologic features.

Antipsychotic Effects

The main effects of the antipsychotic drugs are to reduce the bizarre behavior, hallucinations, and irrational thought disorders of psychosis without significantly depressing other intellectual functions. The antipsychotic effects usually require several weeks to fully develop. With drug therapy, patients usually demonstrate decreased interest in the surroundings and less behavioral activation. However, routine daily activities can be carried out, and patients are able to communicate more rationally. Although the psychosis is not cured, it is possible to control it adequately with the proper medication. In addition, patients are usually more amenable to psychotherapy and other treatment measures.

Adverse Effects

Common adverse effects, such as dry mouth, constipation, visual disturbances, and sedation, are due to anticholinergic and antihistaminic actions. Alpha-blocking actions may reduce blood pressure and cause postural hypotension. Because antipsychotic drugs block the effects of dopamine, a number of neurological side effects involving the basal ganglia can occur. Dopamine functions as a neurotransmitter in the basal ganglia of the brain. The basal ganglia are important in the regulation of skeletal muscle tone and movement (see Chapter 17). In addition, blockade of dopamine receptors also may increase prolactin levels, which can cause menstrual irregularities in women and gynecomastia in males.

Blockade of DA receptors in the basal ganglia may cause a number of movement disorders. These disorders are usually referred to as the extrapyramidal syndrome (EPS). **Dystonic reactions** are characterized by muscle spasms, twitching, facial grimacing, and torticollis (wryneck). **Akathisia** refers to continuous body movement in which the individual is restless or constantly paces about. **Parkinsonism** involves development of muscular rigidity, tremors, and other disturbances of movement. Reducing the dosage, stopping the drug, or administering centrally acting anticholinergic drugs usually improves these three neurological conditions.

Tardive dyskinesia is a more serious condition that may develop after long-term antipsychotic therapy. This condition involves involuntary movements of the

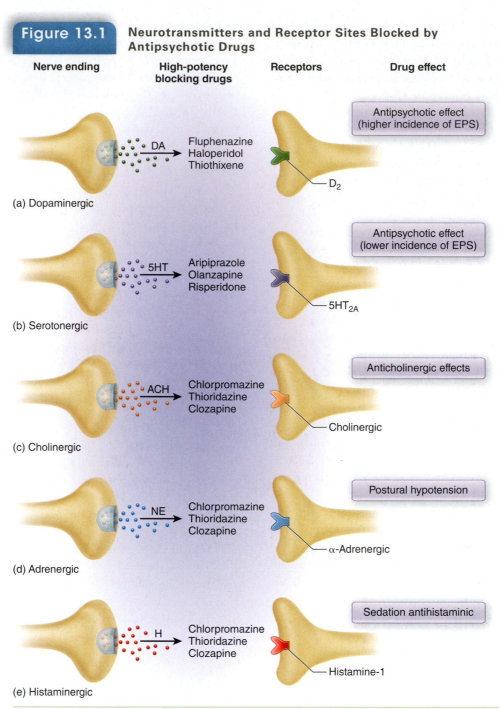

Figure 13.1 Neurotransmitters and Receptor Sites Blocked by Antipsychotic Drugs

Nerve ending	High-potency blocking drugs	Receptors	Drug effect

(a) Dopaminergic — DA — Fluphenazine, Haloperidol, Thiothixene — D₂ — Antipsychotic effect (higher incidence of EPS)

(b) Serotonergic — 5HT — Aripiprazole, Olanzapine, Risperidone — 5HT₂ₐ — Antipsychotic effect (lower incidence of EPS)

(c) Cholinergic — ACH — Chlorpromazine, Thioridazine, Clozapine — Cholinergic — Anticholinergic effects

(d) Adrenergic — NE — Chlorpromazine, Thioridazine, Clozapine — α-Adrenergic — Postural hypotension

(e) Histaminergic — H — Chlorpromazine, Thioridazine, Clozapine — Histamine-1 — Sedation antihistaminic

(a) Phenothiazine, butyrophenone, and thioxanthene drugs primarily block D₂ receptors to produce the antipsychotic effect, and also significant EPS. (b) Atypical antipsychotics primarily block 5HT₂ₐ receptors to produce antipsychotic effects and less EPS. (c) Antipsychotic drugs with prominent anticholinergic effects. (d) Antipsychotic drugs with increased alpha-adrenergic-blocking actions that cause postural hypotension. (e) Antipsychotic drugs with antihistaminic actions and that promote sedation.

lips, jaw, tongue, and extremities. The symptoms of tardive dyskinesia often appear when antipsychotic drug treatment is stopped. The symptoms can be suppressed by reinstituting the drug or by increasing the dose of the antipsychotic drug. However, the condition of tardive dyskinesia continues to progress and will be worse when the drug is stopped.

A serious and potentially fatal condition, **neuroleptic malignant syndrome (NMS),** is also associated with the use of antipsychotic drugs. This syndrome is characterized by hyperthermia, muscular rigidity, catatonia (patient appears frozen in position), and autonomic nervous system instability. Treatment is immediately required and involves stopping antipsychotic

Representative Antipsychotic Drugs and Their Main Pharmacologic Features

Drug (*Trade Name*)	Potency	Sedation	EPS	AC	PH
Phenothiazines					
Chlorpromazine (*Thorazine*)	Low	High	Medium	High	High
Fluphenazine (*Prolixin*)	High	Low	High	Medium	Low
Thioridazine (*Mellaril*)	Low	High	Medium	High	High
Trifluoperazine (*Stelazine*)	High	Medium	High	Medium	Low
Butyrophenones					
Haloperidol (*Haldol*)	High	Low	High	Low	Low
Thioxanthenes					
Thiothixene (*Navane*)	High	Medium	High	Medium	Low
Atypical antipsychotics					
Aripiprazole (*Abilify*)	High	Low	Low	Low	Low
Clozapine (*Clozaril*)	Medium	Medium	Low	High	High
Iloperidone (*Fanapt*)	Medium	Low	Low	Low	Medium
Olanzapine (*Zyprexa*)	High	Medium	Low	Low	Low
Quetiapine (*Seroquel*)	Low	Medium	Low	Medium	Medium
Risperidone (*Risperdal*)	High	Low	Low	Low	Medium
Asenapine (*Saphris*)	Medium	Medium	Low	Low	Medium
Ziprasidone (*Geodon*)	Medium	Low	Low	Low	Low

EPS – extrapyramidal syndrome, AC – anticholinergic effects, PH – postural hypotension

drug administration and symptomatic treatment of the symptoms.

Drug allergy is an infrequent but potentially dangerous complication of phenothiazine therapy. Allergic symptoms usually involve skin rashes and photosensitivity, blood disorders, and liver toxicity (cholestatic jaundice). Other miscellaneous adverse effects include skin pigmentation, ocular deposits (lens and cornea), and various endocrine disturbances.

Butyrophenones

The butyrophenones are high-potency drugs that differ chemically from the phenothiazines but that produce the same type of antipsychotic effects. The main drug of this group is haloperidol (*Haldol*).

Actions and Clinical Uses

On a milligram basis, the butyrophenones are more potent than the phenothiazines. Like the phenothiazines, the butyrophenones block D_2 receptors more than $5HT_{2A}$ receptors. The butyrophenones produce a lower incidence of peripheral effects (alpha-adrenergic blockade, anticholinergic, and antihistaminic), but greater movement disturbances. Haloperidol is especially useful in the treatment of highly agitated and manic patients. In addition, haloperidol is indicated to suppress the motor tics and vocalizations that characterize Gilles de la Tourette's syndrome.

Adverse Effects

The adverse effects of the butyrophenones are similar to those of the phenothiazines. However, the butyrophenones, haloperidol in particular, produce the highest incidence of extrapyramidal symptoms (EPS). There is also the potential for development of tardive dyskinesia and neuroleptic malignant syndrome.

Thioxanthenes

Thioxanthenes have chemical structures very similar to those of phenothiazines. Like phenothiazines and butyrophenones, thioxanthenes exert antipsychotic effects by blocking D_2 receptors more than $5HT_{2A}$ receptors. The most important thioxanthene is thiothixene (*Navane*).

Actions

The pharmacologic actions of thiothixene are similar to those of the phenothiazines. Thiothixene is a high-potency drug that is associated with higher incidences of EPS. Thiothixene generally causes less sedation and fewer anticholinergic and alpha-blocking effects than those of chlorpromazine.

Adverse Effects

The most frequent adverse effects of the thioxanthenes include drowsiness and postural hypotension. Patients who become allergic to these drugs may develop dermatitis, obstructive jaundice, or blood disorders (anemia and leukopenia). Like other antipsychotic drugs, the thioxanthenes may cause parkinsonian symptoms and other extrapyramidal disturbances of movement.

Atypical Antipsychotic Drugs

Unlike the phenothiazine, butyrophenone, and thioxanthene drugs, the atypical antipsychotic drugs affect and reduce the activity of $5HT_{2A}$ receptors more than they interfere with D_2 receptors. Because they have less effect on D_2 receptors, they are associated with a lower incidence of EPS, which is the main reason they are considered atypical. However, as with all antipsychotic drugs there is the potential for development of EPS, tardive dyskinesia, and neuroleptic malignant syndrome. Atypical drugs are associated with several metabolic disturbances such as weight gain, elevated triglycerides (hyperlipidemia), and development of diabetes mellitus. The atypical drugs and their main pharmacologic features are summarized in Table 13:1.

Aripiprazole (*Abilify*)

Aripiprazole is one of the newer atypical drugs that affects a number of DA and 5HT receptors. The main action of aripiprazole is antagonism of both D_2 and $5HT_{2A}$ receptors. Aripiprazole is a high-potency drug that is associated with low incidences of sedation, EPS, and autonomic and metabolic disturbances. Common side effects include dizziness, headache, constipation, anxiety, and sleep disturbances. Aripiprazole may decrease sweating and cause increased body temperature and fever, especially during physical exertion.

Clozapine (*Clozaril*)

Clozapine provides moderate antipsychotic potency along with a low incidence of EPS. However, the use of clozapine is associated with higher incidences of sedation, seizures, weight gain, and agranulocytosis. The latter effect involves a decrease in white blood cells (WBCs), which may increase infections and requires periodic WBC monitoring. Anticholinergic effects and postural hypotension also are prominent. Because of the higher incidence of adverse effects, other atypical drugs are usually preferred.

Risperidone (*Risperdal*)

Risperidone is a high-potency drug that antagonizes $5HT_{2A}$ more than D_2 receptors. The drug is mildly sedating and produces a low incidence of EPS, although the incidence of sedation and EPS increases at higher doses. Postural hypotension and some weight gain also may occur. The drug is also available for IM injection (*Risperdal Consta*).

Olanzapine (*Zyprexa*)

Olanzapine is a high-potency drug associated with a low incidence of EPS. In addition to regular tablets, there is a tablet formulation of *Zyprexa* (*Zyprexa Zydis*) that rapidly dissolves in the mouth and an injectable preparation for IM administration. Adverse effects include dizziness, sedation, weight gain, and postural hypotension. Olanzapine also has shown effectiveness in the treatment of acute mania and bipolar disorder.

Cautions and Contraindications
Pregnancy

Most antipsychotic drugs are designated either Food and Drug Administration (FDA) Pregnancy Category B or C; a few of the drugs have not been rated. As always, the use of drugs during pregnancy should be avoided if at all possible and used only when the benefits outweigh the risks.

Drug Interactions

As previously discussed, many of the antipsychotic drugs produce anticholinergic, alpha-blocking, antihistaminic, and central nervous system (CNS) depressing effects. Therefore, these drugs will interact with all other drugs that also produce these pharmacologic effects.

Anticholinergic drugs (atropine-like) decrease the activity of the urinary and intestinal tracts and increase cardiac activity. They also tend to cause CNS depression and mental disturbances, especially in the elderly. Remember also that anticholinergic drugs are *contraindicated* or used with caution in individuals with glaucoma, prostate hypertrophy, and urinary and intestinal obstruction (see Chapter 7). Many antihistamine drugs possess anticholinergic activity and also cause sedation. Consequently, other anticholinergic drugs taken together with antipsychotic drugs will increase the frequency and severity of anticholinergic adverse reactions.

Alpha-blocking activity (blocks alpha effects of norepinephrine and epinephrine) produces a lowering of blood pressure. Individuals taking alpha-blockers for hypertension, or taking other antihypertensive medication, may experience hypotension, orthostatic hypotension, fainting, and the other adverse effects of alpha blockade (see Chapter 6).

The CNS depressant effects of antipsychotic drugs will be increased by all other drugs that also cause sedation, hypnosis, and depression. These include alcohol, barbiturates, benzodiazepines, antihistamines, tricyclic antidepressants, anticholinergics, and narcotics. When taken together these drugs may cause excessive CNS depression leading to coma, respiratory depression or arrest, and death.

Preferred Therapy for Schizophrenia and Psychosis

Due to the complex nature of schizophrenia and the different degrees of psychotic behavior, it is difficult to select one or two drugs as the drugs of choice. However, with regard to antipsychotic drug classes, the atypical drugs are now the preferred therapy. The advantages of these drugs include lower incidences of EPS, sedation, and other neurologic disturbances. In addition, with the exception of clozapine, the atypical drugs do not cause significant anticholinergic, alpha-adrenergic-blocking, or antihistaminic actions compared to some of the other drugs. The other antipsychotics usually serve as alternatives to the atypical drugs when patient conditions or contraindications exist. Often there is a trial period where different drugs are tried in order to find the most suitable drug for a particular patient.

LO 13.6
ANTIANXIETY DRUGS

Anxiety, tension, and nervousness are effects caused by uncertainty and various situations that are interpreted as being threatening or potentially dangerous. The perceived dangers may be real or due to personal insecurities or unconscious psychological conflicts. Physiologic and behavioral changes—trembling, sweating, nausea, loss of appetite, rapid heartbeat, and emotionalism—are caused by activation of the limbic and sympathetic nervous systems. The limbic system is a group of brain areas (amygdala, hippocampus, hypothalamus, lower parts of the cerebral cortex, others) that are interconnected by a neural pathway. The limbic system is involved with emotional and behavioral responses associated with reward, punishment, anger, fear, and anxiety. An important inhibitory neurotransmitter that functions to keep our emotions and behavior under control is gamma-aminobutyric acid, GABA (see Chapter 12).

When an anxiety condition is prolonged, there are significant behavioral and emotional changes. Antianxiety drugs, also referred to as anxiolytics, are used to calm individuals and reduce the unpleasant aspects of anxiety and hyperemotionalism. In addition, the benzodiazepine antianxiety drugs also are used as sedatives, hypnotics, anticonvulsants, and skeletal muscle relaxants (see Chapters 9, 12, and 16).

Benzodiazepines

The most important antianxiety drugs belong to a chemical class known as the benzodiazepines. Diazepam (*Valium*) and chlordiazepoxide (*Librium*) were the first benzodiazepines introduced and have been available for almost 50 years. A number of the benzodiazepines are marketed as hypnotics and were discussed in Chapter 12. Additional benzodiazepine drugs are listed in Table 13:2.

Mechanism of Action

The benzodiazepines decrease the excitability and the functional activity of specific areas of the brain and spinal cord. As previously discussed in Chapter 12, gamma-aminobutyric acid (GABA) is an inhibitory neurotransmitter in the CNS that, when released from nerve endings, binds to receptors (called GABA receptors) located on the membranes of other neurons. GABA appears to allow more chloride ions (Cl^-) to pass into the neurons, which makes the inside of the neuron more negatively charged (hyperpolarization). Hyperpolarization of the neuron reduces neuronal excitability and consequently produces a depressant effect on those neurons.

The benzodiazepine drugs bind to neuronal membranes at receptor sites (referred to as the benzodiazepine receptors) that are actually a part of the GABA receptors. When both GABA and a benzodiazepine drug are bound to their receptors, more chloride ions pass into the neuron than when only GABA is bound alone (Figure 13.2). Consequently, a greater degree of hyperpolarization and neuronal depression is produced. Simply stated, benzodiazepines are believed to increase the inhibitory actions of GABA, which results in reduced activity (depression) of specific areas of the CNS.

Sites of Action

There are four main areas of the CNS where the benzodiazepines exert their inhibitory effects: the limbic system, reticular formation, cerebral cortex, and spinal cord.

The limbic system is involved with regulation of emotional and behavioral responses. Any emotional or anxiety-producing situation increases the activity of the limbic system. GABA normally functions to inhibit excess stimulation of the limbic system. When anxiety becomes excessive and contributes to neurotic behavior, benzodiazepines are prescribed to decrease the activity of the limbic system. Anxious individuals usually calm down, are less emotional, and are in a better mental state

Table 13:2

Benzodiazepine Drugs

Drug (*Trade Name*)	Main use	Usual dose (mg/day)
Long acting		
Chlordiazepoxide (*Librium*)	Antianxiety, alcohol withdrawal	10–100
Clonazepam (*Klonopin*)	Antianxiety, anticonvulsant	0.5–12
Clorazepate (*Tranxene*)	Antianxiety, alcohol withdrawal	15–60
Diazepam (*Valium*)	Antianxiety, pre-op medication, alcohol withdrawal, anticonvulsant, muscle relaxer	2–40
Flurazepam (*Dalmane*)	Hypnotic	15–30 mg at bedtime
Short acting		
Alprazolam (*Xanax*)	Antianxiety, panic disorder, sedation	0.5–10
Lorazepam (*Ativan*)	Antianxiety, sedation, anticonvulsant	2–6
Oxazepam (*Serax*)	Antianxiety, sedation	30–120
Temazepam (*Restoril*)	Hypnotic	15–30 mg at bedtime
Triazolam (*Halcion*)	Hypnotic	0.25–0.5 mg at bedtime

Figure 13.2

Diagrammatic Representation of the Chloride Channel

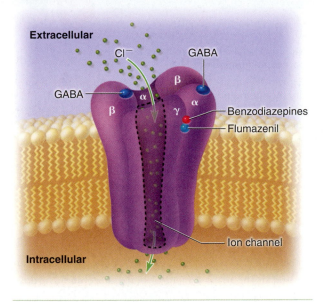

This diagram shows the location of the receptor sites for gamma-aminobutyric acid (GABA) and for the benzodiazepine drugs used to treat anxiety. Both GABA and the benzodiazepine drugs increase the influx of chloride ions that makes the inside of the neuron more negative (hyperpolarization) and inhibits neuronal activity in the limbic system. Flumazenil is a benzodiazepine receptor antagonist used to reverse the effects of the benzodiazepine drugs.

to deal with the situations that cause the anxiety. This is referred to as the antianxiety effect.

The reticular formation regulates the degree of wakefulness and alertness. Amphetamines and other CNS stimulants increase the activity of the reticular formation, which causes increased wakefulness and hyperactivity. GABA normally functions to decrease the activity of the reticular formation. Benzodiazepines, which increase the inhibitory actions of GABA, are used to produce sedation and hypnosis (sleep). A few of the benzodiazepines, those previously discussed in Chapter 12, are used primarily as hypnotics.

Excessive stimulation of the cerebral cortex can cause convulsions and other types of seizures. When administered parenterally, benzodiazepines exert an anticonvulsant effect on the cerebral cortex and are very effective in stopping convulsions. They are believed to exert the anticonvulsant effect by increasing the inhibitory actions of GABA. Diazepam (*Valium*), lorazepam (*Ativan*), and clonazepam (*Klonopin*) are the benzodiazepines that are considered to be the drugs of choice to stop convulsions. In these situations, drugs are administered by IM or IV injection.

GABA has an important function in the spinal cord. It helps regulate the degree of skeletal muscle tone and the responsiveness of spinal reflexes that also maintain skeletal muscle activity. By increasing the inhibitory actions of GABA, benzodiazepines decrease skeletal muscle tone. Relaxation of skeletal muscle is helpful in treating back injuries, spinal cord injuries, muscular dystrophy, and cerebral palsy, where muscle spasticity is usually present. Relaxation of skeletal muscle also is believed to contribute to the antianxiety effect, since increased muscle tension is a common finding in anxious individuals.

Pharmacokinetics

Benzodiazepines are well absorbed from the GI tract, and oral administration is the normal route. Diazepam, chlordiazepoxide, and lorazepam also can be given IM or IV when a rapid response is required. The main differences among the various benzodiazepines are in the duration of action. The benzodiazepines are divided into two groups: the long acting and the short acting (Table 13:2).

The long-acting benzodiazepines have half-lives of more than 20 hours. Also, during metabolism by the liver, they form active metabolites, which generally have long half-lives. When taken on a daily basis, these drugs produce effects that can last several days, due to accumulation of active metabolites in the body. Eventually, the active metabolites are conjugated with glucuronic acid. This step inactivates them and allows them to be excreted in the urine.

The short-acting benzodiazepines have half-lives that range from 5 to 20 hours. Either they do not form active metabolites, or, if they do, the active metabolites do not contribute significantly to the pharmacological effect.

Clinical Indications

The antianxiety drugs are used to relieve nervous tension and anxiety caused by neuroses or other life situations. Patients are made calm and relaxed without being excessively sedated. This state of mind is desirable before surgery, and antianxiety drugs are widely used as preoperative medications. The antianxiety drugs also are used to produce skeletal muscle relaxation in various musculoskeletal disturbances, as anticonvulsant and antiepileptic drugs, and as sedatives and hypnotics. Diazepam and chlordiazepoxide also are used in alcohol withdrawal, where they prevent the withdrawal syndrome and aid in the treatment of alcoholism.

Adverse Effects

The most frequent side effects are drowsiness, confusion, ataxia, minor GI disturbances (nausea and constipation), and rashes. Patients should be warned that performance in operating machinery may be impaired, especially driving an automobile.

Elderly individuals are more susceptible to the CNS depressant effects of these drugs. Other adverse effects, which occur with less frequency, include menstrual irregularities, changes in libido, agranulocytosis (decrease in nongranulated leukocytes), and changes in liver function. Chronic use of benzodiazepines, especially at higher dosages, may interfere with memory and recall of events.

Drug Dependency

There is increasing recognition of the liability of patients to become dependent on the antianxiety drugs. This problem occurs with patients who have been taking an antianxiety drug for a long time and for whom use is abruptly terminated. Hyperactivity, tremors, nervousness, and increased anxiety are common findings. Patients are usually weaned off the benzodiazepines when the decision to stop therapy has been determined. There are also individuals who abuse the benzodiazepines (nonmedical use), consume larger-than-therapeutic doses, and develop a more severe drug dependency. These individuals exhibit hyperexcitability, tremors, and anxiety and may experience a more intense withdrawal reaction that can include the development of seizures. An important point to remember is that antianxiety drugs are not curative. They only allay the symptoms and help patients manage until the real cause of the anxiety is discovered and eliminated. Too often, antianxiety drugs are used as a crutch to avoid the discomforts of stress or personal unhappiness.

Cautions and Contraindications

Pregnancy

The benzodiazepines used for the treatment of anxiety have been designated FDA Pregnancy Category D, and should be avoided during pregnancy.

Drug Interactions

Additive effects occur with other CNS depressants, such as the barbiturates and in particular with alcohol. Several cases of coma and permanent brain damage have occurred after the simultaneous ingestion of diazepam and alcohol.

Cimetidine (*Tagamet*) inhibits the microsomal drug metabolizing enzymes and has been shown to inhibit the metabolism of diazepam and other benzodiazepines. When taken together, the effects of the benzodiazepines are increased and prolonged.

Use of Flumazenil (*Romazicon*)

Flumazenil is a benzodiazepine receptor antagonist that may be administered intravenously to reverse the

Patient Administration and Monitoring

Monitor vital signs and patient response during parenteral administration.

Explain to patient the common side effects: sedation, dry mouth, mental confusion, and GI disturbances.

Warn patient not to drive or attempt hazardous activities during treatment.

Warn patient not to take alcohol, barbiturates, and other CNS depressants unless authorized by his or her physician.

Instruct patients to report excessive sedation, mental disturbances, or loss of memory.

depressant effects of the benzodiazepine drugs. It can be used in the management of benzodiazepine overdose to antagonize the effects of excessive CNS and respiratory depression. Flumazenil also may be used in cases where one of the benzodiazepines has been administered to induce anesthesia. Midazolam (*Versed*) is an injectable benzodiazepine anesthetic (see Chapter 18) often used for induction of general anesthesia or for short medical procedures like endoscopy where the state of "conscious sedation" is desired. In this condition, the patient is awake but sedated to the point where unpleasant procedures can proceed without discomfort. Flumazenil is then used to reverse the effects of midazolam after the procedure is completed.

In individuals who are dependent on benzodiazepine drugs (chronic use or abuse), flumazenil may precipitate a withdrawal reaction and, in some cases, seizures.

Buspirone (*BuSpar*)

Buspirone is a drug that is used primarily as an antianxiety drug. It does not demonstrate useful sedative, hypnotic, anticonvulsant, or skeletal muscle relaxant actions like the benzodiazepines. The usual dosage for anxiety is 5–10 mg administered 2–3 times daily. Although the mechanism of action is still unclear, buspirone appears to produce its antianxiety effect by acting on serotonin receptors. Serotonin is a neurotransmitter in the brain involved in the regulation of anxiety. Anxiety is increased by high levels of serotonin. By binding to and blocking certain serotonin receptors, buspirone reduces the activity of serotonin and the level of anxiety. The potential for the development of drug tolerance and dependency with buspirone is low. Common adverse effects include dizziness, lightheadedness, rash, and tiredness. Buspirone is classified as an FDA Pregnancy Category B drug.

In general, buspirone is well tolerated and there appear to be few contraindications for its use. It serves as a suitable alternative to the benzodiazepines, especially when drug dependence and drug abuse problems with the benzodiazepines are an issue. Buspirone is indicated mainly for the treatment of general anxiety disorder (GAD). Some individuals display a high level of anxiety and nervousness about life in general and this is classified as GAD.

Preferred Therapy for Anxiety Disorders

The benzodiazepines are usually the drugs of choice for treatment of general anxiety disorder (GAD) and panic disorder. Depending on the degree of anxiety and patient profile, the preferred drugs are usually one of the long-acting drugs such as diazepam (*Valium*) and chlordiazepoxide (*Librium*) or one of the shorter-acting drugs such as alprazolam (*Xanax*) or lorazepam (*Ativan*). Other drug classes are also effective in the treatment of anxiety disorders. The selective serotonin reuptake inhibitors (SSRIs, Chapter 14) are antidepressant drugs also effective for most types of anxiety. They are usually preferred for treatment of obsessive-compulsive disorder (OCD) and posttraumatic stress disorder (PTSD). Tricyclic antidepressants (TCAs, Chapter 14) also are useful in treating GAD, panic disorder, and OCD. The TCAs cause more side and adverse effects than the SSRIs and are less preferred.

Chapter Review

Understanding Terminology

Answer the following questions.

1. Explain the terms *antipsychotic* and *antianxiety*. **(LO 13.1, 13.6)**
2. What is the difference between akathisia and dystonia? **(LO 13.2)**
3. Define the term *parkinsonism*. **(LO 13.2)**

Match the definition or description in the left column with the appropriate term in the right column. **(LO 13.1, 13.2, 13.6)**

___ 4. A condition characterized by muscular rigidity, tremors, and disturbances of movement.

___ 5. A major form of psychosis.

___ 6. A condition causing individuals to have continuous body movement.

___ 7. Drug-induced involuntary movements of the lips, jaw, tongue, and extremities.

___ 8. Drugs used to treat schizophrenia.

___ 9. Drugs used to calm and reduce excessive nervousness.

___ 10. An inhibitory neurotransmitter in the CNS.

a. akathisia
b. antianxiety drugs
c. antipsychotic drugs
d. GABA
e. parkinsonism
f. tardive dyskinesia
g. schizophrenia

Acquiring Knowledge

Answer the following questions.

1. Describe the areas of the brain and neurotransmitters that are involved in psychosis. **(LO 13.1)**
2. What is the mechanism of action of the phenothiazine antipsychotic drugs? **(LO 13.2)**
3. List the main classes of antipsychotic drugs and give an example of each. **(LO 13.2, 13.3, 13.4, 13.5)**
4. What pharmacological properties do the phenothiazines possess, and how do these properties relate to clinical use and adverse effects? **(LO 13.2)**
5. Describe a few of the more serious neurological adverse effects of the phenothiazine drugs. **(LO 13.2)**
6. List the major sites of action of the benzodiazepines and the clinical effects produced at each site. **(LO 13.6)**
7. Describe the clinical uses of diazepam (*Valium*). **(LO 13.6)**
8. List the adverse effects and drug interactions that may occur with the antianxiety drugs. **(LO 13.6)**

Applying Knowledge on the Job

Use your critical-thinking skills to answer the following questions.

1. For each adult patient described, identify a suitable drug for treatment.
   a. Patient A has been brought to the emergency room (ER) exhibiting extremely agitated and manic behavior. **(LO 13.3)**
   b. Patient B is in intensive care following an episode of bizarre delusions and hallucinations. **(LO 13.2)**
   c. Patient C has suffered severe anxiety ever since being diagnosed with a terminal illness. **(LO 13.6)**
   d. Patient D just presented at the ER with tonic-clonic epileptic convulsions in progress. **(LO 13.6)**
   e. Patient E has open-heart surgery scheduled for tomorrow and is experiencing presurgical anxiety. **(LO 13.6)**
   f. Patient F is in alcohol withdrawal in the local Veterans Administration (VA) hospital detoxification unit. **(LO 13.6)**

2. Each of the following patients is suspected of having adverse effects to a drug prescribed for psychosis or neurosis. Identify the type of drug most likely involved in each case.
   a. Patient A has been experiencing dry mouth, constipation, and EPS. **(LO 13.2)**
   b. Patient B complains of a rash, nausea, drowsiness, confusion, and poor coordination (ataxia). **(LO 13.6)**
   c. Patient C presents with high fever and muscular rigidity and appears unable to move. **(LO 13.2)**

Multiple Choice

Use you critical-thinking skills to answer the following questions.

1. The main action of phenothiazines in the treatment of schizophrenia is **(LO 13.2)**
   A. stimulation of $5HT_{2A}$ receptors
   B. stimulation of D_2 receptors
   C. blockage of $5HT_{2A}$ receptors more than D_2 receptors
   D. blockage of D_2 receptors more than $5HT_{2A}$ receptors

2. Extrapyramidal symptoms (EPS) are caused mainly by **(LO 13.2)**
   A. stimulation of GABA receptors
   B. stimulation of dopamine receptors
   C. blockage of dopamine receptors
   D. blockage of serotonin receptors

3. Increased triglycerides, weight gain, and diabetes are adverse effects associated with **(LO 13.5)**
   A. phenothiazines
   B. butyrophenones
   C. thioxanthenes
   D. atypical drugs

4. The site of action of diazepam (*Valium*) to relieve anxiety is the **(LO 13.6)**
   A. spinal cord
   B. limbic system
   C. reticular formation
   D. basal ganglia

5. The antianxiety effect of buspirone (*BuSpar*) is associated with **(LO 13.6)**
   A. stimulation of DA receptors
   B. stimulation of serotonin receptors
   C. blockage of serotonin receptors
   D. blockade of dopamine receptors

6. Flumazenil (*Romazicon*) is used to reverse the depressant effects of **(LO 13.6)**
   A. clozapine (*Clozaril*)
   B. alprazolam (*Xanax*)
   C. haloperidol (*Haldol*)
   D. chlorpromazine (*Thorazine*)

Multiple Choice (Multiple Answer)

Select the correct choices for each statement. The choices may be all correct, all incorrect, or any combination.

1. What are the main goals of antipsychotic drug therapy? **(LO 13.1)**
   A. increase dopamine
   B. block the D_2 receptor
   C. decrease serotonin
   D. increase akathisia

2. Select the additional effects of phenothiazine drugs. **(LO 13.2)**
   A. antiemetic
   B. anticholinergic
   C. antihistaminic
   D. antitussive

3. Select the advantages of butyrophenones over phenothiazines. **(LO 13.3)**
   A. greater incidence of antihistaminic activity
   B. suppression of motor tics
   C. greater movement disturbances
   D. lower incidence of EPS

4. Select the adverse effects of atypical antipsychotics. **(LO 13.5)**
   A. postural hypotension
   B. dermatitis
   C. obstructive jaundice
   D. weight gain

5. What are the main areas at which benzodiazepines exert their effects? **(LO 13.6)**
   A. limbic system
   B. cerebral cortex
   C. hypothalamus
   D. medulla oblongata

Sequencing

Place the following in order from most serious to least serious adverse effects. **(LO 13.2)**

_____   _____   _____   _____

Most Serious   **Least**
neuroleptic malignant syndrome
akathisia
dry mouth
tardive dyskinesia

Classification

Place the following drugs in their appropriate classification. **(LO 13.2, 13.5, 13.6)**

triazolam   olanzapine
thioridazine   chlordiazepoxide
risperidone   chlorpromazine
trifluoperazine   aripiprazole
oxazepam

Phenothiazines	Benzodiazepines	Atypical antipsychotics

Labeling

Fill in the missing labels. **(LO 13.2, 13.3, 13.4, 13.5)**

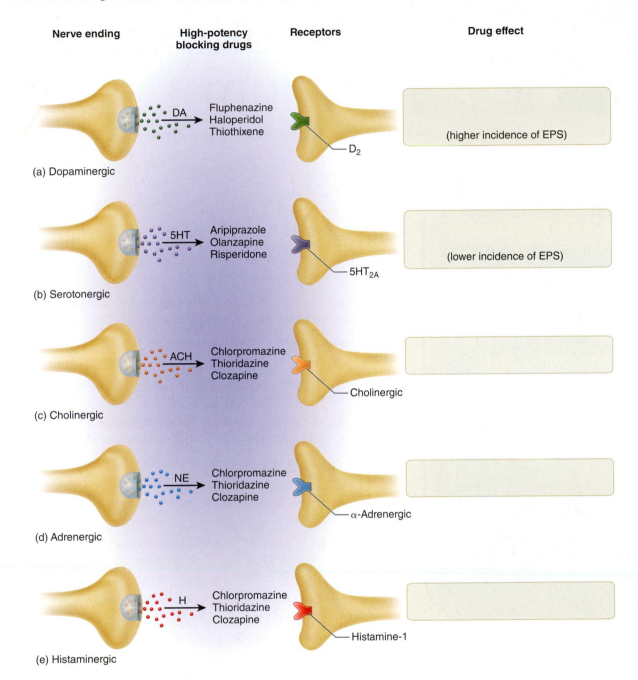

Nerve ending	High-potency blocking drugs	Receptors	Drug effect

(a) Dopaminergic — DA → Fluphenazine, Haloperidol, Thiothixene → D₂ → (higher incidence of EPS)

(b) Serotonergic — 5HT → Aripiprazole, Olanzapine, Risperidone → 5HT₂A → (lower incidence of EPS)

(c) Cholinergic — ACH → Chlorpromazine, Thioridazine, Clozapine → Cholinergic

(d) Adrenergic — NE → Chlorpromazine, Thioridazine, Clozapine → α-Adrenergic

(e) Histaminergic — H → Chlorpromazine, Thioridazine, Clozapine → Histamine-1

For interactive animations, videos, and assessment, visit:

www.mcgrawhillconnect.com

Chapter 14

Antidepressants, Psychomotor Stimulants, and Lithium

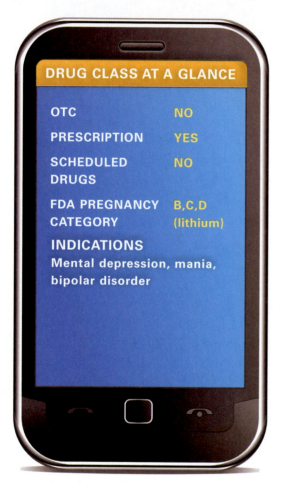

DRUG CLASS AT A GLANCE

OTC	NO
PRESCRIPTION	YES
SCHEDULED DRUGS	NO
FDA PREGNANCY CATEGORY	B,C,D (lithium)

INDICATIONS

Mental depression, mania, bipolar disorder

KEY TERMS

bipolar mood disorder: mood disorder where episodes of mania and depression occur alternately.

depression: mental state characterized by depressed mood, with feelings of frustration and hopelessness.

exogenous, or reactive, depression: depression caused by external factors or life events.

lithium: an element similar to sodium that is used in the treatment of mania and bipolar mood disorder.

major depressive disorder (MDD): depression that arises from within an individual and requires psychotherapy and drug treatment.

mania: mental state of excitement, hyperactivity, and excessive elevation of mood.

monoamine oxidase (MAO): enzyme that inactivates norepinephrine and serotonin.

Monoamine Theory of Mental Depression: theory that mental depression is caused by low brain levels of norepinephrine and serotonin (monoamines).

psychomotor stimulant: amphetamine or related drug that increases mental and physical activity.

SSRIs: selective serotonin reuptake inhibitors, a class of antidepressant drugs.

TCAs: tricyclic antidepressants, a class of antidepressant drugs.

After studying this chapter, you should be able to

14.1 identify the different types of depression and the importance of neurotransmitter function in the cause and treatment of depression.

14.2 describe the mechanism of action and adverse effects profile of the selective serotonin reuptake inhibitors (SSRIs).

14.3 explain the major difference between the SSRIs and the atypical SSRI antidepressants.

14.4 describe the mechanism of action and the adverse effects profile of the tricyclic antidepressants (TCAs).

14.5 explain the mechanism of action of the MAO inhibitors and describe the adverse effects and dietary restrictions relating to these drugs.

14.6 discuss the use of psychomotor stimulants in the treatment of narcolepsy, hyperkinetic syndrome, and obesity.

14.7 explain the use of lithium in mania and bipolar disorder and the adverse effects associated with its use.

14.8 identify the preferred therapies for depression, mania, and bipolar disorder.

Introduction

Mental depression is a common illness that affects most people at one time or another. During **depression,** there are changes in mood and behavior, along with feelings of frustration and hopelessness. Decreased appetite and difficulty in sleeping are also common signs of depression. Depressed individuals appear unable to cope with the demands or stresses of living. In severe depression, when a person feels there is no escape, he or she may come to think of suicide as an acceptable solution. Early recognition and treatment are essential for prevention of the serious consequences of depression.

Evidence accumulated over the years indicates that deficiencies of norepinephrine (NE) and serotonin (5HT) in the brain are involved in the cause of mental depression. Drugs that increase levels of NE and 5HT are used to treat depression.

The causes of mood disorders such as mania and bipolar disorder are not clearly understood. It is believed that hyperactivity in certain areas of the brain and excessive activity of neurotransmitters may be involved. These conditions often require a combination of drug therapies.

LO 14.1

TYPES OF DEPRESSION

There are several different types of depression. Depression that is caused by external factors (death or unemployment) is referred to as **exogenous,** or **reactive, depression.** Usually, there is a period of shock and depression, which is followed by a period of readjustment and a resolve that life must go on. In this sense, a reactive depression is self-limiting and usually does not require drug therapy. The love and understanding of family or friends support the individual through the crisis.

The second major type of depression is referred to as **major depressive disorder (MDD).** MDD is frequently more serious and usually requires both psychotherapy and drug treatment. This type of depression originates from within the individual and may not be associated with easily recognized causes. Psychological disturbances and maladjustments or biochemical defects in the brain are thought to be involved. Episodes of MDD may occur at intervals throughout one's lifetime.

In some cases of depression, there are alternate periods of hyperexcitability and elation known as **mania.** Individuals who experience these alternating

Figure 14.1

Illustration of the Site and Mechanism of Action of the SSRIs, Atypical SSRIs, and Tricyclic Antidepressants to Block the Reuptake of Serotonin (5HT) Back into Serotonergic Nerve Endings

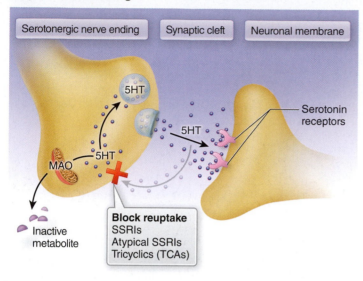

This action increases the concentration of 5HT in the synaptic cleft, resulting in increased stimulation of serotonergic receptors in the brain.

cycles of depression and mania are classified as manic-depressive. Another term for this condition is **bipolar mood disorder.**

LO 14.2 | LO 14.3 | LO 14.4 | LO 14.5

DRUGS USED TO TREAT DEPRESSION

An important advance in understanding depression occurred with the discovery that the levels of norepinephrine and serotonin (5HT) in the brain can influence mental behavior. Low levels of norepinephrine and/or serotonin are associated with mental depression, while high levels of norepinephrine and/or serotonin may be involved in mania. This concept involving norepinephrine and serotonin (referred to chemically as monoamines) is known as the **Monoamine Theory of Mental Depression.**

Drugs that can increase the level of norepinephrine or serotonin in the brain are useful in the treatment of mental depression. They are referred to as antidepressants, or mood elevators. The major antidepressant drug classes include the selective serotonin reuptake inhibitors (SSRIs), atypical SSRIs, tricyclic antidepressants (TCAs), and monoamine oxidase inhibitors (MAOIs).

The psychomotor stimulants are generally amphetamines or amphetamine-like drugs that produce a generalized CNS stimulation, usually increased wakefulness and alertness. These drugs are not true antidepressants and have limited therapeutic uses.

Lithium is referred to as a mood stabilizer and is used to treat individuals who experience wide shifts of mood, mania, or the alternating cycles of depression and mania (bipolar mood disorder). Some anticonvulsant drugs (Chapter 16) are also effective in treating mania and bipolar disorder.

Selective Serotonin Reuptake Inhibitors (SSRIs)

The **SSRIs** are a group of drugs that have a very selective action to block the reuptake of serotonin (5HT) back into the serotonergic nerve endings. This action increases the concentration of 5HT in the synaptic cleft, which results in increased stimulation of serotonin receptors (Figure 14.1). The increase in 5HT activity in the limbic and cerebral cortical areas of the brain is believed to contribute to the antidepressant effect. The SSRIs usually stimulate and activate CNS activity. However, there are differences among the SSRI drugs in the degree of CNS activation; fluvoxamine is an exception and produces a sedating effect. Fluoxetine was the first SSRI to be introduced and it will be discussed in more detail. The other SSRIs produce similar actions and are compared in Table 14:1.

Fluoxetine is well absorbed after oral administration. It is metabolized in the liver into an active metabolite that has a half-life that ranges from several days to a week or more. The metabolites are primarily excreted in the urine. Fluoxetine also has been shown to be an inhibitor of the metabolism of other drugs such as anticoagulants and benzodiazepines.

Clinical Indications

The SSRIs have become preferred therapy for treatment of major depression. All SSRIs are usually administered 1–2 times per day. SSRIs are also effective in the treatment of most anxiety disorders such as posttraumatic stress disorder (PTSD) and obsessive-compulsive disorder (OCD). In OCD, individuals have repetitive and excessive impulses to perform some physical or behavioral action. These impulses can interfere with and disrupt the normal daily routine of work and living. Fluoxetine and sertraline also are approved for premenstrual dysphoric disorder, where mood disturbances occur in relation to the menstrual cycle.

Adverse Effects

Unlike the tricyclic antidepressants, the SSRIs have little action to block cholinergic, adrenergic, or histamine receptors. Consequently, SSRIs and atypical SSRIs (see below) produce fewer side and adverse effects, and currently have become the most widely used antidepressant drugs.

All the SSRIs listed cause GI disturbances including nausea, diarrhea, dry mouth, and anorexia. SSRIs also have been associated with sexual dysfunction, most commonly reduced sexual interest and delayed orgasm. Other CNS effects include headache, nervousness, insomnia, and tremors.

The most common symptoms of overdosage include confusion, fever, tremor agitation, restlessness, and other signs of CNS excitation; seizures also have been reported. These symptoms are referred to as the "serotonin syndrome" and may lead to coma and death if not treated. Sudden discontinuation of SSRI treatment has been associated with a discontinuation syndrome. Symptoms include dizziness, nausea, insomnia, and anxiety. The dosage of SSRIs and related drugs should be gradually reduced over time when treatment is stopped.

Atypical SSRI Antidepressants

The atypical SSRI antidepressant drugs block reuptake of serotonin like the SSRIs but have additional actions on other neurotransmitters and receptors (Figures 14.1 and 14.2). These drugs have been classified by different names and chemical classifications; they will be referred to in this text as atypical SSRI antidepressants. Like the SSRIs, they have little effect in blocking cholinergic, adrenergic, or histamine receptors. The atypical drugs affect serotonin and other neurotransmitters such as norepinephrine and dopamine. The pharmacologic actions of these drugs are complex; only the main features are presented. The atypical SSRI antidepressants are listed in Table 14:2.

The major pharmacologic actions of bupropion (*Wellbutrin*) are to increase the release of and inhibit the reuptake of norepinephrine and dopamine. Bupropion has minimal effect to inhibit the reuptake of serotonin. The antidepressant effects are useful in the treatment of bipolar disorder, where it is claimed to prevent the

switch over into mania. Bupropion is highly activating and and may cause seizures. Bupropion also is prescribed for patients who are trying to quit the smoking habit. Nefazodone (*Serzone*) and trazodone (*Desyrel*) are drugs that are weak reuptake inhibitors of serotonin and norepinephrine but potent antagonists of serotonin $5HT_{2A}$ receptors. This action also provides some

Table 14:1

Selective Serotonin Reuptake Inhibitors

Drug (*Trade Name*)	Daily dosage range	CNS activation
Citalopram (*Celexa*)	20–40 mg PO	Low
Escitalopram (*Lexapro*)	10–20 mg PO	Low
Fluoxetine (*Prozac*)	20–40 mg PO	High
Fluvoxamine (*Luvox*)	50–200 mg PO	Sedating
Paroxetine (*Paxil*)	20–40 mg PO	Low
Sertraline (*Zoloft*)	50–200 mg PO	Low

Figure 14.2

Illustration of the Site and Mechanism of Action of Atypical SSRIs and Tricyclic Antidepressants to Block the Reuptake of Norepinephrine (NE) Back into the Adrenergic Nerve Ending

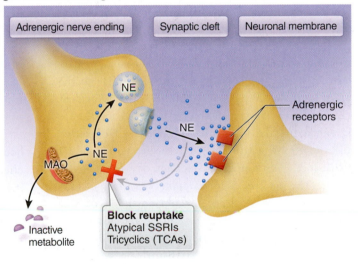

This action increases the concentration of NE in the synaptic cleft resulting in increased stimulation of adrenergic receptors in the brain.

Atypical SSRI Antidepressant Drugs

Drug (*Trade Name*)	Daily dosage range	CNS activation
Bupropion (*Wellbutrin*)	150–450 mg PO	High
Desvenlafaxine (*Pristiq*)	50–200 mg PO	Moderate
Duloxetine (*Cymbalta*)	40–60 mg PO	Low
Mirtazapine (*Remeron*)	15–45 mg PO	Sedating
Nefazodone (*Serzone*)	100–600 mg PO	Sedating
Trazodone (*Desyrel*)	200–600 mg PO	Sedating
Venlafaxine (*Effexor*)	75–375 mg PO	Moderate

The chemistry of these antidepressants is beyond the scope of this book. However, a simple method of classification involves the chemical substitutions (usually methyl groups) on the nitrogen molecule, which is present in all of the drugs. Most of the drugs can then be classified as being either secondary amines (two substitutions on the nitrogen) or tertiary amines (three substitutions on the nitrogen). Another interesting generalization is that secondary amines mainly increase brain levels of norepinephrine more than serotonin while the tertiary amines mainly increase brain levels of serotonin more than norepinephrine. The key to effective therapy is to identify which neurotransmitter should be increased in each patient; however, this step is not always easy. Frequently, several drugs must be tried with each patient before the most effective drug is found.

antipsychotic activity. Adverse effects include sedation, orthostatic hypotension, and liver toxicity. Trazodone also is associated with priapism, which is the development of sustained and painful penile erections. Venlafaxine (*Effexor*), desvenlafaxine (*Pristiq*), and duloxetine (*Cymbalta*) are drugs that block the reuptake of both serotonin and norepinephrine. Venlafaxine is moderately activating and has adverse effects similar to the SSRIs. Increases in diastolic blood pressure are evident at higher doses. Desvenlafaxine is the active metabolite of venlafaxine and has similar properties. Duloxetine causes low CNS activation; adverse effects include GI disturbances, insomnia, and feelings of weakness and fatigue. The actions of mirtazapine (*Remeron*) include the increased release of norepinephrine and serotonin, blockade of $5HT_2$ and $5HT_3$ receptors, and potent histamine receptor blocking actions. Mirtazapine is sedating and usually does not cause GI disturbances or sexual dysfunction. Weight gain has been associated with this drug.

Tricyclic Antidepressants

Tricyclic antidepressant drugs (**TCAs** or tricyclics) are so named because of the characteristic triple-ring structure that they possess. Recently, some new antidepressants, which produce pharmacological effects similar to those of the tricyclics, have been introduced with two rings (bicyclics), four rings (tetracyclics), and others with quite different chemical structures (nontricyclics).

Mechanism of Action

The main action of the tricyclics and related antidepressant drugs is to block the reuptake of norepinephrine and serotonin back into the neuronal nerve endings. As a result there is an accumulation of these neurotransmitters in the synaptic clefts (Figures 14.1 and 14.2). This action increases the level of neuronal activity of norepinephrine and serotonin and alleviates the symptoms and dysfunction of depression.

The pharmacological actions occur within a few hours of administration. However, the full antidepressant effect requires 2 to 4 weeks to develop. Consequently, it is believed that tricyclics and related antidepressant drugs may produce additional pharmacologic actions that are not yet completely understood. However, increasing the concentrations of norepinephrine and serotonin in the brain does appear to be involved in the antidepressant effect.

Pharmacological Actions

In addition to the antidepressant effect, the tricyclics and related drugs produce varying degrees of sedation, anticholinergic effects, and alpha-adrenergic blockade. The degree of sedation, anticholinergic, and alpha-blocking effects among the various drugs is compared in Table 14:3. Generally, the tertiary amines produce more sedation than do the secondary amines. Sedation is often a valuable effect, especially in patients who suffer insomnia along with their depression. The anticholinergic and alpha-blocking effects are associated with many of the side effects of these drugs.

The tricyclics, like the MAO inhibitors discussed later, require 2 to 4 weeks to produce their maximum effect. The antidepressant effects of the tricyclics also continue for approximately 2 weeks after drug administration is terminated. Therefore, extreme caution should be exercised when patients are switched from MAO inhibitors to tricyclics, or vice versa, to prevent drug interaction. Tricyclic and related antidepressants are listed in Table 14:3.

Adverse and Toxic Effects

The tricyclics possess significant anticholinergic activity, which is responsible for many of the adverse effects. Anticholinergic effects include dry mouth, constipation, urinary retention, and rapid heartbeat. Alpha-blocking actions may cause postural hypotension, blurred vision, and drowsiness. Like the MAO inhibitors, the tricyclics stimulate the CNS and may produce restlessness, tremors, convulsions, or mania.

In addition, the tricyclics may produce toxic effects in the heart and liver. In the heart, the effects can be detected by an electrocardiogram. Alterations in the T wave and ST segment, which may lead to serious cardiac arrhythmias, are the most common changes. In the liver, the tricyclics may cause an obstructive type of jaundice, which is relieved when drug treatment ends.

One of the dangers of antidepressant drug treatment is the risk of patients attempting suicide by overdosing on antidepressant drugs. In toxicity the anticholinergic effects, alpha-blocking effects, cardiac disturbances, and CNS stimulation of the TCAs can result in lethal cardiac arrhythmias, seizures, and death.

Table 14:3

Representative Tricyclic and Related Antidepressants

Drug (*Trade Name*)	Sedation	AC	Alpha blockade	Daily dosage range
Secondary amines				
Clomipramine (*Anafranil*)	High	High	High	150–250 mg PO
Desipramine (*Pertofrane*)	Low	Low	High	75–200 mg PO
Nortriptyline (*Aventyl*)	Moderate	Moderate	Moderate	50–150 mg PO
Tertiary amines				
Amitriptyline (*Elavil*)	High	High	High	75–300 mg PO
Doxepin (*Sinequan*)	High	High	High	75–300 mg PO
Imipramine (*Tofranil*)	Moderate	Moderate	High	75–300 mg PO

AC—Anticholinergic activity; alpha blockade reflects postural hypotension

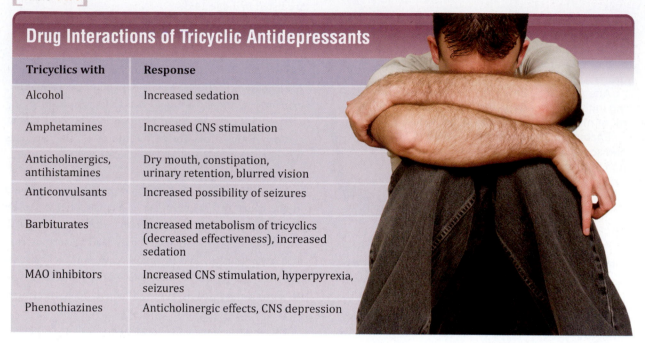

Drug Interactions of Tricyclic Antidepressants

Tricyclics with	Response
Alcohol	Increased sedation
Amphetamines	Increased CNS stimulation
Anticholinergics, antihistamines	Dry mouth, constipation, urinary retention, blurred vision
Anticonvulsants	Increased possibility of seizures
Barbiturates	Increased metabolism of tricyclics (decreased effectiveness), increased sedation
MAO inhibitors	Increased CNS stimulation, hyperpyrexia, seizures
Phenothiazines	Anticholinergic effects, CNS depression

Drug Interactions

The tricyclic antidepressants interact with a number of other drugs, as indicated in Table 14:4.

MONOAMINE OXIDASE INHIBITORS

Monoamine oxidase (MAO) is an enzyme found in most body cells but particularly in the adrenergic and serotonergic nerve endings. The normal function of MAO is to break down norepinephrine and serotonin into metabolites that are then excreted by the kidneys. MAO prevents the buildup of excessive levels of norepinephrine and serotonin in the brain and other body tissue.

In mental depression, there appears to be an abnormal decrease in the levels of brain norepinephrine and serotonin. Drugs that inhibit, or block, MAO are called appropriately MAO inhibitors. By inhibiting MAO, these drugs decrease the amounts of norepinephrine and serotonin that are destroyed. Consequently, the MAO inhibitors permit the levels of norepinephrine and serotonin in the brain to increase. This increase is usually accompanied by clinical improvement of the depression. Like the TCAs, the MAO inhibitors require 2 to 4 weeks to produce their maximum effect. After a week or so of treatment, there is usually an improvement in appetite and sleep, followed by an elevation of mood and an overall improvement in mental state. These effects continue

for approximately 2 weeks after termination of treatment. The MAO inhibitors are infrequently used today and primarily indicated when other antidepressant drugs are not effective.

The MAO inhibitors are involved in many drug interactions. Caution must be exercised if other drugs, especially other antidepressants, are administered during administration of MAO inhibitors and while MAO inhibitors remain in the system. Serious drug interactions can occur.

Dietary Restrictions

One of the main disadvantages of MAO inhibitor therapy is the dietary restrictions. Many foods contain a substance known as tyramine, which causes the release of norepinephrine from storage granules located inside the adrenergic nerve endings. When MAO is inhibited, tyramine may produce a massive release of norepinephrine, which can result in serious consequences, such as hypertensive crisis or cerebral stroke. Foods that normally contain tyramine include wine, beer, herring, and certain cheeses. In addition, certain sympathetic drugs used in the treatment of cold symptoms (decongestants and bronchodilators) interact with the MAO inhibitors, causing potentiation of the effects of the sympathetic agents. Patients receiving MAO inhibitors must be thoroughly instructed with regard to the foods and other medications to avoid. The most frequently used MAO inhibitors are listed in Table 14:5.

Monoamine Oxidase (MAO) Inhibitors	
Drug (*Trade Name*)	Daily dosage range
Isocarboxazid (*Marplan*)	10–20 mg PO
Phenelzine (*Nardil*)	45–90 mg PO
Tranylcypromine (*Parnate*)	30–60 mg PO

Adverse Effects

The MAO inhibitors are capable of producing a wide variety of adverse effects. Common adverse effects include dry mouth, urinary retention, constipation, blurred vision, hypotension, weight gain, and sexual dysfunction. A variety of CNS disturbances including restlessness, dizziness, insomnia, tremors, and seizures may occur. These effects are intensified with overdosage. In addition, they can produce a type of liver damage that may be fatal. Because of the high incidence of adverse effects, many physicians believe that these drugs should be reserved for patients who do not respond to other antidepressant drugs.

LO 14.6

PSYCHOMOTOR STIMULANTS

The **psychomotor stimulants** include the amphetamines and other closely related drugs, which are really not classified as antidepressants. Their role in the treatment of depression is extremely limited. Because of the delayed therapeutic effects of MAO inhibitors and tricyclics, psychomotor stimulants are occasionally used during the first few weeks of treatment to elevate mood and increase psychomotor activity.

Amphetamines also are used to treat narcolepsy (uncontrolled tendency to fall asleep) and hyperkinesis in children. Amphetamines stimulate the reticular formation, which increases wakefulness and alertness and reduces the number of attacks of narcolepsy. In hyperkinetic children, amphetamines increase alertness and attention span, which are important in improving learning ability. Also, amphetamines seem to calm down the hyperactivity. This result is opposite to what would be expected and is referred to as a paradoxical effect. The reason for this effect is not fully understood.

In addition to mental stimulation, amphetamines stimulate motor, or physical, activity. This stimulation causes individuals who are trying to delay fatigue and stay awake to use amphetamines inappropriately. Amphetamine stimulation of the CNS is also associated with a decrease in appetite, and weight reduction presents another area of amphetamine abuse. Because the therapeutic benefits of amphetamines are low and the abuse potential high, there are very few situations where use of amphetamines is warranted.

Mechanism of Action

The amphetamines stimulate the CNS by increasing the activity of norepinephrine and dopamine in the brain. Amphetamines increase neurotransmitter activity by several different mechanisms. They act directly to stimulate norepinephrine and dopamine receptors, they stimulate the release of norepinephrine and dopamine from the nerve endings, and they inhibit the reuptake of these neurotransmitters back into the nerve endings. These actions produce CNS stimulation and an elevation of mood. Psychomotor stimulants are listed in Table 14:6, but it should be emphasized that the psychomotor stimulants are not true antidepressant drugs and their use as such is extremely limited.

Amphetamines have the disadvantage of producing drug tolerance and drug dependence. The amphetamines are among the leading "street drugs" that are abused and illegally marketed. Drug abuse of amphetamines is discussed in Chapter 15.

Adverse and Toxic Effects

The psychomotor stimulants increase the activity of the sympathetic nervous system, producing dry mouth,

Psychomotor Stimulant Drugs	
Drug (*Trade Name*)	Daily dosage range
Amphetamine	10–60 mg PO
Dexmethylphenidate (*Focalin*)	5–20 mg PO
Dextroamphetamine (*Dexedrine*)	5–30 mg PO
Methamphetamine (*Desoxyn*)	5–60 mg PO
Methylphenidate (*Ritalin*)	10–60 mg PO

Selective Serotonin Reuptake Inhibitors

Explain to patient the common side effects: headache, nervousness, insomnia, nausea, loss of appetite, diarrhea.

Instruct patient to report excessive GI and CNS stimulation (agitation, seizures).

Instruct patient not to suddenly stop taking these drugs on his or her own.

Tricyclic Drugs

Monitor vital signs when drugs are administered parenterally with particular attention to blood pressure and heart rate.

Explain to patient the common side effects due to anticholinergic, alpha-blocking, and antihistaminic actions: dry mouth, constipation, low blood pressure, drowsiness.

Instruct patient to report increased pulse rate, excessive difficulties with urination or defecation, excessive CNS stimulation (tremors, restlessness, seizures).

Remember that these drugs may be contraindicated in patients with glaucoma and prostatic hypertrophy, and that the elderly are more sensitive to anticholinergic drugs.

Instruct patient not to take other drugs unless this is checked with the physician or pharmacist.

MAO Inhibitors

Provide patient with a list of tyramine-containing foods and over-the-counter drugs that must be avoided while taking MAO inhibitors.

Explain to patient the common side effects: dizziness, low blood pressure, dry mouth, constipation and other GI disturbances, blurred vision, impotency in males.

Instruct patient to report excessive dizziness or feelings of faintness, difficulty with urination, CNS stimulation or agitation, yellowing of skin (liver jaundice).

---

rapid heartbeat, increased blood pressure, restlessness, and insomnia. Toxic doses may produce severe agitation and a paranoid type of psychosis.

LO 14.7

LITHIUM

Lithium is used for the treatment of **mania** and **bipolar mood disorder.** It is often used in combination with antidepressant drugs in the manic-depressive or bipolar form of psychosis. In mania, there appears to be an excess of norepinephrine and possibly other monoamines (opposite to the situation in depression) in the brain, which produces excitement, hyperactivity, and excessive elevations of mood. Mania is characterized by periods of hyperactivity and excitement combined with excessive elevations of mood. Manic individuals are usually very talkative, but their thoughts and ideas are most often unrealistic. Lithium appears to reduce the hyperactivity and the excitement and also allows better organization of thought patterns.

Several anticonvulsant drugs, including vaproate, carbamazepine, and lamotrigine, also provide mood stabilizing effects and are used in the treatment of mania and bipolar disorder. These drugs are discussed in Chapter 16.

Mechanism of Action

Lithium is an element similar in chemical properties to sodium. The body utilizes lithium as if it were sodium.

Both lithium (Li^+) and sodium (Na^+) exist in body fluids as charged particles, or ions. However, whereas Na^+ is normally required for conduction of nerve impulses, Li^+ interferes with nerve conduction. As a result, there is a decrease in the excitability of nerve tissue. The mechanism of action of lithium is not clearly understood. Actions that decrease the levels of norepinephrine and other transmitters have been suggested.

Pharmacokinetics

Lithium is administered as a salt, lithium carbonate, in the form of capsules (*Eskalith*) or controlled release and slow-release tablets (*Eskalith CR, Lithobid*). Usually 1 to 2 weeks of treatment are required before therapeutic effects are observed.

Lithium can be an extremely toxic drug. Therefore, blood levels are periodically measured to prevent the development of excessive levels of lithium in the body. Lithium and sodium ions compete with each other for renal elimination. Adequate sodium intake is necessary for proper urinary excretion of lithium. Decreased sodium intake and hyponatremia (low sodium levels) promote the retention of lithium and can lead to toxicity.

Adverse and Toxic Effects

Side effects are common with lithium, even at therapeutic doses. Initially, most patients experience some nausea or tremors that usually disappear with continued treatment.

Explain to patient that the therapeutic effects of lithium may require 1 or 2 weeks of treatment.

Explain to patient that side effects are common and usually include nausea and tremors.

Explain to patient that lithium is a salt and that increased thirst and frequency of urination are common.

Instruct patient on the importance of adequate fluid and sodium intake.

Instruct patient to report excessive nausea or vomiting, excessive CNS stimulation, dizziness, abnormal muscle movements, low blood pressure, ringing in the ears.

Explain to patient that periodic drug blood levels may be required.

With overdose, vomiting, diarrhea, drowsiness, loss of equilibrium, ringing in the ears, and frequent urination are common. At toxic levels, the heart and kidneys may be damaged, leading to the development of cardiac arrhythmias or nephritis. Therefore, extreme caution is observed when treating cardiac or renal patients. In addition, lithium occasionally produces disturbances of the thyroid gland, and it is therefore contraindicated in patients with an existing thyroid condition. In acute overdoses, muscle fasciculations, convulsions, and circulatory collapse leading to death are possible. Treatment is aimed at increasing the excretion of lithium by forcing fluids and increasing the intake of sodium.

Cautions and Contraindications
Pregnancy
Lithium has been designated FDA Pregnancy Category D and therefore should not be used during pregnancy.

PREFERRED THERAPY FOR DEPRESSION, MANIA, AND BIPOLAR DISORDER

Due to the complex nature of depression and individual variations in mental and psychological states, it is difficult to select a single drug as preferred therapy for treatment of depression. However, the SSRIs are currently considered the preferred drugs for major depression. The advantages of the SSRIs are the lower incidence of adverse and toxic effects. Unlike the TCAs, the SSRIs do not cause significant anticholinergic, alpha-adrenergic-blocking, or antihistaminic actions. The atypical SSRIs are also usually preferred over the TCAs for the same reason. The atypical SSRIs also produce additional actions on other neurotransmitters and receptors that can benefit patients who are not experiencing sufficient antidepressant relief from SSRIs. The use of TCAs and MAO inhibitors has significantly decreased and these drugs mainly serve as alternates when SSRIs and related drugs are contraindicated or ineffective.

The preferred treatment for mania and bipolar disorder has changed over the years. Previously lithium was the preferred drug for mania and in combination with antidepressants for bipolar disorder. However, a number of anticonvulsant drugs have shown effectiveness, particularly in bipolar disorder. These drugs cause fewer side, adverse, and toxic effects. Valproate (*Depakene*) is now considered to be equal to and in some bipolar conditions more effective than lithium. Currently lithium and valproate are considered the two first-line mood stabilizers. Other mood-stabilizing anticonvulsants include carbamazepine (*Tegretol*) and lamotrigine (*Lamictal*). Often in acute manic episodes antipsychotic drugs also are administered if there are psychotic symptoms.

Chapter Review

Understanding Terminology

Answer the following questions.

___ 1. Differentiate between mania and depression. **(LO 14.1)**

___ 2. Explain the Monoamine Theory of Mental Depression. **(LO 14.1)**

___ 3. List the two main types of depression and define each. **(LO 14.1)**

Acquiring Knowledge

Answer the following questions.

1. What neurotransmitters are deficient in mental depression? **(LO 14.1)**

2. How do the MAO inhibitors increase the levels of norepinephrine and serotonin in the brain? **(LO 14.5)**

3. Explain the mechanism of action of the tricyclic antidepressants. **(LO 14.4)**

4. What are the main pharmacological differences between the secondary and tertiary amine antidepressants? **(LO 14.4)**

5. What adverse effects are associated with the tricyclic antidepressants? **(LO 14.4)**

6. How do the selective serotonin reuptake inhibitors produce their antidepressant effect? **(LO 14.2)**

7. What are the adverse effects of the selective serotonin reuptake inhibitors? **(LO 14.2)**

8. What are some of the clinical uses of psychomotor stimulants? **(LO 14.6)**

9. Explain the mechanism of action and major adverse effects of lithium. **(LO 14.7)**

10. Which antidepressant drug classes are considered to be the preferred therapy for depression. **(LO 14.8)**

Applying Knowledge on the Job

Use your critical-thinking skills to answer the following questions.

1. Assume that one of your duties in the mental health clinic where you work is to note for each patient any contraindications or potential drug interactions for current medications. You also assist with drug overdose emergencies.
   a. Patient A has been diagnosed with major depressive disorder. He's been taking *Elavil* for several weeks, but it makes him excessively drowsy, so his medication is being changed to an MAO inhibitor. The patient also is taking a prescription decongestant for allergies. What should you note on the patient's chart regarding adverse effects and drug interactions? **(LO 14.4, 14.5)**
   b. Patient B appeared at the clinic suffering from a possible overdose of lithium. She appeared drowsy and complained of dizziness and ringing in her ears. What should be done to help rid her body of the excess lithium? **(LO 14.7)**

2. Joe works as a volunteer on a depression hotline. What type of depression is experienced by each of the following anonymous callers?
   a. Caller A says he has no particular reason to feel down, but he's feeling really depressed anyway. He says he gets down-and-out a lot, but it doesn't usually get quite this bad. He wonders if there's any kind of treatment or drug for how he feels. **(LO 14.1)**
   b. Caller B says she's usually a happy-go-lucky sort of person, but she's been feeling depressed since her mother died last month. She thinks she should be over the worst of her grief by now and wonders if she should get counseling. **(LO 14.1)**

3. Janet has just been prescribed lithium for her manic states. What should be included in her medication counseling? **(LO 14.7)**

4. Robyn's physician has just prescribed *Nardil* for severe depression. What foods does Robyn need to avoid and why? **(LO 14.5)**

Multiple Choice

Use your critical-thinking skills to answer the following questions.

1. The main pharmacologic effect of the SSRIs is **(LO 14.2)**
   A. increase levels of norepinephrine
   B. increase levels of serotonin
   C. decrease levels of norepinephrine
   D. decrease levels of serotonin

2. The pharmacologic effects of TCAs include **(LO 14.4)**
   A. alpha-adrenergic blockade
   B. antihistaminic
   C. anticholinergic
   D. all statements are true

3. The serotonin syndrome is mainly associated with overdosage of **(LO 14.2)**
   A. tricyclic antidepressants
   B. monoamine oxidase inhibitors
   C. selective serotonin reuptake inhibitors
   D. psychomotor stimulants

4. The main pharmacologic effects of TCAs on neurotransmitter activity is **(LO 14.4)**
   A. increase norepinephrine
   B. increase acetylcholine
   C. increase serotonin
   D. all statements are true
   E. only A and C are true

5. Venlafaxine (*Effexor*) is classified as **(LO 14.3)**
   A. MAOI
   B. TCA
   C. SSRI
   D. atypical SSRI

6. Clinical uses of bupropion (*Wellbutrin*) include **(LO 14.3)**
   A. treatment of depression
   B. bipolar disorder
   C. cessation of smoking
   D. all statements are true

7. Serious adverse effects of TCAs include **(LO 14.4)**
   A. liver toxicity
   B. cardiac arrhythmias
   C. excess CNS stimulation
   D. all statements are true

Multiple Choice (Multiple Answer)

Select the correct choices for each statement. The choices may be all correct, all incorrect, or any combination.

1. Which of the following is true of depression? **(LO 14.1)**
   A. it can be self-limiting
   B. treatment is aimed at increasing serotonin
   C. it can be caused by biochemical defects
   D. it may not require drug therapy to relieve

2. Which of the following are restrictions for patients taking MAOIs? **(LO 14.5)**
   A. liver
   B. cheese
   C. beer
   D. tuna

3. Select the main actions of TCAs. **(LO 14.4)**
   A. block reuptake of NE
   B. decrease the destruction of NE
   C. decrease the reuptake of serotonin
   D. block MAOIs

4. Which of the following are true of SSRIs? **(LO 14.2)**
   A. preferred treatment for major depression
   B. used to treat mania disorders
   C. anorexia is an adverse effect
   D. has a half-life of 12 hours

5. Select the main pharmacologic actions of bupropion. **(LO 14.3)**
   A. maximum effect on reuptake of serotonin
   B. decreases release of NE
   C. promotes the reuptake of NE
   D. inhibits reuptake of dopamine

Sequencing

Place the following in order of CNS activation. **(LO 14.3)**

_____   _____   _____   _____

High   **Moderate**   **Low**   **Sedating**

Effexor

Wellbutrin

Cymbalta

Serzone

Classification

Place each drug under the appropriate classification. **(LO 14.2, 14.3, 14.4, 14.5)**

Elavil   *Desyrel*

Parnate   *Remeron*

Cymbalta   *Celexa*

Paxil   *Nardil*

Marplan   *Zoloft*

Aventyl   *Sinequan*

SSRI	TCA	MAOI	Atypical SSRI

Matching

Match the following drug classifications with their main mechanism of action. **(LO 14.2, 14.3, 14.4, 14.5, 14.6, 14.7)**

   a. monoamine oxidase inhibitors
   b. tricyclic antidepressants
   c. SSRIs
   d. atypical SSRIs
   e. psychomotor stimulants
   f. lithium

   1. _____block reuptake of NE
   2. _____interferes with nerve conduction
   3. _____block reuptake of 5HT
   4. _____increase wakefulness
   5. _____decrease the destruction of serotonin
   6. _____increase release of NE

Documentation

Using the prescription below, answer the following questions. **(LO 14.7)**

Wellness Clinic
Practice RX

12345 Main Avenue
Anytown, USA   12345
360-555-1000

NAME: ___George Sims_____   DATE: _____

ADDRESS: _____

RX   Eskalith 300mg

Sig: 1 po tid

Dr. Joanna Joans_____ M.D. _____M.D.

   Substitution Permitted   Dispense as written

DEA #: _____   REFILL: NR   1   2   3   4

---

   a. For what condition is Mr. Sims most likely being treated?
   b. How long will it be before the patient sees any therapeutic effects from this treatment?
   c. What precautions or tests should the patient be taking for treatment with this drug?
   d. When is this drug contraindicated?

Labeling

Fill in the missing labels. **(LO 14.2, 14.4)**

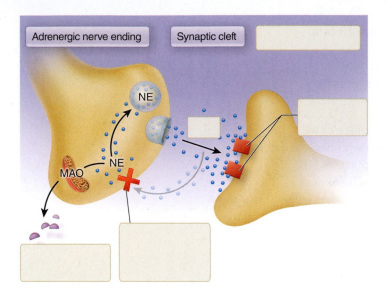

For interactive animations, videos, and assessment, visit:

www.mcgrawhillconnect.com

Chapter 15

Psychotomimetic Drugs of Abuse

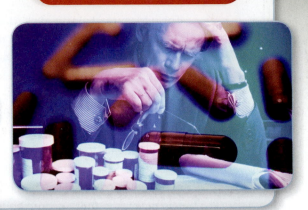

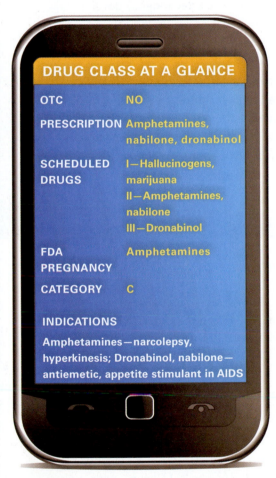

DRUG CLASS AT A GLANCE

OTC	NO
PRESCRIPTION	Amphetamines, nabilone, dronabinol
SCHEDULED DRUGS	I—Hallucinogens, marijuana
	II—Amphetamines, nabilone
	III—Dronabinol
FDA PREGNANCY CATEGORY	Amphetamines
	C

INDICATIONS

Amphetamines—narcolepsy, hyperkinesis; Dronabinol, nabilone—antiemetic, appetite stimulant in AIDS

KEY TERMS

cannabinoid: pharmacologically active substance obtained from the marijuana plant.

cross-tolerance: drug tolerance that develops between similarly acting drugs.

dependency: requirement of repeated drug consumption in order to prevent onset of withdrawal symptoms.

designer drug: chemically altered form of an approved drug that produces similar effects and that is sold illegally.

drug tolerance: requirement of larger doses to be consumed in order to obtain the desired effects.

flashback: phenomenon occurring long after the use of LSD in which the hallucinogenic effects are relived in some type of memory flash.

hallucinogenic drug: a drug or plant substance that produces psychotomimetic effects and sensory distortions.

hashish: resin from the marijuana plant that contains higher levels of THC.

psychotomimetic drug: drug or substance that can induce psychic and behavioral patterns characteristic of a psychosis.

synesthesia: distortion of sensory perception; usually associated with the use of LSD.

tetrahydrocannabinol (THC): active ingredient of the marijuana plant.

After studying this chapter, you should be able to

15.1 identify the mechanisms of action of hallucinogenic drugs and the psychotomimetic effects produced.

15.2 explain the dose-related hallucinogenic phases and the treatment for intoxication.

15.3 identify the mechanism of action, effects, and treatment for intoxication with psychomotor stimulants.

15.4 describe the mechanism of action, effects, and treatment for intoxication with PCP.

15.5 explain the mechanism of action, pharmacokinetics, and pharmacological actions of marijuana.

The widespread abuse of psychoactive drugs has become an unfortunate reality in today's society. Whereas most drugs are used to alleviate disease and human suffering, a few drugs are abused for their mind-altering effects. Although they may provide pleasure, they are not solutions to life's problems and can cause other health or social problems.

Initially, the use of a psychoactive drug can provide the novelty of an experience that is often interpreted as pleasurable and exciting. After initial experimentation, many individuals realize the dangers of continued drug consumption and avoid further abuse. For other individuals, drug abuse appears to provide "the answer" for which they have been searching. With continued drug use, some individuals focus all of their attention and available resources on obtaining and consuming illicit drugs. They begin to feel that as long as they have the drug, nothing else really matters or is important. As drug abuse continues, **drug tolerance** develops and with some drugs larger doses must be consumed in order to attain previous drug effects. The euphoria and good feelings that were the reason for abusing the drug are no longer experienced. As drug **dependency** develops, consumption of larger doses may be necessary to prevent the onset of psychological and physical withdrawal symptoms, forming a vicious cycle from which it is difficult to escape without professional help and a major personal decision to avoid further drug abuse.

This chapter examines the pharmacology of the psychotomimetic and related drugs of abuse. The abuse of narcotic analgesics, barbiturates, benzodiazepines, and alcohol is presented in other chapters. The psychotomimetic drugs of abuse have few therapeutic uses and do not form a distinct drug class. Psychoactive drugs of abuse can be divided into the lysergic acid diethylamide (LSD-type) hallucinogens; the psychomotor stimulants, which include the amphetamines, cocaine, and related designer drugs; and a miscellaneous group of drugs that includes phencyclidine (PCP) and marijuana.

LO 15.1 LO 15.2

LSD-TYPE HALLUCINOGENS

Lysergic acid diethylamide (LSD) is a synthetic drug that was first prepared in 1938. It remains one of the most potent hallucinogenic drugs yet discovered. LSD and other **hallucinogenic,** or **psychotomimetic, drugs** produce similar pharmacological effects. At one time, LSD and other hallucinogenic drugs were investigated for the treatment of alcoholism and mental illness. Currently, these drugs have no therapeutic uses and are classified as Schedule I drugs under the Controlled Substances Act. The prototype of this group is LSD, and it will be discussed in greater detail.

Mechanism of Action

How LSD produces its hallucinogenic effects is not exactly known. Evidence suggests that LSD and the other hallucinogens interact with serotonin receptors in the brain, primarily the $5HT_{2A}$ receptors. The hallucinogens appear to have a mixed action referred to as partial agonism. A partial agonist binds to a receptor and weakly stimulates it. The drug (hallucinogen) then remains on the receptor and acts as an antagonist to block the actions of the neurotransmitter, in this case serotonin. These actions disrupt normal brain activity and contribute to the sensory distortions and hallucinogenic effects.

Pharmacological Effects

Lysergic acid diethylamide (LSD) is readily absorbed from the gastrointestinal tract. The average hallucinogenic dosage ranges from 50–100 mcg. The psychic effects of LSD usually last about 12 hours, with peak effects occurring 1 to 2 hours after oral administration.

Common psychotomimetic effects include sensory distortions and pseudohallucinations. Moving objects appear to be followed by a stream of color or appear as vividly colored geometric patterns. **Synesthesia** may occur, where sensory perceptions are distorted and individuals perceive they are "seeing sounds" or hearing visual images. Perceptual distortions in the size of objects and parts of the body are common. Feelings of separation of part of the body, or loss of a part of the body, or failure to recognize a part as one's own body also occur.

In addition to the psychotomimetic effects, hallucinogenic drugs are potent stimulants of the central nervous system. Piloerection, pupillary dilation, and increased neuromuscular reflex activity can be observed. Cardiovascular effects include tachycardia and increased blood pressure.

Lysergic acid diethylamide is also associated with the occurrence of flashbacks. A **flashback,** which can occur at any time after exposure to LSD, is characterized by many of the psychotomimetic effects of LSD without readministration of the drug. Flashbacks often occur after use of other psychoactive drugs, which somehow trigger flashback episodes.

Tolerance and Physical Dependency

Tolerance develops rapidly to the psychotomimetic effects of LSD, usually within a few doses of continuous use. Also, **cross-tolerance** exists between LSD and the other drugs of this group, so subsequent doses of one drug taken shortly after another drug produce decreased effects. The tolerance is not accompanied by physical dependency, and abrupt discontinuance after chronic use does not precipitate withdrawal symptoms.

Intoxication and Treatment

The signs and symptoms of LSD intoxication include elevated body temperature and blood pressure, tachycardia, hyperreflexia, dilated pupils, anxiety, hallucinations, and psychotic behavior. LSD has a high therapeutic index, and virtually no known causes of death have been related to overdose toxicity by LSD alone. Consequently, treatment is aimed at protecting patients from accidental injury until the drug effects subside. Individuals should be placed in a quiet, nonthreatening environment and given reassurance that everything will be all right. Benzodiazepine antianxiety agents or barbiturates can be used for their sedative effects. This approach to treatment is considered standard therapy for most hallucinogenic drug intoxication.

Other LSD-Type Hallucinogens

In addition to LSD, two other categories of drugs produce similar effects.

Tryptamine Derivatives

Psilocybin and N,N-dimethyltryptamine (DMT) are obtained from natural sources. Psilocybin is found in the *Psilocybe* mushroom species, which have been eaten ceremonially by native cultures for centuries. Psilocybin is converted to an active metabolite, psilocin, which is believed to be responsible for the majority of psychotomimetic effects. The hallucinogenic dose of psilocybin is approximately 25 mg, which produces effects lasting 3 to 6 hours.

N,N-dimethyltryptamine (DMT) occurs in many plants and has been used as a snuff by various Native American cultures. It is ineffective when taken orally; it must be inhaled or administered parenterally. The usual hallucinogenic dose given by injection is 1 mg per kg of body weight, which produces psychotomimetic effects lasting approximately 1 hour.

Phenethylamine Derivatives

Mescaline and 2,-5-dimethoxy-4-methylamphetamine (DOM) are phenethylamine derivatives similar in structure to norepinephrine and amphetamine (Figure 15.1). Central nervous system stimulation and sympathomimetic effects are prominent features of both drugs. Mescaline, found in the peyote cactus, is among the least potent of the hallucinogenic drugs. It is readily absorbed from the gastrointestinal (GI) tract and produces effects that last about 6 hours. DOM, or STP ("Serenity, Tranquility, Peace"), is a synthetic compound. The usual hallucinogenic dose is 3–5 mg, which produces effects lasting 6 to 8 hours.

LO 15.3
PSYCHOMOTOR STIMULANTS

Amphetamine and cocaine are potent CNS stimulants that are widely used. At higher doses, these drugs produce prominent psychotomimetic effects. The central

Figure 15.1

Chemical Structure of the Adrenergic Neurotransmitter Norepinephrine Illustrating the Chemical Similarity to the Hallucinogens Mescaline and DOM, and to the Psychomotor Stimulant Amphetamine

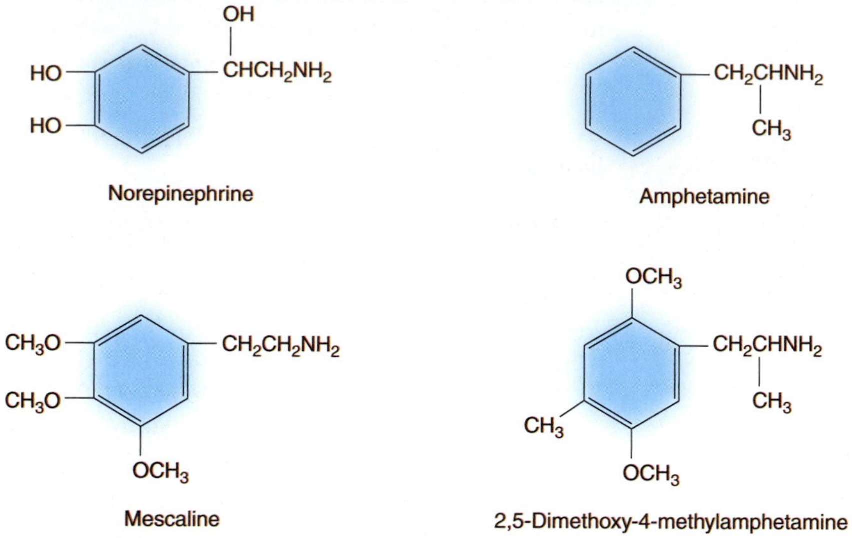

Norepinephrine

Amphetamine

Mescaline

2,5-Dimethoxy-4-methylamphetamine

Pharmacokinetics

In comparison to NE and DA, the amphetamines are lipid soluble and are not affected by the enzymes and inactivation mechanisms that quickly terminate the effects of the neurotransmitters. Consequently, the amphetamines are well absorbed orally, readily pass into the brain, and produce effects lasting several hours. Intravenous injection of amphetamines, especially methamphetamine ("speed"), has become a significant problem. Large amounts are often injected over several days, and during these sustained high-dosage bouts, the psychotomimetic effects of the drug frequently occur.

Pharmacological Effects

Abuse of amphetamines is based on the action of these drugs to influence physical performance and psychological mood. After oral administration, people feel more confident, alert, talkative, and generally hyperactive. Amphetamines increase endurance and reduce feelings of fatigue. Following intravenous administration, users experience the initial "rush," which has been described as orgasmic. The euphoria and excitement produced by amphetamines are important reinforcing properties on behavior. Compulsive behavior drives users to repeat the drug again and again in order to maintain the good feelings, the "reward."

After discontinuance of the drug, profound sleep usually occurs. Upon awakening, users experience disagreeable, depressed feelings ("crash") and want to resume drug taking immediately.

Initially, the hyperactivity may stimulate users to be more industrious and diligent, but eventually, performance deteriorates. Activity may continue for hours, but it may also become compulsive and highly stereotyped. Users get "hung up" doing one thing over and over again. As amphetamine usage increases and dosages become larger, the psychotomimetic effects become apparent and can lead to psychotic behavior. Amphetamine psychosis is similar to paranoid schizophrenia. Although users may feel elated, they appear glum, depressed, and withdrawn. Suspicion, hostility, and aggressive behavior may lead to violent acts. Sensory illusions, auditory and visual hallucinations, and distortions of body image may occur. Psychosis can occur after only a few doses, but it usually occurs after chronic use of high doses.

actions and pharmacological effects of these drugs are very similar. A number of drugs related to the amphetamines are known as "designer drugs." A **designer drug** is a slightly altered derivative of an approved drug, such as amphetamines or narcotics. The effects are similar to those of the approved drug, but they are usually more intense and mind-altering. Designer drugs are synthesized by illegal laboratories and sold "on the street" for great profit.

The major actions of amphetamines and cocaine occur within the brain. Both increase the amounts of norepinephrine (NE) and dopamine (DA) within the brain. The increased levels of NE produce prominent peripheral and central sympathomimetic effects. The higher levels of DA influence behavioral activity, particularly that involving the limbic system. The behavioral actions account for the ability of these drugs to act as potent reinforcers of behavior. This reinforcement acts to compel drug abusers to take the drug repeatedly.

Amphetamines

A number of drugs are referred to as "amphetamines." These include amphetamine itself, dextroamphetamine, methamphetamine ("speed"), and a few related drugs. The amphetamines are basically sympathomimetic amines with chemical structures very similar to NE and DA. There are, however, some important pharmacokinetic differences between the drugs and the neurotransmitters.

Tolerance and Dependency

Tolerance to amphetamines, especially after prolonged intravenous administration, develops rapidly, and larger amounts are usually administered with continuous use. Tolerance develops to the euphoria and to the appetite suppressant effect. Abrupt discontinuance of amphetamines after chronic use results in mild to moderate physical withdrawal symptoms. Withdrawal effects appear to be predominantly psychological in nature and include extreme fatigue, mental depression, and a strong desire for the drug.

Intoxication and Treatment

A number of adverse effects and potential complications are caused by overstimulation of the sympathetic and central nervous systems. The psychotomimetic effects of the paranoid psychosis have already been described. Sympathetic stimulation produces hyperthermia and profuse sweating, respiratory difficulties, tremors, and various cardiovascular effects. Intense cardiovascular stimulation results in tachycardia, arrhythmias, and hypertension, which may contribute to intracranial hemorrhage and sudden death. After prolonged intravenous use, severe fatigue and exhaustion may be followed by convulsion, coma, and death. Chronic intoxication can produce all of these conditions, and, in addition, there may be extreme weight loss from lack of appetite.

Treatment of amphetamine intoxication is aimed at supporting vital functions and providing symptomatic therapy. Acidifying the urine will increase excretion. Adrenergic blockers and vasodilators can be administered to control excessive sympathetic and cardiovascular stimulation. Diazepam is generally preferred to control seizures and also can be used for sedation when necessary. Highly agitated individuals can be given antipsychotic drugs, which reduce psychotic symptoms by antagonizing the actions of DA and NE.

Cocaine

Cocaine was isolated from the leaves of *Erythroxylon coca* in 1855. Native Indians of South America have chewed coca leaves for centuries to ward off fatigue and hunger. In the late nineteenth century, cocaine was considered a "wonder drug" and advocated for treatment of numerous medical conditions, including morphine and alcohol addiction. After recognizing the potential dangers of cocaine abuse, the government enacted legislation in 1914 that restricted and controlled the use of cocaine. Cocaine was "rediscovered" in the 1970s when the phenomenon of recreational drug use dramatically increased. In recent years, the widespread abuse of cocaine has generated major social and medical problems.

The pharmacological effects of cocaine are similar to those of the amphetamines. However, cocaine possesses a number of features that make it more popular with drug users. Cocaine is prepared in different forms that can be administered by a variety of methods. The intensity and duration of drug effects are highly dependent on the preparation used and the route of administration.

Preparations of Cocaine

Cocaine base is extracted from coca leaves and converted to a water-soluble hydrochloride salt. It is in this form that cocaine is exported and adulterated with other substances, such as sugars and local anesthetics. Cocaine hydrochloride can be administered orally, intranasally, and intravenously. It is destroyed, however, by the high temperatures generated during smoking. Several methods exist for conversion of cocaine hydrochloride back into free-base (without hydrochloride) form. Free-base cocaine possesses greater lipid solubility and a lower melting point. Consequently, it can be smoked, which allows almost instantaneous delivery of cocaine to the brain in a concentrated bolus. The intensity of effect is greatly increased. One form of free-base cocaine, "crack," is prepared by an alkalinization-water process that forms a crystalline, rocklike substance that makes a cracking sound when it is smoked.

Pharmacokinetics

Cocaine is absorbed from the intestinal tract and from all mucous membranes. Pharmacological effects are delayed (30 to 60 minutes) and are less intense after oral administration, compared to other routes. Drug effects are detectable 3 to 5 minutes after intranasal administration, peak in 20 to 30 minutes, and last 60 to 90 minutes. Plasma levels measured an hour or more after oral or intranasal administration are comparable; however, it is the concentration of cocaine in the brain that is important. Intranasal administration provides higher drug levels in the brain within a shorter period of time; therefore, the effects are more intense (Figure 15.2). Intravenous injection and smoking both provide immediate effects of high intensity but of shorter duration. Peak effects by these routes occur in minutes and last about 20 minutes. Smoking cocaine is the most popular route of administration; it is more convenient than making injections, and there is less nasal irritation (and no septal perforation) than when taken intranasally. The half-life of cocaine is about 30 to 40 minutes; the metabolites of cocaine are excreted in the urine.

Pharmacological Effects

Cocaine is a powerful CNS stimulant, producing marked euphoria, self-confidence, and heightened feelings of

Figure 15.3

Marijuana Leaves from *Cannabis Sativa*

3 to 4 hours. Tetrahydrocannabinol is widely distributed throughout the body, and the highly lipid-soluble THC is taken up by peripheral body compartments and sequestered in adipose tissue. Biotransformation of THC occurs predominantly in the liver by the microsomal enzyme system. Metabolic degradation is complex, with approximately 80 different metabolites already identified. The primary metabolite is active and equipotent with THC. This compound is subsequently biotransformed to a number of inactive metabolites, which are then eliminated, via the bile, into the feces, with the remainder excreted in the urine.

Mechanism of Action

The mechanism of action of the cannabinoids is not well understood. However, a receptor has been identified in the brain that has been shown to bind cannabinoids. The receptor is referred to as the cannabinoid receptor (CB1). In addition, an endogenous substance, named anandamide, has been identified in the brain that is believed to bind to the cannabinoid receptor. This suggests that there may be cannabinoid-like substances that play some role in activities of the brain. These findings may lead to a better understanding of the actions of the cannabinoids in the future.

Pharmacological Effects

Conjunctival reddening and increases in heart rate have been the most consistently reported effects of marijuana. Heart rate increases of 20 to 50 beats per minute may occur and are dose-related. Tolerance develops to this effect with chronic use. After one marijuana cigarette, the user usually experiences physical and mental relaxation, feelings of euphoria, and increased sociability. These feelings come and go as if in waves. Conversation and ideas tend to concentrate on the "here and now" and not on past or future circumstances. There is a sense that time is passing slowly. With moderate intoxication, there may be drowsiness, lapses of attention, and impairment of short-term memory. At high levels of intoxication, reflexes are slowed, muscle coordination decreases, ataxia is evident, and speech and the ability to concentrate become more difficult. Performance of a variety of tasks deteriorates. The more complex the task, the greater the degree of disruption produced. Dream-like states with alterations of auditory and visual perceptions reflect the psychotomimetic actions of marijuana. Psychic effects also may include dysphoria, acute panic-anxiety reactions, and psychotic episodes. Marijuana psychosis may, in part, be caused by unmasking of latent psychiatric disorders. It appears to occur under conditions of unusually heavy drug use. Symptoms are delirium, disorientation, and schizophrenic-like behavior.

At low doses, marijuana produces a slight bronchodilation. However, marijuana smoke contains higher concentrations of tar and some carcinogens than does tobacco smoke. Chronic use can produce hoarseness, cough, and bronchitis. Heavy use results in increased airway resistance and has been associated with precancerous changes in the respiratory epithelium.

Marijuana alters the plasma levels of some reproductive hormones. In males, lower testosterone levels decrease the sperm count and motility. In females, levels of luteinizing hormone (LH) and prolactin are suppressed, resulting in sporadic ovulation and irregular menstrual cycles. Tetrahydrocannabinol readily crosses the placenta, and teratogenic effects have been demonstrated in animal studies. Specific birth defects have not been observed in humans, but lower birth weights have been recorded in mothers who smoked marijuana during pregnancy.

Experimental studies have shown marijuana to cause a mild, transitory immunosuppressant effect. Decreased levels of T-lymphocytes have been observed in some chronic users. The clinical significance of this effect has not been determined.

Tolerance and Dependency

Tolerance to marijuana—that is, diminished response to a given dose when repeated—has been demonstrated. However, the development of tolerance usually occurs only after prolonged use of higher amounts of marijuana. The tolerance is variable and develops to a greater degree for some effects, such as tachycardia, CNS depression, and euphoria. Tolerance is rapidly reversed after cessation of marijuana use. Some of the tolerance may be metabolic in origin and caused by induction of microsomal enzymes. As with chronic tobacco smoking, tars and residues in marijuana smoke stimulate the drug microsomal enzyme system. However, this effect on metabolism does not explain all of the tolerance that develops. Cross-tolerance with other psychoactive drugs has not been demonstrated.

Abrupt cessation of marijuana after prolonged use has indicated some dependency. The dependency appears to be more psychological than physical and of considerably less intensity than that observed with cocaine and amphetamines. Withdrawal symptoms are mild and not unlike those observed in individuals who quit the tobacco habit. Symptoms include dysphoria, anxiety, tremors, eating and sleeping disturbances, and increased sweating.

Intoxication and Treatment

The most common intoxication reaction requiring treatment is acute panic-anxiety reaction, where users appear to lose control and feel as if they are losing their mind. This reaction occurs most frequently with inexperienced users, who are unfamiliar with the effects of marijuana. The effects rarely last more than a few hours. Diazepam may be administered to individuals who are particularly agitated. Psychotic reactions, which were discussed previously, occur after high doses or prolonged use and may require hospitalization and treatment with antipsychotic drugs.

Therapeutic Potential of THC

Tetrahydrocannabinol and various derivatives have been investigated for treatment of nausea and vomiting, glaucoma, pain management, and other medical conditions. Dronabinol (*Marinol*), a drug formulation of THC, and nabilone (*Cesamet*), an analog of THC, are approved for use to combat the nausea and vomiting associated with chemotherapy. The capsules are administered several hours before and after administration of chemotherapy. Dronabinol also has been approved for the stimulation of appetite and prevention of weight loss in patients with a confirmed diagnosis of acquired immunodeficiency syndrome (AIDS). Dronabinol capsules are administered twice daily, before lunch and dinner.

Chapter Review

Understanding Terminology

Match the definition or description in the left column with the appropriate term in the right column. **(LO 15.1, 15.2, 15.3, 15.5)**

____ 1. Because of this, doses of one drug taken shortly after another drug produce decreased effects.

____ 2. Because of this, one consumes larger and larger doses of a drug in order to get the desired effects.

____ 3. Pharmacologically active substance found in the marijuana plant.

____ 4. Because of this, larger and larger doses of a drug are necessary to prevent withdrawal.

____ 5. A distortion of sensory perception that occurs with the use of LSD.

____ 6. Hallucinogenic effect of LSD relived long after the use of LSD.

a. cannabinoid
b. cross-tolerance
c. dependency
d. flashback
e. synesthesia
f. drug tolerance

Acquiring Knowledge

Answer the following questions.

1. Briefly describe the psychotomimetic syndrome. **(LO 15.1)**

2. List the pharmacological effects produced by LSD. What is synesthesia? **(LO 15.1, 15.2)**

3. Describe the development of tolerance to LSD. What does the term *cross-tolerance* refer to? **(LO 15.1)**

4. What is the usual treatment for LSD and other hallucinogenic drug intoxication? **(LO 15.2)**

5. What mechanism of action is common to both amphetamines and cocaine? **(LO 15.3)**

6. Characterize the development of tolerance and dependency with the psychomotor stimulants. **(LO 15.3)**

7. Describe the pharmacological effects produced by phencyclidine (PCP). **(LO 15.4)**

8. What do the terms *marijuana, cannabinoid, tetrahydrocannabinol (THC),* and *hashish* refer to? **(LO 15.5)**

9. List the common pharmacological effects produced by marijuana. **(LO 15.5)**

10. What adverse effects are associated with the chronic use of marijuana? **(LO 15.5)**

Match the descriptions in the left column with the appropriate phase of hallucinogen use in the right column. **(LO 15.1, 15.2)**

____ 11. Produces the effects desired by the user.

____ 12. Occurs right after absorption of the hallucinogen.

____ 13. A "bad trip".

____ 14. Consists of CNS stimulation and autonomic changes that are predominantly sympathomimetic in nature.

____ 15. Produces sensory distortions and pseudohallucinations.

____ 16. Characteristic of a maximum drug effect.

____ 17. Produces disruption of thought, depersonalization, hallucinations, and psychotic episodes.

a. psychic phase
b. sensory phase
c. somatic phase

Applying Knowledge on the Job

Use your critical-thinking skills to answer the following questions.

1. Mark works in an emergency room (ER) that gets lots of illicit-drug-overdose cases. What treatment recommendations would be appropriate for the following patients?
   a. Patient A presents with LSD toxicity, experiencing anxiety, paranoia, and real hallucinations (as opposed to pseudohallucinations, which the individual knows are not real). **(LO 15.2)**
   b. Patient B presents with cocaine intoxication, following a prolonged binge on the drug. She has had a mild seizure and shows psychotic behavior, hyperthermia, and exhaustion. **(LO 15.3)**

2. Assume you work a drug abuse hotline. What aspect of drug abuse does each of the following callers exhibit?
   a. Caller A says he needs help quitting cocaine. His main reason for wanting to quit is that he can no longer afford to buy the amount of cocaine he needs to get high. He says it seems that he uses more every day, and he still doesn't get as high as he did when he first started using the drug. **(LO 15.3)**
   b. Caller B says he thinks he needs to get medical help with his cocaine problem. He's been using cocaine for months now, and he needs larger and larger doses just to keep from feeling sick and strung out. He can't imagine going without the cocaine, but he knows things can't go on this way, either. **(LO 15.3)**

Questions 3–5 are designed for classroom discussion.

3. A coworker confides in you that working full time, going to school, and taking care of a child and husband are exhausting, so occasionally she takes amphetamines to help her get through it all. She doesn't feel it is a problem because she only uses them when she needs to. What do you do? **(LO 15.3)**

4. You are over at a coworker's house and she brings out some marijuana. What do you do? **(LO 15.5)**

5. A coworker suffers from chronic sinus problems. After many months, this coworker confides in you that she indulges in recreational use of cocaine. What do you do? **(LO 15.3)**

Multiple Choice

Use your critical-thinking skills to answer the following questions.

1. Select the neurotransmitter receptor interaction that explains the mechanism of action of LSD and other hallucinogens. **(LO 15.1)**
   A. norepinephrine
   B. dopamine
   C. serotonin
   D. acetylcholine

2. LSD is associated with the following pharmacologic effects when taken repeatedly: **(LO 15.2)**
   A. rapid development of drug tolerance
   B. drug dependency and withdrawal symptoms
   C. cross-tolerance with other hallucinogens
   D. only A and C are true

3. Intravenous administration and abuse of psychomotor stimulants, such as methamphetamine, is associated with the following: **(LO 15.3)**
   A. increased sympathomimetic actions
   B. development of drug tolerance
   C. behavioral and psychotomimetic effects
   D. all statements are true

4. The drug that possesses anesthetic properties and that acts by blocking glutamate receptors is **(LO 15.4)**
   A. cocaine
   B. methamphetamine
   C. phencyclidine
   D. MDMA

5. Select the statement(s) that are true concerning the use of marijuana. **(LO 15.5)**
   A. active ingredient referred to as THC
   B. believed to bind to a specific receptor in the brain
   C. frequent use associated with development of drug tolerance
   D. all statements are true

Multiple Choice (Multiple Answer)

Select the correct choices for each statement. The choices may be all correct, all incorrect, or any combination.

1. Select all of the following procedures that apply to treatment of cocaine intoxication **and** dependency. **(LO 15.3)**
   A. antagonizing DA and NE
   B. placement in a quiet room
   C. behavior modification
   D. tricyclic antidepressants

2. Select the drugs that increase the levels of NE and DA. **(LO 15.3)**
   A. amphetamines
   B. lysergic acid diethylamide
   C. phencyclidine
   D. marijuana

3. What are the signs of PCP intoxication? **(LO 15.4)**
   A. hyperthermia
   B. hyperreflexia
   C. convulsions
   D. nystagmus

4. Which phases of dose-related effects include hallucinations? **(LO 15.2)**
   A. somatic phase
   B. sensory phase
   C. flashback phase
   D. psychic phase

5. Select the pharmacological effects of marijuana. **(LO 15.5)**
   A. disorders of body image
   B. increased heart rate
   C. mental relaxation
   D. conjunctival reddening

Sequencing

Place the following drugs in order of shortest duration of psychic effects to longest duration. (LO 15.1, 15.3, 15.4)

_____   _____   _____   _____   _____

Shortest   **Longest**

LSD

DMT

PCP

STP

psilocybin

Classification

Place the following drugs into the appropriate category. (LO 15.1)

MDEA   DOM   DMT

psilocybin   mescaline   MDMA

Tryptamine derivatives	Phenethylamine derivatives	Amphetamine derivatives

Documentation

Based on the symptoms experienced by the patient upon arrival at the hospital, answer the following questions. (LO 15.1)

Symptoms:
Elevated body temperature
Dilated pupils
Seeing sounds
Increased heart rate

a. What psychotomimetic drug is the patient most likely intoxicated with?

b. What additional symptoms could be experienced by this patient?

c. If we were to administer a drug to help with this intoxication, which class of drugs would be most appropriate?

d. What symptom would we be treating with the use of the above drug?

e. What other treatments would be appropriate?

For interactive animations, videos, and assessment, visit:

www.mcgrawhillconnect.com

Chapter 16

Antiepileptic Drugs

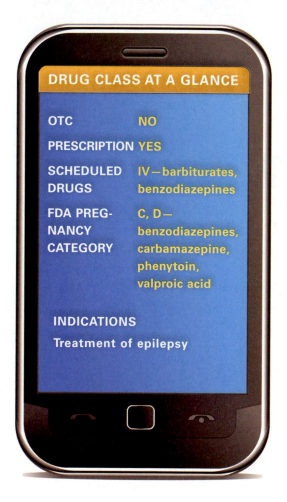

DRUG CLASS AT A GLANCE

OTC	NO
PRESCRIPTION	YES
SCHEDULED DRUGS	IV—barbiturates, benzodiazepines
FDA PREGNANCY CATEGORY	C, D— benzodiazepines, carbamazepine, phenytoin, valproic acid

INDICATIONS

Treatment of epilepsy

KEY TERMS

absence seizure: generalized seizure that does not involve motor convulsions; also referred to as petit mal.

anticonvulsant: drug usually administered IV that stops a convulsive seizure.

antiepileptic drug: drug usually administered orally to prevent epileptic seizures.

atonic seizure: generalized-type seizure characterized by a sudden loss of muscle tone.

clonic: convulsive muscle contraction in which rigidity and relaxation alternate in rapid succession.

convulsion: involuntary muscle contraction that is either tonic or clonic.

epilepsy: CNS disorder characterized by uncontrolled nerve cell discharges and manifested by recurring, spontaneous seizures of any type.

generalized seizure: seizure originating and involving both cerebral hemispheres that may be either convulsive or nonconvulsive.

grand mal: older term for a generalized seizure characterized by full-body tonic and clonic motor convulsions.

myoclonic: generalized seizures that are usually brief and often confined to one part of the body.

partial seizure: seizure originating in one area of the brain that may spread to other areas.

seizure: abnormal discharge of brain neurons that causes alteration of behavior and/or motor activity.

status epilepticus: continuous series of generalized tonic and clonic seizures, a medical emergency requiring immediate treatment.

tonic: convulsive muscle contraction characterized by sustained muscular contractions.

tonic-clonic: generalized seizure characterized by full-body tonic and clonic motor convulsions and loss of consciousness.

After studying this chapter, you should be able to

16.1 describe the main clinical features of generalized and partial epileptic seizures.

16.2 compare the mechanism of action and uses of phenobarbital with those of phenytoin, carbamazepine, and valproic acid.

16.3 identify the mechanism of action of the drugs primarily effective for partial seizures.

16.4 identify the mechanism of action of ethosuximide and drugs used in the treatment of absence seizures.

16.5 describe the treatment of status epilepticus.

16.6 identify the preferred therapies for the different types of epileptic seizures.

A **seizure** is defined as an abnormal electrical discharge of brain neurons that results in alterations in behavior and/or involuntary movements. There can be many different causes of seizures including fever, metabolic disturbances, brain tumors, and drug toxicity. **Epilepsy** is a medical condition involving recurrent seizures that are caused by some underlying disturbance in the activity of neurons in the brain. The neuronal disturbance increases the excitability of neurons, which then discharge uncontrollably. The result is high-frequency repetitive firing of action potentials that cause an alteration of consciousness and that may be accompanied by some form of muscular twitching or **convulsion**. The characteristics and symptoms of the different types of seizures depend on the area of the brain that is experiencing the abnormal electrical discharge. **Generalized seizures** usually involve both hemispheres of the brain, while **partial seizures** are usually localized to specific areas. However, partial seizures can spread and become generalized. Successful treatment of epilepsy with antiepileptic drugs depends upon accurate neurological examination and identification of the type of seizure. There are a variety of **antiepileptic drugs** used to treat epilepsy. Some drugs are effective for multiple types of epileptic seizures, while other drugs are primarily indicated for a specific type of seizure.

TYPES OF EPILEPSY

There are different types of epilepsy, and proper diagnosis is essential to selection of proper treatment. An important diagnostic tool aiding in the detection of epilepsy is the electroencephalogram (EEG), which records the electrical activity of the brain. Specific types of epilepsy produce characteristic electrical patterns. These patterns can be readily recorded by the EEG and identified. Classification of the different epilepsies is based on a neurological examination and EEG evaluation. Epileptic seizures are classified as either generalized or partial.

Generalized Seizures

Generalized seizures originate in and involve both cerebral hemispheres. They are classified as **tonic, clonic,** **tonic-clonic, myoclonic, atonic,** and **absence seizures.**

Tonic-Clonic Seizures

Tonic-clonic **(grand mal)** seizures are the most dramatic in appearance and involve loss of consciousness. They usually begin with tonic followed by clonic muscle contractions. The individual appears to jerk around due to the alternating muscle contractions and relaxations. Increases in blood pressure and heart rate, urination, defecation, and tongue biting are common. A seizure usually lasts several minutes. Following the seizure there is confusion, fatigue, and muscle soreness. A series of generalized seizures, particularly tonic-clonic, without cessation is referred to as **status epilepticus.** Status epilepticus is a major medical emergency and demands immediate treatment.

Myoclonic Seizures

Myoclonic seizures produce muscle contractions that are usually brief and often confined to one part of the body; however, these seizures may spread and become generalized.

Atonic Seizures

Atonic seizures involve a sudden loss of muscle tone. The individual usually falls and can suffer head and other bodily injuries.

Absence Seizures

Absence seizures are generalized seizures that are usually confined to a brief impairment of consciousness. This may involve a form of staring into space or rapid eye blinking that lasts anywhere from a few seconds to less than a minute. Although there is impairment of consciousness, individuals usually do not fall or experience motor convulsions. After a seizure, activity often continues as if nothing had happened. There is usually a characteristic 3-second electrical spike wave that can be observed on the EEG. This type of epilepsy is also known as petit mal.

Partial Seizures

Partial seizures are classified as either simple or complex.

Simple Partial Seizures

Simple partial seizures may be sensory or motor in nature. These seizures usually involve a limited area of the brain and are often manifested by a sensory change (numbness) or muscular twitch that is confined to one body part. The seizures are brief in duration and usually there is no loss of consciousness.

Complex Partial Seizures

Complex partial seizures involve impairment of consciousness, usually not longer than a minute or two, and are accompanied by some type of characteristic movement. These movements have been described as "purposeless" because they are not goal-directed and involve such things as lip smacking or other repetitive movements. Following the attack, the individual usually has no memory of what occurred during the seizure. Complex partial seizures may spread and include other areas of the body, or also may become tonic-clonic and involve the entire body.

LO 16.2

DRUGS EFFECTIVE FOR BOTH GENERALIZED TONIC-CLONIC AND PARTIAL SEIZURES

All of the primary drugs used to treat epilepsy possess anticonvulsant properties. An **anticonvulsant** is defined as a drug, usually administered IM or IV, that terminates convulsive seizures. The term **antiepileptic** infers that the drug, usually administered orally, can be used prophylactically to reduce or prevent epileptic seizures. Not all drugs with anticonvulsant activity can be used in epilepsy; many anticonvulsant drugs produce a significant degree of sedation that interferes with performance of daily activities.

Antiepileptic drugs decrease the excitability of brain cells and, consequently, reduce the incidence and severity of seizures. This action enables affected individuals to have greater control over their daily lives. Several different drug classes possess antiepileptic properties. Each of these will be discussed in relationship to the type of epilepsy for which it is used. The most frequently used antiepileptic drugs and their main indications are summarized in Table 16:1.

Barbiturates

The barbiturates, previously discussed with respect to their sedative and hypnotic properties, are excellent anticonvulsant drugs. All barbiturates have anticonvulsant properties, but only a few, such as phenobarbital and mephobarbital, have the additional property of being antiepileptic. They have a selective effect at lower doses to prevent seizures. Sedation and hypnosis are common pharmacological effects produced by barbiturates. However, in the treatment of epilepsy, excessive sedation or hypnosis is an unwanted side effect. Fortunately, tolerance to the sedative and hypnotic effects develops with chronic use. The barbiturates are used alone or in combination with other antiepileptic drugs.

Mechanism of Action

As previously discussed in Chapter 12, one of the actions of the barbiturates is to increase the inhibitory effects of the inhibitory neurotransmitter gamma-aminobutyric acid (GABA). In the brain, this suppresses the excitability of epileptogenic neurons and makes them less likely to discharge and initiate a seizure. The effect on GABA occurs at lower doses and therefore limits the sedative and depressant effects of the barbiturates.

Clinical Indications

Barbiturates, like phenobarbital, are currently used as alternatives to other more preferred drugs in the treatment of both generalized and partial seizures.

Sudden discontinuation of barbiturates can produce convulsions. Therefore, when barbiturate withdrawal is desired, a patient's dose should be gradually reduced over the course of 1 to 2 weeks. The pharmacology of the barbiturates can be reviewed in Chapter 12.

Antiepileptic Drugs

Drug (*Trade Name*)	Primary mechanism of action	Dosage form
Drugs used for generalized tonic-clonic and partial seizures		
Carbamazepine (*Tegretol*)	Prolongs inactivation of Na+ channels	Tablets, capsules, suspension
Phenobarbital (*Luminal*)	Increases inhibitory actions of GABA	Tablets, elixir, IM, IV
Levetiracetam (*Keppra*)	Mechanism not clearly understood	Tablets, oral solution, IV
Phenytoin (*Dilantin*)	Prolongs inactivation of Na+ channels	Tablets, capsules, suspension, IV
Topiramate (*Topamax*)	Prolongs inactivation of Na+ channels	Tablets, capsules
Zonisamide (*Zonegran*)	Interference with Na+ and Ca++ channels	Capsules
Valproic acid (*Depakene*)	Prolongs inactivation of Na+ channels	Tablets, capsules, syrup, IV
Drugs effective primarily for partial seizures		
Felbamate (*Felbatol*)	Interference with Na+, Ca++, glutamate	Tablets, suspension
Gabapentin (*Neurontin*)	Blockade of Ca++ channels, decreased release of glutamate	Capsules, oral solution
Lacosamide (*Vimpat*)	Enhances slow inactivation of Na+ channels	Tablets, IV
Lamotrigine (*Lamictal*)	Prolongs inactivation of Na+ channels	Tablets
Pregabalin (*Lyrica*)	Same as gabapentin (above)	Capsules
Tiagabine (*Gabitril*)	Blocks neuronal reuptake of GABA	Tablets
Drugs effective for absence seizures		
Clonazepam (*Klonopin*)	Increases inhibitory actions of GABA	Tablets
Ethosuximide (*Zarontin*)	Inhibits thalamic T-type Ca++ currents	Capsules, syrup
Lamotrigine (*Lamictal*)	Prolongs inactivation of Na+ channels	Tablets
Trimethadione (*Tridione*)	Inhibits thalamic T-type Ca++ currents	Chewable tablets, capsules
Valproic acid (*Depakene*)	Prolongs inactivation of Na+ channels	Capsules, syrup, IV
Drugs effective for status epilepticus		
Clonazepam (*Klonopin*)	Increases inhibitory actions of GABA	IM, IV
Diazepam (*Valium*)	Same as above	IM, IV
Lorazepam (*Ativan*)	Same as above	IM, IV

Hydantoins

The most important drug from this class is phenytoin (*Dilantin*). Phenytoin is a very potent antiepileptic drug, and it can be used in several types of epilepsy (Figure 16.1). It is one of the most important antiepileptic drugs available. A significant advantage of phenytoin is that it produces little sedation. Ethotoin (*Peganone*), mephenytoin (*Mesantoin*), and fosphenytoin (*Cerebyx*) are other hydantoins. Fosphenytoin is a more soluble prodrug of phenytoin that is administered by IM or IV injection.

Mechanism of Action

The mechanism of action of phenytoin and the other hydantoins is complex and affects the activity of both neuron ion channels (Na^+, K^+, Ca^{++}) and neurotransmitter functions. The primary effect of phenytoin is believed to prolong the inactivation period of sodium (Na^+) channels in the nerve membrane. The result is a reduction in generation of the high-frequency repetitive firing of action potentials from neurons involved in initiating seizures. Figure 16.2 compares some normal EEG brain waves with those recorded during an epileptic seizure.

Clinical Indications

Phenytoin is used for all types of partial seizures and for tonic-clonic generalized seizures. It also can be administered IV in acute situations to arrest convulsive seizures including the treatment of status epilepticus.

Adverse Effects

The adverse effects of the individual hydantoins are similar. The most common adverse effects involve the cerebellum. The symptoms are dizziness, ataxia, visual disturbances, and postural imbalance. Other adverse effects include skin rashes, hirsutism, and gingival hyperplasia. Good dental hygiene may prevent the overgrowth of the gums. Phenytoin has been associated with birth defects referred to as the "fetal hydantoin syndrome." Defects include craniofacial abnormalities, growth retardation, cardiac defects, learning and developmental problems, and limb defects. It is listed as FDA Pregnancy Category D.

Carbamazepine (*Tegretol*)

Carbamazepine is structurally related to the tricyclic antidepressants. The mechanism of action is similar to that of phenytoin and involves an action to prolong the

Figure 16.1

Drug Label for Phenytoin (*Dilantin*)

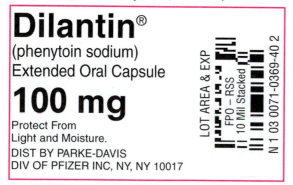

Phenytoin is one of the most important antiepileptic drugs available that is effective for both generalized and partial seizures, and the treatment of status epilepticus.

Figure 16.2

Comparison of Normal Brain Waves with the High-Frequency Repetitive Firing of Action Potentials Observed During an Epileptic Seizure

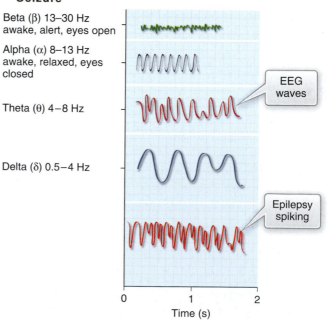

inactivation of Na$^+$ channels. This decreases the neuronal influx of sodium ions and inhibits high-frequency and repetitive firing of neurons.

Clinical Indications

Carbamazepine is used in the treatment of all types of partial seizures and generalized tonic-clonic seizures. It also is indicated for the treatment of mania and bipolar disorder (Chapter 14). Carbamazepine possesses analgesic properties and also is indicated for treatment of trigeminal neuralgia.

Adverse Effects

Common side effects include nausea, vomiting, diplopia, drowsiness, and dizziness. More serious effects involve liver disturbances, jaundice, and bone marrow depression, which may lead to aplastic anemia. In overdosage, carbamazepine may cause convulsions and respiratory depression. Carbamazepine is listed as FDA Pregnancy Category D and has been associated with spina bifida, craniofacial defects, and developmental delay.

Valproic Acid (*Depakene*)

Valproic acid is one of the few drugs that can be used in all types of epilepsy. Like carbamazepine and phenytoin, valproic acid decreases the influx of Na$^+$ ions and inhibits high-frequency firing of neurons (Figure 16.3). In addition, valproic acid blocks excitatory glutamate (NMDA) receptors and increases the inhibitor effects of GABA. These multiple actions are most likely the reason for its effectiveness in almost all types of epilepsy. Valproic acid administered alone produces very little sedation.

Clinical Indications

Valproic acid is very effective against absence seizures and generalized tonic-clonic seizures. In addition, it is effective for treatment of partial seizures. Valproic acid is also effective in the treatment of bipolar disorder.

Adverse Effects

The most common side effects of valproic acid are nausea, vomiting, diarrhea, and tremor. The most serious problem with valproic acid has been the development of a potentially fatal liver toxicity, especially in young patients. The cause of the liver toxicity has been linked to the metabolites of valproic acid, which are hepatotoxic. Valproic acid has been associated with birth defects such as spina bifida and both facial and digital abnormalities. The FDA has listed this drug as Pregnancy Category D.

Primidone (*Mysoline*)

Primidone is chemically related to the barbiturates. Most of the drug is metabolized and converted in the body into phenobarbital, which is believed to account for most of its antiepileptic effects. Primidone is effective against both generalized and partial seizures but is primarily an alternate choice to drugs such as carbamazepine, phenytoin, and valproic acid. Common adverse effects include sedation and gastrointestinal disturbances; other adverse effects are similar to those of phenobarbital.

Levetiracetam (*Keppra*)

The mechanism of action of levetiracetam is poorly understood. The main indication is as adjunctive therapy in the treatment of partial seizures in adults and the treatment of generalized tonic-clonic seizures in children. The drug may be taken without regard to meals and significant drug interactions have not been reported. The most frequently reported adverse effects include sleepiness, dizziness, headache, tiredness, and nervousness.

Figure 16.3 **The Effect of Several Antiseizure Drugs on Voltage-Induced, Sustained, High-Frequency Firing of Neuronal Action Potentials**

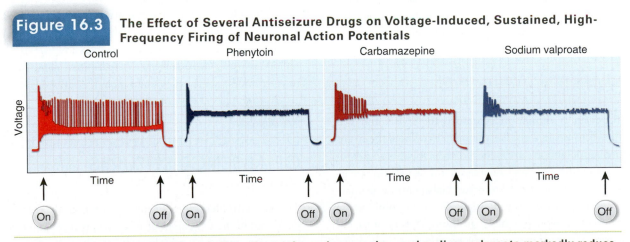

When compared to the control recording, phenytoin, carbamazepine, and sodium valproate markedly reduce the number of voltage-induced action potentials.

Topiramate (*Topamax*)

The actions of topiramate are not clearly understood but are believed to interfere with the action of Na$^+$ ions and generation of high-frequency action potentials. The drug also may increase the inhibitory actions of GABA. Topiramate is indicated for therapy of both tonic-clonic and partial seizures. The drug is absorbed well, is excreted mostly unchanged, and does not appear to cause significant drug interactions. Adverse effects include sleepiness, dizziness, tiredness, mental confusion, and, less frequently, formation of renal stones. Studies have demonstrated teratogenic effects in animals and it is classified as FDA Pregnancy Category C.

Zonisamide (*Zonegran*)

The mechanism of action of zonisamide involves interference with both Na$^+$ and Ca^{++} ion channel activity to inhibit the high-frequency firing of neurons. Indications are for generalized tonic-clonic and partial seizures; it also has shown activity against some myoclonic seizures. Zonisamide is well tolerated. Adverse effects involve minor CNS disturbances, sleepiness, rashes, and occasional development of renal stones.

LO 16.3

DRUGS EFFECTIVE PRIMARILY FOR PARTIAL SEIZURES
Felbamate (*Felbatol*)

Felbamate is indicated for the treatment of partial seizures. Mechanisms of action include interference with sodium (Na$^+$) ions, blockade of calcium (Ca^{++}) channels, and blockade of glutamate receptors. Unfortunately, felbamate has been associated with the development of aplastic anemia and liver failure. Consequently, the drug is reserved for patients who do not respond to other drugs and whose epilepsy is so severe that the benefits of therapy outweigh the risks of developing these serious adverse effects.

Gabapentin (*Neurontin*), Pregabalin (*Lyrica*)

Gabapentin is similar in structure to GABA and was designed to act in a similar manner. However, the major antiepileptic actions are believed to involve blockade of Ca^{++} ion channels and decreased release of the excitatory neurotransmitter glutamate. Gabapentin is primarily used in patients over 12 years of age in combination with other antiepileptic drugs in the treatment of partial seizures. The most common adverse effects include sleepiness, headache, dizziness, ataxia, tremor, and tiredness.

Pregabalin is also related to GABA and similar to gabapentin in pharmacologic properties. It is indicated for adjunctive therapy of partial seizures. In addition, it is approved for treatment of neuralgia (nerve pain) and related conditions such as fibromyalgia.

Lacosamide (*Vimpat*)

Lacosamide is a newer drug that is indicated for add-on therapy with other drugs in the treatment of partial seizures in patients age 17 or older. The mechanism of action of lacosamide is believed to involve enhancement of the slow inactivation of voltage-sensitive Na$^+$ channels, which inhibits the repetitive firing of neurons. Common adverse effects include blurred vision, headache, dizziness, and ataxia. Hypersensitivity reactions and disturbances of the electrical activity of the heart also may occur.

Lamotrigine (*Lamictal*)

The mechanism of action of lamotrigine includes inactivation of Na$^+$ ion channels to decrease high-frequency firing of neurons and inhibition of Ca^{++} ion channels. The drug is used alone and in combination with other antiepileptic drugs in the treatment of partial seizures. Lamotrigine also has demonstrated activity against absence, myoclonic, and atonic seizures. In addition, it is one of the antiseizure drugs indicated for treatment of bipolar disorder. The most common adverse effects include dizziness, ataxia, sleepiness, headache, visual disturbances, and allergic rash. The rash usually develops during the first few weeks of treatment and in some cases has progressed to Stevens-Johnson syndrome, a severe type of dermatitis that can be life-threatening.

Tiagabine (*Gabitril*)

Tiagabine is believed to block the neuronal reuptake of the inhibitory transmitter GABA back into its nerve endings. This increases synaptic GABA levels that are now available for receptor stimulation. The drug is indicated for the treatment of partial seizures alone or in combination with other drugs. Common adverse effects include nausea, GI disturbances, abdominal pain, dizziness, tremors, nervousness, and mental confusion.

LO 16.4

DRUGS USED IN THE TREATMENT OF ABSENCE SEIZURES
Succinimides

The succinimides are a group of compounds that are only used in the treatment of absence seizures. The most important and most widely used succinimide is ethosuximide (*Zarontin*). Ethosuximide has a long half-life that usually allows twice-a-day dosing. The mechanism of action is related to the ability of ethosuximide to decrease specific calcium currents (T-type currents) in the thalamus. These calcium currents are believed to play an important role in causing absence seizures.

The succinimides commonly produce GI disturbances such as nausea, vomiting, and diarrhea. In addition, some drowsiness and dizziness may occur. Less frequently there may be decreases in white blood cells and platelets.

In addition to ethosuximide, lamotrigine and valproic acid (both previously discussed) are the drugs most frequently used for treatment of absence seizures.

Oxazolidinediones

The oxazolidinediones are another class of drugs indicated for absence seizures. The main drug of this class is trimethadione (*Tridione*). The mechanism of action is similar to that of ethosuximide, reduction of T-type calcium (Ca^{++}) currents.

The oxazolidinediones are considerably more toxic than the succinimides. One of the adverse effects characteristic of the oxazolidinediones is hemeralopia, or "snow blindness," a visual disturbance in which patients seem to be looking at everything as if through a snowfall. Hypersensitivity reactions such as rashes and blood disorders usually necessitate alternate therapy. In addition, cases of liver and kidney damage have been reported. Trimethadione is rarely prescribed today because of the higher incidence of adverse effects and toxicities.

Benzodiazepines

As discussed in Chapter 13, the benzodiazepines possess anticonvulsant activity. These drugs act by increasing the inhibitory effects of GABA. Diazepam (*Valium*), clonazepam (*Klonopin*), and lorazepam (*Ativan*) are the drugs used as anticonvulsants. Diazepam and lorazepam are usually administered intravenously to stop seizures that are in progress, usually tonic-clonic seizures, and for the treatment of status epilepticus (see below). Clonazepam also is used as an antiepileptic drug in the treatment of myoclonic and akinetic seizures, and in cases of absence seizure unresponsive to ethosuximide or other drugs. The main side effect of these drugs in the treatment of seizures is sedation. The adverse effects of the benzodiazepines were presented in Chapter 13.

LO 16.5

TREATMENT OF STATUS EPILEPTICUS

Status epilepticus is a medical emergency where a series of seizures occur without interruption. Tonic-clonic-type seizures, in particular, require immediate treatment in order to prevent severe CNS, cardiovascular, and respiratory depression. Lorazepam is currently considered the drug of choice to treat status epilepticus. Diazepam (Figure 16.4) is equally effective but has a shorter duration of action when administered IV and may require additional administration. Parenteral administration of fosphenytoin or phenytoin is also effective for treatment of status epilepticus. Once status epilepticus is under control, other antiepileptic drugs used in the chronic treatment of epilepsy can be administered orally to prevent further seizures.

LO 16.6

PREFERRED THERAPY FOR EPILEPTIC SEIZURES

There are a large number of antiepileptic drugs and the choice of treatment often depends on the age, seizure type, and individual patient characteristics.

Generalized Tonic-Clonic Seizures

Phenytoin (*Dilantin*) is usually considered the drug of choice. Valproic acid (*Depakene*) and carbamazepine (*Tegretol*) are also first-line drugs. Lamotrigine (*Lamictal*) and topiramate (*Topamax*) are also effective and particularly useful in children because of the lower incidence of adverse effects.

Partial Seizures

There are a number of drugs that are equally effective for partial seizures. Phenytoin (*Dilantin*), carbamazepine (*Tegretol*), and valproic acid (*Depakene*) are usually the preferred drugs. Newer drugs such as lamotrigine (*Lamictal*) and topiramate (*Topamax*) are also effective and serve as alternate therapy.

Figure 16.4

Drug Label for Diazepam

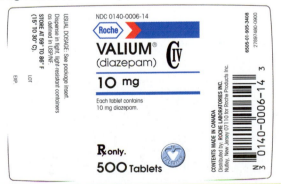

IV administration of diazepam is considered to be one of the drugs of choice for the treatment of status epilepticus.

Absence Seizures

Ethosuximide (*Zarontin*) has usually been the drug of choice for these seizures, especially in children. Valproic acid (*Depakene*) and lamotrigine (*Lamictal*) are also effective drugs and may be preferred in adults, especially when other seizure types are also present.

Status Epilepticus

The drug of choice to arrest status epilepticus is now considered to be lorazepam (*Ativan*) administered IV. Diazepam is equally effective but has a shorter duration of action when administered IV and may require additional administrations. Depending on the situation, administration of lorazepam may be followed with IV administration of phenytoin (*Dilantin*) or fosphenytoin (*Cerebyx*).

Antiepileptic Drug Interactions

There are a variety of drug interactions involving the antiepileptic drugs. When used in combination, these drugs often produce drug interactions with each other. Carbamazepine, phenobarbital, and phenytoin cause microsomal enzyme induction and increase the rate of metabolism of any other drug requiring microsomal metabolism. This results in reduced drug effects and duration of action of the drugs requiring metabolism. Valproic acid inhibits the microsomal enzymes and will therefore increase the effects of drugs requiring microsomal metabolism. Cimetidine (*Tagamet*) and other drugs that inhibit microsomal enzymes will increase the concentrations and effects of anticonvulsant drugs requiring microsomal metabolism, especially carbamazepine.

Some antiepileptic drugs, such as phenytoin and valproic acid, are highly plasma protein bound. They can displace and be displaced by other drugs that are also highly protein bound. This increases the free drug concentration (unbound fraction) of the drug displaced and produces greater pharmacologic effects.

Chapter Review

Understanding Terminology

Match the definition or description in the left column with the appropriate term in the right column. (LO 16.1)

___ 1. Drug that prevents or stops a convulsive seizure.

___ 2. Drug that prevents epileptic seizures.

___ 3. Condition characterized by periodic seizures or convulsions.

___ 4. Generalized seizure only involving a brief impairment of consciousness.

___ 5. Seizures characterized by full-body tonic and clonic convulsions.

___ 6. Continuous series of generalized seizures.

___ 7. Seizure characterized by some purposeless body movement or sensory change.

a. anticonvulsant

b. antiepileptic

c. epilepsy

d. generalized seizure (grand mal)

e. absence seizure

f. complex partial seizure

g. status epilepticus

Acquiring Knowledge

Answer the following questions.

1. Describe what occurs to the brain cells in epilepsy. (LO 16.2, 16.3)

2. List the common types of epilepsy and describe the characteristics of each. (LO 16.1)

3. In what types of epilepsy is phenytoin most useful? (LO 16.2)

4. What is the mechanism of action of phenytoin (*Dilantin*)? (LO 16.2)

5. List the adverse effects of phenytoin. (LO 16.2)

6. What drugs are used primarily to treat absence seizures? (LO 16.4)

7. List the adverse effects of trimethadione (*Tridione*). (LO 16.4)

8. What is the drug of choice for treating status epilepticus? (LO 16.5)

Applying Knowledge on the Job

Use your critical-thinking skills to answer the following questions.

1. Assume that you assist with medications in a busy neurological practice and you've been asked to deal with each of the following cases.
   a. Patient A is a 14-year-old female who frequently has short periods when she loses consciousness. After each seizure, she continues what she was doing as though nothing happened. How would you characterize the type of epilepsy this patient has? (LO 16.4)
   b. Patient B has absence epilepsy. What drug is usually considered the preferred therapy? (LO 16.4, 16.6)
   c. How would you advise Patient C about adverse effects for the antiepileptic drug trimethadione? (LO 16.4)
   d. Patient D has tonic-clonic convulsions in progress. What should be done? (LO 16.5)

2. Freddy suffers from absence seizures. *Zarontin* has not adequately controlled them. His physician has decided to add a benzodiazepine to his drug therapy. Which one would be appropriate? (LO 16.4)

3. What are the additional clinical indications for carbamazepine other than epilepsy? (LO 16.2)

Multiple Choice

Use your critical-thinking skills to answer the following questions.

1. The type of seizure characterized by sustained muscle spasms is **(LO 16.1)**
   A. absence
   B. clonic
   C. tonic
   D. simple partial

2. The preferred drug for treatment of absence seizures is **(LO 16.4)**
   A. primidone
   B. ethosuximide
   C. phenobarbital
   D. trimethadione

3. Hirsutism, gingival hyperplasia, and rash are adverse effects associated with **(LO 16.2)**
   A. valproic acid
   B. carbamazepine
   C. lamotrigine
   D. phenytoin

4. The drug of choice for treatment of status epilepticus is **(LO 16.5)**
   A. fosphenytoin
   B. phenobarbital
   C. lorazepam
   D. valproic acid

5. Fetal hydantoin syndrome is associated with **(LO 16.2)**
   A. diazepam
   B. topiramate
   C. ethosuximide
   D. phenytoin

6. Carbamazepine, phenytoin, and valproic acid all share a common mechanism of action to **(LO 16.2)**
   A. decrease the release of GABA
   B. prolong inactivation of Na^+ channels
   C. increase T-type calcium currents
   D. increase influx of Ca^{++} ions

Multiple Choice (Multiple Answer)

Select the correct choices for each statement. The choices may be all correct, all incorrect, or any combination.

1. Select the main symptoms of a generalized seizure. **(LO 16.1)**
   A. numbness
   B. muscle twitch in the arm
   C. loss of consciousness
   D. purposeless movement

2. What are the mechanisms of action of phenobarbital? **(LO 16.2)**
    A. increase inhibitory effects of GABA
    B. prolong inactivation of sodium channels
    C. block excitatory glutamate receptors
    D. decrease neuronal influx of Na^+

3. Which of the following are mechanisms of action for drugs used for partial seizures? **(LO 16.3)**
    A. inhibit Ca^{++} channels
    B. block neuronal reuptake of GABA
    C. interfere with sodium ions
    D. decrease release of glutamate

4. Which drugs would be considered in the treatment of status epilepticus? **(LO 16.5)**
    A. felbamate
    B. lorazepam
    C. levetiracetam
    D. phenobarbital

5. Select all of the drugs used in the treatment of absence seizures. **(LO 16.4)**
    A. *Zarontin*
    B. *Tridione*
    C. *Paradione*
    D. *Valium*

Classification

Place each drug under the type of seizure for which it is the preferred treatment. **(LO 16.6)**

   Dilantin

   Zarontin

   Ativan

   Valium

   Neurontin

   Keppra

   Felbatol

   Tridione

Generalized tonic-clonic	Partial seizures	Absence seizures	Status epilepticus

Documentation

Using the label provided, answer the following questions.

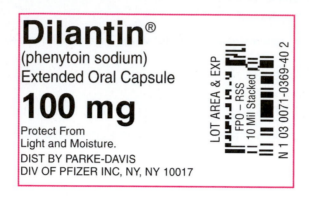

a. What different type of seizures can be treated with this medication?

b. What is the mechanism of action for this medication?

c. If our patient cannot swallow capsules, are there other dosage forms available? What are they?

Labeling

Fill in the missing labels. **(LO 16.2)**

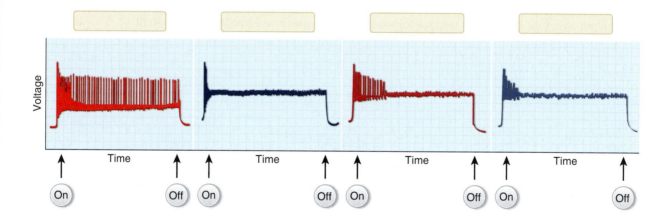

For interactive animations, videos, and assessment, visit:

www.mcgrawhillconnect.com

Chapter 17

Antiparkinson Drugs

DRUG CLASS AT A GLANCE

OTC	NO
PRESCRIPTION	YES
SCHEDULED DRUGS	NO
FDA PREGNANCY CATEGORY	B, C

INDICATIONS
Parkinson's disease, parkinsonism

KEY TERMS

acetylcholine (ACH): excitatory neurotransmitter in the basal ganglia.

basal ganglia: group of cell bodies located within the cerebrum involved in regulation of skeletal muscle tone and body movement.

bradykinesia: slowed body movements.

dopamine: inhibitory neurotransmitter in the basal ganglia.

dyskinesia: abnormal involuntary body movements.

dystonia: muscle spasms, facial grimacing, and other involuntary movements and postures.

on-off phenomenon: alternating periods of movement mobility and immobility.

parkinsonism: symptoms of Parkinson's disease, which include resting tremor, muscle rigidity, and disturbances of movement and postural balance.

Parkinson's disease: movement disorder of the basal ganglia caused by a deficiency of dopamine.

rigidity: a stiffness and inflexibility of movement.

tremor: a trembling and involuntary rhythmic movement.

Learning Outcomes

After studying this chapter, you should be able to

17.1 list the major symptoms of Parkinson's disease.

17.2 explain the relationship between dopamine and acetylcholine in the basal ganglia.

17.3 explain the mechanism of action of levodopa and understand the common adverse effects and different movement disorders that occur over time with this drug.

17.4 identify the mechanism of action of the MAO-B and COMT inhibitors and how they affect levodopa metabolism.

17.5 list the dopamine receptor agonist drugs and explain their mechanism of action and adverse effects.

17.6 explain the therapeutic role of amantadine and the anticholinergic drugs.

The **basal ganglia** are a group of cell bodies (gray matter) located within the white matter of the cerebrum. The major function of the basal ganglia is to help regulate skeletal muscle tone and body movement. The most common disease involving the basal ganglia is **Parkinson's disease**. Parkinson's disease is caused by degeneration of neurons in the substantia nigra (one of the basal ganglia) that produce **dopamine** (DA). The deficiency of DA is the main cause of the symptoms and progression of Parkinson's disease. Some antipsychotic drugs (Chapter 13) that block DA receptors also can cause symptoms of Parkinson's disease; this is referred to as **parkinsonism**. The reason for degeneration of the dopaminergic neurons in Parkinson's disease is not known. However, with aging there is a gradual loss of DA neurons. Environmental factors, genetic predisposition, and destruction by free radicals are a few of the factors that have been linked to the increased destruction of DA neurons. In individuals who develop Parkinson's disease there appears to be an accelerated loss of DA neurons. Parkinson's disease is treated primarily by drug therapy. Although drug treatment is effective in reducing the symptoms of the disease, the disease continues to progress because of the continued destruction of the neurons that produce dopamine. Individuals may eventually become physically disabled, wheelchair bound, and bedridden in the later stages of the disease. In addition to the movement disturbances, there are also a variety of other symptoms. These include hypotension, increased sweating, salivary drooling, and urinary and intestinal disturbances. Also, patients may experience mental depression, anxiety, and other behavioral changes. Several different classes of drugs are used to treat Parkinson's disease. The main therapeutic aim is to administer drugs that increase the activity and concentration of dopamine in the basal ganglia.

LO 17.1 LO 17.2
NEUROTRANSMITTERS AFFECTING THE BASAL GANGLIA

Normal function of the basal ganglia depends mainly upon the interaction between two neurotransmitters: **acetylcholine (ACH)** and dopamine (DA). ACH and DA help regulate the activity of the motor nerves that control voluntary muscle movements. ACH is an excitatory neurotransmitter released by neurons from one of the basal ganglia known as the corpus striatum. ACH increases muscle tone and activity. DA is an inhibitory neurotransmitter released by neurons from another of the basal ganglia, known as the substantia nigra. DA inhibits muscle tone and activity. Parkinson's disease is caused by destruction of the DA neurons in the substantia nigra. The location of the corpus striatum, substantia nigra, and other basal ganglia within the cerebrum can be seen in Figure 17.1.

Normally, the activity of ACH and that of dopamine are balanced, allowing smooth and well-controlled body movements. The deficiency of dopamine in Parkinson's disease disturbs the balance between ACH and dopamine in favor of ACH. The increased activity of ACH produces excessive motor nerve stimulation, resulting in **tremors, muscle rigidity, bradykinesia,** and the other symptoms of Parkinson's disease.

The earliest symptoms of Parkinson's disease are usually **tremor** and muscular rigidity, followed by bradykinesia. The tremors are referred to as "resting tremors" because they only occur when the patient is not moving. Often the initial symptoms appear only on one side of the body but eventually affect both sides. As the disease progresses, the ability to maintain normal posture and balance is affected and the patient may fall. In late-stage disease, the patient may be physically disabled, wheelchair bound, or bedridden. Figure 17.2 summarizes the clinical features, symptoms, and approach to management of an individual with Parkinson's disease.

Several different classes of drugs are used to treat Parkinson's disease and are classified according to their mechanisms of action (Table 17:1).

LO 17.3
LEVODOPA (*DOPAR, LARODOPA*)

In Parkinson's disease, there is a deficiency of dopamine in the basal ganglia. When administered as a drug, dopamine does not readily cross the blood-brain barrier to enter the brain. However, the precursor of dopamine, l-dihydroxyphenylalanine (levodopa or L-DOPA), does cross the blood-brain barrier into the brain. Levodopa is

Figure 17.1 Coronal Brain Section through the Forebrain Showing the Position of the Striatum, Substantia Nigra, and Related Structures

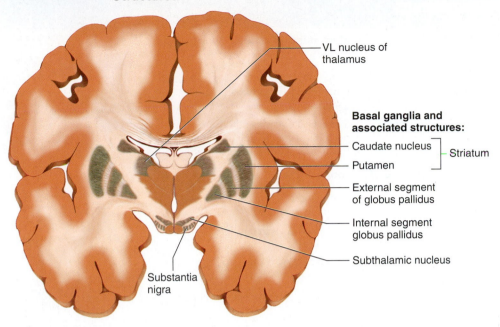

VL nucleus of thalamus

Basal ganglia and associated structures:

Caudate nucleus ⎤ Striatum
Putamen ⎦

External segment of globus pallidus

Internal segment globus pallidus

Subthalamic nucleus

Substantia nigra

Figure 17.2 Summary of the Clinical Features, Symptoms, and Nursing Management Approach for a Patient with Parkinson's Disease

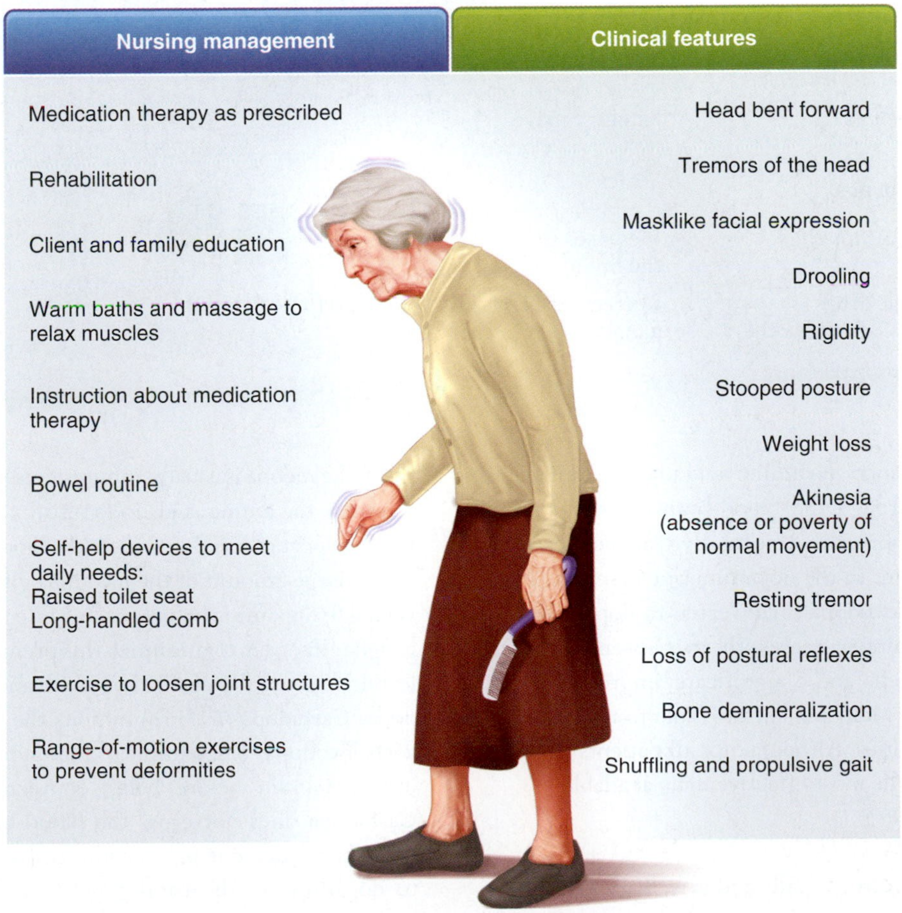

Nursing management	Clinical features
Medication therapy as prescribed	Head bent forward
Rehabilitation	Tremors of the head
Client and family education	Masklike facial expression
	Drooling
Warm baths and massage to relax muscles	Rigidity
Instruction about medication therapy	Stooped posture
	Weight loss
Bowel routine	Akinesia (absence or poverty of normal movement)
Self-help devices to meet daily needs: Raised toilet seat Long-handled comb	Resting tremor
Exercise to loosen joint structures	Loss of postural reflexes
	Bone demineralization
Range-of-motion exercises to prevent deformities	Shuffling and propulsive gait

Antiparkinson Drugs

Drug (*Trade Name*)	Mechanism of action
Drugs that form dopamine	
Levodopa (*Dopar, Larodopa*)	Converted to dopamine in basal ganglia
Levodopa/carbidopa (*Sinemet*)	Same as above plus inhibition of peripheral conversion of l-dopa to DA, more l-dopa enters brain
Drugs that inhibit metabolism of levodopa or DA	
Carbidopa (*Lodosyn*)	Inhibits peripheral conversion of l-dopa to dopamine
Selegiline (*Eldepryl*)	Inhibits MAO-B to increase DA levels in the brain
Rasagiline (*Azilect*)	Inhibits MAO-B to increase DA levels in the brain
Tolcapone (*Tasmar*)	Inhibits COMT in the periphery and brain
Entacapone (*Comtan*)	Inhibits COMT in the periphery
Dopamine receptor agonist	
Bromocriptine (*Parlodel*)	Directly stimulates DA receptors in basal ganglia
Pramipexole (*Mirapex*)	Same as above
Ropinirole (*Requip*)	Same as above
Miscellaneous drugs	
Amantadine (*Symmetrel*)	Increases concentrations of DA in the brain
Anticholinergic drugs benztropine (*Cogentin*), others	Decrease excessive cholinergic activity in basal ganglia

structurally similar to the amino acid phenylalanine and is transported through the blood-brain barrier by the amino acid transporter that normally transports amino acids into the brain. In the dopaminergic neurons of the substantia nigra, levodopa is converted to dopamine. As the level of dopamine increases, there is lessening of parkinsonian symptoms and a significant improvement in physical mobility. Many patients are able to resume normal physical activities. Although not all patients respond to levodopa, it is the most effective drug available.

Pharmacokinetics

Levodopa is administered orally and is well absorbed from the GI tract. The plasma half-life varies between 1 and 3 hours. Levodopa is usually administered on an empty stomach since the amino acids in foodstuffs can interfere with the transport of levodopa across the blood-brain barrier.

A large amount of the levodopa given is rapidly converted to dopamine before passing into the brain and basal ganglia. In order to minimize this premature conversion, levodopa is usually given along with another drug, carbidopa. Carbidopa (*Lodosyn*) inhibits the enzyme that converts levodopa to dopamine so that more levodopa passes into the brain before being converted to dopamine. Carbidopa does not cross the blood-brain barrier and, therefore, does not prevent the conversion of levodopa to dopamine in the basal ganglia. When administered alone without carbidopa, levodopa is mostly metabolized

Figure 17.3

Estimation of the Percentage of Levodopa That Reaches the Brain When Administered Alone (1–3%) versus the Percentage That Reaches the Brain When Administered with Carbidopa (10%)

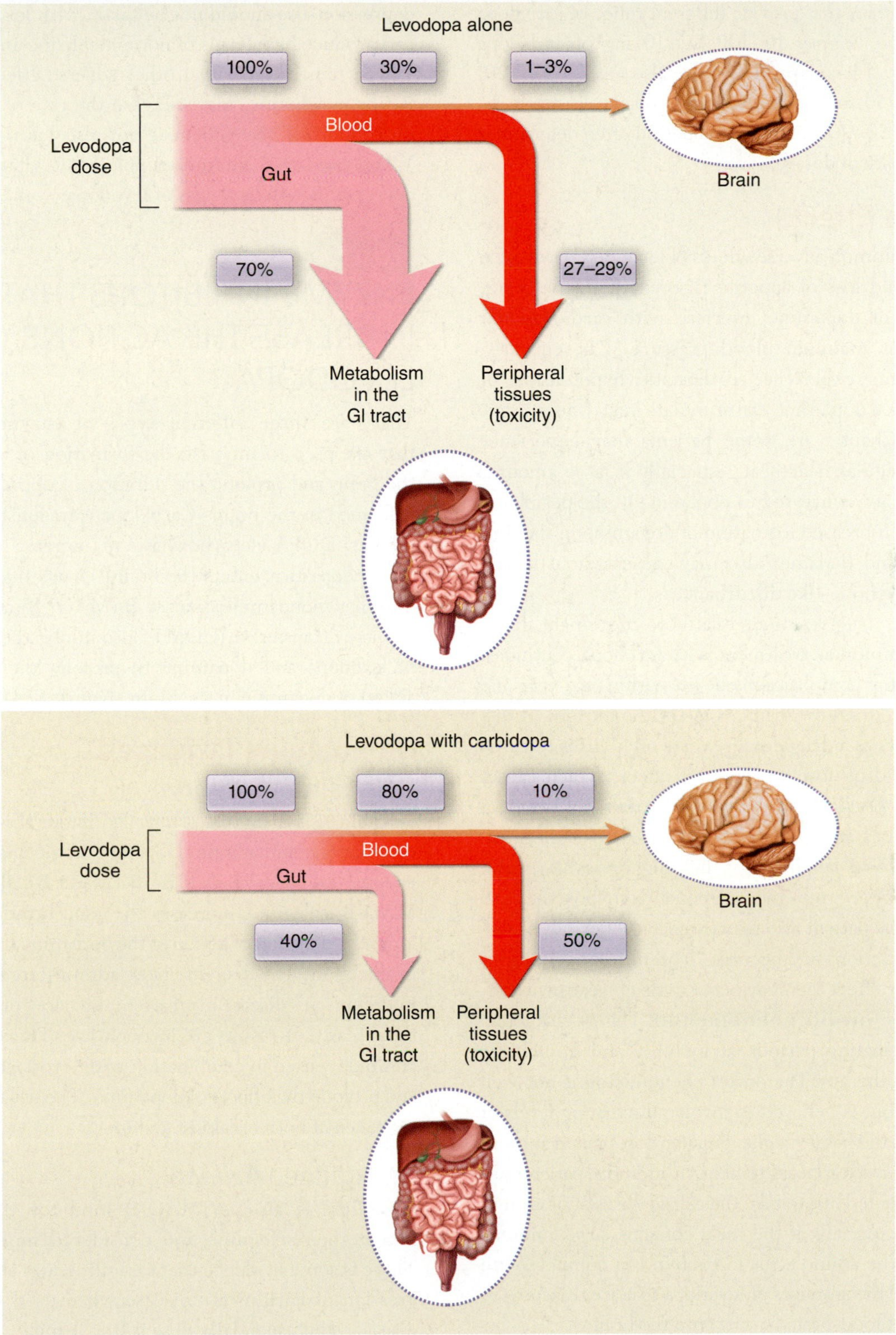

Levodopa alone

| 100% | 30% | 1–3% |

Levodopa dose

Blood

Gut

Brain

70% → Metabolism in the GI tract

27–29% → Peripheral tissues (toxicity)

Levodopa with carbidopa

| 100% | 80% | 10% |

Levodopa dose

Blood

Gut

Brain

40% → Metabolism in the GI tract

50% → Peripheral tissues (toxicity)

in the GI tract and only 1–3 percent of the drug enters the brain. When carbidopa is added, which is standard therapy, the amount of levodopa entering the brain rises to about 10 percent (Figure 17.3). The addition of carbidopa also allows the dosage of levodopa to be reduced, which lowers the incidence of adverse effects.

A combination of levodopa and carbidopa is available under the trade name of *Sinemet,* and is the most widely used drug preparation. There are several different preparations of *Sinemet* that provide different ratios of carbidopa and levodopa. *Sinemet* 10–100 has 10 mg of carbidopa and 100 mg of levodopa. There are also *Sinemet* 25–100, *Sinemet* 25–250, and *Sinemet* CR (controlled release tablets) 25–100 and 50–200. A drug trial period often determines the proper patient dosage.

Adverse Effects

The most common adverse effects of levodopa are nausea, vomiting, and loss of appetite (anorexia). In the brain, high levels of dopamine interfere with cardiovascular reflexes that maintain blood pressure. Consequently, some patients experience orthostatic hypotension or fainting. Since dopamine can stimulate beta-1-adrenergic receptors (Chapter 6), some patients may experience rapid or irregular heartbeat, especially if large amounts of levodopa are converted to dopamine in the peripheral circulation. Increased formation of dopamine in the limbic system and thalamus also may cause various behavioral and psychotic-like disturbances.

Adverse drug reactions related to movement disorders are common as treatment with levodopa continues. Usually motor complications begin within one year and gradually progress over time. One of the movement disorders occurs as a drug dosage wears off. This is referred to as the end-of-dose wearing-off effect, which causes immobility. **Dyskinesias** and **dystonias** can occur at different times but particularly when drug concentrations in the basal ganglia are at their highest levels (peak). These involuntary movements frequently involve the head and neck. The patient also may experience periods of sustained contractions and become "frozen" in one position.

Another effect that may occur as drug treatment progresses is the **on-off phenomenon.** This is characterized by alternating periods of mobility and immobility during drug therapy. The on-off phenomenon is not well understood but is believed to involve fluctuating levels of dopamine in the basal ganglia. Smaller doses taken at more frequent intervals appears to help. In addition, patients are usually instructed not to take their drug doses at or around meal time, especially if the meal contains large amounts of protein. The amino acids in protein can compete with and decrease the amounts of levodopa that are transported through the blood-brain barrier into the brain.

Drug Interactions

A number of drugs interfere with the action of levodopa. The antipsychotic drugs (phenothiazines, haloperidol, drugs that block DA) decrease the effectiveness of levodopa because they block dopamine receptors. This may cause symptoms of Parkinson's disease, referred to as parkinsonism. MAO-A inhibitors used in treating mental depression also should not be taken with levodopa. They can produce high levels of norepinephrine and may cause a hypertensive crisis and other adverse effects. Vitamin B_6, or pyridoxine, may increase the rate of metabolism of levodopa if the patient is not also taking carbidopa. When used as a vitamin supplement, vitamin B_6 may decrease the effectiveness of levodopa.

LO 17.4

ENZYME INHIBITORS THAT INCREASE THE ACTIONS OF LEVODOPA

There are three different types of enzyme inhibitors that are used to increase the formation of dopamine in the brain and prolong the duration of dopamine once it is formed in the brain. Carbidopa (previously discussed) inhibits DOPA decarboxylase to increase the amount of levodopa that enters the brain. Drugs that inhibit the enzymes monoamine oxidase-B (MAO_B) and catechol-O-methyltransferase (COMT) also inhibit the metabolism of levodopa and dopamine to prolong the duration of action of dopamine in the brain (Figure 17.4).

Monoamine Oxidase-B
Selegiline (*Eldepryl*)

Selegiline is a drug that primarily inhibits the metabolism of dopamine in the brain. Dopamine is metabolized by the enzyme monoamine oxidase-B (MAO-B). By inhibiting MAO-B, selegiline increases the concentration and prolongs the duration of action of the dopamine that is formed in the brain. The drug has been administered alone early in Parkinson's disease in an attempt to slow progression of the disease but results are inconclusive. The drug is more commonly used in combination with levodopa to increase and prolong the effects of dopamine. The usual dosage is 5 mg taken at both breakfast and lunch.

Rasagiline (*Azilect*)

Rasagiline is also an MAO-B inhibitor that is more potent then selegiline and considered more effective. There is some evidence that rasagiline may slow the progression of Parkinson's disease when used early in the disease. The usual daily dose is 0.5–1 mg.

Adverse effects of selegiline and rasagiline are associated with increased dopamine levels and are similar to those of treatment with levodopa, but occur with less frequency and intensity. At very high doses these drugs also can inhibit monoamine oxidase-A (MAO-A). MAO-A is the enzyme that primarily metabolizes norepinephrine, epinephrine, and serotonin. Serious drug interactions may occur when selegiline or rasagiline is administered together with either the MAO-A inhibitors or the selective serotonin reuptake inhibitors (SSRIs) used to treat mental depression (Chapter 14).

Catechol-O-Methyltransferase

Catechol-O-methyltransferase (COMT) is another enzyme that normally is involved in the metabolism of dopamine both peripherally and in the brain. Drugs such as tolcapone (*Tasmar*) and entacapone (*Comtan*) inhibit COMT in the periphery and increase the amounts of levodopa that reach the brain. Tolcapone also inhibits COMT in the brain. These drugs are administered with levodopa to increase drug levels and prolong the duration of action of dopamine. A triple combination of levodopa, carbidopa, and entacapone is available under the trade name of *Stalevo;* this combination reduces the number of pills that a patient must take each day.

Adverse effects caused by these drugs are due mostly to increased levodopa and dopamine levels and include nausea, orthostatic hypotension, mental disturbances, and dyskinesias. Tolcapone also can increase liver enzymes, hepatic toxicity, and possible hepatic failure. Use of tolcapone requires a signed patient consent and periodic monitoring of liver function.

Figure 17.4 Inhibition of the Metabolism of Levodopa (L-DOPA) and Dopamine by Drugs That Inhibit Monoamine Oxidase-B (MAO-B), Catechol-O-Methyltransferase (COMT), and DOPA Decarboxylase

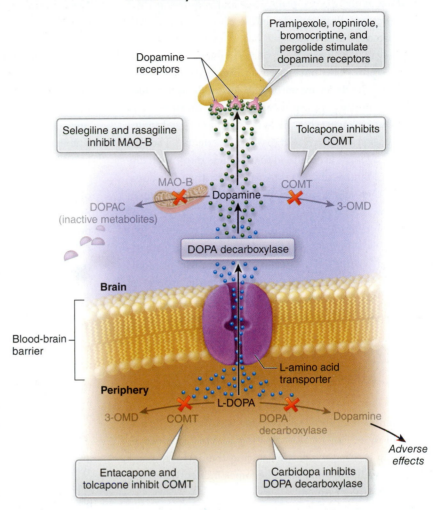

Carbidopa inhibits DOPA decarboxylase, while entacapone and tolcapone inhibit COMT to allow more L-DOPA to enter the brain. Tolcapone also inhibits COMT in the brain. Selegiline and rasagiline inhibit MAO-B to slow the metabolism of dopamine in the brain. Bromocriptine, pramipexole, and ropinirole are dopamine agonists that stimulate dopamine receptors. O-methyldopa (OMD) and dihydroxyphenylacetic acid (DOPAC) are inactive metabolites of L-DOPA and dopamine.

LO 17.5

DOPAMINE RECEPTOR AGONISTS

Dopamine receptor agonists are drugs that enter the brain and bind to and stimulate dopamine receptors in the basal ganglia. These drugs act like levodopa but have longer durations of action. They can be used alone early in treatment or in combination with levodopa as Parkinson's disease progresses. Compared to levodopa, these drugs cause a lower incidence of movement disturbances and dyskinesias. Also, when used with levodopa, there is usually less incidence of the on-off phenomenon and other motor disturbances caused by levodopa.

Bromocriptine (*Parlodel*) was the first DA agonist used in Parkinson's disease and it produces a variety of other pharmacologic effects. In addition to stimulating DA receptors, bromocriptine also stimulates alpha-adrenergic and serotonin receptors, which can cause additional side effects. It is less effective than newer drugs and therefore rarely used today.

Newer dopamine receptor agonists pramipexole (*Mirapex*) and ropinirole (*Requip*) have become the preferred DA receptor agonists. These drugs can be used alone early in Parkinson's disease or in combination with levodopa as the disease progresses and requires greater drug therapy. Pramipexole and ropinirole are usually administered three times per day; however, ropinirole is also available as extended release tablets (*Requip XL*), which requires only once-a-day administration.

Adverse effects are similar to levodopa and include nausea, vomiting, postural hypotension, dizziness, and CNS disturbances that include sleepiness, delusions, hallucinations, and related psychotic effects. The DA receptor agonists are claimed to cause less movement disturbances but more mental disturbances than levodopa. Most of these effects are related to excess stimulation of dopamine receptors.

Apomorphine (*Apokyn*) is another DA receptor agonist that is administered subcutaneously when patients are experiencing the off periods of the on-off phenomenon. Often these patients may be stuck or "frozen" in one position for extended periods of time. Use of this drug requires the supervision of a physician.

LO 17.6

MISCELLANEOUS DRUGS

Amantadine (*Symmetrel*)

Amantadine is an antiviral drug that was accidentally discovered to be beneficial in treating Parkinson's disease. The drug is usually indicated during the early stages of Parkinson's disease and often becomes ineffective after a few months of treatment.

Mechanism of Action

The mechanism of action of amantadine is unclear but believed to involve increased neuronal release of DA and decreased reuptake of DA back into the nerve endings. Both actions increase the amount of DA available to stimulate DA receptors. Amantadine, in oral doses of 100 to 200 mg per day, appears to work best when it is used in the early stages of the disease and in combination with other antiparkinson drugs.

Adverse Effects

The main adverse effects of amantadine are dry mouth, gastrointestinal (GI) disturbances, and a number of CNS effects, usually visual disturbances, dizziness, and confusion. In addition, some patients experience a peculiar type of skin discoloration that clears up when the drug is stopped. The discoloration is referred to as *livedo reticularis*.

Anticholinergic Drugs

Over a century ago, it was observed that anticholinergic drugs such as atropine and scopolamine relieved some of the symptoms of Parkinson's disease. Before the discovery of levodopa, anticholinergic drugs were the main treatment for parkinsonism. When there is a deficiency of dopamine in the basal ganglia, there is excess ACH (cholinergic) activity. By blocking ACH actions, the anticholinergic drugs decrease the level of cholinergic activity. The main therapeutic effects of anticholinergic drugs are to reduce the symptoms of tremor and muscular rigidity.

Atropine and scopolamine produce a high incidence of peripheral anticholinergic side effects. The anticholinergic drugs that act primarily in the brain and that produce a lower incidence of peripheral side and adverse effects are the drugs used. These include benztropine (*Cogentin*), trihexphenidyl (*Artane*), and others. The anticholinergic drugs are listed in Table 17:2.

Clinical Indications

Anticholinergic drugs are less effective than levodopa and the dopamine agonists. In some patients, the combination of levodopa and an anticholinergic drug provides improved results. Anticholinergic drugs also are used in patients treated with antipsychotic drugs who develop parkinsonism. By blocking cholinergic receptors in the basal ganglia, these drugs lower the effects of acetylcholine and help restore the acetylcholine/dopamine balance that is important for normal basal ganglia function. The basic pharmacology of the anticholinergic drugs was previously discussed with the parasympathetic nervous system in Chapter 7. It might be helpful to review this information at this time.

[Table **17:2**]

Anticholinergic Drugs Used in Parkinson's Disease	
Drug (*Trade Name*)	Common daily oral dosage range
Benztropine (*Cogentin*)	0.5–4 mg
Biperiden (*Akineton*)	6–10 mg
Procyclidine (*Kemadrin*)	7.5–15 mg
Trihexyphenidyl (*Artane*)	1–10 mg

Patient Administration and Monitoring

Measure vital signs when possible to detect decreases in blood pressure or increases in heart rate caused by drugs that act through dopamine.

Instruct patients on the importance of following dosing schedules and that missed doses will result in movement difficulties and an increase in parkinsonian symptoms.

Explain to patient the expected side effects of drugs that increase dopamine activity: nausea, dizziness, sleepiness, and occasionally CNS disturbances such as vivid dreams or hallucinations.

Explain to patient the side effects of anticholinergic drugs: dry mouth, constipation, visual disturbances, difficulties

with urination. Remember that these drugs are used with caution in patients with glaucoma, those with prostate hypertrophy, and the elderly.

Warn patients about the end-of-dose effect and the on-off phenomenon that may occur, and to report these occurrences since adjustments in dosage or diet may be helpful.

Warn patients to be extremely careful when engaged in activities where impairment or temporary loss of movement could endanger their safety.

Adverse Effects

The main adverse effects associated with anticholinergic drugs are caused by a decrease in parasympathetic activity. They include dry mouth, constipation, urinary retention, rapid heartbeat, and pupillary dilation (mydriasis).

LO 17.3 LO 17.4 LO 17.5 LO 17.6
PREFERRED THERAPY FOR PARKINSON'S DISEASE

The most effective drug for treatment of Parkinson's disease is the combination of levodopa and carbidopa. However, because of the movement disorders that occur with levodopa over time, levodopa therapy is often delayed in favor of other drugs until symptoms require more effective medications. Age is also a factor; older patients over 65 are often started with levodopa, while younger patients are often started with other drugs.

Treatment of Tremor as Predominant Symptom

In early stages of parkinsonism, tremor and rigidity may be the only symptoms. Often one of the anticholinergic

drugs or amantadine may control these symptoms. In addition, rasagiline (MAO-B inhibitor) also may be considered. Initial treatment with these drugs allows the use of the more potent and effective drugs to be postponed until they are required to treat the more severe symptoms of the disease.

Treatment of Mild-Moderate Disease

As initial symptoms of tremor, rigidity, and bradykinesia worsen, either one of the dopamine receptor agonists or levodopa/carbidopa are added to treatment. Low doses of these drugs are initiated and increased until symptoms are controlled. COMT and MAO-B inhibitors also may be added to levodopa to increase brain drug levels and duration of action.

Treatment of Advanced Disease

In advanced disease increased dosages and more frequent administrations of levodopa/carbidopa are usually required. COMT and MAO-B inhibitors are added if not already prescribed. Dopamine receptor agonists also can be added to the treatment. The severity of disease and patient response often determine which drugs are prescribed.

Chapter Review

Understanding Terminology

Answer the following questions.

___ 1. How are the terms *parkinsonism* and *Parkinson's disease* related? (LO 17.1)

___ 2. Define the terms *dyskinesia* and *dystonia*. (LO 17.3)

Acquiring Knowledge

Answer the following questions.

1. What two neurotransmitters normally control the activity of the basal ganglia? What happens in Parkinson's disease? (LO 17.2)

2. Describe the main symptoms of Parkinson's disease. (LO 17.1)

3. What is the mechanism of action of levodopa? Carbidopa? Selegiline? (LO 17.3, 17.4)

4. List the adverse effects associated with levodopa. (LO 17.3)

5. What drug interactions are possible with levodopa therapy? (LO 17.3)

6. Why are anticholinergic drugs useful in the treatment of Parkinson's disease? (LO 17.6)

7. What side effects are produced by anticholinergic drugs? (LO 17.6)

8. What is the mechanism of action of amantadine (*Symmetrel*)? (LO 17.6)

9. Describe the mechanism of pramipexole (*Mirapex*). (LO 17.5)

Applying Knowledge on the Job

Use your critical-thinking skills to answer the following questions.

1. The local university hospital has a neurological clinic that treats many patients with Parkinson's disease. Why might each of the following patients treated this week at the clinic be prescribed a drug other than *Sinemet*?
   a. Patient A has been taking *Sinemet* for 2 weeks and complains of fainting when getting out of bed, a racing heart, and loss of appetite. (LO 17.3)
   b. Patient B is a self-confessed "health nut" who takes multiple vitamin supplements every day, including all of the B vitamins. (LO 17.3)
   c. Patient C is taking *Marplan* for depression. (LO 17.4)

2. Why might each of the following patients be prescribed a drug other than *Artane*?
   a. Patient A has been taking *Artane* for a week and presents with nausea, constipation, rapid heartbeat, and fever. (LO 17.6)
   b. Patient B is taking haloperidol for Tourette's syndrome. (LO 17.4)

3. Explain why the combination product *Sinemet* is so commonly used in treating Parkinson's disease. (LO 17.3)

4. How do you think taking the combination tablet *Sinemet* would increase patient compliance over taking *Dopar* and *Lodosyn* separately? (LO 17.3)

Multiple Choice

Use your critical-thinking skills to answer the following questions.

1. Symptoms of Parkinson's disease would be increased by **(LO 17.1)**
   A. excess levels of acetylcholine
   B. treatment with some antipsychotic drugs
   C. decreased levels of dopamine
   D. all statements are true

2. The drug classified as a dopamine receptor agonist is **(LO 17.5)**
   A. amantadine (*Symmetrel*)
   B. benztropine (*Cogentin*)
   C. ropinirole (*Requip*)
   D. entacapone (*Comtan*)

3. Select the drugs that increase the duration of action and/or the amount of levodopa that enters the brain. **(LO 17.3, 17.4)**
   A. carbidopa (*Lodosyn*)
   B. tolcapone (*Tasmar*)
   C. selegiline (*Eldepryl*)
   D. all statements are true

4. In Parkinson's disease, slowed movements are defined as **(LO 17.1, 17.2)**
   A. rigidity
   B. bradykinesia
   C. tremor
   D. dystonia

5. *Sinemet* is the trade name of a drug combination that contains **(LO 17.3)**
   A. levodopa, carbidopa, and entacapone
   B. levodopa and entacapone
   C. levodopa and carbidopa
   D. levodopa and selegiline

6. The COMT inhibitor that has been associated with causing liver toxicity is **(LO 17.4)**
   A. ropinirole (*Requip*)
   B. entacapone (*Comtan*)
   C. pramipexole (*Mirapex*)
   D. tolcapone (*Tasmar*)

Multiple Choice (Multiple Answer)

Select the correct choices for each statement. The choices may be all correct, all incorrect, or any combination.

1. Select the symptoms of Parkinson's disease. **(LO 17.1)**
   A. hypertension
   B. decreased sweating
   C. salivary drooling
   D. movement disturbances

2. Choose the correct statements about acetylcholine and dopamine. **(LO 17.2)**
   A. DA inhibits muscle activity
   B. ACH and DA are normally balanced
   C. ACH is an inhibitory neurotransmitter
   D. DA increases muscle tone

3. Which of the following drugs would be used to decrease ACH? **(LO 17.6)**
   A. amantadine
   B. levodopa
   C. bromocriptine
   D. procyclidine

4. Select the mechanisms by which levodopa works. **(LO 17.3)**
   A. crosses blood-brain barrier by an amino acid transporter
   B. converted to dopamine in the neurons
   C. increases level of dopamine
   D. inhibits monoamine oxidase B

5. Select the actions of *Parlodel*. **(LO 17.5)**
   A. stimulates DA receptors
   B. inhibits alpha-adrenergic receptors
   C. inhibits decarboxylase
   D. stimulates serotonin receptors

Sequencing

Place the following mechanisms of action for levodopa in order of the first step to the last. **(LO 17.3)**

_____   _____   _____   _____

First   **Last**

levels of dopamine increase

crosses blood-brain barrier

converted to dopamine

lessening of parkinsonism symptoms

Classification

Put each drug under the correct mechanism of action. **(LO 17.3, 17.4, 17.5)**

entacapone	ropinirole
pramipexole	rasagiline
selegiline	tolcapone

Inhibit MAO-B	Inhibit COMT	Stimulate DA receptors

Matching

Match the following drugs with their correct classifications; each classification may be used more than once (LO 17.4, 17.5)

    a. dopamine receptor agonists
    b. monoamine oxidase inhibitors
    c. catechol-O-methyltransferase inhibitors

1. _____ *Mirapex*
2. _____ *Eldepryl*
3. _____ *Tasmar*
4. _____ *Comtan*
5. _____ *Parlodel*
6. _____ *Azilect*
7. _____ *Requip*

Documentation

Using the prescription below, answer the following questions. (LO 17.5)

Falls Clinic
Practice RX

1000 River Avenue
Anytown, USA   12345
931-555-1000

NAME: ___Bob Jones_____   DATE: _____

ADDRESS: _____

RX   Mirapex 0.25mg   #30

Sig: 1 tablet once daily

Dr L. Hayden_____ M.D.   _____M.D.

  Substitution Permitted   Dispense as written

DEA #: _____   REFILL: NR 1 2 3 4

---

a. What is the drug classification for this particular drug?
b. What is the mechanism of action of this drug?
c. What other medications in this class could be used for once-a-day dosing?

Labeling

Fill in the missing labels. **(LO 17.4)**

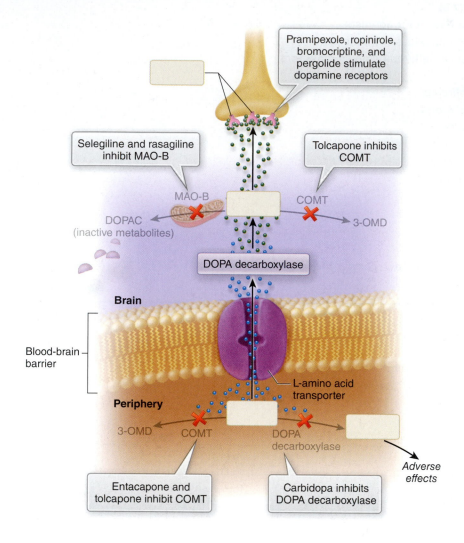

Pramipexole, ropinirole, bromocriptine, and pergolide stimulate dopamine receptors

Selegiline and rasagiline inhibit MAO-B

Tolcapone inhibits COMT

MAO-B

COMT

DOPAC (inactive metabolites)

3-OMD

DOPA decarboxylase

Brain

Blood-brain barrier

L-amino acid transporter

Periphery

3-OMD

COMT

DOPA decarboxylase

Adverse effects

Entacapone and tolcapone inhibit COMT

Carbidopa inhibits DOPA decarboxylase

For interactive animations, videos, and assessment, visit:
www.mcgrawhillconnect.com

Chapter 18

General Anesthetics

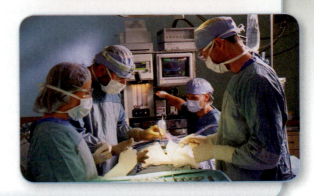

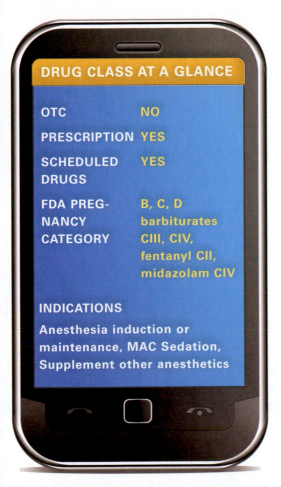

DRUG CLASS AT A GLANCE

OTC	NO
PRESCRIPTION	YES
SCHEDULED DRUGS	YES
FDA PREGNANCY CATEGORY	B, C, D barbiturates CIII, CIV, fentanyl CII, midazolam CIV

INDICATIONS

Anesthesia induction or maintenance, MAC Sedation, Supplement other anesthetics

KEY TERMS

adipose tissue: tissue containing fat cells.

akathesia: continuous body movement in which an individual is restless or constantly paces about.

akinesia: loss of voluntary muscle movement; restless leg movement.

analgesia: decreased response to pain; condition in which painful stimuli are not consciously interpreted (perceived) as hurting.

cation: positively charged ion.

dehiscence: busting open or separation of a wound, usually along sutured line.

dissociative anesthesia: form of general anesthesia in which patients do not appear to be unconscious.

dyskinesia: uncontrollable, involuntary repetitive movements, spastic.

emetogenic: a substance that causes vomiting.

euphoria: feeling of well-being or elation; feeling good.

expectorate: eject from the mouth; spit.

extrapyramidal syndrome: movement disorders such as akathisia, dystonia, and parkinsonism caused by antipsychotic drug therapy.

general anesthesia: deep state of unconsciousness in which there is no response to stimuli, including painful stimuli.

halogenated hydrocarbon: compound that contains halogen (chlorine, fluorine, bromine, iodine) combined with hydrogen and carbon.

hyperpolarized: a change in the cell membrane potential that makes the inside of the cell even more negative, so it can't respond to stimulation.

hyperthermia: abnormally high body temperature.

hypothalamus: center of the brain that influences mood, motivation, and the perception of pain.

hypoxia: reduction of oxygen supply to tissues below the amount required for normal physiological function.

induction of general anesthesia: time required to take a patient from consciousness to Stage III of anesthesia.

maintenance of general anesthesia: ability to keep a patient safely in Stage III of anesthesia.

medullary depression: inhibition of automatic responses controlled by the medulla, such as breathing or cardiac function.

medullary paralysis: condition in which overdose of anesthetic shuts down cardiovascular and respiratory centers in the medulla, causing death.

microcilia: tiny hairs that line the respiratory tract and continuously move, pushing secretions toward the mouth.

neuroleptanalgesia: condition in which a patient is quiet and calm and has no response to pain after the combined administration of an opioid analgesic (fentanyl) and a tranquilizer (droperidol).

neuroleptanesthesia: state of unconsciousness plus neuroleptanalgesia produced by the combined administration of nitrous oxide, fentanyl, and droperidol.

neurotransmitter-gated ion channel: receptor-ion complex in the membrane that opens and allows rapid transmission of signal.

preferred anesthetic: produces adequate anesthesia with minimal side effects.

prodrug: an inactive precursor of a drug, converted into its active form in the body by normal metabolic processes.

synergism: when the action resulting from a combination of drugs is greater than the sum of their individual drug effects.

therapeutic dose: dose at which the desired effect is produced.

Learning Outcomes

After studying this chapter, you should be able to

18.1 identify the various stages of general anesthesia with the physical responses as the central nervous system (CNS) is depressed and define balanced anesthesia and monitored anesthesia care.

18.2 name two classes of general anesthetics by their routes of drug administration and describe the physiological effects associated with their use.

18.3 explain how anesthetics modulate CNS neuronal conduction.

18.4 explain why more than one anesthetic may be administered to provide muscle relaxation without totally depressing the brain.

18.5 describe how volatile liquid anesthetics are excreted from the body and how this differs from the way local anesthetics are excreted.

18.6 explain what an adjunct to anesthesia is and cite two examples of drug adjuncts used with general anesthetics.

18.7 list three side effects and contraindications that may be associated with anesthetic use.

18.8 list the preferred uses of anesthetics.

Introduction

Mild inhibition of cortical activity reduces anxiety, whereas more intense depression of the limbic and reticular systems produces sleep. Sleep is a state of unconsciousness in which stimulation such as yelling or shaking will arouse an individual. **General anesthesia** is a deeper state of unconsciousness (sleep), in which an individual cannot respond to stimulation. During general anesthesia, all sensations are inhibited. Because sensations are suppressed, general anesthesia is used primarily to prevent the reactions to painful stimuli associated with surgery.

GENERAL ANESTHESIA

Drugs discussed in the previous chapters selectively depress the central nervous system (CNS). General anesthesia agents are a diverse group of drugs that abolish pain by modulating the function of the CNS at various sites.

The extent of CNS depression under general anesthesia is much greater than that produced by other CNS depressant drugs (tranquilizers, sedatives, and hypnotics) at **therapeutic doses.** All of the major areas of the CNS are suppressed except for the medullary centers that regulate the vital organs (heart and lungs). An anesthesiologist controls the delicate balance between the beneficial effects of anesthesia and **medullary depression,** which can result in medullary paralysis and death.

Signs and Stages of Anesthesia

General anesthesia is produced by gradually depressing the CNS. The sequence of depression is divided into four stages, as illustrated in Figure 18.1. During Stage I, the cerebral cortex is gradually inhibited. This stage is characterized by a decreased response to pain **(analgesia),** a

Note to the Health Care Professional

Because the anesthetics used today move quickly from Stage I to Stage III, most patients will not exhibit signs of the excitation phase. Occasionally this phase may be observed in children during induction and emergence from anesthesia when mask induction anesthesia is used. Being aware of this keeps the observer alert to potential safety issues in the recovery period.

feeling of **euphoria** (well-being or elation), and a loss of consciousness (sleep).

Once the cerebral cortex is fully depressed, Stage II is achieved and the **hypothalamus** assumes control of body functions. Stage II is known as the "excitement phase" because there is an overall increase in sympathetic tone. Blood pressure, heart rate, respiration, and muscle tone increase during this stage. During Stage II, cardiac arrhythmias may occur. Eventually, respiration becomes

---

Figure 18.1   **Signs and Stages of Anesthesia with CNS Depression**

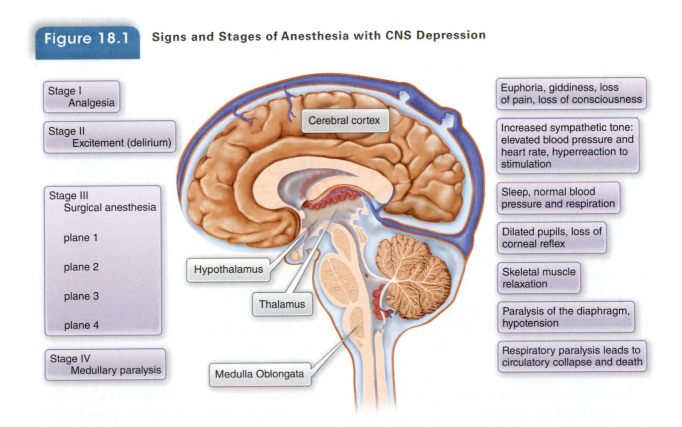

Stage I
Analgesia

Stage II
Excitement (delirium)

Stage III
Surgical anesthesia

plane 1

plane 2

plane 3

plane 4

Stage IV
Medullary paralysis

Cerebral cortex

Hypothalamus

Thalamus

Medulla Oblongata

Euphoria, giddiness, loss of pain, loss of consciousness

Increased sympathetic tone: elevated blood pressure and heart rate, hyperreaction to stimulation

Sleep, normal blood pressure and respiration

Dilated pupils, loss of corneal reflex

Skeletal muscle relaxation

Paralysis of the diaphragm, hypotension

Respiratory paralysis leads to circulatory collapse and death

more regular as excitation is inhibited. This change in respiratory pattern is an indication that patients are in Stage III.

Stage III is usually referred to as surgical anesthesia because surgery is most efficiently performed at this level of general anesthesia. Stage III is divided into four planes (1–4) that reflect the progressive depth of CNS depression. During this stage, cardiovascular and respiratory functions return to normal, spinal reflexes are inhibited, and skeletal muscles are relaxed. Surgical incisions can be made throughout Stage III without producing pain or skeletal muscle contraction.

Stage IV is the phase of **medullary paralysis.** This stage represents an overdose of general anesthetic, in which cardiovascular and respiratory centers in the medulla are inhibited and death occurs.

The clinical signs associated with each stage of general anesthesia vary with the general anesthetic being used. Some anesthetics produce excellent analgesia at Stage I, while others do not produce any analgesia until Stage III. However, most anesthetics used today are capable of producing Stages III and IV anesthesia as just described. An anesthetic that produces all stages of general anesthesia (I, II, III, and IV) is a *complete* anesthetic. To be clear, Stage IV is not a therapeutic objective. To keep the patient in Stage III and not Stage IV reflects the skill and experience of the anesthesiology team.

Induction and Maintenance

Induction of general anesthesia is the time required to take a patient from consciousness to Stage III. **Maintenance of general anesthesia** is the ability to keep a patient safely in Stage III. The depth of anesthesia is continually monitored by vital signs, body temperature, ECG, EEG, and general observation of the patient. The methods of continuous monitoring may include computer-assisted devices. The ideal general anesthetic would produce rapid induction and slow maintenance without entering Stage IV anesthesia. In addition, recovery from the ideal general anesthesia would occur rapidly without side effects.

Unfortunately, there is no ideal general anesthetic. Some anesthetics are excellent for induction (nitrous oxide, thiopental, and fentanyl citrate-droperidol), whereas others are better for maintenance of general anesthesia. Also, all anesthetics are associated with side effects. Today, anesthesiologists usually employ a combination of anesthetics to meet the needs of surgeons and to minimize patient reaction. (See balanced anesthesia below.) Rapid, smooth induction with well-controlled maintenance is the key to good general anesthesia.

Types of Anesthesia

There are three major categories of anesthesia: local anesthesia, Monitored Anesthesia Care (MAC), and general anesthesia.

Local anesthesia inhibits pain sensation in a specific area of the body. (See Chapter 10 for detail including regional anesthesia and nerve block.) The individual remains conscious; sensory nerve conduction is inhibited, but motor neurons are not affected; and sensory nerve function returns to normal (reversible) within minutes to hours of administration.

Monitored Anesthesia Care refers to intravenous sedation with midazolam, followed by propofol and/or fentanyl. These drugs rapidly induce a sleepy state where the patient is calm and less responsive to pain before or during a procedure. Diagnostic and surgical procedures that do not require the patient to be unconscious also may use local anesthetics for nerve block to facilitate completion of the procedure. *Conscious sedation* is a specific term that describes the state where the patient can speak and answer questions but has an altered state of awareness and minimal response to pain when intravenous opioid analgesics and sedatives are administered. The depth of sedation can be light enough to permit patient interaction to instructions or questions, or deep enough that the patient cannot be aroused easily during the procedure. The critical word in this type of anesthesia is *monitored*. The intravenous anesthetics used in this ambulatory setting have special instructions to alert medical personnel to the need for specific observation, evaluation, and electronic monitoring of the patient through the recovery period. For methohexital and midazolam, continuous monitoring of respiratory (e.g., pulse oximetry) and cardiac function is recommended. Resuscitative drugs and age- and size-appropriate equipment for bag/valve/mask ventilation and intubation must be immediately available and personnel trained in their use and skilled in airway management should be present. Monitored Anesthesia Care is used in ambulatory surgical centers for minor fracture repair, foot surgery, dental and cosmetic reconstructive surgery, biopsy, and endoscopy (colonoscopy).

General anesthesia produces a loss of consciousness in which the patient is totally unaware of pain and does not remember (amnesic) the surgical events or diagnostic procedures on awakening. Another commonly used term to describe anesthesia is *balanced anesthesia*. Balanced anesthesia is a strategy whereby more than one anesthetic plus muscle relaxants and antianxiety drugs are used to induce and maintain anesthesia. The objective is that each drug complements the action of the anesthetic acting at different target sites and requires less absolute CNS depression than a single anesthetic used alone.

The anesthesia team and surgical environment in the "not too old days" was a picture of a physician-trained anesthesiologist and a designated room within a hospital specially equipped with monitors and inhalation delivery systems (see Figure 18.2). While this still can be appropriate today, there are many different opportunities for surgery to be performed and general anesthetics to be used outside the hospital. It is fairly common today for anesthesia to be administered for surgical and diagnostic procedures in three areas: a hospital or medical center, an ambulatory surgical center, or a doctor's or dentist's office.

The type and complexity of the surgical procedures that have moved from the hospital to ambulatory care centers are, in part, a result of improvement in office-based technology (equipment, advanced trained staff) and the need to accommodate patient same-day return to home. It certainly reflects the tremendous increase in elective and cosmetic surgi-centers. The anesthesiology team may be a physician, probably Board certified (American Board of Anesthesiology), nurse, and anesthesia technician. Or it may be a graduate-level advanced trained nurse anesthetist (CRNA, Certified Registered Nurse Anesthetist) or a dental professional. License to administer this class of drugs varies from state to state and continues to be debated, specifically about non-anesthesiologist administration of propofol (see Internet Connection www.endonurse.com). This evolution in the anesthetic arena is important to mention because it points to many places the full range of anesthetics are experienced and employed today.

This chapter will focus on drugs with a primary therapeutic action to produce general anesthesia and those drugs that are used in Monitored Anesthesia Care and balanced anesthesia.

Figure 18.2

Inhalation Anesthesia

GENERAL ANESTHETICS

General anesthetics are administered by inhalation or intravenous injection. These routes provide rapid delivery of the drug into the blood, which facilitates a smooth induction into anesthesia. General anesthetics' lipid solubility allows them to dissolve in the blood for distribution to other tissues. Eventually, general anesthetics are carried to the CNS, where lipid solubility permits access across membranes so that the primary pharmacological effect can be produced. The degree of CNS depression resulting in anesthesia is related to the concentration of the anesthetic in the brain.

Inhalation Anesthetics

Inhalation anesthetics include volatile liquids such as ether and **halogenated hydrocarbons** and gases such as nitrous oxide (see Table 18:1). It's worth mentioning that ether and chloroform appear in Table 18:1 because of their special place in the anesthesiology hall of fame. For example, the signs and stages of anesthesia were worked out from observation of ether's gradual CNS depression. If sevoflurane had been the anesthetic prototype, the elaborate stages and planes would not have been observed because sevoflurane moves so rapidly to Stage III. By the way, many of the volatile anesthetics used today are ethers. Chloroform is interesting because many murder mysteries and horror films still show the villain placing gauze soaked in something over the victim's nose and mouth to subdue him or her. It's chloroform, not sevoflurane! While ether and chloroform have been replaced by newer, relatively more manageable anesthetics, their legacy is still with us. The volatile liquids (halogenated hydrocarbons) are vaporized for inhalation. Those routinely used as general anesthetics include enflurane (*Ethrane*), desflurane (*Suprane*), halothane (*Fluothane*), isoflurane (*Forane*), and sevoflurane (*Ultane*). These anesthetics are inhaled through the nose and mouth by means of a face mask (see Figure 18.2). Air (oxygen) must be included in the anesthetic mixture or patients will rapidly develop **hypoxia.** Anesthesiologists control the anesthetic mixture and rate of delivery of throughout the surgical procedure. Inhalation anesthetics are delivered to the alveoli and then to the blood for distribution to the tissues.

These drugs have solubility characteristics where some drugs are more soluble in the blood and like staying there (volatile liquids), or they are not very soluble

Side Effects and Uses of General Anesthetics

Anesthetic (*Trade Name*)	Use	Effect on respiratory system	Nausea & vomiting
Inhalation anesthetics—volatile liquids			
Chloroform—prototype historical reference	Obsolete	Seldom	Moderate
Desflurane (*Suprane*)	Maintenance	Highly pungent, irritating, laryngospams in children, bronchodilating	Low
Ether—prototype historical reference	Maintenance	Frequently, increases secretions	High
Enflurane (*Enflurane, Ethrane*)	Maintenance	Less pungent, some irritation and secretions; bronchodilator	Low
Isoflurane (*Forane*)	Maintenance	Less pungent, some irritation and secretions; bronchodilator	Low
Halothane (*Fluothane*)	Maintenance	Less pungent, some irritation and secretions; bronchodilator	Low
Sevoflurane (*Ultane*)	Maintenance	Bronchodilator, no pungency	Low
Inhalation anesthetics—gases			
Nitrous oxide	Induction	—	Low
Injectable anesthetics			
Etomidate (*Amidate*)	Induction	Bronchospasm, laryngospasm, coughing	High
Fentanyl citrate and droperidol—CII*	Induction	Seldom secretions, laryngospasms	Low
Fospropofol (*Lusedra*)	MAC** sedation	Increased salivation seldom	Low
Ketamine (*Ketalar*)—CIII	Induction maintenance MAC	Salivation and laryngospasm	High
Methohexital (*Brevital, Methohexital*)—CIV	Induction maintenance MAC	Bronchial secretions, bronchospasms, laryngospasms	Moderate
Midazolam (*Versed*)—CIV	Preoperative sedation induction MAC	Increased salivation and bronchospasm seldom	Low
Propofol (*Diprivan*)	Induction maintenance MAC	Increased salivation seldom	**Antiemetic**
Thiopental (*Pentothal*)—CIII**	Induction	Coughing, bronchospasm, salivation	Low–moderate

*Scheduled drug indicated by CII, CIII, or CIV. **MAC is monitored anesthesia care.*

in the blood and can't wait to move out of the blood (nitrous oxide, desflurane, sevoflurane). This solubility characteristic is called the blood:*gas partition coefficient.* The greater the number value of this coefficient (halothane 2.3, enflurane 1.8), the more soluble the drug is in the blood. Nitrous oxide and desflurane are 0.47 and sevoflurane is 0.69. The less soluble drugs have a quicker onset of action because the drugs are ready to cross into the CNS as soon as the circulation gets them there. The more soluble anesthetics have a longer onset of action because they require more anesthetic to dissolve in the blood before enough drug molecules are available to cross into the brain. Once in the CNS, the anesthetics modulate neuronal membranes to produce a state of anesthesia.

All of the inhalation anesthetics except nitrous oxide produce all stages of general anesthesia; therefore, they can be used for induction and maintenance of general anesthesia. Nitrous oxide ("laughing gas"), although it gets there faster, is not potent enough to maintain Stage III, Plane 3 anesthesia. (That's just the way it is!) It can be used only for induction of general anesthesia. However, nitrous oxide produces such good analgesia that it is frequently used alone for dental procedures or in combination with other anesthetics.

Potency of these drugs is measured by the amount of drug (concentration of drug) in the alveoli that produces a specific effect. The smallest alveolar concentration of drug that keeps the patient immobile reflects the potency of the drug. The standard reference for inhaled anesthetics is MAC or median minimum alveolar concentration that keeps 50 percent of the patients from moving in response to a surgical stimulus (e.g., incision). Of course, the objective is to keep 100 percent of the patients from moving during surgery and this is what the anesthesiologist controls. Remember nitrous oxide? It is not a potent *anesthetic* because it requires more than 100 percent minimum alveolar concentration to immobilize 50 percent of patients, but it can be incorporated with other anesthetics because it's a terrific analgesic and less of the second anesthetic would be needed. The volatile liquids all have small MAC numbers like 0.75 percent or 2 percent, indicative of their greater potency. This is an oversimplified description of MAC and blood:gas partition coefficient. It is not intended to explain the physics of gas exchange but to introduce terminology associated with inhalational anesthetics.

At the end of the procedure, the face mask is removed and patients quickly exhale the inhalation anesthetics. As a result of exhalation, the blood drug level falls and the patients begin to recover from anesthesia.

Injectable Anesthetics

Injectable anesthetics include the barbiturates (methohexital, thiopental), etomidate (*Amidate*), ketamine (*Ketalar*), midazolam (*Versed*), diazepam (*Valium*), lorazepam (*Ativan*), and propofol (*Diprivan*) (see Table 18:1 for injectable anesthetics). Propofol has a significant record of acceptance as an agent for induction, sedation, and maintenance of general anesthesia. It has supplanted the contribution barbiturates made for many years because it has a rapid onset of action and a relatively uncomplicated recovery period. The barbiturate anesthetics can be used for induction or maintenance of general anesthesia. These drugs are usually administered intravenously because extravascular injections cause pain, swelling, and ulceration. The other injectable drugs in this group (etomidate, midazolam, diazepam, lorazepam) are primarily used for sedation or analgesia (ketamine).

Barbiturates

Two drugs are used for rapid intravenous induction of anesthesia and prior to face mask placement for inhalation anesthesia to avoid patient discomfort and experiencing irritation of the upper airway. Thiopental (*Pentothal*) and methohexital (*Brevital*) are ultrashort-acting barbiturates that induce general anesthesia within 30 seconds. Because thiopental is highly fat soluble, it is redistributed to fatty tissues. The drug accumulates in **adipose** (fat) **tissue** and leaves the tissue so slowly that it takes some time for these anesthetics to become metabolized and excreted into the urine. As the anesthetic leaves the adipose tissue, it is redistributed to other organs. Redistribution of the drug leads to residual CNS depression (hangover), mental disorientation, and nausea during the recovery period. Methohexital is more efficiently cleared by the liver and does not result in the same degree of tissue redistribution. It has a shorter elimination half-life and a quicker complete recovery than thiopental. It is the preferred drug among the barbiturates used for anesthesia.

Barbiturate anesthetics do not produce analgesia at any dose. In fact, they have been associated with an increased sensitivity to pain when pain is present called hyperalgesia. They are associated with the same side effects and contraindications as other barbiturates (their adverse effects were discussed in Chapter 12). Barbiturate anesthetics may cause laryngospasm or bronchospasm during the postoperative recovery period. It is important to observe patients carefully because they may choke or aspirate fluid into the lungs. An absolute contraindication to the use of thiopental or methohexital is a history or predisposing evidence of *status asthmaticus* or porphyria.

Methohexital is a Schedule IV and thiopental a Schedule III controlled substance because the drugs have a lower potential for abuse, dependence, or addiction relative to the drugs in Schedules I or II and there is an accepted medical use in the United States.

Benzodiazepines

Midazolam: Midazolam (*Versed*) is a more potent short-acting CNS depressant in the benzodiazepine family (diazepam [*Valium*], chlordiazepoxide [*Librium*], and lorazepam [*Ativan*]). It is the drug of choice when a parenteral benzodiazepine is required. It is available for intravenous or rectal administration. The rectal route of administration is particularly useful with uncooperative or agitated children to avoid exacerbating the emotional state because of a fear of needles.

Midazolam is frequently administered intravenously prior to short diagnostic or endoscopic procedures to produce conscious sedation and is a standard component in Monitored Anesthesia Care. Midazolam is used for sedation and amnesia and given with neuromuscular blocking drugs for endotracheal intubation. Midazolam is also used for induction of general anesthesia before administration of other anesthetics or to supplement nitrous oxide.

Midazolam has been used to reduce emergence agitation following sevoflurane anesthesia. It is chosen over lorazepam and the other benzodiazepines because it has a shorter half-life and no active metabolites to extend the pharmacological effects. Metabolism occurs in the liver and is inhibited by concomitant use of grapefruit juice or ethanol. Midazolam has a rapid onset of action and rapid redistribution to tissues other than the CNS. It produces no analgesia even at anesthetic doses but does provide adequate amnesia. It is metabolized to active metabolites in the liver, which increases its duration of action. Postoperative sedation may be less than the other benzodiazepines; however, it is dependent on the duration of administration, which is directly related to accumulation in tissue during long procedures. Midazolam is given as an oral preanesthetic medication for regional anesthesia and brief therapeutic procedures. Because of the CNS depressant action, preanesthetic opioid medications will potentiate the hypnotic effect of all benzodiazepines. All of these drugs are Schedule IV controlled substances because the drugs have a low potential for abuse, dependence, or addiction relative to the drugs in Schedules I, II, and III and there is an accepted medical use in the United States.

The benzodiazepines are the only anesthetic class that have a specific receptor antagonist, flumazenil (*Romazicon*). Flumazenil competitively inhibits the activity at the benzodiazepine recognition site on the GABA receptor. It does not antagonize the effects of any other drugs interacting at other sites on the GABA receptor (barbiturates, volatile anesthetics, or propofol). Flumazenil will reverse the sedative effects of benzodiazepines when an overdose has occurred. Although it has been well tolerated in healthy volunteers and patients who are not dependent on benzodiazepines, it will precipitate withdrawal symptoms in patients who are benzodiazepine dependent. It has caused seizures that are treatable with barbiturates. The association with seizures is a special boxed warning to alert medical personnel to customize the dose to the patient and be prepared to manage seizures if they occur. It is completely metabolized and excreted within 72 hours.

Nonbarbiturates

Etomidate: Etomidate (*Amidate*) is a nonbarbiturate hypnotic drug used for intravenous induction of anesthesia. It is not used for continuous infusion or maintenance anesthesia. Etomidate has no analgesic activity and produces postoperative nausea and vomiting (PONV); however, it exerts less depressant effects on the heart and respiratory centers than do the barbiturates. Because of its cardiorespiratory profile, this drug may be advantageous for use in high-risk surgical patients who cannot tolerate tissue depression. Etomidate is not water soluble and is, therefore, prepared in propylene glycol. This solvent is responsible for causing intense pain on injection. Lidocaine application at the injection site can eliminate this reaction. Etomidate has a rapid onset of action and tissue redistribution limits the duration of action. It is metabolized in the liver to inactive metabolites and excreted by the kidney. While this might contribute to less hangover effect during recovery, etomidate produces nausea and vomiting. Also, it inhibits an enzyme required for the biosynthesis of cortisol in the adrenal gland and cortisol blood levels are reduced during exposure to etomidate. There does not appear to be a significant impact on cortisol synthesis after recovery; however, these side effects often limit the selection of the drug as a maintenance anesthetic. Etomidate is not a restricted drug on the Controlled Substances List.

Ketamine: Ketamine (*Ketalar*) is a short-acting nonbarbiturate **dissociative anesthetic** that produces good analgesia even at nonanesthetic doses and loss of memory (amnesia) but does not relax skeletal muscles. In fact, ketamine increases muscle tone. Patients appear to be awake, eyes are open with alternating smooth and fast object tracking (nystagmus), limbs may move, but they do not respond to painful stimulation. Ketamine inhibits the excitatory pathway by a direct interaction with the NMDA receptor (see Mechanism of Action). It is thought to act primarily upon the limbic system so that very little respiratory and cardiovascular depression is produced. In fact, ketamine stimulates the sympathetic nervous system so blood pressure and heart rate may be elevated during the anesthesia. (See Physiological Effects below for ketamine's cardiovascular activity). Ketamine is not the anesthetic of choice in patients where a significant increase in blood pressure would be hazardous. Ketamine relaxes bronchioles and is a good anesthetic for patients with asthma or bronchospasms.

Ketamine has an onset of action within 3 minutes and a duration of 20 minutes from a single administration. Low-dose ketamine combined with either midazolam or propofol is administered before injection of local anesthetics in outpatients undergoing a variety of surgical procedures. This short-acting anesthetic is rapidly metabolized in the liver to mildly active metabolites. It can be given intramuscularly or intravenously to induce anesthesia. Vivid dreams and hallucinations usually occur during the recovery period and can last for 24 hours after ketamine administration. This occurs most often in adults. Children experience this less frequently and with a milder reaction. Other ketamine-induced effects include out-of-body experiences, increased auditory sensitivity, and euphoria. In a small percentage of patients, delirium occurs (emergence delirium). This is a sudden state of severe confusion with rapid changes in brain function, sometimes associated with hallucinations. Severe reactions are treated with benzodiazepines or short-acting barbiturates. Another ketamine-induced effect is an increase in intraocular pressure, making it not the anesthetic of choice for ocular surgery. Ketamine is chemically related to phencyclidine, a hallucinogen of high abuse potential. Ketamine does appear as a street drug for nonmedical, recreational use. Ketamine is a Schedule III drug because its potential for abuse is less than the drugs in Schedules I and II, it has an accepted medical use in the United States, and abuse of the drug may lead to moderate or low physical dependence or high psychological dependence.

Propofol: Propofol (*Dipravan*) is the most commonly used parenteral anesthetic in the United States. Propofol was first introduced as a sedative-hypnotic and has since frequently replaced barbiturates as the sedative-hypnotic of choice in the anesthesia forum. Propofol is used to initiate and maintain MAC sedation during diagnostic and surgical procedures. It is used for MAC sedation in conjunction with local or regional anesthesia. It is also used for induction or maintenance of anesthesia as part of a balanced anesthetic technique for inpatient and outpatient surgery in adults and children at least 3 years of age. As a complete anesthetic it is able to fully depress the medulla, resulting in death. Like all complete anesthetics, it has a narrow margin of safety; the pharmacologic dose is only a few cc's from the lethal dose. This is especially true to propofol.

Propofol is not water soluble and, therefore, is prepared as an emulsion in soybean oil, glycerol, and purified egg phosphatide. The drug rapidly reaches the CNS with an onset of action in a few seconds. Propofol is used in subanesthetic doses for conscious sedation, but it is not regarded as an analgesic. Occasionally, during induction, there is muscle twitching attributed to an invoked excitatory response. Propofol does depress cardiovascular and respiratory activity similar to or greater than the barbiturates. Hypotension is more prominent than with other anesthetics because it decreases vascular resistance by inhibiting sympathetic tone on vascular smooth muscle, depresses the baroreceptor response to hypotension, and depresses cardio contractility. When used in subanesthetic doses for conscious sedation, propofol depresses the reflex response to increased carbon dioxide and reduced oxygen. These are expected effects with a complete anesthetic and not the reason it is the most used parenteral anesthetic.

Propofol does not rely on tissue redistribution for recovery but is cleared by the liver to inactive metabolites and excreted by the kidney. The duration of action is short, being controlled by readministration of the drug at safe intervals or continuous infusion. There is no hangover effect from tissue redistribution and active metabolites. Recovery to a clear mental state with no nausea and vomiting and minimal respiratory or cardiac depression is shorter compared to other anesthetics. Unique among the anesthetics, propofol is the only anesthetic that is antiemetic. Evidence in the literature demonstrates that patients who received propofol don't develop nausea and vomiting up to 72 hours after exposure, and analgesic consumption and recovery time are reduced. This profile makes propofol an excellent anesthetic for outpatient procedures in all types of surgical settings and contributes to its popularity.

There are some undesirable effects associated with propofol such as pain on injection attributed to a reaction to the emulsifiers. This can be avoided by administering lidocaine with propofol. Strict aseptic technique during handling is required because the vehicle is capable of supporting bacterial growth. Fever, infection, life-threatening illness, and death have occurred due to contamination and patient inoculation. Sodium metabisulfite or EDTA has been added to propofol prefilled syringes and single-use vials to inhibit bacterial growth. The sodium metabisulfite may produce an allergic reaction in sensitive individuals and asthma patients.

At this time, propofol is not a controlled substance; however, the abuse among medical health care professionals has been the basis for placing a brand new sedative-hypnotic, fospropofol, into Schedule IV.

Fospropofol (*Lusedra*) has recently (December 2008) been introduced for MAC sedation in patients undergoing diagnostic or surgical procedures. It is a water-soluble **prodrug** for propofol prepared in a preservative-free solution. The goal was to replace the lipid base and the associated irritant reaction and microbial growth environment yet retain adequate delivery of the active drug. Following intravenous injection, alkaline phosphatases, present in all tissues, convert fospropofol to propofol. While there is a molecule-for-molecule conversion, it appears that the converted propofol is more potent (on EEG and clinical signs of hypnosis) than the one delivered in a lipid emulsifier. Liberated propofol has shorter distribution and elimination half-lives compared to the lipid-formulated propofol. There is variability in the response to a given dose so that dose titration to the drug effect is needed, but there is a delay in observation of the pharmacological effect. This provides an opportunity for administering more drug too soon and overdosing the patient.

Fospropofol is a water-soluble intravenous preparation; however, it might be taken orally as a liquid, making it much easier to abuse than the propofol emulsion, especially as a potential street drug. This is the reason the FDA recommended fospropofol be classified as a controlled substance. Studies investigating the recovery profile of propofol have reported that patients anesthetized with propofol wake up elated, euphoric, and feeling refreshed. Laboratory studies confirm that subanesthetic doses of propofol increase dopamine in the areas of the brain associated with reward and reinforcement behavior, like other Schedule IV drugs. Because of the shorter half-life, repeat dosing may be reinforced, creating a "stacking effect" and potential overdose.

Medical professionals don't usually take the drug to get high because it puts them instantly to sleep. Instead, it is taken to relieve stress; users wake up feeling refreshed. Dependence from propofol is mostly psychological, characterized by craving, loss of control over the amount and frequency of drug required to achieve the desired effect, and continued use despite adverse consequences. Physical dependence has not been identified, although withdrawal phenomena have been reported after prolonged use.

Alpha$_2$ Adrenergic Agonist

Dexmedetomidine (*Precedex*) is a novel drug that is used for short-term procedural sedation. It is a potent α_2 adrenergic agonist. Receptors for alpha$_2$ are found in the peripheral and central nervous systems, platelets, and a variety of organs, including the liver, pancreas, kidney, and eye. Responses mediated by these receptors vary with location. Presynaptic activation of the alpha$_2$ adrenergic receptor suppresses calcium entry into the nerve terminal and inhibits the release of norepinephrine, terminating the propagation of pain signals. Postsynaptic activation of α_2 adrenergic receptors in the CNS inhibits sympathetic activity, resulting in decreased blood pressure and heart rate. Together these effects produce analgesia, sedation, and reduced anxiety. When used during induction, dexmedetomidine potentiates the anesthetic effects of intravenous, volatile, and regional block anesthetics. It also reduces the requirement for supplement opioid analgesics and midazolam. This means less individual sedative, analgesic, or anesthetic is required to achieve the good anesthesia and without additional respiration depression.

The benefits of dexmedetomidine continue in its activation of receptors in other areas. Decreased salivation, decreased GI secretion and bowel motility, increased glomerular filtration, and decreased insulin release from the pancreas are some of its stress-reducing effects in the perioperative period. This drug is administered by continuous infusion so the onset of action is fast and the duration of action after termination of the infusion can be up to 4 hours. The drug is completely metabolized in the liver and its metabolites excreted in the urine and feces. The most frequent adverse effects that occur with dexmedetomidine are hypotension, bradycardia, and dry mouth, which warrant close monitoring through the recovery period.

Dexmedetomidine is used for procedural sedation. It is also used for sedation of initially intubated and mechanically ventilated patients during treatment in an intensive-care setting. It should be administered by continuous infusion not to exceed 24 hours.

Opioids and Droperidol

When a mixture of an opioid analgesic (fentanyl) and a tranquilizer (droperidol) is administered, **neuroleptanalgesia** is produced. This type of anesthesia provides excellent analgesia while patients remain conscious. This combination cannot produce unconsciousness (**neuroleptanesthesia**) unless a third anesthetic (nitrous oxide) is added. Fentanyl is one of the drugs selected for use in balanced anesthesia and conscious sedation. Fentanyl is a rapid-acting synthetic opioid effective in blunting the sympathetic reflex response to laryngoscopy and intubation. Fentanyl and droperidol are eventually metabolized by the liver. Unusual side effects that occur with the use of droperidol are extrapyramidal symptoms. Occasionally, a parkinsonian syndrome—uncontrolled movements of the tongue and head—occurs. The fentanyl and droperidol may be administered intramuscularly or by slow intravenous injection. If an opioid analgesic is prescribed following this kind of anesthesia, the dose of the opioid may be significantly reduced to one-fourth of the recommended dose because these drugs have a synergistic action on the CNS. Droperidol has a special warning (black box) associated with its use because it has been reported to lengthen the QT interval in the heart, potentially predisposing patients to the development of fatal cardiac arrhythmias. Fentanyl is a Schedule II drug because it has a high potential for abuse and may lead to severe psychological or physical dependence. It has a currently accepted medical use in the United States.

LO 18.3

MECHANISM OF ACTION

All general anesthetics are CNS depressants, but how neuronal function is modulated differs with each drug. This class is so dissimilar in chemical structure that it was believed for a long time that these drugs could not interact with receptors, certainly not an individual receptor. In fact, it was held that interference with CNS conduction by anesthetics was probably due to the ability of the drug to cross the blood-brain barrier (lipid solubility) and alter the membrane dynamic (perturb the membrane). During the past several years, there has been a dramatic change in understanding of the mechanism of action of anesthetics. Not only do anesthetics interact with a variety of receptors, the interaction at multiple receptors can **synergize** (enhance) the anesthetic effect when drugs are used in combination to maintain anesthesia.

There is considerable evidence that most general anesthetics inhibit CNS activity by interacting with membrane ion channels **(neurotransmitter-gated ion channels),** especially through activation of gamma-amino butyric acid (GABA) receptors. GABA is the principal inhibitory neurotransmitter within the brain, and glycine is the inhibitory transmitter in the brainstem and spinal cord. The GABA receptors are a superfamily of membrane-bound proteins (see Figure 18.3). When GABA and glycine bind to their respective receptors, pores (ion channels) open through the lipid membrane, allowing passive movement of small ions. This ion movement changes the potential across the membrane, affecting conductivity of the cell.

General anesthetics bind with the $GABA_A$ (inhibitory) receptor and cause chloride ions (Cl^-, negative ion) to move across the membrane into the cells, making the membrane **hyperpolarized** (can't respond to stimulation). This decreases neuronal membrane "excitability." $GABA_A$ receptors are continually active, so anything that interacts with them has a continual response. Inhaled anesthetics, benzodiazepines, barbiturates, etomidate, and propofol bind with $GABA_A$ receptors and enhance the GABA hyperpolarization. The barbiturates and propofol also may directly increase the chloride ion channel opening sustaining the GABA inhibitory action. These anesthetics enhance the inhibitory (GABA, glycine) pathways.

Besides the inhibitory GABA receptor system, anesthetics may interface with membrane pore proteins that facilitate potassium ion (K^+) movement. Throughout the CNS are potassium ion channels. When potassium ions move out of the cell, membranes are hyperpolarized, inhibiting depolarization.

Another way to depress CNS function is to inhibit the excitatory neurotransmitter, glutamate, in the brain. The NMDA (*N*-methyl *D*-aspartate) receptor is a glutamate receptor that facilitates positive ion (**cation,** Na^+, Ca^{++}, K^+) movement through its channel, depolarizing the postsynaptic cell (excitation). Nitrous oxide, propofol, and ketamine antagonize NMDA receptors, thereby blocking cation movement and depolarization.

Figure 18.3

General Anesthetic Sites of Drug Action on GABA and NMDA Receptors

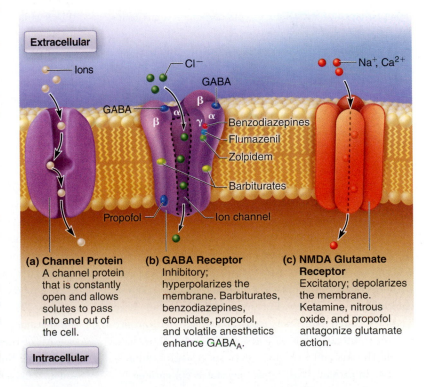

(a) Channel Protein A channel protein that is constantly open and allows solutes to pass into and out of the cell.

(b) GABA Receptor Inhibitory; hyperpolarizes the membrane. Barbiturates, benzodiazepines, etomidate, propofol, and volatile anesthetics enhance $GABA_A$.

(c) NMDA Glutamate Receptor Excitatory; depolarizes the membrane. Ketamine, nitrous oxide, and propofol antagonize glutamate action.

These drugs also enhance the opioid mu receptors, which will be discussed in Chapter 19 on opioid analgesics.

Volatile anesthetics modulate both excitatory and inhibitory synaptic transmission. The most potent inhaled agents and most intravenous agents enhance the inhibitory $GABA_A$ and glycine receptors and depress other excitatory neuronal nicotinic acetylcholine (ACH) receptors. When intravenous and inhalation anesthetics are used together, there is a clinical benefit to the patient. The minimal alveolar concentration of the volatile anesthetics required to induce anesthesia is less when intravenous anesthetics are enhancing the inhibitory receptors and antagonizing excitatory receptors.

LO 18.2 | LO 18.7

PHYSIOLOGICAL EFFECTS OF ANESTHETICS

The primary therapeutic action of inhalation and injectable anesthetics is on the CNS, for the patient to be in an anesthetic state. At low doses or low concentrations in the blood, these drugs relieve anxiety and produce sedation. At the appropriate drug level to produce anesthesia, however, all of these drugs also influence a variety of other tissues. Selection of the proper anesthetic may depend on evaluating the drug's spectrum of actions such as alteration of cardiac, respiratory, or hepatic function.

Central Nervous System

The primary nonanesthetic effects of general anesthetics on the CNS involve regulation of cerebral blood flow, change in intracranial pressure, and seizure induction.

Inhalation Anesthetics

In general, all nervous tissue is depressed by inhalation general anesthetics. Voluntary (motor) and involuntary (autonomic) systems are inhibited in the state of surgical anesthesia. These drugs dilate cerebral blood vessels and may increase intracranial pressure. This group of anesthetics might not be a good choice for use in patients who already have increased intracranial pressure from cerebral edema or tumors, except that the drugs vary in their effect on cerebral blood flow. Halothane produces the greatest increase in intracranial pressure. Isoflurane, desflurane, enflurane, and sevoflurane are associated with less intracranial pressure elevation and are drugs of choice for neurosurgery. Enflurane and sevoflurane have been associated with increased seizure activity and are not recommended for patients with seizure disorders, but desflurane and isoflurane have successfully reduced seizures in patients with refractory status epilepticus.

Injectable Anesthetics

Methohexital, propofol, etomidate, midazolam, diazepam, and lorazepam decrease intracranial pressure and cerebral blood flow. With barbiturates this is considered a protective effect against local cerebral ischemia. It may be an advantage with any of these drugs when used in neurosurgery. Ketamine increases intracranial pressure and cerebral blood flow. This may be a contraindication to its use in patients with increased intracranial pressure. Only ketamine, barbiturates, and benzodiazepines have anticonvulsant activity because they hyperpolarize neuron membranes through their respective receptor interactions (see Figure 18.3). This has a beneficial seizure suppressant action during surgery.

Respiratory System

Respiratory function is depressed through a central action by most anesthetics (but not ketamine). With inhalation anesthetics oxygen deprivation during the procedure does not occur because ventilation is controlled by the anesthesiologist. Residual effects of anesthetics may result in postoperative ventilatory failure and hypoxia. Impaired respiratory control may be caused by depression of central ventilatory control, by depression of peripheral sensory organs (carotid body chemoreceptors), or by impaired control of the pharynx and the upper airways. On the other side the discussion is how muscle spasms within the respiratory system impact other critical tissues such as the brain. Stimulation of the airway causes a sympathomimetic reflex response, whether there is physical contact with implements (laryngoscope) or an anesthetic-induced spasm. This stimulation can result in a transient increase in intracranial pressure (ICP). Simply coughing and gagging may facilitate transmission of intrathoracic pressure to the cranium. The principal issues with drug-induced interference in the respiratory system involve residual postoperative hypoxia, the production of secretions, and muscle spasms along the respiratory tract.

Inhalation Anesthetics

All of the volatile liquid anesthetics are good bronchodilators because they directly relax bronchiolar smooth muscle. They inhibit smooth muscle contractility and interrupt neural conduction involved in the reflex spasticity. This can be of value for patients with a history of chronic obstructive pulmonary disease, bronchitis, or asthma. These anesthetics have been used to treat status asthmaticus when other treatments were not effective.

All of these anesthetics *except sevoflurane* irritate the respiratory lining, causing coughing, increased salivary and mucus secretions, and laryngospasm. Pungency is the term used to describe this characteristic ability to irritate the respiratory tree. Desflurane is the most pungent, strong airway irritant in conscious patients. Studies have reported that study participants pull off the mask and complain about the irritation after a few breaths. For this reason, an intravenous anesthetic is used to induce anesthesia, and then desflurane maintenance follows.

All of the drugs in this class *except sevoflurane* stimulate mucus secretion. Increase in saliva and mucus secretions is important because secretions can interfere with the transfer of gases from the alveoli to the blood and impact oxygenation. These drugs also inhibit the **microcilia** that line the respiratory tract to move secretions. This further complicates the clearance of secretions. Sevoflurane is an anesthetic of choice for induction with an inhalation agent because it lacks pungency, has no irritating effects on the respiratory tree, and does not promote secretion production. It also doesn't depress the heart (see below).

Injectable Anesthetics

Benzodiazepines and barbiturates produce a dose-dependent respiratory depression. These drugs decrease respiratory rate and tidal volume. Benzodiazepines (midazolam) exert relatively less depression than the barbiturates, which can produce transient apnea. Barbiturates can cause a deep depression of the medullary respiratory center. Patients with underlying chronic obstructive pulmonary disease are more susceptible to the depression, even at doses that would be considered therapeutic in healthy individuals. Fatality from barbiturate and benzodiazepine overdose is usually secondary to respiratory depression. Reflex responses to increased carbon dioxide (hypercarbia) and decreased oxygen (hypoxia) are depressed. This effect persists in the postoperative recovery period so patients must be closely monitored to ensure adequate ventilation is not compromised. Barbiturates lightly depress laryngeal reflexes so that any stimulation (secretions, intubation) can result in coughing and laryngospasm. Histamine, released from mast cells by these drugs, produces bronchospasm. These drugs are used with caution in patients with preexisting airway resistance conditions. Etomidate has the same respiratory profile as the barbiturates.

Propofol is a respiratory depressant just as described for barbiturate anesthetics. It dampens the response to hypoxia and hypercarbia and can produce apnea. Unlike the other drugs, it is not associated with histamine release and it depresses reflexes associated with coughing and spasms. This means wheezing, coughing, and bronchospasm are less common with this drug and it can be safely used in asthmatic patients.

Ketamine dilates bronchial smooth muscle and maintains muscle tone and respiratory reflexes. This is valuable in the recovery period as the patient's chemoreceptors will respond appropriately to stimuli of hypoxia or hypercarbia. Ketamine does not produce respiratory depression, unlike all the other anesthetics, and is often selected as an alternative to opioids (respiratory depressants) when analgesia is required. Ketamine does increase tears and salivation, which could precipitate laryngospasms, but this is not a significant problem with its use. Ketamine is the induction agent of choice in patients with bronchospasm. Studies have shown that when ketamine is used in patients with asthma who are dependent on ventilators, respiratory acidosis and airway pressures are decreased.

Cardiovascular System

The myocardium (heart muscle) and blood pressure may be depressed by general anesthetics. However, the degree of depression varies with the anesthetic used. Blood pressure may decrease because sympathetic tone is inhibited, whereas heart rate may increase due to vagal inhibition. Occasionally, catecholamines are secreted from the adrenal medulla in response to the stress of surgery. These circulating catecholamines may counteract the myocardial depression of the anesthetic or ventricular arrhythmias may occur because some anesthetics sensitize the heart to the catecholamine stimulation.

Cardiovascular depression may occur following depression of the medullary vasomotor centers; patients with underlying congestive heart failure (CHF) are more susceptible to these effects. At higher doses, cardiac contractility and vascular tone are compromised, which may cause cardiovascular collapse.

Inhalation Anesthetics

In general, all of these drugs produce peripheral vasodilation and decrease blood pressure. The decrease in blood pressure is proportional to the amount of drug in the lung (alveolar concentration). To decrease blood pressure, either the heart is depressed (reduced cardiac output) or the peripheral vascular musculature is relaxed (peripheral vasodilation). Desflurane, sevoflurane, and isoflurane depress the peripheral vasculature to reduce blood pressure. With these drugs there is no reduction in cardiac output. In fact, these drugs may produce a transient increase in heart rate. Isoflurane and desflurane can cause transient tachycardia and hypertension through stimulation of the sympathetic nervous system. This can be a positive factor for selection of these anesthetics in patients already predisposed to hypotension. Enflurane and halothane have a primary effect on the cardiac muscle. These drugs depress cardiac contractility and cardiac output, resulting in lower blood pressure. Halothane directly sensitizes the myocardium to catecholamine stimulation, which can predispose the patient to cardiac arrhythmias. Nitrous oxide produces less myocardial depression than the volatile anesthetics and desflurane and sevoflurane are associated with minimal to no myocardial depression.

Injectable Anesthetics

Benzodiazepines have little effect on the cardiovascular system or autonomic nervous system compared to other anesthetics. Methohexital and propofol produce a decrease in blood pressure because of peripheral vasodilation and decreased myocardial contraction. The decrease in blood pressure is dose related and produced whether using a large single dose or continuous infusion of the drug. The change in blood pressure is usually counteracted by autoregulation (baroreceptor reflex) through the sympathetic nervous system; however, barbiturates and propofol also depress the baroreceptor reflex. This contributes to the development of hypotension. Propofol causes more pronounced hypotension than the barbiturates. In healthy patients, this is generally manageable and without significant sequelae. Etomidate has a different profile. Etomidate has no depressant effect on blood pressure or cardiac output and mildly increases heart rate. It also decreases oxygen consumption by the heart but does not alter coronary perfusion. This means the heart isn't working as hard. This drug may be favored for its cardiostability and, for this reason, can be selected for patients with coronary artery disease or cardiomyopathy. The unique property of acutely decreasing intracranial pressure while maintaining normal hemodynamics places etomidate in a class by itself among induction agents.

Ketamine increases heart rate, blood pressure, and cardiac output by stimulating the sympathetic nervous system. It also increases oxygen consumption of the myocardium.

Skeletal Muscle

Depression of pyramidal systems and spinal reflexes causes skeletal muscle relaxation in Stage III (Plane 3) anesthesia. Certain anesthetics produce additional skeletal muscle relaxation by inhibiting neuromuscular function. Acetylcholine is prevented from interacting with skeletal muscle membrane–bound receptors.

Inhalation Anesthetics

All volatile anesthetics produce a dose-related relaxation of skeletal muscle. When used alone, inhalation anesthetics facilitate muscle incision and manipulation through relaxed tone exerted at the muscle receptor level. They potentiate the neuromuscular blockade of concomitantly administered depolarizing and nondepolarizing neuromuscular blocking drugs. This may delay recovery of muscle function and coordination. In the postoperative period, assisted ventilation may be required if muscle weakness persists, with the potential for causing airway obstruction and aspiration. Nitrous oxide does not relax skeletal muscle; it has been reported to increase skeletal muscle tone.

Injectable Anesthetics

Benzodiazepines inhibit spinal afferent pathways to produce skeletal muscle relaxation. These drugs are used to interrupt excessive contractions in spasticity disorders and dyskinesias. The site of interaction on the GABA receptor is at a locus separate from that which produces sedation and hypnosis. Propofol does not potentiate neuromuscular blockade of the neuromuscular blocking drugs, while ketamine increases skeletal muscle tone.

Nausea and Vomiting (PONV)

Postoperative nausea and vomiting (PONV) are the most common side effects associated with the use of general anesthetics. PONV is evaluated as three types of patient responses. *Nausea* is the feeling or urge to vomit without **expectorating.** *Vomiting* is oral expulsion of gastric contents. *Retching* is an unproductive effort to vomit. These events can range from mildly annoying nausea to increasing severity of muscle involvement (contraction of the stomach, abdomen, intercostals, larynx, and pharynx) accompanied by increased salivation, vasomotor disturbance, and sweating. The importance of controlling or avoiding these physiological responses ranges from making the patient more comfortable to interruption of potential cardiovascular and vasomotor changes resulting from vomiting-induced dehydration and electrolyte changes.

Anesthetic agents increase the sensitivity of the vestibular center in the inner ear. Rapid position change or movement of a sensitive patient may lead to the development of PONV. When a person becomes disoriented due to motion, the vestibule sends a signal through nerves to the vomiting center in the brain, and vomiting occurs. These effects frequently occur during recovery, making patients uncomfortable and predisposing the patient to potential aspiration. There is evidence that volatile anesthetics are **emetogenic** (induce vomiting) and that there are no meaningful differences between halothane, enflurane, isoflurane, sevoflurane, and desflurane.

Among the injectable anesthetics, etomidate is the most likely to produce PONV.

Propofol is the only anesthetic to have evidence of reducing PONV. Used alone or in combination with other inhalation or intravenous anesthetics, propofol has been reported to reduce the incidence of PONV. It is characterized as an antiemetic among anesthesiologists, although it is not used for that purpose in other medical areas. (See further discussion of antiemetics under Adjuncts to General Anesthesia).

Hepatic and Renal Systems

Inhalation Anesthetics

While volatile anesthetics are exhaled as a route of elimination from the body, most of these drugs and the intravenous anesthetics are metabolized to some extent in the microsomal enzyme system of the liver. The volatile anesthetics temporarily reduce renal and hepatic blood flow, glomerular filtration, and urine output. Other than the temporary inhibition in urine output, there are usually no significant residual effects associated with anesthetic use and renal and hepatic functions. These drugs are used in patients with renal or hepatic disease.

The most significant and *not frequent* event associated with volatile anesthetics is hepatitis. There are two types of postoperative residual effects on liver function: Type I, mild, and Type II, severe hepatitis. Type I is a self-limiting event associated with elevated liver transaminases, lethargy, fever, and nausea in 10 to 20 percent of patients. This mild hepatitis is attributed to an alteration in hepatic blood flow during surgery reducing oxygenation to the hepatocytes. Type II is a life-threatening condition in which liver necrosis occurs and death may ensue. Type II is an immunologic-mediated condition that requires that the patient had to have previously been exposed to a volatile anesthetic resulting in antibody production. The volatile anesthetics, except for sevoflurane, are metabolized in the liver to trifluoroacetate (TFA). In the rare case (1 in 30,000 patients), TFA irreversibly binds to hepatocyte proteins and becomes recognized as a foreign agent to which antibodies are made. There is no diagnostic test to determine which patients are predisposed to developing hepatitis. The occurrence is unrelated to the type or duration of surgery and occurs more frequently in women over 40 years old. Fever, rash, and jaundice may not appear for up to 2 weeks after exposure. A thorough medical history indicating prior evidence of hepatic dysfunction during the course of the recovery on exposure to volatile anesthetics is the only way to identify a potential occurrence of hepatitis. Volatile anesthetics are contraindicated in patients with a known sensitivity to these anesthetics. Despite the infrequent occurrence of hepatitis (first associated with halothane), the availability of other anesthetics has virtually replaced halothane use. Desflurane and sevoflurane have very little association with drug-induced Type II hepatitis.

Injectable Anesthetics

Most of these drugs are metabolized to some degree by the microsomal enzyme system in the liver. Elimination of the drug and its effects depends on the liver and kidneys. In general, there is little effect on these organs. Barbiturates reduce the glomerular filtration rate and hepatic blood flow during their anesthetic activity, but organ function returns to its preexposure state at the end of the procedure.

LO 18.6

ADJUNCTS TO GENERAL ANESTHESIA

In addition to the anesthetic agents, a variety of different drugs are routinely used before and after surgical procedures, as outlined in Table 18:2. Preanesthetic and postanesthetic medications are administered to aid induction of general anesthesia, counteract the side effects of anesthetics, or make recovery safe and more comfortable for patients. Many people approach surgery with fear and apprehension; usually there is intense anxiety about the existing medical problem and concern about the outcome of the operation. Some individuals also experience severe pain as a result of their medical condition. Anxiety and CNS stimulation tend to counteract a smooth induction into anesthesia. Therefore, CNS depressants, such as opioid analgesics, benzodiazepines, tranquilizers, or sedative-hypnotics may be administered before surgery. Often, these adjunct medications are given the evening before so that patients are groggy and unaware of the preparations being carried out prior to surgery. For procedures in an ambulatory or dental surgery setting, the preanesthetic protocol, other than fasting, bowel cleansing, or discontinuance of medications, may begin on site.

Postoperative Nausea and Vomiting (PONV)

Postoperative nausea and vomiting are definitely unwanted events associated with the anesthesia. It is reported to occur in 70 to 80 percent of patients at high risk to develop PONV, and up to 35 percent of all patients. Many patients complain about PONV from a prior procedure or surgery, ranking it among the top three postoperative events they do not want to experience again. Efforts to optimize the prophylactic treatment (preanesthesia) for PONV have identified several

Adjunct Medications Used with Anesthetics

Pharmacological class	Administration	Reason for use
Analgesics (opioid)	Preanesthesia, postanesthesia	Relieve pain and produce sedation
Antianxiety agents (benzodiazepines)	Preanesthesia	Decrease apprehension
Antiarrhythmic drugs	During surgery	Control arrhythmias
Antibiotics	Preanesthesia	Decrease infection
Anticholinergics	Preanesthesia, during surgery	Decrease salivary and bronchial secretions, prevent bradycardia
Antiemetics	Preanesthesia, postanesthesia	Block postoperative nausea and vomiting
Cholinergic drugs	Postanesthesia	Relieve urinary retention
Sedative-hypnotic drugs (short-acting agents)	Preanesthesia	Decrease apprehension
Skeletal muscle relaxants	Beginning of procedure, During surgery	Facilitate endotracheal intubation Sustain skeletal muscle relaxation
Tranquilizers	Preanesthesia, postanesthesia	Sedation, control nausea and vomiting

factors associated with patients at risk: female gender, obesity, a history of PONV or motion sickness, anticipated use of opioids or large doses of neostigmine, type of surgery and anesthetic, and duration of the procedure. PONV is almost always self-limiting and nonfatal, but it can induce dehydration, electrolyte imbalance, suture tension and **dehiscence,** and life-threatening airway compromise. Each vomiting episode delays discharge from the recovery room and, when ambulatory care centers are considered, may result in an unplanned overnight admission rather than a same-day return to home. This impacts patient satisfaction, comfort, and procedural expense.

Induction of vomiting is a well-orchestrated interaction involving two control centers (vomiting center and chemoreceptor trigger zone) and at least five neurotransmitters such as serotonin, acetylcholine, dopamine, histamine, and substance P and their respective receptors located in the control centers (see Figure 18.4). Among the afferent inputs to the vomiting center is direct information from the vagus (cholinergic) nerve relaying conditions in the gastrointestinal tract (distension), the vestibular system relaying conditions from the inner ear regarding balance and motion, and the chemoreceptor

trigger zone (CTZ) assessing noxious chemicals in the circulation. Information about a harmful environment, ingestion of toxic substances, or accumulation of metabolic toxins triggers the release of these neurotransmitters in the vomiting center and CTZ. This may bring about coordinated contraction of abdominal and respiratory muscles to expel the culprit through the mouth.

Dopamine D_2 Antagonists

The drugs that have shown the best efficacy as antiemetics in the perioperative period antagonize specific receptors in the vomiting center or CTZ. For years, droperidol was the gold-standard preanesthetic antiemetic. It is effective in low doses as a single agent antiemetic for prophylaxis and treatment and inexpensive compared to the newer receptor-specific alternatives such as serotonin antagonists. Droperidol is a tranquilizer sedative that is a strong dopamine D_2 receptor antagonist. The hypothesis is that droperidol occupies the postsynaptic GABA receptor so that dopamine accumulates in the synapse. This alters the normal balance between acetylcholine and dopamine and inhibits CTZ transmission to the vomiting center. It is extensively metabolized and excreted in the urine and feces. The best antiemetic

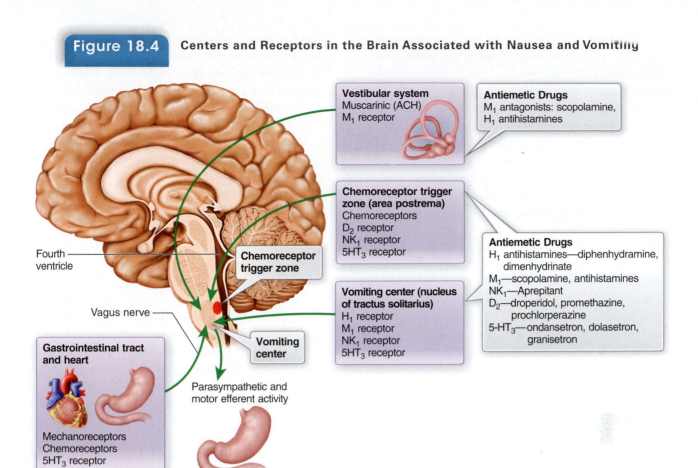

Vestibular system
Muscarinic (ACH)
M_1 receptor

Antiemetic Drugs
M_1 antagonists: scopolamine,
H_1 antihistamines

Chemoreceptor trigger zone (area postrema)
Chemoreceptors
D_2 receptor
NK_1 receptor
$5HT_3$ receptor

Antiemetic Drugs
H_1 antihistamines—diphenhydramine,
    dimenhydrinate
M_1—scopolamine, antihistamines
NK_1—Aprepitant
D_2—droperidol, promethazine,
    prochlorperazine
$5\text{-}HT_3$—ondansetron, dolasetron,
    granisetron

Vomiting center (nucleus of tractus solitarius)
H_1 receptor
M_1 receptor
NK_1 receptor
$5HT_3$ receptor

Fourth ventricle

Chemoreceptor trigger zone

Vagus nerve

Vomiting center

Gastrointestinal tract and heart

Mechanoreceptors
Chemoreceptors
$5HT_3$ receptor

Parasympathetic and motor efferent activity

Nausea, vomiting

effect is observed when droperidol is given at the end of surgery, rather than as a preanesthetic medication. Its onset of action after intramuscular injection is 3 to 5 minutes and its duration of action is 4 to 12 hours.

Although still available as a generic formulation, droperidol use has declined since its cautionary warning regarding a potential association with fatal cardiac arrhythmia. It should be noted that challenges were made to distance the potential of life-threatening cardiac arrhythmia from droperidol through its otherwise relatively uneventful history of fatal arrhythmia during its use estimated as fewer than 10 fatal arrhythmias in 1 million patients treated. While the caution remains in the drug labeling instruction for use, droperidol is still considered among the choices for first-line therapy of PONV. Droperidol is not the antiemetic of choice for patients predisposed to developing cardiac arrhythmia or changes in cardiac function. Otherwise the adverse effects include drowsiness, sedation, and hypotension; because it's an alpha-adrenergic receptor blocker in the vascular smooth muscle and CNS, **akathesia** and, rarely, **extrapyramidal syndrome (dyskinesias, akinesia)** occur. The akithesia and extrapyramidal symptoms are related to the dopamine effect.

Serotonin ($5HT_3$) Antagonists

The serotonin antagonists, first-line therapy for PONV, include ondansetron (*Zofran*), dolasetron (*Anzemet*), and granisetron (*Kytril, Granisol*). These serotonin receptors are located on vagal nerve terminals, neurons in the GI tract, where they regulate GI secretions, colon motility, and transmission of visceral pain, and centrally in the CTZ (see Figure 18.4). There is a high degree of receptor specificity as the ($5HT_3$) antagonists do not interact with other serotonin receptors, or with cholinergic or dopamine receptors. Ondansetron has an effective duration of 4 to 6 hours, whereas granisetron has a duration of about 12 to 14 hours. An oral disintegrating tablet has been developed for ondansetron to be used at home following discharge. This class of drugs seems to have a ceiling effect so that continued dosing in the presence of unresolved PONV does not further reduce the symptoms. Subsequent treatment strategy is to move to another type of antiemetic agent. These drugs are well absorbed orally, metabolized in the liver, and excreted in the urine and feces. Dolasetron has an effect on cardiac conduction observed as prolongation of the PR and QT_c intervals (as with droperidol) and QRS widening, all attributed to blockade of sodium channels. It is worth noting that there is no cautionary warning (black box) that accompanies the use of this drug. Nevertheless, patients with hypokalemia or hypomagnesemia, patients taking diuretics with the potential for inducing electrolyte abnormalities, patients with congenital QT syndrome, and patients taking antiarrhythmic drugs or other drugs that might lead to QT prolongation are not candidates for receiving dolasetron. The other (5HT$_3$) antagonists exhibit this blockade of sodium channels and delayed conduction to a lesser degree. The most common side effects of the 5HT$_3$ receptor antagonists are sedation, headache, dizziness, and anxiety.

Neurokinin (NK$_1$) Antagonists

A new area in antiemetic drug design is inhibition of substance P (neurokinin, NK$_1$) receptors. Substance P mediates a number of biological effects including nausea, anxiety, pain, and vasodilation. It is found in areas of the brain that regulate emotion, in the spinal cord, and in endothelial cells in the small intestine. For sure there are substance P and NK$_1$ receptors in the vomiting center. It's a major neurotransmitter along with acetylcholine and serotonin. Aprepitant (*Emend*), an antiemetic, is the first of this kind of receptor antagonist to be approved for PONV. It also is used in prevention of nausea and vomiting from highly emetogenic cancer chemotherapy agents like cisplatin. Aprepitant is highly selective for the NK$_1$ receptor and has no ability to block serotonin, cholinergic, dopamine, or steroid receptors. Yet, even with this high degree of selectivity, the drug has to be taken before nausea and vomiting begin. This drug is for prevention, not treatment, of nausea and vomiting. A single dose of 40 mg is given orally within 3 hours of induction. The drug is metabolized in the liver to several weakly active metabolites and excreted in the urine and feces. Side effects may include fatigue, dizziness, headache, constipation, and hiccups.

Miscellaneous Antagonists

More recent evidence has shown that propofol (*Diprivan*) or dexamethasone (*Decadron*) is effective prophylaxis for PONV. Dexamethasone is a corticosteroid that is at least as effective as droperidol and the serotonin antagonists when used as a single agent early in the anesthesia regimen. It is given orally, 8 mg, within 2 hours of anesthesia and prevents PONV up to 72 hours. There do not appear to be significant side effects with its short-term use. It offers a replacement for droperidol when it comes to PONV prophylaxis, but it has no role in the treatment of established nausea and vomiting. The combination of a 5HT$_3$ receptor antagonist and dexamethasone when used for prophylaxis has been reported to be 90 percent effective (PONV free).

Dopamine (D$_2$) receptor antagonists (promethazine and prochlorperazine), antihistamines (diphenhydramine, dimenhydrinate), and anticholinergics (scopolamine, atropine) are inexpensive antiemetics used alone or in combination with the first-line drugs. These drugs act on multiple receptor types; antihistamines inhibit acetylcholine receptors in the vestibular center and histamine receptors in the area of the vomiting center. Promethazine and prochlorperazine are anticholinergic and antihistaminic as well. Acetylcholine is a chemical that nerves use to transmit messages to each other. Any anticholinergic character will interrupt the communication between the vomiting center and the CTZ. Scopolamine prevents communication between the nerves of the vestibule and the vomiting center in the brain by blocking the action of acetylcholine and acting directly on the vomiting center. Unfortunately, none of these drugs has the efficacy when used alone that the serotonin antagonists offer. Undesirable anticholinergic side effects such as dry mouth, confusion, constipation, and agitation often accompany these drugs.

The concept of multimodal therapy for PONV used today relies on combination therapy (antiemetic drugs that have different mechanisms of action) such as dexamethasone plus a serotonin antagonist. Selection of total intravenous anesthesia, avoiding medications known to cause PONV (opioids, inhalational agents, nitrous oxide, reversal agents for muscle relaxants), or the use of regional anesthesia for pain control instead of general anesthesia is all part of the strategy.

Analgesics

Alfentanil (*Alfenta*), fentanyl (*Sublimze*), sufentanil (*Sufenta*), and remifentanil (*Ultiva*) are all potent analgesics in the opioid family. Opioids are analgesics that produce pharmacologic effects similar to morphine by acting on one of three major endogenous opioid receptors, mu, kappa, or delta (see Chapter 19). These drugs are considered strong analgesics because they are able to suppress transmission of sensory information associated with moderate to severe pain of any origin. They depress transmission in the spinal cord by interacting with mu opioid receptors.

These drugs are the analgesic component for monitored anesthesia care. Opioids are frequently used during MAC because they block pain associated with the procedure and/or condition undergoing surgery. These drugs are not anesthetics at any dose. Unlike midazolam and propol, opiates do not produce amnesia even at doses that create sedation. Sedation is more of a liability than a clinical benefit with opioid analgesics because the dose to produce sedation usually requires some degree of CNS and respiratory depression. For this reason, and because they produce nausea and vomiting, opioid analgesics are seldom used alone in MAC. When given IV or IM their onset of action is rapid. The duration of analgesia will depend on the characteristics of the specific drug. The more lipid-soluble opioid analgesics (alfentanil, fentanyl, sufentanil, and remifentanil) will undergo redistribution and may have a duration of about 1 hour or less. Additional drug administration or infusion can saturate tissues and prolong the recovery period with side effects. These drugs are CNS depressants and synergize with other depressant drugs. The most significant issue with these drugs is respiratory depression, especially if it continues in the postoperative period.

In the event a patient is unresponsive to physical stimulation accompanied by shallow breathing (less than 8 breaths/minute) and has pinpoint pupils, as a result of overdose or unusual patient sensitivity to the opioid, there is a receptor-specific antagonist that may be used to reverse the respiratory depression. Naloxone (*Narcan*) is a pure opioid receptor antagonist used to reverse respiratory depression, sedation, and hypotension caused by opioid overdose. It does not stimulate the receptors; it does not produce any opioid response. In fact, in the absence of opioid-induced activity, naloxone does not exhibit any pharmacological response. It has to be used with caution in patients who are opioid dependent because it can precipitate withdrawal symptoms in these individuals.

These opioid analgesics are used in the maintenance of anesthesia with the protocol of barbiturate and nitrous oxide/oxygen. They can be used as a continuous infusion with nitrous oxide/oxygen in the maintenance of general anesthesia.

Ketorolac is a potent, parenterally active nonopioid analgesic (NSAID). It has been used both as an analgesic supplement to propofol sedation during local anesthesia and as an alternative to fentanyl for the treatment of intraoperative pain refractory to the administration of local anesthetic alone during MAC. A decided advantage of ketorolac over fentanyl is the absence of nausea and vomiting in the intraoperative and postoperative periods. However, ketorolac has a number of serious effects for consideration before it can be used. It is contraindicated in patients with a history of or active peptic ulcer disease or GI bleeding because it inhibits platelet function. It cannot be used in patients at risk for renal failure or in surgeries where there is an increased risk of bleeding.

Muscle Relaxation

Most general anesthetics that take patients into Stage III, Plane 3 anesthesia produce skeletal muscle relaxation. However, it may be advantageous in certain operations (abdominal and thoracic) to have skeletal muscle relaxation for a long time with minimal CNS depression. For this purpose, neuromuscular blocking drugs, also called paralytics, such as succinylcholine, may be administered during surgery. These drugs produce adequate skeletal muscle relaxation by interfering with acetylcholine-modulated nerve conduction at the synaptic site while patients are maintained in early Stage III anesthesia. The neuromuscular blocking drug succinylcholine is a standard for rapid sequence induction (RSI) used briefly at the beginning of some procedures to facilitate endotracheal intubation. Succinylcholine is the only depolarizing agent used for RSI. Because of its rapid onset, ultrashort duration of action, and safety, it is the paralytic of choice in almost all cases of RSI in adults. For more detail on succinylcholine and other muscle relaxants, see Chapter 8.

Antisecretory/Antispasm

Anticholinergic drugs may be used as preanesthetic medications to prevent the increase in salivary and bronchial secretions induced by some anesthetics. Bronchial secretions of mucus usually line the respiratory tract and may impair the transfer of oxygen and anesthetic across the lungs. If the secretions are not controlled, hypoxia may develop.

LO 18.7
SPECIAL CONSIDERATIONS AND CAUTIONS

Many patients are not aware of possible allergies or hypersensitivities that they have. This lack of awareness is especially likely if patients have not previously encountered surgery or preanesthetic medications. Therefore, patients should be carefully observed for any unusual reactions to medications before and after general anesthesia. Anaphylactoid reactions are rare with anesthetics. Special Type II hepatitis associated with volatile liquid anesthetics has been described. It is more usual that the patient may experience itching and redness due to histamine release (barbiturates, etomidate); this is not an allergic reaction.

Vital signs should be monitored frequently before, during, and after anesthesia. During the postoperative recovery period, patients' airways must be kept unobstructed. It is important to check patients for signs of hypoxia (skin discoloration), laryngospasm, or gagging, which can precipitate aspiration of fluid into a patient's lungs. Patients should be positioned so that the potential for aspiration of secretions is minimized. Intravenous fluids and vasopressor drugs should be kept available for the treatment of hypotensive episodes. Patients should be monitored and positioned to avoid redistribution of anesthetic to the CNS, which may precipitate severe hypotension and respiratory arrest during the recovery period.

Most of the problems that arise following general anesthesia result from residual depression of the CNS. Patients frequently feel "hung over," dizzy, or nauseous, and should be assisted, since mental disorientation may lead to impaired judgment and incoordination. Three drugs in this chapter—methohexital, midazolam, and droperidol—have a special cautionary instruction for their use, called a black box warning. The recommendation that patients be fully monitored, electronically and by third-party observation (not the attending physician or surgeon), is identified for methohexital and midazolam because of the potential to cause respiratory and cardiac depression. Close attention to monitoring patient signs should be the standard of care with the use of all anesthetics. Postanesthetic medications such as analgesics, muscle relaxants, and tranquilizers will potentiate the residual CNS depression of general anesthetics. Antibiotics such as streptomycin, kanamycin, and erythromycin will potentiate the skeletal muscle relaxation to produce muscle weakness and fatigue.

Because propofol is an emulsion, it should be used with caution in patients with lipid metabolism disorders such as primary hyperlipoproteinemia, diabetic hyperlipidemia, and pancreatitis. Elevations in serum triglycerides may occur when it is administered for extended periods of time. Patients at risk of hyperlipidemia should be monitored for increases in serum triglycerides or serum turbidity. The drug is contraindicated in patients with a known hypersensitivity to propofol or its components.

Several of the inhalation anesthetics and surgical adjuncts (skeletal muscle relaxants) produce malignant hyperthermia in certain individuals. The intravenous anesthetics do not cause malignant hyperthermia. This acute toxicity is due to a genetic defect. Malignant hyperthermia is associated with a drastic increase in body temperature, acidosis, electrolyte imbalance, and shock. The mechanism by which **hyperthermia** occurs is believed to be related to the anesthetic-induced potentiation of calcium hyperreactivity in susceptible individuals. The hyperactive biochemical reactions progress so quickly that treatment must be started immediately to reduce the risk of death. Treatment of hyperthermia includes reducing body temperature with ice packs and controlling arrhythmias and acidosis with appropriate drugs. Unfortunately, the incidence of fatality in malignant hyperthermia is high. Prevention is primarily directed at obtaining a good family history about other episodes of difficulty during operative procedures. Dantrolene is the drug of choice in managing the sequelae of malignant hyperthermia.

Solution Incompatibilities

The injectable anesthetics, as their name implies, must be prepared as solutions to facilitate parenteral administration. Frequently, parenteral medications are given in combination for convenience and efficient drug handling and to minimize patient discomfort by reducing the number of injections. Considering the variety of drugs that may be used during an operation, it is understandable why combining medications might be useful. Drug admixture may be performed by adding solutions to an existing intravenous line or by mixing two or more drugs in the same syringe prior to injection. *Note:* Not all drugs can be mixed in the same syringe without compromising the activity of the active components. Some drug combinations result in discoloration of the solution, haze formation, or even precipitation. These are signs of drug incompatibility that should alert medical personnel to discard the solution and avoid such combinations in the future.

Neither the fentanyl-droperidol combination product nor ketamine should be combined in the same syringe with a barbiturate because drug precipitation results. Methohexital and thiopental have been reported to be incompatible with several antibiotics, antihistaminics, and opioid analgesics. Examples of drugs that should not be combined with the barbiturate anesthetics are chlorpromazine, kanamycin, lidocaine, promazine, streptomycin, tetracycline, methyldopa, and prochlorperazine. Thiopental should not

Note to the Health Care Professional

In an ambulatory surgical setting, patients must be monitored through the recovery period. Because of the depressant nature of anesthetics, especially causing residual mental confusion, and the potential for adverse effects to occur with any anesthetic, patients should be alerted to the "Do's and Don'ts" after anesthesia.

- Don't rely on memory for spoken instructions (written instructions should be given to the patient in addition to spoken instructions).
- Do leave the health care facility accompanied by a responsible adult.
- Don't operate complex equipment for at least 24 hours (someone else should be driving the patient home).
- Don't make any important decisions or sign any legal documents for the day.
- Don't take any medications unless prescribed by or discussed with the patient's physician.
- Don't drink alcohol for at least 24 hours.
- Do remain quietly at home for the day and rest.
- Do arrange for someone to take care of any small children for the day.
- Do take liquids first and slowly progress to a light meal.
- Do call the designated medical professional, nurse anesthetist or physician, or the surgery center if any questions arise.

be combined with amikacin, codeine, meperidine, morphine, penicillin G, promethazine, succinylcholine, and tetracycline because precipitation will occur.

Solutions containing barbiturates are usually alkaline (pH greater than 10). As a rule, these alkaline solutions should not be mixed with acid solutions because the barbiturate will precipitate. Such incompatible acid solutions include atropine, scopolamine, and succinylcholine. Methohexital undergoes a specific interaction with silicone and rubber, which dictates that it should never be in contact with rubber stoppers or parts of syringes that have been treated with silicone. Propofol should not be used if there is evidence of separation of the emulsion phases. Unused portions of propofol or solutions containing propofol at the end of the anesthetic procedure or by 6 hours, for longer procedures/ICU use, should be discarded.

LO 18.8
PREFERRED USE OF ANESTHETICS

The volatile anesthetics are used for maintenance anesthesia in an operating room. They are easy to administer, have the benefit of additional skeletal muscle relaxation, and can be controlled by the anesthesiologist as needed to keep the patient oxygenated and away from medullary depression. The frequently used inhalational agents are nitrous oxide, enflurane, sevoflurane, and isoflurane. Sevoflurane is an anesthetic of choice for induction or maintenance anesthesia in inpatient and outpatient procedures because of its minimal respiratory effects.

For most procedures, surgical or diagnostic, it's standard practice to begin with an intravenous agent, either to calm the patient or to make a smooth transition to another maintenance anesthetic.

Propofol is the most frequently used induction anesthetic today. It is used with confidence in the operating room and ambulatory surgical centers. It is a **preferred anesthetic** among the drugs used for balanced anesthesia and as a maintenance anesthetic. It has frequently replaced barbiturates as a sedative-hypnotic. Propofol is an anesthetic of choice for procedures requiring conscious sedation and continuous sedation of mechanically ventilated patients in the intensive care (ICU) setting. Its profile—no nausea and vomiting, no tissue accumulation or neuromuscular blocker potentiation—makes for a reliable, uncomplicated, and satisfactory recovery period.

For Monitored Anesthetic Care, the most frequently used drugs include midazolam, propofol, ketamine, fentanyl, alfentinil, and lidocaine. Depending on the type of procedure, another anesthetic also may be added.

Patient Administration and Monitoring

Patients are usually exposed to these drugs in an operating room environment. For such procedures it is expected that the patient will be closely monitored during and after surgery to ensure adverse reactions are minimized. Even for diagnostic procedures, the patient is kept for observation until it is clear there is no immediate risk. The opportunity for adverse effects is more likely to occur when information on patient medical history is inadequate prior to the selection of the anesthetics and premedication regimen. Patient history is extremely important to ascertain which drugs are most appropriate. Patient interview will provide information that is critical to minimizing adverse reactions to anesthetics. Go to www.anesthesiapatientsafety.com and select "About Anesthesia" in the left side panel. Click on "Preanesthetic Questionnaire" for an excellent sample of what may be covered during a patient history.

Alcohol consumption, blood pressure medication, antibiotic, and OTC product use should be thoroughly reviewed. Intravenous anesthetics will be potentiated by CNS depressants, including alcohol in cough/cold preparations.

Midazolam is contraindicated in patients with acute narrow-angle glaucoma, although it may be used in open-angle glaucoma.

Hypersensitivity to anesthetics and/or premedications from previous exposure, or knowledge of a family member experiencing difficulty during surgery, may provide evidence of a contraindication to specific anesthetics. This is especially valuable as an indication of predisposition to malignant hyperthermia.

Use in Pregnancy

Midazolam is Food and Drug Administration (FDA) Pregnancy Category D because an increased risk of congenital malformations associated with the use of benzodiazepine drugs (diazepam and chlordiazepoxide) has been suggested in several studies. Patients should be apprised of the potential hazard to the fetus if this drug is used for more than a single exposure during pregnancy. Single exposure as an adjunct to anesthesia is less likely to be an issue when administration is warranted during pregnancy. Other general anesthetics are classified as having been designated FDA Pregnancy Category B or C.

Chapter Review

Understanding Terminology

Answer the following questions.

1. Name the brain center that influences mood, motivation, and the perception of pain. **(LO 18.1)**
2. Differentiate among *analgesia, general anesthesia, dissociative anesthesia, medullary depression,* and *medullary paralysis.* **(LO 18.1)**
3. Explain the difference between induction of anesthesia and maintenance of anesthesia. **(LO 18.1, 18.2)**
4. Explain the concept of balanced anesthesia. **(LO 18.1)**
5. Explain when propofol is a preferred anesthetic. **(LO 18.8)**

Acquiring Knowledge

Answer the following questions.

1. How does general anesthesia differ from sleep? **(LO 18.1)**
2. How is general anesthesia produced? **(LO 18.1)**
3. How do the effects of general anesthetics on the CNS differ from those of lesser anesthetics? **(LO 18.1, 18.4, 18.5)**
4. What do the various stages of anesthesia represent? **(LO 18.1)**
5. What effects do general anesthetics have on the cardiovascular and respiratory systems? **(LO 18.1, 18.5)**
6. How may the general anesthetics produce skeletal muscle relaxation? **(LO 18.4)**
7. How do the inhalation anesthetics differ from the injectable anesthetics? **(LO 18.2, 18.4, 18.5)**
8. What is neuroleptanesthesia? **(LO 18.2)**
9. For what purpose are the various adjunct medications administered? **(LO 18.5)**
10. What types of drug interactions may occur in postsurgical patients? **(LO 18.6, 18.7)**

Multiple Choice

Use your critical-thinking skills to answer the following questions.

1. Which of the following anesthetics exhibits potent analgesic properties? **(LO 18.1)**
   A. lidocaine
   B. halothane
   C. ketamine
   D. nitrous oxide and ketamine

2. What is the best reason for using a balanced anesthesia strategy? **(LO 18.1, 18.7)**
   A. producing complementary effects using a few drugs avoids unnecessary intense (deep) CNS depression with one anesthetic to achieve the same effect
   B. the concentration of volatile anesthetic in the alveoli is balanced against the amount of anesthetic in the blood
   C. less monitoring of anesthesia is required
   D. fewer patients experience emergence delirium

3. Why is propofol a drug of choice for induction and maintenance of anesthesia? **(LO 18.2, 18.8)**
   A. it is a potent analgesic at all doses
   B. it slowly brings the patient to the stage of surgical anesthesia
   C. it is a complete anesthetic with a quick onset of action and recovery period uncomplicated by nausea and vomiting
   D. it is administered by special vaporizer to avoid mask delivery

4. Which of the following drugs is associated with its correct pharmacological effect? (LO 18.6, 18.7)
    A. ketamine: nausea
    B. sevoflurane: skeletal muscle relaxation
    C. methohexital: hallucinations and colorful dreams
    D. etomidate: hepatitis

5. Which of the following is true about laryngospasms? (LO 18.7)
    A. they rarely occur because volatile anesthetics depress the CNS
    B. they involve stimulation of the bronchiolar smooth muscle
    C. drug-induced increased salivary secretion can trigger them in pediatric patients
    D. they can be avoided by using a volatile anesthetic with ketamine

6. Which of the following drugs is matched correctly with its use or action? (LO 18.1, 18.4)
    A. chlorpropamide: induction anesthesia
    B. ondansetron: maintenance anesthesia
    C. droperidol: maintenance anesthesia
    D. ketamine: dissociative anesthesia

7. Which of the following is not correct? (LO 18.3)
    A. ketamine causes chloride ions to flow out of the nerve cell by binding to GABA
    B. propofol binds to the $GABA_A$ receptor and enhances hyperpolarization of the neuron
    C. barbiturates and propofol act on the receptor and directly on the chloride channel
    D. potent anesthetics enhance $GABA_A$ and glycine receptors

8. The major routes that remove etomidate and midazolam from the body are which of the following? (LO 18.3, 18.5)
    A. hepatic metabolism and renal excretion
    B. excretion through the lungs and sweating
    C. accumulation in fat tissue and redistribution
    D. increased salivation and bile production

Multiple Choice (Multiple Answer)

Select the correct choices for each statement. The choices may be all correct, all incorrect, or any combination.

1. Select the types of anesthesia in which there is a loss of consciousness. (LO 18.1)
    A. local anesthesia
    B. Monitored Anesthesia Care
    C. general anesthesia
    D. balanced anesthesia

2. Choose the different classes of general anesthetics. (LO 18.2)
    A. injected
    B. inhaled
    C. oral
    D. topical

3. Which of the following is a route of excretion for volatile liquid anesthetics? (LO 18.5)
    A. renal
    B. GI tract
    C. exhalation
    D. sweating

4. Select the mechanisms by which anesthetics inhibit CNS activity. **(LO 18.3)**
   A. bind to GABA receptors
   B. Cl⁻ ions move across membrane
   C. membrane is depolarized
   D. ion channels open

5. Which drugs would be used as adjunct therapy to anesthesia during surgery? **(LO 18.6)**
   A. analgesics
   B. antiarrhythmics
   C. antianxiety
   D. anticholinergics

Sequencing

Place the following stages of anesthesia in order from first symptoms experienced to last. **(LO 18.1)**

_____   _____   _____   _____

First   **Last**

medullary paralysis

analgesia

excitement

surgical anesthesia

Classification

Place each indication under the appropriate stage of anesthesia. **(LO 18.1)**

elevated blood pressure   respiratory paralysis

circulatory collapse   return to normal heart functions

giddiness   euphoria

skeletal muscle relaxation   elevated heart rate

Stage I	Stage II	Stage III	Stage IV

Matching

Match the following drugs with the type of anesthesia for which they are preferred; each classification may be used more than once **(LO 18.2, 18.8)**

   a. maintenance anesthesia
   b. induction anesthesia
   c. monitored anesthesia

1. _____ ketamine   5. _____ sevoflurane
2. _____ nitrous oxide   6. _____ fentanyl
3. _____ midazolam   7. _____ enflurane
4. _____ propofol

Documentation

Using the doctor's notes below, answer the following questions. (LO 18.2)

> One dose of Ketamine administered at 08:00
> Procedure begun at 08:15
> Procedure should take 30 minutes to complete.

a. What type of anesthetic is ketamine?
b. Should the doctor have started the procedure earlier or later, or was this an appropriate amount of time to wait before starting?
c. What is the normal duration of action of ketamine? Will another dose be needed?
d. For what type of side effects should the patient be monitored?

Labeling

Fill in the missing labels. (LO 18.1)

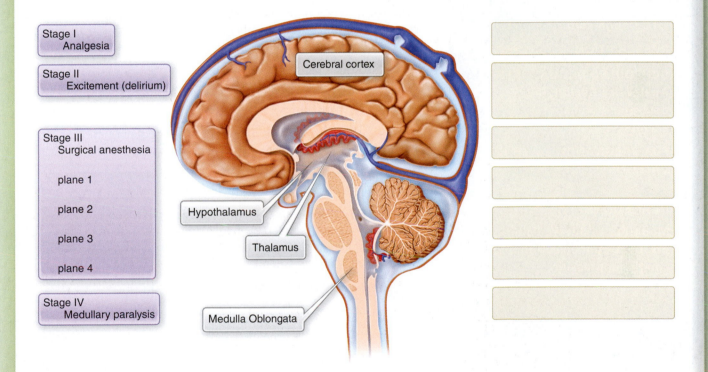

Stage I
   Analgesia

Stage II
   Excitement (delirium)

Stage III
   Surgical anesthesia

   plane 1

   plane 2

   plane 3

   plane 4

Stage IV
   Medullary paralysis

Cerebral cortex

Hypothalamus

Thalamus

Medulla Oblongata

Chapter 19

Opioid Analgesics

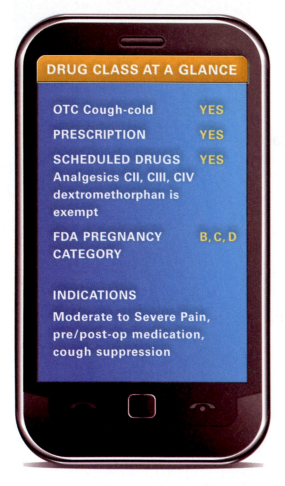

DRUG CLASS AT A GLANCE

OTC Cough-cold	**YES**
PRESCRIPTION	**YES**
SCHEDULED DRUGS	**YES**

Analgesics CII, CIII, CIV
dextromethorphan is
exempt

FDA PREGNANCY CATEGORY	**B, C, D**

INDICATIONS

Moderate to Severe Pain,
pre/post-op medication,
cough suppression

KEY TERMS

addiction: a chronic neurobiologic disease in which genetic, psychosocial, and environmental factors induce changes in the individual's behavior to compulsively use drugs despite the harm that may result.

agonist: drug that attaches to a receptor and initiates an action.

analgesia: relief from pain.

analgesic: substance (synthetic or naturally occurring) that inhibits the body's reaction to painful stimuli or perception of pain.

antagonist: drug that attaches to a receptor, does not initiate an action, but blocks an agonist from producing an effect.

antidiuretic hormone (ADH): substance produced in the hypothalamus and secreted by the pituitary gland that modulates urine production and allows the kidneys to reabsorb water in order to conserve body water.

antitussive: a drug that suppresses coughing.

anuria: condition in which no urine is produced.

dysphoria: feeling of discomfort or unpleasantness.

emesis: vomiting.

endogenous: naturally occurring within the body.

endorphins: neuropeptides produced within the CNS that interact with opioid receptors to produce analgesia.

expectorant: substance that causes the removal (expulsion) of mucous secretions from the respiratory system.

hyperalgesia: an abnormally painful response to a stimulus.

neuropathic pain: pain resulting from a damaged nervous system or damaged nerve cells.

nociceptor: specialized peripheral nerve cells sensitive to tissue injury that transmit pain signals to the brain for interpretation of pain.

nonopioid analgesic: formerly known as nonnarcotic analgesics, such as NSAIDs and COX-2 inhibitors.

oliguria: condition in which very small amounts of urine are produced.

opiate: drug derived from opium and producing the same pharmacological effects as opium.

opioid: drug that produces the same pharmacological effects as opium and its family of drugs or the neuropeptides (enkephalin, endorphin) produced by the body.

opioid analgesics: chemically related to morphine or opium and used to relieve pain.

opioid antagonist: a drug that attaches to opioid receptors and displaces the opioid analgesic or opioid neuropeptide.

peripheral nerve: part of the nervous system that is outside the central nervous system (the brain or spinal cord), usually near the surface of the tissue fibers or skin.

phlegm: secretion from the respiratory tract; usually called mucus.

physical dependence: condition in which the body requires a substance (drug) not normally found in the body in order to avoid symptoms associated with withdrawal, or the abstinence syndrome.

referred pain: origin of the pain is in a different location than where the individual feels the pain.

spasmogenic: causing a muscle to contract intermittently, resulting in a state of spasms.

synthetic drug: drug produced by a chemical process outside the body.

tolerance: ability of the body to alter its response (to adapt) to drug effects so that the effects are minimized over time.

Learning Outcomes

After studying this chapter, you should be able to

19.1 explain the pathway for pain recognition and how opioids produce analgesia.

19.2 describe the sources of opioid analgesics.

19.3 discuss the pharmacological effects of these drugs.

19.4 discuss administration, absorption, and metabolism of these drugs.

19.5 list the adverse effects of these drugs.

19.6 explain acute opioid poisoning.

19.7 discuss the actions of opioid antagonists.

19.8 list drug interactions.

19.9 discuss the specific terms associated with pain, analgesia, addiction, cough, and opioid receptors.

Introduction

Pain functions primarily as a protective signal. Pain may warn of imminent danger (fire) or the presence of internal disease (appendicitis or tumors). On the other hand, pain may be part of the normal healing process (inflammation). Relief from pain is desirable when the duration and intensity of pain alter the ability of an individual to function efficiently. In such situations, analgesic drugs are useful because these agents relieve pain without producing a loss of consciousness.

There are two major classes of analgesics: the opioid analgesics and the nonopioid analgesics. Opioid analgesics are usually referred to as strong analgesics, whereas nonopioid drugs are considered mild analgesics. This classification suggests the type of pain that can be alleviated by each group. Opioid analgesics are capable of inhibiting pain of any origin. However, these drugs are used primarily to relieve moderate to severe pain of trauma, pain associated with myocardial infarction, pain associated with terminal illness, and postoperative pain.

PAIN

The sensation of pain is comprised of at least two elements: the local irritation (stimulation of **peripheral nerves**) and the recognition of pain (within the CNS). Free nerve endings called **nociceptors** are located in the skin, muscle, joints, bones, and viscera. Nociceptors respond to tissue injury and painful stimuli. When there is no injury, there is no pain stimulus, so the nociceptors are quiet. When a pain-generating event happens, biochemical changes occur within the localized area of the injury. Usually, prostaglandins, histamine, bradykinins, serotonin, and Substance P are among the peripheral neurotransmitters released that trigger nociceptors. Substance P is a neuropeptide released from specific sensory nerves in the brain and spinal cord. It is associated with inflammation and pain. In nociception, Substance P transmits information about tissue injury at the peripheral receptors to the CNS, where the sensation of pain is recognized. Nociceptors alert the brain to the intensity of the pain by increasing the frequency of signals sent to the spinal cord and then to specialized areas within the CNS (Figure 19.1).

The signals travel through the spinal cord into the area called the dorsal horn, where they are routed to the appropriate area of the brain that can interpret the intensity and quality of pain present. Pain signals arrive in the spinal cord through A-delta nociceptor and C-nociceptor fibers. The continuing signal is transmitted in the ascending pathways to the brain. If the originating (point-of-injury) signal is transmitted through the A-delta fibers (myelinated), the pain is consciously experienced as sharp. If the signal is passed through C fibers (unmyelinated), dull, aching pain is felt.

Nociceptive pain can only occur when all neural equipment (nerve cells, nerve endings, spinal cord, and brain) is working properly. When pain results from abnormal signals or nerves damaged by entrapment, infection (herpes zoster or HIV), amputation, or diabetes, it is called **neuropathic pain.**

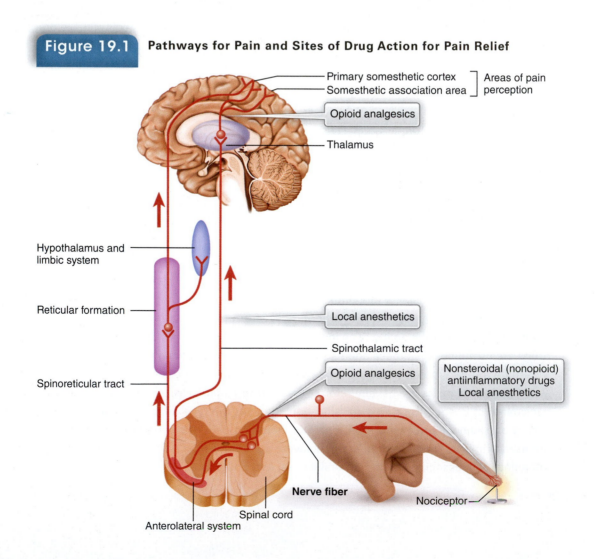

Figure 19.1   **Pathways for Pain and Sites of Drug Action for Pain Relief**

Pain duration is either acute or chronic. Acute pain usually appears in association with an observable injury (e.g., sunburn, broken foot, muscle sprain, or headache) and disappears when the injury heals. Chronic pain persists for weeks, months, or years even with **analgesic** therapy. Nociceptive pain can be either acute or chronic. Neuropathic pain is chronic, even though it may be intermittent. If an injury doesn't heal or the pain is not adequately inhibited, nociceptors get "really irritated," a condition known as peripheral sensitization, and send so many signals through the CNS that the patient overresponds to even normal stimuli, such as a feather or brush touched to the area. In neuropathic conditions sensitization also can occur within the spinal neurons observed as overresponsiveness **(hyperalgesia),** prolonged pain, or the spread of pain to an uninjured area **(referred pain).**

No matter what type of pain is present, relief from pain **(analgesia)** is the therapeutic goal. The specialized medical discipline of pain management has changed the spectrum of therapy and the types of drugs used, especially to achieve satisfactory analgesia as soon as possible. Inadequate control of pain can delay healing. With chronic pain, psychological and emotional changes occur that cause the patient to become tired and irritable; patients develop insomnia, significant stress responses such as increased heart rate and blood pressure, depression, impaired resistance to infection, and even increased sensitization to pain. The psychological component associated with the inability to permanently relieve the pain intensifies the response to pain by stimulating the CNS.

Pain management and selection of the most appropriate analgesic depend on the type and duration of pain present. In other chapters, pain relief (analgesia) has been shown to be the primary therapeutic action of local anesthetics and nonsteroidal antiinflammatory drugs (NSAIDs). By inhibiting sodium and potassium ion movement through the nerves, local anesthetics block nerve conduction and the sensation of pain is avoided (Chapter 10). Analgesia also is produced by interrupting the metabolic pathway of inflammation, such as inhibition of prostaglandins by NSAIDs (Chapter 20). Local anesthetics and NSAIDs act at the site of injury or at the level of the peripheral nerves (Figure 19.1). Because some antiepileptic drugs and tricyclic antidepressants depress neuronal excitability and suppress abnormal discharges, these drugs also play an important adjunct role in pain management. Even though local anesthetics and antiepiletic drugs are used to reduce or ameliorate pain, the NSAIDs, acetaminophen, and COX-2 inhibitor drugs are most often referred to as the **nonopioid analgesics.** The nonopioid analgesics are discussed in the following chapter.

Although the terminology used to describe the mechanism of analgesia is relatively new, the drugs discussed in this chapter, **opioid analgesics,** in their natural plant form, have been medicinally used for 5000 years.

LO 19.1	LO 19.2	LO 19.3
LO 19.5	LO 19.7	LO 19.9

OPIOID ANALGESICS
Clinical Indications

Opioid analgesics are first-line therapy for pain associated with procedures (bone marrow biopsy), pain due to trauma (burns, vehicular accident), cancer, or visceral pain (pancreatitis, appendicitis). It is held that opioid analgesics can relieve virtually any type of pain. Certainly, all opioid analgesics relieve moderate to severe acute and chronic pain. Such pain is often associated with myocardial infarction, post-trauma injury, and cancer. Occasionally the root cause of chronic pain remains unidentified. Opioid analgesics are the drug of choice in treating acute postoperative pain, including dental pain (oral analgesia), because there is no increased risk of bleeding (as with NSAIDs).

The majority of the opioid analgesics are used for the relief of acute and chronic pain. A few, such as fentanyl (*Sublimaze, Duragesic*), alfentanil (*Alfenta*), and sufentanil (*Sufenta*), are primarily indicated for preoperative sedation to reduce patient apprehension. In making the patient less apprehensive, physiological mechanisms are no longer poised to fight the anesthesia. As a result, premedication with opioids often reduces the amount of anesthetic required and facilitates induction of anesthesia.

Other opioids, such as codeine, hydrocodone, and dextromethorphan, are widely used to suppress coughing, while difenoxen/atropine (*Motofen*) and loperamide (*Immodium*) are the active agents in antidiarrheal medications. The antitussive opioids are presented at the end of this chapter. The antidiarrheal opioids are presented in Chapter 34 with other drugs that affect GI motility.

Source of Opioids

Until recently, drugs that were extracted from opium **(opiates)** or synthetic chemicals that produced the same pharmacological effects as opium were called narcotic analgesics. While this name still applies to the laws that govern the use of this class of drugs, current medical and research terminology refers to these drugs as **opioid** analgesics. The naturally occurring opiates (derivatives of opium) include morphine and codeine. Morphine is the largest component of the chemicals (alkaloids) extracted from the poppy plant. The term *opioids* is used today for any molecule, whether natural or **synthetic,** that acts on opioid receptors. Morphine is the prototype or standard opioid analgesic. Because it has been used for centuries as a medicinal drug, its clinical effects are well established and its dose-response has been well documented. This allows morphine to be the standard by which the potency of all the other opioid analgesics is measured. The opioids vary in their potency, onset of action, and incidence of opioid side effects (Table 19:1).

Tolerance and physical dependence are factors that influence opioid use. **Tolerance** (decreasing effects) develops to all opioids. When tolerance develops to the annoying side effects of the drug (sedation), it is considered a therapeutic benefit. However, when tolerance results in the need for a larger dose of drug to produce a CNS action (euphoria, analgesia), that is not a beneficial outcome. In fact, more drug to reach a state of good feeling may reinforce behavior in certain individuals associated with abuse or addiction. **Physical dependence** develops with long-term daily use of all strong opioids.

Because of the potential for abuse, opioid analgesics are federally restricted (controlled) substances. These drugs can be obtained only by prescription from a physician registered and licensed with the Drug Enforcement Agency (DEA). This status obligates strict maintenance

[Table **19:1**]

Pharmacological Effects of Opioid Analgesics

Drug	Addiction potential	Analgesic potency	Antitussive activity**	Incidence of nausea and vomiting**	Respiratory depression**
Alfentanil	*	Same as morphine	*	*	*
Codeine	Low	Less than morphine	3	1	1
Heroin	Highest	Greater than morphine	?	1	2
Hydrocodone	Low	Less than morphine	3	?	1
Hydromorphone	High	Greater than morphine	3	1	2
Levorphanol	High	Same as morphine	2	1	2
Meperidine	High	Same as morphine	1	2	2
Methadone	Low	Same as morphine	2	1	2
Morphine	High	Good	3	2	2
Oxycodone	High	Same as morphine	3	2	2
Oxymorphone	Highest	Greater than morphine	1	3	3
Pentazocine	Moderate	Less than morphine	*	2	2
Propoxyphene	Low	Less than morphine	*	1	1
Sufentanil	*	Greater than morphine	*	*	*

*Not rated. **3 = high; 2 = moderate; 1 = low.*

of records and specific procedures for secure storage of the drugs. Because of their high abuse potential, most opioids used as analgesics or adjuncts to anesthesia are restricted to Schedule II. Schedule II (CII) requires that listed drugs must have a new prescription written for each refill.

In the late nineteenth century, morphine was chemically converted into heroin under the good intention of producing an analgesic that was less addicting than morphine. Unfortunately, heroin is three times more potent than morphine and more rapidly addicting. Heroin is fully restricted to Schedule I (CI) because it has a high abuse potential and no medically sanctioned use in the United States. This means it cannot be legally prescribed in the United States.

Opioids with less abuse potential, such as codeine, appear in Schedules III and V according to the strength (amount of codeine) of the preparation. Opioids with the least abuse potential such as opiates used as antidiarrheals are Schedule V drugs. Select opioid analgesics—codeine, dextromethorphan,and hydrocodone—are approved for use alone or in combinations to suppress coughing. Dextromethorphan does not require a prescription for cough preparation sold over-the-counter, but hydrocodone, under Schedule III, does. Dextromethorphan is under a great deal of scrutiny because of the misuse and abuse of OTC products by minors. Efforts to restrict access and/or sale to individuals under 18 years of age are ongoing. The classification schedules (CI to CV) associated with various opioid controlled substances are indicated in Table 19:2 along with the usual adult doses for analgesia. Codeine, especially, is in combination products for the treatment of cough and cold symptoms. This is presented in Table 19:4 under the Antitussive section.

Site and Mechanism of Action

Pain recognition involves a component that intensifies the response to pain because the CNS anticipates how painful the injury will be or how the continuing chronic pain will feel. This recognition leads to anxiety and apprehension (CNS stimulation), which heightens the reaction to pain. Opioid analgesics are called central analgesics because they selectively act within the CNS to reduce the reaction to pain. Opioid analgesics do not impair the function of peripheral nerves. The pain is still present (especially in chronic conditions), but patients respond differently than before as though they can tolerate the pain.

Several different types of opioid receptors have now been identified within the spinal cord and brain. Morphine was thought to interact with membrane-bound receptors as long as 50 years ago. However, it wasn't until the 1970s that evidence for an opioid receptor in the body was confirmed by the discovery of the **endogenous** peptides. These peptides include endorphin, enkephlin, dynorphin, and the newest ones, nociceptin and nocistatin. The word **endorphin** is derived from the words *endo*genous and m*orphine.* These peptides are believed to be important for survival because, when released, they provide pain relief that allows the injured person to move away from the harmful stimulus. Endorphins have been shown to be more than four times more potent than intravenous morphine. Eventually, the peptides are metabolized, levels decrease, and the pain signal returns, causing the person to seek help to reduce the continuing pain.

Three opioid receptors are the most clinically important—**mu, kappa,** and **delta.** These receptors are G-protein receptors. There are two types of mu receptors. Mu_1, located outside the spinal cord (CNS), "interprets pain." Mu_2, found throughout the CNS, is responsible for respiratory depression, analgesia, euphoria, and physical dependence. Each of the endogenous opioid peptides has a preference for one of the opioid receptors, although they may interact with multiple receptors. Endorphins are produced within the pituitary and hypothalamus and are selective for mu receptors. Enkephlins, produced throughout the CNS and peripheral nerve endings, prefer delta receptors, while dynorphins, primarily found in pain nerve endings, interact with kappa receptors. Reduction in the awareness and reaction to pain is controlled through a combination of mu, kappa, and delta receptors within the brain.

Morphine and the other opioid analgesics act by binding to opioid receptors and mimicking **(agonist)** the effects of the analgesic peptides. The therapeutically important opioid analgesics interact with mu and kappa receptors. These drugs inhibit neurotransmitter release such as Subtance P, inhibit nociceptor signals from reaching the spinal cord, reduce nerve excitability, and alter pain perception (see Figure 19.2). Opioid analgesics reduce pain by more than one action. When opioids bind to their G-protein (mu) receptors, calcium ion channels on presynaptic neurons close. Calcium ions cannot flow into the cells and facilitate neurotransmitter release such as acetylcholine, Substance P, catecholamines, and glutamate. Glutamate is an excitatory neurotransmitter that sends the pain signal along the nerve. So opioids prevent pain transmission when glutamate release is inhibited. Next, opioids bind to the postsynaptic mu receptors and open potassium ion channels. Potassium ions move out of the cell, producing a hyperpolarized state in which the nerve cannot respond to pain signals so further transmission to the brain is interrupted. Opioids interact with their receptors at different CNS levels.

Analgesic Doses of Centrally Acting Analgesics

Drug (*Trade Name*)	Schedule	Adult dose analgesia	Intramuscular onset (min)	Administration duration (hr)
Opiates				
Codeine	II	15–60 mg PO, SC, IM, IV*	15–30	4–6
Heroin	I	No recognized medicinal value in the United States		
Hydromorphone (*Dilaudid*)	II	2 mg PO, 1–2 mg SC, IM, IV*	15–30	4–5
Hydromorphone ER (*Exalgo*)	II	8–64 mg PO QD	—	24
Morphine	II	5–20 mg IM, SC**	15–20	3–7
Opium tincture	II	0–6 ml QID	—	—
Oxycodone (*Roxicodone*)	II	5 mg PO*	15–30	4–6
Oxymorphone (*Numorphan*)	II	1–1.5 mg IM, SC*; 0.5 mg IV	5–10	3–6
Opioids				
Alfentanil (*Alfenta*)	II	8–75 mcg /Kg IV	—	30–60
Buprenorphine (*Buprenex*)*** (*Suboxone*)***	III	0.3 mg (1 ml) deep IM or slow IV 12–16 mg maintenance dose PO	— —	— 4–8
Butorphanol***	III	0.5–2 mg IM**, IV	10	3–4
Butorphanol nasal spray	IV	1 mg (1 spray in one nostril); repeat if needed in 90 min	—	3
Fentanyl (*Sublimaze*)	II	0.05–0.1 mg/kg IM	5–15	1–2
Fentanyl transdermal (*Duragesia-12, 25*)	II	Individualized dose		
Fentanyl transmucosal (*Actia, Fentora, Onsolis*)	II	200–1800 mcg lozenge on a stick; buccal tablets 200–800 mcg or film 200–1200 mcg	—	1.5
Levorphanol (*Levo-dromoran*)	II	2–3 mg PO, SC	30–90	6–8
Meperidine (*Demerol*)	II	50–150 mg PO, SC, IM**	10–15	2–4
Methadone (*Dolophine, Methadone*)	II	2.5–10 mg PO, IM, SC**	10–15	4–6
Nalbuphine (*Nubain*)***	***	10 mg/70 kg SC, IM, IV*	15	3–6
Oxycodone (*Oxycontin*)	II	10–30 mg PO* Immediate release tablets 5 mg *	— —	— —
Pentazocine (*Talwin*)***	IV	50–100 mg PO; 30 mg IM, SC**	20	3
Propoxyphene (*Darvon, Dolene*)	IV	65 mg PO**	15–30	4–6
Remifentanil (*Ultiva*)	II	Continuous infusion		
Sufentanil (*Sufenta*)	II	8–30 mcg/kg IV	—	1.5
Central analgesic (Nonopioid receptor active)				
Tramadol (*Ultram*)		50–100 mgPO*	15–30	2–4

*Dose repeated every 6 hours. **Dose repeated every 3–4 hours.
***These drugs are partial agonist analgesics. Nalbuphine is not a scheduled controlled substance.

Figure 19.2 **Sites of Opioid Receptor Interaction to Produce Analgesia**

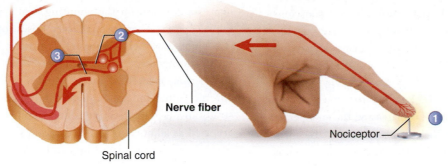

Nerve fiber

Nociceptor

Spinal cord

(a) ① Peripheral nociceptors, ② Presynapse, and ③ Postsynapse correspond to the same areas in part (b)

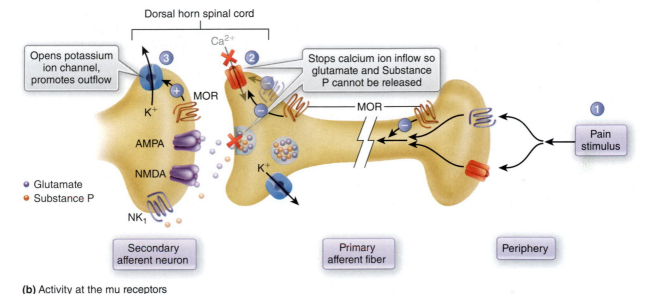

Dorsal horn spinal cord

Ca^{2+}

Opens potassium ion channel, promotes outflow

Stops calcium ion inflow so glutamate and Substance P cannot be released

MOR

K^+

AMPA

NMDA

MOR

Pain stimulus

- Glutamate
- Substance P

NK_1

K^+

Secondary afferent neuron

Primary afferent fiber

Periphery

(b) Activity at the mu receptors

(a) Location of opioid receptor activity. (b) Mu receptors (MOR) in the periphery (1) and presynaptic (2) neurons of the dorsal horn inhibit pain signals (nerve transmission) by decreasing calcium movement into the cell. In the postsynaptic (3) neurons of the spinal cord, mu receptors open potassium channels (outflow of potassium ions) resulting in hyperpolarization so the nerve cannot respond to additional pain signals.

All of these agonist actions contribute to pain relief. Most of the traditional opioids (morphine, oxymorphone, oxycodone, methadone, fentanyl) are pure agonists referred to as mu agonists. This means they bind to the receptor and produce a response. Agonists for different opioid receptors are believed to relieve different types of pain. This would explain why morphine may not work as well for pancreatic pain, but another opioid analgesic does.

Other opioids (nalbuphine, butorphanol) are partial agonists because they initiate kappa receptors but partially block mu receptors. Buprenorphine (*Suboxone*) is a partial agonist combined with naloxone that is only approved for use in the treatment of opioid dependence. Other partial agonist opioids are identified in Table 19:2. Finally, drugs like naloxone and methylnaloxone are

pure **antagonists.** These drugs do not produce effects but bind to the receptor so that other agonists cannot and, in this way, reverse the mu effects of opioids.

Pharmacological Effects

Like the endogenous peptides, opioid analgesics produce effects on a variety of tissues. Opioid receptors are widely distributed outside the CNS, such as in the gastrointestinal and urinary tract. In addition to modifying pain perception, the endogenous peptides modify mood, and regulate cardiovascular, respiratory, and endocrine function. This explains how the opioid analgesics produce their classic side effects of sedation (mu, kappa), euphoria (mu), dysphoria (kappa), constipation (mu), urinary retention (mu), miosis (mu, kappa), and respiratory depression (mu).

Effects on CNS

Opioid analgesics may influence CNS function by increasing or decreasing certain CNS activity. For example, opioid analgesics do not cause a loss of consciousness at therapeutic doses. However, these drugs do alter mental behavior. In particular, opioid analgesics produce changes in mood and decrease mental alertness. Some individuals experience a feeling of well-being—a warm glow—known as euphoria. By activating mu receptors in certain areas of the brain, opiates and the endogenous opioid peptides inhibit the release of GABA (the principal inhibitory neurotransmitter in the brain). Removing GABA allows dopaminergic neurons to fire more vigorously. The release of extra dopamine causes the intensely pleasurable experience of euphoria. This pleasant experience may entice the individuals to use the drug continually, thus contributing to the development of drug dependency. This is a highly variable response because other individuals may experience **dysphoria,** an unpleasant reaction, which enhances anxiety and fear. Dysphoric individuals are less likely to abuse these drugs.

In low doses, most opioid analgesics produce nausea and vomiting. **Emesis** (vomiting) is a direct result of activation of delta or kappa receptors causing CNS stimulation of the chemoreceptor trigger zone, which in turn leads to direct stimulation of the vomiting center in the medulla. In some individuals, the frequency of vomiting increases when the patient is standing or moving. As the dose of opioid is increased, the drug exerts a depressant action on the vomiting center by activating mu receptors. Therefore, at large doses, opioid analgesics counteract their own emetic response by inhibiting the vomiting center (Figure 19.3). Vomiting may not be a serious side effect incurred with the treatment of chronic pain. Understanding the mechanisms and substrates involved in vomiting is important because opiates are used as adjuncts to anesthesia and for postoperative pain control where vomiting can be detrimental to the procedure and recovery process.

One of the most important CNS effects produced by these analgesics is respiratory depression. All dose levels of opioid analgesics depress respiratory activity. Activation of **mu_2 receptors** directly inhibits the respiratory centers in the medulla and the pons. Respiratory rate and volume are reduced so that carbon dioxide (CO_2) is retained in the blood. Mild retention of CO_2 may produce headaches because CO_2 increases cerebral fluid pressure and intracranial pressure. As respiratory depression increases, so does CO_2 retention. However, the suppressed medulla cannot respond to CO_2 stimulation, and hypoventilation persists. The depth of respiratory depression increases as the dose of the

| Figure 19.3 | Opioid Analgesic Effects on the Vomiting Reflex: Chemoreceptor Trigger Zone (CTZ), Vomiting Center (VC), and Stomach |

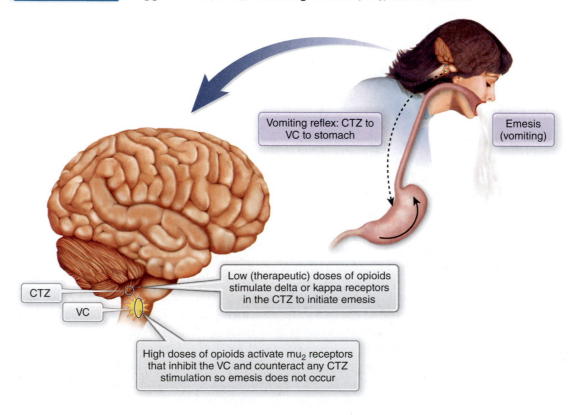

Vomiting reflex: CTZ to VC to stomach

Emesis (vomiting)

CTZ

VC

Low (therapeutic) doses of opioids stimulate delta or kappa receptors in the CTZ to initiate emesis

High doses of opioids activate mu_2 receptors that inhibit the VC and counteract any CTZ stimulation so emesis does not occur

drug increases. Death due to opioid poisoning is usually attributed to respiratory arrest.

Effects on Smooth Muscle

Opioids have **spasmogenic** activity through a direct action on smooth muscle and mu$_2$ receptors in the GI tract. Opioid analgesics increase smooth muscle tone, causing intermittent muscle contractions or spasms. When spasms occur within the intestinal smooth muscle, peristalsis is inhibited. These analgesics inhibit parasympathetic stimulation of the intestines by blocking the release of acetylcholine. Both of these effects can result in constipation, which frequently occurs with the use of opioid analgesics. Three opioid derivatives—loperamide (*Immodium*), diphenoxylate (*Lomotil*), and difenoxin (*Motofen*)—are used in the treatment of persistent diarrhea. Difenoxin (*Motofen*) is a mu receptor agonist, chemically related to meperidine, that stimulates mu receptors in the myenteric plexus to decrease peristalsis and constrict sphincters. It also has a direct effect on circular smooth muscle of the bowel that prolongs gastrointestinal transit time. Diphenoxylate is metabolized to difenoxin, which produces the effect. These drugs will be discussed further in Chapter 34.

Many opioid analgesics, especially morphine, produce spasm of the common bile duct, which causes pressure to increase in the gallbladder. Usually, this effect is accompanied by intense pain. However, in the presence of an opioid, the painful warning may be eliminated, although the pressure continues to increase. For this reason, opioids such as morphine should be used with caution in patients with possible biliary obstruction.

Opioid analgesics affect bronchial smooth muscle by two actions. In addition to their spasmogenic action, these analgesics cause the release of histamine, which directly constricts the bronchioles (see Chapter 31). Constriction of the bronchioles narrows the respiratory passages, making breathing more difficult. This response is dangerous in individuals who already have respiratory difficulties, such as chronic bronchitis, obstructive lung disease, and asthma. Asthmatic patients may be unusually sensitive to histamine release, to the point that opioid analgesics may induce an asthmatic attack.

Urine formation and urination are both decreased by opioid analgesics, since these drugs stimulate the secretion of **antidiuretic hormone (ADH),** which allows the kidneys to reabsorb water. This decreases the volume of urine produced. In addition, spasmogenic activity (mu receptors) of the ureters and sphincter muscles inhibits urine from passing out of the bladder. The combination of these effects usually produces **oliguria** (a smaller than normal amount of urine) rather than **anuria** (no formation of urine).

Effects on Cardiovascular System

Opioid analgesics do not depress cardiac function in therapeutic doses. This lack of effect is important because it allows these drugs to relieve the pain accompanying myocardial infarction without worsening the condition. Although the cardiac muscle is not affected, bradycardia may occur via mu receptors. Hypotension may occur due to histamine release and medullary vasomotor depression. Hypotension is frequently encountered when changing from a sitting position to a standing position (orthostatic hypotension).

Effects on Eyes

Most opioid analgesics produce miosis. This effect is caused by stimulation of the mu receptors in the brain. Most opioid analgesics produce pinpoint pupils in toxic doses. However, meperidine produces mydriasis (dilation). Therefore, the pupil size cannot be used to determine what drug was used by unconscious (overdose) patients.

LO 19.4
DRUG ADMINISTRATION

Opioid analgesics are frequently administered on a repeated schedule (every 4 to 8 hours) to relieve moderate to severe pain. To be effective, these analgesics must be given before intense pain is present. It is important, therefore, that these analgesics be administered on time, as scheduled. Adherence to the prescribed schedule ensures that patients have an adequate blood level of drug to sustain an analgesic effect. If the next dose of drug is significantly delayed, the pain will recur and may be enhanced by psychological factors associated with anticipation of discomfort.

The opioids are available for oral and parenteral administration. Parenteral formulations are used more in surgery and postsurgical recovery. Oral preparations are used to treat acute and chronic pain. All of the oral formulations should be swallowed, never chewed. The amount of drug that can be released as a burst from chewing the tablet could achieve a higher blood level than expected with an increase in side effects. Oral preparations are available for extended release (ER) and immediate release (IR). Morphine capsules (*Avinza*), hydromorphone (*Exalgo*), and oxymorphone (*Opana ER*) are modified-release formulations that permit once-a-day dosing for moderate to severe pain in patients requiring 24-hour pain relief. Immediate-release tablets provide the fastest blood levels from oral absorption. Once the effective analgesic blood level is achieved, the patient may be switched to a controlled-release formulation that releases drug over 8 to 12 hours. In this way the duration of analgesia is increased. Even with sustained-release formulations, patients often experience breakthrough pain that requires immediate attention. Immediate-release formulations and the ultra-rapid-acting fentanyl buccal tablets and lozenges treat breakthrough pain.

Recently there has been a significant change in the attitude and methods regarding the treatment of chronic severe pain. Specialists in pain and symptom management use aggressive drug treatment schedules where dosing is often under the control of the patient. In order to ensure the drug is being taken before intense pain has developed, in hospitals, patients may be using patient-controlled analgesia (PCA). PCA allows the patient to use the lowest effective dose of opioid before the pain intensity becomes unbearable. In effect, the patient minimizes the opportunity for dependence through lower dose exposure and a customized administration schedule.

Drug delivery systems also have improved. Examples of opioid preparations are presented in Figure 19.4. A transdermal patch and transmucosal lozenge are now available forms of fentanyl that are used for the treatment of chronic pain. Transmucosal lozenges are sucked rather than swallowed or chewed. An absorbable film that sticks to the inside of the cheek delivers fentanyl (*Onsolis*) to the oral mucosa. The formulation is indicated for the management of severe flares of breakthrough pain in patients already taking opioids. Because fentanyl is subject to abuse and misuse, *Onsolis* was approved for use in accordance with a risk management program and is restricted to eligible prescribers participating in the program.

Figure 19.4   **Opioid Analgesics Available as Tablets, Nasal Spray, and Transdermal Patches**

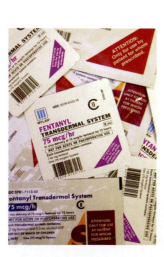

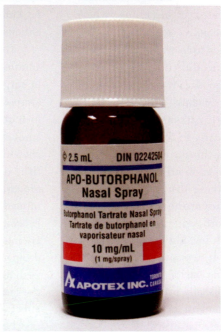

Opioid analgesics are CNS depressants at any dose. It is therefore important to monitor vital signs when patients, especially the elderly, are receiving these drugs. Indications of decreased blood pressure or respiration may be a clue that patients have been overmedicated and are experiencing cardiovascular or respiratory depression.

Absorption and Metabolism

Since these analgesics are weak bases, these drugs are not well absorbed in the acid environment of the stomach. They are absorbed in the intestines, where the pH is more alkaline. Regardless of the route of administration, metabolic inactivation of the opioid eventually occurs in the hepatic drug microsomal metabolizing system. Heroin is a particularly dangerous drug because it is not metabolized to an inactive product. Heroin is rapidly changed into a very active molecule, morphine. Several opioids are metabolized to products that produce analgesia. A clinical benefit is maintained because the circulating active metabolites increase the duration of analgesic activity.

Eventually, the kidneys excrete the metabolic products. Anything that causes the urine to become alkaline, such as alkalosis and diuretics (see Chapter 24), increases

Figure 19.5

Site of Action of Methylnaltrexone

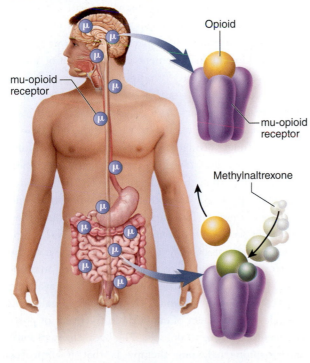

This opioid antagonist stops opioid agonists (analgesics) from interacting with the mu receptor in the intestines.

tubular reabsorption of the opioids. This action elevates the concentration of drug in the blood and increases the risk of developing drug toxicity.

LO 19.5   LO 19.7   LO 19.9

ADVERSE EFFECTS, TOLERANCE, AND PHYSICAL DEPENDENCE

The most common effects produced by these analgesics include mental confusion, nausea, vomiting, dry mouth, constipation, and urinary retention. Constipation is bothersome, especially in the treatment of cancer patients. An opioid antagonist, methylnaltrexone (*Relistor*), is used to reverse such GI effects. Methylnaltrexone bromide selectively blocks peripheral mu-opioid receptors without affecting receptors in the CNS. It is approved for treatment of opioid-induced constipation in patients with advanced illnesses or palliative care who receive opioids for pain relief. (See Figure 19.5.) One subcutaneous injection every other day, but no more frequently than every 24 hours, is the recommended dosing frequency. Dosage is individualized to the patient by weight. In sensitive individuals, histamine release produces hypotension and allergic reactions ranging from itching, skin rashes, and wheals to anaphylaxis. Therefore, it is important to determine whether patients are allergic to any opioid before administering one.

Several, but not all, opioids have black box warnings in their instructions for use. Fentanyl, hydromorphone, methadone, morphine, oxycodone, oxymorphone, and propoxyphene have special cautionary warnings that emphasize the level of abuse liability is highest among these opioids. Deaths from respiratory depression have occurred. Patients must not consume alcohol or medications containing alcohol while on these products because of the synergy to depress the CNS, especially respiration. Certain preparations, for example, morphine capsules (*Kadian*) 100 and 200 mg, are not recommended for treatment of non-opioid-dependent patients. The extended-release formulations hydromorphone (*Exalgo*) and oxymorphone (*Opana ER*), the transmucosal fentanyl (*Onsolis*), and the dosage strength *Kadian* are intended only for the management of opioid-tolerant patients. These drugs are not for the management of acute or postoperative pain.

Tolerance

The effects associated with the chronic use of opioid analgesics are the development of tolerance and physical dependence. Tolerance may result from several changes in the opioid receptors. Desensitization of mu and kappa receptors may be involved, where the G protein does not couple with the opioid as before. The neurotransmitter glutamate and the NMDA receptor may regulate the amount of opioid receptors so that fewer are available for coupling. Although the opioid is present in increasingly larger amounts, it has fewer competent receptors to produce the responses. Tolerance develops to the euphoria, analgesia, sedation, and respiratory depression produced by the opioid analgesics. Tolerance does not develop equally to all opioid effects. When tolerance develops to sedation, drowsiness, or respiratory depression, this is a beneficial response. If, however, the degree of pain has not changed, but the dose of drug must be increased to achieve relief of pain, this is analgesic tolerance, which is not beneficial to the patient. (If pain increases, as occurs with cancer patients, and the dose of opioid is increased to cover the escalating pain, this is not tolerance.) At sufficiently large doses, even tolerant individuals will die from severe respiratory depression (arrest). The onset of tolerance varies with the analgesic. On the other hand, tolerance seldom develops to the annoying spasmogenic effects such as constipation and urinary retention.

Cancer patients usually take larger doses of opioids and may experience intolerable opioid side effects. Opioid rotation is a term used to indicate a change of opioid analgesic that may produce fewer side effects. Therefore, cross-tolerance to opioid effects is relative to the patient's condition and the specific opioid.

Physical Dependence and Addiction Treatment

Physical dependence upon any opioid can develop with chronic use of the analgesic. This means that with sustained use the body reacts (withdrawal syndrome) to sudden removal or rapid dose reduction of the drug. Many people, including medical professionals and patients who have access to opioid drugs (especially meperidine), develop physical dependence. Even infants who are exposed to opioids through the placental blood can be born physically dependent upon these drugs. Controlled gradual tapering of the medication over time (days to a week) enables the person to move off the medication with little withdrawal effect.

Physical dependence is not the same as addiction. **Addiction** is a complex interaction of genetic, psychological, and socioenvironmental factors that describe behaviors in the individual and lack of control over drug use. Pain management with opioids, especially under adequate medical supervision, does not by itself cause addiction. The mechanism by which addiction occurs is not fully understood; however, it is now considered a primary disease rather than a side effect of drug usage.

Once addiction is established, the opioid is required to avoid the onset of withdrawal (abstinence syndrome).

The abstinence syndrome associated with these analgesics gradually develops over the 72 hours following the last exposure. During the initial period of withdrawal, sweating, yawning, restlessness, insomnia, and tremors occur. As the syndrome reaches its peak, blood pressure and irritability increase, accompanied by vomiting and diarrhea. Excessive sweating, gooseflesh, chills, and skeletal muscle cramps develop toward the end of the withdrawal period. Individuals who are addicted to these analgesics usually survive the withdrawal period. Administration of an opioid at any time during the withdrawal period will suppress the abstinence syndrome. Administration of an opioid antagonist in a patient with addiction will precipitate a withdrawal reaction. Other CNS drugs such as barbiturates, alcohol, or amphetamines cannot suppress opioid withdrawal.

Methadone is particularly useful in the treatment of addiction because it satisfies the opioid hunger so that the individual actually becomes acclimated to methadone. Methadone does not produce severe withdrawal symptoms and the symptoms occur gradually during the 6- to 7-week maintenance compared to 72 hours for other opioids. Since oral methadone is half as potent as parenteral methadone, it is easier to withdraw patients from methadone gradually without incurring a severe abstinence syndrome. Levomethadyl acetate is another drug that is only used for the management of opiate addiction.

The newest drug to treat addiction is buprenorphine. Buprenorphine is a partial agonist/antagonist that is used for the management and treatment of addiction. It has a high affinity (binding) for mu receptors so it pushes other opioids out of the way, blocking their attachment to receptors. As a partial agonist, it exerts a limited opioid effect, enough to reverse the withdrawal effects without producing euphoria. Buprenorphine is available for oral (*Subutex*) or parenteral (*Buprenex*) administration, but the preferred choice for maintenance therapy is the combination buprenorphine and naloxone (*Suboxone*). Treatment begins (induction) when the patient has begun to experience withdrawal symptoms. Buprenorphine alone is given 8 mg on the first day and 16 mg the second day. Thereafter, during maintenance, the patient takes the combination drug available with 0.5 or 2 mg of naloxone. The presence of naloxone precludes development of euphoria in the event of post-treatment exposure to opioids. The breakthrough with buprenorphine/naloxone therapy is that it improves patient acceptance and compliance. It permits induction in the physician's office with maintenance at home by prescription. Currently, this drug is limited to use by specially certified physicians who conduct treatment programs in accordance with the Drug Addiction Treatment Act of 2000.

Cautions and Contraindications

Opioid analgesics should not be used in patients with bronchial asthma, heavy pulmonary secretions, convulsive disorders, biliary obstruction, or head injuries. In these cases, opioids may worsen the existing condition. Ambulatory and elderly patients should be warned about the drowsiness that may accompany the use of opioid analgesics.

Since opioid analgesics will cross the placental barrier and affect fetuses, use of these drugs during pregnancy should be minimized. Short-term exposure of the fetus at term (from use of these drugs at parturition) presents relatively little potential danger to the newborn.

Opioid analgesics should never be used when a nonopioid analgesic is indicated to relieve the pain. Whenever opioid analgesics are to be administered intravenously, naloxone should be readily available.

OPIOID ANTAGONISTS AND RESPIRATORY DEPRESSION

Opioid antagonists are drugs that attach to the opioid receptors and displace the analgesic. Displacement rapidly reverses life-threatening respiratory depression. There are two types of antagonists—pure antagonists and partial antagonists (Table 19:3). Pure antagonists, such as naloxone and nalmefene, are competitive blocking drugs. Naloxone occupies the mu, delta, and kappa opioid receptors but has no agonist activity (stimulation). Naloxone inhibits the analgesic from attaching to the receptors but does not produce any pharmacological action of its own. Methylnaltrexone bromide (*Relistor*) is a relatively new drug that selectively blocks peripheral mu-opioid receptors without affecting receptors in the CNS. It is approved for treatment of opioid-induced constipation in patients with advanced illnesses or palliative care who receive opioids for pain relief. One

[Table **19:3**]

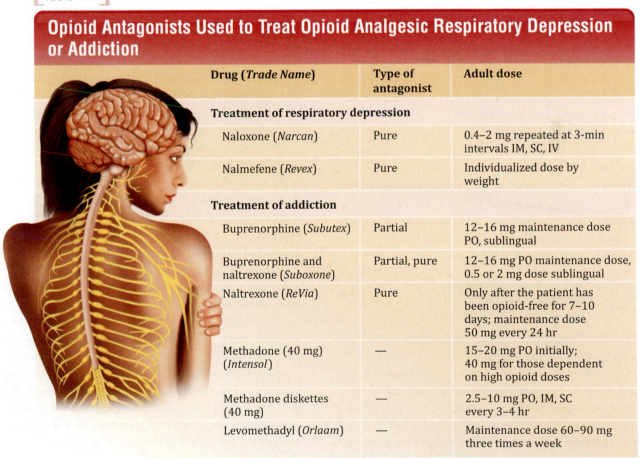

Opioid Antagonists Used to Treat Opioid Analgesic Respiratory Depression or Addiction

Drug (*Trade Name*)	Type of antagonist	Adult dose
Treatment of respiratory depression		
Naloxone (*Narcan*)	Pure	0.4–2 mg repeated at 3-min intervals IM, SC, IV
Nalmefene (*Revex*)	Pure	Individualized dose by weight
Treatment of addiction		
Buprenorphine (*Subutex*)	Partial	12–16 mg maintenance dose PO, sublingual
Buprenorphine and naltrexone (*Suboxone*)	Partial, pure	12–16 mg PO maintenance dose, 0.5 or 2 mg dose sublingual
Naltrexone (*ReVia*)	Pure	Only after the patient has been opioid-free for 7–10 days; maintenance dose 50 mg every 24 hr
Methadone (40 mg) (*Intensol*)	—	15–20 mg PO initially; 40 mg for those dependent on high opioid doses
Methadone diskettes (40 mg)	—	2.5–10 mg PO, IM, SC every 3–4 hr
Levomethadyl (*Orlaam*)	—	Maintenance dose 60–90 mg three times a week

subcutaneous injection every other day, but no more frequently than every 24 hours, is the recommended dosing frequency. Dosage is individualized to the patient by weight.

Partial antagonists such as butorphanol, nalbuphine, and pentazocine have two actions on the respiratory system. These drugs produce weak morphine-like effects in normal individuals, resulting in respiratory depression. In cases of acute opioid poisoning, however, partial antagonists reverse the respiratory depression. Partial antagonists bind with the receptors and produce little or no stimulation of the receptors which mediate respiratory depression.

Today, the drug of choice in the treatment of acute opioid poisonings is naloxone because it does not produce any respiratory depression.

Opioid overdose, or acute poisoning, frequently occurs from accidental ingestion (children), attempted suicide, or exposure of a fetus during pregnancy. The symptoms of poisoning include coma, decreased respiration, cyanosis, hypotension, and a fall in body temperature. Once patients are adequately ventilated with a respirator, the poisoning can be treated with specific opioid antagonists such as naloxone.

LO 19.3 LO 19.4 LO 19.9

OPIOID ANTITUSSIVES

Codeine, hydrocodone, and dextromethorphan are **antitussive,** which means they effectively suppress the cough reflex at therapeutic doses. Dextromethorphan and codeine are the most commonly used antitussives. They are considered to be much less potent analgesics than morphine and possess a lower addiction liability. The antitussive effect is produced by direct inhibition of the coughing center in the medulla. These drugs do not cure the underlying cause of the irritation; they merely decrease the intensity and frequency of the cough. Once the cough reflex has been suppressed, patients become less irritable and less anxious and are usually able to sleep comfortably.

Among the antitussive drugs, codeine and hydrocodone are natural derivatives of opium, whereas dextromethorphan is a synthetic product. Dextromethorphan or very small amounts of codeine have a recognized therapeutic value associated with a lower addiction potential compared to other opioid analgesics when used in recommended doses for short periods. Codeine and dextromethorphan have come under close scrutiny because of the potential for misuse, especially among people under 18 years of age. Dextromethorphan is an active ingredient in more than 100 OTC products. Nonprescription products containing these drugs have been used to achieve a "cheap high" among some people under 18. Concern has prompted attempts to change current regulations in order to restrict the sale of such products to minors. While a change in the current regulations to restrict dextromethorphan has not yet occurred, proposals are ongoing at the federal and state levels. Meanwhile, some stores have voluntarily moved dextromethorphan products behind the counter to alter access. Codeine alone and hydrocodone (*Dicodid*) are Schedule II drugs (recognized medical benefit although associated with high abuse potential with severe dependence liability). Codeine in mixtures or combination, depending on the amount present, may be Schedule III or V. Dextromethorphan is the only opioid that is not a scheduled drug. It is exempt (not included in the list) from the Controlled Substances Act.

The adult antitussive dose of codeine is 10 to 20 mg every 4 to 6 hours. For dextromethorphan, a dose of 15 to 30 mg is recommended over the same time interval. For children 6 to 12 years of age, one-half the adult dose is usually recommended. Table 19:4 compares antitussive doses for the opioid antitussive drugs. These drugs are considered effective for the treatment of a nonproductive cough that is unable to mobilize **phlegm** (mucus). Dextromethorphan is frequently found as the principal drug in over-the-counter cough and cold preparations.

The more potent antitussive drugs (hydrocodone) are not a sole ingredient in over-the-counter cough suppressant remedies. Cough suppression may be only one objective in relieving the symptoms of a cold. Additional objectives of therapy include relieving nasal congestion, reducing pain and fever, and promoting bed rest through sedation. It is not surprising, therefore, that agents such as expectorants, antihistaminics, sympathomimetics, and alcohol are present in various combinations in

Analgesic Combination Products

Trade Name	Schedule	Antitussive dose	Other active ingredients
Fioricet with codeine	III	30 mg codeine	325 mg acetaminophen, 50 mg butalbital
Lortab elixir	III	2.5 mg hydrocodone	167 mg acetaminophen, 7% alcohol
Percocet	II	2.5 mg oxycodone	325 mg acetaminophen
Percocet, Roxicet	II	2 or 5 mg oxycodone	325 mg acetaminophen
Percodan, Roxiprin	II	4.5 mg oxycodone hydrochloride and 0.38 mg oxycodone terephthate	325 mg aspirin
Tylenol with codeine elixir	V	12 mg codeine	120 mg acetaminophen, 7% alcohol
Tylenol with codeine tablets	III	15 mg codeine sulfate	300 mg acetaminophen
Vicodin ES tablets	III	7.5 mg hydrocodone	750 mg acetaminophen
Vicodin tablets	III	5 mg hydrocodone	500 mg acetaminophen
Vicoprofen tablets	III	7.5 mg hydrocodone	200 mg ibuprofen

over-the-counter cold and cough preparations. These other active ingredients (for example, antihistaminics, sympathomimetic amines) may counteract the potential for abuse.

Expectorants (ammonium chloride, guaifenesin, and terpin hydrate) are often combined with antitussive drugs to alter the volume and viscosity of mucus retained in the respiratory tract. Expectorants promote the discharge of mucus from the respiratory tract, thus reducing chest irritation and congestion. Sympathomimetic amines (ephedrine, phenylephrine, phenylpropanolamine, and pseudoephedrine) are combined with antitussive drugs to produce nasal decongestion by constricting nasal blood vessels. The antihistamines that are H_1-antagonists, such as chlorpheniramine and pyrilamine, exert an anticholinergic action, which may decrease secretion of mucus, whereas alcohol may act as a CNS depressant.

It is not unusual to find that liquid preparations contain alcohol, some in excess of 15 percent. (Consider the possible CNS interactions that may occur when these products are used in addition to other prescription medications.) Table 19:5 lists examples of combination over-the-counter preparations that contain an opioid antitussive as the principal active drug. Examples of OTC products containing dextromethorphan are shown in Figure 19.6. Note the concentration of the antitussive product as well as the types of additional pharmacological agents in each preparation. Although this is not an exhaustive list of available products, notice the various amounts of alcohol present in even pediatric liquid preparations. No wonder some of these products are recommended for bedtime use; they certainly can promote sleep.

LO 19.8
DRUG INTERACTIONS

A few specific drug interactions occur with these analgesics. Opioid analgesics potentiate the depression of any CNS depressant drug (sedative-hypnotics, alcohol, and general anesthetics). Meperidine undergoes an unusual, potentially fatal, reaction when used in the presence of monoamine oxidase (MAO) inhibitors. Sweating, hypotension, or hypertension may occur in patients taking meperidine with pargyline, phenelzine, or tranylcypromine concomitantly. Dextromethorphan has been reported to undergo a similar interaction with

Combination Over-the-Counter Preparations Containing Opioid Antitussive Drugs*

Trade Name	Antitussive	Liquid concentration	Other ingredients	Amount of alcohol
Benylin cough	10 mg dextromethorphan	2.0 mg/ml	Ammonium chloride, sodium citrate	5%
Children's Nyquil	5 mg dextromethorphan**	1.0 mg/ml	Pseudoephedrine, chlorpheniramine	—
Cheracol D	10 mg dextromethorphan	2.0 mg/ml	Guaifenesin	4.8%
Dimacol caplets	10 mg dextromethorphan	—	Guaifenesin, pseudoephedrine	—
Multisymptom Tylenol Cold	15 mg dextromethorphan	1.0 mg/ml	Chlorpheniramine, pseudoephedrine,	—
Naldecon-DX child's syrup	10 mg dextromethorphan	1.0 mg/ml	Guaifenesin, phenylpropanolamine	5%
Novahistine DH liquid	10 mg codeine***	0.4 mg/ml	Pseudoephedrine, chlorpheniramine, guaifenesin	5%
Novahistine DHX syrup	10 mg dextromethorphan	2.0 mg/ml	Pseudoephedrine	10%
Nyquil nighttime cold medicine	5 mg dextromethorphan**	1.5 mg/ml	Pseudoephedrine, doxylamine, acetaminophen	25%
Robitussin A-C	10 mg codeine**	2.0 mg/ml	Guaifenesin	3.5%
Robitussin-CF liquid	10 mg dextromethorphan**	2.0 mg/ml	Guaifenesin, phenylpropanolamine	4.8%
Tylenol cold medication, non-drowsy	15 mg dextromethorphan	—	Pseudoephedrine, acetaminophen	—
Vicks Formula 44D	10 mg dextromethorphan**	2.0 mg/ml	Pseudoephedrine	10%
Vicks Formula 44M	10 mg dextromethorphan**	1.5 mg/ml	Pseudoephedrine, chlorpheniramine, acetaminophen	—

*Not an all-inclusive list of available products. **Dose of dextromethorphan reduced from earlier formulation. ***Dose of codeine increased from earlier formulation.

phenelzine. As a result, dextromethorphan should not be given to patients who are receiving MAO inhibitors. Rifampin and phenytoin have been associated with reduction in the plasma concentrations of methadone sufficient to induce withdrawal symptoms.

Certain opioid analgesics may be administered as parenteral solutions; therefore, it is important to be aware of incompatibilities that may result in drug inactivation.

Codeine, levorphanol, meperidine, and morphine have been reported to be physically incompatible when mixed in solution with aminophylline, barbiturates, chlorothiazide, heparin, methicillin, phenytoin, sodium bicarbonate, or sulfisoxazole. Pentazocine is incompatible with solutions of aminophylline, barbiturates, glycopyrrolate, and sodium bicarbonate. Meperidine should not be mixed with solutions containing morphine.

Although opioid analgesics are frequently used in a controlled environment such as a hospital or rehabilitation center, there is considerable opportunity for outpatient use of prescription as well as over-the-counter analgesics. This potentiates the possibility for adverse reactions and/or drug interactions to occur. Patient vital signs should be monitored, especially respiration rate, to determine whether dose adjustment is required. Elderly patients require careful instruction for identifying adverse effects and contacting the physician. Specific signs such as confusion, drowsiness, forgetfulness, and impaired coordination or vision may be ignored as part of the aging process when, in fact, the degree of debilitation may be caused by the dose, frequency, or combination of medications. Written instructions for contacting the physician should be provided in large, easy-to-read type, in a format that can be carried with the patient for easy reference.

Patient Instruction

Patients must be instructed not to chew, break, or crush medications. Oral formulations must be swallowed intact to avoid bursts of drug absorption. *Avinza* (morphine) capsules may be opened and sprinkled on applesauce prior to ingestion, but the individual beads should not be crushed or mashed to avoid rapid release of the drug. As a class, these drugs cause drowsiness, sedation, dizziness, and blurred vision in therapeutic doses. Patients should be interviewed to determine whether they perform tasks that require special equipment or machinery (such as operating a sewing machine, drill press, or assembly tools), coordination, or physical dexterity. As coordination and judgment may be impaired during therapy, extra caution must be in place, including identifying a relative, coworker, or on-site medical person who is aware of the medication schedule. If necessary, alternate transportation may be advisable, particularly in older patients.

Patients should be instructed to move slowly and cautiously when getting out of bed or walking. Postural hypotension as well as drowsiness may contribute to unsteady conditions, particularly in elderly patients.

Dose Adjustment

Advise patients to check with the physician before taking over-the-counter preparations, particularly cough/cold preparations. Alcohol and CNS depressants enhance the opioid depressant effects.

Advise patients to take the drugs as prescribed. Patients should be advised not to change dose or dose interval unless instructed by the physician. **For full analgesic effect, the drug must be taken before intense pain occurs.**

Oral preparations should be swallowed, not chewed, except for fentanyl lozenge and buccal film, which are to be dissolved in the mouth.

Gastrointestinal Effects

If gastrointestinal upset occurs after oral administration, the patient can be advised to take the medication with meals or milk. If nausea, vomiting, or constipation persists, the physician should be notified for further evaluation.

Constipation, a common problem with older patients, may be potentiated with the opioid analgesics, including over-the-counter preparations. The patient should be evaluated to assess bowel function so that appropriate stool softeners or laxatives may be recommended.

Special Formulations

Patients must be instructed on the use of nasal sprays or transdermal patches. Practice in preparation and application using these systems is essential to obtaining good compliance, especially in older patients. For transdermal patch application, the area should be clear of hair. Shaving is not the method of choice because it could irritate the skin and promote absorption of greater amounts of drug. Creams, lotions, and soaps that could irritate the skin or prevent patch adhesion should not be used. Fever or high temperatures of climate can cause the patch to release more drug, resulting in toxicity. Patients should be instructed to clearly identify those times when they may be in hotter climates than usual so that dose adjustment can be considered.

Notify the Physician

Shortness of breath or difficulty breathing should be reported to the physician immediately. Hypersensitivity to these drugs is a contraindication for their use. Patients with depressed respiratory function such as chronic obstructive pulmonary disorder (COPD), emphysema, or severe asthma will exhibit respiratory distress from opioid-induced respiratory depression.

Any elevation in body temperature, such as fever, that is not associated with flu or cold should be considered as a potential side effect and should be reported to the physician.

Use in Pregnancy

Drugs in this class have been designated Food and Drug Administration (FDA) Pregnancy Category C or NR, not rated. Adequate studies in humans have not been conducted so that safety in pregnancy has not been established. However, these drugs may be used when the potential benefit to the pregnant patient outweighs the risks.

Chapter Review

Understanding Terminology

Answer the following questions.

1. What is an opioid? **(LO 19.2)**
2. Describe an antitussive effect. **(LO 19.3)**
3. Define *opioid antagonist.* **(LO 19.2, 19.7)**

Match the definition or description in the left column with the appropriate term in the right column.

___	4. The opposite of euphoria. **(LO 19.3)**	a.	ADH
___	5. Mucus. **(LO 19.3, 19.9)**	b.	analgesic
___	6. Production of only a small amount of urine. **(LO 19.3, 19.5, 19.9)**	c.	anuria
___	7. Vomiting. **(LO 19.3, 19.5)**	d.	dysphoria
___	8. Production of no urine. **(LO 19.3, 19.5, 19.9)**	e.	emesis
___	9. A substance that inhibits one's reaction to pain. **(LO 19.1, 19.9)**	f.	oliguria
___	10. Antidiuretic hormone. **(LO 19.3, 19.5)**	g.	phlegm

Acquiring Knowledge

Answer the following questions.

1. What types of pain are relieved by opioid analgesics? **(LO 19.1, 19.2, 19.3)**
2. What are the therapeutic uses of opioid analgesics? **(LO 19.3, 19.7)**
3. What is the proposed mechanism of action of opioid analgesics? **(LO 19.1, 19.3)**
4. What effects do the opioid analgesics have on the CNS? **(LO 19.3, 19.5)**
5. How might these effects be involved in other drug interactions? What drugs might potentiate CNS respiratory depression? **(LO 19.8)**
6. What is the spasmogenic action of the opioid analgesics? **(LO 19.3, 19.5, 19.9)**
7. Why does urine retention occur with the use of opioid analgesics? **(LO 19.3, 19.5)**
8. Are all opioid analgesics administered orally? Why or why not? **(LO 19.4)**
9. What adverse effects are associated with opioid analgesics? **(LO 19.5, 19.6)**

Applying Knowledge on the Job

Use your critical-thinking skills to answer the following questions.

1. One of your jobs as a pharmacy assistant is to alert the pharmacist about patients with potential contraindications or drug interactions. What's wrong with each of the following prescriptions for the patients in question?
   a. Patient A has been prescribed codeine for severe headaches. Pharmacy records indicate that the patient also takes *Metaprel,* a bronchodilator prescribed for bronchial asthma. **(LO 19.2, 19.3, 19.8)**
   b. Patient B has been prescribed morphine for severe postoperative pain. You note in reviewing his chart that he also takes the drug *Moduretic,* a diuretic, for hypertension. **(LO 19.2, 19.3, 19.8)**
   c. Patient C has been prescribed *Demerol* for a muscle injury. She's already taking *Nardil* for depression. **(LO 19.2, 19.3, 19.8)**

2. For each of the following adult patients, how much opioid is needed to produce the desired effect? **(LO 19.2, 19.4)**
   a. Patient A has been prescribed codeine for dental pain.
   b. Patient B has been prescribed a cough preparation containing codeine.
   c. Patient C has been prescribed *Dilaudid* for pain associated with cancer.
   d. Patient D has bronchitis and has been prescribed *Dilaudid* for his painful cough.

Use the appropriate reference book(s) if needed to answer the following questions.

3. Plain pentazocine was once available in a tablet form. Naloxone was later added to the tablet. Does this interfere with the pharmacological action of pentazocine when taken orally? Why was this added? **(LO 19.2, 19.4, 19.7)**

4. For several months Jack has been getting *Vicodin* (hydrocodone 5 mg/acetaminophen 500 mg) from his regular pharmacy. In the last 30 days he has received #280 *Vicodin* from several different doctors. Would you suspect possible addiction? Would you expect the pharmacy to contact the doctor(s)? Why? **(LO 19.2, 19.5)**

5. It is not uncommon for drug abusers to alter prescriptions for opioids. Common alterations to watch for include changing the quantities (i.e., 10 to 40, 30 to 80, or adding a 1 in front of the number—20 to 120) and adding refills where none were indicated. Prescribers can help deter this practice by spelling out the quantities and refills or by writing *no refill* or *non rep* if no refills are desired. Look at the following prescriptions and see if you notice anything that seems out of place. Then explain what, if anything, is out of place and what you think the pharmacy might do. **(LO 19.2, 19.4)**
   a. dental—*Vicodin* #42—1 po q6h prn dental pain—refill 4 times.
   b. bone break—*Tylenol*/codeine 30mg #30—1–2 po q3–4h prn leg pain—refill 4 times.
   c. cancer patient—morphine *Intensol* 20mg/ml #120ml—0.25 to 1 ml po q1–2h prn breakthru pain—no refill
   d. emergency room—*Demerol* 50mg tablets #110—1 po q4–6h prn migraine pain—0 refills

Multiple Choice

Use your critical-thinking skills to answer the following questions.

1. Which of the following is a correct statement? **(LO 19.3, 19.4, 19.5, 19.7, 19.9)**
   A. opioid analgesics produce little or no respiration depression with long-term use of analgesic doses
   B. opioid antagonists include endorphins
   C. all drugs in the opioid analgesic group are controlled substances, Schedule III
   D. in low doses, opioids produce nausea and vomiting

2. Oxycodone in therapeutic doses can stimulate mu receptors to cause **(LO 19.3, 19.5, 19.7, 19.9)**
   A. hyperventilation and deep breathing
   B. bronchospasms
   C. spasmogenic activity in the ureters and sphincter muscle
   D. relaxation of the skeletal muscles controlling posture (spasmolytic)

3. Opioid analgesics are used in which of the following settings? **(LO 19.1, 19.2, 19.3, 19.4)**
   A. induction of Monitored Anesthesia Care and treatment of chronic severe pain
   B. routine treatment of migraine
   C. unmonitored treatment of chronic severe pain
   D. analgesia for patients with paralytic ileus

4. Which of the following is not a pure opioid agonist analgesic? **(LO 19.2, 19.3, 19.6, 19.7)**
   A. nalbuphine (*Narcan*)
   B. butorphanol (*Stadol*)
   C. fentanyl transmucosal (*Actiq*)
   D. sufentanil (*Sufenta*)

5. Which of the following is a correct statement? (LO 19.1, 19.2, 19.9)
   A. endorphin is an abbreviation from the terms meaning inside the organ
   B. endogenous opioid receptors include mu, alpha-2 adrenergic, and delta receptors
   C. agonism means the drug occupies the receptor and causes a response
   D. opioid agonism means the drug occupies the receptor and stops endorphins from binding to them

6. Which of the following drugs has a recognized medical therapy and does not interact with opioid receptors? (LO 19.2, 19.3)
   A. heroin
   B. codeine
   C. methadone
   D. acetaminophen

7. All opioid analgesics are associated with which of the following? (LO 19.2, 19.4, 19.5)
   A. reversal of respiratory depression from barbiturates
   B. use only for the relief of acute pain
   C. cough suppression alone or in combination with other analgesics over-the-counter
   D. tolerance develops to the analgesic response

8. Fentanyl is an opioid analgesic that (LO 19.1, 19.2, 19.4, 19.9)
   A. can be used for relief of cancer pain
   B. has many formulations (lozenge, film) because it is used routinely in dental surgery
   C. induces neuropathic pain
   D. primarily works on peripheral nerve endings rather than higher centers

Multiple Choice (Multiple Answer)

Select the correct choices for each statement. The choices may be all correct, all incorrect, or any combination.

1. Sharp pain is transmitted through which type of nerve fibers? (LO 19.1)
   A. unmyelinated
   B. myelinated
   C. A-delta
   D. C fibers

2. Which opioids are used as antitussives? (LO 19.3)
   A. sufentanil
   B. fentanyl
   C. codeine
   D. dextromethorphan

3. Opioid drugs are derived from which of the following? (LO 19.2)
   A. poppy
   B. opium
   C. chemical synthesis
   D. alkaloids

4. Select the adverse effects of opioid analgesics. (LO 19.5)
   A. constipation
   B. polyuria
   C. convulsions
   D. bradycardia

5. During tolerance to opioid analgesics, the following is happening. (LO 19.9)
   A. fewer receptors are available to produce a response
   B. increased pain by the patient requires greater doses of medication
   C. the body reacts to removal of the opioid analgesic
   D. histamine release causes hypotension

Sequencing

Place the following in order from the most addiction potential to the least addiction potential. **(LO 19.3, 19.5, 19.9)**

_____	_____	_____		_____
Most				**Least**

meperidine

heroin

methadone

pentazocine

Classification

Place the following under the appropriate analgesic potency. **(LO 19.3)**

sufentanil	levorphanol	propoxyphene
pentazocine	heroin	meperidine
oxycodone	hydrocodone	alfentanil
codeine	oxymorphone	hydromorphone

Less than morphine	Same as morphine	Greater than morphine

Documentation

Using the prescription below, answer the following questions. **(LO 19.4)**

Falls Clinic
Practice RX

12345 Main Avenue
Anytown, USA   12345
931-555-1000

NAME: ___Marge Nester_____   DATE: _____

ADDRESS: _____

RX   **Morphine 40mg**

Sig: inject subcutaneously

Dr. Warren Fisk_____ M.D.   _____M.D.

  Substitution Permitted   Dispense as written

DEA #: _____   REFILL: NR 1 2 3 4

---

a. What is the adult dose for morphine injection?
b. Is the dose prescribed within the adult dosing guidelines?
c. What is the duration of action of this medication?
d. How often would this medication likely be administered?

Labeling

Fill in the missing labels. **(LO 19.3, 19.4, 19.9)**

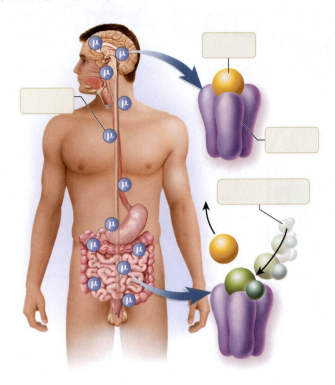

For interactive animations, videos, and assessment, visit:

www.mcgrawhillconnect.com

Chapter 20

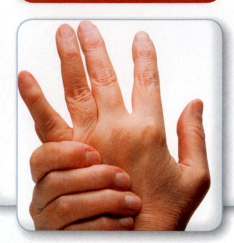

Nonopioid Analgesics, Nonsteroidal Antiinflammatories, and Antigout Drugs

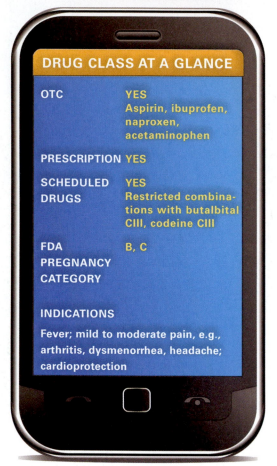

DRUG CLASS AT A GLANCE

OTC	YES Aspirin, ibuprofen, naproxen, acetaminophen
PRESCRIPTION	YES
SCHEDULED DRUGS	YES Restricted combinations with butalbital CIII, codeine CIII
FDA PREGNANCY CATEGORY	B, C
INDICATIONS	

Fever; mild to moderate pain, e.g., arthritis, dysmenorrhea, headache; cardioprotection

KEY TERMS

analgesia: inhibition of the perception of pain.

anaphylaxis: condition in which the body develops a severe allergic response; this is a medical emergency.

anemia: condition in which the number of red blood cells or the amount of hemoglobin inside the red blood cells is less than normal.

antiinflammatory: minimizing or stopping the response to tissue injury by reducing the pain, localized swelling, and chemical substances released at the site of injury.

antipyresis: reducing an elevated body temperature.

arthralgia: joint pain.

arthritis: inflammation of the joints.

COX: cyclooxygenase, a family of enzymes that produce prostaglandins.

dysmenorrhea: difficult or painful menstruation.

erythema: abnormal redness of the skin, caused by capillary congestion.

inflammation: condition in which tissues have been damaged, characterized by swelling, pain, heat, and sometimes redness.

intoxication: state in which a substance has accumulated to potentially harmful levels in the body.

ischemia: reduction in blood supply and oxygen to localized area of the body or tissue.

lavage: washing with fluids or flushing of a cavity such as the stomach.

leukopenia: condition in which the total number of white blood cells circulating in the blood is less than normal.

megaloblastic anemia: condition in which there is a large, immature form of the red blood cell, which does not function as efficiently as the mature form.

myalgia: pain associated with muscle injury.

petechia: small area of the skin or mucous membranes that is discolored because of localized hemorrhages.

phagocyte: circulating cell (such as a leukocyte) that ingests waste products or bacteria in order to remove them from the body.

prophylaxis: treatment or drug given to prevent a condition or disease.

prostaglandin: substance naturally found in certain tissues of the body; can stimulate uterine and intestinal muscle contractions and may cause pain by stimulating nerve endings.

rheumatic fever: condition in which pain and inflammation of the joints or muscles are accompanied by elevated body temperature usually a complication of untreated Strep throat.

salicylism: condition in which toxic doses of salicylates are ingested, resulting in nausea, tinnitus, and delirium.

selective COX-2 inhibitors: drugs that only interact with one of the enzymes in the cyclooxygenase family.

After studying this chapter, you should be able to

20.1 explain the inflammatory process and identify sites where drugs interrupt inflammation.

20.2 identify situations in which it is appropriate to select a nonopioid drug for pain relief.

20.3 describe the advantage of selecting acetaminophen over aspirin.

20.4 explain why nonopioid analgesics are particularly effective against inflammation.

20.5 describe the primary side effects associated with long-term aspirin and antiinflammatory drug use.

20.6 explain why probenecid, febuxostat, and colchicine are specifically useful in the treatment of gout.

Nonopioid analgesics, also known as mild analgesics, relieve mild to moderate pain without altering consciousness or mental function. In particular, these drugs relieve the low-intensity pain associated with **inflammation,** including that from **arthritis** and gout, and associated with dull aches, including headaches, **arthralgia** (joint pain), and **myalgia** (muscle pain). In addition to reducing mild pain **(analgesia),** the nonopioid analgesics reduce fever **(antipyresis)** and reduce inflammation (are **antiinflammatory**). These three pharmacological effects (analgesia, antipyresis, and antiinflammatory), known as the "three As," are characteristics of this class.

LO 20.1

INFLAMMATION AND ANTIINFLAMMATORY DRUG ACTION

The inflammatory process is a normal response to injury. When tissues are damaged, substances (histamine, bradykinin, prostaglandins, and serotonin) are released that produce vasodilation and increased permeability of the capillary walls (see Figure 20.1). Pain receptors are stimulated, and proteins and fluid leak out of the injured cells. As blood flow to the damaged area increases, **phagocytes** (leukocytes) migrate to the area to destroy harmful substances introduced by the injury. These effects result in the development of the cardinal signs of inflammation: redness, swelling (edema), warmth, pain, and loss of function.

Inflammation is usually considered the first step in the process of healing. However, in some instances, the inflammatory process becomes exaggerated or prolonged, which results in further tissue damage. In these situations, inflammation itself becomes a disease process and requires treatment with antiinflammatory drugs,

Figure 20.1 Inflammatory Tissue Injury

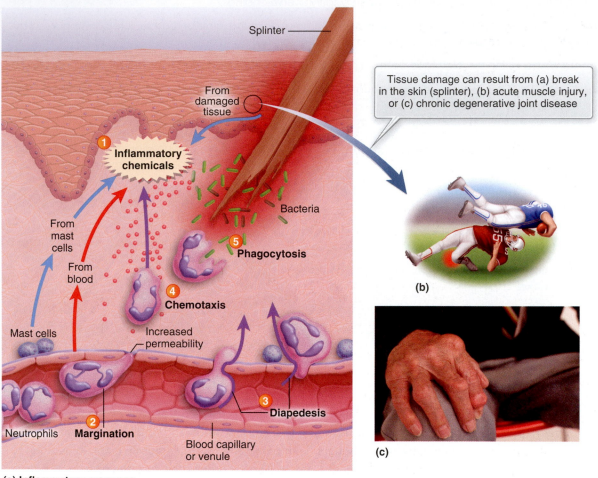

Splinter

From damaged tissue

Tissue damage can result from (a) break in the skin (splinter), (b) acute muscle injury, or (c) chronic degenerative joint disease

1 **Inflammatory chemicals**

From mast cells

From blood

Bacteria

5 **Phagocytosis**

4 **Chemotaxis**

Mast cells

Increased permeability

(b)

Neutrophils 2 **Margination**

3 **Diapedesis**

Blood capillary or venule

(c)

(a) Inflammatory response

(1) Chemical messengers are released by damaged tissue, basophils, and mast cells. These inflammatory chemicals stimulate white blood cell activity such as (2) adhesion to the capillary wall (margination), (3) diapedesis (crawling through the capillary wall), (4) chemotaxis (movement toward the source of the inflammatory chemicals), and (5) phagocytosis (engulfing bacteria or other pathogens).

which interrupt the inflammatory response. These drugs inhibit prostaglandin synthesis so that nocioceptors (free nerve endings) do not have to respond to painful, irritating stimuli, and tissue edema is resolved.

Prostaglandins are mediators of the inflammatory response (Figure 20.2). Prostaglandins are formed in the cell membranes of most organs. Prostaglandins do not travel great distances (like hormones) to their receptors. The target tissue where prostaglandin receptors are located is usually in the same general location as prostaglandin production. Enzymatic conversion of membrane phospholipids forms the parent of all prostaglandins, arachidonic acid, a fatty acid. This fatty acid undergoes further conversion through the enzyme cyclooxygenase to form prostaglandins G_2 and H_2. These intermediates are converted to several prostaglandins (Figure 20.3) that

are amazingly similar but different enough to interact with 10 unique receptors. Prostaglandins in conjuction with histamine and bradykinin are capable of stimulating peripheral pain receptors, constricting (PGE_2) or dilating ($PGF_{2\alpha}$) blood vessels, elevating body temperature (fever PGE_1), and contracting ($PGF_{2\alpha}$) or relaxing (PGE_2) smooth muscles of the bladder, intestines, bronchioles, and uterus. Prostaglandin PGE_2 is involved in the production of **erythema** (abnormal redness), edema, and pain that accompany the inflammatory process; $PGF_{2\alpha}$ is associated with uterine contraction and vasodilation.

Figure 20.2 indicates two major enzyme locations (phospholipase A_2 and cyclooxygenase) where prostaglandin synthesis can be interrupted to minimize the local inflammatory response. The site of inhibition

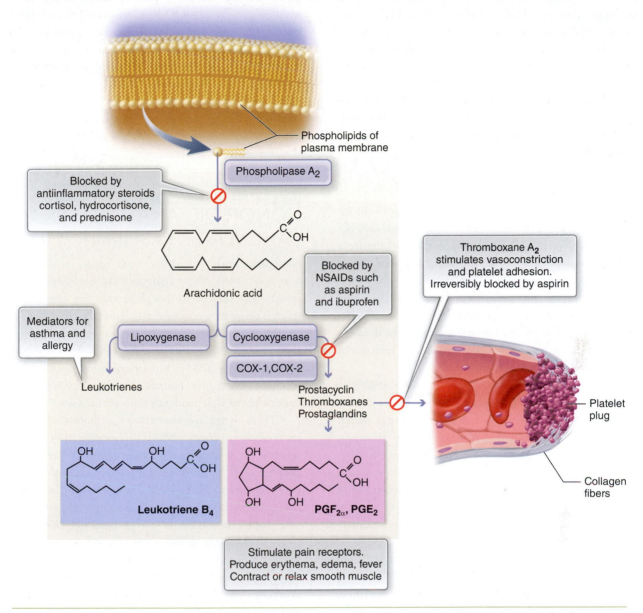

Phospholipids of plasma membrane

Phospholipase A_2

Blocked by antiinflammatory steroids cortisol, hydrocortisone, and prednisone

Arachidonic acid

Blocked by NSAIDs such as aspirin and ibuprofen

Thromboxane A_2 stimulates vasoconstriction and platelet adhesion. Irreversibly blocked by aspirin

Mediators for asthma and allergy

Lipoxygenase

Cyclooxygenase

COX-1, COX-2

Leukotrienes

Prostacyclin Thromboxanes Prostaglandins

Platelet plug

Collagen fibers

Leukotriene B$_4$

PGF$_{2\alpha}$, PGE$_2$

Stimulate pain receptors. Produce erythema, edema, fever Contract or relax smooth muscle

(a) Production of arachidonic acid through phospholipase A_2. Site of steroid inhibition of prostaglandin synthesis. (b) Production of prostaglandins from arachidonic acid through cyclooxygenase. Site of nonsteroidal antiinflammatory drug (NSAID) inhibition of prostaglandins.

differentiates one antiinflammatory drug class from another. Steroidal antiinflammatory substances (cortisol, hydrocortisone, prednisone) inhibit the formation of arachidonic acid. NSAIDs selectively inhibit the cyclooxygenase enzymes.

Cyclooxygenase (COX) is a family of enzymes required to make prostaglandins from arachidonic acid. These enzymes are also called "prostaglandin synthetase," but COX is the newer terminology. The type of prostaglandin produced is dependent upon the specific cell (e.g., platelets versus uterine muscle) and the type of cyclooxygenase present. Two subtypes of cyclooxygenase have been identified: COX-1 and COX-2. COX-1 is believed to always be available in all cells, especially in the platelets, kidneys, and gastrointestinal tract, so that homeostasis in these cells is maintained. COX-2, on the other hand, appears to be manufactured in activated macrophages in response to injury or damage to local tissues. Aspirin affects the cyclooxygenase pathway, reducing inflammatory prostaglandins, and it inhibits the thromboxane pathway, making it useful as an anti-coagulant (see Figure 20.2). NSAIDs ease the pain and headache of dysmenorrhea. Ibuprofen has been reported to suppress uterine PGF_2 even more than PGE_2, making it useful in the treatment of dysmenorrhea. Ocular NSAIDs are used after corneal surgery to block disruption of aqueous humor blood barrier and reduce intraocular pressure.

Nonsteroidal antiinflammatory drugs ease the symptoms associated with inflammation because they inhibit prostaglandin synthesis in many different tissues in the inflammation pathway.

Clinical Indications

Nonsteroidal antiinflammatory drugs are approved for the relief of mild to moderate pain where opioids are not indicated or warranted. This includes pain arising from local inflammatory responses including headache, dental extraction, soft tissue injury, sunburn, musculoskeletal, and joint overexertion and strain. Because of the direct action on regional prostaglandin production, NSAIDs also are indicated for the chronic treatment of dysmenorrhea, and for controlling the signs and symptoms of osteo- and rheumatoid arthritis.

Antiinflammatory drugs vary in their ability to reduce all types of inflammation, which may be indicative of a selective interference at enzymatic sites within the prostaglandin synthesis pathway. Sulindac (*Clinoril*), tolmetin (*Tolectin*), meclofenamic acid (*Ponstel*), meclofenamate (*Meclomen*), and piroxicam (*Feldene*) are antiinflammatory drugs used in the treatment of a variety of inflammatory conditions, such as tendinitis, bursitis, rheumatoid arthritis, osteoarthritis, and **dysmenorrhea** (difficult or painful menstruation).

Nonsteroidal antiinflammatory drugs may be used for short periods (up to 7 days) for the relief of acute inflammation. It is not uncommon, however, for these drugs to be taken for longer periods. In osteoarthritis, a degenerative joint disease, joint movement may be compromised so that movement is painful and difficult (stiff). Pain may occur in the absence of overt signs of inflammation. Although analgesics such as aspirin are indicated, it is still advisable to have patients avoid stressing the involved joints (take weight off the joints and rest).

Rheumatoid arthritis, also a degenerative joint disease, is associated with inflammation of the joint cartilage. Often, inflamed joints are noticeably warm to the touch, are difficult to move (especially in the morning), and become immobile or deformed through the course of the disease. For the treatment of osteoarthritis, spondylitis (inflammation of the vertebrae), and gout, aspirin can be the drug of choice.

The treatment of dysmenorrhea has markedly improved with the advent of the NSAIDs. Also known as menstrual cramps, dysmenorrhea is characterized by uterine contractions, local vasoconstriction (**ischemia**), and pain. In addition, headache, nausea, vomiting, and diarrhea may occur. Evidence suggests that women who suffer the discomfort of dysmenorrhea may have higher levels of uterine prostaglandins, especially $PGF_{2\alpha}$ and PGE_2, than nondysmenorrheic women. Nonsteroidal antiinflammatory drugs are effective in relieving the symptoms of dysmenorrhea and are much better than low doses of aspirin.

LO 20.1 | LO 20.3 | LO 20.4 | LO 20.5

NONOPIOID ANALGESICS: SALICYLATES (ASPIRIN)

Nonopioid analgesics differ from opioid analgesics in four ways. First, these analgesics are not chemically or structurally related to morphine (nor are they related to each other by a common structure). Second, they are not effective against severe, sharp (visceral) pain. Third, they produce analgesia through both a central (central nervous system [CNS]) and a peripheral (site of injury) mechanism of action. Fourth, they do not produce tolerance or physical dependency with chronic use.

These drugs are also known as nonsteroidal antiinflammatory drugs (NSAIDs) because they are not structurally related to cortisone (adrenal steroid) and produce their antiinflammatory action through a different mechanism. Cortisone is a potent antiinflammatory hormone used in specific inflammatory diseases, often when other nonsteroidal agents have not been effective. (Cortisone is discussed in Chapter 36.) There are three groups of nonopioid analgesics: salicylates and aspirin (the original NSAIDs), acetaminophen, and the synthetic NSAIDs such as ibuprophen, indomethacin, and ketoprofen. Several nonopioid analgesics are listed in Table 20:1. Nonsteroidal antiinflammatory drugs (NSAIDs) are the largest class of nonopioid analgesics. There are three groups within this class, distinguished by their prominent pharmacologic action: salicylates, traditional NSAIDs, and COX-2 selective inhibitors. This large class of drugs will be presented in two parts: salicylates and traditional NSAIDs.

The salicylates, represented by aspirin and salicylic acid, are the oldest and most frequently used nonopioid analgesic drugs that are analgesic, antipyretic, and antiinflammatory. This group will be presented first because of its historical prominence in pain management and because it is the most widely used drug in the United States.

Recommended Adult Oral Doses of NSAID (Nonopioid) Analgesics

Drug (*Trade Name*)	Analgesic and antipyretic (including dysmenorrhea)	Antiinflammatory (osteoarthritis, rheumatoid arthritis, ankylosing spondylitis)
N-acetyl-p-aminophenol		
Acetaminophen (*Tylenol*)*	325–650 mg every 4 hr 1300 mg every 8 hr, maximum daily dose 4 g	Not specifically antiinflammatory; used as short-term adjunct to other therapy
Salicylates		
Aspirin (*Ascriptin, Bayer, Bufferin, Ecotrin*)*	325–1000 mg every 4–6 hr	In divided doses; maximum daily dose 4 g
Aspirin (extra strength)	500 mg every 3 hr	1000 mg every 6 hr
Salicylic acid (*Amigesic, Arthra-G, Salflex*)**	1500 mg BID	3 g/day TID
Synthetic nonsteroidal antiinflammatory drugs ***		
Diclofenac (*Cataflam, Voltaren, Zipsor*)**	50 mg TID	100–200 mg/day
Diflunisal (*Dolobid*)**	500–1000 mg every 8–12 hr	500 mg BID; 500–1000 mg/day
Etodolac**	200–400 mg every 6–8 hr	600–1200 mg/day
Fenoprofen (*Nalfon*)**	200 mg every 4–6 hr	300–600 mg TID, QID
Flurbiprofen (*Ansaid*)**	Not indicated for this	200–300 mg up to QID
Ibuprofen (*Advil, Motrin, Nuprin*)* (available by prescription in 300 mg or more)**	200–400 mg every 4–6 hr	600 mg QID; 300–800 mg QID
Indomethacin (*Indocin*)**	Not indicated for this	25–70 mg TID
Ketoprofen**	25–50 mg every 6–8 hr	300 mg/day for immediate release; 200 mg/day for extended release
Ketorolac tromethamine (only used after IV/IM therapy)**	Short-term management of moderate to severe acute (surgical) pain, 10 mg every 6 hr; not to exceed 5 days. Black box warning for use	—
Meclofenamate (*Meclomen*)**	50–100 mg every 4–6 hr	200–400 mg/day
Meclofenamic acid, meclofenamate (*Ponstel*)**	250 mg every 6 hr; dysmenorrhea also. NSAID class warning	
Meloxicam (*Mobic*)	Not indicated for this	7.5–15 mg/day (long half-life 20 hrs)
Nabumetone**	Not indicated for this	1000 mg QD, BID (long half-life 26 hrs)
Naproxen (*Aleve, Midol, extended relief*)*	200 mg every 6–8 hr	550 mg BID or 275 mg every 6–8 hrs; maximum daily dose 1100 mg
Naproxen (*Anaprox, Naprelan, Naprosyn*)**	200 mg every 6–8 hr dysmenorrhea also	250–500 mg BID

(Continued)

Drug (*Trade Name*)	Analgesic and antipyretic (including dysmenorrhea)	Antiinflammatory (osteoarthritis, rheumatoid arthritis, ankylosing spondylitis)
Oxaprozin (*Daypro*)**	Not indicated for this	1200–1800 mg QD (long half-life 58 hrs)
Piroxicam (*Feldene*)**	Not indicated for this	20 mg/day (long half-life 57 hrs)
Sulindac (*Clinoril*)**	Not indicated for this	200 mg BID; 400 mg/day
Tolmetin**	Not indicated for this	400 mg TID up to 1800 mg/day
Selective COX-2 Inhibitors		
Celecoxib (*Celebrex*)**	Not indicated for this	200 mg/day

*Available over the counter. **Available by prescription. ***These drugs are antipyretic and analgesic but are primarily used for their antiinflammatory actions. All NSAIDs have a class warning for use in patients with myocardial infarction, CABG (coronary artery bypass graft), and gastrointestinal bleed potential.*

The traditional NSAIDs, represented by ibuprofen and naproxen, and the sole COX-2 inhibitor, celecoxib, will follow. Traditional NSAIDs are primarily used for their antiinflammatory action. Finally, the analgesic and antipyretic drug acetaminophen will be presented, followed by the drugs used for the clinical management of gout.

Salicylates were discovered centuries ago as a natural product of the willow tree bark. Native Americans drank teas and beverages made from willow bark to relieve headaches and toothaches. The salicylates used today include sodium salicylate, aspirin (acetylsalicylic acid), salicylamide, and methyl salicylate. Methyl salicylate (oil of wintergreen, *Ben-Gay, Deep-Heat*) is the only salicylate that is a poison when taken orally. Methyl salicylate is used topically (creams) to produce cutaneous irritation, which increases blood flow and warmth at the site of application. The other salicylates (aspirin) are weak acids that are rapidly absorbed from the stomach and small intestine following oral administration.

Analgesia and Antipyresis

The centers of the brain that regulate pain and temperature are located in the hypothalamus. Nonopioid analgesics, including salicylates, are thought to produce analgesia and antipyresis by selectively affecting the hypothalamic centers, reducing an elevated body temperature but not affecting normal body temperature. The mechanism of the central action involves blockade of prostaglandin stimulation of the central nervous system (CNS). In addition to the central action, these drugs increase peripheral blood flow (vasodilation) and sweating, permitting a greater loss of excess heat from the body.

Analgesia is produced by affecting both the hypothalamus and the site of injury. In response to tissue injury, joint damage, or edema, active substances such as bradykinin, prostaglandins, and histamine are released. **Prostaglandins** and bradykinin, in particular, stimulate peripheral nerve endings, which carry pain impulses to the CNS. Nonopioid analgesics inhibit the synthesis of prostaglandins and prevent bradykinin from stimulating pain receptors. Since prostaglandins also affect hypothalamic centers, nonopioid analgesics inhibit the recognition of pain impulses centrally and peripherally. Aspirin is the most potent inhibitor of prostaglandin synthetase in the salicylate group. Headache is caused by a variety of stimuli; it can result from vascular, allergic, or local pain triggers. (See Figure 20.3.) Aspirin is particularly useful in the treatment of headache because inhibition of COX inhibits the formation of prostaglandins thus reducing vascular permeability and release of other neurotransmitters involved in pain generation.

Antiinflammatory Action

Salicylates are excellent antiinflammatory drugs. They are effective in reducing inflammation because they inhibit a primary pathway in prostaglandin synthesis. These drugs are antiinflammatory, inhibiting both COX-1 and COX-2. The development of inflammation and the action of the salicylates upon this response was presented in the section on Inflammation and Antiinflammatory Drug Action.

Figure 20.3

Headache Caused by Prostaglandin-Mediated Pain and Vascular Permeability (Edema)

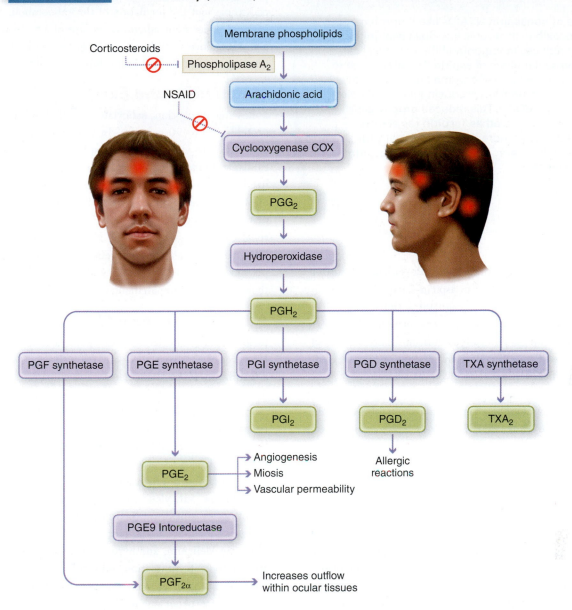

Gastrointestinal Effects

Salicylates directly irritate the stomach mucosal lining. Many people are sensitive to this action and experience nausea after taking aspirin. In addition, salicylates inhibit prostaglandin synthesis. In the stomach, prostaglandins are an integral part of the normal cytoprotective mechanisms. Prostaglandins mediate secretion of mucus and bicarbonate, which protect the lining of the stomach from erosion by gastric acid. When COX-1 is blocked, the protective environment within the stomach is altered, leading to gastric distress and ulcers. In some individuals, vomiting occurs as a result of gastrointestinal (GI) irritation and CNS stimulation. Salicylates stimulate the medullary center known as the chemoreceptor trigger zone. This zone directly excites the vomiting center so that emesis may occur.

Anticoagulant and Cardiovascular Benefit

Aspirin and salicylamide irreversibly inhibit the aggregation of platelets necessary for blood clot formation. Aspirin permanently hinders the access of arachidonic acid to the active site on the COX-1 enzyme (see Figure 20.2). As a result, even low doses of aspirin increase bleeding time. In large doses, salicylates may depress the formation of other coagulation factors (prothrombin), thus increasing bleeding time. **Petechial** (localized) hemorrhages that occur in aspirin-sensitive patients are partially due to the anticoagulant actions. With doses of aspirin greater than 6 g per day, prolongation of pro-thrombin time is clinically significant. This may be significant and requires close monitoring in patients with clotting disorders.

Of therapeutic significance is the fact that aspirin reduces the risk of death and reinfarction following myocardial infarction (MI). Low-dose aspirin daily lowers the risk of heart attack and prevents heart disease and a second heart attack in women over 65 years old and men at any age. Women benefit from aspirin therapy because the risk of first stroke also is reduced. This has not been shown to occur in men. The results of many studies conclude that this cardiovascular benefit warrants its prophylactic daily use. This prophylactic action is directly related to irreversible inhibition of platelet aggregation and has no effect once a clot has formed. Decreased platelet aggregation (prophylaxis against clots and stroke) is mediated by COX-1. Aspirin is unique because it covalently (tight bonding) modifies COX so that new COX enzymes must be synthesized to replace the bound inactive complex. (This is why relatively small amounts of aspirin affect platelets for more than a day. As aspirin is being absorbed, platelets moving through the intestines have their COX permanently blocked. New COX forms only with the synthesis of new platelets.) In patients with atrial fibrillation who cannot take warfarin (oral anticoagulant), adult-strength aspirin daily may be used to provide anticoagulant protection.

These anticoagulant effects increase the potential for hemorrhage in certain patients—that is, those sensitive to salicylates or receiving other anticoagulants or those predisposed to intestinal ulcers. In specific cardiovascular-compromised patients where ulcers are present, chronic administration of aspirin may be beneficial to prevent the formation of thromboemboli. While it does appear contradictory, the use of aspirin in such a circumstance would reduce the greater risk of emboli forming or reaching the brain, lung, or heart.

Metabolism and Excretion

Following absorption, salicylates readily bind to plasma proteins (80 to 90 percent). In this way, salicylates are distributed to various tissues, especially the CNS, joint fluids, and kidneys. Eventually, these drugs are metabolized in the liver and excreted into urine. Plasma levels of salicylates are affected by the pH of the urine. Acidic urine permits these weak acids to be reabsorbed by the renal tubules and reenter the blood. In contrast, alkaline urine increases the excretion of salicylates. Urine pH can change in response to acid-base imbalance, drug therapy, or renal impairment.

Adverse and Toxic Effects

In low doses, salicylates relieve pain, aches, and fever. However, to relieve the pain of arthritis, gout, and **rheumatic fever,** salicylates must be used in large doses for long periods of time. Large-dose therapy is more frequently associated with toxic reactions (chronic **intoxication**). However, acute salicylate intoxication also may occur from accidental ingestion of large amounts of drug. Accidental overdose is more likely to occur with children than with adults.

Chronic salicylate intoxication produces nausea, vomiting, or salicylism. **Salicylism** is a series of symptoms that include nausea, ringing in the ears (tinnitus), headache, delirium, and hyperventilation. These effects are due to CNS stimulation and subside when the dose is reduced or the drug is terminated. In addition, hyperglycemia may occur due to increased sympathetic tone.

A cultural contribution to the development of salicylate intoxication may come from the patient's diet. Many foods are known to contain salicylates naturally, such as curry powder, paprika, licorice, prunes, raisins, tea, and gherkins. It has been estimated that the American diet may contain 6 to 200 mg of salicylates per day.

Hypersensitivity to aspirin may produce skin rashes, laryngeal edema, and asthma. Such reactions may be life-threatening, so that hypersensitive patients must avoid all products containing aspirin. Salicylates are readily available as over-the-counter (OTC) drugs, either alone or in combination with other products. Examples of drug mixtures that contain nonopioid analgesics are presented in Table 20:2. Such products are present in almost every home, and many times they are found by adventurous

Drug Mixtures That Contain Nonopioid Analgesics***

Trade Name	Amount of nonopioid analgesic	Other active drugs	Schedule
Alka-Seltzer, Ascriptin, Bufferin	325–500 mg aspirin	1700–2085 mg sodium bicarbonate 1000 mg citric acid	—
Aspirin	650 mg aspirin	—	—
Bromo-Seltzer	325 mg acetaminophen	2781 mg sodium bicarbonate 2224 mg citric acid	—
Bufferin Extra Strength	500 mg aspirin	—	—
Darvocet-N 50*	325 mg acetaminophen	50 mg propoxyphene	IV
Darvocet-N 100*	650 mg acetaminophen	100 mg propoxyphene	IV
Darvon Compound-65*	389 mg aspirin	32.4 mg caffeine, 65 mg propoxyphene	IV
Equagesic*	325 mg aspirin	Meprobamate 200 mg	IV
Fiorinal*	325 mg aspirin	40 mg caffeine, 50 mg butalbital (barbiturate)	III
Midol IB, Advil, Menadol, Pamprin-IB	200 mg ibuprofen	—	—
Maximum Strength Midol PMS capsules and gelcaps	500 mg acetaminophen	25 mg Pamabrom**, 15 mg pyrilamine	—
Pamprin Maximum Cramp Relief	500 mg acetaminophen	Pamabrom**, pyrilamine	—
Panacet 5/500	500 mg acetaminophen	5 mg hydrocodone	III
Panadol Children's	80 mg acetaminophen	—	
Percodan*	325 mg aspirin	4.5 mg oxycodone HCl, 0.20 mg oxycodone terephthalate	II
Percocet*	325 mg acetaminophen 500 mg acetaminophen 650 mg acetaminophen	2.5, 5, 7.5, or 10 mg oxycodone 7.5 mg oxycodone 10 mg oxycodone	II II II
Tylenol with Codeine* No. 2, No. 3, and No. 4	300 mg acetaminophen	15, 30, or 60 mg codeine	III
Tylox capsules*	500 mg acetaminophen	5 mg oxycodone	II
Vanquish**	204 mg acetaminophen	227 mg aspirin, 33 mg caffeine, magnesium hydroxide and, aluminum hydroxide	
ZORprin*	800 mg aspirin	—	—

*Available by prescription only. **Over-the-counter diuretic. ***Not an all-inclusive list of available products.

children. Attracted by the colored tablets or candy flavor, children often ingest a toxic amount of analgesic. There is a cautionary safety warning associated with the use of salicylates specifically directed at its use in children. Children and teenagers should not use salicylates for chickenpox or flu symptoms before a doctor is consulted because of the possibility for Reye's syndrome to occur.

Acute Toxicity

The dangerous and often fatal reactions of acute salicylate poisoning involve respiratory depression and acidosis. Toxic doses of salicylates depress the medullary respiratory centers so that individuals cannot remove carbon dioxide (CO_2) rapidly, leading to respiratory acidosis. Other acids accumulate in the blood because renal function is impaired. Salicylates and tissue waste products (lactic acid) cannot be cleared from the body. Individuals enter respiratory and metabolic acidosis, and the blood and urine pH values fall. Profuse sweating causes dehydration, and sodium, potassium, and protein excretion in the urine may increase. Cardiovascular function is depressed, resulting in vasodilation and hypotension. The acute lethal dose is estimated to be 10 to 30 g for adults and 4 g for children.

Treatment of salicylate poisoning includes administration of sodium bicarbonate to correct the acidosis and to increase salicylate excretion (increase urine pH). In addition, fluid and electrolytes are infused to correct the hypotension and acid-base balance. Treatment of salicylate poisoning is not always successful. Coma and death may result from dehydration, extensive CNS depression, and renal failure.

Clinical Indications

Salicylates, especially aspirin, are used in mild to moderate pain. This is pain that is not associated with the need for opioids. Inflammation contributing to headache and to muscle and joint pain, including osteoarthritis and rheumatoid arthritis, is reduced and often eliminated by these drugs.

Aspirin is the cornerstone in treatment and prevention of cardiovascular disease. Low-dose aspirin (50 to 100 mg daily) reduces the risk of developing myocardial infarction, transient ischemic attacks (TIAs), and stroke. Clinical management of acute myocardial infarction and stroke requires doses greater than 160 mg daily. Because of the special action on platelet aggregation, aspirin is indicated for use in patients with unstable angina pectoris, TIAs, and stroke, and to reduce the risk of death in men and women with MI. For years patients have been told to take low-dose aspirin to reduce the risk of stroke and myocardial infarction. More recently the data

from long-term studies in patients taking daily aspirin have been reevaluated. The consensus is that long-term aspirin therapy reduces the development of adenomatous polyps and colorectal cancer. As any long-term therapy may be associated with the onset of side effects, patients who have more than average risk for developing colorectal cancer may be the primary group to benefit from this aspirin treatment strategy.

Salicylates that are related to or metabolized to 5-ASA (acetylsalicylic acid) are widely used in the management of ulcerative colitis. Balsalazide (*Colozal*), mesalamine (*Asacol, Pentasa, Rowasa*), olsalazine (*Dipentum*), and sulfadiazine (*Azulfidine, Azulfidine EN tabs*) are administered orally to act within the colon to influence prostaglandin production and activity there. The mechanism of action of these drugs is not specifically known.

Dose and Formulation Availability

Because of its long-standing use, aspirin has become widely acceptable as safe for use in adults and children. To accommodate the wide spectrum of use, aspirin and salicylates are available in a variety of oral formulations ranging from tablets, capsules, and gum to solutions and liquids more easily swallowed by children. While aspirin is available over-the-counter (OTC) alone or in combination with a wide variety of other active ingredients, a prescription is required for products containing greater than 650 mg of aspirin per tablet (see Table 20:1 for examples). Pediatric dosing is based on age and weight, with two 81-mg pediatric tablets (age 2 to 3 years) equal to one-half of a 325-mg adult tablet, every 4 hours. At age 6 to 8 years, the dose is four 81-mg tablets or one adult tablet (325 mg). By age 12 to 14 years, dosing is at the recommended adult level of two (325-mg) tablets (see Table 20:3).

Note to the Health Care Professional

Aspirin use in children, including teenagers, who have active viral infections or chickenpox has been associated with the development of Reye's syndrome. Although rare, this condition can be life-threatening. The symptoms range from vomiting and belligerence to delirium and coma. Death has occurred in some children. Although the mechanism has not been fully characterized, various professional and government organizations advise against the use of aspirin in young adults or children with active flu or chickenpox.

Pediatric Oral Dosing Guidelines for Aspirin and Acetaminophen — Dose Every 4–6 Hours

Age	Acetaminophen	Aspirin
0–3 months	40 mg	—
4–11 months	80 mg	—
1–2 years	120 mg	—
2–3 years	160 mg	162 mg
4–5 years	240 mg	243 mg
6–8 years	320 mg	324 mg
9–10 years	400 mg	405 mg
11 years	480 mg	486 mg
12–14 years	640 mg	648 mg
14 years	650 mg	650 mg

LO 20.1   LO 20.2   LO 20.3   LO 20.4   LO 20.5

ACETAMINOPHEN

Acetaminophen is often considered an aspirin substitute. However, this assumption is not entirely correct. Acetaminophen (*Datril, Panadol, Tylenol*) produces adequate analgesia for the relief of a minor headache and antipyresis but has no proven antiinflammatory activity. It reduces elevated body temperature by a direct action on the heat regulation centers in the hypothalamus, postulated to occur through the COX-3 receptors. Acetaminophen has been a puzzle because it suppresses pain and fever but has relatively little effect on inflammation or the secretion of stomach acid. More recent evidence suggests that it may act on another COX, tentatively called COX-3, that is mainly found in the brain. Acetaminophen is effective against the pain of headache because it inhibits prostaglandin synthetase within the CNS but is not a drug of choice in the treatment of pain associated with muscle aches and inflammation, especially arthritis. Acetaminophen does not significantly inhibit the synthesis of prostaglandins in peripheral systems, which accounts for the lack of antiinflammatory activity. For the relief of headache or the symptomatic relief of cold and flu, aspirin-sensitive patients may substitute acetaminophen because acetaminophen does not produce GI irritation or ulceration in therapeutic doses. Acetaminophen does not affect platelet aggregation or prothrombin response.

Clinical Indications

Acetaminophen is approved to reduce fever, headache, minor musculoskeletal pain, and discomfort associated with the common cold and flu. It is particularly indicated for use in patients allergic to aspirin, those receiving anticoagulant therapy for coagulation disorders, or patients who have upper GI disease and for whom aspirin therapy is not an option. It is recommended for use in patients who experience GI upset from aspirin or nonsteroidal antiinflammatory drugs (NSAIDs); however, it is not interchangeable with these products for chronic therapy of inflammatory conditions such as osteoarthritis. No benefit has been associated with the use of this drug in stroke or infarction.

Dose and Formulation Availability

Acetaminophen is available in OTC products in doses ranging from 80 mg (pediatric) to 650 mg per tablet, capsule, or caplet. Dosing guidelines are available for infants 0 to 3 months (40 mg), 4 to 11 months (80 mg), and 1 to 2 years of age (120 mg). The pediatric and adult doses of 325 mg every 4 hours coincide at the recommendation for 6 to 8 years of age. It is recommended that the adult daily dose not exceed 4000 mg, while the pediatric exposure should not exceed 5 doses in 24 hours (Table 20:3). Because of its acceptability for use in children, acetaminophen is available in a variety of formulations ranging from suppository to solution, elixir, suspension, and syrup. At all doses and formulations, acetaminophen is available without prescription, OTC. For best shelf-life, suppositories should be refrigerated between use.

Adverse Effects

Although remarkably safe when taken in recommended doses, acetaminophen is not a harmless drug. Toxicity may develop from chronic use of large doses of acetaminophen (more than 4 g/day in adults and 75 mg/kg/day in children with febrile illnesses) as well as acute overdose from a single episode of ingestion of a large dose (such as an accidental overdose of 200 mg/kg in children and 6 g in adults). There are no specific early warning signs of acetaminophen toxicity. The course of poisoning may follow several stages. During the first 24 hours after ingestion, the patient may be asymptomatic; then nausea and vomiting may occur. This period often resembles "flu-like" feelings to the patient and is, therefore, ignored as evidence of toxicity. During the next 24 hours, hepatic serum enzymes may rise (AST/SGOT, ALT/SGPT, bilirubin, thrombin). Elevations in AST/SGOT may exceed 20,000. Within 36 hours of ingestion of a toxic dose, hepatic damage may result. Deaths have occurred following acetaminophen overdose. Overdose of acetaminophen also produces acidosis and respiratory complications similar to those described for salicylate poisoning.

Treatment for acetaminophen poisoning includes gastric aspiration and **lavage** (washing with fluids) as well as maintenance of fluid balance through conventional measures. Activated charcoal has been used for decades as a general sequestrant of oral poisons; it will decrease the absorption of acetaminophen if administered within hours of the ingested overdose.

There is, however, an approved antidote for toxic acetaminophen overdose. N-acetylcysteine (NAC, *Acetadote*) is the antidote for toxic acetaminophen overdose. It is usually given by mouth; however, the odor is particularly foul and has to be mixed with palatable liquids or juices to get patient compliance and to minimize its irritation on the stomach lining. Otherwise, it

is given intravenously. The oral dose is repeated over 72 hours to ensure maximal detoxification of the active metabolite, whereas the intravenous route may complete the effect in half the time. N-acetylcysteine stimulates the metabolic system (glutathione) that binds (conjugates) the toxic metabolite and removes it from the body. NAC also facilitates the metabolism of the remaining acetaminophen to a nontoxic product. N-acetylcysteine successfully prevents liver damage when administered intravenously or orally within 10 hours of acetaminophen poisoning. The intravenous route may be preferred over the oral route of administration because detoxification can be accomplished in 24 hours with fewer dosings. The intravenous route has been associated with **anaphylactoid reactions** (allergic reaction) such as flushing, rash, urticaria, hypotension, and bronchospasm. These effects are seen more often in patients with a history of asthma or obstructive airway disease after the initial loading dose of NAC and can be medically managed with intravenous administration of an antihistamine. N-acetylcysteine has been available for years as a mucolytic in cystic fibrosis patients; however, a specific intravenous formulation has been prepared for use in toxic overdose of acetaminophen.

Special Considerations

Acetaminophen is used in more combination products than any other drug in doses from 160 to 500 mg per dose. It has been estimated that one-third of the people in the United States take acetaminophen in some form at least once a month. While taken within the recommended doses for appropriate indications, it is still *relatively* safe and effective. There is an expectation for the over-the-counter products that relatively safe means more is better without risk. When patients take acetaminophen (*Tylenol*) for pain and then use multiple OTC products for relief of cold and flu symptoms, especially in addition to alcohol, there is an increased risk of developing liver toxicity. The excessive use of acetaminophen causes metabolites of the drug to bind to tissue groups in the kidney and liver, causing hepatotoxicity. Liver transplantation is often the only treatment to prevent death. People who consume more than three alcoholic beverages per day have potential hepatic sensitivity that becomes compromised with increased exposure to acetaminophen.

The FDA has continued to express a concern that adults and children are at risk for developing an acetaminophen toxicity through overdose because flavored medications attract children to these medications and adults frequently take "more than the recommended dose striving to eliminate moderate to severe pain." Acetaminophen has been reported to be associated with liver failure in children. Among adults, there is a risk of increased exposure because the large daily doses used by some patients for arthritis (4 to 6 g/day) are compounded by frequent use of the "nonaspirin" headache or cold and flu remedies. Also, the risk of exposure is increased with use of opioid analgesic combination drugs like *Vicodin, Tylox,* or *Percocet.*

Finally, in 2009 the FDA took action to require stronger language in the label for acetaminophen, warning about the risk of developing liver injury with acetaminophen use. This will be required of any acetaminophen-containing product whether an over-the-counter or prescription product, or a single entity or combination product. There is also a recommendation to remove acetaminophen from all combination products, especially those containing strong opioid analgesics, or to place a cautionary boxed warning in the labeling for these products. There is a recommendation to reduce the maximum allowed daily dose of acetaminophen from 4 to 2.6 g per day. Reducing the recommended maximum individual dose from 1000 to 650 mg will not change habits of patient use where more than two or three tablets are taken, exposing the patient to the same total drug exposure.

Organ-specific safety information and dose recommendations are directed to the attention of the consumer/patient, not just medical personnel. This also will be the case for identifying the known drug interaction of acetaminophen with warfarin. Acetaminophen has been reported, in doses of 2 g/day for a week, to increase the anticoagulant effect of warfarin. The mechanism—inhibition of the liver enzyme metabolism of warfarin, resulting in increased circulating anticoagulant—also has been reported to occur with lower-dose exposure (e.g., several 325-mg tablets). For patients taking warfarin, acetaminophen should be taken at the lowest effective dose for short-term therapy only. Coagulation status should be monitored via INR one to two times per week when starting or stopping acetaminophen therapy of more than 2 g per week.

LO 20.1 LO 20.3 LO 20.4 LO 20.5
OTHER NONSTEROIDAL ANTIINFLAMMATORY DRUGS (NSAIDS)

Although many of the drugs listed in Table 20:1 produce the same actions as the salicylates, some drugs are only employed for their antiinflammatory effects.

All NSAIDs have the ability to interact with cyclooxygenases. Older NSAIDs like aspirin, ketoprofen, and indomethacin are considered nonselective—that is, any COX will do. To develop better NSAIDs that relieve pain and inflammation but do not cause gastric problems, drugs were designed that selectively interacted with COX-2. The newest generation of NSAIDs, celecoxib (*Celebrex*), is a **selective COX-2 inhibitor** that alleviates pain and reduces inflammation by inhibiting only COX-2. Pain relief is not superior to that of the older NSAIDs; it is equal to that of the other NSAIDs. While the incidence of ulcers and gastric bleeding is less, patients have reported gastrointestinal effects similar to those of aspirin.

Drug Administration, Absorption, and Metabolism

NSAIDs are available primarily for oral administration. Only ibuprofen (*Advil*) and naproxen (*Aleve, Midol Extended Relief*) are currently available OTC (see Figure 20.4). These nonprescription preparations are extremely popular with the general public for the treatment of osteoarthritis (mild to moderate pain, including rheumatoid complications). For the same spectrum of indications, these NSAIDs require a prescription for tablet strengths greater than 300 mg (ibuprofen) and 250 mg (naproxen). Other NSAIDs are available only by prescription. Only three NSAIDs are available for parenteral administration: ibuprofen (*Neoprofen*), indomethacin (*Indocin IV*), and ketorolac. Only ketorolac (IM, IV, ophthalmic drops or intranasal spray) is used for the treatment of acute moderate to severe pain "at the opioid level" around surgery (see Figure 20.5). Parenteral ibuprofen and indomethacin are used for a nonanalgesic action: to induce closure of the atrial opening in premature infants with patent ductus arteriosis.

The NSAIDs are well absorbed from the stomach following oral administration. Although food may delay drug absorption, it is not uncommon for these drugs to

Figure 20.4

Nonprescription (OTC) Products Containing Aspirin, Acetaminophen, Ibuprofen, and Naproxen

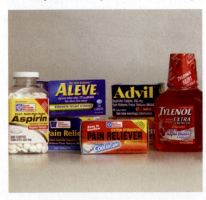

Figure 20.5

NSAID ketorolac Preparations: Injection Vial, Eye Drops and Intranasal Spray

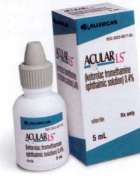
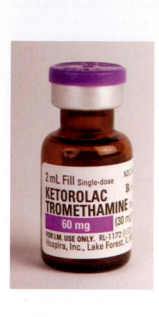

not exactly known. However, these drugs are thought to inhibit the synthesis of substances (mucopolysaccharides) that protect the stomach from hydrochloric acid erosion. Although ibuprofen has been reported to produce less gastric distress than do other antiinflammatory drugs, any of these drugs may produce ulceration with chronic use. The most serious complication of ulceration is massive hemorrhage, leading to shock and death (see drug warning label for ibuprofen, Figure 20.6).

Through CNS stimulation, antiinflammatory drugs may produce vertigo, vomiting, mental confusion, and headaches. Hypersensitivity reactions may include mild rashes, fever, hepatic damage, and respiratory distress in asthmatic individuals. **Anaphylaxis** has occurred in aspirin-sensitive patients. Aspirin intolerance may occur in patients with a history of nasal polyps, asthma, or rhinitis. In such patients, angioedema and severe rhinitis result from exposure to aspirin-containing products. **Megaloblastic anemia,** signaled by large, immature red blood cells, has occurred with these drugs because the intestinal absorption of folic acid has been impaired, whereas iron deficiency **anemia** may occur as a result of blood loss through hemorrhage. Bone marrow suppression leading to blood disorders also has been reported to occur in patients who received NSAIDs. Adverse effects are more likely to occur in patients receiving large doses in the chronic treatment of arthritis, especially rheumatoid arthritis. Overdose of the antiinflammatory drugs produces toxicity similar to that described for salicylates. Treatment is primarily supportive because there is no specific antidote for these agents.

The NSAIDs, which include aspirin in large doses (2 to 5 g), will reduce the inflammatory response of various types of arthritis. At these doses, especially in elderly patients, signs of overdose may be present. Primary signs to watch for include ringing in the ears (tinnitus), gastric upset, and GI bleeding (black, tarry stools). To minimize GI side effects, medication may be given with meals, milk, or antacids. Alcohol should be avoided, since it may enhance the adverse gastric action of these drugs.

be administered with meals, especially in patients who are susceptible to drug-induced gastric irritation. Following oral administration, most of these drugs exert their analgesic action within 30 minutes, with a 4- to 6-hour duration of action. The NSAIDs are highly (more than 90 percent) bound to plasma proteins. For this reason, these drugs undergo many drug interactions due to displacement of other drugs from protein-binding sites. Eventually, these drugs are metabolized by the drug microsomal metabolizing system in the liver prior to renal excretion. Acidification of the urine may result in renal reabsorption of these acidic drugs.

Adverse Effects

All antiinflammatory drugs may produce nausea, GI distress, and ulceration. The mechanism of ulceration is

Figure 20.6   **Warning Label for Nonprescription (OTC) Ibuprofen**

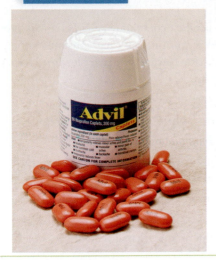
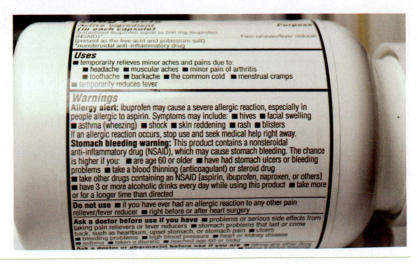

The label indicates the potential for stomach bleeding when taken concurrently with other NSAIDS, anticoagulants, and social alcohol intake more than three times a week. The risk of bleeding increases with patients over 60 years of age or who have stomach ulcers.

Age and underlying condition of the patient do influence the onset of adverse effects. The larger dose in combination with patient age over 65 years appears to predispose to the onset of unwanted effects. The best strategy in elderly patients, therefore, requires using the lowest effective dose. Specific newer potent NSAIDs such as ketorolac tromethamine have a special warning that recommends dosage adjustment for patients over 65 years old and/or less than 110 pounds of body weight. Because ketorolac tromethamine is cleared from the body slowly, this may be exaggerated in older patients and patients with renal impairment, as evidenced by elevated serum creatinine levels.

In 2009, the American Geriatric Society took a bold step in their guidelines for the use of pain medications in elderly patients. Guidelines were originally issued several years ago promoting the use of NSAIDs to improve pain management and quality of life in older patients. Because patients over 75 years of age often have multiple chronic conditions associated with pain and are usually more susceptible to the adverse effects of NSAIDs, especially the cardiovascular and gastrointestinal effects, the newest guidelines specifically recommend *against* the use of NSAIDs in elderly patients. It is recommended that patients with moderate-to-severe pain or diminished quality of life due to pain should be considered for opioid treatment rather than NSAIDs.

The selective COX-2 inhibitors exhibit potentially more serious cardiac or renal adverse effects than do other NSAIDs because they focus only on one group of enzymes. Two large clinical studies in 8000 patients each suggest that more patients experience an increase in blood pressure (aggravated hypertension), bradycardia, irregular heartbeat, or chest pains than patients taking other NSAIDs. Evaluation of these clinical data resulted in the removal of two COX-2 inhibitors, rofecoxib (*Vioxx*) and valdecoxib (*Bextra*). At present, the only available COX-2 inhibitor is celecoxib (*Celebrex*). Selective COX-2 inhibitors do not have the antithrombotic (clot prevention) protective action of aspirin and other COX-1 inhibitors because platelets are predominately a COX-1 pathway.

NSAIDS and COX-2 inhibitor drugs promote sodium and water retention. This can result in peripheral edema and increase stress on the cardiovascular system in patients with heart failure and hypertension. In the elderly, it can lead to the development of heart and renal failure.

Celecoxib should not be taken by patients who have a history of sensitivity to sulfonamides. All selective COX-2 inhibitors have been associated with exacerbating allergic reactions.

Special Considerations

Because the therapeutic benefits of NSAIDs are extremely important, the risks are under continual scrutiny by the FDA and medical professionals for appropriate indication and duration of use. When NSAIDs are used in patients receiving certain antihypertensive drugs, blood pressure should be monitored throughout the duration of therapy. NSAIDs reduce the antihypertensive effects of ACE inhibitors (captopril, losartan) on diastolic blood pressure.

There is a special cautionary boxed warning for the entire NSAID class of drugs. A boxed warning appears in all nonaspirin NSAID labeling that says that all (nonaspirin) NSAIDs may cause an increased risk of serious cardiovascular thrombotic events, myocardial infarction, and stroke, which can be fatal. This risk may increase with duration of use. Patients with cardiovascular disease (CAD, CVD) or risk factors for cardiovascular disease (history of TIA) may be at greater risk. Nonaspirin NSAIDs are contraindicated for the treatment of perioperative pain (up to 10 to 14 days postoperative) from coronary artery bypass graft (CABG) surgery.

NSAIDs cause an increased risk of serious gastrointestinal adverse reactions, including bleeding, ulceration, and perforation of the stomach or intestines, which can be fatal. These events can occur at any time during use and without warning symptoms. Elderly patients are at greater risk for serious gastrointestinal events.

The FDA has just required NSAID manufacturers to display visibly prominent labels accompanying these drugs that identify the risks of stomach bleeding. The term "NSAID" must be highlighted on the front label of every product.

Every OTC product containing an NSAID will have to include a bolded warning advising consumers about the potential risks for "severe stomach bleeding," especially in people who

- Are aged 60 years or older.
- Have had stomach ulcers or bleeding problems.
- Take a blood thinning or steroid drug.
- Take other drugs containing prescription or nonprescription NSAIDs.
- Have three or more alcoholic drinks a day while using the product.
- Take more of the product than directed.

Figure 20.7 Uric Acid Formation and Allopurinol Mechanism of Action

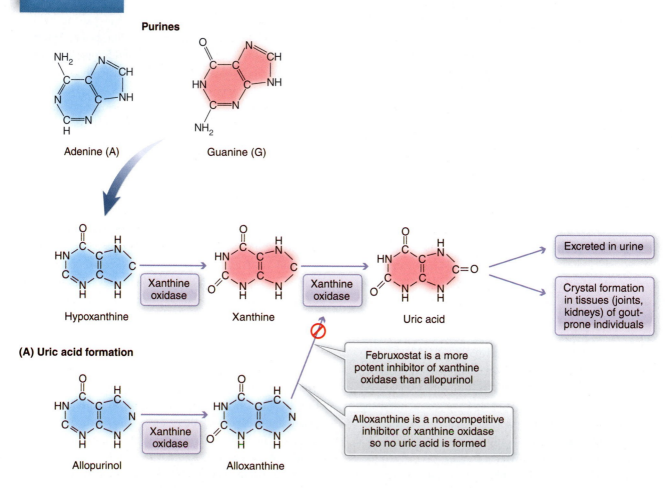

(A) Uric acid formation

(B) Allopurinol and februxostat inhibition of uric acid formation

(A) Breakdown of purines (adenine and guanine) from DNA and RNA to hypoxanthine. Then xanthine oxidase converts hypoxanthine to xanthine and finally to uric acid. (B) Allopurinol is a noncompetitive inhibitor of xanthine oxidase so uric acid formation is blocked.

This effort is directed at patients to alert them to the recommended limited dose and duration of treatment in accordance with package instructions. The new labeling requirements were warranted because many consumers are not aware of the risks associated with overdosing of NSAIDs. More importantly, many OTC products contain individual NSAIDs not recognized as an NSAID by the consumer.

LO 20.1   LO 20.6

DRUGS USEFUL IN TREATING GOUT

Gout is a special inflammatory disease. It is associated with the deposition of uric acid in joint fluid (big toe, knees, and elbows) and soft tissue. Uric acid is formed every day from the metabolism of nucleic acids by the liver (see Figure 20.7). If the liver produces 80 percent of daily uric acid, the remaining uric acid load comes from certain foods, such as alcohol, beer, wine, cheeses, beans, anchovies, sardines, liver, kidneys, and cream, that contain a high purine content, which increases the uric acid level of blood (hyperuricemia).

Humans cannot use uric acid, so it is normally secreted into the urine by the renal tubules. People who suffer from gout may overproduce uric acid or may not excrete it efficiently. If the uric acid level in the blood exceeds uric acid excretion, resulting in more than 7 mg uric acid/dl blood, a condition of hyperuricemia occurs. Causes of hyperuricemia can be either primary (increased uric acid levels due to purine metabolism and diet) or secondary (high uric acid levels due to another disease or condition). Secondary hyperuricemia occurs in patients with renal disease, where uric acid cannot be excreted and, therefore, accumulates in the blood. It occurs in certain diabetic acidosis conditions that promote changes in cellular (pH) environment and the formation of uric acid crystals. Most importantly, hyperuricemia results from certain cancers, leukemia, and lymphoma where there is a high rate of cell turnover and metabolism contributing to changes in pH that predispose to uric acid crystal formation and deposition in the tissues. Chemotherapy in which there is significant cell death and release of metabolic waste also provides an environment for uric acid crystal deposition.

For some unknown reason, uric acid crystals spontaneously accumulate in the joint fluid of gout-prone individuals. Phagocytes (nucleophils, white blood cells) enter the area and attack the uric acid crystals, and this activity leads to a decrease in pH (acid) of the joint fluid, causing more uric acid to accumulate in the joint. This vicious cycle of inflammation produces the edema, redness, and severe pain characteristic of acute gout. In chronic gout, uric acid slowly deposits in soft tissue, causing bulging, deformed joints known as tophi. (Tophaceous deposits may take years to develop; see Figure 20.8.) Uric acid also may accumulate in the kidneys, producing urate stones, which may appear in the urine as sand or gravel. Drugs that are useful in the treatment of gout either relieve the acute inflammatory response or reduce the uric acid levels (uricosuric) in chronic gout. It is worth noting that some patients who suffer intense recurrent bouts of pain with this condition do not have elevated circulating uric acid levels. These agents are listed in Table 20:4.

Treatment of Acute Gout

Colchicine's therapeutic value in the management of gout goes back centuries. It is extremely useful during the first 48 hours of an acute attack. Colchicine, a drug that comes from the crocus plant, specifically alters the ability of the phagocytes to attack uric acid crystals. As a result, the pH of the joint fluid does not fall. Therefore, the cycle of uric acid deposition is interrupted, and the gouty attack eventually subsides.

| **Figure 20.8** | **Deposits of Uric Acid in Patients with Chronic Gout** |

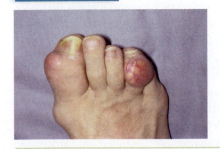 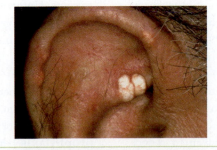 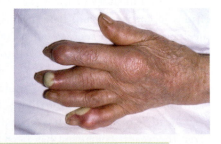

Tophaceous deposit on the (a) toe, (b) ear, and (c) hand of a patient with end-stage chronic renal disease.

Drugs Effective in the Treatment of Gout

Drug (*Trade Name*)	Adult oral dose
Antigout (*Acute*)	
Colchicine	0.5–1.2 mg every 1–2 hr* or 0.5–1.8 mg/day**
Antiinflammatory analgesics	
Aspirin***	3–5 g/day
Choline salicylate (*Arthropan*)***	870 mg every 3–4 hr
Indomethacin (*Indocin*)	50 mg TID
Naproxen (*Naprosyn*)	750 mg followed by 250 mg every 8 hr
Sodium thiosalicylate (*Rexolate*)	100 mg every 3–4 hr
Sulindac (*Clinoril*)	200 mg BID
Hypouricemic	
Allopurinol (*Zyloprim*)	200–400 mg/day (mild); 400–600 mg/day (severe); 600–800 mg/day (uric acid nephropathy; neoplasias)
Uricosuric	
Aspirin	Doses greater than 4 g
Febuxostat (*Uloric*)	40 or 80 mg once daily
Probenecid	250–500 mg BID
Mixtures	
Colchicine (0.5 mg) and probenecid (500 mg)	One tablet daily for 1 week followed by one tablet BID

*Until pain is relieved. **Prophylactic dose. ***OTC; prescription required for all others.

The drug is readily absorbed orally and has good plasma levels within 2 hours. It is excreted into the feces and urine. Colchicine is not an analgesic; it is not a general antiinflammatory drug for the relief of other forms of muscle and joint pain. It is antiinflammatory in the specific condition of acute gout. In 2009, a new colchicine product, *Colcrys,* was approved to treat acute gout flares as well as for prophylaxis.

There is a genetic autoinflammatory condition, Familial Mediterranean Fever (FMF), in which patients periodically experience high fever and abdominal pain. Over the years, colchicine has been given to reduce the acute attack. A significant percentage of FMF patients have received relief with colchicine although the mechanism of action is not understood. Colchicine also prevents the recurrence of aphthous ulcers in these patients. Unfortunately, colchicine frequently produces nausea, vomiting, and diarrhea. Abdominal cramps and blood in the urine (hematuria) also may occur.

Prophylactic Treatment of Gout

Prophylactic therapy involves the long-term use of drugs to prevent the occurrence of gouty attacks and tophi. Two major classes of drugs are used in long-term **prophylaxis**—hypouricemic agents and uricosuric agents.

Allopurinol and febuxostat (*Uloric*) are hypouricemic drugs. Allopurinol is also known as an antimetabolite because it resembles the structure of hypoxanthine. Allopurinol inhibits the enzyme xanthine oxidase, which is necessary to turn hypoxanthine into uric acid (see Figure 20.7). Therefore, no uric acid is formed, and hypoxanthine is excreted into the urine. Eventually, the uric acid in the blood decreases, preventing the future development of tophi and urate stones in the kidneys. Allopurinol also can be used to reduce the hyperuricemia associated with certain malignancies and other drug therapy (thiazide diuretics). The most common side effects associated with the use of allopurinol are fever, rash, and **leukopenia** (low white blood cell count).

Febuxostat is the first selective xanthine oxidase inhibitor that is not a purine analog. It is used for the chronic management of hyperuricemia in patients with gout. More potent than allopurinol, it inhibits the production of uric acid. This once-daily oral medication is effective at 40 and 80 mg per day. Food and antacids do not affect the absorption of febuxostat. Febuxostat is metabolized by the liver and excreted by the kidney, but dose adjustment is not necessary when used in patients with concomitant conditions of reduced organ function.

Colchicine or NSAIDs may be used with febuxostat when a gout flare occurs while establishing the treatment regimen. The flare is a result of uric acid being mobilized from tissue storage sites. Addition of colchicine minimizes or prevents the inflammatory flare. Usually flares can be managed without interrupting the febuxostat regimen.

Immunosuppressants mercaptopurine and azothiaprine and the bronchodilator theophylline are drugs metabolized by xanthine oxidase. These drugs should not be given concurrently with febuxostat therapy. Concurrent drug administration would cause an increase in the blood levels of these drugs, potentially leading to adverse effects and toxicity.

There have been a few nonserious adverse effects associated with febuxostat, including dizziness, rash, nausea, and temporary elevation in liver enzymes. Monitoring of liver function tests is recommended at two and four months after initiation of therapy and periodically thereafter. The drug is not recommended for use in patients with secondary hyperuricemia. While not contraindicated in patients with myocardial infarction and stroke, it is recommended that patients be monitored while on febuxostat. A higher incidence of cardiovascular thromboembolic events was observed in patients treated with febuxostat compared with allopurinol during clinical trials; however, a causal relationship has not been established.

Probenecid is a uricosuric drug used in the chronic management of gout. Uricosuric drugs enhance the renal excretion of uric acid without altering the formation of uric acid, leading to a rapid clearance of uric acid from the blood. Probenecid inhibits the renal tubule mechanism for handling organic acids like uric acid and it inhibits the renal reabsorption of uric acid so that it passes into the urine. Probenecid is rapidly absorbed following oral administration and is metabolized by the liver and excreted through the kidneys. Often, probenecid is administered in combination with colchicine, which reduces the blood urate level, while colchicine protects against the onset of an acute gouty attack.

Probenecid causes GI disturbances, including nausea and vomiting. It is recommended that it be taken with meals, milk, or antacids to avoid GI upset. Other adverse effects reported with probenecid include arthralgias, skin rash, and fever. To reduce the likelihood of developing renal urate stones, any person taking an antigout drug should drink 10 to 12 eight-ounce glasses of water daily.

Clinical Indications and Preferred Therapy

The clinical management of gout, even with diet adjustment, is a life-long process. For the treatment of acute gout attacks, relief of pain, and interruption of the inflammatory process, colchicine and specific NSAIDs (indomethacin, naproxen) and sodium thiosalicylate are indicated.

For the treatment of hyperuricemia associated with gout and gouty arthritis, probenecid has been a longstanding drug of choice. Because of its ability to inhibit the renal tubular secretion of most penicillins and cephalosporins, probenecid elevates and prolongs the plasma levels of these antibiotics. Probenecid is therefore also approved for use as an adjunct to antibiotic therapy.

Allopurinol is approved for the management of primary and secondary gout, acute gout attacks, tophi, joint destruction, uric acid stones, or nephropathy. Because of its mechanism of action, it also is recommended for reduction of serum and urinary uric acid resulting from the treatment of malignancies, leukemia, and lymphoma.

LO 20.5
DRUG INTERACTIONS

Nonopioid analgesics and antiinflammatory drugs undergo a variety of drug interactions. The major area of interaction includes drug displacement from protein-binding sites. This displacement usually results in an increased toxicity of the displaced drug. Inhibition of uric acid excretion is the next most frequent drug interaction. Since most of these drugs are weak acids, they compete with uric acid for sites of excretion along the renal tubules. This competition, especially low doses of probenecid concurrent with aspirin, may cancel the uricosuric effect desired in the treatment of chronic gout. Of noteworthy importance is the potential for serious interaction with acetaminophen because of its ubiquitous use. The hepatotoxicity associated with acetaminophen may increase with the long-term use of drugs that induce microsomal enzymes. The concomitant use of acetaminophen with several drugs ranging from alcohol to rifampin is associated with decreased analgesic therapeutic effect to hepatotoxicity. Clinically significant drug interactions among the classes of drugs represented in this chapter are presented in Table 20:5.

[Table 20:5]

Drug Interactions with the Nonopioid Analgesics and Antigout Drugs

Pharmacological agents	Interact with	Response
Acetaminophen	**Alcohol, barbiturates, carbamazepine, hydantoins, isoniazid, rifampin**	**Increased risk of hepatotoxicity**
Acetaminophen	**Warfarin**	**Increases anticoagulant effect of warfarin; increases circulating warfarin levels**
Allopurinol	Cyclophosphamide	Increased bone marrow depression
Allopurinol	Ampicillin	Skin rash has occurred with concurrent use of these drugs
Allopurinol	Thiazides, ACE inhibitors	Higher risk of hypersensitivity to allopurinol
Aspirin	Antacids, corticosteroids, urinary alkalinizing drugs	Decrease the effects of aspirin (salicylate) by increasing renal excretion, decreasing tubular reabsorption
Aspirin (doses > 2 g/day)	Sulfonylureas, insulin	Potentiate glucose lowering effect; hypoglycemia
Aspirin	**Heparin**	**Increased risk of bleeding**
Diflunisal	**Indomethacin**	**Decreased renal clearance of indomethacin; fatal GI hemorrhage has occurred**
Febuxostat	Mercaptopurine, azathioprine, theophylline	Increases the blood levels of these drugs by blocking their metabolism via xanthine oxidase
NSAIDs	**Alcohol**	**Increased risk for GI ulceration**
NSAIDs	Lithium	May elevate the plasma level of lithium
Indomethacin Oxyphenbutazone Phenylbutazone Salicylates	Anticonvulsants, methotrexate, oral anticoagulants, oral hypoglycemics	Increased bleeding, toxicity due to protein binding, displacement or additive effect of depressing prothrombin
Salicylates	Uricosuric agents	Decreased renal excretion of uric acid
Indomethacin	Furosemide, thiazide diuretics	Decreased sodium excretion and antihypertensive action
Indomethacin	Lithium	May elevate plasma lithium concentrations
Probenecid	Acyclovir, clofibrate, oral hypoglycemics, methotrexate, NSAIDs, penicillins, sulfonamides	Decreases renal excretion, increases plasma concentrations of these drugs

Abbreviations: ACE, angiotensin-converting enzyme.

PREFERRED THERAPY

For the relief of fever, headaches, pains, and inflammation of any nature, including arthritis, and prophylaxis for prevention of heart attack or stroke, aspirin is still the drug of choice. Because of their availability in OTC products, ibuprofen and naproxen are frequently used to relieve aches, pains, and inflammation. There is no cardio protection associated with any dose of these NSAIDs.

Acetaminophen is a preferred drug for reducing fever. In aspirin-sensitive patients or children and teenagers with symptoms of active viral infections or chickenpox, to relieve fever, acetaminophen may be the appropriate drug.

Acetaminophen is not an antiinflammatory drug. The NSAIDs are primarily used to treat inflammatory conditions, notably those associated with arthritis. The condition of the patient and the status of the inflammatory condition to be treated will determine which NSAID is selected.

Treatment for acute gout attacks is colchicine. If hyperuricemia is the trigger for the gout, the drugs of choice to block the production of uric acid are allopurinol and febuxostat. For prophylactic treatment of gout through increased urinary excretion of uric acid, probenecid is warranted. In many patients, a combination of colchicine and probenecid or allopurinol may be needed to bridge management of the acute attack while the uric acid is being processed.

Patient Administration and Monitoring

The drugs in this class are so widely available as OTC preparations and are used by such a broad group of patients that there is more opportunity for inappropriate use to occur. Children and the elderly may be more susceptible to inappropriate exposure, in part, because the drugs are not seen as harmful—that is, as strong, serious medications. After all, prescriptions are not required for the vast majority of the preparations. Therefore, patients benefit from an opportunity to hear clear instruction about the use of these drugs.

Patient Instructions

Whether the active analgesic or antiinflammatory is OTC or prescription, the potential for adverse effects to occur increases with dose and chronic use. Explain to patients that too frequent readministration of OTC preparations can equal the mg amount available by prescription.

Patients should be clearly instructed to take solid oral formulations with a full glass of water to avoid the possibility of the pill or capsule lodging in the esophagus. Probenecid and allopurinol must be accompanied by 10 to 12 full glasses of water daily in order to maintain a neutral to slightly alkaline urine and prevent the formation of kidney stones. Large doses of vitamin C may acidify the urine and increase the potential for kidney stone formation.

Patients may be told that GI irritation can be reduced by taking the medication with milk or with meals. Sustained-release formulations should not be crushed or chewed because more drug is delivered earlier than the formulation intended.

Notify the Physician

With any of the analgesic, antiinflammatory drugs, the patient should call the doctor if fever continues more than 3 days, if pain persists more than 5 days, or if redness or swelling develops. Severe or recurrent pain, or high or continued fever, may indicate serious illness requiring medical attention.

With any of these drugs, the patient should notify the doctor if ringing in the ears (tinnitus), dizziness, hearing impairment, or dimmed vision occurs and discontinue the medication as directed.

Bronchospasm and/or rhinitis may indicate the development of aspirin intolerance. The physician should be notified for further evaluation. Patients with acute asthma, urticaria, and nasal polyps should avoid aspirin and NSAIDs.

These drugs may cause drowsiness that will reduce the coordination and attention required for driving, operating machinery, or performing tasks requiring manual dexterity. Elderly patients should not exceed the recommended daily doses of NSAIDs; this includes exposure to OTC preparations while taking prescribed NSAIDs.

Special Caution with Aspirin and Acetaminophen

Aspirin, alcohol, and alcohol-containing products should be avoided during NSAID therapy.

When possible, aspirin should be avoided 1 week prior to surgery because of the possibility of postoperative bleeding. Standard procedure for discontinuation of aspirin and NSAIDs prior to surgery may vary from 5 to 10 days in different institutions. Patients allergic to tartrazine dye should avoid aspirin.

Acetaminophen should be used at the lowest effective dose for the shortest period necessary in patients who take warfarin. Coagulation status, INR, should be monitored

(Continued)

more frequently in these patients while they are taking acetaminophen. Patients should be educated to read the active ingredients for all over-the-counter medication before they take the cold, headache, or analgesic medication to be sure additional acetaminophen does not impact their current anticoagulant therapy. If the patient is in doubt about the possible ingredient, he or she should be instructed to call the doctor, nurse, or pharmacist to confirm the safety of taking the additional medication.

Use in Pregnancy

All of these drugs are designated Food and Drug Administration (FDA) Pregnancy Category B or C except for aspirin (D). Aspirin causes effects in the mother, including anemia, bleeding, and delayed labor. Since salicylates cross the placenta, prostaglandin synthesis in the fetus may be suppressed. The recommendation is to avoid salicylates during pregnancy, especially during the third trimester. Acetaminophen is the alternative analgesic at all stages of pregnancy. It appears safe for short-term use.

Understanding Terminology

Answer the following questions.

1. How do the nonopioid analgesics differ from the opioid analgesics? (LO 20.1, 20.2)
2. Define *analgesia.* (LO 20.1)
3. Explain the term *inflammation.* (LO 20.1)

Match the description in the left column with the appropriate term in the right column.

___ 4. Joint pain. (LO 20.1, 20.2)

___ 5. Pain associated with muscle injury. (LO 20.1, 20.2)

___ 6. Inflammation of the joints. (LO 20.1, 20.2)

___ 7. Small area of skin or mucous membrane that is discolored because of localized hemorrhages. (LO 20.5)

___ 8. Condition in which pain and inflammation of joints are accompanied by elevated body temperature. (LO 20.1, 20.2)

___ 9. Painful menstruation. (LO 20.1)

___ 10. Condition in which toxic doses of salicylates result in nausea, tinnitus, and delirium. (LO 20.5)

a. arthralgia
b. arthritis
c. dysmenorrhea
d. myalgia
e. petechia
f. rheumatic fever
g. salicylism

Acquiring Knowledge

Answer the following questions.

1. What are the three major pharmacological effects produced by the salicylates? (LO 20.3)
2. How do the nonopioid analgesics relieve pain? (LO 20.1)
3. Why do some people experience nausea and vomiting after taking aspirin? (LO 20.5)
4. Why do the salicylates potentiate the action of the oral anticoagulant drugs? (LO 20.4)
5. What physiological changes might occur during acute salicylate toxicity? (LO 20.5)
6. Why is acetaminophen recommended for patients who are aspirin sensitive? (LO 20.3)
7. How do antiinflammatory drugs interrupt the process of inflammation? (LO 20.1)
8. Which antiinflammatory drugs should not be administered over long periods of time (such as 2 months)? (LO 20.5)
9. What metabolic imbalance is associated with the production of gout? (LO 20.6)
10. How does colchicine alleviate the acute inflammatory reaction of gout? (LO 20.6)
11. How do allopurinol and probenecid differ in their antigout mechanism of action? (LO 20.6)

Applying Knowledge on the Job

Use your critical-thinking skills to answer the following questions.

1. Assume that you work in an emergency room of a hospital. For each of the following patients who come to the ER tonight with a nonopioid drug overdose, determine the probable drug and what should be done to treat the overdose.
   a. Patient A presents with respiratory acidosis, low blood and urine pH values, profuse sweating, vasodilation, and hypotension. (LO 20.5)

b. Patient B presents with nausea and vomiting. Liver enzymes (AST, ALT, bilirubin, and thrombin) are all high and rising. Liver damage seems imminent. (LO 20.5)

2. For each of the following adult patients, how much nonopioid analgesic drug is required to produce the desired effect?
   a. Patient A wants to take aspirin to relieve the fever, aches, and pains of the flu. (LO 20.3)
   b. Patient B wants to take aspirin as an antiinflammatory agent for osteoarthritis. (LO 20.4)
   c. Patient C wants to take ibuprofen for dysmenorrhea. (LO 20.4)
   d. Patient D wants to take ibuprofen for osteoarthritis inflammation. (LO 20.4)
   e. Patient E wants to take naproxen for menstrual pain. (LO 20.4)
   f. Patient F wants to take naproxen for inflammation associated with rheumatoid arthritis. (LO 20.4)

3. A mother of a 26-month-old child calls. Her child is coughing, has nasal congestion, and is running a fever. She would like to know how much aspirin she should give her child. The child weighs 22 pounds. (LO 20.3)

4. John is 62 years old and is currently taking *Coumadin, Tenormin,* and *Micronase.* He wants to know if he can take *Anacin* for his headache. (LO 20.5)

5. Your office receives a frantic call from a young mother. Her 1-1/2 year old accidentally got ahold of children's chewable *Tylenol*. She is not sure how many she ate, but thinks there were at least 20 tablets in the bottle, and now it is empty. She feels that her daughter must have gotten into this within the last 1-1/2 hours. What should she do? (LO 20.5)

Multiple Choice

Use your critical-thinking skills to answer the following questions.

1. Which of the following is pharmacologically considered an all-around antiinflammatory drug? (LO 20.3, 20.5)
   A. febuxostat
   B. allopurinol
   C. ibuprophen
   D. probenecid

2. Cyclooxygenase (COX) is a family of enzymes that (LO 20.1, 20.3)
   A. increase uric acid production and deposition
   B. make various prostaglandins from arachidonic acid
   C. metabolize NSAIDs
   D. are inhibited by allopurinol and febuxostat

3. Which of the following is correct about NSAIDs? (LO 20.1, 20.5)
   A. they are a large class of antiinflammatory drugs that inhibit more than one type of cyclooxygenase (COX-1, 2)
   B. there are no gastrointestinal side effects associated with this group of drugs
   C. the class includes cortisone
   D. there is no association with gastrointestinal bleeding with chronic use of these drugs

4. Acetaminophen (LO 20.1, 20.3)
   A. is an aspirin substitute for the management of severe arthritis
   B. is an aspirin substitute for analgesia and antipyresis in aspirin-sensitive patients
   C. has no associated liver toxicity with chronic use of large doses (> 4 g/day)
   D. is not given to children because it causes flu-like symptoms

5. NSAIDs are **(LO 20.2, 20.4)**
   A. represented by probenecid
   B. used for the clinical management of hyperprostaglandinemia
   C. not to be used in the management of rheumatoid arthritis
   D. highly bound to plasma proteins

6. Which of the following is correct? **(LO 20.4, 20.5)**
   A. gout is a condition of oxalate crystal deposition in the joints
   B. uricosuric drugs can be given with hypouricemic drugs to lower uric acid concentrations
   C. aspirin never causes petechial hemorrhages
   D. COX-2 inhibitors (celecoxib) have greater antiplatelet activity than aspirin and NSAIDs

7. The COX-2 selective NSAID celecoxib (*Celebrex*) **(LO 20.1, 20.4, 20.5)**
   A. produces more effective analgesia than older NSAIDs
   B. is used for its effectiveness in relieving minor headache
   C. inhibits xanthine oxidase to relieve pain and inflammation
   D. is primarily an antiinflammatory drug

8. Antiinflammatory drugs **(LO 20.2, 20.3, 20.4)**
   A. include acetaminophen
   B. vary in their ability to reduce all types of inflammation
   C. have no effect on uterine contraction or vasoconstriction associated with dysmenorrhea
   D. do not require special cautionary warnings about likely adverse effects with their use

Multiple Choice (Multiple Answer)

Select the correct choices for each statement. The choices may be all correct, all incorrect, or any combination.

1. Select all of the following that are part of the inflammatory process. **(LO 20.1)**
   A. prostaglandins are released
   B. phagocytes migrate to area
   C. vasodilation
   D. proteins leak out of injured cells

2. Under which circumstances would nonopioid drugs be the appropriate treatment?
   (LO 20.2)
   A. for pain from broken bones
   B. in the elderly with moderate to severe pain
   C. for treatment of pain from cancer
   D. for acute postoperative pain

3. Which of the following is not a reason to choose acetaminophen? **(LO 20.3)**
   A. for aspirin-sensitive patients
   B. for low GI irritation
   C. for its antiinflammatory effects
   D. for its anticoagulant properties

4. Choose the reasons why probenecid is useful in treating gout. **(LO 20.6)**
   A. enhances the renal excretion of uric acid
   B. decreases the uric acid clearance from the blood
   C. increases reabsorption of uric acid
   D. alters the formation of uric acid

5. Select the indications for aspirin. **(LO 20.2)**
   A. analgesia
   B. antipyresis
   C. anticoagulation
   D. dysmenorrhea

Sequencing

Place the following in order of gouty attack and colchicine's mechanism of action to alleviate symptoms. **(LO 20.6)**

First					Last

pH of joint does not fall

increase in uric acid levels

uric acid crystals accumulate in joint fluid

phagocytes enter joint

phagocytes unable to attack uric acid crystals

Classification

Place the following drugs into the appropriate category. **(LO 20.1, 20.6)**

allopurinol   ibuprofen
colchicine   indomethacin
etodolac   naproxen
febuxostat   probenecid

Gout treatments	Nonsteroidal antiinflammatories

Labeling

Label the structures indicated. **(LO 20.1)**

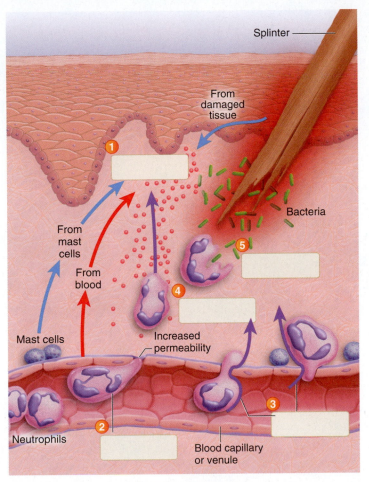

Inflammatory response

For interactive animations, videos, and assessment, visit:

www.mcgrawhillconnect.com

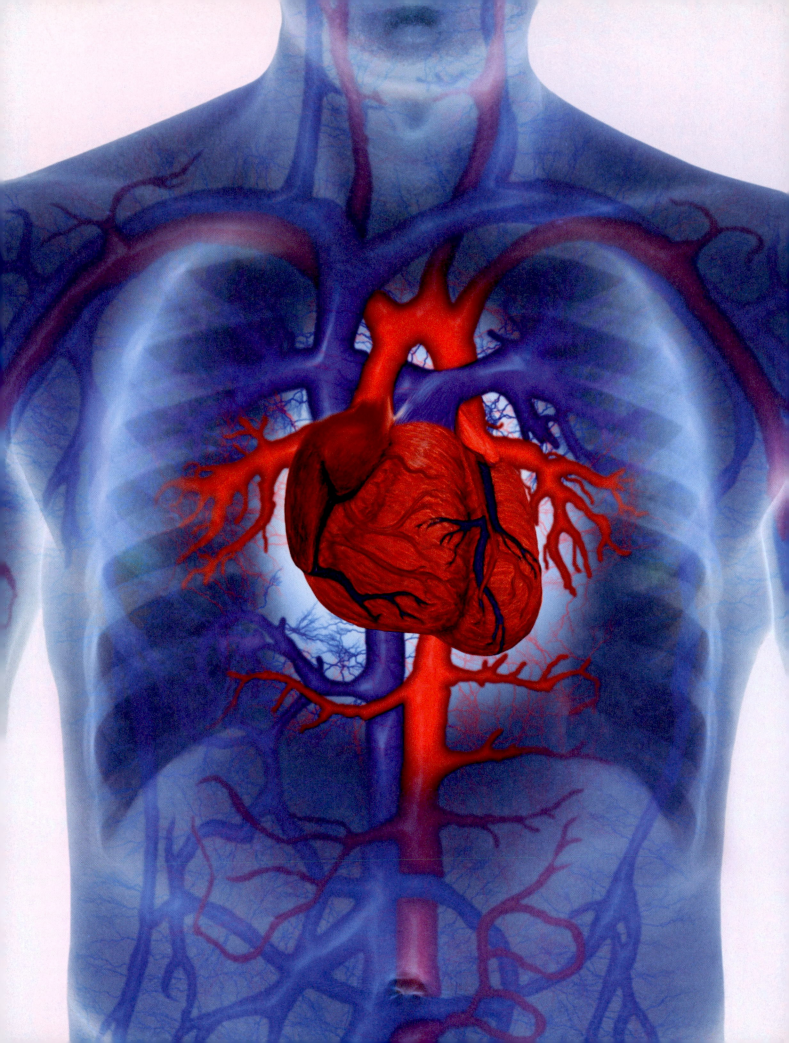

Pharmacology of the Heart

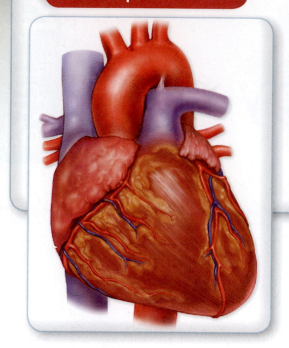

Chapter 21

Review of Cardiac Physiology and Pathology

KEY TERMS

angina pectoris: chest pain caused by insufficient blood flow to the heart.

arteriosclerosis: hardening or fibrosis of the arteries.

atherosclerosis: accumulation of fatty deposits in the walls of arteries.

AV: atrioventricular, as in the AV node.

chronic heart failure (CHF): heart disease caused by weakness of the contractile force of the myocardium.

conduction system: specialized cardiac tissue that transmits electrical impulses and regulates the activity of the heart.

coronary artery disease (CAD): disease of the coronary arteries that decreases blood flow to the heart.

depolarization: the decrease in electrical potential across a cell membrane that results in excitation and generation of an action potential.

electrocardiogram (ECG): recording of the electrical activity of the heart.

ischemia: condition of insufficient tissue blood flow.

myocardial infarction (MI): sudden death of an area of heart muscle, commonly referred to as a heart attack.

myocardium: the muscular layer of the heart.

repolarization: return of the electrical potential across a cell membrane to its resting state following depolarization.

SA: sinoatrial, as in the SA node.

After studying this chapter, you should be able to

21.1 describe the normal flow of blood through the chambers and blood vessels of the heart.

21.2 identify the different parts of the conduction system and how the flow of electrical impulses coordinates contraction of the cardiac chambers.

21.3 explain autonomic nervous system regulation of the heart.

21.4 recognize the different wave forms of the ECG and how they relate to the electrical activity of the heart.

21.5 identify the clinical features of chronic heart failure (CHF), coronary artery disease (CAD), and myocardial infarction (MI).

Introduction

The circulatory system is responsible for supplying blood flow to all the tissues and organs of the body. The heart is a muscular organ whose main function is to generate the force that pumps the blood through the circulatory system. The heart is composed of four muscular chambers, two atria and two ventricles. Contraction of cardiac muscle, the **myocardium,** generates the arterial blood pressure, which is necessary to distribute blood throughout the body. Blood flow to the heart itself is supplied by the coronary arteries, which branch off the aorta immediately after leaving the heart. Within the walls of the heart are specialized cells that make up the **conduction system.** The function of the conduction system is to coordinate the contractions of the atria and ventricles. There are a number of disease conditions that can affect the function of the myocardium, conduction system, and coronary arteries. These diseases, **chronic heart failure (CHF), coronary artery disease (CAD),** and **myocardial infarction (MI),** are among the leading causes of death in this country.

LO 21.1 | LO 21.2 | LO 21.3 | LO 21.4

CARDIAC FUNCTION

To understand cardiac physiology, it is convenient to divide the heart into three functional parts: cardiac muscle, conduction system, and nerve supply.

Cardiac Muscle

The pumping ability of the heart is due to the arrangement of heart muscle (myocardium) into a system of four chambers. Contraction of the chambers increases pressure within the ventricles and forces the blood through a system of valves and blood vessels. The superior and inferior venae cavae receive all the venous blood from the body and drain it into the right atrium. The blood then passes through the tricuspid valve into the right ventricle. The right ventricle pumps the blood through the pulmonary arteries to the lungs, where it gets oxygenated. From the lungs the blood passes through the pulmonary veins back to the left atrium.

Blood then passes through the bicuspid valve into the left ventricle. The left ventricle pumps the blood out of the heart into the aorta, where it then gets distributed to the rest of the body. The path of blood flow is shown in Figure 21.1.

The blood supply to the myocardium is through the coronary arteries that branch off the aorta immediately after the aorta leaves the heart. Under normal conditions, blood flow in the coronary arteries is dependent upon the force of myocardial contraction. Any interference with the normal function of the myocardium or with the normal flow of blood to the myocardium results in **ischemia** and a decreased capacity of the heart to contract.

Conduction System

The conduction system of the heart is composed of a specialized type of nervous tissue that is located in specific areas of the heart. The conduction system is shown in

Figure 21.1   Description of Blood Flow through the Heart

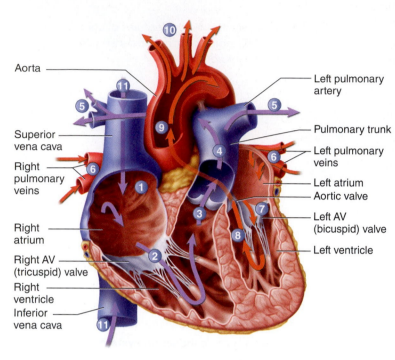

1. Blood enters right atrium from superior and inferior venae cavae.

2. Blood in right atrium flows through right AV valve into right ventricle.

3. Contraction of right ventricle forces pulmonary valve open.

4. Blood flows through pulmonary valve into pulmonary trunk.

5. Blood is distributed by right and left pulmonary arteries to the lungs, where it unloads CO_2 and loads O_2.

6. Blood returns from lungs via pulmonary veins to left atrium.

7. Blood in left atrium flows through left AV valve into left ventricle.

8. Contraction of left ventricle (simultaneous with step 3) forces aortic valve open.

9. Blood flows through aortic valve into ascending aorta.

10. Blood in aorta is distributed to every organ in the body, where it unloads O_2 and loads CO_2.

11. Blood returns to heart via venae cavae.

Figure 21.2   Description of the Cardiac Conduction System and Transmission of an Electrical Impulse

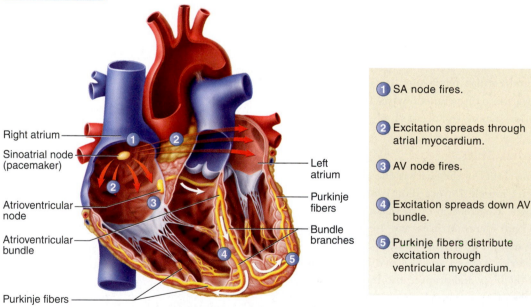

1. SA node fires.

2. Excitation spreads through atrial myocardium.

3. AV node fires.

4. Excitation spreads down AV bundle.

5. Purkinje fibers distribute excitation through ventricular myocardium.

Figure 21.2. Conduction tissue has a unique property known as *autorhythmicity*. This property enables the heart to initiate its own electrical stimulation. Normally, an electrical impulse is generated within the sinoatrial **(SA)** node, referred to as the pacemaker. This impulse continues through both atria to the atrioventricular **(AV)**

Figure 21.3

Electrocardiogram Recording from Lead II

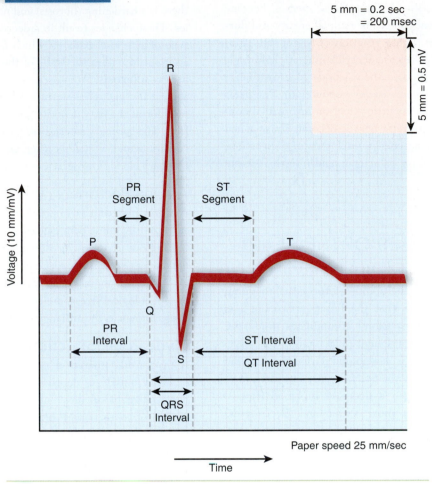

The recording shows ECG waves, segments, intervals, and standard calibrations for time and voltage.

node. The AV node transmits the impulse down through the AV bundle (bundle of His) and through the left and right bundle branches and Purkinje fibers. This impulse conduction results in electrical excitation and subsequent contraction of both atria, followed by excitation and contraction of both ventricles. Consequently, the contractions of both sides of the heart are coordinated by the conduction system and each side pumps the same amount of blood at the same time.

A recording of the electrical activity of the heart results in a characteristic waveform known as the **electrocardiogram (ECG).** An ECG records the electrical activity of the heart from 12 different body locations or leads. Each lead position provides a different electrical view of the heart. This is important for detecting abnormalities and cardiac arrhythmias. The pattern of the ECG reflects **depolarization** and **repolarization** of cardiac tissue. Depolarization of the atria produces the P wave of the ECG. The PR interval, measured from the beginning of the P wave to the beginning of the R wave,

is the time required for passage of an electrical impulse from the SA node through the AV node. Depolarization of the ventricles produces the QRS wave (AV node through Purkinje fibers). Repolarization of the ventricles is represented by the T wave. The QT interval represents the time required for both depolarization and repolarization of the ventricles. Figure 21.3 illustrates the normal wave forms, intervals, and segments recorded from Lead II of the electrocardiogram. Normal values have been established for the different wave forms and intervals and measurements outside of the normal ranges suggest disturbances of conduction.

Nerve Supply

The heart receives its nerve supply from both divisions of the autonomic nervous system. Since the heart possesses the ability to initiate its own heartbeat, the function of the autonomic nervous system is to regulate the rate and force of contraction of the heart. Sympathetic nerves release norepinephrine at adrenergic nerve endings that go to the SA node (increase heart rate), AV node (increase AV conduction), and myocardium (increase contractility). Sympathetic nerves become active when the body needs to expend energy and during the "fight or flight" reaction (Chapter 5). Parasympathetic nerves release acetylcholine at cholinergic nerve endings that go to the SA node (decrease heart rate) and AV node (decrease AV conduction). The parasympathetic system has little effect on myocardial contraction. Parasympathetic nerves become active when the body is restoring energy during eating, digestion, sleep, and elimination of urinary and intestinal waste products.

LO 21.5

MAIN DISEASES OF THE HEART
Chronic Heart Failure (CHF)

In CHF, the contractile ability of the heart to pump blood is decreased so that the heart pumps out less blood than it receives. Blood accumulates inside the chambers, causing enlargement (dilatation) of the heart. Consequently, there is less blood circulating in the blood vessels to supply the body organs. The kidneys—particularly sensitive to a decrease in blood flow—respond by retaining more water and electrolytes, leading to fluid retention and edema.

When the left side of the heart fails, fluid accumulates in the lungs (pulmonary edema) and interferes with gas exchange, resulting in shortness of breath. When the right side fails, fluid accumulates in the abdominal organs (ascites) and lower extremities. Failure in one side of the heart is usually followed by failure of the other side, resulting in total heart failure. Heart failure is treated with diuretics, vasodilators, beta blockers, and cardiac glycosides (Chapter 22).

Coronary Artery Disease

Coronary artery disease (CAD) is a general term for several cardiac conditions. An insufficient flow of blood through the coronary arteries to the heart is a common factor in arteriosclerosis, atherosclerosis, and angina pectoris. These disease conditions are the major contributors to development of a myocardial infarction.

Arteriosclerosis

Arteriosclerosis is a disease of the aging process in which there is a hardening (fibrosis) and narrowing of the arteries. These changes result in a decreased blood flow. One type of arteriosclerosis, in which fatty deposits (plaques) accumulate within the walls of the arteries, is known as **atherosclerosis.** Atherosclerosis is primarily caused by abnormally high cholesterol levels in the blood. Cholesterol forms the fatty deposits (plaque) that decrease blood flow. The coronary arteries are particularly prone to both conditions and, as stated earlier, any abnormal decrease in coronary blood flow decreases the function of the heart.

Angina Pectoris

Angina pectoris refers to the clinical condition characterized by chest pain caused by insufficient coronary blood flow. Arteriosclerosis, atherosclerosis, and coronary artery spasms are the major causes of angina pectoris. Attacks of angina, usually caused by physical exertion or psychological stress, are relieved by rest and a class of drugs known as the antianginal drugs (Chapter 24).

Myocardial Infarction

A myocardial infarction or MI occurs when an area of heart muscle is deprived of blood flow. The area deprived of blood dies unless immediate treatment is administered to restore blood flow. Blockage of blood flow is caused by the formation of a blood clot in one of the coronary arteries. The clot usually forms in a vessel where there are atherosclerotic plaques. Anticoagulant and fibrinolytic drugs (Chapter 27) can be administered to dissolve the clot and prevent further blockage.

Large infarcts usually result in sudden death, whereas lesser infarcts undergo a healing process in which the dead muscle cells are replaced by connective tissue. Consequently, after an attack, the amount of contractile tissue of the heart is reduced. Secondary complications commonly involve the development of heart failure and disturbances of the conduction system (cardiac arrhythmias). Treatment for a myocardial infarction is aimed at allowing the heart to rest and undergo its normal healing process while treating any complications. Patients then undergo a period of physical rehabilitation and exercise to strengthen the heart and improve cardiovascular conditioning.

Understanding Terminology

Answer the following questions.

1. What is the difference between angina pectoris and myocardial infarction? **(LO 21.5)**
2. What do the following abbreviations stand for: AV, CAD, CHF, ECG, SA? **(LO 21.2, 21.4, 21.5)**
3. Differentiate between arteriosclerosis and atherosclerosis. **(LO 21.5)**

Acquiring Knowledge

Answer the following questions.

1. Describe the path of blood flow through the cardiac chambers. Which ventricle forces the blood into the general circulation (aorta)? **(LO 21.1)**
2. How is the blood supplied to the myocardium? **(LO 21.1)**
3. What makes the cardiac conduction system unique? Where is the conduction system located? **(LO 21.2)**
4. Describe the path of an electrical impulse that is generated at the SA node. **(LO 21.2)**
5. Name the characteristic parts of a normal ECG. What can an ECG tell you about cardiac functions? **(LO 21.2)**
6. What would a lengthened PR interval indicate? What does a widened QRS complex suggest? **(LO 21.2)**
7. How do the divisions of the autonomic nervous system (ANS) affect cardiac function? **(LO 21.3)**
8. How might congestive heart failure affect the function of the heart? **(LO 21.5)**
9. How can coronary heart disease contribute to the development of a myocardial infarction? **(LO 21.5)**

Applying Knowledge on the Job

Use your critical-thinking skills to answer the following questions.

1. A patient is brought into the emergency room in a collapsed state. She has shortness of breath, low blood pressure, and is making a gurgling sound with each breath. What is your preliminary diagnosis? **(LO 21.5)**

2. During a scheduled office visit Mrs. Jones explains that after she climbs stairs she has to sit down and rest for a while. One day last week when there was no place to sit, she felt some pain and discomfort in her chest. What condition is most likely causing these symptoms? **(LO 21.5)**

3. Your grandfather is complaining of extreme weakness and fatigue. You notice that his ankles are swollen and that he can't put his shoes on. What cardiac condition is associated with peripheral edema? **(LO 21.5)**

4. Mr. Smith's pulse is irregular and a subsequent ECG reveals that his QRS waves have an abnormal appearance and the T wave is inverted. What part of the heart do you think is affected? **(LO 21.5)**

5. The rescue squad brings in a patient who is complaining of a sharp pain radiating down his left arm. He is extremely fatigued, is short of breath, and has a very rapid heart rate. The ECG records a serious cardiac arrythmia. What cardiac condition causes these symptoms? **(LO 21.5)**

Multiple Choice

Use your critical-thinking skills to answer the following questions.

1. Select the direction of normal blood flow that is correct. **(LO 21.1)**
   A. left ventricle to pulmonary artery
   B. left atrium to pulmonary veins
   C. left ventricle to aorta
   D. right ventricle to pulmonary veins

2. The QRS wave on the ECG represents **(LO 21.4)**
   A. depolarization of the atria
   B. depolarization of the ventricles
   C. repolarization of the atria
   D. repolarization of the ventricles

3. Increased heart rate is caused by **(LO 21.3)**
   A. sympathetic stimulation of the SA node
   B. parasympathetic stimulation of the ventricles
   C. sympathetic stimulation of the ventricles
   D. parasympathetic stimulation of the SA node

4. Angina pectoris can be caused by **(LO 21.5)**
   A. arteriosclerosis
   B. atherosclerosis
   C. coronary artery spasm
   D. all statements are true

5. Select the true statement(s) concerning the conduction system. **(LO 21.2)**
   A. the SA node is located in the wall of the right atrium
   B. the Purkinje fibers are located in the atria
   C. the AV node is located between the atria and ventricles
   D. only A and C are true

Multiple Choice (Multiple Answer)

Select the correct choices for each statement. The choices may be all correct, all incorrect, or any combination.

1. Select all of the following that apply to the cardiac conduction tissue. **(LO 21.2)**
   A. it is nervous tissue
   B. its electrical impulse is recorded on an EEG
   C. it requires outside stimulation
   D. it has autorhythmicity

2. The functions of the sympathetic nervous system in heart activity include **(LO 21.3)**
   A. increases in heart rate
   B. increased AV conduction
   C. increased contractility
   D. increased vasoconstriction

3. Which of the following is true of an electrocardiogram? **(LO 21.4)**
   A. the P wave is measuring the repolarization of the atria
   B. the PR interval measures the time of impulse passage from SA node through the AV node
   C. the QRS wave is measuring the depolarization of the ventricles
   D. the QT wave represents the repolarization of the ventricles and Purkinje fibers

4. Choose the clinical features of chronic heart failure. **(LO 21.5)**
   A. hardening of the arteries
   B. fatty deposits in the arteries
   C. blood accumulation in the heart
   D. fluid retention

5. Which of the following are indications of a myocardial infarction? **(LO 21.5)**
   A. decreased blood flow to heart muscle
   B. area of dead heart tissue
   C. development of scar tissue in the heart
   D. cardiac arrhythmias

Sequencing

Place the following in order of which is touched first as blood flows through the heart. **(LO 21.1)**

_____   _____   _____   _____   _____

First   **Last**

bicuspid valve
right atrium
tricuspid valve
left atrium
right ventricle

Classification

Place the following symptoms into the appropriate category. **(LO 21.1)**

hardening of the arteries   decrease in overall blood circulation
enlargement of the heart   decreased contractile ability of the heart
decrease in coronary blood flow   plaque deposits in arteries

CHF	CAD

Matching

Match the following terms with the correct definitions. **(LO 21.5)**

a. angina pectoris   e. chronic heart failure
b. arteriosclerosis   f. ischemia
c. atherosclerosis   g. myocardial infarction
d. coronary artery disease

1. ___ accumulation of fatty deposits in the walls of arteries
2. ___ sudden death of an area of heart muscle
3. ___ disease of the coronary arteries that decreases blood flow to the heart
4. ___ condition of insufficient tissue blood flow
5. ___ heart disease caused by weakness of the contractile force of the myocardium
6. ___ chest pain caused by insufficient blood flow to the heart
7. ___ hardening of the arteries

Labeling

Fill in the missing labels. **(LO 21.2)**

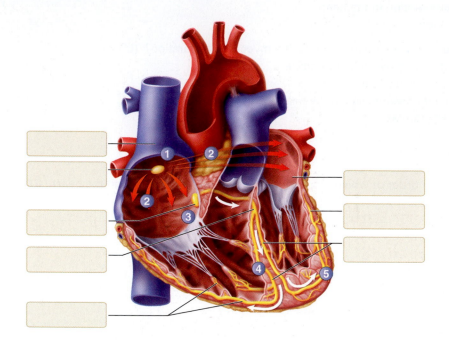

Chapter 22

Treatment of Heart Failure

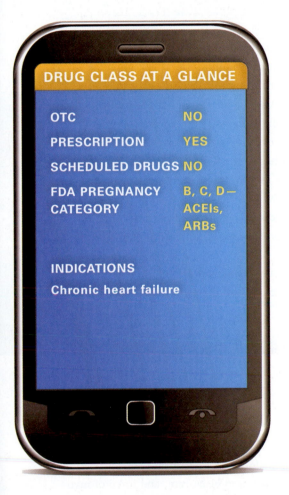

DRUG CLASS AT A GLANCE

OTC	NO
PRESCRIPTION	YES
SCHEDULED DRUGS	NO
FDA PREGNANCY CATEGORY	B, C, D— ACEIs, ARBs

INDICATIONS

Chronic heart failure

KEY TERMS

afterload: a measure of the vascular resistance that the left ventricle must overcome in order to eject blood during contraction.

cardiac glycoside: drug obtained from plants of the genus *Digitalis*.

cardiac output (CO): the amount of blood pumped per minute by the heart.

chronic heart failure (CHF): condition in which the heart is unable to pump sufficient blood to the tissues of the body.

digitalization: method of dosage with cardiac glycosides that rapidly produces effective drug levels.

ectopic beat: extra heartbeat, a type of cardiac arrhythmia.

hypercalcemia: high serum calcium.

hyperkalemia: high serum potassium.

hypokalemia: low serum potassium.

maintenance dose: daily dosage of cardiac glycoside that maintains effective drug levels in the blood.

Na/K adenosine triphosphatase (Na/K ATPase): enzyme that energizes the sodium/potassium pump and is inhibited by cardiac glycosides.

preload: refers to venous return, the amount of blood returning to the heart that must be pumped.

After studying this chapter, you should be able to

22.1 describe the symptoms of chronic heart failure and understand the compensatory activation of the sympathetic nervous system and the renin-angiotensin-aldosterone mechanism.

22.2 recognize the mechanisms of action and uses of diuretics in CHF.

22.3 describe how vasodilator drugs reduce preload and afterload and understand the

mechanisms of action of the different types of vasodilator drugs.

22.4 explain the use of beta adrenergic blockers in the treatment of CHF.

22.5 describe the mechanism of action of digoxin and list the adverse effects and potentially serious toxicities of this drug.

Introduction

Heart failure occurs when the heart is unable to pump sufficient blood to the tissues of the body. The main causes of heart failure are untreated hypertension, myocardial infarction (MI), valvular defects, and other conditions that weaken the contractile force of the heart. Blood accumulates in the heart and subsequently backs up into the lungs and large veins. This causes dilation of the heart, pulmonary edema, and peripheral edema of the lower extremities. The accumulation of blood in the heart, lungs, and tissues is referred to as congestion. When the heart is in failure, the **cardiac output (CO),** the amount of blood pumped by the heart per minute, is significantly reduced. This in turn causes a reduction in blood pressure. The result is that the cardiovascular system is unable to meet the demands of the body for blood flow and delivery of oxygen. Heart failure is a chronic disease and commonly referred to as **CHF, chronic heart failure.** Individuals with CHF display the following symptoms: tiredness, fatigue, shortness of breath, rapid heartbeat, and pulmonary and peripheral edema.

The treatment of CHF involves the use of several different drug classes that include the diuretics, vasodilators, beta blockers, and the cardiac glycoside digoxin. Two or more drugs may be required to effectively treat CHF.

LO 22.1

CHRONIC HEART FAILURE (CHF)

Chronic heart failure is described as a failure of the heart to adequately pump enough blood to supply the tissues and organs of the body with oxygen and other nutrients. In untreated CHF there are compensatory mechanisms that are activated by the body that attempt to overcome the heart failure. Cardiac muscle undergoes hypertrophy, where the walls of the heart chambers increase in size and undergo structural remodeling in an attempt to generate more forceful contractions. In addition, neurohumoral compensatory reflexes involving the sympathetic nervous system and kidneys are activated (Figure 22.1).

Sympathetic activation stimulates the release of norepinephrine and epinephrine from adrenergic nerves and the adrenal medulla. This produces vasoconstriction (alpha-1 effect), increased heart rate, and force of myocardial contraction (beta-1 effects). These actions are an attempt by the body to increase blood pressure and increase cardiac output.

The kidneys respond by releasing a substance called renin. Renin stimulates the enzymatic conversion of a precursor protein from the liver, angiotensinogen, to angiotensin I. An enzyme produced by the lungs, angiotensin-converting enzyme (ACE), converts angiotensin I into angiotensin II. Angiotensin II is a potent vasoconstrictor and also stimulates the release of aldosterone from the adrenal cortex and antidiuretic

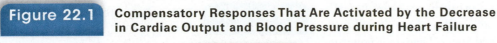

Figure 22.1 **Compensatory Responses That Are Activated by the Decrease in Cardiac Output and Blood Pressure during Heart Failure**

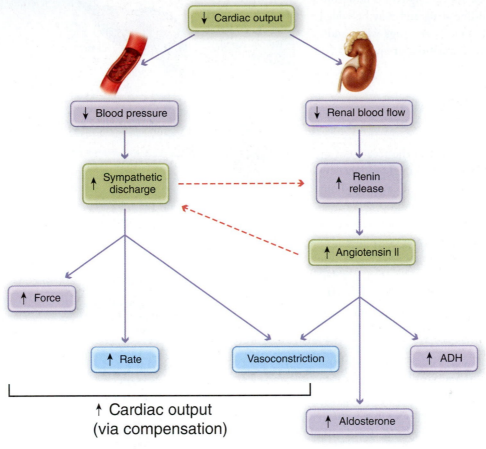

Sympathetic activation increases heart rate, force of contraction, and vasoconstriction. Release of renin leads to the formation of angiotensin II, which causes vasoconstriction, and the release of both aldosterone and antidiuretic hormone (ADH).

hormone (ADH) from the hypothalamus and pituitary gland. This sequence of actions is referred to as the renin-angiotensin-aldosterone (RAA) mechanism (Figure 22.2). Aldosterone is a hormone that causes retention of sodium by the kidneys and ADH acts on the hypothalamus to stimulate thirst and on the kidney tubules to retain water. These actions attempt to increase blood volume and blood pressure. Unfortunately the compensatory responses do not usually reverse heart failure. Over time, these compensatory mechanisms cause "remodeling" of the heart, where the heart enlarges (hypertrophy) and becomes weaker and less efficient.

The treatment of CHF has evolved over the years away from the use of drugs such as the cardiac glycosides (also referred to as digitalis glycosides) that stimulate myocardial contraction to other drugs such as the vasodilators that relax vascular smooth muscle. Vasodilator drugs increase cardiac output by dilating blood vessels,

which reduces the workload on the heart. Vasodilators that primarily dilate veins and decrease venous return are said to decrease **preload.** Preload is the amount of blood returning to the heart (venous return). Vasodilators that dilate arteries reduce blood pressure and peripheral resistance and are said to decrease **afterload.** Afterload is the force (force of ventricular contraction) that the heart must generate in order to overcome vascular resistance (open the aortic valve) and eject blood out of the left ventricle. Decreasing preload, afterload, or both decreases the workload of the heart (volume of blood the heart must pump) and allows the heart to contract more efficiently. This increases cardiac output in CHF and is the main therapeutic effect of vasodilator drugs. Diuretics have always been very useful in CHF and primarily prevent the retention and accumulation of fluid that is the cause of edema and congestion. Beta blockers reduce the heart rate and sympathetic activation, which is usually excessive in CHF. Digoxin is the only cardiac glycoside still available in the United States. Digoxin is now considered a second-line drug and may be added to diuretics and vasodilator drugs when additional myocardial stimulation is required.

LO 22.2

DIURETIC THERAPY OF CHF

Diuretics are widely used in the treatment of CHF. The main therapeutic effect produced by diuretics is the elimination of excess sodium and water by the kidneys. Sodium and water retention are the main cause of edema and congestion in CHF. The excretion of sodium also produces a vasodilating effect, which also can contribute to the therapeutic effect. There are three different types of diuretics used in CHF: the thiazides, organic acids (loop diuretics), and aldosterone antagonists (Table 22:1).

The thiazide and thiazide-like diuretics are similarly acting drugs that block the reabsorption of sodium in the distal tubules of the kidney nephrons. The potency of these diuretics is considered moderate and they are most effective in mild to moderate CHF in patients with normal renal function. Thiazides increase the excretion of sodium, but they also cause the loss of potassium and can cause **hypokalemia.** The main difference among the thiazides is the potency, which determines dosage, and the duration of action.

The organic acids are commonly referred to as the loop diuretics because the site of diuretic action in kidney nephrons is the thick ascending limb of the loop of Henle. Loop diuretics are the most potent diuretics and primarily indicated for patients with impaired renal function or severe heart failure. Like the thiazides, these diuretics increase the excretion of sodium and water and also cause loss of potassium. Loop diuretics can be administered intravenously in acute heart failure to rapidly relieve edema and pulmonary congestion. Furosemide (*Lasix*), bumetanide (*Bumex*), and torsemide (*Demadex*) are the most widely used loop diuretics and indicated when a more potent diuretic effect is required. The duration of action of these drugs averages 4 to 8 hours.

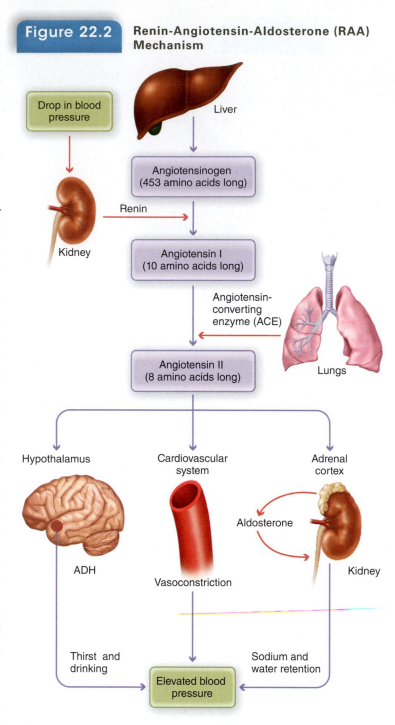

Figure 22.2 Renin-Angiotensin-Aldosterone (RAA) Mechanism

A drop in systemic blood pressure or a decrease in renal blood flow stimulates the release of renin from the kidneys. In the blood, renin initiates enzymatic reactions that lead to the formation of angiotensin II. Angiotensin II causes vasoconstriction and the release of aldosterone (sodium retention) and ADH (water retention). These actions normally function to maintain normal blood pressure and blood volume. In CHF, there is excessive activation of the RAA mechanism. Drugs that reduce the actions of the RAA mechanism, angiotensin-converting enzyme inhibitors (ACEIs) and angiotensin receptor blockers (ARBs), are used to treat CHF.

The aldosterone antagonists are weak diuretics that act on the collecting ducts of the nephron. Aldosterone is a steroid from the adrenal cortex that normally causes the retention of sodium ions and excretion of potassium ions. The main effects of the aldosterone antagonists are to increase excretion of sodium and cause retention of potassium. In CHF there can be excessive activity of aldosterone and studies have shown that treatment with these drugs reduces mortality. Spironolactone (*Aldactone*) is a competitive antagonist of the aldosterone receptor and is only effective when aldosterone levels are increased. Eplerenone (*Inspra*) is an analog of aldosterone that produces fewer adverse effects. Two other drugs, amiloride (*Midamor*) and triamterene (*Dyrenium*), reduce aldosterone activity by blocking the sodium channel in the collecting ducts of the nephron. These drugs are also more effective when aldosterone levels are increased. Because these diuretics increase potassium levels in the blood, they are often referred to as "potassium-sparing diuretics." The potassium-sparing diuretics are frequently combined with thiazide and loop diuretics to counterbalance the loss of potassium by these diuretics.

The adverse effects of the thiazides and loop diuretics are similar and include nausea, hypotension, hypokalemia, hyperuricemia, and hyperglycemia. The main adverse effect associated with the potassium-sparing diuretics is hyperkalemia. More detailed information on the mechanisms of action and adverse effects of the diuretics is discussed in Chapter 25.

Table 22:1

Diuretics Used in Heart Failure

Drug (*Trade Name*)	Duration of action (hrs)
Thiazides	
Chlorothiazide (*Diuril, Diuregen*)	6–12
Hydrochlorothiazide (*HydroDIURIL*)	6–12
Methyclothiazide (*Enduron, Aquatensen*)	24
Thiazide-like diuretics	
Chlorthalidone (*Hygroton*)	24–72
Indapamide (*Lozol*)	24–36
Metolazone (*Zaroxolyn*)	12–24
Organic acids (loop diuretics)	
Bumetanide (*Bumex*)	4–6
Ethacrynic acid (*Edecrin*)	6–8
Furosemide (*Lasix*)	6–8
Torsemide (*Demadex*)	6–8
Potassium-sparing diuretics	
Amiloride (*Midamor*)	24
Eplerenone (*Inspra*)	12–24
Spironolactone (*Aldactone*)	48–72
Triamterene (*Dyrenium*)	12

LO 22.3
VASODILATOR THERAPY OF CHF

The main effect of vasodilator drugs is to relax or dilate blood vessels. Vasodilation lowers peripheral resistance and blood pressure. These changes decrease cardiac work and oxygen consumption. The heart is able to pump more efficiently (increased cardiac output) with less effort. Drugs that primarily dilate arteries have a greater effect to lower arterial blood pressure. This effect is referred to as decreasing the afterload of the heart, which simply stated means that the heart doesn't have to work as hard to pump blood after the blood pressure has been lowered. Drugs that primarily dilate veins (venodilators) mainly decrease the venous return of blood back to the heart. This is referred to as decreasing preload, which also reduces cardiac work. Some drugs dilate both arteries and veins and produce a "balanced" vasodilation that decreases both pre- and afterload.

Vasodilator therapy of CHF has been shown to be very beneficial, especially with the drug classes known as the angiotensin-converting enzyme inhibitors (ACEIs) and angiotensin receptor blockers (ARBs). These drugs have become the preferred agents for the treatment of CHF. There is less risk of toxicity with these vasodilators than with drugs such as digoxin. Vasodilator drugs are used alone and in combination with other drugs. The vasodilators can be divided into different subtypes—arterial dilators, venous dilators, and balanced dilators—based on their sites and mechanisms of action.

Arterial Dilators

Hydralazine is a drug that produces arterial vasodilation, decreased blood pressure, and a reduction in afterload. The mechanism of action is believed to involve the formation of nitric oxide (NO), a substance normally produced in the vasculature that produces vasodilation. By reducing systemic blood pressure, the force (afterload) that the left ventricle must generate in order to eject blood is reduced. The result in CHF is an increase in CO. Adverse effects are mostly due to excessive decreases in blood pressure and include nausea, postural hypotension, headache, and reflex tachycardia.

Venodilators

Nitrate drugs such as nitroglycerine and isosorbide dinitrate (also discussed in Chapter 24) primarily cause venodilation, especially of the larger veins and vena cava. When the heart is congested and overloaded with blood, the contractile force is greatly reduced. Venodilators reduce venous return and preload. The amount of blood returning to the heart is decreased, which allows the heart to pump more forcefully to increase CO. Adverse effects of the nitrates include headache, dizziness, vasomotor flushing, postural hypotension, and reflex tachycardia.

Balanced Vasodilators

These drugs dilate both arteries and veins. Angiotensin-converting enzyme inhibitors (ACEIs) and angiotensin receptor blockers (ARBs) are two rather large classes of drugs that produce this effect. These drugs inhibit the actions of angiotensin II, which causes vasoconstriction, release of aldosterone, and release of ADH. Aldosterone and ADH cause retention of sodium and water. ACEIs have two mechanisms of action. First, they inhibit the angiotensin-converting enzyme (ACE), which reduces the formation of angiotensin II. This action promotes

vasodilation and excretion of sodium and water from the kidneys. Second, inhibition of ACE also decreases inactivation of bradykinin. Bradykinin is an endogenous vasodilator and this action increases bradykinin levels in the plasma and contributes to the vasodilation produced by the ACEIs.

ARBs bind to and block the angiotensin II receptor, referred to as the angiotensin-1 (AT_1) receptor. This blocks the actions of angiotensin II and results in vasodilation and increased excretion of sodium and water. ARBs do not affect bradykinin. Figure 22.3 illustrates the sites of action of the ACEIs and ARBs. Both drug classes produce a balanced vasodilatation that reduces both pre- and afterload. These drugs have become the preferred therapy for CHF and can be combined with diuretics and other drugs indicated for CHF. The major difference between the ACEIs and the ARBs is that the ARBs do not increase bradykinin concentrations. While bradykinin contributes to the vasodilation, it also increases adverse respiratory and allergic reactions.

Adverse effects of both ACEIs and ARBs include headache, dizziness, hypotension, hyperkalemia, and GI disturbances. The ACEIs also can cause a dry cough and allergic reactions that may include angioedema. The cough and allergic reactions are thought to be related to the increased levels of bradykinin, which can increase the formation of allergic and inflammatory chemical mediators. The vasodilator drugs are summarized in Table 22:2.

LO 22.4

USE OF ADRENERGIC BETA-BLOCKERS IN CHF

The pharmacology of beta-blockers was presented in Chapter 6; a brief review of the mechanism of action and adverse effects of these drugs may be helpful. Beta-blockers bind to beta adrenergic receptors and block the actions of norepinephrine and epinephrine. The therapeutic action of beta-blockers in CHF is to block beta-1 receptors on the heart; this decreases heart rate and force of contraction. These actions would seem to be opposite to the effects required in CHF. However, in CHF, there is excessive activation of the sympathetic nervous system that causes tachycardia and increased stress on the heart. By slowing the heart rate, beta-blockers allow the heart to fill and function more efficiently. There are also beta-1 receptors on specialized cells in the kidneys, the juxtaglomerular cells that release renin. Remember that the renin-angiotensin-aldosterone mechanism causes vasoconstriction and

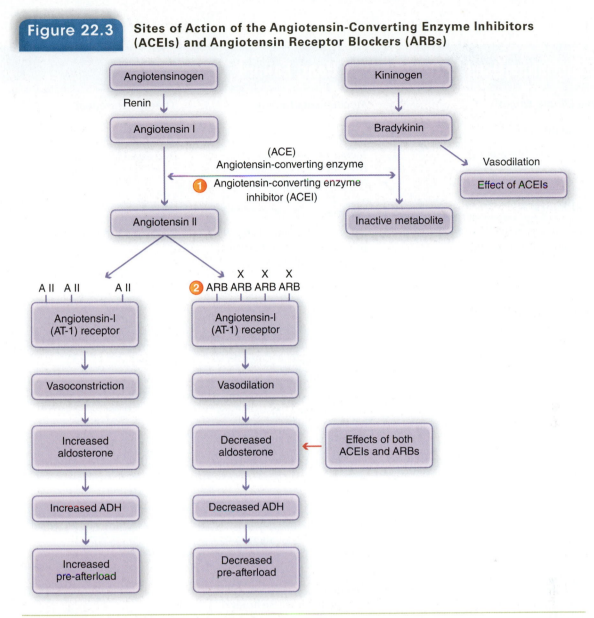

Figure 22.3 Sites of Action of the Angiotensin-Converting Enzyme Inhibitors (ACEIs) and Angiotensin Receptor Blockers (ARBs)

(1) ACEIs inhibit the enzyme ACE and decrease the formation of angiotensin II. This produces vasodilation and decreased release of aldosterone and ADH. In addition, by inhibiting ACE, ACEIs increase the concentration of bradykinin and vasodilation. **(2)** ARBs bind to the angiotensin-1 (AT$_1$) receptor and block angiotensin II from producing its effects. ARBs block the actions of angiotensin II but do not increase bradykinin concentrations.

retention of sodium and water. Therefore, blocking these beta-1 receptors reduces the release of renin and activation of the RAA mechanism. Any of the beta-blockers will produce the desired therapeutic effects, but metoprolol (*Lopressor*) and carvedilol (*Coreg*) are usually the preferred drugs for treatment of CHF. In addition to blocking beta receptors, carvedilol also produces vasodilation by blocking adrenergic alpha-1 receptors. The dosages of beta-blockers in CHF are usually in the lower therapeutic range and it is important not to cause excessive beta blockade of cardiac

function, which would then decrease contractility and cardiac output.

LO 22.5

CARDIAC GLYCOSIDES

The **cardiac glycosides** are a group of compounds originally obtained from the plant leaves of *Digitalis purpurea* and *Digitalis lanata*. The term *digitalis* also refers to these drugs. The major action of these drugs is to increase cardiac contractility. Digoxin (*Lanoxin*) is the

Vasodilators Used to Treat Chronic Heart Failure

Drug (Trade Name)	Mechanism of action	Therapeutic effect
Arterial dilators		
Hydralazine (*Apresoline*)	Increases endothelial release of NO* to produce relaxation of arteriolar smooth muscle	Decreased afterload, increased CO**
Venodilators		
Isosorbide dinitrate (*Isordil*) Nitroglycerine (generic)	Leads to formation of NO, which primarily causes relaxation of venous smooth muscle	Decreased preload, increased CO
Balanced vasodilators		
Angiotensin-converting enzyme (ACE) inhibitors		
Benazepril (*Lotensin*) Captopril (*Capoten*) Enalapril (*Vasotec*) Fosinopril (*Monopril*) Lisinopril (*Prinivil, Zestril*) Ramipril (*Altace*) Trandolapril (*Mavik*)	ACE inhibitors block the enzymatic conversion of angiotensin I to angiotensin II, decrease the release of aldosterone and ADH. This produces a balanced vasodilation of both arteries and veins and reduces sodium and water retention. ACEIs also increase bradykinin levels which contributes to the vasodilating effect	Decreased pre- and afterload, increased CO, reduction of cardiac remodeling
Angiotensin receptor blockers (ARBs)		
Candesartan (*Atacand*) Irbesartan (*Avapro*) Losartan (*Cozaar*) Telmisartan (*Micardis*) Valsartan (*Diovan*)	All ARBs block the binding of angiotensin II to angiotensin receptor sites. The angiotensin receptor is referred to as the AT_1 receptor. Effects are similar to the ACE inhibitors, except that ARBs do not increase bradykinin	Decreased pre- and afterload, increased CO, reduction of cardiac remodeling

*NO-nitric oxide. **CO-cardiac output.*

only drug of this class that is still available in the United States, so this discussion will focus on the pharmacology of digoxin.

Pharmacological Effects

The unique and main pharmacological effect of digoxin is to increase the force of myocardial contractions (also referred to as a positive inotropic effect) in CHF without causing an increase in oxygen consumption. The efficiency of the heart is improved, restoring normal blood circulation. Kidney function increases due to the increased cardiac output and renal blood flow. This increase in kidney function contributes to the elimination of the excess fluid and electrolytes associated with edema.

A second action of digoxin is to stimulate the vagus nerve (parasympathetic effect), which slows the activity of the SA and AV nodes. This slows the heart rate (also referred to as a negative chronotropic effect) and decreases AV conduction. On the electrocardiogram (ECG) this is observed as a lengthening of the PR interval. At higher doses, the decreased conduction through the AV node can lead to various degrees of heart block.

Heart block occurs when conduction of electrical impulses from the atria through the AV node to the ventricles is delayed or blocked. A slight delay in AV conduction is useful in the treatment of atrial flutter and atrial fibrillation. In these conditions, digoxin reduces the ventricular rate by slowing conduction through the AV node. This causes prolongation of the PR interval and is referred to as first-degree heart block. Second-degree heart block is characterized by failure of some impulses to get through the AV node. The result is that every P wave is not followed by a QRS wave. When every other P wave is blocked the arrhythmia is referred to as 2:1 AV block. Other ratios also can be seen, for example, 3:1, 4:1, and so on. In third-degree or complete heart block, no impulses go through the AV node and the atria and ventricles beat independently. Second- and third-degree heart block are arrhythmias that require treatment. ECG tracings of the different degrees of heart block can be seen in Chapter 23, Figure 23.1.

Special Considerations

Before administering glycosides, a patient's pulse should be taken to ensure that the heart rate is between 60 and 100 beats per minute. If the rate is below 60 or above 100, the attending physician should be consulted before the drug is given. In addition, the heart rhythm should be normal.

Mechanism of Action

Digoxin increases the force of myocardial contractions by increasing the concentration of calcium ions inside cardiac muscle cells. First, digoxin inhibits the enzyme **Na/K adenosine triphosphatase (Na/K ATPase),** which energizes the sodium/potassium pump. Normally, the sodium/potassium pump removes sodium from inside the cell (depolarization) and brings potassium back into the cell (after repolarization). Inhibition of Na/K ATPase leads to accumulation of sodium ions inside heart muscle cells. Second, the increase of sodium ions inside heart muscle reduces the activity of another ion exchange mechanism, the sodium-calcium (Na/Ca) exchanger. Normally the Na/Ca exchanger brings Na^+ into the cell and pumps Ca^{++} out of the cell. Inhibition of the Na/K ATPase increases the concentration of Na^+ inside the cell. The increased intracellular Na^+ slows the Na/Ca exchanger and slows the loss of intracellular Ca^{++}. The resulting increased intracellular calcium concentrations increase the formation of the contractile protein actinomyosin, resulting in greater myocardial contraction. After treatment with digoxin, the heart contracts more forcefully to increase cardiac output and

relieve the symptoms of heart failure. Figure 22.4 illustrates the mechanism of action of digoxin.

Pharmacokinetics

In acute CHF, the administration of digoxin normally follows a sequence known as digitalization and maintenance. During **digitalization,** digoxin is administered (PO or IV) at doses and intervals that rapidly produce an effective blood level. Subsequent daily **maintenance doses** are lower and adjusted to maintain a therapeutic level of glycoside in the blood.

Digoxin can be administered orally or intravenously, depending on the urgency of the situation. Food

Figure 22.4

Mechanism of Action of Digoxin

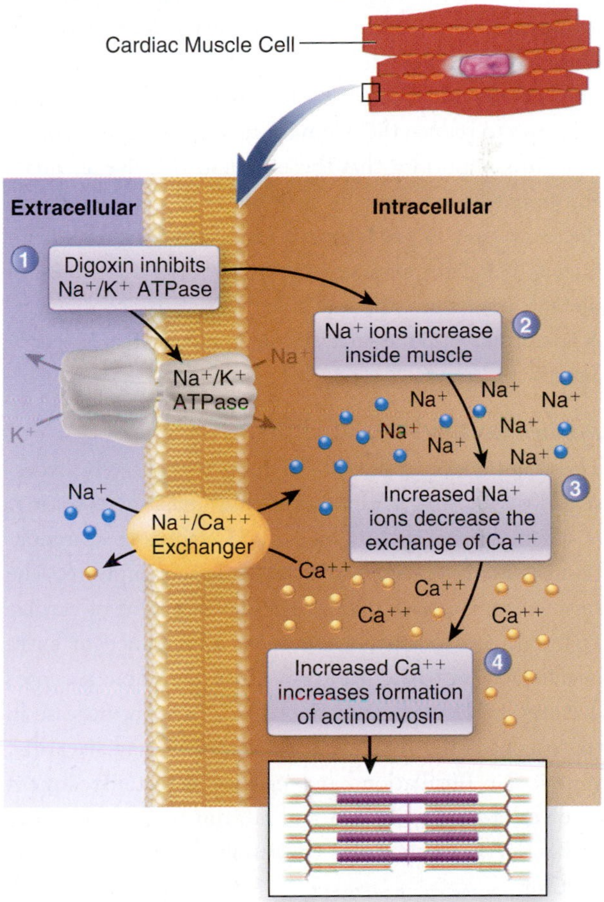

(1) Digoxin binds to and inhibits Na/K ATPase. (2) Inhibition of Na/K ATPase increases intracellular concentration of Na^+ ions. (3) Increased intracellular Na^+ decreases the Na^+/Ca^{++} exchanger and allows intracellular Ca^{++} concentrations to increase. (4) Increased intracellular Ca^{++} increases the formation of actinomyosin and increases the force of myocardial contractions.

may delay absorption but usually does not interfere with the extent of absorption. Digoxin is not bound significantly to plasma proteins and is excreted mostly unmetabolized by the urinary tract. The half-life of digoxin is normally 1.5 to 2.0 days, but it may be prolonged in older patients.

The Effects of Serum Electrolyte Levels on Digoxin

The actions of digoxin are affected by changes in the serum electrolytes, particularly potassium and calcium. **Hypokalemia** (low serum potassium) sensitizes the heart to the toxic effects of digoxin. Decrease in serum potassium may cause an increased incidence of arrhythmias, which can lead to ventricular fibrillation and sudden death. Administration of potassium salts is required to restore normal electrolyte levels during these crises. In contrast, **hyperkalemia** (high serum potassium) antagonizes the therapeutic effects of digoxin. **Hypercalcemia** (high serum calcium) enhances the action of digoxin and can lead to arrhythmias.

Many patients with CHF also are treated with diuretics to reduce the edema associated with this condition. It is important that these patients receive adequate amounts of potassium in their diets to counterbalance the excretion of potassium caused by diuretics. Fruit juices, bananas, and vegetables are good sources of dietary potassium. In addition, there are commercial preparations of potassium supplements such as *K-Lyte* or *Slow-K*.

Adverse and Toxic Effects

The major adverse effects of digoxin are caused by excessive dosage. Mild symptoms include nausea, vomiting, headache, visual disturbances, and rashes. Dose reduction is usually sufficient to relieve these symptoms. The serious toxic effects involve the development of cardiac arrhythmias. Usually, there is an appearance of extra heartbeats **(ectopic beats).** Most common are premature ventricular contractions (PVCs). An increase in these contractions can lead to ventricular tachycardia, ventricular fibrillation, and cardiac arrest. Treatment involves stopping digoxin and administering potassium and antiarrhythmic drugs to restore the normal cardiac rhythm.

In overdose toxicity, an antidote is available to reduce the severity of toxicity. Digoxin Immune Fab (*Digibind*) is a preparation of antidigoxin antibodies that is administered parenterally. The antibodies bind up digoxin and make it unavailable for producing its pharmacological effects. The symptoms and severity of toxicity are usually reduced within 30 to 60 minutes. The antibody-digoxin complex is eliminated in the urine. The main indication for Digoxin Immune Fab is treatment of life-threatening digoxin intoxication.

Clinical Indications

The main use of digoxin is the treatment of CHF, to increase the force of contractions. Digoxin also is used in some cases of atrial flutter and atrial fibrillation. The intent is to produce first-degree heart block and slow AV conduction. This reduces the ventricular rate and prevents the ventricles from excessive stimulation.

Drug Interactions

Antacids, laxatives, kaolinpectin (*Kaopectate*), and cholestyramine (*Questran*) can decrease the absorption of digoxin from the GI tract. The antiarrhythmic drug quinidine increases digoxin plasma levels. Reduction in digoxin dosage is usually required when these two drugs are used together. The calcium channel blockers verapamil and diltiazem and any of the beta-blockers decrease heart rate and force of contraction. These drugs may depress cardiac function and precipitate CHF; this can counteract the therapeutic effectiveness of digoxin. Diuretics (thiazides and loop diuretics) cause loss of potassium; hypokalemia can increase digoxin toxicity.

Other Drugs That Increase Myocardial Contraction

There are several drugs that are administered by IV infusion in the treatment of acute heart failure. Dopamine and dobutamine (*Dobutrex*) are adrenergic drugs (see Chapter 6) that stimulate beta-1 receptors and increase the force of contraction. Amrinone and milrinone (*Primacor*) are drugs that increase contractility by increasing calcium concentrations in heart muscle; these drugs also produce vasodilation. The use of these drugs is limited and administered primarily in the hospital setting during the initial treatment of acute heart failure until the patient is stabilized and other therapeutic decisions can be made.

Preferred Therapy for Chronic Heart Failure

Chronic heart failure can be caused by a variety of conditions including hypertension, coronary artery disease, and myocardial infarction. Consequently, drug selection for CHF also must consider the drugs required to treat these conditions. In mild CHF, restriction of sodium intake and diuretic therapy may be sufficient to control the edema, congestion, and decreased cardiac output. As CHF becomes more severe, the preferred drugs to

Patient Administration and Monitoring

Monitor vital signs during administration of digoxin, especially during digitalization and parenteral administration. Pay particular attention to heart rate.

Monitor the ECG for cardiac arrythmias and signs of digoxin toxicity such as excessive ST segment and T wave depression or heart block.

Always measure the pulse rate before administering digoxin. The physician should be notified when the heart rate is below 60 or above 100 beats per minute.

Instruct patient on the importance of adequate potassium intake and that fruit juices, bananas, and vegetables are good sources.

Explain to patient that common over-the-counter drugs such as antacids and laxatives may reduce drug absorption.

Explain to patient the common side effects: nausea, headache, dizziness, and visual disturbances.

Instruct patient to report excessive vomiting, visual disturbances (halo effect around lights), irregular pulse rates, or heart palpitations.

---

add are usually the angiotensin-converting enzyme inhibitors (ACEIs) or the angiotensin receptor blockers (ARBs). These drugs produce multiple actions to produce a balanced vasodilation and inhibit the retention of sodium and water. If there is tachycardia and evidence of increased sympathetic activation, low-dose beta-blocker therapy can be added. Digoxin is considered when diuretic and vasodilator therapy are unable to effectively control symptoms and when myocardial contractility is weak and unable to maintain cardiac output.

Chapter Review

Understanding Terminology

Answer the following questions.

1. Define *CHF*. **(LO 22.1)**

2. What are ectopic beats? **(LO 22.5)**

3. Differentiate between hyperkalemia and hypokalemia. **(LO 22.5)**

Acquiring Knowledge

Answer the following questions.

1. What is the main action of digoxin on heart rate and force of myocardial contraction? **(LO 22.5)**

2. Explain the use of aldosterone antagonists in treatment of CHF. **(LO 22.2)**

3. Explain the clinical importance of digitalization and tell how digitalization differs from maintenance. **(LO 22.5)**

4. Compare the pharmacologic effects of the arterial dilators and venodilators. **(LO 22.3)**

5. What precautions should be observed prior to administration of digoxin? **(LO 22.5)**

6. Why are beta-blockers useful in CHF? **(LO 22.4)**

7. What is the mechanism of action of angiotensin receptor blockers? **(LO 22.3)**

8. What role do thiazide and loop diuretics play in the treatment of congestive heart failure? **(LO 22.2)**

9. Explain why balanced vasodilator drugs are beneficial in the treatment of congestive heart failure. **(LO 22.3)**

Applying Knowledge on the Job

Use your critical-thinking skills to answer the following questions.

1. Mrs. McNally is a 65-year-old female who presents at the clinic where you're working with complaints of increased shortness of breath and swelling of her feet. Her past medical history includes a diagnosis of hypertension and moderate degree of renal failure. Pertinent laboratory tests show a slightly decreased potassium level of 3.2 M/l (normal 3.5–5 M/l) and an increased serum creatinine of 2.1 mg/dl (normal 0.8–1.5 mg/dl). The physician's diagnosis is acute congestive heart failure. The physician's course of therapy includes doubling Mrs. McNally's dose of hydrochlorothiazide from 25 mg to 50 mg daily and prescribing digoxin 0.25 mg twice daily for 2 days and then 0.25 mg daily.
   a. What is the most likely electrolyte disturbance that may occur in this patient? **(LO 22.5)**
   b. What does the increased level of serum creatinine suggest about this patient's renal function? **(LO 22.5)**

2. Outline the steps to be taken in severe cardiac glycoside intoxication. **(LO 22.5)**

3. Explain the rationale behind the use of digoxin in the treatment of atrial fibrillation. **(LO 22.5)**

Multiple Choice

Use your critical-thinking skills to answer the following questions.

1. The therapeutic actions of angiotensin-converting enzyme (ACE) inhibitors include **(LO 22.3)**
   A. arterial dilation
   B. elimination of sodium
   C. venous dilation
   D. all statements are true

2. The mechanism of action of triamterene (*Dyrenium*) is to **(LO 22.2)**
   A. block aldosterone receptors
   B. increase sodium excretion at loop of Henle
   C. block sodium channels at nephron collecting ducts
   D. increase the release of aldosterone

3. The actions of digoxin (*Lanoxin*) include **(LO 22.5)**
   A. decreased heart rate
   B. inhibition of Na/K ATPase
   C. increased calcium inside heart muscle
   D. all statements are true

4. The actions of carvedilol (*Coreg*) include **(LO 22.4)**
   A. blockade of beta receptors
   B. increased force of myocardial contraction
   C. blockade of alpha-1 receptors
   D. only A and C are true

5. The most effective drug to relieve edema and congestion in acute heart failure would be **(LO 22.2)**
   A. hydralazine (*Apresoline*)
   B. furosemide (*Lasix*)
   C. metoprolol (*Lopressor*)
   D. hydrochlorothiazide (*HyroDIURIL*)

Multiple Choice (Multiple Answer)

Select the correct choices for each statement. The choices may be all correct, all incorrect, or any combination.

1. Select all of the following that are causes of heart failure. **(LO 22.1)**
   A. untreated hypertension
   B. weakening of contractile force
   C. myocardial infarction
   D. valvular defects

2. Which medication reduces edema by blocking the reabsorption of sodium in the distal tubules? **(LO 22.2)**
    A. eplerenone
    B. torsemide
    C. triamterene
    D. chlorothiazide

3. Vasodilators increase afterload work on which part of the circulatory system? **(LO 22.3)**
    A. veins
    B. arteries
    C. cardiac nervous tissue
    D. myocardium

4. Select the adverse effects of digoxin. **(LO 22.5)**
    A. atrial tachycardia
    B. hypokalemia
    C. ventricular fibrillation
    D. angioedema

5. The main effects of beta blockers include **(LO 22.1, 22.4)**
    A. slowing the heart rate
    B. reducing the release of renin
    C. decreasing vasoconstriction
    D. decreasing sodium retention

Classification

Place the following drug effects under the correct type of vasodilator. **(LO 22.3)**

reduce venous return
inhibit angiotensin II
reduce systemic blood pressure
decrease aldosterone
reduce preload
dilate both veins and arteries
increase release of NO
leads to formation of NO
reduce afterload

Arterial dilators	Venodilators	Balanced dilators

Matching

Match the following terms with their correct definition. **(LO 22.1, 22.2, 22.3, 22.4, 22.5)**
    a. hyperkalemia
    b. hypercalcemia
    c. hypokalemia
    d. preload

e. afterload

f. digitalization

g. cardiac output

h. ectopic beat

1. _____ method of dosage with digoxin that rapidly produces effective drug levels

2. _____ high serum calcium

3. _____ extra heartbeat

4. _____ measure of vascular resistance

5. _____ high serum potassium

6. _____ amount of venous return

7. _____ low serum potassium

8. _____ amount of blood pumped per minute

Documentation

Using the prescription below, answer the following questions. **(LO 22.2)**

**Riverview Cardiology
Practice RX**

12345 Main Avenue

Anytown, USA   12345

931-555-1000

NAME: ___Kathy Hart_____   DATE: _____

ADDRESS: _____

RX   **hydrochlorothiazide 25mg**

Sig: **Take one tablet by mouth once daily**

Dr. Craig River_____ M.D. _____M.D.

 Substitution Permitted   Dispense as written

DEA #: _____   REFILL: NR 1 2 3 4

---

a. What symptom of CHF is being treated with this drug?

b. What condition can this medication cause?

c. What is the duration of action of this medication?

d. Is this medication the best choice for someone with renal impairment? If not, what class of diuretics would be?

Labeling

Fill in the missing labels. **(LO 22.1)**

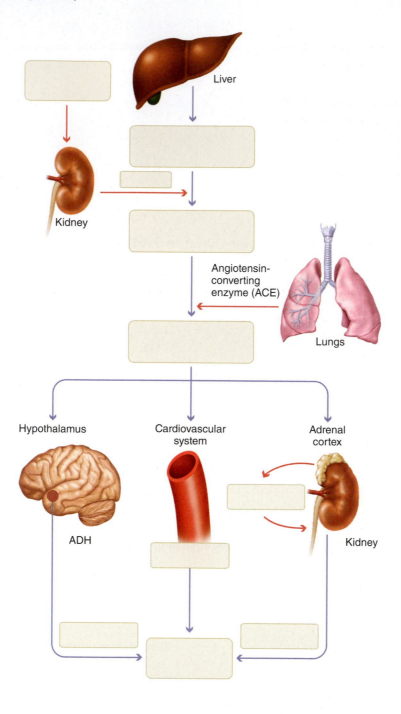

Liver

Kidney

Angiotensin-
converting
enzyme (ACE)

Lungs

Hypothalamus

Cardiovascular
system

Adrenal
cortex

ADH

Kidney

For interactive animations, videos, and assessment, visit:

www.mcgrawhillconnect.com

Chapter 23

Antiarrhythmic Drugs

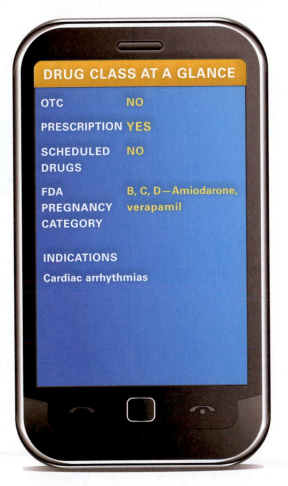

DRUG CLASS AT A GLANCE

OTC	NO
PRESCRIPTION	YES
SCHEDULED DRUGS	NO
FDA PREGNANCY CATEGORY	B, C, D—Amiodarone, verapamil

INDICATIONS

Cardiac arrhythmias

KEY TERMS

antiarrhythmic drug: drug used to restore normal cardiac rhythm.

arrhythmia: disorder of cardiac conduction and electrical impulse formation.

cinchonism: quinidine toxicity, which is characterized by ringing in the ears (tinnitus), dizziness, and headache.

ectopic focus: area of the heart from which abnormal impulses originate.

premature atrial contraction (PAC): premature contraction of the atria, usually caused by an ectopic focus.

premature ventricular contraction (PVC): premature contraction of the ventricles, usually caused by an ectopic focus.

proarrhythmia: an arrhythmia caused by administration of an antiarrhythmic drug.

supraventricular arrhythmia: arrhythmia that originates above the AV node in the atria.

torsade de pointes: a type of proarrhythmia that causes ventricular tachycardia and fainting.

ventricular fibrillation: the most serious arrhythmia; usually a terminal event where ventricular contractions are no longer able to effectively pump blood.

Learning Outcomes

After studying this chapter, you should be able to

23.1 identify the basic terminology and descriptions associated with cardiac arrhythmias.

23.2 describe the phases of the cardiac action potential in relationship to the activity of Na, K, and Ca ions.

23.3 explain the mechanism of action and main differences between the IA, IB, and IC antiarrhythmic drugs.

23.4 describe the antiarrhythmic actions and uses of the beta-blockers.

23.5 explain the mechanism of action of the class III antiarrhythmic drugs and describe the most serious adverse effects of amiodarone.

23.6 describe the antiarrhythmic actions of the calcium channel blockers and their clinical uses.

23.7 recognize the special precautions required with the use of antiarrhythmic drugs.

Introduction

An **arrhythmia** is any abnormality in heart rate or rhythm of electrical conduction through the heart. Arrhythmias disturb the electrical activity of the heart and interrupt the normal sequence of atrial and ventricular activation and contraction. The physiologic consequences of arrhythmias are usually a decrease in cardiac output and blood pressure. In addition, the electrical disturbances can lead to life-threatening arrhythmias such as **ventricular fibrillation** and cardiac arrest. The type of arrhythmia depends on the location in the heart and the severity of the electrical disturbance. The causes of arrhythmias are numerous and include ischemic conditions such as coronary artery disease (CAD), electrolyte disturbances (Na, K, Ca) caused by diuretics and drug toxicities, myocardial infarction, and other pathological conditions. Arrhythmias are identified and classified by evaluation of the electrocardiogram (ECG). The clinical management of arrhythmias involves the use of **antiarrhythmic drugs** that primarily affect the activity of sodium (Na), potassium (K), and calcium (Ca) ions. These ions normally regulate the electrical activity of the heart. The therapeutic aim of antiarrhythmic drugs is to modify the activity of these ions so that normal heart rhythm is restored.

LO 23.1 **LO 23.2**

TYPES OF ARRHYTHMIAS

Arrhythmias are often caused by electrolyte disturbances and overstimulation of the heart. Arrhythmias can originate anywhere in the heart, in the atria, ventricles, or conduction system. The most common types of arrhythmias include tachycardias, premature contractions, flutters, and fibrillations. Electrocardiogram recordings of various cardiac arrhythmias are illustrated in Figure 23.1.

Arrhythmias that originate in the atria and atrioventricular (AV) nodal areas are referred to as **supraventricular arrhythmias** (above the ventricles).

Paroxysmal atrial tachycardia, atrial flutter, and atrial fibrillation are common supraventricular arrhythmias. Paroxysmal atrial tachycardia is characterized by atrial rates of 150 to 200 beats per minute. This arrhythmia is unpredictable and can suddenly develop; it also can spontaneously terminate. The individual may experience anxiety, heart palpitations, and symptoms of heart failure if the arrhythmia persists. In atrial flutter the atrial rate is between 250 and 350 beats per minute. Instead of normal P waves, the ECG shows smaller waves with a sawtooth-like pattern. The ventricles cannot keep up with the atria and contract at a slower rate. In atrial fibrillation the atrial rate is over 350 beats per minute and the ventricular rhythm is irregular. On the ECG the atrial waves are described as a "bag of worms" and there are no effective atrial contractions. This predisposes the atria to the development of blood clots (thromboembolism).

Arrhythmias that originate below the AV node are referred to as ventricular arrhythmias. **Ectopic foci,** areas of abnormal impulse generation, may appear when electrical impulses traveling through the conduction system are delayed or blocked. In this situation, another area of the heart (atrium or ventricle) may become excitable and produce an abnormal heartbeat. Ectopic foci that originate in the atria are referred to as **premature atrial contractions (PACs).** A PAC would be classified as a supraventricular arrhythmia. Ectopic foci that originate in the ventricles are referred to as **premature ventricular contractions (PVCs).** Figure 23.2

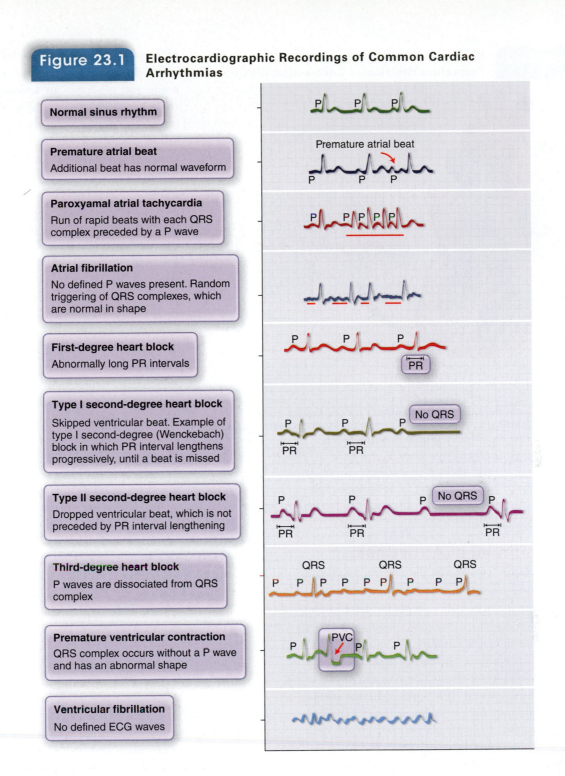

Normal sinus rhythm

Premature atrial beat
Additional beat has normal waveform

Paroxyamal atrial tachycardia
Run of rapid beats with each QRS complex preceded by a P wave

Atrial fibrillation
No defined P waves present. Random triggering of QRS complexes, which are normal in shape

First-degree heart block
Abnormally long PR intervals

Type I second-degree heart block
Skipped ventricular beat. Example of type I second-degree (Wenckebach) block in which PR interval lengthens progressively, until a beat is missed

Type II second-degree heart block
Dropped ventricular beat, which is not preceded by PR interval lengthening

Third-degree heart block
P waves are dissociated from QRS complex

Premature ventricular contraction
QRS complex occurs without a P wave and has an abnormal shape

Ventricular fibrillation
No defined ECG waves

shows the appearance of a PVC produced by a ventricular ectopic focus. In this arrhythmia the PVC depolarizes the ventricle before the SA node and atrium. The electrical impulse travels up the conduction system (instead of down) toward the atrium. The result is a QRS wave that is inverted and that disrupts normal ventricular contraction. Ventricular tachycardia is a rapid ventricular rhythm where three or more PVCs occur consecutively. Ventricular tachycardia can cause significant circulatory impairment and may lead to ventricular fibrillation.

The most serious arrhythmia is **ventricular fibrillation,** which constitutes a medical emergency. During fibrillation, the electrical activity of the ventricles is severely disturbed and the ventricles cannot

Figure 23.2

Illustration of a Ventricular Ectopic Focus or Premature Ventricular Contraction (PVC)

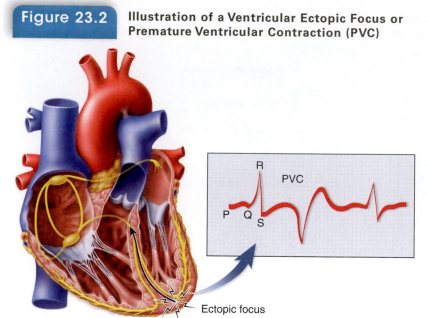

Ectopic focus

The ectopic focus depolarizes the ventricle before the SA node and atrium. The electrical impulse travels up the conduction system and the QRS wave is inverted and abnormal in appearance.

contract efficiently enough to maintain adequate circulation. If not treated immediately, cardiac arrest and death will result.

ECG Monitoring of Arrhythmias

The characteristic pattern of an electrocardiogram (ECG) was reviewed in Chapter 21, Figure 21.3. Electrocardiograms are extremely valuable for determining abnormalities in cardiac rhythm and conduction. Heart rate can be determined by counting the number of QRS waves that occur within a 1-minute period. Abnormalities in the appearance of the ECG waves and measurements of the ECG intervals (PR, QRS, QT) that are not within normal limits indicate abnormalities of conduction. The duration of the PR interval reflects the time required for conduction from the SA to the AV node, the duration of the QRS wave reflects the time for depolarization and conduction through the ventricles, and the QT interval reflects the time for depolarization and repolarization of the ventricles.

Electrophysiology of the Heart

One of the most important aspects of the heart is the function of several ions that regulate the electrophysiological properties of the heart. The ions are sodium (Na^+), potassium (K^+), and calcium (Ca^{2+}). Each ion has a specific role in generation of the cardiac action potential. During Phase 0 influx of Na^+ ions depolarizes the cardiac membrane and generates an action potential. During Phases 1–3 the membrane is undergoing repolarization as K^+ ions efflux out of the cardiac membrane. During Phase 2 (plateau) calcium channels open and Ca^{++} ions pass into the muscle cell and function in myocardial contraction. In Phase 4 the membrane potential has returned to its resting level and is ready for the next action potential. In the SA and AV nodes, the slope of Phase 4 increases upward and functions to automatically generate an action potential. This property is referred to as automaticity. Ventricular muscle does not normally display automaticity. However, it can develop automaticity when there is ischemia, excessive sympathetic stimulation, or other abnormal conditions. When this occurs ventricular muscle can depolarize and generate a premature ventricular contraction (PVC).

The heart possesses several important electrophysiologic properties, including conduction, refractoriness, and automaticity. Table 23:1 describes these properties and correlates them with the phases (0–4) of the ventricular action potential (Figures 23.3 and 23.4). An ECG recording is an electrical summation of all the individual cardiac action potentials. On the ECG, Phase 0 corresponds to the ventricular QRS wave. The time required for Phases 0–4 represents the QT interval.

Antiarrhythmic drugs that slow Phase 0, prolong Phases 1–3, or decrease Phase 4 automaticity produce effective antiarrhythmic actions. Most antiarrhythmic drugs affect the movement of one or more specific ions and exert their major antiarrhythmic action on a specific phase of the action potential.

When some part of the heart develops an arrhythmia, the properties of the heart and the movement of the ions are disturbed. The therapeutic effects of antiarrhythmic drugs rest in their ability to affect the electrophysiological properties of the cardiac membrane and the movement of ions so that the properties of the heart are restored to normal or are at least improved. One cautionary note should be mentioned: all antiarrhythmic drugs have the potential to make any existing arrhythmia worse. In addition, antiarrhythmic drugs can cause new arrhythmias. A new or different

Figure 23.3

Phases of the Cardiac Action Potential of Ventricular Muscle

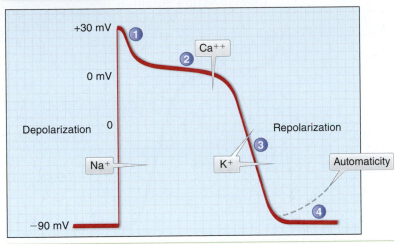

During Phase 0, sodium ions influx into the muscle cell and depolarize the membrane. This generates an action potential that is conducted along the membrane and throughout the ventricles. During Phases 1–3, potassium ions pass out of the muscle cell and the membrane is repolarized. During Phase 2, calcium channels open and calcium ions pass into the muscle and are involved in muscle contraction. Phase 4 reflects the property of automaticity, which is normally absent in ventricular muscle; however, ischemia and excessive sympathetic stimulation can increase ventricular automaticity (dashed line) and cause premature ventricular contractions (PVCs).

arrhythmia caused by administration of an antiarrhythmic drug is referred to as a **proarrhythmia.** One of the most common proarrhythmias is referred to as **torsade de pointes.** This arrhythmia occurs with drugs that cause excessive prolongation of the QT interval, which can lead to hypotension, fainting, and ventricular arrhythmias.

Antiarrhythmic drugs are usually classified according to the Vaughn-Williams classification system, which organizes the antiarrhythmic drugs into four major classes based on their major mechanism of action. These drug classes and their main pharmacologic features are summarized in Table 23:2.

CLASS 1 ANTIARRHYTHMIC DRUGS: SODIUM CHANNEL BLOCKERS

One of the common features of the Class 1 antiarrhythmic drugs is that they possess local anesthetic activity. Like local anesthetics, the Class 1 drugs block the influx of Na ions during depolarization of nerves and excitable membranes like those of the heart. The primary effect of Class 1 antiarrhythmic drugs is to slow depolarization and conduction during Phase 0 of the action potential. Class IA antiarrhythmics also slow the efflux of K ions during repolarization, which prolongs the refractory period. These actions suppress arrhythmias in cardiac cells that are hyperexcitable and arrhythmogenic (giving rise to arrhythmias). The Class I drugs are subdivided into three groups (IA, IB, IC) based on the degree to which they block Na ions during depolarization (Phase 0). IAs produce a moderate block; IBs, a mild block; and ICs, a marked block of Na influx (Phase 0). Each Class I drug also produces a different effect on the refractory period (Figure 23.4).

Quinidine (IA)

Chemically related to quinine, quinidine is a natural product obtained from the bark of the cinchona tree. The use of quinidine for cardiac disorders dates back to the eighteenth century, when patients suffering from malaria were treated with extracts of the cinchona bark. The presence of quinidine in these concoctions resulted in improvement in patients in which malaria and atrial flutter occurred simultaneously. In the past quinidine has been used to treat supraventricular arrhythmias, such as atrial flutter and fibrillation, and also ventricular arrhythmias. However, quinidine is a cardiac depressant that decreases myocardial contraction. In addition, quinidine produces anticholinergic and alpha-blocking effects. Consequently, quinidine can cause a wide range of adverse effects and potential toxicities and is rarely used.

The adverse effects of quinidine include nausea, vomiting, and diarrhea due to irritation of the GI tract. **Cinchonism** is an adverse syndrome produced by quinidine in overdosage or in patients who are sensitive to the drug. This condition is characterized by ringing in the ears (tinnitus), dizziness, salivation, headache, and hallucinations.

Quinidine also depresses smooth and skeletal muscle function. Depression of arteriolar smooth muscle may cause hypotension. Depression of skeletal muscle results in weakness and fatigue, which may interfere with respiration (dyspnea).

Evidence of quinidine's electrophysiologic effects can be observed on the ECG. The durations of the PR, QRS, and QT intervals are all increased as a result of the slowed conduction and prolongation of the refractory period. These changes may cause premature contractions of the atria and ventricles or pro-arrhythmias like torsade de points.

Less frequently there may be hypersensitivity reactions involving the development of hepatitis and thrombocytopenia. The latter condition can lead to bleeding problems.

Procainamide (*Procanbid*) (IA)

A synthetic drug related to procaine (a local anesthetic), procainamide produces similar antiarrhythmic actions as quinidine. However, procainamide produces less anticholinergic and alpha-blocking actions than quinidine. Procainamide causes fewer adverse effects and toxicities and is the most frequently used IA antiarrhythmic drug. Procainamide may be administered orally or parenterally; however, rapid IV administration may cause a sudden drop in blood pressure. Procainamide has a short half-life and is administered in extended-release tablets (*Procanbid*) that allow a 12-hour dosing interval. The drug forms an active metabolite, N-acetylprocainamide (NAPA), that also contributes to the therapeutic effect. Procainamide is effective for both supraventricular and ventricular arrhythmias. However, it is primarily indicated for outpatient treatment of ventricular arrhythmias.

Common adverse effects of procainamide include nausea, diarrhea, anorexia, and skin rash. Following chronic use of procainamide, a large percentage of patients develop an antibody referred to as antinuclear antibody. Approximately 20–30 percent of these patients develop a rash and arthralgia similar to the symptoms seen in lupus erythematosus. The development of these symptoms requires that procainamide be discontinued. Procainamide is also capable of producing changes

(a) Class IA antiarrhythmic drugs produce a moderate decrease in conduction (Phase 0) and prolong the refractory period (Phases 1–3) (dashed line). (b) Class IB drugs produce a mild decrease in conduction and shorten the refractory period. (c) Class IC drugs produce a marked decrease in conduction but do not prolong the refractory period.

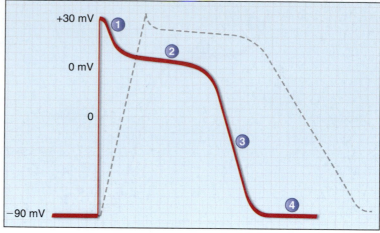

(a)

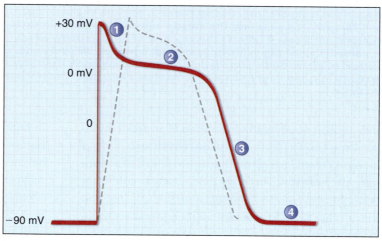

(b)

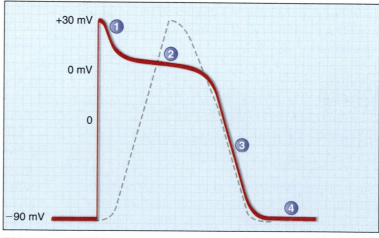

(c)

Correlation of Electrophysiological Properties of the Heart with the Phases of the Cardiac Action Potential and the Movement of Ions

Property	Phase	Ionic movement
Conduction	0	Na^+ rapidly moves to the inside of the cell, causing reversal of the membrane potential (-90 mV to $+30$ mV, and depolarization)
Refractory period (RP)	1–3	K^+ moves to the outside of the cell, bringing the membrane potential back (repolarization) to its resting level (-90 mV)
Plateau phase	2	Ca^{2+} moves to the inside of the cell and is involved in regulating the force of muscle contraction
Automaticity	4	A latent property of ventricular muscle; in pacemaker cells (SA and AV nodes), there is a slow inward movement of Na^+ and Ca^{2+} and an outward movement of K^+, which "automatically" excites the membrane and begins another membrane depolarization (Phase 0)

Table **23:2**

Vaughn-Williams Classification of Antiarrhythmic Drugs

Class	Mechanism of action	Main effects	Drug examples
IA	Moderate block of sodium (Na) channels	Moderate decrease in Phase 0 depolarization; QRS and QT intervals prolonged	Quinidine, procainamide, disopyramide
IB	Mild block of sodium (Na) channels	Mild decrease in Phase 0 depolarization, decrease in ventricular automaticity	Lidocaine, mexiletine
IC	Marked block of sodium (Na) channels	Marked decrease in Phase 0 depolarization, prolongation of QRS interval	Flecainide, propafenone
II	Blockade of adrenergic beta-1 receptors	Decrease in heart rate, AV conduction, and ventricular automaticity; increased PR interval	Propranolol, acebutolol, esmolol
III	Blockade of potassium (K) channels	Prolongation of ventricular repolarization (Phases 1–3), prolongation of QT interval	Amiodarone, dofetilide, ibutilide, sotalol
IV	Blockade of calcium (Ca) channels in SA and AV nodes	Decrease in heart rate and AV conduction, increase in PR interval	Diltiazem, verapamil

in ECGs similar to those produced by quinidine. Usually, increased duration of the PR, QRS, and QT waves occurs. Excessive dosage can cause the development of premature contractions and proarrhythmias. At higher doses procainamide is also a cardiac depressant. A less frequent adverse reaction is agranulocytosis (decrease in granulocytic white blood cells), which can increase the incidence of infection.

Disopyramide (*Norpace*) (IA)

The actions of disopyramide (*Norpace*) on the heart are similar to those of quinidine and procainamide. Disopyramide produces a decrease in conduction and prolongation of the refractory period. This drug is only approved for treating ventricular arrhythmias. Like quinidine, disopyramide depresses myocardial contractility and is considered a second-line drug with limited clinical usage. In addition, disopyramide produces significant anticholinergic effects that account for the common side effects such as dry mouth, visual disturbances, constipation, and urinary retention. At higher doses or with the development of toxicity, the cardiac depressant effects can cause heart failure.

Lidocaine (*Xylocaine*) (IB)

A synthetic drug used primarily as a local anesthetic agent, lidocaine (*Xylocaine*) is widely used for ventricular arrhythmias, especially those resulting from a myocardial infarction or arrhythmias occurring during surgery. As a rule, lidocaine is ineffective in atrial arrhythmias and is therefore not recommended for use in these conditions. Although lidocaine suppresses ectopic foci associated with ventricular arrhythmias, it does not depress normal impulse conduction. The main effect of lidocaine, prevention of ventricular arrhythmias, is attributed to its ability to depress automaticity (Phase 4).

The major disadvantage of lidocaine is that it must be administered parenterally (IV or IM). Since a single administration results in a very short antiarrhythmic response, lidocaine is usually given as an intravenous infusion to maintain the antiarrhythmic action. Usually, a bolus injection of lidocaine (50 to 100 mg) is initially administered over a 2-minute period, followed by continuous infusion at a rate of 1 to 4 mg per minute.

Since lidocaine is rapidly metabolized in the liver, impaired liver function will result in elevated blood levels of lidocaine. At higher concentrations, lidocaine produces a mixed picture of CNS stimulation (tremors, restlessness, convulsions) and CNS depression (confusion, slurred speech, paresthesias). Toxic blood levels of lidocaine usually produce CNS depression (anesthetic effect), and possible cardiac and respiratory arrest.

Mexiletine (*Mexitil*) (IB)

Mexiletine is a derivative of lidocaine that has been structurally modified so that it can be administered orally. Mexiletine produces cardiac effects similar to lidocaine and is used for treatment of outpatient ventricular arrhythmias. Adverse effects are similar to those of lidocaine: lightheadedness, tremors, and other CNS disturbances.

Class 1C Antiarrhythmic Drugs

Flecainide (*Tambocor*) and propafenone (*Rythmol*) are drugs that are usually reserved for treatment of arrhythmias that are unresponsive to other antiarrhythmic drugs. These drugs markedly depress cardiac conduction (Phase 0). Drug trials with the ICs have shown that these drugs can increase the risk of mortality in patients with preexisting arrhythmias and other cardiac conditions. The IC drugs also depress myocardial contractility and may cause heart failure. Flecainide and propafenone are primarily indicated for treatment of supraventricular arrhythmias. Adverse effects include GI disturbances, bradycardia, heart block, and the potential for heart failure.

LO 23.4

CLASS 2 ANTIARRHYTHMIC DRUGS: BETA-BLOCKERS

The beta-adrenergic blockers are classified as Class 2 antiarrhythmic drugs. Frequently, in heart disease, there is increased sympathetic activity with increased release of norepinephrine and epinephrine. These *adrenergic neurotransmitters* increase heart rate, excitability, conduction, and automaticity, particularly of ventricular muscle. In addition, they shorten the refractory period, all of which can contribute to the development of various arrhythmias.

By antagonizing the effects of norepinephrine and epinephrine at the beta-1 receptors, beta-blockers decrease heart rate, AV conduction, and automaticity of the SA and AV nodes, and of atrial and ventricular muscle. Beta-blockers are mainly indicated for supraventricular arrhythmias and for prevention of recurrent myocardial infarction. Propranolol, acebutolol, and esmolol are the beta-blockers most frequently used to treat cardiac arrhythmias. The beta-blockers were previously discussed in Chapter 6.

Propranolol (*Inderal*)

Propranolol is widely used as an antiarrhythmic drug. In addition to its beta-blocking effect, propranolol produces a depressant effect on cardiac membranes that slows conduction and prolongs repolarization. Propranolol can be administered orally and intravenously in emergency situations.

The most common cardiovascular adverse effects are hypotension and bradycardia. In overdosage, propranolol, and other beta-blockers, may cause heart failure and possible cardiac arrest. Skin rashes, mental confusion, and visual disturbances also may occur.

Esmolol (*Brevibloc*)

Esmolol is a selective beta-blocker that mainly affects beta-1 receptors in the heart. It is administered by intravenous infusion in emergency situations when rapid beta-blockade is desired to lower heart rate. The duration of action is very short, only a few minutes, because of rapid metabolism by esterase enzymes in the blood and liver. Excessive bradycardia, delayed AV conduction, and hypotension are adverse effects associated with overdosage.

LO 23.5

CLASS 3 ANTIARRHYTHMIC DRUGS: POTASSIUM CHANNEL BLOCKERS

The main antiarrhythmic action of the Class 3 drugs is to block potassium channels and interfere with the efflux of potassium ions (K^+) during repolarization Phases 1 through 3. This action prolongs the refractory period of the heart and decreases the frequency of arrhythmias. Amiodarone is the most important drug in this class and has become one of the most frequently prescribed antiarrhythmic drug.

Amiodarone (*Cordarone*)

Amiodarone is a very potent antiarrhythmic drug that has multiple sites of action. In addition to blocking potassium channels, amiodarone blocks sodium (Class 1) and calcium (Class 4) channels. It also has blocking actions on both beta- (Class 2) and alpha-adrenergic receptors. The result is a drug that can be used for most supraventricular and ventricular arrhythmias. When administered IV, the alpha-blocking effect can produce vasodilation and hypotension. The major antiarrhythmic effect is prolongation of the refractory period. On the ECG this is observed by an increase in the duration of the QT interval. The other actions of amiodarone decrease both heart rate and AV conduction; consequently the PR and QRS intervals also are prolonged. Amiodarone is structurally similar to the thyroid hormone thyroxine, contains iodine, and can interfere with thyroid function.

The pharmacokinetics of amiodarone are complex. Amiodarone can be administered both orally and intravenously. Oral absorption is incomplete and variable. Drug metabolism produces an active metabolite, desethylamiodarone. The half-life of amiodarone is long and also variable, ranging from 1 to 3 months. Dosages must be carefully regulated and periodic monitoring of serum drug levels is advised.

Amiodarone causes numerous adverse effects and potentially serious toxicities. CNS effects include dizziness, tremors, and ataxia. Disturbances of thyroid function, either hypo- or hyperthyroidism, are possible. Pulmonary fibrosis is one of the more serious problems that can occur and can be fatal. Cardiac toxicities include bradycardia, heart block, heart failure, and generation of proarrhythmias such as torsade de pointes. Other adverse effects include a blue-gray skin discoloration, corneal microdeposits, and GI disturbances. Amiodarone is designated Food and Drug Administration (FDA) Pregnancy Category D and should not be used in pregnancy or in nursing mothers.

Sotalol (*Betapace*)

Sotalol is a nonselective beta-blocker that also has Class 3 antiarrhythmic activity. The main effects are prolongation of the refractory period, slowed AV conduction, and decreased automaticity of the heart. Sotalol is primarily indicated for treatment of ventricular arrhythmias and atrial fibrillation. Adverse effects are similar to those of beta-blockers. The major concern with sotalol is its ability to cause torsade de pointes that leads to ventricular tachycardia and fainting.

Dofetilide (*Tikosyn*) and Ibutilide (*Corvert*)

Dofetilide and ibutilide are two Class 3 drugs whose actions are limited to blocking potassium channels. Dofetilide is administered orally; ibutilide is administered intravenously. Dofetilide is indicated for the treatment of atrial fibrillation; ibutilide is indicated for the conversion of atrial flutter and atrial fibrillation to normal sinus rhythm. Like other Class 3 drugs, excessive prolongation of the QT interval may cause proarrhythmias such as torsade de pointes.

LO 23.6

CLASS 4 ANTIARRHYTHMIC DRUGS: CALCIUM CHANNEL BLOCKERS

The Class 4 antiarrhythmic drugs are referred to as the calcium channel blockers. These drugs decrease the entry of calcium into cells whose electrophysiologic actions depend on the influx of calcium through the slow-type calcium channels. In the heart, the depolarization of SA and AV nodal cells is highly dependent on the influx of calcium ions.

The effect of calcium channel blockers on the SA node is to slow depolarization and decrease the heart rate. The effect on the AV node is to slow conduction. These actions reduce the ventricular rate during fast supraventricular arrhythmias.

The calcium channel blockers also affect the contraction of cardiac and smooth muscle. As indicated in Table 23:1, entry of calcium during Phase 2 of the action potential is important for regulating the force of myocardial contractions. Interference with calcium entry into cardiac muscle reduces myocardial contractility. This is usually not a desired therapeutic action and may precipitate heart failure in patients with CHF. The calcium channel blockers also relax smooth muscle and cause vasodilation, which is useful in the treatment of angina pectoris and hypertension. While all calcium channel blockers produce vasodilation, only verapamil (*Calan*) and diltiazem (*Cardizem*) have direct actions on the heart and are used for their antiarrhythmic actions.

Verapamil (*Calan*)

The major effect of verapamil is on the SA and AV nodes of the heart. Verapamil decreases SA node activity, resulting in a slight decrease in heart rate. More important, verapamil decreases AV node conduction. This effect makes it very useful in treating various types of

rapid AV nodal arrhythmias and other supraventricular tachycardias. Verapamil is administered PO (40 to 120 mg TID) and IV (5 to 10 mg) in emergency situations. Verapamil also produces vasodilation and is used in the treatment of angina pectoris and hypertension (see Chapters 24 and 26).

Common adverse effects of verapamil include headache, dizziness, and minor GI disturbances, especially constipation. The vasodilating effect can produce hypotension, especially when patients change position. More serious complications include cardiac depression leading to heart failure and various degrees of heart block, especially if verapamil is taken with other cardiac depressant drugs such as the beta-blockers. Verapamil is usually contraindicated in patients with existing SA and AV node disturbances or with heart failure.

Diltiazem (*Cardizem*)

The pharmacologic actions, uses, and adverse effects of diltiazem are similar to verapamil. The cardiac depressant effects of diltiazem are slightly less than those of verapamil, but diltiazem is generally considered to be a more potent vasodilator than verapamil.

Adenosine (*Adenocard*)

Adenosine is considered a miscellaneous antiarrhythmic drug that is only used in emergency and acute situations. Adenosine is the naturally occurring metabolite of adenosine triphosphate (ATP). The drug is administered intravenously to terminate episodes of paroxysmal supraventricular tachycardia. The main effect of adenosine is to decrease the activity of calcium ions in the SA and AV nodes. This causes a slowing of the heart rate and AV conduction, which usually terminates the episode of tachycardia. The duration of action of adenosine is extremely short, 15 to 30 seconds, and may require repeated administrations. Adverse effects are brief, but include asystole, respiratory difficulties (bronchospasm), and hypotension.

LO 23.7

SPECIAL CONSIDERATIONS AND PREFERRED THERAPY FOR SELECTED ARRHYTHMIAS

The control of arrhythmias can be a difficult task and patients are often in a precarious situation. Sudden changes in ECGs and the development of life-threatening arrhythmias, like ventricular fibrillation, are always a possibility. In the hospital, ECGs constantly monitor heart patients. It is important to be aware of ECG monitors, to check them frequently, and to be alert for sudden changes in the appearance of ECGs or the condition of patients.

Antiarrhythmic drugs are frequently administered in the hospital by IV infusion. Dosages (drips per minute) are carefully adjusted to deliver the proper amount of drug. Other medications frequently are administered through the same IV line; and procedures, like measuring the central venous pressure (CVP), require turning off or adjusting the infusion. It is extremely important that when these other procedures are completed, the infusion rate of the antiarrhythmic drug is adjusted back to its proper rate of delivery. Failure to do this can result in serious consequences for patients.

It is important to be aware of the adverse effects of the various antiarrhythmic drugs and to be alert for their appearance. Many of the antiarrhythmic drugs are cardiac depressants and can produce heart failure or any variety of cardiac arrhythmias themselves.

Preferred Therapy for Selected Cardiac Arrhythmias

Cardiac arrhythmias are complex and involve a variety of electrophysiologic disturbances. Use of antiarrhythmic drugs carries the risk of causing additional arrhythmias (proarrhythmias) and other serious adverse reactions. The selection of drug therapy is dependent upon the cause of the arrhythmia if it can be determined and other cardiovascular conditions that the patient may be experiencing.

Treatment of Sinus Bradycardia

Sinus bradycardia is defined as a heart rate below 60 beats per minute. The most effective drug for this condition is the anticholinergic drug atropine. Atropine increases heart rate and AV conduction, and also contributes to an increase in blood pressure. Nonpharmacologic therapy involves the use of cardiac pacemakers.

Treatment of Atrial Flutter and Atrial Fibrillation

The atrial rate in atrial flutter is between 250 and 350 beats per minute and there is usually a regular ventricular rhythm. The atrial rate in atrial fibrillation is over 350 beats per minute and the ventricular rhythm is irregular. The ventricles are being overstimulated by these two conditions and slowing of the ventricular rate is usually the first consideration. Beta-blockers, calcium channel blockers, and digoxin, which slow AV conduction, are the preferred drugs to stabilize and protect the ventricles. The second concern is to prevent formation of blood clots in the atria (thromboembolism), which involves the use of anticoagulants. The third approach is to terminate the arrhythmia, often with electrical cardioversion. Pharmacologic drugs of choice for chronic treatment to control the ventricular rate are usually beta-blockers, calcium channel blockers, and digoxin.

Treatment of Paroxysmal Supraventricular Tachycardia

This arrhythmia involves the sudden onset and termination of supraventricular tachycardia that most commonly involves the AV node. In the acute setting, adenosine (*Adenocard*) is the preferred drug. It provides the fastest onset and shortest duration of action. Electrical cardioversion and vagal maneuvers are alternate therapies in acute situations. For chronic therapy of this arrhythmia, there are several choices depending on the patient and other existing conditions. Drugs that slow AV conduction, beta-blockers, calcium channel blockers (verapamil or diltiazem), and digoxin are the preferred drugs.

Treatment of Supraventricular Tachycardia

This arrhythmia usually originates in the SA node and causes sustained increases in heart rate over 100 beats per minute. If there is increased sympathetic tone, beta-blockers such as propranolol (*Inderal*) or metoprolol (*Lopressor*) are generally preferred. The calcium channel blockers verapamil (*Calan*) and diltiazem (*Cardizem*) are also very effective and may be preferred depending on the patient and clinical situation.

Treatment of Ventricular Arrhythmias

Premature ventricular contractions (PVC) are the most common type of ventricular arrhythmia. PVCs are also the major cause of ventricular tachycardia.

Ventricular tachycardia is defined as three or more consecutive PVCs. Since this is a serious condition that can lead to ventricular fibrillation, immediate treatment is required. In the acute setting, the preferred drug is IV administration of amiodarone (*Cordarone*); IV administration of lidocaine (*Xylocaine*) is an alternate choice. For the chronic control of ventricular arrhythmias and ventricular tachycardia, amiodarone is usually the preferred drug. Sotalol (*Betapace*) and beta-blockers are alternate choices.

Understanding Terminology

Match the definition or description in the left column with the appropriate term in the right column. **(LO 23.1)**

___ 1. Arrhythmia that originates below the AV node.

___ 2. A drug used to restore normal cardiac rhythm.

___ 3. Heart area of abnormal electrical impulse generation.

___ 4. Premature ventricular contraction.

___ 5. The most serious type of arrhythmia.

___ 6. Arrhythmia that originates in the atrial or AV nodal area.

___ 7. A disorder of cardiac conduction.

a. antiarrhythmic

b. arrhythmia

c. ectopic foci

d. ventricular arrhythmia

e. PVC

f. supraventricular arrhythmia

g. ventricular fibrillation

Acquiring Knowledge

Answer the following questions.

1. When would the use of an antiarrhythmic drug be indicated? **(LO 23.1)**

2. For what arrhythmias are quinidine and lidocaine used? **(LO 23.3)**

3. What electrolyte ion is active during the plateau phase of the ventricular action potential? **(LO 23.2)**

4. What pharmacological effect do the Class 1 antiarrhythmic drugs have in common? **(LO 23.3)**

5. What is cinchonism? **(LO 23.3)**

6. Describe the procedure for the administration of lidocaine. **(LO 23.3, 23.7)**

7. Explain the mechanism of action of propranolol. **(LO 23.4)**

8. What is a special consideration when administering lidocaine by IV drip? **(LO 23.7)**

9. Explain two important effects of verapamil on the cardiovascular system. **(LO 23.6)**

10. What are the adverse effects associated with amiodarone? **(LO 23.5)**

Applying Knowledge on the Job

Use your critical-thinking skills to answer the following questions.

1. Mr. Wise is a 75-year-old, otherwise healthy male who was admitted to the hospital for a total right knee replacement. On postoperative day 2, a ventricular arrhythmia was diagnosed. The cardiologist was consulted and prescribed *Norpace* 150 mg QID. On the fourth day postoperatively, Mr. Wise complains he cannot urinate and is ordered by the house physician to be catheterized. The house physician asks what medications the patient is on. What do you think the physician is thinking about the cause of the urinary difficulties? **(LO 23.3)**

2. You are working in a pulmonologist's office when a patient comes in for a refill prescription on her *Proventil* inhaler, which she uses as needed for her asthma. She mentions that her asthma seems to have worsened over the past couple of months. Upon reading her chart, you notice that she was referred to a cardiologist 3 months ago. While waiting for the physician to approve the refill, you ask what the cardiologist said. The patient states that the cardiologist started her on propranolol for an irregular heartbeat. Is this important information to tell the pulmonologist? Explain. **(LO 23.4)**

3. Mr. Able has been taking verapamil for treatment of his hypertension. At a recent checkup his family physician noticed that Mr. Able had sustained tachycardia. The physician asks you to get some of those free samples of propranolol that were dropped off by the drug sales representative. Could there be a potential problem if the patient takes these two drugs together? **(LO 23.4, 23.6)**

Multiple Choice

Use your critical-thinking skills to answer the following questions.

1. Select the ion movement that is associated with depolarization of ventricular muscle. **(LO 23.1)**
   A. Na ions move out of the cell
   B. K ions move out of the cell
   C. Na ions move into the cell
   D. Ca ions move into the cell

2. According to Vaughn-Williams, procainamide is classified as Class **(LO 23.3)**
   A. IA
   B. IB
   C. IC
   D. II

3. The antiarrhythmic drug with the shortest duration of action that is administered IV in the emergency treatment of supraventricular tachycardia is **(LO 23.6)**
   A. lidocaine
   B. adenosine
   C. propranolol
   D. amiodarone

4. Ataxia, pulmonary fibrosis, skin discoloration, and thyroid disturbances are potential adverse effects of **(LO 23.5)**
   A. verapamil
   B. procainamide
   C. amiodarone
   D. disopyramide

5. The pharmacologic effects of verapamil include **(LO 23.4)**
   A. decreased heart rate
   B. decreased force of myocardial contraction
   C. slowed AV conduction
   D. all statements are true

Multiple Choice (Multiple Answer)

Select the correct choices for each statement. The choices may be all correct, all incorrect, or any combination.

1. Select all of the ions that regulate heart activity. **(LO 23.1)**
   A. Cl
   B. Ca
   C. Na
   D. K

2. A class IB antiarrhythmic drug does which of the following? **(LO 23.3)**
   A. moderate decrease in Phase 0 depolarization
   B. prolongation of ventricular repolarization
   C. decrease in AV conduction
   D. increase in PR interval

3. Which of the following are types of supraventricular arrhythmias? **(LO 23.1)**
   A. premature atrial contractions
   B. premature ventricular contractions
   C. paroxysmal atrial tachycardia
   D. atrial flutter

4. Select the actions of beta-blockers. **(LO 23.4)**
   A. decrease heart rate
   B. increase AV conduction
   C. decrease automaticity of atrial muscle
   D. increase automaticity of SA nodes

5. Select the adverse effects of amiodarone **(LO 23.5)**
   A. pulmonary fibrosis
   B. torsade de pointes
   C. blue-gray skin discoloration
   D. corneal microdeposits

Sequencing

Place the following in order of least beats per minute to greatest beats per minute. **(LO 23.1)**

_____   _____   _____   _____

Least   **Greatest**

atrial flutter

sinus bradycardia

atrial fibrillation

supraventricular tachycardia

Classification

Place the following medications under the correct antiarrhythmic class. **(LO 23.3)**

flecanide	lidocaine
disopyramide	esmolol
ibutilide	quinidine
verapamil	mexiletine
propranolol	dofetilide
diltiazem	propafenone

IA	IB	IC	II	III	IV

Documentation

Using the following symptoms observed during a hospital admission, answer the following questions.
(LO 23.1, 23.3, 23.4, 23.5)

Symptoms
Heart rate of 375 beats per minute
ECG atrial waves look like a "bag of worms"

a. What type of arrhythmia is the patient suffering?
b. What other conditions might be of concern?
c. What types of medications would be best for short-term treatment of this patient?
d. Is there a recommendation for chronic treatment of this disorder?

Labeling

Fill in the missing labels. **(LO 23.2)**

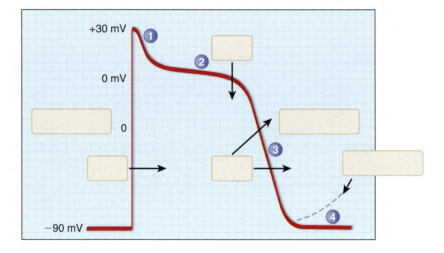

For interactive animations, videos, and assessment, visit:
www.mcgrawhillconnect.com

Chapter 24

Antianginal Drugs

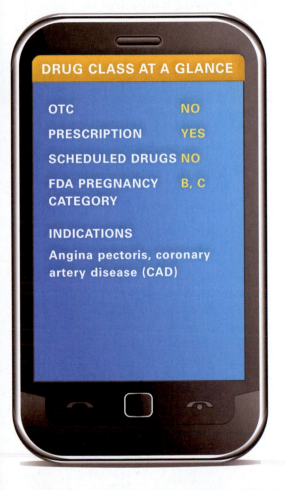

DRUG CLASS AT A GLANCE

OTC	NO
PRESCRIPTION	YES
SCHEDULED DRUGS	NO
FDA PREGNANCY CATEGORY	B, C

INDICATIONS

Angina pectoris, coronary artery disease (CAD)

KEY TERMS

angina pectoris: chest pain due to decreased blood flow (ischemia) to the heart.

atherosclerosis: fatty degeneration of arteries due to accumulation of cholesterol plaques.

coronary artery: artery that supplies blood flow to the heart.

coronary artery disease (CAD): condition due to atherosclerosis and insufficient blood flow to the heart.

exertional angina: angina pectoris caused by increased physical exertion.

ischemia: insufficient blood flow to a tissue.

variant or Prinzmetal angina: angina pectoris caused by vasospasm of the coronary arteries.

Learning Outcomes

After studying this chapter, you should be able to

24.1 describe the main types of angina pectoris and the usual cause of each type.

24.2 discuss the mechanism of action of the nitrate drugs and compare routes of administration and onset of action of the different nitrate preparations.

24.3 explain the mechanism of action of beta-blockers in the treatment of angina and CAD.

24.4 recognize the pharmacologic effects produced by the different calcium channel blockers.

24.5 discuss the preferred therapies for the different types of angina.

The **coronary arteries** branch off the aorta immediately after leaving the heart and deliver blood to the myocardium (Figure 24.1). The coronary arteries are very susceptible to the development of fatty deposits, commonly referred to as plaque. The fatty substance in plaque is mainly cholesterol. Individuals with high blood cholesterol levels are subject to the formation of these cholesterol-laden plaques that reduce coronary blood flow. **Atherosclerosis** is the term used to describe the fatty degeneration of the coronary arteries. The reduction in coronary blood flow caused by atherosclerosis is referred to as **ischemia**. Individuals who develop atherosclerosis and experience cardiac ischemia are classified as having **coronary artery disease (CAD)**. Angina pectoris, described as pain in the chest, is caused by CAD. The pain is due to insufficient blood flow and oxygen supply to the myocardium. Complete blockage of one or more of the coronary arteries results in a myocardial infarction (MI) or heart attack. The treatment of CAD is aimed at reducing the number and severity of anginal attacks, limiting progression of atherosclerosis, and preventing the occurrence of myocardial infarction and possible death. Important nondrug components to the treatment of CAD include diets that limit fat and cholesterol, exercise, elimination of smoking, and weight control. The three classes of drugs used in the treatment of angina pectoris and CAD are the nitrates, beta-adrenergic blockers, and calcium channel blockers.

LO 24.1

CLASSIFICATION OF ANGINA PECTORIS

There are several different types of angina pectoris. The most common type is caused by exercise, overexertion, or stress. This type is classified as **exertional angina** and its occurrence is usually predictable. It is caused by insufficient coronary blood flow due to atherosclerotic plaques. Individuals with this type of angina usually know the activities that will bring on the anginal attack. Stopping the activity and resting often provides some relief.

The second type of angina is referred to as **variant** or **Prinzmetal angina.** The cause is vasospasm of one or more of the coronary arteries. This type of angina is variable because it is unpredictable and can occur at any time, even during sleep. Drugs that relax arterial smooth muscle and produce arteriolar dilation are effective in relieving the vasospasm. Some individuals have both the exertional and variant type of angina.

Unstable angina is a more serious condition that usually occurs with advanced coronary artery disease. It usually occurs in coronary arteries that are almost

Figure 24.1   **Coronary Vessels of the Heart Showing Both the Arterial and Venous Circulation**

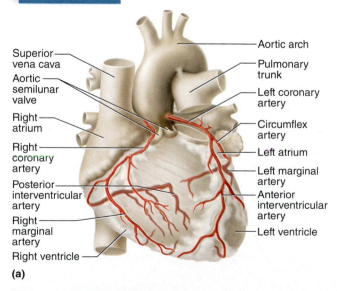

Superior vena cava
Aortic arch
Aortic semilunar valve
Pulmonary trunk
Right atrium
Left coronary artery
Right coronary artery
Circumflex artery
Left atrium
Posterior interventricular artery
Left marginal artery
Right marginal artery
Anterior interventricular artery
Right ventricle
Left ventricle
(a)

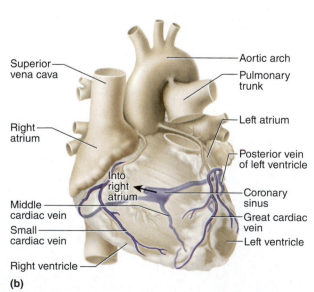

Superior vena cava
Aortic arch
Pulmonary trunk
Right atrium
Left atrium
Into right atrium
Posterior vein of left ventricle
Middle cardiac vein
Coronary sinus
Small cardiac vein
Great cardiac vein
Right ventricle
Left ventricle
(b)

completely blocked (Figure 24.2). In this situation there is the risk that blood platelets will become activated and initiate formation of a blood clot that can completely block the artery and cause a myocardial infarction. Unstable angina requires aggressive therapy with antianginal, anticoagulant, and antiplatelet drugs in order to prevent blood clot formation. This is also the point in treatment when various procedures such as angioplasty and coronary artery bypass are considered.

LO 24.2

NITRATES

The nitrates were once known as coronary dilators, but research has shown that during angina these drugs do not produce significant effects on coronary arteries that are atherosclerotic and hardened by arteriosclerosis. Ischemia itself is a potent vasodilator so that during attacks of angina the coronary arteries are already maximally dilated. The main effect of the nitrates is to produce a general vasodilation of systemic veins and arteries. This reduces cardiac work and oxygen consumption. Reduction of cardiac work and oxygen consumption provides relief of ischemia and pain.

The nitrates are used in two ways. First, they are administered during attacks of angina to relieve the intense pain. The most common route of administration is sublingual. The drugs in this group have an almost immediate onset of action, although their duration is short. Second, they are administered prophylactically on a daily basis to prevent attacks of angina.

Figure 24.2

Cross Section of Diseased Coronary Artery

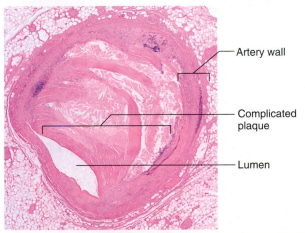

- Artery wall
- Complicated plaque
- Lumen

A plaque has reduced the lumen to a very small space that can easily be blocked by formation of a blood clot or by vasospasm.

Mechanism of Action

The mechanism of action of these drugs is to relax vascular smooth muscle. This effect is caused by nitrate ions, which are enzymatically released from nitrate drugs. These nitrate ions are converted by enzymes in blood vessels to nitric oxide (NO). Nitric oxide is a potent vasodilator that relaxes vascular smooth muscle. Venodilation (dilation of veins) is greater than arteriolar dilation at the lower dosage ranges of these drugs.

The main effects produced by vasodilation are a decrease in venous return to the heart (decrease in preload) and a decrease in blood pressure (decrease in afterload). Consequently, cardiac work is reduced. With a reduction in cardiac work, less oxygen is required by the heart, and relief of pain is accomplished. In the vasospastic form of angina, the vasodilating effect of the nitrates is effective in relieving vasospasm of the coronary arteries.

Clinical Use of Nitrate Drugs

Nitroglycerin, isosorbide dinitrate, and isosorbide mononitrate are the three available nitrate drugs used to treat angina and CAD. They can be administered in several different forms. Table 24:1 summarizes the different nitrate preparations and their durations of action.

Sublingual Nitroglycerin

Nitroglycerin is available as a sublingual tablet and as a sublingual spray for relief of acute anginal attacks. Patients place the nitroglycerin tablet under the tongue and allow the tablet to dissolve without swallowing. Use of the sublingual pump involves one or two sprays under the tongue. The effects of sublingual administration usually occur within 1 to 3 minutes, with the peak effect occurring at about 5 minutes. The duration of action is approximately 30 minutes. Sublingual administration avoids first-pass metabolism by the liver. This method of administration provides the fastest relief for acute angina.

Nitroglycerin Ointment 2%

The ointment is applied topically to an area of the chest or abdomen and is covered with a plastic dressing. Absorption occurs through the skin, with an onset of action of 30 minutes and a duration of 4 to 8 hours, depending on the amount applied. Each inch of ointment squeezed from the tube contains approximately 15 mg of nitroglycerin. Nitroglycerin ointment is used prophylactically to prevent the occurrence of angina.

Nitroglycerin Extended-Release Capsules

Nitroglycerin is available in capsules of 2.5, 6.5, and 9.0 mg that release the drug gradually over a prolonged period. Duration of action is 8 to 12 hours. The

period. Transdermal use is indicated for the prevention of angina. Continuous daily exposure to nitrates, especially throughout the 24-hour period, can lead to rapid development of drug tolerance. It is recommended that there should be a 10- to 12-hour drug-free period each day. Consequently, patients who use the transdermal patch are advised to remove the patch at night during sleep.

Nitroglycerin for Intravenous Infusion

Nitroglycerin can be administered intravenously in emergency and surgical situations in the hospital. The onset of action is rapid, but the duration of action of IV nitroglycerin is short and drug effects quickly wear off once the infusion is stopped.

Adverse Effects

The main adverse effects of the nitrates are related to the vasodilating action. Cutaneous flushing, dizziness, headache, weakness, and fainting may be experienced. Sudden or excessive drops in blood pressure can cause reflex tachycardia.

Patient Education

Since anginal attacks are unpredictable, it is important for patients to carry the prescribed medication at all times. Nitroglycerin is volatile, and tablets lose potency

extended-release capsules are used daily to prevent the occurrence of anginal attacks (prophylaxis).

Transdermal Nitroglycerin (*Transderm-Nitro*)

This nitroglycerin is contained within an adhesive patch that is applied on the torso. The nitroglycerin is slowly and uniformly released into the bloodstream over a 24-hour

[Table **24:1**]

Nitrate Drugs Used in Angina Pectoris and Coronary Artery Disease

Drug (*Trade Name*)		Common dosage	Onset (min)	Duration (hr)
Isosorbide dinitrate	(*Isordil*)	2.5-, 5-, 10- mg sublingual tablets	2–5	2–3
		5-, 10-, 20-, 30-, 40- mg tablets	30	4–6
		40- mg CR tablets, capsules	30	8–12
	(*Sorbitrate*)	5-, 10- mg chewable tab	30	2–3
Isosorbide mononitrate	(*ISMO*)	20- mg tablets	30	6–8
	(*Imdur*)	30-, 60-, 120- mg ER tablets	30	12
Nitroglycerin	(*Nitrostat*)	0.3-, 0.4-, 0.6- mg sublingual tablets	1–3	30 min
	(*Nitrolingual Pump Spray*)	0.4 mcg per spray	1–3	30 min
	(*NitroBid IV*)	5- mcg/min IV infusion	1–3	—
	(*Nitro-bid*)	2% ointment	30	4–8
	(*Transderm-Nitro*)	0.2–0.4- mg/hr transdermal patch	30	24
	(*Nitrogard*)	1-, 2-, and 3- mg extended-release buccal tablets	30	6–8

Abbreviations: *CR—controlled release, ER —extended release.*

if exposed to air or light. Therefore, it is important that tablets be carried in light-resistant, airtight containers. Also, standard practice is not to use nitroglycerin tablets that are more than 6 months old since there may be significant loss of potency.

When patients experience angina, they should be instructed to sit down, place a nitroglycerin tablet under the tongue, and allow it to dissolve without swallowing. Relief should occur within 5 minutes. If it does not, they should repeat the process with another tablet. If there is no relief after three tablets, patients should notify the physician or seek medical assistance.

Patients should be aware of the common side effects, such as cutaneous flushing, headache, and dizziness. They should be advised to lie down if they feel faint. These effects are expected and only last for a few minutes. In addition, patients should become aware of the activities that cause angina (overexertion, emotional upset, or overeating) and try to avoid these situations if possible.

LO 24.3

BETA-ADRENERGIC BLOCKING DRUGS

The beta-blockers antagonize or reverse the effects of sympathetic activation caused by exercise and other physical or mental exertions. In the heart, sympathetic stimulation (beta-1 receptors) increases heart rate, force of myocardial contractions, and oxygen consumption. The therapeutic action of beta-blockers in the treatment of angina lies in the ability of these drugs to decrease heart rate and force of contractions. These changes decrease cardiac work and therefore oxygen consumption. Decreasing oxygen consumption often prevents development of myocardial ischemia and pain.

Beta-blockers are indicated for the long-term (chronic) management of angina pectoris. Patients taking beta-blockers usually have less frequent anginal attacks or a delayed onset of pain during physical exertion. This is another way of saying that they have increased work capacity or exercise tolerance. While all beta-blockers decrease cardiac work and oxygen consumption, propranolol and the drugs listed in Table 24:2 are usually the preferred beta-blockers for the treatment of angina and CAD.

Beta-blockers can be used in combination with nitrates in patients who require more than one drug to control angina. When used in combination with nitrates, blockade of beta-1 receptors will usually prevent the reflex tachycardia that may occur with the nitrates.

Adverse effects of beta-blockers include drowsiness, tiredness, and GI disturbances such as nausea and diarrhea. Excessive drug dosage can cause bradycardia, hypotension, and possible development of heart failure.

[Table 24:2]

Beta-Adrenergic Blocking Drugs Used in CAD

Drug (*Trade Name*)	Main uses	Daily dosage range
Nonselective blockers		
Nadolol (*Corgard*)	Angina pectoris, hypertension	80–240 mg PO
Propranolol (*Inderal, Inderal LA*)	Angina pectoris	80–320 mg PO
	Hypertension, migraine	80–240 mg PO
	Arrhythmias	40–120 mg PO
	Life-threatening arrhythmias	1–3 mg IV
	Post-myocardial infarction	180–240 mg PO
Selective beta-1 blockers		
Atenolol (*Tenormin*)	Angina pectoris, hypertension	50–100 mg PO
Metoprolol (*Lopressor, Toprol XL*)	Angina pectoris, hypertension	100–400 mg PO

Nonselective beta-blockers, like propranolol, should not be given to individuals with asthma or COPD. Blockade of beta-2 receptors in the respiratory tract can cause bronchoconstriction. The pharmacology of the beta-blockers was previously discussed in Chapter 6.

LO 24.4

CALCIUM CHANNEL BLOCKERS

Mechanism of Action

The most important action of calcium channel blockers in the treatment of angina and CAD is to block the influx of calcium ions into vascular smooth muscle. Contraction of vascular smooth muscle is very dependent on calcium influx (movement from extracellular to intracellular sites), which normally occurs during membrane depolarization (action potential) of smooth muscle. At the doses used in angina, the calcium channel blockers relax arterial smooth muscle and have little effect on veins. The primary effect is arteriolar vasodilation and reduction of blood pressure. This reduces cardiac work (afterload) and oxygen consumption. The calcium channel blockers are primarily taken on a daily basis to prevent angina and are also the preferred drugs for treatment of variant or Prinzmetal angina. They are the most effective drugs to relieve vasospasm.

In addition to arteriolar dilation, two of the calcium channel blockers, verapamil and diltiazem, also block the influx of calcium ions in cardiac muscle and in the SA and AV nodes. As previously discussed in Chapter 23 with the antiarrhythmic drugs, these actions decrease heart rate, AV conduction, and the force of myocardial contraction. The cardiac actions of verapamil and diltiazem also reduce cardiac work and can contribute to the antianginal effect. The remaining calcium channel blockers are arterial dilators with very little direct actions on the heart. Table 24:3 summarizes the calcium channel blockers and their cardiovascular indications.

Verapamil (*Calan, Isoptin*)

Verapamil is used to treat supraventricular arrhythmias (see Chapter 23). In addition, its vasodilating properties allow it to be considered for the treatment of angina. Because of its prominent effects on the heart, verapamil also can decrease heart rate, AV conduction, and the force of myocardial contraction. These actions decrease cardiac work and oxygen consumption. However, excessive depression of cardiac function can precipitate heart failure.

Diltiazem (*Cardizem*)

The vasodilating and cardiac effects of diltiazem are similar to those of verapamil. However, diltiazem is considered to have slightly less cardiac depressant effects but greater vasodilating actions than verapamil.

[Table 24:3]

Calcium Channel Blocking Drugs

Drug (*Trade Name*)	Cardiovascular actions	Main clinical uses
Verapamil (*Calan, Calan SR*)	Arterial vasodilation, decreased HR, AV conduction, and myocardial contraction	Angina pectoris, cardiac arrhythmias, hypertension
Diltiazem (*Cardizem, Cardizem SR*)	Same as above	Same as above
Amlodipine (*Norvasc*)	Arterial vasodilation	Angina pectoris, hypertension
Felodipine (*Plendil*)	Arterial vasodilation	Hypertension
Isradipine (*Dynacirc, Dynacirc CR*)	Arterial vasodilation	Hypertension
Nicardipine (*Cardene, Cardene SR*)	Arterial vasodilation	Angina pectoris, hypertension
Nifedipine (*Procardia, Procardia XL*)	Arterial vasodilation	Angina pectoris, hypertension

Nifedipine (*Procardia*)

Nifedipine has very little effect on heart rate and myocardial contraction, but it is a very potent arterial vasodilator that lowers blood pressure (decreases afterload) and causes relaxation of coronary artery spasm.

Nicardipine (*Cardene*)

Nicardipine is similar to nifedipine in that the main pharmacological effects are vasodilation and relaxation of coronary artery spasm.

Other Calcium Antagonists

Amlodipine (*Norvasc*), felodipine (*Plendil*), and isradipine (*DynaCirc*) are additional calcium antagonists. These drugs have little or no direct actions on the heart and are primarily arterial vasodilators with actions and adverse effects similar to nifedipine.

Adverse Effects

Common adverse effects of the calcium antagonists include headache, facial flushing, dizziness, hypotension, and minor gastrointestinal (GI) disturbances. Constipation is one of the more common side effects of verapamil. The calcium channel blockers that do not have direct cardiac effects, like nifedipine, are potent vasodilators that can cause reflex tachycardia if blood pressure drops below normal. With overdosage, verapamil and diltiazem can cause bradycardia, AV block, and decreased myocardial contraction that can lead to heart failure. The use of either verapamil or diltiazem with beta-blockers is generally contraindicated; the combination can cause excessive cardiac depression and heart failure.

LO 24.5

PREFERRED THERAPY FOR TREATMENT OF ANGINA PECTORIS

All patients with CAD should carry with them one of the sublingual nitrate drugs for immediate treatment of a sudden attack of angina.

Exertional, Fixed, or Stable Angina

The nitrates, beta-blockers, and calcium channel blockers are all very effective in controlling the exertional type of angina. The choice often depends on other cardiovascular conditions that the patient may have. For example, patients with hypertension are best treated with calcium channel blockers or beta-blockers since both drug classes are effective in the treatment of hypertension. If there is increased sympathetic activation, then beta-blockers would be the better choice. If combination therapy is required, it should be guided by patient response.

Variant or Prinzmetal Angina

Vasospasm is the major feature of this type of angina. The calcium channel blockers, which relax arterial smooth muscle, are the preferred drugs. The nitrates are also effective. However, chronic use of nitrates requires a drug-free interval, usually at night, in order to avoid drug tolerance. Consequently, the patient would not be protected from vasospasm during this period. The combination of a calcium blocker and nitrate is often the preferred choice when additional treatment is required.

Unstable Angina

Patients with unstable angina are at serious risk of developing a myocardial infarction. Antiplatelet and anticoagulant therapy is essential to prevent formation of a blood clot at the site of arterial blockage. This also is the point when coronary artery bypass grafting or percutaneous coronary interventions, such as stent implantations, are considered. While antianginal drugs are useful for prevention of anginal attacks, the patient needs to reevaluate lifestyle, diet, lipid profile, exercise, and smoking habit in order to prevent progression of disease.

Patient Administration and Monitoring

Monitor vital signs when these drugs are administered during the treatment of acute angina.

Instruct patient on the proper self-administration of sublingual nitroglycerin or similar preparations.

Explain to patient the common side effects of the drugs that dilate blood vessels: dizziness, headache, flushing, faintness, nausea.

Instruct patient to report excessive changes in blood pressure and pulse rate, or other significant changes.

Explain to patient the importance of weight control, diets low in fats and cholesterol, eliminating smoking, and exercise if approved by the physician.

Help patient to identify the situations or stresses that trigger angina and establish mechanisms for avoidance.

Chapter Review

Understanding Terminology

Answer the following questions.

1. What are two main types of angina pectoris? How do they differ? **(LO 24.1)**
2. Write a short paragraph using the following terms: *coronary arteries, atherosclerosis, angina pectoris, exertional angina,* and *vasospastic angina.* **(LO 24.1)**

Acquiring Knowledge

Answer the following questions.

1. What is the mechanism of action of the nitrates? **(LO 24.2)**
2. What are the different routes of administration for nitroglycerin? When is each indicated? **(LO 24.2)**
3. Explain the mechanism of action of propranolol in the treatment of angina. **(LO 24.3)**
4. What is the effect of the calcium channel blockers on vascular smooth muscle? **(LO 24.4)**
5. Compare the adverse effects of the nitrates and the calcium channel blocker drugs. **(LO 24.2, 24.4)**

Applying Knowledge on the Job

Use your critical-thinking skills to answer the following questions.

1. While doing your afternoon assessment of your patients in cardiac care, you ask Mr. Horn if he has had a bowel movement today. He states he has not moved his bowels in 3 days. You review the chart and see that 4 days ago, on admission, he was started on *Lasix, Transderm-Nitro* patch, verapamil, and a potassium supplement. Which drug is most likely causing the constipation? **(LO 24.4)**

2. Mrs. George was just started on *Procardia* and *Nitro-Bid* upon her admission to the cardiac care unit. She has also just been allowed to get out of bed. What precautions might you give her? **(LO 24.2, 24.4)**

3. Instruct Mrs. Smith (or one of your classmates) on the proper procedure for administering sublingual nitroglycerin. What should she do if the first tablet does not provide relief? Second tablet? Third tablet? **(LO 24.2)**

4. Prepare a short oral presentation for a patient with unstable angina that describes the various nondrug modalities that are important to halt progression of the disease. **(LO 24.5)**

Multiple Choice

Use your critical-thinking skills to answer the following questions.

1. The nitroglycerin dosage form providing the longest duration of action is **(LO 24.2)**
   A. sublingual nitroglycerin tablets
   B. nitroglycerin ointment
   C. transdermal nitroglycerin
   D. IV nitroglycerin (bolus injection)

2. The therapeutic actions of propranolol to prevent anginal attacks include **(LO 24.3)**
   A. decreased heart rate
   B. reduced force of myocardial contraction

C. decreased oxygen consumption

D. all statements are true

3. The pharmacologic actions of verapamil include **(LO 24.4)**
   A. decreased AV conduction
   B. increased myocardial contraction
   C. decreased heart rate
   D. only A and C are true

4. In the treatment of variant angina, the drug that is an arterial dilator without direct effects on the heart is **(LO 24.4)**
   A. nitroglycerin
   B. metoprolol
   C. nifedipine
   D. verapamil

5. The drug that is best described as a venodilator that decreases preload (venous return) in the treatment of angina is **(LO 24.2)**
   A. propranolol
   B. verapamil
   C. nifedipine
   D. isosorbide dinitrate

Multiple Choice (Multiple Answer)

Select the correct choices for each statement. The choices may be all correct, all incorrect, or any combination.

1. Angina pectorls is caused by which of the following? **(LO 24.1)**
   A. insufficient blood flow
   B. lack of oxygen to the myocardium
   C. decreased heartbeat
   D. reduction of cardiac work

2. The main mechanisms of action of nitrates include **(LO 24.2)**
   A. increasing the venous return to the heart
   B. reducing atherosclerosis in the arteries
   C. increasing cardiac work and oxygen consumption
   D. relaxation of systemic veins and arteries

3. Beta-blockers work by doing which of the following? **(LO 24.3)**
   A. decreasing heart rate
   B. decreasing cardiac work
   C. decreasing force of contractions
   D. decreasing oxygen consumption

4. Select all of the different types of angina. **(LO 24.1)**
   A. nystagmic
   B. unstable
   C. Prinzmetal
   D. exertional

5. Variant angina is treated with what types of medication? (LO 24.5)
   A. calcium channel blockers
   B. beta-blockers
   C. nitrates
   D. anticoagulants

Sequencing

Place the following in order of longest duration of action to shortest duration of action. (LO 24.2)

_____   _____   _____   _____

Longest   **Shortest**

Nitro-Bid ointment

Nitrostat

Isordil CR tablets

Sorbitrate

Classification

Place the following medications under the disease they are used to treat. (LO 24.5)

beta-blockers

nitrates

antiplatelets

anticoagulant

calcium channel blockers

Stable angina	Variant angina	Unstable angina

Matching

Match the following mechanisms of action with the corresponding class of drug. Answers may be used more than once. (LO 24.2, 24.3, 24.4)

   a. beta-blocker
   b. nitrate
   c. calcium channel blocker

1. ___ relax vascular smooth muscle
2. ___ decrease heart rate
3. ___ decrease in venous return
4. ___ decrease in blood pressure
5. ___ decrease force of contraction
6. ___ relax arterial smooth muscle

Documentation

Using the prescription below, answer the following questions. **(LO 24.2)**

**Riverview Cardiology
Practice RX**
12345 Main Avenue
Anytown, USA   12345
931-555-1000

NAME: Doug Coronado _____   DATE: _____

ADDRESS: _____

RX   **Isosorbide dinitrate 2.5mg**

Sig: **Take one tablet by mouth as directed**

Dr. Craig River _____ **M.D.**   _____ **M.D.**
  Substitution Permitted   Dispense as written

DEA #: _____   REFILL: NR   1   2   3   4

---

a. What type of angina is being treated with this drug?
b. In this milligram strength, what is the likely dosage form?
c. What is the onset of this particular medication?
d. Are there other medications that could be used to treat this type of angina? If so, what are they?

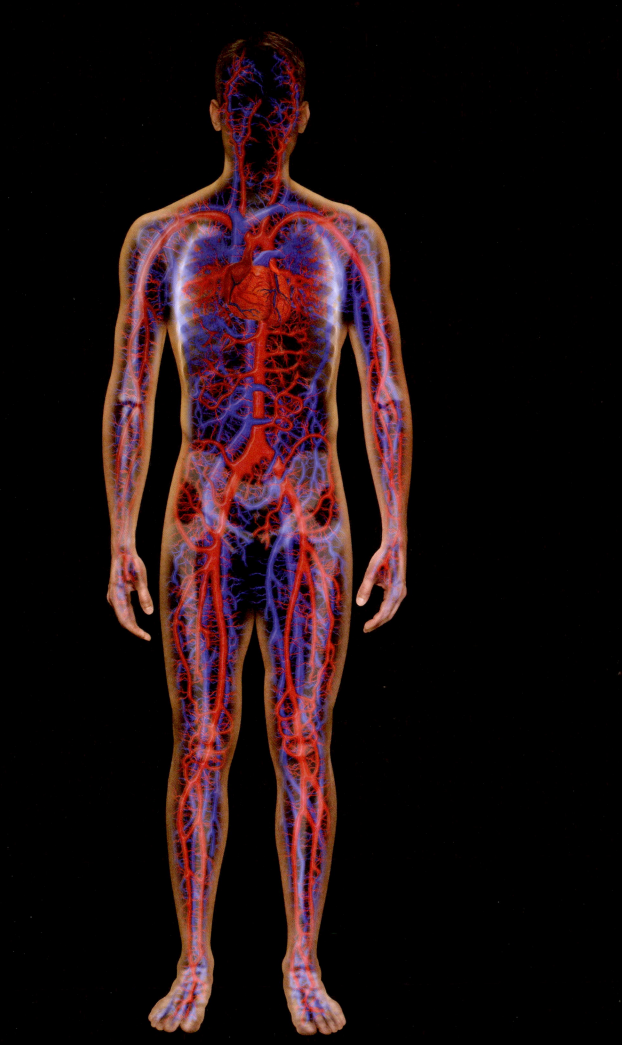

Pharmacology of the Vascular and Renal Systems

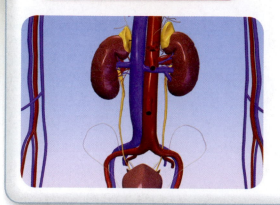

Chapter 25

Diuretics

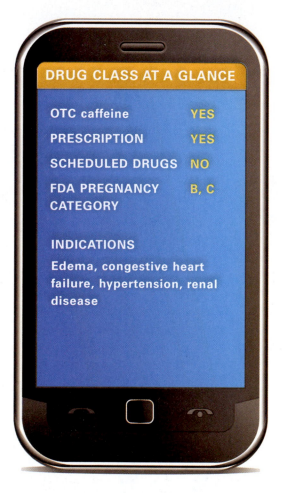

DRUG CLASS AT A GLANCE

OTC caffeine	**YES**
PRESCRIPTION	**YES**
SCHEDULED DRUGS	**NO**
FDA PREGNANCY CATEGORY	**B, C**

INDICATIONS

Edema, congestive heart failure, hypertension, renal disease

KEY TERMS

acidification: process that alters the pH to less than 7.

acidosis: pH less than 7.45 or a condition in which the tissues have relatively more acid or acid waste than normal.

alkalosis: pH greater than 7.45 or a condition in which the tissues have less acid than normal.

anuria: condition in which no urine is produced.

aquaporins: specialized proteins that form pores (channels) in the cell membrane that allow water to pass through but not small molecules like ions.

aquaresis: renal excretion of water without electrolytes.

aqueous humor: ocular fluid; watery substance that is located behind the cornea of the eye and in front of the lens.

ascites: excess fluid in the space between the tissues lining the abdomen and abdominal organs (the peritoneal cavity), usually associated with organ failure.

convoluted: coiled or folded back on itself.

distal convoluted tubule (DCT): part of the nephron that is closest to the collecting duct.

diuresis: condition that causes urine to be excreted, usually associated with large volumes of urine.

edema: swelling caused by fluid in body tissue.

euvolemia: state of normal body fluid volume.

extracellular: area outside the cell.

hyperchloremia: abnormally high level of chloride ions circulating in the blood.

hypertonic: a condition where the concentration of salt (sodium, electrolytes) is greater than that found inside the cells.

hypochloremia: abnormally low level of chloride ions circulating in the blood.

hypokalemia: abnormally low level of potassium ions circulating in the blood.

hyponatremia: abnormally low level of sodium ions circulating in the blood.

hypotonic: a condition where the concentration of salt (sodium, electrolytes) is less than that found inside the cells.

metabolic waste products: substances formed through the chemical processes that enable cells to function; usually, these substances are excreted by the body.

miotic: a drug that causes constriction of the pupil of the eye.

nephritis: inflammation of the glomeruli often following a streptococcus infection.

oliguria: condition in which very small amounts of urine are produced.

osmolality: the concentration of particles dissolved in a fluid.

osmoreceptors: specialized cells in the hypothalamus that respond to changes in sodium concentration (osmolarity) in the blood.

proximal convoluted tubule (PCT): part of the nephron that is closest to the glomerulus.

refractory: unable to produce an increased response even though the stimulation or amount of drug has been increased.

tubular reabsorption: process in which the nephrons return to the blood substances (ions, nutrients) that were filtered out of the blood at the glomerulus.

tubular secretion: process in which the nephrons produce and release substances (ions, acids, and bases) that facilitate sodium ion reabsorption and maintain acid-base balance.

uremia: accumulation of nitrogen waste materials (for example, urea) in the blood.

Learning Outcomes

After studying this chapter, you should be able to

25.1 explain the role of the kidneys in water excretion.

25.2 describe the difference between renal filtration and renal reabsorption.

25.3 identify two areas of the renal tubules where sodium and water transport are connected.

25.4 explain the function of the kidney in maintaining acid balance.

25.5 explain how the action of each diuretic differs from that of thiazide diuretics.

25.6 explain what happens when a diuretic becomes refractory.

25.7 explain how diuretics affect organs like the eye and liver.

25.8 describe three major side effects of each diuretic.

25.9 explain the clinical use and clinically significant terms associated with diuresis and diuretics.

Introduction

The primary functions of the kidneys are to maintain water, electrolyte, and acid-base balance. In order to accomplish this, the kidneys receive a large portion of the cardiac output (25 percent). As blood flows through the kidneys, substances are constantly filtered from the blood. Large molecules, such as plasma proteins, cannot pass through renal membranes, so only small molecules (ions, water, and glucose) and cell waste products are cleared from the blood.

The body requires ions and water to function. For example, electrolytes—sodium (Na^+), potassium (K^+), and chloride (Cl^-)—preserve the stability of cell membranes, whereas bicarbonate ions (HCO_3^-) buffer the blood to maintain the pH at 7.35–7.45. Therefore, the kidneys must reabsorb the essential elements and eliminate the waste products. This balance between renal reabsorption and excretion results in the formation of urine. When this balance is altered by disease or circumstance, the kidneys cannot process essential ions and water and fluid accumulate in the body tissues.

CLINICAL INDICATIONS AND RENAL FUNCTION

Diuretics are primarily used in the management of anuria, hypertension, and **edema.** These are conditions in which the kidneys have stopped making urine (anuria), or there is an accumulation of fluid in other tissues (edema). For example, CHF and liver cirrhosis are associated with an accumulation of fluid in body tissues as a result of acute or chronic organ disease. Edema also may result from local inflammation in the brain, eyes (glaucoma), and kidneys (nephritis). As long as the kidneys are functioning, urine production and renal water excretion can be stimulated in order to eliminate the accumulated fluid. This is accomplished either by increasing the blood flow to the kidneys (glomerular filtration) or by decreasing the renal reabsorption of water. Some diuretics stimulate urine production by increasing glomerular filtration. Other diuretics reduce the excess fluid associated with hypertension and edema by decreasing renal sodium and water reabsorption. As water reabsorption decreases, urine volume and flow increase (diuresis).

There are six classes of diuretics: osmotic agents, carbonic anhydrase inhibitors, thiazide and thiazide-like compounds, organic acids, potassium-sparing diuretics,

and ADH antagonists (Table 25:1). Each of these classes of diuretics produces diuresis by inhibiting water and/or sodium ion reabsorption in the kidneys. Because these drugs inhibit water reabsorption at different sites along the nephrons, the intensity of the diuresis varies with each class of drugs. In general, the intensity of diuresis is dependent upon the extent to which sodium ions are excreted into the urine. To know which drugs are the most effective diuretics and which adverse effects result from the diuretic action, one needs to have an idea of how the renal tubules in the kidneys work.

RENAL PHYSIOLOGY

Urine formation is essential for normal body function because it enables the blood to reabsorb necessary nutrients, water, and electrolytes. In addition, **metabolic waste products** are eliminated from the body through the urine. These processes take place in the working units of the kidneys known as the nephrons. The kidneys contain millions of nephrons, and each nephron is composed of several segments: the glomerulus, the **proximal convoluted tubule (PCT),** the loop of Henle, the **distal convoluted tubule (DCT),** and the

[Table **25:1**]

Classes of Diuretics

Class	Drugs	Adverse effects*
Carbonic anhydrase inhibitors	Acetazolamide, methazolamide	Anorexia, drowsiness, GI distress, headache, **metabolic acidosis**
Organic acids (loop diuretics)	Bumetanide, ethacrynic acid, furosemide, torsemide	**Hyperglycemia, hypokalemia, hypotension, tone deafness**
Osmotic (lumenal) diuretics	Glycerin, isosorbide, mannitol, urea	Chills, dizziness, headache, nausea, **strain on cardiac function** (plasma volume expansion), vomiting
Potassium-sparing diuretics	Amiloride, eplerenone, spironolactone, triamterene	Gynecomastia**, **hyperkalemia,** nausea, vomiting
Thiazide and thiazide-like diuretics	Chlorothiazide, chlorthalidone, hydrochlorothiazide, hydroflumethiazide, indapamide, methychlothiazide, metolazone	Dizziness, headache, **hyperglycemia, hyperkalemia, hyperuricemia, hypotension,** lightheadedness, nausea
Xanthine derivatives (active ingredients of over-the-counter diuretic products)	Caffeine, pamabrom, theobromine, theophylline	Diarrhea, insomnia, irritability, nervousness, restlessness, tachycardia

This is not a comprehensive list of adverse effects. Adverse effects are presented in alphabetical order and not according to any order of incidence. The most clinically significant adverse effects are bolded.

** Spironolactone only.*

Figure 25.1

Nephron Showing the Glomerulus, the Proximal Convoluted Tubule (PCT), Nephron Loop (Loop of Henle), the Distal Convoluted Tubule (DCT), and Collecting Duct

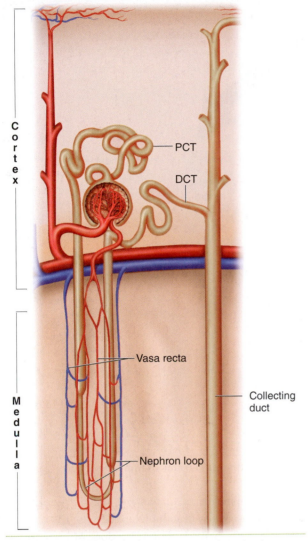

The vasa recta is a network of blood vessels that serves each nephron.

collecting duct (Figure 25.1). Urine is produced in the nephrons through the processes of filtration, reabsorption, and secretion.

Filtration

Filtration of substances from the blood into the nephrons occurs in the glomerulus. The blood pressure entering the glomerulus is high compared to the pressure within the glomerulus, which facilitates movement of small molecules and fluid into the glomerular filtrate. As shown in Figure 25.2, vitamins, amino acids, and electrolytes pass into the glomerular filtrate (which ultimately becomes urine), but large molecules like RBCs and plasma proteins do not. The remaining segments (renal tubules) are involved with reabsorption and secretion. The proximal tubule, loop of Henle (nephron loop), and distal tubule contain specialized transport systems that pull ions out of the tubule lumen and transport them back into the blood **(tubular reabsorption).** One of the most important tubular reabsorption mechanisms is the transport of sodium ions into the circulation. These segments also secrete substances (ions, acids, and bases) that facilitate sodium ion reabsorption and maintain acid-base balance **(tubular secretion).**

Tubular Reabsorption

Most of the ions and nutrients that are filtered at the glomerulus are reabsorbed by the renal tubules. The renal tubules reabsorb as much sodium as possible (99 percent). Sodium ions are extremely important because they are the principal cations (positively charged ions) in the **extracellular** fluid, and their large extracellular concentration creates an osmotic gradient that attracts water molecules. Thus, the renal mechanism for water conservation (balance) is directly dependent upon the tubular reabsorption of sodium ions.

Along the nephron, sodium ions are reabsorbed by two mechanisms: cation exchange and chloride ion transport. In the proximal and distal convoluted tubules, sodium ions (Na^+) are reabsorbed in exchange for hydrogen ions (H^+). Hydrogen ions are produced in the tubular cells through the action of the enzyme carbonic anhydrase (CAH). In the presence of this enzyme, carbon dioxide (CO_2) and water (H_2O) combine to form carbonic acid (H_2CO_3). Carbonic acid rapidly breaks down into hydrogen ions (H^+) and bicarbonate ions (HCO_3^-). See Figure 25.3.

$$CO_2 + H_2O \underset{}{\overset{CAH}{\rightleftharpoons}} H_2CO_3 \rightarrow HCO_3^- + H^+$$

The hydrogen ions are secreted by the proximal and distal tubules in exchange for sodium ions (see Figure 25.4). Subsequently, the sodium and bicarbonate ions are transported into the blood.

In addition to the hydrogen ion exchange, the distal convoluted tubules secrete potassium ions (K^+) in exchange for sodium. The secretion of potassium ions is primarily controlled by the adrenal mineralocorticoid aldosterone. Within these tubules are aldosterone receptors. By interacting with its receptors, aldosterone causes intracellular potassium ions to enter the tubular fluid (urine). As the potassium ions are secreted, sodium ions are reabsorbed (Figure 25.5).

In the loop of Henle, sodium ions are reabsorbed, but not through an ion-exchange mechanism. Sodium

Figure 25.2   Urine Formation

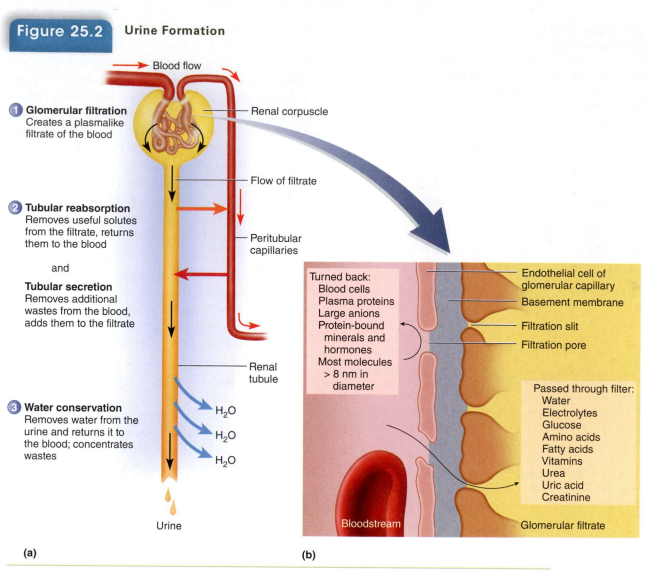

Blood flow

1 Glomerular filtration
Creates a plasmalike filtrate of the blood

— Renal corpuscle

— Flow of filtrate

2 Tubular reabsorption
Removes useful solutes from the filtrate, returns them to the blood

and

Tubular secretion
Removes additional wastes from the blood, adds them to the filtrate

— Peritubular capillaries

— Renal tubule

3 Water conservation
Removes water from the urine and returns it to the blood; concentrates wastes

H₂O

H₂O

H₂O

Urine

(a)

Turned back:
Blood cells
Plasma proteins
Large anions
Protein-bound minerals and hormones
Most molecules > 8 nm in diameter

Endothelial cell of glomerular capillary
Basement membrane
Filtration slit
Filtration pore

Passed through filter:
Water
Electrolytes
Glucose
Amino acids
Fatty acids
Vitamins
Urea
Uric acid
Creatinine

Bloodstream

Glomerular filtrate

(b)

(a) Basic steps in the formation of urine. (b) Filtration of substances at the glomerular membrane.

ions are reabsorbed in the loop of Henle in conjunction with chloride ions (Cl^-). In other words, chloride ions are actively reabsorbed and sodium ions follow (Figure 25.5).

When the renal tubules reabsorb sodium ions through these mechanisms, an osmotic gradient is established along the nephron. More sodium ions are present in the blood, and fewer sodium ions are present inside the renal tubules. Therefore, water molecules migrate toward the sodium ions and into the blood (water reabsorption). Water is primarily reabsorbed within the proximal convoluted tubules and the collecting ducts. Under the influence of the pituitary hormone antidiuretic hormone (ADH), the pores **(aquaporins)** of the collecting ducts open, and water rushes toward the sodium ions. As a result, water is removed from the urine, and urine volume decreases. The renal reabsorption of sodium and water maintains the plasma volume and water balance.

It is important to understand the mechanisms of tubular reabsorption of sodium ions because these mechanisms are the basis of diuretic action. Most diuretics increase urine flow **(diuresis)** by inhibiting the renal tubular reabsorption of sodium ions and water.

Tubular Secretion

The major secretory functions of the nephrons involve the tubular secretion of hydrogen ions, potassium ions, weak acids, and weak bases. Part of the tubular secretory process (cation exchange) has already been mentioned, since it directly results in sodium reabsorption. However, the tubular secretion of hydrogen ions serves another important role in the regulation of acid-base balance. This effect is accomplished through **acidification** of the urine (reducing the pH level to less than 7). Certain renal tubular mechanisms (carbonic anhydrase system) maintain the pH of the blood between 7.35 and 7.45 by altering the pH of the urine. As described,

Figure 25.3 **Dissociation of Carbonic Acid (H_2CO_3) into Bicarbonate (HCO_3^-) and Hydrogen (H^+) Ions**

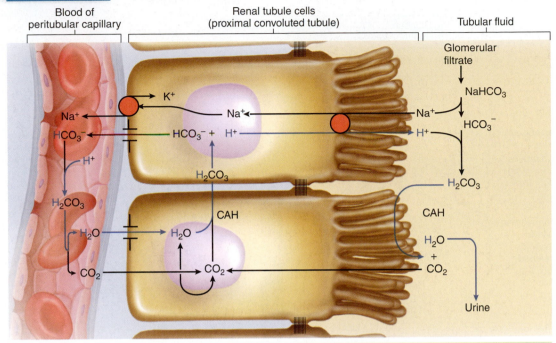

The H^+ ions are exchanged for sodium ions (Na^+) from the tubular fluid so Na^+ are reabsorbed. Formation of (H_2CO_3) is accomplished through the enzyme carbonic anhydrase (CAH).

Figure 25.4 **Ion Reasborption in the Proximal Convoluted Tubule**

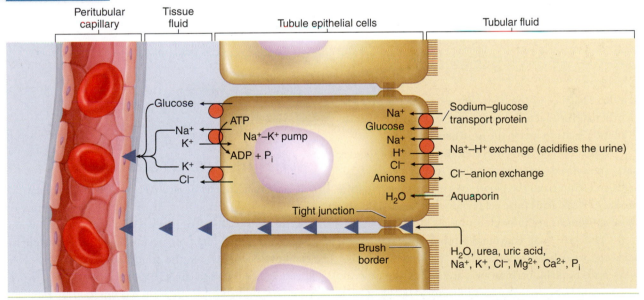

Water and solutes (glucose) in the tubular fluid (right) are carried through the tubule epithelium by various means including aquaporins and ion exchange.

the carbonic anhydrase system produces hydrogen ions (H^+) and bicarbonate ions (HCO_3^-) from CO_2 and water. The bicarbonate is transported into the blood, where it neutralizes (buffers) cell waste products, such as lactic acid. As a result, the pH of the blood remains relatively neutral as long as bicarbonate is available. At the same time, hydrogen ions secreted into the renal tubular fluid acidify the urine (to a pH between 4 and 6). See Figure 25.4. Any condition that impairs the renal production of hydrogen and bicarbonate ions alters the

Figure 25.5

Reabsorption and Secretion in the Nephron and Sites of Diuretic Drug Actions

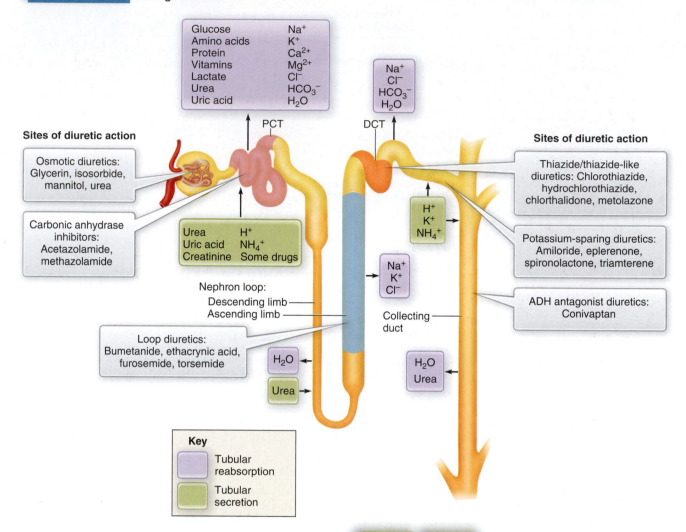

acid-base balance of the body. For example, insufficient bicarbonate production because of carbonic anhydrase inhibition leads to metabolic **acidosis.**

As part of their excretory function, the renal tubules have specialized transport systems that remove weak acids and bases from the blood. Normal cell metabolism produces weak acids (uric acid) and weak bases. Usually, these substances are presented to the kidneys for excretion. The proximal convoluted tubules secrete weak acids and weak bases into the urine. Many drugs are also weak acids (aspirin, barbiturates, and penicillin) or weak bases (opioid analgesics and antihistamines), which also are secreted into the tubular fluid through the proximal convoluted tubules. Metabolic waste products (weak acids, weak bases) compete for the same transport sites that excrete these drugs. This competition can result in altered drug excretion—for example, accumulation in the blood. As long as the kidneys continue to produce urine, the blood is cleared of waste products and toxic (drug) substances.

LO 25.1   LO 25.2
LO 25.3   LO 25.4   LO 25.9

CONDITIONS ASSOCIATED WITH RENAL DYSFUNCTION

Renal function may be altered by renal disease or cardiovascular dysfunction. Usually, infection or inflammation in the renal tissues **(nephritis)** reduces renal function. Reduced renal function occurs in glomerulonephritis and pylonephritis. On the other hand, circulatory problems associated with chronic heart failure (CHF), hypertension, and shock decrease renal function by reducing blood flow to the kidneys. Such circulatory disorders are often severe enough to produce renal failure.

Whether the renal tissue is damaged or the blood flow is reduced, the ultimate result is decreased urine flow, decreased urine volume **(oliguria),** or no urine production at all **(anuria).** As a result, the blood is not adequately filtered, and toxic products and ions accumulate. Such an accumulation can lead to uremia, edema, and hypertension.

Uremia (toxemia) is an accumulation of nitrogenous waste products in the blood due to impaired renal filtration. Edema and hypertension are associated with fluid (water) retention in the circulatory system, often as a result of insufficient sodium clearance. Fluid accumulates in the extracellular spaces of the body when too much sodium is retained in the circulation and tissue fluid. Circulating sodium ions create an osmotic gradient, which pulls water molecules into the circulation. This action causes the blood volume to expand, producing an increase in blood pressure (hypertension). The same phenomenon occurs with edema, in that water migration into the tissues causes swelling, especially in the legs and feet. The increased fluid retention and pressure put a greater strain on the failing heart and kidneys.

LO 25.5	LO 25.7	LO 25.8	LO 25.9

OSMOTIC DIURETICS

Clinical Indications

Of the osmotic diuretics, glycerin, isosorbide, mannitol, and urea, mannitol (*Osmitrol*) is the most frequently used. These drugs are used to stimulate urine flow in the treatment of anuria and oliguria before irreversible renal damage occurs. Mannitol may be indicated for acute renal failure or in cardiovascular surgeries in which renal function is severely compromised. Increased urine flow is also valuable in the treatment of drug toxicity or overdose. Mannitol-induced diuresis maintains renal function and keeps the flow of dilute urine so that renal excretion of the toxic substance is achieved. Mannitol also is used in the treatment of cerebral edema and glaucoma. Localized swelling, edema, and pressure (intraocular, cerebral) can be reduced with mannitol. The route of administration and low intensity of diuresis produced limit the clinical use of mannitol.

Mechanism of Action

Osmotic diuretics are compounds that can be filtered by the glomerulus but not reabsorbed by the renal tubules. These drugs cannot penetrate cell membranes; they must be given intravenously (Table 25:2). Once inside the circulation, the drugs act osmotically, attracting fluid from edematous tissues. Since these drugs cannot cross tubular

[Table 25:2]

Uses and Dose Range of Osmotic Diuretics and Carbonic Anhydrase Inhibitors

Drug name (*Trade Name*)	Use	Adult daily dose
Osmotic diuretics		
Glycerin (*Osmoglyn*)	Reduce intraocular pressure; interrupt acute glaucoma attacks (glaucoma)	1–2.0 g/kg (4–6 oz) PO 1–1.5 hr prior to surgery
Isosorbide (*Ismotic*)	Reduce intraocular pressure; interrupt acute glaucoma attacks (glaucoma)	1–5 g/kg (1–3 g/kg) BID, QID
Mannitol (*Osmitrol*)	Oliguria	50–100 g in 24hr 15% or 25% solution, IV
	Reduce intracranial or intraocular pressure	1.5–2 mg/kg of a 15%, 20%, or 25% solution, IV
	Excretion of toxic substances	5–25% solution infused IV (maximum 200 g)
	Urologic irrigation	2.5% solution IV
Urea (*Ureaphil*)	Reduce intracranial or intraocular pressure	1–1.5 g/kg (3.3–5 ml) solution slow IV infusion (maximum 120 g/day)
Carbonic anhydrase inhibitors		
Acetazolamide (*Diamox*)	Glaucoma	250–1000 mg/day PO, IV in divided doses every 4 hr
	Edema	250–375 mg PO
	Epilepsy	375–1000 mg PO in divided doses
Methazolamide	Glaucoma	50–100 mg PO BID, TID

membranes, osmotic diuretics become trapped in the tubular lumen and create an osmotic gradient within the renal tubule lumen (Figure 25.6). Water molecules tend to migrate toward the diuretic molecules. Consequently, this water is not reabsorbed and is excreted into the urine along with the diuretic. Although water reabsorption is inhibited, there is no major alteration of sodium reabsorption. Therefore, this class of diuretics produces a mild diuresis with no alteration in electrolyte or acid-base balance. Mannitol and urea are administered intravenously. Glycerin and isosorbide, administered orally, produce diuresis up to 6 hours.

Adverse Effects

Mannitol is expected to be administered under close observation so that relatively few adverse effects occur. Most often nausea, dizziness, headache, and chills occur. The most serious reaction is an extension of its osmotic effect in the circulation. Mannitol may produce a strain on cardiac function because it increases the plasma

volume (expansion). This effect is important in individuals who have impaired cardiac function (CHF). Therefore, mannitol is contraindicated for the treatment of chronic edema due to cardiovascular insufficiency, pulmonary edema, or active intracranial bleeding.

| LO 25.5 | LO 25.7 | LO 25.8 | LO 25.9 |

CARBONIC ANHYDRASE INHIBITORS

Clinical Indications

Acetazolamide (*Diamox*) and methazolamide are carbonic anhydrase inhibitor diuretics used as an adjunct treatment in CHF or drug-induced edema. These drugs are individually used because they reduce the pressure and edema associated with chronic simple (open-angle) or narrow-angle (angle-closure) glaucoma. Ocular fluid **(aqueous humor)** is formed through the action of carbonic anhydrase; hence, acetazolamide inhibits the production of aqueous humor and reduces painful pressure. In the treatment of glaucoma, the intravenous route of administration may be selected to ensure a rapid reduction in intraocular pressure. Carbonic anhydrase inhibitors may be used with **miotic** and osmotic drugs in patients with chronic simple (open-angle) glaucoma. Carbonic anhydrase inhibitors are also useful in the treatment of epilepsy. The induction of acidosis apparently decreases the seizure activity in some epileptic states (petit mal and unlocalized seizures). Although it produces adequate diuresis, acetazolamide has been largely replaced by other diuretics as an individual treatment of other edema.

Acetazolamide has the interesting distinction of being approved for the treatment of acute mountain sickness. This is a response to significant change in altitude with inadequate time for the body to adjust to the change in atmosphere, as occurs with mountain climbers and rescue and paramilitary operations. Doses of 500–1000 mg/day taken 48 hours before and after ascent relieve symptoms of oxygen deficit, muscle weakness, cramping, and headache.

Mechanism of Action

Acetazolamide (*Diamox*) is a diuretic that increases sodium and water excretion by inhibiting the enzyme carbonic anhydrase.

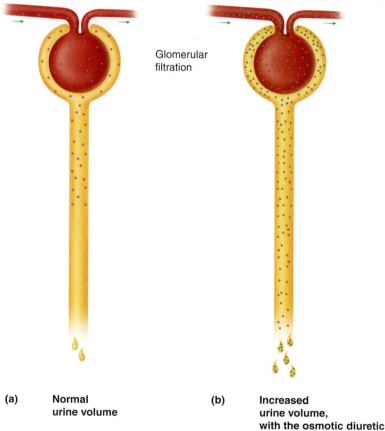

Figure 25.6

Osmotic Diuretics Remain in the Renal Tubule Lumen

Glomerular filtration

(a) Normal urine volume

(b) Increased urine volume, with the osmotic diuretic

The amount of diuretic solute in the tubule creates an osmotic gradient that attracts water. The diuretic cannot be reabsorbed because it cannot move through the tubule membranes so it is excreted along with the water.

As explained in the beginning of this chapter, this enzyme produces hydrogen ions and bicarbonate ions from CO_2 and water. This reaction occurs in the proximal and distal convoluted tubules (Figure 25.3). Acetazolamide inhibits the action of carbonic anhydrase so that very little hydrogen and bicarbonate are produced. Therefore, no hydrogen ions are available for exchange with sodium ions (decreased sodium reabsorption). As a result, sodium ions are excreted into the urine along with increased amounts of water.

Additional Renal Effects

Since the hydrogen ion exchange is blocked, the distal convoluted tubules attempt to reabsorb sodium ions by increasing the potassium ion exchange. The increased secretion of potassium ions causes an increased loss of potassium in the urine. Eventually, this loss of potassium leads to **hypokalemia** (decreased potassium ions in the blood). Inhibition of carbonic anhydrase not only inhibits sodium and water reabsorption but also affects the acid-base balance of the body. Sodium ions always have to be accompanied on their journey; therefore, they are excreted with bicarbonate ions. This "wastes" bicarbonate because it is excreted into the urine. Bicarbonate makes the urine more alkaline (pH increases). The pH of urine is close to neutral (7) but can normally vary between 6.5 and 7.4. Since carbonic anhydrase is inhibited, little or no bicarbonate is produced to buffer the blood. This situation results in metabolic acidosis. The available hydrogen ions get into the bloodstream accompanied by chlorine (Cl^-, since bicarbonate isn't available). This produces **hyperchloremic** metabolic acidosis.

Route of Administration

Acetazolamide and methazolamide are well absorbed following oral administration. They are not metabolized in the body but excreted totally by the kidneys. Since they are weak acids, they are secreted by the proximal convoluted tubules into the urine.

In the presence of metabolic acidosis, excretion is enhanced, and diuresis decreases. Because the drug action is inhibited when the acid-base balance is altered, acetazolamide is considered a **refractory** diuretic. The dose range of acetazolamide for the treatment of edema, glaucoma, and epilepsy is presented in Table 25:2. In some cases, patients are started on the lowest dose and titrated upward until successful results are achieved.

Intramuscular administration should be avoided because the alkaline solution causes pain on injection. However, when rapid relief is required to reduce ocular pressure, the drug can be administered intravenously.

Adverse Effects

The most common adverse effects produced by this group include drowsiness, anorexia, gastrointestinal distress, headache, depression, allergic rash, and acidosis. Hypokalemia and hyperuricemia also may occur. Hyperuricemia, which is too much uric acid in the blood due to impaired urate excretion, is usually a problem only in individuals who are predisposed to gout.

Contraindications

Patients who have metabolic acidosis due to renal failure or severe respiratory acidosis should not receive carbonic anhydrase inhibitors. These drugs aggravate acidosis. Therapy should be avoided in glaucoma patients who have renal disturbances, mental depression, or electrolyte imbalances.

LO 25.5 | LO 25.7 | LO 25.8 | LO 25.9

THIAZIDE AND THIAZIDE-LIKE DIURETICS

Clinical Indications

Thiazide and thiazide-like drugs are the largest group of diuretics. These drugs are widely used in the treatment of edema with hypertension and can alleviate edema of any cause, including the chronic edema associated with CHF or renal disease. These diuretics are particularly useful in the management of mild to moderate hypertension because they reduce the plasma volume and relax vascular smooth muscle. While the antihypertension action requires 4 to 6 weeks to establish, the diuretic action begins immediately.

Thiazide diuretics such as metolazone are often added to the loop diuretic regimen in refractory heart failure due to systolic dysfunction. The thiazide diuretic in addition to the loop diuretic is able to stimulate diuresis, remove sodium and water, and reduce the volume workload on the heart in these patients.

Although they are not chemically related, thiazide and thiazide-like diuretics produce the same pharmacological action in the renal tubules. Both groups can be administered orally to produce a diuretic response. These diuretics differ only in potency and duration of action (see Table 25:3). Commonly used drugs in this class include chlorothiazide (*Diuril*), chlorthalidone (*Hygroton*), and metolazone (*Zaroxolyn*).

Mechanism of Action

This class of diuretics was originally synthesized to produce a potent carbonic anhydrase inhibitor that did not

Recommended Doses of Thiazide and Thiazide-like Diuretics

Drug (*Trade Name*)	Duration of action	Adult daily oral dose	
		Hypertension	Edema
Thiazides			
Chlorothiazide (*Diuril*)	6–12 hr	500–2000 mg	500–2000 mg
Hydrochlorothiazide (*Ezide, HydroDIURIL, Hydro-par*)	6–12 hr	25–50 mg	25–100 mg
Methyclothiazide (*Enduron, Aquatensen*)	24 hr	2.5–5.0 mg	2.5–10 mg
Thiazide-like Diuretics			
Chlorthalidone (*Hygroton, Thalitone*)	24–72 hr	15–50 mg	30–120 mg
Indapamide (*Lozol*)	Up to 36 hr	1.25–5.0 mg	2.5–5 mg
Metolazone (*Zaroxolyn*)	12–24 hr	2.5–5.0 mg	5–20 mg

cause acidosis. These diuretics are only weak carbonic anhydrase inhibitors. They produce diuresis primarily by inhibiting sodium transport in the distal portion of the nephron. This inhibition causes a substantial loss of sodium and water and produces intense diuresis (Figure 25.5). The potent mobilization of sodium causes chloride and potassium excretion to increase. As a result, these drugs usually produce **hypochloremic alkalosis** and **hypokalemia.** The thiazide and thiazide-like diuretics are not refractory. As long as these drugs are continually administered, diuresis will occur even in the presence of alkalosis. As an extension of their renal action, thiazide-induced **hyponatremia** (low sodium level) has been reported to occur in elderly patients. This group of diuretics reduces the renal excretion of calcium ions. It does not produce hypercalcemia, although there is a mild elevation in serum calcium levels with chronic therapy. Calcium homeostasis is tightly regulated by the parathyroid gland so that bone resorption (release of calcium ions from bones) is reduced. This has been postulated as a bone-saving effect in the presence of osteoporosis.

Adverse Effects

Because thiazide and thiazide-like diuretics rapidly remove water and sodium from the body, the plasma volume may decrease, causing a drop in blood pressure. Patients receiving these diuretics often experience orthostatic hypotension, which is a sudden drop in blood pressure when they quickly change from a sitting position to a standing position. The rapid fall in blood pressure causes individuals to become dizzy, lightheaded, and faint. In addition to hypotension, these diuretics produce hypokalemia, hyperuricemia, and hyperglycemia. The hyperglycemia may be due to a decreased glucose utilization. This effect can upset the blood sugar level in individuals with diabetes mellitus. Because of the effective mobilization of electrolyte excretion, it is not surprising that the patient may experience muscle spasms or cramps.

Short-term thiazide diuretic therapy can elevate total serum cholesterol levels, low-density lipoprotein (LDL) cholesterol, and triglyceride levels in a dose-dependent manner. This appears to occur with diuretic doses large enough to produce a vigorous diuretic response and reduction in plasma volume. It is postulated that the volume depletion triggers a reflex response through the sympathetic nervous system and renin-angiotensin-aldosterone system that effects a change in the cholesterol levels. Long-term thiazide use shows little change in cholesterol from prediuretic exposure. Indapamide has not been shown to affect the cholesterol and lipoprotein profile in long- or short-term treatment.

Hypersensitivity reactions, such as skin rashes, also have been reported with the use of these drugs. These diuretics may produce nausea, diarrhea, constipation, anorexia, headache, impotence, and elevation of blood urea nitrogen or serum creatinine levels. The spectrum and intensity of adverse effects encountered will be related to the general health and condition of the patient. Usually reducing the dose or withdrawing therapy will terminate the adverse effect.

LO 25.5   LO 25.6
LO 25.7   LO 25.8   LO 25.9

ORGANIC ACID DIURETICS

Clinical Indications

The organic acid diuretics, which have a greater diuretic action than do the thiazides, are often used to relieve edema in patients who have become resistant to the thiazide diuretics. The organic acid diuretics are also useful in severe peripheral edema and pulmonary edema where greater diuretic activity is needed. Otherwise, the primary use is reduction of edema associated with CHF, liver cirrhosis, and renal disease. Ethacrynic acid is used in the short-term management of **ascites** due to malignancy and lymphedema. Parenteral administration is indicated when a rapid response is required or when GI absorption is impaired, making oral administration unfeasible.

Mechanism of Action

Bumetanide (*Bumex*), ethacrynic acid (*Edecrin*), furosemide (*Lasix*), and torsemide (*Demedex*) are organic acid, or loop, diuretics (see Table 25:4). These drugs are known as loop diuretics because they promote diuresis by inhibiting sodium and chloride ion transport in the loop of Henle. This action results in a tremendous loss of sodium, chloride, and water. The intense diuresis is usually accompanied by hypochloremic alkalosis. The organic acid diuretics continue to produce an increased urine flow in spite of the acid-base changes; therefore, **they are not refractory.** Hypokalemia may occur with the use of organic diuretics. It is not uncommon for furosemide or ethacrynic acid to be added to other diuretic regimens, especially metolazone. Heart failure is a common clinical syndrome associated with the end stage of a number of different cardiac diseases. It can result from any cardiac disorder in which the ventricle cannot fill with blood or eject blood. In heart failure from systolic dysfunction, the heart cannot move (eject) the volume of blood to meet the body's needs. Loop diuretics, ethacrynic acid or furosemide, may be used to promote water removal through diuresis and lessen the workload on the failing heart. Some patients become refractory to the loop diuretic action. Adding a thiazide diuretic like chlorothiazide or metolazone has proven useful in continuing the process of diuresis. This synergistic diuretic response increases the opportunity for adverse reactions to occur. These drugs are highly bound to plasma proteins, which increases the potential for drug interactions during concomitant therapy from plasma protein displacement. All of the drugs are metabolized to some extent in the liver and excreted in the urine.

Adverse Effects

The effects produced by organic acid diuretics are similar to those of the thiazide diuretics and include nausea, hypotension (due to plasma volume contraction), hypokalemia, hyperuricemia, and hyperglycemia. In addition, the organic acid diuretics have produced tone deafness (ototoxicity) in some patients. These diuretics should not be administered in conjunction with aminoglycoside antibiotics (amikacin, kanamycin, neomycin, or streptomycin) because aminoglycoside antibiotics may potentiate the ototoxicity of the loop diuretics.

Loop diuretics have a special cautionary boxed warning to alert medical personnel that these drugs are *potent* diuretics and can lead to profound diuresis with water and electrolyte depletion. Careful medical supervision is required and dosage must be individualized.

Loop diuretics are contraindicated in patients who are unable to make urine (anuria) or have severe electrolyte depletion. Such conditions have to be adjusted through standard procedures for the existing condition before these potent diuretics can be used.

LO 25.5   LO 25.6   LO 25.8   LO 25.9

POTASSIUM-SPARING DIURETICS

Clinical Indications

The potassium-sparing diuretics are useful in the management of edema when combined with thiazides and loop diuretics. Amiloride, spironolactone, and triamterene inhibit the hypokalemia produced by the other potent diuretics. These three diuretics, therefore, conserve potassium. These diuretics are often used to control potassium depletion in patients who cannot tolerate oral potassium supplements (see "Special Considerations"). Spironolactone and triamterene are routinely used in the treatment of hypertension as an adjunct diuretic. Since hypertension requires life-long therapy, often with thiazide and thiazide-like diuretics, the potassium-sparing drugs are added to prevent the development of hypokalemia. Spironolactone also is used in primary hyperaldosteronism to reduce potassium loss.

Uses and Doses of Organic Acid and Potassium-Sparing Diuretics

Drug (*Trade Name*)	Duration of action, oral doses	Use	Adult oral dose
Organic acids (*loop diuretics*)			
Bumetanide (*Bumex*)	4–6 hr	Edema associated with congestive heart failure, renal disease, or cirrhosis of the liver and nephrotic syndrome; short-term management of ascites	0.5–10 mg/day
Ethacrynic acid (*Edecrin*)	6–8 hr		50–200 mg/day >200 mg/day for refractory patients
Furosemide (*Lasix*)	6–8 hr	Also used in the management of hypertension and acute pulmonary edema	20–80 mg/day
Torsemide (*Demadex*)	6–8 hr	Same as ethacrynic acid Cirrhosis	10–20 mg/day 5–10 mg/day
Potassium-sparing diuretics			
Amiloride (*Midamor*)	24 hr	Hypertension Adjunctive therapy with thiazide or loop diuretics in congestive heart failure; to restore potassium in hypokalemic patients; prevent hypokalemia	5–20 mg/day
Eplerenone (*Inspra*)	12–24 hr	Congestive heart failure, hypertension	25–50 mg QD, BID
Spironolactone (*Aldactone*)	48–72 hr	Edema, hypertension Hyperaldosteronism, hypokalemia	50–100 mg/day 100–400 mg/day
Triamterene (*Dyrenium*)	12–16 hr	Edema, hypertension	100–200 mg/day
Combination products			
Spironolactone (50 mg) and hydrochlorothiazide (50 mg) (*Aldactazide*)	48–72 hr	Hyperaldosteronism, edema, hypertension	50–200 mg/day (1–4 tablets/day)
Triamterene (37.5 mg) and hydrochlorothiazide (25 mg) (*Dyazide*)	12–16 hr	Edema, hypertension	1 or 2 tablets once daily
Triamterene (50 mg) and hydrochlorothiazide (50 mg) (generic brand)	12–16 hr	Edema, hypertension	1 or 2 tablets BID
Triamterene (75 mg) and hydrochlorothiazide (50 mg) (*Maxzide*)	48–72 hr	Edema, hypertension	1 tablet/day

Mechanism of Action

The potassium-sparing diuretics include amiloride (*Midamor*), spironolactone (*Aldactone*), and triamterene (*Dyrenium*) (Table 25:4). Following oral administration, these drugs produce diuresis by inhibiting potassium secretion in the distal convoluted tubules (Figure 25.7). Spironolactone blocks aldosterone receptors located in these tubules. Because aldosterone receptors partially control potassium secretion, the exchange for sodium is inhibited by spironolactone. Although not aldosterone antagonists, amiloride and triamterene inhibit sodium reabsorption by altering the membranes of the distal convoluted tubules so that potassium cannot be secreted. These three drugs produce a mild diuresis without inducing electrolyte changes or acid-base disturbances.

Adverse Effects

The side effects associated with amiloride, spironolactone, and triamterene include nausea, diarrhea, and hyperkalemia. Spironolactone and triamterene also can cause gynecomastia. Unlike the other diuretics, potassium-sparing diuretics promote potassium retention in the blood (hyperkalemia). This effect often occurs in patients who have impaired renal function or who are diabetic. Potassium supplementation, either in the form of medication or as a diet rich in potassium, should not ordinarily be given in patients taking these diuretics. The incidence of hyperkalemia is minimized in most individuals receiving spironolactone and triamterene because these drugs are seldom administered alone.

Amiloride has a special cautionary warning in its label (boxed warning) specifying that hyperkalemia occurs in about 10 percent of patients when amiloride is used without a potassium-excreting diuretic. This incidence is greater in patients with renal impairment,

in patients with diabetes mellitus (with or without recognized renal insufficiency), and in the elderly. When amiloride is used concomitantly with a thiazide diuretic in patients without these complications, the risk of hyperkalemia is reduced to about 1 to 2 percent. It is thus essential to monitor serum potassium levels carefully in any patient receiving amiloride, particularly when it is first introduced, at the time of diuretic dosage adjustments, and during any illness that could affect renal function.

The special warning for spironolactone reminds the prescriber to use this drug only in the recommended conditions because there have been reports of tumor development in long-term high-dose animal studies.

LO 25.5 | **LO 25.8** | **LO 25.9**

ADH ANTAGONISTS AND MISCELLANEOUS DIURETICS

Antidiuretic hormone (ADH) is a substance that regulates water balance in the body by controlling water loss in the urine. **Osmoreceptors** in the hypothalamus detect changes in the salt (sodium) concentration in the plasma that indicate whether more or less water needs to be conserved. Serum sodium is maintained in the normal range (135–145 mEq/L) despite wide fluctuations in fluid intake. If there is too much sodium in the blood (**hypertonic**, serum sodium > 145 mEq/L), ADH will be secreted from the posterior pituitary gland (see Chapter 40). The target organs for ADH are the kidneys, where ADH binds to receptors in the collecting ducts of the renal tubules. ADH increases the reabsorption of water into the blood by causing the collecting duct cells to synthesize specialized proteins called water channels. Free water (without sodium) flows out of the urine into the blood through channels known as aquaporins. These channels appear to be exclusively water channels and do not permit ions or other small molecules to pass through. As a result, there is a decrease in blood **osmolarity,** the osmoreceptors are no longer activated, ADH secretion is inhibited (negative feedback), and water is conserved. The blood compartment, as a result, contains more water. While water is reabsorbed, the urine becomes more concentrated because less water and more ions/sodium are excreted.

When the plasma compartment has a decreased osmolarity (**hypotonic,** serum sodium < 135 mEq/L), indicating there is too much water retained in the circulatory system, ADH secretion is inhibited. Conditions associated with an increase in retained water include

Figure 25.7

Examples of Diuretic Drugs

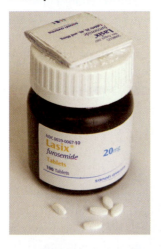
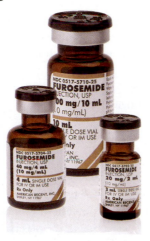

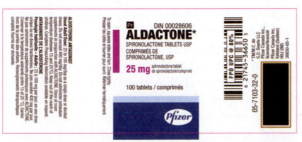

cirrhosis, cardiac failure, severe vomiting, and diarrhea and would inhibit ADH secretion.

Hyponatremia often occurs in patients who are hospitalized or in long-term-care nursing facilities. Age-related or disease-induced changes in kidney function, coupled with medications that alter renal function, can reduce circulating sodium levels even though the circulatory volume is unchanged **(euvolemia).** Sometimes the hyponatremia is corrected by reducing water intake and monitoring the use of diuretics. Chronic conditions such as liver cirrhosis, heart failure, and renal failure can cause excess water to be retained in the circulation. Sometimes drug intervention like the diuretics is required to pull excess water out of the circulation without pulling sodium out of the blood. This resets the sodium concentration in the blood toward the normal range. Conivaptan (*Vaprisol*) is the first ADH receptor antagonist approved for use in patients to conserve sodium and water. Conivaptan antagonizes ADH receptors (V_{1a} and V_2) in the collecting ducts. The circulating level of ADH is critical for the regulation of water and electrolyte balance. Inhibition of the ADH receptors in the renal collecting ducts causes excretion of free water, **aquaresis,** without electrolyte loss.

Conivaptan is currently approved for intravenous infusion; however, it is an orally active nonpeptide antagonist. Other oral ADH antagonists (lixivaptan and tolvaptan) are in development. The oral route would facilitate patient self-treatment. At this time conivaptan must be administered by trained medical personnel as a 20-mg loading dose followed by 20 mg infused over the next 24 hours. Conivaptan is highly bound to plasma proteins, metabolized by the liver, and excreted primarily into the feces. The most common adverse effects are injection site reactions, but headache, hypotension, vomiting, and constipation also have been reported to occur.

Conivaptan should not be given when the patient is receiving ketoconazole, itraconazole, clarithromycin, ritonavir, and indinavir because these drugs block the hepatic enzyme system that metabolizes conivaptan.

The xanthine derivatives (caffeine, pamabrom, theobromine, and theophylline) are naturally occurring drugs that produce a mild diuretic response. These drugs stimulate urine flow by increasing the blood flow through kidneys, resulting in an increased glomerular filtration rate and urine formation. Most often, xanthine diuretics are used in combination with other diuretics. Side effects associated with the xanthine diuretics include CNS stimulation, hypotension, and headache. Caffeine is the active ingredient in over-the-counter diuretics.

LO 25.8   LO 25.9

SPECIAL CONSIDERATIONS

Most of the diuretics, especially the most potent, produce changes in electrolyte and acid-base balance with chronic use. Therefore, the serum electrolytes should be monitored periodically to follow the effects of the diuretics. The serum potassium level is particularly important because changes in potassium can alter cardiovascular and skeletal muscle function. Potassium depletion (hypokalemia) can produce muscle weakness, fatigue, and cardiac arrhythmias.

Hypokalemia

Clinical estimates of diuretic-induced hypokalemia vary between 10 and 40 percent of patients chronically receiving diuretic therapy. Potassium is essential for maintaining pH balance in body fluids and normal function in muscles, nerves, and bones. To avoid the potassium reduction, or hypokalemia, produced by the potent diuretics, patients usually are encouraged to follow a supplementation schedule. Orange juice and bananas supply a large amount of dietary potassium. These fruits should be eaten daily to compensate for the diuretic-induced potassium loss. Additional foods considered to be potassium rich are dates, figs, prunes, apricots, raisins, sweet and white potatoes, as well as grapefruit and prune juices. See Table 25:5 for a larger list of potassium-rich foods across many food groups.

In severe edema, which requires stronger diuretic therapy, oral potassium salt supplements (*K-Lyte* or *Slow-K*) may be required. These potassium supplements often produce GI irritation, which reduces patient compliance. Therefore, the potassium-sparing diuretics are useful as an adjunct drug to reduce potassium depletion during diuretic therapy.

Orthostatic Hypotension and Dehydration

Since diuretics remove salt and water from the circulation, blood pressure may be altered, resulting in orthostatic hypotension. Removal of salt and water can cause contraction of the plasma volume. This is what produces the hypotension. Patients taking a diuretic should be cautioned about potential changes in blood pressure, since the hypotension can lead to dizziness and fainting. The vital signs should be monitored periodically in order to follow effects on circulation and blood pressure.

Often, the use of diuretics is directed toward reducing the sodium level in the blood. Therefore, many patients receiving diuretics also must restrict their dietary sodium intake. As the frequency of urination

Potassium-Rich Foods*

Fruits	Vegetables	Dairy	Other
Apple w/skin	Artichoke, cooked	Cottage cheese, 2%	Almonds
Apple juice, unsweetened	Asparagus, cooked	Ice cream, vanilla	Beef, lean cooked
Apricots, dried sulfured	Beet greens, cooked	Milk, 2%	Brazil nuts
Avocado	Broccoli	Ricotta cheese	Bread, wheat
Banana	Brussel sprouts, fresh	Yogurt	Eggs
Cantalope, cubed	Cabbage, cooked		Halibut
Dates	Carrots, fresh		Hamburger
Figs, dried	Cauliflower, fresh		Molasses
Kiwi	Garbanzo beans		Peanut butter, natural
Mango	Green beans, fresh		Peanuts, salted
Orange	Kidney beans, cooked		Rice, brown
Orange juice	Lettuce, iceburg		Rice, white
Papaya	Mushrooms, cooked		Salmon, baked or steamed
Peach	Pinto beans, cooked		Salmon, canned
Pear	Potato, baked with skin		Tuna, cooked yellowfin
Prune juice, unsweetened	Spinach, steamed		Turkey, roasted dark meat
Raisins	Sweet potato, with skin		
Strawberries, raw	Tomato, fresh		
Watermelon	Tomato juice		

Source: USDA national nutrient database —potassium content of selected foods.

increases, the urine volume should be recorded to determine the effectiveness of the diuretic. The potent diuretics can produce weight loss and dehydration due to intense removal of water from the body.

Blood Glucose Monitoring

Diabetic patients who require long-term diuretic therapy should have their blood glucose levels monitored periodically. Patients sensitive to sulfonamide drugs may develop allergic reactions to furosemide or thiazide diuretics.

Overdose

Diuretics will produce an exaggeration of their clinical effects when the dose exposure is greater than therapeutically required. Plasma volume depletion contributes to hypotension, dizziness, and drowsiness. Electrolyte deficiency produces confusion, muscle weakness, and gastrointestinal disturbances. There is no antidote for any diuretic. Gastric lavage and vomiting may be necessary while maintaining hydration and electrolyte balance parenterally, and supporting respiration as necessary.

LO 25.8 **LO 25.9**

DRUG INTERACTIONS AND INCOMPATIBILITIES

Diuretics are involved in a number of drug interactions because they bind to plasma proteins, alter acid-base balance, and stimulate renal excretion. The most important interaction is the potentiation of digoxin toxicity. Diuretics are frequently used in combination with digoxin in the treatment of CHF. Diuretic-induced hypokalemia increases the toxic effect of digoxin on the myocardium, resulting in the production of arrhythmias. Therefore, it is important to maintain the potassium balance during diuretic therapy. Another important interaction occurs when diuretics are used concomitantly with lithium. Diuretics may decrease the renal clearance of lithium, thus increasing the risk of lithium toxicity.

Carbonic anhydrase inhibitors potentiate potassium depletion in the presence of corticosteroids and increase the excretion of acidic drugs.

Alcohol, antihypertensive drugs, barbiturates, and opioid analgesics increase the possibility of orthostatic hypotension when taken with the potent diuretics such as thiazides and organic acids. Diazoxide potentiates hypotension, hyperglycemia, and hyperuricemia when taken with thiazide diuretics.

Aminoglycoside antibiotics potentiate hearing loss (otoxicity) caused by organic acid diuretics.

Some diuretics can be prepared as solutions for parenteral administration. Usually, the intramuscular route is associated with pain or local irritation, so direct intravenous injection or intravenous infusion is the parenteral route of choice. Since diuretics may be given slowly through the tubing of a running infusion, it is important to avoid mixing solutions that will result in drug incompatibility. Drug incompatibility may be associated with drug precipitation, complex formation, or discoloration of the solution, any of which may alter total drug activity or potency. Mannitol (*Osmitrol*), chlorothiazide (*Diuril*), ethacrynic acid (*Edecrin*), and furosemide (*Lasix*) have been reported to be incompatible with specific solutions or infusions.

Mannitol (*Osmitrol*) should not be mixed with whole blood because agglutination may occur. Advanced premixing of mannitol and cisplatin (antineoplastic drug) may result in complex formation. Chlorothiazide (*Diuril*) has been reported to be incompatible when mixed in solution with amikacin, chlorpromazine, codeine, insulin, methadone, morphine, procaine, promethazine, streptomycin, tetracycline, and vancomycin. Ethacrynic acid has been reported to be incompatible with solutions of drugs with a final pH of less than 5 and should never be mixed with whole blood for infusion. Furosemide may precipitate if combined with ascorbic acid, epinephrine, norepinephrine, or tetracycline solutions.

LO 25.9

PREFERRED TREATMENT

ADH antagonists are indicated for the clinical management of euvolemic and hypervolemic hyponatremia in hospitalized patients.

Carbonic anhydrous inhibitors are used in glaucoma, edema with alkalosis, and mountain sickness.

Loop diuretics are used in pulmonary edema, peripheral edema, hypertension, acute hypercalcemia, or hyperkalemia, and acute renal failure.

Thiazides are preferred therapy in hypertension, mild heart failure, nephrolithiasis, and nephrogenic diabetes insipidus.

Osmotic diuretics are used to improve renal failure due to increased load (rhabdomyolysis, chemotherapy), reduce increased intracranial pressure and remove fluid and reduce pressure in glaucoma.

Potassium-sparing diuretics are used for hypokalemia due to other diuretics and postmyocardial infarction. Spironolactone is specific for the treatment of aldosteronism from any cause.

The term *diuretic* or "water pill" is so familiar to patients that it may be prudent to remind them how effective these drugs are. Certain unpleasant effects may be annoying, but do not warrant interrupting therapy, while other actions require the doctor's attention. Diuretic activity will begin immediately, so the pills should be taken early in the day to minimize urinary urgency (nocturia) during sleep. Medication should be taken as directed "even if the patient is feeling well." Body weight should be periodically (even daily) measured, particularly in elderly patients, who are especially susceptible to excessive diuresis.

Drug Administration

Patients who experience GI upset after taking oral diuretics may be advised to take the medicine with meals or milk.

Patient Instruction

Alcohol, including over-the-counter (OTC) preparations for cold/flu, coughs, and hay fever that contain alcohol, should be avoided while on diuretics. The alcohol inhibits ADH secretion and thereby potentiates dehydration, drowsiness, and dizziness, which may occur with the diuretics.

Diabetic patients may experience a change in their blood sugar values during home monitoring or glucose testing. If the patient is seeing another physician or specialist (diabetologist, endocrinologist) for diabetes, remind the patient to have the diuretic added to that medication history.

Special dose adjustment for elderly patients is not necessary; however, patients should be advised to move slowly when rising from bed or chairs because of the orthostatic hypotension.

Photosensitivity may occur with triamterene. Patients should be advised to avoid unnecessary exposure to the sun while on therapy.

Notify the Physician

Patients should notify physician if muscle pain, weakness or cramps, nausea, vomiting, diarrhea, or palpitations occur.

Sudden joint pain should be reported to the physician immediately for further evaluation. This could be indicative of developing gout.

Use in Pregnancy

Drugs in this class have been designated Federal Drug Administration (FDA) Pregnancy Category B or C. Safety for use during pregnancy has not been established. Routine use of diuretics during normal pregnancy is inappropriate. They are not useful in treating toxemia. These drugs are indicated for use during pregnancy only when the underlying conditions of the patient, such as CHF or renal disease, warrant treatment. These drugs will cross the placental barrier and affect the fetus. These drugs should be used only when clearly needed and the potential benefits are greater than the risks.

Chapter Review

Understanding Terminology

Answer the following questions.

1. Compare the terms *tubular reabsorption* and *tubular secretion*. **(LO 25.1, 25.3)**
2. What is meant by the term *refractory*? **(LO 25.9)**
3. Explain the difference between the terms *acidosis* and *alkalosis*. **(LO 25.4, 25.9)**

Match the definition or description in the left column with the appropriate term in the right column.

_____ 4. A condition in which no urine is produced. **(LO 25.9)**

_____ 5. Watery substance behind cornea of the eye and in front of the lens. **(LO 25.5, 25.9)**

_____ 6. An inflammation or infection in the kidneys. **(LO 25.9)**

_____ 7. A condition that causes very small amounts of urine to be produced. **(LO 25.9)**

_____ 8. An accumulation of urea in the blood. **(LO 25.9)**

_____ 9. A condition that causes a large volume of urine to be excreted. **(LO 25.9)**

a. anuria
b. aqueous humor
c. diuresis
d. nephritis
e. oliguria
f. uremia

Acquiring Knowledge

Answer the following questions.

1. What are the main functions of the kidneys? **(LO 25.1, 25.2, 25.3, 25.4)**
2. Describe the mechanism of sodium reabsorption from the renal tubules. **(LO 25.2)**
3. What is the mechanism of action of most diuretic drugs? **(LO 25.1)**
4. How does the mechanism of action of the osmotic diuretics differ from that of other diuretic drugs? **(LO 25.5)**
5. How can acetazolamide produce metabolic acidosis? **(LO 25.5)**
6. What adverse effects are common to both the thiazide and the organic acid diuretics? **(LO 25.6, 25.8)**
7. How do amiloride, spironolactone, and triamterene affect potassium secretion by the distal convoluted tubules? **(LO 25.4, 25.5)**
8. When are diuretics used? Why are they useful in the treatment of hypertension? **(LO 25.1, 25.3, 25.5)**

Multiple Choice

Use your critical-thinking skills to answer the following questions.

1. Diuretics like organic acids and thiazides are therapeutically useful because they **(LO 25.5, 25.7, 25.8, 25.9)**
   A. can be used in the treatment of refractory heart failure
   B. antagonize antidiuretic hormone at the receptors in the collecting duct
   C. block carbonic anhydrase in the loop of Henle, causing hypochloremic alkalosis
   D. waste potassium at doses that cause diuresis

2. Ototoxicity is a unique side effect of which group of diuretics? **(LO 25.8)**
   A. loop/organic acid diuretics
   B. thiazide diuretics
   C. potassium-sparing diuretics
   D. osmotic diuretics

3. Which of the following actions is related to thiazide diuretics? **(LO 25.3, 25.5, 25.8, 25.9)**
   A. hyperuricemia
   B. hyperkalemia
   C. hypernatremia
   D. hypercalcemia

4. Which of these is **NOT** true with regard to loop diuretics? **(LO 25.3, 25.5, 25.8, 25.9)**
   A. can cause hyperuricemia
   B. can cause hyperglycemia
   C. can be used to reduce ascites due to malignancy
   D. can cause metabolic acidosis

5. The primary site of action of thiazide diuretics in the nephron is **(LO 25.1, 25.3, 25.5)**
   A. the proximal tubule
   B. the loop of Henle
   C. the distal tubule
   D. the capsule area of glomerular filtration

6. Which diuretic is useful in reducing intraocular pressure during acute attacks of glaucoma? **(LO 25.5)**
   A. loop diuretic ethacrynic acid
   B. thiazide diuretic indapamide
   C. potassium-sparing diuretic amiloride
   D. osmotic diuretic mannitol

7. Which drugs are **NOT** routinely used in the clinical management of hypertension? **(LO 25.5)**
   A. thiazide diuretics
   B. chlorthalidone
   C. isosorbide
   D. triamterene

8. Loop diuretics increase the excretion of all of the following **EXCEPT** **(LO 25.3, 25.5)**
   A. sodium
   B. uric acid
   C. water
   D. potassium

9. All of the following are true **EXCEPT** **(LO 25.2, 25.3, 25.5, 25.9)**
   A. anuria is a state where no urine is formed
   B. the major tubular secretory function of the nephron involves hydrogen and potassium ions
   C. uremia is an accumulation of nitrogen waste products
   D. tubular reabsorption of water is diuresis

10. All potassium-sparing diuretics **(LO 25.2, 25.5, 25.9)**
    A. produce a mild diuresis without acid/base disturbance
    B. inhibit aldosterone receptors
    C. produce hypokalemia
    D. produce similar adverse effects to thiazide diuretics

Multiple Choice (Multiple Answer)

Select the correct choices for each statement. The choices may be all correct, all incorrect, or any combination.

1. Tubular reabsorption involves which of the following? **(LO 25.2)**
   A. movement of small molecules into the glomerulus
   B. nephron production of acids
   C. transport of ions into the blood
   D. movement of sodium ions into circulation

2. Select the areas of the kidneys where water is reabsorbed. **(LO 25.3)**
   A. glomerulus
   B. proximal convoluted tubule
   C. distal convoluted tubule
   D. collecting ducts

3. Kidneys maintain acid balance in the body by which of the following actions? **(LO 25.4)**
   A. tubular secretion of hydrogen ions
   B. increasing the pH of the urine
   C. neutralizing cell waste products
   D. decreasing the production of bicarbonate ions

4. When a diuretic is refractory, it does which of the following? **(LO 25.6)**
   A. produces a decreased response to a decreased amount of drug
   B. produces an increased response to an increased amount of drug
   C. doesn't produce a greater response to an increased amount of drug
   D. doesn't produce any response to a decrease in the amount of drug

5. Which of the following are side effects of osmotic diuretics? **(LO 25.8)**
   A. nausea
   B. dizziness
   C. headache
   D. chills

Sequencing

Place the following kidney processes in order of how they occur. **(LO 25.1, 25.2, 25.3)**

_____   _____   _____   _____

First   **Last**

glomerular filtration

tubular secretion

water conservation

tubular reabsorption

Classification

Place the following conditions under the preferred treatment. **(LO 25.5)**

euvolemic hyponatremia	mild heart failure	mountain sickness
pulmonary edema	hypervolemic	acute hypercalcemia
intracranial pressure	hyponatremia	post myocardial infarction
hypokalemia	renal failure from chemo	
edema with alkalosis	nephrolithiasis	

ADH antagonists	Carbonic anhy-drase inhibitors	Loop diuretics	Thiazides	Osmotic diuretics	Potassium-sparing diuretics

Labeling

Fill in the missing labels. **(LO 25.2, 25.3)**

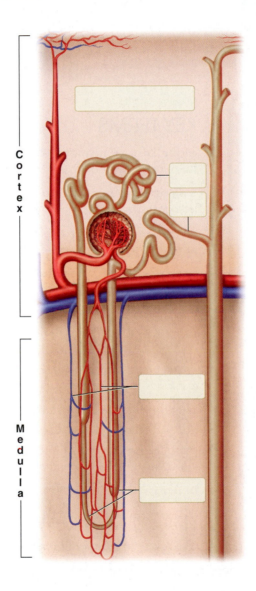

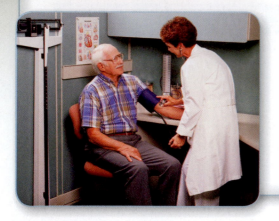

Chapter 26

Antihypertensive Drugs

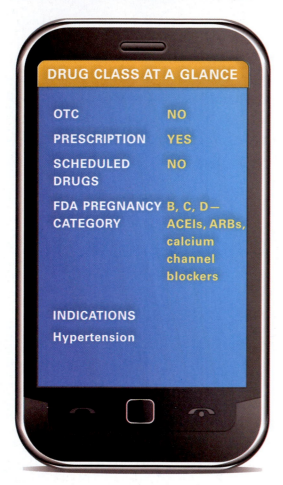

DRUG CLASS AT A GLANCE

OTC	NO
PRESCRIPTION	YES
SCHEDULED DRUGS	NO
FDA PREGNANCY CATEGORY	B, C, D— ACEIs, ARBs, calcium channel blockers

INDICATIONS

Hypertension

KEY TERMS

aldosterone: hormone released from adrenal cortex that causes the retention of sodium from the kidneys.

angiotensin-converting enzyme inhibitor (ACEI): drug that inhibits the enzymatic conversion of angiotensin I to angiotensin II.

angiotensin receptor blocker (ARB): drug that blocks receptors for angiotensin II.

angiotensin II: potent vasoconstrictor that also stimulates release of aldosterone and antidiuretic hormone.

antidiuretic hormone (ADH): hormone from the posterior pituitary gland that causes retention of water from the kidneys.

blood pressure (BP): the pressure of the blood within the arteries; depends primarily on the cardiac output and the peripheral resistance.

cardiac output (CO): the amount of blood pumped per minute by the heart.

essential hypertension: major form of hypertension for which the cause is unknown.

heart rate (HR): number of heartbeats per minute.

hypertension: abnormally high blood pressure.

malignant hypertension: hypertensive crisis associated with inflammation and vascular damage.

peripheral resistance (PR): resistance generated by the flow of blood through the arteries.

renin: enzyme released by the kidneys that converts angiotensinogen into angiotensin I.

secondary hypertension: form of hypertension in which the cause is known.

stroke volume (SV): amount of blood pumped per heartbeat.

After studying this chapter, you should be able to

26.1 describe the major physiological factors that regulate blood pressure.

26.2 understand the role of the kidneys and renin-angiotensin-aldosterone system in blood pressure regulation.

26.3 explain the antihypertensive actions of thiazide and loop diuretics.

26.4 compare the pharmacologic actions of the different classes of drugs that reduce sympathetic nervous system activity.

26.5 describe the mechanism of action of the vasodilator drugs.

26.6 compare the pharmacologic actions of the ACE inhibitors and the angiotensin receptor blockers.

26.7 describe the treatment of hypertensive crisis.

26.8 explain some of the important factors involved in patient education concerning hypertension.

26.9 list the drug classes that are usually preferred for the treatment of hypertension.

Introduction

Hypertension, a condition in which blood pressure (BP) in the arterial system is abnormally high, is one of the leading causes of cerebral strokes, heart attacks, and chronic heart failure (CHF). In CHF, hypertension causes the left ventricle to hypertrophy, which decreases cardiac function and leads to heart failure (Figure 26.1). An estimated 10 to 15 percent of the American population has hypertensive disease. The symptoms of hypertension usually appear years after the disease is well established and permanent organ damage may have occurred.

It is estimated that only half of the people with hypertension are aware of their disease and many individuals under treatment for hypertension are not adequately controlled. This situation is difficult to understand, since the measurement and detection of high blood pressure is relatively easy (Figure 26.2). There are many different types of antihypertensive drugs and most cases of hypertension can now be controlled with one or two drugs.

In the majority of hypertensive cases (approximately 90 percent), the cause of hypertension is unknown. This type of hypertension is referred to as **essential hypertension**. When the cause of hypertension is known, the hypertension is referred to as **secondary hypertension**. Since the cause of essential hypertension is unknown, the goal of drug therapy is to lower the blood pressure back within the normal range to prevent or at least reduce the serious consequences of hypertension.

LO 26.1 | LO 26.2

PHYSIOLOGICAL FACTORS CONTROLLING BLOOD PRESSURE

Blood pressure is mainly determined by two factors: cardiac output (CO) and peripheral resistance (PR).

Cardiac Output

Cardiac output (CO) is the amount of blood that is pumped out of the heart per minute. Two factors determine cardiac output: the **heart rate (HR)** in beats per minute and the **stroke volume (SV),** the amount of blood pumped per beat. The formula for cardiac output (CO) is

$$CO = HR \times SV$$

Peripheral Resistance

The **peripheral resistance (PR)** is the resistance or friction that the arterioles have against the flow of blood (Figure 26.3). The main factor that increases the

Figure 26.1

Cross Section of a Heart with Systemic Hypertension

Left ventricular hypertrophy

The patient had high blood pressure, which increasesd the afterload of the left ventricle and resulted in hypertrophy of the left ventricular myocardium. The increased afterload caused cardiac myocytes to increase their content of contractile proteins, resulting in hypertrophy, reduced cardiac function, and heart failure.

Figure 26.2   Measuring Blood Pressure with a Sphygmomanometer

1 No sound is heard because there is no blood flow when the cuff pressure is high enough to keep the brachial artery closed

2 Systolic pressure is the pressure at which a korotkoff sound is first heard. When cuff pressure decreases and is no longer able to keep the brachial artery closed during systole blood is pushed through the partially opened brachial artery to produce turbulent blood flow and a sound. The brachial artery remains closed during diastole

3 As cuff pressure continues to decrease, the brachial artery opens even more during systole. At first, the artery is closed during diastole: but, as cuff pressure continues to decrease, the brachial artery partially opens during diastole. Turbulent blood flow during systole produces korotkoff sounds, although the pitch of the sounds changes as the artery becomes more open

4 Diastolic pressure is the pressure at which the sound disappears. Eventually, cuff pressure decreases below the pressure in the brachial artery and it remains open during systole and diastole. Nonturbulent flow is reestablished and no sounds are heard

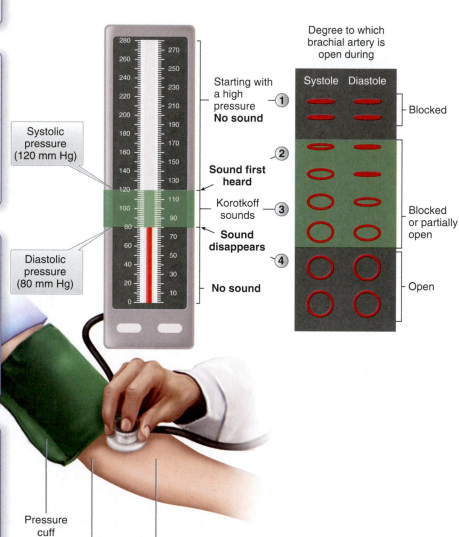

Systolic pressure (120 mm Hg)

Diastolic pressure (80 mm Hg)

Starting with a high pressure **No sound** — 1

Sound first heard — 2

Korotkoff sounds — 3

Sound disappears

No sound — 4

Degree to which brachial artery is open during

Systole   Diastole

Blocked

Blocked or partially open

Open

Pressure cuff

Elbow

Arm

Figure 26.3

Blood Pressures throughout the Systemic Vasculature

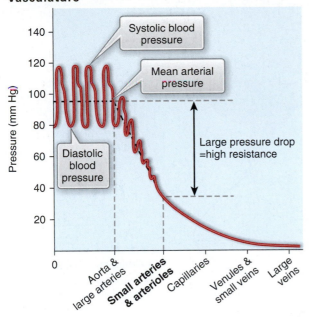

Pressure is highest in the large arteries and lowest in the large veins. The largest pressure decrease occurs across the arterioles, indicating that they are the site of highest vascular resistance.

peripheral resistance is vasoconstriction. Vasoconstriction and a rise in BP are produced by sympathetic stimulation (norepinephrine, epinephrine), **angiotensin II,** and other vasoactive factors. Drugs that cause vasodilation reduce peripheral resistance.

Blood Pressure

Blood pressure (BP) is a result of all of the factors that regulate cardiac output (CO) and peripheral resistance (PR). The formula for BP is

$$BP = CO \times PR$$

Increasing any of the factors (HR, SV, or PR) will cause the blood pressure to rise, and stimulation of the sympathetic nervous system increases all of them. In most cases of essential hypertension, there is increased activity of the sympathetic nervous system, so this factor is important in the control of blood pressure.

Factors That Contribute to High Blood Pressure

A number of factors have been shown to affect BP. While these factors are not believed to be the cause of hypertension, controlling these factors can produce modest decreases in BP. These factors include sodium restriction, weight loss, elimination of smoking, regular physical exercise, and various relaxation techniques aimed at reducing stress. Successful control of these factors may eliminate the need for drug therapy or reduce the dosage and number of drugs required.

Role of Kidneys in Hypertension

With hypertension, there is increased peripheral resistance, and blood flow through the kidneys is reduced. The kidneys play an important role in maintaining sodium and water balance in the body. When renal blood flow is reduced, the enzyme **renin** is released by the kidneys into the bloodstream. As previously discussed in Chapter 22 and Figure 22.2, release of renin activates the renin-angiotensin-aldosterone (RAA) mechanism. Activation of the RAA mechanism causes vasoconstriction, and sodium and water retention, which increases blood pressure and is an important factor in hypertension.

Antihypertensive Therapy

The therapeutic aim in hypertension is to lower blood pressure to within the normal range. This has been shown to reduce the damage to blood vessels, heart, kidneys, and other organs. Importantly, controlling hypertension increases life expectancy. There are a variety of antihypertensive drugs that can effectively lower blood pressure. These include diuretics, sympatholytics, vasodilators, calcium channel blockers, **angiotensin-converting enzyme inhibitors (ACEIs), angiotensin receptor blockers (ARBs),** and renin inhibitors. Figure 26.4 provides an overview of the sites of action of the major classes of antihypertensive drugs. The diuretics and beta-blocking drugs have been considered among the most effective drugs to control blood pressure and reduce mortality. Consequently, these are the drugs usually recommended for initial treatment of hypertension. The more advanced stages of hypertension may require two or even three drug combinations. Classification of the different stages of hypertension is presented in Table 26:1.

LO 26.3
DIURETICS

Diuretics were discussed in Chapter 25, so only applications related to the treatment of hypertension will be discussed here. It has been known for many years that a salt-restricted diet lowers BP. Salt-restricted diets were used to treat hypertension before the discovery of the modern drugs. The diuretics, which increase the excretion of sodium from the kidneys, have been shown to lower blood pressure. Both salt restriction and diuretic therapy are effective measures to reduce BP.

Figure 26.4
The Sites of Action of the Major Antihypertensive Drugs

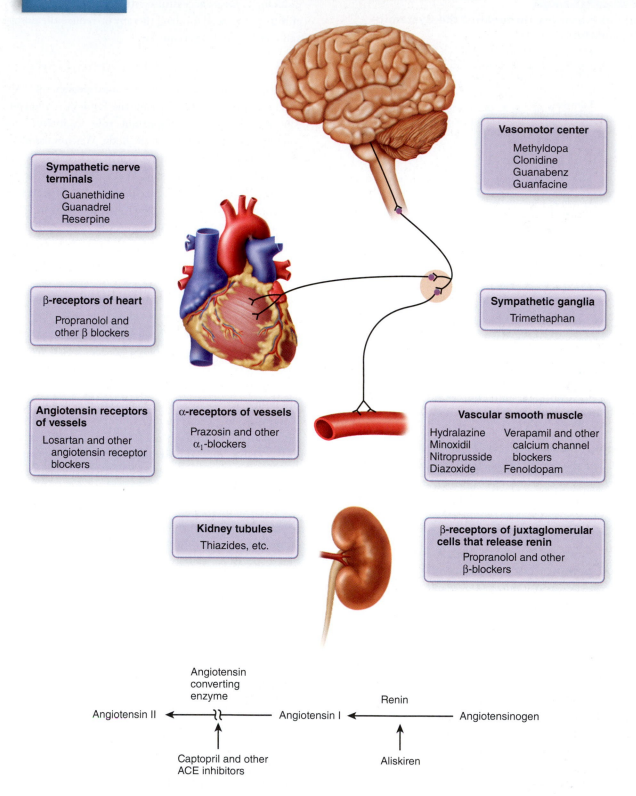

Vasomotor center

Methyldopa
Clonidine
Guanabenz
Guanfacine

Sympathetic nerve terminals

Guanethidine
Guanadrel
Reserpine

β-receptors of heart

Propranolol and
other β blockers

Sympathetic ganglia

Trimethaphan

Angiotensin receptors of vessels

Losartan and other
angiotensin receptor
blockers

α-receptors of vessels

Prazosin and other
α_1-blockers

Vascular smooth muscle

Hydralazine   Verapamil and other
Minoxidil   calcium channel
Nitroprusside   blockers
Diazoxide   Fenoldopam

Kidney tubules

Thiazides, etc.

β-receptors of juxtaglomerular cells that release renin

Propranolol and other
β-blockers

Angiotensin
converting
enzyme

Renin

Angiotensin II ⟵ ⟵ Angiotensin I ⟵ Angiotensinogen

Captopril and other
ACE inhibitors

Aliskiren

Mechanism of Action

The thiazides and thiazide-like drugs are the preferred diuretics used to treat hypertension. The hypotensive effect of these drugs is initially caused by increased excretion of sodium and water, which reduces blood volume and cardiac output. With continued use of diuretics, the cardiac output readjusts back to normal. However, over the course of several weeks, a second

Classification of Hypertension

Classification	Blood pressure (mm Hg)
Normotensive	<120/80
Prehypertension	120–139/80–89
Hypertension	>140/90
Stage 1	140–159/90–99
Stage 2	>160/100

longer-term antihypertensive effect develops. The long-term antihypertensive effect of diuretics involves a reduction of intracellular sodium concentration inside vascular smooth muscle. This reduces the sensitivity of vascular smooth muscle to the vasoconstrictive effects of circulating norepinephrine, epinephrine, angiotensin II, and other vasoconstrictors. The result is a gradual decrease in peripheral resistance and blood pressure. The antihypertensive effect of thiazide and thiazide-like diuretics occurs at low dosages. Higher diuretic dosages do increase urine output but do not result in greater decreases in peripheral resistance.

Diuretics are used alone in mild hypertension. Usually several weeks of treatment are required for the vasodilating effect to fully develop. In moderate or severe hypertension, the diuretics are combined with other antihypertensive drugs. The effects of thiazide-like diuretics (chlorthalidone and quinethazone) are identical to the effects of the thiazides. Recent studies have demonstrated that once-a-day, low-dose therapy with thiazide and thiazide-like diuretics provides effective antihypertensive treatment and patient compliance.

The organic acid diuretics, such as furosemide (*Lasix*) and bumetanide (*Bumex*), are used in patients who have reduced kidney function, where a more potent diuretic effect is required. The potassium-sparing diuretics are usually combined with the other diuretics and indicated when loss of potassium is of concern. For example, *Aldactazide* is the combination of hydrochlorothiazide and spironolactone; *Dyazide* is the combination of hydrochlorothiazide and triamterene. In addition, there are many drug combinations of thiazides with other drug classes such as beta-blockers, ACEIs, and ARBs. Table 26:2 lists some of the thiazide and thiazide-like diuretics used in hypertension. Refer to the drug tables in Chapter 25 for a more complete listing and review of all the diuretic drugs.

Adverse Effects

Most of the adverse effects of the thiazide and loop diuretics are caused by excessive loss of water, sodium, and potassium (hypokalemia), which usually results

Thiazide and Thiazide-like Diuretics Used in Treatment of Hypertension

Drug (*Trade Name*)	Common daily oral dosage range
Thiazide diuretics	
Chlorothiazide (*Diuril*)	500–2000 mg
Hydrochlorothiazide (*HydroDIURIL*)	12.5–50 mg
Thiazide-like diuretics	
Chlorthalidone (*Hygroton, Thalitone*)	12.5–50 mg
Indapamide (*Lozol*)	1.25–5 mg
Metolazone (*Zaroxolyn*)	2.5–5 mg

in dehydration, muscle weakness, and fatigue. These diuretics also interfere with the renal excretion of uric acid. In some patients, increased uric acid levels cause gout. In addition, thiazide and loop diuretics can interfere with the action of insulin and may cause glucose intolerance, which can be significant in diabetic patients. The main concern with the use of potassium-sparing diuretics is the development of hyperkalemia, especially in patients who are also taking ACEIs, ARBs, or potassium supplements.

LO 26.4

DRUGS THAT REDUCE SYMPATHETIC ACTIVITY

The sympathetic division of the autonomic nervous system has a vital function in the control of blood pressure. In hypertension there is often increased sympathetic activation. The adrenergic neurotransmitters norepinephrine and epinephrine stimulate alpha-1 and beta-1 receptors to cause vasoconstriction and increased

cardiac output. Alpha-blockers, beta-blockers, adrenergic neuronal blockers, and drugs that act on the vasomotor center in the brain reduce sympathetic activity and lower BP (Table 26:3). The pharmacology of the alpha-blockers, beta-blockers, and adrenergic neuronal blockers was presented in Chapter 6. Only the aspects of these drugs related to the treatment of hypertension will be discussed here.

Centrally Acting Sympatholytic Drugs

There are several drugs that decrease sympathetic activity and BP by an action in the central nervous system. These drugs include clonidine (*Catapres*), guanabenz (*Wytensin*), guanfacine (*Tenex*), and methyldopa (*Aldomet*). Clonidine is the preferred drug of this group and will be used to describe the actions of this drug class. Methyldopa was previously presented in Chapter 6.

Clonidine is a centrally acting drug used in the treatment of hypertension. The main action of clonidine is exerted on the vasomotor center located in the

[Table **26:3**]

Drugs That Reduce the Activity of the Sympathetic Nervous System

Drug (*Trade Name*)	Mechanism of antihypertensive action
Centrally acting drugs	
Clonidine (*Catapres*) Guanabenz (*Wytensin*) Guanfacine (*Tenex*) Methyldopa (*Aldomet*)	Stimulates inhibitory alpha-2 receptors in the vasomotor center of the medulla oblongata, which decreases sympathetic stimulation to the heart, kidneys, and blood vessels Methyldopa forms alpha-methylnorepinephrine (false transmitter), which stimulates the inhibitory alpha-2 receptors in the vasomotor center
Alpha-1 adrenergic blockers	
Doxazosin (*Cardura*) Prazosin (*Minipress*) Terazosin (*Hytrin*)	Blocks alpha-1 adrenergic receptors in vascular smooth muscle to cause vasodilation and reduction of peripheral resistance
Beta blockers	
Atenolol (*Tenormin*) Metoprolol (*Lopressor*) Nadolol (*Corgard*) Propranolol (*Inderal*)	Blocks beta-1 receptors in the heart to decrease cardiac output and blood pressure; also blocks beta-1 receptors in the kidneys, which decreases the release of renin and activation of the RAA mechanism
Others	
Carvedilol (*Coreg*) Labetalol (*Normodyne*) Nebivolol (*Bystolic*)	Same as above. In addition these drugs produce direct vasodilating actions on vascular smooth muscle, which contributes to the reduction in blood pressure
Adrenergic neuronal blockers	
Guanadrel (*Hylorel*) Guanethidine (*Ismelin*)	Blocks release of and causes depletion of norepinephrine from adrenergic nerve endings to cause general inhibition of all sympathetic activity

medulla oblongata. Clonidine and the other centrally acting drugs stimulate inhibitory alpha-2 receptors. This reduces the activity of the sympathetic nerves that travel from the vasomotor center to the heart (decrease heart rate and cardiac output), kidneys (decrease release of renin), and blood vessels (vasodilation), resulting in a reduction of blood pressure. Clonidine can be administered orally and parenterally and is also available as a weekly transdermal patch (*Catapres-TTS*). The adverse effects of clonidine include dry mouth, constipation, and drowsiness. If clonidine is abruptly discontinued, a withdrawal reaction may occur, with patients experiencing rebound sympathetic activity and hypertensive crisis. To avoid withdrawal symptoms of clonidine, the dose should be reduced gradually over a 2-week period.

Alpha-, Beta-, and Adrenergic Neuronal Blockers

The alpha-blockers doxazosin, prazosin, and terazosin selectively block the alpha-1 receptors located on vascular smooth muscle. The main antihypertensive effects are vasodilation and decreased peripheral resistance. After administration of the first dose, patients may experience dizziness, fainting, or postural hypotension. This is referred to as "the first-dose phenomenon." Patients should be advised to take the first dose at bedtime. Common adverse effects include dizziness, headache, blurred vision, and feelings of tiredness. Overdosage can produce hypotension and reflex tachycardia.

The beta-blockers produce two actions that are of benefit in the treatment of hypertension. First, they block beta-1 receptors in the heart, lowering blood pressure by decreasing CO, especially when there is increased sympathetic activity. Second, they block the release of renin from the kidneys, which reduces activation of the renin-angiotensin-aldosterone (RAA) mechanism. There are also several beta-blockers that have additional vasodilating properties. In addition to blocking beta receptors, labetalol and carvedilol also block alpha-1 receptors. Nebivolol blocks beta-1 receptors and produces vasodilation that may be due to increased nitric oxide formation. These drugs provide a more balanced blockade of sympathetic activity and are indicated for the more advanced stages of hypertension. The most common adverse effect caused by beta-blockers is excessive depression of cardiac function. This includes bradycardia, decreased AV conduction, and symptoms of heart failure. Also, nonselective beta-blockers can cause bronchospasm in patients with asthma and COPD.

Guanethidine and guanadrel are adrenergic neuronal blockers that cause a significant inhibition of sympathetic activity. First, these drugs prevent the release of NE from adrenergic nerve endings. Second, they deplete the storage vesicles of NE. Adrenergic neuronal blockers are only indicated for the treatment of severe hypertension that is unresponsive to other preferred drugs. The main adverse effects are caused by the profound decrease in sympathetic activity and include diarrhea, bradycardia, orthostatic hypotension, and impotency in males.

LO 26.5
VASODILATOR DRUGS

The vasodilator drugs act directly on vascular smooth muscle to cause relaxation. This results in vasodilation and a reduction in BP. Vasodilators are often used in combination with diuretics and beta-blockers. This is necessary because vasodilators often cause fluid retention and reflex tachycardia.

Hydralazine (*Apresoline*)

Hydralazine is an arteriolar dilator used in moderate to severe hypertension in combination with both diuretics and beta-blockers (triple therapy). The main adverse effects are nausea, headache, hypotension, and reflex tachycardia. Long-term use may produce rheumatoid arthritis or a systemic lupus erythematosus–like syndrome.

Minoxidil (*Loniten*)

Minoxidil is a more potent arteriolar dilator than hydralazine, and it is indicated for patients who do not respond to triple therapy with other drug combinations. The usual dose is 10 to 40 mg per day in combination with a diuretic and beta-blocker. Minoxidil has the potential to produce a number of serious adverse effects, including myocardial ischemia and pericardial effusion. Minoxidil also may cause hirsutism (growth of hair); the topical preparation *Rogaine* is marketed specifically for this purpose.

Calcium Channel Blockers

As discussed in Chapters 23 and 24, calcium channel blockers are drugs that interfere with the influx of calcium in cardiac and vascular smooth muscle. The primary action of calcium channel blockers in the treatment of hypertension is arteriolar vasodilation. This lowers peripheral resistance and blood pressure. The calcium channel blockers are usually thought of as composed of two subclasses. Verapamil and diltiazem are vasodilators that also have direct actions to decrease heart rate, AV conduction, and myocardial contractility. They are particularly useful in hypertensive patients who also

Calcium Channel Blockers

Drug (*Trade Name*)	Cardiovascular actions	Clinical uses
Diltiazem (*Cardizem, Cardizem SR*)	Arterial dilation, decreased HR, AV conduction, and myocardial contractility	Hypertension, CAD/ angina pectoris, cardiac arrhythmias
Verapamil (*Calan, Calan SR*)	Arterial dilation, decreased HR, AV conduction, and myocardial contractility	Hypertension, CAD/angina pectoris, cardiac arrhythmias
Amlodipine (*Norvasc*)	Arterial dilation	Hypertension, CAD/angina pectoris
Clevidipine (*Cleviprex*)	Arterial dilation	Hypertension, IV injection
Felodipine (*Plendil*)	Arterial dilation	Hypertension, CAD/angina pectoris
Isradipine (*Dynacirc, Dynacirc CR*)	Arterial dilation	Hypertension, CAD/angina pectoris
Mibefradil (*Posicor*)	Arterial dilation	Hypertension, CAD/angina pectoris
Nicardipine (*Cardene, Cardene SR*)	Arterial dilation	Hypertension, CAD/angina pectoris
Nifedipine (*Procardia, Procardia XL*)	Arterial dilation	Hypertension, CAD/angina pectoris
Nisoldipine (*Sular*)	Arterial dilation	Hypertension, CAD/angina pectoris

SR—slow release, CR—controlled release, XL—long-acting

have coronary artery disease (CAD) or supraventricular arrhythmias. Nifedipine, amlodipine, and related drugs are considered arteriolar dilators that do not have direct actions on the heart. These drugs are indicated for the treatment of hypertension and patients with CAD, particularly the variant or Prinzmetal form of angina pectoris. The calcium channel blockers and their main uses are summarized in Table 26:4.

LO 26.6

DRUGS THAT REDUCE THE ACTIVITY OF ANGIOTENSIN II

There are several drug classes that interfere with the activation of the renin-angiotensin-aldosterone (RAA) mechanism. Angiotensin-converting enzyme inhibitors (ACEIs) and the angiotensin receptor blockers (ARBs) are effective reducers of BP. These drugs have previously been discussed in Chapter 22 with the treatment of heart failure.

A newer class of drugs that reduce the activity of angiotensin II and RAA activation is the renin inhibitors. The first approved drug of this class is aliskiren (*Tekturna*). Aliskiren inhibits the enzymatic activity of renin. This action decreases the conversion of angiotensinogen to angiotensin I and reduces the formation of angiotensin II. Aliskiren is indicated for the treatment of hypertension and produces antihypertensive effects similar to those of ACEIs and ARBs. Aliskiren can be used alone or in combination with diuretics and other antihypertensive drugs. Adverse effects include GI disturbances such as dyspepsia, abdominal pain, and diarrhea. Also, peripheral edema, rash, increased uric acid levels that may cause gout, and formation of renal stones are possible. Table 26:5 summarizes the drugs that reduce the activity of angiotensin II and RAA activation.

Angiotensin-Converting Enzyme Inhibitors

The ACE inhibitors are an important class of drugs and are among the preferred therapies for treatment of hypertension. Captopril has the shortest plasma half-life and duration of action of all the ACEIs and is administered two to three times daily. The remaining ACEIs have longer half-lives and usually require only once-daily dosing.

Mechanism of Action

Angiotensin II is involved in the normal regulation of blood volume and pressure. It is a potent vasoconstrictor that also stimulates the release of aldosterone and ADH. As previously illustrated in Chapter 22, Figure 22.3, the ACEIs inhibit the formation of angiotensin II and decrease the release of aldosterone and antidiuretic hormone. These actions lower blood pressure by causing a balanced vasodilation of both arteries and veins. In addition, ACEIs also inhibit inactivation of bradykinin, which also produces vasodilation.

The ACEIs are well tolerated and cause less interference with mental and physical performance when compared to some of the adrenergic blockers. Also, the ACEIs do not increase plasma lipids or interfere with insulin and blood glucose regulation. Renal function is usually increased in patients with kidney disease.

Adverse Effects

Common adverse effects associated with the ACE inhibitors include headache, dizziness, gastrointestinal disturbances, and rash. Overdosage can cause hypotension and reflex tachycardia. Since the ACE inhibitors decrease the actions of aldosterone, they cause retention of potassium and possible hyperkalemia. Less frequent is the development of a nonproductive cough and allergic reactions, which can include angioedema (swelling) of the face and oral cavity. The cough and allergic reactions are thought to be related to increased bradykinin levels. ACEIs are contraindicated in pregnancy due to the risk of infant renal failure and death.

Angiotensin Receptor Blocking Drugs

The receptor for the vascular effects of angiotensin II is the angiotensin-1 (AT_1) receptor. Angiotensin receptor blockers (ARBs) bind to the AT_1 receptor and competitively antagonize the actions of angiotensin II. This inhibits activation of the RAA mechanism to produce vasodilation and increased excretion of sodium and

[Table **26:5**]

Drugs That Reduce the Activity of Angiotensin II

Drug (*Trade Name*)	Mechanism of action	Therapeutic effects
Angiotensin-converting enzyme (ACE) inhibitors		
Benazepril (*Lotensin*) Captopril (*Capoten*) Enalapril (*Vasotec*) Fosinopril (*Monopril*) Lisinopril (*Prinivil, Zestril*) Moexipril (*Univasc*) Perindopril (*Aceon*) Quinapril (*Accupril*) Ramipril (*Altace*) Trandolapril (*Mavik*)	ACE inhibitors block the enzymatic conversion of angiotensin I to angiotensin II, decrease the release of aldosterone and ADH. This produces a balanced vasodilation of both arteries and veins and reduces sodium and water retention. ACEIs also increase bradykinin levels, which contributes to the vasodilating effect	Vasodilation, decreased peripheral resistance/BP. In CHF, ACEIs decrease pre- and afterload, increase CO, and reverse cardiac remodeling
Angiotensin receptor blockers (ARBs)		
Candesartan (*Atacand*) Irbesartan (*Avapro*) Losartan (*Cozaar*) Olmesartan (*Benicar*) Telmisartan (*Micardis*) Valsartan (*Diovan*)	All ARBs block the binding of angiotensin II to the angiotensin-1 (AT_1) receptor. Effects are similar to the ACE inhibitors, except that ARBs do not increase bradykinin levels	Vasodilation, decreased peripheral resistance/BP. In CHF, ACEIs decrease pre- and afterload, increase CO, and reverse cardiac remodeling
Renin inhibitors		
Aliskiren (*Tekturna*)	Inhibits the enzymatic activity of renin and decreases the formation of angiotensin I and angiotensin II	Vasodilation, decreased peripheral resistance/BP

water, effects similar to those of the ACEIs. A comparison of the sites of action and main effects of both ACEIs and ARBs is illustrated in Chapter 22, Figure 22.3. Unlike the ACEIs, the ARBs do not increase bradykinin concentrations. Losartan (*Cozaar*) was the first drug of this class to be approved. Unlike the other ARBs, losartan is partially metabolized into an active metabolite that is a more potent ARB than the parent drug. The ARBs are orally active drugs and usually require only once-daily dosing.

Adverse effects of ARBs are similar to those of the ACEIs and include headache, dizziness, hypotension, hyperkalemia, and GI disturbances. Because the ARBs do not increase bradykinin concentrations, they do not usually cause the dry cough and allergic reactions associated with the ACEIs. Like the ACEIs, the ARBs are contraindicated during pregnancy.

LO 26.7
TREATMENT OF HYPERTENSIVE CRISIS

Hypertensive crisis is a condition in which severe hypertension suddenly develops, usually in individuals who have untreated hypertension or in response to some acute disease state. When BP is extremely high and there is vascular inflammation and necrosis of blood vessels, the condition is referred to as **malignant hypertension.** Immediate parenteral therapy is usually required to reduce BP and avoid serious complications. Several vasodilator drugs produce rapid effects when administered IV. These include diazoxide and sodium nitroprusside.

Diazoxide (*Hyperstat*)

Structurally, diazoxide is similar to the thiazide diuretics. It is a very potent vasodilator, but it has no diuretic activity. It is used in hypertensive emergencies when a rapid reduction of BP is essential. Diazoxide is administered via IV injection. A 300-mg bolus is injected over a 10-minute interval. The hypotensive effects usually last 6 to 12 hours. The main adverse effects of diazoxide involve fluid retention, tachycardia, and hyperglycemia.

Sodium Nitroprusside (*Nipride*)

Sodium nitroprusside is a potent vasodilating agent used in hypertensive emergencies. Administered by slow intravenous infusion, the normal dose is approximately 3 mcg per kg per minute. Since the drug becomes chemically altered when exposed to light, precautions, such as wrapping the bottle with foil, are necessary. The duration of action is short, usually 1 to 5 minutes.

LO 26.8
PATIENT EDUCATION AND MONITORING

Essential hypertension is a chronic disease. It requires lifelong treatment and medical supervision. Often, people who are told they have high BP have experienced no symptoms. However, once drug therapy begins, they may experience some drug side effects and often claim they were better off before they began treatment. Patients frequently skip doses or take only one medication of a multiple-drug regimen in order to reduce side effects or save money. Patients must understand the importance of taking all of their medications at the proper times. It is also important for hypertensive patients to have regular medical checkups to ensure that their BP is under control and that the medications are not producing any deleterious effects.

LO 26.9
PREFERRED THERAPY FOR TREATMENT OF HYPERTENSION

As with most cardiovascular conditions, the selection of therapy often depends on other existing disease conditions that the patient may have. The drugs with the longest record of proven effectiveness to reduce high blood pressure and prevent mortality are the diuretics and beta-blockers. These drugs are often the preferred therapy of mild to moderate uncomplicated hypertension. The ACEIs and ARBs have a proven record of effectiveness and along with diuretics and beta-blockers have become the most frequently prescribed antihypertensive drugs. The ability of ACEIs and ARBs to improve renal function makes them a preferred choice for most patients with renal disease. Use of calcium channel blockers or beta-blockers in hypertensive patients who also have ischemic heart disease or cardiac arrhythmias can effectively treat both conditions. Adrenergic blocking drugs (alpha-blockers, beta-blockers, adrenergic neuronal blockers, and centrally acting drugs) would be indicated in patients where excessive sympathetic activation is present. Consequently the choice of drugs and preferred therapy depend on the clinical condition of the individual patient and consideration of the potential adverse effects any drug might cause to the patient. Since different patients often respond differently to different drugs, there is often a trial period to determine the drug or drugs that will be most effective in any one patient.

Note to the Health Care Professional

Patients must be aware that untreated or uncontrolled hypertension is the leading cause of death and disability in the United States. Complications include stroke, heart disease, kidney disease, and blindness. Nonpharmacological measures are important for controlling blood pressure. Dietary measures (sodium restriction), attaining normal body weight, elimination of smoking, exercise, and reducing stress can often lower blood pressure and reduce the amount of drug required.

Patient Administration and Monitoring

Monitor vital signs during parenteral administration of antihypertensive drugs, especially during the treatment of hypertensive crisis.

Explain to patient the nondrug factors that can lower blood pressure and the importance of taking all medications exactly as prescribed.

Explain to patient the common side effects of the prescribed drugs (review individually).

Instruct patient to report extreme weakness, faintness, or other signs of excessive reduction of blood pressure and to report significant changes in pulse or respiratory rate.

Instruct patient to check with the physician or pharmacist before taking over-the-counter drugs.

Explain to patient that excessive alcohol consumption may intensify the effects of blood pressure medication, and to check with the physician regarding the use of alcohol.

Chapter Review

Understanding Terminology

Match the definition in the left column with the appropriate term in the right column. **(LO 26.1)**

___ 1. Measured in beats per minute.

___ 2. Hypertension with no known cause.

___ 3. Amount of blood pumped by the heart per minute.

___ 4. Abnormally high blood pressure.

___ 5. Resistance generated by the flow of blood through the arteries.

___ 6. Blood pressure.

___ 7. Hypertension with a known cause.

a. BP

b. CO

c. essential hypertension

d. HR

e. hypertension

f. PR

g. secondary hypertension

Answer the following questions.

8. Define the following terms and explain their relationship: *CO, HR, SV.* **(LO 26.1)**

9. What is the relationship between *BP, CO,* and *PR?* **(LO 26.1)**

Acquiring Knowledge

Answer the following questions.

1. Describe the antihypertensive action of the diuretics. **(LO 26.3)**

2. What role do the kidneys play in hypertension? **(LO 26.2)**

3. What is the mechanism of action of each of the drug classes to lower blood pressure? **(LO 26.3, 26.4, 26.5, 26.6)**

4. Briefly describe the function of the renin-angiotensin-aldosterone (RAA) mechanism. What drugs decrease the actions of this system? **(LO 26.2, 26.6)**

5. What are the two main effects of propranolol to lower blood pressure? **(LO 26.4)**

6. What effect do all sympathetic blocking drugs have in common? **(LO 26.4)**

7. Where is the site of action of clonidine? What are the adverse effects of clonidine? **(LO 26.4)**

8. List two adverse effects associated with each antihypertensive drug class. **(LO 26.3, 26.4, 26.5, 26.6)**

9. What is hypertensive crisis? What drugs are used to treat it? **(LO 26.7)**

10. What two preferred antihypertensive drug classes have been shown to reduce mortality? **(LO 26.9)**

Applying Knowledge on the Job

Use your critical-thinking skills to answer the following questions.

1. During a regular physical exam Mr. Johnson, who is moderately overweight and claims to smoke 10 to 15 cigarettes per day, records a blood pressure reading of 141/91. What might you tell Mr. Johnson concerning his blood pressure? Should he be put on antihypertensive medication? **(LO 26.8)**

2. Mrs. Cox is brought into the emergency room after passing out. She is sweating profusely and claims to have a pounding headache. You take her vital signs, and her blood pressure reads 215/125. **(LO 26.7)**
   a. What is your diagnosis?
   b. What needs to be done?
   c. What are some of the drugs that may be indicated?

3. Mrs. Goodman has stage 2 hypertension and has been prescribed chlorothiazide (*Diuril*) and lisinopril (*Prinivil*) for several years. Her blood pressure reads 155/97. Upon questioning she admits that she usually only takes the diuretic and skips the other drug since it is so expensive. **(LO 26.8)**
   a. What should you tell Mrs. Goodman?
   b. Is there anything that could be done to increase her drug compliance?

Multiple Choice Questions

Use your critical-thinking skills to answer the following questions.

1. The desired antihypertensive effects of adrenergic beta-blocking drugs include **(LO 26.4)**
   A. decrease in heart rate
   B. decrease in cardiac output
   C. decrease in release of renin
   D. all statements are true

2. The antihypertensive action of hydrochlorothiazide includes **(LO 26.3)**
   A. reduction of blood volume
   B. blockade of alpha adrenergic receptors
   C. relaxation of vascular smooth muscle
   D. only A and C are true

3. A decrease in the formation of angiotensin II and an increase in the concentration of bradykinin explains the vasodilator action of **(LO 26.6)**
   A. alpha-blockers
   B. beta-blockers
   C. angiotensin-converting enzyme inhibitors
   D. angiotensin receptor blockers

4. The drug that is classified as an arterial vasodilator and that also has a direct effect to decrease heart rate and cardiac contractility is **(LO 26.5)**
   A. verapamil
   B. propranolol
   C. prazosin
   D. captopril

5. The antihypertensive drug that decreases sympathetic activity by an action on the vasomotor center in the medulla oblongata is **(LO 26.4)**
   A. hydralazine
   B. clonidine
   C. diltiazem
   D. losartan

Multiple Choice (Multiple Answer)

Select the correct choices for each statement. The choices may be all correct, all incorrect, or any combination.

1. The release of renin causes which of the following? **(LO 26.2)**
   A. activation of RNA mechanism
   B. vasodilation
   C. water excretion
   D. decreased blood pressure

2. Thiazide diuretics help treat hypertension by doing what? **(LO 26.3)**
   A. decreasing blood volume
   B. increasing cardiac output
   C. decreasing peripheral resistance
   D. increasing secretion of sodium

3. Clonidine works to reduce blood pressure by which of the following actions? **(LO 26.4)**
   A. increasing sympathetic nerve activity
   B. stimulating inhibitory alpha-2 receptors
   C. dilating blood vessels
   D. decreasing the release of renin in the kidneys

4. Verapamil is used to treat hypertension in individuals who also suffer from which ailments? **(LO 26.5)**
   A. CAD
   B. CHF
   C. supraventricular arrhythmias
   D. tachycardia

5. Select the medications used to treat malignant hypertension. **(LO 26.7)**
   A. guanabenz
   B. diazoxide
   C. carvedilol
   D. terazosin

Sequencing

Place the following in order of lowest blood pressure to highest. (LO 26.1)

_____	_____	_____	_____	_____
Lowest				**Highest**

large veins

aterioles

aorta

capillaries

venules

Classification

Place the following medications under the correct mechanism of action. (LO 26.7)

fosinopril	enalapril	valsartan
telmisartan	losartan	olmesartan
irbesartan	ramipril	lisinopril
quinapril		

Block conversion of angiotensin I to angiotensin II	Block binding of angiotension II to AT$_1$ receptor

Documentation

Using the following symptoms in a patient's chart, answer the following questions. (LO 26.7)

Symptoms

Blood pressure is extremely high

Vascular inflammation

Necrosis of blood vessels

a. What medical condition is this patient suffering from?

b. Should this patient be treated immediately or can we wait for additional tests?

c. What medications would most likely be used to treat this patient?

d. What adverse effects should the patient be aware may occur after dosing?

Labeling

Fill in the missing labels. (LO 26.1, 26.3, 26.4, 26.5, 26.6)

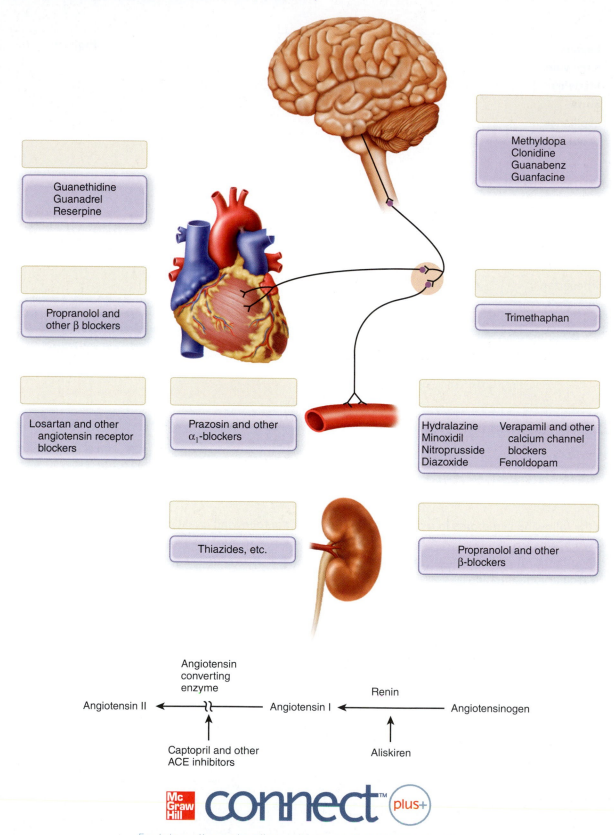

Methyldopa
Clonidine
Guanabenz
Guanfacine

Guanethidine
Guanadrel
Reserpine

Propranolol and
other β blockers

Trimethaphan

Losartan and other
angiotensin receptor
blockers

Prazosin and other
α₁-blockers

Hydralazine   Verapamil and other
Minoxidil   calcium channel
Nitroprusside   blockers
Diazoxide   Fenoldopam

Thiazides, etc.

Propranolol and other
β-blockers

Angiotensin
converting
enzyme

Renin

Angiotensin II ← Angiotensin I ← Angiotensinogen

Captopril and other
ACE inhibitors

Aliskiren

Chapter 27

Anticoagulants and Coagulants

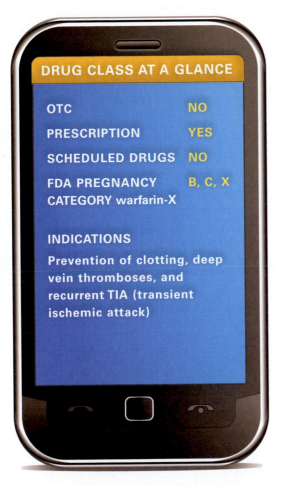

DRUG CLASS AT A GLANCE

OTC	NO
PRESCRIPTION	YES
SCHEDULED DRUGS	NO
FDA PREGNANCY CATEGORY warfarin-X	B, C, X

INDICATIONS

Prevention of clotting, deep vein thromboses, and recurrent TIA (transient ischemic attack)

KEY TERMS

acute coronary syndrome: term used to cover any group of clinical symptoms compatible with acute myocardial ischemia.

acute myocardial ischemia: chest pain due to insufficient blood supply to the heart muscle that results from coronary artery disease.

agranulocytosis: condition in which the number of white blood cells, in particular the granulocytes, is less than normal.

alopecia: baldness or hair loss.

coagulation: process by which the blood changes from a liquid to a solid "plug" as a reaction to local tissue injury; normal blood clot formation.

deep vein thrombosis (DVT): a blood clot that forms in a vein deep inside the body.

hematuria: appearance of blood or red blood cells in the urine.

hemorrhage: loss of blood from blood vessels.

infarction: area of tissue that has died because of a sudden lack of blood supply.

mucopolysaccharide: naturally occurring substance formed by the combination of protein with carbohydrates (saccharides).

peripheral arterial disease (PAD): Narrowing and hardening of the arteries that supply the legs and feet.

thrombocyte: cell in the blood, commonly called a platelet, that is necessary for coagulation.

thromboembolism: clots that jam a blood vessel; formed by the action of platelets and other coagulation factors in the blood.

thrombophlebitis: inflammation of the walls of the veins, associated with clot formation.

thrombus: clot formed by the action of coagulation factors and circulating blood cells.

27.1 describe the mechanism by which a blood clot forms and is dissolved.

27.2 explain the two ways the commonly used anti-coagulants inhibit clot formation.

27.3 explain why heparin must be administered by injection.

27.4 describe the primary response to anticoagulant overdose and routine tests used to monitor anticoagulants.

27.5 explain when clot dissolution is clinically useful.

27.6 explain the action for drugs that are useful to promote clotting.

27.7 describe the adverse effects of anticoagulants and fibrinolytic drugs.

27.8 explain terminology associated with drugs that affect coagulation.

Introduction

Clot formation is essential to survival. Usually, a blood clot acts as a seal that prevents the further loss of blood, oxygen, and nutrients from a wounded area. In addition, factors present in the clot promote wound healing by signaling other cells (phagocytes) to carry off waste products and dead cells that accumulate at the site of injury. This protective mechanism (hemostasis) is always functioning to maintain homeostasis. Occasionally, the mechanism of clot formation becomes too active or the blood vessels become too narrow (atherosclerosis) to allow the clots to pass through easily. As a result, clots may become jammed in blood vessels, forming a **thromboembolism,** which prevents the normal flow of blood to other tissues. The heart, the lungs, and the brain are especially susceptible to damage caused by a loss or reduction in blood flow subsequent to thrombosis. Anticoagulants are used to prevent venous clotting in patients who have thromboembolic disorders because these drugs interfere with the ability of the blood to form stable clots.

COAGULATION

Drugs that affect the coagulation pathway (anticoagulants, antiplatelets, and thrombolytics) are the mainstay of clot prevention, whether given prophylactically prior to a thrombotic episode or to reduce recurrence of thrombi in the management of peripheral vascular disease or following heart attack. To understand how any of these drugs work, the process of normal blood clot formation **(coagulation)** must be understood. Platelets and clotting factors are responsible for initiating coagulation.

When an injury occurs, platelets **(thrombocytes)** immediately migrate to the damaged area. Because platelets stick to each other (aggregation) and to the vessel walls (adhesion), they form a plug around the injured tissue as depicted in Figure 27.1. Plasma clotting factors reach the platelet plug and interact with each other to form a stable blood clot. Hemostasis is the balance between clot formation and clot breakdown that occurs throughout the day. This process occurs in four stages.

A stable blood clot is produced in three stages:

Stage 1. A substance known as thromboplastin is produced.

Thromboplastin is produced by two different mechanisms—the intrinsic and extrinsic systems (see Figure 27.2). The intrinsic system requires many clotting factors and platelets to stimulate production of thromboplastin. In contrast, the extrinsic system requires factor VII and tissue extract, a substance that is released from injured cells. Regardless of the pathway involved, once thromboplastin is produced, clotting proceeds automatically.

Stage 2. Thromboplastin converts prothrombins to thrombin.

Stage 3. Thrombin converts fibrinogen to fibrin and activates several clotting factors (V, VIII, XIII,

Figure 27.1   Hemostasis

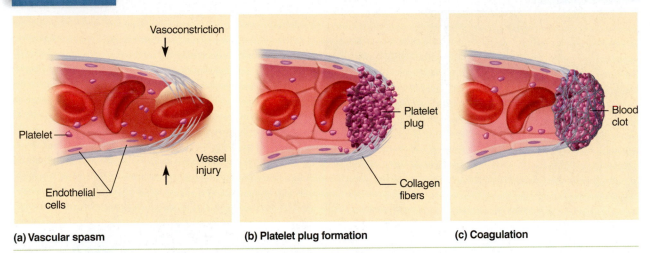

(a) Vascular spasm

(b) Platelet plug formation

(c) Coagulation

(a) Vasoconstriction of a broken vessel reduces bleeding. **(b)** A platelet plug forms as platelets adhere to exposed collagen fibers of the vessels. **(c)** A blood clot forms as platelets become enmeshed in fibrin threads. This forms a longer-lasting seal and gives the vessel a chance to repair itself.

Figure 27.2   Clotting Factor Cascades

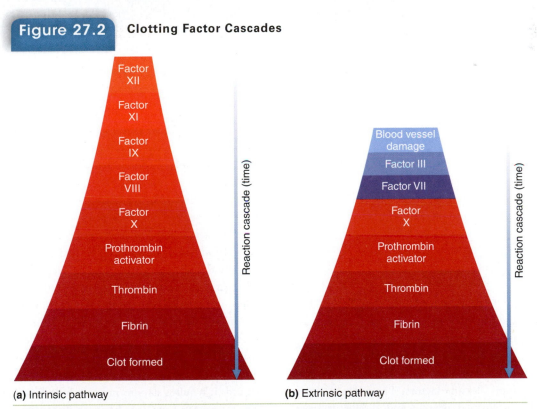

(a) Intrinsic pathway

(b) Extrinsic pathway

Two pathways through which clots are formed. Each clotting factor produces many molecules of the next one, so the number of active clotting factors increases rapidly and a large amount of fibrin is quickly formed.

and protein C). Fibrin is the primary element of a blood clot, and these activated factors build a fibrin mesh that holds the platelets (developing clot) together. Figure 27.3 shows platelets and red blood cells entangled in sticky fibrin threads that form the fabric for clot formation. The factors necessary for clot formation require calcium ions in order to function efficiently. Vitamin K is required for the synthesis of many of the factors in the coagulation pathway, specifically, prothrombin (factor II), proconvertin (factor VII), plasma thromboplastin component (factor IX), and Stuart factor (X).

Figure 27.3 A Blood Clot (SEM, Scanning Electron Micrograph)

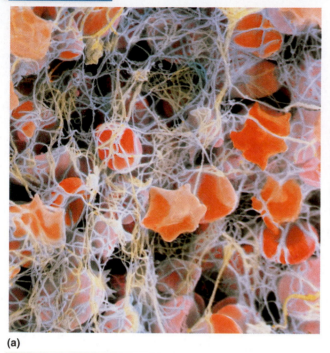

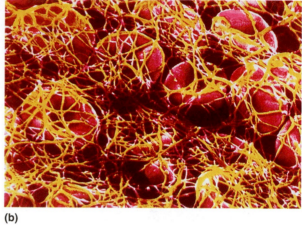

(a)

(b)

(a) Platelets (orange) and (b) red blood cells are seen trapped in a sticky fibrin protein mesh.

Usually, the clot is dissolved once its function has ended.

Stage 4: Plasmin is formed from the conversion of plasminogen by tissue plasminogen activator (tPA). Plasmin is an enzyme that acts upon the fibrin elements to produce a more soluble product.

ANTICOAGULANT MECHANISMS OF ACTION

The clinically useful anticoagulants produce their pharmacological response by interfering with plasma clotting factors, inhibiting platelet aggregation, or dissolving clots.

Heparins, antithrombins, and warfarin anticoagulants inhibit plasma clotting factors. These drugs either attach to the preformed protein and disable it from performing its normal function or alter the formation of special proteins that are essential to the coagulation process.

Heparin and the antithrombin inhibitors prevent thrombin formation by binding to circulating clotting factors, thromboplastin and glycoprotein IIa. This prevents the coagulation cascade that thrombin activates (Table 27:1). The oral anticoagulant, warfarin, prevents the synthesis of several vitamin K–dependent clotting factors, in particular factors VII, IX, X, and prothrombin. Vitamin K is essential for activation of these factors so they can bind to the epithelial walls of blood vessels. If vitamin K is removed, the factors remain inactive precursors and clot formation is inhibited. Warfarin targets the enzyme that permits vitamin K to participate in the biochemical activation pathway.

The mechanism of anticoagulation determines the onset and duration of drug action. Heparin has a quick onset and duration of action because the anticoagulant effect occurs as soon as the thromboplastin-drug complex is formed. Warfarin has a long onset and duration of action because it takes days to clear the normal clotting factors from the circulation before an effect can be observed. Similarly, once normal protein synthesis has been interrupted, it requires days to produce fully functioning clotting factors after the drug has been discontinued.

Antiplatelet drugs include aspirin, dipyridamole, clopidogrel, and ticlopidine. These drugs inhibit platelet aggregation so the platelet plug does not form, or they block platelet adhesion so the plug does not attach to the wall of the blood vessel and block blood flow. These drugs make the platelets less sticky by directly inhibiting adenosine diphosphate (ADP)–mediated platelet aggregation. The onset of action varies from a few hours to a few days.

Anticoagulant Drug Effect on Clotting Factors

Anticoagulant drug	Clotting factor affected		Vitamin K dependent
Heparins	II	Thrombin	No
	III	Antithrombin	No
	X	Stuart–Prower factor	Yes
	XIII	Fibrin stabilizing factor	No
Oral anticoagulants warfarin, sodium	II	Prothrombin	Yes
	VII	Proconvertin	Yes
	IX	Plasma thromboplastin component	Yes
	X	Stuart–Prower factor	Yes
	—	Protein C and S	Yes
Thrombin inhibitors argatroban, bivalirudin, lepirudin	IIa	Thrombin	No
Chelators	IV	Calcium ions	No
Antiplatelet drugs aspirin, clopidogrel, dipyridamole, ticlopidine	—	Platelet viscosity, aggregation and adhesion	No

Thrombolytics either are complex with the plasminogen activator proteins (streptokinase) or *are* the activator protein, tPA, tissue plasminogen activator (alteplase, reteplase, tenecteplase). While the onset of action begins as soon as they are distributed to the site, it is slower for those drugs that must complex with plasminogen activator proteins.

[LO 27.2] [LO 27.3]
[LO 27.4] [LO 27.7] [LO 27.8]

HEPARINS

The class of heparins is comprised of two groups: standard heparin and low-molecular-weight (LMW) heparins (enoxaparin, dalteparin). Heparin is a naturally occurring **mucopolysaccharide** first identified in 1928. Then, as now, the main source of heparin was extraction from the lungs and intestines of cattle and pigs. Standard heparin, also called unfractionated heparin, contains the full complement of saccharides of endogenous heparin. Recently, several low-molecular-weight heparins have become available. These LMW heparins are derived from porcine heparin but only contain an active anticoagulant fraction of heparin. This accounts for their smaller, lower molecular weight. The LMW heparins

interfere with the coagulation cascade, but they cannot produce the same spectrum of interference as standard heparin. For this reason, the LMW proteins are not interchangeable with standard heparin.

Heparins, including LMW heparins, are considered peripherally acting anticoagulants because their anionic (negatively charged) character complexes with circulating clotting factors. As long as heparin is in contact with the clotting factors, coagulation is depressed and clot formation is inhibited. All heparins bind antithrombin and increase the speed of its inactivation of factor X. The LMW heparins are more effective at binding active factor X, but standard heparin is more effective at inactivating factor XIII (fibrin-stabilizing factor) and binding thrombin (active factor II). This advantage with standard heparin is due to the additional chain of saccharides the LMW heparins don't have. Standard heparin also depresses platelet aggregation, which the LMW heparins cannot do.

Lipolysis

In addition to the anticoagulant action, heparin has the ability to clear fatty molecules from the plasma. Heparin stimulates an enzyme (lipoprotein lipase) that hydrolyzes the triglycerides in the blood. This enzyme reaction reduces large fat molecules in the plasma. This effect has no influence on heparin's anticoagulant action, and its physiological importance is not fully understood. Eventually, heparin is metabolized by the liver or excreted unchanged into the urine. Patients with renal impairment or kidney disease tend to accumulate heparin because they cannot efficiently clear it from the blood. Due to the size of the molecules, the heparins do not cross the placenta and cannot affect the developing fetus. Heparin is always the preferred drug when an anticoagulant must be given to a pregnant woman.

Route of Administration

No heparin can be administered by mouth because gastric acid would destroy the mucopolysaccharide. Standard heparin, therefore, is usually administered intravenously or subcutaneously. LMW heparins are only administered subcutaneously. Intramuscular injection should be avoided because painful hematomas can occur. The advantage of the LMW heparins is that the bioavailability is almost complete (90 percent) following subcutaneous administration compared to standard heparin (30 percent). In addition, in patients with normal renal function, the LMW heparins can be dosed based on body size without coagulation test monitoring. Standard heparin requires periodic coagulation monitoring to adjust the therapeutic dose, minimizing the bleeding potential and maintaining adequate clot suppression.

Onset of Action

The onset of action for all heparins is rapid, within 5 minutes, and the duration of action is usually 2 to 5 hours. Drugs derived from animal sources must undergo a standard biological assay to determine their purity, quality, and potency. Drugs such as heparin are administered in units of activity rather than milligrams. One hundred United States Pharmacopeia (USP) units correspond to approximately 1 mg of commercially prepared heparin. Because bioequivalence problems have been encountered with heparin products, products from different manufacturers should not be interchanged in an individual patient. Although the LMW heparins are fragments from the same parent, these drugs cannot be interchanged with standard heparin due to the variability in the anticoagulant activity. Moreover, there is no conversion that would predict a bioequivalent dosing to standard heparin.

Despite the newer heparins, standard heparin use is increasing. Standard heparin is indicated for arterial and venous thrombotic conditions.

Adverse Effects

The major toxicity associated with the use of heparin is **hemorrhage.** At high levels, heparin causes bleeding to occur in mucous membranes (petechiae) and open wounds, such as scratches, cuts, and abrasions. If hemorrhage occurs in the gastrointestinal (GI) membranes, patients' blood pressure and hematocrit may fall even though there are no external signs of bleeding. The dose and frequency of administration should be reduced when hemorrhage is evident. Use in elderly patients requires special attention because enoxaparin elimination may be delayed. Anemia has been reported with enoxaparin.

Other side effects seen with any chronic heparin use include hypersensitivity, fever, **alopecia** (hair loss), osteoporosis, and thrombocytopenia (decrease in the number of blood platelets). Thrombocytopenia occurs occasionally in patients receiving heparin who are undergoing orthopedic or cardiopulmonary bypass surgery. The occurrence is dose-related and occurs more frequently with bovine heparin than porcine heparin. The thrombocytopenia is confirmed by a reduction in platelets by 50 percent (fewer than 50,000 mm^3) within 2 weeks of initiating treatment. As the thrombocytopenia develops, the patient may have no symptoms such as bleeding that would indicate the evolving condition. The decrease in platelets appears to be mediated through an immune response; however, it is not the heparin molecule that stimulates the development of antibodies. Rather, heparin complexes with platelet factor 4 (PF-4) and binds to the platelet membrane. It is this complex that is immunogenic.

LMW heparins have a black box cautionary warning in the product use label that identifies a potential risk of developing epidural or spinal hematomas when these anticoagulants are administered to patients concurrently receiving epidural or spinal anesthesia. The risk of irreversible paralysis from the spinal hematoma is increased when the patient is also receiving additional anticoagulants, or with the use of indwelling catheters for the administration of analgesics, nonsteroidal antiinflammatory drugs, or other platelet inhibitors. Patients are to be monitored for signs and symptoms of neurological impairment.

Heparin Antidotes

Protamine sulfate is the specific antidote in heparin toxicity. Each milligram of protamine sulfate will neutralize 90 to 120 USP units of heparin, 1 mg of enoxaparin, or 100 International Units (IU) of dalteparin. Protamine binds to the heparin molecules and inhibits the anticoagulant action. Administration of heparin or protamine should always be accompanied by coagulation tests to determine the degree of clot suppression that is present.

Thrombin inhibitors (argatroban and bivalirudin) reversibly bind with thrombin and reduce the thrombin-catalyzed activations of factors V, VIII, XIII, protein C, and platelet aggregation. Lepirudin irreversibly binds these clotting factors. These inhibitors are highly selective for thrombin and are indicated specifically for the prophylaxis and treatment of heparin-induced thrombocytopenia. Coagulation is suppressed while heparin is withdrawn. Thrombin inhibitors are synthetic (argatroban) or recombinant rDNA hirudin (lepirudin) that mimics the anticoagulant activity of polypeptides extracted from leech saliva. Bivalirudin is approved for use in patients with unstable angina who are undergoing percutaneous transluminal coronary angioplasty (PTCA) and concurrently taking aspirin for platelet inhibition.

LO 27.2 LO 27.4 LO 27.7 LO 27.8

ORAL ANTICOAGULANT: WARFARIN SODIUM (COUMADIN)

The oral anticoagulants are represented by one drug: warfarin sodium (Coumadin, Jantoven) (see Table 27:2). Because the drug has been used for so long, it is known to patients as Coumadin. Historically, this class was originally discovered as a product of spoiled sweet clover. Cattle that grazed on the contaminated clover developed hemorrhagic disease. In addition, people who drank the milk from these cows developed hemorrhages because they ingested the active anticoagulant substance. Warfarin sodium is significantly different from heparin because it can be administered orally.

Note to the Health Care Professional

Mechanism of Action

Warfarin has no effect on preformed clots, but it may prevent secondary thromboembolic complications. Anything that decreases the availability of vitamin K (certain antibiotics, vitamin E, fish oils) enhances the anticoagulant action of warfarin.

The onset of anticoagulant activity with warfarin is slow, 12 to 72 hours. Several days may be required to produce a significant amount of nonreactive clotting factors. Similarly, the duration of action is long (2 to 10 days), even after drug administration has been discontinued. Warfarin is highly bound to plasma proteins and eventually metabolized by the liver. Both of these factors are responsible for the many drug interactions that occur with warfarin. See Table 27:3.

Adverse Effects

Side effects accompanying the use of an oral anticoagulant include nausea, diarrhea, urticaria, hypotension, fatigue, headache, and alopecia. To reduce gastrointestinal (GI) distress, the oral anticoagulant may be administered in divided doses.

Hemorrhage is always the most significant toxicity associated with the use of an anticoagulant. **Hematuria** (blood or red blood cells in the urine), bleeding of the gums, and petechiae are common side effects that reflect a nonfatal localized bleeding.

There is a boxed cautionary warning for warfarin describing risk factors associated with major or fatal hemorrhage. These factors include patients over 65 years of age, with a history of GI bleeding, serious heart or cerebral vascular disease, INR greater than 4, and long-term warfarin therapy. The recommendation is for more frequent monitoring of coagulation status to optimize dose adjustment of warfarin (see Monitoring Coagulation for INR). In the presence of more significant bleeding, that is, hemorrhage, the action of warfarin cannot be rapidly reversed by merely discontinuing the drug. In severe hemorrhage, prothrombin complex concentrate or fresh frozen plasma may be given with vitamin K to provide a full complement of normal clotting factors. The antidote for overdose, synthetic vitamin K_1 (phytonadione) 2.5 to 25 mg, is given parenterally (usually IM, SC). The parenteral vitamin gains access to the enzyme that puts it into the activation pathway. Phytonadione's response is evident within 2 hours after the antidote is given by monitoring prothrombin time. Phytonadione has the same degree of activity as the naturally occurring vitamin. Depending on the coagulation status of the patient, a small dose of oral vitamin K_1 may be sufficient. The oral formulation of synthetic vitamin K_1 phytonadione is *Mephyton*. It requires the presence of bile salts for absorption to occur.

Warfarin crosses the placenta and may produce hemorrhaging in the fetus. The fetus is dependent on the mother for its source of vitamin K and coagulation factors. Administration of oral anticoagulants during pregnancy will result in a phenomenon known as hemorrhagic

Comparison of Anticoagulant and Thrombolytic Drugs

Drug (*Trade Name*)	Daily maintenance dose	Indication*	Coagulation test used to monitor therapeutic response
Anticoagulants, oral			
Warfarin sodium (*Coumadin, Jantoven*)	2–10 mg PO	DVT and recurrent MI	Prothrombin time (protime, PT) or INR
Antiplatelet drugs			
Anagrelide (*Agrylin*)	0.5 mg QID or 1 mg BID PO	Thrombocytopenia	Routine blood and platelet counts
Cilostazol (*Pletal*)	100 mg BID before meals PO	Intermittent claudication	Routine blood and platelet counts
Clopidogrel (*Plavix*)	75 mg daily PO	Reduction of athrosclerotic events Acute coronary syndrome, MI, PAD	Routine blood and platelet counts
Dipyridamole (*Persantine*)	75 to 100 mg QID	In combination with aspirin for prevention of myocardial reinfarction	Routine blood and platelet counts
Prasugrel (*Effient*)	5–10 mg once daily with food PO	Acute coronary syndrome	Routine blood and platelet counts
Ticlopidine (*Ticlid*)	250 mg BID PO	Stroke patients intolerant to aspirin	Routine blood and platelet counts
Anticoagulants, parenteral heparins			
Dalteparin (*Fragmin*)	2500 IU/day SC, 1–2 hrs before surgery, up to 10 days postsurgery	DVT, prophylaxis and treatment of venous thrombi with or without pulmonary emobolism	Routine blood and platelet counts
Enoxaparin (*Lovenox*)	30 mg BID SC pre-knee surgery, up to 12 days postsurgery 40 mg QD SC for abdominal surgery 40 mg SC for DVT		Routine blood and platelet counts
Heparin sodium injection	10,000–12,000 units initially followed by 15,000–20,000 units every 12 hr SC; 5000–10,000 units every 4–6 hr IV		Whole blood clotting time; activated partial thromboplastin time (APTT)
Heparin sodium lock flush solution (*Heparin Lock Flush*)	**Not intended for therapeutic use; used for maintenance of indwelling IV catheters**		—
Tinzaparin (*Innohep*)	Individualized dosing SC		Routine blood and platelet counts
Thrombolytic/fibrinolytic agents			
Urokinase (*Abbokinase*)	4 ml/min (6000 units) IV up to 2 hours	Coronary artery thrombosis Catheter clearance	Periodic angiography during infusion

(Continued)

Drug (*Trade Name*)	Daily maintenance dose	Indication*	Coagulation test used to monitor therapeutic response
Tissue plasminogen activators			
Alteplase recombinant (*Activase, Cathflo Activase*)	2 mg/ml IV	Management of acute MI	Attention to all potential bleeding sites
Reteplase recombinant (*Retavase*)	10 + 10 unit double bolus injection	Acute ischemic stroke	
Tenecteplase (*TNKase*)	Individualized dosing by body weight	Acute MI	

DVT—deep venous thrombosis; MI—myocardial infarction; PAD—peripheral arterial disease.

disease of the newborn (HDN). Vitamin K_1 (phytonadione) is administered to the mother (prophylaxis) or to the newborn (treatment) when HDN is anticipated. A single intramuscular dose of 0.5 to 1 mg can be administered to the newborn within 1 hour after birth. The mother may be given oral or parenteral prophylaxis 12 to 24 hours before delivery. Intramuscular injection of 1 to 5 mg or oral doses of 2 mg have been successfully used. When an anticoagulant is required during pregnancy, the heparins are the drugs of choice because they do not cross the placenta.

LO 27.1 LO 27.2 LO 27.7 LO 27.8

ANTIPLATELET DRUGS

The class of oral antiplatelet drugs includes aspirin, dipyridamole, clopidogrel, and ticlopidine. All of these drugs are well absorbed following oral administration. Aspirin was presented in the chapter on nonsteroidal antiinflammatory drugs (NSAIDs) as a powerful inhibitor of the prostaglandins. In platelets, this enzyme pathway produces thromboxane A_2, a potent platelet aggregator and vasoconstrictor. When platelets release thromboxane A_2, it constricts blood vessels and slows blood flow so the platelets have an opportunity to stick to each other and to the wall of the blood vessel. Prostacyclin, another product of the cyclooxgenase pathway released from the blood vessel membrane, counteracts the action of thromboxane by dilating the vessels and inhibiting platelet aggregation. Normally, this balance between prostacyclin and thromboxane A_2 activity keeps the platelet plugs from significantly blocking blood flow and oxygenation of the tissues. In conditions such as arterial thrombosis, deep vein thrombosis, myocardial **infarction,** and stroke, platelets increase thromboxane

production and demonstrate an increased sensitivity to aggregate.

Aspirin in doses from 81 mg (baby aspirin) to 325 mg (adult analgesic dose) irreversibly alters platelet cyclooxygenase. Platelets do not have a nucleus and, therefore, do not have the internal machinery to make new cyclooxygenase. Thromboxane cannot be generated until new platelets are formed. Although aspirin also blocks prostacyclin, the blood vessels are able to synthesize new cyclooxygenase within a few hours.

Clopidogrel (*Plavix*), cilostazol (*Pletal*), prasugrel (*Effient*), and ticlopidine (*Ticlid*) inhibit platelet aggregation by blocking adenosine diphosphate (ADP) binding to membrane receptors and preventing ADP activation of glycoproteins IIa/IIIB in the coagulation cascade. They do not have any effect on the cyclooxygenase pathway like aspirin. These drugs irreversibly modify the receptor so the platelet cannot respond to ADP for the rest of its life span (8 to 11 days).

Dipyridamole (*Persantine*) and the combination of dipyridamole and aspirin (*Aggrenox*) are weak platelet inhibitors. They reversibly interfere with platelet aggregation by increasing adenosine, an inhibitor of platelet reactivity, and inhibiting phosphodiesterase within the platelets. Cilostazol (*Pletal*) and its metabolites are phosphodiesterase inhibitors (PDE).

Aspirin is the most inexpensive, effective antiplatelet drug recommended by physicians to reduce the incidence of clots that might injure the heart. Aspirin in doses not greater than 325 mg a day is recommended for the prevention of thrombi, stroke, and heart attack. Aspirin also prevents transient ischemic attacks (TIAs) in stroke patients but has no action on the formed clot. Aspirin is considered as effective or more effective with fewer serious adverse effects compared to the newer antiplatelet drugs. Doses of aspirin greater than 1000 mg daily are no more effective as an antithrombotic and usually increase the side effects. Clopidogrel is significantly more costly than aspirin and is used to reduce myocardial infarction, stroke, and death, especially in patients who are sensitive to the gastrointestinal bleeding induced by aspirin. Dipyridamole is used for prevention of thromboembolism after heart valve replacement surgery. The antiplatelet drugs are used in combination to produce clinically significant reductions in reinfarction and death following myocardial infarction.

Adverse Effects

Common less serious side effects associated with antiplatelet drugs are similar to aspirin and include headache, vomiting, rash, diarrhea, and dizziness. Cilostazol is contraindicated in patients with congestive heart failure. Ticlopidine and clopidogrel can produce severe thrombocytopenia, a dramatic reduction in platelets that does not allow the patient to clot so internal bleeding occurs. Because ticlopidine causes life-threatening anemias including neutropenia, **agranulocytosis,** thrombotic thrombocytopenic purpura (TTP), and aplastic anemia, this drug has a special boxed cautionary warning for its use.

LO 27.7 | **LO 27.8**

SPECIAL CONSIDERATIONS AND CONTRAINDICATIONS WITH ANTICOAGULANTS

Ideally, anticoagulant therapy should be administered at the same time daily. Whenever medications are added to or deleted from the regimen of patients receiving an anticoagulant, the patients' coagulation status is subject to change. Patients should therefore be carefully observed for signs of increased bleeding or hemorrhage. Fever or rash that develops during anticoagulant therapy should be regarded as an indication of potential complication. Patients must be advised to adhere strictly to the prescribed dose schedule for oral anticoagulants. Oral medication should not be discontinued unless on the specific advice of the treating physician.

All heparin vials should be examined carefully to confirm the correct strength has been selected prior to administration of the drug. Heparin Sodium Injection should not be used as a "catheter lock flush" product. Heparin sodium injection is supplied in vials containing various concentrations of heparin, ranging from 1,000 to 40,000 units per ml. The catheter lock flush vials (*Heparin IV Flush, Heparin Lock Flush*) range in concentration

from 1 to 100 units/ml, a tremendous difference in concentration compared to HIS. Fatal hemorrhages have occurred in pediatric patients due to medication errors in which 1 ml Heparin Sodium Injection vials were confused with 1 ml "catheter lock flush" vials. Heparin packaging has changed, and many hospitals are working to tighten up dispensing techniques. To minimize the opportunity for error, prefilled heparin syringes are color-coded and labeled to indicate the contents as shown in Figure 27.4.

Heparin is often administered by intermittent intravenous infusion. Concomitant parenteral medications should not be administered into the heparin infusion line (piggyback) to avoid potential incompatibility reactions that would inactivate the anticoagulants. The low-molecular-weight anticoagulants should not be mixed with other injects or infusions. Drug solutions known to be physically incompatible with heparin are presented in Table 27:3.

Contraindications

Anticoagulants of any type are contraindicated in patients with subacute bacterial endocarditis, ulcerative lesions (GI), visceral carcinoma, threatened abortion, severe hypertension, and recent surgery on the brain or spinal cord. Any patient with active bleeding tendencies should not receive anticoagulants.

All heparins are contraindicated in patients with a hypersensitivity to individual heparins, pork products, sulfites, benzyl alcohol, or heparin-induced thrombocytopenia.

The oral anticoagulants should not be used in patients known to be vitamin K deficient. The most important contraindication for the oral anticoagulants is the use of these drugs during pregnancy. Remember warfarin crosses the placenta and can produce hemorrhaging in the fetus.

LO 27.4 | **LO 27.8**

MONITORING COAGULATION

The dosage of any anticoagulant is individualized to the patient. The therapeutic dosage is established and maintained by evaluation of the patient's clotting time. Once a patient is stabilized, coagulation may be monitored every 4 to 6 weeks. To avoid the danger of hemorrhage due to too much anticoagulant, the coagulability of the blood should be measured before more drug is administered. Among the tests used to monitor coagulation status are whole blood clotting time, partial thromboplastin time (PTT), prothrombin time (PT), and the international normalized ratio (INR). The INR is being used because

| Figure 27.4 | Prefilled Saline and Heparin Flush Syringes |

Saline
White tip cap & label

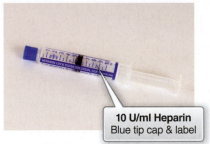

10 U/ml Heparin
Blue tip cap & label

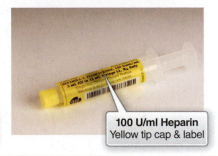

100 U/ml Heparin
Yellow tip cap & label

The prefilled syringes have distinctive colored caps and labels for the contents and heparin concentration to minimize errors in dose handling.

commercial thromboplastin response to anticoagulants varies greatly between batches. The INR calibrates the commercial rabbit thromboplastins against an international human reference standard.

The effect of heparin is most frequently assessed with the whole blood clotting time and the activated partial thromboplastin time (APTT). These tests are usually performed 1 hour prior to the next scheduled dose of heparin. When patients are on a heparin IV drip, PTT is monitored daily. Generally, the PTT is maintained at twice the normal value when heparin is employed. When drawing blood, especially for the purpose of evaluating patients' coagulation status, samples should always be taken from the opposite arm (non-IV line) to avoid false activated partial thromboplastin time (APTT) values. Because of their selective inhibition of coagulation factors that are associated with the APTT monitoring reagents, the LMW drugs cannot be monitored accurately. The therapeutic effect of the LMW drugs is assessed by routine total blood and platelet counts, and urinalysis throughout therapy. The target adjusted platelet count varies according to the overall clinical picture of the patient. As a rule, adjusted platelet counts should not drop below 30 to 50 percent of the normal range.

The oral anticoagulants must be monitored with the one-stage prothrombin time, or protime (PT) or the INR. Because of the long onset of action of these drugs, the initial dose cannot be changed for 3 to 5 days. It takes this long to achieve the peak anticoagulant response. During this time, periodic protime evaluation indicates the degree of clot suppression. People who are not taking oral anticoagulants will have a protime value of 12 seconds and an INR of 1. In the presence of an oral anticoagulant, the blood takes longer to clot so the protime value is a larger number (15 to 18 seconds). The protime may be maintained at 1.2–1.5 times the control,

which may be a 2–4 INR value. An INR of 2 to 3 is the target value for confirmation of warfarin's therapeutic effect. The National Library of Medicine maintains an interactive Web site that has a tutorial showing the relationship between PT and INR monitoring on warfarin/Coumadin at www.nlm.nih.gov/medlineplus/tutorials/coumadinintroduction/htm/lesson.htm. Heparin is known to interfere with accurate protime determinations when it is administered in conjunction with oral anticoagulants. When needed, oral anticoagulants should be given at least 5 hours after the last IV heparin dose or 24 hours after the last SC dose in order to achieve an accurate PT result.

Drug Interactions

Heparin undergoes fewer drug interactions than does the oral anticoagulant warfarin. Examples of clinically important drug interactions with heparins are presented in Table 27:3. Any drugs that are known to affect

Note to the Health Care Professional

All heparin vials should be examined carefully to confirm the correct strength has been selected prior to administration of the drug. Heparin Sodium Injection should not be used as a "catheter lock flush" product because the concentration of the heparin can be 10 to 4000 times greater than a flush preparation, resulting in a life-threatening situation.

Drug Interactions with Heparins

Heparins interact with	Response	Heparins interact with	Response

Aspirin, NSAIDs
Cephalosporins
Dextran
Oral anticoagulants
Platelet inhibitors
Penicillin (high doses)
Ticlopidine
	Increased bleeding	Antibiotics
		  Amikacin
		  Aminoglycosides
		  Cephaloridine
		  Erythromycin
		  Penicillins
		  Polymyxins
		  Tetracyclines
		Dopamine
		Hydrocortisone
		Hydroxyzine
		Methylprednisolone
		Opioid analgesics
		  Codeine
		  Morphine
		  Meperidine
		  Methadone
		Prochlorperazine
		Promethazine
		Vitamins (multiple)
			Incompatible when mixed with these solutions for parenteral infusion

Antihistamines Digitalis Nicotine Nitroglycerin IV Tetracyclines	Decreased anticoagulant action		

platelet aggregation will probably cause increased bleeding when taken concomitantly with heparin. Such drugs include nonsteroidal antiinflammatory drugs (aspirin, ibuprofen, indomethacin, phenylbutazone), dextran, and high doses of penicillin. Digitalis and tetracyclines have been reported to counteract the anticoagulant action of heparin. The mechanism of this action is not known. Diazepam plasma levels have been reported to increase with concomitant heparin therapy. Heparin is an acidic mucopolysaccharide and will precipitate when added to alkaline drugs.

Warfarin has the greatest potential for clinically significant interactions with other medications (see Table 27:4). These drugs are associated with three major sites where interaction may occur. Oral anticoagulants may be displaced from plasma protein binding sites, which may increase their plasma concentrations and toxicity. In addition, any drug that interferes with liver metabolism may increase or decrease the response of warfarin. Finally, because it is taken by mouth, absorption may be inhibited by other oral medications that bind to the anticoagulants. Several drugs, some available over the counter, such as acetaminophen, have been associated with increased bleeding with warfarin

but the mechanism or site of action has not yet been determined.

Because it is so inexpensive and available without a prescription, aspirin is arguably one of the most frequently used medications anyone can take as needed. Cardiac prophylaxis is dependent upon aspirin's antiplatelet effect sustained by taking low doses of aspirin every day. Daily use of aspirin and ibuprofen, also available over the counter, can cancel the antiplatelet effects of aspirin. The reason is that ibuprofen, a COX-1 inhibitor, can occupy the same enzymatic site in the platelets but does not have the ability to alter the active site on cyclooxygenase (COX) or inhibit thromboxane production. During this time, the patient does not have the cardioprotection of altered platelets. This interaction may extend to other COX-1 inhibitors, such as naproxen and ketoprofen. Occasional ibuprofen use does not present the liability; however, another choice of NSAID may be better to take when daily NSAID and daily aspirin prophylaxis is indicated. In general, aspirin should be taken 2 hours prior to ibuprofen so that aspirin has the opportunity to interact with the platelets first.

Tables 27:3 and 27:4 describe numerous drug interactions that occur with anticoagulant drugs. Careful

Drug Interactions with Oral Anticoagulant Warfarin

Warfarin interacts with	Response	Warfarin interacts with	Response
Chloral hydrate Loop diuretics Penicillins Salicylate, diflunisal	Increased bleeding via protein binding displacement	Amiodarone Azole antifungals Chloramphenicol Cimetidine Ifosfamide Methylphenidate Omeprazole Phenylbutazone Propafenone Quinidine Quinine Statins HMG-CoA reductase inhibitors Sulfinpyrazone Sulfamethoxazole–trimethoprim	Increased bleeding due to decreased liver metabolism of warfarin

Antibiotics
    Kanamycin
    Neomycin
    Sulfonamides
Tetracyclines
Vitamin E, fish oil
	Increased bleeding time due to decreased availability of vitamin K		

Aspirin, NSAIDs Cephalosporins Heparin Olsalazine Steroids Sulfinpyrazone Ticlopidine	Increased bleeding due to decreased platelet aggregation or interference with other clotting mechanisms		
Acetaminophen Androgens Beta-blockers Chlorpropamide Clofibrate Corticosteroids Cyclophosphamide Dextrothyroxine Disulfiram Erythromycin Glucagon Hydantoins Influenza vaccine Isoniazid Quinolone antibiotics Propoxyphene Ranitidine Tamoxifen Thyroid hormone	Increased bleeding by unknown mechanism	Cholestyramine Sulcralfate	Decreased anticoagulant effect via decreased warfarin absorption
		Oral contraceptives Estrogens Vitamin K	Decreased anticoagulant effect via stimulation of clotting factor synthesis
		Aprepitant Barbiturates Carbamazepine Griseofulvin Nafcillin Terbinafine	Decreased anticoagulant effect via increased liver metabolism of warfarin
		Ascorbic acid Ethanol Spironolactone Thiazide diuretics Vitamin K Sucralfate	Decreased anticoagulant effect by a variety of mechanisms
Adrenal corticosteroids Ethacrynic acid Phenylbutazone Potassium products Salicylates, NSAIDs	Ulcerogenic effects		

monitoring and appropriate dosage adjustments will ensure the safety of combination drug therapy in patients who receive anticoagulants.

Chelators

Several drugs inhibit coagulation by interfering with essential ions in the blood. Chelating drugs, such as edetic acid (ethylenediaminetetraacetic acid [EDTA]) and oxalic acid, bind calcium ions so that the coagulation scheme is interrupted. These agents are not routinely employed as systemic anticoagulants. However, oxalic acid in particular is present in commercially prepared test tubes to prevent the coagulation of blood taken for routine hematological tests.

LO 27.1 LO 27.5 LO 27.6 LO 27.8

FIBRINOLYTIC/THROMBOLYTIC DRUGS

Fibrinolytic drugs dissolve preformed blood clots and, therefore, are called "clotbusters." Since they work on the formed **thrombus** or fibrin clot, they are referred to as fibrinolytic or thrombolytic drugs. These enzymes convert plasminogen to active plasmin, which breaks the clot into soluble products. This class of drugs includes urokinase (*Abbokinase*), streptokinase (*Streptase*), alteplase (*Activase*), tenecteplase (*TNKase*), and reteplase (*Retavase*). Alteplase, also referred to as tissue plasminogen activator (tPA), and reteplase are thrombolytic enzymes produced through the biotechnology of recombinant DNA. Alteplase is a purified glycoprotein (527 amino acids) that binds to fibrin within the clot, stimulates conversion of plasminogen to plasmin, and initiates clot dissolution (fibrinolysis). Reteplase, derived from the alteplase glycoprotein, contains 355 of the 527 amino acids.

Thrombolytic enzymes are used to lyse pulmonary emboli and coronary artery thromboses during acute myocardial infarction. To receive maximum benefit, the enzymes must be administered as soon as possible following indications that a clot or infarct has occurred. For the treatment of acute myocardial infarction, the timing of drug administration for successful clot resolution is usually within 1 to 6 hours from the onset of symptoms. For pulmonary embolism, the time for initiation of therapy may be up to a few days. There is evidence that streptokinase is as effective as alteplase, even though the cost of alteplase therapy is tremendously more expensive than that of streptokinase. The cost of the product reflects the biotechnical development process of the drug and not necessarily a clinically significant improvement in treatment over existing products.

Dose Administration

Because thrombolytic enzymes are proteins, they are administered by parenteral infusion, usually intravenous. As proteins derived from natural sources or recombinant technology, the amount of active substance is provided as International Units (bioassay) or the milligram equivalent. Streptokinase is administered intravenously 250,000 IU over 30 minutes followed by 100,000 IU per hour up to 72 hours for the treatment of deep vein or arterial thrombosis. For the treatment of acute myocardial infarction, the available 1,500,000 IU vial diluted to 45 ml is administered as a total dose within 60 minutes. Streptokinase (and urokinase) is also used (250,000 IU per 2 ml) to clear occluded arteriovenous cannulae. Alteplase is administered as 100 mg (58 million IU) in divided doses over a 2- to 3-hour period. With tenecteplase, the entire dose is delivered over a single 5-second bolus, infusion or second bolus is not necessary.

At the end of the streptokinase or urokinase infusion, treatment usually continues with heparin infusion. Heparin is begun only after the thrombin time has decreased to less than 2 times the normal control (usually 3 to 4 hours after completion of urokinase infusion). After constant intravenous infusion (4400 units per kg per hour) urokinase is cleared (within 20 minutes) by the liver. The mechanism of streptokinase elimination is not known. Alteplase and reteplase are rapidly cleared from the blood within 5 to 10 and 15 minutes, respectively, after the infusion is terminated. Tenecteplase is metabolized by the liver and has an initial half-life of 22 minutes and a terminal half-life of 90 minutes.

Adverse Effects

The major adverse effect associated with the use of thrombolytic enzymes is hemorrhage. Concomitant use of heparin, oral anticoagulants, or drugs known to alter platelet function (aspirin and nonsteroidal antiinflammatory drugs) is not recommended because of the increased risk of bleeding. Since these drugs are protein enzymes, mild allergic reactions have occurred in patients during use. Allergic reactions include skin rash, itching, nausea, headache, fever, bronchospasm, or musculoskeletal pain. Although severe allergic reactions to enzyme therapy may require discontinuation of therapy, milder reactions are usually controlled with antihistamine or corticosteroid therapy. Contraindications to the use of thrombolytic drugs include conditions such as active internal bleeding, cerebral vascular accident (CVA) within the past 2 months, intracranial or intraspinal surgery, or intracranial tumors. Alteplase and reteplase have been associated with cardiogenic shock, arrhythmias, and recurrent ischemia among the reported adverse effects; however, these are frequent sequelae of myocardial infarction and may or may not be attributable to the drug.

Thrombolytic enzymes are available as powders (or lyophilized powders) containing varying amounts of active substance, which must be reconstituted prior to infusion. These products are stored in powder form at room temperature (15° to 30°C) or refrigerated (2° to 8°C) prior to reconstitution.

Reconstitution should occur just before use, although urokinase solution is stable for up to 24 hours, and streptokinase may be used up to 8 hours after reconstitution. Unused solutions should be discarded after that time. Alteplase has the added requirement that it be protected from excessive exposure to light. *None of these enzyme infusion solutions should have other medications added to them.*

LO 27.2 | LO 27.4 | LO 27.5 | LO 27.8

PREFERRED TREATMENT WITH ANTICOAGULANTS AND THROMBOLYTICS

The antiplatelet and anticoagulant drugs are the mainstay of clot prevention, whether given prophylactically prior to a thrombotic episode or to reduce recurrence of thrombi in the management of peripheral vascular disease or following heart attack.

Heparins

Among the heparins available today, the full mucopolysaccharide referred to as heparin is approved for the broadest spectrum of use. Heparin is approved for the prophylaxis and treatment of venous thrombosis and emboli associated with peripheral arteries and atrial fibrillation. It also is indicated for prevention of postoperative **deep vein thrombosis (DVT)** and pulmonary embolism in patients undergoing major abdominal surgery or who are at risk of developing thromboembolic disease. It is used to prevent clotting during cardiovascular surgery, transfusions, dialysis, and extracorporeal circulation, and in the diagnosis and treatment of disseminated intravascular coagulation.

Standard heparin is always the preferred drug when an anticoagulant must be given to a pregnant woman. Due to its size, standard heparin does not cross the placenta and cannot affect the developing fetus.

Low-molecular-weight heparins are approved for use in prevention of DVT in selective procedures as follows: dalteparin (abdominal surgery) and enoxaparin (knee and hip replacement and abdominal surgery). For these parenteral anticoagulants, the dose must be customized to the patient within recommended guidelines for time of administration.

Patients who are recuperating from surgery (hip and knee replacement) or have chronic inflammatory illnesses such as Crohn's disease, or vascular injury (stroke, ischemic heart disease), and women during pregnancy are more likely to develop DVT. These patients often have a period of inactivity during which the blood flow may pool or slow down, creating a stasis in the circulation that encourages clotting factors and platelets to initiate coagulation. Localized coagulation is also likely to occur when additional risk factors such as smoking or hypertension are present. The localized thrombi may be associated with vascular spasms, pain, tenderness in the legs, swelling and warmth; in half the patients, however, there are no symptoms to warn of impending danger. The most significant clinical risk in DVT is that thrombi will break loose, enter the circulation in the lungs, and block critical blood flow within the pulmonary system. This blockade could lead to tissue death due to stagnant blood flow and interrupted oxygenation of the tissues (ischemia). Pulmonary embolism can be a life-threatening condition.

Recently the risk of DVT has been extended to situations where people are confined or sitting motionless for long periods. "Economy Class" syndrome is a genuine condition associated with inactivity especially during long air flights, but it is not restricted to the economy section of the plane. Dehydration, through increased alcohol intake or reduced water consumption, reduces the blood volume (makes it relatively thicker) and fosters an environment of stasis and local clot formation.

Warfarin

Warfarin is approved for prophylaxis and treatment of venous thrombosis, **thrombophlebitis** (inflammation of the walls of the veins), pulmonary embolism, and atrial fibrillation with embolization. The oral anticoagulant is the drug of choice because warfarin is relatively inexpensive, can be easily taken by patients, and is not associated with painful administration. Other uses of warfarin include clot suppression prior to blood transfusion and during open heart surgery.

Antiplatelet Drugs

Anticoagulants and antiplatelet drugs also are indicated in coronary artery disease, to prevent heart attack, stroke, or angina. Clopidogrel and aspirin have been shown to reduce mortality and decrease the incidence of reinfarction or stroke. This includes reducing the onset of new ischemic stroke and new myocardial infarction. Antiplatelet drugs are routinely used in angioplasty and coronary stents to keep arteries previously obstructed by blood clots clear.

Cilostazol is not used in this broad range of conditions. It is approved only for intermittent claudication. Due to poor circulation in the arteries of the leg, patients experience aching, cramping, and burning sensations in the legs that come and go. It usually occurs with walking and subsides with rest, although severe cases are symptomatic at rest as well.

Because of the incidence of life-threatening blood dyscrasias associated with its use, ticlopidine should be reserved for patients who are intolerant or allergic to aspirin therapy or who have failed aspirin therapy.

Thrombolytics

Thrombolytic enzymes are approved for use in the management of acute myocardial infarction, acute ischemic stroke, and pulmonary embolism to reduce the development of congestive heart failure and death. Only alteplase is approved for acute ischemic stroke to improve neurological recovery. Streptokinase also is approved for lysis of deep vein thrombi. Streptokinase and urokinase have been used for clearance of occluded arteriovenous cannulae or IV catheters obstructed by clotted blood or fibrin.

LO 27.1 **LO 27.8**

COAGULANTS/HEMOSTATICS

There are occasions when an agent is required to decrease the incidence or severity of hemorrhage. The use of vitamin K_1 and protamine sulfate as specific antidotes for anticoagulant overdose has been discussed. A limited number of substances may be useful in arresting bleeding arising from other causes. In particular, aminocaproic acid (*Amicar*) inhibits fibrinolysin activation in situations when excessive clot dissolution is occurring. At a dose of 5 g orally or IV, aminocaproic acid promotes clotting and

appears to concentrate in the newly formed **thrombus** (clot) so no dissolution can occur. The major danger with the use of aminocaproic acid is the production of a generalized thrombosis. Otherwise, the side effects include headache, diarrhea, cramps, and rash.

Thrombin (*Thrombin-JMI, Thrombin*), obtained from cattle or recombinant DNA technology (*Recothrom*), is a direct activator of fibrin formation. This plasma protein initiates clot formation when applied topically to actively oozing injuries. It is available in vials containing 5,000, 10,000, or 20,000 units of sterile powder. The recombinant thrombin is significantly less antigenic; that is, antibody production occurs infrequently compared with bovine sources. Thrombin is never administered intravenously due to the potential danger of generalized thrombosis or antigenic reactions. Syringes containing reconstituted thrombin such as the prefilled recombinant thrombin product must be carefully labeled "Recothrom—DO NOT inject" to avoid a potentially life-threatening accident.

Hemostatic Sponges

Three popular preparations of gelatin or cellulose sponges are employed to soak up excess blood and fluids and control bleeding in procedures in which suturing is ineffective or impractical. Such procedures include oral, dental, ophthalmic, and prostatic surgery. Gelatin sponge (*Gelfoam*), gelatin film (*Gelfilm*), fibrous absorbable collagen (*Hemopad*), and oxidized cellulose (*Oxycel, Surgicel*) expand in contact with large amounts of blood. These gauze or sponge preparations also permit clotting to occur along their surfaces when used as wound dressings and surgical packings. These agents are applied topically to control hemorrhage in situations such as amputation, resection of the internal organs, and certain neurologic surgery. Most of these packings ultimately are absorbed by the body with little or no deleterious effect. Oxidized cellulose, in particular, cannot be used as a permanent implant because it interferes with bone regeneration. It also may produce cyst formation and reduce epithelialization (healing) of surface wounds.

Patient Administration and Monitoring

Since many of the anticoagulants are used in a controlled hospital setting, close patient observation minimizes the risk associated with the onset of adverse reactions. In the hospital environment it is assumed that drug interactions that potentiate bleeding such as platelet inhibitors (aspirin, nonsteroidal antiinflammatory drugs [NSAIDs]) are minimized by frequent chart review by the medical-pharmacy team. Patients certainly may continue to take oral anticoagulants on an outpatient basis for chronic prophylaxis of emboli. Therefore it becomes necessary to provide clear instruction not only to the patient, but to relatives and friends who may participate in home care of the patient. Adverse reactions with this class of drugs are potentially life-threatening and need to be communicated to the doctor immediately.

Patient Instructions

As a general safety precaution, patients taking anticoagulants should carry identification that indicates the medication, reason for use, and potential for bleeding to occur.

Patients should clearly be told that dosing is highly individual and may have to be adjusted several times to achieve the best result. For this reason patients are urged to comply with the medication schedule and follow-up appointments during which coagulation status will be monitored. Oral anticoagulants should be taken at the same time each day.

Patients receiving anticoagulant therapy should be instructed to be attentive to the appearance of bruises, bleeding gums, hematuria, or unusually heavy menstrual flow because these are signs of an increased bleeding tendency. In addition, patients should be cautioned to avoid the concomitant use of alcohol or drugs that alter platelet function, such as over-the-counter products containing aspirin or salicylates. Before undergoing dental work or other surgery, the patient should confer with the physician monitoring anticoagulant therapy.

Concomitant Medications

Patients should be reminded not to discontinue other medications unless directed by the physician. Abrupt withdrawal of other medications may alter the dynamics of the oral anticoagulant.

Patients should be instructed to avoid aspirin and over-the-counter (OTC) preparations that contain products known to interfere with platelet aggregation such as ibuprofen.

Notify the Physician

Patient and family should be instructed to report signs of bleeding to the physician immediately for evaluation. When dosage is changed or stopped for any reason, the patient should be instructed to look for signs that may indicate a change in clotting status such as bleeding gums, bruises, petechiae, nosebleeds, hematuria, hematemesis, or menses that is heavier than usual. Patients may need to change to a soft toothbrush or electric razor to avoid irritation that could predispose the patient to bleed.

Use in Pregnancy

The oral anticoagulant warfarin is designated Food and Drug Administration (FDA) Pregnancy Category X.

Any plan to become pregnant or discovery that the patient has become pregnant must be reported to the physician immediately.

Warfarin crosses placental barriers, resulting in hemorrhage, and possibly fetal brain and eye abnormalities and central nervous system (CNS) abnormalities among others.

Parenteral anticoagulants including thrombolytics are designated Pregnancy Category B and C. Use during pregnancy is recommended only when the potential benefit justifies the potential risk to the fetus.

Chapter Review

Understanding Terminology

Match the description in the left column with the appropriate term in the right column.

_____ 1. Several blood clots together that form a plug. **(LO 27.1, 27.8)**

_____ 2. Hair loss or baldness. **(LO 27.1, 27.8)**

_____ 3. Inflammation of the walls of the veins due to blood clots. **(LO 27.1, 27.8)**

_____ 4. The appearance of red blood cells or blood in the urine. **(LO 27.1, 27.8)**

_____ 5. A blood clot. **(LO 27.1, 27.8)**

a. alopecia

b. hematuria

c. thromboembolism

d. thrombophlebitis

e. thrombus

Acquiring Knowledge

Answer the following questions.

1. What are the major stages of coagulation? **(LO 27.1)**

2. Explain the action of antithrombotic drugs. **(LO 27.1, 27.2)**

3. How does heparin differ from the oral anticoagulants? **(LO 27.1, 27.2)**

4. What factors permit heparin to have a rapid onset of action? **(LO 27.1, 27.2, 27.3)**

5. How do the oral anticoagulants exert an antithrombotic effect? What coagulation factors are affected? Why do the oral anticoagulants have a long onset of action? **(LO 27.1, 27.2, 27.6)**

6. Name two specific contraindications to the use of warfarin sodium. **(LO 27.7)**

7. What effects does aspirin have on anticoagulant therapy? **(LO 27.7)**

8. Explain the major toxicity associated with anticoagulant therapy. **(LO 27.7)**

9. Why isn't vitamin K_1 useful in heparin overdose? **(LO 27.2, 27.7)**

10. How can the effects of the oral anticoagulants or heparin be monitored prior to giving the next scheduled dose? **(LO 27.6)**

11. When is heparin preferred over Coumadin? **(LO 27.6, 27.7)**

12. What are three contraindications to the use of anticoagulants? **(LO 27.4, 27.6, 27.7)**

Applying Knowledge on the Job

Use your critical-thinking skills to answer the following questions.

1. Anticoagulants of any type are contraindicated in patients with certain health conditions. List those conditions. **(LO 27.4, 27.7)**

2. Because the duration of action with warfarin is long, 2 to 10 days, hemorrhage due to toxicity requires the use of an antidote. If phytonadione is used, when would you expect to start seeing results using prothrombin time? **(LO 27.4, 27.7)**

3. Because warfarin interacts with a large array of medications, patients should be advised to withhold their current medications. What should they be advised regarding additions or deletions of medications? What might they expect to happen? **(LO 27.6, 27.7)**

Multiple Choice

Use your critical-thinking skills to answer the following questions.

1. All of the following are correct about coagulation EXCEPT **(LO 27.1)**
   A. calcium ions are required for clotting factors to be activated
   B. platelets adhere to the epithelial cells in the walls of blood vessels
   C. there is no process for clot resolution in the body
   D. chelators (EDTA) bind calcium ions and inhibit coagulation in blood samples

2. Warfarin is therapeutically useful because it **(LO 27.1, 27.2, 27.6)**
   A. can be used to prevent the formation of venous thrombi
   B. has a quick onset of action within 2 hours
   C. does not synergize with aspirin to increase the anticoagulant response
   D. can be given intravenously

3. Which of the following is classified as a fibrinolytic? **(LO 27.1, 27.2, 27.6)**
   A. enoxaparin
   B. warfarin
   C. ticlopidine
   D. alteplase, tissue plasminogen activator

4. All of the following are correct about heparins EXCEPT **(LO 27.6, 27.7)**
   A. they are a chain of mucopolysaccharides
   B. LMW heparins stand for low molecular weight
   C. they complex with vitamin K
   D. they are recommended when anticoagulation is required during pregnancy

5. Which of the following is correct? **(LO 27.1, 27.6, 27.7)**
   A. tissue plaminogen activator is the third step in the coagulation cascade
   B. local hemorrhage does not occur with the oral anticoagulants
   C. hemorrhagic disease of the newborn occurs with fibrinolytic drugs
   D. any anticoagulant is contraindicated in patients with active bleeding disorders

6. Which of the following makes the platelets less sticky so a clot cannot form? **(LO 27.2, 27.6)**
   A. warfarin
   B. clopidogrel and aspirin
   C. standard heparin
   D. urokinase

7. Which of the following is not an adverse effect of heparins? **(LO 27.7, 27.8)**
   A. hematuria
   B. petechiae
   C. increased urination
   D. thrombocytopenia

8. Which of the following is correct? **(LO 27.3, 27.4, 27.6)**
   A. heparin is a peripherally acting anticoagulant
   B. LMW heparins can be taken by mouth with food
   C. standard heparin can be added to other intravenous lines (piggyback)
   D. heparins may produce extreme hemorrhage in the fetus
   E. the onset of action of heparins is 10 to 14 days

9. Each of the following is correctly matched to its therapeutic effect EXCEPT (LO 27.5, 27.6)
   A. heparin: stop bleeding in ulcer patients
   B. LMW heparins: knee and hip replacement surgery
   C. fibrinolytic alteplase: coronary artery disease
   D. warfarin: treatment of deep venous thrombosis

10. Which mechanism of anticoagulant action is correct? (LO 27.1, 27.2, 27.5)
    A. warfarin blocks vitamin K from the biochemical path that activates factors II, VIII, IX, and X
    B. dalteparin lyses the thrombi within a few hours of symptom onset
    C. warfarin binds to factors II, VIII, IX, and X
    D. heparin complexes with tissue plasminogen

Multiple Choice (Multiple Answer)

Select the correct choices for each statement. The choices may be all correct, all incorrect, or any combination.

1. The process of clot formation includes which steps? (LO 27.1)
   A. a thrombocyte is formed
   B. platelets migrate to area
   C. injury to an area
   D. a plug is formed

2. Choose the ways in which anticoagulants inhibit clot formation. (LO 27.2)
   A. interfering with plasma clotting factors
   B. inhibiting platelet aggregation
   C. making platelets less sticky
   D. increasing adenosine diphosphate function

3. Which of the following are true of standard heparin? (LO 27.2, 27.3)
   A. binds to clotting factors
   B. gastric acid destroys its mucopolysaccharides
   C. is administered subcutaneously
   D. has a long onset of action

4. Select the adverse effects of warfarin. (LO 27.7)
   A. osteoporosis
   B. thrombocytopenia
   C. hematuria
   D. petechiae

5. Thrombolytic enzymes are used to treat which conditions? (LO 27.5)
   A. pulmonary embolism
   B. acute ischemic stroke
   C. acute myocardial infarction
   D. deep vein thrombosis

Sequencing

Place the following in order of which happens first in the clot formation cascade. (LO 27.1)

_____ _____ _____ _____ _____

First   **Last**

prothrombin converted to thrombin
fibrinogen converted to fibrin
plasmin is formed
activation of clotting factors
thromboplastin is produced

Classification

Place the following drugs under the correct tests used to monitor their therapeutic response. **(LO 27.4)**

dipyridamole   warfarin   heparin

Prothrombin time	INR	Routine blood/platelet counts	Whole blood clotting time

Labeling

Fill in the missing labels for the intrinsic pathway of clot formation. **(LO 27.1)**

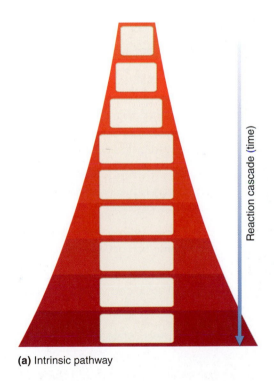

Reaction cascade (time)

(a) Intrinsic pathway

For interactive animations, videos, and assessment, visit:

www.mcgrawhillconnect.com

Chapter 28

Nutrition and Therapy

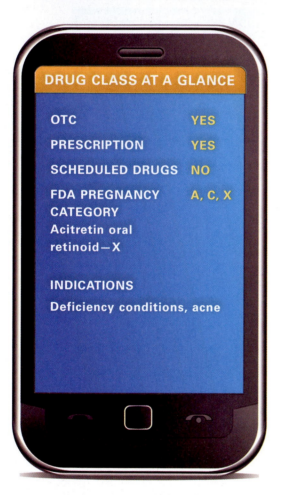

DRUG CLASS AT A GLANCE

OTC	YES
PRESCRIPTION	YES
SCHEDULED DRUGS	NO
FDA PREGNANCY CATEGORY	A, C, X

Acitretin oral retinoid—X

INDICATIONS
Deficiency conditions, acne

KEY TERMS

acidosis: disturbance of acid-base balance; when the pH of the blood is below 7.35.

alkalosis: disturbance of acid-base balance; when the pH of the blood is above 7.5.

anion: negatively charged ion.

cation: positively charged ion.

electrolyte: dissolved mineral that can conduct an electrical current and that exists as an ion.

essential amino acids and fatty acids: substances that are required for critical body function to sustain life and cannot be produced by the body.

hypervitaminosis: the accumulation of vitamins (fat soluble) in storage tissues that creates a deleterious condition related to the excess substance.

isotonic: normal salt concentration of most body fluids; a salt concentration of 0.9 percent.

IV fluid therapy: the infusion of large amounts of fluid into a vein to increase blood volume or supply nourishment.

percent composition: common measure of solution concentration; refers to grams of solute per 100 ml of solution.

TPN: Total parenteral nutrition; a combination of nutrients that may include amino acids, carbohydrates, vitamins, and minerals (electrolytes) that is infused into patients who cannot absorb these substances from the gastrointestinal tract because of condition or disease. The combination and concentration of nutrients vary according to patient need.

After studying this chapter, you should be able to

28.1 describe the difference between an energy-producing substance and minerals and list an example of each.

28.2 describe the role of vitamins in tissue function.

28.3 list the water-soluble vitamins and describe at least three diseases resulting from vitamin deficiency.

28.4 list the fat-soluble vitamins and two ways deficiency can occur.

28.5 list two main body fluid compartments and the major cation found in each compartment.

28.6 explain the main functions of sodium, potassium, and calcium.

28.7 describe the importance of hydrogen in relation to acidosis and alkalosis of the blood.

28.8 list three different intravenous solutions and their main uses.

Introduction

In Chapter 1 a drug was defined as a substance that alters the function of a living system. The substances covered in this chapter are traditionally not regarded as drugs even though they alter the function of living systems. In fact, these substances—vitamins, minerals, and water—are required for maintaining normal function and, more importantly, they are essential for life!

LO 28.1 LO 28.2
LO 28.3 LO 28.4 LO 28.6

NUTRIENTS

The body can make tissues, build and repair organs, and maintain activity and growth as long as vitamins, minerals, energy-producing substrates, and water are available. The body cannot synthesize vitamins and minerals and must therefore rely on an outside source to provide daily requirements. Energy-producing substrates, which include proteins, carbohydrates, and fats, can be synthesized by the body; however, the body relies on an outside source to provide "essential" building blocks. Nine of the 20 amino acids and two fatty acids that the body cannot produce from scratch are termed **essential amino acids and fatty acids.** These essential energy substances, presented in Table 28:1, are found in foods that are complete proteins such as meats, poultry, eggs, and fish. See Figure 28.1.

Figure 28.1

Examples of Complete Proteins

Meat, fish, poultry, eggs, and milk contain all the essential amino acids.

Essential Amino and Fatty Acids

Amino acids	Fatty acids
Arginine*	Linolenic (polyunsaturated omega-3 fatty acids)
Histidine	
Isoleucine	
Leucine	Linoleic (polyunsaturated omega-6 fatty acids)
Lysine	
Methionine	
Phenylalanine	
Threonine	
Tryptophan	
Valine	

Arginine is essential under some conditions.

Diet and Disease

Even before their biochemical importance was identified, it was assumed that diet provided ample quantities of vitamins, minerals, and energy foods to sustain day-to-day activity. The content of the diet, however, varies with the culture, the ethnic group, and geographical location because eating patterns develop according to the type of food available in the region. People living at the Arctic Circle eat a different spectrum of food than those in Central America or Southeast Asia. Nevertheless, all diets must satisfy the daily demands for fuel and essential amino and fatty acids that are absorbed from plant or animal products.

It is difficult (but not impossible) to develop a deficiency to most vitamins and minerals in healthy people under the age of 70 in the United States. Poorly balanced diets or poverty level diets certainly can limit the opportunity for adequate absorption of essential amino acids, vitamins, and minerals. Even in the presence of affluence and abundance, dietary composition can vary so widely that the quantities of some vitamins and minerals absorbed do not meet the level to support normal activity. In addition, decreased organ function associated with aging, medications, and disease can accelerate depletion of some elements. The value of vitamins, minerals, and substrates is easily observed in the conditions that result from deficiency, ranging from dull, brittle hair to malformed red blood cells, chronic anemias, and neuritis. Table 28:2 presents conditions that have been correlated with vitamin deficiency. Research has continually supported a relationship between diet and disease, including certain cancers.

International studies have confirmed that large amounts of fat or salt-cured or smoked meats are associated with high cancer rates for prostate, stomach, and esophageal cancers, respectively. In addition, diets that provide natural antioxidants (vitamins A, C, E) are associated with lower incidences of cancer.

Recommended Dietary Allowance and U.S.-Recommended Daily Allowance

Suggestions for the daily amount of each element needed to prevent deficiency conditions were established years ago in the U.S.-Recommended *Daily* Allowance (U.S.-RDA) and the RDA, Recommended *Dietary* Allowance. The U.S.-RDA and the RDA are not interchangeable. While both provide information, the U.S.-RDA (previously called the Minimum Daily Requirement) is used by the Food and Drug Administration to monitor the claims for quality of food processing destined for human consumption. Standards for nutrition advertising presented in product labels must meet legal requirements represented by the U.S.-RDA.

The National Research Council–National Academy of Sciences, Food and Nutrition Board publishes the Recommended *Dietary* Allowance (RDA). This is not a requirement, but a suggestion for daily intake of elements that are not produced by the body. The recommendations are derived from healthy individuals consuming a 2000-calorie daily diet balanced from the six basic food groups. Standard referenced healthy men weigh 70 kg (150 to 160 pounds), the women weigh 60 kg (130 to 148 pounds), and both are between 20 and 50 years old. Diet and muscle mass of many elderly people are significantly different from younger adults; however, recommendations of dietary allowances for this population have not yet been established.

Dietary Recommendations

Except for conditions (osteoporosis, pernicious anemia, iron deficiency anemia, myelin degeneration) that result from a confirmed deficiency in vitamins or minerals, oral and parenteral supplements are not usually recommended. Conventional medical advice suggests that

Vitamins and Minerals: Recommended Dietary Allowances and Conditions Related to Deficiency

	RDA*	Conditions resulting from deficiency	Chapter**
Fat-soluble vitamins			
Vitamin A	1900 (700) mcg	Night blindness, dry skin, decrease in epithelial cell growth	—
Vitamin D	200 (200) IU	Bone loss, serum calcium	38
Vitamin E	12 (15) IU	Possible anemia	—
Vitamin K	80 (65) mcg	Hemorrhage, decreased coagulation	27
Water-soluble vitamins			
Thiamine (B$_1$)	1.5 (1.1) mg	Anorexia, constipation, peripheral neuritis	—
Riboflavin (B$_2$)	1.7 (1.3) mg	Glossitis, ocular itching, vascularization	—
Niacin (B$_3$)	15 (19) mg	Insomnia, delusions, confusion	29
Pyridoxine (B$_6$)	2 (1.6) mg	Anemia, convulsions	—
Cyanocobalamin (B$_{12}$)	2 (2) mcg	Macrocytic anemia, muscle incoordination	30
Vitamin C	60 (60) mg	Bleeding gums, bruising, loose teeth	—
Folate (folic acid)	200 (180) mcg	Macrocytic anemia, neuropathy	30
Minerals			
Calcium	1200 (1200) mg	Bone loss	38
Chloride	2300 mg	Hypochloremic alkalosis	—
Iron	10 (15 mg)	Microcytic anemia, fatigue, brittle nails, sore tongue, pica	30
Phosphorus	1200 mg	Hypophosphatemia, muscle weakness, bone pain, rickets, osteomalacia	—
Potassium	4700 mg	Hypokalemia, fatigue, muscle weakness, leg cramps, irregular heartbeat	—
Sodium	1200 mg	Hyponatremia, weakness, muscle cramps, nausea, mental apathy	—

Recommended dietary allowances for 70-kg males (60-kg females) 20 to 50 years old.

**Additional information presented in other chapters of this textbook.*

adequate daily requirements of vitamins and minerals can be supplied through a healthy diet. Recommended servings for healthy adults and senior adults from a diet balanced to provide nutrition, energy, and essential vitamins and minerals are presented in Table 28:3. Specific conditions such as pregnancy and athletic performance increase the demand for some of these elements and benefit from diet supplements. In addition, there is

Recommended Daily Food Consumption for Healthy Adults and Senior Adults

Food groups	Minimum servings per day	
	Healthy adults	**Senior adults**
Milk, cheese, dairy	2	3–5
Meat, poultry, fish, beans	2	2–3
Vegetable, fruit	4	3–5
Bread, cereal, whole grain (enriched or fortified cereal)	4	4–6

mounting evidence that adult vitamin supplements may be beneficial in preventing cancer (prostate, vitamin E), minimizing the toxicities of chemotherapy (vitamins A, E, C), and bone demineralization (elderly, vitamin D).

Food Guide Pyramid

A well-balanced diet is one that incorporates servings from all of the recommended food groups daily. The U.S. Department of Agriculture (USDA) developed a nutritional guide, called the food pyramid (see Figure 28.2), that visually describes the relationship of the food groups required to provide the essential vitamins, minerals, and fiber each day. The new food pyramid is designed to balance nutritional and physical activity needs. The pyramid is color-coded for each food group:

- Orange represents grains
- Green represents vegetables
- Red represents fruits
- Yellow represents oils
- Blue represents milk products
- Purple represents meat and beans

Research on obesity has led to changes in the recommendations for serving sizes and the need for exercise. The action figure climbing the stairs in Figure 28.2 reminds us to include physical activity along with a healthy diet. At www.mypyramid.gov an animation walks the viewer through the use of the pyramid as a menu planner and nutrition guide. Ideally, 3 to 9 ounces of breads and grains should be eaten daily. Three to four cups each from fruits and vegetables, and two to three

servings from dairy products (milk, cheese, yogurt), and 4 to 5 ounces from protein such as meat, fish, poultry, and nuts are recommended daily. Individual food groups cannot be substituted for another because no single group contains the recommended full complement of vitamins, minerals, or fuel substances (carbohydrates, protein, fat). Notice the skinny yellow group of the food pyramid contains fats, oils, and sweets. Fats are an essential part of daily food consumption; however, the high number of calories and limited nutritional value associated with this group warrant special attention in daily consumption.

Recommended serving sizes vary with each food group based on the age, gender, and weight of the individual. One serving includes

Breads, cereals, rice, pasta, and other grains

- *1 slice of bread*
- *½ hamburger bun, bagel, or English muffin*
- *1 nine-inch flour tortilla*
- *½ cup cooked pasta, rice, or cereal*
- *1 ounce of ready-to-eat cereal*
- *2 to 4 crackers*

Fruits or vegetables

- *½ to ¾ cup of raw berries or chopped fruits or vegetables*
- *¾ cup of vegetable or fruit juice*
- *1 cup of leafy raw vegetables such as lettuce*
- *a medium apple, banana, orange, or ½ grapefruit*

Figure 28.2   U.S. Department of Agriculture's Food Guide Pyramid

Grains
Make half your grains whole

- Eat at least 3 ounces of whole grain bread, cereal, crackers, rice, or pasta every day

- Look for "whole" before the grain name on the list of ingredients

Vegetables
Vary your veggies

- Eat more dark green veggies

- Eat more orange veggies

- Eat more dry beans, peas

Fruits
Focus on fruits

- Eat a variety of fruit

- Choose fresh, frozen, canned, or dried fruit

- Go easy on fruit juices

Oils
Know your fats

- Make most of your fat sources from fish, nuts, and vegetable oils

- Limit solid fats like butter, stick margarine, shortening, and lard

Milk
Get your calcium-rich foods

- Go low-fat or fat-free

- If you don't or can't consume milk, choose lactose-free products or other calcium sources

Meat & Beans
Go lean on protein

- Choose low-fat or lean meats and poultry

- Bake it, broil it, or grill it

- Vary your choices—with more fish, beans, peas, nuts, and seeds

Meat, fish, poultry, beans, eggs

- 2 to 3 ounces of cooked lean meat, poultry, or fish
- 1 cup of cooked (dried) beans or lentils
- 2 eggs
- 4 tablespoons of peanut butter

Milk, yogurt, cheese

- 1 cup milk or yogurt
- 1½ ounces natural cheese
- 2 ounces of processed cheese
- 1¾ cup of ice cream

For processed foods, the number of servings and the contribution to the recommended daily intake of fat, protein, carbohydrates, and sodium, for example, are identified on the label as Nutrition Facts. The serving size is the basis for the nutrition information provided. A container of soup, fruit, vegetables, or ice cream is one container but may contain 2 or more servings, as shown in Figure 28.3. The percent (%) Daily Value section shows how many grams or milligrams of each nutrient are contained in *one serving*. For the ice cream product label shown in Figure 28.3, the percentage of saturated fat intake in a ½ cup serving is 28 percent of the total recommended fat intake for a day. Review of nutrition facts on labels develops an understanding of the concept of serving size and contribution of nutrient components to overall calorie intake.

The amount of food eaten daily will supply calories, or fuel, for normal physiological function. Of course, the number of calories needed by each individual is dependent upon age, gender, and the level of daily activity. A moderately active person may be one who is working, including household maintenance, but doesn't perform a great deal of exercise in addition to work activities. An inactive person is one who does not exercise and engages in very little daily exertion such as walking but prefers to ride in the car or sit at home. When caloric intake from any food combination (even healthy choices) is greater than energy expenditure (burn-up), body weight will increase.

LO 28.2

VITAMINS

Vitamins have traditionally been considered "natural substances" and food additives rather than drugs. Although vitamin K and niacin are used in doses that produce pharmacologic effects (blood clotting, cholesterol reduction), vitamins are principally associated with routine tissue activity. Vitamins act as cofactors (coenzymes) that facilitate biochemical reactions in all tissues, yet the spectrum of their importance is still under discovery. A cofactor is a nonprotein substance that is bound to a protein (enzyme) and is required for the protein to function. More than 300 metabolic or enzyme reactions are known to require vitamins in order to function properly.

Vitamins are categorized as fat soluble (A, D, E, K) or water soluble (C and B vitamins). Fat-soluble vitamins characteristically are well stored in the liver and fatty tissues. They are affected by conditions that limit fat absorption such as biliary obstruction, pancreatic disease, liver cirrhosis, and absorbent resins (cholestyramine). These vitamins are absorbed in a provitamin state and metabolically converted in the intestine or kidney to the active compound that produces a specific action. Water-soluble vitamins are readily absorbed from the intestinal tract and are not influenced by biliary

Figure 28.3

Food Label Nutritional Facts

This label provides facts on the ingredients and nutrients contained in this regular ice cream container.

function. Since these vitamins are not stored in the body, they are more easily depleted through renal excretion. The recommended daily amount of each vitamin can be achieved with a well-planned diet; however, balanced supplements are readily available OTC to complement or augment dietary intake.

LO 28.2   LO 28.4

FAT-SOLUBLE VITAMINS

Vitamin A

Source

Beta-carotene (provitamin A) is the most important member of a group of biologically active compounds known as vitamin A. Vitamin A$_1$ (retinol) is found in fish liver oils, animal liver, yellow vegetables, palm oil, parsley, spinach, and dandelion leaves. Synthetic retinol provides more consistent blood levels than do dietary sources. Vitamin A activity is expressed as retinol activity equivalents (RA), where one RA equals 1 mcg of retinol or 12 mcg of beta-carotene.

Function in the Body

Vitamin A is absolutely required for the production of the protein visual purple (rhodopsin). Dietary beta-carotene (provitamin A) is converted to retinol in the intestine. Retinol combines with a protein, opsin, to form rhodopsin. This protein enables specialized retinal cells (rods) to adapt to very low-intensity light (dark adaptation). Without beta-carotene, the rods cannot respond, resulting in "night blindness." Vitamin A is also involved in the synthesis of ribonucleic acid (RNA), cholesterol, and proteins and preserves the integrity of epithelial cells. Through these pathways, vitamin A deficiency retards cell growth and results in thickened, dry skin.

Clinical Indication

Vitamin A is administered orally as replacement therapy in deficiency conditions resulting from biliary, pancreatic, and hepatic disease; partial gastrectomy; and cystic fibrosis. Parenteral vitamin A is also available for conditions such as anorexia, malabsorption syndrome, or vomiting where oral administration is not possible.

Vitamin A is used topically for skin abrasions, minor burns, sunburn, diaper rash, and noninfected skin irritation resulting from indwelling drains as with colostomy or ileostomy.

Vitamin A acid (13-retinoic acid, *trans*-retinoic acid) is used in the management of acne vulgaris. By reducing sebum (oil) production and stimulating epithelial cell turnover, retinoic acids improve cystic acne and prevent the skin thickening (keratinization) that occurs in chronic acne.

Treatment of Deficiency

The daily RDA for vitamin A is 900 mcg (RAE) in men, 700 mcg (RAE) in women, and 800 to 1300 mcg (RAE) in pregnant and nursing women. Treatment of adult deficiency ranges from 100,000 to 500,000 IU per day up to 2 weeks. Treatment beyond 2 weeks may range between 10,000 and 20,000 IU daily for 2 months. Oral preparations of beta-carotene are available over the counter (OTC) alone or in multivitamin products containing beta-carotene and vitamin A. OTC products usually contain 5000 IU/capsule or less. Significantly larger amounts of vitamin A are also available by prescription (25,000 IU/capsule oral; *Aquasol A,* 50,000 IU/ml injection). Oral and injectable forms of vitamin A are also available by prescription.

Treatment of Acne

Retinoic acid (isotretinoin) is available as an oral formulation taken twice daily for up to 20 weeks and a topical gel applied once a day. The topical cream or liquid preparations will adhere to the hands and therefore necessitate thorough washing after application to avoid inappropriate exposure to other sensitive tissues; for example, the eyes.

Products

The number of available vitamin A products is numerous. Among the oral and parenteral preparations of vitamin A alone are *Aquasol A* and *Palmitate-A 5000.* Topical OTC preparations for the skin are combinations of vitamin A with vitamin D and/or vitamin E and include *A and D, Desitin, Lobana Peri-Garde, Lazer Creme,* and *Aloe Grande.* Retinoic acids are available by prescription for topical application (*Retin-A*) and oral administration.

Overdose

Hypervitaminosis can occur because healthy individuals should have adequate stores of vitamin A within the liver. Toxicity observed will vary with the age and condition of the person and the dose ingested. Acute toxicity may produce headache, irritability, and vertigo associated with an increase in cranial pressure. Symptoms of chronic toxicity may include lethargy; desquamation (shedding epithelial lining); dry, cracked skin; arthralgia; and cirrhotic-like liver syndrome. Prolonged daily administration over 25,000 IU can produce signs of vitamin A toxicity. It has been suggested that individuals taking daily doses greater than 5000 IU should be monitored for signs of vitamin A toxicity. Following accurate diagnosis of the condition, the vitamin A supplement should be discontinued and, if necessary, supportive treatment with prednisone begun. Liver function enzymes may be monitored until the clinical profile improves.

Overdose characteristic of hypervitaminosis A can result from overuse of the oral formulation, and from accidental oral ingestion of the topical creme or liquid formulations. Symptoms include headache, vomiting, facial flushing, dizziness, and abdominal pain. Once treatment is discontinued, the symptoms stop.

Contraindication

Vitamin A in doses greater than the RDA are contraindicated in women who are pregnant. Human fetal malformations have occurred and there may be an increased risk of spontaneous abortion following treatment in women who received retinoic acid while pregnant. *This product used in doses greater than the RDA is classified as Food and Drug Administration (FDA) Pregnancy Category X* because there is the potential for all exposed fetuses to be affected by maternal circulating retinoic acid. The topical formulation of retinoic acid is not associated with fetal malformation; however, use in pregnancy should be considered only when the benefit justifies the potential risk. The topical formulation is classified as FDA Pregnancy Category C.

Vitamin D (see Chapter 38 for additional information)

Source

Vitamin D is a term for a group of compounds with similar activity. Vitamin D provitamins are found in fish liver oils, egg yolks, and fortified commercial dairy products such as whole milk, butter, bread, and cereals. Following absorption of two provitamins, active forms of vitamin D are produced by metabolic conversion in the liver or by the action of ultraviolet (UV) irradiation converting cholesterol to vitamin D in the skin. The liver and kidney further convert vitamin D into the more active forms of vitamin D_3, 25-hydroxydihydrotachysterol, and calcitriol. Vitamin D activity is expressed as international units (IU) of vitamin D_3.

Function in the Body

Vitamin D is essential for the metabolism of bone and cartilage. Vitamin D regulates serum calcium levels in conjunction with parathormone and calcitonin. It increases absorption of dietary calcium and phosphate in the large intestine (duodenum) and raises the level of calcium in the blood. Figure 28.4 shows that a prohormone form of vitamin D is converted in the skin by sunlight (UV) to vitamin D_3. The liver and kidneys each modify the vitamin D form until the calcitriol is produced. In response to a drop in blood calcium

parathyroid hormone (PTH) is secreted. PTH stimulates the kidneys to secrete calcitriol, the most potent form of vitamin D. It then facilitates calcium and phosphate absorption. Vitamin D deficiency produces a condition of weakened skeletal structure known as rickets in children and osteomalacia in adults. Indirectly, vitamin D affects the status of muscle contraction, nerve conduction, and blood clotting through its influence on serum calcium ions. Calcium deficiency manifests as sustained muscle contraction (tetany) or impaired nerve conduction.

Clinical Indication

Various forms of the vitamin are administered orally and parenterally in the treatment of conditions resulting from or associated with low serum calcium such as metabolic bone disease, postoperative tetany, hypoparathyroidism, and renal dialysis. It is increasingly recognized that elderly people may develop vitamin D deficiency in a number of ways. Age- or disease-related renal changes may decrease the amount of active vitamin D produced in people over 70 years old. In this age group, people may be house-bound, incapacitated, or institutionalized so that exposure to sunlight for vitamin D conversion in the skin is not a daily routine. It has been suggested that this may be complicated by the use of sunscreen products (SPF), which decrease the UV activity on the skin. Finally, conditions of lactose intolerance, avoidance of dairy products because of potential constipation, or decreased appetite may contribute to an overall decrease in vitamin D absorption in older people.

As a topical cream containing vitamins A, E, and D, vitamin D is applied to the skin for the temporary relief of minor burns, chafed or dry skin, sunburn, abrasions, and noninfected irritated areas including diaper rash. Topical preparations may be applied to irritated areas resulting from ostomy connections.

Treatment of Deficiency

The daily RDA for vitamin D is 200 IU for men and women. Newer research suggests that this is much too low, especially with the use of sunblock and inadequate exposure to UV light. The literature suggests that 2000 to 5000 IU are appropriate (compared to 200 IU). Treatment of adult deficiency ranges between 12,000 and 500,000 IU of vitamin D activity daily. Therapy is continued with calcium supplementation until serum calcium, phosphorus, and blood urea nitrogen (BUN) indicate improvement. Ergocalciferol (D_2) and cholecalciferol (D_3) are used in the treatment and prophylaxis of vitamin D deficiency.

Figure 28.4

Sites of Vitamin D Conversion to Calcitriol and Vitamin D Activity in Calcium Absorption

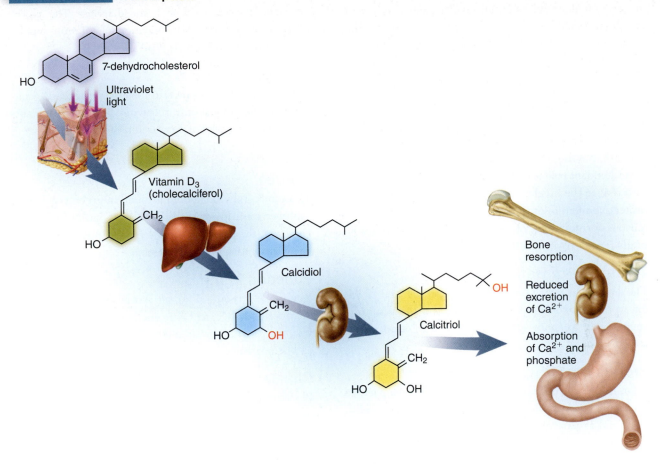

7-dehydrocholesterol

Ultraviolet light

Vitamin D₃ (cholecalciferol)

CH₂

Calcidiol

CH₂

OH

Calcitriol

CH₂

Bone resorption

Reduced excretion of Ca²⁺

Absorption of Ca²⁺ and phosphate

Other forms of vitamin D are used in the management of serum calcium disorders, tetany, hypophosphatemia, and hypoparathyroidism.

Products

Ergocalciferol (D₂) is available orally and parenterally. Oral formulations include *Calciferol Drops, Drisdol Drops, Vitamin D,* and *Deltalin Gelseals.* Cholecalciferol (D₃) is available OTC as *Delta-D* and *Vitamin D₃.* Dihydrotachysterol (*DHT, Hytakerol*), calcitriol (*Rocaltrol, Calcijex*), and calcifediol (*Calderol*) are available only by prescription.

Overdose

Hypervitaminosis can occur from administration to patients in excess of their daily needs. Acute toxicity may produce weakness, headache, nausea, vomiting, constipation, muscle or bone pain, and a metallic taste. Later changes in renal and liver function may be observed by elevations in BUN, aspartate aminotransferase (AST), alanine aminotransferase (ALT), and albumin in the urine. Finally, levels of calcium and phosphate may be elevated in the blood or urine. Bone demineralization can occur in adults, persisting after vitamin treatment

has been discontinued. Death following cardiovascular or renal failure has occurred.

Drug Interactions

Patients receiving renal dialysis are predisposed to experiencing drug interactions with vitamin D preparations. Antacids containing magnesium may contribute to hypermagnesemia in combination with vitamin D therapy. Hypercalcemia resulting in atrial fibrillation has occurred with patients receiving vitamin D and verapamil or digoxin.

Vitamin E
Source

Vitamin E, alpha-tocopherol, is found in vegetable oils, eggs, cereals, milk, meat, and leafy vegetables, and is available synthetically. Like all fat-soluble vitamins, absorption depends on the availability of bile salts. Vitamin E absorption is related to ingestion of polyunsaturated fatty acids (linoleic acid). Fatty tissue, liver, and muscle store most of the alpha-tocopherol absorbed from the intestine.

Function in the Body

The mechanism of vitamin E activity is not fully known; however, it does act as an antioxidant and cofactor in metabolic reactions. As an antioxidant it prevents the formation or accumulation of toxic metabolites. In addition, vitamin E is essential to the maintenance of red blood cell (RBC) membranes.

Clinical Indication

Vitamin E is used topically for the temporary relief of minor burns and chapped or chafed skin, especially diaper rash. Vitamin E is used in the treatment of cancer. Its antioxidant role is attributed to the ability of vitamin E to reduce the incidence of certain cancers and act as a protective agent in oxygen therapy in premature infants. Various formulations of alpha-tocopherol are available orally for the treatment of vitamin E deficiency.

Treatment of Deficiency

The daily RDA for vitamin E is 12 IU for men and 15 IU for women. Deficiency of vitamin E and the resulting anemia are rare since adequate amounts are available in foods.

Products

Vitamin E activity is expressed as IU of alpha-tocopherol. Vitamin E is available orally OTC as an individual supplement and as part of multivitamin preparations. Among the products available are *Aquasol E, E-200 I.U. Softgels, Amino-Opti-E,* and *E-Complex 600.* Topical OTC products intended for skin application only include *E-Vitamin, Vitec,* and *Vite E Creme.* Vitamin E is also available for topical use in combination with vitamins A and/or D as *Lobana-Peri Garde, Lazar Creme, Lobana Derm-Ade,* and *Aloe Grande.* See Figure 28.5.

Figure 28.5

Vitamin E as Gel Capsules and "Wrinkle-Free" Age-Defying Lotion

(a)   (b)

Overdose

Hypervitaminosis may produce symptoms of fatigue, headache, nausea, weakness, and diarrhea. The appropriate treatment is discontinuation of vitamin supplement until symptoms disappear.

Drug Interactions

Because vitamin E suppresses platelet aggregation, concomitant use in patients receiving oral anticoagulants may lead to episodes of increased bleeding.

Vitamin K (see Chapter 27)
Source

Vitamin K_1 (phytonadione) is found in green vegetables, cabbage, cauliflower, fish, liver, eggs, milk, and meat. However, the primary source of vitamin K in humans is bacterial synthesis in the intestine.

Function in the Body

Vitamin K is required for the synthesis of blood clotting factors II, VII, IX, and X in the liver. Interference with vitamin K synthesis or metabolism results in bleeding and hemorrhage.

Clinical Indication

Bleeding resulting from suppressed coagulation due to malformation of vitamin K–dependent clotting factors warrants vitamin K replacement therapy. Conditions that impair or eliminate bacterial vitamin K synthesis, such as antibiotic therapy, or interfere with vitamin K metabolism are also indications for vitamin K therapy. Vitamin K is given in the prophylaxis and management of hemorrhagic disease of the newborn where the mother received oral anticoagulants, anticonvulsants, or antibiotics during pregnancy that interfered with vitamin K–dependent clotting mechanisms. ***Note: Vitamin K will not reverse the bleeding associated with heparin overdose.***

Treatment of Deficiency

The RDA for vitamin K is 80 mcg for men and 65 mcg for women. Deficiency of vitamin K and the resulting coagulation disorder do not usually result from dietary limitations.

Replacement is achieved through oral and parenteral administration of vitamin K. Individualized doses ranging between 2.5 and 25 mg of vitamin K are taken until coagulation returns to normal or to the previous therapeutic level. Continuation of treatment is based on the protime (PT) evaluation.

Products

Vitamin K as phytonadione is available orally as *Mephyton* and parenterally by prescription as *Aqua-Mephyton.*

Overdose

Hypervitaminosis is not likely to occur with oral preparations. However, patients may experience adverse reactions to parenteral vitamin K administration. Symptoms, which may include flushing, dizziness, and brief hypotension, do not necessarily obligate cessation of treatment. Pain and swelling at the injection site with repeated injections may occur. Severe allergic reactions including death, however, have occurred after intravenous administration of vitamin K.

LO 28.2 | LO 28.3

WATER-SOLUBLE VITAMINS

Water-soluble vitamins include all the B vitamins and vitamin C. These vitamins are not stored in fatty tissues, are readily used up following absorption, and are easily excreted with water into the urine. Chronic inadequate intake of these vitamins through the diet, therefore, can lead to deficiency. Among adults the condition most commonly associated with vitamin deficiency is alcoholism. Decreased appetite, decreased food intake, and damage to digestive and metabolic systems that occur with alcoholism contribute to a deficiency state. Other conditions such as anorexia nervosa, prolonged fasting, and intravenous feeding also can precipitate vitamin deficiency. Even when diets include appropriate sources of water-soluble vitamins, overcooking and boiling food products cause the vitamins to break down (heat labile) or leach into the cooking water, making vitamin deficiency possible. Except for vitamin B_{12} and folate, it is unusual for deficiency of one vitamin to occur. As a rule, conditions that predispose an individual to vitamin deficiency will reduce the levels of multiple B vitamins concurrently.

Vitamins B_1 (Thiamine), B_2 (Riboflavin), B_3 (Niacin, Nicotinic Acid), B_5 (Calcium Pantothenate), B_6 (Pyridoxine), B_9 (Folic Acid), B_{12} (Cyanocobalamin)

Source

The family of B vitamins is available in yeast, whole grains, soybeans, liver, milk, egg yolks, leafy green vegetables, and fruit. The daily RDA for the B vitamins is presented in Table 28:2 on page 439.

Function in the Body

All of the B vitamins have coenzyme activity or are integral to cell reproduction and maturation. Thiamine combines with adenosine triphosphate (ATP) to form a coenzyme that is critical for carbohydrate metabolism. As carbohydrate intake increases in the diet, so does the requirement for thiamine. Riboflavin combines with proteins to form coenzymes in the respiratory system. Niacin forms two coenzymes in oxidation-reduction reactions. Pyridoxine forms a coenzyme in the metabolism of carbohydrates, fats, and protein. When dietary protein increases, the requirement for pyridoxine increases. Pantothenate is a precursor of coenzyme A associated with synthesis of fatty acids and steroid hormones. Cyanocobalamin and folic acid are essential for cell growth, reproduction, and hematopoiesis. A full discussion of the activity of vitamin B_{12} and folic acid is presented in Chapter 30.

Clinical Indication

Thiamine is indicated in the treatment of vitamin B_1 deficiency, known as beriberi. Symptoms range from weakness, paresthesia, and hypotension to sensory and motor dysfunction. In severe cases, psychosis, ataxia, confusion (Wernicke's encephalopathy), and cardiovascular damage can occur.

Riboflavin, pantothenate, and pyridoxine are indicated for the treatment of vitamin B_2 deficiency. In the absence of riboflavin, changes occur in the cornea (vascularization) accompanied by itching, burning, and photophobia, and glossitis and seborrheic dermatitis develop.

Pantothenate deficiency induced experimentally has been shown to cause fatigue, headache, sleep disturbances, muscle cramps, and impaired coordination.

Niacin is used in the treatment and prevention of pellagra and, pharmacologically, to reduce hyperlipidemia (see Chapter 29). Pellagra is characterized by the three "Ds": diarrhea, dermatitis, and dementia.

Treatment of Deficiency

Few nutrients play such a critical role and deserve the special attention as the need to increase folic acid intake before conception and during pregnancy. One month prior to conception and during pregnancy, it is recommended that women take 400 to 800 mcg of folic acid daily. The requirement for nonpregnant women is 400 mcg daily. This is achieved with oral vitamin supplements. Research indicates that folic acid is better absorbed from the vitamin supplements than from foods containing folic acid such as lentils; dried beans and peas; dark green vegetables and citrus fruit. In addition, the FDA authorized the addition of folic acid to many grain foods (such as bread and cereal).

For thiamine deficiency replacement is achieved through oral and parenteral administration of thiamine (10 to 20 mg IM) until symptoms resolve. Then oral vitamin supplement is continued for a few months. In severe cases precipitated by other chronic conditions, symptoms may not fully improve.

Riboflavin deficiency is easily corrected with daily oral doses of 25 mg. While parenteral niacin is available, deficiency is usually corrected with 100 to 500 mg of niacin orally a day.

Products

Thiamine is available OTC as *Thiamilate,* and by prescription for injection as *Biamine.* Riboflavin, pantothenate, niacin, and pyridoxine are available OTC alone under the generic names, or within multivitamin supplements available under numerous labels.

Overdose

Hypervitaminosis is not likely to occur with B vitamins, although adverse reactions to individual vitamin preparations do occur. In large doses, thiamine produces a sensation of warmth, sweating, urticaria, tightness in the throat, and gastrointestinal bleeding (hemorrhage). Niacin may cause gastrointestinal distress, diarrhea, generalized flushing (vasodilation that has not been confirmed to be therapeutically useful), decreased glucose tolerance, and elevated uric acid and liver function tests.

Cautions

Parenteral administration of vitamins has caused severe hypersensitivity reactions, even death. Prior to intravenous administration of thiamine, an intradermal sensitivity test should be performed to assess potential reactivity.

Riboflavin may cause orange discoloration of the urine that is inconsequential. However, patients should be alerted to the potential for this coloration to occur.

Vitamin C (Ascorbic Acid)
Source

Vitamin C is plentiful in citrus fruits, green vegetables, tomatoes, potatoes, strawberries, and green peppers.

The daily Recommended Dietary Allowance (RDA) for vitamin C is 60 mg a day for adults.

Function in the Body

Vitamin C is essential in the formation of collagen, catecholamines, and steroids, and conversion reactions such as folic acid to folinic acid.

Clinical Indication

Although vitamin C has been recommended for use in a wide range of conditions from the common cold to cancer, the only clinically recognized use of ascorbic acid is in the prevention and treatment of vitamin C deficiency, or scurvy.

Treatment of Deficiency

Scurvy is characterized by degenerative changes in soft tissue and bones. Bleeding gums, loose teeth, and poor bone development have been identified with vitamin C deficiency for more than two centuries. Deficiency is readily reversed through diet as well as oral supplements in doses ranging from 70 to 500 mg daily. See Figure 28.6.

Products

Ascorbic acid is available OTC alone or in combination with multivitamin supplements.

Special Consideration

There is no overdose potential with vitamin C. Doses up to 10 g daily have been used for prophylaxis of colds, as adjuncts in cancer treatment, and to improve wound healing. While these uses are still under debate, it has provided evidence that large doses of vitamin C do not produce significant adverse effects. At most, vitamin C may cause diarrhea and precipitate renal stones because it acidifies the urine. Patients prone to renal stones should not take megadoses (greater than 2 g) of vitamin C.

Figure 28.6   **Vitamin C (Ascorbate) Can Be Found in a Wide Variety of Foods**

Prior to performing an amine-dependent stool occult blood test, ascorbic acid should not be taken for 48 to 72 hours to avoid a false-negative response.

LO 28.5

BODY WATER

The body can tolerate acute deficiencies in food, vitamins, and minerals, but water deprivation is incompatible with life. Water is the most abundant constituent of the body, representing about 60 to 70 percent of total body weight. Many substances in the body normally exist in solution, being dissolved in water. Body water is distributed between two main compartments: the intracellular (intracellular fluid, ICF) and the extracellular (plasma and interstitial fluid, extracellular fluid [ECF]) compartments. The fluid in these compartments is normally maintained at relatively constant amounts. Loss of body water produces dehydration, whereas retention of water produces edema. In turn, the substances dissolved within the fluid compartments are directly affected by the shift or change in fluid volume.

Figure 28.7

Typical Water Intake and Output in a State of Water Balance

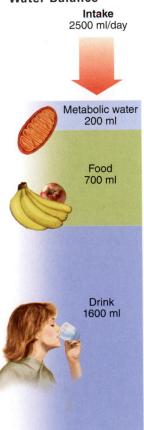
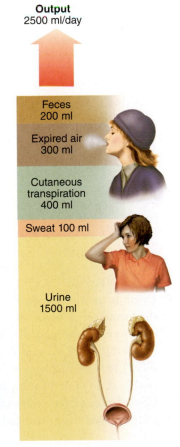

Intake
2500 ml/day

Output
2500 ml/day

Metabolic water
200 ml

Food
700 ml

Drink
1600 ml

Feces
200 ml

Expired air
300 ml

Cutaneous
transpiration
400 ml

Sweat 100 ml

Urine
1500 ml

Fluid Balance

The normal daily intake of fluids by an average-size adult is approximately 2500 ml, or about 3 quarts. This amount includes fluids from drinking, fluids in food, and water formed by body metabolism. The normal daily output of fluids is about the same as fluid intake. Fluid output is water that is normally lost in urine, sweat, and feces and through respiration. During illness, additional fluid may be lost by hemorrhage, vomiting, or diarrhea. See Figure 28.7.

When a large amount of fluid is lost by the body, it must be replaced. Usually, adequate fluid intake is accomplished by drinking. In disease states or medical emergencies, fluid loss may be so great that fluid intake must be accomplished by other methods. Intravenous **(IV) fluid therapy** is commonly employed in these situations. It involves the infusion of large amounts of fluid into a vein to increase blood volume or supply nourishment.

LO 28.1 LO 28.6 LO 28.7 LO 28.8

MINERALS

Minerals, such as sodium (Na), potassium (K), and chloride (Cl), are important constituents of body composition. When dissolved in body fluids, they exist as acids, bases, and salts. These dissolved minerals are referred to as **electrolytes** because they are able to conduct an electrical current. The electrolytes form charged particles called ions. Ions that have a positive charge are known as **cations.** Ions possessing a negative charge are called **anions.**

$$NaCl \xrightarrow{dissolved} H_2O + Cl^- + Na^+$$

Electrolytes are involved in many important body functions. Water is the solvent, electrolytes are the solutes, and together they form the normal salt (isotonic) concentration of the body fluids. **Isotonic** refers to a salt concentration of 0.9 percent. Alterations of water or salt levels result in fluid concentrations (hypotonic or hypertonic) that will destroy body cells (lysis or crenation). A common measure of solution concentration is **percent composition,** or grams of solute per 100 ml of solution. A 5 percent dextrose solution contains 5 g of dextrose in 100 ml of water.

Electrolytes
Sodium (Na⁺)

Sodium, the main cation of extracellular fluid, plays a major role in maintaining normal fluid balance. The average diet is sufficient to meet body requirements for

Intravenous Solutions and Their Main Uses

IV solution	Use
Saline	
Sodium chloride 0.45%	Fluid and electrolyte replacement (Na, Cl)
Sodium chloride 0.9%	Fluid and electrolyte replacement (Na, Cl)
Dextrose in saline	
5% dextrose in 0.45% saline 5% dextrose in 0.9% saline 10% dextrose in 0.9% saline	Fluid and electrolyte replacement, provides carbohydrate calories
Dextrose in water	
5 and 10% dextrose in water 20 and 50% dextrose in water	Fluid replacement, TPN carbohydrate calories
Multiple electrolyte solutions	
Ringer's solution	Fluid and electrolyte replacement (Na, Cl, K, Ca)
Lactated Ringer's solution	Same as Ringer's plus lactate, which provides buffer action in acidosis
Plasma expanders	
10% dextran 40 in 0.9% saline	Increases plasma volume when hypovolemia is present
Parenteral nutrition	
Amino acid solutions (*Aminosyn, Travasol*)	Provides protein calories
Fat emulsions 10%, 20% (*Intralipid, Liposyn*)	Provides essential fats and calories

sodium. The kidneys help maintain normal levels of sodium in plasma and other body fluids. Significant loss of sodium (vomiting and diarrhea) reduces ECF volume. Excessive use of diuretics also causes sodium depletion. Consequently, fluid moves out of the intracellular compartment in an effort to maintain blood volume. If the lost sodium and water are not replaced, blood volume and blood pressure decrease, and circulatory collapse may occur. Sodium is administered intravenously in various concentrations, as seen in Table 28:4.

Potassium (K⁺)

Potassium, the main cation of intracellular fluid, is important in maintaining cell structure and function. Potassium is also vital in the regulation of muscle function, especially heart muscle. Loss of potassium can produce a loss of muscle tone, weakness, and paralysis.

Excessive potassium levels can produce cardiac arrhythmias, especially heart block. The normal concentration of potassium in the serum ranges between 3.5 and 5.0 milliequivalents per liter (mEq/l). Potassium is administered IV as potassium chloride in various concentrations. Table 28:5 shows the effect of changes in potassium on acid-base balance.

Calcium (Ca²⁺)

Calcium, another cation that is usually associated with the formation of bone, also plays a vital role in muscle contraction and blood coagulation. The normal serum concentration of calcium ranges between 9.0 and 10.5 mEq/l (8.4 to 10.2 mg/dl). A deficiency of calcium in the blood results in hyperexcitability of nerve and muscle fibers (tetany). Excess calcium produces muscle weakness and may lead to cardiac and respiratory failure. When

Relationship Among Fluid, Electrolyte, and Acid-Base Imbalances

If the following occurs		Potential effect	Reason
Acidosis	K^+	Hyperkalemia	H^+ diffuses into cells and displaces K^+. As K^+ leaves the ICF, K^+ concentration in the ECF rises
Hyperkalemia		Acidosis	High K^+ concentration in the ECF causes less K^+ to diffuse out of the cells than normally. H^+ diffuses out to compensate, and this lowers the extracellular pH
Alkalosis	K^+	Hypokalemia	H^+ diffuses from the ICF to ECF. More K^+ remains in the ICF to compensate for the H^+ loss, causing a drop in ECF K^+ concentration
Hypokalemia		Alkalosis	Low K^+ concentration in the ECF causes K^+ to diffuse out of cells. H^+ diffuses in to replace K^+, lowering the H^+ concentration of the ECF and raising its pH
Acidosis	Cl^-	Hypochloremia	More Cl^- is excreted as ammonium chloride (NH_4Cl) to buffer the excess acid in the renal tubules, leaving less Cl^- in the ECF
Alkalosis		Hyperchloremia	More Cl^- is reabsorbed from the renal tubules, so ingested Cl^- accumulates in the ECF rather than being excreted
Hyperchloremia		Acidosis	More H^+ is retained in the blood to balance the excess Cl^-, causing hyperchloremic acidosis
Acidosis	Ca^{++}	Hypocalcemia	Acidosis causes more Ca^{2+} to bind to plasma protein, lowering the concentration of free, ionized Ca^{2+} and causing symptoms of hypocalcemia
Alkalosis		Hypercalcemia	Alkalosis causes more Ca^{2+} to dissociate from plasma protein and citrate ions, raising the concentration of free Ca^{2+}
Hypovolemia	Na^+	Alkalosis	More Na^+ is reabsorbed by the kidney. Na^+ reabsorption is coupled to H^+ secretion in the renal tubule so more H^+ is secreted and pH of the ECF rises
Hypervolemia		Acidosis	Less Na^+ is reabsorbed, so less H^+ is secreted into the renal tubules. H^+ retained in the ECF

ICF is intracellular fluid; ECF is extracellular fluid.

given intravenously, calcium is usually administered in the form of calcium chloride or calcium gluconate.

Hydrogen (H^+)

The major source of hydrogen is from the dissociation of water, protein, bicarbonate, and phosphate buffer systems.

$$CO_2 + H_2O \rightleftarrows H_2CO_3 \rightleftarrows HCO_3^- + H^+$$

In the bicarbonate buffer system, carbonic acid (H_2CO_3) forms by the hydration of carbon dioxide and then dissociates into bicarbonate (HCO_3^-) and H^+. When the lungs blow off CO_2, the reaction moves to the left and hydrogen ion is neutralized (tied up). If there is a need to generate hydrogen ions (to lower the pH in the

extracellular fluid), the kidneys can excrete HCO_3^- and keep the H^+ reaction moving to the right.

$$H_2PO_4^- \rightleftarrows HPO_4^{2-} + H^+$$

The phosphate buffer system works predominately in the renal tubules and intracellular fluid.

This reaction regulates the acidity or alkalinity of body fluids. Normal pH of blood is tightly regulated between 7.35 and 7.45. When the pH of the blood falls below 7.35, a condition known as **acidosis** occurs. A pH higher than 7.45 indicates a state of **alkalosis.** The body has several buffer systems to maintain normal body pH. When these buffer systems are not able to maintain pH, acid-base disturbances occur. There are different types of acidosis and alkalosis. See Figure 28.8.

Figure 28.8

The Relationship of Bicarbonate–Carbonic Acid Ratio to pH

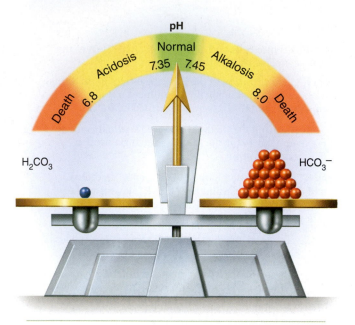

At a normal pH of 7.40, there is a 20 to 1 ratio of bicarbonate ions (HCO_3^-) to carbonic acid (H_2CO_3) in the plasma. An excess of HCO_3^- tips the balance toward alkalosis, whereas an excess of H_2CO_3 tips it toward acidosis.

Metabolic Acidosis

Metabolic acidosis occurs when there is excessive loss of bases, such as bicarbonate (HCO_3^-) or sodium. Such losses can occur with diarrhea, starvation, or diabetic coma. Treatment involves the administration of sodium bicarbonate along with fluids and other electrolytes, if necessary.

Respiratory Acidosis

Respiratory acidosis is associated with increased levels of carbon dioxide (CO_2) in the blood, occurring when there is interference with respiratory gas exchange. Carbon dioxide combines with water to form carbonic acid (H_2CO_3). Carbonic acid can dissociate into hydrogen ions, which will lower the pH of the blood (acidosis).

Metabolic Alkalosis

Metabolic alkalosis is usually associated with excessive loss of potassium (K^+) or chloride (Cl^-). This kind of loss is most often caused by severe vomiting (Cl^- loss) or diarrhea (K^+ loss).

Respiratory Alkalosis

Respiratory alkalosis is produced by hyperventilation (salicylate poisoning or artificial respirator), which lowers the carbon dioxide (CO_2) levels of the blood.

The treatment of acidosis or alkalosis involves administering the appropriate electrolyte solutions so that serum electrolyte levels are returned to normal.

Intravenous Therapy

In addition to the various electrolyte solutions, a number of intravenous solutions are used as plasma expanders or to provide parenteral nutrition (Table 28:4). Patients who are unable to take fluids or food by mouth must depend on intravenous administration to ensure adequate fluid and caloric intake. Intravenous solutions usually contain some form of carbohydrate, such as dextrose, fructose, or dextran. In addition, electrolytes, vitamins, amino acids, proteins, and fat emulsions can be included. Total parenteral nutrition (**TPN**) may be used during chemotherapy in order to improve patient outcome. TPN does not influence tumor growth but may reverse the negative aspect of cancer treatment—weight loss. Its greatest value has been demonstrated in patients responding with increased white blood cell counts, improved immunocompetence, improved wound healing, and, overall, a better-than-expected response to chemotherapy. TPN may increase the blood sugar level in the diabetic patient.

Review of the patient history should provide evidence of eating disorders, alcohol abuse, or poor dietary habits that could contribute to nutrition imbalance. Especially among elderly patients, the psychological state resulting from being socially isolated or continually worried often causes the patient to stop eating. Reassurance is the best therapy, followed by dietary adjustment and appropriate nutritional supplements. During treatment patients should be monitored for development of sensitivity reactions.

Patient Instructions

Instruct patients to take nutritional supplements with meals to avoid gastrointestinal upset.

Extended-release formulations of vitamins should not be crushed or chewed. This formulation is designed to deliver the active substance over a controlled period of time rather than all at once. Chewing will dump the vitamin into the stomach and may cause nausea or irritation depending on the vitamin; however, the patient will not experience harmful effects from the change in delivery.

Vitamin A

If being taken as an individual supplement, the recommended maximum daily dose should not be exceeded. Pregnant women should be cautioned to stay within the recommended dose range to avoid potential excess storage and adverse effects.

Vitamin D

Remind patients, especially elderly adults, that brief periodic exposure to sunlight (10 minutes a day, up to 3 days each week) is beneficial to maintain a normal level of active vitamin D.

Calcium Supplements

Vitamin D and calcium are often taken together as part of a nutritional program. This may occur more frequently today due to patient anxiety about developing osteoporosis. Remind patients that calcium supplements without an adequate vitamin D level will not permit calcium to be utilized by the body. Moreover in the absence of vitamin D and estrogen, calcium supplementation (especially *Tums)* alone does not correct osteoporosis in postmenopausal women.

Niacin

Patients should be told that niacin may cause flushing and a sensation of warmth in the neck and face and tingling or itching. These effects usually subside within a few days.

Riboflavin

During treatment, patients may observe a change in urine color to deeper orange-yellow. This is not harmful and will subside when the supplement is discontinued.

Vitamin C

Daily doses in excess of 2 g may change the acidity of the urine, causing stones to develop. Patients with a history of renal stones should avoid megadose exposure of vitamin C.

Notify the Physician

Patients should be told to notify the physician if they experience weakness, headache, weight loss, vomiting, and abdominal or muscle cramps. Such symptoms may indicate an adverse reaction to the supplement or hypersensitivity.

Use in Pregnancy

Folic Acid

Folic acid has been shown to be essential in the prevention of certain birth defects that affect the brain and spinal cord. Spina bifida is a condition in which the embryonic neural tube does not completely close during early development (within 4 weeks after conception). This is called a neural tube deficit. This tissue, which eventually becomes the brain and spinal cord, may later push through the vertebrae, meninges or the skin. Depending on the severity of the condition, the brain and spinal cord may be at risk of infection while exposed, bowel and bladder function may be impaired, and, in the most severe cases, death can occur. Research has shown that women who take folic acid supplement especially in early pregnancy dramatically reduce the risk of having a baby with such neural tube defects.

Few nutrients play such a critical role and deserve the special attention as the need to increase folic acid intake before conception and during pregnancy. One month prior to conception and during pregnancy, it is recommended that women take 400 to 800 mcg of folic acid daily. The requirement for nonpregnant women is 400 mcg daily. This is achieved with oral vitamin supplements. Research indicates that folic acid is better absorbed from the vitamin supplements than from foods containing folic acid such as lentils; dried beans and peas; dark green vegetables and citrus fruit. In addition, the FDA authorized the addition of folic acid to many grain foods (such as bread and cereal).

Except for folic acid, pyridoxine, and thiamine (FDA Pregnancy Category A), it is suggested that vitamin supplements not exceed the recommended maximum daily amounts. Vitamins are usually found classified as FDA Pregnancy Category C. Therapy that obligates larger doses should be monitored during prenatal evaluation.

Oral retinoic acid and excessive doses of vitamin A should be avoided during pregnancy. Vitamin A is classified as FDA Pregnancy Category C because safety for use during pregnancy has not been established. **Retinoic acid, oral not topical, is classified as FDA Pregnancy Category X because of its direct deleterious actions on the developing fetus at any time during pregnancy.**

Chapter Review

Understanding Terminology

Answer the following questions.

1. Explain what is meant by the term *essential amino acid*. **(LO 28.1)**
2. Why are vitamins considered essential? **(LO 28.2)**
3. What information does *RDA* convey to the reader? **(LO 28.2)**
4. Explain what *hypervitaminosis* is and which substances are potentially involved. **(LO 28.1, 28.2, 28.4)**
5. Explain what is meant by *percent composition* as a measure of solution concentration. **(LO 28.8)**
6. Write a short paragraph using these terms: *electrolytes, ions, cations, anions*. **(LO 28.5, 28.6, 28.7)**
7. What is the purpose of TPN? **(LO 28.8)**

Acquiring Knowledge

Answer the following questions.

1. List the different forms of body fluids and their locations. **(LO 28.5)**
2. What are the usual sources of fluid intake and the means of fluid output? **(LO 28.5)**
3. What is the function of vitamin D? **(LO 28.2, 28.4)**
4. Explain why elderly adults are more likely to experience vitamin D and calcium deficiency. **(LO 28.2, 28.4)**
5. Why is it easier to develop a deficiency of the B vitamins than to develop a deficiency of vitamin A? **(LO 28.2, 28.3, 28.4)**
6. Which vitamins have a therapeutic role beyond the treatment of vitamin deficiency? **(LO 28.2, 28.3, 28.4)**
7. What are the main functions of Na^+, K^+, and Ca^{++}? **(LO 28.5, 28.6)**
8. List the various types of acidosis and alkalosis and the common causes of each. **(LO 28.5, 28.7)**
9. What solutions would be appropriate for the treatment of metabolic acidosis? **(LO 28.5, 28.7)**
10. When is IV therapy indicated? **(LO 28.8)**

Applying Knowledge on the Job

Use your critical-thinking skills to answer the following questions.

1. *Accutane* is contraindicated in women who are or may become pregnant. What should be included in the medication counseling when *Accutane* is prescribed to a female patient? **(LO 28.4)**

2. What are the symptoms of vitamin D overdose? **(LO 28.3)**

3. Pregnant women or women who are of childbearing age should take 400 to 800 mcg of folic acid daily. Why is this important? What disorder is commonly associated with folic acid deficiency? **(LO 28.3)**

Multiple Choice

Use your critical-thinking skills to answer the following questions.

1. Pellagra is common in people whose diet consists primarily of corn. Which vitamin deficiency causes pellagra? **(LO 28.1, 28.2, 28.3)**
   A. niacin
   B. B_{12}
   C. vitamin C
   D. folic acid

2. A good food source of ascorbic acid is **(LO 28.1, 28.2, 28.3)**
   A. meat
   B. lettuce
   C. black beans
   D. citrus fruits

3. Which of the following are correct categories of vitamins? **(LO 28.1, 28.2)**
   A. water soluble and water insoluble
   B. antioxidant and prodrug
   C. synthetic and natural
   D. low molecular weight and fat soluble

4. Which of the following vitamins is essential for vision? **(LO 28.4)**
   A. vitamin D
   B. vitamin D_3
   C. vitamin A
   D. vitamin B_6

5. Which of the following vitamin preparations is contraindicated in pregnancy? **(LO 28.4)**
   A. ergocalciferol
   B. phytonadione
   C. retinoic acid
   D. pyridoxine

6. Which of the following cations are lost (taken out of the body) in metabolic acidosis? **(LO 28.6, 28.7)**
   A. chloride
   B. calcium
   C. iron
   D. potassium

7. Which of the following is correct? **(LO 28.8)**
   A. parenteral nutrition provides protein and calories
   B. saline solution provides carbohydrate calories
   C. plasma expanders are used to immediately replace sodium and chloride
   D. parenteral fluid therapy requires intra-arterial administration

8. Antibiotics can kill bacteria living in the gut that synthesize vitamin **(LO 28.4)**
   A. C
   B. B_{12}
   C. D
   D. K

9. Which of the following vitamins is required for collagen synthesis? **(LO 28.3)**
   A. K
   B. D
   C. C
   D. B_1

10. Fat-soluble vitamins include **(LO 28.3, 28.4)**
    A. B, A, C, K
    B. D, A, K, E
    C. C, A, K, E
    D. B_1, B_6, B_{12}, E

11. Which of the following is the term for vitamin involvement in biochemical reactions? **(LO 28.1, 28.2)**
    A. coenzyme
    B. modifier
    C. precursor
    D. obligatory

12. This vitamin is essential to absorb calcium. **(LO 28.3, 28.4)**
    A. beta-carotene
    B. vitamin E
    C. cholesterol
    D. vitamin D

13. Under the influence of sunlight (UV), which of the following occurs? **(LO 28.3, 28.4)**
    A. vitamin B_6 generates nucleic acids
    B. vitamin D is formed from cholesterol in the skin
    C. vitamin C reduces carbohydrates
    D. vitamin A generates retinol

14. Which of the following is NOT associated with vitamin E? **(LO 28.4)**
    A. cofactor and antioxidant
    B. essential to maintenance of red blood cell membrane
    C. hypervitaminosis produces nausea, weakness, and diarrhea
    D. hypervitaminosis produces dry cracked skin, desquamation, and cirrhotic-like liver

Multiple Choice (Multiple Answer)

Select the correct choices for each statement. The choices may be all correct, all incorrect, or any combination.

1. Which of the following are energy-producing substances? **(LO 28.1)**
    A. proteins
    B. electrolytes
    C. water
    D. fats

2. Choose the true statements about vitamins. **(LO 28.2)**
    A. water-soluble vitamins are stored in the liver
    B. vitamins act as cofactors for biochemical reactions
    C. fat-soluble vitamins are metabolically converted in the intestines
    D. water-soluble vitamins are influenced by biliary function

3. Which of the following are ways in which fat-soluble vitamin deficiency can occur? **(LO 28.4)**
    A. antibiotic therapy
    B. pancreatic disease
    C. hypoparathyroidism
    D. cystic fibrosis

4. Select all of the fat-soluble vitamins. **(LO 28.3, 28.4)**
    A. thiamine
    B. ascorbic acid
    C. pyridoxine
    D. phytonadione

5. Select the main electrolytes present in intracellular fluid. **(LO 28.5)**
    A. calcium
    B. potassium

C. sodium

D. hydrogen

Sequencing

Place the following steps in order as they happen in the body from first to last. **(LO 28.2, 28.4)**

_____   _____   _____   _____

First   **Last**

rods are able to adapt to low light

retinol combines with opsin

beta-carotene converted in the intestine

rhodopsin is formed

Classification

Place the following vitamins under the appropriate classification. **(LO 28.3, 28.4)**

niacin

vitamin D

beta-carotene

riboflavin

ascorbic acid

alpha-tocopherol

folic acid

phytonadione

Fat soluble	Water soluble

Matching

Match the following vitamins with their correct function in the body. **(LO 28.2, 28.3, 28.4)**

a. vitamin A

b. vitamin B

c. vitamin C

d. vitamin D

e. vitamin E

f. vitamin K

1. _____ cofactor in metabolic reactions

2. _____ cell production and maturation

3. _____ production of rhodopsin

4. _____ formation of catecholamines

5. _____ synthesis of blood clotting factors

6. _____ metabolism of bone

Documentation

Using information from the doctor's chart below, answer the following questions. **(LO 28.3)**

Patient presents with the following symptoms:

hypotension

weakness

motor dysfunction

1. What type of deficiency is this patient suffering from?
2. What additional symptoms could this patient experience?
3. What is the recommended treatment for this type of deficiency?
4. In addition to medications, are there any other sources for this substance?

Labeling

Fill in the missing labels. **(LO 28.2, 28.4)**

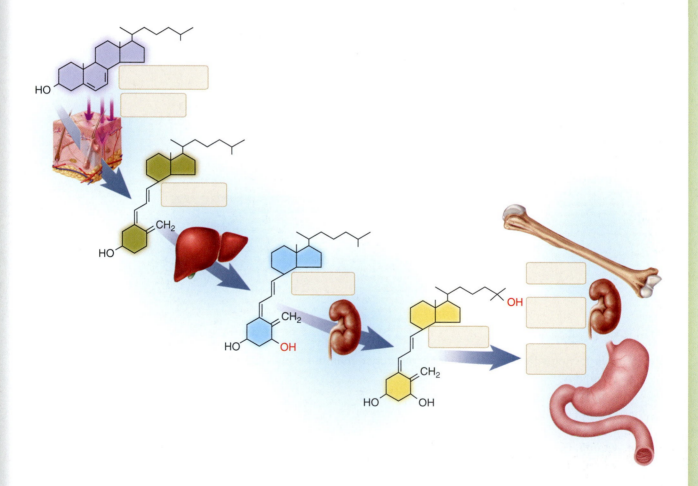

Chapter 29

Hypolipidemic Drugs

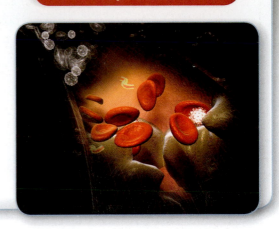

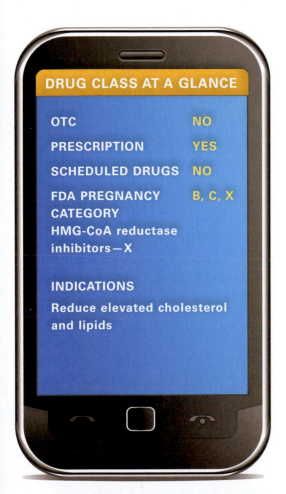

DRUG CLASS AT A GLANCE

OTC	NO
PRESCRIPTION	YES
SCHEDULED DRUGS	NO
FDA PREGNANCY CATEGORY	B, C, X

HMG-CoA reductase inhibitors—X

INDICATIONS

Reduce elevated cholesterol and lipids

KEY TERMS

aneurysm: an abnormal widening or ballooning of a portion of an artery due to weakness in the wall of the blood vessel.

angina: chest pain or discomfort that occurs when the heart muscle does not get enough blood and oxygen.

anti-atherogenic: the ability to prevent or stop atherosclerosis, the deposition of lipid-containing plaques on the innermost layers of the arteries.

antilipemic drug: a drug that reduces the level of fats in the blood.

apoprotein: a protein that is attached to a second molecule that is not a protein.

atherogenic: the ability to start or accelerate the deposition of fats and calcium in the walls of arteries, called atherosclerosis.

cholesterol: a fat (lipid) normally synthesized by the liver; essential for the structure and function of cells.

chylomicron: A microscopic particle of blended fat found in the blood and lymph; formed during the digestion of fats.

coronary artery disease (CAD): narrowing of small arteries that supply blood and oxygen to the heart.

C-reactive protein (CRP): a protein produced by the liver but only found in the blood in conditions of acute inflammation; an inflammation marker.

endocytosis: process by which cells absorb molecules (such as proteins) from outside the cell by engulfing them with their cell membrane.

endogenous: originating or produced within an organism, tissue, or cell.

exogenous: originating or produced outside the organism or body.

foam cells: a type of cell formed after macrophages in the artery wall digest LDL-cholesterol; a transformed macrophage.

high-density lipoprotein (HDL): One of the forms of cholesterol transported in the blood with lipoprotein known as "good" cholesterol.

hyperlipidemia: abnormally high fat (lipid) levels in the plasma.

hypolipidemic drug: drug used to lower plasma lipid levels also referred to as an antilipemic drug.

intermittent claudication: severe pain in the calf muscles that occurs while walking, but subsides with rest.

ischemia: insufficient blood supply (and oxygen) to meet the needs of the tissue or organ.

lipoprotein: a molecule that contains a protein and a lipid (fat).

low-density lipoprotein (LDL): One of the forms of cholesterol transported in the blood with lipoprotein known as "bad" cholesterol.

peripheral artery disease (PAD): any disease caused by the obstruction of blood flow in the large arteries of the arms and legs.

plaque: substance containing cholesterol, dead cell products, and calcium that accumulates in the innermost layer of the arteries.

rhabdomyolysis: the rapid breakdown of skeletal muscle (rhabdomyon) due to muscle injury.

stable plaque: plaque formed in the artery wall that remains in the wall.

stroke: loss of brain function due to a loss of blood supply.

transient ischemic attack (TIA): an interruption of blood flow to the brain for a short period of time; a mini-stroke that produces stroke-like symptoms but no lasting damage.

triglyceride: a fat formed by three fatty acids into one molecule that supplies energy to muscle cells.

unstable plaque: plaque formed in the artery wall that can break away and obstruct blood flow or form a clot.

very-low-density lipoprotein (VLDL): Molecules made of cholesterol, triglycerides and protein that carry cholesterol from the liver to organs and tissues; also serves as a precursor to low density lipoproteins (LDL).

Learning Outcomes

After studying this chapter, you should be able to

29.1 explain the importance of triglycerides and cholesterol and their role in atherosclerosis.

29.2 discuss the treatment of hyperlipidemia.

29.3 explain the mechanism of action of five different hypolipidemic drugs.

29.4 explain why the HMG-CoA inhibitors are more effective than other hypolipidemic drugs.

29.5 discuss the main adverse effects of each hypolipidemic drug class and how liver function tests are affected.

29.6 explain the essential terminology associated with atherosclerosis and hypolipidemic drugs.

Introduction

It is often stated "you are what you eat." A balanced diet includes carbohydrates, proteins, and lipids (fats). The important dietary lipids include fatty acids, **triglycerides,** and **cholesterol.** These substances are necessary for the formation of cell membranes, nerve tissue, and plasma lipoproteins. Excess dietary lipids are stored as fat in adipose tissue, where they serve as a reserve form of energy. Cholesterol is stored in the gallbladder as a component of bile acids. The metabolism of fat, especially excess dietary fat, can contribute to other fatty deposits that line blood vessels and impede normal circulation and tissue perfusion.

ATHEROSCLEROSIS AND ARTERIAL DISEASE

The drugs in this chapter are referred to as the **hypolipidemic** or **antilipemic drugs** (lower the fats). The primary drug action is to reduce elevated circulating lipids (fats), but the therapeutic focus is to prevent coronary heart disease and associated heart attack and stroke. Atherosclerosis is a progressive condition that leads to **coronary artery disease (CAD)** and **peripheral artery disease (PAD).** It is the leading cause of illness and death in the United States.

Atherosclerosis is a disease that begins in early adulthood, even childhood, in which fat builds up inside the smooth lining of the arteries. This accumulated fat, called **plaque,** is mostly cholesterol with calcium, cell debris, and other substances found in the blood. The plaque begins as streaks of fat in the arterial wall. When a vessel is damaged through infection, smoking, diabetes, or high blood pressure, a specific type of cholesterol, LDL-cholesterol, migrates to the injured area. In the wall of damaged arteries the LDL becomes oxidized and sends chemical signals directly to macrophages to "come and get me." As the macrophages consume the LDL, they transform into cholesterol-rich **foam cells.** The oxidized LDL triggers more macrophage influx and inhibits their mobility so macrophages accumulate and form more foam cells. This is the beginning of fat streaks in the artery. Foam cell production is part of a local inflammatory response that continues over time, causing plaque to build up. There are two kinds of plaque. **Stable plaque** has a cholesterol core with a fibrous cap and may contain calcium that hardens as it builds up within the cell wall. Eventually this plaque pushes into the space where the blood flows through the artery. This may reduce the local blood flow and oxygen supply to the tissues. Because plaque builds slowly over years, there are usually no symptoms until the artery becomes drastically narrowed or blocked, reducing oxygen to the tissues **(ischemia).** It is now known there is another kind of plaque. **Unstable plaque** also has a cholesterol core but it is more dangerous because it has a thin cap that can erode, rupture and break away. The ruptured material released into the bloodstream can form a clot (thrombus) that blocks blood flow and oxygenation of the tissues. The development of plaque in an artery is depicted in Figure 29.1.

When blockage occurs in the heart, it can cause arrhythmias or an acute, life-threatening heart attack. Blockage in the arteries supplying the heart causes CAD;

Figure 29.1

Plaque Formation

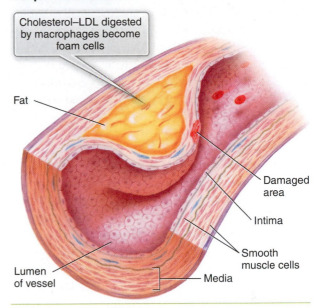

Cholesterol–LDL digested by macrophages become foam cells

Fat

Damaged area

Intima

Smooth muscle cells

Lumen of vessel

Media

Deposition of cholesterol attached to low-density lipoprotein (LDL) within the wall of an artery is known as plaque.

the characteristic symptom of an attack is crushing chest pain called **angina.** Blockage also can occur in other parts of the body like the carotid artery, which supplies the brain, resulting in a **TIA (transient ischemic attack)** or a debilitating **stroke.** When the wall of an artery weakens, it may bulge out, forming an **aneurysm,** which can leak or hemorrhage, thereby removing blood and oxygen from the tissues. When blood flow to the legs, pelvis, or arms is compromised in PAD, it causes numbness and pain in the limbs, called **intermittent claudication.**

Lipids and Lipoproteins
Cholesterol

Understanding how cholesterol is processed in the body and the impact of dietary cholesterol on plaque formation is critical to understanding how the hypolipidemic drugs work. Cholesterol is a critical substrate for the body because it is the fundamental building block of steroid hormones (sex hormones, glucocorticoids, aldosterone). It is essential for building cell membranes, the myelin sheath that provides the insulation for nerves, and the brain and it is a core component of bile salts secreted by the gallbladder to digest dietary fats. A precise amount of cholesterol is required in cells so the body is finely tuned to balance cholesterol circulation and storage (homeostasis).

With a balanced nutritional diet, the body absorbs 20 to 25 percent of its daily cholesterol from the diet and produces 75 to 80 percent through cellular synthesis (**endogenous**) in the liver and the small intestine. Endogenous cholesterol is synthesized through a complicated biochemical pathway starting with a 2-carbon molecule acetyl CoA and ending with 27 carbon atoms in cholesterol. (An early step in this process, which is a target for drug therapy, will be presented under the section on statin drugs.)

Lipoproteins

From the liver, cholesterol is stored in the gallbladder or it is transported to cells that need it. Because it is a fat (not water soluble), it can't float in the bloodstream by itself. It has to be transported by specialized proteins called **apoproteins.** When apoproteins join cholesterol, they are called **lipoproteins.** The lipoprotein surrounds the fatty cholesterol core (like a hard-boiled egg, where cholesterol is the yolk). These lipoproteins come in different densities according to the amount of protein in the combined molecules (Figure 29.2). Although there are five lipoproteins, only three will be mentioned now. There is a **low-density lipoprotein (LDL)** formed from apoprotein B-100 and cholesterol, a **very-low-density lipoprotein (VLDL),** and a **high-density lipoprotein (HDL)** comprised of apoproteins A-1 and E and cholesterol. Apoproteins B (LDL) and E (HDL) not only transport fat, they are recognized by LDL receptors on cell surfaces that allow the lipoproteins to enter the cells (receptor-mediated **endocytosis**). See Figure 29.3. Cholesterol is then extracted from the lipoprotein for cell-specific biosynthesis.

LDL cholesterol is bad cholesterol (remember it as **l**ousy **LDL**) because, as you already know, it transports cholesterol to damaged areas in the arteries and forms plaque. LDL is **atherogenic.** Good cholesterol is the HDL cholesterol because it goes looking for cholesterol to return to the liver for disposal (remember it as **h**ealthy **HDL**). HDL actually retrieves cholesterol from the artery walls, inhibits the oxidation of LDL, and inhibits platelet aggregation at plaque sites. HDL is a protective lipoprotein. It is **anti-atherogenic.**

Triglycerides

One other fat has to be mentioned in order to understand how cholesterol is clinically monitored. Triglycerides are another type of fat found in the blood. Triglycerides are the main form of fat from diet regardless of the source—carbohydrate, fat, or protein. The body converts any calories it doesn't need to use right away into triglycerides and stores them in fat cells (adipose tissue). Triglycerides provide your body with energy. **Chylomicrons** are very large lipoproteins produced by the intestines to transport dietary (**exogenous**) cholesterol and triglycerides. They are mostly a triglyceride core (85 percent) (Figure 29.2). In the circulation, chylomicrons deliver triglycerides to muscle and fat tissue but return to the liver with a full complement of cholesterol that was absorbed by the intestine. When circulating chylomicrons become anchored to blood capillaries of muscle and adipose tissue, the triglycerides are hydrolyzed by the enzyme lipoprotein lipase. The triglycerides are made into free fatty acids to be used by the muscle as energy or stored as fat. During times when dietary lipids are not available, the liver produces cholesterol and triglycerides itself (endogenous). The liver packages triglycerides into VLDL. Triglycerides transported by VLDL are hydrolyzed by lipoprotein lipase to provide energy to the target tissues. Moderately elevated plasma

---

Figure 29.2   **Lipoprotein Types Showing the Composition of Phospholipid, Protein, and Cholesterol**

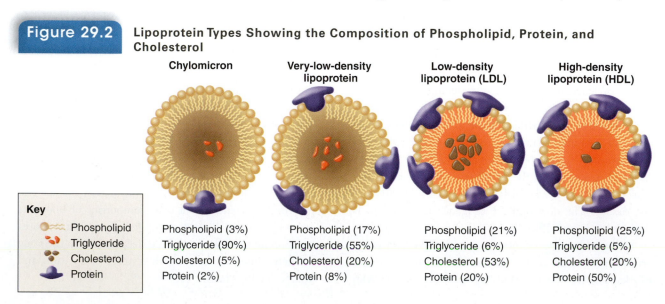

Chylomicron

Very-low-density lipoprotein

Low-density lipoprotein (LDL)

High-density lipoprotein (HDL)

Key
- Phospholipid
- Triglyceride
- Cholesterol
- Protein

Phospholipid (3%)
Triglyceride (90%)
Cholesterol (5%)
Protein (2%)

Phospholipid (17%)
Triglyceride (55%)
Cholesterol (20%)
Protein (8%)

Phospholipid (21%)
Triglyceride (6%)
Cholesterol (53%)
Protein (20%)

Phospholipid (25%)
Triglyceride (5%)
Cholesterol (20%)
Protein (50%)

Figure 29.3   Pathways of Lipoprotein Processing

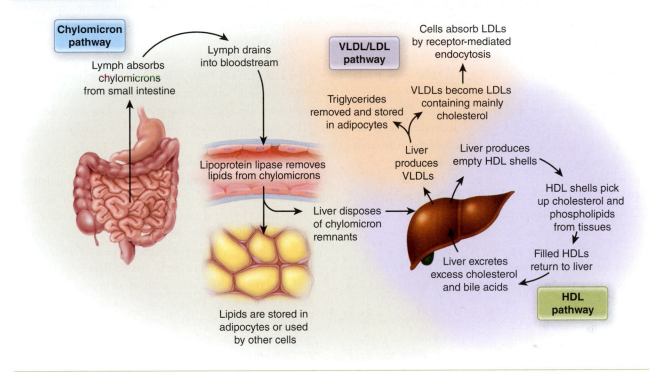

Chylomicrons, formed in the small intestine, pass to the bloodstream, where lipoprotein lipase breaks them into free fatty acids. The chylomicron remnant is broken down in the liver. The liver is the central station for lipoprotein processing. Very-low-density lipoproteins (VLDL) made in the liver carry lipids to adipose tissue for storage or become low-density lipoproteins (LDL) that contain mostly cholesterol. High-density lipoproteins (HDL), produced in the liver as a protein shell, pick up cholesterol and phospholipids from other organs. HDL brings them to the liver, where cholesterol is removed and put into the bile as cholesterol or into bile acids.

triglyceride levels contribute to increased risk for cardiovascular disease and severe hypertriglyceridemia is associated with an increased risk of pancreatitis.

Lipoprotein Levels, Monitoring, and Disease

There is a dynamic communication among the liver, intestines, and lipoproteins that balances the cholesterol synthesis needed day-to-day. Although lipids are essential for cell structure and function, unusually high lipid levels in the plasma have been correlated with several diseases such as diabetes mellitus, lupus erythematosus, lipodystrophies, hypothyroidism, and premature atherosclerosis. There are hereditary conditions that predispose some individuals to elevated serum cholesterol (hypercholesterolemia) or triglyceride levels (hypertriglyceridemia), but mostly it's the dietary lifestyle that contributes to elevated lipid levels.

The average American diet provides large amounts of cholesterol from meat, eggs, and dairy products. Consequently, the plasma cholesterol level of many Americans can be several times higher than needed for daily

metabolic balance. Since excess calorie intake from food products is turned into triglycerides and fatty acids, it's also possible to develop elevated plasma levels of triglycerides. It is therefore not surprising that there is a significant incidence of atherosclerosis in this culture.

Risk factors associated with the development of atherosclerosis are

- Age (men over age 45; women over age 55)
- History of smoking, hypertension, premature menopause, obesity, antihypertension medications
- Hormone imbalance (diabetes mellitus, hypothyroidism)
- Weight (>30 percent overweight)
- **Lipoprotein status (low HDL, high LDL)**

Lifestyle intervention, especially diet adjustment, can dramatically improve many of the risk factors (obesity, diabetes mellitus, and lipoprotein levels). The treatment of **hyperlipidemia** involves dietary restriction of saturated fats, cholesterol, and carbohydrates. Diet control is always the first line of defense. The American

Heart Association recommends a stepped approach to diet adjustment toward a goal of 100 to 150 mg of cholesterol intake daily, and fat limited to 20 percent of the total calories. Overall health status is evaluated by reviewing the levels of lipids and lipoproteins in the circulation. Routine lipid analysis includes fasting values of total cholesterol, triglycerides, and HDL-cholesterol. Quantitative analysis of serum cholesterol is not a routine assay and must be specifically ordered. This analysis identifies the circulating levels of free cholesterol and cholesterol esters. Triglycerides and cholesterol are measured from fasting (12 to 14 hours) blood samples where the patient has not consumed alcohol for the previous 24 hours. Although the literature speaks of plasma lipid levels, or plasma lipoproteins, blood samples used for analysis are serum samples. Serum, fluid that remains after the blood has been allowed to clot, is the preferred fluid because it provides the greatest amount of (previously circulating) cholesterol and triglyceride for measurement.

Lipoprotein electrophoresis is the separation of lipoproteins in a blood sample. It is performed to characterize the lipoprotein profile in a test called the lipid panel or lipid profile. Actually, the lipid panel measures total cholesterol, HDL-cholesterol, and triglycerides. LDL-cholesterol is calculated from the values for total cholesterol (TC), HDL-cholesterol (HDL), and triglycerides (TG) as follows: $LDL = TC - HDL - TG/5$. The recommended serum values to prevent heart disease for these lipoproteins are presented in Figure 29.4. Cholesterol values in the population range from 120 to 330 mg/dL. When cholesterol levels rise, the liver makes more LDL for transport. Circulating triglyceride values vary with age, ranging from 10 to 190 mg/dL. The clinical strategy is to keep the bad cholesterol (**LDL**) as **low** as possible by reducing total serum cholesterol and triglycerides and raising the good cholesterol (**HDL**) as **high** as possible.

HDL levels can be elevated through vigorous exercise, a diet that includes fish and/or diet supplementation with omega-3-polyunsaturated fatty acids (fish oils), and moderate alcohol consumption. Factors that decrease HDL include smoking, obesity, liver damage, uremia, and starvation.

Significant elevations in lipid levels that occur as a result of genetic disorders are *primary* hyperlipidemias. One or more lipids may be affected (hypercholesterolemia, hypertriglyceridemia, or mixed lipidemias). *Secondary* hyperlipidemias also involve one or more lipids, but they are caused by any of the three D's: diet, drugs, or disease. Diet—cholesterol and triglycerides increase as a function of age, diets rich in saturated fats, and a nonactive lifestyle. Drugs—acute alcohol intoxication, thiazide and loop diuretics, beta-blockers, retinoic acid, progesterone, and steroids can elevate cholesterol and/or triglycerides and LDL. Disease—acute pancreatitis, chronic renal failure, diabetes mellitus, hypothyroidism, gout, and liver disease can elevate cholesterol and/or triglycerides. Secondary hyperlipidemias arising from diet or disease are risk factors that contribute to the development of atherosclerosis and heart disease.

Whether treating primary or secondary hyperlipidemia, diet control is always initiated first. Saturated fat raises the LDL-cholesterol level more than anything else in a diet. *Trans* fatty acids (*trans* fats), made when vegetable oil is hydrogenated, also raise cholesterol levels.

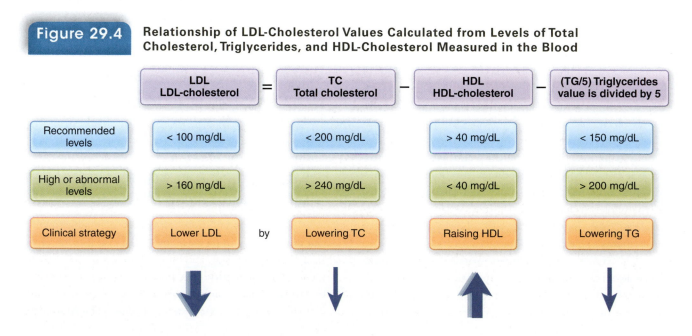

Figure 29.4 Relationship of LDL-Cholesterol Values Calculated from Levels of Total Cholesterol, Triglycerides, and HDL-Cholesterol Measured in the Blood

	LDL LDL-cholesterol	=	TC Total cholesterol	−	HDL HDL-cholesterol	−	(TG/5) Triglycerides value is divided by 5
Recommended levels	< 100 mg/dL		< 200 mg/dL		> 40 mg/dL		< 150 mg/dL
High or abnormal levels	> 160 mg/dL		> 240 mg/dL		< 40 mg/dL		> 200 mg/dL
Clinical strategy	Lower LDL	by	Lowering TC		Raising HDL		Lowering TG

Genetics can't be changed, but diet can be restructured to take in more unsaturated fats and eliminate trans fats. If diet adjustment does not adequately lower the target lipid, drugs may be added to reduce the bad lipid and raise the good cholesterol levels. Reduction in cholesterol has been demonstrated in large clinical trials to be associated with a 20 to 30 percent reduction in CAD. Combined diet and drug therapy reduces **morbidity** and CAD-related mortality.

LO 29.2 | LO 29.3 | LO 29.4 | LO 29.5 | LO 29.6

HYPOLIPIDEMIC/ANTILIPEMIC DRUGS

There are five groups of drugs that are used alone or as adjunctive treatment to diet:

- in the management of hyperlipidemias
- for the prevention of coronary events in patients at risk
- for the treatment of clinically evident coronary heart disease
- to slow the progression of atherosclerosis

The groups are the HMG-CoA reductase inhibitors (known as the statins), cholesterol absorption inhibitors, bile acid sequestrants, fibric acid derivatives, and nicotinic acid. Each group works at a specific location within the liver or intestine and has a different mechanism of action to affect cholesterol, triglycerides, and lipoproteins.

HMG-CoA Reductase Inhibitors: Statins

Lovastatin (*Mevacor*) was the first in the class of novel drugs that alter cholesterol synthesis in the liver by inhibiting the enzyme HMG-CoA reductase. Lovastatin was discovered in the fungus known as red yeast rice. Four of these drugs are derived from a variety of different fungi and three are synthetically (*) made. All drugs in this class—atorvastatin (*Lipitor**), fluvastatin (*Lescol**), lovastatin (*Mevacor*), pravastatin (*Pravachol*), pitavastatin (*Livalo**), rosuvastatin (*Crestor**), and simvastatin (*Zocor*)—have the same site of action and effectively reduce total cholesterol and LDL plasma levels.

Mechanism of Action

Remember the cholesterol pathway starts as two acetyl-CoA molecules (see Figure 29.5). An early, very important step in this process is the conversion of acetyl-CoA molecules into HMG-CoA, which is then converted to mevalonic acid by *HMG-CoA reductase*. Mevalonic acid is a rate-limiting pivotal step in steroid and cholesterol synthesis. Drug action in the synthetic pathway has a significant impact on circulating cholesterol levels because the liver makes two-thirds of the daily cholesterol requirement. This reduces the need to make apolipoproteins B and E to form LDL for cholesterol transport so circulating LDL drops. The plasma levels of LDL and cholesterol are reduced. Similarly, VLDL also is reduced by the statins so plasma levels of triglycerides decrease. At the same time, levels of HDL-cholesterol are increased in the circulation. These are very effective hypolipidemic drugs. The effect on circulating lipids is observable within 2 weeks of treatment; the maximum effect requires up to 6 weeks of drug therapy. When the medication is stopped, the reduction in lipoprotein plasma levels disappears within 6 weeks. Maintenance of therapeutic benefit requires diet adjustment and continued drug treatment for years. Of course, the most appropriate drug and dose may be adjusted during this time.

Comparative Effects

While each drug in this class can lower cholesterol levels, they differ by how greatly they can reduce total cholesterol, LDL, and triglyceride levels. All of the statins reduce LDL up to 30 percent. When a greater reduction of LDL is required, simvastatin (*Zocor*), atorvastatin (*Lipitor*), and rosuvastatin (*Crestor*) reduce more than 45 percent; in fact, rosuvastatin and atorvastatin have been demonstrated to reduce up to 60 percent. All of these reductions are patient and dose dependent and most individuals would not require reductions above 40 percent. All of the statins raise the HDL level up to 20 percent. Again, simvastatin (*Zocor*), atorvastatin (*Lipitor*), and rosuvastatin (*Crestor*) increase HDL more than 30 percent. (See comparison with other lipid-lowering drugs later in the chapter in Table 29:2).

Antiinflammatory Effect

Remember that LDL initiates an inflammatory response when it begins the plaque-building process. The recruitment of macrophages and development of foam cells are part of the local inflammation in the atherosclerotic artery. **C-reactive protein (CRP)** is a protein released during injury and inflammation, and in some chronic conditions such as arthritis. High levels of CRP in the blood may raise the risk for atherosclerosis. Statins lower CRP while performing lipid-lowering tasks, which may have an additional clinical benefit. Extensive research is being done on this antiinflammatory action. Meanwhile, simvastatin and atorvastatin are being used in

Figure 29.5 **HMG-CoA Site of Action in the Biosynthesis of Cholesterol: Pathway from Acetoacetyl CoA to Mevalonate**

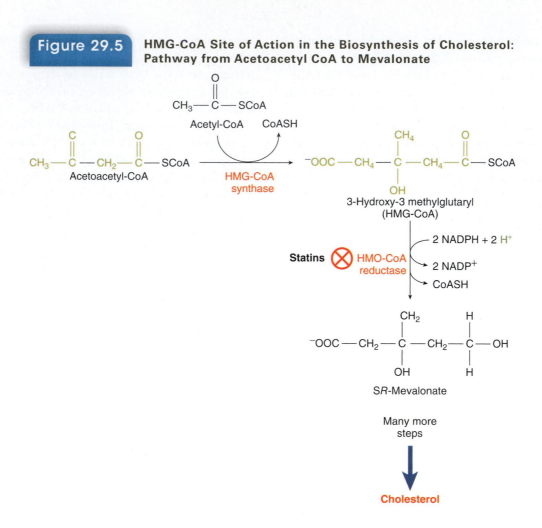

patients with multiple sclerosis and adult and juvenile arthritis.

Administration

All of these drugs are well absorbed following oral administration. However, lovastatin is better absorbed when administered with meals. Lovastatin is metabolized in the liver to active metabolites. All of the other drugs in this class may be taken with or without meals without affecting the therapeutic effect. Except for pravastatin, all are highly bound (95 to 98 percent) to plasma protein. Recommended maintenance doses for HMG-CoA reductase inhibitors are presented in Table 29:1. Generally, it is recommended to take the statins in the evening because the majority of cholesterol is produced by the body at night. Atorvastatin (*Lipitor*) can be taken at any time of the day.

Combinations

Lovastatin and simvastatin have been used successfully in combination with other lipid-lowering drugs. Two products are now available that combine a statin with another lipid-lowering drug. *Advicor* combines niacin (500, 750,

or 1000 mg) with 20 mg of lovastatin. *Vytorin* combines 10, 20, 40 or 80 mg simvastatin (*Zocor*) with 10 mg of ezetimibe (*Zetia*). Lovastatin and simvastatin can be used with cholestyramine to lower cholesterol. Any of these combination treatments dramatically reduces cholesterol and LDL to levels that cannot be attained by the individual drugs alone. When using combination therapy with cholestyramine, the statin should be taken 4 to 6 hours after the bile acid sequestrant to avoid the possibility of the sequestrant binding the statin while in the intestinal tract.

Adverse Effects

The range of adverse effects includes headache, dizziness, alteration of taste, insomnia, diarrhea, flatulence, abdominal cramping, and photosensitivity. Some people experience memory loss or an inability to concentrate as well. Because the HMG-CoA reductase inhibitors are absorbed and are able to affect lipid metabolism in a variety of tissues, the spectrum of adverse effects is greater than other hypolipidemic drugs. In general, any of these adverse effects occur in less than 3 to 5 percent of patients taking the drugs. The statins do cause myalgias,

Hypolipidemic Drugs

Drug (*Trade Name*)	Usual oral daily dose
Bile acid sequestrants	
Cholestyramine (*Prevalite, Questran*)	4–16 g
Colestipol (*Colestid*)	5–20 g
Colesevelam (*Welchol*)	2.6–8 g
HMG-CoA enzyme inhibitors	
Atorvastatin (*Lipitor*)	10–80 mg
Fluvastatin (*Lescol, Lescol XL*)	20–80 mg
Lovastatin (*Altoprev, Mevacor*)	20–80 mg/day
Pitavastatin (*Livalo*)	2–4 mg
Pravastatin (*Pravachol*)	20–80 mg
Rosuvastatin (*Crestor*)	5–40 mg
Simvastatin (*Zocor*)	20–80 mg
Alteration of lipid and lipoprotein metabolism	
Gemfibrozil (*Lopid*)	600 mg BID 30 min before meals
Fenofibrate (*Antara, Lofibra, Tricor, Trilipix*)	54–160 mg
Niacin (*Niacor*)	2–6 g
Cholesterol absorption inhibitor	
Ezetimibe (*Zetia*)	10 mg
Combination drugs	
Ezetimibe and simvastatin (*Vytorin*)	10 mg/10–80 mg
Niacin and lovastatin (*Advicor*)	500–1000 mg/20–40 mg
Niacin extended release and simvastatin (*Simcor*)	500–1000 mg/20 mg

leg ache, and muscle weakness in some patients that are not serious conditions and may not require a change in treatment.

There is a rare adverse effect that affects muscle metabolism. Cerivastatin (*Baycol*) was removed from the market due to safety concerns. In long-term treatment, patients on cerivastatin showed evidence of muscle breakdown (**rhabdomyolysis**). The incidence of this life-threatening side effect was significantly higher with cerivastatin alone than with other statin drugs. Rabdomyolysis is a condition in which the contents of the skeletal muscle cells (enzymes, creatinine, myoglobin) leak into the circulation. The patient experiences muscle pain and weakness and renal failure develops when the large molecules of myoglobin obstruct normal renal flow. Transient elevations in creatine phosphokinase (CPK) may occur before and during the myalgia. Depending on the medical profile of the patient, periodic monitoring of serum enzymes including liver function (AST, ALT) and CPK will indicate the need for dose adjustment or discontinuation.

Rhabdomyolysis is a very rare adverse event with the use of the other statins. The chance of it occurring is less than one per million statin prescriptions. It is worth understanding the difference between rhabdomyolysis and the less serious myalgias statins do cause. Patients should be instructed to report muscle tenderness or weakness to their physician. Sometimes the leg pain is only a leg pain, but it's important to the patient. There is *no* special boxed warning with the use of the HMG-CoA reductase inhibitor class of drugs.

Prior to initiation of treatment, or increase in dosage, liver function tests may be performed to confirm the status of alanine aminotransferase (ALT) and aspartate aminotransferase (AST) in the patient. The drugs are contraindicated in patients who have *unexplained persistent* elevations in these liver enzymes (and, as just described, elevated CPK). This class of drugs can elevate liver enzymes and enzymes can return to normal in some patients on chronic therapy. The serum levels should be repeated every 6 to 12 weeks as needed. Accidental overdose (up to 6 g) has occurred in adults and children (being treated for primary hyperlipidemias) with these drugs. There is no specific antidote. Using general supportive measures for overdose of any medication, these patients recovered without complication.

Contraindications

Clinical manifestations of hypersensitivity, active liver disease, or persistent elevation in liver function enzymes are contraindications to the use or continued use of these drugs. Statins are *absolutely contraindicated* during pregnancy because of their ability to inhibit essential lipid metabolism in the developing fetus. While no human data are available, skeletal malformations have occurred in animals.

Drug Interactions

There are significant drug interactions that occur with nicotinic acid, antifungal drugs, and grapefruit juice. See Table 29:3 and the drug interaction section at the end of the chapter.

Cholesterol Absorption Inhibitors: Ezetimibe

The statin drugs exert their lipid-lowering effects specifically on liver metabolism. Two of the other groups of hypolipidemic drugs, bile acid sequestrants and ezetimibe, interfere with dietary cholesterol absorption.

Mechanism of Action

Ezetimibe (*Zetia*) is the first of a novel class of *selective* cholesterol-absorption inhibitors. It has a mechanism of action unlike all the other hypolipidemic drugs. Ezetimibe acts at the surface of the small intestine called the brush border to block absorption of dietary cholesterol (see Figure 29.4). This decreases the content of cholesterol in chylomicrons so the amount of cholesterol delivered to the liver is reduced. This results in a decrease in VLDL particles that are precursors to LDL, thereby decreasing circulating LDL-cholesterol. This drug is very selective in its action and does not prevent absorption of other dietary fats or fat-soluble vitamins.

Ezetimibe is metabolized in the intestinal wall to an active metabolite that is even more potent than ezetimibe. The metabolite is taken directly to the liver and then passed back to the small intestine to continue reducing cholesterol absorption. This cycle of recirculation between the intestine and liver continues to give ezetimibe its long half-life (22 hours) and allows it to be used once a day. Remember cholesterol balance (homeostasis) is very tightly controlled. Well, when cholesterol from the intestine decreases and the liver isn't seeing dietary cholesterol, it starts making cholesterol. This does partially offset the total cholesterol decrease from ezetimibe. This may be why ezetimibe produces a less dramatic reduction in the lipid profile compared to the statins (see Table 29:2).

Combinations

Ezetimibe (10 mg) taken once daily will modestly reduce total cholesterol, LDL, and triglyceride blood levels. Its mechanism, site of action, and safety profile make it an ideal drug to combine with other

[Table **29:2**]

Comparative Effects of the Hypolipidemic Drugs on Cholesterol and Lipoproteins

Drug	Decrease in TC Total cholesterol	Decrease in LDL Low-density lipoproteins	Decrease in TG Triglycerides	Increase in HDL High-density lipoproteins
HMG-CoA reductase inhibitors (statins)*	19–37%	25–50%	14–29%	4–12%
Absorption inhibitors				
Ezetimibe	13%	18%	9%	1%
Bile acid sequestrants	7–10%	10–18%	**	3%
Other				
Nicotinic acid	10–20%	10–20%	30–70%	14–35%
Fibric acid derivatives	19%	4–8%	30%	12%

These are reported changes in cholesterol and lipoproteins at 40 mg doses of the statin under study.
***There is a little increase or no change.*

hypolipidemic drugs. This drug primarily stays within the blood between the liver and intestine (the enterohepatic circulation). It does not interact with other organs and produces very few side effects. When combined with other lipid-lowering drugs, it has a complementary mechanism of action without increasing potential adverse effects. In fact, it has been demonstrated that when added to the statin drugs, circulating LDL has been reduced an additional 20 percent or more. This therapeutic success led to the preparation of a fixed-dose combination of ezetimibe with simvastatin (*Vytorin*). Ezetimibe can be used with any of the hypolipidemic drugs. The only significant dosing sequence issue is when it is given with a bile acid sequestrant; it must be taken 2 to 4 hours after the bile acid sequestrant to avoid an absorption interaction. The mechanism of the bile acid sequestrants could bind ezetimibe and keep it from acting in the small intestine.

Adverse Effects

The range of adverse effects reported by patients taking *Zetia* or *Vytorin* includes abdominal pain, fatigue, coughing, diarrhea, back pain, and arthralgia. With *Vytorin*, adverse effects associated with statins, especially myalgias, may be expected to occur.

There are few drug interactions that occur with ezetimibe.

Bile Acid Sequestrants: Cholestyramine, Colestipol, and Colesevelam

Mechanism of Action

Bile salts are synthesized from cholesterol and released into the duodenum as a part of bile. The main function of bile salts is to break down fats ingested in the diet into absorbable forms. The bile salts are recycled by intestinal absorption and stored within the gallbladder through the enterohepatic circulation. Cholestyramine (*Questran*) is an ion-exchange resin that combines with the bile salts and cholesterol in the intestinal tract. This insoluble binding prevents the absorption of the bile salts and cholesterol. The result is an increased elimination of bile salts, cholesterol, and other fats in the feces. Low-density lipoprotein and cholesterol levels decrease during treatment. Liver synthesis of cholesterol may increase, however—the circulating cholesterol concentration decreases because cholesterol is cleared from the plasma (see Table 29:2). Changes in LDL levels may be observed within 1 week of treatment, while changes in circulating cholesterol may require 1 month. The action of colestipol (*Colestid*) is similar to that of cholestyramine. Colestipol interferes with the absorption of bile acids and cholesterol from the intestinal tract.

Administration

Cholestyramine, 4 to 6 g per dose, is mixed with liquid and taken twice a day before meals. Cholestyramine is a powder that must be mixed with water, fruit juice noncarbonated beverages, or fluid soups (broth, not cream). Applesauce or crushed pineapple also may be used to suspend the powder. The daily oral dose of colestipol tablets is 2–16 g/day given once or in divided doses. Patients are often started at 2 g once or twice daily and raised 2 g once or twice daily at 1–2 month intervals until the lipid profile is acceptable. Colestipol comes as tablets or granules.

Colesevelam (*Welchol*) is recommended to start with three tablets twice daily or six tablets once daily with a meal. Each tablet contains 625 mg of active drug so the maximum dose is more than 3 g daily.

Adverse Effects

Cholestyramine is not absorbed from the gastrointestinal tract so systemic effects do not usually occur. Because it remains within the intestinal lumen, GI disturbances are the most common adverse effect, notably constipation. Some patients may experience severe constipation accompanied by fecal impaction. The most serious adverse effect with the bile acid sequestrants is intestinal obstruction. Because of the large doses required, nausea and vomiting may occur. With continued use of the drug, constipation, flatulence, and nausea may disappear. Headache, dizziness, drowsiness, and anxiety have been reported to occur in some patients. Colestipol has produced transient elevations in aspartate aminotransferase (AST), alanine aminotransferase (ALT), and alkaline phosphatase.

There are significant drug interactions that occur with nicotinic acid. See Table 29:3 and the drug interaction section at the end of the chapter.

| LO 29.3 | LO 29.5 | LO 29.6 |

OTHER HYPOLIPIDEMIC DRUGS

Nicotinic Acid, Niacin (*Niacor, Niaspan*)

Niacin, vitamin B_3, is a general term that refers to nicotinic acid and its derivatives nicotinamide and inositol nicotinate. It is an important vitamin in the metabolism of carbohydrates. A deficiency of niacin that causes severe dermatitis, peripheral neuritis, and photosensitivity is known as pellagra. However, in very large doses (2000 mg, compared to the daily vitamin requirement of 15 mg), niacin, in the form of nicotinic acid, lowers plasma lipid levels.

Mechanism of Action

Nicotinic acid reduces the level of the VLDL and LDL, lipoproteins responsible for carrying triglycerides and cholesterol in a dose-dependent manner. The mechanism of action is unclear, but it appears to affect cholesterol synthesis in the liver through a recently discovered G protein–coupled receptor for nicotinic acid. HDL is significantly increased as well (see Table 29:2 and Figure 29.6). At the same time, fat metabolism in adipose tissue is affected. In adipose tissue, nicotinic acid inhibits triglyceride lipase and stimulates lipoprotein lipase, which decreases free fatty acid release and removes triglycerides. Consequently, the plasma lipid level is significantly reduced. The effects of nicotinic acid on lipoproteins are evident within 4 days of treatment and maximum effects occur within 3 to 5 weeks. The other forms of niacin, nicotinamide and inositol nicotinate, do not lower cholesterol.

Niacin is available over the counter in strengths up to 500 mg per tablet. *Niacor* (500 mg) and *Niaspan* (500, 750, and 1000 mg) are available by prescription. Although these are all taken orally, these formulations are not interchangeable. *Niaspan* is a once-daily extended-release tablet. Interestingly, the formulations of the vitamin affect circulating lipids differently. The immediate-release preparation increases HDL, while the sustained-release product reduces total cholesterol and LDL preferentially. Nicotinic acid (*Niacor*), an immediate-release tablet, is administered orally several times per day. Initial doses (100 mg TID) are gradually increased to 1 to 2 g three times a day. The maximum dose is usually 8 g per day. Because niacin has a good effect on raising HDL, it complements other hypolipidemic drug action. It has been successfully used in combination with colestipol and lovastatin, leading to the preparation of a fixed-dose combination product with lovastatin (*Advicor*). See Table 29:1 for dose availability. For patients that require an aggressive lipid-lowering strategy, the triple combination is more effective in reducing LDL than dual combination of nicotinic acid with one of the others.

Adverse Effects

Common adverse effects include nausea, vomiting, diarrhea, and vasodilation. Nicotinic acid produces vasodilation that manifests as flushing of the skin. The flushing is accompanied by a sensation of warmth on the face and upper body, sometimes with tingling, itching, or headache. This effect is not harmful but may not be well tolerated by patients who experience a persistent flushing. Patients should be advised to avoid drinking hot liquids just before and after dosing to avoid the potential for producing more vasodilation from the liquids. Aspirin taken 30 minutes before dosing also mitigates the vasodilation in many patients.

Figure 29.6 **Site of Hypolipidemic Drug Actions**

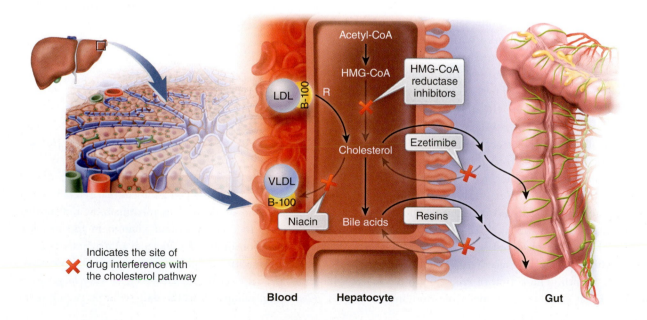

Nicotinic acid also may increase uric acid levels in the blood (hyperuricemia). Individuals with high uric acid levels may develop symptoms of gout. The sustained-release product in doses greater than 2 g per day may promote jaundice, increased bilirubin, nausea, and prolonged prothrombin time. These effects appear to be mediated by an alteration of liver function. Periodic monitoring of liver enzymes every 6 to 12 weeks for the first year, especially if combined with a statin drug, will provide adequate indication of liver status. There had been concern that nicotinic acid might compromise blood sugar control if used in patients with elevated blood glucose or diabetic patients. As diabetes is a significant risk factor for atherosclerosis, diabetic patients are likely to be recipients of nicotinic acid therapy. Results from recent studies with immediate-release nicotinic acid and a new once-daily extended-release form show that effects on glucose control are minimal at doses commonly used for the treatment of lipidemia (i.e., up to 2 g daily). For patients treated with the new once-daily formulation, the adverse event and tolerability profile, including flushing, liver function test elevations, and occurrence of myopathy, is the same among those with and without diabetes, and no special or additional monitoring is required. Moreover, nicotinic acid reduces the risk of cardiovascular events and long-term mortality similarly among patients at all levels of baseline glucose, including those patients with elevated fasting glucose, metabolic syndrome, or glucose values in the overtly diabetic range. Nicotinic acid may be considered as a therapeutic option in these patients, alone or in combination with a statin, as part of a comprehensive program of cardiovascular risk factor reduction. There are significant drug interactions that occur with nicotinic acid. See Table 29:3 and the drug interaction section at the end of the chapter.

Fibric Acid Derivatives

Gemfibrozil (*Lopid*) and fenofibrate (*Tricor*) are derivatives of fibric acid that decrease triglyceride and VLDL, and increase HDL. The mechanism of action is directed at triglyceride production. It inhibits triglyceride lipolysis in adipose tissue, decreases free fatty acid uptake by the liver, and decreases hepatic VLDL-triglyceride synthesis. Overall there is a modest cholesterol-lowering effect.

Both drugs are well absorbed from the intestinal tract. The oral dose of gemfibrozil is usually 600 mg BID, while the dose of fenofibrate is 54–160 mg daily. Fenofibrate is a micronized formulation of fibric acid, meaning the particles are reduced to a very small size to facilitate absorption. These drugs are approved for use in hypertriglyceridemia patients who do not respond to diet where triglyceride levels can exceed 1000 mg/dl (compared to the normal range of 10 to 190 mg/dl) to prevent pancreatitis, an inflammation of the pancreas. They also can be used in combination with other cholesterol-lowering drugs to facilitate a further reduction in triglycerides. Gemfibrozil is usually taken twice a day, 30 minutes before the morning and evening meals.

Common adverse effects involve the GI tract and include nausea, vomiting, diarrhea, and flatulence. They also may produce dizziness and blurred vision that may interfere with the ability to perform intricate hand work or operate equipment. Since this class of drugs—fibrates—can produce muscle pain and weakness, combination with HMG-CoA reductase inhibitors potentiates the development of myopathy and elevated creatine phosphokinase levels. Gemfibrozil may increase cholesterol excretion into the bile, leading to gallstone formation. The drug must be discontinued in the presence of cholelithiasis or elevated creatine phosphokinase.

LO 29.2

PREFERRED THERAPY

All of the hypolipidemic drugs are indicated as adjunctive therapy for the reduction of elevated cholesterol in patients with primary hypercholesterolemia and elevated LDL who do not adequately respond to diet. This class of drugs is used to decrease mixed lipidemias of primary or secondary origin, especially where high-risk patients (diabetic and nephrotic lipidemia) have not responded to other treatments.

The HMG-CoA reductase inhibitors atorvastatin (*Lipitor*) and simvastatin (*Zocor*) are among the top 10 most prescribed drugs in the United States in adults ages 18 to 64. Atorvastatin is third in number of prescriptions written. They are used for the treatment of primary hyperlipidemias and to slow the progression of atherosclerosis to reduce the risk of acute coronary episodes and sudden death.

In clinical practice, the role of ezetimibe (*Zetia*) as monotherapy is for patients who require modest reductions in their LDL level or who cannot tolerate other lipid-lowering agents. Its major benefit, however, is seen when administered in combination with a statin in patients who cannot tolerate high statin dosage alone or who need further LDL reductions despite treatment with the maximum statin dosage.

Cholestyramine is also recommended in the management of partial biliary obstruction. Examples of these hypolipidemic drugs appear in Figure 29.7.

Figure 29.7   **Examples of Cholesterol-Lowering Drugs**

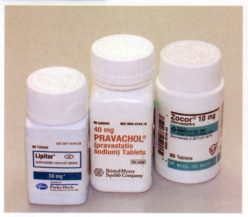

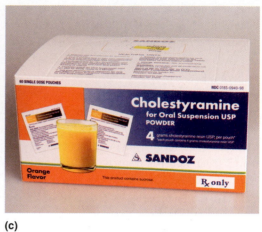

(a) (b) (c)

(a) HMG-CoA reductase inhibitors (statins). (b) Combination simvastatin and ezetimibe. (c) Cholestyramine resin.

LO 29.5 LO 29.6

CONTRAINDICATIONS AND PREGNANCY

For the systemically absorbed drugs (all but the bile acid sequestrants), clinical manifestations of hypersensitivity, active liver disease, or persistent elevation in liver function, enzymes are contraindications to the use or continued use of the hypolipidemic drug. The bile acid sequestrants should not be used in patients who are hypersensitive to the drug or have biliary or intestinal obstruction. Nicotinic acid is contraindicated in patients with gallbladder disease, glaucoma, impaired liver function, or peptic ulcer.

HMG-CoA reductase inhibitors are absolutely contraindicated during pregnancy because of their ability to inhibit essential lipid metabolism in the developing fetus. Hypolipidemic drugs have been designated as FDA Pregnancy Category B or C, except for HMG-CoA reductase inhibitors, which are designated Category X. The safety for use of hypolipidemic drugs during pregnancy has not been clearly established through well-controlled clinical trials. Even niacin at the doses used to lower cholesterol has not been studied. The usual recommendation is to discontinue treatment once pregnancy is confirmed and restart after breast-feeding has been discontinued. The risk of temporarily interrupting hypolipidemic treatment is usually far less than the potential for harm to the fetus.

LO 29.6 LO 29.7

DRUG INTERACTIONS

The bile acid sequestrants stay in the lumen of the intestine and trap other subtances during transit through the intestine. Cholestyramine binds with fat-soluble vitamins (A, D, and K), folic acid, and many drugs, thus reducing their GI absorption. Supplementation at time intervals when the bile acids are no longer in the absorption area may be necessary to avoid vitamin deficiencies. It is recommended that any other medications be taken 1 hour before or at least 4 hours after cholestyramine to avoid interaction within the intestinal tract that would delay or inhibit absorption of the concomitant medication.

Often drug metabolism occurs in the liver by forms of P-450 enzymes. There is a cytochrome P-450 enzyme CYP3A4 in the wall of the small intestine that metabolizes many drugs. This enzyme has become well known in recent years because it can be inhibited by grapefruit pulp and grapefruit juice. Eating one whole grapefruit causes the same effect as a juice serving because both contain the compound bergamottin that is the enzyme inhibitor. That means taking some medication in the presence of grapefruit juice can significantly decrease drug metabolism at the intestinal wall and increase its bioavailability. For example, the bioavailability of simvastatin is about 5 percent, meaning that a dose of simvastatin is about 95 percent metabolized before it reaches the blood. Imagine how powerful this drug is if only 5 percent can reduce lipoproteins. This large amount of normally metabolized drug can be systemically available if an inhibitor of CYP3A4, such as grapefruit juice, is present. Increasing a drug's bioavailability will increase risk of developing adverse effects. Grapefruit juice interacts only with drugs that are administered orally. The degree of inhibition varies among patients, but it may last up to 24 hours after a single glass of juice and up to 72 hours after multiple glasses of juice. Atorvastatin, lovastatin, and simvastatin are definitely affected by grapefruit. Although the studies concerning grapefruit interactions with pravastatin, fluvastatin, or rosuvastatin were not as significant, it probably would be prudent not to consume grapefruit a few hours before or after taking these medications. Orange juice does not have any effect on absorption of these drugs.

Drugs that are potent inhibitors of CYP3A4 and also cause an increase in statin blood levels include cyclosporine, itraconazole, ketoconazole, erythromycin, clarithromycin, and HIV protease inhibitors. For patients who require antifungal therapy, the statins should be stopped until the fungal treatment is discontinued.

Gemfibrozil should not be administered with the statins because this combination was used in patients who developed rhabdomyolysis. The combination may predispose patients to develop severe myopathy. Similarly severe myopathy has occurred in patients taking nicotinic acid in doses over 1 g with statin drugs. A list of specific drugs that have been shown to interact with hypolipidemic drugs is presented in Table 29:3.

[Table 29:3]

Drug Interactions with Hypolipidemic Drugs

Hypolipidemic	Interact with	Response
Bile acid sequestrants	Anticoagulants (oral), aspirin, clindamycin, clofibrate, dextrothyroxine digitalis glycosides, furosemide, glipizide, imipramine, methyldopa, niacin, penicillin, phenytoin, tetracyclines, thiazides, diuretics, tolbutamide, ursodiol, vitamins A, D, K, E	Decrease drug absorption
Cholestyramine	HMG-CoA reductase inhibitors	Decrease bioavailability of the enzyme inhibitors when taken within 1 hour
	Anticoagulants	Increase bleeding
Gemfibrozil, fenofibrate	HMG-CoA reductase inhibitors	Severe myopathy
	Oral anticoagulants	Increase blood levels of anticoagulants
HMG-CoA reductase inhibitors (statins)	Alcohol	Increase blood level of enzyme inhibitors
	Cycloprorine, clarithromycin, erythromycin, grapefruit/grapefruit juice, itraconazole, ketoconazole, oral contraceptives, protease (HIV) inhibitors	Increase statin blood level by inhibiting CYP3A4 enzymes; potential for myopathy to occur
	Digoxin, warfarin	Increase blood levels of digoxin and warfarin
	Rifampin	Decrease plasma clearance of fluvastatin
	Nicotinic acid, propranolol, digoxin	Decrease fluvastatin levels
	Propranolol	Decrease statin hypolipidemic effect
Nicotinic acid	Alcohol	Increase vasodilation, flushing
	Antihypertensive drugs	Increase hypotension
	Ganglionic blocking drugs	

Compliance with drug therapy is critical to achieving the long-term benefit of reduced blood levels of cholesterol and low-density lipoproteins and prevention of CHD.

Patient Instruction

To assist patients in developing compliance habits for proper drug use, the medication, dosing schedule, and specific adverse reactions should be reviewed with the patient.

Drug Administration

Medication is usually taken before meals. Lovastatin should be taken with meals in order to absorb the maximum therapeutic amount. Niacin may be taken with meals for those patients who experience GI upset with dosing. Powders can be mixed with beverages, soups, cereals, or pulpy fruits; however, colestipol tablets should be swallowed whole, not crushed or chewed. *Niaspan* preparations should not be substituted for equivalent doses of immediate-release (crystalline) niacin.

Drug Interactions

Inquire about the consumption of juices, especially around medication time. If the patient drinks grapefruit juice, suggest a dosing schedule that will not interfere with statin drug metabolism. Recommend limiting the amount of juice and extending the interval between taking the juice at breakfast and taking the drug several hours later (bedtime). Review other medications with the patient because beta-blockers will decrease the blood level of the statin drugs and impact therapy. Antifungals, warfarin, or oral contraceptives will increase the level of the statin drugs and may induce adverse effects. Since medication may interfere with other drugs, concomitant medications should be taken 1 hour before or 6 hours after bile acid sequestrants. HMG-CoA reductase inhibitors used as combination therapy with bile acid sequestrants should be taken 4 to 6 hours after the bile acid sequestrant.

Notify the Prescribing Physician

The patient should be told that a serum chemistry panel will be performed periodically during treatment to determine whether cholesterol and the LDL/HDL ratio are within the normal range. Liver function enzymes, AST, ALT, and alkaline phosphatase are evaluated to ensure the patient is not developing undesirable changes during treatment. The patient should be instructed to notify the physician if unusual bleeding from the gums or rectum occurs. Muscle pain, tenderness, weakness, malaise, or fever while taking these medications should be reported to the doctor immediately. Statin-related muscle problems *usually* appear within a few weeks of starting the drug. Be aware of muscle pain, cramps, stiffness, spasms, and weakness that can't be explained by arthritis, recent strenuous exercise, a fall, or other common causes.

Gemfibrozil may cause dizziness and blurred vision that could impair judgment in tasks requiring focused concentration or coordination. This should be reviewed with patients who need to drive or operate heavy equipment.

Patients who experience flushing (sensation of warmth on the face and upper body) with niacin treatment should avoid hot liquids immediately before and after dosing to minimize triggering of vasodilation. Patients experiencing persistent flushing may benefit from aspirin 300 mg 30 minutes before niacin dosing.

Use in Pregnancy

3-Hydroxy-HMG-CoA reductase inhibitors ***should not be taken*** during pregnancy because of their ability to affect metabolism and critical growth factors in the developing fetus. Patients who may become pregnant should be advised to notify the physician immediately so that the medication can be discontinued and another appropriate treatment begun.

Understanding Terminology

Match the terms in the right column with the appropriate definitions in the left column.

___ 1. A dietary lipid normally synthesized in the body. **(LO 29.6)**

___ 2. A protein in the plasma that transports triglycerides and cholesterol. **(LO 29.6)**

___ 3. Abnormally high levels of lipids in the plasma. **(LO 29.6)**

___ 4. A dietary lipid normally used by the body. **(LO 29.6)**

___ 5. A drug used to lower plasma lipid levels. **(LO 29.6)**

a. cholesterol

b. hyperlipidemia

c. hypolipidemic

d. lipoprotein

e. triglyceride

Acquiring Knowledge

Answer the following questions.

1. What diseases are associated with hyperlipidemia? **(LO 29.1, 29.2)**

2. What is the major approach to the treatment of hyperlipidemia? **(LO 29.1, 29.2)**

3. How does lovastatin (*Mevacor*) produce its hypolipidemic effect? **(LO 29.3, 29.4)**

4. List the adverse effects of niacin. **(LO 29.5)**

5. How does the mechanism of action of fenofibrate (*Tricor*) differ from that of cholestyramine (*Questran*)? **(LO 29.3)**

6. What is the primary indication for the use of gemfibrozil (*Lopid*)? **(LO 29.3)**

Applying Knowledge on the Job

Use your critical-thinking skills to answer the following questions.

1. The HMG-CoA reductase inhibitors may affect liver function. Liver function tests (ALT and AST) should be done at certain points during therapy using these medications. Explain when these tests should be done. **(LO 29.5)**

2. Some patients may experience persistent flushing when taking niacin. What advice might be helpful for the patients who find this to be intolerable? **(LO 29.5)**

3. What are the adverse effects listed for lovastatin? **(LO 29.5)**

Multiple Choice

Use your critical-thinking skills to answer the following questions.

1. Which of the following is correct: 75 to 80 percent of total cholesterol in the body **(LO 29.1, 29.2)**
   A. is synthesized in the liver
   B. enters the body as dietary cholesterol
   C. is transported as chylomicrons in the blood
   D. is transported as HDL

2. All of the following are correct about "bad" cholesterol EXCEPT **(LO 29.1, 29.2)**
   A. it is a high-density lipoprotein
   B. high levels of LDL contribute to atherosclerosis
   C. it is a lipoprotein
   D. it contains more fat and less protein than "good cholesterol"

3. Chronically elevated blood lipid levels may cause **(LO 29.1, 29.2)**
   A. pancreatitis when cholesterol is 80 to 100 mg/dL
   B. plaque when HMG-CoA reductase is 80 to 100 mg/dL
   C. plaque when LDL cholesterol exceeds 160 mg/dL
   D. arthritis and edema

4. All of the following are correct about cholesterol and these hypolipidemic drugs EXCEPT **(LO 29.1, 29.2, 29.3)**
   A. cholesterol is lowered by a diet rich is saturated fats
   B. cholesterol is elevated in people with primary hypercholesterolemia
   C. nicotinic acid is used to treat *hyper*cholesterolemia
   D. fenofibrate primarily affects VLDL and triglycerides

5. Which of the following mechanisms of action is correct? **(LO 29.3)**
   A. ezetimibe (*Zetia*) acts in the intestinal lumen to bind and trap cholesterol
   B. fibric acid derivatives act at the brush border of the intestine wall
   C. nicotinamide stimulates lipoprotein lipase to lower triglycerides
   D. lovastatin (*Mevacor*) inhibits an enzyme in the cholesterol synthetic pathway

6. All of the following are correct about the statin drugs EXCEPT **(LO 29.3, 29.4)**
   A. all drugs in this class have the same mechanism of action
   B. dosing is recommended for the evening because the patient won't experience adverse effects while sleeping
   C. these are systemic drugs meaning they have to be absorbed into the blood
   D. they are used as adjunct treatment to diet adjustment

7. The greatest reduction in circulating LDL is associated with which hypolipidemic drug? **(LO 29.3, 29.4, 29.5)**
   A. gemfibrozil (*Lopid*)
   B. nicotinic acid (*Niacor*)
   C. atorvastatin (*Lipitor*)
   D. colesevelam (*Welchol*)

8. Which of the following is NOT correctly matched to its adverse effect? **(LO 29.5, 29.6)**
   A. niacin/nicotinic acid causes cutaneous vasodilation (flushing)
   B. fenofibrate (*Tricor*) causes nausea and flatulence
   C. cholestyramine (*Questran*) causes rhabdomyolysis
   D. rosuvastatin (*Crestor*) causes muscle pain, weakness

9. Which of the following is correct? **(LO 29.1, 29.2, 29.5)**
   A. TC (total cholesterol) = HDL – LDL – TG
   B. periodic monitoring of liver enzymes (AST, ALT) is not recommended with systemic hypolipidemic drugs
   C. grapefruit consumption may reduce the blood level of the statin drugs
   D. grapefruit inhibits the same enzyme in the cholesterol pathway as the statin drugs

10. All of the following are correct EXCEPT **(LO 29.1, 29.2)**
    A. LDL pulls cholesterol out of plaque and returns it to the liver
    B. VLDL transports triglycerides
    C. apolipoproteins B and E contain a cholesterol core to form LDL and HDL, respectively
    D. foam cells are cholesterol-rich macrophages

Multiple Choice (Multiple Answer)

Select the correct choices for each statement. The choices may be all correct, all incorrect, or any combination.

1. Select all of the following that make cholesterol so important for the body. **(LO 29.1)**
   A. building block for glucocorticoids
   B. essential for building cell membranes
   C. needed to help form myelin sheath
   D. helps in digestion of dietary fats

2. Which of the following are not risk factors for atherosclerosis? **(LO 29.1)**
   A. male over the age of 45
   B. smoker
   C. hypothyroidism
   D. low HDL levels

3. Select all of the medications used to treat hyperlipidemia. **(LO 29.2)**
   A. statins
   B. thiazides
   C. nicotinic acid
   D. fibric acid derivatives

4. HMG-CoA reductase inhibitors work by doing which of the following? **(LO 29.3)**
   A. blocking the intestinal absorption of cholesterol
   B. inhibiting triglyceride lipase
   C. inhibiting the production of mevalonic acid
   D. decreasing hepatic VLDL-triglyceride synthesis

5. The main effects of the statins include **(LO 29.4)**
   A. reducing LDL levels
   B. reducing HDL levels
   C. reducing CRP levels
   D. reducing acetyl CoA levels

Sequencing

Place the following in order from greatest reduction in total cholesterol to least reduction. **(LO 29.3)**

_____   _____   _____   _____

Greatest   **Least**

HMG-CoA reductase inhibitors

ezetimibe

bile acid sequestrants

fibric acid derivatives

Classification

Place the following medications under the correct classification. **(LO 29.2)**

fluvastatin	fenofibrate
niacin	rosuvastatin
colestipol	cholestyramine

Bile acid sequestrants	HMG-CoA reductase inhibitors	Alter lipid and lipoprotein metabolism

Documentation

Using the prescription below, answer the following questions. **(LO 29.2, 29.3, 29.5)**

Riverview Cardiology Practice RX

12345 Main Avenue
Anytown, USA 12345
931-555-1000

NAME: _Gary Stanton_____   DATE: _____

ADDRESS: _____

RX   Lescol 200mg

Sig: Take one tablet by mouth once daily

Dr. Georgia Hart_____ M.D.   _____M.D.
  Substitution Permitted   Dispense as written

DEA #: _____   REFILL: NR 1 2 3 4

a. What type of hypolipidemic drug has been prescribed?
b. What is the usual daily dose for this medication? Is the dose prescribed within the usual daily dose?
c. List the tests that should be performed before beginning this medication.
d. How often should these tests be repeated?

Labeling

Fill in the missing labels. **(LO 29.1)**

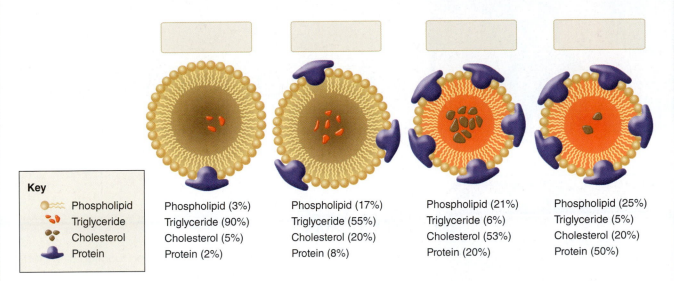

Key

- Phospholipid
- Triglyceride
- Cholesterol
- Protein

Phospholipid (3%)
Triglyceride (90%)
Cholesterol (5%)
Protein (2%)

Phospholipid (17%)
Triglyceride (55%)
Cholesterol (20%)
Protein (8%)

Phospholipid (21%)
Triglyceride (6%)
Cholesterol (53%)
Protein (20%)

Phospholipid (25%)
Triglyceride (5%)
Cholesterol (20%)
Protein (50%)

Chapter 30

Antianemics

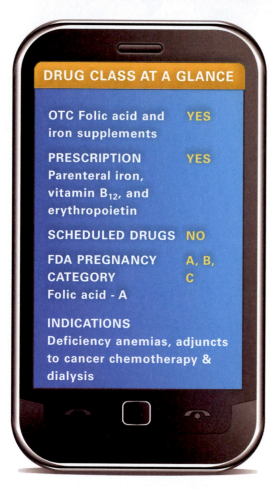

DRUG CLASS AT A GLANCE

OTC Folic acid and iron supplements	YES
PRESCRIPTION Parenteral iron, vitamin B$_{12}$, and erythropoietin	YES
SCHEDULED DRUGS	NO
FDA PREGNANCY CATEGORY Folic acid - A	A, B, C

INDICATIONS
Deficiency anemias, adjuncts to cancer chemotherapy & dialysis

KEY TERMS

anemia: condition in which the oxygen-carrying function of the red blood cells to the tissues is decreased.

aplastic anemia: anemia caused by defective functioning of the blood-forming organs (bone marrow).

CERA: stands for continuous erythropoietin receptor activator.

chelate: chemical action of a substance to bond permanently to a metal ion.

-chromic: suffix meaning color.

chronic: condition of long duration, usually months or years.

-cytic: suffix meaning cells.

enteric-coated: type of tablet or pill with a coating that enables it to pass through the stomach without being dissolved, so the stomach lining will not be irritated; the drug is then released in the intestine.

ESA: stands for erythropoietin stimulating agent.

gastric lavage: flushing of the stomach.

hematinic: medications containing iron compounds, used to increase hemoglobin production.

hemoglobin: protein in red blood cells that transports oxygen to all tissues of the body.

hypochromic: condition in which the color of red blood cells is less than the normal index.

intrinsic factor: protein necessary for intestinal absorption of vitamin B$_{12}$; lack of intrinsic factor leads to pernicious anemia.

malabsorption: inadequate ability to take in nutrients through the intestine.

mega-: prefix meaning large.

megaloblast: large, immature cell that cannot yet function as a mature red blood cell (RBC).

micro-: prefix meaning small.

morphology: shape or structure of a cell.

normocytic anemia: anemia in which RBCs are normal size and usually contain normal hemoglobin but are insufficient to carry adequate oxygen to the tissues; low RBC count.

pernicious: disease of severe symptoms, which could be fatal if left untreated.

RBC: red blood cell.

Introduction

Hemoglobin is a protein found in red blood cells **(RBCs)** that gives blood its color. See Figure 30.1. Because the main function of hemoglobin is to transport oxygen to all tissues of the body, anything that alters the function of the RBCs or the production of hemoglobin causes a deficiency in oxygen transport, thus producing a condition known as **anemia**. In response to oxygen deficiency, the body develops the characteristic symptoms of anemia, including weakness, fatigue, irritability, and pallor.

LO 30.1   LO 30.2   LO 30.3

CAUSES OF ANEMIA

Certain anemias are inherited because the synthesis of hemoglobin is genetically controlled. Cooley's anemia and sickle cell anemia are inherited diseases in which the hemoglobin is abnormal and cannot efficiently carry oxygen. Inherited anemias are **chronic** illnesses and cannot be successfully treated or cured with drug replacement therapy. Anemia also may be caused by deficiency in the amount of hemoglobin, occurring when the number of circulating red blood cells is decreased. Loss of blood (hemorrhage), increased destruction of RBCs (hemolysis), or decreased production of RBCs reduces the amount of circulating hemoglobin. The production of normal blood cells may be impaired when the bone marrow is poisoned by chemicals, such as benzene or anticancer drugs. More commonly, however, blood cell production is decreased when essential vitamins and minerals are deficient in the diet. The most commonly occurring deficiency anemias are produced by a lack of iron, cyanocobalamin (vitamin B_{12}), or folic acid. Besides decreasing RBC production, deficiency anemias may be associated with changes in the size and shape of

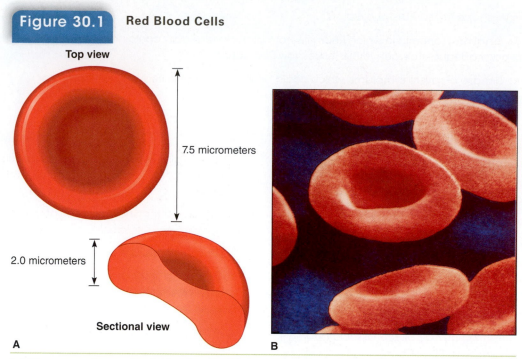

Figure 30.1 Red Blood Cells

Top view

7.5 micrometers

2.0 micrometers

Sectional view

A

B

(a) Biconcave shape of red blood cells. (b) Scanning electron micrograph of red blood cells.

the red and white blood cells. For this reason, deficiency anemias are also classified according to the shape, or **morphology,** and color of the blood cells.

Microcytic (**micro-** means small and **-cytic** refers to cells) anemias are characterized by unusually small RBCs. When mycrocytic anemia is associated with a hemoglobin deficiency, the RBCs appear pale (**hypochromic**— *hypo-* refers to less than normal and **-chromic** means color). Macrocyte (*macro-* means large) anemias have unusually large blood cells. When blood cell production is interrupted, large immature cells known as **megaloblasts** (**mega-** also means large) are released into the circulation. In megaloblastic anemias, the blood cells may appear larger, but the RBCs are normochromic (no change in color). Morphological changes associated with several different anemias are compared in Table 30:1. Unlike inherited anemias, deficiency anemias are very responsive to replacement therapy. Once the missing substance is identified and restored to the diet, the symptoms of the anemia subside. In addition, the morphology and production of blood cells return to normal.

LO 30.2 | LO 30.3 | LO 30.4
IRON DEFICIENCY ANEMIA

The amount of iron in the body is maintained at a relatively constant level between 2 and 5 g. Diets that include meat, fish, or soy products should supply an adequate amount of iron. Iron is primarily distributed in the RBCs in association with hemoglobin or stored in tissues

such as the bone marrow, spleen, and liver. Ferritin is an iron-binding protein that acts as a storage site for iron in these tissues. The amount of ferritin in the blood reflects the amount of stored iron in the body.

The plasma protein manufactured by the liver that delivers iron to tissues is called transferrin. It reversibly binds two ferric ions (Fe^{+3}) absorbed from the intestine and macrophage activity and delivers them to other tissues. Iron transport is very efficient; transferrin even recycles iron from aging RBCs. Transferrin interacts with a transferrin receptor, located in the target cells, and ferric ions are carried into the cells (see Figure 30.2). Since the body excretes very little iron each day, iron stores are efficiently conserved. (This is why dietary sources of animal organ meat such as liver provide the greatest amount of iron.) Iron deficiency occurs when the internal iron stores become depleted.

Development of Deficiency

To maintain an adequate iron balance, the National Academy of Sciences Research Council suggests that the Recommended Dietary Allowance (RDA) for iron should be between 10 and 18 mg. The RDA varies with the age, sex, and health of the individual. After age 20, healthy males require less iron intake than do females. Depletion of iron reserves in adult males does not readily occur. Most often, when it does occur, it is caused by internal bleeding (including NSAID-induced GI bleeding), chronic disease (carcinoma or ulcers), or dialysis rather than a dietary deficiency of iron.

Origin and Treatment of RBC Anemias

Origin	Cause	RBC characteristics	Treatment
Excessive blood loss	Hemorrhage	Normocytic normochromic	Stop bleeding, blood transfusion
Decreased RBC production			
Deficiency anemia	Lack of iron Lack of copper	Microcytic hypochromic	Replace iron or copper in the diet
	Lack of folic acid Lack of cyanocobalamin	Macrocytic (megaloblastic) normochromic	Replace folic acid or cyanocobalamin in diet
Bone marrow failure	Chemicals Anticancer drugs Irradiation	Normocytic normochromic	Blood transfusion
Increased RBC destruction	Defective RBC Metabolism Microbial toxins Drug allergy	Normocytic normochromic	Blood transfusion
Altered RBC production and destruction	Defective hemoglobin synthesis	Sickle shape microcytic	Blood transfusion
	Chronic infection Liver disease	Hypochromic Normocytic normochromic	Blood transfusion

Figure 30.2   **Iron Transport in the Blood**

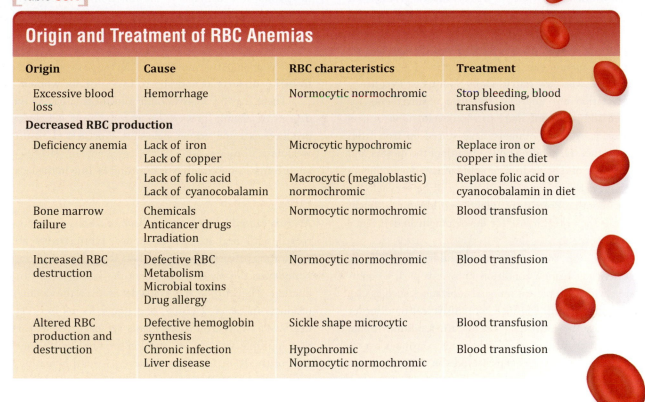

Iron is transported in the blood by transferrin. Most of the iron is involved in red blood cell production, while some is stored in the liver.

Chronic disease and internal bleeding also deplete iron in women; however, women are always predisposed to iron deficiency, primarily as a result of the constant loss of blood during each menstrual period (in which 1 to 20 mg of iron may be lost). For this reason, iron deficiency anemia can easily develop in women, especially those who have nutritionally poor diets. Pregnancy and lactation also increase the iron requirements for women and may contribute to the development of iron deficiency. At birth, infants have stored-up iron from their mother. Depending on the health of the mother and the amount of dietary iron or supplements taken during pregnancy, the infant's stored iron will be available for 4 to 6 months. Premature infants and low-birth-weight babies are at a greater risk for developing iron deficiency anemia.

In addition, women and young children may become iron deficient from a condition known as pica, a condition in which people eat unusual substances such as clay and laundry starch. This is a compulsive eating disorder that makes the individual crave eating nonnutritional items such as dirt or soap. When this continues over a long time, the clay and starch bind the dietary iron so that no iron is absorbed. Eventually, internal iron stores become depleted, and anemia results. Children exposed to lead by swallowing water, paint chips, or dust containing lead can develop an anemia. Lead interferes with the hemoglobin production.

Chronic iron deficiency from any cause results in a microcytic hypochromic anemia. See Figure 30.3. The RBCs and hemoglobin are affected because iron is essential for normal oxygen transport. Oxygen molecules are carried by the iron, which is bound to hemoglobin. In chronic iron deficiency, the function of hemoglobin is severely impaired. This is reflected in the amount of hemoglobin measured in the blood. Normal adult levels of hemoglobin are 14 to 18 g/dL for men and 12 to 16 g/dL for women. After middle age, the range drops to 12.4 to 14.9 g/dL for men and 11.7 to 13.8 g/dL for women.

There may be no symptoms in mild anemia. As the degree of anemia progresses, chronic iron deficiency produces extreme fatigue, pale skin, shortness of breath, weakness, dizziness, and restless legs syndrome (RLS)—an uncomfortable tingling or crawling feeling in the legs.

Hematinics

Anemia caused by a nutritional lack of iron is easily corrected with oral iron supplements. **Hematinics** are medications that primarily contain iron (ferrous) compounds for the purpose of increasing hemoglobin production. Hematinics are available as over-the-counter products in tablet, capsule, and liquid forms (see Figure 30.4). Many iron supplements are packaged as part of a multiple vitamin preparation containing 100 percent of the RDA for iron. However, several hematinics listed in Table 30:2 contain 5 to 20 times the RDA for iron. Ferrous compounds such as fumarate, sulfate, and gluconate are equally well absorbed orally and are the agents of choice. The addition of ascorbic acid (vitamin C) enhances the intestinal absorption of iron. Long-term iron-deficient patients may require 100 to 200 mg of iron TID for at least 6 months. In comparison, iron deficiency associated with pregnancy, especially in the last trimester, may be corrected with 20 to 50 mg of iron per day.

Figure 30.3

Iron Deficiency Microcytic Anemia

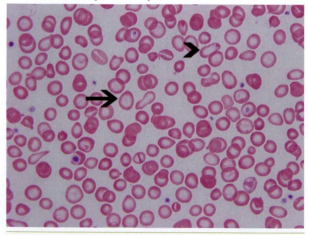

The majority of the red blood cells have a central pallor (hollow, no color, arrow) (1000X magnification).

Figure 30.4

Iron Preparations: Oral Tablets and Parenteral Iron

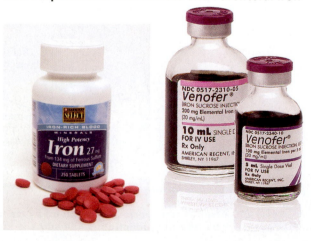

Iron Preparations*

Trade Name	Iron	Other ingredients
Parenteral iron preparations		
Feraheme (ferumoxytol)	30 mg/ml elemental iron	Mannitol 44 mg, preservative free
INFeD	50 mg/ml iron dextran	—
Venofer	20 mg/ml iron sucrose	—
Oral iron preparations		
Femiron	63 mg ferrous fumarate	—
Chromagen	70 mg elemental iron	intrinsic factor and vitamins B12 and C
Feosol Tablets	200 mg ferrous sulfate	—
Fergon Tablets	225 mg ferrous gluconate	—
Fer-in-Sol Drops	75 mg ferrous sulfate/0.6 ml	0.02% alcohol
Fero-Gradumet 500	525 mg ferrous sulfate	500 mg ascorbic acid
Ferro-Sequels	150 mg ferrous fumarate	Docusate sodium
Geritol tonic liquid	18 mg iron ammonium citrate	Niacin, thiamine, pyridoxine, choline, cyanocobalamin, methionine, 12% alcohol
Mol-Iron Tablets	195 mg ferrous sulfate	—
Mol-Iron with Vitamin C	39 mg ferrous sulfate	Ascorbic acid
Tri-Tinic Capsules	36.3 mg ferrous fumarate	Ascorbic acid, folic aid, cyanocobalamin, intrinsic factor concentrate
Vitron-C	66 mg ferrous fumarate	Ascorbic acid, tartrazine

This is not an inclusive list of available oral iron products.

Occasionally, iron deficiency is caused by an inability to take oral medications or to absorb iron **(malabsorption).** In these situations, iron dextran (*InFeD*) may be administered intramuscularly or intravenously. The intravenous route is usually preferred because there is less pain at the injection site. Also, staining of the skin may occur at the injection site. The manufacturer's suggested dose is based upon the patient's weight and hemoglobin value. The parenteral use of iron dextran has resulted in anaphylactic-type reactions. Patients must be tested for sensitivity prior to administering iron dextran to avoid an anaphylactic reaction. Iron dextran should only be used in patients for whom there is a clearly established indication of lack of tolerance of oral supplements or for whom gastrointestinal (GI) absorption is impaired. Iron dextran is *incompatible* in solutions containing oxytetracycline.

New Treatment

A novel new iron product is available for the treatment of iron deficiency in chronically ill patients. Ferumoxytol (*Feraheme*) is a parenteral iron formulation specifically for iron deficiency anemia in patients with chronic kidney disease. This is a superparamagnetic iron oxide with a carbohydrate covering. This means iron combined with oxygen is in solution as very, very tiny particles known as nanoparticles (sizes in the range of billionths of the conventional molecule). The iron is released from the iron-carbohydrate complex after ingestion by macrophages. Then iron either resides in the ferritin storage form or is transferred to plasma transferrin as needed for incorporation into hemoglobin. View an excellent animation at www.feraheme.com/about/mechanism.html that shows how iron is transported and stored.

Supplied as a solution for intravenous injection, *Feraheme* is given as an initial dose of 510 mg followed by a second 510-mg intravenous injection 3 to 8 days later. *Feraheme* should be administered as an undiluted intravenous injection.

Clinical Indications

Iron supplementation, including parenteral administration, is approved for the prevention and treatment of iron deficiency anemia from any source. Ferumoxytol is specifically indicated for the treatment of iron deficiency in patients with chronic kidney disease.

Adverse and Toxic Effects

The most frequently occurring side effects associated with oral hematinics are gastric irritation, nausea, and constipation. Supplements are recommended to be taken on an empty stomach to optimize absorption. In sensitive patients, however, the gastric irritation may be intense. When gastric irritation occurs, the dose of the iron supplement may be reduced or taken with meals. Delayed release and **enteric-coated** iron preparations reduce the gastric irritation by releasing the iron in the lower intestine. Unfortunately, the iron in these preparations is not well absorbed, and the products usually are more expensive than are other iron supplements. Patients should be cautioned not to chew or crush these preparations prior to swallowing. Overall, the special formulations offer no significant advantage over other hematinic formulations available. Some hematinics contain a stool softener to counteract constipation, whereas others contain an antacid to alleviate the nausea.

Liquid iron preparations are recommended to be taken with juice or water to avoid staining the teeth. Patients may be advised to take such liquid preparations through a drinking straw to decrease the potential for staining.

Parenteral iron, ferumoxytol, causes the same spectrum of adverse effects, although the incidence may be less. These effects include rash, gastric irritation, dizziness, diarrhea, and hypotension. Because iron is magnetic, there is a special consideration for patients who receive this drug. As a superparamagnetic iron oxide, ferumoxytol can alter magnetic resonance imaging (MRI) studies for up to 3 months after the last dose. X-ray, CAT (computed tomography), and PET (positron emission tomography) scans and ultrasound imaging are not affected.

In therapeutic doses, unabsorbed iron is excreted into the feces, causing stools to become black and tarry. This effect should not be mistaken for blood in the stool, since both iron therapy and occult bleeding produce the same fecal appearance. Iron overload (excessive iron storage) rarely occurs with oral iron therapy. However, acute iron toxicity may occur as a result of accidental overdose or poisoning. Usually, iron poisoning occurs in children who are attracted by the colored tablets and flavored liquids containing iron. In toxic doses (0.3 to 1 g), iron erodes the stomach lining, causing pain, bleeding, and vomiting. In severe cases, acidosis, hypotension, and cardiovascular collapse occur. Treatment of acute iron toxicity includes **gastric lavage** (flushing the stomach) with deferoxamine mesylate (5 to 10 g). The deferoxamine binds, or **chelates,** the iron so that none can be absorbed.

Drug Interactions

Drug interactions with hematinics are few. However, tetracyclines and antacids taken simultaneously with oral iron supplements decrease iron absorption because they chelate iron. Tetracycline absorption also decreases. Cimetidine through a different mechanism of action also decreases iron absorption. These products should not be taken within 2 hours of each other. Iron salts will decrease the absorption of penicillamine, quinolones, methyldopa, and levodopa. Allopurinol (*Zyloprim*) has been reported to increase oral iron absorption, and ascorbic acid (vitamin C—200 mg per 30 mg iron) enhances the absorption of iron from the GI tract. Coffee, tea, milk, and eggs decrease the absorption of dietary iron. The clinical effect associated with these foods and oral iron supplements is not known.

LO 30.1 LO 30.2
LO 30.3 LO 30.4 LO 30.5

COBALAMIN DEFICIENCY ANEMIA

Cobalamin (vitamin B$_{12}$), also known as cyanocobalamin, is available in dietary products such as meats, eggs, milk, and seafood. The synthetic vitamin is known as cyanocobalamin, although it does not occur in nature. Nursing infants receive an adequate supply of cobalamin (0.3 to 2 mcg) in mother's milk. The adult RDA is 3 mcg.

Development of Deficiency

Deficiency of cobalamin in adults due to a decreased dietary intake is difficult to produce. Cobalamin is so efficiently stored in the liver that depletion of internal reserves usually takes 6 to 10 years. However, individuals who follow strict vegetarian diets may require vitamin supplementation. Pregnancy and lactation also increase the requirement for cobalamin. Deficiency of this vitamin usually occurs when the absorption process is interrupted by lack of ability to synthesize **intrinsic**

factor, disease, surgery, or infection. Dietary cobalamin complexes with proteins (R-proteins) secreted in the gastric juice and saliva. In the duodenum, pancreatic proteases metabolize the R-proteins and release cobalamin to bind with another glycoprotein, intrinsic factor. Gastric parietal cells secrete a protein intrinsic factor along with hydrochloric acid that carries cobalamin to the ileum, where it is absorbed. In the epithelial cells of the ileum are intrinsic factor receptors that allow cobalamin to enter the cells. Cobalamin then complexes with another transport protein, transcobalamin II. This protein readily releases cobalamin at the target tissues such as bone marrow. The intestinal absorption of cobalamin is dependent upon the presence of intrinsic factor. See Figure 30.5.

Some individuals lack the ability to synthesize intrinsic factor. As a result, these people are cobalamin deficient and develop **pernicious** anemia. The presence of pernicious anemia implies a deficiency in cobalamin absorption specifically due to lack of intrinsic factor. Pernicious anemia may occur in adults following gastrectomy (removal of the stomach) or when the secretory portions of the stomach have been damaged by gastric

---

Figure 30.5   Dietary Vitamin B$_{12}$ (Cobalamin) Is Transported by Specialized Proteins

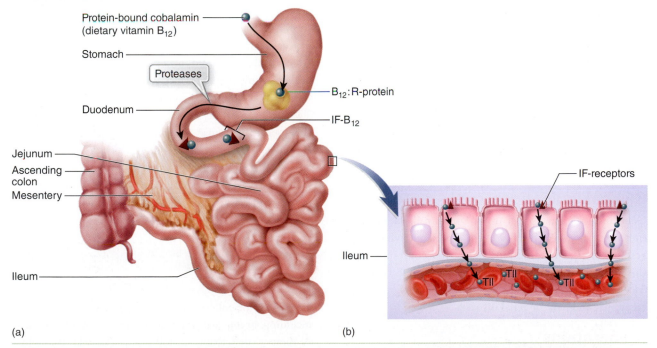

(a)   (b)

(a) First are proteins secreted by the saliva and gastric juices (R-proteins). Next is intrinsic factor (IF) secreted from the parietal cell with hydrochloric acid (HCL). The IF-B$_{12}$ complex is absorbed on the brush border of the epithelial cells in the terminal ileum. (b) Finally, cobalamin binds to transcobalamin II in the blood for transport to target cells like bone marrow and nerves.

carcinoma or have been removed surgically. Cobalamin absorption also may be decreased when there is a chronic overgrowth in intestinal bacteria or tapeworm, and the bacteria or parasites utilize the vitamin before intestinal absorption can occur.

Characteristics of Deficiency

The anemia resulting from cobalamin deficiency is a megaloblastic anemia. Many tissues are affected because cyanocobalamin is essential for the normal synthesis of nucleoprotein (deoxyribonucleic acid [DNA]). In particular, DNA synthesis and cell division require cobalamin and folic acid. Both of these vitamins contribute to the formation of N^{10}-methyltetrahydrofolic acid (FH_4), which is needed to synthesize nucleoprotein precursors of DNA. Cobalamin (and folic acid) deficiency causes changes in all dividing cells, resulting in the production of macrocytes and megaloblasts. The blood-forming system (hematopoiesis) reflects these changes by circulating giant platelets and large red and white blood cells with short life spans.

Cobalamin is essential for the formation of the myelin sheaths that surround the peripheral nerves and spinal cord. This biochemical process involves fatty acids and lipids, which are incorporated into the myelin sheath. In cobalamin deficiency, the myelin sheaths are not properly formed, leading to nerve degeneration and neurological changes. Degeneration first occurs along peripheral nerves so that paresthesia (numbness, "pins and needles" feeling) is produced. Eventually portions of the spinal cord degenerate, resulting in poor muscle coordination and weakness. Optic atrophy and glossitis (smooth, sore, beefy red tongue) occur. Deficient patients may undergo mood changes ranging from nervousness to psychosis. If the deficiency of this vitamin persists for several years, the neurological changes become irreversible.

Clinical Indications

Cobalamin is approved for use in vitamin B_{12} deficiency (pernicious anemia) or to prevent deficiency where disease or physical condition increases the requirement for this vitamin. The most common medical indications for use are pregnancy, hemorrhage, malignancy, postgastrectomy, and liver or renal disease.

Preparations

Cobalamin (vitamin B_{12}) is available in tablets, nasal sprays, and injectable solution. Oral preparations containing less than 50 mcg are primarily supplements for nutritionally based deficiencies. Injectable solutions of cobalamin are administered intramuscularly or subcutaneously 30 mcg per day for up to 10 days, followed by 100 to 200 mcg per month until remission occurs. Thereafter, 100 mcg per month may be sufficient to maintain remission. Patients who have pernicious anemia should be advised that they will require monthly injections for the rest of their lives. For any of the parenteral formulations, intravenous administration should be avoided because it is associated with excretion of the vitamin before the therapeutic response can be achieved.

Several over-the-counter preparations, primarily multiple vitamins, contain cobalamin varying from 1 to 25 mcg per tablet. The trade names of some commercial preparations are listed in Table 30:3. In malnourished individuals and geriatric patients, oral supplements (1 mcg per day) may be beneficial. The only recognized therapeutic value of cobalamin is in the treatment of pernicious anemia or cobalamin deficiency. It has not been proved to cure hepatitis, poor appetite, allergies, sterility, psychosis, and aging, for which it is often administered. There is no known toxicity to this vitamin. The kidneys excrete all of the vitamin that cannot be used.

Drug Interactions

Cobalamin absorption has been reported to be decreased due to drug interactions with colchicine, neomycin, aminosalicylic acid, and timed-release potassium. Chronic heavy alcohol intake (for more than 2 weeks) may produce malabsorption of cobalamin. Chloramphenicol and other drugs that suppress the bone marrow may interfere with red blood cell maturation so that vitamin B_{12} cannot function in these cells. The result may be seen in patients as an inadequate therapeutic response to vitamin B_{12}. Antiulcer drugs (H_2-receptor antagonists, cimetidine) decrease gastric acid so that vitamin B_{12} cannot combine with available gastric intrinsic factor, impairing but not totally inhibiting absorption of vitamin B_{12}.

LO 30.1 LO 30.2 LO 30.4 LO 30.5

FOLIC ACID DEFICIENCY

The RDA for folic acid (400 mcg) can be satisfied by including green leafy vegetables and meat in the diet. A dietary deficiency of folic acid (folates) frequently occurs because people do not adequately supplement their diet with vegetables. In addition, even well-balanced diets become folate deficient because the heat required for canning and cooking destroys folic acid. For this reason, folates are considered to be heat labile. Many

Cobalamin (Vitamin B$_{12}$) Preparations*

Trade Name	Dose form	Unit dose	Other ingredients
Prescription preparations			
CaloMist	Nasal spray	25 mcg per actuation	—
Nascobal	Nasal spray	500 mcg per actuation	—
Hydroxocobalamin	Injection	1000 mcg/ml	—
Vitamin B$_{12}$	Injection	1000 mcg/ml	—
Over-the-counter preparations			
Enviro-Stress Tablets	Oral	25 mcg	Ascorbic acid, niacin, riboflavin, thiamine
Feminins	Oral	10 mcg	Ascorbic acid, folic acid, iron, niacin, pantothenic acid, pyridoxine, riboflavin, thiamine, and vitamins A, D, and E
Geritol Complete	Oral	6 mcg	Ascorbic acid, iron, niacin, pantothenic acid, pyridoxine, riboflavin, thiamine, vitamin K, and assorted minerals
Geritonic Liquid	Oral	9 mcg /15 ml	Iron, desiccated liver, niacin, pyridoxine, riboflavin, thiamine, yeast concentrate, assorted minerals, **20% alcohol**
Golden Bounty B Complex	Oral	25 mcg	Ascorbic acid, niacin, riboflavin, thiamine
Multi 75 Tablets	Oral	75 mcg	Ascorbic acid, niacin, riboflavin, thiamine, and assorted minerals
One-A-Day	Oral	6 mcg	Ascorbic acid, folic acid, niacin, riboflavin, thiamine, pyridoxine, and vitamins A and D
Livitamin Liquid	Oral	5 mcg/15 ml	Iron, desiccated liver, niacin, pyridoxine, riboflavin, thiamine, and copper
Rogenic	Oral	25 mcg	Ascorbic acid, desiccated liver, iron, and pyridoxine
Surbex-T Filmtabs	Oral	10 mcg	Ascorbic acid, niacin, pantothenic acid, pyridoxine, riboflavin, thiamine

This is not an inclusive list of commercially available products.

conditions increase the requirement for folic acid. In particular, pregnancy, hemolytic anemia, rheumatoid arthritis, and hyperthyroidism are conditions associated with an increased production of blood cells that require folic acid for synthesis.

Role of Folic Acid

Folic acid is essential for cell growth and reproduction because it is necessary for protein synthesis. Folic acid is utilized in the synthesis of thymidine, an essential element in the nucleoprotein DNA. Also, synthesis of amino acids requires an activated form of folic acid known as FH$_4$. Therefore, folic acid and cyanocobalamin deficiencies produce identical anemias. Folate deficiency is associated with a macrocytic (megaloblastic) anemia. Oral preparations of folic acid in doses of 0.1 to 1 mg per day are used to treat folate deficiency. These folic acid products are available by prescription (called folic acid or *Folvite*) or as over-the-counter preparations (called folic acid). Parenteral (IM, IV, SC) formulations are available (folic acid, *Folvite*) for patients in whom the anemia is severe or gastrointestinal absorption is severely impaired. There are no known toxicities to folic acid, and allergic reactions rarely occur.

Clinical Indications

Folic acid is approved for use in megaloblastic anemia due to folate deficiency. Deficiency may arise from inadequate nutrition in infants, children, or adults, or increased requirement due to pregnancy. Folic acid is designated Food and Drug Administration (FDA) Pregnancy Category A because of its critical role in fetal development. Folate status in pregnancy is directly related to proper neural development. Folate deficiency increases the potential for neural tube deficit (NTD).

Contraindications

Folic acid should never be given for treatment of cobalamin (vitamin B_{12}) deficiency anemia. Administration of folic acid in a cobalamin deficiency will reverse the production of the megaloblastic cells. Therefore, the anemia will be corrected. However, folic acid has no effect on the synthesis of myelin. Thus, folic acid cannot reverse the neurological changes associated with cobalamin deficiency, and the damage may continue until it becomes irreversible. When megaloblastic anemia is present, patients must undergo tests that specifically diagnose the cause of the anemia so that proper replacement therapy can be initiated. Folic acid is not effective in the treatment of **aplastic** and **normocytic anemias.**

Drug Interactions

Drug interactions with folic acid may result in decreased absorption of folate or decreased production of FH_4. Anticonvulsants such as phenytoin (*Dilantin*), primidone (*Mysoline*), barbiturates, and oral contraceptives interfere with (decrease) the intestinal absorption of folic acid by an unknown mechanism. This decrease in folic acid absorption infrequently results in clinically significant megaloblastic anemia. However, increase in seizure frequency and decrease in serum phenytoin concentrations have been reported in patients receiving 15 to 20 mg of folic acid per day. Long-term use of aspirin, salicylamide, and caffeine also has been associated with impaired folate absorption.

Certain drugs, such as methotrexate (antineoplastic), trimethoprim (*Septra*), and pyrimethamine (antimalarial) block the formation of FH_4 because they inhibit the enzymes that convert folic acid to tetrahydrofolic acid.

The treatment for anemias caused by decreased folic acid utilization (interference with the metabolic pathway that produces FH_4) is leucovorin calcium (folinic acid), a derivative of FH_4. This compound, also known as citrovorum factor, is available only by prescription and can be given orally or intramuscularly. For the treatment of megaloblastic anemia, up to 1 mg of leucovorin per day may be given IM. This compound is *contraindicated* in the treatment of pernicious anemia and other vitamin B_{12}–associated anemias because folinic acid does not influence vitamin B_{12}–dependent myelin pathways. Leucovorin also is used to prevent or treat the severe toxicity of massive methotrexate doses in the clinical management of resistant neoplasms.

LO 30.6 | LO 30.7 | LO 30.8

ERYTHROPOIETIN STIMULATING AGENTS

Erythropoietin is a protein normally produced by the kidneys that participates in red blood cell homeostasis. Responding to changes in tissue oxygenation, erythropoietin stimulates production of red blood cells in the bone marrow. This provides more vehicles to transport oxygen to the tissues, thus improving oxygenation. Production of endogenous erythropoietin is impaired in patients with chronic renal failure. The resulting anemia is due to the erythropoietin deficiency. Erythropoietin stimulating agents **(ESAs),** synthetic proteins that mimicked erythropoietin, were introduced with epoetin alfa. Epoetin alfa (EPO) is a synthetic glycoprotein produced through recombinant DNA technology. Its 165 amino acids mimic the activity of endogenous erythropoietin to stimulate red blood cell production, and increase hematocrit and hemoglobin in anemic patients. Darbepoetin alfa (*Aranesp*), another synthetic erythropoietin, and epoetin alfa (*Epogen, Procrit*) have the same mechanism of action.

MIRCERA is the trade name for ethoxy polyethylene glycol-epoetin beta. This is a third-generation ESA referred to as a continuous erythropoietin receptor activator **(CERA).** *MIRCERA* interacts with the erythropoietin receptor on special cells in the bone marrow to stimulate the production of RBCs and hemoglobin. *MIRCERA* gets on and off the receptors easily so it continues to interact with the receptors and sustain a therapeutic response. *MIRCERA* is as effective as the other ESAs, but it has the longest half-life (22 hours) of all ESAs. It is six times longer than darbepoetin alfa and more than 20 times longer than epoetin alfa. This long half-life promotes hemoglobin building and allows an extended period between dosing intervals to maintain hemoglobin levels.

Clinical Indications

Erythropoietin (*Epogen, Procrit, Aranesp*) is approved for use in chronic renal failure, cancer chemotherapy, or dialysis patients where the hematocrit and hemoglobin confirm an anemic condition exists. The receptor activator *MIRCERA* is only approved for use in chronic renal failure. Zidovudine-related anemia in HIV patients is another use for erythropoietin. In such cases the anemia represents a threat to patient health and/or obligates frequent transfusions to maintain adequate hematocrit and hemoglobin. The goal of therapy is to reduce the need for frequent transfusions as well as providing adequate tissue oxygenation.

Dose Administration

Erythropoietin is given either IV or SC injection, 100 to 300 units/kg, three times a week IV or 40,000 units SC weekly. The dose varies according to the medical indication for treatment. Darbepoetin has a longer half-life and can be given once a week, whereas epoetin alfa is given 2 to 3 times a week for the same clinical response. The initial dose for darbepoetin is 0.45 mcg/kg IV or SC. For patients not receiving dialysis, the initial dose can be 0.75 mcg/kg every 2 weeks. The standard indicator for monitoring ESAs and CERAs is the hemoglobin level in whole blood. Hemoglobin is monitored to ensure the level has risen and stabilized to the target range, usually 10 to 12 g/dL. Increased hemoglobin levels are not generally observed until 2 to 6 weeks after initiating treatment. At this point the dose may be adjusted. Dose adjustment, based on the monitored hematocrit and hemoglobin, can be made if the hemoglobin level is sufficient to avoid transfusion or 2 weeks since the last adjustment. Patients who do not respond to the 300 units/kg dose after 8 weeks of treatment are probably nonresponders to erythropoietin. The starting dose of *MIRCERA* is 0.6 mcg/kg IV or SC every 2 weeks until the hemoglobin target has been achieved. At 10 g/dL hemoglobin, the monthly maintenance regimen may begin.

Special Considerations

Severe anemias, or anemias resulting from deficiencies in iron, folate, and/or vitamin B_{12}, are not candidates for erythropoietin treatment. These anemias obligate appropriate replacement of the deficient factor until the red blood cell morphology and total count are returned to normal.

Preparations of erythropoietin cannot be frozen or vigorously shaken because the mechanical action will break (denature) the glycoprotein. In general, erythropoietin should not be added to any other drug solution; however, benzyl alcohol 0.9 percent may be added to minimize the discomfort of injection and act as a bacteriostatic.

Adverse Effects

The spectrum of adverse effects associated with erythropoietin reflects symptoms of the underlying disease and cannot always be directly attributed to erythropoietin. Among the most common effects are headache, arthralgia, nausea, hypertension (dialysis patients), and diarrhea. A significant number of patients who receive erythropoietin are on dialysis schedules. Such patients have hypertension as part of their chronic condition. Skin rashes, indicative of hypersensitivity, are mild and transient. Antibodies do not develop to erythropoietin, minimizing the potential for hypersensitivity reactions. There is a cautionary box warning for any ESA or CERA drug. More deaths, and serious cardiovascular events, occurred when patients were administered ESAs to hemoglobin levels above 13 g/dL. This is the basis for the target therapeutic hemoglobin range of 10 g/dL to 12 g/dL.

MIRCERA is not indicated for the treatment of anemia caused by cancer chemotherapy.

ESAs have shortened overall survival and/or increased the risk of tumor progression or recurrence in some clinical studies in patients with breast, non–small cell lung, head and neck, lymphoid, and cervical cancers. While the ESAs are used in cancer chemotherapy, the dose should be the lowest possible one that avoids transfusion.

Patient Administration and Monitoring

Compliance with diet recommendations to improve borderline deficiencies is not always successful. Thus, supplementation becomes a significant factor in treating anemias, especially those not just outside the range of normal. Patients often need direction in developing a medication schedule that fosters compliance and, therefore, consistent improvement in the blood profile. The following suggestions are helpful in encouraging patients to stick with the treatment schedule.

- Oral iron formulations may irritate the stomach lining when taken on an empty stomach. Taking the supplement with meals reduces the incidence of nausea and irritation.

- Sustained-release preparations should not be chewed or crushed because they will deliver more or all medication at once rather than over an extended period. This will foster GI irritation because of the larger amount of iron released.

- Remind patients who cannot take pill or capsule formulations to drink liquid iron formulations with a straw. This will avoid discoloration of the teeth.

- Review the medication history of the patient to confirm whether antacids, tetracyclines, or quinolones are being taken. These drugs should be taken at least 2 hours before iron supplements to avoid chelation.

- For vitamin B_{12} supplementation, make clear that treatment of pernicious anemia is for life. Monthly injection is necessary to avoid irreversible nerve damage.

- Caution patients taking multiple supplements that folic acid cannot substitute for vitamin B_{12}. Medication schedules must be followed as directed.

- Supplements used in the treatment of anemias are designated as Food and Drug Administration (FDA) Pregnancy Category C. Safety of parenteral formulations in pregnant women has not been established through controlled clinical trials. Nevertheless, when a clear benefit to the mother outweighs the risk to the fetus, these supplements are used. Folate, in particular, is designated Category A because of its absolute requirement in the fetus for normal development of the nervous system.

Chapter Review

Understanding Terminology

Match the definition or description in the left column with the appropriate term in the right column.

___ 1. Shape or structure of a cell. **(LO 30.1)**

___ 2. A condition in which the oxygen-carrying function of the RBCs is decreased. **(LO 30.1)**

___ 3. A tablet with a coating that enables it to pass through the stomach without being dissolved. **(LO 30.6)**

___ 4. A disease with severe symptoms; could be fatal if left untreated. **(LO 30.1, 30.3, 30.5)**

___ 5. Protein in RBCs that transports oxygen to all tissues of the body. **(LO 30.1, 30.2, 30.3, 30.6)**

___ 6. Large, immature RBC. **(LO 30.3, 30.5, 30.6)**

___ 7. Medications containing iron compounds, used to increase hemoglobin production. **(LO 30.6)**

a. anemia

b. enteric-coated

c. hematinic

d. hemoglobin

e. megaloblast

f. morphology

g. pernicious

Match the definition in the left column with the appropriate prefix or suffix in the right column.

___ 8. Prefix meaning large. **(LO 30.6)**

___ 9. Prefix meaning small. **(LO 30.6)**

___ 10. Suffix meaning cells. **(LO 30.6)**

___ 11. Suffix meaning color. **(LO 30.6)**

a. chromic

b. cytic

c. mega

d. micro

Acquiring Knowledge

Answer the following questions.

1. How are anemias produced? **(LO 30.1, 30.2, 30.3, 30.5)**

2. Describe the cell changes that may be produced in anemic individuals. **(LO 30.1, 30.2, 30.3, 30.5)**

3. What types of anemias are responsive to drug therapy? **(LO 30.3, 30.5)**

4. What is the most common cause of microcytic hypochromic anemia? **(LO 30.1, 30.2, 30.3)**

5. How can the gastric irritation associated with oral hematinics be alleviated? **(LO 30.4)**

6. What is the antidote for acute iron toxicity? **(LO 30.4)**

7. How is cyanocobalamin absorbed? How can a deficiency be produced? **(LO 30.1, 30.3, 30.5)**

8. Describe the anemia associated with cyanocobalamin deficiency. **(LO 30.1, 30.3, 30.5)**

9. How can cyanocobalamin deficiency be diagnosed? **(LO 30.3, 30.5)**

10. When is cyanocobalamin therapy of value? **(LO 30.3, 30.5)**

11. How does folic acid deficiency anemia differ from cyanocobalamin deficiency? **(LO 30.3, 30.5)**

12. Are folic acid and cyanocobalamin interchangeable in the treatment of megaloblastic anemia? Why? **(LO 30.3, 30.5)**

13. How can a folate deficiency be produced? **(LO 30.3, 30.5)**

14. When is leucovorin calcium therapeutically useful? **(LO 30.5)**

Applying Knowledge on the Job

Use your critical-thinking skills to answer the following questions.

1. One of your jobs is to remind patients of the potential for interactions with other medications the patient is taking. Why is it recommended not to take iron supplements with tetracyclines? **(LO 30.3, 30.4)**

2. Ms. Benson, who has been treated for epilepsy since 1989, has been placed on a folic acid supplement. Why do you ask whether she is still taking *Dilantin?* How can this medication affect the folate treatment? **(LO 30.4, 30.5)**

3. Explain the reason for not routinely administering vitamin B_{12} for any patient presenting with chronic symptoms of anemia and a hematology profile of large immature cells consistent with vitamin B_{12} deficiency? **(LO 30.5)**

4. A patient has just received a prescription for *Procrit.* What adverse effects are associated with this medication? **(LO 30.8)**

5. Iron toxicity usually occurs with a specific group of people. Which group is most susceptible and why? **(LO 30.3)**

6. In an effort to increase patient compliance, what suggestions would you make? **(LO 30.3)**

Multiple Choice

Use your critical-thinking skills to answer the following questions.

1. Which of the following is correct about developing iron deficiency anemia? **(LO 30.1, 30.2, 30.3)**
   A. iron is lost through internal bleeding (ulcers, NSAID-induced bleeding, carcinoma)
   B. it cannot occur in middle-age men
   C. megaloblastic red blood cells are typically present
   D. hemoglobin is not affected, so there is no blood test to confirm the diagnosis

2. Which blood plasma protein delivers iron to the cells? **(LO 30.1, 30.2)**
   A. ferritin
   B. creatinine
   C. hemoglobin
   D. transferrin

3. What is the cause of pernicious anemia? **(LO 30.1, LO 30.2, LO 30.5)**
   A. folic acid deficiency
   B. vitamin B_{12}
   C. overproduction of intrinsic factor
   D. gastrectomy removing the secretory portion of the stomach and intrinsic factor

4. Which of the following is correct about deficiency anemias? **(LO 30.1, 30.2, 30.5)**
   A. megaloblasts are immature RBCs produced in folic acid and cyanocobalamin deficiency
   B. vitamin B_4 can be substituted for cyanocobalamin and reverse the anemia
   C. deferoxamine is a chelator used to treat iron deficiency
   D. microcytic means large RBCs that carry extra oxygen

5. All of the following are correct about erythropoietin **EXCEPT (LO 30.7)**
   A. it is produced in kidneys
   B. severe deficiencies of iron or folic acid are reversed by synthetic erythropoietin
   C. the primary use is clinical management of cancer chemotherapy or chronic renal failure
   D. an objective of treatment is to reduce the need for blood transfusion

6. All of the following are correct about ESA or CERA **EXCEPT** (LO 30.6, 30.7)
   A. ESAs are erythropoietin stimulating agents
   B. CERA cannot be used in chronic renal failure anemia
   C. ESAs and CERA increase hemoglobin levels in chronic renal failure patients
   D. ESAs are synthetic erythropoietins

7. Which of the following is correct? (LO 30.3, 30.4, 30.6)
   A. folic acid is a B vitamin found in green vegetables and meats
   B. methotrexate is a rescue factor for megaloblastic anemia
   C. folic acid reverses aplastic anemia
   D. cyanocobalamin can only be given by injection (IV or SC)

8. Which of the following is correct? (LO 30.8)
   A. anticonvulsants and oral contraceptives increase folic acid absorption
   B. tetracyclines and antacids taken with oral iron supplements decrease iron absorption
   C. long-term aspirin use increases folic acid absorption
   D. NSAID-induced internal bleeding does not cause anemia

Multiple Choice (Multiple Answer)

Select the correct choices for each statement. The choices may be all correct, all incorrect, or any combination.

1. Anemia can be caused by which of the following? (LO 30.1)
   A. lack of iron
   B. genetic heredity
   C. increase in folic acid
   D. malabsorption

2. Select the terms that relate to RBC shape. (LO 30.6)
   A. hypochromic
   B. microcytic
   C. megaloblast
   D. hypochronic

3. In males, what are the most common causes of iron deficiency anemia? (LO 30.1)
   A. internal bleeding
   B. poor diet
   C. carcinomas
   D. eating clay

4. Select all of the symptoms of toxic levels of iron. (LO 30.4)
   A. nausea
   B. constipation
   C. hypotension
   D. acidosis

5. Which of the following is true in the use of folic acid to treat anemia? (LO 30.5)
   A. it is useful in the treatment of aplastic anemia
   B. it reverses the neurological changes of B_{12} deficiency
   C. it increases the synthesis of myelin
   D. it increases the production of megaloblastic cells

Sequencing

Place the following in order of occurrence in the body. **(LO 30.1)**

_____	_____	_____	_____
First			**Last**

fatigue

oxygen transport diminished

reduction in RBC production

poisoning of bone marrow

Classification

Place the following medications under the drug with which they have a drug-drug interaction. **(LO 30.8)**

quinolones	colchicine	cimetidine
phenytoin	antacids	neomycin
oral contraceptives	primidone	barbiturates
time-released potassium	aminosalicylic acid	tetracyclines

Folic acid	Cyanocobalamin	Iron

Labeling

Fill in the missing labels. **(LO 30.2)**

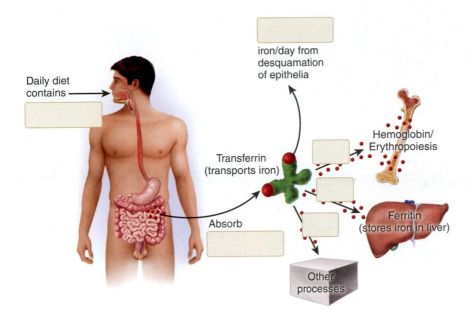

Daily diet
contains

iron/day from
desquamation
of epithelia

Transferrin
(transports iron)

Hemoglobin/
Erythropoiesis

Absorb

Ferritin
(stores iron in liver)

Other
processes

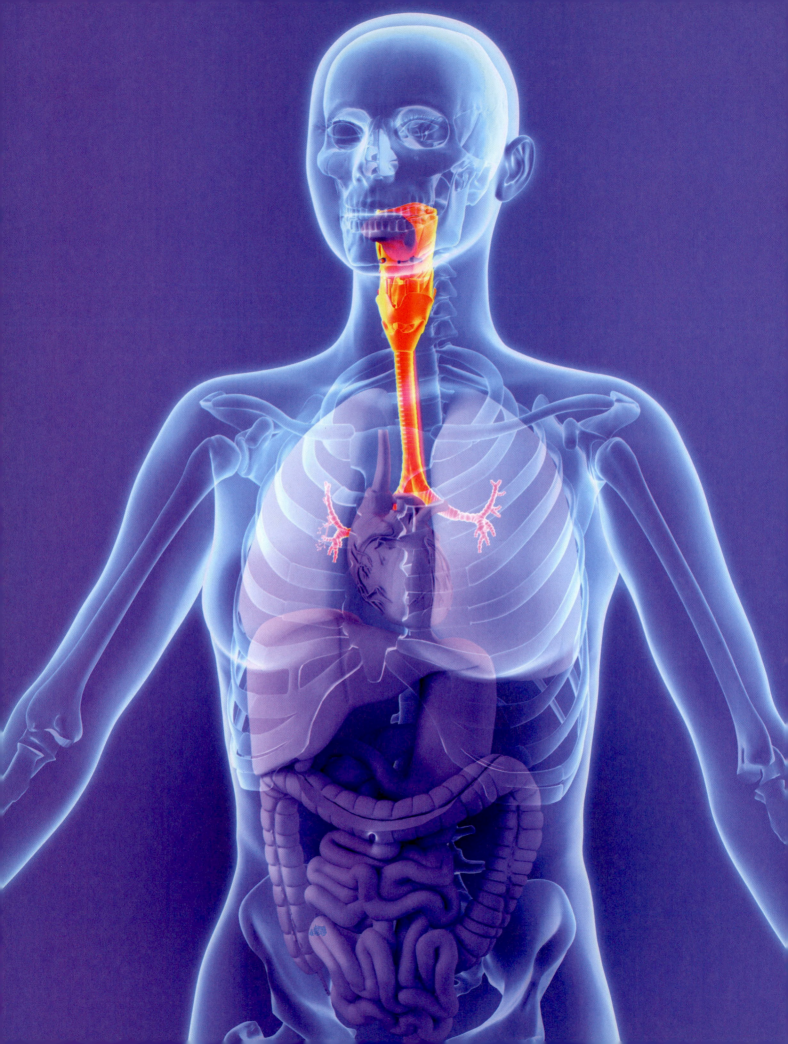

Drugs That Affect the Respiratory System

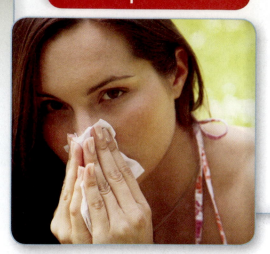

PART 6

Chapter 31

Antihistaminic Drugs and Mast Cell Release Inhibitors

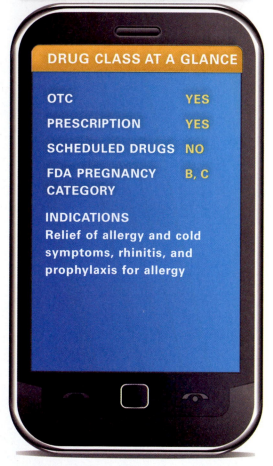

DRUG CLASS AT A GLANCE

OTC	YES
PRESCRIPTION	YES
SCHEDULED DRUGS	NO
FDA PREGNANCY CATEGORY	B, C

INDICATIONS
Relief of allergy and cold symptoms, rhinitis, and prophylaxis for allergy

KEY TERMS

allergen: a substance capable of producing an allergic reaction.

angioedema: edema and swelling beneath the skin.

antiallergic: drug that prevents mast cells from releasing histamine and other vasoactive substances.

antibody: a specialized protein (immunoglobulin) that recognizes the antigen that triggered its production.

antigen: substance, usually protein or carbohydrate, that is capable of stimulating an immune response.

antihistaminic: drug that blocks the action of histamine at the target organ.

asthma: inflammation of the bronchioles associated with constriction of smooth muscle, wheezing, and edema.

dermatitis: inflammatory condition of the skin associated with itching, burning, and edematous vesicular formations.

eczematoid dermatitis: condition in which lesions on the skin ooze and develop scaly crusts.

erythema: redness of the skin, often a result of capillary dilation.

excoriation: an abrasion of the epidermis (skin) usually from a mechanical (not chemical) cause; a scratch.

histamine: substance that interacts with tissues to produce most of the symptoms of allergy.

hives: a skin condition characterized by intensely itching wheals caused by an allergic reaction; also called urticaria.

hyperemia: increased blood flow to a body part like the eye; engorgement.

nonselective: interacts with any subtype receptor.

prophylactic: process or drug that prevents the onset of symptoms (or disease) as a result of exposure before the reactive process can take place.

selective: interacts with one subtype of receptor over others.

sensitize: to induce or develop a reaction to naturally occurring substances (allergens) as a result of repeated exposure.

urticaria: intensely itching raised areas of skin caused by an allergic reaction; hives.

wheal: a firm, elevated swelling of the skin often pale red in color and itchy; a sign of allergy.

xerostomia: dryness of the oral cavity resulting from inhibition of the natural moistening action of salivary gland secretions or increased secretion of salivary mucus, rather than serous material.

Learning Outcomes

After studying this chapter, you should be able to

31.1 explain the reactions produced by histamine released in response to allergic reactions.

31.2 describe the difference in action between an antihistaminic and a mast cell release inhibitor.

31.3 describe two specific therapeutic uses of antihistaminics that result from an action on the central nervous system (CNS) yet are not associated with allergic responses.

31.4 describe three side effects of antihistaminics.

31.5 describe three examples of first- and second-generation antihistamines and the characteristic difference between the two groups.

31.6 explain terminology associated with allergy and these drugs.

Introduction

Sneezing, coughing, itching, headache, and nasal congestion often indicate that people are experiencing an allergic reaction. Severe allergic reactions can result in respiratory and cardiovascular failure (anaphylaxis). The symptoms of an allergic reaction indicate that individuals have become **sensitized** to certain antigens in the environment. **Antigens** are substances such as pollen, mold, dust, and insect venom that stimulate the production of **antibodies** in the blood and tissues. In sensitized people, repeated exposure to these antigens results in allergic reactions due to antigen-antibody interactions. People who suffer from **asthma,** a chronic obstructive lung disease, are highly sensitive to antigenic stimulation. Allergic reactions that occur in asthmatic people severely restrict their ability to breathe. (See Chapter 32 for the treatment of asthma.)

Once an antigen has initiated an allergic reaction, certain cells in the body (mast cells) release active substances into the blood. In other chapters, the role of mast cells in inflammation has been presented. This chapter will focus on the mast cell in allergy. One of the substances released is **histamine,** which interacts with histamine receptors located on other cells to produce most of the symptoms of allergy. Drugs that block histamine receptors and stop histamine's responses are known as **antihistamines.** Such drugs alleviate the annoying discomfort that accompanies most allergic reactions.

In contrast, drugs that prevent mast cells from releasing histamine are considered **antiallergic** agents. Antiallergic drugs also block the action of other active substances (serotonin and bradykinin). Antiallergic drugs are valuable in the prophylactic therapy of asthma because they help prevent future allergic reactions.

ACTION OF HISTAMINE

Histamine is found throughout the body in the mast cells and basophilic white blood cells. Mast cells usually found alongside blood vessels contain granules of bioactive substances. The largest concentrations of mast cells are in the lungs, the gastrointestinal (GI) tract, and the skin. See Figure 31.1. The first time a person comes into contact with tree pollen, dust mites, or other **allergens** (antigens), white blood cells produce antibodies, specifically IgE immunoglobulin. During this first encounter, there are no symptoms. The IgE attaches to the surface of mast cells. On the repeated exposure, when an antigen comes into contact with the skin or lungs or enters the bloodstream of sensitized individuals, the allergen binds to the IgE and triggers a release of mast cell contents. This is called degranulation of the mast cell. Among the substances immediately released into the blood are histamine, heparin, serotonin, prostaglandins, leukotrienes, platelets, and eosinophil-activating factors. While all of these substances produce a variety of effects, this chapter will focus on the actions of histamine. Histamine interacts with the membrane receptors in certain tissues to produce the symptoms of allergy (itching, redness, **urticaria,** stuffy nose). This is a Type I (acute) hypersensitivity reaction because the response is immediate (not delayed). By the way, some drugs, antibiotics, and opioid analgesics (morphine) cause the release of histamine from mast cells, resulting in allergy-like symptoms.

There are four types of receptors associated with histamine: H_1-, H_2-, H_3-, and H_4-receptors. Histamine interacts with postsynaptic H_1-receptors, located on blood vessels, bronchiolar smooth muscle, and intestinal smooth muscle, to mediate allergic reactions. The intensity of the allergic symptoms is proportional to the amount of histamine released.

Figure 31.1 Mast Cells

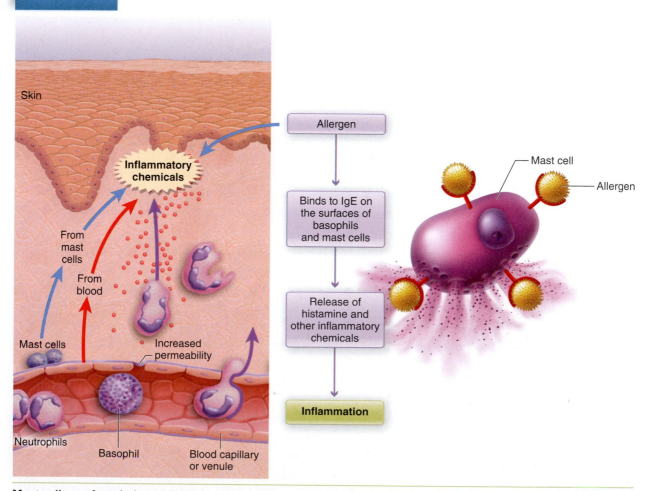

Mast cells are found along blood vessels or in the circulation as basophils. In response to an allergic stimulus, mast cells release histamine.

The postsynaptic H₂-receptors are located within the stomach, heart, blood vessels, and uterine tissue. The most important response mediated by H_2-receptors is increased secretion of gastric acid in the stomach. This response is not usually associated with allergies. However, the action of H_2-receptors is clinically important in the management of GI ulcers and will be discussed in Chapter 33. H_3- and H_4-receptors have a role in modulating the body's response to pain and inflammation. H_3-receptors have been identified in neurons and presynaptic areas of the brain, while H_4-receptors are associated with white blood cells (neutrophils, CD_4, and T cells).

Vascular Effects

Histamine usually produces a transient drop in blood pressure because it dilates small blood vessels and capillaries. With large histamine concentrations, this drop can result in hypotension and circulatory collapse. Dilation of cerebral blood vessels stimulates pain receptors in the skull. This action explains the throbbing headache known as histaminic cephalgia. Capillary dilation in the skin results in a localized redness called **erythema.** Localized dilation and redness in the eye are the hallmark of allergic conjunctivitis.

Histamine causes fluids and proteins to leak out of the capillaries. H_1-receptors cause a separation of the endothelial cells in the capillaries. This allows the fluid and plasma proteins to leak into the space around the vessels. When capillary leakage occurs in the nasal mucous membranes, nasal congestion occurs. See Figure 31.2. When capillary leakage occurs in the skin, edema, **wheals,** or **hives** are produced. See Figure 31.3. Itching and pain occur because histamine binds to receptors on local sensory nerve endings and causes itch-specific fibers to send information to the spinal cord and brain (spinothalamic tract). The erythema and edema produced by histamine in the skin are known as the Response of Lewis. When the edema and swelling are beneath the skin rather than on the surface, it is **angioedema.** Histamine also increases the production of nasal and bronchial mucus.

Extravascular Smooth Muscle Effects

Histamine produces contraction of the smooth muscle of the intestine and bronchioles by stimulating H_1-receptors. Contraction of intestinal smooth muscle results in disturbances of intestinal activity like increased peristalsis and diarrhea. Contraction of the bronchiolar smooth muscle results in bronchoconstriction, which makes breathing difficult.

Humans are more sensitive to the bronchiolar constriction produced by histamine than to the disturbances of intestinal activity. In particular, people who have pulmonary diseases (asthma and emphysema) may be

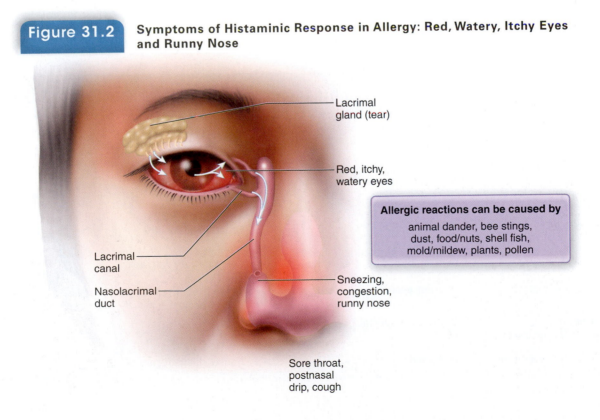

Figure 31.2 **Symptoms of Histaminic Response in Allergy: Red, Watery, Itchy Eyes and Runny Nose**

Lacrimal gland (tear)

Red, itchy, watery eyes

Lacrimal canal

Nasolacrimal duct

Allergic reactions can be caused by
animal dander, bee stings, dust, food/nuts, shell fish, mold/mildew, plants, pollen

Sneezing, congestion, runny nose

Sore throat, postnasal drip, cough

Figure 31.3

Hives from an Allergic Reaction

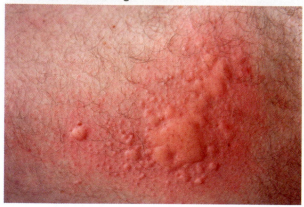

1000 times more sensitive to the respiratory actions of histamine. Antihistamines are not therapeutically useful in asthmatics because the intensity and nature of the allergic response requires an antiallergy approach (see Chapter 32).

Cardiac Effects

Histamine produces several effects on the heart that are directly related to the amount of histamine present. Histamine usually produces rapid heartbeat. However, at high levels of histamine (histamine shock), cardiac conduction is impaired. Such impairment may lead to the development

of arrhythmias and cardiovascular collapse. The major effects of histamine are summarized in Table 31:1.

LO 31.2 **LO 31.6**

MAST CELL RELEASE INHIBITORS

Allergic reactions can be blocked in two ways. Mast cells can be prevented from releasing their contents or the postsynaptic H_1-receptors can be blocked from interacting with histamine. Cromolyn sodium is a drug that selectively prevents the release of histamine from the mast cells. See Figure 31.4. Cromolyn sodium is not a bronchodilator, a smooth muscle relaxant, or a histamine-receptor antagonist. It is one of the drugs known as mast cell release inhibitors. Since this drug has no effect on histamine receptors, cromolyn sodium must be administered before histamine release has begun.

Drugs like cromolyn sodium, which prevent the onset of symptoms or disease as a result of exposure before the reactive process can take place, are called **prophylactic** drugs. Cromolyn sodium is ingested or applied topically to the mucous membranes of the nose and eyes. The drug reaches the mast cells before any antigens can induce an allergic reaction.

Routes of Administration

Cromolyn is available as ampoules of liquid concentrate for oral administration (*Gastrocrom*) and as a dilute solution for intranasal and intraocular use. See Figure 31.5

[Table **31:1**]

Physiological Responses Following Histamine Stimulation

System or tissue	Histamine effect	Receptor	Physiological response
Blood pressure	Decreased	H_1, H_2	Hypotension
Heart rate	Increased	H_2	Rapid heartbeat
Bronchioles	Constriction	H_1	Breathing difficulty
Intestine	Contraction	H_1	Constipation/diarrhea
Skin capillaries	Dilation, edema	H_1	Triple Response of Lewis : redness, flare, wheal
Nerves in spinothalamic tract	Trigger itch-specific fibers	H_1	Itching
Gastric acid secretion	Increased	H_2	Nausea, heartburn

Figure 31.4

Cromolyn Sodium Nasal Spray

Figure 31.5

Application of Antiallergic Drugs Using a Nasal Spray

for the proper technique for using a nasal spray. Indications for use and dosages are presented in Table 31:2. See Figures 31.4 and 31.5. The oral ampoule formulation (*Gastrocrom*), which contains a measured dose, is opened and the liquid dissolved into a glass of hot water. The full glass of liquid must be consumed to receive the proper dose. Fruit juice, milk, or food will inhibit dissolution and absorption of the drug and therefore should not be consumed until 0.5 hour after dosing.

Ophthalmic Mast Cell Release Inhibitors

There are four drugs in addition to cromolyn that inhibit the release of histamine and other mediators of inflammation from mast cells. Bepotastine (*Bepreve*), cromolyn (*Crolom*), lodoxamide (*Alomide*), nedocromil (*Alocril*),

and pemirolast (*Alamast*) are only available by prescription as ophthalmic solutions. None of these drugs have any activity on postsynaptic histamine receptors or inflammatory pathways such as cyclooxygenase or prostaglandin synthesis. The mechanisms of action aren't fully known, but mast cells do not release histamine or leukotrienes after antigen stimulation in the presence of these drugs. They all inhibit eosinophil chemotaxis, which blocks recruitment of specialized white blood cells that increase the inflammatory response. All of these are indicated for the treatment of allergic conjunctivitis and keratoconjunctivitis.

Conjuctivitis is an inflammation of the conjunctiva, the thin, clear, outermost membrane that lies over the white part of the eye and lines the inside of the eyelid as well as the exposed parts of the eye, except the cornea. Sometimes this is due to mechanical (dust or sand) or chemical (shampoos, dirt, smoke, and pool chlorine) irritation. When an infectious virus or bacteria are the cause, it is called "pink eye." Most often it is due to an allergic response to pollen or some other antigen in sensitized individuals or contact lens wearers.

Note to the Health Care Professional

If a rash develops while patients are taking cromolyn sodium, the drug must be discontinued before further sensitivity occurs. Cromolyn sodium cannot be used in acute allergies in which histamine has already been released.

Indications for Use of Mast Cell Release Inhibitors

Formulation	Prophylaxis indication	Daily dose
Cromolyn		
Nasal solution	Allergic rhinitis	One spray in each nostril 3–6 times a day at regular intervals
Oral	Mastocytosis	200 mg 4 times a day 30 min before meals and at bedtime
Ophthalmic drugs		
Bepotastine (*Bepreve*)	Allergic conjunctivitis	1 drop (1.5% solution) into the affected eye BID
Cromolyn (*Crolom*)	Vernal keratoconjunctivitis, vernal conjunctivitis, and vernal keratitis	1 to 2 drops in each eye 4 to 6 times at regular intervals
Lodoxamide (*Alomide*)	Vernal keratoconjunctivitis, vernal conjunctivitis, and vernal keratitis	1 to 2 drops in each affected eye QID for up to 3 months
Nedocromil (*Alocril*)	Allergic conjunctivitis with itching	1 to 2 drops (2% solution) in each eye BID
Pemirolast (*Alamast*)	Allergic conjunctivitis with itching	1 to 2 drops (0.1% solution) QID

Keratoconjunctivitis is an inflammation of the cornea and conjunctiva at the same time. It is characterized by hard, elevated, cobblestone-like bumps on the upper eyelid. There also may be swellings and thickening of the conjunctiva. Symptoms include redness of the white or inner eyelid; yellow, green, or white discharge from the eye; itching; burning; and increased sensitivity to light. Severe cases may develop corneal ulcers that can scar if not properly healed.

Mast cell release stabilizers are effective in reducing itching, **hyperemia** (red-looking eye), and mucous discharge. In severe cases, they may be used concurrently with mild corticosteroids. Drops of each drug are placed (instilled) into the affected eye. The duration of treatment usually continues until symptoms resolve. Doses and indications of mast cell release inhibitors are presented in Table 31:2.

Clinical Indications

Cromolyn is currently used as a prophylactic adjunct in the management of chronic allergic rhinitis to prevent bronchospasms and ocular allergy. See Figures 31.4 and 31.8. Pulmonary function tests must demonstrate that the patient has a bronchodilator reversible component to the airway obstruction for cromolyn to be of any benefit. Patients must be compliant with dosing at regular repeated intervals; otherwise the drug cannot achieve a satisfactory response. All of the ophthalmic drugs are indicated for the treatment of allergic conjunctivitis and keratoconjunctivitis. Vernal keratoconjuctivitis is a special condition that occurs in warm dry areas only between April and August, meaning vernal. Oral cromolyn improves diarrhea, flushing, headaches, urticaria, abdominal pain, and nausea in some patients with mastocytosis. In this condition, mast cells accumulate in organs and tissues in excessive amounts. Patients may experience symptoms associated with excessive histamine release from pruritis to peptic ulcer and chronic diarrhea.

Adverse Effects and Contraindications

Adverse effects to mast cell release inhibitors are minimal and include wheezing, nasal itching, nasal burning, nausea, drowsiness, and headache with cromolyn nebulization. All of these drugs are contraindicated in patients who develop hypersensitivity to the drug. The usual side effects for the ophthalmic solutions include stinging or burning of the eyes, which resolves; hypersensitivity; nausea; and dryness in the nose.

ANTIHISTAMINE H₁ ANTAGONISTS

Antihistaminic drugs are used to relieve the signs and symptoms of acute reactions in which histamine has already been released. All of the antihistamines discussed in this chapter block histamine from interfacing with its H_1-receptors. Therefore, the H_1-mediated allergic responses of histamine are prevented. Antihistaminic drugs are usually administered orally (see Table 31:3) because they are absorbed well from the intestinal tract. These drugs are rapidly metabolized by the liver, necessitating repeated drug administration (usually two to four times a day) to maintain a therapeutic response. First-generation antihistamines include brompheniramine, chlorpheniramine (*Chlor-Trimeton*), clemastine (*Tavist*), diphenhydramine (*Benadryl*), dimenhydrinate, meclizine, and promethazine (*Phenergan*). These characterstically have a **nonselective** interaction with peripheral and central (CNS) histamine receptors. For this reason these early antihistamines produce the same spectrum of therapeutic responses, varying only in their degree of activity. These drugs can be used interchangeably and frequently cause sedation (CNS) along with relief of allergy symptoms. In addition to inhibiting the actions of histamine, these drugs possess local anesthetic and anticholinergic activity. Diphenhydramine has been shown to be a sodium channel blocker, which accounts for its local anesthetic action. Antihistamines can relieve itching and local surface pain of bites, stings, and **excoriations.** Diphenhydramine (*Benadryl*) is still considered an antihistamine of choice.

Dimenhydrinate (*Dramamine Chewable*) and meclizine (*Antivert*) exert a unique action in the brain to relieve vertigo and motion sickness and the nausea that accompanies it. Cyproheptadine (*Periactin*) inhibits the actions of histamine and serotonin. For this reason, it often offers a wider range of relief or another therapeutic alternative in highly sensitized individuals.

The second generation of antihistamines began with astemizole and terfenadine. These two drugs were removed from the market for safety reasons (see Cautions and Contraindications for further explanation). The current generation, which includes cetirizine (*Zyrtec,* now OTC only), fexofenadine (*Allegra*), desloratadine (*Clarinex*), levocetirizine (*Xycal*), and loratadine (*Alavert,* now OTC only), appears to be more **selective** for peripheral H_1-receptors. These agents are not as sedating or drying and demonstrate equal antiallergic activity to the first-generation drugs. These drugs have much less anticholinergic activity than the first-generation antihistamines. The proposal that patients who were refractory to first-generation drugs would find relief with the newest antihistamines has not proven to be a significant advantage. The new antihistamines are not superior in antihistamine activity to first-generation drugs, but they are truly less sedating. Recently, levocetirizine (*Xycal*) was added to the class of antihistamines. It is the first new oral antihistamine in a number of years and is a third-generation antihistamine. It has a similar chemical structure to cetirizine, but it has twice the affinity for the receptors. This means it fits the receptors better and is expected to work at least as well as cetirizine. It is expected to cause less drowsiness than other antihistamines, but some people will still experience slight adverse effects.

A few antihistamines have made the move from prescription to OTC status. The most recent are cetirizine (*Zyrtec*) and loratadine as *Claritin* and *Alavert* OTC preparations. It is tough to keep track of all these drugs; seven are available OTC. See Table 31:3. Cetirizine, loratadine, and *Actifed* are OTC only. Clemastine, dimenhydrinate, diphenhydramine, and meclizine are OTC and prescription depending on the dose and label. All the others listed in Table 31:3 are prescription only. The cost of OTC medications is expected to be significantly less than the equivalent prescription product. Extensive effort has been spent by the FDA and the product manufacturers to provide the consumer/patient with detailed instructions for use, which has contributed to the interest in moving these drugs into the OTC market. See Figure 31.6.

Routes of Administration

These drugs are usually taken orally, whether as single agents or combined with other drugs in cough-cold and allergy preparations. Only a few antihistamines are available for parenteral administration: dimenhydrinate (*Dramamine*), diphenhydramine (*Benadryl*), and promethazine. See Table 31:3 for doses and routes of administration.

There are topical formulations, ointments, creams, lotions, and sprays available for application to the skin and mucous membranes. Diphenhydramine (0.5% to 2%) is the antihistamine contained in most topical products to relieve itching and manage symptoms of insect bites. Topical products containing antihistamines often contain multiple additional ingredients. Examples of

Frequently Used H₁ Antagonist Antihistaminic Drugs*

Drugs (*Trade Name*)**	Recommended doses			
	Adult oral	**Child oral**	**Adult parenteral**	**Sedative dose**
Brompheniramine (*BroveX*)	12–24 mg every 12 hr	12–24 mg once a day	2.5–10 mg IM, SC	—
Cetirizine (*Zyrtec*)	10 mg once a day			—
Chlorpheniramine (*Allerclor, Chlor-Trimeton*)	4 mg every 4–6 hr	2 mg every 4–6 hr		—
Clemastine (*Tavist*)***	1.34–2.68 mg BID	0.67–1.34 mg BID	—	—
Cyproheptadine	4–6 mg/day	2–4 mg BID, TID	—	—
Dexchlopheniramine	2 mg every 8–10 hr	4 mg at bedtime	—	—
Desloratadine (*Clarinex*)	5 mg/day	2.5–5 mg/day	—	—
Dimenhydrinate*** (*Dramamine Chewable*)	50–100 mg every 4–6 hr	12.5–50 mg every 6–8 hr up to 150 mg/day	50 mg IV, IM	—
Diphenhydramine*** (*Benadryl Allergy, Triaminic Multi Symptom*)	25–50 mg every 4–6 hr	6.25–25 mg TID, QID	10–50 mg IV, deep IM to 400 mg/day	50 mg at bedtime
Doxylamine (*Aldex, Doxytex AN*)	2 tablets 4–6 times/day	1–2 tablets 4–6 times/day	—	—
Fexofenadine (*Allegra*)	60 mg BID or 180 mg once daily	30–60 mg BID	—	—
Hydroxyzine (*Atarax, Vistaril*)	25 mg TID, QID	50–100 mg daily in divided doses		50–100 mg before anesthesia
Loratadine (*Claritin, Alavert*)	10 mg/day	5 mg/day	—	—
Levocetirizine (*Xycal*)	2.5–5 mg in evening	2.5–5 mg in evening	—	—
Meclizine*** (*Antivert, Bonine*)	25–50 g/day	—	—	—
Promethazine (*Phenergan, Phenadoz*)	12.5 mg TID or 25 mg at bedtime	6.25–12.5 mg TID or 25 mg at bedtime	25 mg deep IM	25–50 mg at bedtime IM,IV
Triprolidine (*Zymine*)	10 ml every 4, 6, or 12 hr	5–10 ml every 12 hr	—	
Triprolidine (2.5 mg), Pseudoephedrine (60 mg)(*Actifed*)	1 dose every 4–8 hr PO	—	—	—

*Not an inclusive list of trade names.
**All drugs are used for acute allergy (urticaria, rhinitis, hay fever, contact dermatitis, and pruritus) except for dimenhydrinate, which is used to prevent motion sickness, and meclizine, which is used for motion sickness and vertigo. Diphenhydramine is also used as an antiemetic and hydroxyzine is used to relieve anxiety and for sedation.
*** These drugs are available OTC and by prescription depending on the dose and the label. All other drugs in this table are prescription only.

Figure 31.6 OTC Antihistamine Products

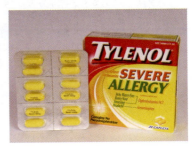

topical products with a variety of antihistaminic drugs is presented in Table 31:4.

Antihistamines are also available as nasal sprays and eyedrops. Azelastine (*Astelin, Astepro*) and olopatadine (*Patanase*) are used for relief of symptoms of allergic rhinitis. The usual dose is 2 sprays in each nostril twice a day.

Ophthalmic (eye instillation) antihistamines relieve the symptoms of hyperemia, tearing, and itching due to immediate (type I) response of histamine release (see Figure 31.7). These drugs are either selective H$_1$-receptor antagonists, emedastine (*Emadine, Zyrtec Itchy Eyes*), or mast cell stabilizers that block the release of histamine in addition to antagonizing the H$_1$-receptor (azelastine, epinastine, olopatadine). Ketotifen (*Zaditor*) is a relatively selective, noncompetitive H$_1$-receptor antagonist and mast cell stabilizer that relieves symptoms of allergic conjunctivitis for up to 12 hours. It has been available by prescription and OTC since 2006. The usual dose is one drop in the affected eye every 8 to 12 hours. The other ophthalmic antihistamines require a prescription. The dose varies with the product from 1 drop in the affected eye once a day (2% olopatadine [*Pataday*]), to 1 drop BID (azelastine [*Optivar*] and epinastine [*Elestat*]) or QID (emedastine [*Emadine*]). Patients with a history of allergy, hay fever, or eczema respond well to mast cell stabilizer antihistamines.

Examples of ophthalmic antihistamines are shown in Figure 31.8.

Clinical Indications

Antihistaminics are frequently used in acute allergic reactions including urticaria, hay fever, insect bites, rhinitis, and **dermatitis.** Because of the inherent sedation, antihistaminics may be used to induce sleep in OTC sleeping aids (for example, *Nytol*) or to relieve motion sickness (*Dramamine Chewables*) or vertigo (*Antivert*). Certain antihistamines—chlorpromazine, perphenazine, prochlorperazine (*Compro*), promethazine (*Phenergan*), and triflupromazine—are extremely effective in reducing nausea and vomiting. These drugs are used as adjunct pre- and postoperative medications to minimize anesthetic irritability and facilitate patient recovery (see Chapter 33). Antihistaminics are frequently found in cold remedies and cough syrups because of their ability to dry nasal secretions. Many of the common OTC analgesic and cough-cold medications contain an antihistamine as an active ingredient. The most common ingredients are chlorpheniramine, brompheniramine, and doxylamine. The anticholinergic component of H$_1$-antagonists provides relief from symptoms associated with the common cold as well as allergic reactions such as runny nose. In addition,

Over-the-Counter Cold and Allergy Preparations That Contain Antihistaminics*

Trade Name	Antihistamine	Form	Other active ingredients
Advil Allergy and Sinus	2 mg chlorpheniramine	Tablet	Ibuprofen 200 mg
Allerest Maximum Strength	12 mg chlorpheniramine	Tablet	Pseudoephedrine 30 mg
Drixoral Plus	3 mg dexbrompheniramine	Tablet, extended release	Acetaminophen 500 mg, pseudoephedrine 60 mg
Nyquil Nighttime Cold/Flu Medicine Liquid	6.25 mg doxylamine/ml	Liquid	Alcohol 10%, acetaminophen 500 mg, dextromethorphan 15 mg
Tussionex Pennkinetic	8.0 mg chlorpheniramine/5 ml	Suspension	Hydrocodone 10 mg
Benadryl Skin Allergy Relief Lotion	1% diphenhydramine	Lotion	Alcohol, camphor, parabens, zinc oxide 2%

Not an inclusive list of available products.

sedation caused by an antihistaminic in a multiingredient cold product aids recovery by promoting bed rest. Examples of over-the-counter cold and allergy products that contain antihistaminics are given in Table 31:4.

Adverse Reactions

Antihistaminics generally produce similar side effects but differ in the predominance or intensity of one side effect over another. The most common side effects produced by the antihistaminics are drowsiness and sedation. Another frequently occurring side effect is dry mouth **(xerostomia).** At any dose, most of these drugs exert an anticholinergic effect that dries the mucous linings of the mouth and nasal passages. This side effect is therapeutically useful in treating a runny nose in the common cold. Other adverse effects include hypotension, rapid heartbeat, anorexia, epigastric distress, and urinary retention. Within the class of antihistamines, diphenhydramine (*Benadryl*), promethazine (*Phenergan*), and hydroxyzine (*Vistaril*) reportedly cause sedation most often, whereas chlorpheniramine (*Chlor-Trimeton*) and cyproheptadine (*Periactin*) are associated with little or no sedation. In unusual circumstances, patients may become nervous and unable to sleep (insomnia) while taking chlorpheniramine. In patients over 60 years of age, paradoxical stimulation rather than sedation can occur and may warrant dose reduction to eliminate this adverse experience.

Cautions and Contraindications

Because of their anticholinergic activity, antihistaminic drugs should be used with caution in patients with cardiovascular disease, hypertension, prostate enlargement, or urinary retention.

Antihistaminics are found as active agents in many ointments, sprays, and cream preparations to be used on the skin. The prolonged indiscriminate use of topical antihistaminic preparations can lead to the development of hypersensitivity in some people. This hypersensitivity may range from rashes to **eczematoid dermatitis,** in which lesions on the skin surface ooze and develop scaly crusts. Antihistaminics also may produce drug fever, which will subside only when the drug is stopped. The mechanism of this drug-induced fever is not known. Antihistaminics are not harmless drugs, even though they may be found in many over-the-counter products (see Table 31:4). The potential for adverse effects increases when any individual takes three to five medications *or more* daily and older patients are likely to be taking multiple medications. Patients taking multiple medications, including the elderly, are more likely to experience dizziness, excessive sedation, paradoxical stimulation, or confusion with these drugs. Medications

Figure 31.7 Allergic Conjunctivitis before and after Treatment with Antihistamine Eyedrops

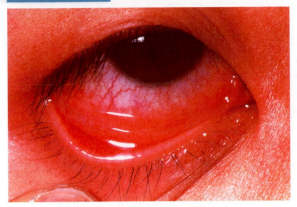

that affect the CNS (sedation) and cardiovascular system (alter blood flow to the brain) predispose patients to develop mental confusion. Patients are often unaware they are taking an antihistamine because it isn't the primary ingredient in the advertisement for cough-cold, headache, or sleep products. Many of these antihistamine combination products for cough-colds, flu, and allergy contain ingredients such as dextromethorphan, ephedrine, pseudoephedrine, and phenylpropanolamine. These products are no longer self-serve OTC because of the incidence of misuse. Dextromethorphan-containing products were used to achieve a "mental high" among school kids. Concern about this misuse prompted regulation that put the drugs behind the pharmacist's counter to be dispensed under stricter control of inventory and distribution. Ephedrine, pseudoephedrine, and phenylpropanolamine were the specific subject of a federal law, the "Combat Methamphetamine Epidemic Act of 2005," which regulates retail over-the-counter sale with

purchase limits, placement of product out of direct customer access, and very detailed recordkeeping of inventory and sales. These drugs are precursor chemicals used in the illegal manufacture of methamphetamine and amphetamine and were being used to make street-grade Schedule II drugs.

Figure 31.8 Ophthalmic Drops: Antihistamine and Mast Cell Stabilizers

QTc Interval Prolongation

Two second-generation antihistamines, astemazole and terfenadine, were removed from the market because they produced serious cardiovascular and hepatic effects that were fatal in some patients. These drugs delayed conduction within the heart and prolonged the QTc interval. On the ECG, prolongation of the QTc interval reflects a change in cardiac conduction that makes it possible for life-threatening ventricular arrhythmias to occur. The mechanism is a direct interaction with selective ion channels (K^+, Na^+, Ca^{++}) in the myocardium that interrupts normal cardiorhythm.

Four antihistamines still on the market prolong the QTc interval but have not been associated with fatalities: desloratadine, diphenhydramine, fexofenadine, and hydroxyzine. Prolongation of the QTc interval as a side effect is a hot topic in drug development. A number of drugs have been confirmed to produce this adverse effect. Because of the potential for serious arrhythmias and death, new drugs in development, no matter what the therapeutic focus (antibiotics, antidepressants, and cancer chemotherapy), have to determine whether QTc prolongation may occur during treatment. The outcome may result in a special cautionary warning in the product label or even the end of product development. (Go to www.azcert.org for a list of drugs that prolong the QTc interval.)

Contraindications

Antihistamines should not be used by patients with a known hypersensitivity to antihistamines or patients with narrow-angle glaucoma, stenosing peptic ulcer, or prostatic hypertrophy.

Hydroxyzine is contraindicated for use in early pregnancy. Antihistamines are not recommended for use during pregnancy because safe use during pregnancy has not been established. Animal studies have demonstrated abnormalities in the offspring with certain antihistamines. Antihistamines should not be used in newborn or premature infants because these patients are more susceptible to the adverse effects. Convulsions in newborns after exposure to antihistamines in the third trimester have been reported. These drugs should not be used by nursing mothers, since they are excreted into breast milk and thus passed into the newborn.

These drugs should not be given to dehydrated children because dystonias (abnormal tissue tone) may occur. Promethazine has a special cautionary warning (black box) in its instructions for use. Promethazine should not be used in children younger than 2 years of age because of the potential for fatal respiratory depression. Phenothiazine antihistamines such as promethazine (*Phenergan*) are contraindicated for use in patients with CNS depression or a history of phenothiazine-induced jaundice.

Drug Interactions

First, the newest antihistamines, cetirizine and levocitirazine, do not appear to undergo drug interactions. In general, other antihistaminics interact with many drugs. Some antibiotics, muscle relaxants (curare), and narcotic analgesics (morphine) cause the release of histamine from mast cells. If patients are taking such a drug, it is not unusual for an antihistaminic to be given to counteract the effects of histamine. Drugs that depress the activity of the CNS (sedatives, tranquilizers, opioid analgesics, and alcohol) increase the incidence of drowsiness when taken with antihistamines, including nasal antihistamines. This synergistic effect is likely to occur with liquid OTC products that contain an antihistaminic in addition to alcohol as an active ingredient.

Antacids, especially those containing aluminum or magnesium, bind drugs like fexofenadine in the intestine, inhibit absorption, and reduce effective drug blood levels. Fexofenadine should not be taken within 1 hour of the antacid. Cimetidine increases the blood level of nasally administered azelastine, which may predispose patients to adverse effects. Antihistamines known to prolong the QT interval (desloratadine, diphenhydramine, fexofenadine, hydroxyzine) should be monitored carefully when patients are receiving antiarrhythmic drugs, antivirals, and antibiotics that also have this effect on the heart to avoid serious arrhythmias and myocardial infarction. (See Table 31:5.) Some of the second-generation antihistamines undergo food interactions. Fexofenadine absorption is delayed when taken closely with high fatty meals or fruit juices including orange and grapefruit juice. Other antihistamines do not appear to be affected by meal timing or composition.

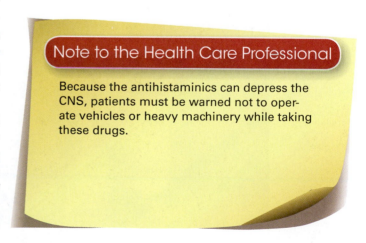

Note to the Health Care Professional

Because the antihistaminics can depress the CNS, patients must be warned not to operate vehicles or heavy machinery while taking these drugs.

Drug Interactions with Antihistaminic Drugs

Drug	Response
Antacids with aluminum or magnesium	Decrease the blood level of fexofenadine
Antibiotics: azithromycin, clarithromycin, erythromycin	Increase plasma concentrations of fexofenadine through inhibition of hepatic metabolism
Anticholinergics: atropine	Increase nervousness, insomnia, and constipation with any antihistamine
Antidepressants: imipramine	Increase anticholinergic effect, urinary retention, and intraocular pressure
Antifungals: azole drugs fluconazole, itraconazole	Increase plasma concentrations of fexofenadine through inhibition of hepatic metabolism
Antivirals: ritonavir	Increase the plasma level and half-life of levocitrizine
Cimetidine	Inhibits the metabolism of hydroxyzine and azelastine
CNS depressants: alcohol, barbiturates, hypnotics, opioid analgesics, phenothiazines, tranquilizers	Increase drowsiness, sedation, and lethargy for first-generation antihistamines, azelastine and olopatadine
Corticosteroids: oral drugs	Increase risk of glaucoma in susceptible patients
MAO inhibitors: amphetamines, tranylcypromine	Intensify the drying effects of first-generation antihistaminics and may cause hypotension with phenothiazines
QT prolongation: amiodarone, chlorpromazine, clindamycin, dofetilide, droperidol, mefloquine, moxifloxacin, oxafloxacin, pentamidine, procainamide, quinidine, sotalol, tacrolimus, and more	An additive effect to prolong the QT interval may occur with desloratadine, diphenhydramine, fexofenadine, hydroxyzine
Theophylline	Decreases cetirizine blood levels, eliminating its effect

Abbreviations: MAO, monoamine oxidase.

Antihistamines provide symptomatic relief for a variety of acute and chronic conditions when used at the recommended dose and at regular, approved intervals. Because these products are widely available OTC, patients frequently assume the drugs have less potential for producing adverse effects. In all cases where the antihistamine is available OTC and prescription, the OTC product contains the same active agent, only in a lower amount per dosage unit than that available by prescription. Therefore, with children, elderly, and hectic working adults, it becomes extremely easy to take multiple OTC doses that are comparable to the prescription antihistamines. Whenever possible it is worthwhile reviewing the following facts with patients who are using antihistamines or cromolyn.

Patient Instruction

Special formulations should be reviewed with patients to ensure the product is delivering the designated amount of drug appropriately.

Sustained-release (SR) preparations should not be chewed or crushed. These capsules should not be opened to divide the dose. The pellets are coated to release the drug at a variety of time intervals that cannot be determined by the patient. Sustained-release preparations should be swallowed intact with water.

Oral cromolyn is designed to be dissolved in water. Patients should be reminded not to take this drug with fruit juice, milk, or food because it will not be absorbed.

Dosing Schedule

The time of dosing should be provided in writing if necessary to ensure adequate drug absorption. Oral cromolyn should be taken 30 minutes before meals to avoid any delay in drug absorption.

Dosing with Meals

Oral antihistamines may cause gastric upset in some patients. Although patients may take most antihistamines with meals to minimize the irritation, remind patients that fexofenadine should not be taken within 60 minutes of an aluminum/magnesium antacid, grapefruit juice, or a high fatty meal. All of these decrease the absorption of fexofenadine.

Adverse Effects

Patients should be instructed to avoid prolonged exposure to sunlight because antihistamines may produce photosensitivity.

Even with nonsedating antihistamines, patients should be reminded to avoid alcohol and CNS depressants that could potentiate adverse effects. This includes OTC preparations for relief of coughs, colds, flu, and allergy. Any product designated "elixir" contains alcohol in amounts that can interact with antihistamine effects.

Notify the Physician

Patients should notify their physician immediately if they develop involuntary muscle spasms, wheezing, or edema. These may be signs of a muscle disorder or hypersensitivity.

Changes in the patient's medical history or onset of signs and symptoms of glaucoma, peptic ulcer, or urinary retention are important to tell the physician because the anticholinergic actions of antihistamine drugs will worsen these conditions.

Use in Pregnancy

Antihistamines are designated as Food and Drug Administration (FDA) Pregnancy Category B or C. They are not recommended for use in pregnancy because the safety for use in humans has not been established. The physician should be notified if the patient becomes pregnant during therapy. Hydroxyzine is contraindicated in early pregnancy.

Chapter Review

Understanding Terminology

Answer the following questions.

1. What is the difference between an antiallergic and an antihistaminic drug? **(LO 31.1, 31.2)**
2. Differentiate between erythema and dermatitis. **(LO 31.6)**
3. Define *prophylaxis*. **(LO 31.6)**
4. Define *xerostomia*. **(LO 31.6)**

Acquiring Knowledge

Answer the following questions.

1. Where is histamine located in the body? What stimulates histamine release? **(LO 31.1)**
2. What are the effects of histamine on various tissues? **(LO 31.1)**
3. How does cromolyn sodium produce its antiallergic response? When is cromolyn sodium used? **(LO 31.2)**
4. How do the antihistaminics prevent the action of histamine? What receptors are involved in allergic reactions? **(LO 31.2)**
5. What other pharmacological actions do antihistaminics produce? **(LO 31.3)**
6. Why are antihistaminics found in over-the-counter products? What are two examples? **(LO 31.3)**
7. What adverse effects are associated with antihistaminic use? **(LO 31.4)**
8. What drugs commonly interact with antihistaminics? **(LO 31.4)**

Applying Knowledge on the Job

Use your critical-thinking skills to answer the following questions.

1. Mrs. Lewis calls the clinic where you are working. She says when she was in the clinic 2 days ago, the doctor diagnosed her with allergic rhinitis and gave her prescriptions for *Nasalcrom* and *Chlor-Trimeton*. She claims she has used *Nasalcrom* for the past 48 hours without any relief of her nasal symptoms. "My nose is running like a faucet with this pollen count so high. I didn't fill the *Chlor-Trimeton* prescription because I have to work and can't tolerate the drowsiness." What should you tell her? **(LO 31.1, 31.2)**

2. Six months later, during cold season, Mrs. Lewis calls the office for a refill on her *Nasalcrom* prescription. She says she has a terrible cold with a runny nose and the *Nasalcrom* worked so well when she used it during hay fever season she wants to use it now. What should you do? **(LO 31.1, 31.2)**

3. A patient has just received a prescription for *Gastrocrom*. What should be included in his instructions for proper administration? **(LO 31.2)**

4. What are contraindications for anticholinergic antihistamines? **(LO 31.4)**

5. Can antihistamines be used safely during pregnancy? Why or why not? **(LO 31.4)**

Multiple Choice

Use your critical-thinking skills to answer the following questions.

1. Histamine **(LO 31.1)**
   A. is classified as a mast cell release inhibitor
   B. is one of the substances released during an allergic response
   C. is found in white blood cells known as neutrophils
   D. does not cause skin reactions

2. Mast cells **(LO 31.1, 31.2)**
   A. are only found in the bloodstream
   B. are coated with immunoglobulins that recognize antigens
   C. have no other role than antiallergy in the body
   D. degranulate when the H_1-receptor is stimulated

3. An allergic response **(LO 31.1, 31.2)**
   A. can be blocked only by histamine
   B. cannot be prophylactically treated
   C. is characterized by itching, sneezing, and edema
   D. is only characterized by wheals and urticaria

4. Antihistamines like chlorpheniramine **(LO 31.2, 31.3)**
   A. are the newest, third-generation drugs
   B. are effective and cause sedation and drowsiness
   C. are not found in OTC products
   D. do not have anticholinergic properties

5. Fexofenadine and cetirizine **(LO 31.3)**
   A. are more selective for peripheral H_1-receptors
   B. bind the H_1-receptors in the brain to produce fewer side effects
   C. are more sedating and drying than diphenhydramine
   D. are mast cell release inhibitors

6. Cromolyn and pemirolast **(LO 31.2)**
   A. are effective oral antihistamines
   B. work best after the mast cells have degranulated
   C. are effective in reducing the symptoms of conjunctivitis
   D. are applied intranasally

6. Adverse effects associated with antihistamine use DO NOT include **(LO 31.4, 31.6)**
   A. eczematoid dermatitis
   B. increased intraocular pressure
   C. urinary retention
   D. heparin reaction on blood clotting

7. Which of the following is NOT correct about drugs used to treat allergy? **(LO 31.2, 31.3, 31.5)**
   A. oral cromolyn should be taken with fruit juices or food
   B. first-generation antihistamines are nonselective in receptor interaction
   C. meclizine is also effective in reducing vertigo
   D. antihistamines should not be used during pregnancy

8. Which of the following is NOT a correct statement? **(LO 31.4, 31.6)**
   A. promethazine is the only antihistamine with a cautionary (black box) warning
   B. antihistamines reduce itching and pain at the sensory nerve endings

C. histamine causes bronchiolar constriction of smooth muscle

D. hypersensitivity does not occur to antihistamines

9. Which of the following is NOT a correct statement? **(LO 31.3, 31.4, 31.6)**

A. antihistamines decrease nausea and heartburn through the H_2-receptors

B. mastocytosis is a condition of excess histamine release and stimulation

C. only a few antihistamines can be administered orally or parenterally

D. levocetirizine is usually administered once a day

10. Levocetirizine (*Xyzal*) **(LO 31.3, 31.5, 31.6)**

A. is only found in OTC products

B. stimulates eosinophil chemotaxis

C. is the newest antihistamine

D. is not related to cetirizine

Multiple Choice (Multiple Answer)

Select the correct choices for each statement. The choices may be all correct, all incorrect, or any combination.

1. The release of histamine causes which of the following symptoms? **(LO 31.1)**

A. itching

B. urticaria

C. stuffy nose

D. redness

2. Mast cell release inhibitors work by blocking **(LO 31.2)**

A. histamine after it is released

B. H_1-receptors from binding histamine

C. histamine release from cells

D. the effect of histamine after it binds

3. Which of the following drug actions of antihistaminic drugs are due to their action on the CNS? **(LO 31.3)**

A. sedation

B. relief of motion sickness

C. reduction of nausea and vomiting

D. relief of local pain

4. Which of the following are side effects of antihistaminic drugs? **(LO 31.4)**

A. increased appetite

B. nausea

C. hypotension

D. xerostomia

5. Select all of the first-generation antihistaminic drugs. **(LO 31.5)**

A. promethazine

B. cetirizine

C. loratadine

D. levocetirizine

Sequencing

Place the following steps of body response in order from first to last. **(LO 31.1)**

_____   _____   _____   _____   _____

First   **Last**

release of mast cells

white blood cells produce antibodies

allergen binds to IgE

histamine interacts with membrane receptors

IgE attaches to surface of mast cell

Classification

Place the following medications under the correct classification. **(LO 31.5)**

clemastine	fexofenadine	loratadine
diphenhydramine	dimenhydrinate	cetirizine

First-generation antihistaminic	Second-generation antihistaminic

Matching

Match the following terms with the correct definitions. **(LO 31.6)**

a. erythema

b. antigen

c. hyperemia

d. nonselective

e. urticaria

f. wheal

g. allergen

h. excoriation

1. _____ firm, elevated swelling of the skin
2. _____ redness of the skin
3. _____ interacts with any subtype receptor
4. _____ an abrasion of the epidermis
5. _____ hives
6. _____ substance that stimulates an immune response
7. _____ substance capable of producing an allergic reaction
8. _____ increased blood flow to a body part

Documentation

Using the following symptoms in the patient's chart, answer the following questions. **(LO 31.2)**

Symptoms
Redness in the white part of the eye
Green discharge from the eye
Itching and burning eyes
Increased sensitivity to light

a. What medical condition is this patient suffering from?
b. What types of medications would be best to treat this patient?
c. How long should the patient continue to use the above medications?
d. What symptoms would this medication be treating?

Labeling

Fill in the missing labels. **(LO 31.1)**

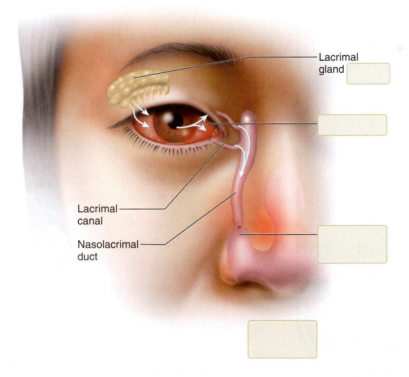

Lacrimal gland

Lacrimal canal

Nasolacrimal duct

Chapter 32

Respiratory Pharmacology, Treatment of Asthma, and COPD

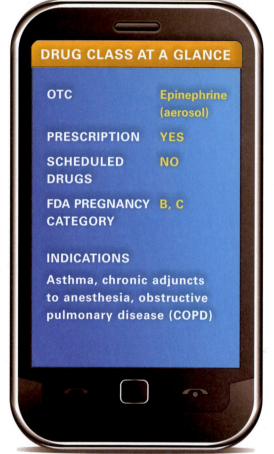

DRUG CLASS AT A GLANCE

OTC	Epinephrine (aerosol)
PRESCRIPTION	YES
SCHEDULED DRUGS	NO
FDA PREGNANCY CATEGORY	B, C

INDICATIONS

Asthma, chronic adjuncts to anesthesia, obstructive pulmonary disease (COPD)

KEY TERMS

asthma: respiratory disease characterized by bronchoconstriction, shortness of breath, and wheezing.

bronchodilator: drug that relaxes bronchial smooth muscle and dilates the lower respiratory passages.

chemical mediator: substance released from mast cells and white blood cells during inflammatory and allergic reactions.

chronic bronchitis: respiratory condition caused by chronic irritation that increases secretion of mucus and causes degeneration of the respiratory lining.

COPD: chronic obstructive pulmonary disease, usually caused by emphysema and chronic bronchitis.

emphysema: disease process causing destruction of the walls of the alveoli.

expectorant: drug that helps clear the lungs of respiratory secretions.

leukotrienes: chemical mediators involved in inflammation and asthma.

mucolytic: drug that liquefies bronchial secretions.

prostaglandins: chemical mediators released from mast and other cells involved in inflammatory and allergic conditions.

Learning Outcomes

After studying this chapter, you should be able to

32.1 describe the effects of chronic obstructive pulmonary disease (COPD) and asthma on respiratory function.

32.2 list the chemical mediators involved in asthma.

32.3 explain the actions of the sympathetic and parasympathetic divisions of the autonomic nervous system on respiratory function.

32.4 describe the mechanism of action and main pharmacological effects of the three types of bronchodilators.

32.5 explain the therapeutic actions of the corticosteroids and leukotriene inhibitors in the treatment of asthma.

32.6 describe the use of cromolyn in the treatment of asthma.

32.7 explain the use of mucolytic and expectorant drugs.

32.8 identify the preferred therapy for asthma and COPD.

Introduction

The respiratory system plays a vital role in the exchange of the respiratory gases, oxygen (O_2) and carbon dioxide (CO_2). Functionally, the respiratory system consists of a series of anatomical tubes (trachea, bronchi, bronchioles, and alveolar ducts) that conduct air to and from the air sacs (alveoli) of the lungs (Figure 32.1). Each alveolus is surrounded by a network of capillaries. Both the alveoli and the capillaries consist of a single cell layer that allows rapid diffusion of O_2 into the blood and equally rapid diffusion of CO_2 out of the blood (Figure 32.2).

The larger respiratory airways such as the trachea and bronchi are composed of smooth muscle and cartilage (C-rings). The C-rings support these airways and prevent them from collapsing. There are no C-rings in the smaller airways such as the bronchioles and alveolar ducts. The diameter of the smaller airways is determined by the tone of bronchiolar smooth muscle. The tone of bronchiolar smooth muscle is regulated by both the sympathetic (bronchodilation) and parasympathetic (bronchoconstriction) divisions of the autonomic nervous system. The lining of the respiratory airways is composed of ciliated epithelial cells. Mucus glands in the lining normally secrete a thin watery layer of mucus that functions to trap inhaled particles and debris. The rapid upward beating of the cilia moves the mucus and debris out of the airways and is an important component of respiratory function. The ciliary mechanism is referred to as the mucociliary escalator system (Figure 32.3). Irritation of the respiratory tract (dust, tobacco smoke, respiratory infection) can increase and cause a thickening of mucus secretions. This can decrease the effectiveness of mucociliary activity and be a factor in the development of pulmonary congestion and infection.

The most common diseases that affect the airways and the exchange of respiratory gases include asthma, chronic bronchitis, and emphysema. Chronic bronchitis and emphysema are primarily caused by tobacco smoking and chronic exposure to other environmental pollutants. These two conditions are collectively referred to as chronic obstructive pulmonary disease (COPD). Drugs used in the treatment of asthma and COPD include bronchodilators and a variety of antiinflammatory and antiallergic agents.

LO 32.1 LO 32.2

RESPIRATORY DISEASES

Any disease process or condition that interferes with respiratory gas exchange causes serious alterations in the concentrations of oxygen and carbon dioxide in the blood. The most common causes of respiratory difficulties are chronic obstructive pulmonary disease (COPD) and asthma.

Chronic Obstructive Pulmonary Disease (COPD)

Chronic obstructive pulmonary disease **(COPD)** is a common respiratory condition that is caused by emphysema and chronic bronchitis. Both conditions cause irreversible changes to the respiratory system. **Chronic bronchitis** is caused by chronic irritation of the respiratory tract. Cigarette smoke and other environmental pollutants increase and thicken respiratory secretions of mucus. Chronic exposure to these pollutants causes degenerative changes in the respiratory lining and mucociliary escalator system. As mucus secretions thicken and accumulate, they can interfere with respiratory gas exchange. Symptoms of chronic bronchitis include a productive cough, difficulty in breathing, increased respiratory infections, and restriction of physical activity. Drug therapy can provide some relief, but it cannot reverse the degenerative changes that have already occurred

Figure 32.1

Anatomic Relationship of the Trachea and Bronchial Airways

Air passageways decrease in size but increase in number

Larynx

Trachea

Carina

Superior lobe

Main (primary) bronchus

Lobar (secondary) bronchus

Segmental (tertiary) bronchus

Bronchiole

Cardiac notch

Inferior lobe

Middle lobe

To terminal bronchiole

Diaphragm

Figure 32.2 **Pulmonary Alveoli**

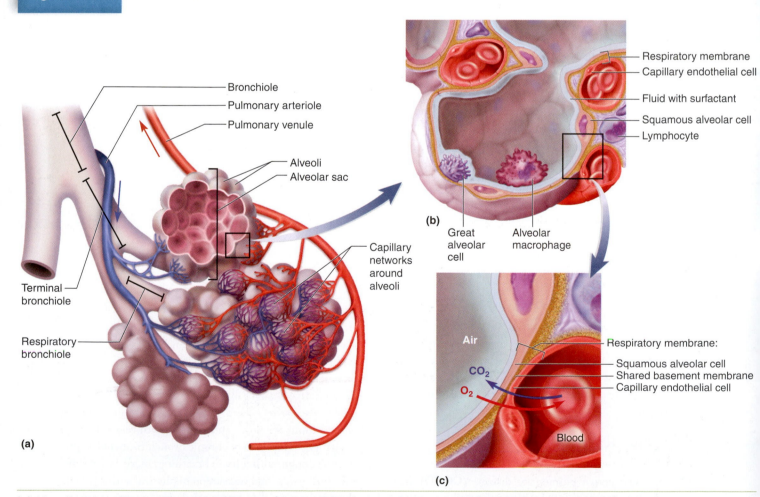

Bronchiole

Pulmonary arteriole

Pulmonary venule

Alveoli

Alveolar sac

Capillary networks around alveoli

Terminal bronchiole

Respiratory bronchiole

(a)

Respiratory membrane

Capillary endothelial cell

Fluid with surfactant

Squamous alveolar cell

Lymphocyte

(b)

Great alveolar cell

Alveolar macrophage

Air

CO_2

O_2

Respiratory membrane:

Squamous alveolar cell

Shared basement membrane

Capillary endothelial cell

Blood

(c)

(a) Alveoli and capillary blood supply. (b) Individual alveolus and capillary endothelial cell. Alveolar macrophages function to keep alveoli free of debris. (c) Exchange of oxygen and carbon dioxide through alveolar and capillary membranes.

Figure 32.3

Inner Lining of the Trachea Showing the Action of the Mucociliary Escalator System

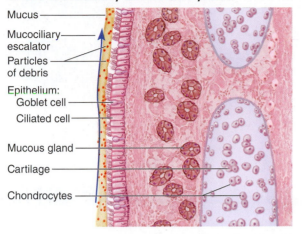

Mucus

Mucociliary escalator

Particles of debris

Epithelium:
Goblet cell
Ciliated cell

Mucous gland

Cartilage

Chondrocytes

---

in the respiratory lining. The most effective treatment for smokers is to stop smoking. Drug therapy, primarily with bronchodilators, is aimed at improving respiratory gas exchange and reducing the volume of mucus secretions.

Emphysema

Emphysema is a disease process involving destruction of the alveoli (air sacs). Protease enzymes that cause destruction of the alveolar walls are increased by air pollution, tobacco smoke, and other respiratory irritants. This causes enlargement of the air spaces within the lungs and leads to hyperinflation. Individuals with emphysema have difficulty expelling air from the lungs. Respiratory exchange is reduced, and shortness of breath occurs. Irreversible lung damage takes place, forcing the individuals to restrict daily activities. Treatment involves respiratory exercises designed to increase the efficiency of respiration, oxygen therapy, and administration of bronchodilators and antiinflammatory agents.

Asthma

Asthma is a respiratory condition characterized by bronchoconstriction, shortness of breath, and wheezing. Asthma is considered an inflammatory disease. Individuals with asthma display a hyperresponsiveness to various environmental factors. Allergens, air pollutants, cold air, certain drugs, infections, and exercise are some of the factors that can trigger an asthmatic attack. These factors stimulate the release of chemical mediators from mast cells and other cells involved in the inflammatory process. The chemical mediators are the cause of the two main components of asthma, bronchoconstriction and inflammation.

In allergic asthma, individuals develop antibodies to the foreign protein (antigen) that is the cause of the allergy. After exposure to the antigen, an antigen-antibody reaction occurs in the respiratory tract that stimulates the release of the chemical mediators. The immediate result is shortness of breath, wheezing, and the terrifying feeling of suffocation. In addition, there is usually mucosal edema and increased production of mucus. Ciliary activity of the respiratory tract is usually depressed. This interferes with the clearing of mucus and other debris from the lower respiratory airways. The combination of bronchoconstriction, edema, and increased mucus significantly reduces the diameter of the airways and the ability to breathe. Relief of acute asthmatic attacks and chronic treatment of asthma involve use of a bronchodilator and a variety of antiinflammatory and antiallergic drugs.

Chemical Mediators

During an inflammatory reaction, **chemical mediators** are formed and released from injured tissue, mast cells, and leukocytes in the respiratory tract. These mediators are responsible for most of the symptoms and complications of asthma. The chemical mediators involved include histamine, eosinophilic chemotactic factor of anaphylaxis (ECF-A), prostaglandins, and leukotrienes. The large number of chemical mediators involved in asthma presents a complicated situation both for the understanding of the disease and for its treatment.

Histamine

Whenever there is injury or insult to body tissue, histamine is rapidly released from mast cells. The pharmacology of histamine was presented in Chapter 31. In the respiratory tract, histamine causes bronchoconstriction, increased vascular permeability that contributes to mucosal edema, and infiltration of leukocytes, particularly eosinophils. Antihistamines are usually of little benefit in the treatment of asthma, and for this reason, histamine is not considered to be the most important mediator in asthma.

Eosinophilic Chemotactic Factor of Anaphylaxis (ECF-A)

Eosinophilic chemotactic factor (ECF-A) is released from eosinophils and mast cells and functions to attract eosinophils to the site of cell injury or irritation. Eosinophils are part of the general inflammatory and allergic reaction that often occurs in the lining of the respiratory tract in asthma. The inflammatory and allergic reactions worsen and prolong the asthmatic process.

Prostaglandins and Leukotrienes

Prostaglandins and **leukotrienes** (LT) are two different chemical mediators that are both derived from arachidonic acid. Arachidonic acid is a substance found in cell membranes, particularly in mast cells and other inflammatory cells. Both prostaglandins and leukotrienes are formed and released in inflammatory conditions, such as asthma. Both mediators can cause bronchoconstriction, edema, and mucus production. During inflammation an enzyme, phospholipase A, stimulates the release of arachidonic acid from the cell membrane. Arachidonic acid is then acted upon by two different enzymes. One enzyme, cyclooxygenase, converts arachidonic acid into several different prostaglandins. Prostaglandins are involved in a variety of physiological functions and also in inflammation and generation of pain. Aspirin and drugs known as the nonsteroidal antiinflammatory drugs (NSAIDs) inhibit the formation of prostaglandins. While prostaglandins are involved in asthma, aspirin and the NSAIDs do not seem to produce significant antiasthmatic effects.

The second enzyme, lipoxygenase, converts arachidonic acid into the leukotrienes. The leukotrienes are potent bronchoconstrictors with long durations of action and considered to be one of the more important chemical mediators in asthma. The different leukotrienes are designated as LTB_4, LTC_4, LTD_4, and LTE_4. LTB_4 is a chemotactic factor that attracts leukocytes, eosinophils, and other inflammatory cells into the area of inflammation. LTC_4, LTD_4, and LTE_4 each stimulate a common leukotriene receptor, designated the cysteinyl leukotriene-1 receptor (LT-1). Activation of this receptor is responsible for causing the bronchoconstriction, edema, and other inflammatory actions. Drugs that inhibit the actions of the leukotrienes, referred to as the leukotriene inhibitors or antileukotrienes, have been developed and are important drugs in the control of asthma. Figure 32.4 illustrates the formation of prostaglandins and leukotrienes from arachidonic acid and the sites of action of drugs that block these chemical mediators.

LO 32.3

ROLE OF THE AUTONOMIC NERVOUS SYSTEM

Bronchiolar smooth muscle tone and secretion of mucus are normally influenced by the sympathetic and parasympathetic divisions of the autonomic nervous system. Sympathetic stimulation by epinephrine (beta-2 receptor) produces bronchodilation. Parasympathetic activation through the release of acetylcholine produces

Figure 32.4

Synthesis of Prostaglandins and Leukotrienes from Arachidonic Acid

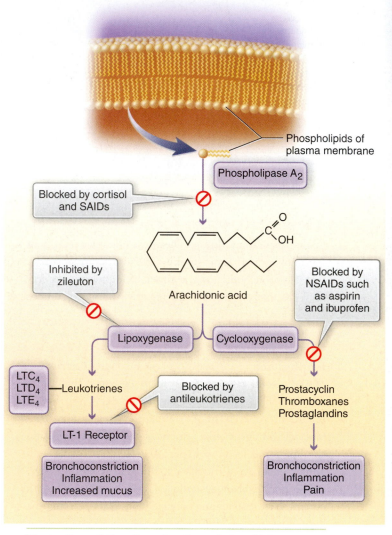

Illustration of the sites of action of steroidal antiinflammatory drugs (SAIDs), nonsteroidal antiinflammatory drugs (NSAIDs), zileuton (lipoxygenase inhibitor), and the antileukotriene drugs (montelukast, zafirlukast) that block the leukotriene-1 (LT-1) receptor.

bronchoconstriction and increased secretion of mucus. Noxious irritants of the respiratory tract stimulate vagal reflexes that result in parasympathetic activation.

Sympathetic activation of beta-2 adrenergic receptors has been shown to increase the formation of an intracellular nucleotide known as cyclic adenosine monophosphate or cyclic AMP. Increased levels of cyclic AMP are responsible for producing relaxation of bronchial smooth muscle (bronchodilation). Also, the formation and release of inflammatory mediators from mast cells are inhibited by increased levels of cyclic AMP.

Consequently in asthma and COPD, the aim of therapy is to administer sympathomimetic drugs that stimulate beta-2 adrenergic receptors or anticholinergic drugs that decrease parasympathetic activity.

LO 32.4
BRONCHODILATOR DRUGS

Bronchodilators are important drugs in the management of both asthma and COPD. There are three different types of bronchodilators: sympathomimetics that stimulate beta-2 adrenergic receptors, anticholinergics that block cholinergic (muscarinic) receptors, and methylxanthines such as theophylline. These drugs are referred to as "relievers" because their main effect is to relieve bronchoconstriction, particularly in asthma. The term "rescue" is applied to those bronchodilators that provide immediate relief of bronchoconstriction. An overview of the mechanisms of action of the bronchodilators is illustrated in Figure 32.5. The bronchodilators and the dosage forms used in the treatment of asthma and COPD are listed in Table 32:1.

Beta-Adrenergic Drugs

Sympathetic stimulation of bronchial smooth muscle causes bronchodilation. This effect is mediated by beta-2 adrenergic receptors, which increase the formation of intracellular cyclic AMP. Epinephrine (normally released from the adrenal gland) and isoproterenol are two potent beta-adrenergic drugs. As previously discussed in Chapter 6, these two drugs are nonselective and stimulate both beta-1 (heart) and beta-2 (relax smooth muscle) adrenergic receptors. When used as bronchodilators, they increase heart rate and may cause tachycardia and cardiac arrhythmias. The duration of action of both drugs is relatively short, approximately one hour. Epinephrine is administered by subcutaneous injection for the treatment of acute asthma and immediate-type allergic reactions such as anaphylaxis. Over-the-counter aerosol preparations of epinephrine are available but not recommended for chronic therapy because of the cardiac stimulation. Isoproterenol is no longer recommended for the chronic treatment of asthma for the same reason.

The selective beta-2 adrenergic drugs are the bronchodilators of choice for the chronic control of asthma

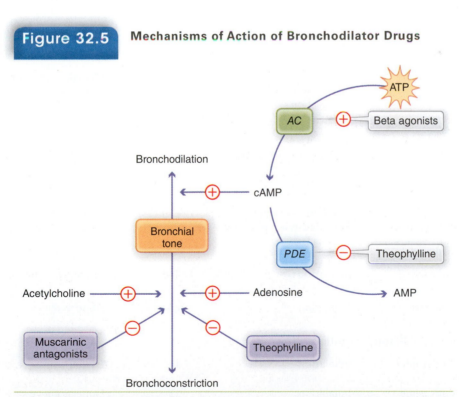

| Figure 32.5 | **Mechanisms of Action of Bronchodilator Drugs** |

Beta adrenergic drugs stimulate the enzyme adenylyl cyclase (AC) to increase cyclic AMP (cAMP) levels, resulting in bronchodilation. Theophylline inhibits the enzyme phosphodiesterase (PDE), which slows the metabolism and inactivation of cAMP. Theophylline also antagonizes adenosine, a bronchoconstrictor. Muscarinic antagonists (anticholinergics) block the effects of acetylcholine and parasympathetic activity to promote bronchodilation.

Bronchodilator Drugs

Drug (*Trade Name*)	Administration	Duration (hr)	Main indications
Nonselective beta drugs			
Epinephrine (*Adrenaline*) (*Primatene Mist*, others) (*Epipen, Epi E-Z Pen*)	SC injection, nebulization Inhalation (OTC) Auto-injector, IM	1 1 1	Acute asthma/allergic reactions Therapy of asthma Acute allergic emergencies
Isoproterenol (*Isuprel*)	SC injection, nebulization	1	Therapy of asthma
Selective beta-2 drugs			
Albuterol (*Proventil, Ventolin*, others)	Inhalation, oral tablets	4–6	Chronic control of asthma/COPD
Arformoterol (*Brovana*)	Nebulization	12	Chronic control of COPD
Formoterol (*Foradil*)	Inhalation	12	Same as above
Isoetharine (*Bronkometer*)	Nebulization	1–2	Therapy of asthma
Levalbuterol (*Xopenex*)	Nebulization	4–6	Same as above
Metaproterenol (*Alupent*)	Inhalation	2–4	Same as above
Pirbuterol (*Maxair*)	Inhalation	4–6	Chronic control of asthma/COPD
Salmeterol (*Serevent*)	Inhalation	12	Same as above
Terbutaline (*Brethaire*) (*Brethine*) (*Bricanyl*)	Inhalation Oral tablets SC injection	4–6 4–6 4–6	Chronic control of asthma/COPD Same as above Acute asthma/allergic reactions
Methylxanthines			
Aminophylline (generic)	Oral tablets, IV injection	6	Therapy of asthma/COPD
Dyphylline (*Lufyllin*)	Oral tablets	6	Same as above
Theophylline (*Elixophyllin*, many) (*Slo-Bid*, many)	Oral tablets/capsules/syrup Extended-release capsules	6–8 8–12	Same as above Same as above
Anticholinergic drugs			
Ipratropium (*Atrovent*)	Inhalation	4–6	Therapy of asthma/COPD
Tiotropium (*Spiriva*)	Inhalation	24	Same as above
Combination bronchodilator/antiinflammatory steroid			
Formoterol/budesonide (*Symbicort*)	Inhalation	12	Chronic control asthma/COPD
Salmeterol/fluticasone (*Advair*)	Inhalation	12	Same as above
Bronchodilator combinations			
Albuterol/ipratropium (*Combivent*)	Inhalation	4–6	Therapy of asthma/COPD

and COPD. At therapeutic concentrations, these drugs produce little or no cardiac stimulation and few systemic drug effects. However, at increased dosages, these drugs can begin to cause cardiac stimulation. The usual route of administration is by metered-dose inhalation. Albuterol, pirbuterol, and terbutaline provide durations of action of 4 to 6 hours. The bronchodilating effects of these drugs begin almost immediately after inhalation and they are considered "rescue" drugs. Several of these drugs (albuterol, metaproterenol, terbutaline) are also available in tablet form for oral administration. Oral administration is usually limited to patients who are unable to use metered-dose inhalers. Oral administration involves larger dosages and increased systemic drug effects. Terbutaline is also available for subcutaneous injection during acute asthmatic attacks.

Salmeterol and formoterol are two long-acting beta-2 drugs with increased beta-2 receptor selectivity. Administration is by inhalation and each provides a duration of action of approximately 12 hours. While these two drugs are "reliever drugs," they are not considered "rescue drugs" because the onset of action usually requires 10 to 20 minutes. These drugs are usually administered in combination with one of the antiinflammatory corticosteroids. Table 32:1 lists the bronchodilator drugs and their main indications.

The selective beta-2 drugs are generally well tolerated and, since they are usually administered by inhalation directly into the lungs, they cause few systemic adverse effects. Nervousness, skeletal muscle tremors, and increased heart rate, especially with oral administration, are effects most frequently reported.

Long-term use of beta adrenergic bronchodilators, especially the longer-acting drugs, has been associated with a small but significant increase in asthma-related mortality. The FDA has issued a "black box" warning to physicians alerting them to this risk. The recommendation is to avoid using high dosages of the long-acting beta drugs. The reasons for the increased risk of mortality are not known.

Methylxanthine Drugs: Theophylline

Caffeine, theophylline, and theobromine are plant compounds found naturally in tea, cocoa, and coffee. These compounds, classified as methylxanthines, produce mild stimulation of the central nervous system, heart, and kidneys. Other physiological actions include relaxation of smooth muscle (bronchodilation) and increased skeletal muscle tone and strength of contraction. Theophylline is the only natural methylxanthine used for its bronchodilating actions. Dyphylline is similar to theophylline but generally considered less potent.

Theophylline inhibits an intracellular enzyme, phosphodiesterase, that normally inactivates cyclic AMP. By inhibiting phosphodiesterase, levels of cyclic AMP increase in bronchiolar smooth muscle and in mast cells. As discussed, cyclic AMP produces bronchodilation and inhibits the release of mediators from mast cells. In addition to bronchodilation, theophylline also has been shown to increase respiratory muscle contractility (respiratory muscles and diaphragm are skeletal muscle) and mucociliary clearance. The actions to increase contractility and mucociliary clearance are important for the treatment of both chronic bronchitis and emphysema (COPD).

Theophylline can be administered orally, or intravenously. There is significant patient variability in regard to absorption and metabolism. Therefore, the dose must be adjusted carefully. Plasma concentrations of theophylline are periodically determined to ensure that theophylline levels are in the therapeutic range (10 to 20 mcg per ml).

Numerous preparations of theophylline, including extended-release tablets, are available. Aminophylline is a water-soluble preparation of theophylline that is used for intravenous administration, usually during acute asthmatic attacks. Theophylline can be administered in combination with sympathomimetics in situations where one drug is unable to control the asthmatic condition alone.

The most frequent side effects from oral administration of theophylline are nausea and vomiting. Theophylline may cause vasodilation, and some patients experience flushing, headache, and hypotension. Caution is necessary in patients with existing cardiovascular disease, since theophylline may cause excessive cardiac stimulation. Theophylline also stimulates the CNS and may cause restlessness, insomnia, tremors, and convulsions, especially when plasma levels are above the therapeutic range.

Anticholinergic Drugs

In the respiratory tract, parasympathetic activation and release of acetylcholine cause bronchoconstriction and increased mucus secretion. By blocking the actions of acetylcholine, anticholinergic drugs produce bronchodilation and also reduce the volume of respiratory secretions. Anticholinergic drugs are not as potent bronchodilators as the beta adrenergic drugs and in asthma are primarily indicated when other bronchodilators are contraindicated or additional bronchodilation is needed. In COPD and especially chronic bronchitis, there appears to be increased cholinergic activity. Consequently, anticholinergic actions are useful in the treatment of COPD and these drugs are considered first-line drugs. The anticholinergic drugs available are administered by oral inhalation. Chemically they are quaternary compounds (charged) and very little drug is absorbed from the lungs into the systemic circulation, which limits anticholinergic side effects.

Ipratropium Bromide (*Atrovent*)

Ipratropium is a quaternary derivative of atropine and is indicated for the treatment of both asthma and COPD. Ipratropium is administered by oral inhalation. It has a slow onset but prolonged duration of action (6 hours). Because it is poorly absorbed into the systemic circulation, it causes few adverse effects. Excessive drying of the mouth and upper respiratory passages may cause discomfort and is the most common side effect. Tiotropium (*Spiriva*) is another anticholinergic bronchodilator that is similar to ipratropium but produces a longer duration of action.

LO 32.5

ANTIINFLAMMATORY DRUGS

The antiinflammatory steroids and other drugs with antiinflammatory actions are referred to as "controller" drugs because they reduce and control the inflammatory response. When inflammation is under control, the actions of the bronchodilator drug are more effective, and often the dosages can be reduced. Lower dosages decrease the incidence and severity of adverse drug effects.

Corticosteroids

The corticosteroids are derivatives of the steroid hormone cortisol, which is normally released from the adrenal cortex. The corticosteroid drugs are considered the most potent antiinflammatory and antiallergic drugs available. They interfere with all stages of the inflammatory and allergic response. Corticosteroids inhibit the activity of inflammatory cells, the release of inflammatory mediators from mast cells, the production of allergic antibodies, edema, and many other antiinflammatory actions. The general pharmacology of the corticosteroids, also known as adrenal steroids and glucocorticoids, is presented in Chapter 36. One of the main uses of these drugs is for treatment of inflammatory and allergic conditions such as asthma. The major effect of steroids in the treatment of asthma is to inhibit the inflammatory response that occurs in the respiratory airways. One of the antiinflammatory actions of steroids is to inhibit the activation of arachidonic acid. This action decreases the formation of prostaglandins and leukotrienes (Figure 32.4).

During acute asthmatic attacks, corticosteroids such as prednisone, prednisolone, and others (Table 32:2) are administered by either the oral or parenteral route. These drugs provide systemic drug effects and are associated with a number of potentially serious adverse effects. Consequently, these steroids are primarily used during the initial acute phase of inflammation. These steroids have durations of action that range from 12 to 48 hours. One method that helps limit adverse effects is to administer these steroids on alternate days.

For the chronic control of asthma and COPD, the preferred route of administration is oral inhalation with metered-dose inhalers. The advantage of inhalation is that lower dosages of steroid are delivered directly into the respiratory tract. Use of this route greatly limits systemic

[**Table 32:2**]

Corticosteroids for Oral or Parenteral Administration

Drug (*Trade Name*)	Administration	Duration of action (hr)
Hydrocortisone (*Cortef, SoluCortef*)	Oral, IM, IV	12–24
Methylprednisolone (*Medrol, Depo-Medrol*)	Oral, IM, IV	24–36
Prednisolone (*Millipred, Flo-Pred*)	Oral, IM, IV	24–36
Prednisone (*Sterapred, Sterapred DS*)	Oral	24–36
Betamethasone (*Celestone*)	Oral, IM, IV	48–72
Dexamethasone (generic)	Oral, IM, IV	48–72

absorption and the adverse effects associated with steroid use. Antiinflammatory steroids also are used in the treatment of upper respiratory inflammatory and allergic conditions caused by pollen (hay fever) and other allergens. Chapter 31 discussed the use of antihistamines in the treatment of these conditions. There are also steroid preparations that are administered by nasal spray. The corticosteroids used for oral inhalation in the treatment of asthma and COPD, and the steroids administered by nasal spray in the treatment of allergic rhinitis, are listed in Table 32:3.

Adverse Effects

Adverse effects associated with systemic steroid use include fluid retention, muscle wasting, metabolic disturbances, and increased susceptibility to infection. These effects are not usually observed with aerosol therapy. However, steroids increase the incidence of oral infections (usually fungal infections) and they can cause hoarseness and other vocal chord disturbances. The incidence of these adverse effects can be reduced by rinsing the mouth with water after inhalation to minimize the amount of steroid that remains in the oral cavity.

Leukotriene Inhibitor Drugs

A major focus of asthma research has been to discover drugs that inhibit the actions of the arachidonic acid derivatives known as leukotrienes. These chemical mediators cause bronchoconstriction, mucus production, and inflammation. Drugs known as leukotriene inhibitors or antileukotrienes have been developed and are indicated for the chronic control of asthma. Zileuton (*Zyflo*) inhibits the enzyme lipooxygenase and prevents the synthesis of all the leukotrienes (Figure 32.4). The usual dosage is 600 mg administered four times per day. Zileuton is also available as extended-release tablets (*Zyflo CR*) administered twice per day. Adverse effects include nausea, diarrhea, rash, and headache. One of the more serious adverse effects involves the liver. An abnormal increase

[Table **32:3**]

Corticosteroids Administered by Oral Inhalation and Nasal Spray

Drug (*Trade Name*)	Preparations	Usual adult dose
Treatment of asthma and COPD		
Beclomethasone (*QVAR*)	Aerosol: 40, 80 mcg/puff	2 inhalations BID
Budesonide (*Pulmicort*)	Aerosol: 200 mcg/puff	200–400 mcg inhalations BID
Ciclesonide (*Alvesco*)	Aerosol: 80, 160 mcg/puff	80–320 mcg inhalations BID
Flunisolide (*Aerobid*)	Aerosol: 250 mcg/puff	2 inhalations BID
Fluticasone (*Flovent*)	Aerosol: 44, 110, 220 mcg/puff	88–220 mcg inhalations BID
Fluticasone (*Flovent Diskus*)	Powder: 50, 100, 250 mcg	100–250 mcg inhalations BID
Triamcinolone (*Azmacort*)	Aerosol: 100 mcg/puff	2 inhalations TID or QID
Treatment of allergic rhinitis		
Beclomethasone (*Beconase AQ*)	Nasal spray: 42 mcg/spray	1 or 2 sprays/nostril BID
Budesonide (*Rhinocort Aqua*)	Nasal spray: 32 mcg/spray	2–4 sprays/nostril once daily
Flunisolide (*Nasarel*)	Nasal spray: 29 mcg/spray	2 sprays/nostril BID
Fluticasone (*Flonase*)	Nasal spray: 50 mcg/spray	1 or 2 sprays/nostril BID
Mometasone (*Nasonex*)	Nasal spray: 50 mcg/spray	2 sprays/nostril once daily

in liver enzymes and the development of fever, dark urine, clay-colored stools, or jaundice are signs of liver toxicity and should be reported to the physician.

Zafirlukast (*Accolate*) and montelukast (*Singulair*) are leukotriene receptor antagonists that block the leukotriene receptor, referred to as the cysteinyl leukotriene-1 receptor (Figure 32.4). The drugs are administered orally, 20 mg BID and 10 mg once/day, respectively for the chronic treatment of asthma. These drugs are generally well tolerated; adverse effects include headache, nausea, and diarrhea. As with zileuton, these drugs also can increase liver enzymes. Although very rare, each of these leukotriene inhibitors has been associated with a form of vasculitis known as Churg-Strauss syndrome.

Note to the Health Care Professional

The Food and Drug Administration (FDA) has recently issued a labeling change for the leukotriene inhibitor drugs zileuton, montelukast, and zafirlukast. The FDA has added a "Precaution" warning that these drugs may cause adverse neuropsychiatric effects. These effects may include behavioral changes, sleep disorders, anxiousness, agitation, aggressiveness, depression, and suicidal ideation. Patients should be warned to contact their physician if any of these effects occur.

LO 32.6
ANTIALLERGIC AGENTS

Cromolyn Sodium

Allergic conditions involve the interaction of an antigen (foreign protein) and an antibody (produced by the body). This interaction causes the release of histamine and other chemical mediators from mast cells that then trigger an asthmatic attack. Cromolyn sodium is a drug that interferes with the antigen-antibody reaction to release mast cell mediators. The drug is taken prophylactically (before allergic exposure) on a daily basis. Cromolyn is also useful in allergic conditions affecting the eyes, nose, and gastrointestinal tract.

In the treatment of asthma, cromolyn is administered by oral inhalation three to four times per day. Several different drug preparations of cromolyn are available for asthma. There is an oral inhalation solution (*Intal*) for nebulization, a metered-dose inhaler (*Intal*), and inhaler capsules (*Intal*) that require a special device that punctures the capsule and allows oral inhalation. Cromolyn is not a bronchodilator, and it has no use in the treatment of acute asthma. The therapeutic effect to prevent asthmatic attacks requires several weeks to fully develop.

Cromolyn is also available as an eye solution (*Opticrom*) for conjunctivitis; cromolyn nasal spray (*Nasalcrom*) is used for allergic rhinitis; and cromolyn oral solution (*Gastrocrom*) is used in gastrointestinal allergies.

The most frequent adverse effects of cromolyn are nasal stinging, nasal irritation, headache, and bad taste. In addition, allergic reactions have occurred involving rash, hives, cough, and angioedema.

Nedocromil (*Tilade*) is a drug similar to cromolyn in mechanism and pharmacological effect. It is administered by oral inhalation, usually two inhalations four times per day.

Omalizumab (*Xolair*)

Omalizumab is an anti-IgE monoclonal antibody indicated for the treatment of asthma. The anti-IgE monoclonal antibody binds to and inactivates the immunoglobulin IgE. IgE is an antibody produced by the body as part of the allergic response to a foreign antigen. IgE sensitizes mast cells to the foreign antigen. During an allergic or asthmatic reaction, the foreign antigen binds to the IgE antibodies to cause mast cell degranulation. This antigen-antibody reaction stimulates the release of mast cell mediators (histamine, prostaglandins, leukotrienes, etc.) responsible for producing the allergic reaction and asthmatic attack. Omalizumab binds up the IgE antibody and decreases the circulating levels of IgE. This reduces the severity and frequency of asthmatic attacks.

Omalizumab is administered subcutaneously every 2 to 4 weeks. The drug is expensive and currently indicated for patients with severe asthma uncontrolled with other medications. Adverse drug effects include pain and inflammatory reactions at the site of injection and allergic reactions to the monoclonal antibody.

LO 32.7
MUCOLYTICS AND EXPECTORANTS

Mucolytics are chemical agents that liquefy bronchial mucus. In various conditions, such as asthma, bronchitis, and respiratory infections, the production of mucus increases. In these situations the mucus thickens and also contains glycoproteins, cellular debris, and inflammatory exudate. During respiratory infections, the mucus becomes purulent. These changes in the mucus make it difficult for the respiratory tract to remove the mucus by way of the mucociliary escalator system. When increased production and thickening of mucus contribute to airway obstructions and interfere with normal respiration, mucolytics are administered by aerosol to thin or liquefy the secretions. Then, the mucus and other respiratory secretions can be removed by coughing or suction apparatus. It is also important that patients be adequately hydrated, since water itself can help liquefy and mobilize secretions.

Acetylcysteine (*Mucosil*) is an effective mucolytic that contains a chemical group (sulfhydryl) that breaks apart the glycoproteins in bronchial secretions. This action decreases the viscosity (resistance to flow) of bronchial secretions and promotes easier mobilization and removal. Acetylcysteine is irritating and can cause bronchospasm. For this reason, a bronchodilator is added to the inhalation mixture. Administration is usually by nebulization, three or four times a day, followed by postural drainage and tracheal suction when necessary.

Expectorants are drugs that facilitate the removal of thickened mucus secretions from the lungs. The primary action of expectorants is to increase respiratory secretions, which lubricate and help liquefy mucus. The expectorants include salts (ammonium chloride and potassium citrate), ipecac syrup, and guaifenesin. Guaifenesin (*Mucinex*) is available over the counter and is the most frequently used expectorant. It is indicated to provide relief of unproductive coughing that occurs with colds, bronchitis, and other respiratory conditions. Expectorants are added to many cough syrups and cold medications.

LO 32.8

PREFERRED THERAPY FOR ASTHMA AND COPD

The therapeutic plan in the treatment of asthma is to allow patients to maintain as near normal pulmonary functions and physical activity levels as possible. Drug selection depends on the severity of disease and frequency of symptoms.

Mild/Intermittent Symptoms

Patients who experience less than two asthmatic episodes per week often do not require daily medication. Selective beta-2 adrenergic bronchodilators for oral inhalation that provide immediate onset of action, such as albuterol, can be carried by the patient and used for any sudden onset of symptoms.

Mild/Persistent Symptoms

Patients who experience more than two asthmatic episodes per week but less than one per day are usually prescribed daily treatment with low-dose inhaled antiinflammatory corticosteroids. Alternate therapies include inhaled cromolyn and oral administration of antileukotriene drugs. One of the inhaled beta adrenergic bronchodilators with immediate onset of action can be carried and used as needed.

Moderate/Persistent Symptoms

Patients who experience daily asthmatic episodes require daily treatment with low-to-moderate-dose inhaled antiinflammatory corticosteroids and inhaled selective beta-2 adrenergic bronchodilators. The selective beta-2 adrenergic drugs, such as albuterol or pirbuterol, or the longer-acting drugs like salmeterol are usually preferred for chronic therapy. The combination of bronchodilator plus corticosteroid (*Advair* or *Symbicort*) provides both drug actions in one preparation.

Severe/Persistent Symptoms

These patients require high-dose inhaled corticosteroids and long-acting beta adrenergic bronchodilators. Oral or parenteral steroids may be required when symptoms intensify. Additional bronchodilators and antileukotrienes may be added depending on the clinical situation and patient response.

The therapeutic aim in COPD is to improve lung function and exercise capacity as much as possible. While bronchoconstriction is not the major symptom of COPD, maximizing respiratory gas exchange is of prime importance. Bronchodilation facilitates gas exchange and bronchodilator drugs are the preferred therapy. The beta adrenergic drugs are the most potent bronchodilators; however, anticholinergic and methylxanthine bronchodilators have additional actions that are useful in COPD. Anticholinergic drugs reduce the production of respiratory secretions, which is particularly useful in chronic bronchitis. The ability of theophylline to improve respiratory muscle contraction and stimulate mucociliary activity improves gas exchange and removal of secretions. Inflammation is a factor in COPD, but the result of treatment with corticosteroids is not as dramatic as with bronchodilators. The inhaled corticosteroids are preferred in COPD, but the recommendation is that a trial of inhaled corticosteroids is used to determine whether or not there is improvement in lung function. If steroid therapy is indicated, the combination preparations (*Advair* and *Symbicort*) provide extended durations of action. Mucolytics and expectorants can be used in COPD to liquefy and help remove secretions, but the benefit of these drugs does not appear to be clinically significant.

Chapter Review

Understanding Terminology

Match the definition or description in the left column with the appropriate term in the right column.
(LO 32.1, 32.2, 32.3, 32.7)

___ 1. Chemical mediator released from mast cells.

___ 2. A disease in which patients have difficulty expelling air from the lungs; causes destruction of the walls of the alveoli.

___ 3. Characterized by shortness of breath and wheezing.

___ 4. A drug that relaxes bronchial smooth muscle and dilates the lower respiratory passages.

___ 5. Chronic obstructive pulmonary disease.

___ 6. A respiratory condition caused by chronic irritation that increases secretion of mucus and causes degeneration of the respiratory lining.

___ 7. A drug that liquefies bronchial secretions.

a. asthma

b. bronchodilator

c. chronic bronchitis

d. COPD

e. emphysema

f. mucolytic

g. histamine

Acquiring Knowledge

Answer the following questions.

1. What are some of the factors that can precipitate an asthma attack? **(LO 32.1)**

2. List four physiological changes that can occur in the respiratory tract during an asthma attack. **(LO 32.1)**

3. What chemical mediators are released from mast cells? What effects do they produce? **(LO 32.1, 32.2)**

4. Discuss the relationship of cyclic AMP to the autonomic nervous system. **(LO 32.3)**

5. What effects does increasing the level of cyclic AMP have on the respiratory tract during asthma? **(LO 32.3)**

6. Compare the pharmacological effects of epinephrine and albuterol. What is the main indication for each? **(LO 32.4, 32.8)**

7. Explain the mechanism of action of theophylline. **(LO 32.4)**

8. Discuss the indications for the use of corticosteroids. What advantage is there to using beclomethasone by inhalation? **(LO 32.5)**

9. Explain the mechanism of action of cromolyn. How is it administered? **(LO 32.6)**

10. How does acetylcysteine liquefy mucus? **(LO 32.7)**

Applying Knowledge on the Job

Use your critical-thinking skills to answer the following questions.

1. Mrs. Willard has been prescribed *Ventolin* plus *Atrovent Inhalation Aerosol* while in the hospital to treat her chronic obstructive pulmonary disease (COPD). When you walk into her room to do your afternoon assessment, you notice she is wheezing more than on admission 3 days ago. She is due to take both inhalers within the next half hour. Which inhaler would you administer first to provide her with the quickest relief? **(LO 32.4)**

2. Mr. Wiblin calls his physician's office complaining of a dry throat, raspy voice, and a couple of white, patchy areas in his throat. He requests a prescription for an antibiotic. You pull his chart and see that he was given new prescriptions for *Azmacort* and theophylline 1 week ago for newly diagnosed asthma. What additional questions would you ask him? Is an antibiotic appropriate for this patient? If not, why? **(LO 32.5)**

3. Following a bee sting, a young boy developed hives and had difficulty breathing. What drug is indicated for immediate treatment of this condition? How should it be administered? **(LO 32.4)**

4. Mrs. Peabody is an elderly woman who has taken theophylline for years for her asthma. Recently she has complained of trouble sleeping and she says her hands are shaking and her heart is pounding. What do you think is happening to her? What would be a logical course of action to take? **(LO 32.4)**

5. Patient compliance is an important factor in the treatment and control of asthma. Of the selective beta-2 drugs listed, assuming that each medication would be equally effective, which medication do you feel would lend itself to better patient compliance? What was the main factor in choosing this medication? **(LO 32.4)**

6. Why is it important to advise patients using corticosteroid inhalers to rinse their mouth with water after inhalation? **(LO 32.5)**

Multiple Choice

Use your critical-thinking skills to answer the following questions.

1. The bronchodilator drug that would provide the longest duration of action is **(LO 32.4)**
   A. epinephrine (*Adrenaline*)
   B. ipratropium (*Atrovent*)
   C. salmeterol (*Serevent*)
   D. theophylline (*Elixophylline*)

2. The drug used in the treatment of asthma that blocks the leukotriene receptor is **(LO 32.5)**
   A. fluticasone (*Flovent*)
   B. cromolyn (*Intal*)
   C. albuterol (*Proventil*)
   D. montelukast (*Singulair*)

3. The only drug class that provides immediate relief of an acute asthmatic attack is **(LO 32.4)**
   A. anticholinergics
   B. beta adrenergics
   C. methylxanthines
   D. corticosteroids

4. The mechanism of action of cromolyn sodium (*Intal*) is to **(LO 32.6)**
   A. produce bronchodilation
   B. increase expectoration of mucus
   C. inhibit release of mast cell mediators
   D. liquefy bronchial secretions

5. The pharmacologic actions of theophylline (*Elixophylline*) in the treatment of COPD include **(LO 32.4)**
   A. bronchodilation
   B. increased contractility of respiratory muscles
   C. increased mucociliary activity
   D. all statements are true

Multiple Choice (Multiple Answer)

Select the correct choices for each statement. The choices may be all correct, all incorrect, or any combination.

1. The symptoms of chronic bronchitis include which of the following? **(LO 32.1)**
   A. wheezing
   B. increased respiratory infections
   C. enlargement of the alveoli
   D. productive cough

2. The chemical mediators involved in asthma include **(LO 32.2)**
   A. prostaglandins
   B. histamine

C. ECF-A

D. leukotrienes

3. Parasympathetic activation of the respiratory tract causes which of the following? **(LO 32.3)**

A. bronchodilation

B. increased cyclic AMP

C. increased mucus secretion

D. stimulation of the beta-2 receptors

4. Select all of the mechanisms of action for bronchodilators. **(LO 32.4)**

A. inhibit release of mediators from mast cells

B. relax smooth muscle

C. decrease skeletal muscle tone

D. inhibit beta-2 receptors

5. Corticosteroids are used in the treatment of asthma in which of the following ways? **(LO 32.5)**

A. increasing activation of arachidonic acid

B. inhibiting the release of inflammatory mediators

C. decreasing the production of allergic antibodies

D. increasing the activity of inflammatory cells

Sequencing

Place the following in order of longest duration of action to shortest duration of action. **(LO 32.8)**

_____   _____   _____   _____

Longest   **Shortest**

Foradil

Spiriva

Isuprel

Alupent

Classification

Place the following medications under their correct classification. **(LO 32.8)**

Decadron	Foradil	aminophylline
Lufyllin	Elixophyllin	Alupent
Xenopex	Celestone	Medrol

Selective beta-2 drugs	Methylxanthines	Corticosteroids

Documentation

Using the prescription on the next page, answer the following questions. **(LO 32.7)**

a. What symptom of COPD would be treated with this medication?

b. How does this medication work to treat these symptoms?

c. How is this medication usually administered?

d. Are there any side effects that would require additional medication to treat? If so, what type of medications would be administered?

Falls Pulmonary Clinic
Practice RX
12345 Main Avenue
Anytown, USA 12345
931-555-1000

NAME: ___Judith Aire_____   DATE: _____

ADDRESS: _____

RX   **Mucosil 10% solution**

Sig: **Use as directed three times daily**

Dr. F. Breathe_____ M.D.   _____ M.D.
   Substitution Permitted   Dispense as written

DEA #: _____   REFILL: NR 1 2 3 4

Labeling

Fill in the missing labels. **(LO 32.4)**

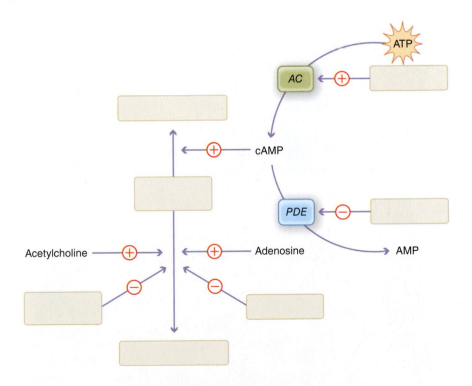

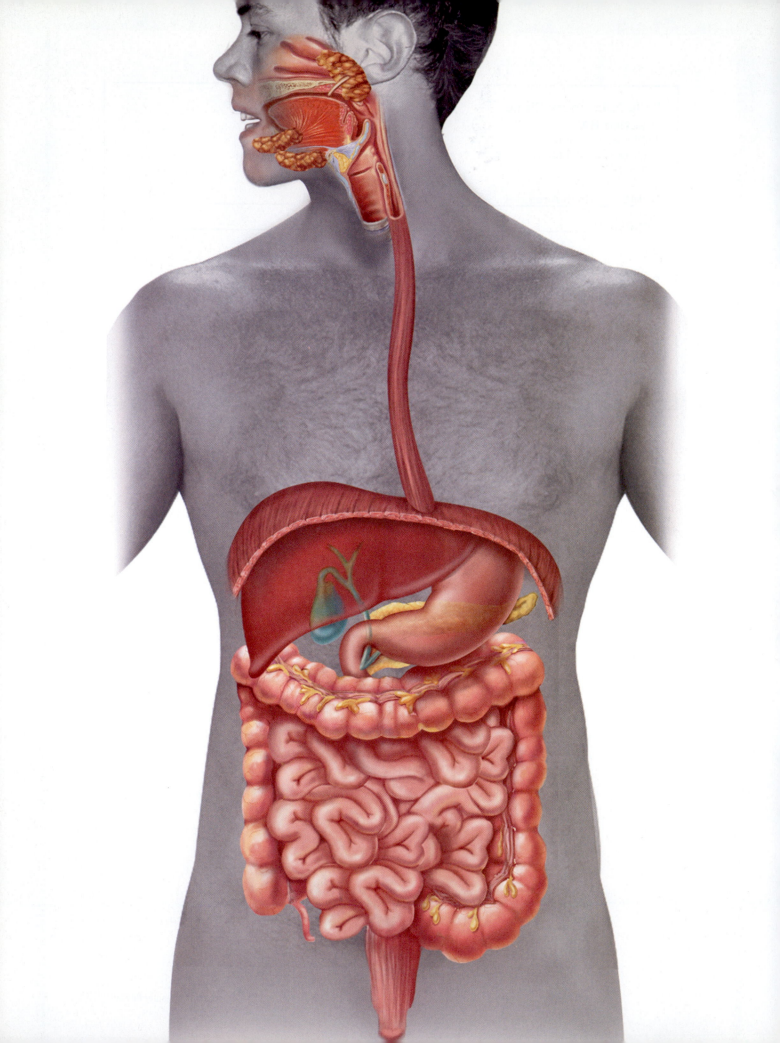

Pharmacology of the GI Tract

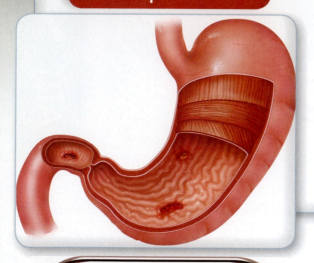

Chapter 33

Therapy of Gastro-intestinal Disorders: Peptic Ulcers, GERD, and Vomiting

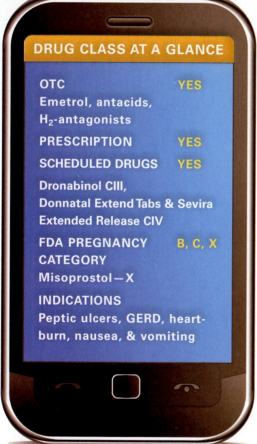

DRUG CLASS AT A GLANCE

OTC	**YES**
Emetrol, antacids, H_2-antagonists	
PRESCRIPTION	**YES**
SCHEDULED DRUGS	**YES**
Dronabinol CIII, Donnatal Extend Tabs & Sevira Extended Release CIV	
FDA PREGNANCY CATEGORY	**B, C, X**
Misoprostol—X	

INDICATIONS
Peptic ulcers, GERD, heartburn, nausea, & vomiting

KEY TERMS

abortifacient: substance that induces abortion.

absorption: the uptake of nutrients from the GI tract.

acid rebound: effect in which a great volume of acid is secreted by the stomach in response to the reduced acid environment caused by antacid neutralization.

antacid: drug that neutralizes hydrochloric acid (HCl) secreted by the stomach.

antisecretory: substance that inhibits secretion of digestive enzymes, hormones, or acid.

chyme: partially digested food and gastric secretions that move into the duodenum from the stomach by peristalsis.

digestion: mechanical and chemical breakdown of foods into smaller units.

dyspepsia: indigestion.

emesis: vomiting.

enterochromaffin-like cells (ECL): cells that synthesize and release histamine.

GERD: gastroesophageal reflux disease.

heartburn (acid indigestion): a painful burning feeling behind the sternum that occurs when stomach acid backs up into the esophagus.

hepatic microsomal metabolism: specific enzymes in the liver (P_{450} family) that metabolize some drugs and can be increased (stimulated) by some medications or decreased (inhibited) by other medications so that therapeutic drug blood levels are altered.

hyperacidity: abnormally high degree of acidity (for example, pH less than 1) in the stomach.

hypercalcemia: elevated concentration of calcium ions in the circulating blood.

hyperchlorhydria: excess hydrochloric acid in the stomach.

hypermotility: increase in muscle tone or contractions causing faster clearance of substances through the GI tract.

538

hypophosphatemia: abnormally low concentrations of phosphate in the circulating blood.

parietal (oxyntic) cell: cell that synthesizes and releases hydrochloric acid (HCl) into the stomach lumen.

pepsin: enzyme that digests protein in the stomach.

perforation: opening in a hollow organ, such as a break in the intestinal wall.

proteolytic: action that causes the decomposition or destruction of proteins.

ulcer: open sore in the mucous membranes or mucosal linings of the body.

ulcerogenic: capable of producing minor irritation or lesions to an integral break in the mucosal lining (ulcer).

Learning Outcomes

After studying this chapter, you should be able to

33.1 explain the three phases of gastric secretion and what stimulates the production of acid and pepsin in the GI tract.

33.2 explain the different causes of peptic ulcer disease and GERD.

33.3 explain the mechanisms of action, route of administration, adverse effects, drug interactions, and clinical indications of H_2-receptor antagonist, antacid, proton pump inhibitor, and antisecretory drugs and give examples of each.

33.4 explain the rationale for using anticholinergic, antiserotonin, and antispasmodic drugs.

33.5 describe GERD and explain the rationale for drugs used in gastroesophageal reflux disease.

33.6 explain the mechanism of action of drugs that inhibit vomiting.

Introduction

The organs of the upper gastrointestinal (GI) tract are concerned primarily with the **digestion** and **absorption** of nutrients. The stomach and small intestine (particularly the duodenum) secrete several hormones and enzymes that aid in the digestion and absorption of nutrients. Secretion of these digestive juices is stimulated by the thought, sight, or smell of food; stretch of the stomach muscles; food entering the stomach; peristalsis; and hormones such as gastrin. Specialized cells in the stomach produce hydrochloric acid (HCl) and **proteolytic** enzymes (for example, pepsin), which break down food particles into an absorbable form.

LO 33.1 LO 33.2

DIGESTION AND ULCER PRODUCTION

Process of Digestion

There are three phases of gastric acid secretion (cephalic, gastric, and intestinal) involved in the digestion of foods. In the cephalic phase, the sight, smell, taste, and thought of food stimulate the release of gastric juices before the bolus of food actually reaches the stomach. Gastric juices are predominately hydrochloric acid (HCl) and an enzyme, **pepsin.** During the gastric phase, the stomach distends when food enters, again stimulating the release of gastric juices. The **parietal cells,** also known as **oxyntic cells,** located in the stomach are responsible for the secretion of gastric acid (HCl). The secretion of HCl decreases the pH, which activates digestive enzymes such as pepsin so it can partially digest proteins in the food. The volume of partially digested foods **(chyme)** entering the duodenum distends it and stimulates the release of gastric juices. The protein by-products (peptides and amino acids) within the chyme also stimulate the secretion of gastric juices. Later in the intestinal phase, the presence of acid and fat inhibit their release. This action prevents excess secretion of HCl and pepsin, which could damage the GI tissue. (See Figure 33.1.)

Acetylcholine (ACH), gastrin, and histamine are the *major stimulators* for the release of gastric juices. ACH is a potent stimulator and binds to receptors on the chief, G, **enterochromaffin-like** (ECL), and parietal cells, stimulating the release of pepsin, gastrin, histamine, and HCl respectively. (See Figure 33.2.) Gastrin binds to receptors on parietal and ECL cells, thus stimulating the release of HCl and histamine, respectively. The histamine receptors located on parietal cells are designated H_2-receptors to distinguish them from the H_1-receptors involved in hypersensitivity and allergic reactions (see Chapter 31). Histamine binds to receptors on the parietal cells and greatly enhances the released volume and concentration of HCl. Drugs that block histamine release and the pump that releases HCl from the parietal cells can drastically diminish the release of HCl. The secretion of HCl causes the contents of the stomach to become extremely acidic (pH 0.8). This acid pH is necessary to activate the digestive enzymes such as pepsin.

Note to the Health Care Professional

Cigarette smoking has been shown to be closely related to ulcer recurrence and reversal of antiulcer drug effectiveness.

Gastric acid is even produced and secreted between meals in response to appropriate stimuli. Acid secretion between meals, during the evening hours, and during sleep reduces bacterial growth in the stomach, thus minimizing the risk of infection. Normally, the cells of the GI tract are protected from the destructive action of acid and pepsin. The mucosal lining of these organs is continuously lubricated with secretions of

Figure 33.1   Regulation of Gastric Function Showing Neural and Hormonal Control of the Gastric Secretions

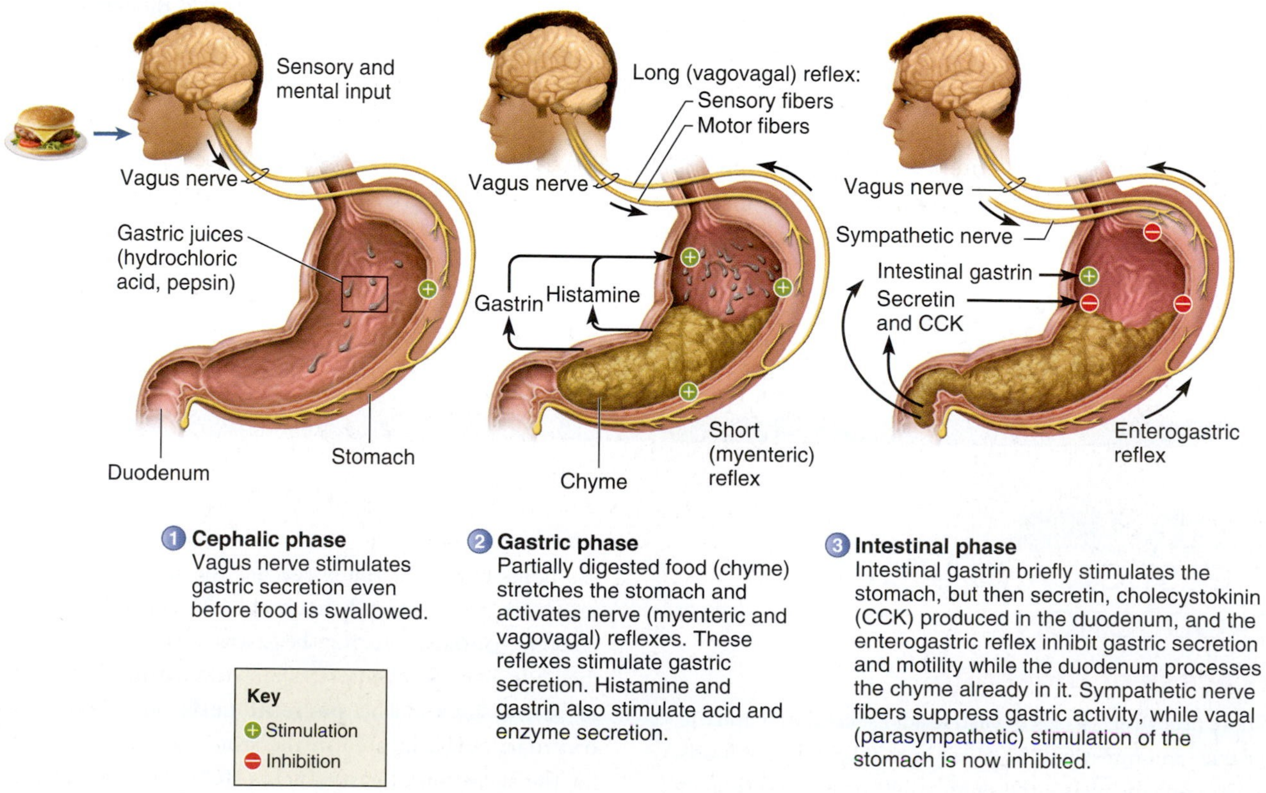

Key
⊕ Stimulation
⊖ Inhibition

① Cephalic phase
Vagus nerve stimulates gastric secretion even before food is swallowed.

② Gastric phase
Partially digested food (chyme) stretches the stomach and activates nerve (myenteric and vagovagal) reflexes. These reflexes stimulate gastric secretion. Histamine and gastrin also stimulate acid and enzyme secretion.

③ Intestinal phase
Intestinal gastrin briefly stimulates the stomach, but then secretin, cholecystokinin (CCK) produced in the duodenum, and the enterogastric reflex inhibit gastric secretion and motility while the duodenum processes the chyme already in it. Sympathetic nerve fibers suppress gastric activity, while vagal (parasympathetic) stimulation of the stomach is now inhibited.

Figure 33.2   **Gastric Secretions**

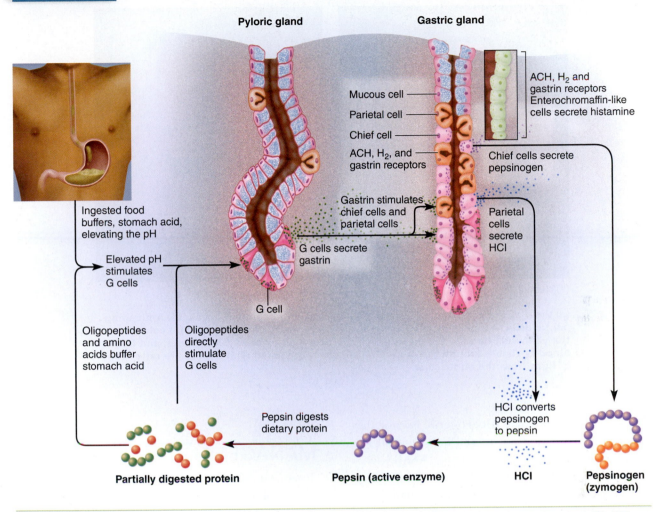

Pyloric gland   **Gastric gland**

Mucous cell

Parietal cell

Chief cell

ACH, H₂, and gastrin receptors

ACH, H₂ and gastrin receptors Enterochromaffin-like cells secrete histamine

Chief cells secrete pepsinogen

Gastrin stimulates chief cells and parietal cells

Parietal cells secrete HCl

G cells secrete gastrin

G cell

Ingested food buffers, stomach acid, elevating the pH

Elevated pH stimulates G cells

Oligopeptides and amino acids buffer stomach acid

Oligopeptides directly stimulate G cells

Pepsin digests dietary protein

HCl converts pepsinogen to pepsin

Partially digested protein   Pepsin (active enzyme)   HCl   Pepsinogen (zymogen)

G cells secrete gastrin; chief cells, pepsinogen; parietal cells, HCl and intrinsic factor; and enterochromaffin-like cells, histamine. Acetylcholine (ACH), histamine (H₂), and gastrin receptors are located on parietal cells. ACH and gastrin receptors, also located on enterochromaffin-like cells, cause histamine secretion, which then stimulates the parietal cells to produce more HCl.

mucus and alkaline fluid to prevent autodigestion (self-destruction). There is also rapid replacement (turnover) of the epithelial cells to help minimize erosion. These protective mechanisms are extremely important during the evening hours, when acid is secreted into an empty stomach. Anything that interferes with the protective function of the mucosal cell barrier may contribute to the production of ulcers.

Production of Ulcers

Peptic **ulcers** are open sores that develop on the mucosal lining of the stomach and duodenum, where acid and pepsin activity are greatest (Figure 33.3).

There is no simple cause of ulcers. The most common cause of peptic ulcers is an infection caused by a bacterium called *Helicobacter pylori* (*H. pylori*). The

Nobel Prize in 2005 was awarded to two scientists who discovered this bacteria. Recent clinical research has confirmed that *H. pylori* bacteria are present in 100 percent of patients with chronic active duodenal ulcers. The Centers for Disease Control has reported that 9 out of 10 cases of GI ulcer are caused by *H. pylori*. Of course, some individuals with or without *H. pylori* present secrete excess amounts of gastric acid (**hyperacidity** or **hyperchlorhydria**) even when food is not present in the stomach. Other individuals may not produce enough protective mucus or inhibitory enzyme to stop acid secretion. In addition, many other factors make individuals susceptible to ulcer production. For example, alcohol, smoking, and increased cholinergic (vagus) activity stimulate the secretion of acid. Drugs, such as the nonsteroidal antiinflammatory drugs

Figure 33.3   **View of the Gastroesophageal Junction by Endoscopy**

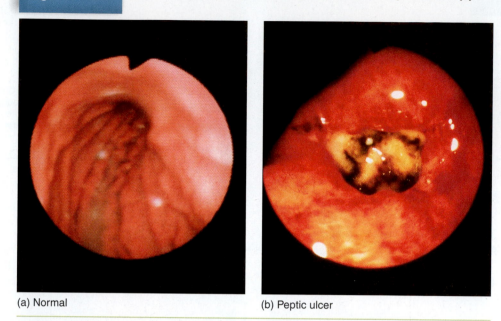

(a) Normal   (b) Peptic ulcer

(a) View of the cardiac opening from above showing healthy mucosa. (b) A bleeding peptic ulcer. A peptic ulcer typically has an oval shape and yellow-white color. Here the yellowish floor of the ulcer is partially obscured by black blood clots, and fresh blood is visible around the margin of the ulcer. The small white spots are reflections of light from the endoscope.

(NSAIDs) and steroids, are **ulcerogenic** because they inhibit the secretion of mucus and interfere with the normal production of the mucosal lining. NSAIDs block the production of certain prostaglandins that inhibit gastric secretions. Thus, if the prostaglandins that inhibit gastric secretions are blocked, more gastric acid is produced, increasing the likelihood of developing an ulcer. In addition, there is evidence that some people are genetically susceptible to ulcer formation. Usually, a combination of ulcerogenic factors is involved in the development of peptic ulcers. Whether gastric or duodenal, peptic ulcers are associated with acid-induced injury to the mucosa.

Regardless of the cause, peptic ulcers may be accompanied by periodic pain, nausea, loss of appetite, and vomiting. The pain is characteristically described as a dull, gnawing, burning sensation, and it often resembles **heartburn** (a burning sensation behind the sternum). Duodenal pain is usually (but not always) relieved by food, whereas gastric pain is brought on by food. In both cases, the pain may be intense enough to awaken patients from sleep. Chronic erosion of the mucosa may produce a **perforation** in the GI wall. Symptoms of a perforation include blood in stools or vomit. The immediate danger is that the GI perforation will lead to hemorrhage, hypotension, and shock.

LO 33.3
MANAGEMENT OF ULCERS

Treatment of peptic ulcers is directed toward the source of the irritation and pain and allowing the mucosal sores to heal. Recommended treatment of active ulcers is short term, 4 to 8 weeks. Frequently, therapy is continued (maintenance therapy) to minimize the risk of ulcer recurrence. Therefore, inhibition of gastric acid and pepsin secretion is a major part of ulcer therapy. Treatment of peptic ulcer disease includes proton pump inhibitors (PPI), H_2-antagonists (antihistamines), prostaglandins, anticholinergic drugs, and antacids. These antiulcer drugs are not always curative. In some instances, recurrent ulcers require surgical repair to avoid further damage, pain, and hemorrhage.

Therapy also involves lifestyle changes. Patients are encouraged to stop smoking, avoid caffeine and alcohol, and reduce psychological stress. NSAIDs should be eliminated, if possible. For patients that need to continue NSAID usage (for example, rheumatoid arthritis), a proton pump inhibitor may be added. While research has shown that dietary restrictions alone are not justified, individual patients are encouraged to eliminate foods that cause dyspepsia or increase their ulcer symptoms.

Peptic ulcer patients with *H. pylori* will require antibiotic therapy in addition to conventional antiulcer therapy. Antibiotics must be administered to eradicate the bacteria. Antibiotic monotherapy is not recommended because bacterial resistance develops. One of the standard regimens recommends at least two antibiotics in combination with bismuth salts. Bismuth is believed to lyse the bacterial cell wall and prevent further adhesion of the bacteria to the gastric mucosa. This provides greater opportunity for the antibiotics to eradicate the bacterial infection. Amoxicillin, tetracycline, metronidazole (*Flagyl*), and clarithromycin (*Biaxin*) are the drugs of choice because *H. pylori* is sensitive to them. A variety of regimens are in use: "dual therapy" refers to the simultaneous administration of two antibiotics; "triple therapy" includes two antibiotics plus bismuth; and "quadruple therapy" is the triple combination plus a proton pump inhibitor. Once the microorganism has been eradicated, chances of reinfection are minimal and ulcer recurrence is dramatically reduced. The wide variety of drugs used in the treatment and management of peptic ulcers is presented in Table 33:1.

LO 33.4
MANAGEMENT OF GASTROESOPHAGEAL REFLUX DISEASE (GERD)

GERD is a disorder characterized by heartburn. Patients frequently describe the symptom as an irritation and/or burning in their chest or throat. While heartburn is a common complaint among otherwise healthy people, in GERD this symptom is part of a chronic disease. In GERD, heartburn occurs after meals, worsens when the patient is lying down, and involves regurgitation of digestive juices into the esophagus. In severe GERD, the patient also may have signs of chronic blood loss, ulcerative esophagitis and strictures, and fibrous tissue bands resulting from the chronic injury to the esophagus.

The normal barriers to regurgitation of acid involve contraction of the lower esophageal sphincter (LES), dilution of acid by swallowed saliva, peristalsis that moves digested material toward the stomach, and, ultimately, resistance by the mucosal lining.

In GERD, the LES relaxes inappropriately such that gastric acid washes back (reflux) into the esophagus. When this occurs out of synchrony with peristalsis, the acid remains in contact with esophageal tissue longer. Certain foods are known to relax this sphincter (reduce lower esophageal pressure) in anticipation of digestion

(see Table 33:2). In GERD, the normal barriers are not able to respond correctly to the damaging triggers. Any additional complication, such as hiatal hernia, that impedes the flow of digestive contents, or drug-induced relaxation of the sphincter, predisposes patients to prolonged acid contact and irritation, even erosion. Once the mucosa is eroded, HCl can directly injure the cells.

The primary therapeutic objectives in the management of GERD are to suppress acid production, prevent erosion, and provide symptomatic relief.

Many people that suffer from infrequent GERD or heartburn take antacids or OTC H_2-receptor antagonists for symptomatic relief. Cimetidine (*Tagamet*), ranitidine (*Zantac*), and famotidine (*Pepcid*) were the first H_2-receptor antagonists approved in the United States and are now sold OTC. The H_2-receptor antagonists have a longer duration of action and greater efficacy than antacid therapy. The H_2-antagonists have brought dramatic relief to many patients with mild to moderate GERD. Where ulcerative damage is present, especially in severe GERD, the proton pump inhibitors are considered the first-line therapy. In severe GERD, especially to avoid lifetime drug therapy, the patient may undergo surgery to remove damaged tissue and delay further erosion. The mechanisms of action of the drugs used in the management of GERD are presented in Table 33:3.

Diet and lifestyle modifications have an important role in GERD maintenance therapy. Patients are encouraged to eat smaller meals and eliminate foods and drugs to reduce symptoms (see Table 33:2). Weight loss is recommended for overweight patients. If patients suffer from symptoms during the night, the head of the bed should be elevated to reduce reflux.

LO 33.1 LO 33.3
LO 33.4 LO 33.5 LO 33.6
ANTISECRETORY DRUGS: RECEPTOR-MEDIATED DRUG ACTION

Two primary mechanisms are involved in drug-mediated ulcer healing: reduction of gastric acidity and enhancement of mucosal barrier defenses. Antihistaminics, prostaglandins, proton pump inhibitors, and anticholinergic drugs reduce the volume and concentration of gastric acid (antisecretory). **Antacids,** on the other hand, neutralize the acid already present. Sucralfate (*Carafate*) is neither an antacid nor an antisecretory drug. It acts to enhance the mucosal defense by a local action at the site of the ulcer.

Antisecretory Drugs/Adult Oral Daily Doses Used in the Clinical Management of Ulcers and GERD

Drug (*Trade Name*)	Duodenal ulcer		Gastric ulcer	GERD	Pathological hypersecretory conditions
	Short-term active ulcer	Maintenance			
Histamine H$_2$-receptor antagonists					
Cimetidine (*Tagamet*)	800 mg at bedtime or 400 mg BID or 300 mg QID	400 mg at bedtime	800 mg at bedtime or 300 mg QID	800 mg BID or 400 mg QID	300 mg QID not to exceed 2400 mg/day
Cimetidine OTC (*Tagamet-HB*)	—	200 mg QD, BID no more than 2weeks	—	—	—
Famotidine (*Pepcid*)	40 mg at bedtime or 20 mg BID	20 mg at bedtime	40 mg at bedtime	20 mg BID or 1 hr before eating	20 mg every 6 hr
Famotidine OTC (*Pepcid-AC*)	—	—	10 mg (1 tablet) BID 1 hr before the meal causing symptoms (do not exceed 2 tablets/day)	—	—
Nizatidine (*Axid Pulvules*)	300 mg at bedtime or 150 mg BID	150 mg at bedtime	300 mg at bedtime or 150 mg BID	150 mg BID	—
Nizatidine OTC (*Axid AR*)	—	—	—	75–150 mg	—
Ranitidine (*Zantac*)	300 mg at bedtime or 150 mg BID	150 mg at bedtime	150 mg BID	150 mg BID	150 mg BID
Ranitidine OTC (*Zantac 75*)	—	—	—	75–150 mg	—
Prostaglandins					
Misoprostol (*Cytotec*)	200 mcg	—	100–200 mcg QID with food for prevention of NSAID-induced gastric ulcers	—	—
Proton pump inhibitors					
Dexlansoprazole (*Kapidex*)	—	—	—	30 mg daily	60 mg daily
Esomeprazole (*Nexium*)	—	—	—	20 or 40 mg daily	—
Lansoprazole (*Prevacid*)	15 mg QD	15 mg QD	—	30 mg/day	60 mg/day up to 120 mg
Lansoprazole OTC (*Prevacid 24*)	—	—	—	150 mg QD for 14 days, treatment of heartburn only	—
Omeprazole (*Prilosec*)	20 mg daily*	—	20 mg daily	20 mg daily	60 mg once a day to 120 mg TID

(Continued)

Drug (*Trade Name*)	Duodenal ulcer		Gastric ulcer	GERD	Pathological hypersecretory conditions
	Short-term active ulcer	Maintenance			
Omeprazole OTC (*Prilosec OTC, Zegerid OTC*)	20 mg*** at least 1 hr before eating	—	20 mg*** at least 1 hr before eating	20 mg*** at least 1 hr before eating	—
Pantoprazole (*Protonix*)	—	—	—	40 mg daily	—
Rabeprazole (*Aciphex*)	20 mg daily	—	—	20 mg daily	60 to 120 mg daily
H. pylori* combination treatment*					
Bismuth subsalicylate plus metronidazole plus tetracycline (*Helidac*)	525 mg 250 mg 500 mg	—	—	—	1 dose (4 tablets) QID
Lansoprazole plus clarithromycin plus amoxicillin (*Prevpac*)	30 mg 500 mg 1 g	—	—	—	1 dose BID
Omeprazole plus clarithromycin	40 mg once a day 500 mg TID	—	—	—	—
Triple therapy***					
Omeprazole or esomeprazole Clarithromycin Amoxicillin	20 mg BID 40 mg daily 500 mg BID 1000 mg BID	—	—	—	—
Lansoprazole Clarithromycin Amoxycillin	30 mg BID 500 mg BID 1 g BID	—	—	—	—
GI stimulants (prokinetic drugs)					
Metoclopramide (*Reglan, Maxolon*)	—	—	—	10–15 mg up to QID 30 minutes before each meal	—

*4–8 weeks. **Not an inclusive list of H. pylori regimens. ***Up to 14 days.

H₂-Receptor Antagonists (Antihistamines)

Histamine is a potent stimulator of gastric secretions in humans. Histamine is located throughout the GI mucosa within mast cells. Histamine receptors are found in the gastric mucosa and mediate the secretion of gastric acid and pepsin. These receptors are designated H_2-receptors to distinguish them from the H_1-receptors involved in hypersensitivity and allergic reactions (see Chapter 31). The **parietal,** or **oxyntic, cells** located in the stomach are responsible for acid production. Evidence suggests that the receptors involved in gastric secretion are located on the parietal cells. These receptors include cholinergic and histamine receptors, which facilitate acid secretion as well as sensitize the cells to gastrin stimulation. Stimulation of these receptors increases the volume and strength (decreases pH) of acid secretion. If either the cholinergic receptors or H_2-receptors are blocked, acid secretion decreases and gastrin-induced secretion is inhibited.

Cimetidine (*Tagamet*), famotidine (*Pepcid*), nizatidine (*Axid),* and ranitidine (*Zantac*) are H_2-receptor

Examples of Drugs and Foods Known to Lower Esophageal Sphincter Pressure

Food	Drugs
Chocolate	Alcohol, calcium channel blockers
Fat	Cigarettes, morphine
Onion	Dopamine
Coffee	Diazepam
Peppermint	Barbiturates
Spearmint	Prostaglandins Digestive hormones

Table **33:3**

Management of GERD: Drug Response

Drug	Response
Antacids	Increase pH of the refluxed fluid Local cytoprotection
GI stimulants/prokinetic drugs	
Bethanechol (*Urecholine*)	Increase lower esophageal pressure through a parasympathetic pathway Induce intestinal peristalsis
Metoclopramide (*Reglan*)	Increase lower esophageal pressure Increase gastric and esophageal peristalsis Increase gastric emptying
H$_2$-receptor antagonists	
Cimetidine (*Tagamet*) Famotidine (*Pepcid*) Nizatidine (*Axid*) Ranitidine (*Zantac*)	Decrease gastric acid secretion Decrease gastric volume
Proton pump inhibitors	
Dexlansoprazole (*Dexilant*) Esomeprazole (*Nexium*) Lansoprazole (*Prevacid*) Omeprazole (*Prilosec*) Pantoprazole (*Protonix*) Rabeprazole (*Aciphex*)	Inhibit gastric acid secretion Decrease gastric volume

antagonists that competitively inhibit the interaction of histamine with H$_2$-receptors (see Figure 33.4). Blockade of these receptors significantly reduces the secretion of acid and pepsin output from the stomach. These drugs are neither anticholinergic nor antispasmodic drugs. Their antiulcer action is directed at the histamine (H$_2$-) receptors. These drugs act to inhibit acid secretion **(antisecretory).** Therefore, in the presence of other acid-promoting (secretory) stimuli, gastric acid secretion is suppressed. These drugs differ in their potency, pharmacodynamic characteristics (bioavailability or protein binding), and ability to influence the **hepatic microsomal metabolism** of other medications. Suppression of acid secretion by an H$_2$-receptor antagonist is less than with a proton pump inhibitor because only the histamine receptor is blocked, whereas a proton pump inhibitor blocks the secretion of HCl. The currently available H$_2$-receptor antagonists are presented in Table 33:1.

Route of Administration

All of the H$_2$-receptor antagonists except nizatidine can be administered orally and parenterally. Following oral administration, these drugs are absorbed into the blood. Peak absorption occurs within 90 minutes for cimetidine and 2 to 3 hours for famotidine, nizatidine, and ranitidine. Overall absorption does not appear to be adversely affected by the presence of food in the GI tract. Therefore, these drugs can be taken with meals. Cimetidine absorption has been reported to be delayed by the concomitant use of antacids, but the data are not as clear for famotidine, nizatidine, and ranitidine. Antacids should be taken 1 hour after cimetidine and ranitidine administration to avoid an interaction resulting in decreased absorption of these drugs. No special precautions are associated with the oral use of other H$_2$-receptor antagonists and antacids. The primary route of drug elimination is the kidneys, although hepatic metabolism occurs to some extent.

Figure 33.4 **Sites of Antiulcer Drug Action**

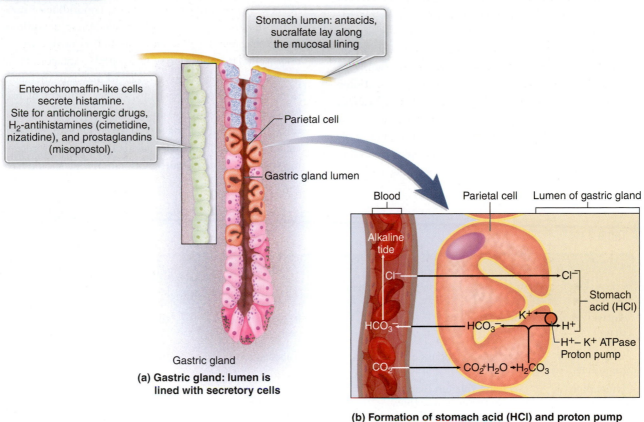

Stomach lumen: antacids, sucralfate lay along the mucosal lining

Enterochromaffin-like cells secrete histamine. Site for anticholinergic drugs, H₂-antihistamines (cimetidine, nizatidine), and prostaglandins (misoprostol).

Parietal cell

Gastric gland lumen

Gastric gland

(a) Gastric gland: lumen is lined with secretory cells

Blood   Parietal cell   Lumen of gastric gland

Alkaline tide

Cl^- Cl^-

Stomach acid (HCl)

HCO_3^- HCO_3^- K^+ H^+

H^+-K^+ ATPase Proton pump

CO_2 $CO_2 + H_2O \rightarrow H_2CO_3$

(b) Formation of stomach acid (HCl) and proton pump in the parietal cell. Bicarbonate (HCO_3^-) ions return to the blood and Cl^- ions enter the cell to combine with H^+ forming HCl. Site for proton pump inhibitors (omeprazole, lansoprazole), anticholinergic drugs, H₂-antihistamines (cimetidine, nizatidine), and prostaglandins (misoprostol) to inhibit HCl formation.

(a) Lumen of the intestine (antacids, sucralfate), parietal cell–inhibition of hydrochloric acid secretion HCl (anticholinergics, H₂-antihistamines, proton pump and prostaglandin inhibitors, gastric stimulants), enterochromaffin-like cells' inhibition of histamine secretion (anticholinergics), prostaglandins, H₂-antihistamines. (b) Formation of stomach acid and proton pump in the parietal cell.

Adverse Effects

The H₂-receptor antagonists are very well tolerated during short-term or chronic maintenance therapy requiring high daily doses. Adverse effects may include headache or constipation. Cimetidine has been associated with reversible central nervous system (CNS) effects, mental confusion, and disorientation, usually in severely ill patients. Liver or renal disease may contribute to elevated circulating levels of cimetidine due to decreased metabolism and excretion and predispose elderly patients to CNS effects. Nizatidine and ranitidine have been associated with elevations in hepatic enzyme levels, in particular, AST (aspartate aminotransferase), ALT (alanine aminotransferase), and alkaline phosphatase. These levels return to normal when the medication is discontinued.

A safety profile in children under 16 years of age has not been established with this class of drugs. A relatively small number of pediatric patients have required antihistaminic therapy, usually for hypersecretory conditions. Since there is little experience with these drugs in infants, and because these drugs are secreted into breast milk, female patients should be cautioned not to nurse their infants while taking H₂-receptor antagonists.

No serious adverse effects have been associated with reported overdose of these drugs. Treatment of overdose is symptomatic and supportive.

Drug Interactions

Cimetidine has been reported to increase blood levels of several drugs by altering their metabolism. The mechanisms of metabolic interference are inhibition of hepatic microsomal systems (binding to cytochrome P_{450}), as well as alteration of hepatic blood flow leading to decreased hepatic clearance of certain drugs. Cimetidine inhibits many enzymes including CYP2C9, CYP2D6, and CYP3A4, which are major contributors to the metabolism of other drugs. Although ranitidine binds to cytochrome P_{450} less than cimetidine, famotidine and nizatidine have no effect on this metabolic pathway.

Since an inhibition of the hepatic microsomal metabolizing system may lead to an elevation in the drug levels of certain concomitant medications, famotidine or nizatidine may be a favored choice under these conditions. Drugs that may be affected by inhibition of the hepatic microsomal metabolizing system with H_2-antagonists are presented in Table 33:4. In order to maintain therapeutic blood levels of these drugs, dosage adjustment may be necessary when concomitant H_2-receptor antagonist therapy is begun or ended. To avoid clinically significant variation in anticoagulant action, patients receiving warfarin concomitantly with cimetidine should have

[Table **33:4**]

Drug Interactions Associated with Antisecretory Drugs

Antisecretory drug	Interacts with	Mechanism of action	Response
Cimetidine or ranitidine	Antacids, sucralfate	Delay absorption	Decreased cimetidine or ranitidine availability
Cimetidine	Caffeine, calcium channel blockers, carbamazepine, chlordiazepoxide, chloroquine, diazepam, labetalol, lidocaine, meperidine, metoprolol, metronidazole, pentoxifylline, phenobarbital, phenytoin, propranolol, quinidine, quinine, sulfonylureas, tacrine, theophylline, triamterene, tricyclic antidepressants, warfarin	Cimetidine inhibits hepatic metabolic enzymes	Increased blood levels of these drugs
Lansoprazole, omeprazole	Sucralfate	Delay absorption	Decrease availability of lansoprazole and omeprazole
Metoclopramide	Alcohol, cyclosporin	Accelerate gastric emptying	Increase absorption of alcohol, cyclosporin
Metoclopramide	Cimetidine	Accelerate gastric emptying	Decrease cimetidine absorption
Metoclopramide	MAO inhibitors	Release catecholamines	Increase potential for hypertension
Nizatidine	Aspirin, doses greater than 3 g/day	Unknown	Increase serum salicylate levels
Omeprazole	Clarithromycin	Unknown	Increase plasma levels of both omeprazole and clarithromycin
Omeprazole, lansoprazole	Diazepam, flurazepam, triazolam, phenytoin, warfarin	Interfere with metabolism	Increased blood levels of these drugs
Ranitidine	Diazepam, midazolam	Ranitidine alters drug absorption	Increased blood levels of midazolam; decreased blood levels of diazepam
Ranitidine, omeprazole	Warfarin	May decrease warfarin clearance	Increased hypoprothrombinemia

their prothrombin time monitored during the treatment period. Ranitidine does not affect the hepatic microsomal system to the same extent as does cimetidine. However, ranitidine has been reported to interact with some of the same types of drugs. Absorption of ranitidine, for example, appears to be decreased by concomitant use of antacids. Other drugs, such as diazepam and metoprolol, are affected by concomitant use of ranitidine (Table 33:4).

Information regarding the compatibility of mixing H$_2$-receptor antagonists with other drug solutions for parenteral administration is available for cimetidine. Cimetidine is incompatible when added to solutions of barbiturates, cefamandole nafate, cefazolin sodium, cephalothin sodium, and theophylline. These drugs should not be mixed in the same syringe with cimetidine because precipitation of cimetidine will occur.

Clinical Indications

H$_2$-receptor antagonists are recommended for the short-term treatment (up to 8 weeks) of benign gastric and duodenal ulcers. This class of agents will heal 60 to 80 percent of ulcers within 4 weeks of treatment. Although patients often take medication beyond 4 weeks, it is not necessarily associated with total cure or eradication of all lesions. In the treatment of active ulcers, the doses of these drugs may vary from a single dose taken at bedtime to BID or QID regimens. Prophylaxis or maintenance therapy may be continued with a single daily dose taken at bedtime (Table 33:1). The specific doses of the H$_2$-receptor antagonists vary because each drug has a different potency. However, all of these drugs are effective in alleviating the symptoms and subsequent tissue damage or complications of peptic ulcer disease to the same extent when used in the recommended regimens. At this time, cimetidine (*Tagamet-HB 200*), famotidine

(*Pepcid-AC*), nizatidine (*Axid AR*), and ranitidine (*Zantac 75, Zantac 150*) are available OTC in strengths (mg per tablet) that are less than most of those available by prescription. (See Figure 33.5.) The dosage of *Tagamet-HB 200* is 200 mg per tablet, compared to the prescribed range of 200–800 mg per dose form, while the dose of *Pepcid-AC,* which has an effect on pepcid acid control, is 10 mg per tablet compared to 20 or 40 mg. OTC nizatidine is available in 75 mg and ranitidine in 75- and 150-mg tablets.

H$_2$-receptor antagonists are used in the treatment of special hypersecretory conditions such as multiple endocrine adenomas, systemic mastocystis (mast cells), or Zollinger-Ellison (ZE) syndrome. Zollinger-Ellison syndrome is a disease characterized by the presence of gastrin-containing tumors (gastrinomas) and ulceration of the GI tract. In most ZE syndrome patients, gastric acid hypersecretion is present. The flood of hydrochloric acid into the intestine ultimately contributes to severe diarrhea, whereas the acid and pepsin erode the GI mucosa, producing peptic ulcers. Zollinger-Ellison syndrome patients are often resistant to other modes of therapy but have successfully responded to the H$_2$-receptor antagonists at doses three times the usual daily dose. Cimetidine and ranitidine have been given to ZE patients in doses of 3 to 6 g per day to control ulcers. In these patients, treatment with H$_2$-antagonist drugs must be continued indefinitely to avoid ulcer recurrence.

At present, most of the H$_2$-receptor antagonists are approved for the short-term management of duodenal ulcers, gastric ulcers, and pathological hypersecretory conditions. However, some of these drugs are also used clinically for the treatment of GERD, stress ulcers induced in critically ill patients (burns, intracranial lesions, trauma), and gastric irritation in susceptible patients requiring nonsteroidal antiinflammatory drugs

| **Figure 33.5** | **Examples of Antacid and Antiulcer Drugs** |

 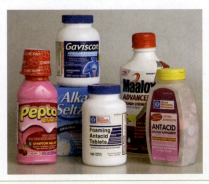 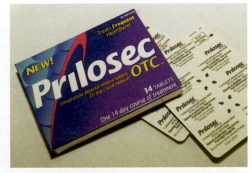

(a) H$_2$-antagonist famotidine *(Pepcid)*. (b) Various antacids. (c) Proton pump inhibitor omeprazole *(Prilosec)*. All products shown are over-the-counter (OTC); no prescription required for purchase.

(NSAIDs) or chronic aspirin treatment. Table 33:1 indicates the recommended doses for the approved uses of each H$_2$-receptor antagonist.

Prostaglandins

Several pathways and receptors are involved in the production and secretion of gastric acid and cytoprotective mucus. Prostaglandins PGE$_2$ and PGI$_2$, which are lipids made from fatty acids, are believed to have specific receptors in the gastric mucosa. These receptors mediate bicarbonate production and secretion of mucus, and therefore they directly influence the protective environment of the stomach. These prostaglandins are potent inhibitors of histamine secretion and local vasodilators that increase blood flow to injured cells and promote healing. Drugs that inhibit prostaglandin synthesis, such as NSAIDs, are known to induce gastric ulcers, presumably by inhibition of the prostaglandin-mediated secretions.

Note to the Health Care Professional

Women who are in their child-bearing years should be instructed about the effects of taking prostaglandins and urged never to give their medication to friends or relatives.

Route of Administration

At present, only one synthetic prostaglandin is approved for use in the management of NSAID- and aspirin-induced gastric ulcers. An analog of prostaglandin E$_1$, misoprostol (*Cytotec*), is available for oral administration (tablets) in doses of 100 to 200 mcg QID. Misoprostol may be taken with meals to minimize any local irritation. For those patients who cannot tolerate the 200 mcg dose, the recommended dose is 100 mcg. Misoprostol is recommended to be taken throughout the duration of NSAID therapy in patients at high risk for developing gastric ulcers, but misoprostol does not appear to prevent duodenal ulcers in patients on chronic NSAID therapy.

Adverse Effects and Contraindications

Prostaglandins mediate a number of physiological effects in the body. Effects produced during misoprostol therapy appear to be related to the effect of prostaglandin on the smooth muscle of the GI and genitourinary (GU)

tract. Misoprostol has been associated with self-limiting diarrhea in men or women on therapy and, to a lesser extent, abdominal pain, headache, flatulence, nausea, and constipation may occur.

Besides their involvement in peripheral pain pathways, prostaglandins are directly involved in the process of uterine contraction. Misoprostol (*Cytotec*) has a special cautionary (black box) warning with its use because it produces uterine contractions **(abortifacient)** and may cause miscarriage. For this reason, misoprostol is contraindicated for use in pregnant women. If a woman becomes pregnant during treatment, the drug should be terminated immediately and the patient should be counseled about the potential hazards to the fetus. Misoprostol should not be given to women of child-bearing potential until the abortifacient risks and sequelae have been thoroughly explained and an effective contraception method begun.

The toxic dose of prostaglandins in humans has not been determined. However, signs of overdose may include sedation, tremor, palpitations, hypotension, bradycardia, and fever.

Proton Pump Inhibitors

Gastric acid secretion may be affected by directly inhibiting the exchange of hydrogen (H$^+$) and potassium (K$^+$) ions within the parietal cells. This exchange of hydrogen and potassium ions is absolutely essential for the production of HCl. (See Figure 33.4.) In 1989, a new class of drugs called proton pump inhibitors was approved, of which omeprazole was the first. This class of drugs directly inhibits the secretory system that releases HCl. Since then, five other PPIs (dexlansoprazole, lansoprazole, rabeprazole, pantoprazole, and esomeprazole) have been introduced. These compounds have no effect on any other receptor-mediated activity.

Omeprazole (*Prilosec*), esomeprazole (*Nexium*), lansoprazole (*Prevacid*), dexlansoprazole (formerly *Kapidex*, now called *Dexilant*), pantoprazole (*Protonix*), and rabeprazole (*Aciphex*), the drugs currently available in this class, are used in the management of ulcers. Omeprazole (*Prilosec*) and lansoprazole (*Prevacid 24*) are also available OTC (see Figure 33.5). A newly FDA-approved proton pump inhibitor, *Dexilant* (dexlansoprazole) is a dual delayed-release formulation that releases the drug in two phases: 1 to 2 hours after administration, followed by a second 4 to 5 hours later. The proton pump inhibitors are approved for the short-term treatment of benign gastric ulcers, active duodenal ulcers, GERD, or long-term therapy in pathological hypersecretory conditions. These drugs are part of the effective combination treatment with antibiotics to eradicate *Helicobacter pylori*, promote ulcer healing, and prevent ulcer recurrence in susceptible patients. When administered with clarithromycin and amoxicillin, the proton pump inhibitors promote ulcer healing.

Adverse Effects

Oral administration of the proton pump inhibitors is generally well tolerated. The more common side effects include headache, abdominal pain, diarrhea, nausea, and constipation. There has been no evidence that omeprazole alters human gastric cell function to predispose patients to develop malignancies. However, because of the ability of this drug to sustain an inhibition of acid production, coupled with cell changes in laboratory animals, caution is indicated in the product labeling, which recommends that the drug be used only under the conditions and dosage described.

In the event of overdose, treatment is symptomatic and supportive, since there is no specific antidote. Because omeprazole is extensively bound to circulating plasma proteins, the drug cannot be dialyzed readily from the blood.

Drug Interactions

Omeprazole (*Prilosec*) is metabolized through the hepatic microsomal system and has been reported to cause elevated blood levels of diazepam, phenytoin, and warfarin when these drugs have been taken concomitantly. Since omeprazole profoundly affects the pH of the gastric contents, it may interfere with the absorption of drugs that depend upon an acid environment for optimal absorption. The FDA has issued a warning about an interaction between clopidogrel (*Plavix*), an anticlotting medication, and omeprazole (*Prilosec/Prilosec OTC*). New data show that when clopidogrel and omeprazole are taken together, the effectiveness of clopidogrel is reduced. Therefore, patients taking clopidogrel to prevent blood clots will not get the full effect of this medicine. Dexlansoprazole is extensively metabolized by the liver by CYP P$_{450}$ enzyme system. Present research data do not rule out an interaction with clopidogrel. Although lansoprazole, pantoprazole, and rabeprazole are metabolized through the hepatic microsomal system, there have been no reported clinically relevant drug interactions at this time.

Gastrointestinal Stimulants

Gastrointestinal stimulants induce contractions within the upper GI tract that prevent reflux of acid into the esophagus and promote gastric emptying. This combination of actions moves the potentially damaging digestive material away from the lower esophagus. Metoclopramide (*Reglan*) stimulates contraction of the lower esophageal sphincter by enhancing the action of endogenous acetylcholine. Metoclopramide increases tissue sensitivity to acetylcholine, but does not interact with cholinergic receptors or stimulate cholinergic nerves. The selectivity of action for upper GI smooth muscle makes the drugs clinically valuable for the treatment of GERD and minimizes the potential for unnecessary stimulation of gastric and biliary secretion.

Metoclopramide (*Reglan*) reduces symptoms best in daytime heartburn, especially meal induced. For this reason the recommended dose schedule is 10 to 15 mg 30 minutes prior to the meal or provocative situation. Metoclopramide is readily absorbed orally. In the treatment of GERD metoclopramide can be taken up to four times a day—that is, at each meal and before bedtime, for 8 to 12 weeks.

Metoclopramide (*Reglan*) is also available for other therapeutic uses and parenteral administration. Diabetic patients may experience delayed gastric emptying. This physiological alteration, known as diabetic gastroparesis, is usually accompanied by a persistent feeling of fullness, nausea, and heartburn. The degree of gastric stasis and intensity of the accompanying symptoms will determine whether intravenous administration is warranted to stabilize the patient.

Metoclopramide (*Reglan*) is also used in the treatment of chemotherapy-induced vomiting.

Adverse Effects and Contraindications

Metoclopramide (*Reglan*) may produce cardiovascular effects such as palpitations and sinus tachycardia. Fatigue, restlessness, nausea, and diarrhea are common adverse effects that are dose related. There is a special cautionary (black box) warning for drugs that contain metoclopramide. It is used as a short-term treatment of GERD in patients who have not responded to other therapies and to treat diabetic gastroparesis (slowed emptying of the stomach's contents into the intestines). It is recommended that treatment not exceed three months. Long-term or high-dose use of metoclopramide significantly increases the risk of tardive dyskinesia, even after the drugs are no longer taken. Tardive dyskinesia is characterized by involuntary, repetitive movements of the extremities, lip smacking, grimacing, tongue protrusion, rapid eye movements or blinking, puckering, pursing of the lips, or impaired movement of the fingers. These symptoms are rarely reversible and there is no treatment. But in some patients, symptoms may lessen or resolve after metoclopramide treatment is stopped. Children and young adults may develop extrapyramidal reactions at the doses used to block vomiting during chemotherapy.

Metoclopramide (*Reglan*) is contraindicated in four conditions. It is contraindicated in patients in whom GI motility may precipitate hemorrhage or perforation. Such patients are those who have active GI hemorrhage, bowel perforation, or bowel obstruction. Patients with pheochromocytoma, tumor of the catecholamine-producing adrenal tissue, may develop hypertension because GI stimulants evoke release of catecholamines from the tumor. Patients who have demonstrated sensitivity or intolerance to the drug should not receive the drug.

In addition, metoclopramide is contraindicated in patients who are epileptic or are receiving drugs that are likely to cause extrapyramidal reactions. In epileptic patients, the severity and frequency of seizures may be increased.

Anticholinergic and Antispasmodic Drugs

The secretion of gastric acid is mediated by several substances including hormones (gastrin), neurotransmitters (acetylcholine), and histamine. There is no question that stimulation of the vagus nerve increases the secretion of gastric acid. Stimulation of the parasympathetic nerves that supply the GI tract increases intestinal motility, and this activity also may enhance gastric secretion. Drugs that inhibit cholinergic activity by blocking the autonomic ganglia or blocking muscarinic receptors directly decrease gastric acid secretion and intestinal motility. Among the anticholinergic drugs, the belladonna derivatives (atropine, hyoscyamine, and scopolamine), glycopyrrolate, isopropamide, and propantheline have been used in the management of peptic ulcers because of their pharmacological effects on acid secretion and intestinal motility (see Table 33:5). Synthetic antispasmodic drugs such as dicyclomine (*Bentyl*) do not exhibit anticholinergic activity, but they are used for their ability to relax intestinal smooth muscle via nonspecific pathways. Drugs with an antispasmodic action are used in the clinical management of irritable bowel syndrome (spastic colon), GI **hypermotility** (increased muscle tone or stimulation of muscle contractions, causing faster clearance of substances through the GI tract), neurogenic colon, and other functional GI disorders. The mechanisms of action of these drugs have been discussed in previous chapters dealing with the parasympathetic nervous system and autonomic ganglia.

The anticholinergic drugs are available as combination preparations that may include a sedative (barbiturate) or an antianxiety drug (chlordiazepoxide). Examples of the available combination products include *Antrocol Elixir, Butibel Elixir, Donnatal,* and *Librax.* Combination products (*Donnatal Extendtabs, Sevira Extended Release*) that contain

<table><tr><td colspan="2">[Table **33:5**]</td></tr></table>

Anticholinergic and Antispasmodic Drugs Used in the Clinical Management of Gastrointestinal Disorders

Drug name (*Trade Name*)	Use	Adult oral dose
Belladonna alkaloids		
Atropine (*Sal-Tropine*)	Bradyarrhythmia, peptic ulcer, stomach inflammation	0.4–0.6 mg every 4 to 6 hr; 0.5 to 1 hr before meals
I-hyoscyamine (*AnaSpaz, Levsin*)	Gastrointestinal disorders	Up to 2 tablets every 4 hr
Scopolamine hydrobromide (*Scopace*)	Sedation preoperative, motion sickness	0.4–1.0 mg every 1–2 hr
Synthetic anticholinergics		
Glycopyrrolate (*Robinul*)	Peptic ulcer	1–8 mg per day
Propantheline (*Pro-Banthine*)	Peptic ulcer	15–75 mg per day
Synthetic antispasmodics		
Dicyclomine (*Bentyl*)	Irritable bowel	80–160 mg/day in four divided doses

48.6 mg of phenobarbital (compared to 16 mg in other products) are Schedule IV (CIV) drugs.

Route of Administration

Oral and parenteral preparations of these drugs are available. In the management of GI disorders, anticholinergic compounds are usually administered orally 30 minutes before meals and at bedtime (see Table 33:5). These drugs must be absorbed (systemically) in order to produce the desired pharmacological effects. Following oral administration, the synthetic anticholinergic compounds are not as readily absorbed as the belladonna derivatives.

Adverse Effects

Because the naturally occurring belladonna alkaloids are easily absorbed and readily cross the blood-brain barrier, they are associated with CNS side effects (dizziness, headache, insomnia, and drowsiness) at therapeutic doses.

Since the synthetic anticholinergic drugs are quaternary compounds (ionized) that cannot cross membranes easily, including the blood-brain barrier, the synthetic anticholinergics are not associated with CNS side effects. The synthetic anticholinergic drugs, however, may produce ganglionic blockade and neuromuscular blockade at toxic doses. Other adverse effects associated with the use of anticholinergic drugs include mydriasis, blurred vision, dry mouth, bradycardia or tachycardia, increased intraocular pressure, and urinary retention. By the nature of their effect on GI motility, these drugs frequently produce constipation. Anticholinergic drugs are eventually metabolized in the liver and are relatively short-acting. The synthetic (quaternary) derivatives have a longer duration of action than do the belladonna alkaloids.

Special Considerations and Contraindications

Anticholinergic and antispasmotic drugs should be used with caution in patients who have wide angle glaucoma, tachyarrhythmias, or bladder obstructions. They are contraindicated in patients who have myasthenia gravis, narrow-angle (acute) glaucoma, or obstructive bowel disease. Elderly patients may be sensitive to the effects of these drugs, as evidenced by episodes of mental confusion and excitement even at low doses.

Drug Interactions

Because of the potential for interaction, these drugs should be used with caution in patients who are receiving cardiac glycosides, antihistaminics, levodopa, or other parasympathomimetic drugs. Any pharmacological agent that has an anticholinergic component will enhance the anticholinergic activity of these drugs. Such drugs include amantadine, antipsychotics, meperidine, and tricyclic antidepressants. Monoamine oxidase (MAO) inhibitors may inhibit the metabolism of these drugs, thus potentiating anticholinergic activity. Since antacids decrease the oral absorption of these drugs, anticholinergics should be given 1 or 2 hours before the antacids.

Clinical Indications

Anticholinergic drugs will affect secretion and muscle contraction within the GI system. The appropriate drug is selected according to the desired site of action. Synthetic anticholinergics are approved as adjunct treatment of peptic ulcer. Synthetic antispasmodics are approved for use in peptic ulcer (oxyphencyclimine) or irritable bowel (dicyclomine). Belladonna alkaloids are used as adjuncts to peptic ulcer treatment, in functional GI disorders (diarrhea, spasm, diverticulitis) and intestinal and biliary colic, including infant colic.

LO 33.1   LO 33.3

ACID NEUTRALIZATION: ANTACIDS

Antacids are used to relieve the pain and indigestion that accompany overeating, hyperacidity associated with heartburn, GERD, gastritis, hiatal hernia, or peptic ulcers. Antacids are usually taken orally as liquids or tablets so that they are readily distributed to the GI tissues. A phenomenal number of antacid products are available over the counter as single or combination products, too many to present in the scope of this chapter. The majority of over-the-counter (OTC) antacid products contain magnesium (Mg^{2+}), aluminum (Al^{3+}), or calcium (Ca^{2+}) ions (see Table 33:6). However, one of the oldest antacids, sodium bicarbonate (baking soda), can be found in almost every home. (See Figure 33.5.)

Mechanism of Action

Antacids neutralize gastric acidity. These drugs react with hydrochloric acid (HCl) to form water and salts (see Table 33:6). Since the hydrogen ions are used to form water, gastric acidity decreases and the pH of the stomach juices increases. When the pH of the stomach contents reaches 4 or 5, pepsin activity is completely inhibited, and the mucosal irritation is removed.

The use of antacids is limited by their short duration of action. When taken on an empty stomach, the duration of action is about 30 minutes. Since food acts as a buffer, most antacids are taken 1 hour after meals so that the buffering activity continues for 2 to 3 hours.

All antacids produce a similar spectrum of effects because they directly neutralize gastric acid. Selection

Neutralization of Gastric Acid (HCl) by Antacids

Antacid	Gastric acid		Insoluble salt
$Mg(OH)_2$ magnesium hydroxide	$+ 2\ HCl$	$\longrightarrow$	$MgCl_2$ magnesium chloride $+ 2\ H_2O$
$CaCO_3$ calcium carbonate	$+ 2\ HCl$	$\longrightarrow$	Ca_2+ calcium ions $+ H_2O + CO_2$ gas
$Al(OH)_3$ aluminum hydroxide	$+ 3\ HCl$	$\longrightarrow$	$AlCl_3$ aluminum chloride $+ 3\ H_2O$

of an antacid may be based on the acid neutralizing capacity. Otherwise, advantages of some OTC products may not be related to their acid neutralization but to the ability of additional ingredients to produce other pharmacological actions. For example, saccharin may be added to increase the palatability (overcome the chalky taste), simethicone may be added as an antigas agent, and aspirin or acetaminophen may be included in varying amounts to ameliorate the symptoms of headache and minor muscle aches associated with tension (Table 33:7).

Special Considerations and Adverse Effects

Most antacid drugs are nonsystemic drugs; they are not intended to be absorbed into the bloodstream to work. The anti-acid action is primarily exerted along the GI tract. Although small amounts of magnesium, aluminum, and calcium ions may be absorbed, these antacid components primarily remain in the GI tract. Cations (Mg^{2+}, A^{3+}, Ca^{2+}), which are absorbed, are usually excreted by the kidneys. The nonsystemic antacids interfere with the intestinal absorption of other elements.

Over-the-Counter Preparations of Antacids

Trade Name	Antacid content	Additional active ingredients	Available preparations
Alka-Seltzer Plus	Sodium bicarbonate	Citric acid, sodium, 325 mg aspirin *Contains 1700 or more mg of sodium*	Effervescent tablets
Extra Strength Alka-Seltzer	Sodium bicarbonate	Citric acid, sodium, 500 mg aspirin	Effervescent tablets
Di-Gel	Aluminum hydroxide, magnesium hydroxide	Simethicone, saccharin, sorbitol	Tablets, liquid
Gaviscon	Aluminum hydroxide, magnesium hydroxide	Alginic acid, magnesium trisilicate	Tablets, liquid
Gelusil	Aluminum hydroxide, magnesium hydroxide	Simethicone, saccharin, sorbitol	Tablets, liquid
Maalox	Aluminum hydroxide, magnesium hydroxide	Simethicone, saccharin, sorbitol	Tablets, liquid
Milk of magnesia	Magnesium hydroxide	—	Tablets, suspension
Riopan	Hydroxymagnesium aluminate (magaldrate)	Simethicone, saccharin, sorbitol	Tablets, suspension, liquid
Rolaids	Dihydroxyaluminum, sodium carbonate	—	Tablets
Tums	Calcium carbonate	—	Tablets, liquid

Constipation is a frequent adverse effect of these drugs because the absorption of water and phosphate ions is inhibited. For this reason, individuals using antacids over a long period of time also may require a laxative to improve bowel function. While constipation may occur with aluminum and calcium antacids, diarrhea is likely to develop with magnesium-containing antacids. **Hypophosphatemia** (phosphate depletion) occasionally occurs with the chronic use of antacids containing aluminum compounds.

Sodium bicarbonate is a systemic antacid that is capable of producing metabolic alkalosis as a result of sodium (Na^{2+}) and bicarbonate (HCO_3^-) ion absorption. This may occur with excess or prolonged use of sodium bicarbonate. The excess bicarbonate absorbed is eventually excreted by the kidneys, causing the urine to become more alkaline. Absorption of sodium ions promotes fluid retention, which can lead to edema or increased blood pressure. Such fluid is particularly important in patients who have renal insufficiency, congestive heart failure, or hypertension. These individuals are usually on a sodium- (salt-) restricted diet, which is counteracted by the systemic antacid.

Chronic use of systemic antacids in combination with milk or calcium may lead to the milk-alkali syndrome. Here, in addition to metabolic alkalosis, **hypercalcemia** (elevated concentration of calcium ions), nausea, headache, weakness, and mental confusion are present. These symptoms subside when the antacids are discontinued.

Chronic use of antacids may produce a condition known as **acid rebound.** As the pH of the stomach increases (more alkaline) in the presence of antacids, the secretory cells respond by increasing the secretion of gastric acid. This eventually counteracts the neutralization potential of the antacids.

Another consideration in the selection or long-term use of antacids involves the sodium content. The sodium associated with the sodium bicarbonate component may be significant for patients with hypertension, congestive heart failure, or other conditions requiring maintenance on a low-sodium diet. Patients are encouraged to read the nutrient content before selecting which antacid to use.

Drug Interactions

Antacids may alter the absorption and excretion of other drugs by forming insoluble complexes or altering the pH of the stomach or urine. Absorption of oral tetracyclines is inhibited by antacids (especially magnesium and calcium compounds) because the antacids bind the tetracyclines into a nonabsorbable form (see Table 33:8).

Alteration of the urinary pH (alkaline) causes increased blood levels of drugs that are weak bases. Drugs such as quinidine, morphine, and pseudoephedrine are reabsorbed into the blood during antacid therapy. Conversely, acid drugs such as aspirin, penicillins, and isoniazid are excreted more quickly in an alkaline urine.

Clinical Indications

Antacids are approved for reduction of hyperacidity associated with peptic ulcer and relief of upset stomach associated with heartburn, GERD, and acid indigestion. Individual antacids have been formulated to be of value in replacement therapy as follows: magnesium deficiency resulting from alcoholism, restricted diet or magnesium-depleting drugs (magnesium hydroxide); treatment of hyperphosphatemia (aluminum carbonate); and calcium deficiency associated with postmenopausal osteoporosis (calcium carbonate).

LO 33.1 LO 33.2

BARRIER ENHANCERS: SUCRALFATE

Sucralfate (*Carafate*) is a complex of aluminum hydroxide and sulfated sucrose that is used to promote healing of peptic ulcers. Similar to the antacids, sucralfate is a nonsystemic drug that exerts its effect locally in the GI tract. Unlike antacids, however, sucralfate does not alter gastric pH.

Mechanism of Action

Sucralfate acts by forming a protective barrier over damaged gastric mucosa. Sucralfate binds proteins, such as albumin and fibrinogen, that are exuded from damaged mucosal cells and are present in the ulcer crater. A coating is formed that prevents further damage by blocking contact with gastric acid and pepsin, allowing healing to occur. In addition, sucralfate inhibits pepsin activity and may absorb bile salts that can cause irritation of the gastric lining. A small amount of sucralfate is absorbed from the GI tract and eventually excreted in the urine. The most common side effect associated with the use of sucralfate is constipation.

Clinical Indications

Sucralfate is recommended for short-term treatment of duodenal ulcers. It is available only in tablet form. The usual dose is 1 g taken four times daily on an empty stomach, 1 hour before meals and at bedtime. Antacids also may be part of the combined antiulcer therapy. However, antacids should not be taken within 30 minutes before or after sucralfate administration.

Drug Interactions Associated with Antacid Drugs

Drugs	Interaction	Response
Allopurinol, anticholinergics, chloroquine, chlorpromazine (phenothiazines), corticosteroids, digoxin, ethambutol, H_2 histamine antagonists, iron, isoniazid, penicillamine, salicylates, tetracyclines, thyroid hormones	Bind with antacids to form insoluble complexes	Decreases the oral absorption of drug
Weak acids		
Pentobarbital, salicylates	Alkaline urine produced by the antacid	Increases the renal excretion of drug (decreases blood drug level)
Weak bases		
Morphine, pseudoephedrine, quinine, quinidine, benzodiazepines	Alkaline urine produced by the antacid (increased toxicity)	Increases renal reabsorption of drugs

Drug Interactions

Concomitant administration of sucralfate has been shown to affect the absorption of digoxin, quinolone, quinidine, ketaconazole, and warfarin, resulting in decreased bioavailability of these drugs. The interaction is believed to be a direct result of sucralfate's binding to the drug, leading to a decrease in absorption from the GI tract. Sucralfate has been reported to reduce the bioavailability of phenytoin. The dose of phenytoin may need to be adjusted to maintain a therapeutic response in patients who are taking sucralfate. Oral administration of any of these drugs should be separated from sucralfate administration by at least 2 hours to avoid drug interaction. Sucralfate may interfere with the absorption of fat-soluble vitamins, possibly resulting in deficiencies with long-term use of the drug. Small amounts of aluminum absorption do occur with sucralfate. Although this is of little clinical significance in most patients, use of sucralfate in patients with chronic renal failure may lead to accumulation of aluminum because of the inability to excrete these ions efficiently. In other patients, the concomitant use of sucralfate and aluminum-containing antacids may result in aluminum accumulation. However, the clinical significance in patients who are not renally compromised is not known.

LO 33.6

MANAGEMENT OF EMESIS

Process of Emesis

Vomiting is a natural defense mechanism that may signal the presence of disease or organ dysfunction, or provide a route for removal of harmful ingested substances. Emesis may be self-induced (bulimia) or involuntary, associated with cold and flu, pregnancy, motion sickness, inner ear infection, or exposure to certain drugs. Induction of vomiting is a well-orchestrated interaction involving two control centers (vomiting center [VC] and chemoreceptor trigger zone [CTZ]) and at least five neurotransmitters such as serotonin, acetylcholine, dopamine, histamine, and substance P and their respective receptors located in the control centers. Among the afferent inputs to the vomiting center is direct information from the vagus (cholinergic) nerve relaying conditions in the gastrointestinal tract (distension), the vestibular system relaying conditions from the inner ear regarding balance and motion, and the CTZ assessing noxious chemicals in the circulation. Information about a harmful environment, ingestion of toxic substances, or accumulation of metabolic toxins triggers the release of these neurotransmitters in the vomiting center and CTZ. This may bring about coordinated contraction of abdominal and respiratory muscles to expel the culprit through the mouth. (See Figure 33.6.)

The VC may be directly triggered by afferent nerves receiving stimulation from visceral distention, increased intracranial pressure, rotation, unequal stimulation of the inner ear (labyrinth), or pain. Even sight, smell, and memory can precipitate activation of the VC. The message is received to reverse peristalsis through stimulation of the salivary glands (increased secretion), the diaphragm, and muscles of the upper GI tract.

Frequently, vomiting is self-limiting and of short duration such as viral-induced symptoms of cold and flu. Even without medication, vomiting will often resolve within 2 to 3 days. Acute and delayed nausea and vomiting are associated with radiation and certain chemotherapy. Acute means they occur within 24 hours after treatment and delayed (or late) occurs more than 24 hours after treatment. Uncontrolled nausea and vomiting can interfere with the patient's ability to receive cancer treatment and care for him/herself at home. Persistent vomiting results in electrolyte, fluid, and acid-base imbalance. Infants and elderly are more susceptible to developing life-threatening electrolyte changes if the vomiting is not controlled. Patients

Figure 33.6   CNS Centers for Nausea and Vomiting

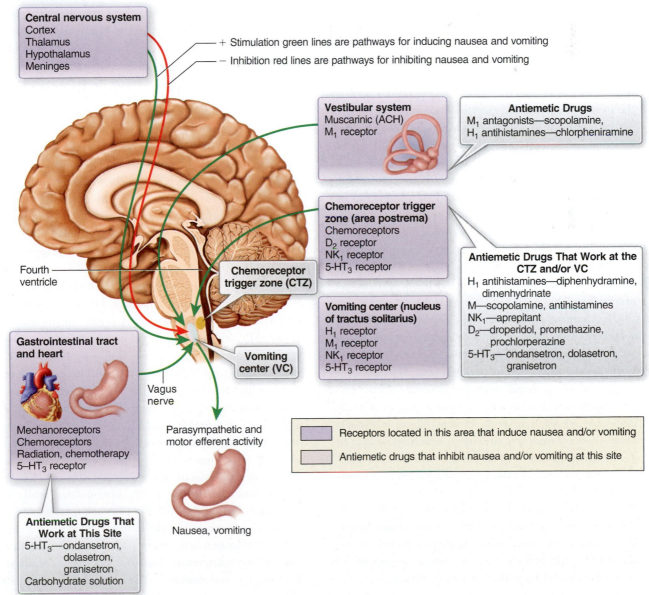

+ Stimulation green lines are pathways for inducing nausea and vomiting
− Inhibition red lines are pathways for inhibiting nausea and vomiting

Central nervous system
Cortex
Thalamus
Hypothalamus
Meninges

Vestibular system
Muscarinic (ACH)
M_1 receptor

Antiemetic Drugs
M_1 antagonists—scopolamine,
H_1 antihistamines—chlorpheniramine

Chemoreceptor trigger zone (area postrema)
Chemoreceptors
D_2 receptor
NK_1 receptor
$5\text{-}HT_3$ receptor

Fourth ventricle

Chemoreceptor trigger zone (CTZ)

Vomiting center (nucleus of tractus solitarius)
H_1 receptor
M_1 receptor
NK_1 receptor
$5\text{-}HT_3$ receptor

Antiemetic Drugs That Work at the CTZ and/or VC
H_1 antihistamines—diphenhydramine, dimenhydrinate
M—scopolamine, antihistamines
NK_1—aprepitant
D_2—droperidol, promethazine, prochlorperazine
$5\text{-}HT_3$—ondansetron, dolasetron, granisetron

Gastrointestinal tract and heart
Mechanoreceptors
Chemoreceptors
Radiation, chemotherapy
$5\text{-}HT_3$ receptor

Vomiting center (VC)

Vagus nerve

Parasympathetic and motor efferent activity

Antiemetic Drugs That Work at This Site
$5\text{-}HT_3$—ondansetron, dolasetron, granisetron
Carbohydrate solution

Nausea, vomiting

Receptors located in this area that induce nausea and/or vomiting

Antiemetic drugs that inhibit nausea and/or vomiting at this site

with advanced cancer may experience chronic nausea and vomiting. Motion sickness is often associated with nausea and vomiting and may require pharmacological intervention because the labyrinthine (inner ear) stimulation may persist well beyond the initial trigger. Other circumstances where vomiting can be detrimental to the patient include the postoperative period where the force of **emesis** could tear sutures or dangerously increase pressure on the organs (eye or cranial surgery).

Emetics

Stimulation of clinical emesis is primarily restricted to removal of noxious substances—that is, drug overdose following oral administration. Gastric lavage has replaced the use of emetics; however, ipecac syrup is still available for home use. Ipecac is a root extract available in pharmacies as an oral solution 1.5 to 2% in alcohol as an antidote for toxic accidental poisoning and in vitamin and herbal shops as a natural remedy. Gastric emptying, when warranted, should occur within the first 2 hours to minimize absorption of the toxic substance. Ipecac syrup given in one or two doses acts on the gastric mucosa locally and on the CTZ centrally to induce vomiting. Oral dosing should be followed by 200 to 300 ml of water. Carbonated beverages should not be given because it may enhance absorption of ipecac. Systemic absorption of ipecac is limited because vomiting removes it from the body as well. Ipecac should not be administered until contact with a trained health professional has been established (for example, emergency service, paramedics, poison control). If vomiting does not occur after 2 doses of 15 to 30 ml (infants 5 ml), the patient should be transported to a proper facility for gastric lavage.

If vomiting does not occur within 30 minutes, absorbed ipecac may produce adverse reactions from diarrhea, hypotension, arrhythmia, and bradycardia to CNS depression. In systemic doses it is cardiotoxic.

Ipecac syrup should never be administered to individuals who are unconscious, semiconscious, or severely inebriated, or who are having seizures. These individuals cannot control muscle contraction, which could lead to aspiration of gastric contents and bronchospasm. Life-threatening pulmonary edema and aspiration pneumonitis can result.

Ipecac is contraindicated when the ingested substance is unknown, caustic (lye), or petroleum based, such as kerosene or gasoline. Regurgitation of caustic substances will damage the esophagus. Vegetable oil delays the absorption of the petroleum substances.

Ipecac syrup is available OTC and by prescription. Unfortunately it is a drug still used by people with bulimia to complete the binge and purge cycle.

Antiemetics: Serotonin 5-HT₃ and NK₁ Receptor Antagonists

Commonly used antiemetics are antihistamines (H_1-antagonists) and phenothiazines that mitigate vomiting by inhibiting receptors such as dopaminergic or cholinergic receptors within the CNS. Drugs that are antidopaminergic such as metoclopramide (*Reglan*) also can inhibit the vomiting reflex. Antihistamines (H_1-antagonists) effective in relieving vomiting also exhibit significant anticholinergic activity and, therefore, affect multiple sites in the CNS. These antihistamines are also effective in relieving the nausea and vomiting associated with motion sickness. The specific mechanism or sites of action have been identified for all these agents used in the clinical management of nausea and vomiting; many are known to act at the CTZ, the VC, or both (see Figure 33:5).

Serotonin (5-HT₃) Antagonists

Serotonin (5-HT₃) antagonists are among the newest drugs that prevent or reduce the nausea and vomiting (NV) produced by highly emetogenic cancer chemotherapy (cisplatin, carboplatin), radiation therapy, and postoperatively. They represent a major development in the treatment of delayed NV. Drugs in this class are granisetron (*Kytril*), ondansetron (*Zofran*), dolasetron (*Anzemet*), and palonosetron (*Aloxi*). These drugs prevent nausea and vomiting by preventing serotonin from initiating afferent signals to the CNS via vagal and spinal sympathetic nerves (see Figure 33.5). Ninety percent of the serotonin is released from enterochromaffin cells in the GI mucosa. The 5-HT₃ antagonists also block serotonin stimulation at the CTZ and VC. There are no major differences in effectiveness with the three first-generation 5-HT₃ receptor antagonists (dolasetron, granisetron, ondansetron) in the treatment of chemotherapy-induced acute nausea and vomiting. The use of both first-generation and second-generation (palonosetron) 5-HT₃ receptor antagonists has not always been optimal. These drugs are more effective when they are given with other medicines, such as dexamethasone and aprepitant (*Emend*). Except for palonosetron, the drugs are administered orally or intravenously (see Table 33:9). They are metabolized in the liver and excreted by the kidney. The drugs are usually well tolerated and adverse effects include diarrhea, constipation, dizziness, headache, fatigue, sleepiness, nervousness, and muscle cramps. Serotonin antagonists

Drugs Used to Relieve Vomiting or Motion Sickness

Drug (*Trade Name*)	Nausea and vomiting	Motion sickness
Antidopaminergic		
Phenothiazines		
Chlorpromazine	10–25 mg every 4–6 hr PO	No
Prochlorperazine (*Compro*)	25 mg BID rectally	No
Promethazine (*Phenergan*)	12.5–25 mg every 4–6 hr PO rectal 25 mg BID initial dose 0.5–1 hr before travel	No No
Other		
Metoclopramide (*Metozolv, Reglan*)	1–2 mg/kg IV 30 min before cancer chemotherapy, repeat every 2 hr for 2 doses, then every 3 hr for 3 doses; 10–20 mg IM near the end of surgery	No
Anticholinergic		
Antihistamines (H$_1$-antagonists)		
Cyclizine (*Bonine for Kids, Marezine***)	50 mg every 4–6 hr PO, initial dose 0.5–1 hr before travel; do not exceed 200 mg daily	Yes
Diphenhydramine (*Benadryl***)	25–50 mg TID, QID PO	Yes
Dimenhydrinate (*Dramamine***)	50–100 mg every 4–6 hr PO; do not exceed 400 mg daily	Yes
Meclizine (*Antivert, Bonine***)	25–50 mg 1 hr before travel; repeat every 24 hr as needed	Yes
Anticholinergics		
Scopolamine (*Transderm-Scop*)	Apply behind the ear 4 hr before effect is required	Yes
Trimethobenzamide (*Tigan*)	250 mg TID, QID PO, rectal	No
Neurokinen antagonist		
Aprepitant (*Emend*) Fosaprepitant (*Emend*)	4-day regimen. 125 mg followed by 80 mg plus dexmethasone and a serotonin antagonist	No
Serotonin antagonists		
Alosetron (*Lotronex*)	1 mg BID PO chemotherapy	No
Dolasetron (*Anzemet*)	100 mg PO an hour before chemotherapy 1.8 mg/kg IV 30 min prior to chemotherapy or 100 mg PO within 2 hr of ending surgery PONV 12.5 mg IV 15 min before end of anesthesia PONV	No
Granisetron (*Kytril*)	10 mcg/kg IV 30 min before chemotherapy or 1 mg over 30 sec before and after anesthesia	No
Granisetron (*Sancuso*) transdermal patch	1 patch 24 to 48 hr before chemotherapy	No
Ondansetron (*Zofran*)	4 mg IV over 2–5 min before and after anesthesia; or 4 mg IM; 24 mg PO 30 min prior to chemotherapy or 8 mg PO BID	No

(Continued)

Drug (*Trade Name*)	Nausea and vomiting	Motion sickness
Palonosetron (*Aloxi*)	0.5 mg PO an hour before chemotherapy 0.25 mg over 30 sec IV 30 min before chemotherapy 0.075 mg IV 30 min prior to anesthesia induction	No
Miscellaneous		
Dronabinol (*C-III Marinol*)	15 mg/m^2 PO 1–3 hr before chemotherapy; then every 2–4 hr after up to 6 doses daily	No
Carbohydrate solution (*Emetrol, Formula EM, Nausea Relief*)** Dextrose, fructose, phosphoric acid	15–30 ml every 15 min for morning sickness up to a maximum of 5 doses; 15 ml for motion sickness	Yes

*For severe nausea and vomiting. **Over-the-counter preparations.*

do not cause spasms or movement problems because they do not affect dopamine, nor are they anticholinergic.

Neurokinin-1 Receptor (NK₁) Antagonists

Aprepitant (*Emend*) is the first drug in the class of NK$_1$-receptor antagonists. Endogenous substance P is an important neuropeptide in neural transmission that binds and activates NK$_1$-receptors. Substance P is associated with afferent nerves that respond to painful stimuli as well as regulation of mood and vomiting. Substance P and its receptors are found in high concentrations in the brainstem along with other neurotransmitters such as dopamine, serotonin, and opioids. No matter what the emetic stimulus is, substance P and its NK$_1$-receptors are the final pathway that regulates vomiting. Aprepitant is a selective high-affinity antagonist for the NK$_1$-receptor that blocks the activity of substance P. It has no affinity for serotonin or dopamine receptors. It is available as an oral formulation and intravenous solution, fosaprepitant (*Emend*). It is metabolized primarily by hepatic enzymes CYP3A4. Aprepitant is a CYP2C9 inducer and has been shown to induce the metabolism of warfarin and tolbutamide, resulting in lower plasma levels. It is a moderate inhibitor of CYP3A4 and can increase plasma concentration of dexamethasone, methylprednisolone, midazolam, alprazolam, triazolam, and paclitaxel because these drugs are metabolized through CYP3A4. Aprepitant or fosaprepitant is combined with dexmethasone and a serotonin HT$_3$-receptor antagonist over a 4-day treatment schedule. Ondansetron, granisetron, or palonosetron is the standard choice of serotonin antagonist.

One effective antiemetic that does not work through specific receptors is carbohydrate solution. This product stands out in this class because it produces its effect directly on the stomach. Phosphorated carbohydrate solution (*Emetrol, Nausea Relief*) is a combination of sugars (fructose, dextrose) and phosphoric acid. Because it is a hyperosmolar solution, it delays gastric emptying, and acts on the wall of the GI tract to reduce smooth muscle contraction. It is safe for use during pregnancy, especially for morning sickness during the first trimester. It is also used in infants and children.

Dronabinol is another noteworthy drug. Dronabinol (*Marinol*), the principal psychoactive substance in *Cannabis sativa,* is indicated for the treatment of nausea and vomiting associated with cancer chemotherapy. Most often dronabinol is only used after conventional antiemetics have failed.

Adverse Effects and Contraindications

For the most part, the adverse effects of the phenothiazines, antihistamines, and serotonin antagonists are extensions of their therapeutic activity. The spectrum of adverse effects presented in previous chapters includes dry mouth, sedation, drowsiness, diarrhea, and blurred vision. The phenothiazines, metoclopramide (*Reglan*), and ondansetron (*Zofran*) have the potential to produce extrapyramidal reactions at antiemetic doses. Diphenidol (*Vontrol*) has anticholinergic activity and has produced hallucinations, disorientaton, or confusion in patients. It is recommended that this drug be used only in a supervised setting; for example, in a hospital.

Dronabinol, although used in patients who have not responded to other therapy, is considered highly abusable, and thus is designated a Schedule C-III drug. Mood changes (euphoria, confusion, depression, dizziness) can develop especially in elderly patients, and irritability, insomnia, and restlessness characteristic of withdrawal syndrome have occurred. Dronabinol may cause an increase in central sympathethic activity and therefore should be used with caution in patients who are hypertensive, manic, or schizophrenic.

Contraindications to the use of these drugs, except for phosphorated carbohydrate, include hypersensitivity or pregnancy. Safety for use in pregnancy has not been established in humans.

Phosphorated carbohydrates should be used with caution in diabetic patients, and should be avoided in patients with a family history of fructose intolerance. Otherwise, the most common adverse effects associated with this product are abdominal pain and diarrhea. These effects are dose related and a direct result of hyperosmotic fluid in the intestine.

Clinical Indications

The drugs in this class provide symptomatic relief ranging from morning sickness in pregnancy to severe nausea and vomiting of cancer chemotherapy. Promethazine is used as preanesthetic medication to prevent nausea and vomiting. Chlorpromazine also inhibits intractable hiccoughs within the antiemetic dose range. Metoclopramide (*Reglan*), ondansetron (*Zofran*), and granisetron (*Kytril*) are specifically used as prophylaxis and treatment in cancer chemotherapy. When given prior to chemotherapy, vomiting can be reduced or prevented so that the patient is able to complete chemotherapy without discomfort or interruption. This predisposes the patient to be compliant with subsequent chemotherapy sessions—that is, to complete the full protocol. Ondansetron (*Zofran*) and granisetron (*Kytril*) also are used for prevention of vomiting postoperatively and with radiotherapy; however, they are not recommended for use where the incidence of emesis is expected to be low. Dronabinol (*Marinol*), a derivative of tetrahydrocannabinol, is an alternative antiemetic when other conventional drugs have proven unsuccessful in cancer chemotherapy.

Severe vomiting should not be treated with antiemetics alone. Because fluids and electrolytes will be affected by severe, protracted vomiting, fluid and electrolyte replacement are essential to stabilizing the patient. The recommended doses for the antiemetic drugs are presented in Table 33:9. Cyclizine (*Marezine*), meclizine (*Antivert*), and diphenhydramine (*Benadryl*) are available in therapeutic doses OTC and by prescription, while phosphorated carbohydrate solution (*Emetrol*) is only OTC.

Patient Administration and Monitoring

Drugs effective in the relief of symptoms associated with acute or recurrent heartburn, nausea, esophagitis, or GI ulcers are often used by patients between physician visits. It is not uncommon for individuals to delay proper evaluation because they fear the worst diagnosis (for example, ulcer and/or need for a change in diet). Since many of these medications are available OTC, patients self-medicate rather than return for periodic reevaluation when symptoms return. With the increasing availability of drugs in this class, especially in the wide variety of formulations (tablet, liquid, suspension, suppository), and the likelihood that concurrent medications can cancel therapeutic effects, it is important that patients receive instructions on proper drug administration.

Rules for Antiulcer Medication

While the drugs in this class are extremely effective, there are two rules essential for successful therapy and patient safety. Rule number one: If symptoms persist, especially when medication has been taken for 1 to 2 weeks, notify the physician for further evaluation. Rule number two: If signs of bleeding occur such as black or tarry stools, or dark material appears in vomited fluids ("coffee grounds"), notify the physician immediately. Adequate evaluation includes changing medication until the appropriate efficacy is attained. Bleeding may herald the recurrence or onset of mucosal damage, which can lead to life-threatening hemorrhage.

Patient Instruction on Formulation

Product formulation should be explained to patients so that active drug is released at the appropriate time and in the designated amount to effectively relieve symptoms.

Chewable tablets should be chewed before swallowing, and followed with a full glass of water. These tablets are not designed to be swallowed whole and the delay in tablet dissolution will reduce or eliminate their effectiveness. Tablets not designated as chewable and capsules should not be chewed when taking medication with meals. Omeprazole, including the OTC formulations *Prilosec OTC* and *Zegerid OTC*, must be swallowed whole, not chewed, crushed, or opened, at least 1 hour before meals. OTC omeprazole is to be taken only once a day with a full glass of water for 14 days. It may take 4 days before a full response is evident. If a dose is missed, the patient should be instructed to take the dose as soon as possible but not to take 2 doses together or 2 doses within 24 hrs. Lansoprazole capsules can be opened and contents put onto applesauce for patients having difficulty taking the medication.

Sustained-release preparations should not be crushed or chewed. This formulation releases drug over a specific period of time to maintain therapeutic blood levels of drug.

(Continued)

Effervescent tablets should dissolve completely before swallowing. Bubbling should have stopped before swallowing.

Hyperosmolar solutions used for nausea and vomiting should not be diluted before dosing. The product exerts its effect through the concentrated sugars. Dilution removes the product's ability to produce a response.

Transdermal patch formulations should be placed on an area of skin that is not covered with hair, sores, or cuts. For scopolamine, the patch is placed directly behind the ear. Patients must be instructed to wash hands thoroughly with soap after handling the patch. Drug that may have transferred to the hands could cause temporary dilation of the pupils or blurred vision if scopolamine comes in contact with the eyes (rubbing).

Antacid Interactions

Patients who are expected to use antacids concurrent with other GI medication should receive clear instructions on the antiulcer dosing regimen to avoid drug incompatibility. Where medications may be prescribed by other physicians (for example, gynecologist, ophthalmologist), patients should be reminded not to take antacids until they have checked with the prescribing physicians for potential interaction or incompatibility.

H_2-antagonists, especially cimetidine and ranitidine, should not be taken with antacids. Dosing should be staggered by at least 1 hour.

Sucralfate should be taken on an empty stomach 1 hour before meals. Antacids should be used 2 hours before or 2 hours after sucralfate.

Magnesium-containing antacids may act as a laxative when taken in large doses, resulting in diarrhea. Aluminum- and calcium-containing antacids may cause constipation.

H. pylori Therapy

All of the combination regimens for *H. pylori* require the patient to drink large amounts of fluid during the treatment. This not only keeps the drugs adequately circulating through the system; it minimizes the potential for irritation of the lower esophagus, especially from the tetracycline component.

When tetracyclines are part of the combination therapy for eradication of *H. pylori* in women, the patient must be asked whether she uses oral contraceptives. Tetracyclines used concomitantly with oral contraceptives reduce the effectiveness of the contraceptive. Patients should be advised to use another form of contraception during the antibiotic therapy.

If metronidazole is part of the antibiotic regimen (*Helidac*), the patient must be instructed to avoid alcohol during therapy. This includes OTC alcohol-containing products. Metronidazole will produce an *Antabuse* (disulfuram) type of reaction—that is, nausea and vomiting—by interfering with alcohol metabolism.

Bismuth salts produce a unique cosmetic effect. It will darken the tongue during treatment. The effect is temporary and does not harm the patient.

Antacids *can be used* while taking lansoprazole.

Common Adverse Effects

Antiemetic drugs may produce drowsiness and sedation, and impair judgment.

Patients should receive instruction to use caution when driving, operating equipment, or performing tasks that require coordination and dexterity.

Patients should be instructed to avoid alcohol or CNS depressants since the antiemetic may enhance sedation, mental confusion, and depression.

Use in Pregnancy

All of the drugs used in the treatment of ulcers or GERD are designated Food and Drug Administration (FDA) Pregnancy Category B or C except for **misoprostol,** which is designated **Category X.** There are no specific studies that have established the safety of these drugs for use during pregnancy. The long-standing availability and use of antacids suggest that there are no deleterious effects to the fetus with short-term therapy. The recommendation during pregnancy is that these drugs be used only when clearly needed.

Misoprostol is designated pregnancy Category X because it causes miscarriage and potentially dangerous bleeding. This drug should never be taken during pregnancy. Female patients should be advised to avoid becoming pregnant while receiving misoprostol. If the patient becomes pregnant, the physician should be notified immediately.

Except for phosphorated carbohydrate solution, antiemetic drugs are not recommended for use in pregnancy. Safety for use in pregnancy has not been established in humans.

Patients who become pregnant while receiving combination *H. pylori* therapy should notify the physician immediately.

Chapter Review

Understanding Terminology

Match the definition or description in the left column with the appropriate term in the right column.

___ 1. A substance that inhibits secretion of digestive enzymes, hormones, or acid. **(LO 33.1)**

___ 2. A substance that causes abortion. **(LO 33.3)**

___ 3. An open sore in the mucous membranes or mucosal linings. **(LO 33.2)**

___ 4. A back splash of gastric juice into the esophagus. **(LO 33.4)**

___ 5. A drug that neutralizes gastric acid. **(LO 33.3)**

___ 6. A cell that produces hydrochloric acid in the gastric mucosa. **(LO 33.1)**

___ 7. An opening in a hollow organ, such as a break in the intestinal wall. **(LO 33.2)**

___ 8. An abnormally high amount of acid secretion. **(LO 33.2)**

___ 9. An action that causes the decomposition of proteins. **(LO 33.1)**

___ 10. A drug that decreases hypermotility. **(LO 33.5)**

___ 11. Another term for vomiting. **(LO 33.6)**

a. abortifacient
b. antacid
c. antisecretory
d. emesis
e. hyperacidity
f. antispasmotic
g. parietal
h. perforation
i. proteolytic
j. reflux
k. ulcer

Acquiring Knowledge

Answer the following questions.

1. What factors contribute to ulcer production? **(LO 33.2)**
2. What stimulates gastric secretion of digestive enzymes and acid? **(LO 33.1)**
3. How does the mechanism of action of an antisecretory drug differ from that of an antacid? **(LO 33.3, 33.5)**
4. How do the H_2-receptor antagonists differ from other antiulcer drugs? **(LO 33.3, 33.5)**
5. How do the H_2-receptor antagonists differ from each other? **(LO 33.3)**
6. What would predictably occur from the administration of prostaglandins to a pregnant woman? **(LO 33.3)**
7. How does the mechanism of action of proton pump inhibitors differ from that of antacids and sucralfate? **(LO 33.3)**
8. How do anticholinergic and antispasmodic drugs affect gastric secretions? **(LO 33.5)**
9. Are all antispasmodic drugs also anticholinergic? **(LO 33.5)**
10. How do systemic antacids differ from nonsystemic antacids? **(LO 33.3)**
11. Can antacids be used in conjunction with antisecretory drugs in the treatment of ulcers? **(LO 33.3, 33.5)**

Applying Knowledge on the Job

Use your critical-thinking skills to answer the following questions.

1. Assume that you work for an internist who treats numerous ulcer patients, many of whom are prescribed *Tagamet* or *Zantac*. For the following patients, decide whether *Tagamet* or *Zantac* is right for them.
   a. Patient A is taking *Toprol* for hypertension. **(LO 33.3)**
   b. Patient B is taking *Coumadin* for thrombosis. **(LO 33.3)**
   c. Patient C is taking *Valium* for anxiety. **(LO 33.3)**
   d. Patient D is taking *Donnatal* for epilepsy. **(LO 33.3)**

2. Jeri works in a hospital pharmacy, where she's responsible for checking patient charts to spot potential drug interaction problems. Yesterday, she checked the following four adult ulcer patients for whom antacids were recommended. In each case, the patient was taking another drug that could affect the bioavailability of the antacid. For each patient, decide whether the antacid dose should be increased or decreased because of the drug interaction.

    a. Patient A is taking quinidine for heart arrhythmias. **(LO 33.3)**

    b. Patient B is taking penicillin for gingivitis. **(LO 33.3)**

    c. Patient C is taking *Trinalin* for allergic rhinitis. **(LO 33.3)**

    d. Patient D is taking *INH* for tuberculosis. **(LO 33.3)**

3. A 25-year-old female patient has been taking NSAIDs on a regular basis for a chronic inflammatory disease of the joints. Her physician has decided to initiate *Cytotec* therapy. What should this patient be advised regarding pregnancy? Why? **(LO 33.3)**

4. A woman calls inquiring about syrup of ipecac. She was told by a friend that every house that has children in it should have syrup of ipecac. What should she be told regarding the administration? **(LO 33.6)**

Multiple Choice

Use your critical-thinking skills to answer the following questions.

1. Which of the three phases of gastric acid secretion is stimulated by the distention of the stomach? **(LO 33.1)**

    A. cephalic

    B. colonic

    C. gastric

    D. intestinal

2. What is the most common etiology of peptic ulcer disease? **(LO 33.2)**

    A. alcohol

    B. GERD (gastroesophageal reflux disease)

    C. NSAIDs (nonsteroidal antiinflammatory drugs)

    D. Helicobacter pylori

3. Which of the following drugs blocks the release of HCl from the parietal gland? **(LO 33.3)**

    A. antacids

    B. H_2-receptor antagonists

    C. proton pump inhibitors

    D. sucralfate

4. A patient is newly diagnosed with GERD. Which of the following medications would you prescribe? **(LO 33.4)**

    A. barbiturates

    B. H_2-receptor antagonists

    C. metoclopramide

    D. Scopalamine

5. Which of the following classes of drugs is useful in the clinical management of GI hypermotility? **(LO 33.5)**

    A. antispasmatic

    B. antacids

    C. sucralfate

    D. misoprostol

6. A patient presents with severe nausea and vomiting after his cisplatin chemotherapy this morning. Which of the following drugs would you prescribe to reduce nausea and vomiting? **(LO 33.6)**
   A. ipecac
   B. serotonin (5-HT$_3$) antagonists
   C. proton pump inhibitors
   D. antisecretory drugs

Multiple Choice (Multiple Answer)

Select the correct choices for each statement. The choices may be all correct, all incorrect, or any combination.

1. Which of the following are not phases of gastric secretion? **(LO 33.1)**
   A. parietal
   B. gastric
   C. intestinal
   D. cephalic

2. The causes of peptic ulcers include **(LO 33.2)**
   A. not enough mucosal lining in the stomach
   B. too much acid production
   C. regurgitation of stomach acids
   D. being genetically predisposed

3. The primary therapeutic goal in treatment of GERD is to **(LO 33.2, 33.5)**
   A. increase mucosal production
   B. suppress acid production
   C. prevent erosion of esophagus
   D. relieve symptoms

4. Select all of the mechanisms of action for 5-HT$_3$ antagonists. **(LO 33.6)**
   A. prevent intestinal stimulation of emesis
   B. prevent serotonin from stimulating the CNS
   C. block stimulation at CTZ and VC
   D. increase secretions from ECL cells

5. Anticholinergic drugs are used to treat which ailments of the GI tract? **(LO 33.4)**
   A. GI hypermotility
   B. irritable bowel syndrome
   C. peptic ulcers
   D. neurogenic colon

Sequencing

Place the following in order of the process that happens last to the one that happens first. **(LO 33.1)**

_____   _____   _____   _____

Last   **First**

partial digestion of proteins

HCl decreases pH

chyme enters duodenum

activation of pepsin

Classification

Place the following medications under their correct mechanism of action. **(LO 33.3)**

Protonix	Pepcid	Riopan
Tagamet	Nexium	Prevacid
Di-Gel	Prilosec	Maalox
Gaviscon	Axid	Zantac

Block H$_2$ receptors	Increase gastric pH	Inhibit exchange of H$^+$ ions

Documentation

Using the prescription below, answer the following questions **(LO 33.4, 33.6)**

Liberty Clinic
Practice RX

12345 Main Avenue
Anytown, USA 12345
931-555-1000

NAME: Gary McDowel _____ DATE: _____

ADDRESS: _____

RX   Anzemet 100mg

Sig: Take one tablet by mouth prior to procedure

Dr. Bryan Misson _____ M.D. _____ M.D.

   Substitution Permitted   Dispense as written

DEA #: _____   REFILL: NR 1 2 3 4

---

a. What is this patient most likely suffering from?
b. What class of medication has been prescribed?
c. What adverse effects could this drug cause?
d. What other classes of drugs could be used to treat this patient's symptoms?

For interactive animations, videos, and assessment, visit:
www.mcgrawhillconnect.com

Chapter 34

Agents That Affect Intestinal Motility

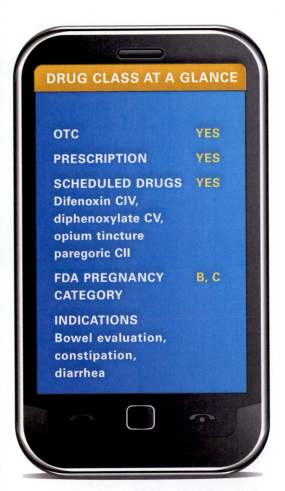

DRUG CLASS AT A GLANCE

OTC	YES
PRESCRIPTION	YES
SCHEDULED DRUGS	YES
Difenoxin CIV, diphenoxylate CV, opium tincture paregoric CII	
FDA PREGNANCY CATEGORY	B, C
INDICATIONS Bowel evaluation, constipation, diarrhea	

KEY TERMS

adsorbent: substance that has the ability to attach other substances to its surface.

cathartic: pharmacological substance that stimulates defecation.

chloride channel activators: a novel class of drugs that stimulate pore-forming receptors in the intestine, causing chloride ions to cross membranes.

constipation: a decrease in stool frequency.

defecation: process of discharging the contents of the intestines, as feces.

diarrhea: abnormal looseness of the stool or watery stool, which may be accompanied by a change in stool frequency or volume.

electrolyte: ion in solution, such as sodium, potassium, or chloride, that is capable of mediating conduction (passing impulses in the tissues).

emollient: substance that is soothing to mucous membranes or skin.

evacuation: process of removal of waste material from the bowel.

hernia: protrusion of an organ through the tissue usually containing it; for example, intestinal tissue pushing outside the abdominal cavity, or stomach pushing into the diaphragm (hiatal hernia).

hypokalemia: decrease in the normal concentration of potassium in the blood.

hyponatremia: decrease in the normal concentration of sodium in the blood.

IBS (irritable bowel syndrome): a functional disorder of the colon with abdominal pain, cramping, bloating, diarrhea, and/or constipation.

laxative: a substance that promotes bowel movements.

mu-opioid receptor antagonist: drugs that block the mu protein receptor for opioids.

osmolality: the concentration of particles dissolved in a fluid.

osmosis: process in which water moves across membranes following the movement of sodium ions.

peristalsis: movement characteristic of the intestines, in which circular contraction and relaxation propel the contents toward the rectum.

transit time: amount of time it takes for food to travel from the mouth to the anus.

After studying this chapter, you should be able to

34.1 describe the process of defecation.

34.2 describe the primary causes of diarrhea.

34.3 identify the consequences of acute and chronic diarrhea.

34.4 explain the mechanisms of action for the drug classes used to treat diarrhea.

34.5 describe the primary causes of constipation.

34.6 explain the mechanisms of action for the drug classes used to treat constipation.

Introduction

The function of the colon is to absorb nutrients and water. Bacteria in the colon digest carbohydrates and proteins by fermentation and produce a significant amount of vitamin K. Approximately 90 percent of the fluid entering the colon is absorbed, producing a semisolid mass (feces). Rhythmic contractions known as **peristalsis** move the intestinal contents through the bowel. See Figure 34.1. In the colon or large bowel, water is absorbed from digested material passing through. Eventually, the digested material that cannot be absorbed further is compacted into a fecal mass.

Figure 34.1 **Formation of Feces**

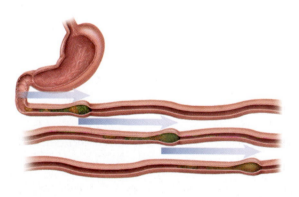

(a) Peristalsis

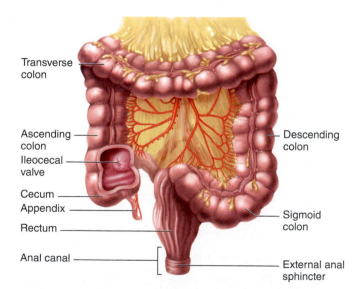

Transverse colon

Ascending colon

Ileocecal valve

Cecum

Appendix

Rectum

Anal canal

Descending colon

Sigmoid colon

External anal sphincter

(b) Gross anatomy of the large intestine (cecum, colon, rectum)

(a) Contractions of the small intestine (peristalsis) move material (digested food, chyme) toward the colon.
(b) The large intestine removes water and minerals from the residual waste product and compresses the waste into a smaller mass (feces) for excretion through the rectum (defecation).

BOWEL FUNCTION

The movement of feces into the empty rectum increases rectal pressure, triggering the defecation reflex, which is under parasympathetic control. The internal anal sphincter relaxes and peristalsis propels the feces into the anus. If the individual determines **defecation** is appropriate (voluntary control), the external anal sphincter relaxes and the feces are expelled. See Figure 34.2. In order to initiate defecation, individuals can voluntarily increase abdominal pressure (straining) to force contraction and **evacuation** (removal of waste matter) of the bowel; however, the bowels are very sensitive to emotional stress or changes in the nervous system. Defecation can be enhanced or inhibited by stimulating the divisions of the autonomic nervous system. Stimulation of the parasympathetic fibers (cholinergic) that innervate the intestines increases intestinal motility, whereas stimulation of the sympathetic fibers (adrenergic) decreases motility.

Occasionally, intestinal motility is drastically altered, so that normal bowel function is impaired. Increased bowel motility may cause the fecal mass to move rapidly through the intestines (decreased **transit time**) and into the rectum. This increased activity does not permit adequate time for colonic water absorption to occur. As a result, frequent defecation of a watery stool (diarrhea) occurs. In contrast, decreased intestinal motility permits the fecal mass to remain in the colon (increased transit time) so that excess water is absorbed. Often, the stool is firmer and more difficult to expel, and defecation is less frequent. This abnormality in bowel function is characteristic of constipation.

ANTIDIARRHEALS

Diarrhea is a symptom of increased intestinal activity. Acute diarrhea is associated with the production of loose stools in otherwise healthy individuals that lasts less than 14 days. Diarrhea that lasts more than 30 days is defined as chronic, and is accompanied by weight loss, muscle weakness, and **electrolyte** imbalance. As diarrhea continues over a long time, large quantities of water, sodium, potassium, and chloride are lost or excreted in the fluid stool. This loss results in dehydration and electrolyte imbalance. Although chronic diarrhea occurs more readily in children, any individuals in poor health or with poor nutrition, especially the elderly, may develop serious effects from chronic diarrhea.

Figure 34.2

Nerve (Voluntary and Involuntary) Control of Defecation

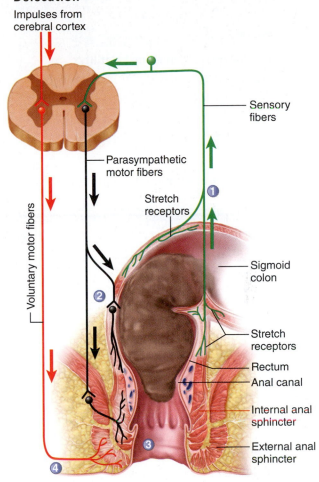

1. Feces stretch the rectum and stimulate stretch receptors, which transmit signals to the spinal cord.

2. A spinal reflex stimulates contraction of the rectum.

3. The spinal reflex also relaxes the internal anal sphincter.

4. Impulses from the brain prevent untimely defecation by keeping the external anal sphincter contracted. Defecation occurs only if this sphincter also relaxes.

Causes of Diarrhea

Diarrheas are classified according to the mechanisms involved: increased motility, secretory, inflammatory or exudative, and osmotic. Increased intestinal motility may be produced by several mechanisms (see Table 34:1). Accurate diagnosis of the underlying cause of diarrhea determines the proper drug therapy to ease the symptoms of diarrhea. For example, microorganisms (bacteria, viruses, or amoebae) may invade the gastrointestinal (GI) tissue, causing local inflammation and irritation. The bowel reacts by increasing its motility in

Factors That Promote Increased Intestinal Activity Resulting in Diarrhea

Contributing factors		Treatment of choice
Agents that increase intestinal motility		
a. Acute GI infections		
Bacteria	Found in contaminated food	Antibiotics appropriate to the microorganism
Salmonella		
Shigella		
Escherichia coli		
Viruses		
Cytomegalovirus	Immunocompromised patients	Antiviral therapy (ganciclovir)
Herpes simplex virus, viral hepatitis		Antiviral drugs (valacyclovir)
Rotavirus (children), norovirus	Stomach flu	Alcohol- and chlorine-based disinfectants
Protozoa		
Entamoeba histolytica	"Traveler's diarrhea" found in contaminated water	Antibiotics
Giardia lamblia		Rifaximin (*Xifaxan*)
b. Drugs		Reduce or discontinue drug use
Antacids		
Antiarrhythmic and blood pressure medications		
Antibiotics		
Chemotherapy medications		
Colchicine		
Nonsteroidal antiinflammatory drugs (NSAID)		
Laxatives		
c. Bile salts malabsorption		Cholestyramine resin (*Questran*)
Increased intestinal motility arising from other medical problems		
a. Chronic gastroenteritis resulting from		Antidiarrheal drugs
Anemia		Loperamide (*Imodium*)
Carcinoma		
Diabetes		
Neuropathies		
b. Colitis, irritable colon resulting from		Antidiarrheal drugs
Emotional stress		Loperamide (*Imodium*)
Colon disorders (IBS, Crohn's disease)		
Increased osmolality within the intestine		
Lactose		Reduce or discontinue use
Sorbitol (artificial sweetener)		
Magnesium-containing antacids		

order to evacuate the noxious organisms. Diarrhea arising from infection may be cured by administering the proper antibiotic or antiviral drug. Fluid and electrolyte supplements may be given (PO or IV) to correct any imbalances that develop during chronic infection.

Certain drug therapy also may produce diarrhea as a side effect. Different drugs produce diarrhea via a different mechanism (increased motility, secretory, exudative,

and/or osmosis). Lactose intolerance produces an osmotic diarrhea, in which lactose particles pull water into the bowel to dilute the concentration of lactose. A high dietary intake of sorbitol (bulk sweetener in sugar-free products) also produces osmotic diarrhea. Drugs that stimulate the parasympathetic nervous system, inhibit the sympathetic nervous system, irritate the bowel directly, or disrupt the normal intestinal bacteria (broad-spectrum antibiotics) will produce diarrhea. Treatment of diarrhea in these cases is accomplished by reducing the dose of the specific drug or stopping the drug completely.

Treatment of Simple Diarrhea

Simple functional diarrhea is most frequently associated with poor dietary habits and emotional stress. The underlying cause of the increased intestinal motility may be difficult or impossible to determine. Therefore, treatment of mild diarrhea is usually symptomatic rather than curative. Drugs useful in the treatment of nonspecific diarrhea include adsorbents, anticholinergics, and an opioid derivative (see Table 34:2). These antidiarrheal drugs either decrease intestinal motility (anticholinergics and opioids) or remove the intestinal irritant (**adsorbents,** antibiotics).

Adsorbents

Kaolin with pectin (*Kapectolin*), attapulgite (*Diasorb, K-Pec*), and bismuth salts (*Pepto-Bismol*) act within the intestine. These drugs are taken orally as tablets or liquid suspension. The drugs do not act on specific receptors and are not intended to be absorbed into the circulation to work. In the lumen of the intestine, adsorbents form a complex (bind up) with irritating substances such as bacteria, digestive enzymes, or toxins, and carry them into the feces. Because of their mechanism of action, adsorbents also complex with vitamins, minerals, and other drugs, thereby impairing systemic absorption of these substances. Hence, adsorbents usually should not be administered with meals or other medications. Separate their administration from other oral medications by

[**Table 34:2**]

Drugs Used in the Clinical Management of Diarrhea

Active components (*Trade Names*)	Schedule	Adult oral dose
Adsorbents		
Attapulgite (*Diasorb, Kaopectate Maximum Strength*)	OTC	2 tablets after each bowel movement up to 6 doses/day or 20 ml up to 3 doses/day
Bismuth subsalicylate (*Pepto-Bismol, Bismatrol, Pepto-Bismol Maximum Strength*)	OTC	2 tablets or 30 ml every 30 min to 1 hr up to 8 doses in 24 hr
Kaolin with pectin (*Kapectolin, Kaodene nonnarcotic*)	OTC	60–120 ml after each bowel movement up to 6 doses/day
Antibiotics		
Rifaximin (*Xifaxan*)	Prescription	One 200-mg tablet 3 times/day for 3 days
Opioid derivatives		
Difenoxin and atropine (*Motofen*)	CIV	2 tablets, then 1 every 3 to 4 hr not to exceed 8 tablets in 24 hr
Diphenoxylate and atropine (*Logen, Lomotil, Lonox*)	CV	5 mg up to QID
Loperamide (*Imodium A-D, K-peck II*)	OTC and prescription	4 mg up to 8 mg/day
Opiates		
Paregoric (*Opium Tincture*)*	CII	5 to 16 drops of liquid mixed in water up to four times a day
Serotonin (5-HT$_3$) antagonists		
Alosetron (*Lotronex*)	Prescription	0.5–1 mg BID

Still available although largely replaced by other medications.

2 to 3 hours. Dosing follows each loose bowel movement usually up to a maximum of 6 to 8 doses per day depending on the product. The suspension product must be shaken well to ensure the active agents are evenly dispersed in every dose. In general, these drugs are well tolerated although stomach upset may occur.

Traveler's diarrhea is the most common illness affecting travelers who have been outside the United States. The onset usually occurs within the first week of travel but may occur even after returning home. Adsorbents like *Pepto-Bismol* are routinely recommended during travel to areas known for their endemic contaminated water sources or inadequate food washing procedures. The adsorbent taken prophylactically (2 tablets or 2 oz. four times a day) lines the intestine to impair microbial transmission and may complex with the organisms, facilitating their removal in the feces. Antibiotics are also the drugs of choice in the treatment of traveler's diarrhea. Rifaximin (*Xifaxan*) is an antibiotic used in the treatment of "traveler's diarrhea," caused by the bacteria *E. coli.* Rifaximin prevents bacteria from growing in the intestinal tract. The recommended oral dose for an adult is 200 mg taken three times a day for three days. It is not used in invasive infection such as *Shigella* or in the

Note to the Health Care Professional

Antidiarrheals should not be used for more than a few days. These drugs should be kept out of the reach of children. Infants and children under the age of 5 are very sensitive to the action of these drugs, particularly the anticholinergic effects. Chronic misuse of these drugs can produce serious alterations in bowel function.

treatment of bloody diarrhea associated with protozoal infections.

Antimotility Drugs

Several drugs useful in the treatment of diarrhea interact with specific receptors, such as cholinergic, serotonergic, or opioid receptors. Anticholinergic drugs inhibit the postganglionic receptors of parasympathetic nerves that control intestinal motility. Figure 34.3 shows the innervation of the myenteric plexus in the large intestine.

Figure 34.3 **Parasympathetic and Sympathetic Innervation of the Large Intestine (Myenteric Plexus)**
The Autonomic Nervous System

Parasympathetic Division

Sympathetic Division

Preganglionic fiber of vagus nerve

Postganglionic fiber

Preganglionic fibers of pelvic splanchnic nerves

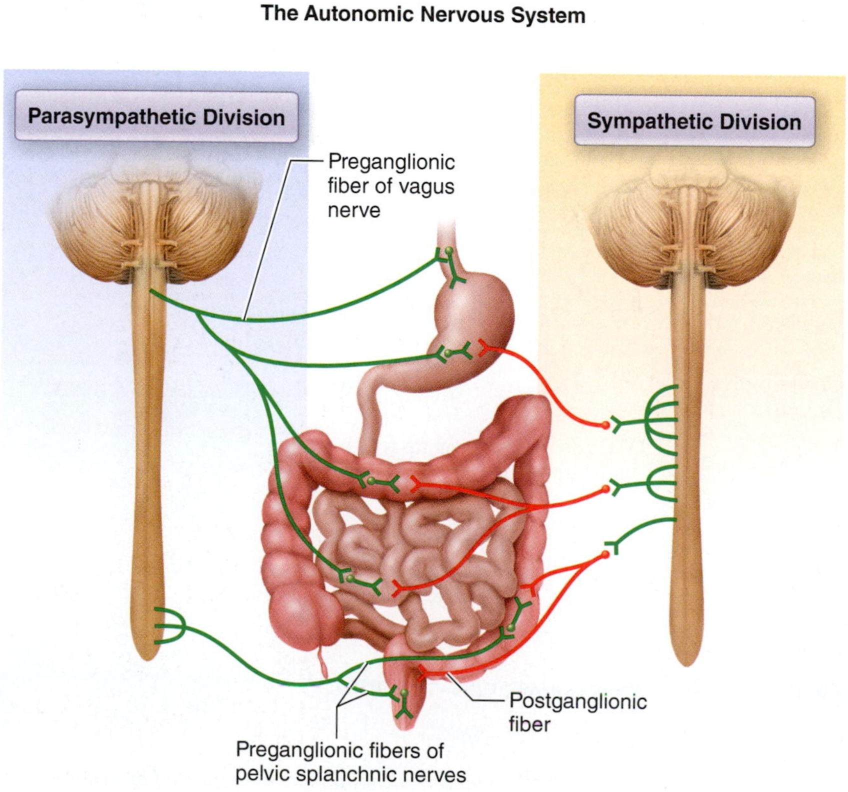

This network of parasympathetic and sympathetic nerves controls motor activity in the muscle and secretomotor activity in the intestinal mucosa. Atropine is an anticholinergic drug that is usually found in combination with an opioid, either diphenoxylate (*Logen, Lomotil, Lonox*) or difenoxen (*Motofen*). Although available as separate products, the active agent in both preparations is difenoxen because diphenoxylate is rapidly metabolized in humans to difenoxen. Difenoxen is a mu receptor agonist that stimulates mu receptors in the myenteric plexus to decrease peristalsis and constrict sphincters. It also has a direct effect on circular smooth muscle of the bowel that prolongs gastrointestinal transit time. Diphenoxylate and difenoxen are chemically related to meperidine (*Demerol*). At therapeutic doses (up to 20 mg/day), the active opioid can produce weak opiate effects, including euphoria. Other opioid-like activity (nausea, vomiting, and hypotension) is seen with larger doses (40 to 60 mg). Long-term use should be avoided so there is no opportunity for dependency to develop; however, the addition of atropine reduces the possibility of drug abuse and dependence.

Diphenoxylate-atropine is a Schedule V drug. Difenoxin-atropine is Schedule IV because it is more potent than its parent.

Loperamide is not a controlled substance and is available OTC and by prescription. The recommended oral dose of loperamide is 4 mg, not to exceed 16 mg per day as a tablet or liquid. This drug is used for nonspecific (noninfection) diarrhea, and acute and chronic diarrhea of **IBS (irritable bowel syndrome).** Loperamide has been used in combination with trimethoprim and sulfamethoxazole to facilitate rapid relief of traveler's diarrhea.

Selective 5-hydroxytryptamine$_3$ (5-HT$_3$) serotonin receptor antagonists are primarily used in the treatment of chemotherapy-induced vomiting. Since more than 90 percent of endogenous serotonin is in the intestines, as are 5-HT$_3$ receptors, some of these drugs have been used in the clinical management of diarrhea-predominant IBS. Alosetron (*Lotronex*) is approved for use in women with IBS who have not responded to conventional therapy. Ondansetron (*Zofran*) and granisetron (*Kytril*), at higher than the standard antiemetic doses, have demonstrated improvement in several diarrhea-predominant IBS symptoms. The effects noted were improved stool consistency and fewer episodes of pain, as well as decreases in bowel frequency.

Cautions and Contraindications

Most of the antidiarrheals are relatively nontoxic to organs other than the intestines because they are not absorbed into the general circulation. The most frequent side effect produced by antidiarrheal drugs is constipation. Since diphenoxylate is absorbed, it may produce rashes, dizziness, blurred vision, and nausea. The diphenoxylate that is absorbed is extensively metabolized by the liver to an active substance, diphenoxylic acid (difenoxine). Ultimately, the metabolite is excreted into the urine. This drug should not be administered to patients with liver disease or severe colitis. Toxic doses of diphenoxylate could produce respiratory depression and coma similar to opiate overdose.

Over-the-counter (OTC) preparations containing anticholinergics should not be used by patients who have glaucoma. Anticholinergic drugs may increase intraocular pressure by reducing anterior chamber drainage in patients with glaucoma. Otherwise, the amount of anticholinergic drug is small enough to avoid the likelihood of the adverse effects usually associated with these drugs in adults.

There is a special cautionary warning with the use of alosetron, the serotonin antagonist. Serious life-threatening reactions have occurred, including ischemic colitis and serious complications of constipation, and, rarely, blood transfusion, surgery, and death. A prescribing program was implemented to educate health care providers and reduce the risks of serious adverse reactions. Alosetron should be discontinued immediately in patients who develop constipation or symptoms of ischemic colitis.

LO 34.5 **LO 34.6**

LAXATIVES AND CATHARTICS

Laxatives and **cathartics** are pharmacological agents that stimulate defecation. Although these terms are often used interchangeably, laxatives produce a mild, gentle stimulus for defecation, whereas cathartics produce a more intense action on the bowel. All laxatives and cathartics act directly on the intestine to alter stool formation. There are only a few valid indications for the use of laxatives. Primarily, these drugs are used to relieve constipation and to evacuate the intestine prior to surgery or diagnostic examination.

The accepted clinical uses of laxatives and cathartics are to

- provide relief of constipation from nonorganic abnormalities, voluntary retention of feces, inadequate fiber in the diet, and emotional disturbances,

- evacuate the bowel contents for adjunct medication in the treatment of intestinal parasites (anthelmintics) and food or drug poisoning; and cleanse the bowel prior to radiographic examination, diagnostic examination, or surgery,

- prevent straining at stool to avoid rupture of existing **hernia,** avoid rupture following a hemorrhoidectomy,

- prevent straining in patients with myocardial infarction.

Constipation is defined differently by patients and health care professionals. Patients commonly describe constipation as hard stools or incomplete emptying, whereas providers define it by stool frequency of fewer than 3 bowel movements per week. Chronic constipation occurs when symptoms last more than 3 months. Poorly developed toilet habits, such as ignoring the intestinal stimulus to defecate (rectal distention) or voluntary retention of feces, may result in constipation. Diets low in fiber also contribute to the development of constipation. Foods that have a low fiber content do not retain water in the intestine. When these foods are digested, they cannot produce adequate colonic distention to initiate a defecation reflex at regular intervals. Constipation also can have a pathophysiologic cause such as Parkinson's disease, spinal cord injury, diabetes, hypothyroidism, and genetic disorders (Hirschsprung's), to name a few. Anxiety, fear, and other emotional disturbances also induce constipation by altering the parasympathetic control of the intestines. Stressful situations usually result in sympathetic stimulation that decreases intestinal motility. All of these factors may lead to the production of hard, dry stools that are difficult to pass.

Laxatives are employed to facilitate defecation without straining, stress, or pain. Their use is especially important in patients who have hemorrhoids or hernias or who have had a myocardial infarction. Resistance to defecation is usually overcome by voluntarily increasing abdominal pressure (straining). Such increases in pressure can affect the workload on the heart or rupture an existing hernia or hemorrhoids.

A major component in the management of constipation is increased dietary fiber. Fiber increases stool bulk and fluid content and decreases transit time. Thus, decreasing the amount of time for stool to move through the colon increases the frequency of defecation. Remember the longer the transit time, the more fluid is reabsorbed from the stool, causing constipation. Patients should be advised to include at least 10 g of crude fiber in their diet. Fruits, vegetables, and unprocessed grains and cereals have the highest fiber content. The patient should be encouraged to continue on the high-fiber diet for at least a month before effects on the bowel can be assessed. Abdominal distention and flatus may occur the first few weeks on a high-fiber diet. These symptoms may resolve as bowel habits improve.

Mechanism of Action

Laxatives can be classified according to their mechanism of action, which includes stimulants, swelling agents, osmotic (saline) laxatives, emollients, chloride channel activators, and mu-opioid receptor antagonists (see Table 34:3). Stimulant laxatives directly irritate the mucosal lining of the intestine. In addition to the irritation, histamine is released, enhancing intestinal motility.

Swelling agents are natural fibers or grains that remain in the intestine, soak up water, and expand (swell). The water, which is retained, softens the stool, whereas the swelling action distends the rectum and initiates defecation. Osmotic, or saline, laxatives are a mixture of sodium and magnesium salts. These ions attract water **(osmosis),** which causes a more liquid stool to be formed. Lactulose is a combination of sugars (galactose, fructose) that promotes the same action because of the amount of sodium associated with the nonabsorbable sugar molecules. Polyethylene glycol-electrolyte solution (PEG-ES) is a nonabsorbable solution containing sodium sulfate that acts in a similar manner to promote complete, thorough bowel evacuation. PEG laxatives are most commonly used as bowel preparation for colonoscopy.

Emollients are laxatives that act on the stool to permit water to penetrate the fecal mass. The oily nature of these laxatives eases the passage of the stool through the rectum.

A novel laxative is a product that is a carbon dioxide–releasing suppository (*Ceo-Two*). The potassium bitartrate and sodium bicarbonate combination releases carbon dioxide gas. The gas pushes against the rectum wall, inducing muscle contraction and stool movement.

Chloride channel activators are the newest class of drugs approved by the FDA specifically for chronic constipation and IBS with constipation. The first drug approved is lubiprostone (*Amitiza*), a fatty acid prostaglandin E1 derivative, that acts locally in the membrane of the intestine. Chloride channels are pore-forming proteins that are critical to fluid transport and maintaining cell volume and pH. Lubiprostone opens these

Laxatives*

Class (onset of action)	Active compound(s)	Trade Name	Adult daily dose	Route of administration
Over-the-counter medications				
Bowel evacuants (0.5–3 hrs)	Polyethylene glycol-electrolyte solution (PEG-ES)	GoLYTELY, Colyte, OCL	4 liters prior to GI exam as 240 ml every 10 min	Oral solution
	Senna extract	X-prep, X-prep Bowel, Fleet Prep Kits (1–6)	As instructed	Oral, tablets, liquids, rectal suppositories
Emollients (6–8 hrs)	Mineral oil	Kondremul	5–45 ml	Oral, liquid
Osmotic (saline) laxatives (0.5–3 hrs)	Magnesium hydroxide	Phillips' Milk of Magnesia	30–60 ml	Oral, suspension
	Magnesium citrate	Citrate of Magnesia	1 glass	Oral, liquid
(2–15 min)	Sodium biphosphate and sodium phosphate	Fleet Enema	118 ml	Rectal, liquid
Stimulants (0.6–10 hrs)	Bisacodyl	Correctol, Dulcolax, Ex Lax Ultra, Fleet Laxative	5–15 mg 1× daily (10 mg) suppository 1× daily	Oral, tablets Rectal suppositories (15–60 min onset)
	Castor oil	Castor Oil, Emulsoil	15–60 ml	Oral, liquid
	Senna preparations	Fletcher's Castoria	10–15 ml	Oral, liquid
		Black Draught Lax Senna, Senokot	2 tablets	Oral, tablets
Stool softeners (12–72 hrs)	Docusate sodium	Colace, D.O.S., Phillip's Liqui-Gels	50–300 mg, increase daily fluid intake	Oral, 1–4 tablets or capsules
	Docusate calcium	Surfak Liqui-Gels, DC-softgels	240 mg daily	Oral, capsules
Swelling agents (12–72 hrs)	Bran, polycarbophil	Equalactin, Fibercon, Fiberlax	2 tablets (1 g) up to QID	Oral, tablets
	Prunes	—	6–12 prunes	—
	Psyllium hydrophilic	Metamucil, Perdiem, Reguloid, Serutan	1 tsp up to QID in 8 oz liquid	Oral, suspension
Mixtures	Mineral oil and magnesium hydroxide	Haley's MO	4–60 ml at bedtime with 8 oz water	Oral, liquid
	Senna concentrate and docusate sodium	Peri-Colace, Senokot-S, Senna Plus Tablets	2–4 tablets	Oral, tablets
CO_2-releasing suppositories	Sodium bicarbonate and potassium bitartrate	Ceo-Two	1 at bedtime	Suppository

(Continued)

Class (onset of action)	Active compound(s)	Trade Name	Adult daily dose	Route of administration
Prescription medications				
Chloride channel activators	Lubiprostone	*Amitiza*	24 mcg BID	Oral, capsules
Hyperosmotic laxative	Lactulose (galactose, fructose)	*Cephulac, Enulose*	15–30 ml	Oral, syrup
Mu-opioid receptor antagonist	Methylnaltrexone bromide	*Relistor*	1 dose alternate days 8 mg for 38 to 61 kg or 12 mg 62 to 114 kg	SC

Not an inclusive list of available preparations.

channels so that chloride enters the lumen; water follows the ions to maintain isotonic balance (pulls fluid into the lumen), accelerating transit time and softening the stool. It has no action on intestinal smooth muscle or prostaglandin receptors. Lubiprostone is broken down in the stomach and small intestine so very little is systemically absorbed. Common adverse effects include headache, diarrhea, and nausea. Dosage for the adult is one 24 mcg gel capsule taken twice daily with food and water.

Mu-opioid receptor antagonists are another drug class used to reduce specific opioid-induced constipation. Methylnaltrexone bromide (*Relistor*) is a new drug that selectively blocks peripheral mu-opioid receptors without affecting receptors in the CNS. See Figure 34.4. It is approved for treatment of opioid-induced constipation in patients with advanced illnesses or palliative care who are receiving opioids for pain relief. One subcutaneous injection every other day, but no more frequently than every 24 hours, is the recommended dosing frequency. Dosage is individualized to the patient by weight.

Route of Administration

Most laxatives are administered orally. The onset of action by this route varies from 6 to 12 hours for the stronger laxatives (osmotic and stimulants) and 12 to 72 hours for the stool softeners and swelling agents. Certain laxatives may be administered rectally as suppositories or as enemas (see Table 34:3). Administration of drug as an enema (traditionally, warm fluid injected rectally) usually has an onset of action from within 5 to 60 minutes.

Hence, enemas are preferred to cleanse the bowel prior to surgery or diagnostic examination. Certain preparations are considered bowel evacuants because of their ability to empty the bowel quickly and thoroughly prior to procedures such as GI examination. Bowel evacuation

Figure 34.4

Site of Action of Methylnaltrexone

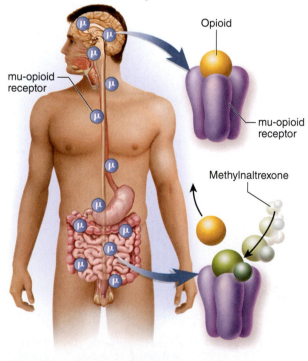

Methylnaltrexone blocks opioids from interacting with the mu-receptor in the intestines.

is particularly successful if patients have fasted for 3 to 4 hours prior to receiving the laxative. Often, patients are given bowel preparations the evening before the GI examination and instructed to abstain from foods, except for clear liquids, until after the procedure has been completed.

> ### Note to the Health Care Professional
>
> Stimulant cathartics may produce dehydration and electrolyte changes (**hypokalemia**—a decrease in potassium—or **hyponatremia**—a decrease in sodium) if used too frequently. The senna preparations produce such an intense response that abdominal cramping (griping) or nausea may accompany their action.

Adverse Effects

Certain laxatives are absorbed when administered orally and therefore produce systemic effects. Such agents include the osmotic laxatives and phenolphthalein. The sodium and magnesium ions that are absorbed from osmotic laxatives are excreted through the kidneys. However, the increased sodium load may be harmful to patients who have impaired renal function, edema, or congestive heart failure. Also, in sensitive or debilitated patients, excess magnesium ions can depress central nervous system (CNS) and muscle function. The osmotic laxatives are not harmless drugs. These agents cause large amounts of water to be lost with the feces. Hence, it is possible to dehydrate patients from overuse of these drugs.

Cautions and Contraindications

Laxatives should be taken with clear liquids; usually a minimum 8 ounces of water is recommended. Chronic use (misuse) of laxatives may result in cathartic colon or laxative dependency. Cathartic colon is a situation in which the intestines do not respond to physiological stimulation (loss of bowel tone), necessitating daily use of cathartics to produce defecation. Although they relieve constipation, laxatives should never be used to treat constipation that occurs because of bowel obstruction (tumor).

> ### Note to the Health Care Professional
>
> Laxatives and cathartics should never be used for long periods of time. These drugs are absolutely contraindicated in individuals with nausea, vomiting, appendicitis, or any undiagnosed abdominal pain.

Drugs affecting the GI tract are widely available without prescription and are a cultural mainstay of self-medication among older people. It often takes a few days for the full therapeutic effect to become evident; meanwhile the patient has probably re-dosed more frequently and not taken sufficient fluid to allow the GI tract to cooperate with the medication. Proper diet incorporating fiber, fruit, and vegetables; adequate daily fluid intake, up to 10 (8 oz.) glasses; and exercise are essential for maintaining normal bowel function.

Patient Instructions

Patients should be reminded to take medication with a full glass of water or fruit juice. Juice will mask the taste of those products that taste bitter.

Discoloration of the urine is expected with the use of cascara and senna (red-brown, yellow-brown) laxatives.

Keep antidiarrheals out of the reach of children, since accidental ingestion may cause respiratory depression.

In adults, therapeutic doses may cause dizziness or drowsiness that can impair coordination and mental alertness required for operating cars or machinery.

Drug Administration

Bismuth should be avoided before GI radiologic procedures because it is radiopaque and may interfere with X-ray.

While OTC laxatives may take more than 1 day to exert an adequate effect, products recommended for bowel evacuation prior to diagnostic procedures or examination will exert their effect promptly, usually within 1 hour. Patients should be advised to take the medication so that planned activities and sleep are not interrupted.

Product Interactions

Bisacodyl-containing products should not be taken within 1 hour of antacids or milk because the enteric coating may dissolve, resulting in gastric irritation.

Docusate sodium should not be taken when mineral oil is being used because of the potential to increase the absorption of mineral oil. Mineral oil should be taken on an empty stomach.

Refrigerate magnesium citrate to retain potency and palatability.

Notify the Physician

These drugs should not be used in the presence of nausea, vomiting, or abdominal pain. Notify the physician if rectal bleeding, muscle cramps, weakness, or dizziness occurs.

Laxatives should not be continued for more than 1 week unless under the supervision of a physician. Unrelieved constipation should be reported to the doctor for further evaluation.

Antidiarrheals should not be continued for more than 2 days if diarrhea persists; physician should be notified for evaluation.

Use in Pregnancy

The drugs in this class are designated Food and Drug Administration (FDA) Pregnancy Category B or C or NR, not rated. Castor oil should not be taken during pregnancy because of the potential for the irritant action to induce labor. Other products should only be taken during pregnancy when there is a clear indication for use and after discussion with the physician.

Chapter Review

Understanding Terminology

Answer the following questions.

1. Differentiate between laxatives and cathartics. **(LO 34.4)**
2. Define *peristalsis.* **(LO 34.1)**
3. Define *osmosis.* **(LO 34.4)**
4. Define *adsorbents.* **(LO 34.4)**

Acquiring Knowledge

Answer the following questions.

1. How do voluntary control and the autonomic nervous system affect the process of defecation? **(LO 34.1)**
2. What is diarrhea? What are the primary causes of diarrhea? **(LO 34.2, 34.3)**
3. What are the consequences of chronic and acute diarrhea? **(LO 34.2, 34.3)**
4. What agents are used for the treatment of simple diarrhea? **(LO 34.4)**
5. How do the adsorbent antidiarrheals differ from the opiates? **(LO 34.4)**
6. What is the mechanism of action of diphenoxylate? **(LO 34.4)**
7. What are the primary causes of constipation? **(LO 34.5)**
8. What are the various types of laxatives? How do they differ? **(LO 34.1, 34.6)**
9. Why are the osmotic laxatives potentially dangerous? **(LO 34.1, 34.5, 34.6)**

Applying Knowledge on the Job

Use your critical-thinking skills to answer the following questions.

1. Assume that your job is physician's assistant in a county health department in a rural area. What would you recommend for each of the following patients presenting with diarrhea at the clinic where you work?
   a. Patient A thinks she ate "something spoiled." **(LO 34.1, 34.3, 34.4)**
   b. Patient B went deer hunting and drank water from a stream in the woods. **(LO 34.1, 34.3, 34.4)**
   c. Patient C is taking an antibiotic for a urinary tract infection. **(LO 34.1, 34.3, 34.4)**
   d. Patient D has irritable bowel syndrome. **(LO 34.1, 34.3, 34.4)**

2. Assume you work an eating disorders hotline. Convince the following two callers of the seriousness of their laxative abuse.
   a. Caller A is anorexic and extremely underweight. She eats very little, exercises a great deal, and takes laxatives nearly daily. She takes the laxatives because, without them, she only has a bowel movement every 2 or 3 days, and that makes her feel fat. **(LO 34.1, 34.5, 34.6)**
   b. Caller B is bulimic and of average weight. Almost every day, she binges on huge quantities of food and then purges by vomiting and taking laxatives. She takes the laxatives because she can't always induce the gag reflex after forcing herself to vomit so many times—and she can't stand the thought of all that food being turned into body fat. **(LO 34.1, 34.5, 34.6)**

Multiple Choice

Use your critical-thinking skills to answer the following questions.

1. The defecation reflex **(LO 34.1)**
   A. is a voluntary process
   B. contracts the external anal sphincter
   C. is initiated by distension of the colon
   D. propels feces into the small intestine

2. A patient presents with severe diarrhea. Upon questioning, the patient mentions that he returned from Thailand a week ago. The patient is diagnosed with "traveler's diarrhea." The drug of choice for this patient would include **(LO 34.2)**
   A. rifaximin
   B. bulk laxatives
   C. lubiprostone
   D. methylnaltrexone

3. Which of the following treatments for simple diarrhea works by forming a complex with the irritant?
   (LO 34.3, 34.4)
   A. antibiotics
   B. opioid derivatives
   C. anticholinergics
   D. adsorbents

4. Which of the following drugs has been approved for treatment of patients with constipation caused by opioid analgesics? **(LO 34.5, 34.6)**
   A. emollients
   B. lubiprostone
   C. stimulants
   D. methylnaltrexone

5. Which of the following laxatives would be ordered before a colonoscopy? **(LO 34.5, 34.6)**
   A. docusate sodium
   B. polyethylene glycol
   C. psyllium hydrophilic
   D. mineral oil

Multiple Choice (Multiple Answer)

Select the correct choices for each statement. The choices may be all correct, all incorrect, or any combination.

1. Select all of the causes of diarrhea. **(LO 34.2)**
   A. increased intestinal motility
   B. inflammation
   C. osmotic imbalance
   D. drug therapy

2. Choose the mechanisms of action of adsorbants. **(LO 34.4)**
   A. kill bacteria
   B. decrease serotonin release
   C. form a complex with irritating substance
   D. absorbed into blood circulation to work on the system

3. Which of the following drugs are used to stimulate defecation? **(LO 34.6)**
   A. 5-HT$_3$ antagonists
   B. adsorbants
   C. antimotility drugs
   D. cathartics

4. Select all of the mechanisms by which swelling agents increase defecation. **(LO 34.6)**
   A. soak up water
   B. irritate the mucosal lining of the intestine
   C. distend rectum
   D. coat the fecal matter

5. What are the main adverse effects of osmotic laxatives? **(LO 34.5)**
   A. depressed CNS
   B. decreased muscle function
   C. dehydration
   D. respiratory depression

Sequencing

Place the following steps of defecation in order from first to last. **(LO 34.1)**

_____   _____   _____   _____   _____

First   **Last**

peristalsis moves feces to anus

feces moves to rectum

external sphincter relaxes

increase in rectal pressure

trigger of defecation reflex

Classification

Place the following mechanisms of action under the correct heading. **(LO 34.4, 34.6)**

soak up water
inhibit postganglionic receptors
block mu-opioid receptors
stimulate mu receptors
open Cl$^-$ channels
bind to digestive enzymes

Relief of diarrhea	Relief of constipation

Matching

Match the following drugs with the correct use. **(LO 34.4, 34.6)**

a. Treatment of diarrhea
b. Treatment of constipation

1. _____ *Kytril*
2. _____ *Amitiza*
3. _____ *Relistor*
4. _____ *GoLYTELY*
5. _____ *Lonox*
6. _____ *Motofen*
7. _____ *Colace*
8. _____ *Imodium*

Documentation

Answer the following questions based on the information given at ER admissions. **(LO 34.2, 34.4)**

Symptoms
severe diarrhea
dehydration
Pt mentions just returning from a vacation

a. What is the probable cause of this patient's diarrhea?
b. What could this patient have done to prevent his diarrhea?
c. What medications can now be used to treat him?
d. What are the recommended dosages of these mediations?

Labeling

Fill in the missing labels. **(LO 34.1)**

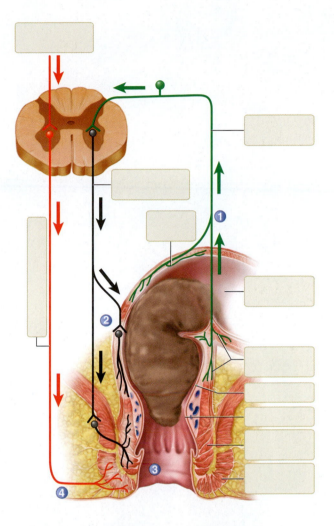

1. Feces stretch the rectum and stimulate stretch receptors, which transmit signals to the spinal cord.

2. A spinal reflex stimulates contraction of the rectum.

3. The spinal reflex also relaxes the internal anal sphincter.

4. Impulses from the brain prevent untimely defecation by keeping the external anal sphincter contracted. Defecation occurs only if this sphincter also relaxes.

For interactive animations, videos, and assessment, visit:

www.mcgrawhillconnect.com

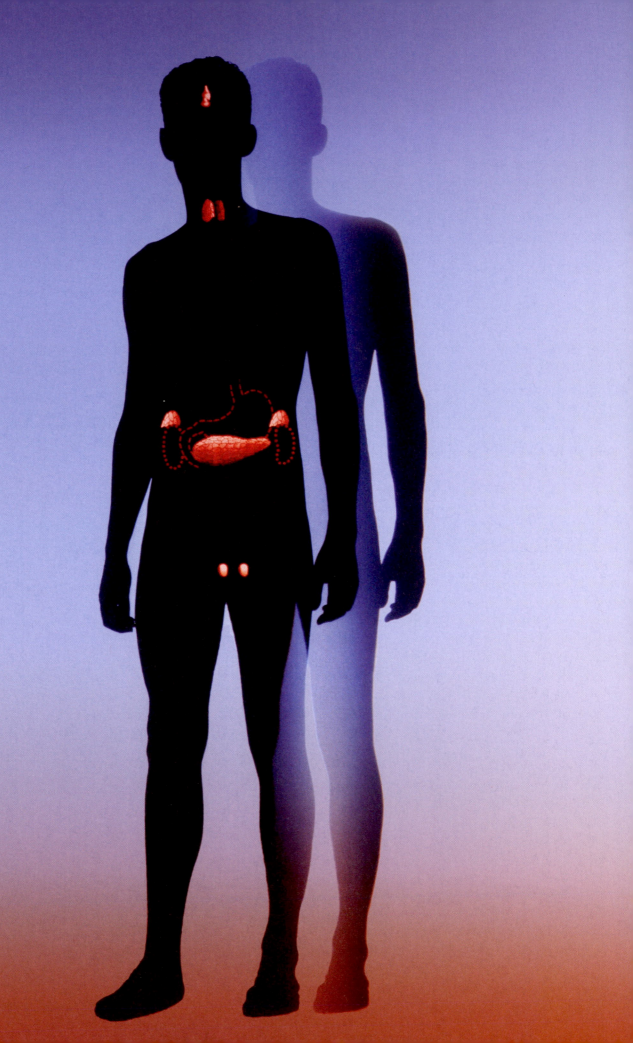

Pharmacology of the Endocrine System

Chapter 35

Introduction to the Endocrine System

DRUG CLASS AT A GLANCE

OTC	NO
PRESCRIPTION	YES
SCHEDULED DRUGS	NO
FDA PREGNANCY CATEGORY	B, C

INDICATIONS

Growth hormone replacement, acromegaly

KEY TERMS

acromegaly: condition usually in middle-aged adults from hyper-secretion of growth hormone.

carcinoid tumor: a slow-growing type of cancer that can arise in the gastrointestinal tract, lungs, ovaries, and testes.

cretinism: condition in which the development of the body and brain has been inhibited.

ductless glands: containing no duct; endocrine glands that secrete hormones directly into the blood or lymph without going through a duct.

dwarfism: inadequate secretion of growth hormone during childhood, characterized by abnormally short stature and normal body proportions.

endocrine: pertaining to glands that secrete substances directly into the blood.

gigantism: increased secretion of growth hormone in childhood, causing excessive growth and height.

gonads: organs that produce male (testes) or female (ovaries) sex cells, sperm or ova.

hormone: substance produced within one organ and secreted directly into the circulation to exert its effects at a distant location.

insulin-like growth factor (IGF): a stimulator of cell growth and proliferation.

somatomedins: peptides in the plasma that stimulate cellular growth and have insulin-like activity.

somatostatin: an inhibitory hormone that blocks the release of somatotropin (GH) and thyroid-stimulating hormone (TSH).

somatotropin: another term for growth hormone (GH).

target organ: specific tissue where a hormone exerts its action.

tropic hormone: hormone secreted by the anterior pituitary that binds to a receptor on another endocrine gland.

After studying this chapter, you should be able to

35.1 describe the basic function of a hormone.

35.2 explain the hypothalamic-anterior pituitary-target organ axis.

35.3 explain how hormones produce their effects (the mechanisms of hormone action for water-soluble and lipid-soluble hormones).

35.4 describe the endocrine functions of the hypothalamus.

35.5 describe the endocrine functions of the anterior pituitary.

35.6 describe negative feedback, and give an example.

The two main systems of the body that function to regulate the others are the nervous system and the endocrine system. The nervous system regulates activity by conducting nerve impulses to various organs. Nerve impulses travel rapidly along specific pathways to produce their effects. The response to nerve stimulation is rapid, and the duration of action is short. An example would be the contraction of skeletal muscle. In contrast to the nervous system, hormones have a slower onset and a longer duration of stimulation. An example of hormone action would be the effect of insulin to lower blood sugar.

LO 35.1   **LO 35.2**   **LO 35.3**

ENDOCRINE SYSTEM

The **endocrine** system, composed of **ductless glands** throughout the body, regulates activity by releasing hormones into the bloodstream to affect a **target organ.** There are eight major endocrine glands: the pineal, pituitary, thyroid, thymus, adrenal, pancreas, ovary, and testis. Each of these glands secretes specific **hormones** in order to regulate growth, metabolism, or reproduction. Categories of hormones include steroids, amines, polypeptides, and glycoproteins. An example of a hormone in each category is presented in Table 35:1 and includes estrogen, melatonin, growth hormone, and follicle-stimulating hormone, respectively. Hormones are divided into two groups based upon their mechanism of action at the target cell. Hormones that are lipid-soluble (insoluble in water) are able to diffuse through the target cell's plasma membrane and bind to receptors in the

nucleus of the cell. Lipid-soluble hormones like steroids and thyroid hormone stimulate gene transcription to synthesize proteins. Water-soluble hormones such as amines and polypeptides cannot diffuse through the cell membrane so they bind to receptors on the plasma membrane and produce their effects by activating second messengers. A second messenger is the chemical that is able to carry out the intended action of the hormone inside the cell. For example, you receive a text message from a friend asking you to tell her sister to pick up milk on the way home. In this case, you are the second messenger. The best-known second messenger is cyclic adenosine monophosphate (cAMP). Some hormones such as glucagon, calcitonin, and catecholamines produce their final response through second messengers.

There are many other substances released into the circulation which effect target tissues such as cholecystokinin

Classification of Hormones

Type of hormone	Hormones presented in Chapters 35 through 40	Examples of other "hormones"
Steroids and sterols		
	Androgens Calcitriol Corticosterone Cortisol Estrogens Progesterone Vitamin D	
Peptides and glycoproteins		
	Adrenocorticotropic hormone Antidiuretic hormone Calcitonin Corticotropin-releasing hormone Follicle-stimulating hormone Glucagon Gonadotropin-releasing hormone Growth hormone Growth hormone–releasing hormone Insulin Luteinizing hormone Oxytocin Parathyroid hormone Prolactin Somatostatin Thyroid-stimulating hormone Thyrotropin-releasing hormone	Angiotensin II Cholecystokinin Erythropoietin Gastrin Ghrelin Thymic hormones
Monoamines		
	Thyroid hormone	Dopamine Epinephrine Melatonin Norepinephrine

and gastrin that are involved in digestion, or erythropoietin associated with red blood cell production. These substances are occasionally referred to as hormones; however, they are not controlled by the hypothalamus or pituitary gland and, therefore, are not discussed in this endocrine section. Some of these "other hormones" (angiotensin II, erythropoietin, dopamine, epinephrine and norepinephrine) have been discussed in earlier chapters. They appear in Table 35.1 because they are sometimes referred to as hormones.

The deficiency of any hormone results in several characteristic disease states. For example, in children, the lack of growth hormone (somatotropin) results in **dwarfism,** whereas lack of thyroid hormone in infancy

produces **cretinism.** There are two major therapeutic uses of hormones. In cases of hormone deficiency, the missing hormone is given as a replacement therapy to fulfill a normal physiological role. On the other hand, in certain disease states (chronic inflammation), various hormones produce beneficial effects when given in large doses. In these situations, the hormones are acting pharmacologically. The main emphasis of this chapter is on the relationship between the hypothalamus and the pituitary gland and how hormones from these organs stimulate other hormone secretions from target tissues located well outside the brain. The role of growth hormone is also presented, but individual endocrine glands (adrenals, gonads, thyroid, parathyroid, pancreas, and posterior pituitary) and the specific target organ hormones they control (cortisol, androgens, estrogens, calcitonin, insulin, and glucagon) will be discussed in the following chapters.

LO 35.3 LO 35.4 LO 35.5

HYPOTHALAMIC-PITUITARY AXIS

Often referred to as the "master gland" of the endocrine system, the pituitary gland controls many of the other glands. Located in the brain and attached to the base of the hypothalamus, the pituitary gland is composed of two main lobes: the anterior lobe (adenohypophysis) and the posterior lobe (neurohypophysis). Each lobe contains a number of hormones that may be released into the general circulation. See Figure 35.1.

The hypothalamus controls the "master gland" and each lobe of the pituitary gland is controlled in a different manner. The hypothalamus and the anterior lobe of the pituitary gland are connected by small blood vessels known as the portal system. The hypothalamus produces releasing and inhibiting hormones, which are secreted into the portal vein to the anterior pituitary. The releasing hormones [thyrotropic-releasing hormone (TRH), corticotropin-releasing hormone (CRH), growth hormone–releasing hormone (GHRH), and gonadotropin-releasing hormone (GnRH)] stimulate the release of the hormones produced in the anterior lobe such as thyroid-stimulating hormone (TSH), adrenocorticotropic hormone (ACTH), growth hormone (GH), and insulin-like growth factor (IGF), respectively. Gonadotropin-releasing hormone (GnRH)

Figure 35.1   **Hypothalamo-Anterior Pituitary Target Organ Relationships**

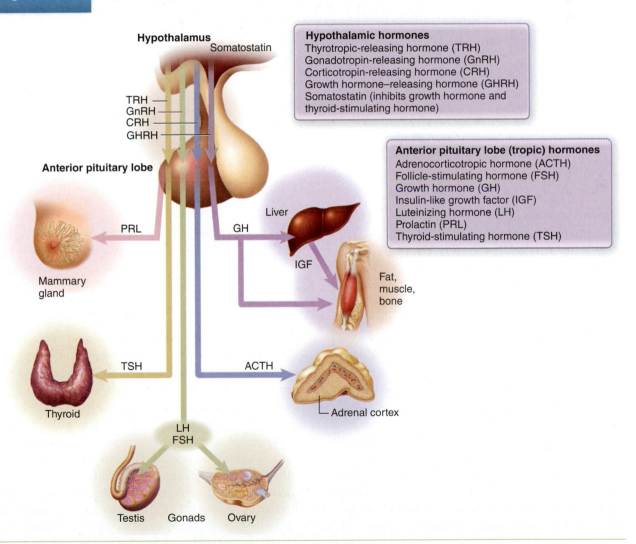

Hypothalamic hormones
Thyrotropic-releasing hormone (TRH)
Gonadotropin-releasing hormone (GnRH)
Corticotropin-releasing hormone (CRH)
Growth hormone–releasing hormone (GHRH)
Somatostatin (inhibits growth hormone and thyroid-stimulating hormone)

Anterior pituitary lobe (tropic) hormones
Adrenocorticotropic hormone (ACTH)
Follicle-stimulating hormone (FSH)
Growth hormone (GH)
Insulin-like growth factor (IGF)
Luteinizing hormone (LH)
Prolactin (PRL)
Thyroid-stimulating hormone (TSH)

Hypothalamus
Somatostatin
TRH
GnRH
CRH
GHRH
Anterior pituitary lobe
PRL
Mammary gland
GH
Liver
IGF
Fat, muscle, bone
TSH
Thyroid
ACTH
Adrenal cortex
LH
FSH
Testis Gonads Ovary

Hypothalamic-releasing hormones (TRH, GnRH, CRH, GHRH) trigger the secretion of all the anterior pituitary hormones (PRL, TSH, GH, ACTH, LH, FSH) except prolactin (PRL).

Hormones of the Anterior and Posterior Lobes of the Pituitary and Their Functions

Anterior pituitary hormones	Target organ	Effect
Growth hormone (GH)	Liver, bone, cartilage, muscle, fat	Stimulates growth and repair in all tissues but especially in the target organs
Thyroid-stimulating hormone (TSH)	Thyroid gland	Thyroid growth and stimulates production and release of thyroxine
Adrenocorticotropic hormone (ACTH)	Adrenal cortex	Stimulates production and secretion of cortisol (glucocorticoids)
Follicle-stimulating hormone (FSH)	Gonads of male and female	Stimulates development of sperm and ova; secretion of estrogen and testosterone
Luteinizing hormone (LH)	Gonads of male and female	Controls production of sex hormones estrogen and testosterone; female—ovulation and maintenance of corpus luteum; male—testosterone secretion
Prolactin	Mammary glands—female Testes	Milk production Testosterone secretion
Posterior pituitary hormones		
Antidiuretic hormone (ADH)	Kidneys	Water retention
Oxytocin (OT)	Uterus, mammary glands	Labor contractions, milk release; possibly involved in ejaculation, sperm transport, sexual affection, and mother-infant bonding

releases hormones (FSH, follicle-stimulating hormone; LH, luteinizing hormone) required for expression of male (testes) and female (ovary) sex cells. These hormones of the anterior lobe are known as the **tropic hormones.** The tropic hormones are released into the general circulation to control the activities of the other endocrine glands. With the exception of growth hormone, each of these hormones stimulates a specific endocrine gland such as the thyroid, ovary, or adrenal gland. Table 35:2 lists the hormones of the anterior lobe of the pituitary gland and the organs that are affected. The hypothalamus produces *inhibiting hormones* that suppress pituitary secretion. Examples are somatostatin (inhibits secretion of GH and TSH) and prolactin-inhibiting hormone (inhibits prolactin secretion).

The hypothalamus also produces the hormones that are retained in the posterior lobe of the pituitary gland. The posterior lobe is an extension of the nerve tissue of the hypothalamus as shown in Figure 35.2. These hormones—oxytocin and antidiuretic hormone (ADH)—travel down nerve axons (axonal transport) to the posterior lobe, where they are stored until needed. Secretion of the posterior pituitary hormones is controlled by nerve reflexes, not releasing hormones (see Chapter 39).

Regulating Hormone Secretion

Three different groups of hormones actually control the endocrine system: the releasing or inhibiting hormones (hypothalamus), the tropic hormones (anterior lobe), and the hormones from each of the other endocrine glands. The mechanism that controls the release of most of these hormones is known as negative feedback because the target organ hormone inhibits or turns off the specific pituitary hormone secretion. Figure 35.3 illustrates this concept, using the thyroid gland as an example. The hypothalamus secretes thyrotropin-releasing hormone (TRH), which then stimulates the release of thyroid-stimulating hormone (TSH) from the anterior pituitary gland. In turn TSH stimulates the

Figure 35.2

Posterior Lobe of the Pituitary Gland

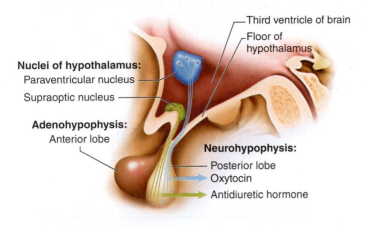

Nuclei of hypothalamus:
Paraventricular nucleus
Supraoptic nucleus

Adenohypophysis:
Anterior lobe

Third ventricle of brain
Floor of hypothalamus

Neurohypophysis:
Posterior lobe
Oxytocin
Antidiuretic hormone

The hormones oxytocin and antidiuretic hormone are produced by two areas (nuclei) in the hypothalamus and later released from the posterior lobe of the pituitary.

Figure 35.3

Negative Feedback Inhibition of the Pituitary Gland by the Thyroid Gland

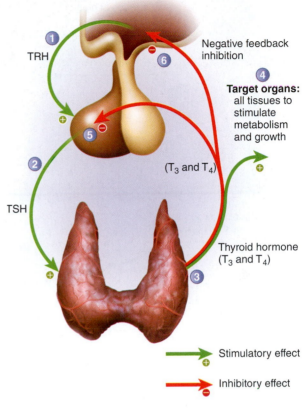

TRH

Negative feedback inhibition

Target organs: all tissues to stimulate metabolism and growth

$(T_3 \text{ and } T_4)$

TSH

Thyroid hormone $(T_3 \text{ and } T_4)$

→ Stimulatory effect

→ Inhibitory effect

(1) The hypothalamus secretes TRH (thyrotropin-releasing hormone); (2) TRH stimulates the anterior pituitary to secrete thyroid-stimulating hormone (TSH); (3) TSH stimulates the thyroid to secrete thyroid hormone (T_3, T_4); (4) thyroid hormone stimulates the metabolism of most cells throughout the body; (5) thyroid hormone also inhibits the release of TSH by the pituitary and also inhibits the release of TRH by the hypothalamus (6).

thyroid gland to release its hormone, thyroxine. Subsequently, the concentration of thyroxine increases in the blood. When the thyroxine concentration rises above a level required to regulate muscle metabolism and cellular growth, further secretion of the releasing factor and TSH is inhibited. Consequently, levels of the various hormones are maintained in the blood within modest limits and sudden severe changes in hormone levels are avoided. Most hormones are controlled through a negative feedback response; however, there also can be a positive feedback response. When a baby suckles on the mother's breast, the hypothalamus gets the message to release oxytocin. Oxytocin causes the breast to eject more milk as the baby continues to feed. This is an example of positive feedback where the end product stimulates more production of the end product. See Figure 35.4.

LO 35.2 | LO 35.4 | LO 35.5 | LO 35.6

ANTERIOR PITUITARY GROWTH HORMONE

Growth hormone **(somatotropin),** or GH, is referred to as a general hormone that regulates the growth and maintenance of all body tissues, especially cartilage, bone muscle, and fat. GH itself directly stimulates these tissues, but it also induces the liver and other tissues

to produce growth stimulants called **insulin-like growth factors (IGF-1, IGF-2),** or **somatomedins,** which go on to stimulate target cells. For example, IGF-1 accelerates bone growth at the epiphyseal plates during childhood. Growth hormone increases plasma glucose, fatty acids, and glycerol by inhibiting glucose uptake by adipose cells. Increasing plasma levels of these nutrients provides the energy needed for growth. Lack of growth hormone in children results in dwarfism, whereas an excess of growth hormone results in **gigantism.** Hypersecretion of growth hormone in adults causes **acromegaly**—thickening of the bones and soft tissues with especially noticeable effects on the hands,

Figure 35.4 Positive Feedback Loop: Oxytocin

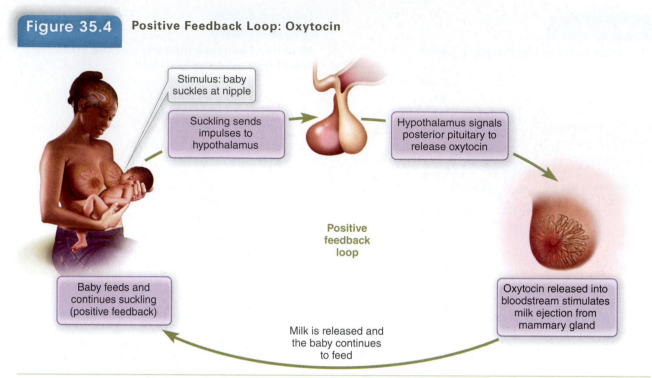

Stimulus: baby suckles at nipple

Suckling sends impulses to hypothalamus

Hypothalamus signals posterior pituitary to release oxytocin

Positive feedback loop

Baby feeds and continues suckling (positive feedback)

Oxytocin released into bloodstream stimulates milk ejection from mammary gland

Milk is released and the baby continues to feed

Stimulation of more milk production following suckling stimulation of the breast.

feet, and face. The cause is almost always a benign pituitary tumor. See Figure 35.5. The main pharmacological use of growth hormone is replacement therapy in cases of suspected dwarfism.

At first, the supply of human growth hormone was limited because it was obtained from human cadaver tissue. However, human growth hormone was withdrawn from the market in 1985 when the National Hormone and Pituitary Program (NIH) linked Creutzfeldt-Jakob's disease to contaminated cadaver tissue. In the same year, purified recombinant growth hormone (rDNA) replaced pituitary-derived human growth hormone for therapeutic use in the United States. Somatropin (*Humatrope, Genotropin,* and *Nutropin*) is identical in amino acid sequence to the hormone produced by the human pituitary. Another recombinant product is mecasermin (*Increlex*). Insulin-like growth factor-1 (IGF-1) is secreted by the liver in response to growth hormone stimulation and mediates the actions of growth hormone. Mecasermin is a recombinant IGF-1 that is indicated for the long-term treatment of growth failure in children with severe primary IGF-1 deficiency or who have developed neutralizing antibodies to GH. IGF-1 is not intended for use of growth hormone deficiency.

Somatostatin is an inhibitory hormone produced by the hypothalamus (and stomach, intestine, and pancreas). Somatostatin inhibits GH and TSH. Two analogs of somatostatin are used in the treatment of acromegaly to reduce blood levels of GH and IGF-1. Octreotide (*Sandostatin, Sandostatin LAR depot*) and lanreotide (*Somatuline depot*) are synthetic proteins used in the management of acromegaly in patients who have had inadequate response to surgery or cannot be treated with surgery. Even with radiation therapy, tumor reduction takes months or years and these analogs may be used to ameliorate clinical symptoms during that time. Figure 35.6 shows the similarity between the somatostatin molecule and octreotide. Octreotide is significantly more potent than somatostatin in inhibiting GH, insulin, and glucagon. The dose may vary from 100 to 500 mcg three times a day administered subcutaneously or intravenously. Octreotide is cleared through the kidneys and has a half-life of 7 to 10 hours. Renal impairment increases the plasma level by decreasing the clearance of octreotide. Lanreotide is only available as a slow-releasing depot formulation. At 4-week intervals, 90 mg is given via deep subcutaneous injection.

Clinical Indication

The current indication for somatropin is long-term treatment of children who have growth failure because of lack of adequate endogenous growth hormone secretion. The hormone is reconstituted from a powder prior to IM or SC injection three times a week.

Mecasermin is a soluble solution intended for SC injection. The dose should be administered 20 minutes before or after the meal. Therapy should be initiated at a low dose and increased only if no hypoglycemia occurs after 7 days of dosing.

Octreopeptide and lanreotide are used to treat acromegaly. Because octreopeptide also inhibits the release of intestinal hormones such as secretin and vasoactive intestinal peptide (VIP), it is clinically valuable in the management of severe diarrhea and flushing associated with metastatic **carcinoid tumors.**

Adverse Effects

Adverse effects associated with the use of recombinant GH and IGF-1 are extensions of the normal physiological action. Changes in blood sugar level (hypoglycemia or hyperglycemia) consistent with insulin fluctuations may occur. Glycosylated hemoglobin should be monitored in all patients taking GH. Headache, muscle weakness, knee and hip pain, and transient edema have been reported. Some patients develop antibodies to the exogenous hormone, but these antibodies do not affect the beneficial effects on growth.

Diagnostic Tests for Abnormal Anterior Pituitary Function

In order to assess the adequacy of anterior pituitary function, the serum concentration of growth hormone or TSH may be analyzed. Secretion of GH and TSH follows a diurnal pattern so that the optimal blood level of hormone is available to the tissues during the active waking state. For evaluation of pituitary and target gland function, blood samples are usually taken between 6 and 8 AM. If the serum levels of the hormones are within normal levels (TSH 0–15 µIU/ml; GH 0–16 ng/ml—the maximum varies with men 3 ng/ml, women 10 ng/ml, children 16 ng/ml), the anterior pituitary and the thyroid gland are functioning normally. Serum TSH would be elevated outside the normal limits if the thyroid gland was not producing thyroxine (hormone feedback).

Since the range of normal for these hormones includes "0" or "undetectable levels," deficiency associated with anterior pituitary function must be further evaluated in conjunction with the patient's clinical profile. Further evaluation may include stimulation of the anterior pituitary to provoke secretion of growth hormone and TSH prior to obtaining an early morning blood sample. An example of a provocative test for thyroid function is the

| Figure 35.5 | **Acromegaly, a Condition Caused by Growth Hormone Hypersecretion in Adulthood** |

Age 16   **Age 33**   **Age 52**

These classic photographs show the same person taken at different ages.

Figure 35.6

Amino Acid Sequence of Somatostatin and Synthetic Octreotide

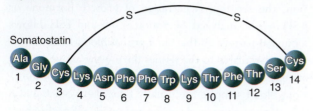

Somatostatin

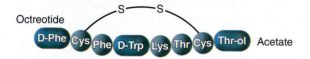

Octreotide

TRH Challenge Test. Thyrotropic-releasing hormone (TRH) is injected intravenously prior to drawing blood at 5, 10, 20, and 60 minutes postinjection. The TSH concentration of the blood samples is analyzed to determine whether a sudden rise in TSH occurs in response to the TRH stimulation. Observation of a spike confirms a normal functioning anterior pituitary. If the TSH level does not rise or remains undetectable, pituitary dysfunction is indicated. Note: if the patient is experiencing excess thyroid hormone secretion (thyrotoxicosis), endogenous TSH secretion should be inhibited through hormone feedback. Consequently, if TRH is injected to a patient with thyrotoxicosis, the TSH level will not rise.

Chapter Review

Understanding Terminology

Answer the following questions.

1. Differentiate among dwarfism, gigantism, and cretinism. **(LO 35.2, 35.3, 35.4, 35.5)**
2. What is a hormone? **(LO 35.1, 35.2)**
3. Define *target organ*. **(LO 35.1, 35.2)**
4. What is GH? **(LO 35.1, 35.4, 35.5)**

Acquiring Knowledge

Answer the following questions.

1. What are the main uses of hormones in medical treatment? **(LO 35.1, 35.3)**
2. What are the functions of the anterior pituitary? **(LO 35.1, 35.2, 35.5)**
3. What is the function of the hypothalamus in the endocrine system? **(LO 35.1, 35.2, 35.4)**
4. What substances are produced in the hypothalamus? **(LO 35.1, 35.4)**
5. Where are the tropic hormones produced? Give two examples of a tropic hormone. **(LO 35.1, 35.4)**
6. What are the functions of growth hormone? **(LO 35.1, 35.5)**
7. How do the releasing hormones get to the anterior pituitary gland? **(LO 35.1, 35.2, 35.5)**
8. What is the function of releasing hormones? **(LO 35.1, 35.4, 35.5)**
9. Explain the concept of negative feedback in the control of hormonal secretion. **(LO 35.1, 35.2, 35.4, 35.5)**

Applying Knowledge on the Job

Use your critical-thinking skills to answer the following questions.

1. As a lab assistant in a hospital lab, explain to a patient why he must receive an injection before his blood is drawn to be tested for thyroid function. **(LO 35.1, 35.2, 35.4, 35.5)**
2. Explain why it is necessary to use a provocative challenge in order to evaluate a deficiency in pituitary function. **(LO 35.1, 35.2, 35.3, 35.4, 35.5)**

Multiple Choice

Use your critical-thinking skills to answer the following questions.

1. A hormone **(LO 35.1)**
   A. rapidly responds to a stimulus
   B. is a neurotransmitter
   C. binds to specific receptors to produce its effects
   D. produces nerve impulses

2. Releasing hormones **(LO 35.2, 35.5)**
   A. travel along axons to the posterior pituitary
   B. affect the secretion of hormones in the anterior pituitary
   C. are released by the target organ to regulate hypothalamus
   D. produce nerve impulses

3. Hormone release by the anterior pituitary is regulated by **(LO 35.1, 35.2, 35.4, 35.5)**
   A. the hypothalamus
   B. the anterior pituitary
   C. the target organ
   D. all of the above

4. Dwarfism is caused by **(LO 35.1, 35.3, 35.4)**
   A. elevated thyroid hormone production
   B. decreased adrenocorticotropic hormone
   C. decreased growth hormone
   D. high plasma glucose concentration

5. A patient newly diagnosed with hyperthyroidism has blood drawn for labs. The physician tells the patient that his TRH function is normal as is the TSH level. Using negative feedback, which location is most likely secreting excess hormone? **(LO 35.2, 35.4, 35.6)**
   A. CNS
   B. anterior pituitary
   C. hypothalamus
   D. target organ (thyroid gland)

6. Which of the following hormone disorders causes mental retardation in infancy? **(LO 35.3)**
   A. cretinism
   B. gigantism
   C. dwarfism
   D. diabetes mellitus

Multiple Choice (Multiple Answer)

Select the correct choices for each statement. The choices may be all correct, all incorrect, or any combination.

1. Select all of the functions of hormones. **(LO 35.1)**
   A. conduct electrical impulses
   B. regulate growth
   C. control metabolism
   D. help in reproduction

2. Which of the following are true of the hypothalamus? **(LO 35.2, 35.4)**
   A. it controls the master gland
   B. it is composed of two main lobes
   C. it is connected by a portal system to the posterior pituitary gland
   D. it releases luteinizing hormone

3. Choose all of the hormones whose target organs are the gonads of males and females. **(LO 35.5)**
   A. TSH
   B. ACTH
   C. LH
   D. FSH

4. Water-soluble hormones work by doing what? **(LO 35.3)**
   A. binding outside the cell
   B. crossing the plasma membrane
   C. sending second messengers
   D. stimulating gene transcription

5. Which of the following is true of the negative feedback system? **(LO 35.6)**
   A. levels of circulating hormone always change suddenly and severely
   B. the target organ turns off pituitary secretion
   C. a baby suckling is an example of negative feedback
   D. most hormones are controlled by this process

Sequencing

Place the following actions of the negative feedback system in order from first action at the hypothalamus to last action. **(LO 35.6)**

_____ _____ _____ _____ _____

First   **Last**

release of thyroxine

release of TSH

secretion of TRH

secretion inhibited

stimulation of thyroid gland

Classification

Classify each hormone by type. **(LO 35.1)**

growth hormone   cortisol   oxytocin
progesterone   prolactin   calcitriol

Steroids and sterols	Peptides and glycoproteins

Matching

Match the following terms with the correct definitions. **(LO 35.1, 35.3)**
   a. gigantism
   b. somatotropin
   c. cretinism
   d. target organ
   e. endocrine
   f. dwarfism
   g. somatostatin
   h. hormone

1. ___ condition of inhibited development of the brain
2. ___ substance that is secreted and then exerts its effects in another location
3. ___ inadequate secretion of growth hormone in childhood
4. ___ pertaining to glands that secrete substance into the blood
5. ___ growth hormone
6. ___ increased secretion of growth hormone in childhood
7. ___ blocks the release of growth hormone
8. ___ specific tissue where a hormone exerts its action

Labeling

Fill in the missing labels. **(LO 35.2)**

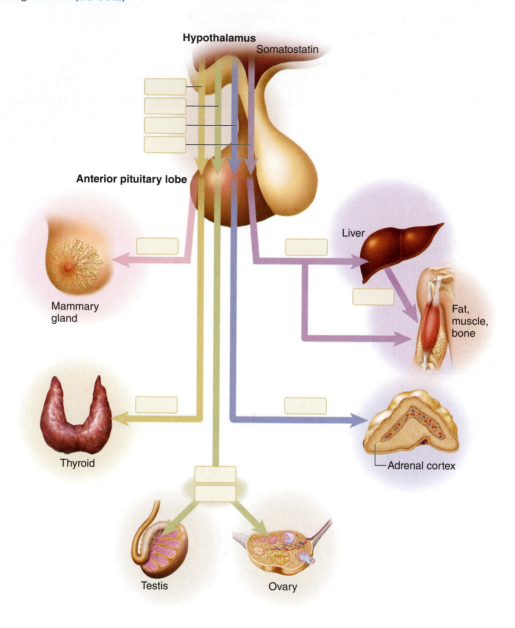

Hypothalamus

Somatostatin

Anterior pituitary lobe

Mammary gland

Thyroid

Liver

Fat, muscle, bone

Adrenal cortex

Testis

Ovary

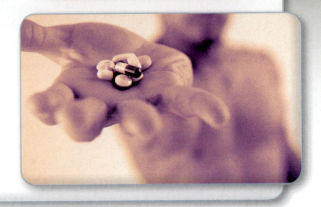

Chapter 36

Adrenal Steroids

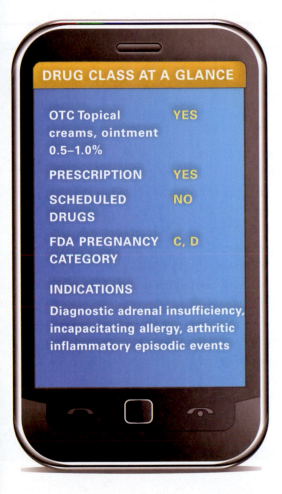

DRUG CLASS AT A GLANCE

OTC Topical creams, ointment 0.5–1.0%	**YES**
PRESCRIPTION	**YES**
SCHEDULED DRUGS	**NO**
FDA PREGNANCY CATEGORY	**C, D**

INDICATIONS

Diagnostic adrenal insufficiency, incapacitating allergy, arthritic inflammatory episodic events

KEY TERMS

Addison's disease: inadequate secretion of glucocorticoids and mineralocorticoids.

ADT: alternate-day therapy.

catabolism: process in which complex compounds are broken down into simpler molecules; usually associated with energy release.

circadian rhythm: internal biological clock; a repeatable 24-hour cycle of physiological activity.

Cushing's disease: excess secretion of adenocorticotropic hormone (ACTH).

glucocorticoid: steroid produced within the adrenal cortex (or a synthetic drug) that directly influences carbohydrate metabolism and inhibits the inflammatory process.

gluconeogenesis: the synthesis of glucose from molecules that are not carbohydrates, such as amino and fatty acids.

intra-articular (IA): joint space into which drug is injected.

isotonic: normal salt concentration of most body fluids; a salt concentration of 0.9 percent.

lymphokine: a substance secreted by T-cells that signals other immune cells like macrophages to aggregate.

lysosome: part of a cell that contains enzymes capable of digesting or destroying tissue/proteins.

mineralocorticoid: steroid produced within the adrenal cortex that directly influences sodium and potassium metabolism.

native: natural substance in the body.

proinflammatory: tending to cause inflammation.

replacement therapy: administration of a naturally occurring substance that the body is not able to produce in adequate amounts to maintain normal function.

repository preparation: preparation of a drug, usually for intramuscular or subcutaneous injection, that is intended to leach out from the site of injection slowly so that the duration of drug action is prolonged.

steroid: member of a large family of chemical substances (hormones, drugs) containing a structure similar to cortisone (tetracyclic cyclopenta-a-phenanthrene).

Learning Outcomes

After studying this chapter, you should be able to

36.1 compare the adrenal medulla and cortex and identify the two main classes of steroids.

36.2 describe the regulation of cortisol secretion.

36.3 explain the functions and the administration of glucocorticoids.

36.4 explain the functions and administration of mineralocorticoids.

36.5 describe adverse effects associated with chronic (routine) use of steroids.

Introduction

The adrenal glands are located on the upper surface of each kidney. The glands consist of an inner part, known as the adrenal medulla, and an outer part, known as the adrenal cortex. In the embryo, the adrenal medulla and cortex develop from different tissue. The adrenal medulla develops from the same tissue as sympathetic ganglia and the cortex develops from mesodermal tissue. The medulla secretes catecholamines during sympathetic activation of the "fight or flight" response. The cortex is composed of three separate tissue layers. Each layer releases one or more hormones that have important physiological functions, as shown in Table 36:1. The precursors for hormones of the adrenal cortex are derived from cholesterol. As shown in Figure 36.1, each of the three areas has different enzymes and, therefore, produces different classes of corticoids (corticosteroids): the glucocorticoids, the mineralocorticoids, and sex steroids.

The hormones of the adrenal cortex are generally referred to as corticosteroids, or just **steroids.** A deficiency in steroid production results in **Addison's disease.** Excess steroid production results in **Cushing's disease.** One of the main pharmacological uses of adrenal steroids is in the treatment of hormone deficiency conditions such as Addison's disease. This type of treatment is usually referred to as **replacement therapy.**

LO 36.1 | **LO 36.2** | **LO 36.3**

REGULATING ADRENOCORTICOID SECRETIONS

From the standpoint of pharmacology, the **glucocorticoids** are very important. In the body, *gluco*corticoids stimulate *gluco*neogenesis (production of *glucose* from amino acids) and lipolysis (breakdown of fat) and inhibit glucose uptake by the cells (increase plasma glucose). Glucocorticoids are all about making energy supplies (glucose) as the body's demands change. As drugs, they are used frequently in the treatment of inflammatory or allergic conditions.

The hypothalamic-anterior pituitary axis controls the production and secretion of cortisol as shown in Figure 36.1. When conditions cause the hypothalamus to secrete cortiocotropin-releasing hormone (CRH), the anterior pituitary responds by secreting corticotropin, also called adrenocorticotropin hormone (ACTH).

Layers of the Adrenal Cortex and the Main Hormones Secreted from Each Layer

Layer	Hormones	Main function
Glomerulosa (outer)	Aldosterone (referred to as a mineralocorticoid)	Regulates blood levels of sodium and potassium
Fasciculata (middle)	Cortisol, cortisone (referred to as glucocorticoids)	Regulates the metabolism of carbohydrates and proteins; also has potent antiinflammatory effects
Reticularis (inner)	Minute amounts of male (dehydroepiandrosterone [DHEA]) and female (estradiol) sex hormones	Normal physiological function of the sex hormones from this layer not clearly understood

ACTH travels in the circulation to the adrenal glands and subsequently stimulates the secretion of cortisol from the adrenal cortex. It is important to know which factors stimulate the hypothalamus to secrete CRH: the sleep-wake cycle (diurnal rhythm, **circadian rhythm**), negative feedback, and stress.

The levels of CRH, and therefore of cortisol, are adjusted to each individual's sleep-wake cycle. Higher

Figure 36.1   **Hypothalamo-Anterior Pituitary-Adrenal Relationship**

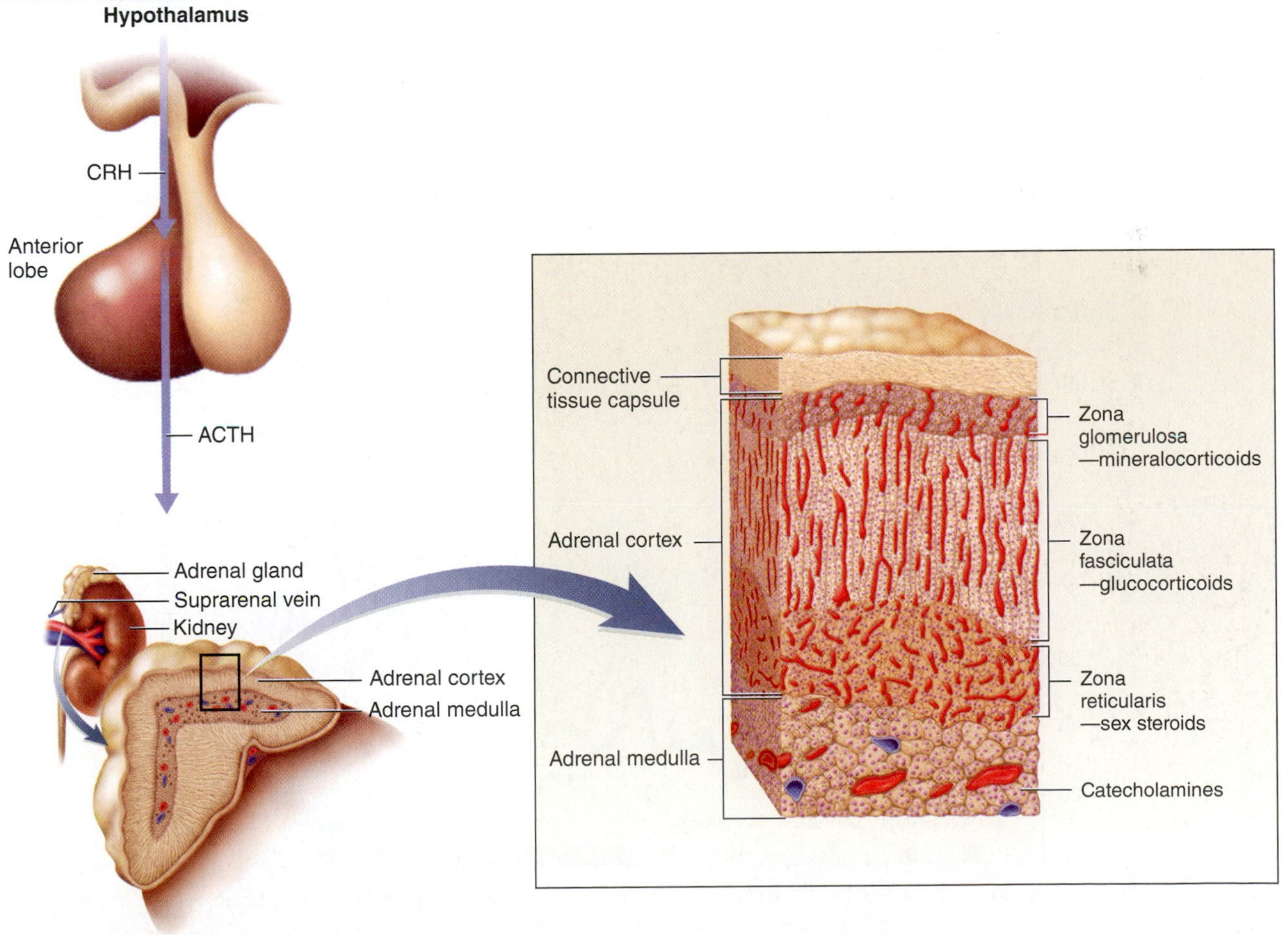

The hypothalamus secretes CRH (corticotropin-releasing hormone), which stimulates the release of ACTH (adreno-corticotropic hormone). ACTH stimulates secretion of glucocorticoids and growth of the adrenal cortex.

amounts of corticotropin and cortisol are secreted during the waking hours, whereas lower amounts are present during sleep. Figure 36.2 shows the fluctuation of ACTH secretion followed by glucocorticoid secretion over a 24-hour period. During the wake period, cortisol regulates body metabolism to meet the requirements of this active period.

Releasing hormone and corticotropin stimulate the release of cortisol into the bloodstream. When the level of cortisol rises above normal, further release of corticotropin (ACTH) and the releasing hormone (CRH) is inhibited. Negative feedback is the very finely tuned control that maintains the day-to-day levels of cortisol at relatively constant amounts.

Stress refers to a situation in which the body is subjected to increased physical or mental demands: exercise, cold weather, infections, surgery, and anxiety are all forms of stress. Stress produces an increase in CRH and ACTH secretion; ACTH stimulates cortisol secretion. The increased amounts of cortisol provide the body with an increased ability to cope with the demands of stress.

LO 36.3

GLUCOCORTICOIDS

The glucocorticoids regulate the metabolism of carbohydrates, proteins, and fats particularly during stress. During periods of stress involving bodily injury (trauma or surgery), there is an increased demand for glucose. Tissues undergoing repair and wound healing use glucose almost exclusively, as does the brain. The main physiological effects of the glucocorticoids are accomplished by two main metabolic processes: gluconeogenesis and protein **catabolism.** Both of these processes are stimulated by the glucocorticoids.

Gluconeogenesis is the process of making "new" glucose in the liver, where amino acids or glycerol are converted into glucose. As a result, plasma glucose concentration rises and can be used by injured tissue or the brain.

Catabolism is the breakdown of proteins into amino acids. This occurs mainly in skeletal muscle. The amino acids that are released can then be used by the liver to make glucose (gluconeogenesis).

Figure 36.2 Fluctuations in Plasma ACTH and Glucocorticoids throughout the Day in a Normal Female

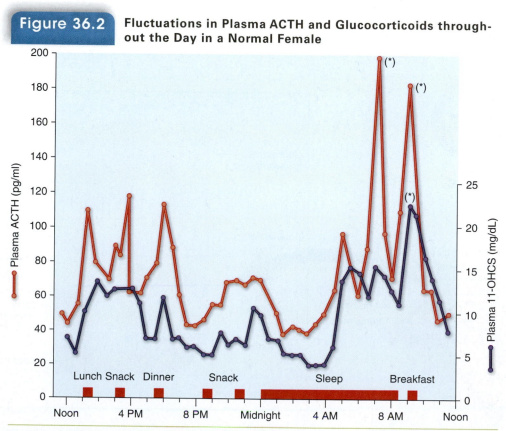

Note the marked rises (*) in ACTH and glucocorticoids in the morning before awakening. Glucocorticoids were measured as 11-oxysteroids (11 OHCS).

The glucocorticoids also have some mineralocorticoid activity—that is, the ability to cause the retention of sodium by the kidneys. Wherever sodium goes, water follows; therefore, water also is retained by the body (fluid retention). At high concentrations of glucocorticoids in the circulation, sodium and water retention may lead to the development of edema and/or hypertension.

Pharmacological Effects

The most important uses of the glucocorticoids are for replacement therapy in adrenocortical insufficiency (Addison's disease) and in the treatment of inflammatory conditions. The steroids that are available include the naturally occurring steroids and various synthetic preparations.

Replacement Therapy

The adrenal steroids are essential to life. In Addison's disease, there is a deficiency of both glucocorticoids and mineralocorticoids. The main symptoms in Addison's disease are dehydration, hypotension, and muscle weakness. Following ACTH administration, plasma cortisol and 17-hydroxycorticosteroids (17-OHCS) are measured. When the plasma levels of these steroids do not rise or cannot be detected, primary adrenal failure—that is, Addison's disease—is present. Cosyntropin is a synthetic peptide that corresponds to an active segment of ACTH. Although it provides the same therapeutic activity as ACTH with less allergenic potential, its formulation limits its use to diagnostic evaluation. Patients with Addison's disease must receive chronic hormone replacement therapy. The naturally occurring glucocorticoids are used most frequently (see Table 36:2). Dosages administered are similar to the levels that normally exist in the body (20 to 30 mg per day). In patients who continue to lose sodium due to a lack of aldosterone, a mineralocorticoid also must be administered along with the glucocorticoid.

Antiinflammatory Effects: Mechanism of Action

Glucocorticoids are the most potent antiinflammatory agents available. Sometimes the normal inflammatory response is too intense (acute inflammatory reaction)

[Table **36:2**]

Comparison of Naturally Occurring and Synthetic Glucocorticoids			
Drug (*Trade Name*)	Equivalent antiinflammatory dose (mg)	Sodium retention	Duration of action (hours)
Naturally occurring short-acting steroids			
Cortisone	25	High	12–24
Hydrocortisone (*Cortef, Solu-Cortef*)	20	High	12–24
Synthetic intermediate-acting steroids			
Methylprednisolone (*Depo-Medrol, Medrol, Solu-Medrol*)	4	None	24–36
Prednisolone (*Millipred, Flo-Pred*)	5	Mild	24–36
Prednisone (*Sterapred, Sterapred DS*)	5	Mild	24–36
Triamcinolone (*Aristospan-IL, Aristospan-IA, Kenalog-40*)	4	None	36–48
Synthetic long-acting steroids			
Betamethasone (*Celestone*)	0. 75	None	48–72
Dexamethasone	0. 75	None	48–72

or is prolonged (chronic inflammatory reaction), and the inflammation itself becomes a disease process. For example, in rheumatoid arthritis, the inflammatory response can lead to permanent joint damage. Therefore, suppression of the inflammatory response becomes the most important therapeutic outcome.

All glucocorticoids interfere with all stages of the inflammatory response. Virtually every cell has glucocorticoid receptors located in the cytoplasm. The glucocorticoid hormone, cortisol (and other corticosteroids), is a hydrophobic molecule that requires a transport protein to carry it in the plasma. At the target cell, however, cortisol passes through the plasma membrane into the cytoplasm, where it binds to the specific, high-affinity glucocorticoid receptor (see Figure 36.3). The activated receptor-glucocorticoid complex goes into the nucleus and binds to specific DNA elements to activate transcription of antiinflammatory proteins or prevent **proinflammatory** protein production. Glucocorticoids have a wide range of influence and affect virtually every cell in the immune system (mast cells, eosinophils, neutrophils, macrophages, and lymphocytes). Macrophages appear to be most sensitive to corticosteroid effects, followed by B-cells, and then the T-lymphocytes. There are almost three times as many glucocorticoid receptors on the macrophages as on B-cells and T-cells. Macrophages, once considered as simple scavenging cells, are today recognized as primary proinflammatory cells, especially when antibodies are involved in mediation of injury. Corticosteroids inhibit the expression of receptors on macrophages and reduce the secretion of proinflammatory **lymphokines** and vasoactive substances. This action reduces the inflammatory reaction by limiting the capillary dilatation and permeability of the vascular structures, thereby preventing edema. The corticosteroids restrict the accumulation of white blood cells and macrophages that would have continued the inflammatory process. They also inhibit the release of destructive enzymes, **lysosomes,** which attack injury debris and destroy normal tissue indiscriminately.

Slight alterations in the structure of the naturally occurring glucocorticoids produce synthetic steroids with greater antiinflammatory potency. The synthetic steroids have a longer duration of action than do the naturally occurring steroids. In addition, they produce fewer undesirable mineralocorticoid effects. Features of the glucocorticoids are shown in Table 36:2. Prednisone and triamcinolone are four times more potent than

Figure 36.3 **Steroid Transport to Target Cell and Receptor Interaction**

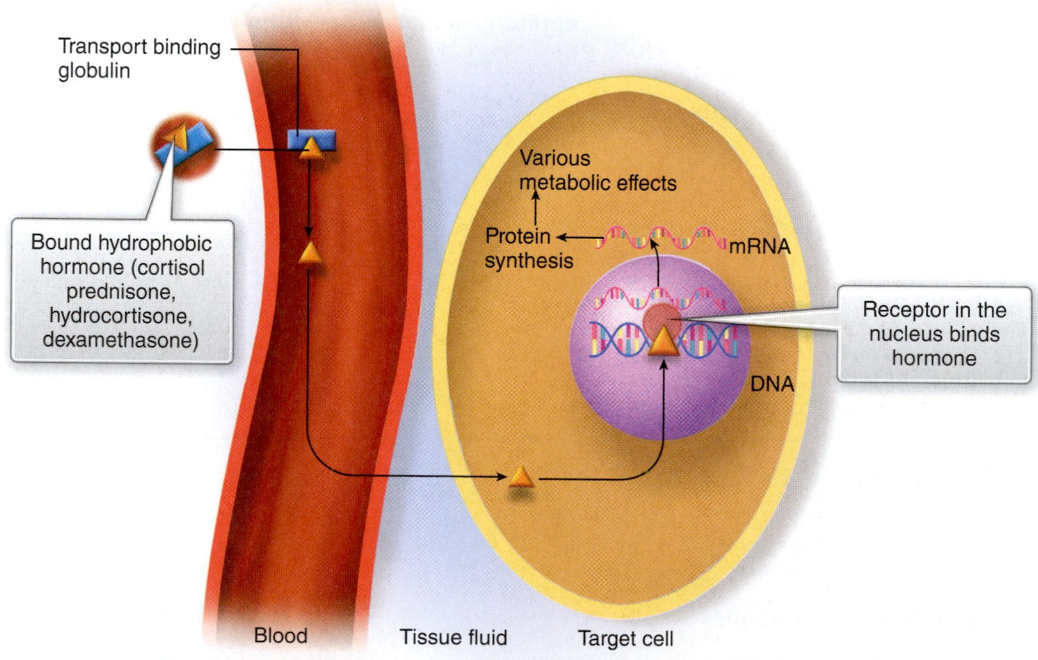

Glucocorticoids (orange triangles) are hydrophobic molecules and must be carried by transport binding globulins, TBG (transcortin), to the target tissue. Upon dissociating from the transport protein, the lipophilic glucocorticoid diffuses into the cell and combines with a receptor that enables it to enter the nucleus and direct transcription of mRNA protein.

the native corticosteroids cortisone and hydrocortisone. They have far less sodium-retaining activity associated with a mineralocorticoid and they have a significantly longer duration of action.

Clinical Indications

Adrenocorticotropic hormone is primarily used for diagnostic evaluation of adrenocortical function. In established disorders, ACTH is used in the constellation of drug therapy for exacerbations of multiple sclerosis and hypercalcemia associated with cancer. Glucocorticoids are the drugs of choice in primary and secondary adrenal cortical insufficiency (conditions where cortisol release is decreased). Glucocorticoids like prednisone are also approved for use in a wide range of inflammatory disorders, including rheumatic disorders, arthritis, collagen disease, specific ulcerative colitis, multiple sclerosis, severe allergic reaction, respiratory disease, and management of leukemias and lymphomas (see Table 36:3). Since inflammation is part of allergic reactions, glucocorticoids are useful in the clinical management of allergies.

Synthetic glucocorticoids are frequently used to treat allergic and nonallergic, irritant-mediated inflammation. High doses of these steroids may be given to interrupt flares of inflammation, often as a temporary measure until another medication takes effect. In low doses, the steroid prevents flares and protects joints, eyes, and internal organs from damage caused by inflammation.

In addition to these FDA-approved uses of corticosteroids, there are other uses that are medically appropriate although not specifically approved by the FDA (off-label use). Such inflammatory conditions include acute mountain sickness, bacterial meningitis, chronic obstructive pulmonary disease (COPD), Graves's ophthalmopathy, respiratory distress syndrome, septic shock, and spinal cord injury.

Administration and Dosage

Glucocorticoids may be administered orally, intranasally, IM, IV, or topically. Methylprednisolone and prednisone are used to achieve prompt suppression of inflammation. In general, the lowest effective dose is used. The initial oral dose is 4 to 48 mg daily for methylprednisolone or 5 to 60 mg daily for prednisone, depending on the disease. A *Medrol Dose Pack* for methylprednisolone is available

[Table **36:3**]

Some Therapeutic Indications for the Use of Glucocorticoids in Non-adrenal Conditions

Condition	Indication
Allergy	Angioneurotic edema, asthma, bee stings, contact dermatitis, serum sickness, urticaria
Collagen disorders	Lupus erythematosus, polymyositis, rheumatoid arthritis
Eye diseases	Acute uveitis, allergic conjunctivitis, optic neuritis
Gastrointestinal disease	Inflammatory bowel disease (ulcerative colitis, Crohn's disease)
Inflammation of bones and joints	Arthritis, bursitis
Neurological disorders	Cerebral edema following brain surgery, multiple sclerosis
Organ transplants	Prevention and treatment of tissue rejection (immunosuppression)
Renal disorders	Nephrotic syndrome
Skin diseases	Atopic dermatitis, pemphigus, seborrheic dermatitis
Thyroid disease	Malignant exophthalmos, subacute thyroiditis
Miscellaneous	Hypercalcemia, mountain sickness, postherpetic neuralgia

with six days of tapered oral dosing. Each unit pack is a card that contains 21 4-mg pills (See Figure 36.4). The patient starts with six pills (24 mg) and takes one less pill each day, until the pack is finished. The pills are taken orally with a full glass of water before breakfast, after lunch, after dinner, and at bedtime (according to the day). The patient gets a strong dose of the steroid on the first day of treatment, and as the dose decreases by the end of the sixth day, the inflammatory problem should subside. Prednisone is also available as a unit pack (5 mg/tablet) for dose tapering over six days.

Intravenous administration is used in emergencies, when prompt effects are needed. The preparations for IM injection include **repository preparations,** in which the glucocorticoid is slowly released within the muscle or joint providing a longer duration of action. Examples of injectable preparations that have a slow onset and long duration of action are methylprednisolone (*Depo-Medrol*), triamcinolone (*Aristospan*), and very new dexamethasone intravitreal implant (*Ozurdex*). These formulations are not water soluble. They are sterile suspensions that release the active corticosteroid by slow hydrolysis in the tissue. Doses and indications for the adrenal steroids are presented in Table 36:4. There is wide variation in the therapeutic dosages of the glucocorticoids (see Table 36:4). Doses must be individualized to the condition under treatment. Short-term treatment with glucocorticoids absorbs scar tissue (keloids) when injected directly into the scarred skin. For exacerbations of chronically inflamed joints and soft tissue, the drugs may be injected into the specific area. For swollen joints, the edematous fluid is removed before the steroid is injected. Too frequent **intra-articular (IA)** administration can damage joint tissues, so patients are advised to decrease all stress on the inflamed joint to minimize the need for reinjection.

Topical use of the glucocorticoids is indicated in the treatment of inflammation and pruritic dermatosis. Topical steroids as ointments, creams, or sprays are available over the counter or by prescription; however, there is only one steroid approved for nonprescription products, hydrocortisone. Over-the-counter preparations are specifically labeled for the temporary relief of minor skin irritations, itching, and rashes due to eczema, dermatitis, insect bites, poison ivy, detergents, and cosmetics, as well as itching in the genital and anal regions (see Figure 36.4). Examples of over-the-counter topical steroids include *Cortaid Maximum Strength, Corticaine, Lanacort Maximum, Corticool gel (45% alcohol),* and *Cortizone-10 Anti-Itch Quickshot Spray.* See Figure 36.4 for examples of OTC hydrocortisone products. These products usually contain 0.5 or 1 percent hydrocortisone, a lesser amount of hydrocortisone than may be obtained by prescription;

Figure 36.4

Examples of a Methylprednisolone Dose Pack and Over-the-Counter Hydrocortisone Products

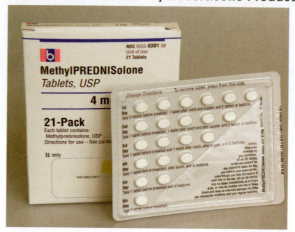

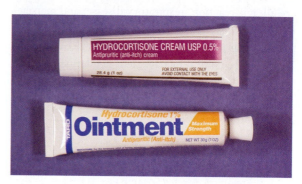

Doses and Indications for Adrenal Steroids

Adrenal steroids	Indication	Dose
Corticotropins		
ACTH	Confirmation of adrenal responsiveness	80 units single injection or 10–25 units diluted IV over 8 hr
Repository corticotropin (*H.P. Acthar gel*)	Confirmation of adrenal responsiveness	40–80 units every 24–72 hr IM, SC
Cosyntropin (*Cortrosyn*)	Confirmation of adrenal responsiveness	0.25–0.75 mg IM or IV
Mineralocorticoids		
Fludrocortisone acetate (*Florinef Acetate*)	Addison's disease	0.2 mg daily PO three times a week
Glucocorticoids		
Betamethasone (*Celestone*)	Antiinflammatory	0.6–7.2 mg daily PO; up to 9 mg per day IV
Budesonide (*Rhinocort*)	Allergic rhinitis	1 spray/nostril daily (64 mcg)
Budesonide (*Entocort E. C.*)	Crohn's disease	9 mg daily up to 8 weeks
Cortisone (*Cortisone Acetate*)	Antiinflammatory	25–300 mg/day PO
Dexamethasone (*Decadron, DexPak Taperpak*)	Allergic disorders Cushing syndrome test suppression	0.75 mg daily PO for 6 days 1 mg at 11 PM or 0.5 mg every 6 hr for 48 hr
	Multiple sclerosis	30 mg/day PO for a week followed by 4 –12 mg on alternate days for 1 month
	Palliative treatment of brain tumor	2 mg PO BID or TID
Dexamethasone (*Hexadrol*)	Allergies, collagen, endocrine, GI, and rheumatic disorders	4 or 8 mg IM
Dexamethasone with lidocaine (*Decadron with Xylocaine*)	Bursitis	0.5–0.75 ml soft tissue injection
Fluticasone (*Flonase*)	Allergic rhinitis	2 sprays/nostril once daily (50 mcg/spray)
Hydrocortisone (*Cortef*)	Antiinflammatory	20–240 mg/day PO
	Multiple sclerosis	200 mg/day PO for a week followed by 80 mg every other day for 1 month
Hydrocortisone sodium succinate (*A-hydroCort, Solu-Cortef*)	Antiinflammatory	100–500 mg every 2, 4, or 6 hr IV
Methylprednisolone (*Medrol*)	Antiinflammatory	4–48 mg/day PO or alternate-day therapy
Methylprednisolone sodium (*A-Methapred, Solu-Medrol*)	Antiinflammatory	10–40 mg IV over several minutes

(Continued)

Adrenal steroids	Indication	Dose
Methylprednisolone acetate (*Depo-Medrol*)*	Adrenocorticoid insufficiency	40 mg IM every 2 weeks
	Asthma, allergic rhinitis	80–120 mg IM weekly
	Bursitis, tendonitis	4–80 mg intra-articular
	Dermatologic lesions	40–120 mg IM weekly for 1 to 4 weeks
	Rheumatoid arthritis	40–120 mg IM weekly
Mometasone (*Nasonex*)	Allergic rhinitis	2 sprays/nostril daily (50 mcg/spray)
Prednisone (*Sterapred-DS, Sterapred*)	Antiinflammatory, immunosuppressive	5–60 mg/day PO
Prednisolone (*Flo-Pred, Millipred, Prelone*)	Allergies, collagen, endocrine, GI, and rheumatic disorders	5–60 mg/day PO or 4–100 mg intralesional, intra-articular
	Exacerbation of multiple sclerosis	200 mg/day PO for a week, followed by 80 mg every other day for 1 month
	Multiple sclerosis	200 mg daily PO for 7 days, then 80 mg every other day for 1 month
Triamcinolone* (*Aristospan, Kenalog-10, Kenalog-40, Trivaris*)	Alopecia areata, keloids, psoriasis	2–100 mg daily intralesional
	Gouty arthritis, bursitis, rheumatoid arthritis	2–15 mg intra-articular depending on joint size
	Hay fever and pollen allergy	40–100 mg IM
	Tuberculous meningitis	32–48 mg PO daily as adjunct treatment

Not an inclusive list of products.

nevertheless, the active component is still a steroid. Misuse of these drugs may be accompanied by adverse effects similar to those described for other steroids. See Adverse Effects for more detail.

Metabolism and Excretion

The **native** and synthetic glucocorticoids are metabolized by the liver and then excreted in the urine. The most common urinary metabolites of cortisol are the 17-hydroxycorticosteroids (17-OHCS). These can be measured from 24-hour urine collections, and they provide an estimate of glucocorticoid secretion from the adrenal cortex. In patients with adrenocortical insufficiency, these metabolites are usually very low.

Adverse Effects

The adverse effects of the glucocorticoids, including prednisone, are related to the amount of drug taken daily and the duration of treatment. Usual adverse effects include increase in appetite, weight gain, indigestion, restlessness, and hirsutism. Less frequently patients may experience a change in skin color, dizziness, increased sweating, flushing of the face, and skin rash. In patients receiving high doses or long-term treatment, the adverse reactions are an exaggeration of the normal steroidal

effects and similar to the symptoms of Cushing's disease (excess corticosteroid production). Figure 36.5 shows the effect of abnormal fat deposition that occurs with

Figure 36.5

Cushing Syndrome

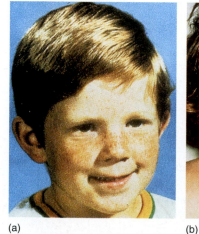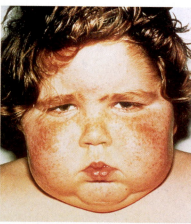

(a)   (b)

(a) Boy before the onset of the syndrome. (b) The same boy four months later showing the "moon face" from abnormal fat deposition in the face that is characteristic of Cushing syndrome.

excess cortisol secretion. Similar changes occur with long-term hydrocortisone therapy. In addition to the rounded "moon face," patients may develop a "buffalo hump" from fat deposition along the shoulders, as shown in Figure 36.6. The adverse effects are summarized in Table 36:5. An important adverse reaction associated with long-term use is steroid addiction, which may manifest as mood changes (euphoria), insomnia, personality changes, and psychological dependency. This is steroid psychosis. The incidence is usually associated with larger steroid doses. Abrupt withdrawal of the steroids can produce severe mental depression. For this reason, discontinuation of long-term or high-dose steroids must be done under medical supervision, gradually, over months in small decrements to avoid precipitating withdrawal symptoms and depression.

Glucocorticoids can definitely be misused and abused. There have been reports of women taking dexamethasone who want to gain weight because they perceive the changes in fat distribution as a pleasant alteration of body features. However, the term *steroid abuse* usually refers to the use of anabolic steroids for bulking up and body-building, rather than glucocorticoids. Anabolic steroids are synthetic substances related to the male sex hormones, called androgens. These steroids are presented in Chapter 37.

Alternate-Day Therapy

Steroid administration is also accomplished by alternate-day therapy **(ADT).** Alternate-day therapy is intended to reduce or eliminate the adverse effects of prolonged steroid treatment. In ADT, a short-acting steroid is administered every other day in the morning. The effects of a single dose of a short-acting steroid will last into the next day. However, during the second day (no steroid administered), the patient's adrenal gland begins to function (that is, is released from negative feedback). On the following day (third day), the steroid is again administered and the patient's adrenal gland is once again suppressed. This therapy prevents adrenal atrophy and permanent destruction of the adrenal gland. There is also a lower incidence of other adverse effects. Doses and indications for the adrenal steroids are presented in Table 36:4.

LO 36.1 LO 36.4

MINERALOCORTICOIDS

The **mineralocorticoids** are hormones secreted by the outer layer of the adrenal gland. The main effect of the mineralocorticoid hormones is to regulate the fluid balance of the body. When there is a deficiency of mineralocorticoids, a condition known as hypoaldosteronism results. This condition usually is caused by adrenalectomy or by adrenal tumors. Replacement therapy is necessary because the mineralocorticoids are essential for life.

Physiological Effects

The most important mineralocorticoid is aldosterone. Its site of action is at the distal tubules of the nephrons. The main function of the nephrons is the formation of urine, during which process many essential nutrients and ions are reabsorbed through the tubules back into the blood. Aldosterone increases the reabsorption of sodium ions. In exchange, potassium ions are transported into the urine. This process is usually referred to as sodium-potassium exchange. Water also is reabsorbed with sodium. Consequently, normal sodium and water levels **(isotonic)** are maintained in the blood and other body tissues.

Administration and Dosage

Fludrocortisone (*Florinef*) is a potent mineralocorticoid and a potent glucocorticoid (greater than cortisone). Although fludrocortisone has dual activity, it is usually administered in conjunction with a glucocorticoid (cortisone, hydrocortisone) to achieve total replacement therapy in primary and secondary adrenocortical insufficiency. Fludrocortisone is administered orally in doses of 0.1 mg three times per week to 0.2 mg per day.

Adverse Effects

Excessive use of the mineralocorticoids results in sodium and water retention and the loss of potassium. The major symptoms are edema, hypertension, arrythmias, and muscle weakness due to the loss of potassium. In certain patients, the edema could lead to congestive heart failure. A physician should be notified if dizziness,

Figure 36.6

An Example of Buffalo Hump Caused by a Redistribution of Body Fat during Prednisone Treatment

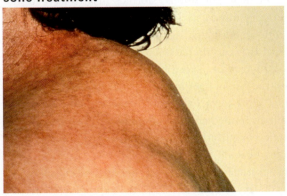

Adverse Effects of Long-Term Steroid Therapy

Metabolic effect	Symptoms and signs
Glucocorticoid	
Increased gluconeogenesis	Obesity, diabetes mellitus
Increased protein catabolism	Muscle weakness and wasting, thinning of skin (ecchymosis, striae), osteoporosis (loss of protein matrix), decreased growth (in children), decreased wound healing, increased infections (in leukopenia), peptic ulceration
Mineralocorticoid	
Sodium and water retention	Edema, increased blood volume, hypertension
Loss of potassium	Muscle weakness and cramps
Miscellaneous effects	
Androgenic effects	Hirsutism, virilism, irregular menstruation
Eye complications	Glaucoma, cataract formation
Psychological changes	Euphoria, steroid addiction, depression

continuing headaches, or swelling in the lower extremities occurs. Dose adjustment usually mitigates adverse effects. Other adverse effects include increased sweating, bruising, and allergic skin rash.

LO 36.1 **LO 36.3** **LO 36.4** **LO 36.5**

SPECIAL CONSIDERATIONS

Steroids are administered for their antiinflammatory activity in patients with normal adrenal function. With continued use (as well as misuse of these drugs), patients may experience changes in appearance and behavior indicative of metabolic alterations. Since steroids universally affect metabolism, patients must be observed carefully for changes in body weight, electrolyte balance, and cardiac function. The sodium retention associated with these drugs may lead to elevated blood pressure, even hypertension, and edema. Patients should be weighed daily to monitor changes in overall body weight. Patients should be questioned about feeling fatigued or experiencing cramps and weakness in the extremities because these may be symptoms of

hypokalemia. Patients with Addison's disease are often sensitive to drug effects and therefore often have an exaggerated response to drug therapy. Patients, especially those on high-dose therapy, should be monitored for changes in sleep patterns and mood, particularly depression or psychotic episodes.

Steroids should be used cautiously in patients who have gastrointestinal (GI) ulceration, renal disease, congestive heart failure, ocular herpes simplex, diabetes mellitus, emotional instability, or psychotic tendencies. In all of these conditions, steroids may exacerbate the underlying disease as a result of their pharmacological actions. Although steroids are ulcerogenic, it is not unusual that certain patients with gastrointestinal ulcer or colitis may be placed on a steroid regimen. In such cases, the risk of continuing degeneration outweighs the risk of short-term exposure to the steroid in order to obtain an immediate antiinflammatory response. Ophthalmic complications during prolonged corticosteroid therapy include posterior subcapsular cataract, glaucoma, possible damage to optic nerves, and enhancement of secondary ocular infections due to fungi or virus.

Contraindications

Steroids are contraindicated for use in patients who have systemic fungal and local viral (especially ocular herpes) infections. Topical steroids should not be applied to the eyes or periorbital area. Steroids and ACTH may reduce the patient's resistance to fight local infection. Live virus vaccinations should not be given during steroid therapy. Patients receiving high-dose steroids may not have the ability to develop antibody immunity, putting them at risk for developing infection and neurological complications. This does not apply to patients receiving physiological steroid doses as replacement therapy.

LO 36.3 **LO 36.4**

DRUG INTERACTIONS

Steroids have been reported to interact with a variety of drug classes (see Table 36:6). Since the glucocorticoids affect carbohydrate metabolism, it is not surprising that diabetics may have an increased insulin or oral hypoglycemic requirement during periods of steroid treatment. Glycosylated hemoglobin should be monitored during steroid treatment. Steroids administered concomitantly with potassium-depleting diuretics, amphotericin B, or digoxin may potentiate the development of hypokalemia. Patients receiving coumarin anticoagulant may have a decreased warfarin response in the presence of steroids. Prothrombin time must be monitored to ensure that patients are adequately covered.

Note to the Health Care Professional

To avoid adrenal insufficiency, patients receiving high-dose or long-term steroid therapy must not discontinue treatment abruptly. These patients should be gradually weaned from the drug under the supervision of a physician.

Phenytoin, phenobarbital, and rifampin enhance the metabolism of corticosteroids, leading to reduced blood steroid levels and a decreased pharmacological response. In patients receiving these drugs chronically, the dose of corticosteroid may require adjustment.

On the other hand, oral contraceptives inhibit steroid metabolism. Concomitant use of these drugs may lead to elevated blood steroid concentrations and may potentiate steroid toxicity.

[Table **36:6**]

Examples of Drug Interactions Associated with Glucocorticoids

Glucocorticoids interact with	Response
Amphotericin B, digitalis, diuretics	Potentiate hypokalemia (possible digitalis toxicity)
Antibiotics, macrolide	Increase methylprednisolone clearance from plasma
Aspirin	Increase GI side effects by an additive effect
Growth hormone	Decrease growth-promoting effect of growth hormone
Insulin, oral hypoglycemics	Increase requirement for insulin or oral hypoglycemics
Isoniazid	Increase requirements for isoniazid
Oral contraceptives, estrogens, ketoconazole	Increase response of glucocorticoid and mineralocorticoid because of decreased steroid metabolism
Phenobarbital, phenytoin, rifampin	Increase steroid requirement due to increased steroid metabolism through CYP34A induction
Warfarin	Inhibit response to the anticoagulants

This class of drugs has a tremendous potential for overuse and overexposure due to the availability of over-the-counter preparations. In addition, steroids may be prescribed by more than one treating physician. It is not unusual for older patients to visit orthopedists, allergists, diabetologists, ophthalmologists, and rheumatologists in addition to their family physician. Therefore, it becomes important to review steroid actions that could be misinterpreted as exacerbations of other underlying conditions.

Time of Dosing

Single steroid doses should be taken before 9 AM to allow distribution of drug to mimic diurnal levels without suppressing available adrenocortical activity. Large doses of steroids may cause GI upset. Patients may take the medication with meals or antacids to minimize the irritation.

Changes in Blood Sugar Levels

Diabetics taking steroids must be properly counseled that steroids increase blood glucose otherwise they may overmedicate as a response to this transient hyperglycemia. Diabetic patients should notify the prescribing (steroid) physician if changes in their monitored blood glucose levels occur. Diabetics may have an increased blood glucose concentration requiring dose adjustment in insulin or oral antidiabetic drugs. Patients should be reminded to give full disclosure of steroid use to other physicians, such as diabetologist or endocrinologist, to keep their medication history current.

Physician Notification

The physician should be notified immediately if significant fluid retention manifests as swelling of lower extremities or unusual weight gain, muscle weakness, abdominal pain, seizures, or headache occur. This may indicate the need for dose alteration or discontinuation if hypersensitivity develops. Topical steroids will more likely produce skin or ocular itching and irritation rather than the spectrum of other effects.

Elderly patients should be reminded to call if they develop signs of hypertension, hyperglycemia, and potassium loss. These include dizziness, muscle weakness, and headaches. Because of the reduced muscle mass, elderly patients are more sensitized to the effects of steroids and should be monitored in the office at least every 6 months.

For patients receiving high doses of steroids, there is a decreased resistance to fight local infection (immunosuppressive response). Patients should notify the prescribing (steroid) physician before immunizations with live vaccines are given.

Stopping Medication

Patients receiving high-dose or long-term therapy should not discontinue steroids without supervision of the prescribing physician to avoid precipitating symptoms of withdrawal.

Use in Pregnancy

Drugs in this class have been designated FDA Pregnancy Category C. Safety for use in pregnancy has not been established through adequate use or clinical trials in pregnant women. Steroids cross the placenta. Chronic maternal steroid use in the first trimester is known to produce cleft palate in newborns (about 1 percent incidence). The benefit to the mother must outweigh risk to the fetus and newborn. When clearly required, maternal steroid administration should be at the lowest effective dose for the shortest duration and the infant should be subsequently monitored for adrenal activity. Where mothers received ACTH, the newborn should be monitored for hyperadrenalism.

Understanding Terminology

Answer the following questions.

1. Define the term *steroid*. (LO 36.1, 36.2, 36.3, 36.4)
2. Differentiate between mineralocorticoids and glucocorticoids. (LO 36.1, 36.3, 36.4)
3. Explain replacement therapy. (LO 36.3, 36.4)

Acquiring Knowledge

Answer the following questions.

1. What are the two main parts of the adrenal gland? (LO 36.1)
2. Which layer of the adrenal cortex secretes the mineralocorticoids? Which layer secretes the glucocorticoids? (LO 36.1)
3. What disease results from a deficiency of the corticosteroids? (LO 36.2, 36.3)
4. What three hormones regulate the release of cortisol? (LO 36.1, 36.2)
5. What is the importance of higher glucocorticoid secretion during injury and wound healing? (LO 36.3)
6. List the two main therapeutic uses of the glucocorticoids. (LO 36.3)
7. What are the main differences between the naturally occurring steroids and the synthetic steroids? (LO 36.3, 36.4)
8. List the major adverse effect of steroid therapy. What is meant by *ADT?* (LO 36.3, 36.5)
9. What is the function of the mineralocorticoids? (LO 36.4)
10. What are the adverse effects of excessive administration of the mineralocorticoids? (LO 36.4, 36.5)

Applying Knowledge on the Job

Use your critical-thinking skills to answer the following questions.

1. Assume you are a pharmacy assistant in a nursing home, screening patients for contraindications and drug interactions. What is the potential drug problem—and its solution—for each of the following cases?
   a. Patient A has hypertension. He has been prescribed hydrocortisone injections for severe bursitis. (LO 36.2, 36.3)
   b. Patient B is diabetic. She has been prescribed prednisolone for osteoarthritis. (LO 36.2, 36.3)
   c. Patient C is taking coumadin anticoagulant. He has been prescribed prednisone for gout. (LO 36.2, 36.3)

2. Assume you are a pharmacy intern in a university hospital. What is the potential drug problem for each of the following patients? How would you resolve the problem?
   a. A 25-year-old woman has been prescribed betamethasone for severe psoriasis. The patient is currently taking oral contraceptives. (LO 36.2, 36.3)
   b. A 16-year-old boy has been prescribed dexamethasone for bronchial asthma. He is an epileptic currently taking phenobarbital for seizure control. (LO 36.2, 36.3)

3. Tom is an 8-year-old who is taking 80 mg of prednisone for inflammation of the liver. He has been diagnosed with chickenpox. Would this affect his prednisone dose? Why or why not? (LO 36.2, 36.3)

4. Ten-year-old Shannon has had a severe allergic reaction to poison oak. Her physician has decided to initiate prednisone therapy. The prescription reads:

Prednisone QS 40 mg qd × 3d, 30 mg qd × 3d, 20 mg qd × 3d, 10 mg qd × 3d, 5 mg qd × 2d then dc. Assume the pharmacy fills this prescription with prednisone 10-mg tablets. How many tablets would the patient receive and how would you expect the label to read? (LO 36.3)

5. Why is it important for patients receiving high-dose or long-term therapy to be taken off prednisone by "tapering" or decreasing the dose gradually? (LO 36.2, 36.5)

Multiple Choice

Use your critical-thinking skills to answer the following questions.

1. Mineralocorticoids are secreted by the (LO 36.1, 36.2, 36.4)
   A. medulla
   B. zona reticularis
   C. zona fasciculata
   D. zona glomerulosa

2. A patient presents with dehydration. Following ACTH administration, plasma cortisol levels cannot be detected. The most likely diagnosis for this patient is (LO 36.1, 36.2)
   A. Addison's disease
   B. Cushing's disease
   C. thyroid disease
   D. rheumatoid arthritis

3. The advantage of a repository preparation of a glucocorticoid is (LO 36.3)
   A. rapid response
   B. slow release from the muscle
   C. oral administration
   D. prevention of edema in the joint

4. A patient diagnosed with rheumatoid arthritis is in remission, and the physician tells the patient to discontinue her prednisone. Which important advice would the physician give to his patient? (LO 36.5)
   A. discontinuing the prednisone will lower your potassium
   B. taper the medication dosage down over the next few months
   C. your immune function will decrease after discontinuing the medication
   D. your skin may bruise more easily

5. A patient presents with Cushing's disease. Which of the following adverse effects would you expect to see upon examination? (LO 36.3, 36.5)
   A. dehydration
   B. hyperpigmentation
   C. muscle weakness
   D. weight loss

Multiple Choice (Multiple Answer)

Select the correct choices for each statement. The choices may be all correct, all incorrect, or any combination.

1. Select all of the true statements about the adrenal medulla. (LO 36.1)
   A. it is the outer part of the adrenal gland
   B. it is composed of three separate tissue layers
   C. it secretes corticosteroids
   D. it secretes catecholamines

2. The regulation of cortisol secretions involves which of the following? **(LO 36.2)**
   A. diurnal rhythm
   B. negative feedback
   C. stress
   D. circadian rhythm

3. Which of the following are not functions of glucocorticoids? **(LO 36.3)**
   A. metabolism of carbohydrates
   B. making new protein
   C. gluconeogenesis
   D. retention of sodium

4. Mineralocorticoids do which of the following? **(LO 36.4)**
   A. increase reabsorption of sodium
   B. cause K^+ ion transport to urine
   C. regulate fluid balance
   D. decrease inflammation

5. Choose all of the effects of long-term steroid therapy. **(LO 36.5)**
   A. obesity
   B. thinning of skin
   C. glaucoma
   D. depression

Sequencing

Place the following medications in order from longest duration of action to shortest. **(LO 36.3)**

_____   _____   _____   _____

Longest   **Shortest**

Flo-pred

Aristospan

Celestone

Cortef

Classification

Place the following medications under the correct type of steroid. **(LO 36.3, 36.4)**

budesonide
cosyntropin
Celestone
ACTH
H.P. Acthar gel
Decadron

Corticotropins	Glucocorticoids

Matching

Match the following terms with the correct definition. **(LO 36.1, 36.2, 36.3, 36.4)**

a. catabolism
b. glucocorticoid
c. gluconeogenesis
d. mineralocorticoid
e. steroid
f. tropic

1. ___ substance that influences sodium and potassium metabolism
2. ___ breaking down of complex compounds into simpler molecules
3. ___ substance containing a similar structure to cortisone
4. ___ substance that influences carbohydrate metabolism
5. ___ having an affinity for a particular organ
6. ___ synthesis of glucose from amino and fatty acids

Documentation

Using the prescription below, answer the following questions. **(LO 36.3, 36.5)**

Lakeside Clinic
Practice RX

12345 Main Avenue
Anytown, USA   12345
931-555-1000

NAME: ___Julie Brown_____   DATE: _____

ADDRESS: _____

RX   **cortisone 200mg**

Sig: **Take by mouth once daily**

__Dr. Frank Lloyd_____   **M.D.**   _____**M.D.**

  Substitution Permitted   Dispense as written

DEA #: _____   REFILL: NR   1   2   3   4

---

a. What condition is likely being treated with this medication?
b. What is the usual daily dose for this medication? Is the dose prescribed within the usual daily dose?
c. What adverse effects might be seen with long-term use of this medication?
d. How should this medication be discontinued?

For interactive animations, videos, and assessment, visit:
www.mcgrawhillconnect.com

Chapter 37

Gonadal Hormones, Oral Contraceptives, and Erectile Dysfunction Drugs

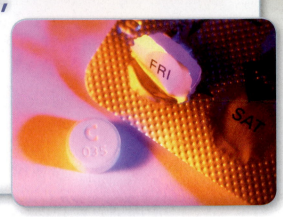

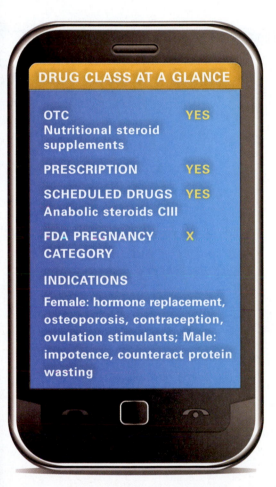

DRUG CLASS AT A GLANCE

OTC Nutritional steroid supplements	YES
PRESCRIPTION	YES
SCHEDULED DRUGS Anabolic steroids CIII	YES
FDA PREGNANCY CATEGORY	X

INDICATIONS

Female: hormone replacement, osteoporosis, contraception, ovulation stimulants; Male: impotence, counteract protein wasting

KEY TERMS

amenorrhea: condition in which monthly menstruation (menses) no longer occurs.

anabolism: process that converts or incorporates nutritional substances into tissue; usually associated with conversion of proteins into muscle mass.

androgen: male sex hormone responsible for the development of male characteristics.

apoptosis: cell death, either due to programmed cell death or other physiological events.

biphasic: two different amounts of estrogen hormone are released during the cycle.

bone mineral density: amount of calcium and phosphorus deposited in bone matrix.

buccal absorption: absorption of drug through the mucous membranes lining the oral cavity.

contraception: preventing pregnancy by preventing either conception (joining of egg and sperm) or implantation in the uterus.

diplopia: condition in which a single object is seen (perceived) as two objects; double vision.

dysmenorrhea: condition that is associated with painful and difficult menstruation.

endometrium: lining of the uterus.

equipotent: when drugs (substances) produce the same intensity or spectrum of activity. Usually, the absolute amount of drug (for example, 5, 10 mg) that produces the response is different for each substance, but the response generated is the same.

erythropoiesis: process through which red blood cells are produced.

fertility drug: drug that stimulates ovulation.

FSH: follicle stimulating hormone. In the female stimulates the development of the follicles, and in the male stimulates spermatogenesis.

germ cells: Cells that become the reproductive cells eggs (in ovary) or sperm (in testes).

GnRH: gonadotropin releasing hormone (also called luteinizing releasing hormone). Hormone released by the hypothalamus that stimulates the anterior pituitary to secrete LH and FSH.

hCG: human chorionic gonadotropin, a glycoprotein hormone produced in pregnancy to maintain progesterone production.

hirsutism: condition usually in women in which body and facial hair is excessive.

lactation: production of milk in female breasts.

LH: luteinizing hormone. In the female stimulates ovulation, and in the male stimulates testosterone synthesis and release; in the male also called ISCH (interstitial cell stimulating hormone).

meiosis: type of cell division where diploid parent cells (46 chromosomes) divide, producing haploid cells (23 chromosomes); occurs only during gamete production.

menarche: first menstruation (endometrial tissue sloughing) during puberty.

menopause: condition in which menstruation no longer occurs, either because of the normal aging process in women (45 years of age and older) or because the ovaries have been surgically removed (any age); the clinical effects of menopause are a direct result of little or no estrogen secretion.

menstruation: shedding of endometrial tissue with accompanying bleeding; the first day of the menstrual cycle.

mitosis: cell division in which two daughter cells receive the same number of chromosomes (46) as the parent cell.

monophasic: a fixed amount (nonchanging) of estrogen is released during the cycle.

oligospermia: reduced sperm count.

oocytes: the immature female reproductive cell prior to fertilization.

oogenesis: formation of ova.

osteoporosis: decrease in the bone mineral density, usually in the elderly, that results in areas predisposed to fracture.

ova: mature eggs (singular ovum).

ovulation: release of an egg from the ovary.

perimenopause: 2 to 10 years before complete cessation of a menstrual period.

pluripotent: ability of a substance to produce many different biological responses.

prohormone (anabolic androgen): after ingestion is converted to the hormone testosterone.

puberty: sequence of physiological changes associated with the expression of sexual characteristics and reproductive function that occur when a child progresses into young adulthood, usually at 12 to 14 years of age.

spermatogenesis: formation of spermatozoa.

spermatogonia: intermediary kind of male germ cell in the production of spermatozoa.

spermatozoa: mature sperm cells (singular *spermatozoon*).

transdermal absorption: absorption of drug (substance) through the skin, usually associated with the application of drug-loaded patches.

triphasic: the estrogen and progestin amounts released may vary during the cycle.

virilization: development of masculine body (hair, muscle) characteristics in females.

After studying this chapter, you should be able to

37.1 explain the hypothalamic-anterior pituitary-gonadal axis.

37.2 correlate the follicular, hormonal, and endometrial changes that occur in the menstrual cycle to the hormones released.

37.3 identify the different classes of contraceptives and explain the mechanisms of action for each class.

37.4 explain the difference between monophasic and multiphasic oral contraceptives.

37.5 describe the Women's Health Initiative, its findings, and the effects this study has had on hormonal replacement therapy in postmenopausal women.

37.6 describe the mechanisms of action for the types of fertility drugs.

37.7 describe the mechanisms of action of the classes of androgenic drugs.

Introduction

The sex hormones are produced and secreted by the gonads, which include the female ovaries and the male testes. The ovaries and testes are under control of the hypothalamic-anterior pituitary-gonadal axis, which releases hormones regulating the synthesis and release of the various sex hormones. Production of the sex hormones is almost entirely inhibited until the time of puberty. During **puberty,** hormone production drastically increases and is responsible for the development and maintenance of the secondary sex characteristics.

At this time, the female sex hormones have a broader spectrum of pharmacological use than the male sex hormones. This is due to the cyclic nature of ovarian function (menstrual cycle) and its role in pregnancy and childbearing, and the evolving protective role of estrogen during the period after the childbearing years.

LO 37.1 | LO 37.2
LO 37.3 | LO 37.4 | LO 37.5

FEMALE SEX HORMONES

The female sex hormones are defined as the steroid hormones produced by the ovaries, including estrogen, progesterone, and testosterone (majority converted to estrogen). These steroid hormones are **pluripotent,** meaning these hormones have a significant role in the physiology and metabolism of target tissues other than those associated with reproduction. The influence of the estrogens on bone and cardiovascular function and insulin sensitivity will be discussed after considering the role of the steroid sex hormones in the reproductive cycle.

Female Reproductive Cycle

During female embryonic development **oogenesis** begins. The **germ cells** in the ovaries multiply, so that by the fifth gestational month the ovaries contain 6 to 7 million **oogonia.** The oogonia begin to differentiate into primary **oocytes** that begin and are arrested in prophase of the first meiotic division **(meiosis).** The primary oocytes undergo **apoptosis,** so by birth there are only about 2 million oogonia left, and by puberty only about 400,000 primary oocytes. This is more than enough to accommodate reproduction needs during the next 45 years. The incidence of birth defects such as Down syndrome increases as the woman ages, one reason being the ovum is as old as the woman, and over the years, chromosomal changes occur in the ova arrested in prophase of the first meiotic division. Each month after menarche, the ovaries are stimulated to develop one dominant follicle from which one egg will be released for fertilization and hormones will be secreted to prepare the uterus to receive the fertilized embryo for continued development.

The reproductive cycle consists of the changes that occur in the ovaries and endometrium, called the ovarian and endometrial cycles. The ovarian cycle consists of the follicular phase, ovulation, and luteal phase. The endometrial cycle phases (menstrual, proliferative,

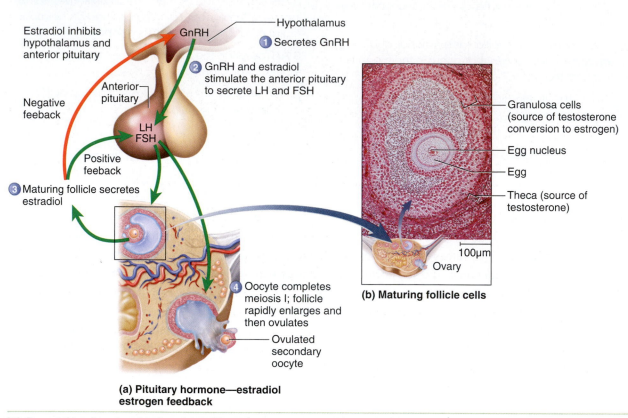

Figure 37.1   Control of Ovulation by the Pituitary and Ovarian Hormones

Estradiol inhibits hypothalamus and anterior pituitary

Negative feeback

Anterior pituitary

Positive feeback

Hypothalamus
1 Secretes GnRH

GnRH

2 GnRH and estradiol stimulate the anterior pituitary to secrete LH and FSH

LH FSH

3 Maturing follicle secretes estradiol

4 Oocyte completes meiosis I; follicle rapidly enlarges and then ovulates

Ovulated secondary oocyte

(a) Pituitary hormone—estradiol estrogen feedback

Granulosa cells (source of testosterone conversion to estrogen)

Egg nucleus

Egg

Theca (source of testosterone)

100µm
Ovary

(b) Maturing follicle cells

(1) Gonadotropin releasing hormone (GnRH) is secreted by the hypothalamus. (2) GnRH stimulates the release of luteinizing hormone (LH) and follicle stimulating hormone (FSH), which are essential for follicle maturation (3). The surge in LH (4) causes ovulation and inhibits further secretion of GnRH.

and secretory) correlate with the release of estrogen and progesterone of the ovarian cycle, as presented in Figure 37.1. The reproductive cycle begins with the hypothalamus. First, the hypothalamus releases **GnRH,** which travels in the portal vein to the anterior pituitary, stimulating the synthesis and secretion of **FSH** and **LH.** FSH stimulates the primary follicle to mature. Next, the follicular cells divide and produce theca and granulosa cells. The theca cells synthesize testosterone, which diffuses into the granulosa cells, which contain an enzyme to convert testosterone to estrogen. As the follicle develops, more and more cells divide, stimulating the release of more and more estrogen. Among the naturally occurring estrogens (estradiol, estriol, estrone), estradiol is the most abundant and most active. Estrogens stimulate the **endometrium** to grow and blood vessels branch into the area to provide nutrients. Estrogens exert a negative feedback effect on FSH and LH, presented as estradiol in Figure 37.2. When estrogens rise to a certain level, a positive feedback effect against LH and FSH occurs (approximately day 14). The surge in FSH stimulates the maturation of the follicle for the next cycle.

Finally, the surge of LH causes **ovulation** to occur (dominant follicle ruptures).

The egg passes into the fallopian tube, where fertilization by a sperm cell may occur. After ovulation, the follicle, which remains in the ovary, undergoes a change. Although estrogens do not induce ovulation, they directly influence the motility of the fallopian tubes and endometrial environment for favorable ovum transport. Under the influence of luteinizing hormone (LH), the follicle is transformed into a corpus luteum. The corpus luteum continues to produce estrogen and begins to produce progesterone, the second major type of female sex hormone.

At ovulation, the follicle is transformed into a corpus luteum in the ovary. If fertilization occurs, the second meiotic division is completed. The corpus luteum secretes mainly progesterone and some estrogen. Progesterone exerts a negative feedback against LH and FSH, and FSH and LH levels drop. The endometrial lining becomes thick, arteries continue to branch, and glycogen is stored for energy if implantation occurs. If implantation occurs, the placenta begins to produce

Figure 37.2   The Female Sexual Cycle

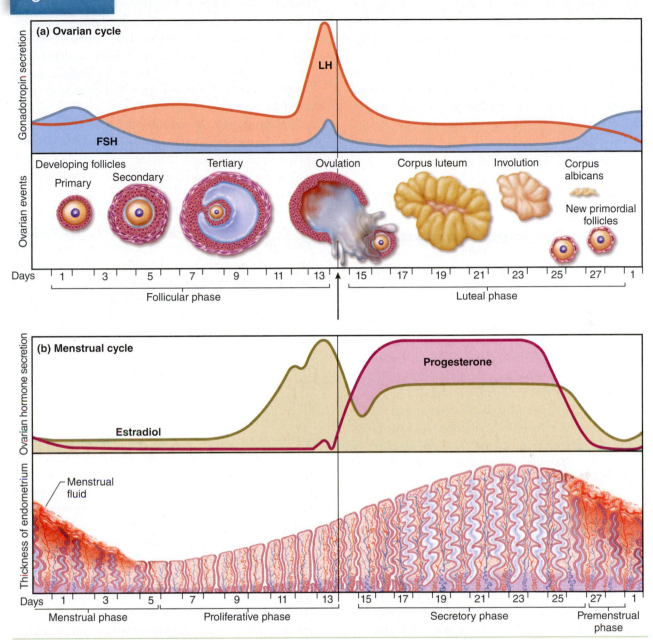

(a) Ovarian cycle

Gonadotropin secretion

LH

FSH

Ovarian events

Developing follicles

Primary   Secondary   Tertiary   Ovulation   Corpus luteum   Involution   Corpus albicans

New primordial follicles

Days   1   3   5   7   9   11   13   15   17   19   21   23   25   27   1

Follicular phase   Luteal phase

(b) Menstrual cycle

Ovarian hormone secretion

Progesterone

Estradiol

Thickness of endometrium

Menstrual fluid

Days   1   3   5   7   9   11   13   15   17   19   21   23   25   27   1

Menstrual phase   Proliferative phase   Secretory phase   Premenstrual phase

(a) Ovarian cycle (events in the ovary). (b) The menstrual cycle (events in the uterus). The two hormone levels in part (a) are drawn to the same scale, but those in (b) are not. The peak progesterone concentration is 17 times as high as the peak estradiol concentration.

hCG; hCG is released into the bloodstream and stimulates the corpus luteum to continue to secrete progesterone until the placenta has developed sufficiently to produce progesterone. If implantation does not occur, the corpus luteum degenerates and rapidly decreases the production of progesterone and estrogen. Progesterone is sometimes called the hormone of quiescence, as it inhibits endometrial muscle contractions. When progesterone levels decrease, the uterine contractions cause the blood vessels to spasm, decreasing blood flow into the endometrial tissue. This causes the sloughing of tissue **(menstruation).** During menstruation there is a temporary anticoagulant action within the uterine tissue and bleeding begins. The duration of menstruation is 4 days (±2 days). Menstruation stops when endometrial cells rich in thromboplastin are shed, contributing to clot formation. At this same time, a new follicle in the ovary begins to develop, and the cycle repeats itself. This monthly cycle continues throughout women's reproductive years.

If the corpus luteum degenerates before the placenta can maintain the hormone level, the uterine lining (with fetus) ruptures, hemorrhages, and sloughs off, resulting in miscarriage. During pregnancy, the levels of estrogen and progesterone are high. Such high levels continue to inhibit (negative feedback) the release of FSH. Therefore, during pregnancy, no other follicles undergo development. Similarly, oral contraceptives maintain high hormone levels in the blood, which prevent the release of FSH (such as during pregnancy). Since no follicle develops, there is no egg for fertilization.

Clinical Indications for Estrogens and Progestins

The main uses of the female sex hormones include hormone replacement therapy (HRT), oral **contraception,** fertility enhancement, and adjunctive therapy of certain cancers (prostate and nonestrogen-dependent breast cancer). Replacement therapy is required in children who have hypogonadism, primary ovarian failure, to complete puberty and permit adequate bone growth. Replacement therapy in adults arises from removal of the ovaries during the active reproductive years (20 to 45 years of age) or cessation of ovarian activity at menopause. The clinical indication for adult HRT is management of vasomotor symptoms associated with menopause. As an outgrowth of adult HRT, estrogens are now also clinically indicated for the prevention and treatment of osteoporosis.

LO 37.1 LO 37.2

HORMONAL REPLACEMENT THERAPY (HRT)

The most frequent causes of female hormonal deficiency are removal of the ovaries (surgical-induced menopause; premature menopause) and menopause. Menopause is an expected but not always anticipated part of the aging process.

The perception of menopause has dramatically changed over the last decade, primarily as a result of the improved lifestyle of women entering menopause and because of women's increased longevity. Average life expectancy for American women who are now 65 years old is 84! Women are entering **perimenopause,** the period leading up to menopause, as early as 40. This means that women can expect to survive 44 more years. More than ever before, the goal is to improve women's quality of life as they age.

Perimenopause is characterized by a significant decrease in female sex hormone production (estrogens,

progestins), frequency of ovulation, and menstruation. Initially, there is a period of physiological and emotional adjustment. During this time, individuals may experience symptoms such as fatigue, hot flashes, vasomotor spasms, nervousness, anxiety, irritability, or depression. Tissue changes in the endometrium and vagina, such as atrophy, decreased metabolism, irritation, and dryness, also take place.

Menopause, clinically defined, is the complete cessation of a menstrual period for 12 months accompanied by a circulating estrogen level less than 50 picograms/ml and an FSH blood level greater than 50 IU/ml. There is a wide variability in the transition from perimenopause to menopause as the decline in estrogen and progesterone production and secretion is such that women can be intermittently symptomatic for a number of years. Even after menopause has been clinically established, an estimated 60 percent of postmenopausal women will experience hot flashes or sweating years later. The hot flashes vary in intensity and duration from woman to woman. The hot flash can range from a rising warm feeling to awakening literally in a pool of sweat, referred to as night sweats. Among the other symptoms that cause women to seek treatment are insomnia, inability to concentrate, and arthritis-like aching joints. Insomnia, which contributes to depression, anxiety, myalgias, and vasomotor symptoms are effectively relieved by HRT.

Administration of estrogen reduces the severity of the symptoms and smooths the transition into this postreproductive period. The options for treatment must be considered because there is no single option that is acceptable for all women. The goal is to individualize the treatment to the symptoms the woman is experiencing and to establish estrogen levels within a "normal acceptable" range (50 to 150 picograms/ml). Estrogen levels that are too high for an individual woman also will produce adverse effects such as sweats, hot flashes, anxiety, irritability, bloating, water retention, breast tenderness, and headaches. (It is worth noting that exogenous progestin quickly relieves these symptoms.) Hormone replacement therapy options include estrogen replacement only, estrogen with cyclic progestin, and continuous estrogen and progestin. Postmenopausal women are monitored by symptoms rather than hormone blood levels, changing HRT combinations until adequate symptom relief occurs. At least 1 month is required to establish whether treatment is effective and acceptable to the patient. Annual follow-up is recommended as the treatment is continued indefinitely. Although not Food and Drug Administration (FDA) approved for this indication, an off-label treatment strategy is that physicians may add an androgen (micronized testosterone or dehydroepiandrosterone [DHEA]) to HRT once androgen deficiency has been confirmed by the laboratory. Androgen replacement is directed at maintaining muscle mass and strength.

HRT is still the most effective treatment for relief of hot flashes, sleep disturbances, and vaginal dryness. The recommendation now is to take the lowest effective dose for the shortest time (i.e., not indefinitely). As always, women are advised to have regular general medical and breast examinations with periodic mammograms during and after hormone therapy.

For women who have not experienced age-induced menopause but become hormone deficient as a result of surgery, estrogen replacement may still be an appropriate therapy. The therapeutic goal after removal of the ovaries in women under 50 years of age is to restore the estrogen and progesterone levels to those that are more representative of endocrine support and provide adequate cyclic feedback to the hypothalamus.

Adverse Effects of Female Hormones

Adverse effects related to estrogen or progestogen use include nausea, vomiting, headache, dizziness, irritability, depression, fluid retention, breast tenderness, and weight gain. Usually, the severity of these effects does not warrant medical intervention or can be ameliorated by reducing the dose or changing to another product. Breakthrough bleeding or amenorrhea usually resolves to a consistent menstrual pattern within 3 months of continuing treatment.

Women who require prolonged hormone therapy for any reason should be monitored closely. The lowest effective dose should be selected and patients should be reevaluated annually. There is no evidence that the naturally occurring hormones are safer than the synthetic drugs—the key is identifying the appropriate lowest effective dose. The dose and length of treatment are two important factors associated with the potential for adverse events after individual patient risk factors have been considered.

Risks of Hormone Replacement Therapy

The Women's Health Initiative (WHI), a very large clinical study involving more than 16,000 women over 50 years old, provided results that have curbed the overwhelming enthusiasm for HRT in postmenopausal women. The study provided evidence that women taking a combination estrogen-progestin daily for at least 5 years had an *increased* risk of nonfatal heart attacks, thromboembolism, stroke, breast cancer, and dementia including Alzheimer's disease. This study confirmed the coronary results of a second large study in postmenopausal women, the Heart and Estrogen/Progestin Replacement Study (HERS). Because the benefits did not outweigh the cardiovascular risks, the estrogen combination therapy part of the WHI study was stopped. The medical community has been advising women to discuss the use of HRT with their physicians and to seek alternative therapeutic options under the direction of a physician.

Women who had a family history or current evidence of hypertension, diabetes, or hypercholesterolemia were not prescribed oral contraceptives or received much lower dose regimens. As a result, the incidence of cardiovascular disorders can be evaluated in risk-free women exposed to high-dose, long-term treatment (50 to 100 mg) versus low-dose, long-term treatment (20 to 35 mcg). This provides a clearer picture of the risks of estrogen exposure without complications from other underlying conditions.

Chronic estrogen use taken unopposed (no progestin) is associated with an increased risk of developing endometrial cancer in postmenopausal women. This risk is one to six times higher than the risk for endometrial cancer in women with an intact uterus who never took endogenous estrogen. When a variety of factors are considered, the risk ranges between 2 and 13 times greater. Progestin, which is now added to estrogen replacement therapy, reduces the risk of endometrial cancer by directly down regulating (decreasing production) estrogen receptors.

Osteoporosis

Some good news from the Women's Health Initiative is that the risk of colon cancer and bone fracture decreased in women taking estrogen. Mounting evidence confirms that estrogen depletion, not specifically aging, contributes to bone loss in postmenopausal women. Estrogen inhibits the hormone PTH (parathyroid hormone). Parathyroid hormone stimulates osteoclasts to release calcium from bone (resorption). If estrogen inhibition of PTH is removed, more bone is resorbed. That means calcium is taken out of the bone. As estrogen declines, bone resorption begins to exceed formation, particularly in trabecular bone. This leads to a reduction in bone mass that is termed **osteoporosis.** In the presence of low calcium intake, and inadequate gravity-resisting exercise, bone fractures occur without apparent severe trauma. The incidence of fracture and osteoporosis is greater in postmenopausal women than men (6:1), but occurs asymptomatically in both. Some complain of acute pain over the fractured area or chronic lower back discomfort; however, most fractures are usually found on X-ray during medical evaluation for some other condition. These patients are not aware that the weakened skeleton has been damaged. The principal bones affected in postmenopausal women are vertebrae (crush fractures) and the distal radius. Mechanical stress or pressure, even rising from a sitting position, is enough strain to produce fractures in postmenopausal women.

Women with established osteoporosis may require a multidisciplinary approach to treatment in order to reduce or eliminate factors predisposing to fracture and to enhance elements that strengthen the body's natural defenses. Predisposing factors that might be eliminated include cigarette smoking, low calcium intake (recommended increase to 1500 mg daily), high caffeine and phosphate intake, sedentary lifestyle, and estrogen deficiency. Calcium can easily be acquired in the diet since one 8 oz glass of skim milk, 1 oz of cheese, or 1 cup of yogurt is 300 to 400 mg of calcium. Otherwise calcium carbonate supplements coupled with vitamin D to facilitate calcium absorption can be taken. Weight-bearing exercises such as walking and swimming are excellent means of building the muscle support to the skeleton, thus minimizing the potential for weight-bearing fractures.

Patients should be encouraged to begin these recommendations in the perimenopausal stage to prevent osteoporosis. Risk factors for developing osteoporosis include women who have a family history of osteoporosis, are Caucasian or Asian, have a lean body mass and short stature, and/or have premature menopause. Because the hormone has an effect on bone metabolism, estrogen has been indicated in the treatment and prevention of osteoporosis in postmenopausal women. Estrogen reduces bone (calcium) loss and is recommended as part of the multifocal therapy of diet, calcium supplement, and exercise. In those women who have developed osteoporosis, estrogen therapy has been shown to increase **bone mineral density** (BMD). When estrogen treatment was discontinued or interrupted, loss of bone density was again accelerated. This beneficial action to reduce bone fracture in postmenopausal women by building bone density has been confirmed in the WHI study. However, estrogen replacement in postmenopausal women who have an intact uterus may not be the first line of treatment because the benefit to the bones may not outweigh the negative effects on the heart. At the same time, drugs known as SERMs, selective estrogen receptor modulators, are in development. Drugs such as raloxifene (*Evista*) are synthetic estrogens targeted for specific estrogen receptors associated with the bones (osteoporosis) but leave other parts of the body unaffected. Postmenopausal women who have not yet developed osteoporosis, either as a result of estrogen deficiency or senile osteoporosis, may be advised to begin calcium supplementation. Those with a family history of osteoporosis or women who begin to develop evidence of bone loss may be directed toward alternative treatment options such as bisphosphonates. (See Chapter 38 for a detailed discussion of osteoporosis and its management.)

Oral Contraception

Oral contraception is the most frequent method of contraception used among women. Combinations of estrogen and progesterone derivatives are used to prevent pregnancy. As mentioned, high hormonal levels of estrogen and progesterone inhibit the release of FSH and LH. Therefore, ovarian follicles do not undergo maturation or ovulation. In addition, changes in the endometrium and cervical mucus militate against sperm penetration as well as egg implantation. This is the most frequent method of contraception among women. If sterilization techniques for men and women are combined (tubal ligation and vasectomy), then oral contraception is second. The usual sequence is that one tablet is taken (beginning on day 5 of the menstrual cycle) for 20 to 21 consecutive days. A few days after the last tablet, bleeding (menses) occurs and the cycle is then repeated. To eliminate the need to count the days between cycles, some products are supplied with seven additional inert tablets or supplemental iron tablets. With such products, individuals take a tablet each day of the cycle. *Seasonale, Jolessa,* and *Quasense* instruct the patient to take one tablet daily beginning on the first Sunday after the onset of menstruation so that 84 days of active pink tablets are followed by 7 days of inert white tablets. Some oral contraceptive preparations are listed in Tables 37:2 and 37:3.

The combination (estrogen-progesterone) oral contraceptives differ in the potency of their components as well as which component exhibits predominant activity. Nevertheless, the mechanism of contraception is similar.

Oral contraceptives that contain only progesterone (progestin) are also available. The mechanism of action is not understood, but it appears that the progesterone-only contraceptives alter cervical mucus and endometrial tissue in a manner that interferes with implantation. Progestin-only contraceptives have a slightly higher failure (pregnancy) rate than do the combination products.

Most oral contraceptives are taken as individual pills each day. Low-dose pills, 20 to 35 mcg of estrogen, are routinely used today compared to doses of 100 to 150 mcg several years ago. The range of progestin dose is more flexible, going from 0.15 mg desogestrel or levonorgestrel to 1.0 mg of norethindrone or ethynodiol diacetate. (*Note:* Estrogen amounts are in microgram quantities and the progestins are always in milligram quantities.) With oral contraceptives, the dosing must be consistent to ensure contraception. For most oral contraceptives, one pill is taken daily, preferably at the same time each day, approximately every 24 hours. If one dose is missed, breakthrough spotting may occur. The potential for ovulation increases with each consecutive daily medication missed. In establishing contraception early on if the woman is sure the regimen was followed precisely yet two menstrual flow periods have not occurred, she should be evaluated for pregnancy before continuing on hormone contraception. After several months of oral contraceptive therapy, the menstrual flow will decrease without being a signal that conception has occurred. Usually dose adjustment to a comfortable level of effectiveness is titrated against the types of unwanted effects the woman is experiencing.

Effectiveness in most cases is directly related to compliance with the daily pill schedule. Anything that facilitates user compliance decreases the chances of failure. The types of long-term contraception available today include drug delivery devices and slow-release products.

Medroxyprogesterone (*Depo-Provera*) is available for a deep IM injection that provides contraception for 3 months.

Among the most recent advances in reversible contraception is the development of contraceptive implants. Etonogestrel (*Implanon*) is a single 4-cm-long implant that contains 68 mg etonogestrel. It releases 60 mcg per day the first month, and then decreases to 30 mcg per day for three years. Etonogestrel should be inserted on day 1 to 5 of the menstrual cycle. If the woman is currently on oral contraceptives, the implant should be inserted within seven days after the last pill (Figure 37.3).

Mirena is a reservoir of progesterone (52 mg levonorgestrol) that is inserted in the uterus (intrauterine). This device releases contraceptive concentrations of progesterone to the local tissue for up to 5 years. The mechanism of action is directed at interrupting pregnancy at the uterine tissue. This product does not prevent ovulation—therefore, there is a greater risk of ectopic pregnancy (ovulation and implantation outside the uterus).

There is an oral progestin available for emergency contraception. Levonorgestrel (*Plan B, Plan B-One Step, Next Choice*) prevents conception when 1.5-mg tablets are taken within 72 hours after unprotected sex. Just two tablets are taken 12 hours apart. It is not intended as a routine contraceptive but protection in the event of contraceptive failure. It is available without prescription for

Figure 37.3

Contraceptive Hormone Delivery

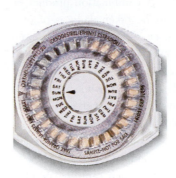 

(a) Birth-control pills   (b) NuvaRing

(a) Birth control pills. (b) *NuvaRing* **etonogestrel and ethinyl estradiol release.**

women 17 years or older but requires a prescription for those under 17.

Hormone contraceptives have been used indefinitely. There is no obligatory requirement to provide a "rest period" from treatment. These contraceptives should be discontinued when a medical condition develops for which hormonal treatment is contraindicated—for example, cancer, thrombophlebitis.

Note to the Health Care Professional

Estrogens and oral contraceptives containing estrogens increase the risk of developing thromboembolic vascular disorders such as thrombophlebitis, pulmonary embolism, stroke, and myocardial infarction. The development of cardiovascular disorders is related to the dose and duration of hormone therapy and is influenced (increased) by the presence of other underlying risk factors: smoking, hypertension, obesity, diabetes, and hypercholesterolemia.

Evidence suggests that women who use oral contraceptives and smoke have a fivefold greater chance of developing a myocardial infarction than do nonsmoking contraceptive users. This risk increases with age (>35 years) and with heavy smoking (15 or more cigarettes/day), indicating that women who elect to use oral contraceptives should not smoke.

Special Considerations

Women interested in using oral contraceptives must be educated about the proper use of these drugs as well as the associated risks. A combination product or progestin-only product must be taken daily as recommended by the manufacturer. Sexually active women should be aware that not taking the drug as scheduled increases the risk of becoming pregnant. If two consecutive menstrual periods are missed while a woman is taking an oral contraceptive, a physician should be consulted immediately. The physician can perform appropriate tests to establish whether conception has occurred. The risks of exposing a developing embryo or fetus to these hormones clearly warrant such caution. Women using oral contraceptives who want to become pregnant should discontinue the oral contraceptive 3 months before trying to conceive and use alternate birth control during that time.

Diabetic women who are receiving hormone therapy may experience changes in glucose tolerance. For this reason, during estrogen therapy, diabetic patients should be alerted to the potential for changes in glucose levels observed during routine glucose monitoring and the symptoms that may accompany these changes. Women who choose to have an intrauterine device inserted should have the placement just after a menstrual flow and a confirmed negative pregnancy test to ensure fertilization has not occurred. The device should be replaced every 12 months. If the retrieval threads are not visible at any time during the year, the device should be removed by the physician and replaced.

Menstrual Bleeding Disorders

In nonmenopausal women, menstrual disorders (**amenorrhea**—no menstruation—and **dysmenorrhea**—painful or difficult menstruation) also may be alleviated by the use of estrogens, progesterone, or estrogen-progestin combinations. Progesterone, 5 to 10 mg IM daily for 8 days, will promote bleeding in amenorrhea and spontaneous normal cycles in dysfunctional uterine bleeding.

Cancer Therapy

Certain cancers—particularly those involving the breast, uterus, and prostate gland—appear to be dependent on the presence of the sex hormones. Removal of the ovaries and testes has produced beneficial results in some cases. In other cases, use of the sex hormones appears to antagonize tumor growth, especially where the sex hormones are applied to a patient of the opposite sex. Megestrol (*Megace*) is only used as a palliative treatment

of advanced breast cancer, whereas medroxyprogesterone (*Depo-Provera*) is used for adjunctive and palliative treatment of inoperable cancer of the endometrium or kidney. Diethylstilbestrol is used in inoperable prostate cancer when patients do not have estrogen-dependent cancer or an active thromboembolic disorder.

Estrogen and Progestin Drug Administration

Estrogens and progestins can be obtained naturally or made synthetically. One of the most available estrogens is estradiol. Conjugated estrogens, obtained from pregnant mare urine, contain a variety of estrogenic substances. These products may contain up to 10 estrogenic substances. Estrogenic substances not normally produced by women—for example, ethinyl estradiol and diethylstilbestrol (DES)—are produced synthetically. Whether naturally occurring or synthetically produced, estrogens produce the same physiological responses and adverse effects when **equipotent** doses are administered. Progestins and progesterone, although related, are different chemicals. Progesterone is the natural hormone made within the ovary after ovulation and in the corpus luteum when present. There is an available progesterone (*Prometrium, Prochieve,* progesterone in oil); however, many progestin products contain the synthetically made medroxyprogesterone, norethindrone, or norgestrel. Examples of some estrogens and progestins and the recommended dosages and uses are presented in Table 37:1.

Estrogen and progestin products are available for use orally, parenterally (IM), vaginally, and topically. Oral estrogen dosing is designed to mimic the physiological pattern of estrogen activity. This is especially true for the oral contraceptives. From days 0 through 21, estrogen is the dominant hormone taken daily. During the last 7 days of the monthly cycle it can be replaced by inert or iron-containing pills, progesterone, or no pill for 7 days. Some oral contraceptives are considered **monophasic**—formulations that release a fixed amount of estrogen (relative to progestin) in each pill from days 0 to 21 (see Table 37:2). With the **biphasic** and **triphasic** formulations, the pill color varies over the cycle and represents different strengths (dose ratio) of estrogens to progestin in the pill (see Table 37:3). Convenient packaging of daily medication for the 28-day cycle (one pill each day for 28 days) improves patient compliance by reducing the potential for missing doses through forgetfulness or confusion (see Figure 37.3). Doses of estrogen are significantly lower today than those pioneered 20 years ago. With these newer low-dose estrogen regimens, there is rarely

Estrogen and the Progestogen Drugs*

Drug (*Trade Name*)	Form	Dose for prostate cancer	Dose for menopausal (vasomotor) symptoms atropic vaginitis	Dose for replacement therapy
Estrogen				
Conjugated estrogens (*Premarin*)	Tablets	1.25–2.5 mg PO TID	0.3–1.25 mg/day PO	0.3–0.625 mg/day PO, 3 wks on 1 wk off
Estradiol (*Estrace, Gynodiol*)	Tablets micronized	1–2 mg PO TID	1–2 mg PO cyclically (21 days on drug, 7 days off drug)	
Estradiol acetate (*Femtrace*)	Tablets	1–2 mg TID	1–2 mg PO once daily	
Estradiol transdermal (*Alora, Estraderm, Vivelle-Dot*)	Patch	—	0.25–0.5 mg patch applied twice a week	
Estradiol transdermal (*Climara, Menostar*)	Patch	—	0.25–0.5 mg patch applied once a week	
Estradiol (*Elestrin, Divigel*) Estradiol (*Evamist*)	Gel topical Spray topical	— —	0.25–1 g/day upper thigh 1–3 sprays on forearm	— —
Estradiol cypionate (*Depo-Estradiol*)	Oil, IM only	—	1–5 mg IM every 3–4 weeks	1.5–2 mg/month IM
Estradiol valerate (*Delestrogen*)	Oil, IM only	30 mg or more/week IM every 1 or 2 wks	10–20 mg IM every 4 weeks	
Combinations**				
Estrogen/Androgen Esterified estrogens and methyltestosterone (*Covaryx, Estratest*)	Tablets	—	0.5/0.1 mg/day PO	—
Estrogen/Progestin Conjugated estrogens and methylprogesterone (*Prempro, Premphase*)	Tablets	—	0.625 mg/2.5 mg or 0.625 mg/5 mg once daily	—
Estradiol and drospirenone (*Angeliq*)	Tablets	—	1.0 mg/0.5 mg once daily	—
Estradiol and norethindrone (*Activella*)	Tablets	—	0.5 mg/1.0 mg once daily	—
Drug (*Trade Name*)	**Form**	**Abnormal bleeding**	**Amenorrhea**	**Endometriosis**
Progestogens				
Progesterone	Oil, IM only	5–10 mg IM for 6–8 days	5–10 mg/day IM for 6 days	—
Norethindrone (*Aygestin*)	Tablets	—	2.5–10 mg/day PO for 5–10 days	5 mg/day for 2 weeks
Medroxyprogesterone (*Provera*)	Tablets	5 or 10 mg PO for 5 to 10 days		10 mg/day PO for 14 consecutive days/month

(Continued)

Drug (*Trade Name*)	Form	Endometrial/Renal Carcinoma***	Contraception	—
Other uses				
Medroxyprogesterone acetate (*Depo-Provera*)	Injection	400 to 1000 mg IM weekly	150 mg every 3 months deep IM	—
(*depo-subQ provera 104*)	Injection	—	104 mg SC every 3 months	—

Not an inclusive list of available products.
**Estrogen amount appears first, e.g., 0.5 mg (estrogen)/1 mg progestin.*
***As adjunctive and palliative treatment in advanced inoperable cases.*

a need to employ more than 50 mcg of estrogen for effective contraception. Products range in dose from 20 to 50 mcg of estrogen daily. This provides the lowest effective coverage and improves the safety profile of estrogen therapy.

HRT is achieved through oral and parenteral administration of estrogen or progestin. Preparation of the hormone in oil makes a "depo" formulation, designed to deliver estrogen as a slow release over a long period of time. Estradiol cypionate (*Depo-Estradiol*) and estradiol valerate (*Delestrogen*) are administered intramuscularly once a month as HRT. Following oral and IM administration, the active hormones are metabolized by the liver and, depending on the type of conjugate formed, the metabolites are excreted into the bile or the urine.

A unique hormone delivery system is the vaginal ring (see Figure 37.3). This estrogen and progestin–loaded device (*NuvaRing*) is pressed into the vaginal canal, continuously releasing drug to the local tissue (ethinyl estradiol 0.015 mg and etonogestrel 0.12 mg per day). The ring remains in place for 3 weeks and then is removed for 1 week to permit withdrawal bleeding to occur. The next ring is placed 1 week after the previous one was removed.

In order to lengthen the onset and duration of estrogen action, the hormone can be administered transdermally. Estrogens are available as "drug-loaded" patches that can be applied to a clean, dry surface of the abdomen or buttocks so that the drug is absorbed through the skin **(transdermal absorption).** The skin minimally metabolizes estradiol so that the estradiol absorbed into the blood is initially greater than that following the oral route. This formulation provides an opportunity for convenient dosing of once or twice a week rather than daily. Another novel delivery system is *Evamist,* an estradiol transdermal spray used to treat the vasomotor symptoms of menopause. One spray to the forearm is the initial dosage, increasing to 2 to 3 sprays per day as needed. *Elestrin* and *EstroGel* are estradiol gels that are applied once daily to the upper arm using a metered-dose pump.

Alternative Estrogen Sources

There are a number of women who believe that estrogen deficiency is the natural order and do not wish to replace estrogen at all, while others at least prefer to use more natural sources of estrogen. Phytoestrogens are estrogens that are extracted from plants or absorbed from foods that contain phytoestrogens, such as spearmint. Soy products in particular are an excellent source of isoflavones, which are phytoestrogens. Soy added to the diet has been shown to decrease total cholesterol and LDL-cholesterol. The most common forms of soy are tofu, soy milk, tempeh, soy flour, and flavored soy protein powders. Such products are found in specialty food stores, health food stores, and stores that carry vitamin and nutritional supplements. It must be cautioned, however, that the effects of natural estrogens in large doses can produce similar physiological and adverse effects as HRT.

Cautions and Contraindications to the Use of Estrogens and Progestins

There is a special cautionary (black box) warning with the use of estrogens and progestins. These drugs should not be used for the prevention of cardiovascular disease. Because of the potentially life-threatening adverse effects (*increased* risk of thromboembolism, stroke, and breast cancer), estrogen and progestins, including oral contraceptives, should not be used in women with a history of thrombophlebitis, liver disease, undiagnosed breast lumps, or unexplained vaginal bleeding. Persistent vaginal bleeding in women with an intact uterus should

Oral Contraceptive Preparations—Monophasic

Trade Name*	Estrogen	Progestin
Desogen, Solia	Ethinyl estradiol 30 mcg	Desogestrel 0.15 mg
Levora, Jolessa, Portia	Ethinyl estradiol 30 mcg	Levonorgestrel 0.15 mg
Loestrin 24 Fe 1/20	Ethinyl estradiol 20 mcg	Norethindrone 1.0 mg plus ferrous fumarate**
Loestrin Fe 1.5/30	Ethinyl estradiol 30 mcg	Norethindrone 1.5 mg
Lo/Ovral	Ethinyl estradiol 30 mcg	Norgestrel 0.3 mg
Lybrel	Ethinyl estradial 20 mcg	Levonorgestrel 0.09 mg
Micronor	—	Norethindrone 0.35 mg
Necon, Ortho-Novum 1/50	Mestranol 50 mcg	Norethindrone 1.0 mg
Norinyl 1 + 35, Necon 1/35	Ethinyl estradiol 35 mcg	Norethindrone 1.0 mg
Nor - Q.D.	—	Norethindrone 0.35 mg
Ortho-Novum 1/35	Ethinyl estradiol 35 mcg	Norethindrone 1.0 mg
Ovcon-35, Balziva, Femcon	Ethinyl estradiol 35 mcg	Norethindrone 0.40 mg
Ogestrel 0.5/50	Ethinyl estradiol 50 mcg	Norgestrel 0.50 mg
Yasmin	Ethinyl estradiol 30 mcg	Drospirenone 3 mg
Yaz	Ethinyl estradiol 20 mcg	Drospirenone 3 mg
Zovia 1/35 E, Kelnor	Ethinyl estradiol 35 mcg	Ethynodiol diacetate 1.0 mg
Zovia 1/50 E	Ethinyl estradiol 50 mcg	Ethynodiol diacetate 1.0 mg

*Not an inclusive list of available products.
**Contains 4 iron tablets to facilitate daily dosing habit.

be monitored to rule out the possibility of carcinoma. Women with a history of diabetes, high blood pressure, or a seizure disorder may not be good candidates for oral contraceptives either. Estrogens and oral contraceptives are contraindicated in women who are pregnant or have an estrogen-dependent cancer. Estrogen use during early pregnancy can affect fetal development. Congenital heart defects and limb formation defects have occurred even with localized intrauterine exposure to female hormones. Estrogens are not indicated for the treatment of postpartum breast engorgement. Estrogens and progestins are designated FDA Pregnancy Category X. The risk of use in pregnant women clearly outweighs any possible benefit.

Diethylstilbestrol (DES) has been linked to alterations in fetal development when given to pregnant women. Female fetuses exposed *in utero* to DES reportedly developed changes in vaginal and cervical tissue (vaginal adenosis and vaginal and cervical cancer) that do not become evident until the offspring reach maturity.

Oral Contraceptive Preparations—Multiphasic

Trade Name	Phase I	Phase II	Phase III
Progestin: Estrogen	**Norethindrone: Ethinyl estradiol**		
Tri-Norinyl	0.5 mg: 35 mcg	1.0 mg: 35 mcg	0.5 mg: 35 mcg
Ortho-Novum 7/7/7	0.5 mg: 35 mcg	0.75 mg: 35 mcg	1.0 mg: 35 mcg
Levonorgestrel: Ethinyl estradiol			
Enpresse	0.05 mg: 30 mcg	0.075 mg: 40 mcg	0.125 mg: 30 mcg
Norgestimate: Ethinyl estradiol			
Ortho-Tri-Cyclen	0.18 mg: 35 mcg	0.215 mg: 35 mcg	0.25 mg: 35 mcg

Congenital abnormalities such as structural problems of the genitourinary tract also have occurred in males exposed *in utero* to DES. It is worth noting that DES is an effective postcoital contraceptive when taken orally within 72 hours after intercourse.

LO 37.1 | **LO 37.2**

FERTILITY DRUGS

Anovulation

Drugs that bring about ovulation are referred to as **fertility drugs.** Currently, there are two chemical types of fertility drugs: one synthetic drug and three protein hormones extracted from human fluids. These drugs are available for patients in whom pregnancy is desired but who, for some reason, are not ovulating or releasing an egg. Anovulation can occur because the ovaries do not function (cannot respond) or do not respond to the level of endogenous anterior pituitary hormones. If the ovaries do not function, the levels of LH and FSH will be elevated due to a continuous attempt to stimulate ovulation. Elevated levels of LH and FSH are indicative of primary ovarian failure. Currently, drugs are not available that will reverse primary ovarian failure. Anovulation other than primary ovarian failure can be treated with exogenous stimulants that induce follicular growth and maturation. In these patients, fertilization and implantation may occur *in utero*. Partners therefore must engage in coitus daily during a narrow window of time after the egg has been released for fertilization to occur. Otherwise, there are a number of assisted reproductive technologies (ART), such as *in vitro* fertilization, in which ovulation may be exogenously stimulated prior to harvesting the egg for fertilization outside the body. Then implantation may be performed in the egg donor or into a surrogate uterus. Drugs used in ART to develop multiple mature follicles or to induce ovulation are presented in Table 37:4.

Synthetic Ovulation Stimulants

Clomiphene (*Clomid, Milophene, Serophene*) is a synthetic nonsteroidal estrogen receptor antagonist that stimulates the release of FSH and LH from the anterior pituitary. Consequently, ovarian follicle development and ovulation are stimulated. Clomiphene binds to estrogen receptors (blocking estrogen from interacting) and through negative feedback inhibition increases LH and FSH secretion. This augmentation in LH, FSH, and gonadotropin secretion results in multifocal stimulation of the ovaries. Occasionally, more than one egg is produced, resulting in an increased incidence of multiple births (twinning) with the use of this drug. Risk of multiple births is decreased if the woman is started on a low dose and increased until ovulation occurs.

Clomiphene cannot produce ovulation in patients with ovary dysfunction that will not respond to normal physiological stimulation. Frequently, this drug is used in women who are 35 to 50 years of age, a population in whom the risk of endometrial cancer or ovulatory

Drugs Used in Assisted Reproductive Technology (ART) to Stimulate Ovulation

Drug (*Trade Name*)*	Indication	Dose
Follicle stimulating agents		
Follitropin alfa (*Gonal f, Gonal f RFF pen*)	Follicle maturation Ovulation induction	75 units/day SC for 14 days
Follitropin beta (*Follistim AQ, Follistim AQ cartridge*)	Follicle maturation Ovulation induction	75–300 units/day SC for 6–12 days
Urofollitropin (*Bravelle*)	Follicle maturation Ovulation induction	150–225 units/day SC for 5 days after GnRH is given
Lutropin (*Luveris*)	Follicle stimulation	75–225 units SC co-administered with follitropin alfa
Menotropins (*Menopur, Repronex*)	Multiple follicle development	225–450 units/day for 12 days (*Repronex*) 225–450 units/day for 20 days (*Menopur*)
Ovulation stimulant		
Clomiphene (*Clomid, Milophene, Serophene*)	Ovulatory failure	50 mg/day PO for 5 days 100 mg/day PO for 5 days
Chorionic gonadotropin recombinant DNA (*Ovidrel*)	ART, follicle maturation Ovulation induction	250 mcg 1 day after last dose of a follicle-stimulating agent
Human chorionic gonadotropin hCG (*Choron-10, Gonic, Novarel, Profasi, Pregnyl*)	Ovulation induction	5,000–10,000 units 1 day after the last dose of menotropin

dysfunction is increased as a function of age. Therefore, clomiphene should not be administered without first conducting a thorough pelvic and diagnostic examination of patients.

Clomiphene is readily absorbed after oral administration. The standard protocol for inducing ovulation is a 5-day treatment beginning on the fifth day of the woman's menstrual cycle. One, two, or three courses of treatment may be required to achieve at least one mature follicle. If ovulation does not occur within 31 days of the first course (50 mg/day for 5 days), the second course of 100 mg/day for 5 days is given. Most women respond. However, if ovulation does not occur after the third course, the patient should be reevaluated for other underlying conditions that may be responsible for the anovulatory condition.

Polypeptide Ovulation Stimulants

Protein hormones extracted from urine are used to induce ovulation in conjunction with a polypeptide produced in placental tissue. Gonadotropin (FSH) can be extracted from postmenopausal women's urine as urofollitropin (*Bravelle*) or purified as menotropins

(*Menopur, Repronex*) from the urine. These proteins act as FSH to stimulate follicles to mature and rupture. After the last dose of these gonadotropins, human chorionic gonadotropin (hCG, *Choron-10, Pregnyl*) is given to act as LH and stimulate production of progesterone from the corpus luteum of the ruptured follicle. If implantation of a fertilized egg occurs, the placenta that develops will then supply an endogenous source of hCG. Gonadotropins are amazing polypeptides. For example, hCG has an amino acid sequence (α subunit) that is identical to endogenous FSH, LH, and TSH. While these protein hormones are primarily used in women, menotropins and hCG also are used in men to stimulate spermatogenesis. In men, hCG stimulates the interstitial (Leydig) cells of the testis to produce androgens, and it permits the testis to descend in certain types of prepubertal cryptorchism and hypogonadism.

Drug Administration

Urofollitropin and menotropin are administered intramuscularly in one to three courses. The first course is 75 IU/day for 7 to 12 days followed by 5000 to 10,000 U

IM of hCG 1 day after the last dose of the tropins. The tropin dose represents 75 IU of LH and 75 IU of FSH. Urine is tested for estrogen concentration to determine whether multiple follicles have developed (>150 mcg in 24 hours) rather than one dominant follicle. Couples should be advised to avoid coitus when multiple follicles have developed because of the significant potential for multiple fertilization. Patient reevaluation is warranted if ovulation does not occur after three courses of treatment. Table 37:4 presents doses of ovulation stimulants.

Risks of Fertility Drugs

Ovarian hyperstimulation syndrome is a significant adverse effect because of the potential for multiple fertilization. Virtually all physicians who engage in assisted reproductive technologies are specialists who are well acquainted with the physical risks to the mother and fetuses. Although these specialists can monitor biochemical activity, only abstinence from intercourse will ensure multiple fertilization will not occur. Other effects during the course of treatment may include bloating, stomach or pelvic pain, enlarged ovaries, ovarian cysts, blurred vision, and hypersensitivity reactions. Hot flashes, breast discomfort, headache, or nausea may be directly related to the antiestrogenic actions of clomiphene. Men may experience gynecomastia, breast pain, and mastitis.

Note to the Health Care Professional

Patients receiving hormone therapy should be instructed to report incidences of pain or alteration in their vision (**diplopia**—double vision—or loss of vision). Pain in the legs, groin, or chest or changes in vision may be associated with thrombosis and may necessitate immediate drug discontinuation. A physician should be alerted if patients experience shortness of breath, abnormal bleeding, breast lumps, or yellowing of the skin or eyes.

Drug Interactions for Estrogens and Progestins

Reports of drug interactions with the use of estrogens or progestogens have been associated primarily with the use of oral contraceptives. Although numerous drugs have been indicated, evidence of a clinically significant interaction is usually not overwhelming. Nevertheless, it is probably prudent for patients taking oral contraceptives to seek an alternate form of contraception if the following drugs also are used: barbiturates, carbamazepine, griseofulvin, neomycin, penicillin, phenytoin, salicylates, tetracyclines, and rifampin. These drugs may increase the metabolism of oral contraceptives, thus reducing their effectiveness. Estrogens not necessarily associated with oral contraceptives have reduced the clearance of corticosteroids, prolonging the steroid action. It also has been hypothesized that contraceptive-induced fluid retention may precipitate seizures in epileptic patients. Although additional evidence is needed to support this proposal, an alternate form of contraception should be used in appropriate patients at risk. Estrogens interact with hydantoins used for seizure control, resulting in breakthrough bleeding, spotting, and pregnancy.

Oral contraceptives have been reported to decrease the anticoagulant response to dicumarol. The mechanism appears to involve hormone-induced stimulation of clotting factors rather than interference with the metabolism of the oral anticoagulant. Oral contraceptives increase the elimination of clofibrate and increase the clearance of benzodiazepines through enhanced metabolism. This may reduce the effectiveness of clofibrate and benzodiazepines in some patients.

LO 37.1   LO 37.6   LO 37.7

MALE SEX HORMONES (ANDROGENS)

During male embryonic development, the germ cells that migrate to the testes are called **spermatogonia.** The male also is born with a specific number of spermatogonia; however, these cells go through **mitosis** continuously. One of the daughter cells does not differentiate so that the male has the ability to produce sperm throughout life. At puberty the secretion of testosterone stimulates **spermatogenesis** in the seminiferous tubules of the testes. The main sex hormone of the male is testosterone, which is produced by the testes. The adrenal cortex of both sexes produces small amounts of other male hormones. Testosterone production is controlled by the hypothalamic-anterior pituitary-testes axis. LH, also known as interstitial cell-stimulating hormone (ICSH) stimulates the synthesis and release of testosterone from the interstitial cells (Leydig) cells (see Figure 37.4). FSH stimulates the secretion of an adrogen-binding protein (ABP), which facilitates spermatogenesis in the presence of testosterone. LH and testosterone are

Figure 37.4 **Hypothalamic-Anterior Pituitary Control of Testosterone Secretion**

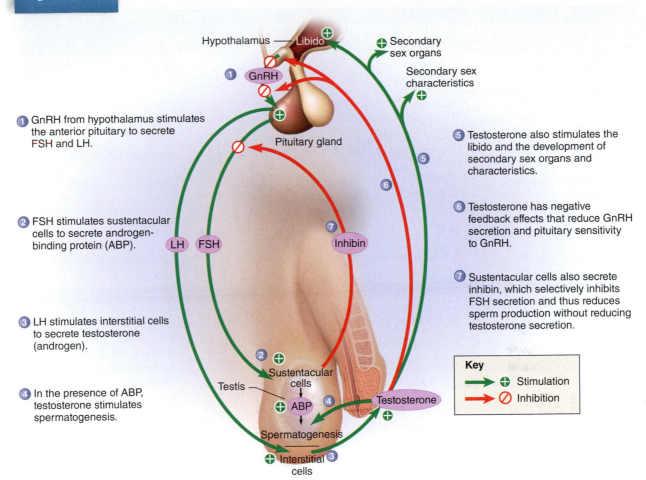

Hypothalamus — Libido

GnRH

① GnRH from hypothalamus stimulates the anterior pituitary to secrete FSH and LH.

Pituitary gland

② FSH stimulates sustentacular cells to secrete androgen-binding protein (ABP).

LH   FSH

③ LH stimulates interstitial cells to secrete testosterone (androgen).

④ In the presence of ABP, testosterone stimulates spermatogenesis.

Testis

Sustentacular cells

ABP

Spermatogenesis

Interstitial cells

Inhibin

Secondary sex organs

Secondary sex characteristics

⑤ Testosterone also stimulates the libido and the development of secondary sex organs and characteristics.

⑥ Testosterone has negative feedback effects that reduce GnRH secretion and pituitary sensitivity to GnRH.

⑦ Sustentacular cells also secrete inhibin, which selectively inhibits FSH secretion and thus reduces sperm production without reducing testosterone secretion.

Testosterone

Key

→ ⊕ Stimulation

→ ⊘ Inhibition

synergistic hormones. Acting together, these hormones cause significant sperm production (300,000 sperm/minute), greater than either hormone alone can produce. In addition to stimulating spermatogenesis, testosterone stimulates the development of male sex organs (prostate, seminal vesicles, scrotum, and penis) and maintains the secondary sex characteristics (hair distribution, vocal cord thickening, and changes in musculature) of the male. In addition, testosterone produces an anabolic effect that promotes synthesis and retention of proteins (muscle and bone) in the body.

Androgens

Male sex hormones are steroids generally referred to as **androgens.** The sex hormone is testosterone and the anabolic androgen drugs are oxandrolone and oxymetholone. Deficiencies of testosterone may be caused by pituitary disorders, testicular failure, or castration. Androgens are administered as replacement therapy to maintain male sex characteristics and organ function.

Testosterone is often the drug of choice over the available synthetic androgens. Testosterone is metabolized in the intestine and liver; therefore, the intramuscular route of administration is preferred to achieve adequate blood levels. Testosterone is available for injection as an aqueous or oil suspension (short acting). In addition, various depo preparations can provide adequate blood concentrations for a period of 4 weeks. *Testopel* (testosterone implant) is a pellet containing 75 mg of testosterone placed subcutaneously for drug delivery over 3 to 6 months. The dose is individualized by implanting multiple pellets as needed. The transdermal testosterone reservoir patch (*Androderm*) is applied to the back, abdomen, arms, or thighs daily until clinical results are adequate. If scrotal descent does not occur within 8 weeks, the patient must be reevaluated for another type of testosterone. The patch remains on the application site for 24 hours. Application sites must be rotated so that the same site is not used for 7 days. Examples of androgenic drugs are listed in Table 37:5.

Examples of Androgenic Drugs, Schedule CIII

Drug (Trade Name)*	Dose	Route	Use
Parenteral short-acting androgens*			
Testosterone transdermal system (Androderm)	1 or 2 patches applied to the skin for 24 hours	Transdermal	Androgen deficiency
Testosterone (Striant)	30 mg BID 1 tablet on gum surface	Buccal	Androgen deficiency
Testosterone (Androgel, Testim)	5 g (1% gel) 1 tube content/day to deliver 50 mg testosterone	Topical, shoulder or arm	Replacement therapy
Parenteral long-acting androgens*			
Testosterone cypionate (oil)	50–400 mg every 2–4 weeks	IM	Deficiency, replacement therapy
(Depo-testosterone)	200–400 mg every 2–4 weeks	IM	Carcinoma of the breast
Testosterone pellets (Testopel)	150–400 mg every 6 months as 2 to 5 pellets	SC implant	Replacement therapy
Oral androgens*			
Fluoxymesterone (Androxy)	5–20 mg/day 10–40 mg/day in divided doses	PO PO	Replacement therapy Carcinoma of the breast
Methyltestosterone (Android, Testred, Virilon)	10–50 mg/day 50–200 mg/day 30 mg/day	PO PO PO	Replacement therapy Carcinoma of the breast Postpubertal cryptorchidism
Anabolic androgens			
Oxandrolone (Oxandrin)	2.5–20 mg BID to QID for 2–4 weeks	PO	Promote weight gain where protein breakdown is part of the underlying condition
Oxymethalone (Anadrol 50)	1–5 mg/kg/day for 3–6 months	PO	Anemias from deficient RBC production

Not an inclusive list of available products.

Clinical Indications

Androgens are approved for use in males as replacement therapy in primary hypogonadism, hypogonadotropic hypogonadism, delayed puberty, and impotence that is the result of androgen deficiency. The hypogonadism may be congenital or acquired. In women, androgens are approved for the treatment of metastatic inoperable breast cancer. Androgen therapy has been beneficial in some cases of metastatic breast cancer. Androgen therapy has inhibited tumor growth while retaining the anabolic effects of increased protein synthesis and weight gain.

Anabolic Action

Many chronic diseases are characteristically associated with significant protein catabolism and weight loss. In some clinical situations, androgens are administered because of their ability to stimulate protein synthesis **(anabolism).** In conjunction with a diet designed to increase caloric intake, patients usually experience an increase in appetite and weight on anabolic therapy.

Androgens have been used to stimulate the production of red blood cells **(erythropoiesis)** in patients with refractory anemia, particularly those with renal disease. Anabolic steroids have been used as adjunctive drugs to improve athletic performance. Anabolic steroids do increase lean muscle mass, partly through the tissue retention of sodium and water. Adverse effects associated with chronic use of these hormones may be serious and irreversible.

An addiction syndrome that is characterized by the inability to stop using the drug and craving the drug after withdrawal has been reported with prolonged use of anabolic androgens. Combined with the increased potential for abuse among athletes, this addiction liability has resulted in reclassification of the anabolic steroids to controlled substance status, Schedule CIII.

Risks of Androgen Use—Schedule CIII Drugs

When reference is made to "super steroids" or "steroid" abuse, the active agent is usually an androgen. Under federal law, the Anabolic Steroid Control Act of 1990 and 2004, anabolic androgens and **prohormones** are classified as Schedule III drugs because of their high potential for abuse and misuse. These drugs are being used by men who believe the anabolic actions maintain strength and virility after the age of 50. Between 40 and 70 years of age, men may lose 10 to 20 pounds of muscle mass, 15 percent of their bone mass resulting in a loss of 2 inches in height, and a drop in testosterone levels of 30 percent. An estimated 15 percent of men are completely impotent by age 70. Testosterone has been shown to increase muscle mass and reduce bone loss through mineral excretion. While moods, libidos, and cholesterol levels improved, testosterone does not correct impotence. In the vast majority of cases, impotence at any age is related to vascular disease, or conditions that impair tissue perfusion such as cardiovascular disease, diabetes, smoking, and alcoholism. Testosterone and its analogs have been used for years by athletes, especially body builders, to increase size, strength, and endurance (see Figure 37.5). These drugs are referred to as roids, juice, hype, weight trainers, gym candy, arnolds, and stackers. Cycling is the pattern of use in which steroids are taken for periods of weeks or months, then stopped for a period of time, and then restarted. Users often combine several different types

Figure 37.5 Anabolic Androgen Effects on Muscle

of anabolic androgenic steroids, known as "stacking," to maximize drug effectiveness.

Testosterone is available by prescription in a variety of convenient formulations, tablets, injection, transdermal patch, topical gel, and pellet implant (see Table 37:4). With the generation of postwar babies entering this zone (age 50 years or older), there is a great likelihood that androgen use will increase during the next 10 to 20 years. Dehydroepiandrosterone (DHEA) is naturally produced by the adrenals and promotes testosterone production. Dehydroepiandrosterone is currently not categorized as a drug but as a nutritional supplement, and is available without prescription for purchase. DHEA is a precursor to male and female sex hormones and can increase levels of androgens. No long-term studies have been conducted to determine if DHEA supplementation will increase the risk of prostate, breast, and ovarian cancers.

The main adverse effects produced by the androgens are caused by overdose or chronic use. In adult males, high testosterone levels inhibit the release of FSH (anterior pituitary), which is needed for sperm production. The result is **oligospermia,** or a reduced sperm count. Adult males also may develop gynecomastia and priapism during androgen therapy. In prepubertal boys, there is a stunting of growth due to premature closure of the bone epiphyses. In females, masculinization occurs, which is characterized by **hirsutism,** menstrual irregularities, changes in the external genitalia, acne, and a deepening of the voice. Other adverse effects include jaundice, nausea, vomiting, and diarrhea. Individuals who abuse anabolic steroids can experience withdrawal symptoms when they stop taking the drug—these include mood swings, fatigue, restlessness, loss of appetite, insomnia, reduced sex drive, and steroid cravings, all of which may contribute to continued abuse. Long-term high-dose testosterone exposure such as that seen with use in athletes has been associated with bouts of aggressive combative behavior known as roid-rage, tumors, and sterility. There is a special cautionary (black box) warning in the label for oxandrolone and oxymetholone because of serious liver changes that have occurred with these drugs. Blood-filled cysts that have the potential for hemorrhage have developed in the liver of some patients as well as benign and malignant tumors. Less immediately life-threatening is the increase in low-density lipoproteins and decrease in high-density lipoproteins that occurs with use of androgens and anabolic steroids.

Drug Interactions

Anabolic steroids have been reported to alter the pharmacological effects of such drugs as oral anticoagulants, antidiabetic drugs, and other steroids. With concomitant androgen therapy, the dose of oral anticoagulants may need to be reduced to maintain coagulation control. It has been proposed that the androgens may decrease the formation of clotting factors, which also are influenced by the oral anticoagulants. By affecting carbohydrate metabolism, androgens may decrease blood glucose levels, necessitating a reduction in insulin or oral antidiabetic dosage to maintain proper glucose levels in diabetic patients. Because androgens are steroids that facilitate the retention of sodium and water, it is not surprising that androgens given in the presence of other steroid therapy enhance the development of edema.

Special Considerations and Contraindications

Androgens are contraindicated in men with carcinoma of the breast or prostate. Androgens should never be used during pregnancy because **virilization** of the female fetus will occur. Although virilization occurs to some extent in female patients being treated for breast carcinoma, these patients should report changes to the physician to avoid irreversible virilizing effects. Androgenic steroids cause the retention of sodium, water, and calcium. In patients with carcinoma, hypercalcemia may be a signal to discontinue androgen therapy.

Since androgenic steroids are metabolized quickly following oral use, patients may be given a buccal formulation. *Striant,* with a mucoadhesive surface, is the first-ever transbuccal (gum surface) treatment for testosterone. The product is placed on the gum gently until it adheres. Moisture in the mouth softens the product and allows it to conform to the shape of the gum. Patients should be instructed not to swallow the tablets and confirm placement has not been disturbed after brushing teeth. **Buccal absorption** enables the drug to bypass intestinal and hepatic metabolism. Diabetic patients receiving androgen therapy should be monitored for alterations in glucose tolerance so that antidiabetic medications can be adjusted to meet their needs. Similarly, patients receiving oral anticoagulants should be observed for petechiae or other signs of hemorrhage. Such signs indicate the need to adjust the oral anticoagulant dose during androgen therapy.

LO 37.1   LO 37.6

ERECTILE DYSFUNCTION

Impotence is the inability to perform sexual function often associated in men as erectile dysfunction (ED) or inability to achieve an erection. Impotence may result from nerve or spinal damage so that stimulatory impulses no longer reach the muscles of the penis to evoke a physical action. It is also an adverse effect of over 200 types of prescription medications (e.g., antianxiety and antidepressant drugs, antihistamines, cardiovascular drugs, chemotherapy medications, and diuretics) that apparently diminish blood flow to the penis, inhibit nerve excitability, or alter psychomotor (brain) activity, any of which eliminates or decreases the normal response during sexual stimulation. Arteriosclerosis, the hardening and narrowing of the arteries, causes a reduction in blood flow throughout the body and can lead to impotence. Other factors that contribute to diminished blood flow include smoking and diabetes mellitus. Diabetes is associated with damage to small blood vessels and nerves as the condition progresses. Although male hormone replacement (the subject of this chapter) is not a recommended or effective treatment for impotence, the importance of effective drug therapy warrants presentation here.

Drugs Used in Erectile Dysfunction

To establish and maintain an erection, there must be increased blood flow through the erectile tissue in the penis. During sexual arousal, the male brain receives a signal to release nitric oxide (NO), an endogenous vasodilator, in the area where the increased blood flow is needed (penis). NO stimulates the enzyme guanylate cyclase that produces cyclic guanosine monophosphate (cGMP), the chemical that relaxes arterial smooth muscle. Once the smooth muscle is relaxed, blood flows into tissue and the penis inflates (erection). The increased blood flow continues as long as cGMP is generated. A local enzyme, phosphodiesterase type 5 (PDE5), metabolizes the cGMP and the blood flow returns to a pre-erection state. In conditions of impotence, where blood flow has been affected, PDE inhibitor drugs selectively block PDE5 in the penis so that cGMP accumulates and a full erection is maintained. Sildenafil (*Viagra*), vardenafil (*Levitra*), and tadalafil (*Cialis*) are selective oral PDE5 inhibitors indicated for use in erectile dysfunction. These drugs do not increase or affect erection in men who are not impotent, and do not affect erection that is not a result of sexual stimulation. The recommended effective doses can be taken "as needed" within 1 hour of anticipated sexual activity. Otherwise, the recommended dose can be taken daily. (See Table 37:6.) Since a physiological dysfunction does also occur in women, the drug is being evaluated for its potential effectiveness in women. At this time, however, the drug is not approved for use in women and is designated as FDA Pregnancy Category B.

Adverse Effects

The effects most frequently reported include headache, flushing of the skin, upset stomach, nasal congestion, diarrhea, and rash. Specific visual effects, color tinged vision, and sensitivity to light or blurred vision also have been reported to occur. PDE6 is responsible for normal color vision in the retina. Prolonged erections lasting longer than 4 hours and priapism (painful erections lasting longer than 6 hours) can occur.

Contraindications

PDE inhibitors should not be used in patients who are taking nitrates because a synergistic decrease in blood pressure may produce severe hypotension and/or other cardiovascular sequelae that are life-threatening. These drugs should be used with caution in patients who may have conditions that predispose them to priapism such as sickle cell anemia, leukemia, or predisposing anatomical conditions.

[Table **37:6**]

Drugs Used in the Management of Erectile Dysfunction

Drug (*Trade Name*)*	As needed dose	Daily dose	Maximum
Sildenafil (*Viagra*)	50 mg 1 hour prior to sexual activity	100 mg PO	100 mg in 24 hrs
Tadalafil (*Cialis*)	10 mg (range 5–20 mg) prior to sexual activity	2.5 mg PO	1 dose in 72 hrs
Vardenafil (*Levitra*)	10 mg 1 hour prior to sexual activity	—	20 mg in 24 hrs

Tadalafil as Adcirca and sildenafil as Revatio are available for the treatment of pulmonary arterial hypertension and are not used for erectile dysfunction.

After hormone therapy has been prescribed, patients should be contacted by phone or office visit within 4 to 12 weeks to review patient concerns, the safety profile, and potential compliance issues. Serum testosterone levels may be taken 4 weeks into treatment to confirm the dose response for male patients. Otherwise, special blood tests are not required unless there is a medical issue to be evaluated. Annually, patients should receive a full evaluation—that is, breast, abdominal, and pelvic exam for women.

Remember, once the appropriate dose is established, replacement of male or female hormones is usually associated with a positive self-image. This encourages patient compliance with the medication schedule, which is critical to the success of contraception, prophylaxis against bone and heart disease, and symptom resolution in male and female patients. The lowest effective dose is the proper choice. More is not better, especially with estrogens, testosterone, and DHEA. It should be kept in mind that the prescribing physician is not always the physician most frequently visited for physical examinations or seasonal problems—for example, flu, allergy. Women may be given hormones by a gynecologist or fertility specialist, while men today may be seen by sports medicine specialists. When interviewing and monitoring patients who are taking hormones, the information that follows should be provided to the patient.

General Information

Encourage patients to disclose all medications with all of their physicians, even if the physician is visited infrequently, so that their medication history at other health care centers is current. This counters the possibility of another medication being given that might decrease the hormone effect or produce a serious adverse effect.

Instruct patients that hormonal contraceptives do not protect them against sexually transmitted diseases and human immunodeficiency virus (HIV). Barriers such as condoms are the only means of protection from microbial transmission during intercourse.

Patients taking clomiphene must be instructed to observe caution when driving, operating heavy machinery, or performing tasks requiring coordination or dexterity because this drug may produce dizziness, visual disturbances, and lightheadedness.

Drug Administration

Oral medications, especially contraceptives, should be taken at the same time every day. To develop compliance, the patient can be instructed to take medication with meals or at bedtime. When just starting oral contraceptive therapy, the patient should be advised to use an alternate form of birth control during the first week in addition to the oral contraceptive. This permits adequate time for the hormones to reach their effective blood levels.

If the patient experiences nausea or gastrointestinal upset when taking oral medication, the medication may be taken with meals to minimize the effect.

Buccal tablets (androgens) should not be swallowed. Instruct the patient to hold the tablet between the gum and cheek until it dissolves completely. While the tablet is in place the patient must avoid eating, drinking, and smoking.

Vaginal gels should not be used concurrently with other intravaginal treatments including douching. For patients who are using other intravaginal products, apply the hormone gel 6 hours before or after other products.

Review the appropriate application of transdermal testosterone patches with the patient. Be clear which patch system is being used (*Transderm* goes on the scrotum, *Androderm* does not go on the scrotom). The skin must be clean and dry shaved if necessary to provide adequate patch to skin contact.

Menopause

There are some changes in diet and environment that are often of help in minimizing the symptom triggers. Vasomotor symptoms may be triggered by a variety of substances such as alcohol, spicy foods, citrus, strawberries, and chocolate, as well as environmental factors, stress, and hot and humid weather. Ice water, chilled fruits, and frozen grapes often relieve the "rising hot feeling" and have minimal negative impact on weight gain. Synthetic fabrics such as polyesters or nylon do not "breathe" and, although feeling lighter in weight, actually trap perspiration against the skin. Natural fibers such as cotton are ideal for air flow. Even in winter, cotton layering is better than heavier wool or acrylic clothing. Layering (camisole, blouse, vest, cardigan) permits easy shedding of clothing for comfort as needed.

Vaginal dryness and painful intercourse may be relieved by using water-based vaginal lubricants (*Replens, Astroglide*).

Patients should be instructed that estrogens may cause photosensitivity so they should avoid prolonged exposure to sunlight. Sunscreens and protective clothing are advisable until it is evident whether the patient is experiencing photosensitivity.

Notifying the Prescribing Physician

Breakthrough bleeding or spotting that lasts for more than a few days or occurs in more than one menstrual cycle while receiving hormones should be reported to the prescribing physician immediately.

Intrauterine devices: Patients should notify the physician immediately if abnormal or excessive bleeding, severe cramping, abnormal vaginal discharge, fever or flu-like symptoms, genital lesions, or sores develop.

Diabetic patients must be instructed to be alert for changes that may occur during estrogen treatment. The prescribing physician should be notified immediately if any of the following occur:

- *pain in the calves or groin*
- *sharp chest pain*
- *shortness of breath*

(Continued)

- *abnormal vaginal bleeding*
- *missed menstrual period*
- *severe headache*
- *numbness in the arms or legs*
- *yellowing of the skin or eyes*
- *severe depression*

Glucose tolerance may be decreased, especially with progestins and anabolic steroids. Alert diabetic patients to the potential for fluctuations in their blood sugar levels during routine monitoring. Patients should report significant changes in glucose levels and associated symptoms to the prescribing physician.

Epileptic patients should notify the prescribing physician immediately if migraine or seizures occur during hormone therapy. Patient evaluation will determine whether the seizures are related to fluid retention associated with the hormone treatment.

Female patients receiving androgens should notify the physician for further evaluation if hoarseness, voice deepening, baldness, hirsutism, acne, or menstrual irregularities occur.

Pregnancy

Patients must be informed that all hormones are contraindicated during pregnancy. If the patient becomes pregnant, the prescribing physician should be notified immediately for appropriate discontinuation of treatment. These products are designated FDA Pregnancy Category X: the risk to the fetus outweighs any possible benefit to the mother.

Chapter Review

Understanding Terminology

Match the definition or description in the left column with the appropriate term in the right column.
(LO 37.1, 37.2, 37.3, 37.4, 37.5, 37.6, 37.7)

___ 1. The development of masculine characteristics, such as muscular frame and body hair, in females.

___ 2. The lining of the uterus.

___ 3. Reduced sperm count.

___ 4. Absorption of a drug through the skin, such as with a patch.

___ 5. A disease that results in a decrease in bone density, usually associated with older women.

___ 6. A process that converts nutritional substances into tissue; usually associated with the conversion of protein into muscle mass.

___ 7. A condition in women in which body and facial hair is excessive.

___ 8. Male sex hormones.

___ 9. A condition in which menstruation ceases.

___ 10. A condition associated with painful menstruation.

___ 11. Absorption of a drug through the mucous membranes lining the cheek.

a. amenorrhea

b. anabolism

c. androgens

d. buccal absorption

e. dysmenorrhea

f. endometrium

g. hirsutism

h. osteoporosis

i. oligospermia

j. transdermal absorption

k. virilization

Answer the following questions.

12. Define *equipotent*. **(LO 37.1, 37.2, 37.3, 37.4)**

13. Differentiate between conception and contraception. **(LO 37.1, 37.2)**

14. Write a short paragraph using the following terms: *lactation, menopause, menstruation, puberty,* and *ovulation*. **(LO 37.1, 37.2)**

Acquiring Knowledge

Answer the following questions.

1. Where are the sex hormones produced? **(LO 37.1, 37.2, 37.7)**

2. Briefly describe the production of the estrogens and progesterone in relation to the ovarian follicle. **(LO 37.1, 37.2)**

3. What is the mechanism of action of the oral contraceptives? **(LO 37.2, 37.3, 37.4)**

4. List the main uses of the female sex hormones in medical treatment. **(LO 37.3, 37.4, 37.6)**

5. What adverse effects are associated with estrogen and oral contraceptive therapy for females? **(LO 37.3, 37.4, 37.5)**

6. How is the production of testosterone regulated in males? **(LO 37.1, 37.7)**

7. Briefly describe the main effects produced by testosterone in males. **(LO 37.1, 37.7)**

8. List the main uses of the androgens. **(LO 37.1, 37.7)**

9. What are the adverse effects of androgen therapy in females? **(LO 37.1, 37.2, 37.7)**

Applying Knowledge on the Job

Use your critical-thinking skills to answer the following questions.

1. Assume you work in an ob-gyn practice. Many of the patients are menopausal and considering estrogen replacement therapy. Which patients should be cautioned against this therapy? **(LO 37.3, 37.4, 37.5)**

2. Assume you work in a family-planning clinic, where many patients consider using oral contraceptives. Which patients should be cautioned to use a different means of birth control? **(LO 37.3, 37.4, 37.5)**

3. DES is contraindicated for use during pregnancy. Why? **(LO 37.3, 37.4)**

4. Should a patient taking oral contraceptives be warned regarding possible drug interactions with antibiotics? **(LO 37.3, 37.4)**

5. What should a patient being placed on oral contraceptives for the first time be told regarding sexual activity? **(LO 37.1, 37.2, 37.3, 37.4, 37.5)**

Multiple Choice

Use your critical-thinking skills to answer the following questions.

1. In both males and females the hypothalamus secretes this hormone to stimulate the release of LH and FSH. **(LO 37.1)**
   A. testosterone
   B. estrogen
   C. GnRH
   D. DHEA

2. In the menstrual cycle which of the following hormones is responsible for ovulation? **(LO 37.1, 37.2)**
   A. progesterone
   B. FSH
   C. hCG
   D. LH

3. A mechanism by which oral contraceptives prevent ovulation includes **(LO 37.3, 37.4)**
   A. inhibiting the corpus luteum's production of progesterone
   B. inhibiting implantation to occur
   C. increasing the levels of estrogen and progesterone
   D. stimulating the release of LH and FSH

4. Clomiphene produces its effects by **(LO 37.6)**
   A. inhibiting the release of LH
   B. inhibiting estrogen's negative feedback
   C. combining estrogen and progesterone
   D. increasing bone mineral density

5. The mechanism of action by which erectile dysfunction is treated causes **(LO 37.7)**
   A. inhibition of phosphodiesterases
   B. inhibition of GnRH
   C. vasoconstriction of the blood vessels in the penis
   D. stimulation of the release of testosterone

Multiple Choice (Multiple Answer)

Select the correct choices for each statement. The choices may be all correct, all incorrect, or any combination.

1. Which of the following are parts of the ovarian cycle? **(LO 37.2)**
   A. ovulation
   B. luteal
   C. endometrial
   D. follicular

2. Which of the following are true about oral contraceptives? **(LO 37.3)**
   A. the hormone is delivered via a vaginal ring
   B. they can be monophasic, biphasic, or triphasic
   C. they can be administered as a spray
   D. the doses of estrogen are at the highest effective coverage dose

3. Choose all of the mechanisms by which clomiphene works. **(LO 37.6)**
   A. stimulates the release of FSH and LH
   B. decreases gonadotropin secretion
   C. acts as a follicular development stimulant
   D. increases estrogen receptors

4. Which of the following is true of monophasic oral contraceptives? **(LO 37.4)**
   A. pill color varies over the cycle
   B. estrogen to progestin ratio changes over the cycle
   C. the last 7 pills of the cycle may be iron supplements
   D. there is a fixed ratio of hormones for days 0 to 21

5. Select all of the anabolic actions of androgens. **(LO 37.7)**
   A. stimulation of protein synthesis
   B. increase in appetite
   C. erythropoiesis
   D. weight gain

Sequencing

Place the following steps of the female reproductive cycle in order from first to last. **(LO 37.2)**

_____ _____ _____ _____ _____

First   **Last**

synthesis and secretion of FSH and LH

the surge of LH causes ovulation to occur

follicular cells divide

the hypothalamus releases GnRH

primary follicle matures

Classification

Place the following adverse effects of androgens under the population in which they would present. **(LO 37.7)**

oligospermia   menstrual irregularities   priapism
hirsutism   gynecomastia   deepening of the voice

Females	Males

Labeling

Fill in the missing labels. **(LO 37.2)**

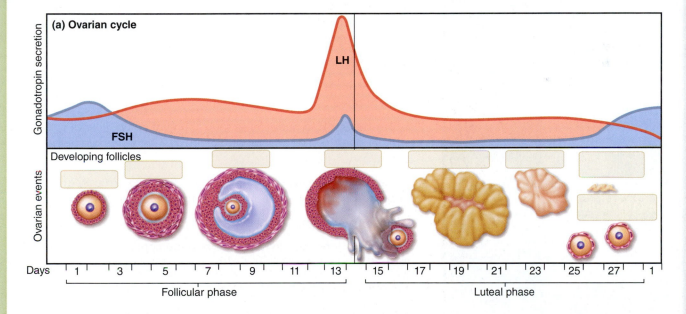

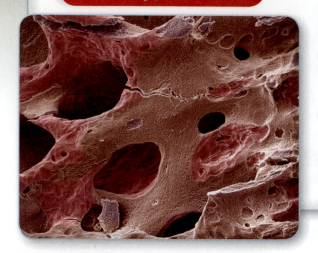

Chapter 38

Drugs Affecting the Thyroid and Para-thyroid Glands and Bone Degeneration

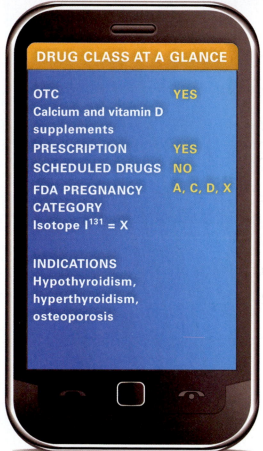

DRUG CLASS AT A GLANCE

OTC	YES
Calcium and vitamin D supplements	
PRESCRIPTION	YES
SCHEDULED DRUGS	NO
FDA PREGNANCY CATEGORY	A, C, D, X
Isotope I^{131} = X	

INDICATIONS
Hypothyroidism, hyperthyroidism, osteoporosis

KEY TERMS

agranulocytosis: acute condition in which there is a reduction in the number of white blood cells (WBCs), specifically polymorphonu-clear cells (granulocytes).

anion: negatively charged ion.

autoimmune disease: condition in which an individual's tissues are damaged by his or her own immune mechanisms.

bone density: a quantitative measurement of the mineral content of bone, used as an indicator of the structural strength of the bone.

bone mass: A measure of the amount of minerals (mostly calcium and phosphorus) contained in a certain volume of bone.

calorigenic: producing heat.

cretinism: condition in which the development of the body and the brain has been inhibited due to congenital hypothyroidism.

euthyroid: having normal thyroid gland function.

exophthalmos: protruding eyeballs out of the socket.

goiter: condition in which the thyroid is enlarged, but not as a result of a tumor.

hypercalcemia: unusually high concentration of calcium in the blood.

myxedema: condition associated with a decrease in thyroid function, caused by removal of thyroid tissue or loss of tissue function because of damage to cells; also associated with subcutaneous edema and slowed metabolism.

osteoblasts: synthesize bone matrix proteins and promote crystal nucleation; contain receptors for PTH, vitamin D_3, and estrogen.

osteoclasts: responsible for bone resorption by binding to bone matrix proteins and releasing enzymes to break down bone.

osteoporosis: condition associated with a decrease in bone density so that the bones are thin and fracture easily.

Paget's disease: condition in older adults in which the bone density is altered so that softening and bending of the weight-bearing bones occurs.

polypeptide: substance, usually large, composed of an indefinite number of amino acids.

T_3 and T_4: hormones (triiodothyronine and thyroxine, respectively) synthesized and released by the thyroid gland. Synthesized T_4 must be converted to T_3 to be utilized by the cell.

thyrotoxic crisis: condition caused by excessive quantities of thyroid hormone, either from a natural source of hypersecretion or exogenous administration of a drug.

TRH: thyroid-releasing hormone, secreted by the hypothalamus.

TSH: thyroid-stimulating hormone, secreted by the anterior pituitary.

Learning Outcomes

After studying this chapter, you should be able to

38.1 explain the terminology associated with the functions and conditions of the thyroid and parathyroid glands.

38.2 explain the functions and hormone regulation of the thyroid gland and the parathyroid glands.

38.3 name two secretions from the thyroid that stimulate tissue growth.

38.4 identify two effects that occur with acute thyroid deficiency in adults and chronic thyroid deficiency in children.

38.5 describe hormonal regulation of calcium.

38.6 explain the bone remodeling process and its relationship to osteoporosis and describe the drug therapy for osteoporosis.

38.7 describe the mechanisms of action of drugs used in the treatment of hypothyroidism and hyperthyroidism.

38.8 explain three adverse effects or drug interactions that occur with hormone replacement or antithyroid drugs.

Introduction

The thyroid gland synthesizes and secretes three hormones that are essential for the growth and development of tissues. These thyroid hormones include triiodothyronine (T_3), thyroxine (T_4), and thyrocalcitonin (calcitonin). All of these hormones directly influence the activity of all peripheral tissues.

THYROID FUNCTION, PHARMACOLOGY, AND DISORDERS

The thyroid hormones triiodothyronine (T_3) and thyroxine (T_4) help regulate tissue growth and mitochondrial metabolism in virtually every cell, especially muscle and nerve tissue. Thyrocalcitonin, however, primarily affects only one peripheral tissue, namely bone.

The secretion of T_3 and T_4 is under the control of the hypothalamic-anterior pituitary-thyroid axis. The hypothalamus secretes **TRH** (thyrotropin-releasing hormone), which travels in the portal vein to the anterior pituitary. The anterior pituitary is then stimulated to secrete **TSH** (thyroid-stimulating hormone) into the bloodstream. TSH binds to receptors on the plasma membrane of the thyroid gland, stimulating the production of T_3 and T_4. As shown in Figure 38.1, sites

---

Figure 38.1   **Formation of Thyroid Hormones (T_3 and T_4) by Follicular Cells***

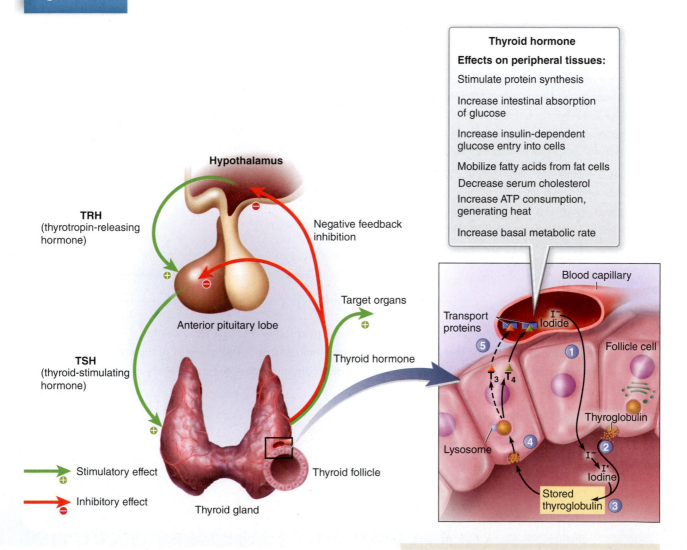

Thyroid hormone

Effects on peripheral tissues:

Stimulate protein synthesis

Increase intestinal absorption of glucose

Increase insulin-dependent glucose entry into cells

Mobilize fatty acids from fat cells

Decrease serum cholesterol

Increase ATP consumption, generating heat

Increase basal metabolic rate

Hypothalamus

TRH (thyrotropin-releasing hormone)

Negative feedback inhibition

Anterior pituitary lobe

Target organs

TSH (thyroid-stimulating hormone)

Thyroid hormone

Stimulatory effect

Inhibitory effect

Thyroid follicle

Thyroid gland

Blood capillary

Transport proteins

I^- Iodide

Follicle cell

T_3 T_4

Thyroglobulin

Lysosome

I^-

I^* Iodine

Stored thyroglobulin

1. Iodide absorption and oxidation
2. Thyroglobulin synthesis and secretion
3. Iodine added to tyrosines of thyroglobulin (stored)
4. Thyroglobulin uptake and hydrolysis
5. Release of T_4 and a small amount of T_3 into the blood

1 through 5, the thyroid follicular cells (site 1) absorb circulating iodide (I^-) obtained from food sources. Thyroid cells are the only cells that can absorb iodide and combine it with the amino acid tyrosine to make T_3 and T_4 (site 3). Follicular cells also synthesize thyroglobulin (site 2). Thyroid hormones stay bound to thyroglobulin (sites 3, 4) until TSH triggers hormone release. Both hormones are carried to their target tissues by transport proteins (site 5). Thyroid hormones are 99 percent bound to transport proteins that protect the hormones from being metabolized along the path to the target cell. The action of thyroid hormones at a target cell is illustrated in Figure 38.2. Thyroid hormone enters the cell and is converted to the more potent hormone T_3 by the removal of an iodine molecule. T_3 enters the nucleus and activates gene transcription for protein synthesis. The new proteins provide metabolic effects that vary with the target cell. For example, T_3 activates the synthesis of the sodium-potassium pump, which then increases ATP consumption and generates heat **(calorigenic).** This increases the basal metabolic rate and balances the loss of body heat in cold weather. To ensure there is oxygen and blood to meet the metabolic demand, T_3 increases

respiration and heart rate and the strength of cardiac muscle contraction.

Thyroid hormone is a permissive hormone, which means it is necessary for other hormones like growth hormone and epinephrine to execute their hormonal actions. Thyroid hormone stimulates protein synthesis; increases carbohydrate breakdown, blood glucose, insulin-dependent entry of glucose into cells, and circulating fatty acids; and decreases serum cholesterol. These substances are essential for cell building, repair, and energy. The balance between thyroid hormone production and secretion is maintained through the negative feedback loop, as shown in Figure 38.1. Thyroid hormone level inhibits TSH and TRH secretion when T_3 interacts with specific receptors.

Drugs are used to alter the action of thyroid hormones in two conditions: hyposecretion of hormone (hypothyroidism) and hypersecretion of hormone (hyperthyroidism).

Hyposecretion of Hormones

Hyposecretion of thyroid hormones may occur as a result of glandular destruction. Glandular damage is produced by excessive exposure to radiation (X-ray), lack of iodine, pituitary dysfunction (lack of TSH), or surgical removal of thyroid tissue. Hypothyroidism (lack of T_3 and T_4) in infants and children produces mental and physical retardation **(cretinism).** Hypothyroidism during gestation and the first 6 months after birth is the most critical period. If the infant is diagnosed and treated before the first month of age, neurological development may almost be restored.

Hyposecretion of thyroid hormone can be caused by iodide deficiency in the diet. The famous image of the Morton Salt package boldly indicates its role in providing iodide for everyone (see Figure 38.3). It worked. Frank iodide deficiency has been virtually eliminated as a cause of thyroid hormone deficiency in the United States since iodinization of commercial salt (iodide supplementation) began in the 1920s. The World Health Organization, however, recognizes that iodine deficiency is still the most common preventable cause of brain damage worldwide. Hyposecretion of T_3 and T_4 in adults results in nontoxic **goiter.** When thyroid hormone secretion is suppressed, the feedback loop (TRH, TSH) stimulates the thyroid to secrete more T_3 and T_4. When little or no T_3 and T_4 circulate in the blood, TSH continues to stimulate the thyroid gland to release hormones that it cannot produce. This constant stimulation of the thyroid results in glandular enlargement (hypertrophy). As the thyroid increases in size, it protrudes from the front of the neck, causing a swollen appearance (see Figure 38.4).

Figure 38.2

Action of Thyroid Hormones (T_3 and T_4) on a Target Cell

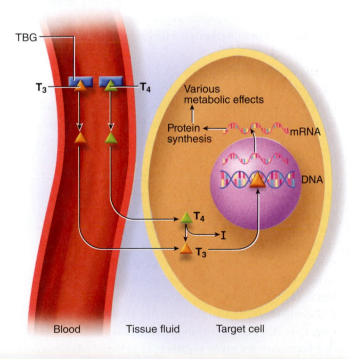

A small amount of T_3 comes from the thyroid, but most T_3 is produced in the target cells by removing an iodine molecule from T_4.

Figure 38.3

Iodized Salt

Iodide added to commercial products must be indicated on the label. Confirmation of no added iodide may say, "No iodide added" as on the left box.

Individuals who have a total absence of T_3 and T_4 develop **myxedema**, which is characterized by a round, puffy face, dry skin, hypotension, bradycardia, and an intolerance to cold temperatures. In severe cases,

Figure 38.4

Endemic Goiter

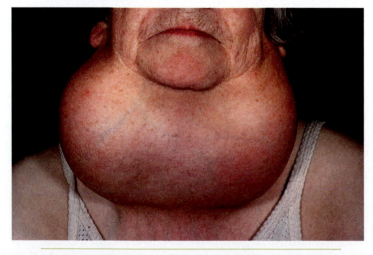

An iodine deficiency in this person's diet resulted in a lack of thyroid hormone and extremely large goiter. For lack of a negative feedback, the pituitary secreted elevated levels of thyroid-stimulating hormone (TSH), resulting in hypertrophy of the thyroid gland.

respiratory acidosis, electrolyte imbalance, and coma may develop (myxedema coma).

Hormone Replacement

Thyroid function is routinely evaluated by measuring circulating TSH and T_4 levels. Primary hypothyroidism is associated with decreased production of total T_4, T_3, and free thyroxine index (FT_4I), but circulating TSH is increased. Secondary hypothyroidism is associated with a decrease in all three hormones. Free thyroxine index is an estimate of free T_4 calculated from total T_4 and thyroid hormone binding ratio. Thyroid deficiency is treated primarily by hormone replacement. To relieve the symptoms associated with thyroid deficiency, various preparations of thyroid hormones can be administered orally.

Thyroid hormones are prepared synthetically or can be extracted from the endocrine glands of pigs (porcine). Although these hormones produce the same spectrum of activity, T_3 and T_4 differ in potency, onset, and duration of action.

Thyroid hormones are usually given in the smallest doses and incrementally raised until a clinically adequate response is reached. This allows individualized dosing and minimizes the potential for adverse responses to occur. Once an adequate dosing schedule is established, the hormone(s) will mimic the action of normal thyroid secretion. The circulating hormone(s) also will inhibit excessive secretion of TSH (negative feedback) so that goiter production is suppressed. Hormone replacement in functionally thyroid-deficient individuals is a lifelong therapy.

Drug Administration

Thyroid hormones are usually administered orally, preferably as a single dose before breakfast. The dose is individualized between 100 and 200 mcg/day (see Table 38:1). These preparations may be administered intravenously in the treatment of myxedema coma at doses between 200 and 500 mcg. These hormones should be taken at the same time each day to maintain a consistent response. Following oral absorption, T_3 and T_4 are bound to a specific plasma protein known as thyroxine-binding globulin (TBG), which transports the hormones to the various target tissues. Triiodothyronine has a quicker onset and a shorter duration of action than T_4 because T_3 is less tightly bound to TBG. Triiodothyronine is also three to five times more potent than T_4 in stimulating metabolic mechanisms. When the two hormones are given together, as in the combination preparations, T_3 acts quickly, whereas T_4 has a lag time. Eventually, both T_3 and T_4 are metabolized in the liver and excreted in the urine.

Table 38:1		

Hormone Replacement Therapy for Thyroid Deficiency

Drug (*Trade Name*)*	Active hormone	Daily adult maintenance dose
Levothyroxine sodium (*Levothroid, Levoxyl, Synthroid*)	T_4	100–200 mcg PO; 50–100 mcg IM, IV
Liothyronine sodium (*Cytomel, Triostat*)	T_3	25–75 mcg PO
Liotrix (*Thyrolar*)	T_3+T_4	1 *Thyrolar-1* tablet to 1 *Thyrolar-2* tablet** (equals 60–120 mg hormone) /day PO
Thyroid (desiccated thyroid) (*Armour Thyroid, Bio-Thyroid, Thyroid USP*)	T_3+T_4	60–120 mcg PO

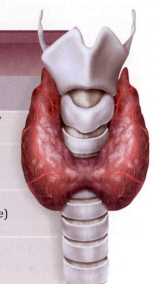

*Not an inclusive list of product names. **Thyrolar tablet strengths vary.*

Note to the Health Care Professional

Iodine *added* to salt has to appear somewhere on the label. Not all salts are iodized. "Iodine-Free" or "Does Not Contain Iodine" can appear on labels where the processor has verified no iodine is present.

Clinical Indications

Thyroid hormones are approved for use in children and adults as replacement or supplement in hypothyroidism from any cause. Thyroid hormones are also used in the treatment of thyroid nodules and thyroid cancer because they suppress TSH, and in the diagnosis of hyperthyroid conditions. Despite their ability to affect metabolism, thyroid hormones are not approved or indicated for use in the treatment of obesity. Doses necessary to effect weight reduction produce serious cardiovascular effects that can be life-threatening to the patient.

Adverse Effects

The majority of adverse effects associated with thyroid hormone result from overdose. The physiological effect of overdose is hyperthyroidism. Symptoms may include psychotic behavior, diarrhea, increased blood pressure and heart rate, fever, and angina attacks. Metabolic stimulation may result in weight loss, menstrual irregularities, and sweating. In addition, tremors, headache, nervousness, and insomnia may occur. These symptoms can be alleviated by temporarily discontinuing the drug or reducing the dose.

Thyroid hormones should be used with extreme caution in patients who have cardiovascular disease (hypertension, congestive heart failure, or angina) or renal disease. Thyroid hormone increases sympathetic tone and may exacerbate the underlying disease. There is a black box cautionary warning with the use of any thyroid hormone product that "in **euthyroid** patients, doses within the range of daily hormonal requirements are ineffective for weight reduction. Larger doses may produce serious or even life-threatening manifestations of toxicity, particularly when given in association with sympathomimetic amines such as those used for their anorectic effects."

Long-term use of thyroxine has been associated with osteoporosis in postmenopausal women. **Bone density** must be evaluated prior to therapy in order to adequately monitor the hormone's effect and adjust the dose to minimize bone demineralization.

Drug Interactions

Cholestyramine (hypolipidemic drug) will bind the thyroid hormones when given together orally. To avoid interference with intestinal absorption of the thyroid hormones, administration of cholestyramine and the hormones should be separated by 4 or 5 hours. Long-term therapy with lithium, chlorpromazine, or imipramine has been reported to produce hypothyroidism. The dose of T_3 and T_4 may therefore require adjustment in patients receiving these drugs chronically. Thyroid hormones (T_4 in particular) enhance the activity of the oral anticoagulant warfarin, leading to increased bleeding and possible hemorrhage. Patients requiring oral anticoagulant therapy should have their thyroid dosing schedule adjusted accordingly.

Thyroid hormone therapy may cause an increase in the required dose of insulin or oral hypoglycemic drugs in diabetic patients because these hormones increase blood glucose levels. Estrogens may increase the requirement of thyroid hormone therapy if given to patients who do not have a functioning thyroid gland. Estrogens increase proteins that bind to circulating thyroid hormone, thus decreasing the amount of hormone available to target tissues.

Special Considerations and Contraindications

Thyroid hormone given as replacement therapy must be taken by patients for life. Patients should not discontinue the drug without their physician's knowledge. Changes in type or brand of medication should be made only after careful examination of the product literature to ensure that the products are bioequivalent. Dosing is often recommended for the morning so that patients will avoid episodes of insomnia (central nervous system [CNS] stimulation).

Note to the Health Care Professional

Thyroid hormone therapy is contraindicated in patients with myocardial infarction or uncorrected adrenal insufficiency. Thyroid hormones should never be administered for the purpose of reducing body weight in obese individuals. These hormones should only be administered to patients who have been accurately diagnosed as being hormone deficient.

Patients, especially the elderly, who experience chest pain, palpitations, sweating, dyspnea (difficult or labored breathing), or tachycardia while receiving thyroid hormones should notify their physician immediately. Thyroid hormone therapy in patients who have diabetes or adrenal insufficiency may exacerbate the underlying disease, leading to an increased requirement of insulin, oral hypoglycemics, and steroids. Once the antidiabetic drug has been adjusted for patients receiving concomitant thyroid therapy, the patients should not discontinue the thyroid drug without their physician's knowledge. Cessation of thyroid therapy may precipitate hypoglycemia unless the antidiabetic medication is readjusted.

Thyroid replacement therapy need not be discontinued during pregnancy. Thyroid hormones administered to pregnant women do not readily cross the placental barrier to affect fetal development. These hormones are designated as Food and Drug Administration (FDA) Pregnancy Category A: adequate studies have not demonstrated a risk to the fetus in the first trimester of pregnancy and there is no evidence of risk in later trimesters.

Hypersecretion of Hormones

Hypersecretion of thyroid hormones may be produced by tumors (thyroid, pituitary, or hypothalamic malignancies), or **autoimmune disease** (Graves' disease). In Graves' disease, the immune system mistakenly attacks the thyroid gland, but instead of destroying the gland, an antibody called thyrotropin receptor antibody (TRAb) stimulates the thyroid to make excessive amounts of thyroid hormone. The patient exhibits physiological responses characteristic of chronic thyroid stimulation and a characteristic protrusion of the eyeballs (**exophthalmos,** see Figure 38.5). The exophthalmos results from swelling of the tissues and muscles behind the eye.

Hyperthyroidism is associated with an increased secretion and circulation of T_3 and T_4, which results in added heat production (fever and sweating), increased cell metabolism, tachycardia, muscle weakness, anxiety, and weight loss. The clinical symptoms resemble excessive stimulation of the sympathetic nervous system.

Hypersecretory conditions may be corrected with antithyroid drugs, irradiation, or surgical removal of the overactive tissue. Treatment of a hyperactive thyroid usually includes a combination of these methods.

Treating Hyperthyroidism with Antithyroid Drugs

Hypersecretory conditions of the thyroid are frequently caused by glandular tumors. Often, these overactive growths can be removed surgically. However, the thyroid mass is frequently treated with antithyroid drugs or irradiation to reduce the tumor, inactivate the tissue, or reduce vascularity (blood flow) prior to surgery (thyroidectomy). Irradiation and antithyroid drug administration in hyperthyroidism are directed toward destroying the overactive tissue or inhibiting the production and secretion of T_3 and T_4.

Figure 38.5

Hyperthyroidism: Characteristic Protruding Eyes (Exophthalmus)

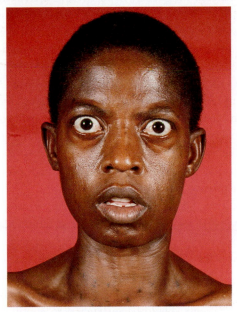

Hyperthyroidism

Route of Administration

Although small amounts of iodide are necessary for hormone synthesis, high levels of iodide inhibit the synthesis and release of thyroid hormones. In large concentrations, iodide inhibits its own uptake and binding within the thyroid gland. Iodide preparations are available in solution as potassium or sodium iodide (see Table 38:2). Strong iodine solution (*Lugol's solution*)

contains 5 percent iodine and 10 percent potassium iodide. These mixtures are taken orally. The thyrotropic effects of iodide solutions are evident in 24 to 48 hours and may last several weeks when the drugs are taken chronically. Strong iodine solution is obtained by prescription. There are over-the-counter potassium iodide tablets; however, these products are different strengths and not indicated for the treatment of hyperthyroid conditions.

Iodide suppression is not useful for long-term treatment of hyperthyroidism because the effects of iodide suppression are not permanent. Eventually, the thyroid escapes the iodide inhibition, resulting in an immediate surge in T_3 and T_4 release, producing a thyroid storm, an acute hyperthyroid condition. Presently, iodide therapy is reserved for short-term treatment (preoperative) because iodide reduces the vascularity of the gland. Lithium carbonate, when given concomitantly with iodide, may enhance the hypothyroid response.

Other side effects produced by iodide therapy include rash, headache, sore gums, hypersalivation, and pruritus.

Radioactive iodide (^{131}I) is used in the diagnosis and treatment of hyperthyroid disorders. Since radioactive iodide behaves like dietary iodide, it rapidly accumulates in the thyroid gland. However, radioactive (unstable) iodide emits two types of radiation: gamma rays and beta rays. Emission of the gamma rays (X-rays) produces a picture of the thyroid that demonstrates abnormal growth or activity. Furthermore, the beta radiation remains in the thyroid cells and destroys the overactive tissue.

[Table 38:2]

Antithyroid Drugs

Drug (*Trade Name*)	Adult oral daily dose
Potassium iodide and iodine (*Lugol's solution*)	2–6 drops PO TID for 10 days prior to surgery
Radioactive iodide (^{131}I) (*Iodotope, Sodium Iodide ^{131}I*)	4–10 millicuries PO or IV (hyperthyroidism) 50 millicuries PO (thyroid carcinoma)
Methimazole (*Tapazole*)	15–60 mg/day PO (initial) TID 5–15 mg/day PO (maintenance) TID
Propylthiouracil	300–400 mg/day PO (initial) TID 100–150 mg/day PO (maintenance) TID

Thus, when ^{131}I is administered to severely hyperthyroid individuals, it reduces the thyroid mass (tumors and nodules) and destroys hormone synthesis. Radioactive iodide is used preoperatively or in the treatment of thyroid carcinoma. Occasionally, patients exposed to ^{131}I become permanently hypothyroid. In these cases, hormone replacement therapy must be administered for life. Because of its destructive potential, ^{131}I should never be used during pregnancy or lactation because permanent damage to the fetal thyroid can develop.

The most frequently used antithyroid drugs include propylthiouracil and methimazole. These agents are thioamide drugs that inhibit the incorporation of iodide into tyrosine and the condensation of monoiodotyrosine and diiodotyrosine. Since these drugs have no effect on hormone release, the antithyroid action cannot be observed until the thyroid stores of T_3 and T_4 become depleted. Thereafter, no new hormones are synthesized.

Long-term treatment with the thioamide drugs usually results in remission of the hyperthyroid condition. These drugs are easily absorbed into the thyroid gland after oral use. Eventually, these drugs are metabolized and excreted in the urine.

Adverse Effects

The usual side effects of thioamide drugs include rash, fever, myalgia, jaundice, and nausea. **Agranulocytosis,** a condition in which white blood cells decrease and fever may develop, also has been reported. Cross-sensitivity occurs for all thioamide drugs in sensitive individuals. Thioamide therapy frequently causes goiter formation because the negative feedback to TSH is removed. If the dose is reduced, some thyroid hormone can be synthesized. The thioamide drugs are primarily used preoperatively or as an adjunct in ^{131}I therapy.

The thioamide drugs are useful in the treatment of **thyrotoxic crisis,** which is associated with an excessive secretion of thyroid hormone. Occasionally, untreated hyperthyroid individuals undergo emotional stress or trauma that results in an intense hyperthyroid reaction. Fever, tachycardia, heart failure, and coma may result. Treatment may include thioamide drugs, iodine, and propranolol. Beta-adrenergic blocking drugs do not affect the thyroid gland but are administered to inhibit the increased sympathetic responses that accompany hyperthyroidism.

Special Considerations and Contraindications

Antithyroid drugs will cross the placenta and inhibit fetal thyroid development, resulting in neonatal goiter and cretinism. Nevertheless, there are situations where the benefit to the mother balances the potential risk to the fetus. In such cases, propylthiouracil is used because placental transfer is much lower than for methimazole. Frequently hyperthyroid activity diminishes during pregnancy. This allows the drug dose to be decreased or discontinued before damage to the fetus can occur. Since these drugs also appear in breast milk, they should not be administered to nursing mothers because the infant will develop hypothyroidism. Again, when necessary, propylthiouracil is the drug of choice to administer to nursing mothers. Propylthiouracil may compromise coagulation, so monitoring prothrombin time may be required for surgical patients. Propylthiouracil may cause bleeding and potentiate anticoagulants.

Patients should be evaluated for sensitivity to iodides, particularly prior to parenteral administration. Hypersensitivity reactions, which may occur immediately or several hours after administration, range from rashes to laryngeal edema. Iodide-containing medications are contraindicated in patients with pulmonary edema. Patients should be instructed to continue their iodide medications as prescribed. Sudden withdrawal of iodides may precipitate thyroid storm. Patients receiving radioactive iodide should be instructed not to expectorate and to use good toilet habits because saliva and urine may be radioactive ("hot") for 24 hours after drug exposure.

Note to the Health Care Professional

Because of their destructive potential, therapeutic doses of sodium iodide ^{131}I should never be administered to patients who are pregnant or lactating. Antithyroid drugs should be avoided during pregnancy.

LO 38.1 LO 38.5
LO 38.6 LO 38.8

PARATHYROID HORMONES

Calcium ions, essential for neuromuscular and endocrine function, enable all muscles to contract and nerves to conduct impulses. Therefore, it is essential that all tissues receive an adequate supply of calcium.

Plasma calcium levels are strictly regulated by the secretion of three hormones: calcitonin, parathyroid hormone (parathormone, PTH), and calcitriol. Calcitonin is secreted by the thyroid gland, whereas PTH is secreted by the parathyroid gland. Normally, plasma calcium is maintained at 9.0 to 10.4 mg/dL (4.5 to 5.2 mEq/L) for men and 8.9 to 10.2 mg/dL (4.4 to 5.1 mEq/L) for women. Elevated plasma calcium (hypercalcemia) stimulates calcitonin secretion while low plasma calcium (hypocalcemia) stimulates the secretion of PTH. Calcitriol is a form of vitamin D that facilitates calcium absorption from the GI tract, thus increasing circulating calcium.

Calcium Homeostasis

Calcitonin and PTH are polypeptide hormones secreted in response to changes in the plasma calcium level. Bone is continually formed throughout life, although the overall mass of bone peaks between the ages of 30 and 40. Bone consists of calcium deposition in a protein matrix. The primary regulator of calcium balance is PTH. Bone consists of four cell types: osteogenic, **osteoblasts,** osteocytes, and **osteoclasts.** Decreases in plasma calcium stimulate the secretion of PTH, which stimulates precursor (osteogenic) cells to differentiate into osteoclasts. Osteoclasts resorb bone. Osteoblasts and osteoclasts balance plasma calcium concentration through

bone remodeling. About 20 percent of bone is remodeled (rebuilt) each year. Bone remodeling consists of two phases: bone resorption and bone deposition. The osteoclasts secrete enzymes that break down bone and release calcium ions. Then the osteoblasts secrete the protein matrix and facilitate calcium ion deposition. A crystalline calcium phosphate salt known as **hydroxyapatite** is the primary substance through which calcium is laid into bone. Calcium homeostasis is illustrated in Figure 38.6. In this metabolic balance, calcium rises and falls, triggering feedback to the sensing hormones, PTH and calcitonin.

PTH increases the intestinal absorption and renal reabsorption of calcium ions. These two physiological processes require calcitriol, an activated analog of vitamin D. Overall, these effects of PTH increase the level of circulating calcium ions in response to hypocalcemia. Estrogen inhibits PTH; thus, after menopause, the negative feedback mechanism to control PTH secretion is lost. As one ages, the amount of time spent in bone deposition decreases and bone resorption increases, causing osteoporosis.

When the plasma calcium level becomes too high (**hypercalcemia,** more than 10.5 mg/dL), calcitonin is secreted. It lowers the circulating calcium level by antagonizing the effect of PTH on bone. Calcitonin directly inhibits bone resorption so that calcium ions are retained

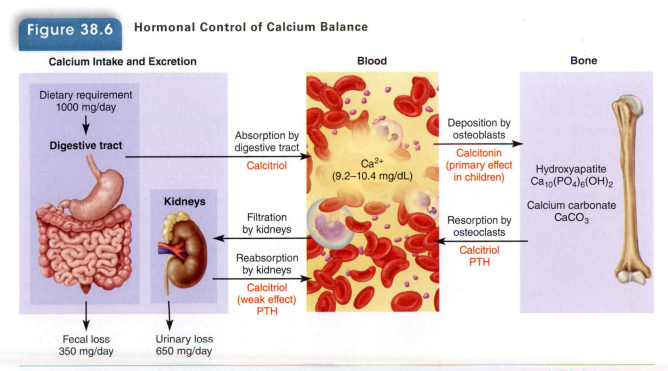

| **Figure 38.6** | **Hormonal Control of Calcium Balance** |

The central panel represents the blood reservoir of calcium and shows its normal (safe) range. Calcitriol (vitamin D analog) and parathormone (PTH) regulate calcium exchanges between the blood and the small intestine and kidneys (left). Calcitonin, calcitriol, and PTH regulate calcium exchanges between blood and bone (right).

in the bone. This is particularly important in children during bone development. It does not affect intestinal and renal calcium absorption, and its action does not require vitamin D.

Treating Calcium Disorders

Hypocalcemia can occur as a result of vitamin D deficiency, thyroid tumors, chronic renal dialysis, diarrhea, and pregnancy, where the calcium is diverted to development of the fetal skeleton. The major endocrine disorder that alters calcium homeostasis is hypoparathyroidism. Hypoparathyroidism may occur by accidental surgical removal of the glands. Since PTH is the predominant controlling factor, lack of PTH produces an imbalance in calcium regulation, and eventually hypocalcemia ensues. Hypocalcemia causes hyperexcitability of the neuromuscular system, resulting in spastic muscle contractions, convulsions, and paresthesia (a pricking, tingling, or creeping sensation). Tetany, the inability of the muscles to relax, occurs when plasma calcium falls to 6 mg/dL. Tetany and hypocalcemia are characterized by a classic sign, carpopedal spasm, shown in Figure 38.7. Treatment of hypoparathyroidism involves the administration of intravenous calcium to quickly raise the calcium level, followed by a combination of oral calcium and vitamin D (cholecalciferol).

Contrary to other endocrine deficiency states, hypoparathyroidism is not usually treated by replacement of the missing hormone. The parathyroid hormone, teriparatide (*Forteo*), is available for subcutaneous injection and is approved for the management of osteoporosis in men and women. The usual dose is 20 mcg SC once a day for up to two years. Hypocalcemia is usually managed by the use of oral calcium salts and vitamin D derivatives (see Table 38:3). Administration of vitamin D enhances intestinal absorption of calcium, thus increasing plasma calcium levels. Through this therapy, calcium ions are immediately available to the tissues without affecting bone resorption. Any excess calcium ions are excreted by the kidneys.

However, calcium salts and vitamin D preparations are not harmless medications. Excessive use of these preparations may lead to hypercalcemia and kidney stone formation. Treatment of drug-induced hypercalcemia may involve the use of edetic acid (ethylenediamine tetraacetic acid [EDTA]), which binds (chelates) the calcium ions and removes them from the blood.

Hypercalcemia

Although hypercalcemia may result from tumors in the parathyroid gland, this is not the most frequent cause of elevated plasma calcium levels. Hypercalcemia is usually associated with certain neoplasms, multiple myeloma, and renal dysfunction. These conditions either accelerate bone resorption or impair renal excretion of calcium. The resultant hypercalcemia produces nausea, vomiting, increased secretion of gastric acid (hyperchlorhydria), headaches, and arrhythmias. Calcium also may be deposited in the cornea and kidneys, producing irreversible tissue damage.

Management of chronic hypercalcemia includes diuretics (thiazides or furosemide), which enhance the renal clearance of calcium, bisphosphonates, and calcitonin.

Figure 38.7

Carpopedal Spasm

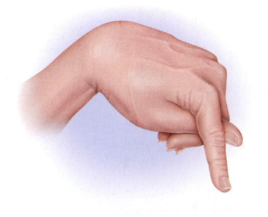

This is a sign of tetany and hypocalcemia.

LO 38.1 | LO 38.6 | LO 38.8

DEGENERATIVE BONE DISEASE: OSTEOPOROSIS

The two most common disorders in bone metabolism are **Paget's disease** and **osteoporosis.** In Paget's disease, bone metabolism is hyperactive in some but not all bones, causing newly laid osteoid to be soft, calcified but fragile. The bones are characterized as thick and weak. Bones most frequently affected are the pelvis, femur, skull, and vertebrae, although any bone can be affected. Microfractures seen on X-ray are usually the first indication of the chronic degenerative process. Though asymptomatic early in development, once it appears, bone pain can range from aching to severe night pain.

Drugs Used in the Treatment of Calcium Disorders

Drug (*Trade Name*)	Use	Adult dose
Calcitonin		
Calcitonin, salmon (*Fortical, Miacalcin*)	Reduce hypercalcemia Paget's disease Postmenopausal osteoporosis	4–8 IU/kg every 12 hr SC or IM 100 IU/day IM, SC 100 IU/every other day SC or IM; 200 IU intranasal
Calcium		
Calcium chloride Calcium gluconate Calcium lactate	Increase plasma calcium Increase plasma calcium Increase plasma calcium	500–1500 mg over 6 to 12 hrs IV 20 ml (10% solution) IV; 15 g/day PO 0.5–2 g QID PO
Bisphosphonates		
Alendronate (*Fosamax*)	Paget's disease Postmenopausal osteoporosis Steroid-induced osteoporosis in women (men)	40 mg/day PO for 6 months 35 mg once a week PO or 5 mg/day 5 or 10 mg once a day (70 mg once a week)
Etidronate disodium (*Didronel*)	Paget's disease Spinal cord injury Total hip replacement	5–10 mg/kg/day PO up to 6 months 20 mg/kg/day PO for 2 weeks, then 10 mg/kg/day for 10 weeks 20 mg/kg/day PO 1 month before and 3 months after surgery
Ibandronate (*Boniva*)	Postmenopausal osteoporosis	150 mg once a month PO; 3 mg IV every 3 months
Pamidronate (*Aredia*)	Hypercalcemia of malignancy Osteolytic bone metastases Paget's disease	60–90 mg IV infusion over 24 hr 90 mg IV infusion over 2 hr every 3–4 weeks 30 mg/day as a 4-hr infusion IV on 3 consecutive days
Risedronate (*Actonel, Atelvia*)	Osteoporosis in postmenopausal women Paget's disease Steroid-induced osteoporosis in women (men)	5 mg daily PO or 35 mg once a week or 75 mg on 2 consecutive days/month 30 mg daily for 2 months 5 mg PO daily (5 mg PO weekly for men)
Tiludronate (*Skelid*)	Paget's disease	400 mg PO with 6–8 oz of water for 3 months
Zoledronic acid (*Reclast, Zometa*)	Prevention of postmenopausal osteoporosis Steroid-induced osteoporosis, Paget's disease Treatment of postmenopausal osteoporosis	5 mg IV infusion every 2 years 5 mg IV infusion once a year 5 mg IV infusion once a year
Vitamin D		
Calcitriol (vitamin D_3)	Increase calcium absorption Management of hypocalcemia Metabolic bone disease	0.25, 0.5 mcg/day PO 1 mcg/ml solution/day PO 1–2 mcg 3 times/week IV
Calcitriol (*Calcijex, Rocaltrol*)	Hypoparathyroidism	0.5–2 mcg daily PO

(Continued)

Drug (*Trade Name*)	Use	Adult dose
Vitamin D		
Cholecalciferol** (*Baby Drops, D-drops, Delta-D*) (D$_3$) (*Depo-Medrol*)*	Inadequate vitamin D	1 tablet or capsule PO daily
Doxercalciferol (*Hectorol*)	Secondary hypoparathyroidism (dialysis)	10 mcg PO 3 times/week
Ergocalciferol* (*Calciferol drops, vitamin D, Drisdol*)	Increase plasma calcium	50,000–200,000 IU (1.25–5 mg) PO
Paricalcitol (*Zemplar*)	Hypoparathyroidism	1–2 mcg daily or 3 times/week PO
Combinations		
Actonel with Calcium 35 mg risedronate, 1250 mg calcium carbonate	Osteoporosis in women	1 *Actonel* tablet/week 1 calcium tablet/day
Fosamax Plus D 70 mg alendronate/70 mcg vitamin D$_3$	Osteoporosis in men	1 tablet/week

* OTC and prescription. ** OTC.

Osteoporosis

Osteoporosis is a condition associated with decreased **bone mass** that affects 55 percent of Americans 50 years of age or older. This condition may result from increased bone resorption, decreased mineral deposition, increased mineral excretion, or a combination of actions that remove calcium from the body. A variety of factors have been associated with the development of osteoporosis, as though predisposing certain individuals beyond the expected age-associated loss. These factors include premature menopause, leanness and short stature in women, Caucasian and oriental race, treatment with corticosteroids or phenytoin, smoking, alcoholism, and family history of osteoporosis. While osteoporosis occurs in elderly men, the incidence in women is greater, related to diminished estrogen availability. The decrease in estrogen correlates with the risk factors of premature menopause and decreased body fat (leanness) in which estrogen could be stored. In addition, calcium absorption decreases as estrogen activity decreases. As women are believed to have a daily dietary intake of calcium well below the recommended level, there is concern that this further contributes to the development of osteoporosis in women.

Bone loss in osteoporosis is associated with reduction in bone density, visualized through X-ray or tomography (see Figure 38.8, the effects of osteoporosis).

These tools are used to evaluate improvement in bone mineral density during therapy. While the objective is to maintain or improve bone mineral density, the goal is to prevent bone fractures. In Paget's disease and osteoporosis fractures result from stress or falls in people over 65 years old. Beyond this age, people more easily fracture vertebrae, hips, and wrists as a result of mechanical stress or pressure.

Drug Therapy: Calcitonin

Calcitonin, available as a synthetic polypeptide hormone, is administered to hypercalcemia patients whose thyroid and parathyroid glands function normally. In Paget's disease, bone turnover is stimulated, causing alkaline phosphatase and hydroxyproline to be excreted as markers of the abnormal bone activity. Calcitonin (*Fortical*), injected subcutaneously or intramuscularly, inhibits the accelerated bone resorption. This hormone, available as a nasal spray (*Miacalcin*), is an extract from salmon, which is identical to human calcitonin but has a greater potency.

Calcitonin has limited clinical use because it produces allergic reactions that require termination of therapy. In addition, some patients develop drug resistance to the **polypeptide.** Drug resistance may be due to the formation of antibodies that neutralize the hormone. However, in patients who have a normal parathyroid,

Figure 38.8

The Effects of Osteoporosis

(a)

(b)

(c)

(a) Spongy bone in the body of a vertebra in good health (left) and with osteoporosis (right). (b) Colorized X-ray of lumbar vertebrae severely damaged by osteoporosis. (c) Abnormal thoracic spinal curvature (kyphosis) due to compression of thoracic vertebrae with osteoporosis.

rebound secretion of PTH occurs when the plasma calcium level falls. This effect may counteract the pharmacological activity of calcitonin. Calcitonin is usually well tolerated by patients. The usual side effects include nausea, vomiting, diarrhea, and inflammation at the injection site. The nasal preparation is associated with rhinitis, insomnia, anxiety, and headache. Overdose with 10 times the daily therapeutic dose has only produced vomiting prior to recovery.

Bisphosphonates

The bisphosphonates are the drugs of choice in the management of osteoporosis because they inhibit normal and abnormal bone resorption in men and women and are effective in steroid-induced osteoporosis. Bisphosphonates are analogs of endogenous pyrophosphates (in ATP) that have a special attraction to calcium in bones. There are two groups of bisphosphonates: one group contains nitrogen atoms and the other does not. Both groups bind to the mineral surface (calcium) of bone in a protective manner, to keep calcium in the matrix. The nonnitrogen drugs [etidronate (*Didronel*), tiludronate (*Skelid*)] compete with osteoclast ATP causing the cells to die; thus, bone resorption decreases. The nitrogen-bisphosphonates are more readily attracted to bone calcium and have greater resorption inhibition potency. These drugs [alendronate (*Fosamax*), pamidronate (*Aredia*), risedronate (*Actonel*), and zoledronic acid (*Reclast*)] prevent protein synthesis in the osteoclast cell membrane by interrupting the HMG CoA-reductase pathway (this important pathway was discussed for the statin drugs in Chapter 29).

These drugs are poorly absorbed in the gastrointestinal tract, not metabolized, and excreted in the urine. Nevertheless, enough drug is absorbed to produce a clinically significant difference in bone mineral density within 3 months of treatment. Improvement in bone density in the spine and hip does not involve demineralization of other bones. The therapeutic effect is presumably conferred to all bones in the management of Paget's disease and osteoporosis. In the treatment of hypercalcemia due to malignancy, plasma calcium levels are dramatically reduced within 24 hours, accompanied by an increase in calcium excretion. To be optimally effective, these medications must be taken with an adequate amount of oral calcium and vitamin D. This includes oral mineral and vitamin supplements for the duration of therapy when necessary.

Drug and Food Interactions

Bisphosphonates have a number of food and drug interactions. Ranitidine and indomethacin increase the bioavailability of alendronate and tiludronate without deleterious effect. Since the absolute absorption of the administered dose is low, it is advisable not to take the bisphosphonates with calcium supplements, caffeine, or antacids. These drugs complex with bisphosphonates and decrease their absorption when taken less than 1 hour before or after the bisphosphonate. Foods and beverages, especially those containing minerals/calcium, interfere with drug absorption. This includes milk, orange juice, and fortified water. All oral bisphosphonates should be taken with a full glass of water (only) 1 hour before meals to minimize absorption effects. While oral bisphosphonates increase the GI irritation of aspirin, aspirin products taken within 2 hours of dosing decrease the bisphosphonate absorption. Because oral bisphosphonates irritate the lining of the esophagus, patients must be able to remain upright for 30 minutes after dosing to avoid extended contact with esophageal tissue. Loop diuretics and aminoglycoside antibiotics may synergize with parenteral bisphosphonates to produce a greater hypocalcemia.

Adverse Effects and Contraindications

The bisphosphonates are well tolerated. The most common adverse effects are flatulence, gastritis, headache, dry mouth, and musculoskeletal pain. Esophageal ulcers have occurred in some patients, so signs of gastrointestinal bleeding should be monitored. The incidence of adverse effects is associated with the highest doses. These drugs are contraindicated in patients with hypocalcemia, hypersensitivity to bisphosphonates, and severe renal disease.

Estrogen

Treatment of osteoporosis had previously been limited to calcitonin and vitamin D supplementation. While still indicated for use in postmenopausal osteoporosis, calcitonin has its primary action on bone resorption, not on bone formation. The bisphosphonates combined with calcium have improved the treatment of osteoporosis, showing a prevention of related fracture incidence after 6 months of therapy. However, the most significant treatment for osteoporosis in postmenopausal women is estrogen replenishment. It has been demonstrated that estrogen receptors are located within bone cells and that estrogen not only increases bone mineral density but reduces the incidence of osteoporotic fracture. Estrogen combined with daily calcium supplementation of 1000 to 1500 mg stimulates bone mineralization even when started up to 10 years after menopause. Estrogen therapy is promoted as a lifelong adjunct to good diet and exercise. The critical factor in achieving patient commitment to estrogen therapy is the concern women voice about the long-term effects of estrogen exposure. Of particular concern is the potential to develop breast cancer. Raloxifene (*Evista*) is an oral selective estrogen receptor modulator (SERM) that has estrogenic actions on bone and anti-estrogenic action on the uterus and breast. Raloxifene has an additional benefit of preventing breast cancer in postmenopausal women at high risk for breast cancer. Recommended dosage is one 60-mg tablet daily. Additional information on the effects of estrogen as a pharmacologic agent is presented in Chapter 37.

Replacement therapy is taken for life; therefore, habits must be developed to ensure good compliance with the dosing schedule. Patients should be alerted to a few critical items that can make lifelong therapy most convenient and safe.

Drug Administration

Hormone products cannot be interchanged. Even the same hormone cannot be substituted among different manufacturers because of the differences in bioavailability or effectiveness. Since dosing is individualized to the patient, using one product consistently maintains therapeutic efficacy with a safety profile commensurate with the dose.

Thyroid hormones may be taken as a single daily dose before breakfast. More levothyroxine, however, will be absorbed if taken on an empty stomach. Patients should be instructed to be consistent in their dosing pattern—that is, with breakfast or not—so that hormone absorption does not fluctuate.

Iodine solution can be diluted with water to make it more palatable.

Calcitonin nasal preparations require demonstration and practice to ensure the patient understands how to prime the pump for initial dosing. Priming is not required again after the initial spray has discharged. The pump and the head should be held upright when spraying the dose into the nostril. For bisphosphonate therapy, patients must be educated to the need to take calcium and vitamin D supplements. Patient surveys indicate that patients believe the bisphosphonate is the only medication required to correct osteoporosis. Patients need to be encouraged to maintain consistent vitamin and mineral supplementation to achieve optimal therapeutic results. Instruct patients that oral bisphosphonates should be taken with a full glass of water (not juices) on an empty stomach or one hour before meals to ensure that adequate absorption occurs. Patients must remain in an upright position (sitting or standing) for 30 minutes after dosing to avoid GI irritation.

Medication should never be discontinued by the patient unless supervised by the prescribing physician.

Patients should be encouraged to disclose a full medication history to all other physicians and medical professionals routinely seen by the patient. Since these drugs can produce cardiovascular changes, or symptoms resembling postmenopausal sweating and flushing, patients must alert other medical personnel that they are taking medication that could produce signs and symptoms that differ from their previous examination.

Notification of Adverse Effects

Thyroid Hormones

Patients should receive clear instruction to call the physician if nervousness, diarrhea, excess sweating, heat intolerance, chest pain, or palpitations occur. These symptoms may warrant thyroid hormone dose adjustment after evaluation by the prescribing physician.

Antithyroid Drugs

Patients should call the physician if fever, sore throat, bleeding or bruising, headache, rash, vomiting, or yellowing of the skin develops while on antithyroid medication. These symptoms may signal the need for dose interruption and further evaluation by the prescribing physician.

Iodine

Patients should call the physician if fever, skin rash, metallic taste, swelling of the throat, burning in the mouth and throat, sore gums and teeth, severe intestinal distress, or enlargement of the thyroid occurs. These signs warrant discontinuation of the drug and further evaluation by the prescribing physician.

Use in Pregnancy

Drugs that inhibit thyroid function are designated FDA Pregnancy Category D: evidence of risk to the human fetus has been demonstrated; however, the benefit of use in pregnancy may make the potential risk to the fetus acceptable. Patients who may become pregnant during therapy should notify the physician immediately for further evaluation and/or dose adjustment.

Drugs that destroy thyroid tissue, such as radioisotope ^{131}I, are designated FDA Pregnancy Category X: the risk to the woman and/or the fetus clearly outweighs any possible benefit. Women who are or may become pregnant should not be treated with ^{131}I.

Bisphosphonates have been designated FDA Pregnancy Category B, C, and D: animal studies indicate abnormalities occur that have not been evaluated in humans. The safe use of these drugs in pregnant women has not been established through appropriate controlled clinical trials. Use in postmenopausal women does not represent a health risk; however, use in women of childbearing age who may become pregnant requires clear evidence that the benefit clearly outweighs potential risk to the fetus.

Chapter Review

Understanding Terminology

Match the definition or description in the left column with the appropriate term in the right column.

_____1. A condition in which there is a significant reduction in the number of WBCs. (LO 38.1)

_____2. A condition characterized by a low level of physical and mental development. (LO 38.1, 38.2)

_____3. A negative ion. (LO 38.1)

_____4. An enlargement of the thyroid that is not a result of a tumor. (LO 38.4)

_____5. A condition in which an individual's tissues are damaged by his or her own immune system. (LO 38.1, 38.4)

_____6. A condition caused by excessive quantities of thyroid hormone. (LO 38.1, 38.2, 38.3)

a. agranulocytosis
b. anion
c. autoimmune disease
d. cretinism
e. goiter
f. thyrotoxic crisis

Acquiring Knowledge

Answer the following questions.

1. What physiological effects are produced by the thyroid hormones T_3 and T_4? (LO 38.1, 38.2)
2. What clinical symptoms reflect the metabolic changes associated with hypothyroidism? (LO 38.1, 38.3)
3. What is the rationale for the treatment of hypothyroidism? (LO 38.2, 38.3, 38.4)
4. What methods are available for treating hyperthyroidism? (LO 38.3)
5. How does the action of the antithyroid drugs differ from the action of radioactive iodide? (LO 38.3, 38.7)
6. What side effects are associated with the use of antithyroid drugs? (LO 38.3, 38.7)
7. What hormones control calcium metabolism? How do these hormones differ? (LO 38.5)
8. What are the side effects of hypoparathyroid therapy? Why? (LO 38.5)
9. When is calcitonin used? (LO 38.6)
10. What drugs might influence thyroid function in normal individuals? (LO 38.7)

Applying Knowledge on the Job

Use your critical-thinking skills to answer the following questions.

1. Assume that you work in the endocrinology clinic of a university hospital. Four patients treated at the clinic today had thyroid conditions. What thyroid condition do you think each of the following patients has? How should it be treated?
   a. Patient A is a 44-year-old male presenting with a round, puffy face, dry skin and hair, hypotension, anemia, drowsiness, and intolerance to cold. (LO 38.2, 38.3, 38.4)
   b. Patient B is an 18-month-old female presenting with growth failure, delayed motor and mental development, delayed tooth eruption, and intolerance to cold. (LO 38.4)
   c. Patient C is a 25-year-old male presenting with anxiety, weight loss, muscle weakness, tachycardia, and intolerance to heat. (LO 38.3, 38.4)
   d. Patient D is a 65-year-old female presenting with nausea, vomiting, headaches, and heart arrhythmia. (LO 38.1, 38.3)

2. The endocrinologist you work for has prescribed thyroid hormones to each of the following adult patients. What is the potential problem in prescribing thyroid hormones to each patient? What should be done to prevent the problem in each case?
   a. Patient A is taking the drug *Questran* for high serum cholesterol. **(LO 38.8)**
   b. Patient B is on long-term *Thorazine* therapy for manic-depressive illness. **(LO 38.8)**
   c. Patient C is an insulin-dependent diabetic. **(LO 38.7, 38.8)**
   d. Patient D takes oral contraceptives. **(LO 38.8)**
   e. Patient E had a heart attack 6 months ago. **(LO 38.8)**

3. Is thyroid replacement contraindicated during pregnancy? Why or why not? **(LO 38.3)**

4. What are the usual side effects with calcitonin? **(LO 38.4, 38.5, 38.6)**

5. Joy has been taking synthetic thyroid replacement medications for 15 years. Her physician has decided to initiate cholestyramine therapy for her high cholesterol. What, if anything, should she be told regarding these two medications? **(LO 38.8)**

Multiple Choice

Use your critical-thinking skills to answer the following questions.

1. A patient has just been diagnosed with hyperthyroidism. You review her labs and find that T_3-T_4 level is elevated; however, TSH level is low, along with TRH. You suspect the problem is occurring at the **(LO 38.1)**
   A. hypothalamus
   B. anterior pituitary
   C. thyroid gland
   D. parathyroid gland

2. If calcium levels decrease below normal, which hormone would be released to compensate? **(LO 38.4)**
   A. calcitonin
   B. PTH
   C. TRH
   D. TSH

3. Which would you utilize for treatment in an infant diagnosed with cretinism? **(LO 38.1, 38.3)**
   A. T_3 and T_4
   B. calcitonin
   C. propylthiouracil
   D. bisphosphonates

4. Therapy for a patient with hypercalcemia would include **(LO 38.4)**
   A. estrogen
   B. irradiation
   C. vitamin D
   D. calcitonin

5. Bisphosphonates **(LO 38.4, 38.6)**
   A. inhibit bone resorption
   B. increase T_3 and T_4 synthesis
   C. inhibit propylthiouracil
   D. stimulate PTH

Chapter Review Continued

Multiple Choice (Multiple Answer)

Select the correct choices for each statement. The choices may be all correct, all incorrect, or any combination.

1. Choose all of the actions of thyroid hormone on the body. **(LO 38.2)**
   A. increases blood glucose
   B. stimulates protein synthesis
   C. decreases serum cholesterol
   D. increases circulating fatty acids

2. Which of the following are hormones secreted from the thyroid gland to help regulate tissue growth? **(LO 38.3)**
   A. TRH
   B. TSH
   C. T_3
   D. T_4

3. Which of the following are symptoms of hypothyroidism? **(LO 38.1, 38.4)**
   A. cretinism
   B. tachycardia
   C. myxedema
   D. goiter

4. Which steps of bone remodeling are affected by menopause? **(LO 38.6)**
   A. bone resorption
   B. PTH regulation
   C. bone deposition
   D. calcium regulation

5. The adverse effects of thioamide drugs include **(LO 38.8)**
   A. psychotic behavior
   B. increased blood pressure
   C. weight loss
   D. insomnia

Sequencing

Place the following steps of bone remodeling in order from first to last. **(LO 38.6)**

_____ _____ _____ _____ _____

First   **Last**

osteogenic cells differentiate into osteoclasts

osteoblasts secrete protein matrix

stimulation of PTH secretion

decrease in plasma calcium

calcium deposition

Classification

Place the following medications under the correct type of thyroid action. **(LO 38.1)**

Synthroid	*Triostat*	*Levoxyl*
Tapazole	*Lugol's solution*	*Iodotope*
Cytomel	*propylthiouracil*	

Hormone replacement for thyroid deficiency	Antithyroid drugs

Documentation

Using the prescription below, answer the following questions. **(LO 38.6)**

Old Bones Clinic
Practice RX

12345 Main Avenue
Anytown, USA   12345
931-555-1000

NAME: ___Heidi Aredia_____   DATE: _____

ADDRESS: _____

RX   Fosamax 40mg

Sig: Take by mouth once daily for 6 months

Dr. Stanley Osteon_____ M.D. _____M.D.

  Substitution Permitted   Dispense as written

DEA #: _____   REFILL: NR 1 2 3 4

---

a. What condition is likely being treated with this medication?
b. What are the symptoms of this condition?
c. How does this drug work to treat this condition?
d. What other medications should be taken with this medication to ensure optimum effectiveness?

Labeling

Fill in the missing labels. **(LO 38.1, 38.4)**

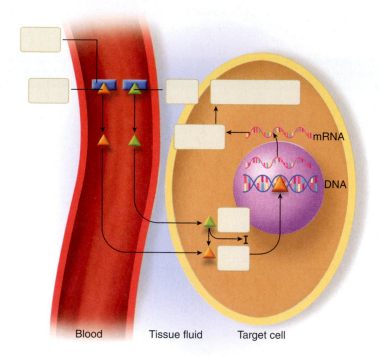

Blood   Tissue fluid   Target cell

For interactive animations, videos, and assessment, visit:
www.mcgrawhillconnect.com

Chapter 39

Pancreatic Hormones and Antidiabetic Drugs

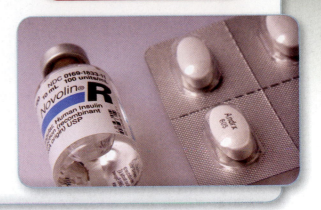

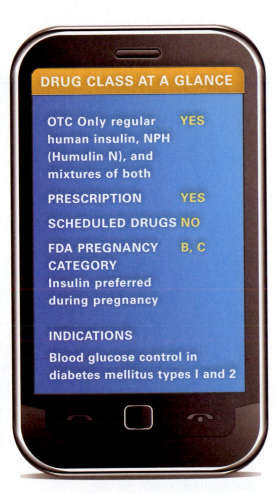

DRUG CLASS AT A GLANCE

OTC Only regular human insulin, NPH (Humulin N), and mixtures of both	YES
PRESCRIPTION	YES
SCHEDULED DRUGS	NO
FDA PREGNANCY CATEGORY	B, C

Insulin preferred during pregnancy

INDICATIONS

Blood glucose control in diabetes mellitus types I and 2

KEY TERMS

adipose tissue: fat.

amylin: peptide of 37 amino acids that is secreted by the pancreas beta cells along with insulin in response to increasing blood glucose levels.

antibodies: normally are produced when a foreign substance such as a pathogen enters the body.

autoantibody: an antibody produced by the immune system against one's own cells.

diabetic neuropathy: nerve disorders caused by diabetes resulting in numbness, pain, and weakness of hands and feet.

DM: diabetes mellitus.

exocytosis: the discharge of substances contained in vesicles by fusion of the vesicular membrane with the outer cell membrane.

gastroparesis: condition, also called delayed gastric emptying, in which the stomach muscles do not function properly.

GIP: glucose-dependent insulinotropic peptide, also known as gastric inhibitory peptide.

GLP-1: glucagon-like peptide-1.

glucagon: hormone released by the alpha cells of the pancreas to increase plasma glucose concentration.

gluconeogenesis: the synthesis of glucose from molecules that are not carbohydrates, such as amino and fatty acids or glycerol.

GLUT: glucose transport proteins.

glycated hemoglobin: form of hemoglobin that is produced when glucose attaches to hemoglobin in the RBC.

glycogen: the storage form of glucose in humans and animals.

glycogenolysis: hydrolysis of glycogen to yield free glucose.

glycosuria: presence of glucose in the urine.

hyperglycemia: higher than normal level of glucose in the blood; fasting blood glucose greater than 126 mg/dl.

hyperinsulinemia: high levels of insulin in the blood often associated with type 2 diabetes mellitus and insulin resistance.

hypoglycemia: lower than the normal range of plasma glucose concentration in the blood; fasting blood glucose below 40 mg/dl in women or 50 mg/dl in men accompanied by symptoms of diabetes.

incretins: a group of gastrointestinal hormones that increase the amount of insulin released.

insulin: hormone secreted by the beta cells of the pancreas to facilitate glucose entry into the cell.

islets: group or island of cells.

ketosis: condition associated with an increased production of ketone bodies as a result of fat metabolism.

lipodystrophy: defective metabolism of fat.

polydipsia: excessive thirst.

polyphagia: excessive hunger.

polyuria: excessive urine production.

postprandial: after a meal.

recombinant: genetically engineered DNA.

suspension: preparation in which undissolved solids are dispersed within a liquid.

type 1 diabetes: insulin-dependent diabetes mellitus.

type 2 diabetes: non-insulin-dependent diabetes mellitus.

After studying this chapter, you should be able to

39.1 describe the factors that affect regulation of blood glucose concentration.

39.2 differentiate between insulin and glucagon and the action of oral antidiabetic drugs.

39.3 discuss the rationale for the symptoms that occur in type I and type 2 diabetes mellitus.

39.4 characterize the different types of insulin.

39.5 differentiate between insulin and glucagon and the action of oral antidiabetic drugs.

The pancreas secretes insulin and glucagon, polypeptide hormones that regulate protein, fat, and carbohydrate metabolism. Although any of these nutrients can be used for tissue fuel, most cells use glucose, which is produced during carbohydrate digestion, as a primary source of energy. Throughout the day and night it is essential to maintain a circulating pool of glucose for the cells and to promote efficient transport of glucose into the cells.

PANCREATIC ENDOCRINE FUNCTION

The pancreas contains clusters of cells called **islets** of Langerhans. Alpha and beta cells are two types of islet cells in the pancreas (see Figure 39.1). The alpha cells secrete **glucagon** and the beta cells secrete **insulin** in response to fluctuations in blood glucose concentration. Insulin and glucagon are antagonistic to each other. When blood glucose concentration increases, the beta cells secrete insulin, and when blood glucose concentration falls below normal range, glucagon is secreted. Thus, blood glucose concentration is maintained within normal range (70−120 mg/dl) by negative feedback (see Figure 39.2). **Amylin** is a peptide that is secreted from the beta cell granules along with insulin. It works synergistically with insulin to lower blood sugar in response to meals. Skeletal muscle is responsible for most of the glucose taken up from insulin stimulation.

Insulin Secretion

The beta cells of a healthy person release a small amount of insulin into the bloodstream throughout the day and night called basal insulin release. An example of the rise and fall of blood glucose over 24 hours in a healthy person is shown in Figure 39.3. The peaks are consistent with glucose absorption and insulin secretion following meals, while the absence of peaks during sleep is consistent with basal insulin activity in a fasting state. Blood glucose rises to a peak usually within 30 minutes of starting a meal. When a healthy person begins to eat a meal, stored insulin is released immediately (phase 1). This insulin should be sufficient to meet the amount of glucose from the meal. If, however, the blood sugar

Figure 39.1   **The Pancreas**

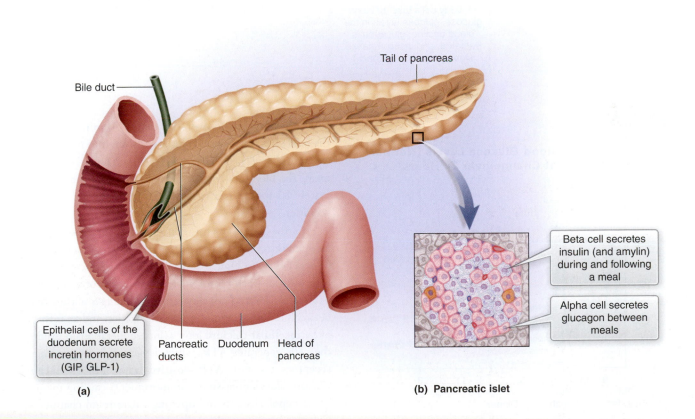

Bile duct

Tail of pancreas

Epithelial cells of the duodenum secrete incretin hormones (GIP, GLP-1)

Pancreatic ducts   Duodenum   Head of pancreas

(a)

Beta cell secretes insulin (and amylin) during and following a meal

Alpha cell secretes glucagon between meals

(b) Pancreatic islet

(a) Gross anatomy and relationship to the duodenum. (b) Cells of a pancreatic islet.

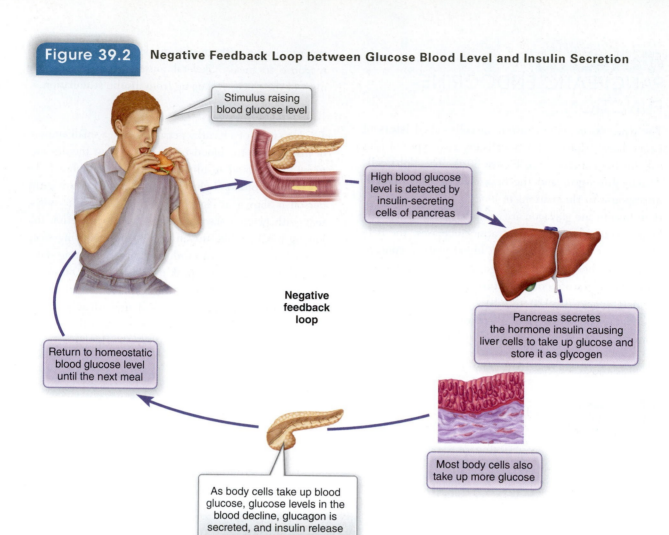

Stimulus raising blood glucose level

High blood glucose level is detected by insulin-secreting cells of pancreas

Negative feedback loop

Pancreas secretes the hormone insulin causing liver cells to take up glucose and store it as glycogen

Return to homeostatic blood glucose level until the next meal

Most body cells also take up more glucose

As body cells take up blood glucose, glucose levels in the blood decline, glucagon is secreted, and insulin release stops (negative feedback)

Figure 39.3

Example of How Blood Glucose Levels (Normal, Nondiabetic) Might Change over 24 Hours

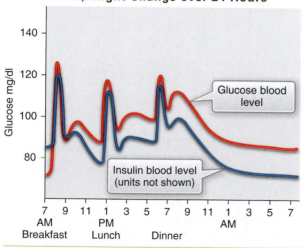

Glucose blood level

Insulin blood level (units not shown)

Blood glucose rises after each meal. Insulin secretion begins as blood glucose levels rise. During sleep, blood glucose levels drop, consistent with the fasting state.

concentration rises to over 100 mg/dl 20 minutes later, the beta cells start secreting more insulin into the bloodstream (phase 2). Usually within 1 to 2 hours after the meal, the blood glucose level should return to approximately 85 mg/dl as a result of the coordinated insulin secretion.

As the blood glucose concentration increases, glucose binds to **GLUT2** receptors on the plasma membrane of beta cells (see Figure 39.4). The GLUT2 receptor is a glucose transporter protein that takes glucose into the beta cell. Elevated concentration of glucose within the beta cell leads to membrane depolarization and an influx of extracellular calcium ions. Glucose metabolism inside the cells generates ATP, which is sensed by membrane receptors to close ATP-sensitive potassium channels. Closure blocks potassium ion movement, causing membrane depolarization and opening calcium ion channels. Calcium ions enter the cell and are one of the primary triggers for **exocytosis** of secretory granules containing insulin and amylin. As blood glucose increases, more

Figure 39.4

Glucose Transporter Receptor (GLUT2) on the Pancreas Beta Cell and Insulin Release

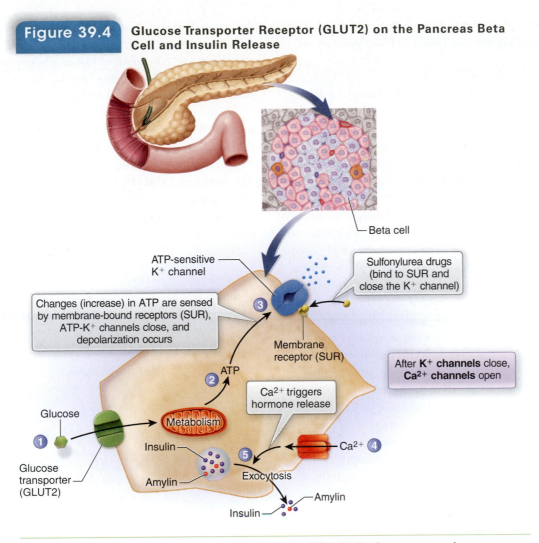

Beta cell

ATP-sensitive K$^+$ channel

Sulfonylurea drugs (bind to SUR and close the K$^+$ channel)

Changes (increase) in ATP are sensed by membrane-bound receptors (SUR), ATP-K$^+$ channels close, and depolarization occurs

③

Membrane receptor (SUR)

After **K$^+$ channels** close, **Ca^{2+} channels** open

② ATP

Ca^{2+} triggers hormone release

Glucose

① Metabolism

Insulin

⑤

Ca^{2+} ④

Glucose transporter (GLUT2)

Amylin

Exocytosis

Amylin

Insulin

Glucose metabolized inside the beta cell generates ATP, which triggers a membrane receptor to close certain potassium channels causing depolarization. This causes calcium channels to open so calcium ions flowing into the cell can trigger hormone release. Sulfonylurea antidiabetic drugs bind (activate) to the membrane-bound receptors and cause the same events resulting in insulin secretion.

glucose enters the beta cell and more ATP causes the receptor to set conditions for more insulin secretion.

Insulin then binds to plasma membrane receptors on skeletal and heart muscle and **adipose tissue.** Insulin causes the translocation of a carrier protein GLUT4. This carrier protein, normally inside the cell, moves to the plasma membrane, where it inserts itself and acts as a channel allowing glucose into the cell. As glucose enters the cell, there are fewer glucose molecules in the bloodstream (decreasing blood glucose concentration). In addition, insulin stimulates **glyconeogenesis** in the liver to store glucose for use between meals or a fast. Insulin also inhibits the liver from releasing more glucose into the bloodstream and inhibits the breakdown of protein and fat for energy. Insulin facilitates the entry of amino acids into the cell for protein synthesis. Thus insulin is an anabolic hormone. Other tissues such as the

brain, red blood cells, and kidneys, do not require insulin for glucose uptake but have specialized glucose transport proteins (GLUT1, GLUT3).

Besides glucose stimulation, there are hormones **(incretins)** that increase insulin secretion: **GIP** (glucose-dependent insulinotropic peptide; also known as gastric inhibitory peptide) and **GLP-1**(glucagon-like peptide-1). Both hormones are secreted by endocrine cells located in the epithelium of the small intestine (Figure 39.1). The endocrine cells sense an increase in the concentration of glucose in the lumen of the digestive tract and hormone secretion is triggered. Incretins are carried through the circulation to the pancreatic beta cells, where they cause more insulin to be secreted and stop the liver from producing glucose. Eventually the incretins are inactivated by the enzyme DPP-4 (dipeptidyl peptidase-4). This is important because it provides unique opportunities for drug intervention in the process of glucose absorption and insulin secretion.

Glucagon Secretion

Glucagon raises blood glucose. Between meals or during a fast, blood glucose concentration falls, stimulating the release of glucagon from the alpha cells of the pancreas. Glucagon binds to its receptors on the plasma membrane of hepatocytes to activate the enzymes that depolymerize (break down) **glycogen (glycogenolysis)** and release glucose. Glucagon is catabolic, stimulating the breakdown of glycogen to glucose. Glucagon stimulates gluconeogenesis in the liver. This is the formation of glucose from amino acids. The breakdown of glycogen to glucose and the formation of glucose from protein maintain blood glucose concentrations within normal range. Glucagon also stimulates the breakdown of triglycerides to make fatty acids available for cells that can use this fuel. As glucose is released into the bloodstream, blood glucose concentration rises to within normal range and glucagon secretion stops (negative feedback) (Figure 39.2). All of this activity occurs in the liver; there are no glucagon receptors on skeletal muscle. The glucagon receptor is in the family of G-protein-coupled receptors that include the incretins glucagon-like peptide-1 (GLP-1) and gastric inhibitory peptide (GIP). Glucagon is administered pharmacologically for emergency treatment of **hypoglycemia.**

LO 39.1 LO 39.2
LO 39.3 LO 39.4 LO 39.5

DIABETES MELLITUS

There are 23.6 million people in the United States who have diabetes mellitus **(DM).** Diabetes mellitus is a syndrome with a deficient secretion of insulin, insulin resistance, or a combination of the two. The two major types of DM are **type 1** (formerly called insulin-dependent diabetes) and **type 2** (formerly called non-insulin-dependent diabetes). Approximately 10 percent of those diagnosed with DM have type 1, and 90 percent have type 2. Diabetes mellitus was named for the glucose in the urine (mellitus, from the Latin word "sweet") and the increased urination (diabetes, from the Greek word "siphon"). Diabetes patients usually have elevated blood glucose levels **(hyperglycemia)** because glucose cannot get out of the blood and into the cells. This occurs when insulin is unable to bind to its receptor so GLUT4 transporter proteins cannot migrate to the membrane and form a glucose channel. Diagnosis of DM is based on blood glucose levels (see Glucose Monitoring). The

American Diabetes Association criteria for diagnosing DM is a repeated blood glucose of 126 mg/dl or more after fasting or 200 mg/dl or higher 2 hours after eating or random sampling during the day accompanied by symptoms of DM (see Table 39:1).

Type 1 DM is an autoimmune disorder in which **autoantibodies** are produced against the beta cells in the pancreas. This destroys the beta cells, the production of insulin decreases, and hyperglycemia ensues. The mechanism that triggers the body to develop autoantibodies against its own tissue is not well understood. Normal immune responses occur if a foreign substance such as a pathogen invades the body. A Coxsackie virus

[Table **39:1**]

Characteristics of Diabetes Mellitus

Insulin deficiency		
Type 1 (absolute)	**Symptoms**	**Type 2 (relative)**
X	Hyperglycemia	X
X	Glucosuria (glycosuria)	X
X	Ketoacidosis	—
X	Polyphagia	X
X	Polyuria	X
X	Polydipsia	X
X	Dry skin	X
X	Dry mouth	X
Juvenile onset common	Onset age	≥40 yrs MOD*: 18 yrs or less MODY
X	Persistent infections	X

MOD is maturity onset diabetes. MODY is maturity onset diabetes of youth.

has been implicated as a "trigger" to initiate the autoimmune response. The rate of destruction of the beta cells is variable, and symptoms do not appear until the body can no longer compensate (90 percent of the beta cells destroyed). Because glucose cannot enter the cell, glycogenolysis occurs, breaking down protein and fat to form glucose. The breakdown of fat produces acetoacetic acid and acetone, which are termed ketone bodies, causing diabetic ketoacidosis.

The cause of type 2 DM is unknown, but it is characterized by a failure of target tissues to respond to insulin (insulin resistance). Initially, the beta cells are releasing insulin and amylin. There are a number of factors that contribute to the development of type 2 DM, including a strong genetic link and obesity, but insulin resistance is a major factor. The insulin receptors in the liver and skeletal muscle have a decreased sensitivity to insulin, and insulin cannot bind as effectively to the receptor. Less glucose enters the cell to provide a source of "fuel." Usually it takes a lot more insulin to push the glucose into the cells. This lack of "fuel" stimulates the beta cells to secrete even more insulin (hyperinsulinemia). The second insulin secretion phase may be prolonged because the beta cells have to work harder to secrete enough insulin to counter the insulin resistance. The nature of how insulin is taken into the target cell (internalized) in receptor binding contributes to the decrease in receptors. After binding, insulin is degraded inside the cell by enzymes that also degrade receptor proteins. The excess production of insulin causes the down regulation (decrease) in the number of receptors and the target cells cannot synthesize enough receptor protein to keep up, further contributing to the problem. Over time, hyperinsulinemia can lead to elevations in blood pressure, cholesterol, and weight, factors predisposing to heart attack and stroke. Eventually the body may not be able to produce enough insulin, beta cells die, and blood glucose levels rise.

The World Health Organization has identified obesity as the major risk factor for development of type 2 DM. Eighty percent of people diagnosed with type 2 DM are obese. Obesity decreases the sensitivity of the receptors to insulin. While the majority of patients diagnosed with type 2 DM are older than age 40, there is an increase in incidence of type 2 DM in obese children and adolescents. This disorder is termed maturity-onset diabetes of youth (MODY). As the number of obese children and adolescents increases, the incidence of MODY will increase.

A subgroup of type 2 DM is gestational diabetes. Gestational diabetes is discovered when the woman is pregnant. Certain hormones produced by the placenta cause insulin resistance. Blood glucose levels in the woman return to normal after delivery; however, she has an increased risk of developing type 2 DM later in life. The high blood glucose levels can cause excessive weight gain in the fetus, increasing the risk for obesity and diabetes.

Symptoms and Complications

The common symptoms of diabetes mellitus reflect an imbalance in carbohydrate metabolism due to insulin deficiency (see Table 39:1). The cardinal feature of diabetes is the high blood glucose concentration (hyperglycemia), which leads to an increase in urine glucose (glycosuria). Since glucose cannot enter the cells in the absence of insulin, the excess glucose is filtered through the kidneys for excretion. However, as the number of glucose molecules increases in the urinary tubules, more water follows (diffuses) into the tubules via osmosis to dilute the urine glucose concentration. As a result, the volume of urine increases (polyuria), and patients lose large amounts of water and become dehydrated. Since dehydration stimulates thirst, the patients usually drink large amounts of fluids (polydipsia).

Diabetics often demonstrate polyphagia (excessive hunger). Although the blood is loaded with sugar, some cells are "starving" because glucose cannot enter the cell and provide the energy needed for the cell to function. Therefore, diabetic patients may increase food consumption in order to avoid fatigue and hunger. Unfortunately, the absorption of dietary glucose only worsens the hyperglycemia.

In the absence of insulin, the cells begin to use protein and fat as sources of fuel. The breakdown of fat produces an increase in ketone bodies in the blood. This condition is called ketosis. As the ketone level increases, metabolic acidosis (ketoacidosis) occurs. Ketoacidosis may increase the loss of electrolytes (sodium, potassium, and chloride) through the urine. The electrolyte concentration in the urine increases and central nervous system (CNS) depression develops. If not diagnosed and treated, diabetic coma and death may ensue. In general, type I diabetics are prone to ketoacidosis, whereas type 2 diabetics are usually resistant. Since patients with either type can develop hypoglycemia leading to a comatose state, ketoacidosis may be differentiated from severe hypoglycemia by blood glucose concentration and acetone in the urine.

Diabetes also is associated with degenerative tissue damage due to the hyperglycemia. As a result, diabetics are at risk of developing atherosclerosis, retinal hemorrhages, blindness, renal dysfunction, and **diabetic neuropathy** (numbness of hands and feet) and antibiotic-resistant skin infections. Inadequate circulation to the extremities coupled with soft-tissue infections that resist healing may lead to necrosis (gangrene) and the need for amputation.

Blood Glucose Monitoring

Blood glucose concentration is used to characterize the body's response to basal insulin secretion during fasting states (FBG, fasting blood glucose) and meal-stimulated insulin secretion (PPG, postprandial glucose). A healthy fasting blood glucose is between 70 and 110 mg/dl. Levels of 111 to 125 mg/dl indicate impaired glucose tolerance (insulin resistance), while levels greater than 126 mg/dl are indicative of diabetes. An oral glucose tolerance test is also used to determine how quickly absorbed glucose (from oral test administration) is cleared from the blood. Prior to glucose administration, the fasting blood glucose should be less than 126 mg/dl; after glucose, the level should be less than 200 (150) mg/dl 1 and 2 hours postdose and less than 120 mg/dl (normal is less than 110 mg/dl) at 3 and 4 hours postdose. Blood insulin is also measured; less than 10 mcIU/ml is normal, while values greater than 10 mcIU/ml indicate insulin resistance.

Once the diagnosis has been confirmed through appropriate tests and medical evaluation, type 1 and type 2 diabetics will monitor their blood glucose throughout the day. This is done to assess hyperglycemia or hypoglycemia, confirm or adjust the dose of insulin needed for glycemic control, and characterize the body's response to antidiabetic medication regimens. Glucose monitoring helps patients adjust their lifestyle (meal planning, exercise) to their condition. Type 1 patients may monitor blood levels with portable glucose meters more than 5 times a day, while type 2 patients may monitor at least once a day. Most glucometers today use an electrochemical method to read the amount of glucose in the blood from the blood-loaded test strip (Figure 39.11).

In addition to daily glucose fluctuations, it is important to follow glucose concentrations over a longer period of time. **Glycated hemoglobin,** called HbA1c, is a form of hemoglobin that has glucose attached to it. Because RBCs do not require insulin to uptake glucose, glucose enters the RBC and readily binds to hemoglobin without the help of enzymes. This is known as nonenzyme glycosylation or glycation. HbA1c identifies the glucose concentration over the past 3 months (the lifespan of the RBC). The physician reviews this as an indication of how well the patient is managing blood glucose over time. In general, the more elevated the blood glucose is, the more HbA1c is formed and the greater the risk that the patient may develop complications such as retinopathy, nephropathy, neuropathy, and cardiovascular disease and stroke. Normal values vary among laboratories, but an HbA1c of 6 percent or less indicates good diabetic control. The HbA1c, performed in the laboratory, is usually evaluated every 3 to 6 months.

LO 39.3 **LO 39.4** **LO 39.5**

TREATMENT OF DIABETES

The immediate objective of therapy is to correct the metabolic imbalance and to restore fluid and electrolytes. Insulin administration rapidly reduces hyperglycemia and its complications and corrects acid/base imbalance (ketosis). Maintenance therapy of diabetes is directed at regulating the blood glucose level through diet control, exercise, and drug administration. In both forms of diabetes, patients' diets are adjusted to limit the intake of carbohydrates. In this way, blood glucose levels can be balanced with insulin administration.

Type 2 diabetics secrete a limited amount of insulin from the pancreas, and strict diet control and physical exercise can balance glucose utilization in many patients. Unfortunately, many people do not adhere to the dietary limitations or cannot use diet alone to control their diabetes. Studies have shown that only 33 percent of people with type 2 diabetes were meeting established targets for blood glucose control. For these reasons, therapy of type 2 diabetics may include insulin and/or antidiabetic drugs.

Drugs used in the treatment of DM are administered parenterally (insulins, amylin analog, incretin mimetics) or they are oral antidiabetic drugs that include

- Secretagogues (sulfonylureas and meglitinides)
- Glucose absorption inhibitors (alpha-glucosidase inhibitors)
- Biguanides (metformin)
- Insulin sensitizers (thiazolidinediones)
- Peptidase inhibitors

The insulins and secretagogues are hypoglycemics—that is, they decrease normal or elevated blood glucose levels. The class of oral antidiabetic drugs is also called antihyperglycemic drugs. Most are glucose-dependent, working to lower or eliminate elevated glucose (hyperglycemic) levels in DM patients. Glucose absorption inhibitors delay dietary glucose absorption or inhibit glucose production in the liver without producing hypoglycemia. The confirmation of specific sites of drug action facilitated the development of new classes of oral medications such as the "insulin sensitizers and the peptidase (DPP-4) inhibitors."

Because of the nature of the disorder, type I diabetics must receive insulin for life and adjust their diets accordingly.

Regardless of the regimen selected, only the symptoms associated with hyperglycemia and ketosis can be controlled. Antidiabetic drugs, even insulin, do not cure diabetes. Although insulin and diet may not prevent vascular or neural damage, they may greatly reduce the severity of the effects.

LO 39.1 | LO 39.3 | LO 39.4

PARENTERAL ANTIDIABETIC DRUGS: INSULIN

Clinical Indications for Insulin

Insulin is indicated for the treatment of type 1 DM and type 2 DM that cannot properly be controlled by diet and exercise. Insulin is the drug of choice for reversing severe ketoacidosis and diabetic coma and for management of gestational DM. Insulin does not cross the placenta and does not produce hypoglycemic effects in the fetus. Insulin is also approved for use in hyperkalemia because the protein naturally provokes a shift of potassium into cells,

lowering circulating potassium levels. Glucose coadministration is necessary to circumvent possible hypoglycemia. Several types of insulin are available primarily for subcutaneous injection. Intravenous and intramuscular use is reserved for emergencies, such as ketoacidosis, or severely ill patients where an immediate onset of action is required. Insulin is not available for oral administration because it is a polypeptide that would be destroyed in the GI tract.

Source of Insulin

In the past, the only active polypeptide hormone was extracted from pork and beef organs. Today, insulin is produced in the United States only by **recombinant DNA** technology. Human insulin produced by recombinant DNA is identical to the protein secreted by the human pancreas. Recombinant insulin analogs are available in which amino acids have been switched (lispro insulin) or replaced (glargine, glulisine), making a "different molecule" that is still recognized by the receptor and fully functional. The sequence of amino acids in the A and B chains that is the active human insulin molecule is shown in Figure 39.5. The location of the amino acid

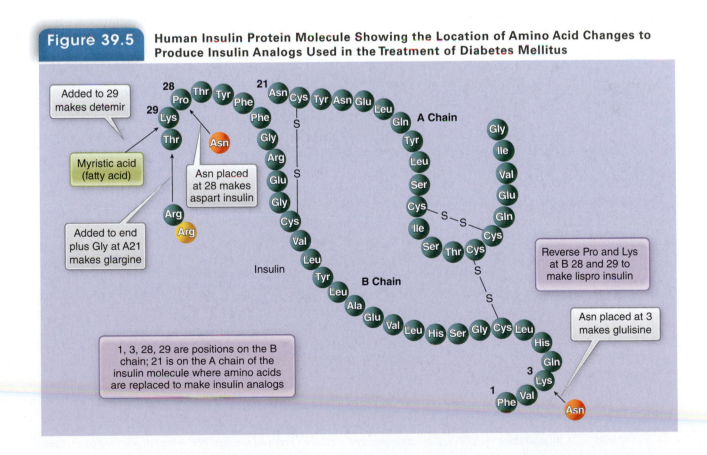

Figure 39.5 Human Insulin Protein Molecule Showing the Location of Amino Acid Changes to Produce Insulin Analogs Used in the Treatment of Diabetes Mellitus

substitution or addition of a fatty acid to form each of the four insulin analogs also is indicated.

The objective in establishing an adequate insulin dose is to imitate a healthy pancreas with a moderate amount of insulin throughout the day and a little more at meal times. The insulin preparations produce similar metabolic effects but vary in their onset and duration of action (see Table 39:2). The insulins can be divided into short-, intermediate-, and long-acting preparations. The duration of action varies with the type of insulin, the buffer, and the amount of protein (protamine) or zinc present.

[Table **39:2**]

Characteristics of Parenteral Antidiabetic Preparations

Drug (*Trade Name**)	Type	Onset (hours)	Duration (hours)	Appearance/Dosers**/Remarks
Amylin analog				
Pramlintide (*Symlin*)	Short-acting analog	0.5	1–2.5	Clear, pen only. **Cannot be mixed with insulins**
Insulin and insulin analogs				
Insulin aspart (*NovoLog*)	Short-acting analog	0.2–0.3	3–5	Clear phosphate buffer MDV, FPS, PFC
Insulin glulisine (*Apidra*)	Short-acting analog	0.3–0.5	1–2.5	Clear sterile water; MDV, OptiClik, pen Compatible with NPH isophane human insulin **Incompatible with other insulin preparations**
Insulin lispro (*Humalog, Humalog Mix*)	Short-acting analog	0.25	2–5	Clear phosphate buffer MDV, PFC, *Kwikpen* (*Humalog Mix*) Compatible with NPH isophane human insulin
Regular human insulin (*Humulin R*)	Short human	0.5–1	8–12	Clear sterile water solution, MDV Compatible with other human insulin preparation
Isophane NPH (human) insulin zinc suspension (*Humulin N, Novolin-N*)	Intermediate human	1–2	18–24	Supension MDV Compatible with any human insulin, glulisine and lispro insulin
NPH and regular insulin (*Humulin 50/50, Humulin 70/30, Novolin 70/30*)	Long human	0.5	24	Suspension, MDV, DP (*Humulin* mix) **Incompatible with other insulin preparations**
Insulin detemir (*Levemir*)	Long analog	1–2	24	Clear aqueous solution MDV, FPS, PFC **Incompatible with other insulin preparations**
Insulin glargine (*Lantus*)	Long analog	1	24	Clear aqueous glycerol solution **Incompatible with any insulin preparation**
Incretin mimetics for type 2 diabetes mellitus. Not insulin substitutes				
Exenatide (*Byetta*)	Short-acting analog	0.6	4	Disposable prefilled *Byetta* pen; 30-day expiration
Liraglutide (*Victoza*)	Long analog	—	24	Disposable prefilled *Victoza* pen

*** MDV = 10- ml multidose vial; DP = disposable pen; FPS = FlexPen prefilled syringe; PFC = PenFill prefilled cartridges.*

Regular human insulin (a clear solution) is a short-acting preparation with an onset of 30 minutes and duration of action up to 12 hours. In order to increase the duration of action, different amounts of protein (protamine) were added to the regular insulin preparation. This addition resulted in the production of isophane NPH insulin zinc suspension (intermediate). NPH stands for neutral protamine Hagedorn insulin. Any preparation containing NPH is a **suspension** (undissolved substance dispersed within a liquid) of insulin and protamine in phosphate buffer. The amount of protein that binds to the insulin reduces the rate of absorption from the injection site. NPH is a drug of choice in gestational diabetes and for newly diagnosed patients.

A preparation of isophane insulin (70 percent) and regular insulin injection (30 percent) provides a rapid onset of action and a prolonged effect (up to 24 hours). This premixture is also available in a 50:50 combination of isophane and regular insulin. A comparison of the blood glucose effects for the human insulins and insulin analogs is presented in Figure 39.6. The early onset of and peaking action with short-acting insulin analogs are compared to regular and NPH insulins.

Figure 39.6   **Types of Insulin: Extent and Duration of Action**

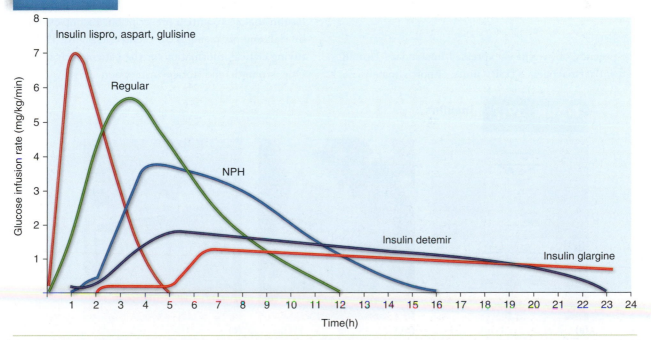

The durations of action are typical of a 0.2–0.3 U/kg dose.

All other insulins are analogs or modified insulin structures. Some of the rapid and short-acting preparations available today have been refined to produce a single peak in glucose blood levels that can be timed to coincide with the individual's meal and daily activity. Insulins are usually injected 30 to 60 minutes before meals except for lispro insulin, which is so quick it is recommended to be injected 15 minutes before meals.

The long-acting recombinant human DNA insulins have been developed to deliver a consistent concentration of insulin over 24 hours after a single subcutaneous injection. These preparations (detemir, glargine) produce "peakless" blood glucose levels throughout 24 hours. They are designed for once-a-day dosing with a consistent level of response. The blood glucose effect over 24 hours is shown for short, intermediate, and long-acting insulins in Figure 39.6. Insulin glargine (*Lantus*) is recommended for patients with type 1 diabetes, or those with type 2 diabetes who require basal control of blood glucose levels. Insulin is released from the injection site at a consistent rate; therefore, blood glucose levels should not rise and fall in response to changing insulin levels. Because the drug is administered at bedtime, the patient will have controlled insulin release during the next day. Although its onset of action is short, insulin glargine cannot be substituted for short-acting insulin preparations. It is not short-acting; once injected, its action lasts 24 hours. In certain patients, this is an advantage over intermediate insulins that require multiple injections to achieve 24-hour glucose control. Insulin glargine is a clear solution that cannot be diluted or mixed with any other insulin preparation. It is not a drug of choice for ketoacidosis.

Dosage

The potency of insulin is expressed in standard United States Pharmacopeia (USP) units. Approximately 25 USP units are contained in 1 mg of insulin. Every preparation of insulin is clearly labeled with the number of units per milliliter and the equivalent potency. There is no standard dose for insulin. Initially, 5 to 10 units of any regular insulin may be given to reduce hyperglycemia. However, the selection of the preparation and the dose must be designed to maintain an adequate blood glucose level. Adequate blood glucose levels vary with individual diabetics and their dietary and exercise (or lack of exercise) patterns. The insulin preparation is usually selected so that the peak effect coincides with patients' peak blood glucose concentrations. All insulin preparations are available in vials of 100 USP units per ml. Today, the 100 USP unit per ml strength is used most often because of the convenience in measurement.

Insulin is administered with specifically calibrated syringes that correspond to the bottle concentration. For example, a U-100 syringe delivers 100 units of insulin when filled with a U-100 preparation. If an insulin syringe is not available, a regular (tuberculin) syringe can be used. However, the dose of insulin must be converted from units to 0.01 ml (0.01 ml = 1 unit of U100 insulin). In most states, all the human insulins (regular, NPH, and combinations of both) are over-the-counter (OTC)—that is, no prescription is required. These products are kept behind the counter because refrigeration is required to maintain their effectiveness. This facilitates diabetic patients' obtaining an emergency source of medication; for example, when they are on vacation or out of town for any reason. A prescription may be required to obtain the syringes or for verification for insurance coverage but not necessarily for the insulin. However, all insulin analogs require a prescription. Examples of insulin vials and packaging are presented in Figure 39.7 identifying critical information for the patient such as insulin type, strength, and storage instruction.

Figure 39.7 Insulins

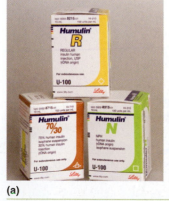 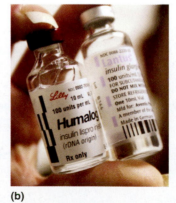 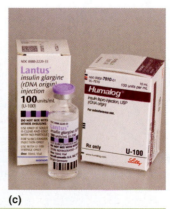

(a)   (b)   (c)

(a) Multidose vials of regular (R), isophane NPH (N), and mixture of 70% NPH/30% R insulin. (b) Lispro insulin (*Humalog*) and glargine (*Lantus*) multidose vials. (c) *Humalog* package.

Usually insulin doses range between 20 and 60 units per day. Some patients who develop resistance to insulin may require 300 to 500 units to achieve adequate glucose control. Specifically indicated for such patients, concentrated insulin (*Humulin R regular U-500*), available in vials of 500 units per ml, is administered by tuberculin syringe. Insulin and other parenteral antidiabetic drugs are usually administered subcutaneously in the arm, thigh, or abdomen. Figure 39.8 illustrates the areas available for administration and the techniques for sub-Q administration with a syringe and insulin pen.

Insulin Pens

Innovation in insulin delivery has been combined with improved safety for correct insulin type with the use of insulin pens (see Figure 39.9). An insulin pen is an

| **Figure 39.8** | **Insulin Injection** |

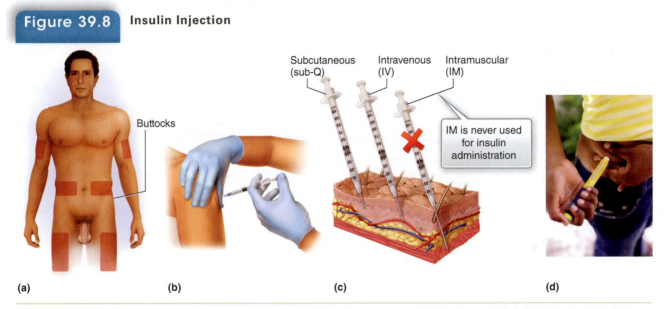

(a) **Locations usually used for subcutaneous injection (arms, abdomen, thighs, buttocks). (b) Syringe administration into pinched skin. (c) Subcutaneous (sub-Q) is within the layers of the skin, not into the muscle. IV insulin is used only for emergency situations. (d) Insulin pen injection held like a dart into the skin fold.**

| **Figure 39.9** | **Insulin Pens** |

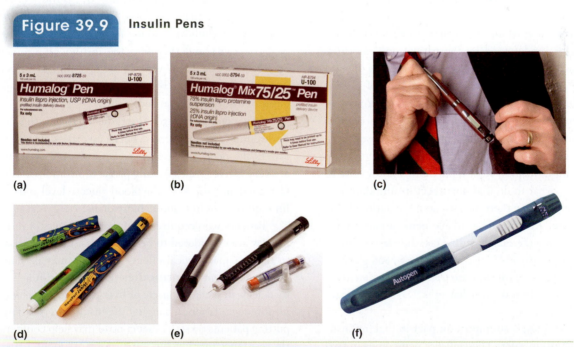

(a) **and (b) Prefilled pens with end trigger: Lilly's *Humalog* (lispro insulin) and *Humalog Mix 75/25*. (c) *Humapen* (Lilly) with end trigger uses insulin cartridges and records date, time, and dose for last 16 doses. (d) *Novopen Junior* with cap removed to show needle and *Novolog* cartridge. (e) Generic insulin pen and cartridge. (f) *Autopens* (Owen Mumford) use 1.5- or 3.0-ml insulin cartridges and have a side trigger instead of an end trigger.**

alternative to a syringe for delivering a precise dose of insulin. The pens increase accuracy in dose delivery and convenience by their design and portability. There are two types of pens, prefilled disposable or durable reusable pens; each has disposable needles. Both types use cartridges, but the prefilled pens are discarded when the cartridge is empty. To administer a dose of insulin with a pen, the patient will affix a new pen needle to the insulin pen. The patient may then dial the control at the end of the pen to the correct dosage. Pressing a button until a drop appears at the tip of the needle ensures that there is no trapped air—this primes the pen. Handling still requires proper technique (washing, alcohol swab) to minimize contamination at the injection site. The pen is held in one hand like a dart; the needle is inserted at a 90° angle into pinched skin and a button is depressed to release medication.

It is recommended that needles not be attached to pens until ready to inject to avoid changes that could affect the dose. Even when capped, air can be introduced in to the cartridge through the needle. For example, moving from outside on a hot day into an air-conditioned room, the change in temperature may cause the volume of insulin to shrink, providing a space for air to move into. With needles attached too early, air may flow into the cartridge and become trapped. On the other hand, going from the cold into a warm environment may cause the insulin to expand and leak through an attached needle. Therefore, needles should only be attached just prior to injection.

It is very important that instructions for pen use be thoroughly understood by the patient and the caregiver because pens from different manufacturers operate differently. Pens vary in the brand and type of insulin compatible with their use and the maximum number of units contained when the pen is full. One pen records the last 16 doses with the date and time of doses; others do not offer a tracking feature but have a large, easy-to-read number display. It is important to know how to set the dose, what to do if an incorrect insulin dose was selected, or whether there is not enough insulin left for the next dose. Among the available pens, aspart (*NovoLog*) and detemir (*Levemir*) insulins use the *FlexPen*, lispro insulin *Humalog Mix 75/25* uses the *Kwikpen*, and glargine (*Lantus*) and glulisine (*Apidra*) use *Opticlick*. The *Autopen* is a multidose injection device that uses 1.5- or 3-ml cartridges of insulin.

Color has played an important part in making insulin administration safer. The *Opticlick* pen comes in two colors so the glargine insulin can go in one and glulisine insulin in the other. This is for patients who are using both insulins to manage their diabetes. The manufacturer (Eli Lilly) of *Humulin R* and *Humalog* introduced a color differentiation system for U-100 insulin products (vials, pens, and individual packaging) available in the United States. The *Humalog* (lispro insulin) products are burgundy: *Humalog* (burgundy), *Humalog Mix 50/50* (burgundy and red), and *Humalog Mix 75/25* (burgundy and yellow). Dark blue is the identifier for *Humulin R* (regular human insulin) products: *Humulin R* (dark blue and light yellow), *Humulin N* (dark blue and bright green), *Humulin 50/50* (dark blue and gray), and *Humulin 70/30* (dark blue and brown).

Check the manufacturer's instructions for insulin storage. Unopened cartridges may be refrigerated. Once a cartridge is loaded and opened, the loaded pen should be kept at room temperature. Open product is not refrigerated (never frozen) because the electronics in the pen may be affected by refrigeration. Some manufacturers have needles for their pen, but there are needles available that are universal for all diabetic pens and dosers (BD products). Insulin pen needles should be disposed of properly. To reduce the risk of injury, used needles should be discarded in an appropriately labeled sharp medical waste container. These containers are puncture-resistant, so that no one can sustain an injury due to contact with a used needle.

Changing Insulin Requirements

Once a successful dosing schedule of insulin has been established, fluctuations in the blood glucose level may still occur periodically. Many factors increase the level of cell activity and therefore the insulin requirement. Such factors as colds, fevers, infections, illness, surgery, and stress increase the blood glucose level so that higher doses of insulin are required.

Other factors may require reducing the insulin dose. For example, heavy exercise burns up excess glucose and lowers the need for insulin. This is why children, who are very active, are especially prone to insulin reactions. Certain drugs also alter the blood glucose level and insulin requirement in diabetic individuals.

Patients who require more than 200 units of insulin per day are considered to be insulin resistant. Resistance to the pharmacological effects of insulin may be due to the development of **antibodies** that inhibit insulin activity defects in skeletal muscle or liver cells, and accelerated insulin degradation. Changing the insulin preparation or putting patients on strict diet control may help counteract the resistance therapy, but it may not work for all patients and, eventually, some patients who respond well for a few years exhibit greater resistance later on.

There are patients who require more than 200 units. In order to minimize the volume of injection, concentrated insulin (*Humulin R Regular U-500*) is required. Concentrated insulin is 500 units/ml so a reasonable SC dose may be given that is titrated to the patient's needs. Accurate measurement of the dose is important because concentrated insulin may produce a response up to 24 hours after injection. This insulin should not be given IM or IV because of the potential for overdose that may cause irreversible insulin shock.

Adverse Effects

Insulin is usually well tolerated by diabetics. However, since the hormone is a polypeptide that is frequently combined with a protein (antigen), patients can develop an allergic reaction, although the incidence may be less than seen with animal insulins previously used. Allergic reactions may include itching, urticarial swelling, or anaphylaxis. Usually, patients can be switched to another species of insulin to avoid the reaction.

Some diabetics develop lipodystrophy, hypertrophy, or abscesses at the site of injection. **Lipodystrophy** is a disappearance of subcutaneous fat at the site of insulin injection. As a result, the skin becomes pitted and concave. Diabetics usually inject the insulin SC into the arms, abdomen, or thighs. To avoid atrophy of the subcutaneous tissue in these regions, a record of injection sites should be kept so that sites can be rotated.

The most common adverse effects of insulin therapy are blurred vision and hypoglycemia. During the initial period of insulin therapy, hyperglycemic changes in the lens result in blurred vision. This effect usually subsides within 1 or 2 weeks. However, hypoglycemia is a result of insulin overdose (insulin shock). When the blood glucose level is depressed, patients often experience hunger, headache, blurred vision, fatigue, anxiety, nervousness, confusion, and paresthesia. In severe cases, fainting or convulsions may occur. Glucagon, candy bars, ginger ale, or fruit juices will supply an adequate amount of glucose to correct the hypoglycemia. In severe cases (diabetic coma), glucagon may be administered (0.5 to 1 mg) intravenously. Glucagon produces a rapid rise in blood glucose that lasts about 1 hour. Once patients' symptoms are controlled, dextrose can be given intravenously.

Special Considerations

Before withdrawing any solution, vials should always be examined to ensure the correct insulin and strength (units/ml) have been selected. Suspension insulin vials and pens should always be rotated gently in the palm of the hand to ensure uniform dispersion of the insulin and avoid foaming. Suspension preparations are not uniformly dissolved, so gentle rotation permits a better dispersion of the insulin in the buffer so that the proper amount can be administered on schedule. Regular insulin, insulin glargine, and glulisine should appear as a clear solution and do not require rotation prior to administration. Discolored or turbid solutions should be discarded.

If not exposed to strong sunlight, insulin is stable at room temperature for up to 1 month. Nevertheless, insulins should be refrigerated (do not freeze) between uses to maintain the activity of the polypeptide. Prior to injection, it is recommended that the solution be warmed to room temperature to reduce the likelihood of producing a reaction at the site of injection. The expiration date should always be checked before administering the medication. Regular insulin that has passed the expiration date, that appears cloudy or discolored, or that has evidence of clumping should be discarded.

When preparing and administering insulin, sterile techniques should be followed. Hands should be washed prior to preparing the drug for administration whether using an insulin pen or a syringe. Using an alcohol wipe to cleanse the top of the pen before attaching the needle will ensure cleanliness. The septum of the insulin bottle should be swabbed with alcohol before the needle is inserted. Air should be injected into the bottle in order for insulin to flow easily into the syringe. The amount of air injected should be equal to the patient's insulin dose (that is, the same volume as the number of units to be given). Once air has been injected, the bottle should be turned upside down with the needle well into the insulin and the desired volume of drug withdrawn. Always check for air bubbles. Although the air is harmless, it is important to remove large bubbles because they reduce the amount of insulin injected. Always double-check the dose to be given prior to injection.

The timing of insulin administration and meals is very important for diabetic patients. The blood glucose level is delicately maintained by manipulating the carbohydrate intake. Therefore, insulin must be taken at the same time each day.

Insulin is usually administered 15 to 30 minutes before meals, although longer-acting preparations are given before breakfast. Variation in an established dosing schedule or diet will result in unstable blood glucose levels. Patients should always be observed (and they should be alert) for signals of insulin shock after receiving an injection. Patients should become aware of the onset and time of peak action of the particular insulin they use. Juice or sugar should be available to ease predictable hypoglycemic symptoms. It is important to remember that the insulin requirement may change when patients become ill and experience episodes of vomiting or fever. Hypoglycemia may occur during the night, as evidenced by restless sleep and sweating.

Regular insulin may be administered intravenously in emergencies or in severely ill patients. Plastic IV infusion sets adsorb insulin, so patients receive less insulin than prescribed. There is no way to predict the amount lost through adsorption. Therefore, following intravenous administration with an infusion setup, patients must be monitored carefully to titrate the insulin dose to the desired response.

Patients who are unconscious or severely hypoglycemic cannot offer accurate information about their medical history and therapy. Always examine patients for identification (tags, bracelets, or cards) that might disclose any insulin allergies. Never administer insulin until a positive diagnosis of insulin deficiency has been established. It is always safe to give sugar first to see if the symptoms subside. Insulin overdose is more critical than the added hyperglycemia resulting from fruit juice or candy.

Drug Interactions

Several drugs affect the action of insulin in diabetic patients (see Table 39:3). Many have a direct effect on glucose metabolism. Salicylates, beta-blockers, adrenergic neuronal blockers, and monoamine oxidase (MAO) inhibitors reduce circulating blood glucose levels; therefore, these drugs potentiate the hypoglycemic action of insulin. In contrast, glucagon, epinephrine, diazoxide, chlorpromazine, and sympathomimetics counteract insulin's action by inhibiting glucose

[Table **39:3**]

Physiological Factors and Drugs That Alter the Actions of Insulin

Factors that increase the insulin requirement (antagonize insulin)	Response
Catecholamine secretion—epinephrine	These factors or agents increase blood gucose concentrations by:
Colds, infections, illness	
Drugs: acetazolamide, AIDS antivirals, chlorpromazine, diazoxide, diltiazem, niacin, nicotine, oral contraceptives, rifampin, sympathomimetics, thiazide diuretics	• Increasing cell activity • Increasing gluconeogenesis
	• Inhibiting insulin release
Hormones: corticotropin, estrogens, glucagon, glucocorticoids, growth hormone, progestogens, thyroid hormones	• Stimulating liver glycogenolysis
Obesity	• Stimulating the sympathetic nervous system
Pregnancy	
Smoking	
Stress	
Surgery	

Drugs that decrease the insulin requirement (potentiate insulin)	Response
Alcohol, ACE inhibitors, adrenergic neuronal blockers, anabolic steroids, oral anticoagulants	These drugs decrease blood glucose concentrations by:
Beta-blockers, propranolol, chloroquine, clofibrate	• Interfering with glucose metabolism
Lithium carbonate, MAO inhibitors, metoprolol, pentamidine, pyridoxine (vitamin B$_6$), salicylates, tetracyclines	• Inhibiting the sympathetic nervous system

utilization. Insulin also can produce a shift in potassium from extracellular to intracellular sites, and this shift effectively reduces the serum potassium concentrations. When insulin is administered concomitantly with cardiac glycosides, patients should be monitored for indications of drug antagonism because of the effect on potassium.

Amylin Analog and Incretin Mimetics
Amylin Analog—Pramlintide (*Symlin*)

Amylin is the hormone co-secreted by the pancreas beta cells with insulin. It is synthesized and kept within the secretory granules of the beta cells. Amylin secretion results from insulin's response to food intake and blood glucose concentration. Amylin slows gastric emptying and suppresses glucagon secretion. This reduces the postmeal **(postprandial)** glucose absorption load and output from the liver (glycogenolysis) stimulated by glucagon. Amylin also modulates appetite as a satiety signal to the brain. The native hormone, called islet amyloid, is a peptide half the size of insulin (37 amino acids) that interacts with at least three receptors, each containing a calcitonin (the bone hormone) core. In DM, types 1 and 2, amylin is deficient to absent consistent with insulin availability. Without enough amylin, glucose from food enters the bloodstream more quickly than normal, causing blood glucose levels to rise.

Because the native hormone is like glue, the molecule was altered (3 proline molecules exchanged for 2 serines and 1 alanine) to make a fully functional analog that can be injected subcutaneously for the treatment of DM. The analog, pramlintide (*Symlin*), is approved as an adjunct treatment in patients who use mealtime insulin and have not achieved glucose control (type 1 DM) or type 2 DM patients who have not achieved glucose control with mealtime insulin and/or sulfonylureas or metformin (oral antidiabetic drugs). It is not approved for use with basal insulin where insulin is not taken with meals.

Since pramlintide is an adjunct treatment, it is expected that insulin and oral antidiabetic drugs be used concurrently. The dose of pramlintide is established while reducing the current dose of insulin. The dose is titrated in the type 1 DM patient beginning with 15 mcg SC immediately before meals up to a 60-mcg maximum maintenance dose. Then concurrent insulin is brought to a dose that achieves glycemic control. Type 2 DM patients begin with a dose of 60 mcg and are titrated in a similar manner to a maximum dose of 120 mcg. Pramlintide has resulted in a decrease in the insulin (up to 50 percent) required to achieve target glycemic control. During the titration process, amylin dose adjustment is based on patient tolerability to nausea that may occur. Pramlintide produces similar effects to exogenous insulin except for nausea that may occur in 30 to 40 percent of patients and a modest decrease in body weight consistent with its satiety signaling action and not a result of nausea. Lowering the starting dose may reduce nausea in many but not all patients, but nausea usually goes away with continued use. Other adverse effects include vomiting, upset stomach, decreased appetite, headache, tiredness, and dizziness.

Pramlintide has a special cautionary black box warning that alerts prescibers and health care professionals to the need for appropriate patient selection, careful patient instruction, and insulin dose adjustments as critical elements for reducing the risk of hypoglycemia. Appropriate patients for pramlintide already use insulin as prescribed but still need better blood sugar control, and will follow their doctor's instructions exactly including frequent follow-up. Alone pramlintide does not cause low blood glucose; however, concurrent use with insulin can cause hypoglycemia. Severe hypoglycemia has occurred within 3 hours after pramlintide dosing. Patients should be instructed about this possible effect, especially with regard to driving or engaging in high-risk activities. Increased frequency of glucose monitoring, especially in patients with a history of hypoglycemia, is recommended. Although pramlintide inhibits glucagon secretion, it does not override the body's glucagon response to hypoglycemia. This drug also has been shown to lower LDL-cholesterol.

Pramlintide is available in multidose disposable pen injectors with a predetermined dose. There are two pens, the *Symlin 60* has fixed dosing for 15, 30, 45, or 60 mcg and *Symlin 120* has 60 or 120 mcg to simplify pramlintide administration. The pen may appear empty because pramlintide is a clear solution. Although it has been studied, pramlintide is not approved for mixing with insulin as a single injection. Pramlintide is given as a second injection of relatively small volume, for example, 120 mcg is only 0.2 ml. Peak action is reached in approximately 20 minutes and diminishes over three hours. Unlike insulin, doses of pramlintide do not need to be adjusted for the amount of carbohydrate in meals or for physical activity. However, if a meal is missed, the dose of pramlintide also should be skipped. Pramlintide vials should be stored in the refrigerator until opened. Opened vials can be refrigerated or kept at room temperature for up to 28 days, after which time they should be discarded even with unused drug. Pramlintide should not be used if it has been frozen or appears discolored.

This drug is contraindicated in patients with **gastroparesis** or with drugs known to affect gastric emptying such as the alpha-glucosidase inhibitors or anticholinergic drugs. Patient medications should be reviewed for potential drug interactions. Beta-adrenergic blocking drugs and clonidine mask the symptoms of low blood glucose, while ACE inhibitors, MAO inhibitors, and salicylates may increase the risk of lowering blood glucose.

Incretin Mimetics: Exenatide (*Byetta*) and Liraglutide (*Victoza*)

Incretins are peptide hormones secreted from the duodenum. Plasma insulin levels were known to be greater after oral glucose administration than after IV glucose administration. This difference is due to the incretins that increase insulin secretion in response to dietary glucose levels in the gut. Incretins are glucose-dependent; that is, insulin secretion is only stimulated when glucose is present. The two main incretin hormones in humans are GIP (gastric inhibitory peptide) and GLP-1 (glucagon-like peptide-1). Both incretins have G-protein receptors located on the beta cells and also in the brain, duodenum, kidneys, liver, lungs, and stomach. Both hormones stimulate insulin secretion, but GLP-1 inhibits glucagon secretion and delays stomach emptying time so absorption is distributed over a longer time. This avoids hyperglycemic peaks. Within seconds, native incretins are metabolized by peptidase enzymes (one of which is dipeptidyl peptidase-4).

Studies have shown that in type 2 diabetics, there is less GLP-1 secretion and beta cells are less responsive to GIP. Two new incretin-based drugs have been approved as adjuncts to diet and exercise for the treatment of type 2 DM, exenatide (*Byetta*) and liraglutide (*Victoza*). Exenatide is a synthetic analog of a peptide found in the saliva of a gila monster lizard and liraglutide is a recombinant DNA GLP-1 analog in which arginine and a fatty acid have been inserted into the GLP-1 peptide. These drugs are incretin mimetics; they are not identical to the native molecules but produce the same effects in the presence of elevated glucose by activating GLP-1 receptors (GLP-1 agonists). They increase insulin, delay stomach emptying, and inhibit glucagon secretion. Both drugs are available in multidose disposable pens for subcutaneous administration into the arm, abdomen, or thighs. Exenatide is dosed BID one hour before morning and evening meals and should not be given after meals. Treatment is initiated as a 5-mcg dose SC BID. Based on glucose monitoring, after one month, the dose may be increased to 10 mcg BID to achieve glycemic control. It is eliminated primarily by renal filtration and proteolytic degradation. The analogs differ in their duration of action and elimination. Liraglutide has a half-life of 13 hours, which

supports its once-daily dosing anytime. Liraglutide is broken down by peptidases (not DPP-4), but it does not appear to be affected by renal elimination. Concurrent dosing with secretagogues should be reduced to avoid the risk of hypoglycemia. Liraglutide is begun with 0.6 mg SC OD and then increased after 1 week as needed to 1.2 or 1.8 mg.

Exenatide and liraglutide are not substitutes for insulin and should not be used in patients with type 1 diabetes or for the treatment of diabetic ketoacidosis. Concurrent use with insulin is not recommended. Adverse effects are similar with these drugs and include nausea, diarrhea, vomiting, headache, and dizziness. Exenatide has been associated with acute pancreatitis, including fatal and nonfatal necrotizing pancreatitis. If pancreatitis is suspected (nausea, pain, and elevated serum lipase and amylase), exenatide treatment should be terminated. Liraglutide has a special cautionary warning because it causes thyroid tumors, some of which were cancerous, in animals. It is not known whether thyroid tumors occur in humans. Patients with a history of medullary thyroid cancer or multiple endocrine neoplasia syndrome type 2 (a disease where people have tumors in more than one gland in their body) should not use this drug.

LO 39.2 **LO 39.3** **LO 39.5**

ORAL ANTIDIABETIC DRUGS: SECRETAGOGUES, HYPOGLYCEMICS

Drugs presented in the following sections have two characteristics in common: they are used in the management of type 2 DM and they are oral medications. There are several different mechanisms of action that make each group useful as monotherapy in responsive patients, and they have the advantage of being able to be used concurrently with other antidiabetic drugs, including insulin. This can be particularly important to counteract insulin resistance. Even though some of these drugs cause the insulin secretion, they are not used in the treatment of type 1 DM, especially not in the treatment of ketoacidosis. The oral antidiabetic drugs are approved for the treatment of type 2 DM in patients where diet and exercise with or without other antidiabetic drugs have not achieved target glycemic control. The advantage of these drugs over insulin is that the trauma and complications of injection, such as lipodystrophy, are avoided. These drugs are effective in maintaining glycemic control. The secretagogues (sulfonylureas and meglitinides) and metformin reduce HbA1c levels up to 2 percent, while the insulin sensitizers lower HbA1c 0.5 to 1 percent.

Secretagogues are the class of oral hypoglycemic drugs that describes the mechanism of action and impact on blood glucose concentration. The drugs in this class include sulfonylureas and nonsulfonylureas (also called meglitinides). These drugs are useful in the treatment of type 2 diabetes, alone or in combination with other antidiabetic drugs. The term "secretagogue" is applied to a substance that induces or causes the secretion of another substance.

These antidiabetic drugs cause the release of insulin. These drugs bind to sulfonylurea receptors in the beta cell membrane (Figure 39.4). The receptor senses ATP and ADP levels and responds by closing ATP-sensitive potassium channels. Potassium ion flow is blocked and the cell is depolarized, which triggers an influx of calcium ions across the membrane that triggers insulin release from the cell. Consequently, the secreted insulin alters (decreases) the blood glucose level. These drugs do not have any insulin-like activity. The hypoglycemic activity of the secretagogues is due to insulin released from the pancreas. Therefore, the secretagogues have no value in the treatment of type 1 diabetes because there is no insulin produced by the beta cells.

Note to the Health Care Professional

Oral contraceptives may alter diabetic control. Patients should be advised to use an alternate form of birth control while receiving antidiabetic therapy.

Characteristics

Three first-generation oral hypoglycemic drugs are still available although less commonly used: chlorpropamide, tolazamide, and tolbutamide (see Table 39:4). Newer, second-generation oral hypoglycemic drugs include glipizide, glimepiride, and glyburide. All of these drugs produce the same action on the pancreas to reduce fasting plasma glucose. However, the onset and duration of action vary because the absorption and metabolism of these drugs differ. There is a delay in the onset of action because the drugs must be absorbed from the intestine and then transported to the pancreas.

Except for tolazamide, the oral hypoglycemics are absorbed relatively quickly from the intestines. Since time is required to induce insulin release from the pancreas, the onset of action varies between 1 and 4 hours. Metabolism by the liver quickly inactivates tolbutamide; therefore, tolbutamide is a relatively short-acting drug. Glyburide and glipizide are more slowly metabolized in the liver to inactive metabolites. Tolazamide and acetohexamide are metabolized to active hypoglycemic compounds so that the effective duration of action is much longer (24 hours). Since chlorpropamide is not metabolized at all, it continues to stimulate insulin release until it is excreted by the kidneys. As a result, the duration of chlorpropamide's action may be up to 60 hours. Chlorpropamide elimination is influenced by changes in the urine pH. Urine alkalinization (pH greater than 6) promotes chlorpropamide excretion.

The nonsulfonylureas are represented by repaglinide (*Prandin*) and nateglinide (*Starlix*). The mechanism of action stimulates insulin secretion similar to the sulfonylureas, but the effect is more rapid with a shortened stimulation of the beta cell. These drugs are more rapidly absorbed than the sulfonylureas. The onset of action is 20 to 30 minutes, with peak insulin levels occurring within 60 minutes and returning to the lower, predrug level before the next meal. For this reason, these drugs must be taken within 1 to 30 minutes before each meal (dose and frequency are based on the patient's glucose-lowering requirement). While they lower postprandial glucose, the TID schedule is less convenient for the patient.

Adverse Effects

Hypoglycemia is the most common side effect of oral hypoglycemics. This effect may be severe in elderly, debilitated, or malnourished patients. Due to the variation in the onset and duration of action, it is easy for patients to become hypoglycemic if meals are not strictly timed and well balanced. The usual treatment is to administer carbohydrates as soon as possible. Subsequent adjustment in dose or meal patterns may be necessary. Because of prolonged action, patients who become hypoglycemic on chlorpropamide must be closely observed for several (3 to 5) days. Hospitalization may be required in profound hypoglycemic episodes. In situations requiring hospitalization, dextrose may be administered by intravenous infusion to maintain an adequate blood glucose concentration.

In the absence of hypoglycemia, the secretagogues occasionally produce gastrointestinal (GI) irritation, nausea, diarrhea, weakness, fatigue, dizziness, and weight gain. Reported hypersensitivity reactions include photosensitivity, rashes, jaundice, and occasional mild-to-moderate elevation in BUN, creatinine, AST, LDH, and

Oral Antidiabetic Drugs: Dose and Duration of Action

Drug (*Trade Name**)	Maximal effective dose	Daily dose range	Onset of action (hours)	Duration action (hours)
Hypoglycemics, secretagogues, sulfonylureas				
Chlorpropamide	750 mg	100–250 mg	1	60
Glimepiride (*Amaryl*)	8 mg	1–4 mg QD	1	24
Glipizide (*Glucotrol, Glucotrol-XL*)	40 mg	5–15 mg QD	1–1.5	10–16
Glyburide (*DiaBeta, Micronase*)	20 mg	1.25–20 mg QD**	2–4	24
Glyburide micronized (*Glynase*)	12 mg	0.75–12 mg QD**	1	12–24
Tolazamide	1000 mg	100–500 mg QD**	4–6	12–24
Tolbutamide (*Orinase*)	3000 mg	250–3000 mg QD	1	6–12
Meglitinides, nonsulfonylureas				
Repaglinide (*Prandin*)	16 mg	0.5–4 mg QID	30 min	4
Nateglinide (*Starlix*)	360 mg	60–120 mg TID	20 min	2
Antihyperglycemics, glucose absorption inhibitors (alpha glucosidase inhibitors)				
Acarbose (*Precose*)	100 mg	25–100 mg TID	Rapid	Short
Miglitol (*Glyset*)	100 mg	25–100 mg TID	Rapid	Short
Dipeptidyl peptidase-4 inhibitors				
Saxagliptin (*Onglyza*)	5 mg	2.5 or 5 mg QD	1	24
Sitagliptin (*Januvia*)	100 mg	100 mg QD	2–3 hours	9–24
Biguanides				
Metformin (*Glucophage, Fortamet*)	2500 mg	500–850 mg TID	—	2–4
Metformin (*Glucophage XR*)	2000 mg	1500–2000 mg	—	2–4
Insulin sensitizers (thiazolidinediones)				
Rosiglitazone (*Avandia*)	8 mg	2–8 mg QD	—	—
Pioglitazone (*Actos*)	45 mg	15–45 mg QD	1–2	24

(Continued)

Drug (*Trade Name**)	Maximal effective dose	Daily dose range	Onset of action (hours)	Duration action (hours)
Combination products*				
Glipizide/Metformin (*Metaglip*)	20/2000 mg	2.5/500 mg QD, BID	—	12–24
Pioglitazone/Metformin (*Actoplus Met*)	45/2550 mg	15/500 mg or 15/850 mg QD	—	12–24
Pioglitazone/Glimepiride (*Duetact*)	45/8 mg	30/2 mg or 30/4 mg QD	—	—
Sitagliptin/Metformin (*Janumet*)	100/2000 mg	50/500 BID	—	12–24

*Not an inclusive list of products. ** Single or divided doses.

alkaline phosphatase. Since there is no cross-sensitivity, patients can usually be placed on another secretagogue to avoid these reactions. Some individuals receiving secretagogue therapy have reportedly developed hemolytic anemia, leukopenia, thrombocytopenia, and aplastic anemia. Leukopenia, thrombocytopenia, and mild anemia return to normal when the drug is discontinued. Oral hypoglycemic drugs have been associated with an increased rate of cardiovascular mortality, compared to treatment with diet alone or diet plus insulin.

Contraindications

Oral hypoglycemic drugs are contraindicated in patients with known hypersensitivity to secretagogues, type 1 diabetes, or a diabetic condition complicated by fever, ketoacidosis, or coma. Secretagogues are not recommended for use in patients who have moderate to severe liver or renal disease. Impairment of liver and renal function decreases the clearance of these drugs and their metabolites from the blood. The nonsulfonylurea drugs may be used with caution and careful observation in patients with mild liver or renal disease.

Special Considerations

Occasionally diabetic patients experience trauma or physiological stress from fever, concomitant disease, or a condition that increases the difficulty in maintaining glucose control. In such situations, insulin may be substituted or added to the drug regimen to stabilize glucose control. Insulin is recommended over the secretagogues during pregnancy. Insulin is also used instead of the secretagogues prior to and during surgical procedures. The insulin level is much easier to control, since the stress of surgery may cause frequent fluctuations in the blood glucose level. Secretagogues should never be used in patients with peptic ulcers or ketosis.

Note to the Health Care Professional

Elderly patients are particularly responsive to the pharmacological effects of oral hypoglycemic drugs. It may be necessary to lower the initial dose to one-half the adult recommended dose in geriatric patients.

When transferring patients from one oral hypoglycemic drug to another, a transitional period of dose adjustment is usually not necessary. With chlorpropamide, however, the prolonged duration of action may potentiate the hypoglycemic effect of the alternate medication. Patients must be observed carefully during the transition from chlorpropamide to another oral hypoglycemic drug. When transferring patients from insulin to an oral secretagogue, the urine can be tested easily for glucose and ketones to monitor blood glucose fluctuation.

Drug Interactions

Oral hypoglycemics are bound to plasma proteins and metabolized in the liver. Therefore, these drugs are involved in several drug interactions. Drugs that inhibit liver enzymes, displace sulfonylureas from protein-binding sites, or inhibit glucose metabolism will potentiate the hypoglycemic actions of the sulfonylureas. Repaglinide should not be started in patients who are on gemfibrozil and itraconazole because prolonged glucose lowering may occur. This is a result of inhibited metabolism of repaglinide. Table 39:5 lists specific drugs that are known to interact with the oral hypoglycemics. Alcohol may produce a disulfiram reaction due to the accumulation of acetic acid in the blood. (See Chapter 10 for discussion of disulfiram.)

Oral hypoglycemic drugs stimulate the hepatic microsomal system and may reduce circulating blood digitoxin levels in patients receiving concomitant cardiac glycoside therapy. Rifampin has been reported to stimulate the metabolism of chlorpropamide and tolbutamide, thus reducing their hypoglycemic activity.

LO 39.2 **LO 39.3** **LO 39.5**
OTHER ORAL ANTIHYPERGLYCEMIC DRUGS

These antidiabetic drugs include four groups that have mechanisms of action that are different from those of the insulins or oral hypoglycemic secretagogues. None

of these drugs is a hypoglycemic. They do not decrease blood sugar levels in nondiabetic patients nor do they effect insulin release. One group influences dietary glucose absorption to maintain lower glucose blood levels; one group decreases glucose output from the liver; another group acts directly on fat, skeletal muscle, and the liver to sensitize the action of insulin on its target tissues and enhance glucose utilization. The fourth group inhibits an enzyme that metabolizes the incretin (GLP-1) so the incretin continues to induce insulin secretion. The sites of action for these drugs are presented in Figure 39.10.

Clinical Indications

All of these antidiabetic drugs are indicated for the management of diabetes mellitus type 2 in combination with diet control and/or secretagogues or insulin.

Glucose Absorption Inhibitors (Alpha-Glucosidase Inhibitors)

Miglitol (*Glyset*) and acarbose (*Precose*) interfere with dietary carbohydrate digestion. Ingested oligosaccharides and disaccharides are broken down to glucose through the enzymes glycoside hydrolase and alpha-amylase. In the membrane of the small intestine, miglitol and

[Table **39:5**]

Drug Interactions with Oral Antidiabetic Drugs

Drugs that potentiate oral hypoglycemic drugs	Reason
Adrenergic neuronal blocking drugs, insulin, MAO inhibitors, ranitidine, salicylates, sympatholytics	Inhibit glucose metabolism or glucose utilization
Alcohol, warfarin, cimetidine, chloramphenicol, MAO inhibitors, itraconazole	Inhibit P450 (CYP 31A) hepatic enymes, sulfonylurea, and repaglinide metabolism
Ethacrynic acid, probenecid, sulfonamide antibiotics	Displace the sulfonylureas from plasma protein-binding sites
Drugs that antagonize oral hypoglycemic drugs or acarbose	**Reason**
Beta-blockers, calcium channel blockers, hormones (estrogen, glucagon, growth hormone, progestogens, thyroid homones), isoniazid, steroids, and sympathomimetics	Alter carbohydrate metabolism, causing increased blood glucose concentrations; loss of blood suger control
Alcohol (chronic), phenothiazines, phenobarbital, phenytoin, rifampin	Increase hepatic metabolism, reducing oral hypoglycemic drug concentration in the blood
Drugs that antagonize carbohyrate absorption inhibitors	**Reason**
Digestive enzymes: amylase, pancreatin, charcoal	Decrease effect of miglitol and acarbose

Figure 39.10   Sites of Antidiabetic Drug Activity

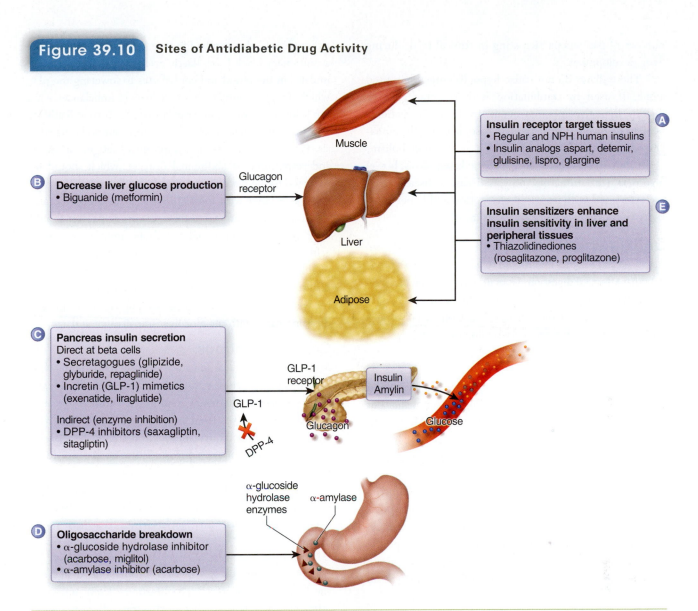

(A) Insulin receptors directly (insulin and insulin analogs); (B) liver glucose production (biguanides); (C) insulin secretion from pancreas beta cells, directly (amylin analog, secretagogues, incretin mimetics) or indirectly (DPP-4 inhibitors); (D) glucose absorption inhibitors (α-glucoside hydrolase and α-amylase inhibitors); (E) insulin sensitizers (thiazolidinediones).

acarbose inhibit glycoside hydrolase so that glucose absorption is delayed, not eliminated. Acarbose is itself an oligosaccharide and also reversibly ties up alpha-amylase (Figure 39.10). What results is a delay in glucose absorption so that the blood glucose level after meals (postprandial) does not immediately peak. This eliminates postprandial hyperglycemia. This mechanism of action is additive to the oral hypoglycemics and insulin.

These drugs are ingested with each meal—that is three times a day—so carbohydrate metabolism can be affected. Acarbose is metabolized within the intestine by enzymes and bacteria. Miglitol is absorbed and excreted through the kidneys unmetabolized. Acarbose can liver

enzymes but miglitol can be used in patients with liver impairment. Dosing may begin with 25 mg and range from 25 to 100 mg TID for both drugs. Dose adjustment is made at 4- to 8-week intervals after glucose monitoring confirms the drug's effectiveness 1 hour after meals.

Adverse Effects

The principal adverse effects are GI flatulence, diarrhea, and abdominal pain, which subside over continued drug use. Even in cases of overdose, only GI symptoms developed. Patients may require periodic evaluation for glycosylated hemoglobin (miglitol) and serum transaminases (acarbose) because such changes were reported in a small number of patients participating in clinical trials during drug development.

These drugs do not cause hypoglycemia when used alone. If used in combination with secretagogues or insulin, hypoglycemia may occur. In this event, patients need to be given glucose (not sucrose) because the alpha-glucosidase inhibitors interfere with sucrose metabolism.

Contraindications include diabetic ketoacidosis, bowel disorders (inflammatory bowel disease), diseases that are associated with impaired absorption and hypersensitivity to the drug or liver cirrhosis (acarbose).

Drug Interactions

Acarbose and miglitol are limited to interactions with products that affect GI digestion. Concurrent ingestion of digestive enzymes such as amylase, pancreatin, or charcoal would inhibit the ability of these drugs to act on carbohydrates within the intestine, thereby decreasing their efficacy.

Biguanides

An antihyperglycemic drug keeps the glucose blood level from rising too fast or too high after meals but does not necessarily "lower" blood glucose. Metformin (*Glucophage*) chemically is a biguanide drug that lowers postprandial glucose levels by decreasing liver glucose production and intestinal glucose absorption. It also appears to enhance glucose utilization by other tissues. Overall, this contributes to a smaller rise in postprandial glucose and smoother distribution to tissues. Unlike the secretagogues, metformin is not a hypoglycemic because it does not drive blood sugar levels down in nondiabetic patients. It has no direct influence on insulin secretion.

The usual dose is 500 mg BID up to a maximum of 2500 mg per day. Metformin is absorbed from the GI tract and excreted unchanged by the kidneys. Elderly patients who have age-related diminution of renal function show decreased plasma clearance of metformin. It is recommended that elderly patients not be titrated to the maximum dose because of increased plasma concentration. Metformin works through pathways complementary to other oral antidiabetic drugs. It is available in a fixed dose combination with glyburide (*Glucovance*), repaglinide (*PrandiMet*), pioglitazone (*Actoplus Met*), rosiglitazone (*Avandamet*), and sitagliptin (*Janumet*) to improve glycemic control. Because of metformin, these products will have a black box warning in their instruction for use (see Adverse Effects).

Adverse Effects

The GI effects of diarrhea, nausea, vomiting, and flatulence are usually tolerable and dissipate with continued use of the drug. Sometimes dose reduction also will ameliorate the adverse effect. There is one adverse effect, although rare, that can be life-threatening and is placed in a cautionary black box—lactic acidosis. Lactic acid accumulates in the blood and contributes to lowering the pH, which directly contributes to electrolyte imbalances. This can lead to respiratory and cardiovascular distress. Patients may present with signs of lactic acidosis but no ketoacidosis. Patients often develop symptoms of fatigue, myalgia, and respiratory or abdominal distress, which should be reported to the physician immediately. Since the GI symptoms associated with initial therapy abate over time and the dose is stable, any GI distress that develops later should be considered a potential metabolic imbalance. Lactic acidosis is a medical emergency that requires patient hospitalization for treatment and observation. Prompt hemodialysis clears metformin from the system and facilitates recovery from the metabolic crisis. The risk of lactic acidosis increases with renal or liver impairment and age.

Contraindications

Metformin is contraindicated for use in patients who have metabolic acidosis, including diabetic ketoacidosis; renal disease; or abnormal creatinine clearance. Because iodine contrast dyes used in radiologic evaluation may cause acute renal failure, metformin should be discontinued at least 48 hours before and after such procedures to avoid the possibility of lactic acidosis.

Alcohol potentiates the action of metformin on lactic acid metabolism. Patients need to be advised to avoid excessive alcohol use during metformin treatment.

Insulin Sensitizers: Thiazolidinedione

Among the new classes of oral antidiabetic drugs are the "insulin sensitizers." Pioglitazone (*Actos*) and rosiglitazone (*Avandia*) enhance peripheral cell response to insulin, allowing glucose to be utilized more efficiently. Although they do not stimulate insulin secretion, these drugs do decrease insulin resistance and increase insulin sensitivity of fat, skeletal muscle, and liver cells by activating receptors inside the cells (nuclear receptors) that regulate insulin activity. Both of these actions contribute to a removal of glucose from the circulation into the target cells. This requires insulin to be present in order to effect a change in glucose distribution. For this reason, they are recommended in the treatment of type 2 DM where there is a deficiency in insulin production. However, if used in type 1 patients receiving insulin, these drugs will produce the conditions for hypoglycemia due to increased insulin sensitivity.

These drugs are rapidly absorbed after oral administration and most of the drugs are excreted unchanged in the feces. Therefore, renal impairment does not affect drug blood levels. The adverse effect profile includes diarrhea and nausea.

Troglitazone, the first drug in this class, has been withdrawn from the market due to safety concerns associated with the increased incidence of liver failure and death in patients taking the drug. The two other drugs in this class are still available for the management of diabetes. There is a special cautionary warning about the use of these drugs in patients with congestive heart failure. Common adverse effects in this class include fluid retention and weight gain. The fluid retention (edema) can exacerbate conditions of heart failure and, therefore, does not make these the drugs of choice for patients with congestive heart failure. There is an increased risk of myocardial ischemic events (angina, MI) and death from cardiovascular causes with rosiglitazone. The FDA has restricted the use of this drug to patients with type 2 DM in whom blood glucose levels cannot be controlled by other medications. Physicians will also be required to enroll patients under a restricted access program (REMS, Risk Evaluation and Mitigation Strategy) to continue rosiglitazone treatment for the patient. Other adverse effects include headache, fatigue, and diarrhea. Reversible elevations in serum liver enzymes have occurred with pioglitazone and rosiglitazone, prompting the recommendation that evaluation of liver function such as serum enzyme profiles should be performed prior to initiating therapy with this class of drugs. Periodically, patients' enzymes should be monitored to confirm that liver injury has not developed during treatment.

Rosiglitazone should be discontinued if ALT levels remain at more than 3 times the upper limit of normal on repeated assay.

Dipeptidyl Peptidase-4 (DPP-4) Inhibitors

The gut hormone incretin GLP-1, which causes the release of insulin from the beta cells, is rapidly metabolized by dipeptidyl peptidase-4 (DPP-4). This provides another opportunity to affect insulin secretion with a specialized antidiabetic drug. The newest class of oral agents for DM includes saxagliptin (*Onglyza*) and sitagliptin (*Januvia*). These drugs inhibit DPP-4 in the intestine so native GLP-1 has more time to stimulate insulin secretion and decrease glucagon secretion. These drugs are approved for the treatment of type 2 DM as monotherapy or in combination with metformin or thiazolidinediones. Saxagliptin is more potent than sitagliptin. The recommended oral dose of saxagliptin is 2 or 5 mg/day and 100 mg/day for sitigliptin. Saxagliptin is metabolized through the hepatic enzymes CYP34A to an active metabolite that also inhibits DDP-IV. Coadministration of drugs known to induce or inhibit CYP34A will affect the drug blood concentration. Sitagliptin does not undergo much metabolism prior to being excreted in the urine. Dosage adjustments are recommended for patients with renal disease. Adverse effects include nasopharyngitis, upper respiratory tract infection, and headache.

This is another group of drugs that demands patient compliance not only with the medication schedule but with diet adjustment. Timing of the dose is critical to circumvent great swings in blood sugar and hypoglycemic episodes that send the patient into sweats, disorientation, pallor, immediate fatigue, and loss of consciousness. Diabetes patients require a significant amount of support to obtain encouragement and maintain a commitment to stick with the program. Fortunately, such support is readily available through community and hospital outreach education programs and the American Diabetes Association. In addition, patients need confirmation that questions can be directed to the treating physician and staff no matter how many times they need to ask. Patients can find adequate treatment from a variety of physicians ranging from family practitioners to endocrinologists or diabetologists. It is not unusual for elderly patients to change physicians because of guilt arising from not achieving the standard of control the physician has set or because they perceive they are not getting sufficient individualized attention. Therefore, diabetes patients need to receive clear, attentive, repetitive instruction in the administration of medication and the formation of new behavior patterns that will make for successful therapy.

The patient should be encouraged to read the patient package insert and instructed about the need for periodic blood glucose monitoring and HbA1c testing. The target values for these glucose assessments should be carefully explained and reviewed at each visit.

In the Event of an Accident or Diabetes Complications

Patients must carry adequate identification that describes their medical condition and clearly identifies which antidiabetic medication they are taking. If possible, the time of usual dosing should be indicated to help medical professionals ascertain the scope of the problem. This is particularly important if the patient is taking metformin, where lactic acidosis can develop.

Patients should be encouraged to disclose their medication to all other physicians who may be evaluating and/or treating the patient.

Patients should be routinely monitoring blood glucose and/or urine ketones to keep their insulin dose at the lowest effective dose.

Patients taking combination therapy should alert family members of the possibility that hypoglycemia could occur so that dextrose or oral glucose is readily available (for example, in the car, in the handbag, on the job). Anxiety, restlessness, and clammy skin often are the first signs that the patient is experiencing low blood sugar. Family members need to be well informed.

Special Note: All sugars are not alike. Table sugar is sucrose and tablets for treating hypoglycemia are dextrose or glucose. Patients taking miglitol or acarbose who experience hypoglycemia *cannot* be given table sugar or sugar cubes because the sucrose is metabolized to glucose by the enzyme that these drugs inhibit. Therefore, the patient would not have rapid absorption of glucose.

Patients and their families must be fully and clearly informed about the possibility of lactic acidosis if the patient is to receive metformin. Symptoms of acidosis need to be understood so that the patient or a relative can notify the physician as soon as symptoms become evident.

Dose Administration

Explain to patients that the parenteral pen medication pramlintide is not insulin, and does not replace insulin. This medication must be injected separately from their insulin. Remind patients to consistently use the same brand of insulin and same type of syringe to avoid errors in medication. If more than one insulin is being administered in the same syringe, tell patients *not to interchange* the order of mixing and not to reinject solution in the syringe into the insulin vial.

Older patients cannot easily distinguish the dose markings on transparent syringes. Recommend the use of syringes with a colored background or magnifiers that attach to the syringe to make the fluid level easier to see.

If insulin is stored in the refrigerator, remind patients to bring it to room temperature before injecting to reduce irritation at the injection site.

Patients taking glucose absorption inhibitors must take the medication at the beginning (with the first bite) of each meal—that means three meals and medication three times a day.

If a patient experiences GI upset when taking the sulfonylureas, advise the dose be taken with food.

Notify the Prescribing Physician

Patients should call the physician *whenever* they develop fever, sore throat, bruising, unusual bleeding, colds, or flu that could alter their medication requirements. Remind the patient to have the last home-monitored glucose values available for the doctor to review (see Figure 39.11).

Call the physician if fatigue, profuse sweating, numbness of the extremities, excessive hunger (hypoglycemia) or excessive thirst, urination, elevation in urine glucose or ketones occurs (hyperglycemia). Evaluation and/or dose adjustment may be indicated. Inform patients using exenatide or liraglutide how to recognize symptoms of pancreatitis. Explain that persistent, severe abdominal pain that may radiate to the back and may or may not be accompanied by vomiting is the hallmark symptom of acute pancreatitis. Instruct patients to promptly discontinue the medication and contact their health care provider if persistent, severe abdominal pain occurs.

Remind patients to avoid alcohol during sulfonylurea treatment because it may produce intense nausea by a disulfiram (*Antabuse*) reaction (buildup of acetaldehye in the blood).

Patients need to be advised to avoid excessive alcohol use during metformin treatment because of its potential to induce metformin lactic acidosis.

Use in Pregnancy

Antidiabetic drugs are designated FDA Pregnancy Category B and C. Overall the safety for use in pregnant women

(Continued)

has not been established through controlled clinical trials although historically women have been exposed to some of these drugs during pregnancy. Animal studies suggest that the oral antidiabetic drugs can cause birth defects so the potential risk to the patient and fetus must be seriously considered before continuing drug therapy during pregnancy. Because abnormal glucose levels during pregnancy have accompanied congenital abnormalities, blood glucose control during pregnancy is imperative in the best interests of the mother and fetus. The universal recommendation is that insulin is the treatment of choice during pregnancy. Patients should be advised to notify the prescribing physician, which is usually not the gynecologist/obstetrician, if they become pregnant while on antidiabetic drugs. Prompt evaluation will determine whether adjustment in dose and/or medication is warranted.

Figure 39.11   Measuring Daily Glucose

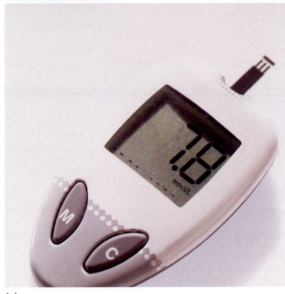

(a)

(b)

(a) Monitoring device with chem strip inserted displays the value of blood glucose concentration.
(b) Patient uses lancet to perform a finger stick for the blood glucose evaluation.

Chapter Review

Understanding Terminology

Match the definitions or descriptions in the left column with the appropriate term in the right column.

___ 1. Numbness of hands and feet. **(LO 39.3)**

___ 2. A higher than normal level of glucose in the blood. **(LO 39.1, 39.2, 39.3)**

___ 3. A preparation in which solid particles of an undissolved drug are dispersed within a liquid. **(LO 39.4)**

___ 4. Excessive thirst. **(LO 39.3)**

___ 5. Fat. **(LO 39.1, 39.2)**

___ 6. Excessive production of urine. **(LO 39.1, 39.2, 39.3)**

___ 7. Excessive eating. **(LO 39.1, 39.2, 39.3)**

___ 8. The presence of glucose in the urine. **(LO 39.1, 39.2, 39.3)**

a. adipose tissue

b. glycosuria

c. hyperglycemia

d. neuropathy

e. polydipsia

f. polyphagia

g. polyuria

h. suspension

Acquiring Knowledge

Answer the following questions.

1. What is the primary deficiency in diabetes? **(LO 39.3)**

2. What is the difference between type 1 and type 2 diabetes? **(LO 39.1, 39.3)**

3. What are the common symptoms of diabetes? **(LO 39.3)**

4. How does insulin control the symptoms of diabetes? **(LO 39.2, 39.3)**

5. What role does glucagon play in diabetes? **(LO 39.2, 39.3)**

6. How do the insulin preparations differ? **(LO 39.4)**

7. Why are some insulins shorter acting than others? **(LO 39.4)**

8. Why do the insulins occasionally produce allergic reactions? **(LO 39.4)**

9. How do the oral hypoglycemic drugs differ from the insulins? **(LO 39.4)**

10. When are the oral hypoglycemics used? **(LO 39.5)**

11. What factors potentiate the hypoglycemic actions of insulin and the oral hypoglycemics? **(LO 39.1, 39.2, 39.4, 39.5)**

12. What factors antagonize the actions of insulin and the oral hypoglycemics? **(LO 39.4, 39.5)**

Applying Knowledge on the Job

Use your critical-thinking skills to answer the following questions.

1. Assume you work in a hospital preparing medications for injection. For each of the following situations, identify the error that has been made in using insulin.

    a. Your coworker on the early shift removed a vial of insulin from the freezer and left it on the counter to thaw so it would be ready for you to use when your shift starts. **(LO 39.4)**

    b. A vial of NPH insulin in your medication refrigerator looks cloudy. You assume that it has gone bad and discard it. **(LO 39.4)**

    c. Your first order of the day calls for a mixture of regular insulin and isophane insulin suspension. Your next order calls for insulin prepared for intravenous injection. **(LO 39.4)**

2. Assume you work in an endocrinology clinic where you screen patients for potential drug interactions. What potential problem(s) do you see in each of the following cases? Should the insulin dose be increased or decreased as a result?
   a. Patient A takes oral contraceptives and is overweight. **(LO 39.4)**
   b. Patient B is taking *Achromycin* for a strep infection. **(LO 39.4)**
   c. Patient C takes *Diamox* for glaucoma. **(LO 39.4)**
   d. Patient D is taking *Lopressor* for hypertension. **(LO 39.4)**

3. Renal impairment is not uncommon in diabetics as the disease progresses. Judy has been taking *Micronase* for 10 years. Her diabetes has been fairly well controlled with diet and medication. She has just been diagnosed with moderate renal impairment due to her diabetic condition. Would you expect to see changes in her medication? Why? **(LO 39.4, 39.5)**

4. Hal, a diabetic, has been taking *Precose* 75 mg three times daily with meals. His diabetes has been well controlled. He has just been diagnosed with liver impairment. Would you expect to see changes in his medication? Why? **(LO 39.5)**

5. Patients taking *Glucophage* should be cautioned to avoid excessive alcohol use during metformin therapy. Why? **(LO 39.5)**

Multiple Choice

Use your critical-thinking skills to answer the following questions.

1. Which of the following parameters would help to differentiate between type 1 and type 2 diabetes? **(LO 39.1, 39.3)**
   A. blood glucose level
   B. hemoglobin A1c level
   C. ketoacidosis
   D. cholesterol level

2. Which of the following insulins would provide a patient diagnosed with type 1 diabetes mellitus a constant release of insulin over a 24-hour period? **(LO 39.4)**
   A. regular insulin
   B. insulin aspart
   C. insulin glargine
   D. insulin lispro

3. Which of the following oral antidiabetic agents increases the incretin's duration of action? **(LO 39.5)**
   A. sitagliptin
   B. acarbose
   C. nateglinide
   D. tolbutamide

4. Which of the following oral agents is categorized as a secretagogue? **(LO 39.5)**
   A. metformin
   B. glipizide
   C. sitagliptin
   D. miglitol

5. Which of the following hormones would be elevated during a fast? (LO 39.1, 39.2)
   A. insulin
   B. glucagon
   C. humulin
   D. GnRH

6. Which of the following is an indicator of glycemic control in type 2 DM patients? (LO 39.1, 39.2)
   A. hourly blood glucose values
   B. HbA1c level
   C. RBC hematocrit
   D. blood insulin of 50 IU/dl

7. Which is NOT a mechanism of action of an oral antidiabetic drug? (LO 39.5)
   A. increased insulin sensitivity in target tissues
   B. inhibit or delay the breakdown of carbohydrates in the intestine
   C. direct action on the beta cell membrane-bound receptors
   D. direct stimulation of insulin receptors in skeletal muscle

8. Which of the following is correct about type 2 DM? (LO 39.1, 39.3)
   A. insulin is secreted by the beta cells and insulin resistance is present
   B. insulin cannot be used in type 2 DM
   C. patients are only prone to persistent infections in type 1 DM
   D. oral antidiabetic drugs cannot be combined to achieve glycemic control

9. Which of the following is correct about polyuria in types 1 and 2 DM? (LO 39.3)
   A. excess glucose spills into the urine and osmotically attracts water into the renal tubule
   B. antidiuretic hormone is no longer secreted in DM
   C. GLUT2 receptors move glucose from the blood into the renal tubule
   D. sulfonylurea drugs interact with their receptors in the kidney to increase urine flow

10. Which of the following when used together have complementary actions that increase insulin secretion? (LO 39.1, 39.2, 39.4, 39.5)
    A. regular human insulin and insulin glargine
    B. DPP-4 inhibitor sitagliptin and metformin
    C. amylin and glucagon
    D. glyburide and incretin mimetics

Multiple Choice (Multiple Answer)

Select the correct choices for each statement. The choices may be all correct, all incorrect, or any combination.

1. Beta cells secrete the following substances: (LO 39.1)
   A. insulin
   B. glucagon
   C. amylin
   D. acetate

2. Choose the true statements about glucagon. (LO 39.2)
   A. incretins increase their secretion
   B. it has receptors on skeletal muscle
   C. it stops the liver from producing glucose
   D. it is an anabolic hormone

3. Which of the following are likely in a person with type 2 diabetes? **(LO 39.3)**
    A. high blood pressure
    B. overweight
    C. hyperthyroidism
    D. increased secretions of insulin

4. Select all of the long-acting insulin preparations. **(LO 39.4)**
    A. *Apidra*
    B. *Novolog*
    C. *Lantus*
    D. *Symlin*

5. Select the causes of type 1 diabetes. **(LO 39.3)**
    A. autoantibody destruction of beta cells
    B. Coxsackie virus
    C. failure of target tissue to respond to insulin
    D. hyperinsulinemia

Sequencing

Place the following in order as they occur after an individual eats a meal. **(LO 39.1, 39.2)**

_____   _____   _____   _____

First   **Last**

exocytosis of secretory granules

membrane depolarization

elevated concentration of glucose within beta cells

closure of ATP-sensitive potassium channels

Classification

Place the following medications under the appropriate classification. **(LO 39.5)**

Prandin	*Novolog*
Onglyza	*Januvia*
Levemir	*Glyset*
Diabeta	*Avandia*
Actos	*Glynase*
Precose	*Starlix*
Glucophage	*Fortamet*

Insulins	Sulfonylureas	Meglitinides	Glucose absorption inhibitors	Biguanides	Insulin sensitizers	Peptidase inhibitors

Labeling

Fill in the missing labels. **(LO 39.1)**

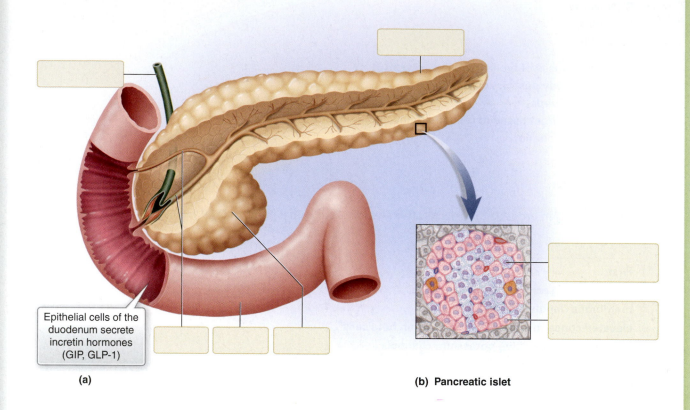

Epithelial cells of the
duodenum secrete
incretin hormones
(GIP, GLP-1)

(a)

(b) **Pancreatic islet**

For interactive animations, videos, and assessment, visit:

www.mcgrawhillconnect.com

Chapter 40

Posterior Pituitary Hormones: Anti-diuretic Hormone and Oxytocin

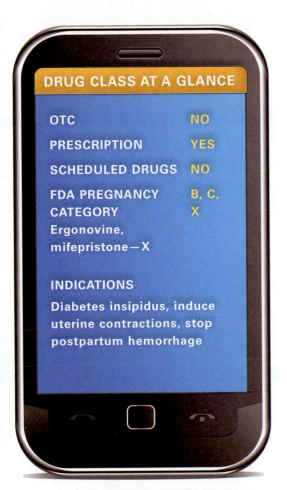

DRUG CLASS AT A GLANCE

OTC	NO
PRESCRIPTION	YES
SCHEDULED DRUGS	NO
FDA PREGNANCY CATEGORY	B, C, X

Ergonovine, mifepristone—X

INDICATIONS

Diabetes insipidus, induce uterine contractions, stop postpartum hemorrhage

KEY TERMS

antidiuretic hormone (ADH): polypeptide substance released within the brain that regulates water balance in the body.

aquaporins: specialized proteins that form pores (channels) in the cell membrane that allow water to pass through but not small molecules like ions.

diabetes insipidus: chronic condition caused by inadequate secretion of antidiuretic hormone, in which individuals are extremely thirsty and produce very large amounts of pale urine.

endogenous: originating within the body.

exogenous: originating outside the body, or administered into the body from outside.

hypertonic: a condition where the concentration of salt (sodium, electrolytes) is greater than that found inside the cells.

hypotonic: a condition where the concentration of salt (sodium, electrolytes) is less than that found inside the cells.

nephrosis: a degenerative disease of the kidneys, characterized by generalized edema, protein in the urine, and an increase in serum cholesterol.

osmolarity: a measure of hydration status; the amount of solute (ions, salts) per liter of solution (blood, plasma).

osmoreceptors: specialized cells in the hypothalamus that respond to changes in sodium concentration (osmolarity) in the blood.

oxytocin: polypeptide substance released within the brain that has specific functions during and after pregnancy, specifically relating to the uterus and the mammary glands.

polydipsia: increased thirst.

polypeptide: substance composed of a number of amino acids.

polyuria: increased urination.

postpartum: after childbirth.

pressor: tending to increase blood pressure.

tetany: a strong sustained muscle contraction.

vasopressin: man-made form of ADH. Because of ADH's fluid reabsorption and vasoconstrictive properties, can elevate blood pressure at higher doses.

After studying this chapter, you should be able to

40.1 explain the functions of ADH.

40.2 explain the functions and clinical use for oxytocin.

40.3 explain the pathophysiology of diabetes insipidus and mechanisms of action of the drugs utilized to treat it.

40.4 differentiate between oxytocic and tocolytic drugs.

The pituitary gland is located at the base of the hypothalamus and has two main lobes: the anterior lobe (adenohypophysis) and the posterior lobe (neurohypophysis). The posterior lobe stores and releases two hormones: antidiuretic hormone (ADH) and oxytocin.

LO 40.1 LO 40.2

POSTERIOR PITUITARY HORMONES

The posterior lobe of the pituitary does not synthesize hormones. The hypothalamus produces the hormones that are stored in the posterior lobe of the pituitary gland. The posterior lobe is an extension of the nerve tissue of the hypothalamus. As shown in Figure 40.1, the paraventricular nuclei and the supraoptic nuclei are neurons where oxytocin and ADH, respectively, are synthesized. Oxytocin is primarily involved with labor contractions before birth and milk ejection after birth, while

ADH is essential for water conservation throughout life. Although they produce markedly different responses, oxytocin and ADH are **polypeptides** that only differ in the placement of two amino acids: isoleucine and leucine in oxytocin versus phenylalanine and arginine in ADH (see Figure 40.2). Each hormone travels down nerve axons (axonal transport) to the posterior lobe, where the hormone is retained until needed. Secretion of the posterior pituitary hormones is controlled by nerve reflexes, that is, release of hormone in response to a nerve signal (not a hormone as with the anterior pituitary).

Figure 40.1   **Anatomy of the Pituitary Gland**

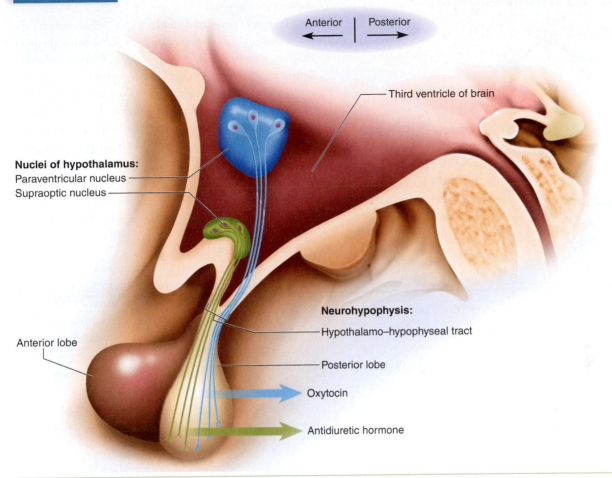

Anterior | Posterior

Third ventricle of brain

Nuclei of hypothalamus:
Paraventricular nucleus
Supraoptic nucleus

Neurohypophysis:
Hypothalamo–hypophyseal tract

Posterior lobe

Oxytocin

Antidiuretic hormone

Anterior lobe

Major structures of the pituitary and hormones of the posterior lobe (neurohypophysis). Note that these hormones (oxytocin and antidiuretic hormone) are produced by two areas (nuclei) in the hypothalamus and later released from the posterior lobe of the pituitary.

LO 40.1   **LO 40.3**

ANTIDIURETIC HORMONE

Water balance, the difference between water intake and water output, is well controlled every day. As shown in Figure 40.3, the typical intake and output of water are about 2500 ml/day. Water intake is largely controlled by thirst, while control of water output is primarily through urine production. **Antidiuretic hormone** is a substance that regulates water balance in the body by controlling water loss in the urine (anti = no; diuresis = urine production/water loss in urine). **Osmoreceptors** in the hypothalamus detect changes in the salt (sodium) concentration in the plasma that indicate whether more or less water needs to be conserved. Serum sodium is maintained in the normal range (135–145 mEq/l) despite wide fluctuations in

fluid intake. If there is too much sodium in the blood (**hypertonic,** serum sodium >145 mEq/l), ADH will be released. The target organs for ADH are the kidneys, where ADH binds to receptors in the collecting ducts of the renal tubules. ADH increases the reabsorption of water into the blood by causing the collecting duct cells to synthesize specialized proteins called water channels. Free water (without sodium) flows out of the urine into the blood through channels known as **aquaporins.** These channels appear to be exclusively water channels and do not permit ions or other small molecules to pass through. As a result, there is a decrease in blood **osmolarity,** the osmoreceptors are no longer activated, ADH secretion is inhibited (negative feedback), and water is conserved. The blood compartment contains more

Figure 40.2

Oxytocin and Antidiuretic Hormone

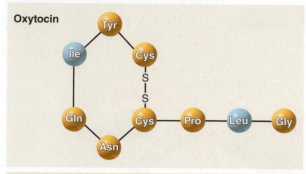

Oxytocin

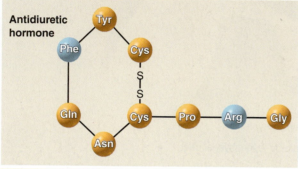

Antidiuretic hormone

The amino acid sequences for oxytocin and antidiuretic hormone differ only in the two amino acids in blue.

Figure 40.3

Typical Water Intake and Output in a State of Fluid Balance

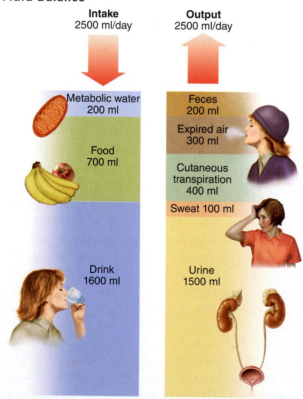

Intake
2500 ml/day

Output
2500 ml/day

Metabolic water
200 ml

Food
700 ml

Drink
1600 ml

Feces
200 ml

Expired air
300 ml

Cutaneous transpiration
400 ml

Sweat 100 ml

Urine
1500 ml

water. While water is reabsorbed, the urine becomes more concentrated because less water and more ions/sodium are excreted.

Triggers associated with water conservation are thirst and significant reduction in blood volume (hemorrhage or dehydration), causing a drop in blood pressure. Thirst also is stimulated via osmoreceptors. A 2 to 3 percent increase in plasma osmolarity makes an individual intensely thirsty so water intake occurs in concert with a decrease in water output for optimal water conservation. Loss of blood in the range of 15 to 20 percent causes significant secretion of ADH so that water is reabsorbed into the blood, blood volume increases, and peripheral blood pressure increases. ADH also is secreted in response to pain, nausea, and vomiting and during the use of certain medications such as morphine during the postoperative period.

When the plasma compartment has a decreased osmolarity (**hypotonic,** serum sodium < 135 mEq/l), indicating there is too much retained water, ADH secretion is inhibited. Conditions associated with an increase in retained water, which include cirrhosis, cardiac failure, and **nephrosis,** would inhibit ADH secretion.

ADH has two names. The **endogenous** compound is called ADH, while the **exogenously** administered synthetic drug is **vasopressin** (see Figure 40.4, vasopressin injection). Vasopressin was named because

Figure 40.4

Vasopressin Injection Multidose Vial

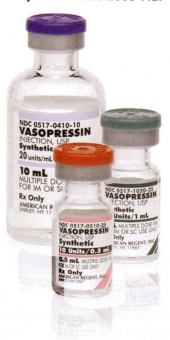

it increases **(pressor)** blood pressure (vaso) and can stimulate smooth muscle vasoconstriction in the control of hemorrhage. ADH in its daily hormonal function in water balance does not produce a similar pressor response. The main use of vasopressin and related synthetic products is in the treatment of diabetes insipidus.

Diabetes Insipidus

In the absence of ADH, the collecting ducts are virtually impermeable to water so all water is excreted into the urine. Individuals who lack ADH have a condition known as **diabetes insipidus,** characterized by the loss of large volumes of body water via the urine **(polyuria).** Diabetes insipidus (DI) may be classified as central or nephrogenic. Central DI is caused by a decreased secretion of ADH, whereas nephrogenic DI is caused by a resistance to ADH in the kidney. Central DI can be caused by head trauma, infections, or tumors of the hypothalamus. Nephrogenic DI usually involves renal disease or gene mutations involved in aquaporin synthesis or ADH receptor formation. Individuals with diabetes insipidus excrete large volumes of dilute urine (3 liters/day) and are unable to maintain fluid balance. Without ADH, the collecting ducts decrease their permeability to water, and water cannot be reabsorbed back into the bloodstream. The condition may not be life-threatening if water intake can balance the output.

Treatment of hypothalamic DI mainly involves replacement therapy with synthetic vasopressin. By the way, diabetes insipidus is not related to the other hormone deficiency condition, diabetes mellitus. In an uncontrolled state, diabetes mellitus can be associated with polyuria because osmotically active glucose molecules spill into the urine; however, diabetes mellitus is due to abnormal insulin activity (see Chapter 39).

Vasopressin Injection (*Pitressin Synthetic*)

Vasopressin (8-arginine vasopressin), obtained from animal sources, contains ADH and oxytocin in a ratio of 20:1. Synthetic vasopressin contains the vital sequence of amino acids that mimics endogenous hormone activity. It is injected SC or IM in the early treatment of diabetes insipidus to stabilize patients' fluid balance. The duration of action of vasopressin injection, 5 to 10 units, is approximately 2 to 8 hours. It is metabolized and excreted by the liver and kidneys.

Desmopressin Acetate (*DDAVP*)

Desmopressin (1-deamino-8-*D*-arginine-vasopressin) is also chemically related to vasopressin. See Figure 40.5 for a comparison of the amino acid composition of

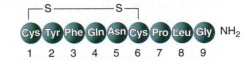

Figure 40.5

Comparison of the Amino Acid Sequences for Oxytocin, Arginine Vasopressin, and Desmopressin

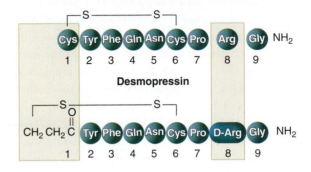

vasopressin and desmopressin. It is administered intranasally usually in two doses, which allows a distribution similar to the normal diurnal response. It has a duration of action of 10 to 20 hours, much longer than the natural vasopressin. Desmopressin is approved for use in conditions other than diabetes insipidus. It is proven effective in the treatment of nocturnal enuresis when administered prior to bedtime. It also is used to prevent or relieve abdominal distention associated with surgical procedures.

Adverse Effects

The most frequent side effects of vasopressin and related substances include nausea, GI cramping, and diarrhea. Tremor, vertigo, and sweating that are transient and usually not serious also have been reported with desmopressin. The physician should be notified if the patient experiences shortness of breath, nasal congestion, or nasal irritation. In higher doses, the pressor effect produces cutaneous vasoconstriction (pallor) and an increase in blood pressure. Caution must be observed with individuals who have coronary artery disease. The natural preparations (animal source) may produce hypersensitivity and allergic reactions. Because these hormones affect water balance, seizures have occurred in some patients. Careful consideration before use is necessary when patients with epilepsy require treatment.

DRUGS AFFECTING UTERINE MUSCLE

Oxytocics

The polypeptide **oxytocin** functions primarily during and after pregnancy. Oxytocin stimulates contractions of the uterus and facilitates delivery. Commercial preparations of oxytocin and related substances are used to induce labor, to control postpartum bleeding, and to induce therapeutic abortions. Drugs that produce contractions of the uterus are referred to as oxytocics. Oxytocin also plays an important role during breast-feeding. For example, oxytocin release occurs through the stimulation of sensory nerve endings in the breast nipple when the baby suckles. The signals travel through the mother's spinal cord and brain to the posterior pituitary. After being released, oxytocin travels in the blood to the myoepithelial cells of the mammary glands, where it causes the ejection of milk for the feeding baby. This neuroendocrine reflex of oxytocin release also can occur when a lactating woman hears a baby cry even though she is not actually breast-feeding her baby.

Oxytocin, also secreted in men, is synthesized in the hypothalamus, testes, and prostate gland. A pulse of oxytocin is produced with ejaculation of sperm and is thought to be associated with sperm transport and maturation. A rise in oxytocin levels correlates with orgasm intensity in men and women. At present, there is no role for oxytocin as a pharmacologic agent beyond labor and delivery.

Labor Induction

Oxytocics are used to induce labor when it does not begin spontaneously. Administering oxytocin stimulates the uterine muscles to contract. The force and duration of uterine contraction are dose dependent. The major problem with the use of oxytocics is the development of violent uterine contractions, which must be avoided because they result in forceful expulsion of the fetus through the undilated birth canal. Naturally occurring oxytocin is no longer available; it has been replaced by synthetic oxytocin. Oxytocin injection (*Pitocin*) is administered by IV infusion, which is carefully adjusted so that birth follows the normal sequence (see Figure 40.6). The major adverse effect of oxytocin is caused by excessive administration, resulting in uterine **tetany,** or rupture, and subsequent fetal distress, injury, or death. Oxytocin has a special cautionary warning to indicate that its administration is for medical induction of labor rather than elective induction of labor.

Figure 40.6

Oxytocin Intravenous Drip in Lactated Ringer's Solution

Postpartum Bleeding

Oxytocics are used after delivery of the placenta **(postpartum)** to cause firm uterine contractions. In this manner, oxytocics decrease uterine bleeding and reduce the possibility of serious hemorrhage. Oxytocin injection can be used as can the ergot alkaloids: ergonovine (*Ergotrate*) and methylergonovine (*Methergine*). The onset of action for these drugs, which can be administered orally or parenterally, is rapid.

The duration of their action (IM) is approximately 6 hours.

Common adverse effects include nausea, vomiting, and constriction of blood vessels, which can produce varying degrees of hypertension. This vascular response combined with contraction of uterine muscle decreases the potential for postpartum hemorrhage and prevents muscle atony. With excessive administration, the pressor effect may be intense and may restrict blood flow to the extremities (fingers and toes). This effect can result in tissue anoxia and the development of gangrene. The ergot alkaloids should never be used to induce labor or abortions.

Therapeutic Abortions

Vigorous contraction of the uterus at any time during pregnancy will dislodge tissues, resulting in abortion. When therapeutic abortion is required, oxytocin may be administered during the first trimester and even up to the 19th week of pregnancy. However, relatively large amounts are required and, in some cases, the drug must be repeatedly administered until the abortion is complete.

The present drug of choice to induce abortion during the second trimester is a prostaglandin. Carboprost tromethamine (*Hemabate*) is a derivative of dinoprost, an $F_{2\alpha}$ prostaglandin, which is administered by deep IM injection. Dinoprostone (*Prostin E₂*), another prostaglandin, is administered by vaginal suppository and mifepristone (*Mifeprex*) is given orally. See Table 40:1 for doses.

Adverse effects of the oxytocics are usually limited after vaginal suppository or gel application. Nausea, vomiting, and diarrhea are common. Other adverse effects include fever, flushing, headache, and dizziness. Constriction of bronchial smooth muscle has been reported and, consequently, these drugs are contraindicated in patients with asthma.

LO 40.2   **LO 40.4**

TOCOLYTICS

Premature Rupture of Obstetrical Membranes

Many women develop premature contractions of the uterus early in the pregnancy that jeopardize their ability to carry the fetus to term. Intense contractions may

[**Table 40:1**]

Indications and Doses for Posterior Pituitary Hormones and Drugs Affecting Uterine Contractions

Drug (*Trade Name*)	Indication	Dose
Urination inhibition		
Vasopressin (*Pitressin Synthetic*)	Diabetes insipidus Postoperative abdominal distention	5–10 units IM 5–10 units IM or SC every 3 or 4 hr
Desmopressin (*DDAVP, Stimate*)	Diabetes insipidus	0.1–0.4 ml daily intranasally or 0.1–1.2 mg PO BID, TID. 0.5–1ml (2–4 mcg) SC
Desmopressin (*DDAVP*)	Enuresis	0.2 to 0.6 mg PO daily at bedtime
Uterine contraction		
Carboprost tromethamine (*Hemabate*)	Abortifacient Postpartum bleeding	250–500 mcg deep IM injection 250 mcg deep IM
Dinoprostone (*Prepidil, Cervidil, Prostin E₂*)	Abortifacient	1 vaginal suppository (20 mg) up to 2 days
	Cervical ripening prior to labor	10 mg vaginal insert for 12 hr or 0.5 mg gel application q 6 hr to the cervix
Oxytocin (*Pitocin*)	Medical induction of labor antepartum	1–2 mU/min IV drip at 15 to 20 ml/min
	Postpartum contraction	Diluted 10–40 units in 1000 ml diluent
Ergonovine (*Ergotrate Maleate*)	Postpartum hemorrhage	1–2 tablets PO BID–QID
Methylergonovine (*Methergine*)	Postpartum hemorrhage	0.2 mg/ml IM repeated in 2 to 4 hr as necessary or 0.2 mg PO TID, QID for 7 days
Mifepristone (*mifeprex*)	Abortifacient	3 tablets (600 mg) single dose PO
Uterine relaxation		
Terbutaline (*Brethine*)	Premature contractions	0.25 mg SC every 20 min to 3 hr up to 48 hr

result in premature rupture of obstetrical membranes (PROM) or preterm PROM, which could lead to premature birth. No single factor is responsible for inducing PROM, although there is a significant link with cigarette smoking. There is no specific preventative medicine, but, where possible, cigarette smoking should be discontinued. When contractions are persistent and strong, the woman is usually confined to bed. Delivery prior to 37 weeks of gestation is associated with significantly underdeveloped fetal organ systems, especially respiratory and neural functions.

Tocolytic drugs inhibit uterine contractions. Magnesium sulfate will slow uterine contractions but also may slow the heart and respiratory rate of the mother. Terbutaline, a beta-adrenergic agonist, also inhibits uterine contractions but increases the heart rates of the mother and fetus. Terbutaline and the calcium channel blocking drug nifedipine are used as tocolytics to control preterm premature contractions. This is an "off-label" use, meaning that these drugs have not been specifically approved by the FDA for this indication; however, clinical practice and the literature support their use under available guidelines for use. Premature infants today often have the availability of "high-tech" neonatal intensive care units where ventilation and cardiovascular support are continually provided. Even though surfactants are now available that can minimize or eliminate time spent on ventilators, there is no substitute for the benefit of having the fetus come to full term *in utero*.

Adverse Effects

Consistent with beta-adrenergic-receptor-mediated activity, fetal tachycardia, increased maternal blood pressure, and increased blood glucose and fatty acids can occur with terbutaline. This is usually dose related and abates on discontinuation of the drug. Nausea, vomiting, headache, anxiety, restlessness, and arrhythmia are among the other adverse effects reported to occur.

Patient Administration and Monitoring

Since this group of drugs has especially restricted use, patients will not have the opportunity to misuse these drugs. Nevertheless, patients require clear instructions on the use of nasal sprays to obtain the optimum therapeutic effect.

Drug Administration for Intranasal DDAVP

Uniform intranasal dosing is achieved when the bottle and the patient's head are held upright. Desmopressin acetate is provided as a 2.5- or 5-ml bottle containing 25 or 50 doses, respectively. Residual contents should never be mixed into another drug bottle. When the total doses have been sprayed, the residual should be discarded to avoid administering an incomplete dose.

Notify the Physician

Patients taking carbamazepine or chlorpropamide may experience an exaggerated response to ADH.

Patients with epilepsy, migraine, asthma, or heart failure may experience exacerbations of these conditions because of an increase in extracellular water with the vasopressins. Patients who experience shortness of breath, nasal congestion, irritation, or severe headache should notify the physician immediately for further evaluation.

Patients who develop skin pallor or abdominal cramping with vasopressin may eliminate the effect if one or two glasses of water are taken with the dose.

Chapter Review

Understanding Terminology

Answer the following questions.

1. Define *polydipsia*. **(LO 40.1)**
2. What is ADH? **(LO 40.1)**
3. Define *postpartum*. **(LO 40.2, 40.4)**
4. What is oxytocin? **(LO 40.2)**
5. What is vasopressin? **(LO 40.1, 40.3)**

Acquiring Knowledge

Answer the following questions.

1. What hormones are released from the posterior pituitary gland? **(LO 40.1, 40.2)**
2. Describe the main functions of ADH and oxytocin. **(LO 40.1, 40.2, 40.3, 40.4)**
3. What condition is associated with a lack of ADH? **(LO 40.1, 40.3)**
4. List some of the preparations that are used to treat diabetes insipidus. **(LO 40.1, 40.3)**
5. List the adverse effects of the drugs used to treat diabetes insipidus. **(LO 40.3)**
6. What are the drugs of choice to induce labor? **(LO 40.4)**
7. What are the drugs of choice after delivery to prevent excessive uterine bleeding? **(LO 40.4)**
8. What is an example of a drug administered to induce therapeutic abortion? **(LO 40.4)**

Applying Knowledge on the Job

Use your critical-thinking skills to answer the following questions.

1. Mr. Jones has just been diagnosed with diabetes insipidus by the physician you work for.
   a. Describe the signs and symptoms Mr. Jones presented with. **(LO 40.1, 40.3)**
   b. What drug should Mr. Jones be prescribed? **(LO 40.1, 40.3)**
   c. Use the *Physicians' Desk Reference* (*PDR*) to advise Mr. Jones about precautions and adverse reactions when taking this drug. **(LO 40.3)**

2. Mrs. Smith has been in labor for 12 hours. Her contractions are frequent and regular but not strong enough to advance the birth process. Mrs. Smith is becoming extremely fatigued. Her doctor has recommended oxytocin.
   a. How should the oxytocin be administered? **(LO 40.4)**
   b. What drugs would you look for in Mrs. Smith's chart to see if there might be drug interactions with the oxytocin? **(LO 40.2, 40.4)**
   c. What signs and symptoms would you look for in Mrs. Smith as you monitor her for adverse reactions? **(LO 40.4)**
   d. What signs of adverse reactions would you look for in the newborn? **(LO 40.4)**

3. Lila has called with an inquiry. Several weeks ago, her physician gave her a prescription for *Diapid* nasal spray. The directions on the label read "Use 1 to 2 sprays in each nostril 3 times a day." Her physician told her that she could increase her dose every week if she needed to, depending on her symptoms. She started using only one spray in each nostril; after a week she used two sprays in each nostril in the

morning and at night and only one spray in the afternoon. After one week she increased it to two sprays in each nostril morning, noon, and night. Now it's been a week and she needs to increase the dose again, but she can't remember how the doctor told her to do it. She wants to know the correct way to increase it. Should she increase it by one or two sprays each dose? What is the most sprays she should use at a time? (LO 40.3)

4. Diabetes insipidus can be treated with *DDAVP*. This is also approved for other indications. What are these indications? (LO 40.3)

5. A patient calls. She thinks she may be experiencing a drug allergy. She was given *Methergine* after her miscarriage. After several doses, her fingers and toes are tingling as if they were falling asleep, and they are cold to the touch. Her bleeding is minimal and she wants to know if she should stop taking the medication and start taking *Benadryl*. She has some at home from when she had an allergic reaction last year. (LO 40.4)

Multiple Choice

Use your critical-thinking skills to answer the following questions.

1. Which hormone is synthesized in the hypothalamus and released from the posterior pituitary? (LO 40.1)
   A. insulin
   B. thyroxine
   C. cortisol
   D. oxytocin

2. Which of these symptoms would lead the physician to diagnose diabetes insipidus? (LO 40.1, 40.3)
   A. edema
   B. low blood pressure
   C. large volume of dilute urine
   D. glucose in the urine

3. During parturition oxytocin (LO 40.2, 40.4)
   A. stimulates uterine muscle contraction
   B. increases urine output
   C. inhibits preterm labor
   D. decreases urine output

4. The route by which desmopressin acetate is administered is (LO 40.1, 40.3)
   A. intramuscular
   B. subcutaneous
   C. orally
   D. intranasally

5. Control of bleeding after delivery is achieved with (LO 40.4)
   A. oxytocics
   B. prostaglandins
   C. dinoprost
   D. methylergonovine

Multiple Choice (Multiple Answer)

Select the correct choices for each statement. The choices may be all correct, all incorrect, or any combination.

1. Choose all of the actions of antidiuretic hormone on the body. **(LO 40.1)**
   A. it increases urine output
   B. it regulates water balance
   C. the kidneys are its target organ
   D. its secretion is controlled by nerve reflexes

2. Which of the following are true? **(LO 40.1, 40.2)**
   A. oxytocin and ADH are both polypeptides
   B. ADH is the only hormone secreted from the posterior pituitary
   C. the release of ADH and oxytocin is caused by another hormone
   D. ADH and oxytocin both travel down nerve axons

3. Which of the following are causes of diabetes insipidus? **(LO 40.3)**
   A. increased ADH
   B. renal disease
   C. tumors of the thyroid gland
   D. head trauma

4. Select the most frequent side effects of vasopressin. **(LO 40.3)**
   A. nausea
   B. diarrhea
   C. nephrosis
   D. polydipsia

5. The uses of oxytocics include **(LO 40.4)**
   A. control of postpartum bleeding
   B. decreasing contractions
   C. inducing therapeutic abortions
   D. uterine tetany

Sequencing

Place the following steps of the breast-feeding response of oxytocin in order from last to first. **(LO 40.2)**

_____   _____   _____   _____   _____

Last   **First**

signal travels through spinal cord

ejection of milk

release of oxytocin

stimulation of nerve endings

oxytocin travels to myoepithelial cells

Classification

Place the following medications under the correct use. **(LO 40.2, 40.3)**

Prostin E$_2$
Ergotrate Maleate
Pitressin
Mefiprex
Methergine
DDAVP

Diabetes insipidus	Abortifacient	Postpartum hemorrhage

Matching

Match the following terms with their correct definitions. **(LO 40.1, 40.2, 40.3, 40.4)**

a. endogenous
b. exogenous
c. hypertonic
d. hypotonic
e. polydipsia
f. polyuria

1. _____ increased urine output
2. _____ originating within the body
3. _____ condition of greater concentration than inside the cells
4. _____ originating from outside the body
5. _____ condition of lesser concentration than inside the cells
6. _____ increased thirst

Documentation

The ER admissions sheet lists the following symptoms:

Symptoms:
Pregnant female
28 weeks gestation
regular contractions

Using the ER symptoms listed, answer the following questions. **(LO 40.2, 40.4)**

a. What condition may result from these premature contractions?
b. What type of medications would likely be administered?
c. How do these drugs work to help this condition?
d. Are there any side effects of these medications that should be monitored?

Labeling

Fill in the missing labels. **(LO 40.1)**

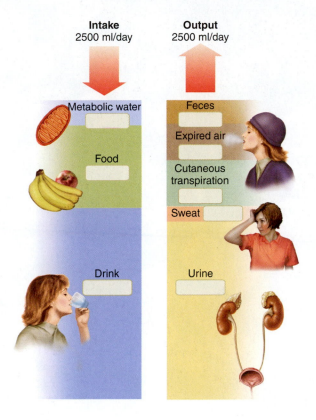

Intake
2500 ml/day

Output
2500 ml/day

Metabolic water

Food

Drink

Feces

Expired air

Cutaneous transpiration

Sweat

Urine

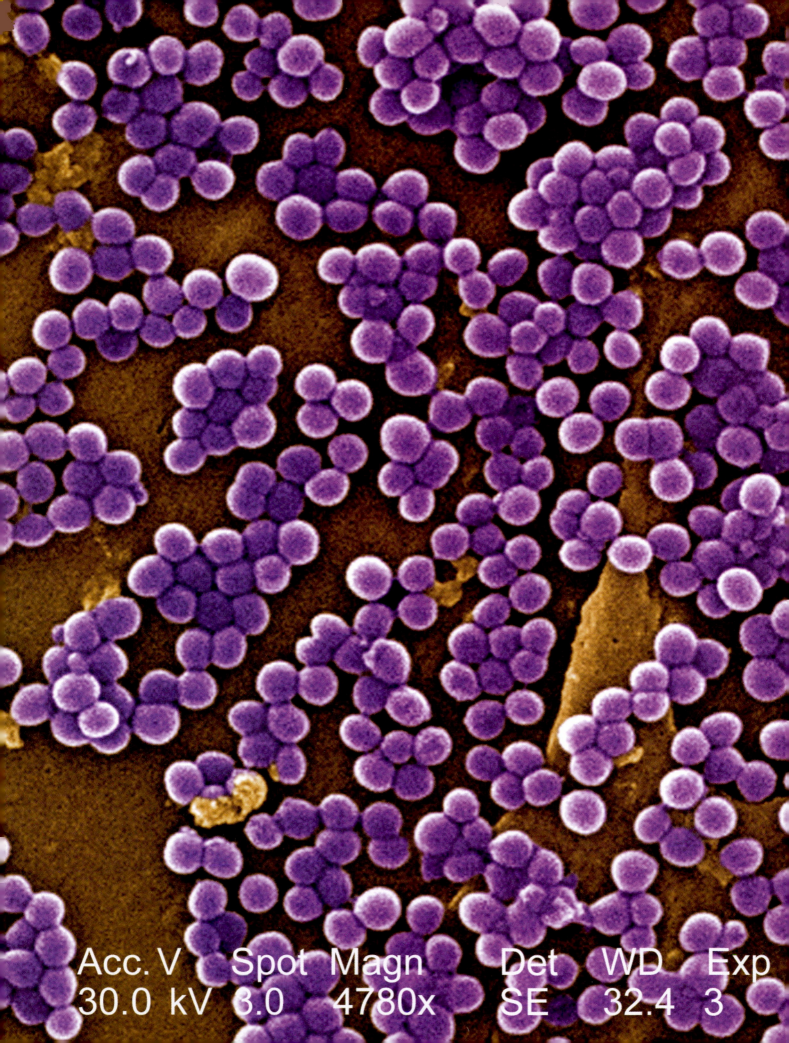

Acc. V   Spot Magn   Det   WD   Exp
30.0 kV   3.0   4780x   SE   32.4   3

Pharmacology of Infectious Diseases

Chapter 41

Antibacterial Agents

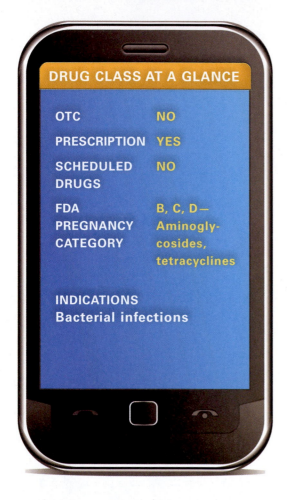

DRUG CLASS AT A GLANCE

OTC	NO
PRESCRIPTION	YES
SCHEDULED DRUGS	NO
FDA PREGNANCY CATEGORY	B, C, D— Aminoglycosides, tetracyclines

INDICATIONS
Bacterial infections

KEY TERMS

antibacterial spectrum: bacteria that are susceptible to the antibacterial actions of a particular drug.

antibiotic: antibacterial drug obtained from other microorganisms.

antibiotic susceptibility: identification of the antibiotics, by bacterial culture and sensitivity testing, that will be effective against specific bacteria.

antimicrobial: antibacterial drugs obtained by chemical synthesis and not from other microorganisms.

bacteria: single-celled microorganisms, some of which cause disease.

bacterial resistance: ability of some bacteria to resist the actions of antibiotics.

bactericidal: antibiotic that kills bacteria.

bacteriostatic: antibiotic that inhibits the growth of, but does not kill, bacteria.

beta-lactamases: bacterial enzymes that inactivate penicillin and cephalosporin antibiotics.

broad-spectrum: drug that is effective against a wide variety of both gram-positive and gram-negative pathogenic bacteria.

cephalosporinases: bacterial enzymes that inactivate cephalosporin antibiotics.

chemoprophylaxis: use of antibiotics to prevent infection, usually before a surgical procedure or in patients at risk for infection.

chemotherapy: use of drugs to kill or inhibit the growth of infectious organisms or cancer cells.

gram negative: bacteria that retain only the red stain in a gram stain.

gram positive: bacteria that retain only the purple stain in a gram stain.

gram stain: method of staining and identifying bacteria using crystal violet (purple) and safranin (red) stains.

pathogenic: type of bacteria that cause disease.

penicillinase: bacterial enzymes that inactivate penicillin antibiotics.

Introduction

Microbiology is the study of microscopic organisms of either animal (bacteria and protozoa) or plant (fungi and molds) origin. **Bacteria** are single-cell organisms that are found virtually everywhere. Bacteria that cause disease are called **pathogenic** and those that do not are nonpathogenic.

There are no bacteria in the internal environment of the body. However, there are many different types of bacteria, including pathogens, in the externally exposed areas, such as the mouth, gastrointestinal (GI) tract, nose, upper respiratory passages, and skin. Therefore, the potential for bacterial invasion always exists. However, even when bacteria enter the body, the normal body defense mechanisms (skin, leukocytes, immune system) function to protect and prevent the development of infection. When the skin or other body tissues break down, bacteria penetrate into the internal body tissues and set up areas of infection. Bacteria produce toxins that cause inflammation, tissue damage, fever, and other symptoms associated with infection. The term *selective toxicity* is often used to describe the mechanisms of action of antibiotic drugs. This refers to the mechanism of action of most drugs to exert harmful effects on bacterial cells without harming human cells. Antimicrobials do cause adverse drug effects, but these are not usually directly related to the antibacterial mechanism of action.

MORPHOLOGY OF BACTERIA

There are thousands of different types of bacteria. Bacteria are generally classified by shape and arrangement. The basic bacterial shapes are spherical (cocci), rod-like (bacilli), and curved rods (spirilla). Some of the bacterial arrangements are in pairs (diplo), chains (strepto), or clusters (staphylo). Table 41:1 illustrates some of the more common bacterial arrangements.

It is necessary to stain bacteria in order to visualize and identify them. One of the most important bacteriological stains is the **gram stain,** which contains two dyes: crystal violet (purple) and safranin (red). Bacteria that retain only the purple stain are classified as **gram**

positive, whereas bacteria that retain only the red stain are **gram negative.** It is important to distinguish gram-positive from gram-negative organisms. The response to antibiotic therapy varies with the type of bacteria involved. Gram stains aid the accurate diagnosis and proper treatment of bacterial infections.

The normal procedure for bacterial identification involves taking some material from the infected area (throat swab, sputum, or urine) and growing the bacteria in a culture medium. After 24 to 48 hours the bacteria are stained. Identification is based on morphology and biochemical procedures. Newer biochemical diagnostic techniques are available for the immediate identification of some organisms.

Bacterial Morphology and Some Common Bacterial Arrangements

Bacterial form	Bacterial arrangement	Classification
Cocci		
Pairs		Diplococci
Chains		Streptococci
Clusters		Staphylococci
Bacilli		
Straight		Bacilli
Short curved		Vibrio
Spirillum		
Twisted		Spirilla
Twisted		Borrelia
Twisted		Treponema

In addition to identification, it is frequently important to determine which chemotherapeutic drugs will be most effective against the specific bacteria that are causing the infection. Identification of the antibiotics that are effective against specific bacteria is referred to as **antibiotic susceptibility.** Two of the simplest methods to determine antibiotic susceptibility are the disk test and serial dilution. In each case, the bacteria are cultured in media that contain various antibacterial drugs. The drug with the greatest sensitivity will produce the greatest inhibition of bacterial growth. This screening method indicates which drug should produce the best clinical results in eradicating the infection. Bacterial identification and determination of antibiotic susceptibility are commonly referred to as culture and sensitivity testing.

LO 41.2

CHEMOTHERAPY

Chemotherapy refers to the use of drugs to kill or to inhibit the growth of infectious organisms or cancerous cells. Antibacterial agents are divided into two main types: bactericidal and bacteriostatic. **Bactericidal** drugs are lethal; that is, they actually kill the bacteria. **Bacteriostatic** drugs inhibit the reproduction (growth) of bacteria. With bacteriostatic drugs, elimination of the pathogenic bacteria is more dependent upon phagocytosis by host leukocytes and macrophages, and other actions of the immune system.

Sources of Antibacterial Drugs

Antibacterial drugs are obtained from two major sources: soil microorganisms and chemical synthesis. Bacteria and other microorganisms naturally produce substances that inhibit the growth of other bacteria. In nature, these substances help protect specific types of bacteria from the harmful chemical substances released by other bacteria. These chemical substances obtained from microorganisms and used in chemotherapy are referred to as **antibiotics.** For example, the mold *Penicillium notatum* produces a substance that inhibits the growth of many gram-positive, pathogenic bacteria. This substance, known as penicillin, is the parent compound of some of the most widely used antibiotic drugs. Some antibacterial drugs, such as the sulfonamides, are produced by chemical synthesis. Antibacterial drugs that are obtained by chemical synthesis and not from other microorganisms are referred to as **antimicrobial** drugs. However, the term *antibiotic* is commonly used to describe all of these drugs.

Antibacterial Spectrum

Very few, if any, antibacterial drugs inhibit the growth of all pathogenic bacteria. Each antibacterial drug is generally effective for only a limited number of pathogenic bacteria. These susceptible bacteria make up the **antibacterial spectrum** for that particular drug. Some drugs are effective against a limited number of bacteria, for example, only some gram-positive or only some gram-negative bacteria. These drugs are characterized as having a narrow antibacterial spectrum. Other drugs are effective against a wide spectrum of both gram-positive and gram-negative bacteria. These drugs are referred to as **broad-spectrum** antibiotics.

Drug Resistance

During chemotherapy, an antibiotic may occasionally lose its effectiveness. This usually occurs when the bacteria undergo some structural or metabolic alteration or mutation that allows the bacteria to survive the actions of the antibiotic. The ability of bacteria to resist the actions of antibiotics is referred to as **bacterial resistance.** One cause of bacterial resistance involves the ability of bacteria to alter the outer cell wall so that antibiotics can no longer penetrate the bacteria. In addition, some bacteria produce enzymes that inactivate the antibiotic (see below). When resistance occurs, the bacteria are able to survive and reproduce in the presence of the drug. Some resistant bacteria may already be present within the infection. As the nonresistant bacteria are eliminated by the antibiotic, the resistant bacteria begin to multiply rapidly and are then responsible for continuation of the infection. When drug resistance occurs, another antibacterial drug that the bacteria are sensitive to must be substituted.

Bacterial Beta-Lactamase Enzymes

Certain bacteria have the ability to produce enzymes that inactivate penicillin and cephalosporin antibiotics. These enzymes are referred to generally as **beta-lactamases.** Beta-lactamases that inactivate penicillins are referred to as **penicillinases.** Beta-lactamases that inactivate cephalosporins are referred to as **cephalosporinases.** Other types of bacterial enzymes are also produced that can inactivate other antibiotics.

Chemoprophylaxis

Chemoprophylaxis refers to the use of antibiotics before bacterial infection has developed in order to prevent infection. Chemoprophylaxis is indicated before certain surgeries that carry a high risk for infection; for example, abdominal surgery, especially after gunshot or stab wounds where the intestines may be ruptured. In addition, individuals who are susceptible to certain infections that may be life-threatening often take antibiotics on a regular basis to prevent infection. Individuals who have had rheumatic fever, heart valve replacement, knee and hip replacement, and other conditions are particularly susceptible to infections that can cause endocarditis and heart valve damage. These individuals should receive chemoprophylaxis before dental, respiratory, urinary, and other invasive medical procedures. In addition, individuals exposed to patients with tuberculosis, meningitis, and other contagious infections are often given chemoprophylaxis to prevent infection. The selection and timing of antibiotic administration depends on the type of infection that is anticipated, patient characteristics, and other considerations related to the specific clinical situation.

Patient Administration and Monitoring

Explain to patients the importance of following the directions on the prescription label for administration of the antibiotic. Many patients skip or stop taking the antibiotic once they start feeling better and their symptoms are no longer present. Completing the full course of therapy is important for preventing recurrence of the infection.

Inform patients of the potential adverse drug effects associated with the antibiotic they have been prescribed. Antibiotics administered orally often cause nausea, vomiting, and diarrhea. Antibiotics can disturb the normal bacterial flora of the large intestines and cause cramps and diarrhea. Uncontrollable diarrhea may indicate development of a superinfection and the patient should be instructed to notify the physician if this or any other serious or unusual adverse effect occurs.

Inform patients if the antibiotic they are prescribed can be taken with food. Small amounts of food may prevent nausea and stomach upset. However, there are food-drug interactions with some of the antibiotics. For example, absorption and bioavailability of tetracyclines and fluoroquinolones can be reduced by dairy products and antacids. The instructions from the pharmacy that accompany the prescription will provide this information.

Warn patients that this prescription is to be used only for the current infection and not for any other infection or condition they may experience.

PENICILLINS

Penicillin is an antibiotic obtained from various species of *Penicillium* mold. Alteration of the basic structure and the addition of various salts have provided numerous penicillin preparations. The main differences between the various preparations involve differences in acid stability (in the stomach), resistance to enzymatic destruction by penicillinase, and antibacterial spectrum.

Mechanism of Action

The term *beta-lactam* is used to classify the penicillin, cephalosporin, carbapenem, and monobactam antibiotics. These antibiotics all contain a four-sided chemical ring, the beta-lactam ring (Figure 41.1). This ring is essential for the bactericidal action of these antibiotics.

Figure 41.1

Comparative Structural Formulas of Beta-Lactam Antibiotics

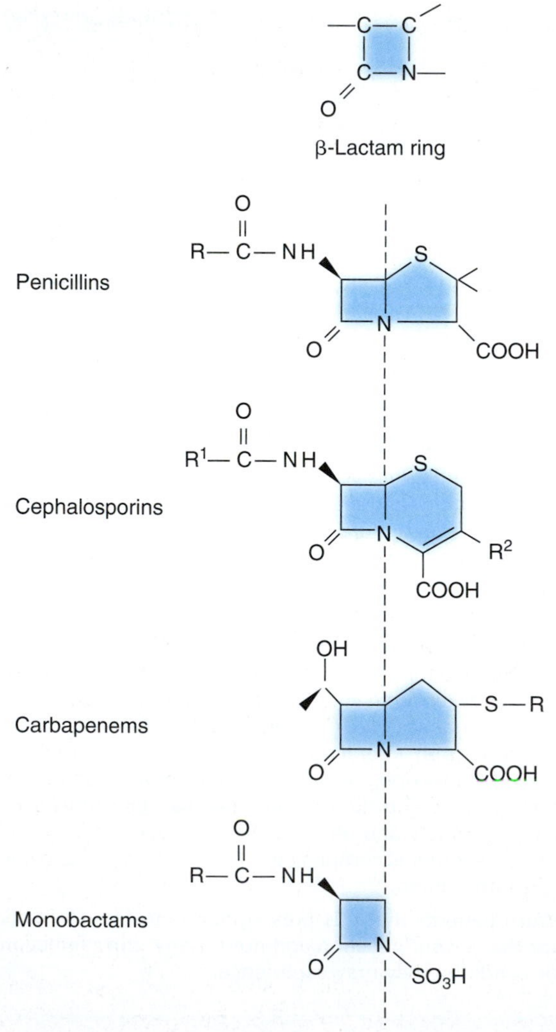

The beta-lactam ring binds to and inhibits bacterial enzymes (referred to as penicillin-binding proteins, PBPs) that are necessary for bacterial cell-wall synthesis. The action of the antibiotics leads to the formation of defective cell walls that cause the bacteria to release autolytic enzymes. These autolytic enzymes cause bacterial cell lysis and death. This mechanism of action is common to all the beta-lactam antibiotics. Resistant bacteria are able to produce enzymes, beta-lactamases, that break open the beta-lactam ring. When this occurs, the antibiotic is no longer able to inhibit the PBPs and the bacteria continue to form new cell walls and multiply.

Antibacterial Spectrum

The penicillins are divided into several different groups based on their spectrum of activity. The current classification system divides the penicillins into four generations (Table 41:2).

First-Generation Penicillins

This group includes penicillin G and penicillin V, which have a narrow antibacterial spectrum. They are effective against common gram-positive staphylococcal and streptococcal organisms. Unfortunately, most *Staphylococcus aureus* bacteria are penicillinase-producers and resistant to most penicillins. Streptococcal bacteria, including *Streptococcus pyogenes* and *Streptococcus pneumoniae* (Figure 41.2), that are often the cause of ear-nose-throat and respiratory infections are usually sensitive to these penicillins. Penicillin G is usually administered parenterally, while penicillin V is taken orally for minor ear-nose-throat infections. First-generation penicillins are not effective against gram-negative bacilli (rods) or organisms that produce penicillinase.

Another subgroup of first-generation penicillins is resistant to penicillinase and is indicated primarily for the treatment of resistant staphylococcal (staph) infections. Staph infections, caused mainly by *Staphylococcus aureus,* cause abscesses and other serious infections (endocarditis and pneumonia). Staph infections are often difficult to treat because there is a high incidence of bacterial resistance due to penicillinase production among staph bacteria. These drugs are listed in Table 41:2 as penicillinase resistant.

Methicillin is a penicillin that in the past was the most effective penicillin against resistant staphylococcal infections. However, a strain of *Staphylococcus aureus* evolved over the years that became resistant to methicillin. The resistance is not due to penicillinase; rather, it is due to alterations in the penicillin-binding proteins (PBPs) that reduce the binding of the beta-lactams. This strain is known as methicillin-resistant *Staphylococcus*

Penicillin, Carbapenem, and Monobactam Antibiotics

Drug (*Trade Name*)	Route	Remarks
First generation		**Main indication: Gram-positive infections**
Penicillin G (*Pfizerpen*)	IM, IV	Produces high plasma levels, short duration of action
Penicillin G benzathine (*Bicillin*)	IM	Penicillin G is slowly released from injection site over 28 days, provides low plasma levels
Penicillin G procaine (*Wycillin*)	IM	Penicillin G is slowly released from injection site over 12–24 hr
Penicillin V (*V-Cillin, Pen-Vee K*)	PO	Resists acid destruction in stomach; used to treat minor throat and ear infections
Penicillinase resistant		**Main indication: Resistant staphylococcal infections**
Cloxacillin (*Tegopen*)	PO	Resistance to the destructive actions of penicillinase; used to treat resistant staphylococcal infections
Dicloxacillin (*Dynapen*)	PO	
Nafcillin (*Unipen*)	IM, IV	
Oxacillin (*Prostaphlin*)	PO, IM, IV	
Second generation		**Main indication: Gram-positive/common gram-negative**
Amoxicillin (*Amoxil*)	PO	**Infections** (e.g., *E. coli, Haemophilus influenzae*)
Amoxicillin/clavulanic acid (*Augmentin*)	PO	Broader spectrum than first generation; amoxicillin
Ampicillin (*Omnipen*)	PO, IM, IV	provides higher plasma levels; *Augmentin* and *Unasyn*
Ampicillin/sulbactam (*Unasyn*)	IM, IV	indicated when penicillinase-producing bacteria present
Third generation		**Main indication: Serious gram-negative infections**
		(e.g., *Proteus vulgaris, Pseudomonas aeruginosa*)
Carbenicillin indanyl (*Geocillin*)	PO	Only for the treatment of urinary tract infections
Ticarcillin disodium (*Ticar*)	IM, IV	Broad spectrum, generally reserved for pseudomonal
Ticarcillin/clavulanic acid (*Timentin*)	IM, IV	and other serious gram-negative infections; *Timentin* for resistant infections
Fourth generation		**Main indication: Serious gram-negative infections**
Mezlocillin sodium (*Mezlin*)	IM, IV	(e.g., *Klebsella pneumoniae, Pseudomonas aeruginosa*)
Piperacillin (*Pipracil*)	IM, IV	Increased effectiveness compared to third-generation
Piperacillin/tazobactam (*Zosyn*)	IV	drugs; also effective against gram-positive and anaerobic infections; *Zosyn* indicated for resistant infections
Carbapenems		**Main indication: Serious gram-negative infections**
Doripenem (*Doribax*)	IV	Also effective against gram-positive and anaerobic
Ertapenem (*Invanz*)	IM, IV	organisms, increased resistance to beta-lactamases;
Imipenem/cilastin (*Primaxin*)	IV	should not be used in patients allergic to penicillins
Meropenem (*Merrem*)	IV	
Monobactams		**Main indication: Serious gram-negative infections**
Aztreonam (*Azactam*)	IV	Aztreonam is not effective against gram-positive and anaerobic organisms, is highly resistant to beta-lactamase enzymes, may be used in patients allergic to penicillins

aureus or MRSA (Figure 41.3). Infections caused by this organism have become a major problem, especially in the hospital setting. None of the penicillins are effective against MRSA and only a few other antibiotics have demonstrated effectiveness against this organism. Because of its toxicity, methicillin is no longer available.

Second-Generation Penicillins

The second-generation penicillins include ampicillin and amoxicillin that have an extended spectrum. The second-generation drugs are effective against the same organisms as penicillin G plus a number of common gram-negative organisms. The gram-negative organisms

Figure 41.2

A Photomicrograph of a Gram Stain from a Patient with Pneumonia due to *Streptococcus pneumoniae*

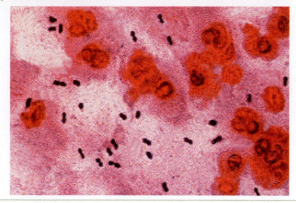

Notice the gram-positive diplococci and the presence of a large number of polymorphonuclear leukocytes (red stain).

Figure 41.3

A Scanning Electron Micrograph of Methicillin-Resistant *Staphylococcus aureus* (MRSA) Bacteria

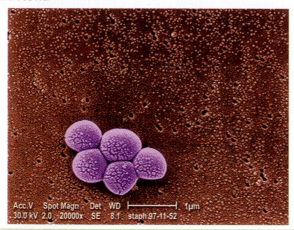

This organism was also resistant to vancomycin. Notice the increase in cell wall material seen as clumps on the organisms' surface.

include *Escherichia coli, Proteus mirabilis,* and *Haemophilus influenzae,* which are responsible for common urinary, respiratory, and ear infections. All second-generation penicillins can be taken orally, which is an important advantage in the treatment of a variety of common gram-positive and gram-negative infections. Amoxicillin is widely used because it is well absorbed from the GI tract and produces higher plasma drug levels than does ampicillin.

When used alone, second-generation penicillins are not effective against penicillinase-producing organisms,

and in recent years, greater numbers and percentages of organisms produce penicillinase, which inactivates the penicillin molecule. However, combinations of the second-generation penicillins with drugs known as beta-lactamase inhibitors are available and are effective against penicillinase-producing bacteria (see below).

Third-Generation Penicillins

The third-generation penicillins include carbenicillin and ticarcillin, which have a broader spectrum than do the second-generation drugs. The main indication for these penicillins is in the treatment of more serious urinary, respiratory, and bacteremic infections caused by gram-negative organisms such as *Pseudomonas aeruginosa* and *Proteus vulgaris.* These infections are often difficult to treat and may require combination therapy with the aminoglycoside antibiotics. Carbenicillin indanyl (*Geocillin*) is administered orally and is only indicated for the treatment of urinary tract infections. Ticarcillin (*Ticar*) is administered parenterally (IM, IV) for the treatment of systemic infections. These drugs are not resistant to penicillinase-producing organisms. Ticarcillin is available in combination with clavulanic acid (beta-lactamase inhibitor) and is effective against penicillinase-producing organisms.

Fourth-Generation Penicillins

These drugs have a wider antibacterial spectrum than do third-generation penicillins, are more effective (potent), and are administered in the form of monosodium salts. This form reduces the amount of sodium ingested compared to the third-generation penicillins that are disodium salts. This may be important for individuals with hypertension or congestive heart failure who are usually on sodium-restricted diets.

The antibacterial spectrum of the fourth-generation drugs includes gram-positive, gram-negative, and anaerobic organisms. The main indication is for serious infections caused by *Pseudomonas aeruginosa, Proteus vulgaris, Klebsiella pneumoniae,* and *Bacteroides fragilis* (anaerobe). These infections also can be difficult to treat and may require combination therapy. The fourth-generation penicillins are not resistant to penicillinase-producing organisms, and they require parenteral administration. Piperacillin is available with tazobactam, another beta-lactamase inhibitor, and is effective against penicillinase-producers.

Beta-Lactamase Inhibitors

There still is not a single penicillin that combines all of the following: can be taken orally, has a broad spectrum, and is resistant to penicillinase. However, several drugs, known as beta-lactamase inhibitors, can be administered along with the various penicillins. These drugs inhibit the penicillinase enzymes and allow the penicillin drug to remain effective. These inhibitors include clavulanic acid, sulbactam, and tazobactam. Combinations of the various penicillins plus inhibitor are marketed together. Amoxicillin plus clavulanic acid is marketed as *Augmentin,* ampicillin is combined with sulbactam in *Unasyn,* and piperacillin is combined with tazobactam in *Zosyn.* These antibiotic combinations are indicated when bacterial resistance is present.

Adverse Effects

As a group, the penicillins are relatively nontoxic. Minor adverse effects, such as nausea or rashes, may occur in some patients. Diarrhea is more common with oral administration. Intramuscular injections of the penicillins are usually painful and may cause inflammation at the site of injection. When used in very high doses, the penicillins can cause central nervous system (CNS) disturbances, including convulsions.

The most serious adverse effect involves individuals who develop an allergy to penicillin. As a drug class, the penicillins cause the highest incidence of drug allergy. Common delayed-type allergic reactions include rashes, fever, and inflammatory conditions. The most serious immediate-type allergic reaction involves anaphylaxis or anaphylactic shock. All patients must be questioned about the possibility of penicillin allergy. In cases of suspected allergy, skin sensitivity testing can be performed to determine whether patients are allergic to penicillin. Patients allergic to one penicillin are considered allergic to all of the penicillin drugs.

Carbapenems and Monobactams

Carbapenems and monobactams are beta-lactam antibiotics structurally similar to the penicillins. The antibacterial spectrum of the carbapenems is broad and similar to the fourth-generation penicillins. In addition, carbapenems have increased resistance to bacterial beta-lactamases. Imipenem is combined with cilastin, a drug that slows the renal metabolism of imipenem. Doripenem, ertapenem, and meropenem are other carbapenem drugs. As with the fourth-generation penicillins, carbapenems are administered parenterally. Adverse effects are similar to those of the penicillins.

Aztreonam is classified as a monobactam and is highly resistant to penicillinase and administered intravenously for resistant gram-negative infections. It is not active against gram-positive or anaerobic organisms. Aztreonam can usually be used in individuals who are allergic to penicillin. Gastrointestinal disturbances and rash are common adverse reactions.

CEPHALOSPORINS

The cephalosporins are bactericidal antibiotics that have chemical structures similar to those of the penicillins. The mechanism of action of the cephalosporins is the same as that of the penicillins. The cephalosporins are usually more resistant than the penicillins to the bacterial beta-lactamase enzymes. They are used as substitutes for penicillins in cases of allergy or bacterial resistance and in the treatment of certain gram-negative infections.

Bacterial Resistance to Cephalosporins

Some organisms, usually gram negative, can produce cephalosporinase. The cephalosporins are ineffective against organisms that produce these beta-lactamase enzymes. The cephalosporins are also classified into four generations and are listed in Table 41:3.

First-Generation Cephalosporins

These antibiotics are considered to be the older cephalosporins. They all have a similar antibacterial spectrum, which includes both some gram-positive and some gram-negative organisms. The cephalosporins are the drugs of choice for treating infections caused by gram-negative *Klebsiella pneumoniae.* Of this group, cephalexin (*Keflex*) and cefazolin (*Kefzol*) are the most frequently used drugs. Cefazolin is also the preferred drug administered for chemoprophylaxis. The first-generation cephalosporins are useful for most of the common gram-positive and gram-negative infections that cause ear, nose, throat, and urinary tract infections.

Second-Generation Cephalosporins

These cephalosporins have a broader spectrum than the first-generation drugs and are generally more potent. They are indicated when first-generation drugs are ineffective. Cefoxitin (*Mefoxin*) is especially useful in treating infections caused by *Bacteroides fragilis* and *Serratia marcescens.* Also, these drugs are often effective in treating respiratory and other infections caused by *Haemophilus influenzae* and *Neisseria gonorrhoeae,* including organisms that produce penicillinase and that are often resistant to penicillins.

Third-Generation Cephalosporins

These drugs have a broader spectrum than do the second-generation drugs. They are more potent antibiotics, and they have longer durations of action than do the other cephalosporins. Ceftriaxone has a half-life of approximately 8 hours and can be administered once daily for

Cephalosporin Antibiotics

Drug (*Trade Name*)	Route	Remarks
First generation		
Cefadroxil (*Duricef*)	PO	Used to treat common gram-positive and gram-negative infections, including *Klebsiella pneumoniae*; cefazolin is preferred for chemoprophylaxis
Cefazolin (*Kefzol*)	IM, IV	
Cephalexin (*Keflex*)	PO	
Cephradine (*Velosef*)	PO, IV	
Second generation		
Cefaclor (*Ceclor*)	PO	Indicated primarily for gram-negative infections; are more resistant to the actions of beta-lactamases; increased activity against *N. gonorrhoeae, H. influenzae,* and *K. pneumoniae*
Cefonicid (*Monocid*)	IM, IV	
Cefotetan (*Cefotan*)	IM, IV	
Cefoxitin (*Mefoxin*)	IM, IV	
Cefprozil (*Cefzil*)	PO	
Cefuroxime (*Ceftin*)	PO, IV	
Loracarbef (*Lorabid*)	PO	
Third generation		
Cefdinir (*Omnicef*)	PO	Indicated for serious gram-negative infections that are resistant to other cephalosporins; increased activity against *K. pneumoniae, P. aeruginosa*; ceftriaxone is lipid soluble and penetrates the blood-brain barrier for use in meningitis; ceftriaxone also has the longest half-life and is the drug of choice for resistant gonorrhea
Cefixime (*Suprax*)	PO	
Cefoperazone (*Cefobid*)	IM, IV	
Cefotaxime (*Claforan*)	IM, IV	
Ceftazidime (*Fortaz*)	IM, IV	
Ceftriaxone (*Rocephin*)	IM, IV	
Fourth generation		
Cefepime (*Maxipime*)	IM, IV	Similar to third generation; broad-spectrum activity; demonstrates greater resistance to beta-lactamase inactivating enzymes; indicated when there is resistance to third-generation cephalosporins

most infections. The third-generation cephalosporins are mainly indicated for the treatment of serious gram-negative infections that are not susceptible to second-generation drugs. These drugs are also more lipid soluble and cross the blood-brain barrier more readily than most other penicillins and cephalosporins. Consequently, they are often used for both gram-positive and gram-negative infections involving the brain (meningitis).

Fourth-Generation Cephalosporins

Cefepime (*Maxipime*) has been classified as the fourth generation of cephalosporins. It is similar in spectrum to the third-generation drugs; the main feature is greater resistance to beta-lactamase inactivating enzymes. It is indicated when the lower generations of cephalosporins are ineffective.

Adverse Effects

Oral cephalosporins may cause GI disturbances, especially diarrhea and rashes. Intramuscular injections with the cephalosporins are usually painful and may cause local inflammation. Intravenous administration may cause phlebitis at the infusion site. The first-generation cephalosporins may cause nephrotoxicity, especially in patients with renal impairment or in patients who are dehydrated. In comparison, the newer cephalosporins are associated with a lower incidence of nephrotoxicity.

Cephalosporins that possess the N-methylthiotetrazone side chain (cefamandole, cefoperazone, cefotetan, others) may interfere with blood coagulation and cause bleeding problems. In addition, these same drugs can cause a disulfiram reaction when combined with alcohol and patients must be warned to avoid any alcohol consumption when taking these drugs (see Chapter 12).

Cephalosporins do cause allergic reactions, but the incidence of allergy with cephalosporins is lower than that with the penicillins. Some individuals are allergic to both penicillins and cephalosporins. Usually, cephalosporins can be used in patients who are allergic to penicillins. The guiding principle is that cephalosporins are not administered to penicillin-allergic individuals who have previously experienced the immediate type of penicillin allergic reaction (hives, anaphylaxis).

AMINOGLYCOSIDES

The aminoglycosides are a group of bactericidal antibiotics whose antibacterial spectrum mainly includes gram-negative bacilli. The aminoglycosides passively diffuse through the outer cell wall of bacteria and are then actively transported through the cell membrane into the cytoplasm. This process requires oxygen and, consequently, the aminoglycosides are not active against anaerobic organisms. Aminoglycosides bind irreversibly to bacterial ribosomes and cause irreversible inhibition of bacterial protein synthesis. The bacteria can no longer produce the enzymes and proteins necessary for survival and reproduction. Aminoglycosides do have some gram-positive activity and are often administered in combination with one of the penicillins or cephalosporins in the treatment of serious gram-positive and gram-negative infections. The combination produces a synergistic bactericidal action.

Pharmacokinetics

The aminoglycosides are poorly absorbed from the GI tract, and this effect is used to advantage before intestinal surgery. Large doses are given orally before abdominal surgery to reduce the number of intestinal bacteria and "sterilize the bowel." The usual route of administration for systemic effects is either IM or IV. These drugs are effective against most gram-negative organisms and generally reserved for the treatment of serious gram-negative infections in hospitalized patients. The aminoglycosides are not significantly metabolized and are excreted mostly unchanged in the urine. Consequently, high urinary concentrations are attained, which can decrease renal function. Patients with renal disease usually require a reduction in dosage. The most frequently used aminoglycosides are listed in Table 41:4.

Adverse Effects

When taken orally, the aminoglycosides may cause nausea, vomiting, and diarrhea. When administered parenterally, the two most serious adverse effects are nephrotoxicity and ototoxicity. Because of the high urinary levels, the aminoglycosides may interfere with normal renal function. Increased casts, albuminuria (protein in the urine), and oliguria (reduced urine output) may occur. The aminoglycosides interfere with the function of the auditory nerve (cranial nerve VIII). The earliest symptoms are tinnitus (ringing in the ears) and temporary impairment of hearing; this is generally referred to as ototoxicity. In some cases, in which the aminoglycosides were taken for extended periods, irreversible damage and permanent hearing loss has occurred.

Cautions and Contraindications
Pregnancy
Aminoglycosides are designated Food and Drug Administration (FDA) Pregnancy Category D and should not be used during pregnancy. The aminioglycosides have

[Table **41:4**]

Aminoglycoside Antibiotics	
Drug (*Trade Name*)	**Remarks**
Amikacin (*Amikin*)	Reserved for treatment of serious gram-negative infections, especially with bacteria resistant to tobramycin or gentamicin
Gentamicin (*Garamycin*)	Reserved for the treatment of serious gram-negative infections; produces a significant incidence of ototoxicity
Kanamycin (*Kantrex*)	Because of toxicity the use of kanamycin is now limited to oral administration before intestinal surgery to cleanse and sterilize the bowel
Neomycin	Used orally before intestinal surgery to cleanse and sterilize the bowel; topical preparations also available for treatment of skin and ocular infections
Spectinomycin (*Trobicin*)	Spectinomycin is structurally related to the aminoglycosides and administered IM for the treatment of resistant gonorrhea
Streptomycin	Used in the treatment of tuberculosis, plague, and tularemia
Tobramycin (*Nebcin*)	Reserved for the treatment of serious gram-negative infections, particularly *Pseudomonas aeruginosa*

been shown to cause fetal harm; in particular, hearing loss and deafness.

Drug Interactions

The aminoglycosides possess some peripheral neuromuscular blocking activity. Administration during surgery or other procedures in which general anesthetics or other neuromuscular blockers also are being used may produce excessive degrees of muscular blockade. The most serious effect would be respiratory arrest due to paralysis of the diaphragm and the other muscles of respiration.

The ototoxic effect of the aminoglycosides is increased when other ototoxic drugs, such as some diuretics (ethacrynic acid and furosemide), are administered at the same time. Combination therapy of other nephrotoxic drugs with cephalosporins may increase nephrotoxicity.

LO 41.6

TETRACYCLINES

The tetracyclines are broad-spectrum antibiotics that are actively taken up by bacteria. The tetracyclines are bacteriostatic; they bind reversibly to bacterial ribosomes to inhibit bacterial protein synthesis. The tetracyclines affect both gram-positive and gram-negative bacteria. However, widespread use over the years has allowed the emergence of bacterial resistance. Consequently, other drugs are now preferred for treatment of common gram-positive and gram-negative infections.

Administration

The tetracyclines are usually administered orally, but IM and IV injection may be used if necessary. Foods, especially those containing calcium (milk) and substances such as antacids and mineral supplements, interfere with the GI absorption of the tetracyclines. Since tetracyclines bind calcium molecules (chelate) and form insoluble compounds, tetracycline should be taken 1 hour before meals or several hours after meals.

Doxycycline and minocycline are more completely absorbed from the GI tract than are the other tetracyclines and are less affected by food. The tetracyclines are listed in Table 41:5.

Clinical Indications

The tetracyclines are occasional alternatives to the penicillins for many of the common gram-positive and gram-negative infections. However, the most important indications for the tetracyclines are for infections caused by *Rickettsiae* (Rocky Mountain spotted fever, typhus), *Mycoplasma pneumoniae, Vibrio cholerae* (cholera), *Chlamydia trachomatis* (urethritis), and *Borrelia burgdorferi* (Lyme disease). Tetracyclines also are used in combination with other antibiotics in the treatment of gastric and duodenal ulcers caused by *Helicobacter pylori.* In addition, the tetracyclines are sometimes used to treat lower respiratory infections that often contribute to chronic bronchitis.

Tigecycline (*Tygacil*) is structurally related to the tetracyclines. It has a broad antibacterial spectrum that includes resistant strains of staphylococcal (MRSA), enterococcal, and other organisms. Tigecycline is only available for IV administration.

Adverse Effects

The most common side effects associated with the tetracyclines are nausea, vomiting, and diarrhea. Suppression of normal intestinal bacteria may result in overgrowth of nonsusceptible organisms (superinfection), especially

[Table 41:5]

Tetracycline Antibiotics

Drug (*Trade Name*)	Usual adult oral dose	Remarks
Demeclocycline (*Declomycin*)	150 mg every 6 hr or 300 mg BID	Highest incidence of phototoxicity
Doxycycline (*Vibramycln*)	100 mg once per day	Most frequently used tetracycline; food does not affect absorption
Minocycline (*Minocin*)	100 mg every 12 hr	Highest incidence of vestibular side effects, dizziness, vertigo
Tetracycline (*Sumycin*)	250–500 mg every 6 hr	Absorption decreased by food, dairy products, and mineral ions
Tigecycline (*Tygacil*)	IV only, 100 mg loading dose, then 50 mg every 12 hr	Active against many resistant strains of gram-positive and gram-negative organisms

fungi (*Candida albicans*). These conditions usually produce diarrhea and various skin rashes. The tetracyclines also produce photosensitivity in some individuals. After ingestion of the tetracyclines and exposure to sunlight, an exaggerated sunburn may occur. The use of outdated tetracycline products may produce a particular type of reaction known as the Fanconi syndrome. The main effects of this syndrome involve the kidneys, where polyuria, proteinuria, and acidosis are most frequently observed.

Cautions and Contraindications
Pregnancy
The tetracyclines bind to calcium and therefore should not be administered to children below the age of 8 and to women who are pregnant or nursing. These drugs are deposited in growing bones and teeth, producing a yellow discoloration (mottling) and possible depression of bone growth. Tetracyclines are designated Food and Drug Administration (FDA) Pregnancy Category D and have been shown to cause growth retardation in relation to infant skeletal development.

LO 41.7
SULFONAMIDES

The sulfonamides are a group of synthetic drugs that were discovered in 1935 as a by-product of the dye industry. The first sulfonamide was sulfanilamide. Alteration of its basic structure produced many other compounds having similar activities. The sulfonamides were initially effective against many gram-positive and gram-negative organisms. Unfortunately, early widespread use of the sulfonamides led to the development of bacterial resistance. After introduction of the penicillins (early 1940s), use of the sulfonamides rapidly declined. Today, the sulfonamides have limited uses in selected infections. Some of the sulfonamides are used topically, especially in burn cases to prevent and treat infection. Other sulfonamides are used primarily for the treatment of urinary and GI tract infections.

Mechanism of Action
Bacteria have an essential requirement for *para*aminobenzoic acid, which is used in the synthesis of folic acid. The sulfonamides are competitive antagonists of *para*-aminobenzoic acid. The sulfonamides block the synthesis of folic acid, which subsequently inhibits bacterial growth, producing a bacteriostatic effect.

Administration
The most common route of administration is oral, although a parenteral route may be used. The main pathway of elimination is renal, and the sulfonamides tend to be concentrated in the urine. The various sulfonamides have different durations of action and generally are classified as short, intermediate, and long acting. In addition, because of their poor oral absorption, some sulfonamides are used to reduce intestinal bacteria before intestinal surgery. The sulfonamides are listed in Table 41:6.

[Table **41:6**]

Sulfonamide Antimicrobial Drugs

Drug (*Trade Name*)	Main uses	Comment
Mafenide (*Sulfamylon*)	In burn cases to prevent infection	Topical
Silver sulfadiazine	In burn cases to prevent infection	Topical
Sulfacetamide (*Sulamyd*)	Ocular infections	Topical
Sulfamethoxazole (generic)	Urinary tract infections	Intermediate acting
Sulfasalazine (*Azulfidine*)	Ulcerative colitis	Long acting
Sulfisoxazole (generic)	Urinary tract infections	Short acting
Trimethoprim-sulfamethoxazole (*Bactrim, Septra*)	Respiratory, urinary infections	Synergistic action

Adverse Effects

Oral administration frequently causes nausea, vomiting, and diarrhea. One of the more serious adverse effects is crystalluria. In the presence of dehydration and acidic urine, the sulfonamides have a tendency to crystallize in the renal tubules, causing cell damage, blood in the urine, and reduced urine output. Therefore, patients must receive adequate fluid intake, and urine should be made alkaline if it is highly acidic.

The sulfonamides also may produce allergic reactions, which usually are limited to the skin and mucous membranes. The most common reactions include rashes, pruritis, and photosensitivity. A very serious type of skin condition, the Stevens-Johnson syndrome, produces a skin reaction that can be fatal. Patients who develop any rash after ingestion of the sulfonamides must receive medical evaluation.

Blood disorders, including anemia, leukopenia, and thrombocytopenia, may develop with sulfonamide therapy. Patients with existing deficiency of glucose-6-phosphate dehydrogenase (G6PD) are particularly susceptible to the development of hemolytic anemia.

Drug Interactions

The sulfonamides may produce a number of drug interactions because of their ability to displace other drugs from inactive plasma protein-binding sites. The most frequent drug interactions involve the coumadin anticoagulants (increased anticoagulant effect) and the oral hypoglycemic drugs (hypoglycemia). Patients receiving sulfonamides and any of these drugs should be closely monitored for bleeding tendencies or hypoglycemic effects.

Trimethoprim-Sulfamethoxazole

This combination, marketed under the trade names of *Septra* and *Bactrim,* has broad-spectrum antimicrobial actions. It is a combination of one of the sulfonamides, sulfamethoxazole, and the drug trimethoprim. Trimethoprim inhibits the enzyme dihydrofolate reductase, which interferes with the further synthesis of folic acid to its activated form. Together, these two drugs exert a synergistic effect to inhibit folic acid production in bacteria that is very effective. Administration is either oral or parenteral in varying concentrations.

Clinical Indications

The sulfamethoxazole-trimethoprim combination is effective against a broad spectrum of gram-positive and gram-negative bacteria. It is often used as an alternative to the penicillins and cephalosporins for respiratory, urinary, GI, and other systemic infections. It is frequently the drug of choice for treatment of *Pneumocystis jiroveci* pneumonial infections, and ear, sinus, and pneumonial infections caused by *Haemophilus influenzae.*

The adverse effects of trimethoprim are generally similar to the sulfonamides; however, trimethoprim does not usually cause crystalluria.

MACROLIDE ANTIBIOTICS

The term *macrolide* refers to the large chemical ring structure that is characteristic of these antibiotics. These antibiotics inhibit bacterial protein synthesis and are considered bacteriostatic. The macrolides include erythromycin and several derivatives that cause less gastric irritation and have a wider antibacterial spectrum than erythromycin. The newer derivatives include azithromycin, clarithromycin, and dirithromycin. The most common adverse effect of these drugs is gastrointestinal irritation.

Erythromycin

Erythromycin is a macrolide antibiotic with an antibacterial spectrum similar to that of penicillin G, but with the addition of a few other organisms. The main use of erythromycin is in the treatment of ear, nose, and throat infections in individuals allergic to penicillins and cephalosporins. Erythromycin is also effective in the treatment of *Legionella pneumophilia* (Legionnaire's disease), *Mycoplasma pneumoniae,* and genital infections caused by *Chlamydia trachomatis.* Because of gastric inactivation and irritation, erythromycin is administered in the form of enteric-coated tablets. The usual oral dose is 250–500 mg 2–4 times per day. Gastrointestinal disturbances such as nausea, vomiting, diarrhea, and minor skin rashes are usually the common adverse effects associated with erythromycin and the other macrolide drugs.

Azithromycin (*Zithromax*)

Azithromycin is administered orally; its longer half-life of 65 to 70 hours allows once-a-day dosing. The drug is eliminated in mostly an unmetabolized state via the biliary-intestinal route. The antibacterial spectrum is similar to erythromycin, but azithromycin has greater activity against gram-negative organisms than erythromycin. It is particularly useful in ear and upper and lower respiratory infections caused by *Haemophilus influenzae.*

Clarithromycin (*Biaxin*)

Clarithromycin is well absorbed after oral administration. The drug forms an active metabolite during first-pass liver metabolism. Clarithromycin has the same antibacterial spectrum as erythromycin, but it is a more potent drug. The main uses are infections caused by *Haemophilus influenzae, Legionella pneumophilia, Chlamydia trachomatis,* and *Borrelia burgdorferi* (Lyme disease).

Dirithromycin (*Dynabac*)

Dirithromycin is a prodrug that is rapidly converted into an active metabolite that is responsible for the antibacterial effect. Oral absorption is increased by food, and administration with meals is recommended. The main indications for dirithromycin are common staphylococcal and streptococcal infections, and gram-negative infections caused by *Mycoplasma pneumoniae, Legionella pneumophilia,* and *Moraxella catarrhalis.*

Telithromycin (*Ketek*)

Telithromycin is structurally related to the macrolides; it is classified as a ketolide. The antibacterial spectrum is similar to that of azithromycin and clarithromycin. In addition, telithromycin is effective against bacterial strains that are resistant to the macrolides. The drug is administered orally, usually 800 mg once per day. The major indication is for upper and lower respiratory infections. Adverse effects are similar to those of the macrolides.

FLUOROQUINOLONE ANTIMICROBIALS

The fluoroquinolones are synthetic antimicrobials that have a broad spectrum of bactericidal activity, especially against gram-negative organisms (Table 41:7). One of their advantages, over other broad-spectrum antibiotics, is that they are well absorbed after oral administration. The mechanism of action of the fluoroquinolones is to inhibit a bacterial enzyme, deoxyribonucleic acid (DNA) gyrase, that is essential for the synthesis of DNA and bacterial replication. Resistance to the fluoroquinolones is most commonly due to mutations in DNA gyrase that reduce the binding of the fluoroquinolones to the enzyme. Also, changes in the outer bacterial membrane can decrease drug penetration.

All the fluoroquinolones are available for oral administration; bioavailability ranges from 70 to 95 percent. However, divalent and trivalent ions such as iron, zinc, and those found in antacids (Mg, Al, Ca) decrease absorption and should be avoided several hours before and after dosing. Several of the drugs also can be administered parenterally. Fluoroquinolones attain effective drug concentrations in most peripheral body tissues and fluids. Renal excretion is the main route of elimination, drug half-lives range from 4 to 10 hours.

[Table **41:7**]

Fluoroquinolone Antimicrobial Drugs

Drug (*Trade Name*)	Administration	Main indications
Ciprofloxacin (*Cipro*)	PO, IV, BID	Highest activity against gram-negative organisms, anthrax, resistant TB
Gemifloxacin (*Factive*)	PO, once/day	Increased gram-positive activity, respiratory infections
Levofloxacin (*Levaquin*)	PO, IV, once/day	Increased gram-positive activity, respiratory and urinary infections
Lomefloxacin (*Maxaquin*)	PO, once/day	Respiratory and urinary tract infections
Moxifloxacin (*Avelox*)	PO, IV, once/day	Increased gram-positive activity, respiratory and anaerobic infections
Norfloxacin (*Noroxin*)	PO, BID	Urinary tract infections
Ofloxacin (*Floxin*)	PO, BID	Urinary tract infections

The fluoroquinolones have broad-spectrum activity, particularly against gram-negative organisms. Ciprofloxacin is the most active drug against gram-negative infections, including those caused by *Pseudomonas aeruginosa*. Fluoroquinolones are also effective against gram-positive staph and strep organisms and some penicillinase producers, but not methicillin-resistant *Staphylococcus aureus* (MRSA). The fluoroquinolones are indicated for urinary, respiratory, abdominal, bone, and soft-tissue infections. Newer fluoroquinolones, gemifloxacin and moxifloxacin, have increased activity against gram-positive, anaerobic, and resistant organisms.

The most common adverse reactions include headache, dizziness, GI disturbances, and rash. Some rashes are related to photosensitivity reactions and patients should avoid excess sun exposure while taking these drugs. The fluoroquinolones are not recommended for children or pregnant women. There is evidence of cartilage defects in animal studies and tendonitis, ruptured tendons, and joint pain in humans. Ciprofloxacin inhibits the metabolism of theophylline and can increase CNS stimulation and may cause seizures. Moxifloxacin and gemifloxacin have been reported to prolong the cardiac QT interval and may interact with some of the antiarrhythmic drugs to cause cardiac arrhythmias.

LO 41.10

MISCELLANEOUS ANTIMICROBIAL DRUGS

Chloramphenicol (*Chloromycetin*)

Chloramphenicol is a broad-spectrum antibiotic that is reserved for serious and life-threatening infections. Two of the main indications for chloramphenicol are the treatment of typhoid fever and certain types of meningitis. The mechanism of action of chloramphenicol is to inhibit bacterial protein synthesis, which produces a bacteriostatic effect. Absorption of chloramphenicol from the GI tract is excellent. The oral dose is 250 to 500 mg every 6 hours.

Adverse and Toxic Effects

Common side effects usually involve nausea, vomiting, and diarrhea. Chloramphenicol is potentially a very toxic drug. One of the most serious effects is bone marrow depression, which usually produces anemia or other blood disorders. In most cases, the effects are reversible. However, in some patients the effects on bone marrow are irreversible and may include aplastic anemia. Frequent blood cell counts should be taken while patients are receiving chloramphenicol. As with all broad-spectrum

antibiotics, suppression of normal intestinal bacteria may result in superinfections.

Cautions and Contraindications

Chloramphenicol should not be administered to infants less than 2 weeks old. Infant livers are unable to metabolize chloramphenicol and accumulation leads to toxic blood levels, resulting in a condition known as the gray baby syndrome, which is characterized by abdominal distention, circulatory collapse, and respiratory failure.

Clindamycin (*Cleocin*)

Clindamycin is a bacteriostatic antibiotic that inhibits bacterial protein synthesis. The drug is effective against most of the common gram-positive organisms and especially against anaerobic organisms, which is its major indication. The most common adverse effects involve the GI tract, usually diarrhea. Occasionally, clindamycin allows the overgrowth of another intestinal organism, *Clostridium difficile*. This can cause a condition known as pseudomembranous colitis, which causes severe diarrhea and abdominal cramps, and can be fatal if untreated.

Metronidazole (*Flagyl*)

Metronidazole is an antimicrobial drug that is bactericidal to both anaerobic bacteria and protozoa. It has no activity against aerobic organisms. Metronidazole was first introduced as an antiprotozoal drug and is considered the drug of choice for infections caused by *Trichomonas vaginalis, Giardia lamblia,* and *Entamoeba histolytica* (see Chapter 43). In addition, it is highly active against anaerobic bacteria such as *Bacteroides* and *Clostridium*. The drug is available for oral, parenteral, and topical administration. Topical application is indicated for the treatment of bacterial vaginosis and acne. Metronidazole is considered the drug of choice for therapy of pseudomembranous colitis caused by *Clostridium difficile*. Adverse effects include GI disturbances, an unpleasant metallic taste, and adverse CNS effects that include dizziness, ataxia, and numbness in the extremities. When mixed with alcohol, metronidazole may cause a disulfiram-like reaction.

Vancomycin (*Vancocin*)

Vancomycin is a bactericidal antibiotic that interferes with cell-wall synthesis. The drug is mainly indicated for treatment of resistant staphylococcal (both penicillinase producers and MRSA) and enterococcal infections. Vancomycin is not absorbed orally and is administered IV for systemic infections. Vancomycin is also effective for treatment of pseudomembranous colitis, an intestinal infection caused by overgrowth of *Clostridium difficile*. Oral administration is effective for this infection. Adverse reactions following IV administration include chills, fever, and phlebitis at the injection site. A condition known as "red man syndrome" may occur when IV administration is too rapid. There is a flushing redness of the neck and upper body due to histamine release. Ototoxicity (deafness) and nephrotoxicity occur less frequently and are usually associated with higher dosages or coadministration with other oto- or nephrotoxic drugs.

Treatment of Vancomycin-Resistant Infections

Within the last several years there has been an increase in the number of gram-positive bacteria that are resistant to vancomycin, especially staphylococcal and enterococcal bacteria. Several newer anti-infective drugs have been approved and are now available for treatment of infections caused by these bacteria.

Quinupristin-dalfopristin (*Synercid*) is a combination of two drugs. It must be administered parenterally and is rapidly bactericidal for most resistant gram-positive organisms. The combination produces a synergistic action to inhibit bacterial protein synthesis. The drug causes pain at the infusion site and an arthralgia-myalgia syndrome.

Linezolid (*Zyvox*) is effective against many gram-positive and some gram-negative bacteria. The drug is administered parenterally and is bacteriostatic against most bacteria. It inhibits bacterial protein synthesis and is indicated for treatment of infections caused by vancomycin-resistant organisms. Adverse effects include gastrointestinal disturbances, headache, and a decrease in platelets and RBCs.

Daptomycin (*Cubicin*) is indicated for treatment of vancomycin-resistant skin infections. The drug is bactericidal and believed to damage the bacterial cell membrane. The antibacterial spectrum is similar to vancomycin except that daptomycin is active against vancomycin-resistant staphylococcal and enterococcal organisms. Daptomycin is administered daily by IV infusion. Adverse effects include GI disturbances, pain at the injection site, and increases in creatine phosphokinase, which can lead to skeletal muscle cramps and pain (myopathy).

Vibativ (*Telavancin*) is a relatively new bactericidal antibiotic indicated for resistant gram-positive staph and strep infections. The drug inhibits bacterial cell-wall synthesis. It is administered once daily by IV infusion. Adverse effects include nausea, vomiting, diarrhea, taste disturbances, rash, and pruritis.

DRUGS USED TO TREAT TUBERCULOSIS

Tuberculosis is an infection caused by *Mycobacterium tuberculosis*. The infection usually involves the lung, but can spread to other body organs, including the brain. The infecting organism can lie dormant within the body, only to reemerge and cause infection years later. Reemergence of the organism often occurs when body resistance to infection is lowered. Infection with human immunodeficiency virus (acquired immunodeficiency syndrome, AIDS) has been one of the factors that accounts for the increased incidence of tuberculosis in recent years. One of the biggest problems in treating tuberculosis has been the dramatic increase in bacterial resistance to drug therapy. Drug therapy usually involves administration of three or four different drugs for prolonged periods of time, often a year or more. The first-line drugs for treating tuberculosis are isoniazid, rifampin, ethambutol, pyrazinamide, and streptomycin. Streptomycin is one of the aminoglycosides; it is sometimes used in initial therapy for the first few weeks. The major disadvantage is that it requires parenteral administration. Isoniazid is also the drug of choice for chemoprophylaxis in individuals at risk for developing tuberculosis or who have become positive skin-test reactors to the purified protein derivative (PPD).

There are a number of drugs referred to as "second-line drugs" that are indicated when there is bacterial resistance to any of the first-line drugs (Table 41:8).

Isoniazid (*INH*)

Isoniazid is a synthetic drug that is bactericidal for reproducing organisms. The drug inhibits the production of mycolic acid, which is essential for bacterial cell-wall synthesis. Isoniazid is well absorbed orally and metabolized by acetylation. This reaction is highly variable among individuals—some are "fast acetylators" while others are "slow acetylators." Slow acetylators usually experience better antibacterial results, but also experience more adverse effects of the drug.

The two most important adverse effects of isoniazid are peripheral neuritis and hepatitis. Peripheral neuritis is characterized by paresthesias (numbness) in the hands and feet. This can be prevented by taking pyridoxine (vitamin B_6) supplementation. Hepatitis is more common in individuals over the age of 35 and those who drink alcohol on a regular basis. Other adverse effects include fever, rash, and central nervous system (CNS) disturbances.

Second-Line Antitubercular Drugs

Drug (*Trade Name*)	Mechanism of action	Toxicity
Aminosalicylic acid (*Paser*)	Bacteriostatic, inhibits folic acid synthesis	GI disturbances, hypersensitivity reactions
Capreomycin (*Capastat*)	Bacteriostatic, inhibits protein synthesis	Ototoxicity, nephrotoxicity
Cycloserine (*Seromycin*)	Bacteriostatic, inhibits cell-wall synthesis	Peripheral neuropathy, CNS disturbances
Ethionamide (*Trecator-SC*)	Bacteriostatic, blocks synthesis mycolic acid	Neurotoxicity, GI disturbances, hepatitis
Fluoroquinolones Ciprofloxacin (*Cipro*) Levofloxacin (*Levaquin*) Moxifloxacin (*Avelox*)	Bactericidal, inhibits DNA gyrase	GI disturbances, phototoxicity, arthropathy, tendonitis

Rifampin (*Rifadin*)

Rifampin is an antibiotic that has a wider antibacterial spectrum than isoniazid. The drug inhibits a bacterial enzyme required for ribonucleic acid (RNA) synthesis. Rifampin is taken orally, undergoes enterohepatic cycling, and induces drug-metabolizing enzymes. This leads to a decrease in the duration of action of both itself and other drugs and may require an increase in drug dosage.

Adverse effects include GI disturbances, hepatotoxicity, rash, and headache. A flu-like syndrome, usually fatigue and muscle ache, may occur when the drug is not taken on a regular basis. Rifampin also stains urine, tears (contact lens), and other body fluids orange-red.

Ethambutol (*Myambutol*)

Ethambutol is a synthetic compound that produces a bacteriostatic effect. The drug is believed to inhibit the incorporation of an essential component, arabinoglycan, into the bacterial cell wall. Ethambutol is generally only used in combination with other drugs. The drug is usually well tolerated; fever, rash, and GI disturbances are common side effects. The most serious concern is the loss of visual acuity due to optic neuritis. It is recommended that visual eye tests be performed before and during therapy to prevent any permanent loss of vision.

Pyrazinamide

Pyrazinamide is a derivative of nicotinamide. Its antibactericidal effects are increased by acidic conditions. The drug is mainly used in initial therapy for the first few months. Its mechanism of action is not well understood.

The most serious adverse effect is development of hepatotoxicity. In addition, some patients develop hyperuricemia and symptoms of gout.

| LO 41.3 | LO 41.4 | LO 41.6 |
| LO 41.7 | LO 41.8 | LO 41.9 |

PREFERRED THERAPY FOR SELECTED INFECTIONS

There are many different factors that determine which antibiotic would be the preferred therapy or drug of choice for any specific infection. The age of the patient, existing drug allergies, location and severity of the infection, drug resistance, and drug cost are just a few of the factors to be considered. There are usually a number of different antibiotics that are effective against most infections. Selecting the drug that is most effective against the organism suspected of causing the infection and the drug that causes the least number of adverse drug reactions are two important considerations. For serious infections, culture and sensitivity testing often determines drug selection. A few of the most common infections and preferred therapies are presented below.

Upper Respiratory Infections

Infections of the nasal cavity (sinusitis), ear (otitis media), and throat (pharyngitis) are most commonly caused by *Streptococcus pneumoniae*, *Streptococcus pyogenes*, *Haemophilus influenzae*, and *Moraxella catarrhalis*. Amoxicillin and amoxicillin plus clavulanic acid PO for 10 days are usually considered the drugs of choice.

Second-generation cephalosporins or azithromycin and clarithromycin (macrolides) are suitable alternatives.

Community-Acquired Pneumonia

The most common cause of infection is with *Streptococcus pneumoniae, Haemophilus influenzae,* and *Mycoplasma pneumoniae.* The recommended treatment for uncomplicated outpatient therapy is with the macrolides, azithromycin, or clarithromycin. Second-generation cephalosporins and doxycycline are alternative choices.

Urinary Tract Infections

Acute uncomplicated urinary tract infections are usually caused by *Escherichia coli, Staphylococcus saprophyticus,* and *Proteus mirabilis.* Trimethoprim/sulfamethoxazole (3-day regimen) or one of the fluoroquinolones (3-day or 7-day regimen) is considered preferred therapy. Complicated infections are usually caused by gram-negative species of *Klebsiella* and *Pseudomonas.* Fluoroquinolones (7–10 days) such as ciprofloxacin and levofloxacin are generally preferred.

Gonococcal Infections

Infections caused by *Neisseria gonorrhoeae* are usually treated with a single dose of one of the cephalosporins, cefixime PO or ceftriaxone IM.

Syphilis Infections

Benzathine penicillin administered as a single dose by IM injection is standard therapy. Alternatives are ceftriaxone IM single dose or doxycycline administered PO twice per day for 14 days.

Chlamydial Infections

Infections caused by *Chlamydia trachomatis* are treated with azithromycin PO administered in a single dose or doxycycline PO for 7 days.

Chapter Review

Understanding Terminology

Answer the following questions.

1. Differentiate between the terms *bactericidal* and *bacteriostatic*. **(LO 41.1, 41.2)**
2. Define the terms *antibacterial spectrum* and *broad-spectrum* drugs. **(LO 41.1, 41.2)**
3. Define the terms *gram stain, gram positive,* and *gram negative.* **(LO 41.1, 41.2)**
4. Define the term *antibiotic susceptibility.* **(LO 41.1, 41.2)**

Acquiring Knowledge

Answer the following questions.

1. What are the major sources of antibacterial drugs? **(LO 41.2)**
2. Why are gram stains important? **(LO 41.1)**
3. Explain the mechanism of action of the penicillin and cephalosporin antibiotics. **(LO 41.3, 41.4)**
4. What are the main advantages of the third- and fourth-generation penicillins? Third-generation cephalosporins? **(LO 41.3, 41.4)**
5. What are the main uses, adverse effects, and drug interactions associated with the aminoglycosides? **(LO 41.5)**
6. Explain how the sulfonamides produce their antibacterial effect. What advantages does trimethoprim-sulfamethoxazole offer? **(LO 41.7)**
7. Explain the mechanisms of action of the tetracyclines, chloramphenicol, and fluoroquinolones. **(LO 41.6, 41.9, 41.10)**
8. What are the contraindications to the use of the tetracyclines? Chloramphenicol? **(LO 41.6, 41.10)**
9. List some of the drugs used in the treatment of tuberculosis (TB). **(LO 41.11)**
10. Explain the mechanisms of action of isoniazid and rifampin. What are the major toxicities of these drugs? **(LO 41.11)**

Applying Knowledge on the Job

Use your critical-thinking skills to answer the following questions.

1. Mrs. Randazzo is an elderly woman admitted to the hospital from a nursing home with a diagnosis of sepsis secondary to a urinary tract infection (UTI). She has been receiving piperacillin (*Pipracil*) for 24 hours and her temperature chart is showing a downward trend. The lab calls you with the initial results of the blood culture and states that gram-negative rods grew in two of three culture tubes. Do you need to call the attending physician for a change in antibiotic? Why or why not? **(LO 41.3)**

2. Mr. Porter is admitted to the hospital with an empiric diagnosis of pneumonia. The emergency room physician prescribed erythromycin IV—piggyback every 6 hours. In the patient's admission history, the patient states he has a penicillin allergy. Is it necessary to call the attending physician for a change in antibiotic because of the penicillin allergy? Why or why not? **(LO 41.3, 41.8)**

3. Mr. Smith has just been diagnosed with a respiratory infection caused by *Pseudomonas aeruginosa.* Which penicillin antibiotic would be appropriate therapy? How is this drug administered? **(LO 41.3)**

4. John is a 22-year-old college student who is taking one of the cephalosporins for a throat infection. Last night at a fraternity party he got violently ill after a few beers. What happened? **(LO 41.4)**

5. Mrs. Evans is a 45-year-old woman who is on a four-drug regimen for treatment of her tuberculosis. At her recent checkup, her liver enzymes were increased and there were signs of jaundice. Which antitubercular drugs could be causing this condition? What other factors may make her more susceptible to this toxicity? **(LO 41.11)**

6. Mrs. Urban was prescribed clindamycin for a minor gram-positive throat infection. After 3 days she was experiencing severe diarrhea and dehydration. The next day she collapsed and was rushed to the hospital. The diagnosis was pseudomembranous colitis. Can you explain how this happened? What drug is indicated for treatment of this condition? **(LO 41.10)**

7. A woman has just presented a prescription at the pharmacy for *Velosef* 500 mg QID × 10d. Upon questioning, she states that she had a severe allergic reaction to penicillin: her throat swelled and she had a hard time breathing. Would you expect the pharmacist to call the physician to change the antibiotic? Why or why not? **(LO 41.4)**

8. A man has just received a prescription for *Bactrim* DS 1 BID × 5d. He told you earlier that he was allergic to *Azulfidine*. Would you ask the patient to wait until you have spoken with the physician about this allergy? Why or why not? **(LO 41.7)**

9. A woman has just received *Zithromax* 250 mg—2 today, then 1 QD × 4d. While talking with the patient, she tells you that she is allergic to erythromycin. When she took it previously, she had stomach cramps, was nauseated, and sometimes vomited. Should the physician be contacted to change the medication? Why or why not? **(LO 41.8)**

Multiple Choice

Use your critical-thinking skills to answer the following questions.

1. The penicillin that provides good oral absorption and that is effective against most common gram-positive and gram-negative bacteria is **(LO 41.3)**
   A. piperacillin
   B. aztreonam
   C. amoxicillin
   D. ticarcillin

2. The bactericidal antibiotic that interferes with bacterial cell-wall synthesis and that may cause "red man syndrome" if injected too rapidly is **(LO 41.10)**
   A. piperacillin
   B. vancomycin
   C. gentamicin
   D. clindamycin

3. The antibiotic that irreversibly inhibits bacterial protein synthesis and whose adverse effects may include ototoxicity and nephrotoxicity is **(LO 41.5)**
   A. doxycycline
   B. clarithromycin
   C. gentamicin
   D. clindamycin

4. Dicloxacillin is **(LO 41.3)**
   A. indicated for gram-negative infections
   B. classified as a third-generation penicillin
   C. indicated for resistant staphylococcal infections
   D. associated with causing "red man syndrome"

5. The antibiotic whose adverse effects include heartburn, photosensitivity, and possible depression of bone growth in young children is **(LO 41.6)**
   A. erythromycin
   B. tetracycline
   C. gentamicin
   D. clindamycin

6. The antibiotic class that is usually considered for the treatment of Rocky Mountain spotted fever, Lyme disease, and cholera is **(LO 41.6)**
   A. aminoglycosides
   B. macrolides
   C. penicillins
   D. tetracyclines

7. Bone marrow suppression, aplastic anemia, and "gray baby syndrome" are associated with **(LO 41.10)**
   A. linezolid
   B. clindamycin
   C. gentamicin
   D. chloramphenicol

8. The main pharmacokinetic feature of aminoglycosides is that they are **(LO 41.5)**
   A. lipid soluble
   B. well absorbed orally
   C. excreted mostly unchanged in the urine
   D. devoid of serious adverse effects

Multiple Choice (Multiple Answer)

Select the correct choices for each statement. The choices may be all correct, all incorrect, or any combination.

1. Which of the following are true of the gram stain? **(LO 41.1)**
   A. gram-positive bacteria will stain red
   B. gram-negative bacteria will stain purple
   C. it is a test to determine antibiotic susceptibility
   D. it contains three dyes

2. Select the true statements about antibacterial spectrums. **(LO 41.2)**
   A. they can be narrow
   B. they can include gram-positive and gram-negative bacteria
   C. they are particular to a specific drug
   D. they are used to classify antibiotics

3. Which bacteria are second-generation penicillins effective against? **(LO 41.3)**
   A. *Pseudomonas aeruginosa*
   B. *Staphylococcus aureus*
   C. *Proteus vulgaris*
   D. *Bacteroides fragilis*

4. Select the correct mechanisms of action for cephalosporins. **(LO 41.4)**
   A. interrupt cell-wall synthesis
   B. interrupt protein synthesis
   C. cause bacteria to release autolytic enzymes
   D. are bactericidal

5. Aminoglycosides cause which adverse effects? **(LO 41.5)**
   A. photosensitivity
   B. nephrotoxicity
   C. crystalluria
   D. permanent hearing loss

Sequencing

Place the following penicillins in order of broadest spectrum to narrowest spectrum. **(LO 41.3)**

_____   _____   _____   _____

Broadest   **Narrowest**

amoxicillin

ticarcillin

penicillin G

piperacillin

Classification

Place the following medications under the correct use. **(LO 41.6, 41.7, 41.8, 41.9)**

Cipro	_Dynabac_	_Tygacil_	_Sulfamylon_
Sumycin	_Minocin_	_Biaxin_	_Vibramycin_
Zithromax	_Avelox_	_Noroxin_	_Erythromycin_
Azulfidine	_Bactrim_	_Levaquin_	_Sulamyd_

Tetracyclines	Sulfonamides	Macrolides	Fluoroquinolones

Matching

Match the following terms with their correct definitions. **(LO 41.1, 41.2)**
   a. antibacterial spectrum
   b. antibiotic
   c. antimicrobial
   d. bactericidal
   e. bacteriostatic
   f. chemoprophylaxis
   g. chemotherapy
   h. pathogenic

1. _____ kills bacteria
2. _____ antibacterial drug obtained from other microorganisms
3. _____ causing disease
4. _____ use of antibiotics to prevent infection
5. _____ bacteria susceptible to a particular medication
6. _____ inhibits growth of bacteria
7. _____ use of drugs to kill infectious organisms
8. _____ antibacterial drug obtained through chemical synthesis

Documentation

A patient's chart indicates confirmed tuberculosis. Using this diagnosis, answer the following questions. **(LO 41.11)**

    a. List the medication used as initial therapy.

    b. List the other medications that are likely to be administered.

    c. Which medication could turn urine and tears red?

    d. Which of these medications can cause conditions of the liver?

Labeling

Fill in the missing labels. **(LO 41.3, 41.4)**

β-Lactam ring

For interactive animations, videos, and assessment, visit:

www.mcgrawhillconnect.com

Chapter 42

Antifungal and Antiviral Drugs

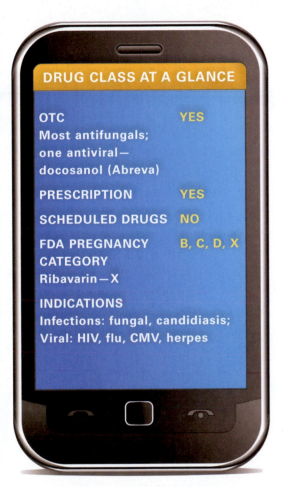

DRUG CLASS AT A GLANCE

OTC	YES
Most antifungals; one antiviral—docosanol (Abreva)	
PRESCRIPTION	YES
SCHEDULED DRUGS	NO
FDA PREGNANCY CATEGORY	B, C, D, X
Ribavarin—X	
INDICATIONS	
Infections: fungal, candidiasis; Viral: HIV, flu, CMV, herpes	

KEY TERMS

acquired immunity: protection from viral reinfection in the form of antibodies produced during an infection (active) or produced after exposure to a vaccine (passive).

acquired immunodeficiency syndrome (AIDS): viral-induced disease characterized by multiple opportunistic infections as a result of depleted lymphocytes involved in the cell-mediated immune process.

albuminuria: the presence of the plasma protein albumin in the urine.

antigen: any substance that stimulates an immune response, i.e., production of an antibody.

antigenic drift and antigenic shift: the ability of viruses to change the composition or structure of their surface proteins (viral coat) that are responsible for producing disease (pathogenicity).

antimetabolite: a drug that is very similar to natural chemicals in a normal biochemical reaction in cells but different enough to interfere with the normal division and functions of cells.

candidemia: infection in the blood caused by the yeast *Candida*.

candidiasis: infection caused by the yeast *Candida*; also known as moniliasis.

dendritic cell: an antigen-presenting white blood cell that is found in the skin, mucosa, and lymphoid tissues and that initiates a primary immune response.

dermatophytic: infection of the skin, hair, or nails caused by a fungus.

fungicidal: substance, chemical solution, or drug that kills fungi.

fungistatic: inhibits the growth of fungi but does not kill off the fungi.

fungus (fungi): a group of microorganisms with a membrane-bound nucleus that includes yeasts and molds.

HIV: human immunodeficiency virus, responsible for producing AIDS.

H1N1: a subtype of the influenza type A virus also referred to as swine flu or pig flu.

immunity: condition that causes individuals to resist acquiring or developing a disease or infection.

immunosuppressed: having inhibition of the body's immune response (ability to fight infection), usually induced by drugs or viruses.

keratinized: composed of a protein substance largely found in hair and nails.

kerion: an inflammation of the hair follicles of the beard or scalp caused by ringworm with swelling and pus.

leukopenia: an abnormal decrease in the number of circulating white blood cells.

mitosis: the process in cell division by which the nucleus divides.

moniliasis: fungal infection previously called monilia, now known to be *Candida albicans*.

mycosis: any disease caused by a fungus.

neutropenia: an abnormally low number of neutrophils (white blood cells).

nucleoside: molecule that contains purine or pyrimidine bases in combination with sugar (ribose or deoxyribose linkage).

onychomycosis: a fungus infection of the nail; *onycho-:* pertaining to a claw or nail.

opportunistic organism: microorganism capable of causing disease only when the resistance (immunocompetence) of the host is impaired.

phlebitis: inflammation of a vein.

porphyria (acute): a genetic disease associated with excessive liver production of delta-aminolevulonic acid and characterized by intermittent hypertension, abdominal cramps, and psychosis.

Reye's syndrome: a potentially fatal illness characterized by vomiting, an enlarged liver, convulsions, and coma, in children and adolescents; linked to the use of salicylates in the management of influenza, usually type B, or chickenpox.

sebum: a lipid substance secreted by glands in the skin to lubricate the skin everywhere but the palms and soles.

thrombocytopenia: an abnormal decrease in the number of circulating platelets.

thrush: term used for *Candida* infection in the mucous membranes of the mouth and pharynx.

Learning Outcomes

After studying this chapter, you should be able to

42.1 describe two drugs that are effective against systemic fungal infections and their mechanism of action.

42.2 describe the mechanism of action of drugs effective against viral infections.

42.3 explain how the treatment of viral infection is different from treatment that kills fungi or bacteria.

42.4 list side effects associated with antifungal drugs and drug interactions.

42.5 describe how pathogenic fungi and viruses gain access to the human host.

42.6 explain terminology associated with these diseases and drug treatment.

Fungi (yeasts and molds) are microorganisms that often produce annoying symptoms in humans (Figure 42.1). Fungi that affect humans can be found in the soil, air, and contaminated food. Certain fungal infections **(mycoses)** occur throughout the body (systemic). These infections usually go undiagnosed and untreated for many months while the fungi infest several tissues (lungs, bones, and meninges). Systemic fungal infections are potentially dangerous in patients who are chronically ill (diabetes mellitus) or immunosuppressed (cancer, leukemia, acquired immunodeficiency syndrome [AIDS]) because resistance to infection is low and recurrence of infections complicates the treatment. The most common mycotic infections that occur in humans involve the hair, skin, nails **(dermatophytic),** and genitals. Dermatophytic and vaginal fungal infections are more annoying than serious, producing symptoms such as intense itching, discolored scaling patches on the skin, inflammation of the scalp, loss of hair, blisters, and broken skin between the toes. Table 42:1 identifies the spectrum of ringworm infections commonly encountered. Vaginal fungal infections are very common and result from an overgrowth of yeast (*Candida albicans*). These sites are considered superficial fungal infections because the fungus invades dead tissue of the mucous membranes, scalp, foot, and nails.

Figure 42.1	Fungi and Molds

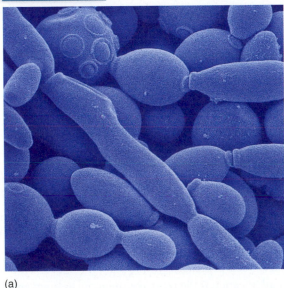 

(a) (b)

(a) Single-celled fungi are called yeasts. (b) Multicelled fungi are called molds.

FUNGAL INFECTIONS AND ANTIFUNGAL DRUGS

There are three principal areas where **fungi** are encountered that require drug intervention: systemic infection, dermatophytic infection, and opportunistic *Candida albicans* causing infections localized in the mouth, vagina, and GI tract (Table 42:1). Systemic or invasive infection is always a serious clinical problem because multiple organs may be involved. Invasive infections clinically manifest as septicemia, endocarditis, and pulmonary and urinary tract infections. Immunocompromised patients may have infections that are particularly difficult to eliminate in any organ or cavity. Systemic fungal infection

Human Fungal Infections

Type	Site	Example	Drug of choice
Systemic infections	Blood, bones, lungs	Aspergillosis, blastomycosis, histoplasmosis, candidiasis, coccidioidomycosis, cryptococcosis, paracoccidioidomycosis	Fluconazole, amphotericin B, or itraconazole, anidulafungin, caspofungin, micafungin; amphotericin B and itraconazole
Dermatophytic infections	Hair, nails, skin	Athlete's foot (*Tinea pedis*), ringworm hair (*Tinea capitis*), body (*Tinea corporis*), nails (*Tinea unguium*), jock itch (*Tinea cruris*)	Griseofulvin Terbinafine Tolnaftate Zinc undecylenate
Candida albicans	Skin, mucous membranes	Vaginal yeast infection, candidiasis, deep mucocutaneous, oropharyngeal infections,	Clotrimazole, econazole, ciclopirox Fluconazole, ketoconazole Miconazole Nystatin
		Miscellaneous subcutaneous infections, sporotrichosis, chromomycosis, leishmaniasis	Amphotericin B and itraconazole

is becoming more common in modern hospitals. Severe systemic fungal infection in hospitals is commonly seen in three major settings: **neutropenic** patients following chemotherapy or with immune suppression; persons immunocompromised by HIV infection; and patients in intensive care who are not necessarily neutropenic but are compromised due to the presence of long-term intravascular (IV) lines, severe systemic illness or burns, and prolonged broad-spectrum antibiotic therapy. Of the 200 species of *Candida* organisms, about 10 contribute to 50 percent or more of the systemic infections referred to as **candidemia.** Invasive aspergillosis can occur in immunocompromised patients following inhalation of *Aspergillus* spores.

Dermatophytic fungal infections usually inhabit a specific location: skin, hair, and nails. These organisms obtain nutrients from **keratinized** material and are usually restricted to the nonliving cornified layer of the epidermis because the immune system blocks penetration to other tissues. These infections are caused by a variety of *Tinea* species such as ringworm (*Tinea capitis*) in the hair or skin. Ringworm occurs almost exclusively in children. Toenail and fingernail infection (*Tinea unguium*), referred to as **onychomycosis,** occurs in about 8 percent of the population (Figure 42.2). Toenail infection is the more common site as fungi enjoy the moist, warm environment of enclosed socks and shoes or inadequately cleaned foot baths at pedicure salons. Of course, there is the ever popular athlete's foot (*Tinea pedis*) on the toes.

Superficial infections of skin and mucosal membranes by *Candida albicans* causing local inflammation and discomfort are very common. This organism is normally present in the oral cavity of 30 to 40 percent of the population. Often as a result of antibiotic use or overuse, normal bacterial flora is removed and the balance shifts in favor of yeast growth. The overall condition of the patient is also a factor. Diabetes

Figure 42.2

Onychomycosis: Fungal Infection of the Toenail

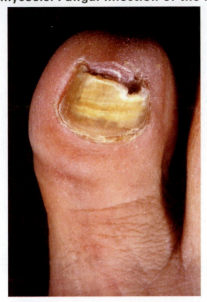

Figure 42.3

Candida albicans

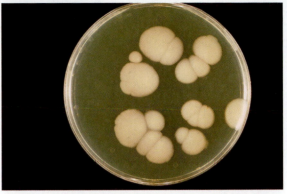

(a)

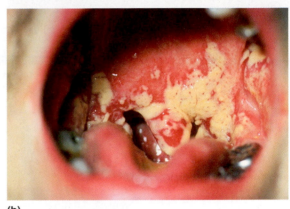

(b)

(a) *Candida* colonies isolated in the lab. (b) *Candida,* the white coating in the throat, is called thrush.

and pregnancy predispose individuals to developing yeast infections. **Candidiasis** is a very common cause of vaginal irritation referred to as a yeast infection or **moniliasis,** but it also occurs in men. *Candida* can thrive in the mouth, pharynx, esophagus, GI tract, and urinary bladder. When it occurs in the mouth or pharynx, it is called **thrush** (see Figure 42.3). Esophageal candidiasis is most commonly diagnosed in patients with HIV, those receiving treatment with antibiotics, those using inhaled corticosteroids, or those receiving chemotherapy.

Many drugs are available for the treatment of mycotic infections. Twenty-six commonly used antimycotic drugs are presented in Table 42:2. Treatment will vary according to the chronic nature of the infection and concomitant medical condition of the patient. Acute superficial infections may require 1 to 2 weeks of treatment, while chronic recurring infections, especially those in nail beds, may take up to 6 months of drug treatment. In the management of fungal infections in immunosuppressed patients, where host resistance to infection is low and recurrence is inevitable, treatment may continue indefinitely.

Antifungal Drugs

In this large class of drugs some were discovered in nature, but most are synthetically made. Griseofulvin (ringworm) is a metabolic product of a *Penicillium* mold; nystatin and amphotericin B (systemic infections) come from *Streptomyces* bacteria; and the newest members, the echinocandins (systemic infections), are

found in *Aspergillus* molds. The echinocandins include three drugs: anidula*fungin,* caspo*fungin,* and mica*fungin.* Undecylenic acid (athlete's foot) is an organic fatty acid derived from natural castor oil from the castor bean plant. The rest of this class is man-made. To make it a little easier to remember, the largest and most frequently used synthetic drugs are the imidazoles and triazoles. This group includes any drug name ending in *azole:* econ*azole,* itracon*azole,* ketocon*azole,* and voricon*azole.* There are 11 azole drugs listed in Table 42:2 with clinical value as antifungal agents. Antifungal drugs are selective in their spectrum of activity and site of action. As a rule, these drugs have no antibacterial or antiviral activity and affect only certain pathogenic fungi.

Mechanism of Action

Drugs useful in the treatment of systemic mycotic infections and candidiasis are usually **fungicidal** (capable of killing fungi). These drugs change cell-wall synthesis, inhibit fungal DNA, or bind to special proteins required by the fungus to survive. The first two mechanisms result in decreased survival (lethal) and

Drugs Effective in the Treatment of Fungal Infections

Drug (*Trade Name*)	Use*	Adult dose
Amphotericin B (*Abelcet, AmBisome, Amphotec*)	Severe progressive fungal infections Systemic infections Severe coccidioidomycosis Cryptococcosis	Adjusted according to the severity of the disease, test dose 1 mg/2 ml dextose solution IV over 20–30 min. Then 0.25–0.35 mg/kg slow IV infusion over 6 hr, total dose of 1.5–2.5 g should be administered over 6 weeks IV
Anidulafungin (*Eraxis*)	Invasive aspergillus or candidemia	500 mg IV infusion over 1 hr for 10 to 30 days
Butenafine** (*Mentax*)	Athlete's foot ringworm, jock itch	1% cream once or twice a day for 4 weeks
Butoconazole** (*Femstat 3*)	Vulvovaginal moniliasis	2% cream 1 applicator (5 g) intravaginally at bedtime for 3–5 days
Caspofungin (*Cancidas*)	Invasive aspergillus or candidemia	50 mg IV infusion over 1 hr for 10 to 30 days
Ciclopirox (*Loprox*)	Superficial dermatophytic infection, *candidia* moniliaisis	1% cream or lotion applied BID up to 4 weeks
Clioquinol/hydrocortisone (*Ala-quin*)	Eczema, itch	3% ointment, cream applied topically 2–3 times a day; do not exceed 1 week
Clotrimazole** (*Cruex**, Desenex**, Gyne-lotrimin,** Mycelex* 7, *Mycelex***)	Candidiasis Athlete's foot and dermatophytic infections	1 tablet (100 mg) intravaginally inserted for 7 days or 1 tablet (500 mg) inserted at bedtime; 1% cream, lotion, solution applied topically BID up to 4 weeks
Econazole (*Spectazole*)	Dermatophytic infections Superficial fungal infections	1% cream applied BID up to 4 weeks
Fluconazole (*Diflucan*)	Candidiasis oroesophageal	200 or 400 mg initially PO followed by 100 mg daily for 2–3 weeks including 2 weeks after resolution
	Candidiasis urinary tract infections	50–200 mg PO daily for 2–3 weeks
	Vaginal candidiasis	150 mg single dose
	Candidiasis in bone marrow transplant	400 mg PO daily for several days before and after transplant
	Cryptococcal meningitis	400 mg initially followed by 200 mg PO once a day for 10–12 weeks
Flucytosine 5-fluorocytosine (*Ancobon*)	Serious infections of *Candidia, Cryptococcus*	50–150 mg/kg in divided doses every 6 hours PO
Gentian violet	Candidiasis	1 and 2% solution apply BID
Griseofulvin (*Grifulvin V*)	Ringworm, *T. Corporis, T. crucis, T. capis*	500 mg/day PO microsize (330–375 mg/day ultramicrosize)
Griseofulvin microsize (*Gris-PEG*)	*T. pedis, T. unguium*	0.75–1 g microsize PO (660–750 mg ultrasize), treatment is 4–8 weeks; treatment for fingernails and toes may be 4–6 months
Itraconazole (*Sporanox*)	Pulmonary and extrapulmonary infections (blastomycosis, histoplasmosis, aspergillosis)	200–400 mg daily PO in divided doses up to several months
	Onychomycosis	200 mg PO daily for 12 weeks

(Continued)

Drug (*Trade Name*)	Use*	Adult dose
Ketoconazole (*Nizoral*)	Blastomycosis, candidiasis Systemic mycosis	200–400 mg PO for 1–2 weeks, can be treated up to 6 months
Micafungin (*Mycamine*)	Invasive aspergillus or candidemia	100 to 150 mg IV infusion over 1 hr for 10 to 30 days
Miconazole (*Lotrimin-AF; Monistat-1, 3 and 7; Neosporin-AF*)	Cutaneous candidiasis, dermatophytic infection	2% cream, powder, or spray BID up to 2 weeks; shampoo twice a week for 4 weeks
Naftifine** (*Naftin*)	Superficial dermatophytic infections	1% cream apply once a day, 1% gel apply BID up to 4 weeks
Nystatin (*Mycostatin, Nilstat*)	Candidiasis intestinal, vulvovaginitis	500,000–1,000,000 units PO TID including 48 hr after resolution of condition; 1 tablet (100,000 units) intravaginally nightly for 2 weeks
Oxiconazole (*Oxistat*)	Dermatophytic infection	1% cream or lotion apply BID up to 2 months
Posaconazole (*Noxafil*)	Oropharyngeal candidiasis and invasive aspergillus and candidemia	100 to 400 mg PO BID for 14 days
Sulconazole (*Exelderm*)	Dermatophytic infection	1% cream or solution apply BID up to 4 weeks
Terbinafine (*Lamisil*)	Dermatophytic infections, onychomycosis	1% cream apply BID up to 4 weeks; 250 mg daily for 6 weeks (fingernails) to 12 weeks (toenails)
Terconazole (*Terazol-3, Terazol-7*)	Candidiasis, vulvovaginal moniliasis	1 suppository (2.5 g) intravaginally at bedtime for 3 days; 0.4%, 0.8% cream 1 applicatorful (5 g) at bedtime for 3 or 7 days
Tioconazole (*Vagistat-1, Monistat-1*)	Candidiasis, vulvovaginal moniliasis	6.5% vaginal ointment; 1 applicator applied at bedtime
Tolnaftate** (*Aftate, Tinactin, Ting*)	Dermatophytic infections, ringworm, athlete's foot	1% cream, powder, liquid spray gel, or solution applied topically BID up to 6 weeks
Undecylenic acid** (*Cruex, Desenex*)*	Athlete's foot, diaper rash	Topical powder or ointment, apply liberally
Voriconazole (*Vfend*)	Serious candidiasis	4 to 5 mg/kg IV every 12 hr; 200 mg PO every 12 hr for 14 days after culture is negative

*Not an inclusive list of uses. **These preparations can be obtained over the counter.*

the third slows propagation of the infecting organism (see Figure 42.4).

Amphotericin B, nystatin, the azoles, and terbinafine produce a change in fungal cell permeability. All of these drugs affect ergosterol, which is a critical substance for fungal cell membrane integrity. Ergosterol is the equivalent of cholesterol in human cells. Amphotericin B and nystatin bind to ergosterol within the cell wall, forming pores that leak electrolytes, especially potassium. The azoles and terbinafine specifically bind enzymes at different locations in the ergosterol pathway that prevent the formation of ergosterol. The azoles inhibit the P450-dependent enzymes midway in the process of the fungal respiration chain, while terbinafine affects squalene epoxidase very early in the process. The result is the same: the cell wall can no longer function as a selective barrier; essential nutrients and inorganic substances (ions) leak out of the cell causing cell destruction. The echinocandins also impair cell-wall synthesis, but they specifically inhibit glucan synthetase, which makes an essential polysaccharide sugar (glucan) substance.

Flucytosine, which is 5-fluorocytosine, is thought to have two actions within the cell body and nucleus but not on the cell wall. Since it is a relative of the anticancer drug 5-fluorouracil (5-FU), it is also an **antimetabolite.** It may be converted to 5-FU by the fungus, allowing it to interrupt RNA synthesis by being incorporated where uracil normally would go. This would make a flawed RNA protein and inhibit the synthesis of other essential proteins. The second mechanism is

Figure 42.4 — Targets of Antifungal Drugs

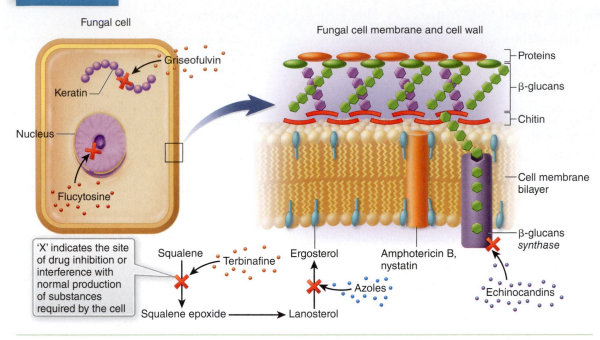

Except for flucytosine and griseofulvin, all currently available antifungal drugs target the fungal cell membrane or wall.

drug conversion to a compound known to inhibit fungal DNA, thus preventing fungal multiplication.

Dermatophytic infections are usually associated with the protein keratin. A drug such as griseofulvin binds to the keratin and prevents the fungi from utilizing the protein. Griseofulvin binds to the keratin for months. As the fungus-infected keratin is shed, it is replaced by new normal, uninfected tissue. Griseofulvin also binds to lipid constituents of the actively growing fungi and inhibits cell **mitosis.** Griseofulvin is **fungi*static*** because its actions are not lethal to the fungi but inhibitory on cell division and nutrient access. Most of the other drugs used in dermatophytic infections are fungicidal.

Systemic Antifungal Drugs

Drugs used in the treatment of systemic infections are always administered intravenously, although often they are combined with an oral medication. Patients are usually hospitalized to receive therapy. Selection of the appropriate drug to reduce or eliminate the infection will depend on characteristics other than excellent antifungal activity (Figure 42.5).

Amphotericin B

For years, amphotericin B was the only drug available to treat serious systemic fungal infections. Deoxycholate-formulated amphotericin B is the conventional drug, but it is insoluble in water. New technology has now made available special lipid-carrying delivery systems. These formulations prolong drug retention through the characteristics of the lipid-carrying vehicle. In the United States only parenteral formulations are available. Amphotericin B has a broad spectrum of fungicidal activity, which makes it clinically valuable, especially against *Aspergillus.* Although highly bound to plasma proteins, it penetrates inflamed tissues to impair fungal colonization. Amphotericin B and nystatin bind to a sterol (ergosterol) in the fungal cell membrane changing cell wall permeability resulting in the leakage of critical intracellular components. Ultimately it is excreted unchanged in the urine, where it can be detected for weeks after treatment has stopped. Presumably, this confers an advantage of continuing coverage for some period of time. Amphotericin B is a first-line therapy, but its adverse event profile is a significant limitation to its use.

Adverse Effects

Drugs used to treat systemic infections are associated with serious side effects. Adverse events with amphotericin B are related either to infusion or prolonged treatment. As amphotericin B is administered by slow IV infusion, all preparations are associated with an infusion reaction. This presents as chills, fever, muscle spasm, headache, vomiting, and hypotension. The effects may be reduced by pretreatment with an NSAID, hydrocortisone, or diphenhydramine; reducing the dose and infusion time of amphotericin B; or using alternate-day drug administration.

Figure 42.5   Examples of Antifungal Drugs

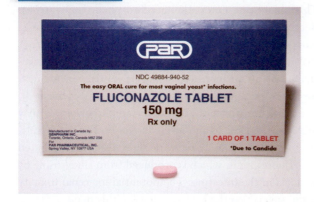

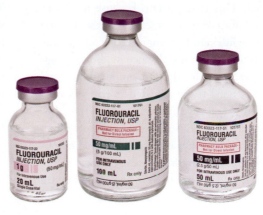

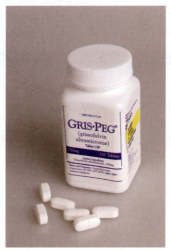

The conventional drug has long been associated with serious renal damage. It decreases renal perfusion and with extended use also damages the renal tubules, causing acidosis and ion wasting (hypokalemia, hypomagnesemia). Patients receiving these drugs must be monitored for hematological, hepatic, and renal function changes. The newer formulations were developed to reduce the nephrotoxicity. All parenteral formulations of amphotericin B have a special cautionary (black box) warning that states the drug should be used primarily for treatment of patients with progressive and potentially life-threatening fungal infections; it should not be used to treat noninvasive forms of fungal disease such as oral thrush, vaginal candidiasis, and esophageal candidiasis in patients with normal neutrophil counts. Exercise caution to prevent inadvertent overdose with amphotericin B. Verify the product name and dosage if dose exceeds 1.5 mg/kg.

Drug Interactions

There is an increased potential for hypokalemia and cardio and renal toxicity with coadministration of any amphotericin B and antineoplastic drugs, steroids, and digitalis glycosides. Combination therapy with azole antifungal drugs may induce fungal resistance to amphotericin B, especially in immunocompromised patients.

Echinocandins

Three of the newest antifungal agents are in the echinocandin class: anidulafungin (*Eraxis*), caspofungin (*Cancidas*), and micafungin (*Mycamine*). The activity of the echinocandins has been extensively studied against *Candida* and *Aspergillus* species. Echinocandins have fungicidal activity against *Candida* species, including triazole-resistant organisms, and fungistatic activity against *Aspergillus* species. All three echinocandins are indicated for the treatment of esophageal candidiasis; anidulafungin and caspofungin are indicated for the treatment of candidemia. All of these drugs are administered by slow IV infusion. The primary difference in the agents is in their route of elimination. While the other two drugs are highly bound to plasma proteins and metabolized in the liver, anidulafungin has a unique nonhepatic degradation. At body temperature, anidulafungin is slowly broken down in the blood to peptide fragments that are excreted. This is important because the other echinocandins exhibit drug interaction in the hepatic enzyme system, while anidulafungin's lack of hepatic metabolism is credited with the absence of clinically significant drug interactions. In addition, anidulafungin and micafungin do not need to be adjusted in patients with renal or hepatic insufficiency. Caspofungin, on the other hand, must reduce the daily maintenance dose by half in patients with moderate hepatic dysfunction. Echinocandins are first-line therapy for systemic fungal infections and candidemia. They are used in combination with amphotericin B or select azole drugs in the treatment of molds. Anidulafungin is primary therapy for invasive candidiasis in non-neutropenic patients, and as alternative therapy to fluconazole in patients with esophageal candidiasis with azole intolerance or triazole-resistance.

Adverse Effects

While adverse events have occurred with this group of drugs, the safety profile is far better than any of the other classes of antifungal drugs. Adverse effects include fever, headache, diarrhea, rash, **phlebitis,** and elevations in liver enzymes (ALT, AST). These drugs do not produce infusion reactions as seen with amphotericin B.

Drug interactions

Drugs that induce cytochrome P450 enzymes, specifically the CYP34A family, may cause a clinically significant reduction in caspofungin plasma levels. Coadministration of drugs such as carbamazepine, dexamethasone, efavirenz, nevirapine, phenytoin, and rifampin may require the dose of caspofungin to be increased to maintain effectiveness. Tacrolimus coadministration requires monitoring of plasma drug level for dose adjustment. Micafungin increases the plasma levels of itraconazole, nifedipine, sirolimus, and cyclosporin. The plasma levels of these drugs should be monitored for toxicity and the dose reduced as needed.

Flucytosine

Flucytosine (*Ancobon*) is a nucleic acid analog, an antimetabolite. Flucytosine is the only available antimetabolite drug with antifungal activity (antimetabolite drugs are more often used in cancer chemotherapy). It is water soluble, well absorbed after oral administration, and mainly excreted unchanged in the urine. This drug is not used alone or as first-line treatment because this frequently results in the emergence of organism resistance. Preexisting or emerging resistance especially among

Candida species to flucytosine is common; however, it is clinically valuable in combination with amphotericin B. This drug can enter the cerebrospinal fluid (CSF). Because flucytosine is cleared primarily by the kidneys, blood levels rise in the presence of renal disease. Drugs that impair glomerular filtration will decrease its excretion, causing an increase in plasma levels. Since flucytosine is commonly combined with amphotericin B, the renal impairment caused by amphotericin B may increase the flucytosine levels in the body and potentiate its toxicity. The toxicity of flucytosine is attributed to 5-fluorouracil, which is produced from flucytosine by bacteria in the intestine. The potential for renal toxicity is the special cautionary warning for this drug. Adverse effects are bone marrow suppression (**thrombocytopenia and leukopenia),** jaundice, abdominal bloating, GI hemorrhage, nausea, vomiting, ulcerative colitis, and elevation in liver enzymes. CNS effects are frequent and include confusion, hallucinations, hearing loss, headache, and paresthesia.

Azoles

The availability of the azole antifungal drugs represents a major advance in the management of systemic fungal infections. Miconazole was the first azole drug to be approved, and then ketoconazole. Ketoconazole could be administered orally and had less toxicity than amphotericin B or miconazole. The third generation of azoles includes the triazoles fluconazole (*Diflucan*), itraconazole (*Sporanox*), posaconazole (*Noxafil*), and voriconazole (*Vfend*). These drugs were introduced to minimize the adverse effects but retain the efficacy of ketoconazole. All of the newer azoles are available as oral formulations; only fluconazole and voriconazole can also be given parenterally.

The azoles have a wide spectrum of activity against common fungal pathogens, although it varies with each member of this group. Itraconazole and fluconazole had been alternatives to amphotericin B before the introduction of the echinocandins. Because of the nature of drug resistance in these organisms, there is still a large role for the azole group in the treatment of serious infections. Fluconazole is a water-soluble drug absorbed almost completely after an oral dose. It is excreted largely unchanged in urine, allowing for single daily dosing. It has high penetration into CSF and has been especially useful in treating cryptococcal and coccidioidal meningitis. It is also one of the first-line drugs for treatment of candidemia patients with normal white blood cells (non-neutropenic). Itraconazole has become the standard treatment for mild or moderately severe histoplasmosis, blastomycosis, and paracoccidioi-domycosis. It is also effective in mild cases of invasive aspergillosis and some types of fungal meningitis. Itraconazole absorption is increased when itraconazole capsules are taken with a full meal. Posaconazole (*Noxafil*), the newest and most potent azole drug, is only available as an oral suspension. It is the broadest spectrum azole and highly active against yeasts and opportunistic infections, which make it clinically valuable in treating immunosuppressed patients (HIV, chemotherapy). Voriconazole, another broad-spectrum triazole, is first-line therapy for serious *Aspergillus* infections. It also has activity against a broader spectrum of *Candida* species than fluconazole.

Adverse Effects

Most adverse effects are similar among the azole antifungal group such as fever, rash, GI (nausea, vomiting, diarrhea), CNS (headache, hallucinations), exfoliative dermatitis (skin peeling), and mild transient elevations in transaminases to clinical hepatitis in rare cases. It is likely that serum enzymes will be evaluated before and during treatment. Visual disturbances such as blurred vision or increased sensitivity to light (photosensitivity) are unique to voriconazole. The effect may last 30 minutes and does not appear to cause residual damage. All of these drugs prolong the QT interval in the heart. This is important because arrhythmias may develop or contractility of the heart can decrease, especially in patients with congestive heart failure (CHF). There is, however, a cautionary (black box) warning *only* for ketoconazole and itraconazole. If symptoms of CHF develop during itraconazole treatment, continuance should be reassessed. When patients were being treated for onychomycosis, some developed CHF; therefore, the drug should not be administered whenever there is a history or evidence of CHF. Ketoconazole, when used orally, has been associated with hepatic toxicity, including some fatalities.

Drug Interactions

All of the azole drugs prolong the anticoagulant action of warfarin. Frequent monitoring of INR and PT is recommended, even after antifungal therapy has finished, to reestablish appropriate anticoagulant levels. Posaconazole and voriconazole inhibit cytochrome P450 enzymes, specifically the CYP34A family. Drugs metabolized through this system will have increased blood levels when taken at the same time as the azoles. The elevated drug blood level is often significant and requires dose adjustment (decrease) of the nonantifungal drugs to avoid toxicity. Examples of the many drugs metabolized through this enzyme system are carbamazepine, oxycodone, rifabutin, ritonavir, tacrolimus, and the statins (HMG-CoA reductase inhibitors). Because of the prolonged QT interval, there is a special cautionary warning for itraconazole and ketoconazole: coadministration of pimozide, quinidine, or dofetilide with itraconazole is contraindicated as serious cardiac arrhythmias and death have occurred.

Additional Antifungal Drugs: Oral and Topical

Nystatin, Griseofulvin, Terbinafine

Nystatin exhibits little or no absorption following oral administration and little adverse effects. It is retained within the intestinal tract and the unmetabolized drug is excreted into the feces. This limits the effective site of action, but it is advantageous in two ways: (1) for the treatment of intestinal candidiasis and (2) in the treatment of pregnant women because the drug cannot affect developing fetal tissues. It is given for nonesophageal intestinal candidiasis. It is also used to cleanse the GI tract as a pre-operative medication in surgical procedures involving the colon. Nystatin is available under prescription for the treatment of vaginal candidiasis as a topical administration in tablets, ointments, creams, and powders. Nystatin is particularly safe (nontoxic). In large doses, oral nystatin has occasionally been associated with diarrhea, nausea, and vomiting.

Griseofulvin binds to keratin in keratin precursor cells and makes them resistant to fungal infections. When hair or skin is replaced by the keratin-griseofulvin complex, the fungi cannot ingest the protein and lose its nutrient. The drug can be taken one, two, or four times a day. Although symptoms may get better in a few days, the drug has to be continued for a long time before the infection is completely gone. It is usually taken for 4 to 6 weeks for hair and scalp infections, 3 to 4 months for fingernail infections, and at least 6 months for toenail infections. The duration of therapy coincides with the pattern of hair or nail growth to incorporate griseofulvin into the keratin. In the scalp, dry patches may develop into a large inflammatory mass (kerion), which is a severe reaction to the fungus. This can result in scarring and hair loss and may require a steroid (prednisone) in addition to the antifungal drug to resolve the inflammation. Food increases the absorption of griseofulvin. This is directly related to the fat content of the meal, as griseofulvin is fat rather than water soluble. Since absorption patterns can be quite variable, the available formulations of griseofulvin have been designed to improve the efficiency of surface contact and absorption from the stomach. Ultramicrosize allows more particles to be in contact with the absorptive surface than the conventional microsize formulation. Although this means less ultramicrosize drug may be taken on each dose compared to the microsized formulation, there is no difference in the clinical benefits derived from either formulation. Adverse effects include rash, urticaria, nausea, vomiting, diarrhea, headache, and photosensitivity. It has been reported to increase protein in the urine **(albuminuria).** Griseofulvin is contraindicated in patients with acute intermittent **porphyria** and hepatic failure, and should not be administered during pregnancy. Itraconazole has been shown to be as effective as griseofulvin in treating dermatophytic infections and may impact the use of griseofulvin in the future.

Terbinafine (*Lamisil*) is an orally and topically active drug that has fungicidal activity against pathogenic fungi. It has been developed as a new class of ergosterol biosynthetic inhibitor for the treatment of interdigital-type *Tinea pedis* (athlete's foot), *Tinea cruris* (jock itch), and *Tinea corporis* (ringworm) due to *Trichophyton* species. Terbinafine is well absorbed after oral administration. Food does not significantly affect absorption. It is distributed to the **sebum** and skin, where there is slow elimination of this drug from skin and adipose tissue. Terbinafine is highly bound to plasma proteins and extensively metabolized, primarily through cytochrome P450 enzymes before being excreted in the urine. Adverse effects include diarrhea, dyspepsia, pruritus, taste disturbances, nausea, abdominal pain, urticaria, rash, and visual disturbances. Serum enzymes may be elevated during terbinafine treatment. Terbinafine hydrochloride tablets are not recommended for patients with chronic or active liver disease or to be taken during pregnancy. Drug interactions include tricyclic antidepressants, selective serotonin reuptake inhibitors, beta-blockers, and antiarrhythmics because these drugs are metabolized through the enzyme system inhibited by terbinafine.

Microorganism Resistance

Before leaving these drugs, it is worth mentioning the significant issue of resistance. Primary resistance is when the organism does not respond to the drug because it doesn't recognize the drug or it has a protective mechanism to destroy the drug on contact. Some species of *Candida* are not sensitive to a particular antifungal drug. Secondary resistance is when the organism initially responds to the drug but then stops responding or requires greater doses to kill the organism. The wide variety of antifungal drugs with different mechanisms of action and target sites provides insurance that

clinical cure is attainable in most situations. When these drugs are used in combination, often it is to delay the development of resistance to a single drug. Studies have shown that resistance may occur because the leaky cell wall caused by an azole drug also causes the azole to leak out until it doesn't have enough intracellular drug concentration to "finish the job." Other studies have shown that as ergosterol synthesis is inhibited, some organisms punch up other enzymes to bypass the metabolic road block. Or the organism undergoes a mutation so that the target area no longer binds the antifungal drug. All of this is important because it explains why older drugs still have value in combination treatment, and why there is a continual research for new antifungal drugs.

Topical Administration

Topical administration includes application of creams, lotions, ointments, tinctures, sprays, and powders to the surface of the skin and mucous membranes. Topical applications are particularly useful in superficial fungal infections of the scalp, skin, nails, and mucous membranes, with special application devices for intravaginal infections. Less than 10 percent of the active drug is absorbed with topical administration. For most of these antifungal drugs, absorption is less than 1 to 5 percent. This permits safe use in pregnant women and may be recommended for use during the second and third trimesters. As a rule, topical antifungal drugs are used to treat less serious fungal infections that occur in the general population. Whether for *Tinea pedis* or diaper rash, these drugs are for external use only. Virtually all of the topical drugs are available over the counter (OTC). These drugs are available under many trade names, but a few have been identified in Table 42:2. A few are available by prescription and OTC (clotrimazole, terbinafine, miconazole), while nystatin and oxiconazole are prescription only. Many of these agents are broad-spectrum antifungals, and a few such as clioquinol are antibacterial as well. These products may have a single antifungal agent or may contain multiple active drugs. Ingredients may include alcohol, emollients, and talc as vehicles or drying agents. Combination products also may contain benzocaine, phenol, coal tar, camphor, chloroxylenol, and salicylic acid. These provide increased absorption, antiseptic activity, or reduced itching when applied liberally to the infected surface. Except for onychomycoses (nail infections), the intended length of use of topical antifungal drugs is usually less than 4 weeks. If symptoms do not resolve within this time frame, the patient should be reevaluated for complicating conditions as well as a more appropriate antifungal drug.

Contraindications

Drug hypersensitivity is the only absolute contraindication for all the antifungal drugs regardless of route of administration. In addition, a few drugs have been associated with specific serious adverse effects mitigating against their use in pregnancy or in combination with particular drugs. Such is the case with the azoles and flucytosine. The U.S. Public Health Service *Guidelines for the Prevention of Opportunistic Infections* include recommendations about using antifungal drugs during pregnancy. In short, the Guidelines recommend that oral azole antifungals should not be used during pregnancy because they have caused birth defects in animal studies. Sexually active women who are taking itraconazole should be using effective contraceptive therapy even up to 2 months after antifungal treatment has been discontinued. In the treatment of onychomycoses, terbinafine is not recommended to be given during pregnancy. The rationale is that these infections often require months of continuous treatment to achieve a cure and the nature of the infection allows it to be postponed until pregnancy has ended.

Patient Administration and Monitoring

Patient Instructions

Serious Fungal Infections

The treatment of serious fungal infections warrants close monitoring of the patient's vital signs, including an electrocardiogram (ECG) for potential evolving cardiac conduction problems. The patient's temperature should be taken frequently during the first 24 hours of treatment. Periodic serum chemistry and hematology tests are warranted to monitor potential elevations in serum creatine (>3 mg/dl) and BUN (>40 mg/dl), indicating changes in renal and liver function that might obligate antifungal dose adjustment or discontinuation of therapy. To minimize the occurrence of thrombophlebitis, indwelling catheters may be rotated to other sites, and heparin may be administered.

Nonserious Fungal Infections

Treatment of less serious though significant fungal infections is dependent upon patient compliance and good hygiene to effect a cure and minimize reinfection. Whether oral or topical formulations are being used, patients must be instructed to complete the entire course of therapy even when signs (cracked skin, redness) and symptoms (itching, burning) have improved. This is particularly true for those infections requiring continuation of medication for 2 weeks after clinical resolution.

Topical Formulations

Creams, ointments, gels, and lotions adhere to skin, providing optimum contact with the infected area. Prior to applying the medication, the skin should always be cleaned with soap and water and dried thoroughly. Hands should always be washed thoroughly after applying medication because of the danger of accidentally touching the eyes or mouth where medication could be deposited. Topical antifungals are for external use only. Application to mucous membranes of the eyes causes intense irritation, burning, and itching. Removal of the offending medication is impossible because of the oily nature of the emollients.

Infected areas that are predisposed to moist conditions, such as the feet, groin, and underarm, may require powder formulations rather than creams or lotions. Powders usually contain talc or cornstarch, which absorbs moisture, so that the medication can perform its action. The advantage of a drier environment has to be balanced against the need to reapply the drug more frequently because the powder does not stay in place. For athlete's foot and jock itch, the cleansed areas should be covered with clean, natural fiber fabric that allows air and moisture to move away from the skin. This means educating patients to the use of cotton socks, preferably white or light colors, whenever wearing shoes. No sockless sneakers or loafers, or polyester briefs, please! Such conditions, usually popular among young adults, are excellent breeding areas for fungi. Patients must be encouraged to change socks, sometimes more than once a day. Occlusive dressings should not be used in lieu of socks.

Discoloration

Certain products may stain clothing, linens, and other fabrics during use. Amphotericin B and clioquinol discolor fabrics and skin but will wash out with soap. Gentian violet, although a lovely color, is a permanent fabric dye. Even when applied to debrided or ulcerative areas, it produces a pattern referred to as "tattooing." This cosmetic effect has caused gentian violet to be replaced by other topical medications even though it is effective.

Drug Interactions

Current medications should be reviewed thoroughly to ascertain whether the patient is taking antacids, cimetidine, or other antiulcer products that could reduce the absorption of oral ketoconazole, fluconazole, or itraconazole. The patient should be instructed to take such medications 2 hours after the antifungal dose.

Adverse Effects

Patients who are using ketoconazole should be alerted that this drug may produce headache, drowsiness, and dizziness

(Continued)

that could impair the coordination and concentration required to drive, operate machinery, or perform tasks requiring manual dexterity.

Oral medications such as the imidazole/triazole drugs or flucytosine may cause nausea or gastrointestinal irritation after dosing. Patients may be encouraged to take these medications with meals, or spread the number of tablets or capsules ingested over 15 to 30 minutes.

Intravaginal Use

Intravaginal application of medication may obligate the patient to refrain from sexual intercourse in order to maintain sufficient drug contact with the infected surface. Depending upon the nature of the infection, abstinence may be warranted throughout the course of treatment (up to 4 weeks).

Intravaginal applicators can be designed for reuse. Product information accompanying the drug will specify whether to dispose of the applicator or reuse it. Patients must be told to wash reusable applicators with soap and water between uses. Oral instruction, whenever possible, is worth the effort because some patients cannot read the print in package inserts.

Notifying the Physician

Patients should be instructed to notify the physician if symptoms of rash, itching, blistering, or swelling occur because this may signal the development of hypersensitivity to antifungal drugs. If such symptoms characterize the infection under treatment and persist for more than 2 to 3 weeks during treatment, the physician should be notified. Change of drug or dose or identification of confounding conditions may be warranted.

The physician should be notified immediately if severe abdominal pain, yellowing of the skin or eyes, dark urine, or diarrhea occurs while taking ketoconazole as this may signal the development of jaundice.

Use in Pregnancy

Nystatin is designated FDA Pregnancy Category A because there has been no evidence of risk to the fetus associated with maternal use in the first, second, or third trimester.

Other antifungal drugs are designated FDA Pregnancy Category B or C because they have not been adequately studied in pregnant women. Among the systemic drugs, safe use in pregnancy has not been established in humans. Nevertheless, there are situations where their use is clearly indicated, and may be used with caution and close patient monitoring. When amphotericin B has been used in pregnant women, harm to the fetus did not occur. Even with topical administration where absorption is extremely low, these drugs are primarily recommended for use in the second and third trimesters.

Itraconazole and flucytosine have produced changes in animals that indicate these drugs should not be used in pregnant women. Women of childbearing age who are receiving itraconazole must be instructed to use effective contraception during antifungal treatment. Effective contraception must be clearly described to the patient and may include oral contraceptives or barrier methods. Women who become pregnant while on itraconazole or flucytosine treatment should notify their physician immediately for further evaluation and discontinuation of antifungal therapy.

LO 42.2 | **LO 42.4** | **LO 42.5** | **LO 42.6**

VIRAL DISEASES

Diseases caused by viruses include influenza, chickenpox, cold sores, mononucleosis, pneumonia, rabies, poliomyelitis, and AIDS. As a rule, viruses occupy specific cells. As shown in Figure 42.6, common respiratory infections (pneumonia, common cold) come from viruses that reside in the nasal canal (rhinoviruses) or lungs (influenza types A [H1N1], B). Adenovirus, norovirus, and rotovirus invade the gastrointestinal tract and produce cramping and diarrhea. Sexually transmitted viruses (STD) can cause skin infections (human papillomavirus—warts) or attack the immune system (HIV).

A virus is a small infectious agent, much smaller than a fungus or bacterium, that must invade a living cell to reproduce. All viruses consist of genetic information, RNA or DNA, surrounded by a protective protein coat. Some viruses also have an outside lipid coat or envelope. Viruses are unique organisms because they cannot reproduce without a host cell. They do not contain the enzymes needed to carry out the chemical reactions for life. Instead, viruses carry only one or two enzymes that decode their genetic instructions.

After contact with a host cell, a virus gets its genetic material into the cell and commandeers the cell's activity. Instead of its usual proteins, the infected host cell produces viral proteins and genetic material (more viruses). Some viruses cause the host cell to die as thousands of new viruses are released into the body. Other viruses are surrounded by the host cell membrane, a process called budding, prior to release. The budding allows the new viruses to leave without damaging the host cell and infect more cells. In the process of virus replication and release, the host may experience symptoms associated with the specific disease.

Virus Exposure and Immunity

Many viral diseases such as chickenpox, measles, and mumps occur during childhood. Usually, these diseases occur only once because antibodies are produced that protect individuals from reinfection. This protection is referred to as active **acquired immunity.** When the

Figure 42.6   Location of Some Common Human Viral Infections

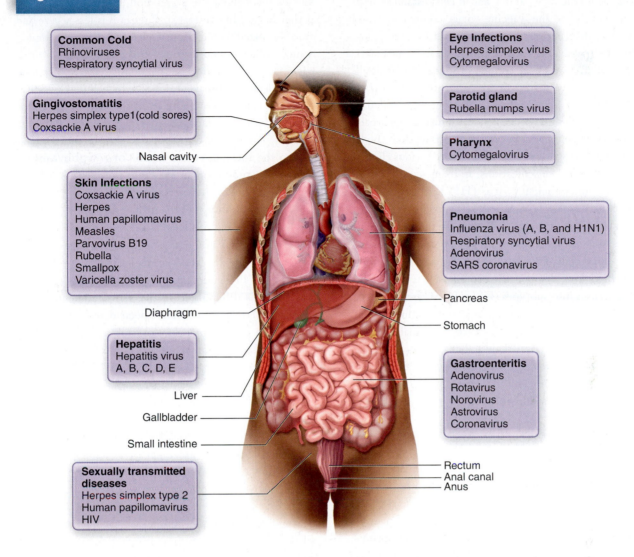

Common Cold
Rhinoviruses
Respiratory syncytial virus

Gingivostomatitis
Herpes simplex type1(cold sores)
Coxsackie A virus

Nasal cavity

Skin Infections
Coxsackie A virus
Herpes
Human papillomavirus
Measles
Parvovirus B19
Rubella
Smallpox
Varicella zoster virus

Diaphragm

Hepatitis
Hepatitis virus
A, B, C, D, E

Liver

Gallbladder

Small intestine

Sexually transmitted diseases
Herpes simplex type 2
Human papillomavirus
HIV

Eye Infections
Herpes simplex virus
Cytomegalovirus

Parotid gland
Rubella mumps virus

Pharynx
Cytomegalovirus

Pneumonia
Influenza virus (A, B, and H1N1)
Respiratory syncytial virus
Adenovirus
SARS coronavirus

Pancreas

Stomach

Gastroenteritis
Adenovirus
Rotavirus
Norovirus
Astrovirus
Coronavirus

Rectum
Anal canal
Anus

virus enters the body for the first time, it is examined by the immune system. Specialized cells (macrophages and **dendritic cells**) engulf the virus, digest its contents, and make samples of the viral **antigens** available for T and B cells (specialized lymphocytes). See Figure 42.7. The T and B cells become familiar with the new antigens so that on the next encounter the B cells will produce antibodies specific for the virus and the T cells (killer T cells) will seek out and destroy cells invaded by the virus. Some of the B and T cells become long-lived memory cells that guard against future infection for years.

Immunity also can be achieved without experiencing the disease through vaccination (passive acquired immunity). For example, with viruses such as smallpox, polio (Sabin), chickenpox, and H1N1 (swine influenza nasal spray), vaccination exposes individuals to a weakened (attenuated) live virus, which stimulates antibody

Figure 42.7

Phagocytes Protect the Body from Infection by Finding, Surrounding, and Digesting Intruding Microorganisms

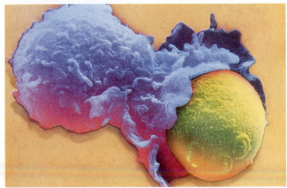

production without producing the disease. The macrophages, dendritic cells, and T and B cells establish virus recognition from the vaccine virus components and retain the destruction memory for future infections. Immunity (passive) also can be achieved using inactivated (killed) virus that cannot produce disease (Salk polio, seasonal influenza) or by exposure to viral fragments. Where possible, vaccines have been developed to provide controlled exposure and immunity to the broadest population or, at least, the most susceptible (high-risk) population who may develop a more serious clinical infection or other complications. In many cases, as with human immunodeficiency virus **(HIV),** it has not been possible to develop a vaccine. HIV rapidly replicates and undergoes mutations so frequently that even small changes in its proteins make the virus unrecognizable to host immune cells. Proteins vary so dramatically among influenza viruses that specific proteins are used to classify the viruses into subtypes (H1–H16). This also means that on exposure immunity develops only to the particular virus subtype. When vaccines are not available, often there are drugs (antiviral drugs) that can interrupt the viral infection process and lessen the course of the disease. Before discussing antiviral drugs, the clinical profile of infections caused by influenza, herpes, and HIV is presented.

Influenza

Flu viruses (e.g., Asian influenza) primarily affect the upper (nasal passages and pharynx) and lower (lungs) respiratory tracts. The virus is spread in the aerosolized droplets from the sneeze or cough of an infected person. The inoculated droplets are inhaled directly or transmitted by contact with the uninfected person who inadvertently delivers the virus into the mouth or respiratory tract (e.g., sucking on contaminated pencils, pens, and fingers).

Influenza is a family of RNA viruses categorized as types A, B, and C. Influenza A and B infect humans, although the alternate host for type A is often birds, such as chickens, or pigs prior to human inoculation. Type A influenza viruses are further typed into subtypes according to different kinds and combinations of virus surface proteins. Among many subtypes of influenza A viruses, currently influenza A (H1N1) and A (H3N2) subtypes are circulating among humans. Influenza viruses circulate in every part of the world. Influenza outbreaks occur every year in the Northern Hemisphere between November and April (and May to October in the Southern Hemisphere) coincident with the winter season. A localized wave of infection confirmed as a high incidence (20 percent) in the general population is considered an epidemic. Influenza A epidemics typically begin

suddenly, last for several months as the wave of infection spreads throughout the population, and end as abruptly as they began. In contrast, influenza B is less severe and more localized, often occurring in schools and nursing homes. When an outbreak of influenza occurs worldwide, it is considered to be "pandemic." Pandemics, like the influenza outbreak of 1918, which killed 675,000 Americans alone (more than in all the wars of the twentieth century), are facilitated by global travel but, fortunately, occur over a greater cycle of 15 to 20 years. (Go to the Internet at **www.pbs.org/wgbh/amex/ influenza/maps** for an excellent presentation on the epidemiology of the influenza pandemic.)

H1N1 is a subtype of the influenza type A virus and was the most recent pandemic viral infection. H1N1, also referred to as swine flu or pig flu, is common in pig populations worldwide. The National Centers for Disease Control and Prevention (CDC), however, has reported that H1N1 is different from the virus found in North American pigs. H1N1 had never been identified as a cause of infection in humans prior to 2009 and genetically it is unrelated to the human seasonal H1N1 virus that has circulated among people since 1977. H1N1 (swine flu) is considered a new emergent influenza A virus to which most people had no immunity. Reported illness of a different kind of flu began in April 2009 in the United States and Mexico and was declared to be pandemic by the World Health Organization (WHO) in June 2009. H1N1 was the predominant laboratory-confirmed influenza virus worldwide (reported in 213 countries). The new virus produced a different pattern of infection, causing infections in the summer (in the northern hemisphere) and greater numbers of infection than seasonal flu in the winter months. Infections and deaths occurred in otherwise healthy young people (under 19 years of age). People over 65 years of age were the least likely to be infected. At risk are pregnant women, very young children, and people of any age with chronic health conditions or compromised immune function.

Clinical Profile

In the general population (relatively healthy individuals), flu viruses usually produce headache, fever, intense fatigue, dry cough, muscle ache, and sensitivity of the eyes to light. The reaction to viral infection is usually mild or moderate with symptom onset within 24 to 72 hours of incubation and resolution after a short period of infection of 7 to 14 days. Flu and its accompanying symptoms are not the same as the constellation of symptoms that occur from "cold" viruses (rhinoviruses). The clinical profile of the common cold differs from flu in that a cold develops gradually, over days, characterized by nasal secretion (rhinorrhea), congestion, and sneezing. Fever (>100.5° F) and muscle and joint aches are usually not associated with a cold but are present with flu.

The problem with flu, especially in children and elderly patients, is that secondary complications may occur, such as bacterial infections, otitis media, or bronchitis, that prolong the duration of illness in spite of treatment. Moreover, in the elderly and chronically ill, the same flu viruses may produce a more difficult or more intense infection such as pneumonia. Because the immune systems of these patients are often less competent to fight the infection, severe reactions such as dehydration, convulsions, and death may occur.

Influenza Vaccine

A vaccine is available for influenza. The influenza vaccine is formulated each year to contain strains of the virus that are expected to produce flu within the population for the following winter. The CDC determines the viral composition of the vaccine for the next year. Because type C influenza cases occur much less frequently, only influenza A and B viruses are included in seasonal influenza vaccines.

Over an 8-month period, viruses are grown in highly purified chicken eggs because the flu virus grows well in eggs. Usually three strains of virus are included in the vaccine—two type A and one type B. To be optimally effective, vaccinations are given in the United States between October and mid-November. Following a single-dose intramuscular injection, antibody production is initiated and continues over a 2-week period, just in time for the onset of the flu season. The immunity conferred by the antibody response is only effective for the strains contained in the vaccine. When the "match" between vaccine and circulating strains is close, the injectable (inactivated) vaccine prevents seasonal influenza in about 70 to 90 percent of healthy persons younger than age 65 years. Elderly, especially those in nursing homes, benefit because severe illness, secondary complications, and deaths related to seasonal influenza are usually prevented. Occasionally, despite vaccination, the population succumbs to the wave of influenza or suffers a more severe course than expected. This resistance (vaccine ineffectiveness) occurs primarily with influenza type A because a strain of virus (in the wild) changed its antigenic nature during the year when the vaccine was in production. As a result, the antibodies produced from the vaccination no longer recognize the wild virus to inactivate it. Small changes in viral surface proteins are known as **antigenic drift** and result in decreased vaccine effectiveness. When the virus undergoes a major change in its surface proteins

such as hemagglutinin and neuraminidase, it is considered an **antigenic shift.** This could obliterate antibody recognition.

The vaccine for H1N1 was produced in the same manner as described above. An inactive virus is administered by injection, while a live attenuated virus is given by intranasal spray. It does not convey immunity to other viruses, including other influenza (seasonal) viruses. To be protected optimally during flu season, it was necessary to receive a flu shot and an H1N1 vaccination. With the 2010–2011 flu season, seasonal flu vaccine will protect against three flu viruses, one of which is a 2009 H1N1-like flu virus. Subsequent production of flu vaccine will be based on the exposure profile of the previous year, as usual.

Despite variability in effectiveness, vaccination is recommended by the CDC for persons over 6 months of age who are at high risk for complications from the flu or who are in a position to transmit the virus to high-risk patients (e.g., health care providers or household members). High-risk persons include persons over 65 years of age, frail elderly, residents of nursing homes or long-term care facilities, adults and children who have chronic pulmonary (asthma, COPD) or cardiovascular disorders, and those who are immunosuppressed, have HIV, and/or require hospitalization. Other high-risk groups include women who are in their second or third trimester of pregnancy during the flu season and children who require long-term aspirin (salicylates) therapy (i.e., at risk for **Reye's syndrome**).

Vaccination in healthy young adults is up to 90 percent effective in preventing or minimizing the clinical symptoms of flu. Vaccination is recommended for healthy individuals to minimize the incidence of febrile upper respiratory tract illness, and to reduce the economic burden from days of lost work and wages, lost productivity, and visits to health care providers.

The most common adverse reaction to vaccination is soreness at the injection site; however, mild fever and myalgia also may occur. Reaction to the live virus includes runny nose, sore throat, chills, fever, and muscle and headache. Vaccines are contraindicated in people known to have allergy to eggs. In addition to the influenza vaccine, there are antiviral drugs that are effective in the clinical management of influenza. See Table 42:5 for a list of these drugs under the section on Antiviral Drugs.

Herpes

There are eight human *Herpes* viruses that are double-stranded DNA viruses. The family of *Herpes* viruses includes *Herpes simplex* (types 1 and 2), *Herpes (varicella) zoster,* cytomegalovirus, Epstein-Barr virus, and herpesvirus 6, 7, and 8. A *Herpes* infection is for life. These viruses infect epithelial mucosal cells or lymphocytes, and then travel up peripheral nerves to a nucleated neuron where they can reside undetected for years. *Herpes simplex* type 1 is responsible for producing innocuous, though unpleasant, skin lesions known as fever blisters or cold sores, yet the same virus can produce encephalitis and severe changes in the eye that can lead to blindness (keratitis and corneal scarring). Cold sores are generally contracted from skin-to-skin contact with an infected area. The fluid in the blisters is full of viruses. The usual incubation period of the virus (time before any symptoms show) is approximately 2 to 12 days after the first exposure to the virus. Once infected with cold sores, the virus remains inside the body in a latent (sleeping) state. Throughout a person's life the virus can then become "activated," causing a cold sore recurrence. *Herpes simplex* type 2 is associated with adult genital infections and neonatal infections through transmission from the mother before, during, or after delivery. Genital herpes is an STD. Each year, 1.5 million new cases are diagnosed. It can be transmitted through direct contact with a *Herpes* infection such as an infected blister or sore. *Herpes* also can be transmitted when there are no symptoms present and be dormant for a long period of time. Symptoms may include blisters or rash in the infected area, itching, burning, genital discharge, and flu-like symptoms of headache, fever, and swollen glands. *Herpes zoster* causes inflammation of nerve roots resulting in a severe painful blistering rash after reactivation of the *Herpes varicella-zoster* virus. The primary infection occurs as chickenpox (varicella), usually during childhood. Like *Herpes simplex,* the virus persists for years in the anterior horn cells before it is reactivated. The reactivation is known as viral shedding. Any *Herpes* virus can be spread from the time the first symptoms are noticed until the skin looks normal again. Even when there are no symptoms, there is a small chance the virus can be spread on contact. Patients with genital herpes should avoid intercourse when prodromal itching symptoms or an active lesion is present. The virus can be spread by contact to other locations on the body, although this is more likely to occur in immunocompromized patients. The lesions on the skin surface from *Herpes zoster* are known as "shingles." Usually, persistent postherpetic neuralgia occurs that may be difficult to treat.

All of the *Herpes* viral diseases are characterized by their high incidence of recurrence because the virus remains within human tissue for years before producing effects. Outside the body, *Herpes* can be killed by washing with acids, detergents, and organic solvents, as might be expected for a virus with a lipid envelope. There is

one available vaccine, *Zostavax,* effective against *Herpes zoster* virus. This vaccine is approved for prevention of shingles in patients over 60 years of age. It is not effective as a treatment once symptoms have occurred. It is administered as a single-dose subcutaneous injection. Antiviral drugs effective in the reatment of *Herpes* infections are presented in Table 42:6 later in the chapter.

Acquired Immunodeficiency Syndrome (AIDS)
Incidence of Infection
Although elderly and immunocompromised patients may die from complications associated with the flu, most people who have been exposed to flu or *Herpes* viruses survive seasonal attacks because the clinical symptoms are usually self-limiting. However, *this is not the case with HIV.* One of the most notorious virus-induced diseases is **acquired immunodeficiency syndrome (AIDS),** caused by the human immunodeficiency virus (HIV). The spread of this disease is still escalating worldwide and the CDC reports that 40,000 new HIV infections occur in the United States each year. Half of these new infections occur in people under 25 years old. Most people live with HIV for several years before developing AIDS. It is a significant cause of death among young adults in the United States and the virus is reaching younger people each year. More than 50 percent of all people who developed AIDS within 10 years of diagnosis have died. The incidence among men has declined slightly since HIV was first identified in 1981; however, the incidence in women continues to escalate. The virus is transmitted through sexual contact, perinatally from an infected mother to the neonate, through infected blood during transfusion, or by injection into the blood through IV drug use. Among all AIDS cases in women in the United States, almost half are due to nonmedical IV drug use. Fortunately, measures to protect against blood bank contamination have succeeded in virtually eliminating this route of infection. While the route of transmission varies among communities, more than 95 percent of HIV infection today occurs through sexual contact and/or needle-borne infection.

Clinical Profile
After exposure to the virus, a person may test HIV positive. This only indicates that the person was infected by the virus at some time. It does not give any indication of what the virus is currently doing. The typical course of infection is characterized by an acute clinical illness that varies in severity followed by a prolonged period of

clinical latency. Hence, the infected individual may go for years (3 to 10 years) without signs or symptoms associated with active infection. During the clinical latency period, the virus is active within the host—preparing conditions for the onset of AIDS. Finally, patients develop opportunistic infections or cancers that manifest a constellation of clinical symptoms announcing the progression to AIDS. Only 5 to 10 percent of HIV-infected people remain asymptomatic 10 years after the initial infection. HIV is a retrovirus. It is an RNA virus that contains the enzyme reverse transcriptase. Retroviruses reverse the normal host cell process and reproduce by transcribing themselves into DNA. The target cells for HIV are macrophages and helper T cells. Once transcription has taken place, the viral DNA gains access to lymphocyte DNA, reproducing along with the cell and its offspring. The viral DNA creates RNA replicas of itself that eventually leave the lymphocytes after coating themselves with a protein. (See Figure 42.8.) Even during the quiet asymptomatic clinical period, HIV is very busy replicating and inducing CD4 T-lymphocyte death. The most significant clinical defect that characterizes AIDS is the profound depletion of T-lymphocytes to less than 200 to 500 cells/mm^3. Patients are monitored for total CD4 cell counts because these numbers reflect the T-lymphocytes available to combat other infections. Some evidence suggests CD4 cells may be a way to quantify viral activity (viral load) in the near future. Signs and symptoms that appear in patients with HIV infection even before the full expression of AIDS-defining illnesses are presented in Table 42:3. Despite the lethal nature of HIV, you might be surprised that outside of a living cell, HIV is considered a "fragile" virus. When left outside living tissue, household bleach is sufficient to kill the HIV virus. This is the recommended disinfectant when cleaning or wiping a surface that has been exposed to fluids containing HIV (for example, infected blood spilled on a countertop).

HIV and Immune System Competence

HIV has made a significant negative impact on the health of young adults because there is no acquired immunity or vaccine that can prevent or interrupt the devastating effects of the chronic infection. HIV is significantly different from other viruses already mentioned. Protection from reinfection is conferred by the final outcome of the disease process—death. HIV attacks the heart of the cell-mediated immune system (lymphocytes) so that the human host is progressively **immunosuppressed** and cannot fight disease. As a result, patients become susceptible to multiple infections such as candidiasis, pneumonia, tuberculosis, and toxoplasmosis. Because these patients are incapable of efficiently fighting infection, they are always susceptible to **opportunistic organisms.** The incompetent immune system, specifically a deterioration of cell-mediated immunity, permits patients to develop secondary cancers, such as Kaposi's sarcoma, non-Hodgkin's lymphoma, or primary lymphoma of the brain. Various HIV vaccines, effective in animal models but not yet demonstrated to be effective in humans, are under development. AIDS patients take a tremendous variety of drugs during the progression of the disease; virtually all of the drugs are directed at eradicating pathogenic organisms (antibiotics), alleviating the symptoms of the AIDS-defining illnesses, and interrupting viral invasion of T-lymphocytes.

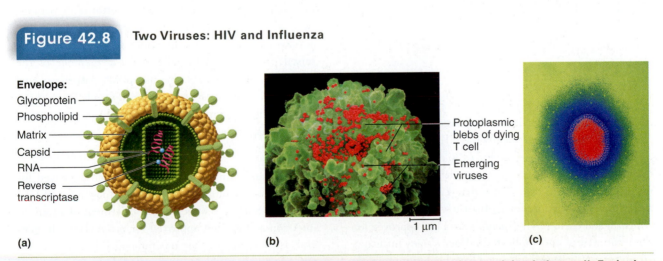

| Figure 42.8 | **Two Viruses: HIV and Influenza** |

Envelope:
Glycoprotein
Phospholipid
Matrix
Capsid
RNA
Reverse transcriptase

Protoplasmic blebs of dying T cell
Emerging viruses

1 μm

(a)   (b)   (c)

(a) Structure of the human immunodeficiency virus (HIV). (b) Viruses emerging from a dying helper cell. Each virus can now invade a new helper T cell and produce a similar number of descendants. (c) The influenza virus.

Signs and Symptoms in Patients with HIV Infection

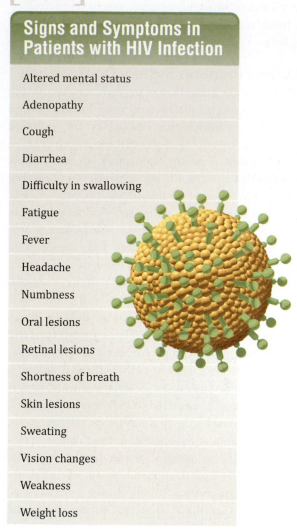

Altered mental status

Adenopathy

Cough

Diarrhea

Difficulty in swallowing

Fatigue

Fever

Headache

Numbness

Oral lesions

Retinal lesions

Shortness of breath

Skin lesions

Sweating

Vision changes

Weakness

Weight loss

LO 42.3 | LO 42.5 | LO 42.6

ANTIVIRAL DRUGS

Clinical Indications and Preferred Treatment

Influenza

Amantadine (*Symadine, Symmetrel*) and rimantadine (*Flumadine*) are used prophylactically to reduce the severity of influenza attacks, specifically the influenza A virus, in susceptible groups. These include the elderly, immunocompromised patients, and patients with chronic diseases predisposing to infection. These drugs are often given in addition to vaccination during the flu season. Zanamivir (*Relenza*) and oseltamivir (*Tamiflu*) are FDA approved for the treatment of uncomplicated influenza (any influenza strain type A or B) in adults who have been symptomatic for less than 3 days. The H1N1 (2009) influenza virus remains susceptible to these drugs. These drugs are not substitutes for annual vaccination and are compatible adjuncts to vaccination. Antiviral drugs effective in the clinical management of respiratory infections are presented in Table 42:4.

Respiratory Syncytial Virus (RSV)

This single-strand RNA virus causes severe bronchitis and pneumonia in infants and children, often leading to death. Although the virus resembles influenza, it responds to treatment as a unique agent. Ribavirin (*Virazole*) is used in the treatment of RSV-induced severe lower respiratory infections in hospitalized children. While ribavirin also has been used to treat influenza A and B, it is not approved for this use in adults.

Herpes simplex Virus (HSV) and Cytomegalovirus (CMV)

Idoxuridine (*Herplex*), vidarabine (*Ara-A, Vira-A*), and trifluridine (*Viroptic*) are used in the treatment of *Herpes simplex* infections of the eye, keratoconjuntivitis, and epithelial keratitis. These compounds can be administered topically (ocular instillation) for treatment of acute viral infections of the cornea and conjunctiva. Acyclovir (*Zovirax*) is approved for the treatment of cutaneous and genital *Herpes* infections. Acyclovir also is used to treat infections of *Herpes* and CMV that occur after bone marrow or renal transplant. Valacyclovir (*Valtrex*) is an analog of acyclovir that is rapidly converted to acyclovir in the tissues. Famciclovir (*Famvir*) is converted to the active antiviral penciclovir and penciclovir itself is available as an antiviral cream. Acyclovir also is given to the mother for fetal prophylaxis at 36 weeks of gestation. Drugs effective for herpes infections are presented in Table 42:5.

Cidofovir (*Vistide*), foscarnet (*Foscavir*), ganciclovir (*Cytovene*), and valganciclovir (*Valcyte*) are approved for use in the treatment of CMV retinitis in patients with AIDS, CMV disease in transplant recipients, and acyclovir-resistant HSV infections in immunocompromised patients. Cytomegalovirus is a member of the *Herpes* group of viruses. In susceptible patients of any age, CMV may cause hepatitis and encephalitis. Exposure during pregnancy may result in abortion or severe brain damage in newborns.

HIV

A significant number of drugs have been approved for use alone or in combination for the management of HIV infection. Some are indicated for treatment of advanced infection and are not approved for prophylaxis. In general, monotherapy is not recommended because it cannot counter the rapid development of drug resistance and missed doses result in a poor clinical response. Among

Drugs Effective in the Treatment of Viral Respiratory Infections

Drug (*Trade Name*)	Black box safety warning	Mechanism of action	Use	Adult dose
Amantadine (*Symmetrel*)	—	Inhibits release of viral DNA into host cells	Influenza A	200 mg PO* daily as single dose or 100 mg BID for at least 10 days
Oseltamivir (*Tamiflu*)	—	Inhibits viral neuraminidase and virus release	Influenza A & H1N1 prophylaxis and treatment	75 mg PO QD for 10 days 75 mg PO QD for 5 days as treatment
Peramivir**	—	Inhibits viral neuraminidase	H1N1 influenza A emergency treatment	600 mg IV over 30 min once daily for 5 to 10 days
Rimantadine (*Flumadine*)	—	Inhibits early viral replication by uncoating the virus	Influenza A prophylaxis	100 mg BID* PO for 7 days
Zanamivir (*Relenza*)	—	Inhibits viral neuraminidase	Influenza A and B prophylaxis and treatment	10 mg (2 inhalations) QD with diskhaler for 10 days
Ribavirin (*Virazole*)	Not for use in adults. Sudden deterioration of respiratory function; monitor continuously	Mechanism unknown; guanosine replacement	RSV syncytial virus; severe lower respiratory infections in infants and young children	20 mg/ml aerosolized (not oral formulation) for 12–18 hr/day 3–7 days

* Dose adjustment to 100 mg/day recommended for elderly and patients with renal or hepatic disease.
** Peramivir is an investigational drug available only through the Centers for Disease Control and Prevention.

the drugs used against HIV are didanosine (*Videx*), enfuvirtide (*Fuzeon*), etravirine (*Intelence*), indinavir (*Crixivan*), maraviroc (*Selzentry*), nelfinavir (*Viracept*), and saquinavir (*Invirase*). Many currently available anti-HIV drugs are presented in Table 42:6.

A current treatment strategy is HAART (highly active antiretroviral therapy). Designed to improve the life expectancy of a HIV-infected person by reducing the amount of virus present in the blood to very low or almost undetectable levels, HAART means administrating more than 2 different kinds of antiretroviral drugs in combination. There are six classes of antiretroviral drugs that interfere with different phases of the HIV cycle (see Mechanisms of Action). Combination drugs introduce multiple obstacles for the virus at each stage of its life cycle, thus reducing the ability of the virus to replicate. The most favored method is the triple-cocktail combining two nucleoside-analogue reverse transcriptase inhibitors (NRTIs) and one nonnucleoside-RTI (NNRTI) or a protease inhibitor. While this has been achieved in the past by taking multiple medications, there are combination drugs now available (*Atripla* and *Trizivir*) as a "triple" cocktail in one pill.

Propagation of Viruses

Unlike other microorganisms, viruses are totally dependent upon the metabolic system of the host's cells. In order to multiply, viruses must enter the cell nucleus. Viruses initially attach to the outer cell membrane and eventually gain access to the nucleus. Viruses have surface proteins (e.g., hemagglutinins) that enable them to attach to the host-cell membrane by binding to specialized structures called receptors. After attaching to the cells, the viruses inject their nucleic acid (RNA or DNA) into the cells. The cells become efficient factories that produce new viruses using host DNA, amino acids, enzymes, bases, and ions. Periodically, the new viruses are expelled into the circulation and more host cells become infected. Drugs have been developed that arrest the infection after symptoms appear. The goal of drug therapy is to destroy the viruses and reduce the severity and length of infection. Since viruses are so closely

Drugs Effective in the Treatment of Herpes Virus Infections

Drug (*Trade Name*)	Black box warning	Mechanism of action	Use	Adult dose
Drugs for influenza virus				
Amantadine (*Symmetrel*)	—	Inhibits release of viral DNA into host cells	Influenza A respiratory tract illness	200 mg PO daily as single dose or 100 mg BID for at least 10 days
Rimantadine (*Flumadine*)	—	Inhibits early viral replication by uncoating the virus	Influenza A respiratory tract illness	100 mg BID PO for 7 days
Drugs for CMV disease				
Cidofovir (*Vistide*)	Acute renal failure, neutropenia	Inhibits viral DNA synthesis	CMV retinitis in AIDS patients	5 mg/kg IV q 12 hr for 14–21 days
Foscarnet sodium (*Foscavir*)	Acute renal failure, seizures	Inhibits viral replication, pyrophosphate binding on DNA	CMV retinitis in immunocompromised patients	90 mg/kg controlled IV* infusion (1–2 hr) q 12 hr, or 60 mg/kg infused IV over 1 hr q 8 hr for 2–3 weeks
Ganciclovir (*Cytovene*)	Granulocytopenia, anemia, thrombocytopenia	Inhibits viral DNA synthesis; guanosine replacement	CMV retinitis, CMV diseases, HIV at risk for CMV; transplant, immunosuppressed patients	5 mg/kg IV infusion* over 1 hr q 12 hr for 14–21 days or 1000 mg PO TID with food or 500 mg PO six times a day
Valganciclovir (*Valcyte*)	Granulocytopenia, anemia, thrombocytopenia	Inhibits DNA synthesis	CMV disease in immunocompromised or immunosuppressed patients	900 mg PO once a day with food*

Drug (*Trade Name*)	Pyrimidine or purine base	Mechanism of action	Use	Adult dose
Drugs for herpes simplex, herpes zoster, and varicella virus diseases				
Acyclovir** (*Zovirax*)	Acycloguanosine; it's a purine nucleoside analog	Inhibits viral DNA replication	Genital herpes, initial; genital herpes, chronic	200 mg PO q 4 hr for 10 days; 400 mg PO BID for up to 12 months
			Herpes zoster (shingles)	800 mg PO q 4 hr for 7–10 days
			Chickenpox (varicella)	200 mq PO QID* for 5 days
Docosanol (*Abreva*)	—	Inhibits viral fusion onto healthy cells	Cold sores (*Herpes labialis*)	5 times/day directly on red or blistered area
Famciclovir (*Famvir*)	Biotransformed to penciclovir, a guanine analog	Inhibits viral DNA replication	Genital herpes, recurrent	1000 mg PO BID for 1 day
			Genital herpes, suppression	250 mg PO BID for 5 days
			Herpes zoster	500 mg PO q 8 hr for 7 days
Idoxuridine (*Dendrid, Herplex*)	5'-iodo-2'-deoxyuridine	Inhibits viral DNA synthesis by blocking incorporation of thymidine	*Herpes simplex* keratitis	1 drop into each infected eye every hour during the day and every 2 hr at night
Penciclovir (*Denavir*)	A guanine analog	Inhibits viral DNA replication	*Herpes labialis* recurrent	Topical cream, apply q 2 hr for 4 days

(Continued)

Drug (*Trade Name*)	Pyrimidine or purine base	Mechanism of action	Use	Adult dose
Trifluridine (*Viroptic*)	Trifluorothymidine	Interferes with viral DNA synthesis	*Herpes simplex* 1 and 2, keratoconjuctivitis, keratitis	1 drop into each infected eye every 2 hr not to exceed 9 drops/day up to 7 days
Valacyclovir (*Valtrex*)	Acyclovir analog; it's a purine nucleoside analog	Inhibits viral DNA replication	Genital herpes, recurrent	500 mg PO BID** for 3 days
			Genital herpes, suppression	0.5 or 1 g PO day
			Herpes labialis	2 g PO BID for 1 day
			Herpes zoster	1 g PO TID for 7 days
			Chickenpox	1 g PO TID

* Doses are adjusted for body weight and/or creatinine clearance. ** Injectable formulation is also available.

involved with cells, it is critical to find a drug that will kill the virus without destroying the host cells.

Mechanisms of Action

Theoretically, viral activity could be interrupted by inhibiting the initial attachment of the virus to the human host cells, injection of viral contents into the host cell, enzymes that transcribe or synthesize viral proteins, and the virus shedding into the circulation to reinfect other cells. Two of these routes (virus attachment and interference with viral protein transcription or synthesis) have proven profitable in the development of antiviral drugs.

The discussion of mechanism and site of antiviral drug action that follows may seem confusing because there are no simple terms for the nucleoproteins and the current cadre of drugs all sound alike. Don't be discouraged! Remember, for the viruses under discussion (HSV, HIV, cytomegalovirus [CMV]), antiviral drugs are effective because they block virus attachment to human cells or they interfere with viral proteins at transcription or synthesis. Figure 42.9 shows the sites of antiviral drug interference with viral entry and replication.

Inhibition of Virus Release or Cell Penetration (Fusion Inhibitors)

Influenza: Amantadine (*Symmetrel*) and rimantadine (*Flumadine*) prevent the virus that causes influenza from uncoating its nucleoside and releasing viral DNA into the cell. When given prophylactically (within 20 hours after exposure to the flu), these drugs reduce the severity of the infection. They have no effect on other viral infections, including other strains of flu, especially H1N1. The drugs are usually recommended for high-risk patients (chronically ill, infants, and elderly) for whom vaccination is contraindicated or for 2 to 4 weeks following vaccination while the antibody response is developing.

In contrast, the neuraminidase inhibitors, oseltamivir (*Tamiflu*) and zanamivir (*Relenza*), have a wide range of therapeutic anti-influenza effectiveness. Neuraminidase and hemagglutinin are present on the surface of *all* influenza viruses. Hemagglutinin is responsible for docking the virus onto host cell membranes by bonding to sialic acid molecules (components of glycoproteins and mucoproteins) and inducing cell penetration. After replication, the viral clones are coated with sialic acid as they emerge from the ruptured cells. During the exodus, neuraminidase on the surface of the viral clones releases the sialic acid connections. This critical step directly affects (increases) viral pathogenicity because it frees the hemagglutinin for docking with new sialic acid molecules on the next host cells to be invaded (and not with the sialic acid-coated viruses).

Neuraminidase inhibitors are designed as sialic acid analogs so that the drug preferentially attaches to the virus surface protein but cannot be released by the enzymatic action of neuraminidase. As a result, the bound sialic acid drug causes the viruses to aggregate and clump together, attaching to each other—sialic acid drug to new virus hemagglutinin. In the end, host cell penetration is inhibited and infection (pathogenicity) is reduced because the "virus-clot" cannot be released from the cell and is unable to connect with host cell receptors. Since the sialic acid-binding site is the same for all influenza virus strains, neuraminidase inhibitors are expected to offer a greater therapeutic advantage in the treatment of influenza.

Drugs Effective in the Treatment of HIV Infections

Drug (*Trade Name*)	Pyrimidine or purine base	Mechanism of action	Black box warning	Adult dose
Didanosine (*ddI, Videx*)	Dideoxvinosine	Inhibits viral DNA replication by interfering with viral reverse transcriptase NRTI*	None	200 mg BID PO tablet (250 mg powder) > 60 kg BW**
Delavirdine (*Rescriptor*)	—	NRTI*	Virus resistance occurs if used as monotherapy. Combine with antiretroviral drug for advanced HIV	400 mg TID PO in combination with nucleoside analogs
Enfuvirtide (*Fuzeon*)	—	Inhibits viral fusion	None	90 mg (1 ml) sub-Q BID
Etravirine (*Intelence*)	—	NNRTI*	None	200 mg PO BID following a meal
Fosamprenavir (*Lexiva*)	—	Protease inhibitor	None	700 mg PO BID plus ritonavir 100 mg BID
Indinavir (*Crixivan*)	—	Inhibits HIV protease	None	800 mg PO every 8 hr
Lamivudine (*3TC, Epivir*)	2'-deoxy-3'-thiacytidine	NRTI*	None	150 mg BID PO** in combination with zidovudine
Nelfinavir (*Viracept*)	—	Inhibits HIV protease	None	750 mg TID PO in combination with nucleoside analogs up to 24 weeks
Nevirapine (*Viramune*)	—	NRTI*	Severe life-threatening hepatotoxicity and skin reactions within first 18 weeks	200 mg BID PO in combination with nucleoside analogs
Maraviroc (*Selzentry*)	—	CCR5 inhibitor	Hepatotoxicity, systemic allergic reaction has occurred	150–600 mg PO BID based on other antiviral drugs used
Raltegravir (*Isentress*)	—	Integrase inhibitor	None	400 mg PO BID
Ritonavir (*Norvir*)	—	Inhibits HIV protease	Coadministration with sedative hypnotics antipsychotics or antiarrhythmics may cause life-threatening reactions due to metabolism interference	600 mg PO BID
Saquinavir (*Invirase*)	—	Inhibits HIV protease	Capsules and tablets cannot be interchanged; not bioequivalent	200 mg PO TID in combination with nucleoside analogs
Stavudine (*d4T, Zerit*)	2', 3'-didehydro-3'-deoxythymidine	NRTI*	None	40 mg BID PO (< 60 kg BW, 30 mg)**

(Continued)

Drug (*Trade Name*)	Pyrimidine or purine base	Mechanism of action	Black box warning	Adult dose
Tipranavir (*Aptivus*)	—	Protease inhibitor	Clinical hepatitis and hepatic decompensation, intracranial hemorrhage	500 mg PO plus ritonavir 200 mg BID
Zalcitabine (*ddC, Hivid*)	2′, 3′-dideoxycytidine	NRTI*	None	0.75 mg PO** every 8 hr
Zidovudine *** (*Retrovir*)	Azidothymidine (AZT)	NRTI*	None	100 mg PO every 4 hr up to 600 mg daily

NRTI = nucleoside reverse transcriptase inhibitor; NNRTI = nonnucleoside reverse transcriptase inhibitor.
**Doses are adjusted for body weight and/or creatinine clearance. ***Formulations for injection are also available.*

HIV: Maraviroc (*Selzentry*) is the first CCR5 antagonist approved for use in HAART. Before HIV can enter the cell, its glycoprotein must bind to the CD4 receptor. Binding initiates changes in the virus that reveal additional specialized receptors known as chemokine coreceptors (CCR5). A strain of the virus CCR5-tropic virus is present during the early stages of HIV infection. Maraviroc selectively binds to the CCR5 receptor and blocks HIV attachment to the host cell. This action effectively prevents HIV infection (penetration) of the

[**Figure 42.9**] **Major Sites of Antiviral Drug Action**

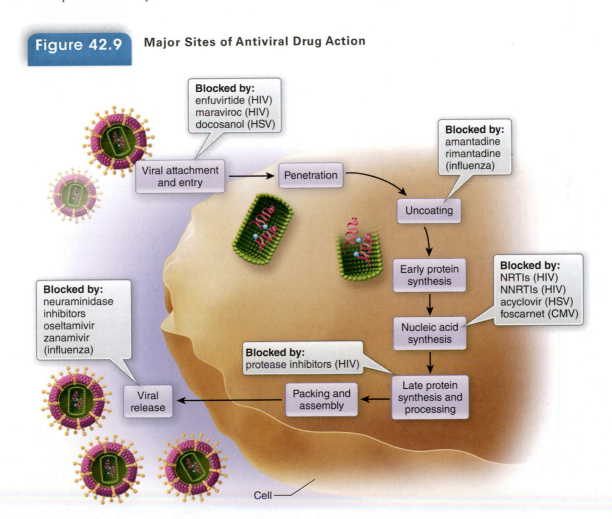

cell. Maraviroc is used in patients who have ongoing viral replication, evidence of CCR5-tropic virus, and are resistant to multiple antiretroviral agents.

Fusion inhibitors: Enfuvirtide (*Fuzeon*) is a 36-amino-acid synthetic peptide that prevents completion of the HIV fusion sequence. As a result a fusion pore by which the viral genetic material enters the CD4+ cell does not form and penetration is blocked.

HSV: Docosanol is used for the external treatment of cold sores and fever blisters. Its mode of action is different from other antiviral drugs because it takes place only in healthy cells. In noninfected cells, docosanol works on the cell membrane to help inhibit the ability of the virus to fuse with the cell membrane so that the virus is less likely to enter the cell to begin the process of infection. Because it works on healthy cells, docosanol is not categorized as an antiviral, but it does shorten the duration of symptoms and has been FDA approved for treatment of cold sores.

Transcription and/or Synthesis Inhibitors

Some antiviral drugs interfere with one or more viral enzymes. Although the target cell may differ—for example, *Herpes* (nervous tissue), cytomegalovirus (CMV; retina, liver, lung), or influenza viruses (respiratory tract), the route of access to host cell nuclei and propagation of viruses are similar. This is simplistically illustrated in Figure 42.9.

HIV: After fusion of the outside viral coat (lipid envelope), the internal contents of the virus enter the lymphocyte cytoplasm. Its single strand of viral RNA is converted to double-stranded DNA to make more retroviruses through a specific enzyme, reverse transcriptase (RT). Newly produced viral DNA enters the host cell nuclei and is incorporated into the host chromosome through a special HIV enzyme, integrase. In this manner, HIV has taken control of cell function so that only production of new viruses can begin.

NRTI: Nucleosides are molecules that contain purine (adenine, guanine) or pyrimidine (uridine, cytidine, thymidine) bases in combination with a ribose or deoxyribose linkage. Nucleosides are the fundamental building blocks of RNA and DNA. Antiviral drugs such as abacavir (*Ziagen*), didanosine (*ddi, Videx*), emtricitabine (*Emtriva*), lamivudine (*3TC, Epivir*), stavudine (*d4T, Zerit*), zalcitabine (*ddc, Hivid*), and zidovudine (*Retrovir*) are purine or pyrimidine nucleoside analogs that become incorporated into the DNA and inhibit reverse transcriptase and synthesis of new virus. Virus replication is decreased and the infection is reduced.

NNRTI: Reverse transcriptase also can be inhibited by drugs that are not nucleosides (nonnucleosides) such as delavirdine (*Rescriptor*), nevirapine (*Viramune*), efavirenz (*Sustiva*), and etravirine (*Intelence*). The nonnucleoside reverse transcriptase inhibitors (NNRTI) directly bind to the enzyme RT and block viral protein synthesis without harming human DNA activity.

Protease Inhibitors: Other anti-HIV drugs, indinavir (*Crixivan*), nelfinavir (*Viracept*), ritonavir (*Norvir*), and saquinavir (*Invirase*), inhibit HIV protease. This is an enzyme essential for the final assembly of the new viruses. The advantage of these drugs is that new viruses cannot be released to infect more lymphocytes. The site and mechanism of action are removed from RT activity so that cocktail combination treatment for HAART effectively reduces the number of viruses in circulation.

HSV: Interference with viral transcription is also an important part of *Herpes* treatment. Nucleoside analogs such as acyclovir (*Zovirax*), idoxuridine (*Herplex*), vidarabine (*Vira-A*), ganciclovir (*Cytovene*), and trifluridine (*Viroptic*) are recognized during the replication process and incorporated into the new viral DNA. However, because the analog is a "false base" (not the "correct match" that would permit synthesis to continue), the viral DNA chain is terminated at the point where the drug was incorporated. These drugs effectively inhibit *Herpes* viral DNA synthesis.

Resistance to Antiviral Therapy

Although all of these mechanisms halt viral replication, these drugs do not cure viral diseases. The primary reason that drug therapy does not yet result in a cure is that HIV rapidly mutates into a drug-resistant agent. HIV replicates so frequently and in such large numbers (viral load) that mutations occur in viral proteins that are clinically significant. Mutations are mistakes that occur accidentally during replication of viral genetic material. When this mistake occurs in the code for HIV enzymes such as protease or RT, the drugs that inhibit these enzymes cannot recognize the mutant enzyme. Therefore, the virus with the mutated genetic material is unaffected by drug treatment and goes on to infect more host cells and replicate new HIV with resistant properties. Despite the inability to cure the disease, each new class of drugs provides substantial improvement in the management of AIDS until a vaccine becomes available.

Administration and Pharmacokinetics

All of the antiviral drugs except docosanol (*Abreva*) are only available with a prescription. Docosanol is for external use only for the treatment of cold sores and fever blisters on the lips and face. It is an OTC product. All of the antiviral drugs presented in this chapter except for those used against CMV and ophthalmic herpes are available as oral formulations.

This facilitates patient adherence to therapy, particularly since the treatment of recurrent genital herpes and HIV may be several months to lifelong. In general, these drugs are well absorbed after oral administration, attaining peak blood drug levels within 1 to 2 hours, are metabolized to some extent, and excreted in the urine. Zanamivir (*Relenza*) is a dry powder administered through a breath-actuated diskhaler. Drug is distributed to the pharynx and lower tracheobronchial tree for an immediate onset of action.

Absorption

Most of the drugs presented in this chapter are absorbed as the active antiviral agent. A few, however, must be converted to the active moiety. Oseltamivir (*Tamiflu*), which has no antiviral activity, is readily absorbed following oral administration and is converted in the liver to the active neuraminidase inhibitor. Similarly, famciclovir (*Famvir*) and valacyclovir (*Valtrex*) are metabolized to the active antiherpes component penciclovir and acyclovir, respectively. A few other antiviral drugs exhibit specific problems that must be circumvented in order to achieve therapeutic concentrations in the tissues.

Anti-HIV drugs indinavir (*Crixivan*), ganciclovir (*Cytovene*), nelfinavir (*Viracept*), ritonavir (*Norvir*), saquinavir (*Invirase*), and didanosine (*Videx*) are affected by the presence of food or changes in gastric pH with oral dosing. Food decreases the absorption and bioavailability of indinavir. AIDS patients experience a general body wasting at some point in the disease process. It is not unusual for these patients to be on nutritional supplements to boost body weight. However, high-caloric, high-protein, and high-fat meals will decrease indinavir absorption. Didanosine is destroyed in an acidic environment so that the formulation is prepared with special buffering agents to permit maximum absorption. Anything that stimulates acid secretion (such as food) will overcome the buffering effect and degrade the active drug. In contrast, oral absorption is enhanced when the doses are accompanied by food with ganciclovir (*Cytovene*), nefinavir (*Viracept*), saquinavir (*Invirase*), and ritonavir (*Norvir*). This is a desirable interaction with these drugs. All

of these actions are the basis of recommendations for drug administration (see Patient Administration and Monitoring) that must be communicated to patients.

Among the other oral antiviral drugs for *Herpes*—acyclovir (*Zovirax*), famciclovir (*Famvir*), valacyclovir (*Valtrex*—or influenza (*Oseltamivir*), oral absorption is good and unaffected by food or meal content.

Hepatic Microsomal Metabolism

The HIV protease inhibitors inhibit the CYP-450 system to varying degrees, such that metabolism of other concomitant medications going through these enzymes might accumulate in the circulation. Saquinavir (*Invirase*), nelfinavir (*Viracept*), indinavir (*Crixivan*), and delavirdine (*Rescriptor*) are expected to affect drugs such as calcium channel blockers, midazolam, triazolam, clindamycin, dapsone, warfarin, and quinidine. This hepatic system also can be induced. Concomitant medications that induce CYP-450 would likely eliminate the circulating antiviral drug through increased metabolism. Nevirapine induces CYP-450 within a few weeks of treatment, increasing its own clearance (removal). The neuraminidase inhibitors do not affect the hepatic microsomal system.

Renal Excretion

Inhibition of glomerular filtration and tubular secretion by any means (drugs, renal impairment) will cause certain antiviral drugs to accumulate. Almost all of the active moieties or their metabolites are excreted via urine. All of the drugs used in the treatment of herpes, CMV (cidofovir, foscarnet), as well as amantidine, stavudine, and zalcitabine, must be dose adjusted in the presence of renal impairment. Anything that decreases renal clearance as evidenced by a creatinine clearance less than 50 ml/min will obligate a reduction in the antiviral dose. Both oral and intravenous doses are reduced. Amantadine and rimantadine are also dose adjusted for patients over 65 years of age in whom renal clearance is decreased with age. This is to avoid precipitation of central nervous system (CNS) adverse effects including seizures.

Cidofovir must be administered in conjunction with oral probenecid in order to maintain adequate blood levels. Cidofovir is excreted by renal tubular secretion that is actively inhibited by probenecid. Probenecid is administered before (2 hours) and after (2 and 8 hours) cidofovir infusion.

Adverse Effects

Antiviral drugs are used in seriously ill patients or in special populations of elderly patients or young children. Often underlying conditions (flu, diabetes, hypertension, arthritis, liver or kidney dysfunction) make it difficult to distinguish the onset of adverse effects from those symptoms associated with the progressing disease. This is

---

Note to the Health Care Professional

Corticosteroids alone are contraindicated for the treatment of acute superficial herpes simplex keratitis (ocular herpes) because of the potential to exacerbate the infection and produce cataract and/or glaucoma.

particularly true in the treatment of AIDS. In this regard, all antiviral drugs may be associated with nausea, gastritis, GI pain, vomiting, diarrhea, headache, confusion, dizziness, insomnia, arthralgia, myalgia, allergic reactions, hypertension, edema, and rash. With a few drugs, more unusual adverse effects may occur. Patients taking acyclovir may develop blurred vision or tinnitus. Patients on ritonavir (*Norvir*) who experience dysgeusia (unpleasant taste) often take the medication with chocolate milk or Ensure to improve the taste so that the medication regimen can be completed. Whether given intravenously or orally, serious adverse effects do occur and may be the reason for black box warnings with certain antivirals (protease inhibitors). These include nephrotoxicity, inhibition of hepatic microsomal metabolism, and various anemias that can jeopardize the patient's ability to fight infection, including neutropenia and granulocytopenia. Tables 42:4 and 42:6 show which drugs have a special cautionary warning and the nature of the event.

Anti-influenza Drugs

The incidence of adverse effects associated with amantadine is relatively low. The most common adverse effects include slurred speech, ataxia, lethargy, dizziness, nausea, and irritability. Hypotension and congestive heart failure also have been reported. Since amantadine produces anticholinergic effects within the CNS, this drug should be used with caution in the presence of other anticholinergic medication (potentiation) or in the elderly. Amantadine (*Symmetrel*) is not indicated for patients who have impaired liver or renal function, epilepsy, or psychosis, and it is not recommended for administration during pregnancy. Rimantadine (*Flumadine*) has a similar profile, and with both drugs elderly patients appear to experience adverse effects more frequently. This does not preclude the use of these drugs in the elderly.

The neuraminidase inhibitors are generally well tolerated. The incidence of adverse effects (nausea, vomiting, diarrhea, abdominal pain, and headache) reported during oseltamivir (*Tamiflu*) treatment is very low and indistinguishable from the clinical course of flu. In addition to the type of adverse effects seen with oseltamivir, zanamivir (*Relenza*) has induced bronchospasm when administered to individuals with mild to moderate asthma. The drug should be discontinued in any patient who develops bronchospasm or reduced pulmonary function.

Anti-herpes Drugs

The adverse effects reported to occur in patients include transient elevations of serum BUN and creatinine. When given concurrently with drugs known to decrease renal clearance, nephrotoxicity will develop. The incidence of nephrotoxicity with famciclovir is dose related.

Downward dose adjustment is recommended when creatinine clearance is less than 60 ml/min. Acyclovir (*Zovirax*) may cause injection site irritation, mainly due to the alkaline pH. Otherwise, the adverse effects usually reported are headache, nausea, vomiting, and fatigue. Blurred vision, when it occurs, can impair the patient's ability to operate machinery or perform tasks requiring dexterity.

Idoxuridine (*Herplex*), trifluridine (*Viroptic*), and vidarabine (*Vira-A*) may produce local irritation on instillation, edema of the eyelids and cornea, and small defects (clouding) in the corneal tissue. Although some drug is absorbed into ocular tissues, systemic absorption is extremely small.

Idoxuridine produces sensitivity to bright light that can be ameliorated by the use of sunglasses. The effect usually resolves within 7 to 14 days. Foscarnet (*Foscavir*) removes ionized calcium from the blood, causing neuromuscular instability. Since foscarnet is a chelating agent, it ties up metal ions. This is a dose-related effect on calcium, as well as several other electrolytes (potassium, phosphates, magnesium). Patients may experience tetany, muscle pain, spasm, or convulsions. Decreasing the infusion rate may delay the occurrence of these effects. Nevirapine (*Viramune*) has caused life-threatening skin reactions, that is, Stevens-Johnson syndrome, while zalcitabine (*Hivid*) and zidovudine (*Retrovir*) induce a state of acidosis with a decrease in serum bicarbonate levels that can be fatal. Zidovudine produces a myopathy that is sometimes indistinguishable from the progression of the AIDS-defining illnesses.

Anti-HIV Drugs

Even with significant zidovudine overdose (50 times the therapeutic dose), the outcome was not fatal and the effects observed were nausea and vomiting. In the treatment of HIV-infected patients, it is important to have a complete blood count performed frequently to monitor lymphocytes (CD4 level), anemia, or granulocytopenia, so that transfusion or dose adjustment can be made as early as possible. The frequency of testing increases with advanced disease. Ganciclovir (*Cytovene*) is also noted to cause a decrease in platelets (thrombocytopenia), chills, fever, and malaise. Intravenous ganciclovir (*Cytovene*) is associated with fewer adverse effects than via oral administration.

Peripheral neuropathy that is dose dependent occurs with stavudine (*Zerit*), didanosine (*Videx*), and zalcitabine (*Hivid*). The symptoms range from tingling to burning sensations in the hands and feet. This is the primary reason for dose interruption with zalcitabine. When the drug is stopped, the effect may resolve, although slowly with zalcitabine. After the effect subsides, the drug may be restarted at a lower dose. Evidence suggests that this adverse effect occurs more frequently in those patients with a history of neuropathy as well as those patients with low CD4 counts (<200 to 300 cells/mm³).

There are two areas affected by these drugs that are always serious and can be life-threatening: nephrotoxicity and neutropenia. Zidovudine (*Retrovir*), lamivudine (*Epivir*), and cidofovir (*Vistide*) produce neutropenia. Frequent blood counts are the principal means of following the onset and severity of this effect. These drugs should be used with caution in patients already compromised by bone marrow suppression showing a granulocyte count <1000 cells/mm³ or hemoglobin, 9.5 mg/dl. Transfusion and/or dose adjustment may be required. Almost all of these drugs produce some degree of interference with renal function in addition to being affected by a decrease in renal clearance. Foscarnet (*Foscavir*) produces nephrotoxicity evidenced by elevated serum creatinine and BUN in most patients, while cidofovir (*Vistide*) may damage the proximal renal tubule. The onset and severity of the renal damage obligates dose adjustment for didanosine (*Videx*), famciclovir (*Famvir*), ganciclovir (*Cytovene*), nevirapine (*Viramune*), stavudine (*Zerit*), and zalcitabine (*Hivid*) when creatinine clearance is less than 50 ml/min, and/or when urine protein is high, for cidofovir. Hydration (1 liter 0.9 percent saline or 5 percent dextrose IV) is recommended with dosing of acyclovir (*Zovirax*), cidofovir (*Vistide*), indinavir (*Crixivan*), and foscarnet (*Foscavir*) to minimize the damage to renal tissue, and to keep the urine flowing and maintain excretion. Renal damage with cidofovir may not return to normal after the drug is discontinued. Lamivudine (*Epivir*) and valacyclovir (*Valtrex*), while not causing renal damage initially, may accumulate in the presence of end organ impairment. Lamivudine and stavudine have special warnings in their directions for use because of their ability to produce lactic acidosis—severe hepatomegaly with elevated liver enzymes. Therefore, these drugs must be used with caution in patients with renal dysfunction and the initial dose reduced.

Special Considerations and Contraindications

Except for the drugs used in the prophylaxis of influenza and treatment of *Herpes zoster*, there is little experience in the use of the antiviral drugs in elderly patients. Specifically for HIV, CMV, and genital herpes, the patient population has been primarily young adults. With the success of the newer treatment strategies and remarkable protease inhibitors, patients may be surviving longer before the onset of AIDS and this will contribute critical information on long-term safety. The newest HIV antiviral drugs are indicated for use in combination with other RT inhibitors such as zidovudine. Experience has shown that monotherapy quickly results in resistance to treatment through viral mutation. Lamivudine (*Epivir*), nevirapine (*Viramune*), delavirdine (*Rescriptor*), and zalcitabine (*Hivid*) are not used as monotherapy for this reason. The combined mechanisms of action reduce the virulent viral load in circulation. However, the incidence and severity of adverse effects such as neutropenia, granulocytopenia, thrombocytopenia, and nephrotoxicity may be potentiated. Therefore, routine chemistry and hematology are performed before all dosing with IV drugs and periodically as determined by the treating physician for oral medication. Absolute contraindication to the use of any of these drugs is hypersensitivity. Otherwise the drugs are used with caution in patients with significant concurrent disease and organ failure.

LO 42.4 | LO 42.6
DRUG INTERACTIONS

The drugs discussed in this chapter are primarily used in patients who are seriously ill and usually have more than one chronic condition. By the nature of this population, patients can easily be exposed to 5 to 15 or more medications daily. This provides ample opportunity for drug interactions to occur, especially with OTC products. Antacids, tetracyclines, and/or H_2-receptor antagonists reduce the absorption of fluconazole, itraconazole, and didanosine when taken concurrently.

Another significant concern is those interactions that predispose patients to decreased renal clearance of drugs and active metabolites or nephrotoxicity. Since these drugs are indicated for combination treatment, either as antivirals plus antivirals or antifungals plus antivirals, there is a significant opportunity to develop nephrotoxicity. Contributors to renal damage are zidovudine (*Retrovir*), cidofovir (*Vistide*), and foscarnet (*Foscavir*), especially taken concurrently with notoriously nephrotoxic drugs such as amphotericin B, aminoglycoside antibiotics, and IV pentamidine. Probenecid-induced inhibition of tubular secretion is beneficial when given to boost cidofovir blood levels; however, probenecid also affects famciclovir (*Famvir*) and ganciclovir (*Cytovene*) in which increased blood levels may precipitate adverse effects.

The potential for elevating drug blood levels of drugs metabolized through the hepatic microsomal system with chronic protease inhibitors therapy is significant. The advantages of drug interaction certainly include the probenecid and cidofovir combination as well as fluconazole, and itraconazole elevation in concomitant cyclosporine blood levels. This interaction has permitted cyclosporine doses to be reduced without jeopardizing clinical effectiveness.

The treatment of HIV, especially advanced stages or with opportunistic infections, warrants close monitoring of the patient's vital signs and body temperature and frequent evaluation of serum chemistry and hematology profiles. Serum analyses forecast changes in electrolytes, liver (ALAT, alanine aminotransferase [AST]), or renal function (serum creatinine, creatine clearance, urine protein) and blood cell production (complete blood count [CBC] with differential, total neutrophil count, hematocrit, hemoglobin, and platelets). The hematology, chemistries, and urine protein should be reviewed prior to each dosing. Patients should be asked frequently about symptoms (tingling, burning sensations) that signal the onset of neuropathy so that dose adjustment or discontinuation of medication can be initiated. Changes in serum bicarbonate (decrease) with or without tachypnea may be an indication of developing acidosis.

Transplant Recipients

Transplant recipients receiving ganciclovir (*Cytovene*) must be evaluated for elevations in serum creatine and BUN, indicating changes in renal function that might obligate dose adjustment or discontinuation of therapy.

Serious Hematologic Changes

The frequency of granulocytopenia and thrombocytopenia obligates frequent complete blood count (CBC) and platelet evaluations. Patients receiving ganciclovir (*Cytovene*) and zidovudine are predisposed to develop severe granulocytopenia.

Medication Review

Current medications should be reviewed thoroughly to ascertain whether the patient is taking products that could potentiate the onset of peripheral neuropathy, hepatitis, or pancreatitis. The prescribing physician may need to adjust or interrupt certain treatments to minimize the potential for serious outcome.

Patient Instruction for Chronic Viral Infections

Treatment of any viral infection, especially HIV, does not produce a cure. Patients with HSV, HIV, or CMV must receive clear instruction that underlying conditions will progress, although more slowly, and opportunistic infections may occur. Medications must be completed as directed whether oral or intravenous. Conversations with patients should present a clear picture of the frequency of clinical evaluation required during treatment and scope of adverse effects so the patient can make a commitment to stay the course of therapy. Pharmacological treatment of HIV or *Herpes is not a substitute for altering lifestyle patterns* that promote the transmission of the virus.

Patients under treatment for genital herpes should receive instructions to avoid sexual intercourse when lesions are visible.

Drug Administration

Patients receiving ganciclovir (*Cytovene*), nelfinavir, ritonavir, or saquinavir must be reminded to take the dose with meals to maximize absorption and bioavailability.

Patients receiving didanosine (*Videx*) and indinavir (*Crixivan*) must be reminded to take the dose on an empty stomach or 2 hours after a meal.

Delavirdine (*Rescriptor*) must be taken 1 hour before antacids to avoid a drug interaction and decreased absorption of delavirdine.

Patients may take ritonavir (*Norvir*) with chocolate milk or Ensure to improve the taste of the medication.

Adverse Effects

Amantadine (*Symmetrel*) may decrease alertness and cause blurred vision that may interfere with driving or performing tasks requiring concentration.

Saquinavir (*Invirase*) may cause photosensitivity so that patients should avoid unnecessary exposure to sunlight until tolerance is evident.

Idoxuridine (*Herplex*) sensitivity to bright light, which should resolve within 7 to 14 days, may be ameliorated by the use of sunglasses.

Notifying the Physician

With any of these drugs, including those for the prophylaxis of cold and flu, patients should receive clear instructions that swelling, edema, shortness of breath, and dizziness should be reported to the prescribing physician.

The physician must be notified immediately if rash, fever, blistering, joint aches, or symptoms of liver dysfunction occur.

Tingling, burning, and pain or numbness in hands or feet may signal the onset of peripheral neuropathy, especially for stavudine (*Zerit*).

With IV administration of foscarnet (*Foscavir*), the physician must be notified immediately if the patient reports feeling numbness or tingling, which may indicate changes in serum calcium and other electrolytes.

Use in Pregnancy

In general, antiviral drugs are designated FDA Pregnancy Category B or C because they have not been adequately studied in pregnant women. Among the systemic drugs, safe use in pregnancy has not been established in humans. Nevertheless, there are situations where their use is clearly indicated and may be used with caution and close patient monitoring. There are registry centers that encourage physicians to provide information on antiviral (HIV, herpes) use during pregnancy in order to accumulate information on maternal-fetal outcome. These centers are supported by the specific drug manufacturers.

Ribavarin (*Copegus, Ribatab*) is contraindicated in pregnancy because it causes teratogenic effects (malformations) in all animals tested. A pregnancy registry has been set up to monitor all pregnancies that occur during treatment or within 6 months of treatment cessation.

Drug Interaction and Pregnancy

Nelfinavir (*Viracept*) counteracts oral contraceptive action by decreasing the blood levels of estrogen and progestins. Patients must be advised to use alternate or additional contraceptives to avoid failure and pregnancy.

Chapter Review

Understanding Terminology

Match the definition or description in the left column with the appropriate term in the right column.

___ 1. A condition that causes individuals to resist acquiring or developing a disease or infection. **(LO 42.6)**

___ 2. A microorganism capable of causing disease only when the resistance of the host is impaired. **(LO 42.6)**

___ 3. The virus that causes AIDS. **(LO 42.6)**

___ 4. A drug that kills fungi. **(LO 42.6)**

___ 5. Infection of the skin, hair, or nails caused by a fungus. **(LO 42.6)**

___ 6. An incurable disease caused by a virus and characterized by multiple opportunistic infections. **(LO 42.6)**

a. AIDS

b. dermatophytic

c. fungicidal

d. HIV

e. immunity

f. opportunistic organism

Acquiring Knowledge

Answer the following questions in the spaces provided.

1. What sites are commonly involved in fungal infections? **(LO 42.5)**

2. What organism is usually associated with common vaginal fungal infections? **(LO 42.1, 42.5)**

3. What is the mechanism of action of amphotericin B? **(LO 42.2)**

4. Why is griseofulvin useful in the treatment of ringworm? **(LO 42.3)**

5. How do some viruses protect the host they infect? **(LO 42.3)**

6. Are vaccines available to treat any virus infection? **(LO 42.3)**

7. Do patients exposed to HIV always test HIV positive? **(LO 42.2)**

8. Why are viral infections difficult to treat with drugs? **(LO 42.3)**

9. How do amantadine and ganclicovir affect viruses without damaging the human cells? **(LO 42.2)**

10. How do the drugs currently available for the treatment of HIV infection work? **(LO 42.2)**

Applying Knowledge on the Job

Use your critical-thinking skills to answer the following questions.

1. Mr. Garcia is admitted to the hospital for treatment of a deep vein thrombosis (blood clot) in his calf. His admitting orders state "Continue meds from home." Upon questioning, Mr. Garcia says he is taking ketoconazole. Warfarin, an oral anticoagulant, is also prescribed. Is there any potential for an adverse reaction? **(LO 42.4)**

2. Can both drugs (in Question 1) be continued safely? **(LO 42.4)**

3. How does food affect the absorption of the following medications and how should they be taken with regard to food? **(LO 42.4)**
   a. ganciclovir _____
   b. famciclovir _____
   c. indinavir _____
   d. valacyclovir _____
   e. didanosine _____
   f. saquinavir _____

4. A 19-year-old female has been prescribed itraconazole. What should she be told regarding sexual activity during therapy? **(LO 42.1, 42.5)**

5. A female patient has been diagnosed with a vaginal yeast infection. Her physician has prescribed *Mycostatin* vaginal tablets—1 pv qhs × 15d. What should this patient be told regarding proper use and handling? **(LO 42.1)**

Multiple Choice

Use your critical-thinking skills to answer the following questions.

1. Griseofulvin is useful in dermatophytic infections because it **(LO 42.2)**
   A. binds to keratin
   B. is fungicidal
   C. forms ergosterol in hair and nails
   D. incorporates itself into fungal RNA

2. Which of the following is NOT correct about antifungal drugs or fungal infection? **(LO 42.1)**
   A. systemic infection may occur in patients who are receiving drugs to suppress their immune system
   B. warts are an example of a dermatophytic infection
   C. the majority of antifungal drugs interfere with fungal cell-wall integrity
   D. amphotericin B is associated with serious renal toxicity

3. Which of the following describes a systemic fungal infection? **(LO 42.1)**
   A. candidemia
   B. vaginal candidiasis
   C. influenza
   D. *Staphylococcus*

4. Which of the following pairs are antifungal drugs? **(LO 42.1)**
   A. fluconazole and micafungin
   B. ritonavir and ketoprofen
   C. dihydroepiandosterone and inositol
   D. mebendazole and gentian violet

5. Which antifungal drug is matched with its correct mechanism of action? **(LO 42.1)**
   A. echinocandins inhibit polysaccharide (glucan) synthesis in the cell wall
   B. flucytosine binds to the cell membrane
   C. ticonazole is an antimetabolite for fungal RNA
   D. amphotericin B binds to a cytochrome P450-dependent enzyme

6. Which of the following is NOT correct about these antifungal drugs? **(LO 42.1, 42.4)**
   A. caspofungin and micafungin are administered by slow IV infusion
   B. voriconozole and posaconazole are man-made drugs (synthetic)
   C. anidulafungin undergoes degradation in the bloodstream to peptide fragments
   D. vaginal yeast infection (candidiasis) can only be treated with prescription drugs

7. Which is the correct fungal infection site of action and common name? **(LO 42.1, 42.5)**
   A. warm moist areas on the feet: onychomycosis
   B. *Candida* in the mouth: thrush
   C. toe- and fingernails: aspergillosis
   D. hair protein: candidiasis

8. Which of the following is correct about viruses? **(LO 42.2, 42.3)**
    A. active infection is the only way to develop immunity to the microorganism
    B. viruses attach to the keratin protein and remain dormant for years
    C. viruses can quickly develop resistance to drugs
    D. viruses die as soon as they land on hard surfaces

Multiple Choice (Multiple Answer)

Select the correct choices for each statement. The choices may be all correct, all incorrect, or any combination.

1. Which drugs are effective against systemic fungal infections? **(LO 42.1)**
    A. griseofulvin
    B. butenafine
    C. gentian violet
    D. clotrimazole

2. The mechanisms of action for antiviral medications include **(LO 42.2)**
    A. changing cell-wall synthesis
    B. binding to ergosterol
    C. inhibiting cell mitosis
    D. inhibiting neuraminidase

3. Which of the following are true of the treatment for viral infections? **(LO 42.3)**
    A. they are difficult to treat due to host cell invasion
    B. immunity can be gained through the attenuated live virus
    C. treatment can be given via an intranasal spray
    D. the vaccines are contraindicated in people allergic to eggs

4. Select all of the side effects of antifungal drugs. **(LO 42.4)**
    A. muscle spasm
    B. renal damage
    C. phlebitis
    D. exfoliative dermatitis

5. What are ways fungi are able to infect their human host? **(LO 42.5)**
    A. antibiotic overuse
    B. poorly cleaned foot baths
    C. inhalation of fungal spores
    D. invasion of host cell

Sequencing

Place the following steps of virus propagation in order from first to last. **(LO 42.5, 42.6)**

_____ _____ _____ _____
First   **Last**

virus attaches to outer cell membrane
virus injects its nucleic acid
host cells replicate viral RNA
viruses are expelled into blood circulation

Classification

Place the following drugs under their appropriate classification. **(LO 42.1, 42.2)**

ribavirin   oxiconazole   naftifine

oseltamivir   nevirapine   idoxuridine

butenafine   foscarnet   tolnaftate

clioquinol

Antifungal	Antiviral

Labeling

Fill in the missing labels. **(LO 42.6)**

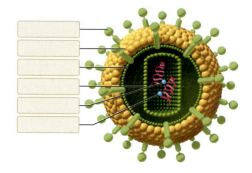

For interactive animations, videos, and assessment, visit:

www.mcgrawhillconnect.com

Chapter 43

Parasitic Infections: Antiprotozoal and Anthelmintic Drugs

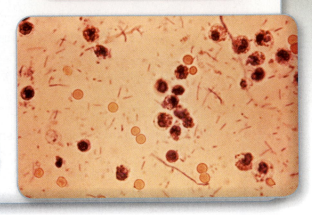

DRUG CLASS AT A GLANCE

OTC	YES
Pyrantel pamoate for pinworms	
PRESCRIPTION	YES
SCHEDULED DRUGS	NO
FDA PREGNANCY CATEGORY	C, D

INDICATIONS

Amebiasis, amebic dysentery, malaria, pinworm, *Giardia lamblia*, trichomonas

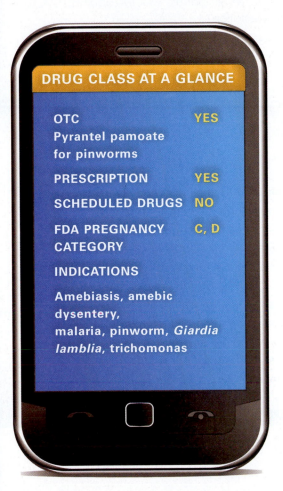

KEY TERMS

asymptomatic: condition in which there is no outward evidence (symptom) that an infection is present.

cinchonism: pattern of characteristic symptoms (central nervous system [CNS] stimulation and headache) associated with the use of cinchona alkaloids (chemicals extracted from the bark of the cinchona tree).

disulfiram-like reaction: reaction to alcohol ingestion characterized by intense nausea as a result of drug-induced accumulation of acetaldehyde, similar to that produced by disulfiram (*Antabuse*).

dysentery: condition characterized by frequent watery stools (usually containing blood and mucus), tenesmus, fever, and dehydration.

dysgeusia: a persistent abnormal sense of taste.

electrolyte: ion in solution, such as sodium, potassium, or chloride, that is capable of mediating conduction (passing impulses in the tissues).

endemic: present continually in a particular geographic region, often in spite of control measures.

hemozoin: crystalline disposal product from the digestion of blood from blood-feeding parasites.

intolerant: not able to continue drug therapy usually because of extreme sensitivity to the side effects.

malaria: protozoal infection characterized by attacks of chills, fever, and sweating.

methemoglobin: an altered hemoglobin that can no longer carry oxygen due to a change (oxidation) in iron from ferrous (Fe^{2+}) to ferric state (Fe^{3+}).

oocyst: a thick-walled structure in which parasitic protozoal sex cells develop for transfer to new hosts.

prophylaxis: procedure or medication to prevent a disease, rather than to treat an existing disease.

protozoacidal: a substance, chemical solution, or drug that kills protozoa.

protozoan: single-celled organism belonging to the genus *Protozoa*.

radical cure: arresting of malaria, in which protozoal parasites are eliminated from all tissues.

suppression therapy: taking the drug daily even when there are no observable acute symptoms.

tenesmus: a painful spasm of the anal sphincter, causing an urgent desire to defecate although little or no material is passed.

trichomoniasis: infection caused by the *Trichomonas* organism; a sexually transmitted disease.

After studying this chapter, you should be able to

43.1 identify three nonbacterial organisms that produce common infections and how they get into humans.

43.2 describe the stages of malaria and the site of protozoal activity in each.

43.3 describe the mechanism by which drugs eradicate protozoal organisms.

43.4 differentiate between the symptoms and infecting organisms of dysentery and malaria.

43.5 describe the side effects produced by each class of protozoal drugs and a significant drug interaction.

43.6 describe how parasitic worms gain access to the human host to develop an infestation.

43.7 describe two drugs that are effective against parasitic worm infestation.

43.8 explain essential terminology associated with these diseases and drug treatment.

This chapter will discuss infections of human tissue by certain common parasites. Parasites are organisms that live on (or in) another organism and take nourishment from that organism. Many microorganisms in addition to bacteria produce infectious disease in humans. Single-cell microorganisms known as **protozoa** produce infection in the circulatory, gastrointestinal (GI), and urogenital systems. The most common diseases associated with protozoal infection in these tissues are malaria, dysentery, and trichomoniasis. Protozoa are frequently introduced into the GI tract through contaminated food and water. However, protozoa also can be transmitted to humans through vectors (mosquitos) or coitus (sexual intercourse). These parasitic microorganisms and drugs effective in their eradication will be presented first. Besides microorganisms, there are whole animals that are parasitic in humans. A variety of worms, some large in size, and common parasites in humans are presented in the second half of this chapter.

LO 43.1

PROTOZOAL INFECTIONS

Dysentery and trichomoniasis are usually not debilitating diseases. These infections produce symptoms that are primarily more annoying than dangerous (for example, diarrhea and itching). In a compromised patient such as a diabetic, elderly or cancer patient, or children, however, dysentery can be life-threatening due to loss of fluid (dehydration) and electrolytes. Malaria produces serious changes in tissue function at any stage of infection. Malaria is characterized by recurrent chills, high fever, sweating, and jaundice. Malaria is a major medical problem throughout many areas of the world (South America, Africa, and Asia). Americans are exposed to malaria as a result of travel or military duty in **endemic** areas. Regions in Mexico and Central America have endemic malaria. While the United States is not a breeding ground for malaria, interest in effective treatment has led to the development and recent approval of new drugs available in this country. Fortunately, all of these protozoal infections, especially malaria, readily respond to drug therapy.

MALARIA

Malaria is a protozoal infection of the circulation system and liver. The malaria parasite is a protozoan known as *Plasmodium*. Although four species of *Plasmodia* infect humans, each species produces the same physiological responses. These parasites (*Plasmodium falciparum, P. vivax, P. ovale,* or *P. malariae*) differ in the severity of the symptoms produced. All *Plasmodia* are transmitted to humans by the *Anopheles* mosquito. Normally, the protozoal parasite inhabits the salivary glands of this mosquito. When the mosquito bites an individual, the parasite is injected directly into the human bloodstream (see Figure 43.1).

Initially, the microorganisms invade the liver, where they mature. During this period, no symptoms are produced to suggest the presence of disease. Some of the mature protozoa eventually leave the hepatic tissue and enter the red blood cells (RBCs). In the RBCs, the protozoa rapidly multiply, often causing the cells to rupture. When the cells rupture, chills and high fever are produced, and many protozoa are released to reinfect more red blood cells. In addition, other mosquitos may suck the infected blood and transmit the microorganisms to the next human.

Antimalarial Drugs

The pharmacological treatment of malaria is directed toward preventing the disease, **prophylaxis,** or eradicating the existing parasites from the body. Antimalarial drugs administered before and during exposure to malaria to prevent the development of disease are known as causal prophylactics (see Table 43:1). Most of the antimalarial drugs used today act prophylactically by destroying the microorganisms as they enter the circulation, thereby preventing the development of liver infection.

Certain antimalarial drugs are also useful when administered during an acute malarial attack (chills and fever). These drugs such as chloroquine, mefloquine, or quinine have a selective action against the parasites that invade the RBCs so multiplication of the organisms is inhibited, and the disease is arrested. **Radical cure** of malaria is produced when the antimalarial drug eliminates the protozoal parasites from all tissues, especially the liver and RBCs. Primaquine is an antimalarial agent used to produce radical cure.

Mechanism of Action

All of the available antimalarial agents are **protozoacidal** drugs. These pharmacological agents destroy *Plasmodia* by interfering with the microorganisms' metabolism or inhibiting normal replication of the protozoa. Pyrimethamine inhibits the conversion of the folic acid to folinic acid in the microorganisms, whereas sulfadoxine inhibits *para*-aminobenzoic acid, a different enzyme essential in the folic acid pathway. Pyrimethamine is a competitive inhibitor of dihydrofolate reductase (DHFR). DHFR is a key enzyme in the production of tetrahydrofolate, a cofactor that is required for the synthesis of DNA and proteins.

Figure 43.1   **Malaria Transmission Cycle in Man**

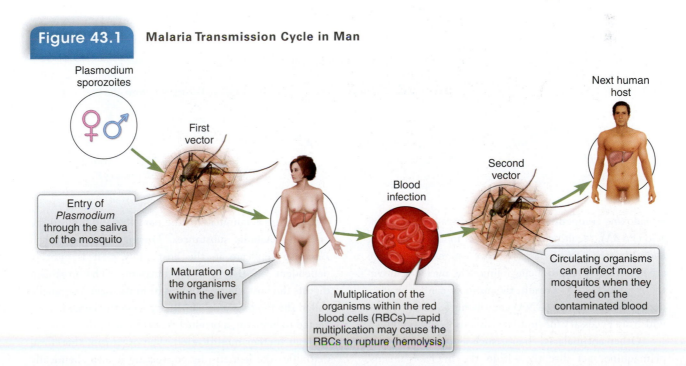

Plasmodium sporozoites

First vector

Next human host

Second vector

Blood infection

Entry of *Plasmodium* through the saliva of the mosquito

Maturation of the organisms within the liver

Multiplication of the organisms within the red blood cells (RBCs)—rapid multiplication may cause the RBCs to rupture (hemolysis)

Circulating organisms can reinfect more mosquitos when they feed on the contaminated blood

Drugs Used in the Treatment of Malaria

Drug (*Trade Name*)	Use	Adult oral dose
Antimalarial drugs		
Chloroquine (*Aralen*)	Acute malarial attacks	500 mg weekly 2 weeks prior to exposure and up to 8 weeks after leaving an endemic area
	Causal prophylaxis	2.5 g over 3 days in specified graduated doses
Doxycycline (*Vibramycin*)	Causal prophylaxis	100 mg daily 1–2 days before, continuously, during, and 4 weeks after travel
Hydroxychloroquine (*Plaquenil*)	Acute attacks and causal prophylaxis	600 mg initially, then 300 mg weekly 2 weeks prior to exposure and up to 4 weeks after leaving an endemic area
Mefloquine (*Lariam*)	Treatment of mild–moderate *P. falciparum, P. vivax*; acute attacks	5 tablets (1250 mg) as a single dose with 8 ounces water
	Causal prophylaxis	250 mg once a week, then every other week before, during, and up to 4 weeks after leaving an endemic area
Primaquine	Radical cure for *P. vivax;* prevent relapses	1 tablet (15 mg) for 14 days
Pyrimethamine (*Daraprim*)	Prophylaxis	25 mg once a week up to 10 weeks
Quinine sulfate (*Qualaquin*)	Treatment of uncomplicated *P. falciparum.* Acute malarial attacks alone or in combination with sulfonamide or tetracyclines	2 capsules (648 mg) every 8 hr for 7 days
Combination antimalarial drugs		
Artemether (20 mg) /lumefantrine (120 mg) (*Coartem*)	Treatment of uncomplicated *P. falciparum*	4 tablets over 3 days
Atovaquone (250 mg) /proguanil (100 mg) (*Malarone*)	Treatment of acute, uncomplicated *P. falciparum*	4 tablets/day for 3 days
	Prophylaxis of *P. falciparum*	1 tablet 1–2 days before, during, and 7 days after return
Sulfadoxine (500 mg) /pyrimethamine (25 mg) (*Fansidar*)	Acute attacks for chloroquine-resistant patients	2–3 tablets daily
	Prophylaxis	1 tablet weekly for up to 6 weeks after leaving an endemic area

Sulfadoxine competitively antagonizes para-aminobenzoic acid (PABA), resulting in disruption of folic acid synthesis and ultimately DNA synthesis. Since the microorganisms are prevented from producing folinic acid, nucleic acid synthesis is blocked. As a result, the protozoa cannot produce deoxyribonucleic acid (DNA) and ribonucleic acid (RNA), which are necessary for protein synthesis to sustain life.

Other antimalarial drugs, such as chloroquine and primaquine, act directly within the microorganisms. These drugs accumulate in the parasites and bind to the critical metabolic substances. During infection, when *Plasmodia* replicate in the host's RBCs, it is entirely dependent on the host for nutrients. The organism digests the host's hemoglobin within its special organelle called the food vacuole. In this process the heme is converted to hematin, a product that is toxic to the *Plasmodia* without further modification. The organism, therefore, detoxifies the hematin by converting it into chemically safe crystals called **hemozoin.** Chloroquine accumulates in the food vacuoles and inhibits the formation of hemozoin. This causes free heme to be released, which lyses *Plasmodia* membranes and kills the organisms. Chloroquine resistance has been associated with a decreased accumulation of chloroquine in the food vacuole, possibly due to impaired transport proteins. Relapse is associated with *P. vivax* because it is able to go into a dormant form for long periods that is asymptomatic until it is triggered to produce symptoms again. The other *Plasmodia* are effectively eradicated with drug treatment so symptoms do not occur unless the patient is reinfected.

Occasionally, patients are **intolerant** to one of the antimalarial drugs or, more frequently, the organism *P. falciparum* is resistant to the effects of chloroquine. In these situations, quinine, tetracycline, and/or pyrimethamine therapy may be initiated alone or in combination.

Drug Administration

Antimalarial drugs include derivatives of quinolone—4-amino quinolones are chloroquine and hydroxychloroquine; 8-amino quinolones are primaquine, mefloquine, quinine, and pyrimethamine. Table 43:1 identifies which agents are used for acute attacks and which are better suited to prophylaxis. Drugs for the treatment of acute malaria exacerbations are usually administered orally for relatively short periods (2 days to 2 weeks). Patients are often given chloroquine to destroy the parasites within the RBCs quickly and end the cycle of chills and fever. This initial course of treatment may be followed by primaquine to eradicate the parasites completely. If the oral route is not available, chloroquine hydrochlorine injection is available for parenteral administration.

Prophylaxis requires a longer duration of treatment. Persons planning to enter an area where malaria is endemic should begin treatment 1 to 2 weeks prior to their arrival. Treatment should continue throughout the stay and for up to 6 weeks after leaving the area. Short-term travelers (1 to 2 weeks) may be advised to begin a course of daily tetracycline (Sumycin) that continues up to 4 weeks following their return home.

Pharmacokinetics

These drugs are well absorbed following oral administration. They are highly bound to plasma proteins and are primarily metabolized in the liver. Mefloquine has a half-life of 3 weeks which supports once weekly dosing. Because these drugs are bases, anything that alkalinizes the urine (acetazolamide, sodium bicarbonate) will enable these drugs to be reabsorbed rather than excreted. Conversely, acidification of the urine will promote excretion.

Miscellaneous Therapeutic Actions

Among the antimalarial drugs, tetracycline and chloroquine have value in the treatment of infection caused by other protozoans, such as amebic dysentery. Quinine is readily available in tonic water but it is no longer available OTC for treating leg cramps. At prescribed doses of 260 to 300 mg taken once or twice before bedtime, quinine (*Qualaquin*) relieves nocturnal leg cramps. Because it exerts a direct action on skeletal muscle to affect calcium ions, muscle excitability is decreased, resulting in muscle relaxation. Quinine, which is related to quinidine (an antiarrhythmic drug), has the ability to depress cardioconduction as well.

Chloroquine, like its close relative quinine, is antiinflammatory. It is used in the management of rheumatoid arthritis and systemic lupus erythematosus.

Adverse Effects

The adverse effects associated with the use of pyrimethamine, the aminoquinolones, and the combination drugs are seldom serious, but the intensity of the effects increases with the dose of the drug and the length of treatment. Chloroquine and primaquine have a special cautionary black box warning that says, "Physicians should completely familiarize themselves with the complete contents of [the drug instructions for use] before prescribing" these drugs. The most common side effects include nausea, diarrhea, headache, blurred vision, vertigo, and rash. Quinine may produce cinchonism in sensitive individuals. **Cinchonism,** a symptom complex characterized by central nervous system (CNS) stimulation, ringing in the ears, and headache, is derived from cinchona, the South American tree from which quinine is obtained.

Primaquine, specifically, produces hemolytic anemia in individuals who are genetically deficient in the enzyme glucose-6-phosphate dehydrogenase (G6PD). This condition, which occurs primarily in Caucasians, is characterized by hemolysis of RBCs. In their metabolism, drugs such as primaquine, salicylates, and sulfonamides produce peroxide, which oxidizes hemoglobin and RBC membranes. The severity of the anemia will vary with the genetic sensitivity of the patient—that is, the degree of G6PD deficiency. Large doses of primaquine and chloroquine also have been associated with **methemoglobinemia** and leukopenia. Therefore, the recommended doses should not be exceeded.

Mefloquine increases the potential for cardiotoxicity when given concurrently with quinine or beta-blocking drugs. Increases in PR and QT intervals, indicative of conduction blockage, are evident on the electrocardiogram (ECG). Mefloquine is a myocardial depressant. Since it is likely to be given in conjunction with other antimalarials in severe cases, mefloquine should be given at least 12 hours after the last dose of quinine. Mefloquine also produces Stevens-Johnson syndrome. "Physicians should completely familiarize themselves with the complete contents of this monograph before prescribing chloroquine phosphate."

Pyrimethamine has a special cautionary (black box) warning on its label. Pyrimethamine has been associated with Stevens-Johnson syndrome. This is a severe inflammatory reaction where lesions on the skin and mucous membranes cause the patient's eyes to be swollen and pruritic, and the patient may not be able to swallow. Since this can be a fatal condition, the offending agent is discontinued immediately and supportive treatment provided. If a rash appears, especially if the RBC count is reduced significantly or an active fungal infection occurs, the drug should be stopped immediately. Chloroquine and primaquine also have cautionary warnings that state, "Physicians should completely familiarize themselves with the complete contents of this drug use label before prescribing chloroquine phosphate."

Overdose

There is no antidote for overdose of the antimalarial drugs. Treatment is supportive according to the evolving symptoms. Children are particularly sensitive to chloroquine and hydroxychloroquine, with death resulting from exposure to even small doses. The symptoms range from headache, drowsiness, nausea, and vomiting to cardiovascular collapse and convulsions. Death is usually a result of respiratory and cardiac arrest.

Contraindications

Antimalarial drugs are contraindicated in patients who are hypersensitive to the drug or known to be hypersensitive to a related compound.

LO 43.1 | **LO 43.3**
LO 43.4 | **LO 43.5** | **LO 43.8**

DYSENTERY

Two protozoal organisms, *Entamoeba histolytica* and *Giardia lamblia,* are frequently responsible for producing **dysentery** in humans. These organisms gain access to the human GI tract through contaminated food and water and irritate the intestinal muscles, causing the inflammation, pain, **tenesmus,** and diarrhea characteristic of dysentery. The severity of the symptoms depends on the organism producing the response. For example, when the infection is limited to the intestinal tract, diarrhea is the primary symptom. Diarrhea may result in loss of body water and **electrolytes,** which leaves patients feeling fatigued and dehydrated. *Entamoeba histolytica* can cause additional damage because it invades hepatic tissue and produces hepatic

amebiasis (amebic hepatitis). In the stages of amebic hepatitis, the organisms burrow into the wall of the liver and create an inflammatory reaction; this usually results in the formation and accumulation of pus (liver abscess) even though no overt symptoms may be present.

Antidysenteric Drugs

Several drugs are useful for the treatment of dysentery. The choice is often based on the site of protozoal infection (see Table 43:2). Acute intestinal amebiasis is currently treated with a combination of drugs.

Mechanism of Action

Paromomycin and tetracyclines are antibiotics that reduce protozoal infections in the intestines by inhibiting the availability of nutrients to the microorganisms. Since the normal intestinal flora (bacteria) provide nutrients that are necessary for the survival of the infectious protozoa, antibiotics such as paromomycin and tetracyclines destroy the intestinal flora. Elimination of intestinal bacteria "starves" the protozoa and decreases the multiplication of the parasites. Paromomycin also has a direct amebicidal action against *Entamoeba histolytica*. Metronidazole and now tinidazole represent a great advance in the treatment of dysentery because they are systemic drugs active against various anaerobic bacteria and protozoa. These drugs are distributed widely to many tissues, including bone, bile, intestines, and abscesses within the liver. They have amebicidal activity in all stages of amebiasis (intestinal and hepatic).

Most of the other agents in this class are useful only in the intestinal protozoal infections. At present, metronidazole and tinidazole are considered drugs of choice in the treatment of acute intestinal dysentery. Tinidazole has a longer half-life and can be given once a day. In moderate to severe cases of amebiasis, iodoquinol and chloroquine are used. Chloroquine is of primary value in the treatment of amebic hepatitis. These drugs probably damage the protozoal DNA so that the organism cannot replicate properly. As a result, these two drugs are direct-acting amebicides.

Pharmacokinetics

Metronidazole, tinidazole, and chloroquine are readily absorbed following oral administration. These drugs can be taken with food to minimize the GI effects without affecting absorption. Chloroquine is very slowly redistributed among tissue, metabolized slightly (30 percent), and excreted into the urine mostly unchanged (70 percent). Metronidazole is metabolized in the liver to active trichomonicidal conjugates. Therefore, the drug may accumulate in patients with severe liver disease. These patients must be monitored more closely; however, the drug can be given. The major route of metronidazole elimination is the

[Table 43:2]

Drugs Effective in the Treatment of Protozoal Infections

Site of infection	Drug (*Trade Name*)	Adult oral dose
Entamoeba histolytica		
Intestine	Iodoquinol (*Yodoxin*)	650 mg TID for 20 days
	Metronidazole (*Flagyl*)	750 mg TID for 5–10 days
	Paromomycin sulfate (*Humatin*)	25–35 mg/kg in three divided doses for 5–10 days
	Tetracyclines (Sumycin)	100 mg once daily as an adjunct to amebicide treatment
	Tinidazole (*Tindamax*)	2 g/day for 3 days
Liver and intestinal wall	Chloroquine (*Aralen*)	1000 mg/day for 2 days, then 500 mg/day up to 3 weeks
	Metronidazole (*Flagyl*)	500–750 mg TID for 5–10 days
	Tinidazole (*Tindamax*)	2 g once a day for 3–5 days
Giardia lamblia		
Intestine	Metronidazole (*Flagyl*)	500 mg every 12 hours for 3 days
	Nitazoxanide (*Alinia*)	500 mg BID for 3 days
	Tinidazole (*Tindamax*)	2 g single dose
Toxoplasmosis gondii		
Genitourinary tract	Pyrimethamine plus sulfonamide	50–75 mg/day for 1–3 weeks
Trichomonas vaginalis		
Genitourinary tract	Metronidazole (*Flagyl*)	375 mg BID for 7 days
	Tinidazole (*Tindamax*)	2 g single dose

urine. Tinidazole is entirely metabolized in the liver prior to excretion. Paromomycin is not absorbed or metabolized within the GI tract. This feature facilitates its contact with the microorganisms within the intestine. Then it is excreted unchanged (100 percent) in the feces.

Metronidazole and tinidazole cross the placenta and are distributed within fetal tissues. Although it has not been associated with human abnormalities, metronidazole has produced mutagenic activity *in vitro* (test tube analyses). For this reason these drugs are not recommended to be used in the first trimester of pregnancy when active cell division and development occur. When necessary, they are given for trichomoniasis during the second and third trimesters.

Adverse Effects

Most of the amebicides produce side effects such as nausea, vomiting, abdominal cramps, and diarrhea. The diarrhea usually subsides once the drug is discontinued and the infectious microorganisms are eradicated. The usual side effects of metronidazole and tinidazole include nausea, diarrhea, vaginal and urethral burning, and headache. Individuals taking metronidazole and tinidazole should not drink alcoholic beverages because metronidazole produces a **disulfiram-like reaction** with alcohol that can be very unpleasant. Acetaldehyde dehydrogenase, an enzyme in the metabolism of alcohol that converts acetaldehyde to acetic acid, is inhibited by disulfiram. This inhibition causes greater accumulation of acetaldehye in the blood, which results in an immediate reaction of flushing, nausea, headache, tachycardia, shortness of breath, and possible collapse. Metronidazole and tinidazole produce a similar condition when taken with alcohol.

Metronidazole and tinidazole have a special cautionary warning in their labeling because metronidazole has been shown to be carcinogenic in mice and rats. Because tinidazole is chemically similar to metronidazole, caution is warranted. Unnecessary use of the drugs should be avoided. Use should be reserved for the conditions for which the drugs are indicated.

The quinoline derivatives, chloroquine and others, are probably the most toxic agents in this class. These drugs have been associated with the production of CNS stimulation, amnesia, peripheral neuropathy, and optic atrophy, which can be permanent. The amebicidal drugs are contraindicated in patients who have liver or renal damage, visual dysfunction, or known hypersensitivity to the drugs.

Paromomycin is an aminoglycoside antibiotic produced by the mold *Streptomyces rimosus*. It is a cousin to neomycin and kanamycin. Since it is not absorbed, it is unlikely to produce the same renal toxicity and impaired hearing produced by the other aminoglycosides. Nevertheless, with protracted use in severe infection, the potential for producing adverse effects should be kept in mind.

Tetracyclines readily cross the placenta, are found in fetal tissues, and can have toxic effects on the developing fetus (retardation of skeletal development). These drugs are contraindicated during pregnancy.

LO 43.1 | LO 43.5 | LO 43.8

OTHER PROTOZOAL INFECTIONS

Giardia lamblia

Giardia infection has become recognized as a common cause of waterborne disease in humans in the United States. *Giardia lamblia* is a flagellated protozoan that resides in the intestine of humans, cats, dogs, and rural wildlife. It gains access to water sources through unsanitary conditions such as sewage entering the local water supply or infected individuals using recreational bathing and swimming facilities. Travelers and children are among the largest groups affected. Backpackers, hikers, and international travelers may unknowingly encounter contaminated drinking water including the ice cubes made from contaminated streams or lakes. See Figure 43.2. Children are most susceptible because everything goes into their mouths, especially dirty hands. *Giardia* comes into humans by way of the mouth; it is not transmitted by blood contact. *Giardia* infection can be highly contagious. The protozoa attach to the membranes of the intestine. As they multiply, they spread into the feces, are excreted into the water, or are transmitted to sex partners through oral-anal contact. The waterborne organisms can exist even in chlorinated water that is not adequately filtered. Characteristic symptoms are diarrhea, flatulence, greasy stools, GI cramps, nausea, and vomiting. The intensity of diarrhea and vomiting may lead to weight loss and dehydration. Prevention involves good hygiene practices: washing hands with soap and water after the toilet and before handling food. For children it is important to establish this frequent habit. *Giardia* can be found in a day-care setting, even among diapered children, and in major camping grounds. Boiling will kill *Giardia* cysts and there are commercially available filters that will remove the cysts from water (for the campers). Three drugs are available for the first-line treatment of *G. lamblia*: metronidazole (*Flagyl*), nitazoxanide (*Alinia*), and tinidazole (*Tindamax*). Each drug is given orally; the duration of treatment is short and varies from one to three days depending on the drug. Usually the medications are well tolerated, but adverse effects may include dizziness, headache, diarrhea, nausea, stomach pain, loss of appetite, constipation,

| **Figure 43.2** | **Source of *Giardia lamblia*** |

Giardiasis is caused by the protozoan *Giardia lamblia*

(a)

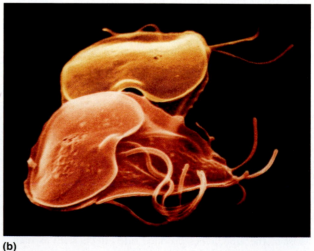
(b)

(a) Man encounters the microorganism through contaminated water sources. (b) Electron micrograph of the flagellated organism.

changes in taste **(dysgeusia),** and dry mouth. Urine may be darkened or discolored but this is not a harmful effect. See Table 43.2 for oral doses and durations of treatment.

Toxoplasma

Toxoplasmosis is caused by another protozoan, *Toxoplasma gondii,* which uses any mammal as a host. Most commonly *Toxoplasma* has been identified in the fecal material of domestic cats. Presumably the animals eat raw or undercooked meat containing the protozoan cysts, which then attach to the intestinal tissue, undergo sexual reproduction, and multiply. The asymptomatic feline host sheds the **oocysts** in the stool and provides an opportunity for children and adults to become exposed to the oocysts by ingestion. The parasite enters macrophages in the intestinal lining and is distributed via the bloodstream throughout the body. Humans access contaminated fecal matter by routinely cleaning pet cat litterboxes and distributing the material into the air, which is then inhaled, or on hands that are not adequately washed after the task. Children also may be exposed to the same contact in play areas where cats have defecated. Women are cautioned not to clean pet litterboxes during pregnancy in order to minimize the opportunity for exposure to potential infection. This also has been termed "cat scratch disease" because of the potential for an infected animal to transmit cysts to a human host by scratching the skin or mucous membranes around the eyes, either in play or aggressive behavior, bringing blood in contact with the organism.

If the patient is infected very early in pregnancy, *Toxoplasma* will induce abortion, viewed in the patient as a miscarriage of the first trimester. Miscarriage, in general, is not uncommon during this period, and in the absence of significant symptomatology toxoplasmosis goes undetected. Pregnant women who contract the infection during the second and third trimesters can pass the organism onto the newborn. Symptoms can range from mild malaise, muscle pain, and low-grade fever that is self-limiting to an acute fulminating infection. The more severe manifestations usually occur in patients who are compromised, such as those with acquired immunodeficiency syndrome (AIDS). In the United States, toxoplasmosis is most commonly encountered as encephalitis.

Pharmacotherapy

Drugs that are effective in the treatment of toxoplasmosis include pyrimethamine, 50 to 75 mg/day PO for 1 to 3 weeks, in conjunction with 1 to 4 g of sulfonamide treatment. Maintenance dose at half the initial dose may continue for 5 weeks. Congenitally infected infants may be given pyrimethamine every 2 or 3 days for up to 1 year.

Similarly, the relapse rate in AIDS patients warrants indefinite drug administration. Because pyrimethamine affects folic acid metabolism, 10 mg of folinic acid is taken daily for the duration of treatment.

Trichomonas

Trichomonas vaginalis is a protozoan that infects the urinary tract of men and women. See Figure 43.3. Since this organism is frequently transmitted to females through sexual intercourse, **trichomoniasis** is considered a sexually transmitted disease (STD). Sexual intercourse with an infected male may result in a vaginal trichomonal infection in the female partner. Usually, the female is made aware of the infection because a pungent vaginal discharge is produced, accompanied by intermenstrual spotting and itching. However, many women harbor the organism without experiencing discomfort (are asymptomatic). Proper treatment of this protozoal infection should include treatment of both partners. If the infected individuals are not treated simultaneously, the infection will rapidly recur in either person.

The drug of choice used to eradicate *Trichomonas vaginalis* is metronidazole (*Flagyl*) or tinidazole (*Tindamax*). It is an effective trichomonacide when administered orally (either 2 g as a single or divided dose in 1 day, or 250 mg TID for 7 consecutive days) to both men and women. Occasionally, metronidazole is used in conjunction with vinegar douches.

The usual side effects of these drugs include nausea, diarrhea, vaginal and urethral burning, and headache. These drugs produce a disulfiram reaction with alcohol so that patients should be cautioned to avoid alcohol consumption during treatment (this includes

Figure 43.3

The Protozoan *Trichomonas Vaginalis* Causes a Venereal Disease in Humans

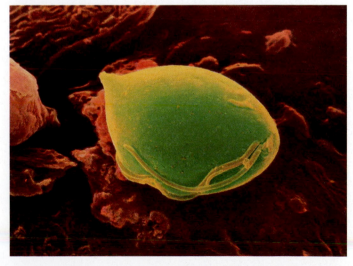

OTC products with any alcohol content). Metronidazole has been suspected of being potentially carcinogenic in animals, so metronidazole should not be used indiscriminately in the treatment of trichomoniasis. But for short-term use, metronidazole is a relatively safe drug valuable in the treatment of trichomoniasis. Although metronidazole has been used during pregnancy with no adverse results, as a precaution metronidazole should not be administered during the first trimester of pregnancy. When given in the second or third trimester, the 7-day schedule should be used rather than the single 2-g dose.

LO 43.6 | LO 43.7 | LO 43.8

ANTHELMINTIC DRUGS

Parasitic worm infestations are a major cause of disease throughout the world. However, in the United States, the most frequently encountered parasitic infestations are limited to pinworms, roundworms, and tapeworms, as shown in Table 43:3. These parasites gain access to the human GI tract when food or soil contaminated with worm eggs is ingested. The worms then mature and multiply in the intestines. Frequently, worms can be seen in the stools when there is a heavy infestation. Occasionally, certain worms also gain access to muscle tissue and burrow into the tissue. See Figure 43.4. Usually parasitic worm infestations produce symptoms such as diarrhea, nausea, loss of appetite, intense itching, and abdominal cramping. Hookworms and tapeworms are especially dangerous because these parasites can perforate the intestinal membranes, resulting in loss of blood, anemia, and hemorrhage. When diagnosed early, most parasitic worm infestations are confined to the intestinal tract. Oral administration of anthelmintic drugs brings the drugs into direct contact with the parasites throughout the GI tract (see Table 43:3).

Mechanism of Action

Most anthelmintic drugs are not well absorbed and, therefore, remain in close contact with the parasites. In general, these drugs produce muscle paralysis in the worms and decrease their motility. They also may inhibit the metabolic functions of the parasites. After the parasites are immobilized, the peristaltic action of the intestine can carry worms and eggs out of the body. Usually, a laxative is administered to increase intestinal activity and facilitate bowel flushing, so that worms and eggs are excreted into the feces. Encysted forms of parasites (in the muscle) may require more intensive drug therapy to remove them.

Two drugs in this class, pyrantel (*Antiminth*) and piperazine (*Antepar*), directly affect muscle contraction in the worms through different mechanisms. Piperazine

Figure 43.4

Parasitic Worms

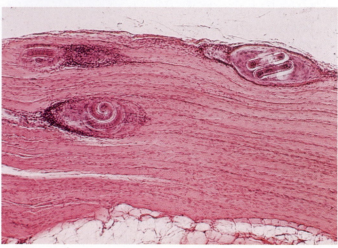

(a)

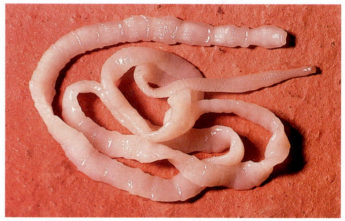

(b)

(a) *Trichinella spiralis* encyst in muscle fibers after being ingested by humans through contaminated meat. (b) Tapeworm.

blocks the worms' responses to acetylcholine (ACH), causing flaccid paralysis, whereas pyrantel inhibits cholinesterases (elevating ACH), leading to depolarizing neuromuscular blockade. These two drugs should not be coadministered to treat roundworms because their mechanisms of action will counteract the therapeutic effect when given together. Drug interactions reported to occur with anthelmintics, antivirals, and antifungal drugs are presented in Table 43:4.

Adverse Effects

Many anthelmintic drugs are derivatives of antimony, which is usually well tolerated by human hosts. The common adverse effects include nausea, fever, headache, cramps, and diarrhea. Tinnitus, hypotension, and paresthesia also have been reported. These drugs must be used

Drugs Effective in the Treatment of Parasitic Worm Infestations

Drug (*Trade Name*)	Use	Oral adult dose
Mebendazole (*Vermox*)	Pinworms Roundworms and hookworms	100 mg one time 100 mg BID for 3 days
Praziquantel (*Biltricide*)	Tapeworm	20 mg/kg TID for 1 day
Pyrantel pamoate (*Pin-Rid, Pin-X*)	Roundworms and pinworms	11 mg/kg of body weight up to maximum does of 1 g
Thiabendazole (*Mintezol*)	Roundworm	22 mg/kg/dose < 70 kg; 1.5 g/dose >70 kg at 2 doses daily for 2–3 days

Drug Interactions Associated with the Use of Antiprotozoal Drugs

Drug (*Trade Name*)	Administered in conjunction with	Result of the interaction
Chloroquine	Kaolin or magnesium trisilicate Cimetidine	Decrease absorption of chloroquine Decrease clearance of chloroquine
Mefloquine	Beta-adrenergic blockers Chloroquine Valproic acid	Cardiac arrest has occurred Increased risk of convulsions Decrease seizure control of valproic acid
Metronidazole	Lithium Alcohol	Increase lithium levels Disulfiram reaction
Pyrimethamine	Methotrexate, sulfonamides Lorazepam	Synergistic folic acid deficiency, increase the risk for bone marrow suppression Mild hepatotoxicity has occurred
Quinine	Antacids with aluminum Antibiotics rifabutin, rifampin Cimetidine Neuromuscular blockers Oral anticoagulant warfarin Urinary alkalinizers acetazolamide, sodium bicarbonate	Decrease quinine absorption Induce hepatic microsomal metabolism of quinine Decrease quinine clearance Quinine may potentiate the neuromuscular blockade, causing respiratory difficulty Quinine may depress the hepatic synthesis of vitamin K clotting factors Increase renal reabsorption leading to toxic levels of quinine
Tinidazole	Alcohol Warfarin	Disulfiram reaction Prolong prothrombin time

with caution in patients who have severe renal, cardiac, or liver disease. Pregnant women and young children may be especially sensitive to the adverse effects of these drugs.

Special Considerations

In the treatment of parasitic worm infestations, all family members must be counseled to wash their hands and fingernails before eating meals and after bowel movements. To avoid reinfection, the family must be reminded to wash the perianal area daily. Usually, all family members receive treatment until there is no evidence that the worms are still present. For some infestations (pinworms), medication is taken as an initial dosage and then repeated 3 weeks later if the worms persist in stool samples. In the treatment of tapeworm, patients are not considered cured until the stools are negative for worms for 3 months.

Drug Interactions

The most critical adverse effects involve precipitation of convulsions or cardiac arrhythmias. Chloroquine and valproic acid must be used with caution if given concomitantly with mefloquine because of the significant risk of producing convulsions. Beta-blocking drugs and cardiac depressants such as quinine administered with mefloquine are apt to induce conduction disorders leading to arrhythmias and potential arrest.

Drugs that decrease the clearance of antiprotozoal drugs, such as cimetidine, increase the blood levels and predispose the patient to possible adverse effects. Cimetidine treatment may be interrupted until the protozoal infection is stabilized. Conversely, antibiotics such as rifampin may induce hepatic metabolism of the quinolines and quinine and therefore reduce their effectiveness.

Antacids containing aluminum can bind these drugs within the intestinal tract when given concurrently, reducing absorption and effectiveness. Metronidazole and tinidazole produce a disulfiram-like reaction when alcohol is taken during treatment and up to 48 hours after the drug is stopped. Tinidazole has prolonged the prothrombin time of warfarin up to 8 days after tinidazole was discontinued. Specific drug interactions are presented in Table 43:4.

Patient Administration and Monitoring

Routine CBC and platelet count should be periodically performed during prolonged therapy. A drop in hematocrit and hemoglobin may indicate the onset of anemia. Quinine and amino-quinolines in particular may induce hemolysis, resulting in hemolytic anemia in susceptible patients. Prior to beginning treatment with the quinolines, the patient interview should interrogate the possibility of G6PD deficiency in the family or personal history. Susceptible individuals should have the drug schedule changed to weekly administration.

Vital signs and ECG should be performed before and during therapy to identify potential changes in cardiac conduction. Especially with mefloquine and quinine, prolongation in conduction may precipitate escape foci leading to arrhythmias, fibrillation, and arrest.

General Instructions to Patients

Patients should be instructed to use caution when driving, operating equipment, or performing tasks requiring coordination and dexterity because quinine and mefloquine may cause blurred vision, dizziness, and confusion.

Instruct patients to keep any of these drugs out of the reach of children. Overdose in children is especially dangerous with the quinolines. In the event of overdose, the patient should be taken to the emergency room for proper symptomatic treatment.

Drug Administration

Patients should be instructed to take these medications at the same time every day whenever possible. For drugs taken more than once daily, the dosing intervals should be evenly spaced. Explain that stopping this medication too early may allow the parasites to continue to grow, which may result in a relapse of the infection. Patients must be told to complete the full course of treatment even if symptoms disappear after a few doses. In order to ensure optimum compliance with the treatment schedule, patients can be instructed to take these drugs with meals. This will minimize any gastric irritation.

Any of the azole drugs, tinidazole or metronidazole, may have a metallic taste that is unpleasant and noticeable to some patients. Encourage patients to continue the medication until it has been used up. These drugs will darken the urine. Although the effect is not harmful, patients should be alerted to this to avoid unnecessary concern and deviation from the treatment schedule.

Notify the Physician

Patients should be clearly instructed to notify the physician immediately for evaluation and potential discontinuation of the drug if they develop itching, rash, or fever (indicative of allergy), or stomach pain, difficulty breathing, severe diarrhea, vomiting, visual disturbances, or ringing in the ears.

Use in Pregnancy

Metronidazole, although designated FDA Pregnancy Category B, should not be given in the first trimester.

Other antiprotozoal and anthelmintic drugs are designated FDA Pregnancy Category B or C because specific evidence of safety has not been established through clinical trials. The drugs can be given if clearly needed.

Chapter Review

Understanding Terminology

Match the definition or description in the left column with the appropriate term in the right column.

_____ 1. Examples include sodium, potassium, and chloride. **(LO 43.8)**

_____ 2. A protozoal infection carried by mosquitos. **(LO 43.1, 43.2, 43.8)**

_____ 3. Procedures or medications to prevent, rather than to treat, an existing disease. **(LO 43.8)**

_____ 4. A condition in which there is no outward evidence that an infection is present. **(LO 43.8)**

_____ 5. A sexually transmitted disease. **(LO 43.8)**

_____ 6. A painful spasm of the anal sphincter. **(LO 43.8)**

_____ 7. Present continually in a particular geographic region. **(LO 43.8)**

_____ 8. A condition characterized by frequent watery stools, tenesmus, fever, and dehydration. **(LO 43.8)**

a. asymptomatic
b. dysentery
c. electrolytes
d. endemic
e. malaria
f. prophylactic
g. tenesmus
h. trichomoniasis

Acquiring Knowledge

Answer the following questions.

1. Which diseases are commonly produced by protozoa? **(LO 43.1, 43.4)**
2. How do these infectious protozoa gain access to the body? **(LO 43.1)**
3. Describe the cycle of infection produced by *Plasmodium.* **(LO 43.2)**
4. What is meant by prophylactic treatment of malaria? **(LO 43.8)**
5. How does prophylaxis differ from radical cure? **(LO 43.3)**
6. Which organisms produce dysentery in humans? **(LO 43.4)**
7. Which drugs are effective against protozoally induced dysentery? **(LO 43.3)**
8. Why is trichomoniasis considered an STD? **(LO 43.8)**
9. What is the drug of choice in the treatment of trichomoniasis? **(LO 43.3)**
10. Why should alcoholic beverages be avoided during metronidazole therapy? **(LO 43.5)**
11. What are the common parasitic worm infestations found in the United States? **(LO 43.6)**
12. Why are tapeworms and hookworms potentially dangerous? **(LO 43.6)**
13. How do anthelmintic drugs act? **(LO 43.7)**
14. Why are laxatives administered as adjunct medication in treating parasitic worm infestations? **(LO 43.7)**

Applying Knowledge on the Job

Use your critical-thinking skills to answer the following questions.

1. Mrs. Bell is leaving her gynecologist's office with prescriptions for herself and her husband for metronidazole because of her diagnosis of trichomoniasis. As she is chatting with you on her way out, she mentions that she and her husband will be going out to a four-star restaurant two nights from now to celebrate their third anniversary. What potential drug interaction should Mrs. Bell be warned of? **(LO 43.5)**

2. Mr. Green calls his physician's office complaining of significant foul-smelling diarrhea, abdominal discomfort, and weight loss. He is requesting a prescription for something, such as *Lomotil,* to control the diarrhea. You recall talking to him several weeks ago about his upcoming trip to Yellowstone Park, where he planned backpacking for a couple of weeks. Could Mr. Green's recent vacation be related to his current diarrhea? **(LO 43.4)**

3. Which is the only antiprotozoal drug that is contraindicated in pregnancy and why? **(LO 43.5)**

4. Susan is traveling to Mexico for a 1-week vacation. She has asked for travel medications in case she develops dysentery during her trip. She is 7 months pregnant. Her physician has decided to prescribe paromomycin. Why is this the medication of choice? **(LO 43.3)**

5. Becky is 5 months pregnant and has just been diagnosed with trichomoniasis. Her physician has decided to medicate her and her partner with *Flagyl.* This may be administered orally as 2 g as a single or divided dose in 1 day, or 250 mg TID × 7 d. Which dosing schedule should be prescribed for Becky? Why? Can her partner be treated with a different dosing schedule? Why or why not? **(LO 43.7)**

Multiple Choice

Use your critical-thinking skills to answer the following questions.

1. Which of the following drugs kills pinworms? **(LO 43.7)**
   A. voriconizole
   B. mebendazole and pyrantel pamoate
   C. ritonovir
   D. flucytocine

2. Protozoal infections include all of the following except: **(LO 43.1, 43.4)**
   A. *Tinea pedis*
   B. *Trichomonas*
   C. *Giardia lamblia*
   D. *Toxoplasma gondii*

3. Amebiasis **(LO 43.1, 43.4)**
   A. causes diarrhea and intense intestinal pain
   B. stops electrolyte loss from the gut
   C. does not exist in contaminated streams and water supply
   D. only affects the lumen of the intestine

4. In the malaria life cycle **(LO 43.1)**
   A. there is no life or stage outside of man
   B. organisms rapidly multiply in the liver
   C. eggs are shed in human feces
   D. chills and fever coincide with bursting red blood cells

5. Which combination is the correct drug and organism? **(LO 43.1, 43.4, 43.7, 43.8)**
   A. metronidazole: *Plasmodium vivax*
   B. primaquine radical cure: *Plasmodium*
   C. paromomycin: *Trichomonas vaginalis*
   D. tinidazole: hepatic malaria

6. Paromomycin **(LO 43.1, 43.4, 43.5, 43.8)**
   A. paralyzes parasitic worms in the intestine
   B. eliminates intestinal bacteria as an antibiotic
   C. is in the chloroquine family of drugs
   D. is the drug of choice for *Giardia*

7. Which of the following is NOT transmitted through contaminated food or water? **(LO 43.1, 43.4, 43.6, 43.8)**
   A. *Trichomonas* and *Toxoplasma*
   B. *Giardia lamblia*
   C. *Entamoeba histolytica*
   D. amebiasis

8. Which of the following is the correct statement? **(LO 43.2, 43.3, 43.5)**
    A. cinchonism is a side effect of paromomycin from tree bark
    B. malaria is symptomatic when it invades the liver
    C. tetracyclines/doxycycline have no place in the treatment of malaria
    D. metronidazole should not be given in the first trimester of pregnancy

Multiple Choice (Multiple Answer)

Select the correct choices for each statement. The choices may be all correct, all incorrect, or any combination.

1. Which of the following are ways protozoa can infect humans? **(LO 43.1)**
    A. via sexual intercourse
    B. via contaminated food
    C. via mosquitos
    D. via contaminated soil

2. Select all of the ways antimalarial drugs work to eradicate protozoan infections. **(LO 43.3)**
    A. interfere with metabolism of protozoans
    B. interrupt protein synthesis
    C. inhibit the formation of hemozoin
    D. inhibit the conversion of folic acid to folinic acid

3. The symptoms of dysentery include **(LO 43.4)**
    A. recurrent chills
    B. sweating
    C. jaundice
    D. high fever

4. Choose the medications effective in treating parasitic worms. **(LO 43.7)**
    A. *Yodoxin*
    B. *Daraprim*
    C. *Flagyl*
    D. *Biltricide*

5. Which of the following are adverse reactions of mefloquine? **(LO 43.5)**
    A. disulfiram-like reaction
    B. cinchonism
    C. Stevens-Johnson syndrome
    D. tenesmus

Sequencing

Place the following steps of protozoal infection in order from first to last. **(LO 43.2)**

_____ _____ _____ _____ _____

First   **Last**

transmission by *Anopheles*

protozoa released

enter RBC

invade liver

cells rupture

Classification

Place the following protozoans under the diseases they cause. **(LO 43.2, 43.4)**

Entamoeba histolytica   *Plasmodia*   *P. falciparum*

Trichomonas vaginalis   *Toxoplasma gondii*   *Giardia lamblia*

Malaria	Dysentery	Other protozoal infections

Documentation

Using the prescription below, answer the following questions. **(LO 43.7)**

Riverside Clinic
Practice RX

12345 Main Avenue
Anytown, USA 12345
931-555-1000

NAME: ___Felicia Kitburg_____   DATE: _____

ADDRESS: _____

RX   Vermox 100mg

Sig: Take by mouth once

Dr. Leslie Granger_____ M.D. _____M.D.

   Substitution Permitted   Dispense as written

DEA #: _____   REFILL: NR   1   2   3   4

---

a. What condition is being treated with this medication?

b. List the possible parasites that cause this condition.

c. What are the common adverse effects of this drug?

d. How do these drugs work on the parasite?

Labeling

Fill in the missing labels. (LO 43.1)

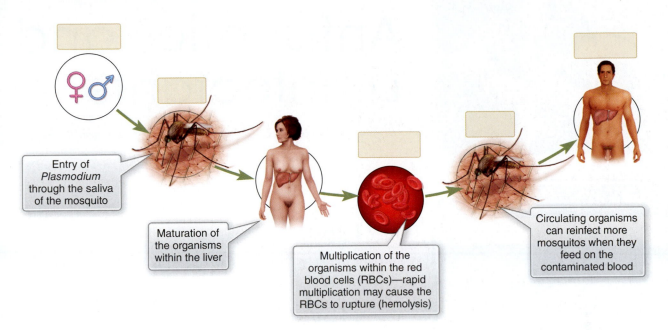

Entry of *Plasmodium* through the saliva of the mosquito

Maturation of the organisms within the liver

Multiplication of the organisms within the red blood cells (RBCs)—rapid multiplication may cause the RBCs to rupture (hemolysis)

Circulating organisms can reinfect more mosquitos when they feed on the contaminated blood

For interactive animations, videos, and assessment, visit:

www.mcgrawhillconnect.com

Chapter 44

Antiseptics and Disinfectants

DRUG CLASS AT A GLANCE

OTC	YES
PRESCRIPTION	NO
SCHEDULED DRUGS	NO
FDA PREGNANCY CATEGORY	Not applicable

INDICATIONS

Surface cleansing, degerm materials, sterilization

KEY TERMS

antiseptic: substance that inhibits the growth of microorganisms on living tissue.

aphthous ulcer: a painful open sore in the mouth or upper throat; also known as a canker sore.

argyria: permanent black discoloration of skin and mucous membranes caused by prolonged use of silver protein solutions.

bactericidal: chemical that kills or destroys bacteria.

bacteriostatic: chemical that inhibits growth or reproduction of bacteria but does not kill bacteria.

-cidal: suffix denoting killing, as of microorganisms.

cold sterilization: Destruction of microorganisms at room temperature without the use of heat or ionizing radiation.

decubitis ulcer: bedsore.

denaturing: causing destruction of bacterial protein function; also adulteration of alcohol, rendering it unfit for drinking.

disinfectant: substance that kills disease-causing microorganisms on nonliving surfaces.

eschar: thick crust or scab that develops after skin is burned.

fungicidal: chemical that kills or destroys fungi.

fungistatic: chemical that inhibits growth or reproduction of fungi but does not kill fungi.

germicidal: Substance, chemical solution, or drug that kills microorganisms.

hypersensitivity: exaggerated response such as rash, edema, or anaphylaxis that develops following exposure to certain drugs or chemicals.

iodophor: compound containing iodine.

irrigation: washing (lavage) of a wound or cavity with large volumes of fluid.

lyse: to disintegrate or dissolve.

nosocomial: infection acquired as a result of being in a hospital.

pathogen(ic): a microorganism that causes disease.

-static: suffix denoting the inhibition of, as of microorganisms.

sterilization: process that results in destruction of all microorganisms.

virucidal: the capacity to destroy or inactivate viruses.

Learning Outcomes

After studying this chapter, you should be able to

44.1 explain the difference between reducing bacterial growth and inhibiting all bacterial growth (eradication).

44.2 describe the mechanisms by which antiseptics reduce bacterial function.

44.3 discuss how four common chemicals are used to inhibit infectious microorganisms.

44.4 explain why these chemicals are not administered by mouth to treat infection.

44.5 explain the differences between antiseptic, disinfectant. and antibiotics.

44.6 describe adverse effects that occur with these chemicals.

44.7 explain essential terminology associated with antiseptics.

Introduction

Antiseptics and disinfectants are used to control and prevent infection. These drugs can be distinguished from other antimicrobials in that they are usually chemical solutions (for example, alcohols, aldehydes, or iodophors) that are topically applied to surfaces such as skin, mucous membranes, or inanimate objects (floors, walls, or instruments) where microorganisms may be present. The primary mode of application is via swab, sponge, scrub solution, or, occasionally, as a mouthwash.

Antiseptics and disinfectants destroy microorganisms on contact. The term **antiseptic,** however, is more frequently associated with the eradication or inhibition of microbial growth on living tissue surfaces. **Disinfectants,** on the other hand, reduce the risk of infection by destroying pathogenic microbes on nonliving surfaces. Unlike antibiotics, antiseptics and disinfectants are not intended to be swallowed, injected, taken internally, or reach the general circulation in order to destroy microorganisms.

| LO 44.1 | LO 44.2 | LO 44.5 | LO 44.7 |

ANTISEPSIS AND DISINFECTION

Microorganisms are everywhere and migrate freely on skin, hair, and furniture and in air currents. Given the right environment, any microbe can produce an infection. Many times an infection is localized on the skin surface where it can be treated with topical drugs. Sometimes, **pathogenic** microorganisms enter the general circulation. At home, simple wounds and skin abrasions provide potential pathogens an access route to the blood. Usually, the immune system is capable of detecting and destroying the pathogen, although it might need some help from an antibiotic. In hospitals and other health care institutions, the risk of infection is complicated by the type of wound—**decubitis ulcer** (bedsore), trauma, or surgical—as well as the potential for contracting a nosocomial infection. **Nosocomial** infections are hospital-acquired infections that develop while patients are in the hospital. These microorganisms characteristically are virulent and difficult to eradicate. Hospital-acquired infections may result from catheterizations (urinary tract or intravenous therapy), which provide a pathway for microorganisms to enter the body. These infections occur with prolonged hospitalization or in high-risk patients with decreased immunoresistance (elderly, malnourished, burned, or immunosuppressed patients). These are all opportunities for bacteria, fungi, and viruses to get comfortable and multiply.

In this era of highly effective systemic antibiotics, it would seem there would be plenty of drugs to stop these opportunistic microorganisms. One problem is that overuse of antibiotics has made some microorganisms "superbugs"; that is, the organism has developed resistance so it isn't destroyed by the standard antibiotic treatments. These microorganisms stay around to continue an existing infection or migrate to another person or place for more opportunity.

A clinical strategy to reduce the onset or frequency of infection is to eliminate potential pathogens from the surfaces they fall on. This is the role of antiseptics and disinfectants: reduce microbial growth and contamination from exogenous (outside the body) sources and reduce the risk of infection. This can be as broad and simple as washing hands, floors, and bed linens to remove potential pathogens or it can be localized to specific tissues or procedures. During surgical procedures, this is particularly important because local infection could significantly delay wound (incision) healing or jeopardize the patient's general health should a systemic (throughout the body) infection develop. (See Figure 44.1.)

Figure 44.1

Surgical Asepsis

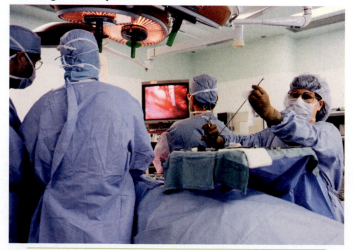

Surgical asepsis must be strictly adhered to even for minor procedures.

The objective of antisepsis and disinfection is to eliminate the opportunity for microorganisms to enter the body in order to permit normal defense mechanisms to work. Table 44:1 lists examples of antiseptics and disinfectants.

Spectrum of Antiseptic Action versus Sterilization

Antiseptics and disinfectants destroy microorganisms by interfering with cell metabolism, damaging nucleic acid, disrupting cell membranes, and **denaturing** protein. These agents can decrease the surface tension of bacterial cell walls causing the cells to swell and **lyse** (disintegrate or dissolve). Chemicals that denature protein or decrease surface tension have a quicker onset of action than chemicals that exert an antimicrobial action through cell metabolism. Solutions of heavy metals (mercury or silver) and hexachlorophene inhibit cell enzyme systems. Silver and mercury ions bind to the microorganism's cell membrane and inhibit its respiration process. Alcohols, formaldehyde, glutaraldehyde, and chlorhexidine directly disrupt cell membrane integrity. Chlorhexidine is incorporated into the bacterial cell wall, which disrupts the membrane and reduces its permeability. It also binds to bacterial DNA, alters its transcription, and causes lethal DNA damage.

Categories of Antisepsis and Disinfection

Chemicals that kill microorganisms **(-cidal)** are termed **germicidal, bactericidal, fungicidal,** or **virucidal,** depending on the type of microorganism they affect. Chemicals that reduce or inhibit growth without eradicating the microorganisms are considered **-static** agents, such as **bacteriostatic** or **fungistatic.** Antiseptics and disinfectant solutions differ in their antimicrobial potency (bactericidal versus bacteriostatic), spectrum of activity (the range of microorganisms they affect), and duration of action. Some of these chemicals are nonselective in their antimicrobial action and have broad-spectrum activity. Formaldehyde, glutaraldehyde, and iodine-containing solutions, which are effective against bacteria, bacterial spores, fungi, viruses, and protozoa, are broad-spectrum agents. More selective chemicals, such as hexachlorophene and benzalkonium chloride, are primarily effective against gram-positive bacteria. Alcohol (40 to 70 percent ethyl alcohol solutions) is bactericidal for vegetative forms of gram-positive and gram-negative bacteria, whereas benzalkonium chloride, cetylpyridinium chloride, and thimerosal may be more bacteriostatic. Examples of commonly used antiseptics and disinfectants are presented in Table 44:1.

Examples of Antiseptics and Disinfectants

Product (*Trade Name*)	Primary antimicrobial activity	Concentration	Disinfectant use	Antiseptic use
Alcohols				
Ethanol, ethyl alcohol, isopropanol, isopropyl alcohol	Vegetative bacteria	40–70% solution 70% solution	Disinfect instruments	Prepare skin prior to injection
Aldehydes				
Formaldehyde	Bacteria, spores, fungi, viruses	10–37% solution **Always dilute the 37% concentrate**	Cold sterilization of equipment, tissue fixative, preserve cadavers Avoid contact with skin or mucous membranes	Never
Glutaraldehyde (*Cidex, Cidex Plus 2*)		2% solution	**Use only on inanimate objects** Cold sterilization of surgical instruments; fumigation (aerosol) of operating rooms	Never
Biguanides				
Chlorhexidine (*Betasept, Dyna-Hex2, Hibiclens liquid, Hibistat*)	Bacteria, spores, fungi, viruses	0.5% wipes 2–4% liquid	—	Cleanse skin wounds, surgical scrub, hand washing, mouthwash for aphthous ulcers; **keep out of ears and eyes**
Halogenated compounds				
Iodine, tincture of iodine	Bacteria, spores, fungi, viruses	2, 5, 7% (Conc) water solution 2.7% in alcohol	—	Topical treatment of skin; germicide; stains skin and linens
Sodium hypochlorite (*Dakin's solution*)		4–6% solution 0.25–0.5% antiseptic	Disinfect walls, floors	Wound irrigation; avoid contact with hair (bleach)
Oxychlorosene (*Chlorpactin-WCS-90*)		0.4% solution	—	Preoperative skin cleanser, local irrigation during surgery, ophthalmic irrigant
		0.1–0.2% ophthalmic solution		
Heavy metals				
Thimerosal (mercurial)	Vegetative forms of bacteria and fungi	1:1000 solution 0.02% ophthalmic	—	Preoperative skin preparation; antiseptic for eyes, nose, throat, urethral membranes, wounds

(Continued)

Product (*Trade Name*)	Primary antimicrobial activity	Concentration	Disinfectant use	Antiseptic use
Silver nitrate		10–25% solution	—	Treatment of conjunctiva and burned skin
Silver sulfadiazine (*Silvadene, SSD, Thermazene*)		1% cream	—	Topical treatment of wound sepsis in second- and third-degree burns
Iodophors				
Povidone-iodine (*Betadine, Betagen, Polydine*)	Vegetative microorganisms and spores	1–10% foam, swab, douche, gel	Disinfect instruments	Preoperative scrub; postoperative antiseptic, often used for bedsores, burns, lacerations; skin preparation prior to injections and hyperalimentation line; whirlpool solution
Oxidizing agents				
Peroxide, hydrogen peroxide	Vegetative microorganisms	1.0–3% solution	—	Wound cleansing, mouthwash for Vincent's infection
Phenols				
Hexachlorophene (*pHisoHex*)	Vegetative gram$^+$ bacteria	0.25–3% foam	—	Surgical scrub, skin cleanser; use soaps, lotions with caution in infants and burn patients where absorption can occur
Triclosan/irgasan (*Septisoft, Septisol*)	Vegetative gram$^+$ and gram$^-$ bacteria	0.20–0.6% liquid, solution, wash	—	Health care skin degermer, handwash
Quaternary ammonium compounds				
Benzalkonium chloride (*Pedi-Pro, Zephiran*)	Vegetative gram$^+$ bacteria	0.13–17% solution, foam, spray, tincture	Preservation of instruments, ampules, rubber articles; disinfect operating room equipment	Preoperative treatment of denuded skin, mucous membranes; irrigation of deep wounds, vagina; topical treatment of acne; preservative in ophthalmic products

The difference between *cidal* and *static* often is related to the concentration of the chemical used and the time it remains in contact with the surface. Specific disinfectant and antiseptic procedures (protocols) have been developed over the last 70 years to identify which chemicals or combinations of chemicals are the most efficient for removing a wide range of microorganisms. If you have ever donated blood, you may have noticed

Figure 44.2

Skin Antiseptic Preparation

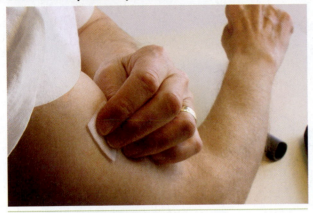

Swabbing to degerm the skin.

how many times the phlebotomist swabbed the injection site with a brown (iodophor) solution, moving in a circular motion a number of times. This is a protocol for removing microorganisms on the skin prior to a needle puncture into the vein, a site for potential infection, where the needle will stay inserted and blood will be drawn over a period of 45 minutes or more. This is much different than giving two or three tubes of blood over 60 seconds for a routine blood test. Here the phlebotomist uses an alcohol or iodophor swab with a short swabbing procedure. (See Figure 44.2.) Contact time and

concentration can be manipulated to meet the demands of the situation.

Sometimes it is absolutely necessary to sterilize equipment or an operating room. **Sterilization** is the complete eradication of *all* microorganisms and spores. It's the biggest gun. Sterilization can be achieved by using high-pressure steam for hours in specialized tanks called autoclaves. (See Figure 44.3.) This is practical for stainless steel surgical instruments, but you can't fit a room or a patient in an autoclave. It is often more practical to chemically disinfect the area. Since microorganisms are affected to different degrees by the available disinfectants, protocol requires that a sequence of disinfectant solutions be applied after precleaning the area.

Cleaning Technique

Surfaces, whether walls, fingernails, or open wounds, must be thoroughly cleaned prior to using disinfectants or antiseptics. Organic matter (pus, mucus, or protein exudate), dirt, or other foreign material reduce the activity of the disinfectant or antiseptic because the active ingredient (iodine, hexachlorophene, or formaldehyde) forms a complex with proteins and isn't available to attack the microorganism. On the other hand, the amount of organic matter or dirt may simply be dense enough to block penetration to an area of microbial activity. Dirt and organic matter can be removed first by washing with medicated soap or detergent. Figure 44.4 shows the proper technique for washing hands, nails, and

Figure 44.3   Sterilization with an Autoclave

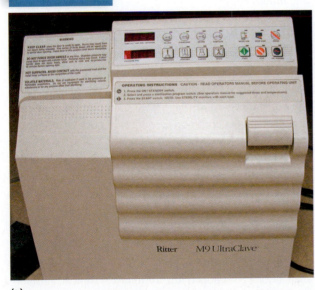

(a)

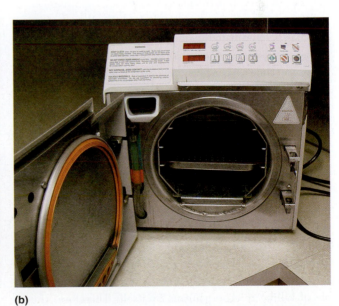

(b)

(a) Steam autoclave is the most common method of sterilizing instruments and equipment. (b) Properly loaded trays allow steam to reach all instruments and equipment.

Figure 44.4 **Hand Washing Technique**

(a)   (b)

(a) Proper hand washing cleans all surfaces including the palms, between the fingers, and under the fingernails. (b) Nails and cuticles require additional attention to ensure all dirt is removed.

cuticles. Depending on the nature of the surface to be treated, a combination of alcohol, phenols, or iodophors may then be generously washed over the area. Some disinfectant combinations are incompatible; for example, quaternary ammonium compounds are inactivated by contact with soaps or cotton. Under optimal conditions (that is, application of an appropriate concentration of chemical solutions to a particular surface for a specified length of time), even narrow-spectrum disinfectants may be effective in *sterilizing* a local area.

Bacterial spores are particularly difficult to destroy and may be eliminated by increasing the disinfectant-to-surface contact time. Various disinfectant-to-surface exposure times have been recommended, particularly prior to surgical procedures. These periods include a 2-minute wash with soap followed by a 2-minute alcohol wash followed by a 5- to 10-minute iodophor scrub. The particular ritual for surgical disinfection varies among individual institutions. Even inherently low- or moderate-potency antiseptics (chlorhexidine, benzalkonium chloride) can increase their antimicrobial efficiency by combining the agent with alcohol. It is not unusual to find ethyl or isopropyl alcohol as an active vehicle for chlorhexidine, benzalkonium chloride, hexachlorophene, and iodine. The term "active vehicle" means that the solution used to dissolve or dilute the antiseptic is capable of killing microorganisms by itself. Therefore, the activity of the active vehicle contributes to the overall germ-killing activity.

Clinical Uses

Antiseptics are used to cleanse and **irrigate** wounds, cuts, and abrasions; to prepare (degerm) patients' skin prior to surgery or injection; and to prepare the surgical team prior to surgery. An ideal antiseptic kills bacteria with a persistent duration of action and does not irritate or sensitize the skin. Antiseptics are also widely available to the public as an active ingredient or preservative in hand washes, face cleansers, eye washes, sanitary wipes, and mouth rinses.

Disinfectants are used to clean and store surgical instruments, to disinfect operating room walls and floors, and to sterilize **(cold sterilization)** objects that cannot tolerate the high temperatures associated with routine steam sterilization procedures. Some of these products are also available to the public as cleaning agents; most common is sodium hypochlorite, better known as chlorine bleach.

Antiseptics and disinfectants do eliminate microorganisms like the drugs we call to mind as antibiotics. The mechanisms of action may be similar, but there are two major differences. Antibiotics, in general, are expected to reach the bloodstream to produce their antimicrobial effects. Antibiotics are frequently targeted at one microorganism during treatment even though they may be a broad-spectrum antibiotic. Topical antibiotics may be applied to the skin like an antiseptic, but they are intended for specific microorganisms such as

Staphylococcus aureus and *Staphylococcus pyogenes* (*gentamycin, Altabax*) in the treatment of impetigo, or *Acne vulgaris* (*Clearasil, Pan Oxyl*). Antiseptics and disinfectants are never intended for internal use; even mouth washes are not expected to be swallowed. When these chemicals are used, it is to eliminate multiple organisms at one time.

LO 44.3   LO 44.4   LO 44.6

ANTISEPTICS AND DISINFECTANTS

Halogenated Compounds

The halogen elements are chlorine, fluorine, bromine, and iodine. The ones used most in antiseptics are iodine and chlorine. Iodine is probably superior to all other antiseptics for degerming the skin. Iodine is a rapid-acting, potent germicide effective against bacteria, protozoa, and viruses. Much more effective than the aqueous solution, iodine tincture is also associated with residual staining and local pain. The stinging sensation is principally due to the alcohol vehicle of the tincture (2 percent iodine in 50 percent ethanol). Iodine complexes **(iodophors)** cause less irritation and staining. Elemental iodine is complexed with a stable compound PVP (polyvinylpyrolidone) to form povidone-iodine. Iodine is slowly released from the complex to inhibit microbial cytoplasmic and membrane function. Povidone-iodine (*Betadine, Polydine*) is used frequently as a surgical prep. In dental practice, povidone-iodine may be swabbed on the oral mucosa prior to injecting a local anesthetic. Preparations containing iodine are for topical use and are never to be taken orally. Povidone-iodine is an external antiseptic known to be a powerful broad-spectrum germicidal agent effective against a wide range of bacteria, viruses, fungi, protozoa, and spores.

Iodophors cannot be mixed with the quaternary ammonium agents because this will inactivate the iodophor.

Of the chlorine compounds, the most cost-effective disinfectant is common chlorine bleach (a 5 percent or 10 percent solution of sodium hypochlorite). See Figure 44.5. This solution is effective against most common pathogens, including such difficult organisms as tuberculosis, hepatitis B and C, fungi, antibiotic-resistant strains of *Staphylococcus* and *Enterococcus,* and viruses. It also has disinfectant action against parasitic organisms. It works at room temperature and breaks down to nontoxic sodium and oxygen. To use chlorine bleach effectively, the surface or item to be disinfected must be clean. A 1-to-20 solution in water is effective simply by being wiped on and left to dry. The user should wear rubber gloves. Chlorine bleach is caustic to the skin, lungs, and eyes. Extreme caution must be taken to avoid contact with eyes and mucous membranes. Protective goggles and good ventilation are mandatory when applying concentrated bleach. Sodium hypochlorite should not be mixed with any product that contains ammonium or vinegar to avoid toxic gas by-products. This is encountered most often in cleaning lavatories where urine containing ammonia may be present. As soon as the container is opened, the solution begins to lose potency and must be used within 28 days.

Alcohol

Ethyl alcohol is an effective antiseptic in concentrations of less than 70 percent, whereas isopropyl alcohol (rubbing alcohol) is bactericidal at all concentrations (50 to 90 percent). Alcohols are not considered to have persistent antimicrobial activity; that is, activity that lasts for hours after application. Alcohol can be used alone or in combination with other topical agents to degerm the skin prior to surgery, placement of intravenous

Figure 44.5   **Examples of Disinfectants (Isopropyl Alcohol, Wipes), Bleach, and Formaldehyde Warning**

   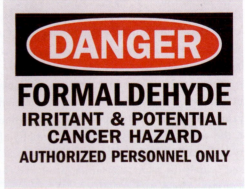

lines, or hypodermic injection. Studies have demonstrated that formulations containing 60 to 95 percent alcohol alone or 50 to 95 percent when combined with limited amounts of a quaternary ammonium compound, hexachlorophene, or chlorhexidine gluconate lower bacterial counts on the skin immediately after scrubbing more effectively than do other agents. Alcohol preparations such as tinctures frequently increase the penetrability of additional antiseptic ingredients, which improves antiseptic efficiency but may lead to increased skin irritation. Most "prep" wipes or swabs contain isopropyl alcohol, which quickly evaporates following topical application and sucks the life out of the bacteria as it evaporates. Because isopropyl alcohol causes local vasodilation, increased bleeding at the venipuncture site occasionally occurs. Note: Alcohols are flammable.

Phenols

Hexachlorophene is a bacteriostatic preparation that is primarily effective against gram-positive bacteria and provides relatively weak activity against gram-negative bacteria, fungi, and mycobacteria. Despite its selectivity, hexachlorophene is useful as a skin cleanser and surgical scrub because potential pathogens that reside on the skin surface are frequently gram-positive bacteria. With repeated use, hexachlorophene accumulates in the skin and maintains its bacterial response.

Hexachlorophene should not be used to bathe patients, especially infants, or patients with burns or extensive areas of susceptible, sensitive skin because it will be absorbed into the circulation. Several years ago, hexacholorophene at a concentration of 6 percent was associated with neurological disturbances when newborn infants were frequently bathed in this antiseptic wash. The concentration of hexachlorophene has been reduced in the currently available products; however, the FDA has recently given a restricted-use status to the 3 percent product. Its instructions for use must clearly state that *phisohex* 3 percent must not be used for bathing infants unless specifically recommended by a physician. Infants may absorb the active compound in *phisohex* more readily than older children and adults. Such absorption has been associated with central nervous system effects such as convulsions.

Triclosan has a broad range of antimicrobial activity, but it is often bacteriostatic. Triclosan activity against gram-negative bacilli is weak. It has persistent activity on the skin and activity is not substantially affected by organic matter. Triclosan as an antibacterial has been used widely in many consumer products (soaps, skin cleansers, deodorants, lotions, creams, toothpastes,

dishwashing liquids, toys, paints, mattresses, clothing, toilet bowls, and furniture fabric) for years.

Peroxides

Hydrogen peroxide is an oxidizing agent that is generally regarded as safe and effective by the FDA. It is used medically for cleaning wounds, for removing dead tissue, and as an oral debriding agent. When used to clean abrasions with slow blood oozing, it rapidly stops capillary bleeding. Peroxide rapidly breaks down to molecular oxygen and water. The standard medicinal solution is a weak antiseptic that contains 3 percent hydrogen peroxide in water. As it oxidizes, oxygen is released and it effervesces (bubbles). In fact, a 3 percent solution releases 10 volumes of oxygen. The effervescence may facilitate mechanical cleansing of debris surrounding a superficial wound. Hydrogen peroxide is recommended as a mouthwash for the treatment of Vincent's infection (trench mouth); however, continued use may produce hypertrophied papillae of the tongue, known as "hairy tongue." This effect subsides when treatment is discontinued. Other uses of peroxide include hair bleaching when mixed with ammonia and treatment of acne. Hydrogen peroxide's cousin, benzoyl peroxide, is a standard ingredient in over-the-counter acne preparations. The bacteria responsible for acne eruptions cannot live in an oxygen-rich (aerobic) environment. Benzoyl peroxide works by releasing oxygen into the pore, destroying the bacteria.

Chlorhexidine is bacteriostatic in low concentrations (0.5 percent) and bactericidal at higher concentrations (2 to 4 percent). It is effective against gram-positive and gram-negative bacteria; yeasts, including *Candida;* and viruses such as influenza, *Herpes,* and HIV. It is not effective against spores. It has a unique method of action: it is incorporated into the bacterial cell wall, disrupting the membrane and reducing its permeability, and alters the nucleic acid, DNA. Chlorhexidine is found in many antiseptic products from oral rinses to hand disinfectants. As an oral rinse it is used to treat redness, swelling, and bleeding of inflamed gums (gingivitis), prevent **aphthous ulcers** (canker sores), and decrease the amount of plaque deposited on teeth. It has been shown to be at least as effective as hexachlorophene and more effective that povidone-iodine. In fact, it was the first surgical scrub to be approved as safe and effective by the FDA. *Hibiclens* and *Betasept* are surgical scrubs in 4 percent alcohol, while *Hibistat* is prepared in 70 percent alcohol. Chlorhexidine is a positively charged (cation) compound and therefore can be combined with other cationic antiseptics (quaternary ammoniums) but not with soap or anionic detergents. This type of detergent is routinely found in toothpaste and mouthwashes, so to remain active chlorhexidine mouth rinsing has to begin 30 to 60 minutes after other dental products have been used.

Quaternary Ammonium Compounds

This is a large group of related compounds that includes the agent benzalkonium chloride (*Bactine, Gold Bond First Aid antiseptic, Zephiran*). They are effective against many bacteria, fungi, and protozoa but not against bacterial spores or molds. They also can be effective disinfectants against enveloped viruses such as influenza, respiratory syncytial virus (RSV), *Herpes* viruses, and HIV. At bactericidal concentrations, these agents attack the microorganism membrane and produce rapid cell leakage, resulting in total depletion of the intracellular potassium. The preparations range from bactericidal surgical hand wash to bacteriostatic eye irrigants, contact lens solutions, and vaginal douches. These cannot be combined with iodophors because the ionic nature of the compound inactivates the iodophor. This agent is inactivated by soaps and anionic detergents; therefore, any prewashed area must be rinsed thoroughly before the product is applied. Otherwise, benzalkonium chloride is combined with menthol, lidocaine, or alcohol to boost the antimicrobial activity in commercial products.

Heavy Metals

Among the heavy metal solutions currently available as antiseptics are organic mercurials and inorganic silver complexes. Silver nitrate is commonly used as an ophthalmic antiseptic in newborns. The practice of placing such a solution in the eyes of newborns shortly after birth is common throughout the world. This revolutionized preventative care for newborn babies because it dramatically decreased the number of infections of neonatal conjunctivitis. Some states mandate this practice by law. The purpose of this is to prevent infection of the tissues surrounding the eyes caused by gonorrhea and *Chlamydia,* which may be present in the birth canal as the baby is being born. Left unchecked, the gonorrhea and *Chlamydia* bacteria can cause permanent visual impairment and spread to other parts of the body. The tissue around the eyes may be irritated but resolves within a few days. Silver nitrate also has been used in the treatment of burn patients. However, it has been displaced by silver sulfadiazine, which penetrates the crust of burns better and does not produce residual skin staining. Prolonged or frequent use of silver solutions will produce **argyria,** a permanent black discoloration of the skin and mucous membranes. Because silver attaches to proteins in the fabric, it will stain clothes and bed linens.

Organomercurials

The bacteriostatic organic mercurial (thimerosal) is not as effective as are other antiseptics, despite its popularity in over-the-counter first aid preparations. Thimerosal is found in eye care and contact lens preparations as a preservative to reduce microflora growth.

Thimerosal has been in the news because it is a mercury-based preservative that has been used for decades in the United States in multidose vials (vials containing more than one dose) of some vaccines to prevent the growth of bacteria and fungi that may contaminate them. Concern was raised by public groups that exposure in children may be associated with developmental or behavioral conditions, specifically autism, because of the number of recommended vaccinations in childhood. The Centers for Disease Control, the National Institutes of Health, and the Food and Drug Administration have reviewed the research and concluded that there is no evidence linking thimerosal to developmental changes in children. Nevertheless, as a precautionary measure, all new vaccines for children under six years of age are thimerosal-free or contain only trace amounts.

Note to the Health Care Professional

Antiseptics in general and disinfectants in particular should never be swallowed or injected in order to destroy microorganisms.

Aldehydes

These are the big guns. This group includes formaldehyde, glutaraldehyde, and ethylene oxide. These chemicals are used to inactivate viruses and toxins (and any other organism) because they add functional groups to the microorganism that are not compatible with its life. *This group is never used as an antiseptic because of the potential damage to human tissue at any concentration.* Glutaraldehyde is used for cold sterilization of equipment, medical devices, and surgical instruments. The preferred methods of sterilization are high pressure and high temperature steam heat (in autoclaves, 250°F 0.5 hour), dry heat for items that can withstand high temperature (350°F, 2 to 4 hours), and ethylene oxide gas (70°F, 12 hours) for items that cannot withstand high temperature. Cold chemical sterilization may be used effectively for many items that cannot stand high temperatures or pressure, or decompose in gas sterilization. Sensitive laboratory or surgical items can be soaked in glutaraldehyde 2 percent (*Cidex*) at room temperature for 12 hours to achieve sterilization, and then rinsed thoroughly with sterile saline or sterile water and wrapped following an aseptic technique for storage prior to the next use. Contact with mucosal surfaces, the eyes, and mouth should be avoided because glutaraldehyde is an irritant and causes skin rash and discoloration.

Formalin is a 37 percent solution of formaldehyde in water. Dilution of formalin to 5 to 8 percent provides an effective disinfectant with good activity against vegetative bacteria, spores, and viruses. Solutions of 8 percent formaldehyde in 70 percent alcohol are considered very good for disinfection purposes because of the effectiveness against vegetative bacteria, fungi, spores, and viruses. Otherwise, formaldehyde is reserved for preserving cadavers and preparing tissue samples for lab evaluation. Formaldehyde gas is primarily used in the decontamination of closed spaces or biological containment equipment like biological safety cabinets. It is highly toxic to microorganisms, and unfortunately also to humans. Formaldehyde is a human carcinogen and creates respiratory problems at low levels of concentration. It must be handled with special ventilation and isolated prep areas. If you are not trained to safely and properly handle formaldehyde, *stay away from it and never breathe it directly.*

Ethylene oxide is a gaseous chemosterilizer especially useful for its penetrating power. The mode of sterilization allows it to penetrate irregular surfaces, nooks, and crannies. It is used to sterilize prepackaged laboratory equipment that otherwise would be destroyed by a heat process.

Adverse and Toxic Effects

The most common side effects associated with the topical use of disinfectants and antiseptics in general are skin dryness, irritation, rash, and **hypersensitivity** at the contacted surface. Chlorhexidine may cause irritation

Figure 44.6

Burns

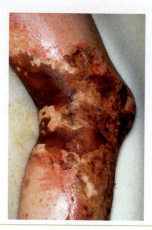

Eschar is a dry scab that forms on the skin that has been burned or exposed to corrosive chemicals.

especially in genital areas. Topical iodine preparations may cause a hypersensitivity reaction. Iodophors have been reported to penetrate the **eschar** of burn patients, leading to increased absorption of iodine. (See Figure 44.6.) Iodine toxicity can manifest as erosion of the gastrointestinal (GI) tract or hypothyroidism. Absorbed iodine crosses the placenta and can cause hypothyroidism and goiter in the fetus and newborn. In cases of accidental iodine ingestion, sodium thiosulfate is the antidote of choice. It can also be used to remove iodine stains.

Antiseptics and certain disinfectants should not be taken orally. Although ethanol is a constituent of alcoholic beverages, ingestion of pure ethyl alcohol (99 percent) can be fatal. Ethyl alcohol and isopropyl alcohol antiseptics are not for consumption because these products contain denaturing agents, methylisobutylketone, and color additives that are poisonous. When taken orally, hexachlorophene can produce anorexia, vomiting, abdominal cramps, convulsions, and death.

Sodium hypochlorite used as a wound irrigant may dissolve blood clots and delay further clotting. In concentrations greater than 0.5 percent (modified *Dakin's* solution) sodium hypochlorite may be irritating to the skin.

Chapter Review

Understanding Terminology

Match the definition or description in the left column with the appropriate term in the right column.

___ 1. Includes responses such as a rash, edema, or anaphylaxis that develop following administration of certain drugs. **(LO 44.5)**

___ 2. Compound that contains iodine. **(LO 44.3, 44.7)**

___ 3. A permanent darkening of skin and mucous membranes caused by prolonged use of silver protein solutions. **(LO 44.6)**

___ 4. A process that kills all microorganisms. **(LO 44.7)**

___ 5. The destruction of bacterial protein. **(LO 44.7)**

___ 6. A scab that develops after skin is burned. **(LO 44.6, 44.7)**

a. argyria

b. denaturing

c. eschar

d. hypersensitivity

e. iodophor

f. sterilization

Answer the following questions.

7. Explain the difference between an *antiseptic* and a *disinfectant*. **(LO 44.2, 44.5)**

8. Differentiate between a *-static* solution and a *-cidal* solution. **(LO 44.1)**

Acquiring Knowledge

Answer the following questions.

1. How are disinfectants and antiseptics similar in their clinical uses? **(LO 44.1, 44.2, 44.5)**

2. How do antiseptics differ from antibiotics? **(LO 44.5)**

3. What is cold sterilization? **(LO 44.7)**

4. What are nosocomial infections? **(LO 44.7)**

5. What are two objectives of antiseptic treatment? **(LO 44.2, 44.5)**

6. Why aren't antiseptics given parenterally or by mouth? **(LO 44.6)**

7. Why is silver nitrate frequently used for newborns? **(LO 44.3)**

8. Why is alcohol frequently a vehicle for other antiseptics such as benzalkonium chloride? **(LO 44.5)**

Multiple Choice

Use your critical-thinking skills to answer the following questions.

1. Which of the following is correct about antiseptics? **(LO 44.1, 44.2, 44.5)**
   A. only bacteria are affected
   B. antiseptics are antimicrobial only in very high concentrations
   C. they can be bacteriostatic and bactericidal
   D. viruses are not affected by them

2. The principal difference between disinfectants and antiseptics is **(LO 44.1, 44.2, 44.3, 44.5)**
   A. a broader spectrum of microorganisms are killed with antiseptics
   B. antiseptics cause skin rashes
   C. disinfectants destroy cell membranes
   D. disinfectants by definition are used on nonliving surfaces

3. Which of the following is NOT correct about aldehyde disinfectants? **(LO 44.1, 44.3, 44.4)**
   A. they are considered antiseptic at diluted concentrations
   B. special handling procedures must be followed because of their inherent toxicity to humans
   C. they are broad-spectrum microbicidal agents
   D. they are used for cold sterilization of instruments

4. All of the following are correct EXCEPT (LO 44.1, 44.2, 44.3, 44.5)
   A. antiseptics are used to reduce contamination in homes, hospitals, and clinics
   B. disinfectants are microbiostatic surgical hand scrubs
   C. iodophors are compounds that have iodine as the active antimicrobial element
   D. antiseptics that contain iodine and silver inhibit cell enzyme (respiration) systems

5. All of the following are correct EXCEPT (LO 44.2, 44.5)
   A. hydrogen peroxide releases oxygen as part of its action
   B. chlorhexidine is antiseptic because it disrupts the cell membrane and inhibits DNA
   C. alcohol can be added to many other antiseptics to increase penetrability and antimicrobial effectiveness
   D. sterilization reduces the number of microorganisms but does not kill them

6. How do general antibiotics differ from antiseptics and disinfectants? (LO 44.5)
   A. antibiotics are usually expected to achieve a certain blood level
   B. antiseptics cover a different spectrum of microorganisms
   C. antibiotics do not lyse cell walls or inhibit protein synthesis in microbes
   D. disinfectants must reach the same blood levels as antibiotics to be effective

7. Which of the following is NOT correct? (LO 44.6)
   A. surfaces must be thoroughly cleaned prior to using antiseptics
   B. organic matter and pus reduce the activity of antiseptics
   C. benzalkonium chloride is a mouthwash that causes "hairy tongue"
   D. argyria is a permanent black stain from prolonged use of silver antiseptics

8. Which is not true concerning nosocomial infections? (LO 44.1, 44.7)
   A. they are caused by bacteria, fungi, or viruses
   B. the patient is responsible for a nosocomial infection
   C. they are acquired in the hospital
   D. the infections are usually virulent and difficult to eradicate

9. Narrow-spectrum disinfection (LO 44.1, 44.5, 44.7)
   A. means the chemical has to be left on the surface for more than 1 hour
   B. cannot be used to sterilize a local surface
   C. does not harm human tissue
   D. means fewer types of microorganisms are affected compared to broad-spectrum agents

10. Which of the following explains what an active vehicle is? (LO 44.7)
    A. the solution used to dilute or dissolve an antiseptic that is also antimicrobial itself
    B. bacterial spores that carry the microorganism into the hospital
    C. a chemical that inhibits bacterial growth but does not eradicate the organism
    D. the term for chlorhexidine's mechanism of action

Multiple Choice (Multiple Answer)

Select the correct choices for each statement. The choices may be all correct, all incorrect, or any combination.

1. Select all of the ways antiseptics and disinfectants can reduce bacterial function. (LO 44.2)
   A. increase surface tension of bacterial cell walls
   B. damage nucleic acid
   C. interfere with cell metabolism
   D. increase cell enzyme systems

2. Select the statements that are correct. (LO 44.5)
   A. antiseptics eradicate microbial growth on living tissue
   B. disinfectants destroy pathogenic microbes on nonliving surfaces

C. antibiotics are used to eradicate systemic microbes

D. sterilization is the complete eradication of all microorganisms

3. Choose the true statements. **(LO 44.4, 44.5)**

   A. antibiotics should not be administered to the skin

   B. antiseptics are used to eliminate multiple microorganisms

   C. antibiotics target several microorganisms

   D. disinfectants are not intended for internal use

4. Choose the adverse effects of topical disinfectants. **(LO 44.6)**

   A. dryness

   B. rash

   C. irritation

   D. hypersensitivity

5. Select all of the following terms that mean to kill a particular microorganism. **(LO 44.7)**

   A. bacteriostatic

   B. fungistatic

   C. germicidal

   D. virucidal

Sequencing

Place the following surgical prep procedures in order from first to last. **(LO 44.2)**

_____   _____   _____

First   **Last**

2-minute alcohol wash

5- to 10-minute iodophor scrub

2-minute wash with soap

Classification

Place the following agents under their correct classification. **(LO 44.5)**

formaldehyde   oxychlorosene   *Cidex*   *phisohex*

Disinfectants	Antiseptics

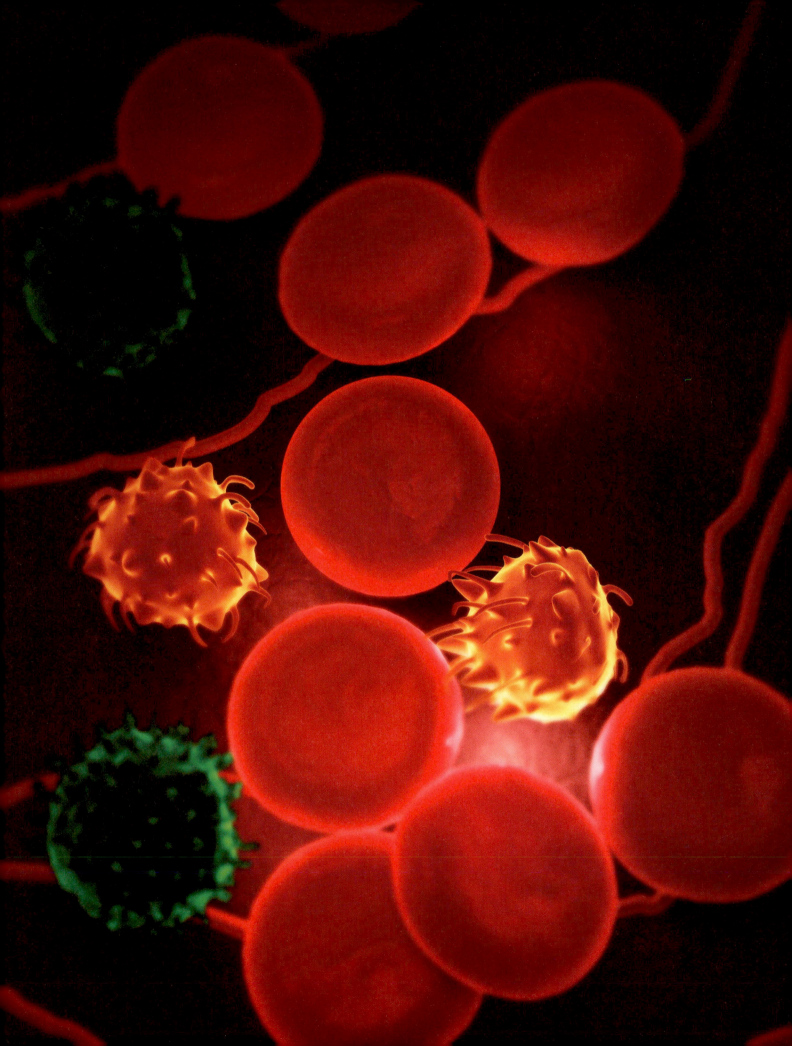

Antineoplastics and Drugs Affecting the Immune System

10

PART

Chapter 45

Antineoplastic Agents

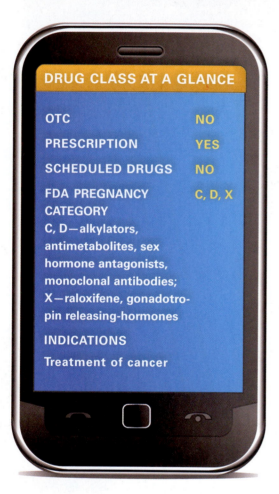

DRUG CLASS AT A GLANCE

OTC	NO
PRESCRIPTION	YES
SCHEDULED DRUGS	NO
FDA PREGNANCY CATEGORY	C, D, X

C, D—alkylators, antimetabolites, sex hormone antagonists, monoclonal antibodies; X—raloxifene, gonadotropin releasing-hormones

INDICATIONS

Treatment of cancer

KEY TERMS

alkylation: irreversible chemical bond that some cancer drugs form with nucleic acids and DNA.

antimetabolite: drug whose chemical structure is similar to that of normal body metabolites and that inhibits normal cell function.

antineoplastic: drug that inhibits the growth and proliferation of cancer cells.

cancer: disease that involves the development and reproduction of abnormal cells.

cell-cycle nonspecific (CCNS): refers to cancer drugs that act in all phases of the cell cycle.

cell-cycle specific (CCS): refers to cancer drugs that only act when the cell is actively dividing.

chemotherapy: use of drugs to inhibit the growth of or to destroy infectious organisms or cancer cells.

drug resistance: lack of responsiveness of cancer cells to chemotherapy.

malignant: life-threatening; refers to growth of a cancerous tumor.

metastasis: spread of cancer cells throughout the body, from primary to secondary sites.

myelosuppression: suppression of bone marrow activity that interferes with the production of all blood cells; causes anemia, increased infections, and bleeding problems.

remission: period when cancer cells are not increasing in number.

teratogenic: capable of causing birth defects or fetal abnormalities or development.

tumor: uncontrolled growth of abnormal cells that form a solid mass; also called a neoplasm.

After studying this chapter, you should be able to

45.1 explain the terms *chemotherapy, metastasis, remission, drug resistance,* and *myelosuppression.*

45.2 describe the mechanism of action of the alkylating drugs and the adverse effects associated with these drugs.

45.3 explain how the different types of antimetabolite drugs inhibit the growth of cancer cells.

45.4 explain the actions of plant extracts, antibiotics, and other natural products to affect cancer cells.

45.5 describe the mechanism of action of the different types of hormone antagonists.

45.6 explain the use of monoclonal antibodies and related drugs in the treatment of cancer.

Introduction

The ability of cells to reproduce (mitosis) is one of the most vital characteristics of living organisms. A frequently stated biological principle is "like produces like," which means that, when a cell reproduces, it forms another cell that is identical to itself. Unfortunately, this is not always true; there is always the possibility for the development of an abnormal cell. **Cancer** is a disease process that involves the development and reproduction of abnormal cells.

There are two consistent findings with cancerous cells. First, regardless of the type of cell (for example, epithelial, muscle), there is structural alteration accompanied by a loss of function. Second, normal cell reproduction is controlled, whereas cancer cell reproduction is uncontrollable. As a result, groups of cells (a **tumor** or neoplasm) that have no useful function are produced. Also, these cells often multiply at a faster rate than many normal body cells. The term **malignant** (life-threatening) tumor, or cancer, is used to describe this situation of abnormal cell growth. As a malignant tumor increases in size, it robs normal body cells of vital nutrients. Therefore, as the tumor increases, the normal body cell population decreases. In the later stages of cancer, there is significant loss of body weight and vitality. Surgery, radiation, and chemotherapy are the three main approaches to the treatment of cancer. The goal of treatment is to rid the body of all cancerous cells. Surgery and radiation exert local effects to eliminate or cause destruction of cancerous cells. Chemotherapy is the only treatment method that exerts a systemic effect throughout the body and can affect cancer cells that have metastasized.

TYPES OF CANCER

The original location of a tumor is referred to as the primary site. As the tumor enlarges, there is an increased likelihood that some of the tumor cells will detach and relocate in other body areas. These new sites of tumor development are referred to as secondary sites. This spread of cancer is referred to as **metastasis.** The route of metastases is usually through the lymphatic system or the circulatory system.

There are many different types of cancer that can affect a variety of body cells. The different forms of cancer can be broadly classified into solid tumors and diffuse tumors. Solid tumors (breast, prostate, and lung) are stationary and can usually be palpated if they are significantly large and accessible. The diffuse tumors (leukemias and Hodgkin's disease)—especially the leukemias that involve cancer of the white blood cells—are not restricted to any one location. The successful treatment of any cancer depends mainly on the type of cancer present and its location.

There are three main approaches to the treatment of cancer: surgery, radiation, and chemotherapy. Surgery is the best method for solid tumors that are surgically accessible. Radiation (X-ray treatments) is used after surgery in an attempt to kill any cancer cells located in the area around where the tumor was located. However, even after surgery and radiation, there is no guarantee that all cancerous cells have been eliminated.

Chemotherapy

Chemotherapy is the use of drugs to kill cancer cells. This form of treatment is the primary therapy for diffuse tumors. In addition, chemotherapy is often used after surgery and irradiation of solid tumors in order to eliminate the possibility of any remaining cancer cells that may have metastasized.

Chemotherapy is administered in cycles that usually vary between 1 and 6 weeks. The time between treatments allows recovery of normal cells. The hope is that normal cells will recover faster than cancerous cells. The growth of cancer cells is logarithmic and the destruction of cancer cells follows first-order kinetics. This means that a constant percentage of cells, not number of cells, are killed with each treatment. This is referred to as the log-kill hypothesis (Figure 45.1).

Many drugs are used to treat cancer. The term **antineoplastic** refers to drugs that inhibit tumor growth or cell reproduction. Unfortunately, most antineoplastic drugs cannot differentiate cancer cells from normal cells. Therefore, antineoplastic drugs usually kill some normal cells and are, in general, very toxic drugs. This is the major problem with cancer chemotherapy—there is very little selectivity of action. The goal of chemotherapy is to kill more cancer cells than normal cells and eventually rid the body of all cancer cells.

Both normal and cancer cells reproduce through the cell cycle known as mitosis. Mitosis is divided into different phases. The M phase (mitosis) is when cells actually divide and form new cells. During the G1 phase, the new cells are growing and synthesizing RNA and proteins. In the S phase, the cells are synthesizing and duplicating DNA in preparation for the next cell division. In the G2 phase, cells are preparing for mitosis. Cells that are not actively dividing (dormant) are in the G0 or resting phase. Anticancer drugs that can kill cells regardless of the phase are referred to as **cell-cycle nonspecific (CCNS).** Drugs that are effective only when the cell is actively dividing (not in G0) are referred to as **cell-cycle specific (CCS).** Figure 45.2 illustrates the phases of the cell cycle where some of the cancer drugs exert their chemotherapeutic actions.

Cells that have the fastest rates of metabolism and reproduction are most affected by antineoplastic drugs.

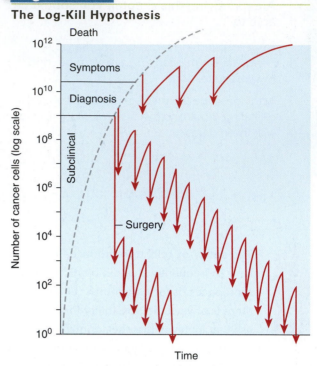

Figure 45.1

The Log-Kill Hypothesis

Relationship of tumor cell number to time of diagnosis, symptoms, treatment, and survival. Three approaches to drug treatment are shown for comparison with the course of tumor growth when no treatment is given (dashed line). In the protocol diagrammed at top, treatment (indicated by the arrows) is given infrequently and the result is prolongation of survival but with recurrence of symptoms between treatments and eventual death of the patient. The combination of chemotherapy treatment diagrammed in the middle is begun earlier and is more intensive. Tumor cell kill exceeds regrowth, drug resistance does not develop, and "cure" results. In this example, treatment has been continued long after all clinical evidence of cancer has disappeared. In the treatment diagrammed near the bottom of the graph, early surgery has been employed to remove the primary tumor and intensive chemotherapy has been administered long enough to eradicate any tumor cells that have metastasized.

Consequently, cancer cells are readily affected by cancer chemotherapy. However, normal cells of the bone marrow, gastrointestinal (GI) tract, and skin have growth rates that are equal to those of most cancer cells. During chemotherapy, there is always some degree of drug toxicity to these tissues. One of the major toxicities is **myelosuppression,** or bone marrow suppression. This can reduce the number of red blood cells (anemia), white blood cells (leukopenia, increased infections), and platelets (thrombocytopenia, bleeding problems). Myelosuppression usually requires 1 to 2 weeks to develop. In addition, disturbances and ulcerations of the skin and GI

Figure 45.2

The Cell Cycle

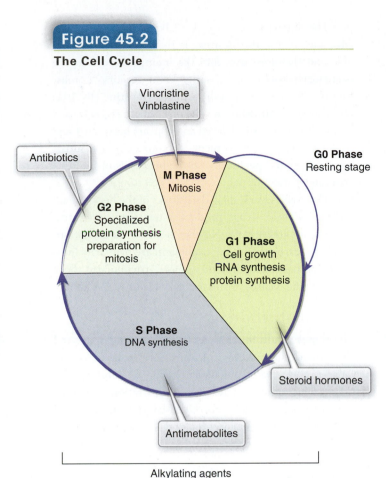

This diagram indicates where some cancer drugs act during the cell cycle. Antibiotics are cell-cycle specific for the G2 phase. Mitotic inhibitors such as vincristine and vinblastine are cell-cycle specific for the M phase. Antimetabolites are cell-cycle specific for the S phase. The alkylating drugs are cell-cycle nonspecific and interfere with cell growth in all phases whether the cell is actively dividing or in the resting stage.

tract are also common. Many of the drugs cause temporary hair loss (alopecia). In order to limit toxicity, the antineoplastic drugs are usually administered in a series of treatments, which allows a drug-free period (1 to 6 weeks) between each treatment.

Remission

One of the early goals of chemotherapy is **remission,** which refers to an inactive period when cancer cells are not actively reproducing and increasing in number. Remission occurs when a drug treatment kills all of the actively dividing cancer cells. Other cancer cells that are dormant (resting) usually become active with time, but during remission the cancer is not growing. Although remission is not a cure, it does offer patients more time and respite from the disease.

Drug Resistance

Drug resistance is a lack of responsiveness of cancer cells to chemotherapy. When this occurs, the cancer cells continue to reproduce even in the presence of the drug. When resistance occurs, alternate drugs must be substituted for those that have lost their effectiveness.

One method used to prevent the development of drug resistance is combination therapy. When two or three different antineoplastic drugs are used in combination, there is usually a significant decrease in the incidence of drug resistance. Drugs with different mechanisms of action are able to attack different areas of the cancer cells and are therefore more efficient in destroying the cells. The classification of antineoplastic drugs is based mainly on the mechanism of action and source of the drug. The main drug classes include the alkylators, antimetabolites, natural products, hormone antagonists, and monoclonal antibodies. The treatment of cancer is a specialty administered by oncologists and hematologists. Combination drug regimens are very specific and dosing schedules very exacting and based on patient body surface area. Some antineoplastic drugs are used in many different types of cancer and in many different drug combinations. Memorizing the different drug combinations and the specific cancers they are used for would be a daunting task and is not recommended for the beginning student. The focus of this chapter is to organize the main classes of antineoplastic drugs and explain general mechanisms of action, primary clinical uses, and the most characteristic adverse or dose-limiting toxicities.

LO 45.2
ALKYLATING DRUGS

One of the frightening developments of World War I was the introduction of chemical warfare. These compounds were known as the nitrogen mustard gases. Individuals who were exposed to these gases and survived were found to have shrunken lymph nodes and low blood cell counts. After the war these compounds were investigated and found to inhibit cell growth, including growth of cancerous cells. The nitrogen mustards were the first cancer drugs developed and stimulated the search for additional drugs. The goal of therapy has always been to discover drugs that rid the body of cancerous cells but that do not harm or affect normal cells.

Mechanism of Action

Nitrogen mustards inhibit cell reproduction by binding irreversibly with the nucleic acids (DNA, RNA) and proteins. The specific type of chemical bonding involved is **alkylation.** Hence, the nitrogen mustards also are referred to as alkylating drugs. Most alkylating drugs contain two chloroethyl side chains (Figure 45.3). Following administration, the chloride molecules separate from the drug and the drug forms a charged compound that binds covalently (alkylation) with DNA. After alkylation, DNA is unable to replicate and therefore can no longer synthesize proteins and other essential cell metabolites. Consequently, cell reproduction is inhibited and the cell eventually dies from the inability to maintain its metabolic and reproductive functions. The nitrogen mustards and other alkylating drugs are considered cell-cycle nonspecific (CCNS) and can cause cell death regardless of the cell cycle. However, they are more effective when cells are actively dividing.

Cyclophosphamide is one of the most important and frequently used alkylating drugs. It can be administered orally or intravenously. The drug is metabolized in the liver to phosphoramide mustard, which is the active metabolite that produces alkylation. Cyclophosphamide is used in the treatment of leukemias, lymphomas, and breast, ovarian, and lung cancers. The dose-limiting toxicity of cyclophosphamide and the other nitrogen mustards is myelosuppression.

The nitrosoureas are also alkylating drugs. The advantage of the nitrosoureas is that they are lipid soluble and therefore pass into the brain, where they are particularly useful for treating brain tumors. Lomustine (CCNU) is taken orally while carmustine (BCNU) requires IV administration. The myelosuppression caused by the nitrosoureas is delayed and appears between 4 and 6 weeks following treatment. Streptozocin is a nitrosourea that acts specifically on the beta cells of the pancreas and is used for pancreatic islet cell tumors.

There are several drug derivatives of the heavy metal platinum. These drugs produce interstrand and intrastrand cross-linking of DNA that is similar to alkylation. Cisplatin, carboplatin, and oxaliplatin are primarily indicated for treatment of solid tumors, particularly those involving the ovaries, testes, urinary bladder, and lungs.

Administration

The routes of administration of the alkylating drugs and their main pharmacologic features are summarized in Table 45:1. Some of the alkylators can be administered orally, while others require IV administration. Mechlorethamine, carmustine, and other drugs require special precautions with preparation and IV administration.

Figure 45.3 **Chemical Structure of the Alkylating Drugs**

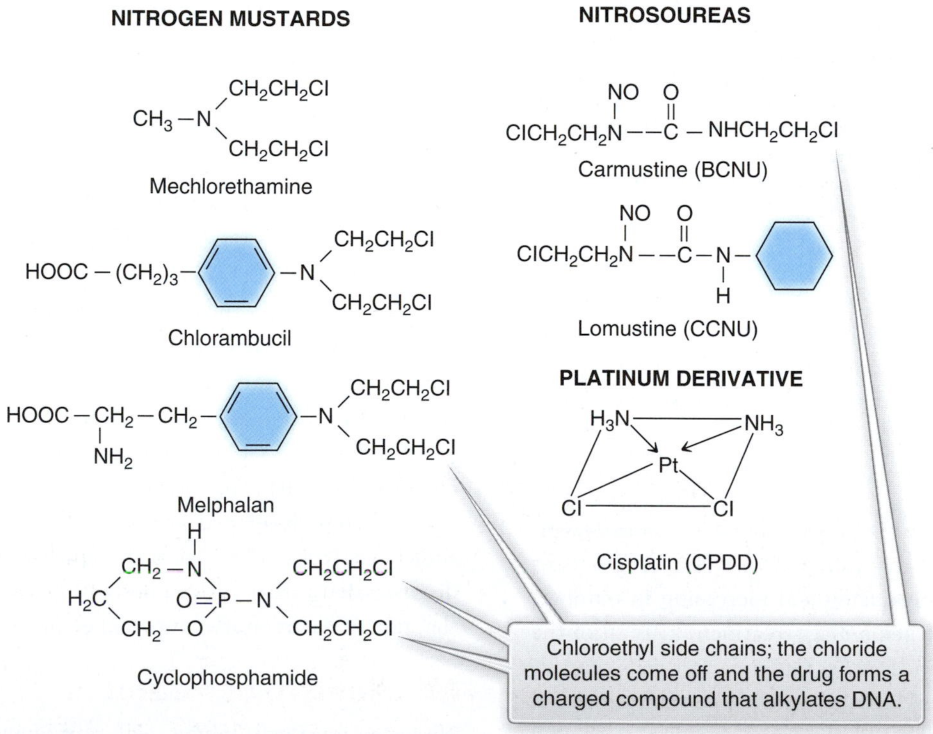

The common feature of most drugs is the chloroethyl side chains that are involved in alkylation with DNA.

Alkylating Drugs

Drug (*Trade Name*)	Route	Main uses	Dose-limiting toxicities
Nitrogen mustards/related drugs			
Bendamustine (*Treanda*)	IV	Chronic lymphocytic leukemia, non-Hodgkin's lymphoma	Myelosuppression, infusion reactions
Busulfan (*Myleran*)	PO	Chronic myelogenous leukemia (CML)	Myelosuppression, pulmonary fibrosis
Chlorambucil (*Leukeran*)	PO	Leukemia, non-Hodgkin's lymphoma	Myelosuppression
Cyclophosphamide (*Cytoxan*)	PO, IV	Breast, ovarian, leukemias, many cancers	Myelosuppression, cystitis
Ifosfamide (*Ifex*)	IV	Testicular, lung, breast cancer	Myelosuppression, cystitis
Mechlorethamine (*Mustargen*)	IV	Hodgkin's disease, leukemia	Myelosuppression
Melphalan (*Alkeran*)	PO	Multiple myeloma, breast, ovarian cancer	Myelosuppression
Procarbazine (*Matulane*)	PO	Hodgkin's, non-Hodgkin's lymphoma	Myelosuppression
Temozolomide (*Temodar*)	PO	Brain tumors, melanoma	Myelosuppression
Nitrosoureas			
Carmustine (*BiCNU*)	IV	Brain tumors, lymphoma, Hodgkin's disease	Myelosuppression, nephrotoxicity
Lomustine (*CeeNU*)	PO	Brain tumors	Myelosuppression, nephrotoxicity
Streptozocin (*Zanosar*)	IV	Pancreatic cancer	Renal toxicity, diabetes mellitus
Platinium derivatives			
Carboplatin (*Paraplatin*)	IV	Ovarian, lung, bladder, breast cancer	Myelosuppression
Cisplatin (*Platinol*)	IV	Testicular, ovarian, lung, breast cancer	Nephrotoxicity, ototoxicity
Oxaliplatin (*Eloxatin*)	IV	Colorectal and pancreatic cancer	Myelosuppression, sensory neuropathy

These drugs are vesicants and will cause blistering and necrosis if accidently exposed to skin.

Adverse Effects

Nausea and vomiting are characteristic adverse effects produced by the alkylating agents and most antineoplastic drugs. These effects occur shortly after drug administration and usually last for 1 or 2 days. Varying degrees of myelosuppression occur (anemia, leukopenia, and thrombocytopenia) in all patients. Blood cell counts (red blood cells [RBCs], white blood cells [WBCs], and platelets) are determined periodically to avoid the development of aplastic anemia. In addition, ulceration of the skin and GI tract and hair loss (alopecia) are common. Because of their growth-inhibiting properties, most antineoplastic drugs have the potential to cause **teratogenic** effects. These drugs should not be used during pregnancy if at all possible, but especially not during the first trimester.

Note to the Health Care Professional

It is important for medical personnel to observe the guidelines for handling cytotoxic drugs. Use protective gloves and eyewear to avoid skin and eye contact; many of these drugs are vesicants and will cause severe blistering.

During IV infusion assess the injection site frequently for signs of extravasation. Antineoplastics often cause thrombophlebitis and extravasation, which can lead to severe tissue necrosis. If this occurs, stop the infusion and try to aspirate back as much drug as possible, apply ice packs, and contact the physician.

Alkylating drugs are also carcinogenic and can cause secondary malignancies, most commonly acute leukemias.

Cyclophosphamide and ifosfamide are metabolized by the liver to a toxic metabolite, acrolein, that can cause hemorrhagic cystitis of the urinary bladder. Pre-drug hydration and administration of mesna disulfide, a chemical that inactivates acrolein, can reduce the incidence of cystitis.

LO 45.3

ANTIMETABOLITES

In order for cells, whether normal or cancerous, to reproduce, they must be able to synthesize and duplicate DNA. The **antimetabolites** are a group of drugs whose chemical structures are similar to those of the purines, pyrimidines, and folic acid normally required for synthesis of DNA. The antimetabolite drug is taken up by both normal and cancerous cells and incorporated into the metabolic pathway for DNA synthesis as if it were the normal metabolite. However, the antimetabolite is a fraud. When activated by the cell, the antimetabolites inhibit enzymes that are essential to the synthesis of DNA and RNA. The antimetabolites are considered cell-cycle specific (CCS) and are most effective when the cell is synthesizing DNA in the S phase. The antimetabolites are classified as folic acid, purine, and pyrimidine antagonists (Table 45:2).

Folic Acid Antagonists

Folic acid is a vitamin that is essential to the synthesis of the nucleic acids. Deficiency of folic acid decreases the production and replication of DNA. The symptoms of folic acid deficiency usually involve the development of various anemias and GI disturbances. The enzyme folic acid reductase converts folic acid into its active form, tetrahydrofolate. Methotrexate is structurally similar to folic acid (Figure 45.4) and, when taken up by the cell, inhibits the enzyme folic acid reductase to block the synthesis of DNA.

Methotrexate is well absorbed following oral administration and this is the preferred route for treatment of choriocarcinoma. In the treatment of acute lymphocytic leukemia, methotrexate is usually administered intravenously. Intrathecal administration is used when the meninges are involved. Intrathecal administration can cause CNS disturbances that include headache, fever, and meningeal inflammation. The main use of methotrexate is in the treatment of choriocarcinoma and acute leukemia.

Overdosage of methotrexate is treated by the administration of folinic acid, referred to as leucovorin rescue, which prevents many of the adverse effects caused by methotrexate therapy. The administration of leucovorin after methotrexate provides the bone marrow with activated folic acid so that blood cell production can resume. The adverse effects of methotrexate include nausea, vomiting, diarrhea, myelosuppression, GI ulceration, and mucositis.

Pemetrexed (*Alimta*) is another antifolate drug indicated for the treatment of mesothelioma and non-squamous non-small cell lung cancer. The drug is administered IV; folic acid and vitamin B_{12} supplementation are usually administered with pemetrexed to limit toxicity. The dose-limiting toxicity is myelosuppression.

Purine Antagonists

The purine bases adenine and guanine are essential to synthesis of DNA. Mercaptopurine (*Purinethol*), a purine antagonist, has a chemical structure similar to that of adenine (Figure 45.4). Mercaptopurine competes with adenine in the formation of the nucleotide adenylic acid. When mercaptopurine is utilized, an abnormal nucleotide is formed that prevents the successful replication of DNA. Consequently, normal cell reproduction does not occur.

Mercaptopurine is administered orally in the treatment of acute lymphocytic leukemia (ALL) and chronic myelogenous leukemia (CML). The major adverse effects include nausea, vomiting, myelosuppression, and liver toxicity.

Additional purine antagonists include cladribine (*Leustatin*), which is used in hairy cell leukemia; fludarabine (*Fludara*), which is used in chronic lymphocytic

Antimetabolite Drugs

Drug (*Trade Name*)	Route	Main uses	Major adverse effects
Folic acid antagonists			
Methotrexate	PO, IV	ALL*, choriocarcinoma	Myelosuppression, nausea, vomiting, diarrhea, stomatitis, mucositis, alopecia, rash
Pemetrexed (*Alimta*)	IV	Nonsquamous non-small cell lung cancer, mesothelioma	
Purine antagonists			
Cladribine (*Leustatin*)	IV	Hairy cell leukemia	Myelosuppression, nausea, vomiting, stomatitis, hyperuricemia
Fludarabine (*Fludara*)	IV	Chronic lymphocytic leukemia (CLL)	
Mercaptopurine (*Purinethol*)	PO	ALL, CML*	
Pentostatin (*Nipent*)	IV	Hairy cell leukemia	
Thioguanine	PO	ANLL*, ALL, AML*	
Pyrimidine antagonists			
Capecitabine (*Xeloda*)	PO	Breast, GI, liver, pancreatic cancer	Myelosuppression, nausea, vomiting, mucositis, diarrhea, arthralgia
Cytarabine (*Cytosar*)	IV	ALL, AML, CML	
Fluorouracil (*5-FU*)	IV	Head/neck, colorectal, breast cancer	
Gemcitabine (*Gemzar*)	IV	Bladder, pancreatic, breast, ovarian, non-small cell lung cancer	

ALL—acute lymphocytic leukemia; CML—chronic myelogenous leukemia; ANLL—acute nonlymphocytic leukemia; AML—acute myelogenous leukemia.

leukemia (CLL); and pentostatin (*Nipent*), which is used in hairy cell leukemia. These drugs are all administered intravenously and produce bone marrow suppression as their major toxicity.

Pyrimidine Antagonists

Three pyrimidine bases are required in the synthesis of deoxyribonucleic acid (DNA) and ribonucleic acid (RNA): cytosine, thymine, and uracil. Two pyrimidine antagonists are fluorouracil (*Adrucil*) and cytarabine (*Cytosar-U*). Fluorouracil competes with uracil, whereas cytarabine competes with cytosine (Figure 45.4). The pyrimidine antagonists prevent the normal synthesis and replication of DNA. Administered orally or intravenously, fluorouracil is used in the treatment of solid tumors involving the colon, stomach, pancreas, breast, and ovaries. The major adverse effects include nausea, vomiting, GI ulceration, bone marrow depression, and hair loss. Cytarabine is administered IV in the treatment of several different leukemias.

Capecitabine (*Xeloda*) is a fluorinated pyrimidine that is metabolized to fluorouracil by tumor enzymes. The drug is administered orally in the treatment of metastatic breast, colorectal, and other GI cancers. Adverse effects are similar to fluorouracil. In the

Figure 45.4 Examples of Antimetabolites Compared with the Corresponding Normal Metabolite

Metabolite

Folic acid (pteroylglutamic acid)

Antimetabolite

Methotrexate
(4-Amino-N^{10}-methylpteroylglutamic acid)

Adenine

Mercaptopurine

Uracil

Fluorouracil

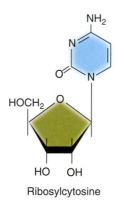

Ribosylcytosine

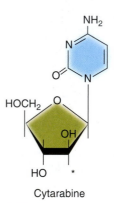

Cytarabine

(The asterisk indicates the structural change.)

treatment of metastatic and advanced breast cancer, a relatively new drug, ixabepilone (*Ixempra*), is used in combination with capecitabine. Ixabepilone is a mitotic inhibitor (M phase) that is administered by IV infusion.

Gemcitabine (*Gemzar*) is an antimetabolite of cytosine that inhibits DNA synthesis. The drug is administered IV for treatment of pancreatic, bladder, breast, and non-small cell lung cancers. Adverse effects include myelosuppression, nausea, vomiting, and a flu-like syndrome.

DRUGS DERIVED FROM NATURAL PRODUCTS

A number of antineoplastic drugs are obtained from natural products such as plants, trees, and bacterial organisms.

Drugs Derived from Plants and Trees

The periwinkle plant (*Vinca rosea*) contains several alkaloids that inhibit tumor growth. The *Vinca* alkaloids include vincristine (*Oncovin*), vinblastine (*Velban*), and vinorelbine (*Navelbine*). These drugs inhibit the process of mitosis by binding to the microtubules to cause metaphase arrest. These drugs are considered CCS and are most effective when cells are dividing in the M phase. The primary toxicity of vincristine is neurotoxicity (paraesthesias and loss of reflexes); the primary toxicity of vinblastin and vinorelbine is myelosuppression. These drugs cause severe pain and local toxicity if there is leakage of drug out of the blood vessels and into the tissues (extravasation).

Etoposide (*VePesid*) and teniposide (*Vumon*) are two derivatives of the extract from the mandrake or mayapple plant. These drugs inhibit an enzyme, topoisomerase II, that is essential for the normal function and resealing of DNA strands. The result is accumulation of DNA strand breaks and eventual cell death. Both drugs are administered intravenously. The dose-limiting toxicity is myelosuppression.

Paclitaxel (*Taxol*) is a drug that was originally isolated from the bark of the yew tree. Docetaxel (*Taxotere*) is a semisynthetic analog of paclitaxel. These drugs bind to the mitotic microtubules and inhibit mitosis (M phase). Both drugs are administered by IV infusion. Myelosuppression and peripheral neuropathy are the main adverse effects.

Irinotecan (*Camptosar*) and topotecan (*Hycamtin*) are synthetic analogs of camptothecin, an alkaloid originally obtained from the extracts of a tree grown in China. The mechanism of action of these drugs is to inhibit an enzyme, topoisomerase I, that is essential to the normal strand breakage and resealing of DNA. Enzyme inhibition causes an accumulation of DNA strand breaks and cell death. Both drugs are administered by intravenous infusion. Myelosuppression and diarrhea are the usual dose-limiting toxicities. The drugs derived from plant/tree extracts and their main uses are summarized in Table 45:3.

Drugs Derived from Bacteria

Certain antibiotics derived from bacteria, such as dactinomycin, doxorubicin, and idarubicin, interfere with the synthesis of DNA. These drugs have multiple actions that include enzyme inhibition, free radical formation, and DNA strand breakage. Although classified as antibiotics, these drugs are too toxic for the treatment of bacterial infections. These drugs are administered by IV infusion and extravasation can cause severe tissue damage. Doxorubicin is particularly effective for many different types of cancer involving the blood and solid organ tumors. Myelosuppression and cardiac disturbances are the usual dose-limiting toxicities produced by these drugs. Acute cardiac disturbances include tachycardia and development of arrhythmias. There is also

a chronic dose-dependent toxicity that can progress to congestive heart failure.

Asparaginase (*Elspar*) is an enzyme derived from the bacterium *Escherichia coli*. The function of asparaginase is to metabolize the amino acid L-asparagine to the inactive L-aspartic acid. In the treatment of acute lymphocytic leukemia, asparaginase depletes the cancer cells of asparagine, which inhibits the ability of the cancer cells to synthesize proteins and nucleic acids. Administration is by IV infusion. Asparaginase is relatively nontoxic; it does not suppress the bone marrow like most other drugs. The development of allergy to the bacterial enzyme and liver disturbances are the most frequent adverse effects observed. The drugs derived from bacteria and their main uses are listed in Table 45:3.

LO 45.5

HORMONE ANTAGONISTS

Tumors that involve the reproductive organs (prostate, testes, breast, uterus, and ovaries) are frequently hormone-dependent. These cancerous cells usually possess the same sex hormone receptors normally found on these organs. The hormones that normally develop and maintain these organs now act as growth factors and stimulate the growth of the cancer cells. Drugs that block or interfere with the actions of these hormones are classified as hormone antagonists. These drugs are primarily indicated after surgery and radiation therapy. Hormone antagonists are not cytotoxic; they do not cause cell death. The function of the hormone antagonists is to inhibit the growth of any cancer cells that remain. The hormone antagonists are summarized in Table 45:4.

Tamoxifen (*Nolvadex*)

Tamoxifen is an estrogen receptor blocker used in the treatment of breast cancer. Tamoxifen is usually administered over a 5-year period following surgical removal of the primary tumor. Studies have shown that this reduces the incidence of tumor recurrence. Tamoxifen is administered orally on a daily basis. This drug also can be taken prophylactically by women who have a family history or predisposition to developing breast cancer. The common side effects of tamoxifen are similar to the postmenopausal syndrome and include nausea, vasomotor hot flashes, rash, and vaginal bleeding. Tamoxifen can increase blood clotting factors and stimulate proliferation of the uterine lining. These actions increase the risk for thromboembolism and

Drugs Derived from Natural Products

Drug (*Trade Name*)	Mechanism of action	Main uses
Plant/tree extracts		
Vinblastine (*Velban*)	Inhibits mitosis/metaphase arrest	Hodgkin's and non-Hodgkin's lymphoma
Vincristine (*Oncovin*)	Inhibits mitosis/metaphase arrest	Hodgkin's and non-Hodgkin's lymphoma, ALL*
Vinorelbine (*Navelbine*)	Inhibits mitosis/metaphase arrest	Non-small cell lung cancer
Paclitaxel (*Taxol*)	Binds/inactivates mitotic microtubules	Ovarian, breast, lung cancer
Docetaxel (*Taxotere*)	Binds/inactivates mitotic microtubules	Breast, lung, prostate cancer
Etoposide (*VePesid*)	Inhibits topoisomerase II/cell death	Testicular tumors, lung cancer
Teniposide (*Vumon*)	Inhibits topoisomerase II/cell death	Acute childhood leukemia
Irinotecan (*Camptosar*)	Inhibits topoisomerase I/cell death	Colorectal, small cell/non-small cell lung cancer
Topotecan (*Hycamtin*)	Inhibits topoisomerase I/cell death	Ovarian, small cell lung cancer
Drugs derived from bacteria		
Bleomycin (*Blenoxane*)	Damages DNA/DNA strand breaks	Head/neck, testicular, ovarian cancer
Dactinomycin (*Cosmegen*)	Damages DNA/forms free radicals	Wilms' tumor, choriocarcinoma
Doxorubicin (*Adriamycin*)	Damages DNA/forms free radicals	Breast cancer, lymphomas, solid tumors
Daunorubicin (*Cerubidine*)	Damages DNA/forms free radicals	AML*, ALL
Idarubicin (*Idamycin*)	Damages DNA/forms free radicals	AML
Asparaginase (*Elspar*)	Deprives cancer cell of essential amino acid asparagine	ALL
Pegaspargase (*Oncaspar*)	Same as asparaginase	ALL in patients allergic to asparaginase

ALL—acute lymphocytic leukemia; AML—acute myelogenous leukemia.

endometrial cancer. Results from animal studies indicate that tamoxifen is hepatotoxic and can cause liver tumors; however, this has not been reported in women taking the drug. Toremifene (*Fareston*) and raloxifene (*Evista*) are additional estrogen antagonists similar to tamoxifen. Raloxifene is used to prevent postmenopausal osteoporosis and for prophylaxis of breast cancer in women with increased risk factors. An advantage of raloxifene is that it does not stimulate proliferation of the uterine lining.

Aromatase Inhibitors

Aromatase is an enzyme involved in the synthesis of estrogens. Anastrozole (*Arimidex*), letrozole (*Femara*), and exemestane (*Aromasin*) are aromatase enzyme inhibitors indicated for the treatment of breast cancer following surgical removal of the tumor. By blocking the synthesis of estrogen, these drugs reduce the amount of estrogen available to stimulate estrogen receptors on cancer cells. Originally these drugs were indicated for women

Hormone Antagonists

Drug (*Trade Name*)	Administration	Main indication
Estrogen antagonists		
Raloxifene (*Evista*)	PO	Prevention of osteoporosis, prophylaxis of breast cancer
Tamoxifen (*Nolvadex*)	PO	Treatment of breast cancer, prophylaxis of breast cancer
Toremifene (*Fareston*)	PO	Treatment of breast cancer, prophylaxis of breast cancer
Aromatase inhibitors		
Anastrozole (*Arimidex*)	PO	
Letrozole (*Femara*)	PO	Treatment of advanced breast cancer
Exemestane (*Aromasin*)	PO	
Gonadotropin antagonists		
Degarelix (*Degarelix*)	SC	
Goserelin (*Zoladex*)	SC	Suppresses production of gonadotropins (FSH, LH) and both female and male sex hormones; treatment of breast, ovarian, and prostate cancers; treatment of endometriosis and uterine fibroids
Leuprolide (*Lupron*)	SC, IM	
Nafarelin (*Synarel*)	Nasal spray	
Triptorelin (*Trelstar*)	IM	
Androgen antagonists		
Bicalutamide (*Casodex*)	PO	
Flutamide (*Eulexin*)	PO	Prostate cancer
Nilutamide (*Nilandron*)	PO	

whose tumors had become resistant to tamoxifen. The aromatase inhibitors are more effective than tamoxifen in reducing the actions of estrogen to stimulate cancer cell growth. Consequently, the aromatase inhibitors have become the preferred therapy to inhibit breast cancer cell growth. The drugs are administered orally on a daily basis. Common adverse effects include nausea, vasomotor flushing or hot flashes, menstrual irregularities, and vaginal bleeding.

Drugs Affecting Gonadotropin-Releasing Hormone

Gonadotropin-releasing hormone (GnRH) is released from the hypothalamus. It travels to the anterior pituitary gland where it stimulates the release of follicle-stimulating hormone (FSH) and luteinizing hormone (LH). In females, FSH and LH are responsible for the development of the ovarian follicle and secretion of estrogen and progesterone. In males, FSH and LH stimulate production of sperm and secretion of testosterone. Gonadotropin-releasing hormone is normally released in a pulsatile manner, that is, not continuously. Leuprolide (*Lupron*) and Goserelin (*Zoladex*) are analogs of GnRH that, when administered as drugs in a continuous manner, inhibit the release of FSH and LH. Additional gonadotropin inhibitors are nafarelin (*Synarel*), administered by nasal spray, and triptorelin (*Trelstar*), administered by IM injection. The main pharmacologic action of these drugs is to inhibit production of estrogen, progesterone, and testosterone.

In males, these drugs are used to block the secretion of testosterone in the treatment of prostate cancer. In females, these drugs can be used in advanced breast and ovarian cancer to block secretion of both estrogen and progesterone. Leuprolide is usually administered by subcutaneous or intramuscular injection. Goserelin is implanted subcutaneously; one preparation delivers the drug over 28 days, another over a 3-month period. Adverse effects are generally those of hormone deficiency and include headache, nausea, vasomotor hot flashes, and other symptoms of hypogonadism.

Androgen Antagonists

Drugs that block androgen receptors in males are indicated for the treatment of prostate cancer. Flutamide (*Eulexin*) is administered orally and competitively blocks the androgen receptor. Adverse effects include GI disturbances, hot flashes, tenderness or swelling of the breasts (gynecomastia), impotency, jaundice, and changes in liver function. Newer antiandrogens include bicalutamide (*Casodex*) and nilutamide (*Nilandron*). These drugs are administered orally, once daily, and generally well tolerated. Hot flashes, GI disturbances, and breast tenderness and swelling are the most common adverse effects. Nilutamide may infrequently cause breathing difficulties and pneumonitis.

LO 45.6

NEW APPROACHES TO CANCER CHEMOTHERAPY

One of the goals of cancer chemotherapy has always been to discover drugs that selectively target cancer cells and do not affect normal cells. Advances in molecular biology have identified specific cell antigens and membrane receptors involved in cellular proliferation and growth

of certain cancer cells. Biological agents are now available that selectively bind to and inhibit the actions of these antigens and receptors. A number of monoclonal antibodies and other drug molecules have been approved for treatment of various cancers. These drugs are administered in combination with other chemotherapeutic drugs and have proven effective in inhibiting cancer cell proliferation. The drugs are usually well tolerated and do not cause myelosuppression. Nausea, vomiting, and rash are common to most drugs. Monoclonal antibodies can cause allergic and infusion reactions, particularly if the antibody was derived from nonhuman sources. Table 45:5 describes the actions and uses of some of these drugs.

Cautions and Contraindications
Pregnancy

Antineoplastic drugs are growth-inhibiting compounds that can interfere with fetal development, especially the alkylating and antimetabolite drugs. These drugs should be used with extreme caution during pregnancy, and women of childbearing age should use contraceptive methods if there is any possibility of pregnancy while taking these drugs. Only in circumstances where the benefits of treatment far outweigh the risks of harm to the fetus should these drugs be considered.

Patient Administration and Monitoring

Monitor vital signs during and after administration of drugs.

During parenteral drug administration, especially prolonged infusions, check the IV site frequently for extravasation of drug. If extravasation occurs, stop the infusion and notify the physician immediately.

Since most cancer chemotherapy causes nausea and vomiting, be prepared to assist the patient.

Observe for and instruct patient to report fever, chills, sore throat, swollen glands, and other signs of infection.

Explain to patient the common side effects of the drugs administered.

Instruct patients to report any significant symptoms such as difficulty with breathing, central nervous system (CNS) effects, sores on the skin or in the mouth, or any other symptoms that suggest drug toxicity.

Antineoplastic Drugs with Specific Molecular Targets

Drug (*Trade Name*)	Description/main use
Monoclonal antibodies	
Alemtuzumab (*Campath*)	Monoclonal antibody used to treat B-cell chronic lymphocytic leukemia in patients who have not responded to alkylating drugs or fludarabine; administered by IV infusion
Bevacizumab (*Avastin*)	Binds to and inhibits vascular endothelial growth factor (VEGF), inhibits formation of new blood vessels in tumors; administered IV in metastatic colorectal cancer
Cetuximab (*Erbitux*)	Binds epidermal growth factor receptor (EGFR) to inhibit tumor growth; administered IV in metastatic colorectal cancer
Gemtuzumab (*Mylotarg*)	Binds a specific protein on leukemic blast cells; preparation includes a cytotoxic drug, ozogamicin; the combination damages DNA, causing cell death; administered IV in acute myelogenous leukemia
Ofatumumab (*Arzerra*)	Anti-CD20 monoclonal antibody used to treat chronic lymphocytic leukemia in patients refractory to fludarabine and alemtuzumab; administered IV
Panitumumab (*Vectibix*)	Human IgG2 monoclonal antibody that binds epidermal growth factor receptor to inhibit cell growth and vascular growth factor production; administered IV
Pazopanib (*Votrient*)	Binds vascular epidermal growth factor receptor (VEGFR) tyrosine kinase; inhibits growth of new blood vessels; used for renal cell carcinoma; administered orally
Rituximab (*Rituxan*)	Binds to an antigen (CD20) on normal and malignant B lymphocytes; causes rapid depletion of B cells; administered IV in B-cell non-Hodgkin's lymphoma and chronic lymphocytic leukemia
Trastuzumab (*Herceptin*)	Binds to human epidermal growth factor receptor protein 2 (HER-2) and inhibits proliferation of cells that express HER-2; administered IV in metastatic breast cancer
Miscellaneous drugs	
Gefitinib (*Iressa*)	Drug that inhibits tumor tyrosine kinase activity associated with epidermal growth factor receptors; administered orally in the treatment of non-small cell lung cancer
Imatinib (*Gleevec*)	Drug that inhibits tumor tyrosine kinase activity and inhibits cell proliferation; administered orally in the treatment of chronic myelogenous leukemia and gastrointestinal stromal tumors

Chapter Review

Understanding Terminology

Match the definition or description in the left column with the appropriate term in the right column.
(LO 45.1, 45.2)

_____ 1. The spread of cancer cells.

_____ 2. A period, usually after chemotherapy, when cancer cells are not increasing in number.

_____ 3. The use of drugs to inhibit the growth of cancer cells.

_____ 4. A disease that involves the development of abnormal cells.

_____ 5. A drug used to treat cancer by inhibiting tumor growth or cancer cell reproduction.

_____ 6. Lack of responsiveness of cancer cells to chemotherapy.

_____ 7. Also called a neoplasm; a group of new cells with no useful function.

_____ 8. Life-threatening; refers to the growth of a cancerous tumor.

_____ 9. Refers to a drug that can cause birth defects.

a. antineoplastic

b. cancer

c. chemotherapy

d. drug resistance

e. malignant

f. metastasis

g. remission

h. teratogenic

i. tumor

Acquiring Knowledge

Answer the following questions.

1. What are two cell changes caused by cancer? **(LO 45.1)**

2. What process occurs with the development of secondary cancer sites? **(LO 45.1)**

3. List three main approaches to the treatment of cancer. **(LO 45.1)**

4. What are three common toxicities caused by alkylating drugs? **(LO 45.2)**

5. What is the mechanism of action of the alkylating drugs? **(LO 45.2)**

6. What is the function of folic acid? How does methotrexate interfere with folic acid utilization? **(LO 45.3)**

7. What is leucovorin rescue, and when is it used? **(LO 45.3)**

8. Give an example of a purine antagonist and a pyrimidine antagonist. What is the mechanism of action of these drugs? **(LO 45.3)**

9. Briefly describe the mechanism of action of the plant extracts, hormone antagonists, and antibiotics in the treatment of cancer. **(LO 45.4, 45.5)**

10. Describe the mechanism of action of monoclonal antibodies. **(LO 45.6)**

Applying Knowledge on the Job

Use your critical-thinking skills to answer the following questions.

1. Cancer drugs are often administered in various combinations and at specific time intervals that allow time periods (usually several weeks) that are drug free. What is the logic behind these two practices? **(LO 45.1)**

2. Mr. White presented at his physician's office with enlarged lymph glands, hepato-splenomegaly, anemia, fever, chills, night sweats, loss of appetite, and loss of weight. The diagnosis was Hodgkin's disease.

Mr. White was administered a combination of drugs referred to as MOPP (mechlorethamine, *Oncovin*, procarbazine, prednisone), which included mechlorethamine (M) and vincristine (*Oncovin*). **(LO 45.2)**

a. What is the major precaution to be observed in the handling and administration of mechlorethamine and vincristine?

b. Mr. White asks you to explain how these drugs are going to get rid of his cancer. What will you tell him?

c. Mr. White complains about feelings of numbness in his hands and feet. Which drug might be causing this?

d. What are the most common immediate adverse effects of mechlorethamine? What is the most serious delayed adverse effect of mechlorethamine?

3. Following the diagnosis of breast cancer and bilateral mastectomy, Mrs. Smith was prescribed tamoxifen and told she would be taking the drug for the next 2 years. **(LO 45.4)**

a. What is this drug and why was it prescribed after the breast tumors were removed?

b. Explain to Mrs. Smith the expected adverse effects and why these particular effects occur.

4. High doses of methotrexate were administered to a young patient for the treatment of acute lymphocytic leukemia (ALL). **(LO 45.3)**

a. How does this drug work to kill these cancer cells?

b. What is the most serious adverse effect that can occur after methotrexate therapy?

c. Eight days after drug treatment, the patient became extremely debilitated with fever, breathing difficulties, blood in the urine, and there was evidence of bacterial infection. What do you suppose is happening?

d. What would be the immediate treatment for the patient's condition? What is this treatment called?

Multiple Choice

Use your critical-thinking skills to answer the following questions.

1. Carmustine functions as an **(LO 45.2)**
   A. antimetabolite
   B. alkylator
   C. hormone antagonist
   D. mitotic inhibitor

2. The antimetabolite that blocks DNA synthesis by interfering with folic acid is **(LO 45.3)**
   A. mercaptopurine
   B. fluorouracil
   C. methotrexate
   D. cytarabine

3. The drug that binds to mitotic tubules to cause metaphase arrest is **(LO 45.4)**
   A. doxorubicin
   B. asparaginase
   C. etoposide
   D. vincristine

4. Enzyme inhibition of aromatase is the mechanism of action of **(LO 45.5)**
   A. tamoxifen
   B. anastrozole
   C. leuprolide
   D. goserelin

5. The monoclonal antibody that inhibits vascular endothelial growth factor and new blood vessel formation is (LO 45.6)
   - A. imatinib
   - B. trastuzumab
   - C. bevacizumab
   - D. gefitinib

Multiple Choice (Multiple Answer)

Select the correct choices for each statement. The choices may be all correct, all incorrect, or any combination.

1. Which of the following is true of chemotherapy? (LO 45.1)
   - A. one of the early goals of chemotherapy is remission
   - B. antineoplastic drugs only attack cancerous cells
   - C. drug resistance is increased with combination therapy
   - D. it is the primary form of treatment for solid tumors

2. Select the correct statements for alkylating drugs. (LO 45.2)
   - A. bind irreversibly with nucleic acids
   - B. decrease cells' ability to synthesize proteins
   - C. are cell-cycle nonspecific
   - D. more effective when cells are actively dividing

3. The mechanisms of actions for the antimetabolites include (LO 45.3)
   - A. inhibiting mitosis
   - B. blocking DNA synthesis
   - C. forming abnormal nucleotides
   - D. preventing DNA replication

4. Select the correct statements about the plant extract treatments for cancer. (LO 45.4)
   - A. they can bind to microtubules
   - B. they increase the DNA strand breakage
   - C. they induce enzymes
   - D. they decrease free radicals

5. Which of the following are correct about hormone antagonists? (LO 45.5)
   - A. they are cytotoxic and cause cell death
   - B. their function is to block hormones
   - C. they are used for hairy cell leukemia
   - D. they are primarily indicated after surgery and radiation therapy

Sequencing

Place the following in order of how they happen in the body. (LO 45.1)

_____   _____   _____   _____

First   **Last**

metastasis

development of abnormal cell

formation of secondary site tumor

reproduction of cancerous cell

Classification

Place the following agents under their correct mechanism of action. **(LO 45.2, 45.3, 45.4, 45.5)**

Xeloda	Nilandron	Leukeran
Oncovin	Alimta	Eloxatin
Velban	Synarel	Arimidex
Taxol	Leustatin	Zanosar

Irreversible binding of nucleic acids	Inhibition of enzymes responsible for DNA synthesis	Inhibition of mitosis	Blockage of hormone receptors

Documentation

Using the prescription below, answer the following questions. **(LO 45.5)**

Valley Clinic
Practice RX

12345 Main Avenue
Anytown, USA   12345
931-555-1000

NAME: ___Karen Wilson_____   DATE: _____

ADDRESS: _____

RX   Arimidex 1mg

Sig: Take one tablet by mouth once daily

Dr. J. McDonaldson_____ M.D. _____M.D.

  Substitution Permitted   Dispense as written

DEA #: _____   REFILL: NR 1 2 3 4

---

a. What type of cancer is being treated with this medication?
b. How does this medication work?
c. What was the original indication for this drug?
d. List the common adverse effects of this drug.

Labeling

Fill in the missing labels. **(LO 45.2, 45.3, 45.4, 45.5)**

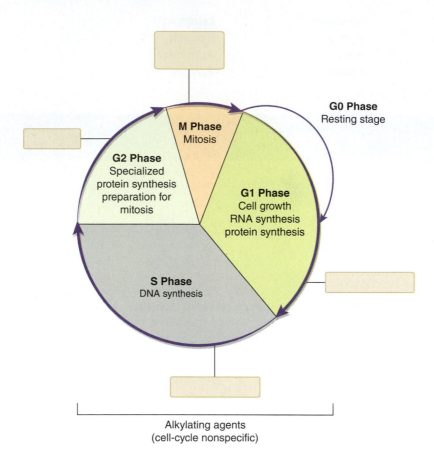

G0 Phase
Resting stage

M Phase
Mitosis

G2 Phase
Specialized
protein synthesis
preparation for
mitosis

G1 Phase
Cell growth
RNA synthesis
protein synthesis

S Phase
DNA synthesis

Alkylating agents
(cell-cycle nonspecific)

For interactive animations, videos, and assessment, visit:
www.mcgrawhillconnect.com

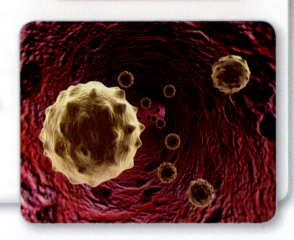

Chapter 46

Immunopharma-cology

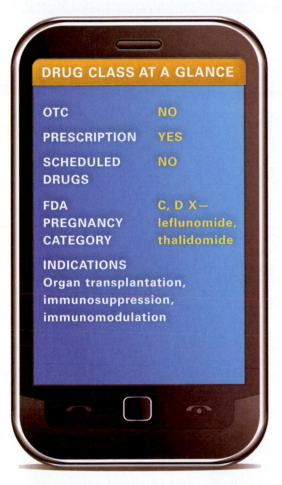

DRUG CLASS AT A GLANCE

OTC	NO
PRESCRIPTION	YES
SCHEDULED DRUGS	NO
FDA PREGNANCY CATEGORY	C, D X— leflunomide, thalidomide

INDICATIONS
Organ transplantation, immunosuppression, immunomodulation

KEY TERMS

antibody: a protein (immunoglobulin) produced naturally or induced by a foreign protein that provides immune protection against infectious organisms and foreign substances.

carcinogenic: causing cancer.

immunomodulation: ability to stimulate and increase immune function.

immunopharmacology: study of drugs with immunosuppressive and immunomodulating actions.

immunosuppression: ability to reduce the activity of the immune system.

interferon: chemical mediator produced by immune cells that increases immune function.

interleukin: chemical mediator produced by immune cells that helps regulate and increase immune function.

lymphopenia: decrease in the number of circulating lymphocytes.

mutagenic: having the ability to cause mutations.

teratogenic: capable of causing abnormal development.

Learning Outcomes

After studying this chapter, you should be able to

46.1 describe the main functions of the macrophages and lymphocytes in the immune response.

46.2 describe the immune response and how immune cells work together to protect the body.

46.3 identify the mechanism of action and uses of the cytotoxic, noncytotoxic, and monoclonal antibodies in immunosuppression.

46.4 identify the mechanism of action and uses of the interferons, interleukins, and colony stimulating factors.

Immunology is the study of how normal body defenses resist and overcome invasion from infectious organisms (bacteria, viruses) and other foreign substances. Recent advances in this field have identified various drugs that affect the activity of the immune system. **Immunosuppression** refers to drugs and biological factors that decrease immune activity. It is used after organ transplantation and in the treatment of severe inflammatory and allergic conditions when the immune system is hyperactive and causing harmful effects. **Immunomodulation** refers to actions or drugs that stimulate the activity of the immune system. Immunomodulating drugs are indicated for the treatment of various cancers, hepatitis, myelosuppression, and other conditions where increasing the activity of the immune system is beneficial. **Immunopharmacology** is the study of drugs that affect the immune system. To understand how drugs act to affect immunity, it is necessary to have a basic understanding of the immune system.

LO 46.1 | LO 46.2

IMMUNE SYSTEM

The immune system is made up of different lymphoid tissues (bone marrow, tonsils, lymph nodes, spleen) and cells (macrophages, lymphocytes) that are found in the blood and most body organs. There are two very important kinds of lymphocytes: T-cells, which mature in the thymus gland, and B-cells, which originate in the bone marrow. When the immune system is activated, these cells multiply and help protect the body. Lymphocytes and macrophages also produce chemical mediators, classified as cytokines, that help regulate the activity of the immune system. Two important classes of cytokines are the **interleukins** and the **interferons.** These mediators act as chemical messengers that regulate and direct the activity of the various immune cells. More than 20 different interleukins have been identified that are involved in regulating immune function.

Cells Involved in the Immune Response

Many different types of cells are involved in the immune response; however, macrophages and several different types of lymphocytes are the most important.

Macrophages

Macrophages are scavenger cells that phagocytize infectious organisms and foreign substances (Figure 46.1). Macrophages are one of the immune cells that first recognize the proteins (antigens) of infectious organisms and foreign substances. Immune cells that can recognize foreign antigens are referred to as antigen-presenting cells (APCs). After recognition and processing of a foreign antigen, the APCs display the antigen to other immune cells, especially helper T-cells.

Figure 46.1

Macrophages Phagocytizing

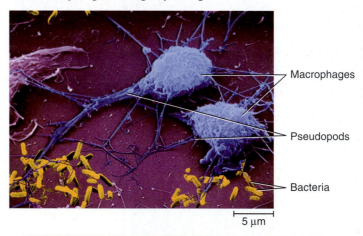

Macrophages

Pseudopods

Bacteria

5 μm

Filamentous pseudopods of the macrophages snare the rod-shaped bacteria and draw them to the cell surface, where they are phagocytized.

Helper T-cells

These T-cell lymphocytes play a key role in regulating the activity of the immune system. The function of helper T-cells is to recognize the foreign antigens presented to them by macrophages and other APCs. Recognition of foreign antigens activates the helper T-cells to multiply and increase in numbers. Helper T-cells then release interleukins and other chemical factors that activate killer T-cells (cytotoxic T-cells) and B-cells to multiply and increase in numbers. Interleukin-1 (IL-1) and interleukin-2 (IL-2) have multiple actions and activate both killer T-cells and B-cells.

Killer T-cells

Killer T-cells are lymphocytes that are cytotoxic and function to attack and kill cells that are infected with foreign organisms. This form of immunity where T-cells

Figure 46.2

The Actions of a Natural Killer (NK) Cell

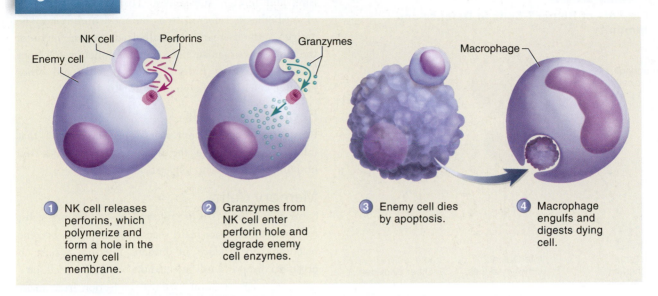

1. NK cell releases perforins, which polymerize and form a hole in the enemy cell membrane.

2. Granzymes from NK cell enter perforin hole and degrade enemy cell enzymes.

3. Enemy cell dies by apoptosis.

4. Macrophage engulfs and digests dying cell.

attack and destroy infected or foreign cells is referred to as cellular immunity. Killer T-cells and natural killer cells are lymphocytes that destroy cells by releasing various cytotoxic chemicals such as perforins, granzymes, and interferons (Figure 46.2).

B-cells

B-cells are lymphocytes that function as APCs and that also can differentiate into plasma cells that function to produce antibodies (Figure 46.3). **Antibodies,** also referred to as immunoglobulins, are proteins that bind

Figure 46.3   B-Cell and Plasma Cell

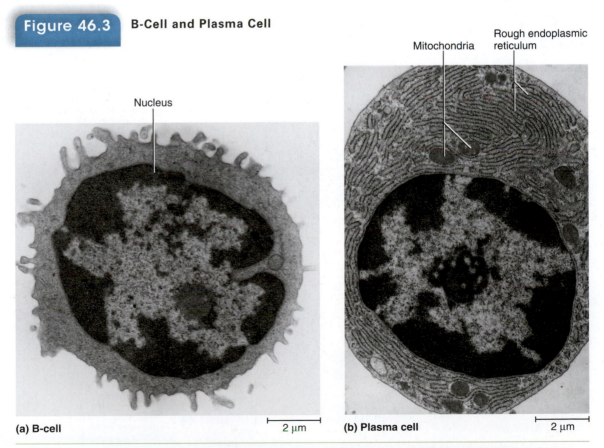

(a) B-cell   2 µm

(b) Plasma cell   2 µm

(a) B-cells have little cytoplasm and scanty organelles. (b) A plasma cell, which differentiates from a B-cell, has an abundance of rough endoplasmic reticulum that synthesizes the antibodies.

Figure 46.4

The Role of Helper T-Cells in Defense and Immunity

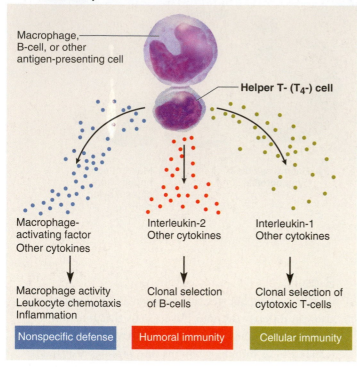

Macrophage, B-cell, or other antigen-presenting cell

Helper T- (T₄-) cell

Macrophage-activating factor Other cytokines

Interleukin-2 Other cytokines

Interleukin-1 Other cytokines

Macrophage activity Leukocyte chemotaxis Inflammation

Clonal selection of B-cells

Clonal selection of cytotoxic T-cells

| Nonspecific defense | Humoral immunity | Cellular immunity |

to and inactivate antigens located on infectious organisms and foreign substances. The immune function of antibodies is referred to as humoral immunity. The antigen-antibody reaction usually leads to destruction of the infectious organism. The immune function of helper T-cells to activate killer T-cells, B-cells, and other immune defenses is shown in Figure 46.4.

Regulatory T-Cells

Regulatory T-cells (suppressors) are lymphocytes that inhibit the activity of the immune system when the immune response is no longer needed.

Memory Cells

Some B-cells and T-cells, referred to as memory cells, remain in the body for many years and can quickly become reactivated to produce an immune response against an organism that previously infected the body. These cells provide long-term immunity against reinfection from many childhood diseases (for example, measles, chickenpox). The purpose of vaccination is to produce memory cells and antibodies against a specific organism in order to produce long-term immunity and protection against infection. Figure 46.5 illustrates the actions of these immune cells during a typical immune response to an infectious organism.

Figure 46.5
   Response of Immune Cells to Viral Infection

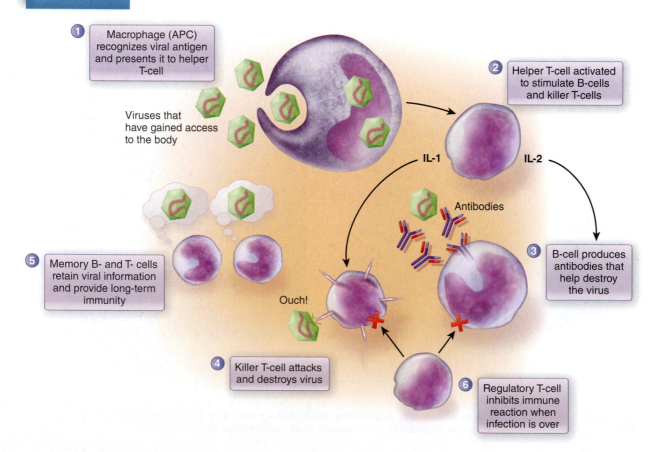

1. Macrophage (APC) recognizes viral antigen and presents it to helper T-cell

2. Helper T-cell activated to stimulate B-cells and killer T-cells

Viruses that have gained access to the body

IL-1

IL-2

Antibodies

3. B-cell produces antibodies that help destroy the virus

5. Memory B- and T- cells retain viral information and provide long-term immunity

Ouch!

4. Killer T-cell attacks and destroys virus

6. Regulatory T-cell inhibits immune reaction when infection is over

IMMUNOSUPPRESSIVE DRUGS

Drugs that have the ability to suppress the immune response are useful in the treatment of severe allergic reactions and immune-based diseases such as multiple sclerosis, myasthenia gravis, and systemic lupus erythematosus. These drugs are also essential in preventing organ rejection following organ transplantation. In these conditions, inappropriate activation of the immune system causes inflammatory reactions that lead to destruction of body tissue and rejection of transplanted organs.

Corticosteroid Drugs

The corticosteroids produce potent antiinflammatory and antiallergic effects (see Chapter 36). Corticosteroids also have the ability to suppress the immune response. Prednisone (*Sterapred, Sterapred DS*) and methylprednisolone (*Medrol*) are two widely used corticosteroid drugs.

Mechanism of Action

One of the main immunosuppressive effects of the corticosteroids is to cause lymphocytes in the blood to be redistributed into the bone marrow. This immunosuppressive effect **(lymphopenia)** occurs 4 to 6 hours following drug administration and significantly reduces the number of circulating lymphocytes in the blood. Lymphopenia decreases the ability of lymphocytes to initiate and participate in an immune response. Corticosteroids also reduce the amount of lymphoid tissue and cells in the lymph nodes and spleen. In addition, the number and activity of macrophages, T-cells, and B-cells is reduced. Corticosteroids also inhibit the synthesis of inflammatory mediators such as the prostaglandins, leukotrienes, and cytokines. These mediators play an important role in inflammation and immune activity and this accounts for much of the immunosuppressant action of the corticosteroids.

Clinical Indications

Corticosteroids are usually used in combination with other immunosuppressive drugs. Initially, a large dose is administered parenterally, followed by smaller oral doses on a daily schedule to maintain the effect. Corticosteroids are used to prevent rejection of transplanted organs, to treat severe allergic reactions, and to control inflammatory responses in other immune-based diseases.

Adverse Effects

Chronic administration of corticosteroids is associated with many serious adverse effects (see Chapter 36).

Azathioprine (*Imuran*)

Azathioprine is a derivative of the antineoplastic drug mercaptopurine. The drug is usually administered orally and following absorption, azathioprine is rapidly converted in the body to mercaptopurine and exerts a similar cytotoxic effect. Azathioprine inhibits the synthesis of purine nucleotides (adenine, guanine) that are required for the synthesis of deoxyribonucleic acid (DNA) and for cell growth and reproduction. Inhibition of DNA synthesis leads to the death of many existing lymphocytes and suppresses the formation of new B-cells and T-cells.

Clinical Indications

Azathioprine is widely used in organ transplantation to prevent rejection. It is usually administered along with corticosteroids. In addition, it is used to control immune-based diseases, such as lupus erythematosus and rheumatoid arthritis.

Adverse Effects

Adverse effects are similar to those observed with mercaptopurine. Gastrointestinal disturbances include nausea, vomiting, diarrhea, and ulceration. Excessive reductions in blood cells and depression of bone marrow function may occur, which, along with the immunosuppressive effect, can increase susceptibility to serious infection. Azathioprine and the other cytotoxic drugs are **mutagenic, carcinogenic,** and **teratogenic;** therefore, the benefits and risks of treatment must be carefully evaluated.

Cyclophosphamide (*Cytoxan*)

Cyclophosphamide is an alkylating drug used in the treatment of certain cancers. Like azathioprine, it is a cytotoxic drug that kills and suppresses the function of lymphocytes. Cyclophosphamide is used in bone marrow transplantation and various autoimmune disorders such as systemic lupus erythematosus and severe rheumatoid arthritis.

Adverse Effects

Similar to other alkylating drugs used to treat cancer, cyclophosphamide causes nausea, vomiting, alopecia (hair loss), and bone marrow depression. During the metabolism of cyclophosphamide, a toxic metabolite is formed, which during urinary excretion may cause hemorrhagic cystitis along with hematuria and bladder dysfunction. Increased fluid intake can minimize the incidence of these adverse effects.

Cyclosporine (*Sandimmune*)

Cyclosporine is a polypeptide metabolite produced by a particular fungus. It is a potent immunosuppressive drug and, unlike azathioprine and cyclophosphamide, is not cytotoxic.

Cyclosporine suppresses T-cell function, especially the activity of helper T-cells. Since helper T-cells play a key role in regulating the activation of other immune cells (killer T-cells and B-cells), the immune response is significantly depressed. Cyclosporine inhibits the production of interleukin-2 (IL-2), a chemical mediator necessary for the growth and multiplication of T-cells.

Clinical Indications

The major use of cyclosporine is to prevent organ rejection after transplantation. The selective action is to suppress T-cell function. The low toxicity compared to that of the cytotoxic drugs has made cyclosporine one of the drugs of choice for this indication. Cyclosporine is usually administered along with corticosteroid drugs. Cyclosporine is also considered for other autoimmune conditions such as rheumatoid arthritis.

Adverse Effects

The major concern is the development of nephrotoxicity, characterized by renal tubule damage. This effect occurs in about one-fourth of individuals treated. Reduction of the dosage usually eliminates tubular damage. Liver toxicity and central nervous system (CNS) disturbances such as paresthesias and seizures occur less frequently. Other adverse effects include tremors, hypertension, gum hyperplasia, and hirsutism.

Tacrolimus (*Prograf*)

Tacrolimus is a macrolide antibiotic that has a similar mechanism of action as cyclosporine—to inhibit T-cell lymphocyte activity. This drug is more potent than cyclosporine and is primarily used in organ transplantation to prevent rejection. Nephrotoxicity and CNS disturbances that include tremors and seizures are the most serious toxicities; other adverse effects are similar to those of cyclosporine.

Mycophenolate Mofetil (*CellCept*)

Mycophenolate mofetil is a cytotoxic drug that inhibits the activity of both T-cells and B-cells. The primary use of this drug is in renal organ transplantation to prevent rejection. Adverse effects include diarrhea, vomiting, myelosuppression, and increased susceptibility to infection.

Leflunomide (*Arava*)

Leflunomide is currently used in the treatment of rheumatoid arthritis. The drug is converted to a long-acting metabolite that inhibits the synthesis of pyrimidines and DNA. This action inhibits the proliferation of both T-cells and B-cells involved in rheumatoid arthritis. Leflunomide is taken orally and has a half-life (on average) of 15 days. Adverse drug effects include diarrhea and other GI disturbances, liver and renal impairment, and the potential to cause birth defects.

Muromonab-CD3 (*Orthoclone OKT3*)

New discoveries in molecular biology have led to the development of commercially prepared monoclonal antibodies designed to attack specific aspects of the immune system. The first of these antibodies to be approved was muromonab-CD3, which was a murine (derived from mouse) antibody. The immunosuppressive effect occurs when the CD3 antibody (administered IV) binds specifically to T-cells. This binding quickly decreases the activity of the T-cells. Since T-cells play a major role in regulating immune activity, the overall activity of the immune system is reduced. The major use of CD3 is to prevent organ rejection after renal transplantation. Nausea, vomiting, fever, shortness of breath, and chest pain are associated adverse effects.

Daclizumab (*Zenapax*)

Daclizumab is a monoclonal antibody that binds to and blocks the interleukin-2 receptor. This action inhibits the activation of lymphocytes and the immune reaction that occurs during the rejection of transplanted organs. The main indication for daclizumab is for the prevention of renal allograft rejection. Common adverse drug reactions include weakness, chills, muscle and joint ache, GI disturbances, and renal impairment.

Infliximab (*Remicade*)

Infliximab is a monoclonal antibody that binds to and inhibits the activity of tumor necrosis factor (TNF-alpha). TNF-alpha is a mediator of inflammation and immune activation. The main indication for infliximab is in the treatment of Crohn's disease, which is an inflammatory condition of the intestinal tract. Administration of infliximab is associated with an infusion reaction that may occur following IV injection. The reaction can include fever, chills, hives, hypotension, and chest pain. There is also an increased incidence of bacterial infection that occurs in infliximab-treated patients. Other adverse effects include headache, nausea, and GI disturbances.

The discovery and development of monoclonal antibodies is a rapidly expanding area of pharmacology. Newer monoclonal antibodies and other immunosuppressive drugs are summarized in Table 46:1.

Immunosuppressive Drugs and Monoclonal Antibodies

Drug (*Trade Name*)	Administration	Mechanism of action/major indications
Cytotoxic drugs		
Azathioprine (*Imuran*)	PO, IV	Antimetabolite/organ transplantation, autoimmune disorders
Cyclophosphamide (*Cytoxan*)	PO, IV	Alkylation/bone marrow transplantation, autoimmune disorders
Leflunomide (*Arava*)	PO	Antimetabolite/rheumatoid arthritis
Mycophenolate (*CellCept*)	PO, IV	Antimetabolite/organ transplantation
Noncytotoxic drugs		
Cyclosporine (*Sandimmune*)	PO, IV	Inhibits IL-2 and T-cell production/organ transplantation
Tacrolimus (*Prograf*)	PO, IV	Inhibits T-cell production/organ transplantation
Sirolimus (*Rapamune*)	PO	Inhibits T-cell production/organ transplantation
Thalidomide (*Thalomid*)	PO	Antiinflammatory, inhibits TNF*/erythema nodosum leprosum
Monoclonal antibodies		
Abatacept (*Orencia*)	IV injection	Blocks activation of T-cells/rheumatoid arthritis
Adalimumab (*Humira*)	SC every other week	Binds and blocks TNF/rheumatoid arthritis
Alefacept (*Amevive*)	IM injection	Inhibits activation of T-cells/plaque psoriasis
Basiliximab (*Simulect*)	IV injection	Blocks interleukin-2/acute organ rejection, renal transplantation
Daclizumab (*Zenapax*)	IV injection	Blocks interleukin-2/acute organ rejection, renal transplantation
Etanercept (*Enbrel*)	SC injection	Binds and blocks TNF/rheumatoid arthritis
Natalizumab (*Tysabri*)	IV injection	Inhibits vascular cell adhesion molecules (VCAM), prevents migration of lymphocytes into GI tract/Crohn's disease
Omalizumab (*Xolair*)	SC injection	Blocks attachment of antibodies on mast cells/asthma
Palivizumab (*Synagis*)	Monthly IM injection	Prevents growth of respiratory syncytial virus/prevents respiratory syncytial virus (RSV) infection
Ranibizumab (*Lucentis*)	Intravitreal injection	Reduces blood vessel formation/age-related macular degeneration

TNF—tumor necrosis factor.

Patients receiving immunosuppressive drugs usually have disease conditions that require hospitalization or they have recently undergone organ transplantation, which also requires prolonged hospitalization.

Consequently, these patients receive intensive care treatment and close clinical observation. Of greatest importance is the detection of any signs that indicate infection or organ rejection. Blood counts are taken periodically to ensure that blood cells do not fall below acceptable levels. It is extremely important to observe all the precautions for infection control.

Monitor vital signs and body temperature during and after drug administration; fever is often the first indication of infection.

Explain to patient the common side effects of the administered drugs.

Instruct patient to report fever, chills, swollen glands, sore throat, tiredness, and malaise or any other symptoms that suggest infection or possible organ rejection, especially after hospitalization.

Instruct other family members on the importance of cleanliness and infection control.

LO 46.4

IMMUNOMODULATING DRUGS

Drugs that increase the activity of the immune system are desirable in the treatment of cancer, AIDS, and other conditions where immunological deficiencies exist. At present, there are a limited number of drugs available. Many of these immunostimulant drugs are commercial preparations of growth factors and mediators that are normally produced by immune cells.

Interferons

Interferons are naturally occurring proteins produced by lymphocytes and other cells of the immune system. The interferons are chemical mediators involved in the immune attack on infectious organisms and other foreign substances. The three types of interferons are classified as alpha, beta, and gamma interferons. Administration is by SC or IM injection. Common adverse effects are flu-like symptoms: chills, fever, muscle aches, and pains. The interferons and their uses are listed in Table 46:2.

Interleukin-2 (*Proleukin*)

Interleukin-2 (IL-2) is one of the chemical mediators known as a lymphokine. It is produced by lymphocytes and other cells. Interleukin-2 is especially important for the activity of helper T-cells. It functions to stimulate B-cell production of antibodies and killer T-cell activity. These actions increase the function and response of the immune system. Killer T-cells, in particular, attack and destroy cancer cells and cells infected with infectious organisms. Consequently, there is a great interest in developing interleukins for the treatment of cancer and other immunosuppressive diseases. Fever, flu-like symptoms, and fluid retention are common adverse effects.

Colony Stimulating Factors (CSF)

Colony stimulating factors are synthetic preparations of naturally occurring proteins that normally stimulate the formation of macrophages and granulocytes. The CSFs stimulate the bone marrow to increase the production of these blood cells. The CSFs are used to speed the recovery in patients with myelosuppression who are undergoing cancer chemotherapy or bone marrow transplantation. Common adverse effects include fever, chills, GI disturbances, and muscle and bone pain. CSF drugs are listed in Table 46:2

Immunomodulating Agents

Drug (*Trade Name*)	Administration	Clinical uses
Interferons		
Interferon alpha-2a (*Roferon-A*)	SC, IM injection	Hairy cell leukemia, Kaposi's sarcoma, chronic myelogenous leukemia, hepatitis C
Interferon alpha-2b (*Intron A*)	SC, IM injection	Hairy cell leukemia, Kaposi's sarcoma, chronic hepatitis B and C, lymphoma, melanoma
Interferon alpha-n3 (*Alferon N*)	SC and intralesional injection	Human papillomavirus (HPV), genital/anal warts
Interferon alfacon-1 (*Infergen*)	SC injection	Chronic hepatitis C
Interferon beta-1a (*Avonex*) (*Rebif*)	Weekly IM injection 3X weekly SC	Multiple sclerosis Multiple sclerosis
Interferon beta-1b (*Betaseron*)	SC injection	Multiple sclerosis
Interferon gamma-1b (*Actimmune*)	3X weekly SC	Chronic granulomatous disease
Interleukins		
Interleukin-2 (*Proleukin*)	SC, slow IV infusion	Renal cell cancer, melanoma
Colony stimulating factors (CSF)		
Filgrastim (G-CSF, *Neupogen*)	SC, IV injection	Increases formation of granulocytes (neutrophils) in patients with myelosuppression undergoing cancer chemotherapy and bone marrow transplantation
Sargramostim (GM-CSF, *Leukine*)	SC, IV injection	Increases formation of macrophages and granulocytes in patients with myelosuppression undergoing cancer chemotherapy and bone marrow transplantation

Chapter Review

Understanding Terminology

Match the definition or description in the left column with the appropriate term in the right column. **(LO 46.1, 46.3)**

___ 1. The study of drugs with immunosuppressive or immunomodulating effects.

___ 2. Proteins that attack and help destroy infectious organisms.

___ 3. The ability to stimulate and increase immune function.

___ 4. Having the capability of causing cancer.

___ 5. Capable of causing abnormal development (birth defects).

___ 6. A decrease in the number of circulating lymphocytes.

___ 7. Capable of causing mutations.

___ 8. A chemical mediator produced by immune cells that helps regulate and increase immune function.

___ 9. Antigen-presenting cell (APC).

___ 10. The ability to suppress or decrease immune function.

a. antibodies

b. carcinogenic

c. immunopharmacology

d. immunostimulation

e. immunosuppression

f. macrophages

g. interleukin

h. lymphopenia

i. mutagenic

j. teratogenic

Acquiring Knowledge

Answer the following questions.

1. In what diseases or conditions is it useful to suppress immune function? **(LO 46.3)**

2. When is it desirable to stimulate immune function? **(LO 46.4)**

3. Briefly describe the function of macrophages, helper T-cells, B-cells, and killer T-cells. **(LO 46.1, 46.2)**

4. What is the function of regulatory (suppressor) T-cells and memory cells? **(LO 46.1)**

5. Describe the main immunosuppressive effects of corticosteroid drugs. **(LO 46.3)**

6. Compare the actions of azathioprine and cyclophosphamide with that of cyclosporine. Is there any advantage with cyclosporine? **(LO 46.3)**

7. What adverse effects are associated with cyclosporine? **(LO 46.3)**

8. What is the mechanism of action of muromonab-CD3? **(LO 46.4)**

9. Explain the immunomodulating actions of alpha-interferon and interleukin-2. **(LO 46.4)**

Applying Knowledge on the Job

Use your critical-thinking skills to answer the following questions.

1. As a nurse, you often get to know your patients personally as well as medically. Mary Peters is one of your patients. You know she feels lucky that a heart was found for her transplant surgery and glad just to be alive, but she still has to deal with organ rejection. **(LO 46.3)**
   a. Mary was prescribed cyclosporine. What is the mechanism of action of this drug?
   b. What adverse effects should Mary be monitored for while being administered this drug?
   c. What can be done to reduce the drug's adverse effects?

2. All patients taking immunosuppressants should be cautioned to watch for and report any signs of infections. Why is this important? **(LO 46.3)**

3. Patients receiving *Imuran* should be warned of the common adverse effects, GI disturbances, etc. What additional adverse effects should they be warned of? **(LO 46.3)**

4. Patients using alpha interferon should be warned of the common adverse reactions. Which adverse reactions are most likely to occur? **(LO 46.4)**

Multiple Choice

Use your critical-thinking skills to answer the following questions.

1. The immune cell that when activated stimulates the activity of killer T-cells and B-cells is **(LO 46.1)**
   A. macrophage
   B. B-cell
   C. helper T-cell
   D. killer T-cell

2. The immunosuppressive drug that inhibits the production of interleukin-2 is **(LO 46.3)**
   A. azathioprine
   B. cyclosporine
   C. cyclophosphamide
   D. infliximab

3. Filgrastim is classified as a(n) **(LO 46.4)**
   A. interleukin
   B. interferon
   C. corticosteroid
   D. colony stimulating factor

4. The immunosuppressive drug that forms a toxic metabolite and that can cause hemorrhagic cystitis is **(LO 46.3)**
   A. cyclosporine
   B. muromonab-CD3
   C. cyclophosphamide
   D. mycophenolate

5. The monoclonal antibody that inhibits tumor necrosis factor-alpha in the treatment of Crohn's disease is **(LO 46.4)**
   A. sargramostim
   B. infliximab
   C. interleukin-2
   D. daclizumab

Multiple Choice (Multiple Answer)

Select the correct choices for each statement. The choices may be all correct, all incorrect, or any combination.

1. Which of the following are roles of macrophages? **(LO 46.1)**
   A. release interleukins
   B. produce antibodies
   C. provide long-term immunity
   D. recognize antigens

2. Select the cells involved in the immune response. **(LO 46.2)**
   A. killer T-cells
   B. B-cells
   C. memory cells
   D. immunocytes

3. Corticosteroids work by doing which of the following? **(LO 46.3)**
   A. inhibit synthesis of purine nucleotides
   B. reduce lymphoid tissue in the spleen
   C. inhibit synthesis of inflammatory mediators
   D. cause lymphopenia

4. Select the cytotoxic drugs. **(LO 46.3)**
   A. azathioprine
   B. cyclophosphamide
   C. cyclosporine
   D. mycophenolate mofetil

5. Which of the following are uses for interferons? **(LO 46.4)**
   A. multiple sclerosis
   B. hairy cell leukemia
   C. lymphoma
   D. AIDS

Sequencing

Place the following steps of the immune response in order of how they happen. **(LO 46.2)**

_____ _____ _____ _____ _____

First   **Last**

killer T-cell attacks and destroys bacteria

macrophage recognizes antigen

regulatory T-cell inhibits immune reaction

B-cell produces antibodies

helper T-cell activated

Classification

Place the following agents under their correct classification. **(LO 46.3)**

Humira	*Sandimmune*	*Cytoxan*
Prograf	*Simulect*	*Imuran*
Amevive	*Rapamune*	*CellCept*
Synagis	*Thalomid*	*Arava*

Cytotoxic	Noncytotoxic	Monoclonal antibodies

Documentation

Using the prescription below, answer the following questions. (LO 46.4)

Freeman Clinic
Practice RX

12345 Main Avenue
Anytown, USA   12345
931-555-1000

NAME: ___Phyliss Kalenia_____   DATE: _____

ADDRESS: _____

RX   Neupogen 5mcg/kg

Sig: Take once daily

Dr. Leonard Wardly_____ M.D.   _____M.D.

   Substitution Permitted   Dispense as written

DEA #: _____   REFILL: NR   1   2   3   4

---

a. What is the clinical use of this medication?
b. How is this medication administered?
c. What is the mechanism of action for this drug?
d. List the common adverse effects of this drug.

Labeling

Fill in the missing labels. **(LO 46.2, 46.4)**

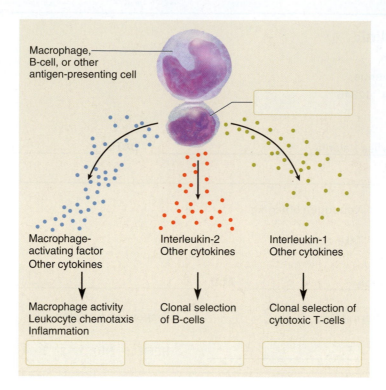

Glossary

A

abortifacient Substance that induces abortion.

absence seizure Generalized seizure that does not involve motor convulsions; also referred to as petit mal.

absorption The uptake of nutrients and drugs from the GI tract.

acetate Compound that contains acetic acid.

acetylcholine (ACH) Neurotransmitter of parasympathetic (cholinergic) nerves; stimulates the cholinergic receptor; excitatory neurotransmitter in the basal ganglia.

acetylcholinesterase An enzyme that inactivates acetylcholine.

acid rebound Effect in which a great volume of acid is secreted by the stomach in response to the reduced acid environment caused by antacid neutralization.

acidification Process that alters the pH to less than 7.

acidosis pH less than 7.45 or a condition in which the tissues have relatively more acid or acid waste than normal; disturbance of acid-base balance; when the pH of the blood is below 7.35.

acquired immunity Protection from viral reinfection in the form of antibodies produced during an infection (active) or produced after exposure to a vaccine (passive).

acquired immunodeficiency syndrome (AIDS) Viral-induced disease characterized by multiple opportunistic infections as a result of depleted lymphocytes involved in the cell-mediated immune process.

acromegaly Condition usually in middle-aged adults from hypersecretion of growth hormone.

acute coronary syndrome Term used to cover any group of clinical symptoms compatible with acute myocardial ischemia.

acute myocardial ischemia Chest pain due to insufficient blood supply to the heart muscle that results from coronary artery disease.

addiction A chronic neurobiologic disease in which genetic, psychosocial, and environmental factors induce changes in the individual's behavior to compulsively use drugs despite the harm that may result.

Addison's disease Inadequate secretion of glucocorticoids and mineralocorticoids.

ADH (antidiuretic hormone) Polypeptide substance synthesized by the hypothalamus and released from the posterior pituitary gland that regulates water balance in the body by altering urine volume at the collecting ducts.

adipose tissue Tissue containing fat cells; fat.

adrenergic neuronal blocker Drug that acts at the neuronal nerve endings to reduce the formation or release of NE.

adrenergic receptor Receptor located on internal organs that responds to norepinephrine and epinephrine.

adsorbent Substance that has the ability to attach other substances to its surface.

ADT Alternate-day therapy.

adverse effect General term for undesirable and potentially harmful drug effect.

afferent nerve Transmits sensory information from peripheral organs to the brain and spinal cord (central nervous system).

afterload A measure of the vascular resistance that the left ventricle must overcome in order to eject blood during contraction.

agonist Drug that attaches to a receptor and initiates an action; drug that binds to a receptor and activates a physiologic response or drug action.

agranulocytosis Acute condition in which there is a reduction in the number of white blood cells (WBCs), specifically polymorphonuclear cells (granulocytes); condition in which the number of white blood cells, in particular the granulocytes, is less than normal.

akathisia Continuous body movement in which an individual is restless or constantly paces about.

akinesia Loss of voluntary muscle movement; restless leg movement.

albuminuria The presence of the plasma protein albumin in the urine.

aldosterone Hormone released from adrenal cortex that causes the retention of sodium from the kidneys.

alkalosis pH greater than 7.45 or a condition in which the tissues have less acid than normal; disturbance of acid-base balance; when the pH of the blood is above 7.5.

alkylation Irreversible chemical bond that some cancer drugs form with nucleic acids and DNA.

allergen A substance capable of producing an allergic reaction.

alopecia Baldness or hair loss.

alpha adrenergic drug Drug that stimulates the alpha adrenergic receptors.

alpha-1 adrenergic blocker Drug that blocks the alpha-1 effects of NE and EPI.

alpha-1 adrenergic receptor Receptor located on smooth muscle that mediates smooth muscle contraction.

alpha-2 adrenergic receptor Receptor located on adrenergic nerve endings that reduces the release of NE.

amenorrhea Condition in which monthly menstruation (menses) no longer occurs.

amide local anesthetic Anesthetic class that includes lidocaine, bupivicaine, and mepivicaine and has a moderate to long duration of action because metabolism occurs in the liver.

amylin Peptide of 37 amino acids that is secreted by the pancreas beta cells along with insulin in response to increasing blood glucose levels.

anabolism Process that converts or incorporates nutritional substances into tissue; usually associated with conversion of proteins into muscle mass.

analgesia Decreased response to pain; condition in which painful stimuli are not consciously interpreted (perceived) as hurting; relief from pain; inhibition of the perception of pain.

analgesic Substance (synthetic or naturally occurring) that inhibits the body's reaction to painful stimuli or perception of pain.

anaphylaxis Condition in which the body develops a severe allergic response; this is a medical emergency.

androgen Male sex hormone responsible for the development of male characteristics.

anemia Condition in which the number of red blood cells or the amount of hemoglobin (the oxygen-carrying substance) inside the red blood cells is less than normal; condition in which the oxygen-carrying function of the red blood cells to the tissues is decreased.

aneurysm An abnormal widening or ballooning of a portion of an artery due to weakness in the wall of the blood vessel.

angina Chest pain or discomfort that occurs when the heart muscle does not get enough blood and oxygen.

angina pectoris Chest pain due to decreased blood flow (ischemia) to the heart; caused by insufficient blood flow to the heart.

angioedema Edema and swelling beneath the skin.

angiotensin-converting enzyme inhibitor (ACEI) Drug that inhibits the enzymatic conversion of angiotensin I to angiotensin II.

angiotensin receptor blocker (ARB) Drug that blocks the receptors for angiotensin II.

angiotensin II Potent vasoconstrictor that also stimulates release of aldosterone and antidiuretic hormone.

anion Negatively charged ion.

antacid Drug that neutralizes hydrochloric acid (HCl) secreted by the stomach.

antagonist Drug that attaches to a receptor, does not initiate an action, but blocks an agonist from producing an effect; drug that binds to a receptor and interferes with other drugs or substances from producing a drug effect.

antagonistic Counteract; oppose.

antiallergic Drug that prevents mast cells from releasing histamine and other vasoactive substances.

antianxiety drug Drug used to treat anxiety; these drugs are also referred to as anxiolytics.

antiarrhythmic drug Drug used to restore normal cardiac rhythm.

anti-atherogenic The ability to prevent or stop atherosclerosis, the deposition of lipid-containing plaques on the innermost layers of the arteries.

antibacterial spectrum Bacteria that are susceptible to the antibacterial actions of a particular drug.

antibiotic Antibacterial drug obtained from other microorganisms.

antibiotic susceptibility Identification of the antibiotics, by bacterial culture and sensitivity testing, that will be effective against specific bacteria.

antibody A specialized protein (immunoglobulin) that recognizes the antigen that triggered its production; a protein (immunoglobulin) produced naturally or induced by a foreign protein that provides immune protection against infectious organisms and foreign substances; normally produced when a foreign substance such as a pathogen enters the body.

anticholinergic Refers to drugs or effects that reduce the activity of the parasympathetic nervous system.

anticonvulsant Drug usually administered IV that stops a convulsive seizure.

antidiuretic hormone (ADH) Polypeptide substance synthesized by the hypothalamus and released from the posterior pituitary gland that regulates water balance in the body by altering urine volume at the collecting ducts; hormone from the posterior pituitary gland that causes retention of water from the kidneys; substance produced in the hypothalamus and secreted by the pituitary gland that modulates urine production and allows the kidneys to reabsorb water in order to conserve body water.

antiepileptic drug Drug usually administered orally to prevent epileptic seizures.

antilipemic drug A drug that reduces the level of fats in the blood.

antigen Substance, usually protein or carbohydrate, that is capable of stimulating an immune response; any substance that stimulates an immune response, i.e., production of an antibody.

antigenic drift and antigenic shift The ability of viruses to change the composition or structure of their surface proteins (viral coat) that are responsible for producing disease (pathogenicity).

antihistaminic Drug that blocks the action of histamine at the target organ.

antiinflammatory Minimizing or stopping the response to tissue injury by reducing the pain, localized swelling, and chemical substances released at the site of injury.

antimetabolite A drug that is very similar to natural chemicals in a normal biochemical reaction in cells but different enough to interfere with the normal division and functions of cells; drug whose chemical structure is similar to that of normal body metabolites and that inhibits normal cell function.

antimicrobial Antibacterial drugs obtained by chemical synthesis and not from other microorganisms.

antineoplastic Drug that inhibits the growth and proliferation of cancer cells.

antipsychotic drug Drug used to treat schizophrenia and other psychotic conditions.

antipyresis Reducing an elevated body temperature.

antisecretory Substance that inhibits secretion of digestive enzymes, hormones, or acid.

antiseptic Substance that inhibits the growth of microorganisms on living tissue.

antitussive A drug that suppresses coughing.

anuria Condition in which no urine is produced.

anxiety A state of anxiousness and hyperemotionalism that occurs with uncertainty, stress, and fearful situations.

aphthous ulcer A painful open sore in the mouth or upper throat; also known as a canker sore.

aplastic anemia Anemia caused by defective functioning of the blood-forming organs (bone marrow).

apoprotein A protein that is attached to a second molecule that is not a protein.

apoptosis Cell death, due to either programmed cell death or other physiological events.

aquaporins Specialized proteins that form pores (channels) in the cell membrane that allow water to pass through but not small molecules like ions.

aquaresis Renal excretion of water without electrolytes.

aqueous humor Ocular fluid; watery substance that is located behind the cornea of the eye and in front of the lens.

argyria Permanent black discoloration of skin and mucous membranes caused by prolonged use of silver protein solutions.

arrhythmia Disorder of cardiac conduction and electrical impulse formation.

arteriosclerosis Hardening or fibrosis of the arteries; accumulation of fatty deposits in the walls of arteries.

arthralgia Joint pain.

arthritis Inflammation of the joints.

ascites Excess fluid in the space between the tissues lining the abdomen and abdominal organs (the peritoneal cavity), usually associated with organ failure.

asthma Inflammation of the bronchioles associated with constriction of smooth muscle, wheezing, and edema; respiratory disease characterized by bronchoconstriction, shortness of breath, and wheezing.

asymptomatic Condition in which there is no outward evidence (symptom) that an infection is present.

atherogenic The ability to start or accelerate the deposition of fats and calcium in the walls of arteries, called atherosclerosis.

atherosclerosis Fatty degeneration of arteries due to accumulation of cholesterol plaques; accumulation of fatty deposits in the walls of arteries.

atonic seizure Generalized-type seizure characterized by a sudden loss of muscle tone.

autoantibody An antibody produced by the immune system against one's own cells; antibodies normally are produced when a foreign substance such as a pathogen enters the body.

autoimmune disease Condition in which an individual's tissues are damaged by his or her own immune mechanisms.

automatism Drug-induced confusion that can cause increased drug consumption.

autonomic nervous system (ANS) System of nerves that innervate smooth and cardiac muscle (involuntary) of the internal organs and glands.

AV Atrioventricular, as in the AV node.

avitaminosis Chronic or long-term vitamin deficiency caused by lack in diet or defect in metabolic conversion in body resulting in a vitamin-specific condition such as beri-beri.

B

bacteria Single-celled microorganisms, some of which cause disease.

bacterial resistance Ability of some bacteria to resist the actions of antibiotics.

bactericidal Antibiotic that kills bacteria; chemical that kills or destroys bacteria.

bacteriostatic Chemical that inhibits growth or reproduction of bacteria but does not kill bacteria; antibiotic that inhibits the growth of, but does not kill, bacteria.

barbiturate CNS depressant drug possessing the barbituric acid ring structure.

basal ganglia A group of cell bodies (gray matter) within the white matter of the cerebrum that helps control body movement; involved in regulation of skeletal muscle tone and body movement.

benzodiazepine Class of drugs used to treat anxiety and sleep disorders.

beta-lactamases Bacterial enzymes that inactivate beta-lactam antibiotics; bacterial enzymes that inactivate penicillin and cephalosporin antibiotics.

beta-1 adrenergic receptor Receptor located on the heart that increases heart rate and force of contraction.

beta-2 adrenergic receptor Receptor located on smooth muscle that relaxes smooth muscle when stimulated.

bioavailability Percentage of the drug dosage that is absorbed.

biphasic Two different amounts of estrogen hormone are released during the cycle.

bipolar mood disorder Mood disorder where episodes of mania and depression occur alternately.

black box warning (boxed warning) A warning that appears in the instructions for use surrounded by a thick black box to alert medical professionals to serious or life-threatening adverse effects associated with the drug usage.

blood pressure (BP) The pressure of the blood within the arteries; depends primarily on the cardiac output and the peripheral resistance.

bone density A quantitative measurement of the mineral content of bone; used as an indicator of the structural strength of the bone.

bone mass A measure of the amount of minerals (mostly calcium and phosphorus) contained in a certain volume of bone.

bone mineral density Amount of calcium and phosphorus deposited in bone matrix.

bradykinesia Slowed body movements.

broad-spectrum Drug that is effective against a wide variety of both gram-positive and gram-negative pathogenic bacteria.

bronchodilator Drug that relaxes bronchial smooth muscle and dilates the lower respiratory passages.

buccal absorption Absorption of drug through the mucous membranes lining the oral cavity.

C

CAD (coronary artery disease) Narrowing of small arteries that supply blood and oxygen to the heart.

calorigenic Producing heat.

cancer Disease that involves the development and reproduction of abnormal cells.

candidemia Infection in the blood caused by the yeast *Candida*.

candidiasis Infection caused by the yeast *Candida*; also known as moniliasis.

cannabinoid Pharmacologically active substance obtained from the marijuana plant.

carcinogenic Causing cancer.

carcinoid tumor A slow-growing type of cancer that can arise in the gastrointestinal tract, lungs, ovaries, and testes.

cardiac arrhythmia Variation in the normal rhythm (motion) of the heart.

cardiac glycoside Drug obtained from plants of the genus *Digitalis*.

cardiac output (CO) The amount of blood pumped per minute by the heart.

catabolism Process in which complex compounds are broken down into simpler molecules; usually associated with energy release.

catecholamine Refers to norepinephrine, epinephrine, and other sympathomimetic compounds that possess the catechol structure.

cathartic Pharmacological substance that stimulates defecation.

cation Positively charged ion.

caudal anesthesia Injection of a local anesthetic into the caudal or subcaudal spinal canal.

cell-cycle nonspecific (CCNS) Refers to cancer drugs that act in all phases of the cell cycle.

cell-cycle specific (CCS) Refers to cancer drugs that only act when the cell is actively dividing.

centrally acting skeletal muscle relaxant Drug that inhibits skeletal muscle contraction by blocking conduction within the spinal cord.

cephalosporinases Bacterial enzymes that inactivate cephalosporin antibiotics.

CERA Stands for continuous erythropoietin receptor activator.

cerebellum Part of the brain that coordinates body movements and posture and helps maintain body equilibrium.

cerebral cortex Uppermost layers of the cerebrum involved in sensory perception, voluntary motor control, and all higher intellectual abilities.

cerebrum Largest and uppermost part of the brain that is divided into right and left cerebral hemispheres.

chelate Chemical action of a substance to bond permanently to a metal ion.

chemical mediator Substance released from mast cells and white blood cells during inflammatory and allergic reactions.

chemical name Name that defines the chemical composition of a drug.

chemoprophylaxis Use of antibiotics to prevent infection, usually before a surgical procedure or in patients at risk for infection.

chemotherapy Use of drugs to inhibit the growth of or to destroy infectious organisms or cancer cells; use of drugs to kill or inhibit the growth of infectious organisms or cancer cells.

chloride channel activators A novel class of drugs that stimulate pore-forming receptors in the intestine, causing chloride ions to cross membranes.

cholesterol A fat (lipid) normally synthesized by the liver; essential for the structure and function of cells.

cholinergic Refers to the nerves and receptors of the parasympathetic nervous system; also refers to the drugs that stimulate this system.

cholinergic receptor Receptor located on internal organs and glands that responds to acetylcholine.

-chromic Suffix meaning color.

chronic Condition of long duration, usually months or years.

chronic bronchitis Respiratory condition caused by chronic irritation that increases secretion of mucus and causes degeneration of the respiratory lining.

chronic heart failure (CHF) Heart disease caused by weakness of the contractile force of the myocardium; condition in which the heart is unable to pump sufficient blood to the tissues of the body.

chylomicron One of the microscopic particles of emulsified fat found in the blood and lymph and formed during the digestion of fats.

chyme Partially digested food and gastric secretions that moves into the duodenum from the stomach by peristalsis.

-cidal Suffix denoting killing, as of microorganisms.

cinchonism Pattern of characteristic symptoms (central nervous system [CNS] stimulation and headache) associated with the use of cinchona alkaloids (chemicals extracted from the bark of the cinchona tree); quinidine toxicity, which is characterized by ringing in the ears (tinnitus), dizziness, and headache.

circadian rhythm Internal biological clock; a repeatable 24-hour cycle of physiological activity.

clonic Convulsive muscle contraction in which rigidity and relaxation alternate in rapid succession.

coagulation Process by which the blood changes from a liquid to a solid "plug" as a reaction to local tissue injury; normal blood clot formation.

cold sterilization Destruction of microorganisms at room temperature without the use of heat or ionizing radiation.

conduction system Specialized cardiac tissue that transmits electrical impulses and regulates the activity of the heart.

constipation A decrease in stool frequency.

contraception Preventing pregnancy by preventing either conception (joining of egg and sperm) or implantation in the uterus.

contraindications Situations or conditions when a certain drug should not be administered.

controlled substance Drug that has the potential for abuse and thus is regulated by law.

convoluted Coiled or folded back on itself.

convulsion Involuntary muscle contraction that is either tonic or clonic.

COPD Chronic obstructive pulmonary disease, usually caused by emphysema and chronic bronchitis.

coronary artery Artery that supplies blood flow to the heart.

coronary artery disease (CAD) Disease of the coronary arteries that decreases blood flow to the heart; narrowing of small arteries that supply blood and oxygen to the heart; condition due to atherosclerosis and insufficient blood flow to the heart.

COX Cyclooxygenase, a family of enzymes that produce prostaglandins.

C-reactive protein (CRP) A protein produced by the liver but only found in the blood in conditions of acute inflammation; an inflammation marker.

creatinine A metabolite of muscle metabolism that is excreted in the urine in proportion to renal function.

creatinine clearance A measure of renal creatinine excretion that is used to evaluate renal function.

cretinism Condition in which the development of the body and the brain has been inhibited due to congenital hypothyroidism.

cross-tolerance Drug tolerance that develops between similarly acting drugs.

CRP (C-reactive protein) A protein produced by the liver but only found in the blood in conditions of acute inflammation; an inflammation marker.

cryoanesthesia Removing the sensation of touch or pain by applying extreme cold to the nerve endings.

Cushing's disease Excess secretion of adenocorticotropic hormone (ACTH).

cutaneous Pertaining to the skin.

-cytic Suffix meaning cells.

D

DCT (distal convoluted tubule) Part of the nephron that is closest to the collecting duct.

decimal Another way to write a fraction when the denominator is 10, 100, 1000, and so on.

decubitis ulcer Bedsore.

deep vein thrombosis (DVT) A blood clot that forms in a vein deep inside the body.

defecation Process of discharging the contents of the intestines as feces.

dehiscence Bursting open or separation of a wound, usually along sutured line.

denaturing Causing destruction of bacterial protein function; also adulteration of alcohol, rendering it unfit for drinking.

dendritic cell An antigen-presenting white blood cell that is found in the skin, mucosa, and lymphoid tissues and that initiates a primary immune response.

denominator Bottom number of a fraction; shows the number of parts in a whole.

dependency Requirement of repeated drug consumption in order to prevent onset of withdrawal symptoms.

depolarization The decrease in electric potential across a cell membrane that results in excitation and generation of an action potential.

depolarizing blocker Produces paralysis by first causing nerve transmission, followed by inhibition of nerve transmission.

depression Mental state characterized by depressed mood, with feelings of frustration and hopelessness.

dermatitis Inflammatory condition of the skin associated with itching, burning, and edematous vesicular formations.

dermatophytic Infection of the skin, hair, or nails caused by a fungus.

designer drug Chemically altered form of an approved drug that produces similar effects and that is sold illegally.

diabetes insipidus Chronic condition caused by inadequate secretion of antidiuretic hormone (ADH), in which individuals are extremely thirsty and produce very large amounts of pale urine.

diabetic neuropathy Nerve disorders caused by diabetes resulting in numbness, pain, and weakness in hands and feet.

diarrhea Abnormal looseness of the stool or watery stool, which may be accompanied by a change in stool frequency or volume.

digestion Mechanical and chemical breakdown of foods into smaller units.

digitalization Method of dosage with cardiac glycosides that rapidly produces effective drug levels.

diplopia Condition in which a single object is seen (perceived) as two objects; double vision.

disinfectant Substance that kills disease-causing microorganisms on nonliving surfaces.

dissociative anesthesia Form of general anesthesia in which patients do not appear to be unconscious.

distal convoluted tubule (DCT) Part of the nephron that is closest to the collecting duct.

disulfiram-like reaction Reaction to alcohol ingestion characterized by intense nausea as a result of drug-induced accumulation of acetaldehyde, similar to that produced by disulfiram (*Antabuse*).

diuresis Condition that causes urine to be excreted; usually associated with large volumes of urine.

DM Diabetes mellitus.

dopamine Inhibitory neurotransmitter in the basal ganglia.

dose A measurement of the amount of drug that is administered.

drug Chemical substance that produces a change in body function.

drug absorption Entrance of a drug into the bloodstream from its site of administration.

drug addiction Condition of drug abuse and drug dependence that is characterized by compulsive drug behavior.

drug compliance Following drug prescription directions exactly as written.

drug dependence Condition of reliance on the use of a particular drug, characterized as physical and/or psychological dependence.

drug distribution Passage of a drug from the blood to the tissues and organs of the body.

drug excretion Elimination of the drug from the body.

drug indications Intended or indicated uses for any drug.

drug metabolism The enzymatic biotransformation of a drug into metabolites.

drug microsomal metabolizing system (DMMS) Group of enzymes located primarily in the liver that function to metabolize (biotransformation) drugs.

drug resistance Lack of responsiveness of cancer cells to chemotherapy.

drug tolerance Requirement of larger doses to be consumed in order to obtain the desired effects; decreased drug effect occurring after repeated drug administration.

ductless glands Containing no duct; endocrine glands that secrete hormones directly into the blood or lymph without going through a duct.

DVT (deep vein thrombosis) A blood clot that forms in a vein deep inside the body.

dwarfism Inadequate secretion of growth hormone during childhood, characterized by abnormally short stature and normal body proportions.

dysentery Condition characterized by frequent watery stools (usually containing blood and mucus), tenesmus, fever, and dehydration.

dysgeusia A persistent abnormal sense of taste.

dyskinesia Distortion in voluntary muscle movement, spastic; uncontrollable, abnormal involuntary repetitive body movements.

dysmenorrhea Difficult or painful menstruation; condition that is associated with painful and difficult menstruation.

dyspepsia Indigestion.

dysphoria Feeling of discomfort or unpleasantness.

dystonia Muscle spasms, facial grimacing, and other involuntary movements and postures.

dystonic reaction Reaction characterized by muscle spasms, twitching, facial grimacing, or torticollis.

E

ECL (enterochromaffin-like cells) Cells that synthesize and release histamine.

ectopic beat Extra heartbeat, a type of cardiac arrhythmia.

ectopic focus Area of the heart from which abnormal impulses originate.

eczematoid dermatitis Condition in which lesions on the skin ooze and develop scaly crusts.

edema Swelling caused by fluid in body tissue.

ED50 Effective dose 50, or dose that will produce an effect that is half of the maximal response.

efferent nerve Carries the appropriate motor response from the brain and spinal cord to the peripheral organs.

electrocardiogram (ECG) Recording of the electrical activity of the heart.

electroencephalogram (EEG) A surface recording of the electrical activity of the brain.

electrolyte Ion in solution, such as sodium, potassium, or chloride, that is capable of mediating conduction (passing impulses in the tissues); dissolved mineral that can conduct an electrical current and that exists as an ion.

emesis Vomiting.

emetogenic A substance that causes vomiting.

emollient Substance that is soothing to mucous membranes or skin.

emphysema Disease process causing destruction of the walls of the alveoli.

endemic Present continually in a particular geographic region, often in spite of control measures.

endocrine Pertaining to glands that secrete substances directly into the blood.

endocytosis Process by which cells absorb molecules (such as proteins) from outside the cell by engulfing them with their cell membrane.

endogenous Naturally occurring within the body; originating or produced within an organism, tissue, or cell.

endometrium Lining of the uterus.

endorphins Neuropeptides produced within the CNS that interact with opioid receptors to produce analgesia.

enteric-coated Type of tablet or pill with a coating that enables it to pass through the stomach without being dissolved, so the stomach lining will not be irritated; the drug is then released in the intestine.

enterochromaffin-like cells (ECL) Cells that synthesize and release histamine.

enterohepatic recycling The process whereby drug is eliminated from the liver/biliary tract into the GI tract and then reabsorbed from the GI tract back to the liver.

enzyme induction Increase in the amount of drug-metabolizing enzymes after repeated administration of certain drugs.

enzyme inhibition Inhibition of drug-metabolizing enzymes by certain drugs.

epidural anesthesia Injection of a local anesthetic into the extradural (outermost part of the spinal canal) space.

epilepsy CNS disorder characterized by uncontrolled nerve cell discharges and manifested by recurring, spontaneous seizures of any type.

epinephrine (EPI) Hormone from adrenal medulla that stimulates adrenergic receptors, especially during stress.

equipotent When drugs (substances) produce the same intensity or spectrum of activity; usually, the absolute amount of drug (for example, 5, 10 mg) that produces the response is different for each substance, but the response generated is the same.

erythema Redness of the skin, often a result of capillary dilation; abnormal redness of the skin, caused by capillary congestion.

erythropoiesis Process through which red blood cells are produced.

ESA Stands for erythropoietin stimulating agent.

eschar Thick crust or scab that develops after skin is burned.

essential amino acids and fatty acids Substances that are required for critical body function to sustain life and are not produced by the body.

essential hypertension Major form of hypertension for which the cause is unknown.

ester local anesthetic Anesthetic class that includes procaine, cocaine, benzocaine, and tetracaine; metabolism is primarily by plasma cholinesterases.

euphoria Feeling of well-being or elation; feeling good.

euthyroid Having normal thyroid gland function.

euvolemia State of normal body fluid volume.

evacuation Process of removal of waste material from the bowel.

excoriation An abrasion of the epidermis (skin) usually from a mechanical (not chemical) cause; a scratch.

exertional angina Angina pectoris caused by increased physical exertion.

exocytosis The discharge of substances contained in vesicles by fusion of the vesicular membrane with the outer cell membrane.

exogenous Originating or produced outside the organism or body; originating outside the body, or administered into the body from outside.

exogenous, or reactive, depression Depression caused by external factors or life events.

exophthalmos Protruding eyeballs out of the socket.

expectorant Substance that causes the removal (expulsion) of mucous secretions from the respiratory system; drug that helps clear the lungs of respiratory secretions.

expectorate Eject from the mouth; spit.

extracellular Area outside the cell.

extrapyramidal syndrome (EPS) Movement disorders such as akathisia, dystonia, and parkinsonism caused by antipsychotic drug therapy.

F

false transmitter Substance formed in nerve endings that mimics and interferes with the actions of the normal transmitter.

fasciculation Twitchings of muscle fiber groups.

fertility drug Drug that stimulates ovulation.

fibrocystic breast disease Condition in which cystic lesions form within the connective tissue of the breasts.

fight or flight reaction Response of the body to intense stress; caused by activation of the sympathetic division of the ANS.

first-pass metabolism Drug metabolism that occurs in the intestines and liver during oral absorption of drugs into the systemic circulation.

flashback Phenomenon occurring long after the use of LSD in which the hallucinogenic effects are relived in some type of memory flash.

foam cells A type of cell formed after macrophages in the artery wall digest LDL-cholesterol; a transformed macrophage.

fraction Part of a whole.

FSH Follicle stimulating hormone. In the female stimulates the development of the follicles, and in the male stimulates spermatogenesis.

fungicidal Substance, chemical solution, or drug that kills fungi; chemical that kills or destroys fungi.

fungistatic Inhibits the growth of fungi but does not kill off the fungi; chemical that inhibits growth or reproduction of fungi but does not kill fungi.

fungus (fungi) A group of microorganisms with a membrane-bound nucleus that includes yeasts and molds.

G

GABA Gamma-aminobutyric acid, an inhibitory neurotransmitter in the CNS.

gametocyte Organism in an immature stage of development.

ganglionic blocker Drug that blocks the nicotinic-neural (Nn) receptors and reduces the activity of the autonomic nervous system.

ganglionic stimulant Drug that stimulates the nicotinic-neural (Nn) receptors to increase autonomic nervous system activity.

gastric lavage Flushing of the stomach.

gastroparesis Condition, also called delayed gastric emptying, in which the stomach muscles do not function properly.

general anesthesia Deep state of unconsciousness in which there is no response to stimuli, including painful stimuli.

general anesthetic Drug that abolishes the response to pain by depressing the central nervous system (CNS) and producing loss of consciousness.

generalized seizure Seizure originating and involving both cerebral hemispheres that may be either convulsive or nonconvulsive.

generic name Nonproprietary name of a drug.

GERD Gastroesophageal reflux disease.

geriatrics Medical specialty that deals with individuals over 65 years of age.

germ cells Cells that become the reproductive cells eggs (in ovary) or sperm (in testes).

germicidal Substance, chemical solution, or drug that kills microorganisms.

gigantism Increased secretion of growth hormone in childhood, causing excessive growth and height.

GIP Glucose-dependent insulinotropic peptide, also known as gastric inhibitory peptide.

GLP-1 Glucagon-like peptide-1.

glucagon Hormone released by the alpha cells of the pancreas to increase plasma glucose concentration.

glucocorticoid Steroid produced within the adrenal cortex (or a synthetic drug) that directly influences carbohydrate metabolism and inhibits the inflammatory process.

gluconeogenesis The synthesis of glucose from molecules that are not carbohydrates, such as amino and fatty acids or glycerol.

GLUT Glucose transport proteins.

glycated hemoglobin Form of hemoglobin that is produced when glucose attaches to hemoglobin in the RBC.

glycogen The storage form of glucose in humans and animals.

glycogenolysis Hydrolysis of glycogen to yield free glucose.

glycosuria Presence of glucose in the urine.

GnRH Gonadotropin releasing hormone (also called luteinizing releasing hormone); hormone released by the hypothalamus that stimulates the anterior pituitary to secrete LH and FSH.

goiter Condition in which the thyroid is enlarged, but not as a result of a tumor.

gonads Organs that produce male (testes) or female (ovaries) sex cells, sperm or ova.

gram negative Bacteria that retain only the red stain in a gram stain.

gram positive Bacteria that retain only the purple stain in a gram stain.

gram stain Method of staining and identifying bacteria using crystal violet (purple) and safranin (red) stains.

grand mal Older term for a generalized seizure characterized by full-body tonic and clonic motor convulsions.

H

half-life Time required for the body to reduce the amount of drug in the plasma by one-half.

hallucinogenic drug A drug or plant substance that produces psychotomimetic effects and sensory distortions.

halogenated hydrocarbon Compound that contains halogen (chlorine, fluorine, bromine, iodine) combined with hydrogen and carbon.

hashish Resin from the marijuana plant that contains higher levels of THC.

hCG Human chorionic gonadotropin. A glycoprotein hormone produced in pregnancy to maintain progesterone production.

heart rate (HR) Number of heartbeats per minute.

heartburn (acid indigestion) A painful burning feeling behind the sternum that occurs when stomach acid backs up into the esophagus.

hematinic Medications containing iron compounds, used to increase hemoglobin production.

hematuria Appearance of blood or red blood cells in the urine.

hemoglobin Protein in red blood cells that transports oxygen to all tissues of the body.

hemorrhage Loss of blood from blood vessels.

hemozoin Crystalline disposal product from the digestion of blood from blood-feeding parasites.

hepatic microsomal metabolism Specific enzymes in the liver (P_{450} family) that metabolize some drugs and can be increased (stimulated) by some medications or decreased (inhibited) by other medications so that therapeutic drug blood levels are altered.

hernia Protrusion of an organ through the tissue usually containing it; for example, intestinal tissue pushing outside the abdominal cavity, or stomach pushing into the diaphragm (hiatal hernia).

high-density lipoprotein (HDL) One of the forms of cholesterol transported in the blood with lipoprotein; known as "good" cholesterol.

hirsutism Condition usually in women in which body and facial hair is excessive.

histamine Substance that interacts with tissues to produce most of the symptoms of allergy.

HIV Human immunodeficiency virus, responsible for producing AIDS.

hives A skin condition characterized by intensely itching wheals caused by an allergic reaction; also called urticaria.

homeostasis Normal state of balance among the body's internal organs.

H1N1 subtype of the influenza type A virus; also referred to as swine flu or pig flu

hormone Substance produced within one organ and secreted directly into the circulation to exert its effects at a distant location.

hyperacidity Abnormally high degree of acidity (for example, pH less than 1) in the stomach.

hyperalgesia An abnormally painful response to a stimulus.

hypercalcemia Unusually high concentration of calcium in the blood; high serum calcium; elevated concentration of calcium ions in the circulating blood.

hyperchloremia Abnormally high level of chloride ions circulating in the blood.

hyperchlorhydria Excess hydrochloric acid in the stomach.

hyperemia Increased blood flow to a body part like the eye; engorgement.

hyperglycemia Higher than normal level of glucose in the blood; fasting blood glucose higher than 126 mg/dl.

hyperinsulinemia High levels of insulin in the blood often associated with type 2 diabetes mellitus and insulin resistance.

hyperkalemia High serum potassium.

hyperlipidemia Abnormally high fat (lipid) levels in the plasma.

hypermotility Increase in muscle tone or contractions causing faster clearance of substances through the GI tract.

hyperpolarized An increase in the amount of electrical charge on either side of a cell membrane so that there is an increase in the electric potential across the membrane usually due to an outflow of potassium ions or an inflow of chloride ions. A change in the cell membrane potential that makes the inside of the cell even more negative, so it can't respond to stimulation.

hypersensitivity Exaggerated response such as rash, edema, or anaphylaxis that develops following exposure to certain drugs or chemicals.

hypertension Abnormally high blood pressure.

hyperthermia Abnormally high body temperature.

hypertonic A condition where the concentration of salt (sodium, electrolytes) is greater than that found inside the cells.

hypervitaminosis The accumulation of vitamins (fat soluble) in storage tissues that creates a deleterious condition related to the excess substance.

hypnotic Drug used to induce and maintain sleep.

hypochloremia Abnormally low level of chloride ions circulating in the blood.

hypochromic Condition in which the color of red blood cells is less than the normal index.

hypoglycemia Lower than the normal range of plasma glucose concentration in the blood; fasting blood glucose below 40 mg/dl in women or 50 mg/dl in men accompanied by symptoms of diabetes.

hypokalemia Abnormally low level of potassium ions circulating in the blood; low serum potassium; decrease in the normal concentration of potassium in the blood.

hypolipidemic drug Drug used to lower plasma lipid levels, also referred to as an antilipemic drug.

hyponatremia Abnormally low level of sodium ions circulating in the blood.

hypophosphatemia Abnormally low concentrations of phosphate in the circulating blood.

hypothalamus Part of the brainstem that regulates functions such as body temperature, water balance, appetite, and the pituitary gland; center of the brain that influences mood, motivation, and the perception of pain.

hypotonic A condition where the concentration of salt (sodium, electrolytes) is less than that found inside the cells.

hypoxia Reduction of oxygen supply to tissues below the amount required for normal physiological function.

I

IA (intra-articular) Joint space into which drug is injected.

IBS (irritable bowel syndrome) A functional disorder of the colon with abdominal pain, cramping, bloating, diarrhea. and/or constipation.

IGF (insulin-like growth factor) A stimulator of cell growth and proliferation.

immunity Condition that causes individuals to resist acquiring or developing a disease or infection.

immunomodulation Ability to stimulate and increase immune function.

immunopharmacology Study of drugs with immunosuppressive and immunomodulating actions.

immunosuppressed Having inhibition of the body's immune response (ability to fight infection), usually induced by drugs or viruses.

immunosuppression Ability to reduce the activity of the immune system.

improper fraction Fraction that has a value equal to or greater than 1.

incompatibility Undesirable interaction of drugs not suitable for combination or administration together.

incretins A group of gastrointestinal hormones that increase the amount of insulin released.

individual variation Difference in the effects of drugs and drug dosages from one person to another.

induction of general anesthesia Time required to take a patient from consciousness to Stage III of anesthesia.

infarction Area of tissue that has died because of a sudden lack of blood supply.

infiltration anesthesia Injection of a local anesthetic directly into the tissue.

inflammation Condition in which tissues have been damaged, characterized by swelling, pain, heat, and sometimes redness.

insulin Hormone secreted by the beta cells of the pancreas to facilitate glucose entry into the cell.

insulin-like growth factor (IGF) A stimulator of cell growth and proliferation.

interferon Chemical mediator produced by immune cells that increases immune function.

interleukin Chemical mediator produced by immune cells that helps regulate and increase immune function.

intermittent claudication Severe pain in the calf muscles that occurs while walking, but subsides with rest.

intolerant Not able to continue drug therapy usually because of extreme sensitivity to the side effects.

intoxication State in which a substance has accumulated to potentially harmful levels in the body.

intra-articular (IA) Joint space into which drug is injected.

intradermal anesthesia Injection of a local anesthetic into the part of the skin called the dermis.

intramuscular (IM) injection Route of drug administration; drug is injected into gluteal or deltoid muscles.

intrathecal Space around the brain and spinal cord that contains the cerebrospinal fluid.

intravenous (IV) injection Route of drug administration; drug is injected directly into a vein.

intrinsic factor Protein necessary for intestinal absorption of vitamin B_{12}; lack of intrinsic factor leads to pernicious anemia.

iodophor Compound containing iodine.

irrigation Washing (lavage) of a wound or cavity with large volumes of fluid.

irritable bowel syndrome (IBS) A functional disorder of the colon with abdominal pain, cramping, bloating, diarrhea, and/or constipation.

ischemia Insufficient blood supply (and oxygen) to meet the needs of the tissue or organ; condition of insufficient tissue blood flow; reduction in blood supply and oxygen to localized area of the body or tissue insufficient blood flow to a tissue.

islets Group or island of cells.

isotonic Normal salt concentration of most body fluids; a salt concentration of 0.9 percent.

IV fluid therapy The infusion of large amounts of fluid into a vein to increase blood volume or supply nourishment.

K

keratinized Composed of a protein substance largely found in hair and nails.

kerion An inflammation of the hair follicles of the beard or scalp caused by ringworm with swelling and pus.

ketosis Condition associated with an increased production of ketone bodies as a result of fat metabolism.

L

lactation Production of milk in female breasts.

lavage Washing with fluids or flushing of a cavity such as the stomach.

laxative A substance that promotes bowel movements.

LD50 Lethal dose 50, or dose that will kill 50 percent of the laboratory animals tested.

leucopenia (leukopenia) An abnormal decrease (less than normal) in the number of circulating white blood cells; condition in which the total number of white blood cells circulating in the blood is less than normal.

leukotrienes Chemical mediators involved in inflammation and asthma.

LH Luteinizing hormone in the female stimulates ovulation, and in the male stimulates testosterone synthesis and release; in the male also called ISCH (interstitial cell stimulating hormone).

limbic system Neural pathway connecting different brain areas involved in regulation of behavior and emotion.

lipodystrophy Defective metabolism of fat.

lipoprotein A molecule that contains a protein and a lipid (fat).

lithium An element similar to sodium that is used in the treatment of mania and bipolar mood disorder.

loading dose Initial drug dose administered to rapidly achieve therapeutic drug concentrations.

local anesthetic Drug that reduces response to pain by affecting nerve conduction. The action can be limited to an area of the body according to the site of administration.

low-density lipoprotein (LDL) One of the forms of cholesterol transported in the blood with lipoprotein; known as "bad" cholesterol.

lymphokine A substance secreted by T cells that signals other immune cells like macrophages to aggregate.

lymphopenia Decrease in the number of circulating lymphocytes.

lyse To disintegrate or dissolve.

lysosome Part of a cell that contains enzymes capable of digesting or destroying tissue/proteins.

M

maintenance dose Dose administered to maintain drug blood levels in the therapeutic range; daily dosage of cardiac glycoside that maintains effective drug levels in the blood.

maintenance of general anesthesia Ability to keep a patient safely in Stage III of anesthesia.

major depressive disorder (MDD) Depression that arises from within an individual and requires psychotherapy and drug treatment.

malabsorption Inadequate ability to take in nutrients through the intestine.

malaria Protozoal infection characterized by attacks of chills, fever, and sweating.

malignant Life-threatening; refers to growth of a cancerous tumor.

malignant hypertension Condition of hypertensive crisis where the high BP is causing vascular inflammation and necrosis of the blood vessels; hypertensive crisis associated with inflammation and vascular damage.

malignant hyperthermia Condition in susceptible individuals resulting in a life-threatening elevation in body temperature.

mania Mental state of excitement, hyperactivity, and excessive elevation of mood.

mechanism of action Explanation of how a drug produces its effects.

medulla oblongata Lower part of the brainstem that controls cardiac, vasomotor, and respiratory functions.

medullary depression Inhibition of automatic responses controlled by the medulla, such as breathing or cardiac function.

medullary paralysis Condition in which overdose of anesthetic shuts down cardiovascular and respiratory centers in the medulla, causing death.

mega- Prefix meaning large.

megaloblast Large, immature cell that cannot yet function as a mature red blood cell (RBC).

megaloblastic anemia Condition in which there is a large, immature form of the red blood cell, which does not function as efficiently as the mature form.

meiosis Type of cell division where diploid parent cells (46 chromosomes) divide, producing haploid cells (23 chromosomes); occurs only during gamete production.

menarche First menstruation (endometrial tissue sloughing) during puberty.

menopause Condition in which menstruation no longer occurs, either because of the normal aging process in women (45 years of age and older) or because the ovaries have been surgically removed (any age); the clinical effects of menopause are a direct result of little or no estrogen secretion.

menstruation shedding of endometrial tissue with accompanying bleeding; the first day of the menstrual cycle.

metabolic waste products Substances formed through the chemical processes that enable cells to function; usually, these substances are excreted by the body.

metastasis Spread of cancer cells throughout the body, from primary to secondary sites.

methemoglobin An altered hemoglobin that can no longer carry oxygen due to a change (oxidation) in iron from ferrous (Fe^{2+}) to ferric state (Fe^{3+}).

micro- Prefix meaning small.

microcilia Tiny hairs that line the respiratory tract and continuously move, pushing secretions toward the mouth.

microfilaments Minute fibers located throughout the cytoplasm of cells, composed of the protein actin, that maintain the structural integrity of a cell.

mineralocorticoid Steroid produced within the adrenal cortex that directly influences sodium and potassium metabolism.

miotic A substance that causes constriction of the pupil or miosis.

mitochondria Normal structures responsible for energy production in cells.

mitosis Cell division in which two daughter cells receive the same number of chromosomes (46) as the parent cell; the process in cell division by which the nucleus divides.

mixed-function oxidase system Drug microsomal metabolizing enzymes (DMMS) that decrease with age and slow the rate of drug oxidation and metabolism.

mixed number Number written with both a whole number and a fraction.

moniliasis Fungal infection previously called monilia, now known to be *Candida albicans*.

monoamine oxidase (MAO) Enzyme that inactivates norepinephrine and serotonin.

Monoamine Theory of Mental Depression Theory that mental depression is caused by low brain levels of norepinephrine and serotonin (monoamines).

monophasic A fixed amount (nonchanging) of estrogen is released during the cycle.

morphology Shape or structure of a cell.

mucolytic Drug that liquefies bronchial secretions.

mucopolysaccharide Naturally occurring substance formed by the combination of protein with carbohydrates (saccharides).

mu-opioid receptor antagonist Drugs that block the mu protein receptor for opioids.

muscarinic receptor An older but more specific term for the cholinergic receptor on smooth and cardiac muscle.

mutagenic Having the ability to cause mutations.

myalgia Pain associated with muscle injury.

mycosis Any disease caused by a fungus.

myelin The fatty substance that covers and protects nerves and allows efficient conduction of action potentials down the axon.

myelosuppression Suppression of bone marrow activity that interferes with the production of all blood cells; causes anemia, increased infections, and bleeding problems.

myocardial infarction (MI) Sudden death of an area of heart muscle, commonly referred to as a heart attack.

myocardium The muscular layer of the heart.

myoclonic Generalized seizures that are usually brief and often confined to one part of the body.

myxedema Condition associated with a decrease in thyroid function, caused by removal of thyroid tissue or loss of tissue function because of damage to cells; also associated with subcutaneous edema and slowed metabolism

N

Na/K adenosine triphosphatase (Na/K ATPase) Enzyme that energizes the sodium/potassium pump and is inhibited by cardiac glycosides.

native Natural substance in the body.

nephritis Inflammation of the glomeruli often following a streptococcus infection.

nephrosis A degenerative disease of the kidneys, characterized by generalized edema, protein in the urine, and an increase in serum cholesterol.

nerve conduction Transfer of impulses along a nerve by the movement of sodium and potassium ions.

neuroleptanalgesia Condition in which a patient is quiet and calm and has no response to pain after the combined administration of an opioid analgesic (fentanyl) and a tranquilizer (droperidol).

neuroleptanesthesia State of unconsciousness plus neuroleptanalgesia produced by the combined administration of nitrous oxide, fentanyl, and droperidol.

neuroleptic malignant syndrome (NMS) Toxic syndrome associated with the use of antipsychotic drugs.

neuromuscular junction (NMJ) Space (synapse) between a motor nerve ending and a skeletal muscle membrane that contains acetylcholine (ACH) receptors.

neuropathic pain Pain resulting from a damaged nervous system or damaged nerve cells.

neurotransmitter Substance that stimulates internal organs to produce characteristic changes associated with sympathetic and parasympathetic divisions.

neurotransmitter-gated ion channel Ion channels that open or close when a neurotransmitter binds to a receptor.

neutropenia An abnormally low number of neutrophils (white blood cells).

nicotine Alkaloid drug in tobacco that stimulates ganglionic receptors.

nicotinic-muscle (Nm) receptor Cholinergic receptor located at the neuromuscular junction of skeletal muscle.

nicotinic-neural (Nn) receptor Cholinergic receptor at the autonomic ganglia; cholinergic receptor located on both sympathetic and parasympathetic ganglia.

NMJ (neuromuscular junction) Space (synapse) between a motor nerve ending and a skeletal muscle membrane that contains acetylcholine (ACH) receptors.

nociceptor Specialized peripheral nerve cells sensitive to tissue injury that transmit pain signals to the brain for interpretation of pain.

nonbarbiturate Refers to sedative-hypnotic drugs that do not possess the barbituric acid structure, such as benzodiazepines and related drugs.

nondepolarizing blocker Produces paralysis by inhibiting nerve transmission.

nonopioid analgesic Formerly known as nonnarcotic analgesics, such as NSAIDs and COX-2 inhibitors.

nonprescription, over-the-counter (OTC) drug Drug that can be purchased without the services of a physician.

nonselective Interacts with any subtype receptor.

nonselective beta-adrenergic blocker Drug that blocks both beta-1 and beta-2 adrenergic receptors.

nonselective beta-adrenergic drug Drug that stimulates both beta-1 and beta-2 receptors.

norepinephrine (NE) Neurotransmitter of sympathetic (adrenergic) nerves that stimulates the adrenergic receptors.

normocytic anemia Anemia in which RBCs are normal size and usually contain normal hemoglobin but are insufficient to carry adequate oxygen to the tissues; low RBC count.

nosocomial Infection acquired as a result of being in a hospital.

NREM sleep Stages of sleep characterized by nonrapid eye movement (NREM).

nucleoside Molecule that contains purine or pyrimidine bases in combination with sugar (ribose or deoxyribose linkage).

numerator Top number of a fraction; shows the part.

O

oligospermia Reduced sperm count.

oliguria Condition in which very small amounts of urine are produced.

on-off phenomenon Alternating periods of movement mobility and immobility.

onychomycosis A fungus infection of the nail; *onycho-*: pertaining to a claw or nail.

oocyst A thick-walled structure in which parasitic protozoal sex cells develop for transfer to new hosts.

oocyte the immature female reproductive cell prior to fertilization.

oogenesis Formation of ova.

opiate Drug derived from opium and producing the same pharmacological effects as opium.

opioid Drug that produces the same pharmacological effects as opium and its family of drugs or the neuropeptides (enkephalin, endorphin) produced by the body.

opioid analgesics Chemically related to morphine or opium and used to relieve pain.

opioid antagonist A drug that attaches to opioid receptors and displaces the opioid analgesic or opioid neuropeptide.

opportunistic organism Microorganism capable of causing disease only when the resistance (immunocompetence) of the host is impaired.

oral administration Route of drug administration by way of the mouth through swallowing.

osmolality The concentration of particles dissolved in a fluid.

osmolarity A measure of hydration status; the amount of solute (ions, salts) per liter of solution (blood, plasma).

osmoreceptors Specialized cells in the hypothalamus that respond to changes in sodium concentration (osmolarity) in the blood.

osmosis Process in which water moves across membranes following the movement of sodium ions.

osteoblasts Synthesize bone matrix proteins and promote crystal nucleation; contain receptors for PTH, vitamin D_3, and estrogen.

osteoclasts Responsible for bone resorption by binding to bone matrix proteins and releasing enzymes to break down bone.

osteoporosis Condition associated with a decrease in bone density so that the bones are thin and fracture easily; decrease in the bone mineral density, usually in the elderly, that results in areas predisposed to fracture.

ova Mature eggs, also termed oogonia. *Ovum* is singular; *ova* is plural.

ovulation Release of an egg from the ovary.

oxyntic (parietal) cell Cell that synthesizes and releases hydrochloric acid (HCl) into the stomach lumen.

oxytocin Polypeptide substance released within the brain that has specific functions during and after pregnancy, specifically relating to the uterus and the mammary glands.

P

Paget's disease Condition in older adults in which the bone density is altered so that softening and bending of the weight-bearing bones occurs.

parasympathetic Refers to nerves of the ANS that originate in the brain and sacral portion of the spinal cord; they are active when the body is at rest or trying to restore body energy and function.

parasympatholytic Refers to drugs (anticholinergic) that decrease activity of the parasympathetic nervous system.

parasympathomimetic Refers to drugs (cholinergic) that mimic stimulation of the parasympathetic nervous system.

parenteral administration Route of drug administration that does not involve the gastrointestinal (GI) tract.

parietal (oxyntic) cell Cell that synthesizes and releases hydrochloric acid (HCl) into the stomach lumen.

parkinsonism Symptoms of Parkinson's disease, which include resting tremor, muscle rigidity, and disturbances of movement and postural balance; disease or drug-induced condition characterized by muscular rigidity, tremors, and disturbances of movement.

Parkinson's disease Movement disorder of the basal ganglia caused by a deficiency of dopamine.

partial seizure Seizure originating in one area of the brain that may spread to other areas.

pathogen(ic) Type of bacteria that cause disease; a microorganism that causes disease.

PCT (proximal convoluted tubule) Part of the nephron that is closest to the glomerulus.

penicillinase Bacterial enzymes that inactivate penicillin antibiotics.

pepsin Enzyme that digests protein in the stomach.

percent Decimal fraction with a denominator of 100.

percent composition Common measure of solution concentration; refers to grams of solute per 100 ml of solution.

perforation Opening in a hollow organ, such as a break in the intestinal wall.

perimenopause Two to ten years before complete cessation of a menstrual period.

peripheral artery disease (PAD) Any disease caused by the obstruction of blood flow in the large arteries of the arms and legs; usually a narrowing and hardening of these arteries that supply the legs and feet.

peripheral nerve Part of the nervous system that is outside the central nervous system (the brain or spinal cord), usually near the surface of the tissue fibers or skin.

peripheral resistance (PR) Resistance generated by the flow of blood through the arteries.

peripheral skeletal muscle relaxant Drug that inhibits muscle contraction at the neuromuscular junction or within the contractile process.

peristalsis Movement characteristic of the intestines, in which circular contraction and relaxation propel the contents toward the rectum.

permissive Enables another hormone to fully function.

pernicious Disease of severe symptoms, which could be fatal if left untreated.

petechia Small area of the skin or mucous membranes that is discolored because of localized hemorrhages.

phagocyte Circulating cell (such as a leukocyte) that ingests waste products or bacteria in order to remove them from the body.

pharmacokinetics Describes the processes of drug absorption, drug distribution, drug metabolism, and drug excretion.

pharmacology Study of drugs.

phlebitis Inflammation of a vein.

phlegm Secretion from the respiratory tract; usually called mucus.

physical dependence Condition in which the body requires a substance (drug) not normally found in the body in order to avoid symptoms associated with withdrawal, or the abstinence syndrome.

plaque Substance containing cholesterol, dead cell products, and calcium that accumulates in the innermost layer of the arteries.

pluripotent Ability of a substance to produce many different biological responses.

polydipsia Excessive thirst; increased thirst.

polypeptide Substance, usually large, composed of an indefinite number of amino acids.

polyphagia Excessive hunger.

polypharmacy The situation in patients whose treatment involves multiple drug prescriptions.

polyuria Excessive urine production; increased urination.

pons Part of the brainstem that serves as a relay station for nerve fibers traveling to other brain areas; also involved in sensory and motor functions.

porphyria (acute) A genetic disease associated with excessive liver production of delta-aminolevulonic acid and characterized by intermittent hypertension, abdominal cramps, and psychosis.

postpartum After childbirth.

postprandial After a meal.

potency Measure of the strength, or concentration, of a drug required to produce a specific effect.

potentiates Produces an action that is greater than either of the components can produce alone; synergy.

preferred anesthetic Produces adequate anesthesia with minimal side effects.

preload Refers to venous return, the amount of blood returning to the heart that must be pumped.

premature atrial contraction (PAC) Premature contraction of the atria, usually caused by an ectopic focus.

premature ventricular contraction (PVC) Premature contraction of the ventricles, usually caused by an ectopic focus.

prescription drug Drug for which dispensing requires a written or phone order that can only be issued by or under the direction of a licensed physician.

pressor Tending to increase blood pressure.

proarrhythmia An arrhythmia caused by administration of an antiarrhythmic drug.

prodrug An inactive precursor of a drug, converted into its active form in the body by normal metabolic processes.

prohormone (anabolic androgen) After ingestion is converted to the hormone testosterone.

proinflammatory Tending to cause inflammation.

proper fraction Fraction that has a value less than 1.

prophylactic Process or drug that prevents the onset of symptoms (or disease) as a result of exposure before the reactive process can take place.

prophylaxis Treatment or drug given to prevent a condition or disease; procedure or medication to prevent a disease, rather than to treat an existing disease.

proportion A mathematical equation that expresses the equality between two ratios.

prostaglandin Substance naturally found in certain tissues of the body; can stimulate uterine and intestinal muscle contractions and may cause pain by stimulating nerve endings; chemical mediators released from mast and other cells involved in inflammatory and allergic conditions.

proteolytic Action that causes the decomposition or destruction of proteins.

protozoacidal A substance, chemical solution, or drug that kills protozoa.

protozoan Single-celled organism belonging to the genus *Protozoa*.

proximal convoluted tubule (PCT) Part of the nephron that is closest to the glomerulus.

psychomotor stimulant Amphetamine or related drug that increases mental and physical activity.

psychosis Form of mental illness that produces bizarre behavior and deterioration of the personality.

psychotomimetic drug Drug or substance that can induce psychic and behavioral patterns characteristic of a psychosis.

puberty Sequence of physiological changes associated with the expression of sexual characteristics and reproductive function that occur when a child progresses into young adulthood, usually at 12 to 14 years of age.

R

radical cure Arresting of malaria, in which protozoal parasites are eliminated from all tissues.

ratio The relationship of one number to another expressed by whole numbers (1:5) or as a fraction ($\frac{1}{5}$).

RBC Red blood cell.

receptor Specific cellular structure that a drug binds to and that produces a physiologic effect.

recombinant Genetically engineered DNA.

referred pain Origin of the pain is in a different location than where the individual feels the pain.

refractory Unable to produce an increased response even though the stimulation or amount of drug has been increased.

regional nerve block Also called nerve block; the injection of a local anesthetic near the nerve root.

REM sleep Stage of sleep characterized by rapid eye movement (REM) and dreaming.

remission Period when cancer cells are not increasing in number.

renin Enzyme released by the kidneys that converts angiotensinogen into angiotensin I.

replacement therapy Administration of a naturally occurring substance that the body is not able to produce in adequate amounts to maintain normal function.

repolarization Return of the electric potential across a cell membrane to its resting state following depolarization.

repository preparation Preparation of a drug, usually for intramuscular or subcutaneous injection, that is intended to leach out from the site of injection slowly so that the duration of drug action is prolonged.

reticular formation Network of nerve fibers that travel throughout the central nervous system that regulates the level of wakefulness.

Reye's syndrome A potentially fatal illness characterized by vomiting, an enlarged liver, convulsions, and coma, in children and adolescents; linked to the use of salicylates in the management of influenza, usually type B, or chickenpox.

rhabdomyolysis The rapid breakdown of skeletal muscle (rhabdomyon) due to muscle injury.

rheumatic fever Condition in which pain and inflammation of the joints or muscles are accompanied by elevated body temperature usually a complication of untreated Strep throat.

rigidity A stiffness and inflexibility of movement.

S

SA Sinoatrial, as in the SA node.

salicylism Condition in which toxic doses of salicylates are ingested, resulting in nausea, tinnitus, and delirium.

sarcolemma A thin membrane enclosing a striated (skeletal) muscle fiber.

sarcoplasm The cytoplasm of a striated (skeletal) muscle fiber.

sarcoplasmic reticulum Specialized organelle in the muscle cell that releases calcium ions during muscle contraction and absorbs calcium ions during relaxation.

schizophrenia Major form of psychosis; behavior is inappropriate.

Schwann cell Any cell that covers the axons in the peripheral nervous system and forms the myelin sheath.

sebum A lipid substance secreted by glands in the skin to lubricate the skin everywhere but the palms and soles.

secondary hypertension Form of hypertension in which the cause is known.

sedative Drug used to produce mental relaxation and to reduce the desire for physical activity.

seizure Abnormal discharge of brain neurons that causes alteration of behavior and/or motor activity.

selective Interacts with one subtype of receptor over others.

selective beta-1 adrenergic blocker Drug that blocks only beta-1 receptors.

selective beta-2 adrenergic drug Drug that stimulates only beta-2 receptors at therapeutic doses.

selective COX-2 inhibitors Drugs that only interact with one of the enzymes in the cyclooxygenase family.

sensitize To induce or develop a reaction to naturally occurring substances (allergens) as a result of repeated exposure.

side effect Drug effect other than the therapeutic effect that is usually undesirable but not harmful.

site of action Location within the body where a drug exerts its therapeutic effect, often a specific drug receptor.

solute Substance dissolved in a solvent; usually present in a lesser amount.

solution Homogeneous mixture of two or more substances.

solvent Liquid portion of a solution that is capable of dissolving another substance.

somatomedins Peptides in the plasma that stimulate cellular growth and have insulin-like activity.

somatostatin An inhibitory hormone that blocks the release of somatotropin (GH) and thyroid-stimulating hormone (TSH).

somatotropin Another term for growth hormone (GH).

spasmogenic Causing a muscle to contract intermittently, resulting in a state of spasms.

spasmolytics Drugs that relieve, interrupt, or prevent muscle spasms (intermittent muscle contractions often associated with pain).

spermatogenesis Formation of spermatozoa.

spermatogonia Intermediary kind of male germ cell in the production of spermatozoa.

spermatozoa Mature sperm cells (singular *spermatozoon*).

spinal anesthesia Injection of a local anesthetic into the subarachnoid space.

SSRIs Selective serotonin reuptake inhibitors, a class of antidepressant drugs.

stable plaque Plaque formed in the artery wall that remains in the wall.

-static Suffix denoting the inhibition of, as of microorganisms.

status epilepticus Continuous series of generalized tonic and clonic seizures, a medical emergency requiring immediate treatment.

sterilization Process that results in destruction of all microorganisms.

steroid Member of a large family of chemical substances (hormones, drugs) containing a structure similar to cortisone (tetracyclic cyclopenta-a-phenanthrene).

stroke Loss of brain function due to a loss of blood supply.

stroke volume (SV) Amount of blood pumped per heartbeat.

suppression therapy Taking the drug daily even when there are no observable acute symptoms.

supraventricular arrhythmia Arrhythmia that originates above the AV node in the atria.

suspension Preparation in which undissolved solids are dispersed within a liquid.

sympathetic Refers to nerves of the ANS that originate from the thoracolumbar portion of the spinal cord; they are active when the body is under stress or when it is exerting energy.

sympatholytic Refers to the action of an adrenergic blocking drug or an action that decreases sympathetic activity.

sympathomimetic Refers to the action of an adrenergic drug or an action that increases sympathetic activity.

synaptic knob Contains vesicles that store and release neurotransmitters.

synaptic vesicles A small membrane-bound structure in the axon terminals of nerve cells that contains neurotransmitters and releases them when an action potential reaches the terminal.

synergistic Complementary or additive.

synergism When the action resulting from a combination of drugs is greater than the sum of their individual drug effects.

synesthesia Distortion of sensory perception; usually associated with the use of LSD.

synthetic drug Drug produced by a chemical process outside the body.

systemic Occurring in the general circulation, resulting in distribution to most organs.

T

T_3 and T_4 Hormones (triiodothyronine and thyroxine, respectively) synthesized and released by the thyroid gland. Synthesized T_4 must be converted to T_3 to be utilized by the cell.

tardive dyskinesia Drug-induced involuntary movements of the lips, jaw, tongue, and extremities.

target organ Specific tissue where a hormone exerts its action.

TCAs Tricyclic antidepressants, a class of antidepressant drugs.

tenesmus A painful spasm of the anal sphincter, causing an urgent desire to defecate although little or no material is passed.

teratogenic Capable of causing birth defects or fetal abnormalities or development; capable of causing abnormal development.

tetany A strong sustained muscle contraction.

tetrahydrocannabinol (THC) Active ingredient of the marijuana plant.

thalamus Uppermost part of the brainstem that regulates sensory and motor impulses traveling to and from the cerebral cortex.

therapeutic dose The amount (dose) of drug required to produce the desired change in the disease or condition.

therapeutic effect Desired drug effect to alleviate some condition or symptom of disease.

therapeutic index (TI) Ratio of the LD50 to the ED50 in animal studies.

thrombocyte Cell in the blood, commonly called a platelet, that is necessary for coagulation.

thrombocytopenia An abnormal decrease in the number of circulating platelets.

thromboembolism Clots that jam a blood vessel; formed by the action of platelets and other coagulation factors in the blood.

thrombophlebitis Inflammation of the walls of the veins, associated with clot formation.

thrombus Clot formed by the action of coagulation factors and circulating blood cells.

thrush Term used for *Candida* infection in the mucous membranes of the mouth and pharynx.

thyrotoxic crisis Condition caused by excessive quantities of thyroid hormone, from either a natural source of hypersecretion or exogenous administration of a drug.

thyroxine (T_4) Hormone synthesized and released by the thyroid gland.

TIA (transient ischemic attack) An interruption of blood flow to the brain for a short period of time; a ministroke that produces stroke-like symptoms but no lasting damage.

tolerance Ability of the body to alter its response (to adapt) to drug effects so that the effects are minimized over time.

tonic Convulsive muscle contraction characterized by sustained muscular contractions.

tonic-clonic Generalized seizure characterized by full-body tonic and clonic motor convulsions and loss of consciousness.

topical application Placing a drug on the surface of the skin or a mucous membrane (for example, mouth, rectum).

torsade de pointes A type of proarrhythmia that causes ventricular tachycardia and fainting.

toxic effect Undesirable drug effect that implies drug poisoning; can be very harmful or life-threatening.

TPN Total parenteral nutrition; a combination of nutrients that may include amino acids, carbohydrates, vitamins, and minerals (electrolytes) that is infused into patients who cannot absorb these substances from the gastrointestinal tract because of condition or disease; the combination and concentration of nutrients vary according to patient need.

trade name Patented proprietary name of drug sold by a specific drug manufacturer; also referred to as the brand name.

transdermal absorption Absorption of drug (substance) through the skin, usually associated with the application of drug-loaded patches.

transient ischemic attack (TIA) An interruption of blood flow to the brain for a short period of time; a ministroke that produces stroke-like symptoms but no lasting damage.

transit time Amount of time it takes for food to travel from the mouth to the anus.

tremor A trembling and involuntary rhythmic movement.

TRH Thyroid-releasing hormone, secreted by the hypothalamus.

trichomoniasis Infection caused by the *Trichomonas* organism; a sexually transmitted disease.

triglyceride A fat formed by three fatty acids into one molecule that supplies energy to muscle cells.

triiodothyronine (T₃) Hormone synthesized and released by the thyroid gland.

triphasic The estrogen and progestin amounts released may vary during the cycle.

tropic Having an affinity for the designated organ; for example, adrenotropic.

tropic hormone Hormone secreted by the anterior pituitary that binds to a receptor on another endocrine gland.

TSH Thyroid-stimulating hormone, secreted by the anterior pituitary.

tubular reabsorption Process in which the nephrons return to the blood substances (ions, nutrients) that were filtered out of the blood at the glomerulus.

tubular secretion Process in which the nephrons produce and release substances (ions, acids, and bases) that facilitate sodium ion reabsorption and maintain acid-base balance.

tumor Uncontrolled growth of abnormal cells that form a solid mass; also called a neoplasm.

type 1 diabetes Insulin-dependent diabetes mellitus.

type 2 diabetes Non-insulin-dependent diabetes mellitus.

U

ulcer Open sore in the mucous membranes or mucosal linings of the body.

ulcerogenic Capable of producing minor irritation or lesions to an integral break in the mucosal lining (ulcer).

unstable plaque Plaque formed in the artery wall that can break away and obstruct blood flow or form a clot.

uremia Accumulation of nitrogen waste materials (for example, urea) in the blood.

urticaria Intensely itching raised areas of skin caused by an allergic reaction; hives.

V

vagolytic action Inhibition of the vagus nerve to the heart, causing the heart rate to increase (counteraction to vagal tone that causes bradycardia).

variant or Prinzmetal angina Angina pectoris caused by vasospasm of the coronary arteries.

vasoconstriction Tightening or contraction of muscles (sphincters) in the blood vessels, which decreases blood flow through the vessels.

vasodilation Relaxation of the muscles (sphincters) controlling blood vessel tone, which increases blood flow through the vessels.

vasodilator Substance that relaxes the muscles (sphincters) controlling blood vessels, leading to increased blood flow.

vasopressin Man-made form of ADH. Because of ADH's fluid reabsorption and vasoconstrictive properties, can elevate blood pressure at higher doses.

ventricular fibrillation The most serious arrhythmia; usually a terminal event where ventricular contractions are no longer able to effectively pump blood.

very-low-density lipoprotein (VLDL) Molecules made of cholesterol, triglycerides, and protein that carry cholesterol from the liver to organs and tissues; also serves as a precursor to low density lipoproteins (LDL).

virilization Development of masculine body (hair, muscle) characteristics in females.

virucidal Substance, chemical solution, or drug that kills viruses; chemical that kills or destroys viruses.

W

wheal A firm, elevated swelling of the skin often pale red in color and itchy; a sign of allergy.

X

xerostomia Dryness of the oral cavity resulting from inhibition of the natural moistening action of salivary gland secretions or increased secretion of salivary mucus, rather than serous material.

Appendix A

LATIN ABBREVIATIONS USED IN MEDICINE

Latin Phrase	Latin Abbreviation	English Meaning
Ad	ad	to, up to
Ad libitum	ad lib	at pleasure
Ante cibum	ac	before meals
Aqua	aq	water
Bis in die	BID	twice a day
Capsulae	caps	capsule
Cum	c̄	with
Dosis	dos	a dose
Ex aqua	ex aq	with water
Gutta	gtt	a drop
Hora somni	hs	at bedtime
Inter cibos	ic	between meals
Nil per os	npo	nothing by mouth
Non repetatur	non rep	do not repeat
Oculus dexter	od	right eye
Oculus sinister	os	left eye
Oculus uterque	ou	both eyes
Ophthalmicus	ophth.	ophthalmic
Pabulum	pab	food
Per	per	by
Per os	PO	by mouth
Post cibum	pc	after meals
Pro re nata	PRN	as needed
Quaque die	QD, q.d.	once a day
Quarter in die	QID	four times a day
Quatum satis	qs	with sufficient amount
Recipe	R_x	take thou
Repetatur	rept	let it be repeated
Sigma	sig.	write on label
Sine	s̄	without
Statim	stat	immediately
Ter in die	TID	three times a day

Appendix B

ABBREVIATIONS AND SYMBOLS COMMONLY USED IN MEDICAL NOTATIONS

Abbreviations

Abbreviation	Meaning	Abbreviation	Meaning
a	before	CP	chest pain
$\overline{aa}$, $\overline{AA}$	of each	CPE	complete physical examination
a.c.	before meals	CPR	cardiopulmonary resuscitation
ADD	attention deficit disorder	CSF	cerebrospinal fluid
ADL	activities of daily living	CT	computed tomography
ad lib	as desired	CV	cardiovascular
ADT	admission, discharge, transfer	d	day
AIDS	acquired immunodeficiency syndrome	D&C	dilation and curettage
a.m.a.	against medical advice	DEA	Drug Enforcement Administration
AMA	American Medical Association	Dil, dil	dilute
amp.	ampule	DM	diabetes mellitus
amt	amount	DOB	date of birth
aq., AQ	water; aqueous	DTP	diptheria-tetanus-pertussis vaccine
ausc.	auscultation	Dr.	doctor
ax	axis	DTs	delirium tremens
Bib, bib	drink	D/W	dextrose in water
b.i.d., bid, BID	twice a day	Dx, dx	diagnosis
BM	bowel movement	ECG, EKG	electrocardiogram
BP, B/P	blood pressure	ED	emergency department
BPC	blood pressure check	EEG	electroencephalogram
BPH	benign prostatic hypertrophy	EENT	eyes, ears, nose, and throat
BSA	body surface area	EP	established patient
$\overline{c}$	with	ER	emergency room
Ca	calcium; cancer	ESR	erythrocyte sedimentation rate
cap, caps	capsules	FBS	fasting blood sugar
CBC	complete blood (cell) count	FDA	Food and Drug Administration
C.C., CC	chief complaint	FH	family history
CDC	Centers for Disease Control and Prevention	Fl, fl, fld	fluid
CHF	congestive heart failure	F/u	follow-up
chr	chronic	Fx	fracture
CNS	central nervous system	GBS	gallbladder series
Comp, comp	compound	GI	gastrointestinal
COPD	chronic obstructive pulmonary disease	Gm, gm	gram

Abbreviation	Meaning		Abbreviation	Meaning
gr	grain		N&V	nausea and vomiting
gt, gtt	drop, drops		NYD	not yet diagnosed
GTT	glucose tolerance test		o-	ortho-
GU	genitourinary		OB	obstetrics
GYN	gynecology		OC	oral contraceptive
HA	headache		OD	overdose
HB, Hgb	hemoglobin		oint	ointment
HEENT	head, ears, eyes, nose, throat		OOB	out of bed
HIV	human immunodeficiency virus		OPD	outpatient department
HO	history of		OPS	outpatient services
h.s., hs, HS	hour of sleep/at bedtime		OR	operating room
Hx	history		OTC	over-the-counter
ICU	intensive care unit		p-	para-
I&D	incision and drainage		p̄	after
I&O	intake and output		P&P	Pap smear (Papanicolaou smear) and pelvic examination
IM	intramuscular			
inf.	infusion; inferior		PA	posteroanterior
inj	injection		Pap	Pap smear
IT	inhalation therapy		Path	pathology
IUD	intrauterine device		p.c., pc	after meals
IV	intravenous		PE	physical examination
KUB	kidneys, ureters, bladder		per	by, with
L1, L2, etc.	lumbar vertebrae		PH	past history
lab	laboratory		PID	pelvic inflammatory disease
lb	pound		p/o	postoperative
liq	liquid		POMR	problem-oriented medical record
LLL	left lower lobe		PMFSH	past medical, family, social history
LLQ	left lower quadrant		PMS	premenstrual syndrome
LMP	last menstrual period		p.r.n., prn, PRN	whenever necessary
LUQ	left upper quadrant			
M	mix (Latin misce)		Pt	patient
m-	meta-		PT	physical therapy
MI	myocardial infarction		PTA	prior to admission
mL, ml	milliliter		PVC	premature ventricular contraction
MM	mucous membrane		pulv	powder
MRI	magnetic resonance imaging		q.	every
MS	multiple sclerosis		q2, q2h	every 2 hours
NB	newborn		q.a.m., qam	every morning
NED	no evidence of disease		q.d., QD	once a day
no.	number		q.h., qh	every hour
noc, noct	night		qhs	every night, at bedtime
npo, NPO	nothing by mouth		q.i.d., QID	four times a day
NPT	new patient		qns, QNS	quantity not sufficient
NS	normal saline		qs, QS	quantity sufficient
NSAID	nonsteroidal antiinflammatory drug		RA	rheumatoid arthritis; right atrium
			RBC	red blood cells; red blood (cell) count
NTP	normal temperature and pressure		RDA	recommended dietary allowance, recommended daily allowance

Abbreviation	Meaning	Abbreviation	Meaning
REM	rapid eye movement	T1, T2, etc.	thoracic vertebrae
RF	rheumatoid factor	T & A	tonsillectomy and adenoidectomy
RLL	right lower lobe	tab	tablet
RLQ	right lower quadrant	TB	tuberculosis
R/O	rule out	tbs., tbsp	tablespoon
ROM	range of motion	TIA	transient ischemic attack
ROS/SR	review of systems/systems review	t.i.d., tid, TID	three times a day
RUQ	right upper quadrant	tinc, tinct, tr	tincture
RV	right ventricle	TMJ	temporomandibular joint
Rx	prescription, take	top	topically
$\bar{s}$	without	TPR	temperature, pulse, and respiration
SAD	seasonal affective disorder	TSH	thyroid-stimulating hormone
SC	subcutaneously	tsp	teaspoon
SIDS	sudden infant death syndrome	Tx	treatment
Sig	directions	UA	urinalysis
sig	sigmoidoscopy	UCHD	usual childhood diseases
SOAP	subjective, objective, assessment, plan	UGI	upper gastrointestinal
SOB	shortness of breath	ung, ungt	ointment
sol	solution	URI	upper respiratory infection
S/R	suture removal	US	ultrasound
ss, $\bar{ss}$	one-half (Latin semis)	UTI	urinary tract infection
Staph	staphylococcus	VA	visual acuity
stat, STAT	immediately	VD	venereal disease
STD	sexually transmitted disease	Vf	visual field
Strep	streptococcus	VS	vital signs
subling, SL	sublingual	WBC	white blood cells; white blood (cell) count
subq, SubQ	subcutaneously	WNL	within normal limits
surg	surgery	wt	weight
S/W	saline in water	y/o	year old
SX	symptoms		

Weights and Measures

Symbol	Meaning	Symbol	Meaning
£	pounds	mμ	millimicron; nanometer
°	degrees	mEq	milliequivalent
′	foot; minute	mL, ml	milliliter
″	inch; second	dL, dl	deciliter
μm	micrometer	mg%	milligrams percent; milligrams per 100 ml
μ	micron (former term for micrometer)		

Mathematical Functions and Terms

Symbol	Meaning	Symbol	Meaning
#	number	$\times$	multiply; magnification; crossed with, hybrid
+	plus; positive; acid reaction	$\div$, /	divided by
−	minus; negative; alkaline reaction	=	equal to
$\pm$	plus or minus; either positive or negative; indefinite	$\approx$	approximately equal to
		>	greater than; from which is derived

Symbol	Meaning	Symbol	Meaning
<	less than; derived from	$^3\sqrt{\ }$	cube root
≮	not less than	∞	infinity
≯	not greater than	:	ratio; "is to"
≤	equal to or less than	∴	therefore
≥	equal to or greater than	%	percent
≠	not equal to	π	pi (3.14159)—the ratio of circumference of a circle to its diameter
√	square root		

Chemical Notations

Symbol	Meaning	Symbol	Meaning
Δ	change; heat	↑	increase
⇌	reversible reaction	↓	decrease

Warnings

Symbol	Meaning	Symbol	Meaning
Ⓒ	Schedule I controlled substance	Ⓒᵥ	Schedule V controlled substance
Ⓒ Ⅱ	Schedule II controlled substance	☠	poison
Ⓒ Ⅲ	Schedule III controlled substance	☢	radiation
Ⓒ Ⅳ	Schedule IV controlled substance	☣	biohazard

Others

Symbol	Meaning	Symbol	Meaning
℞	prescription; take	†	one
□, ♂	male	††	two
○, ♀	female	†††	three

Photo Credits

FRONT MATTER

Page i: © Levent Ince/iStockphoto RF; p. iii: © spxChrome/iStockphoto RF; p. v: © Brand X Pictures/PunchStock RF; p. vi: © M. Freeman/PhotoLink/Getty Images RF; p. vii: © Image DJ/Alamy RF; p. x: © Getty Images RF; p. xi: © Photodisc/Getty Images RF; p. xii: © Science Photo Library RF/Getty Images RF; p. xiii: © The McGraw-Hill Companies; p. xiii: © M. Freeman/PhotoLink/Getty Images RF; p. xv: CDC/Janice Carr; p. xvi: © MedicalRF.com/Getty Images RF; p. xvii: © Don Wilkie/iStockphoto RF; p. xviii–xxi: © pixhook/iStockphoto RF; p. xxiii: © Levent Ince/iStockphoto RF.

CHAPTER 1

Opener: © Brand X Pictures/PunchStock RF; p. 3: © Leigh Schindler/iStockphoto RF; p. 4: © Jason Reed/Getty Images RF; Table 1:1: © Stockdisc/PunchStock RF.

CHAPTER 2

Opener: © Digital Vision RF; Table 2:2: © Brand X Pictures/Jupiterimages RF; Table 2:4: © Diana McDonald/Getty Images RF.

CHAPTER 3

Opener: © Royalty-Free/CORBIS; Table 3:1: © Dynamic Graphics/Jupiterimages RF; Table 3:2: © Ryan McVay/Getty Images RF; 3.1: © Creatas/PunchStock RF.

CHAPTER 4

Opener: © Royalty-Free/CORBIS; 4.2: © Keith Brofsky/Getty Images RF.

CHAPTER 5

Opener: © M. Freeman/PhotoLink/Getty Images RF; p. 59: © Photodisc/Getty Images RF.

CHAPTER 6

Opener: © Photodisc Collection/Getty Images RF; 6.2: © Scott Camazine/Photo Researchers, Inc.

CHAPTER 7

Opener: © John Miles/Getty Images RF; 7.4: © McGraw-Hill Higher Education, Inc./Rick Brady, photographer; 7.5: © Corbis RF.

CHAPTER 8

Opener: © Stockdisc/PunchStock RF; Table 8:1: © Corbis RF; 8.2: © S. Pearce/PhotoLink/Getty Images RF.

CHAPTER 9

Opener-Table 9:2: © Royalty-Free/CORBIS.

CHAPTER 10

Opener: © Photodisc Collection/Getty Images RF; 10.3: © The McGraw-Hill Companies, Inc./Jill Braaten, photographer.

CHAPTER 11

Opener: © Image DJ/Alamy RF; p. 147: © Royalty-Free/CORBIS; p. 148: © Brand X Pictures/PunchStock RF.

CHAPTER 12

Opener: © Royalty-Free/CORBIS; 12.2: © The McGraw-Hill Companies, Inc./Bob Coyle, photographer; 12.3: © Stockbyte/PunchStock RF.

CHAPTER 13

Opener: © Royalty-Free/CORBIS.

CHAPTER 14

Opener: © Ralf Schultheiss/Corbis RF; Table 14:4: © Richard Nelson/Cutcaster RF.

CHAPTER 15

Opener: © Dynamic Graphics/PictureQuest RF; 15.2: © Medioimages/PictureQuest RF; 15.3: © travelib india/Alamy RF.

CHAPTER 16

Opener: © The McGraw-Hill Companies, Inc./Rick Brady, photographer.

CHAPTER 17

Opener: © Keith Brofsky/Getty Images RF; Table 17:1: © Andersen Ross/Photodisc/Getty Images RF.

CHAPTER 18

Opener: © Photodisc Collection/Getty Images RF; 18.2: © Digital Vision RF; Table 18:2: © Photolink/Getty Images RF.

CHAPTER 19

Opener: © Brand X Pictures/PunchStock RF; 19.4(top): © L. Steinmark/Custom Medical Stock Photo; 19.4(left): © Tom Gannam/AP Photo; 19.4(right): Photo courtesy Apotex Inc.; Table 19:5: © Photodisc/Getty Images RF; 19.6(left, right): © The McGraw-Hill Companies, Inc./Jill Braaten, photographer.

CHAPTER 20

Opener: © Comstock/Alamy RF; 20.1c: © Image Source/Getty Images RF; Table 20:3: © Pixtal/agefotostock RF; 20.4-20.5(top-left): © The McGraw-Hill Companies, Inc./Jill Braaten, photographer; 20.5(top-right, right): © Allergan, Inc.; 20.5(bottom): Photo courtesy ROXRO Pharma, Inc.; 20.6(left): © The McGraw-Hill Companies, Inc./Photo by Eric Misko, Elite Images Photography; 20.6(right): © Barbara Nagle; 20.8a: © Dr. Ken Greer/Visuals Unlimited; 20.8b: © SPL/Photo Researchers, Inc.; 20.8c: © Dr. M.A. Ansary/Photo Researchers, Inc.

CHAPTER 21

Opener: © Getty Images RF; p. 321: © Leigh Schindler/iStockphoto RF; p. 322-Fig.21.3: © The McGraw-Hill Companies, Inc.

CHAPTER 22

Opener: © Getty Images/Brand X RF; Table 22:1: © Comstock/Alamy RF; Table 22:2: © Stockbyte/PunchStock RF.

CHAPTER 23

Opener: © Comstock Images/PictureQuest RF.

CHAPTER 24

Opener: © The McGraw-Hill Companies, Inc./Rick Brady, photographer; 24.2: © Ed Reschke.

CHAPTER 25

Opener-p. 375: © Photodisc/Getty Images RF; p. 376: © Purestock/Getty Images RF; 25.7(left): © The McGraw-Hill Companies, Inc./Jill Braaten, photographer; 25.7(right): Courtesy American Regent, Inc.; 25.7(bottom): Used with Permission from Pfizer Inc.; Table 25:5: © Comstock/PunchStock RF.

CHAPTER 26

Opener: © Royalty-Free/CORBIS; 26.1: © The McGraw-Hill Companies, Inc.

CHAPTER 27

Opener: © Science Photo Library RF/Getty Images RF; 27.3a: © Professor Pietro M. Motta/Photo Researchers, Inc.; 27.3b: © CNRI/SCIENCE PHOTO LIBRARY/Photo Researchers, Inc.; 27.4a(all): © The McGraw-Hill Companies, Inc./Jill Braaten, photographer.

CHAPTER 28

Opener: © Thinkstock/PunchStock RF; 28.1: © The McGraw-Hill Companies, Inc./Jill Braaten, photographer; Table 28:3: © Royalty-Free/CORBIS; 28.3: © The McGraw-Hill Companies, Inc./Jill Braaten, photographer; 28.5a: © Brand X Pictures/PunchStock RF; 28.5b: © The McGraw-Hill Companies, Inc./Jill Braaten, photographer; 28.6(left): © David Tietz/Editorial Image, LLC RF; 28.6(middle): © Pixtal/SuperStock RF; 28.6(right): © The McGraw-Hill Companies, Inc./Jill Braaten, photographer; Table 28:4: © Getty Images/Steve Allen RF.

CHAPTER 29

Opener: © MedicalRF.com/Getty Images RF; Table 29:2: © BananaStock/Alamy RF; 29.7a: © Yoav Levy/Phototake; 29.7b-c: © The McGraw-Hill Companies, Inc./Jill Braaten, photographer.

CHAPTER 30

Opener: © Getty Images/Brand X RF; 30.1b: © Bill Longcore/Photo Researchers, Inc.; 30.3: © The McGraw-Hill Companies, Inc.; 30.4(left): © The McGraw-Hill Companies, Inc./John Flournoy, photographer; 30.4(right): Courtesy American Regent, Inc.; Table 30:2: © Thinkstock Images/Jupiterimages RF.

CHAPTER 31

Opener: © Science Photo Library RF/Getty Images RF; p. 499: © Royalty-Free/CORBIS; p. 500: © Mina Chapman/Corbis RF; 31.3: © PHANIE/Photo Researchers, Inc.; 31.4: © Pharmascience Inc.; 31.5: © Peter Jobst/Alamy RF; 31.6(all): © The McGraw-Hill Companies, Inc./Jill Braaten, photographer; Table 31:4: © Stockdisc/PunchStock RF; 31.7(left): © Dr. P. Marazzi/Photo Researchers, Inc.; 31.7(right): © LADA/Photo Researchers, Inc.; 31.8(left, right): © The McGraw-Hill Companies, Inc./Jill Braaten, photographer.

CHAPTER 32

Opener: © Kenneth C. Zirkel/Getty Images RF; Table 32:2: © Footage supplied by Goodshoot/PunchStock RF.

CHAPTER 33

Opener: © The McGraw-Hill Companies; p. 537: © Leigh Schindler/iStockphoto RF; p. 538: © The McGraw-Hill Companies, Inc.; 33.3a-b: © CNRI/Photo Researchers, Inc.; 33.5a-b: © The McGraw-Hill Companies, Inc./Jill Braaten, photographer; 33.5c: © Al Behrman/AP Photo; Table 33:6-Table 33:8: © Royalty-Free/CORBIS.

CHAPTER 34

Opener: © Ingram Publishing/agefotostock RF; Table 34:2: © Ingram Publishing/SuperStock RF.

CHAPTER 35

Opener: © M. Freeman/PhotoLink/Getty Images RF; p. 585: © Photodisc/Getty Images RF; p. 586: © The McGraw-Hill Companies, Inc./Joe DeGrandis, photographer; 35.5(all): From "Clinical Pathological Conference Acromegaly, Diabetes, Hypermetabolism, Protein Use and Heart Failure," in *American Journal of Medicine*, 20:133, 1986. Copyright © 1986 by Excerpta Media, Inc.

CHAPTER 36

Opener: © TRBfoto/Getty Images RF; 36.4(top): © The McGraw-Hill Companies, Inc./Jill Braaten, photographer; 36.4(middle): © Leonard Lessin/Photo Researchers, Inc.; 36.4(bottom): © The McGraw-Hill Companies, Inc./Jill Braaten, photographer; 36.5a-b: From: *Atlas of Pediatric Physical Diagnosis, 3/e,* by Zitelli & Davis, fig 9-17, 1997, with permission from Elsevier; 36.6: © Custom Medical Stock Photo.

CHAPTER 37

Opener: © Royalty-Free/CORBIS; 37.1b: © Manfred Kage/Peter Arnold, Inc.; 37.3a: © The McGraw-Hill Companies, Inc./Bob Coyle, photographer; 37.3b: © A. Wilson Photo/Custom Medical Stock Photo; Table 37:3: © Photodisc Collection/Getty Images RF; 37.5(top): © Corbis Premium RF/Alamy RF; 37.5(right, bottom): © Nick Dolding/Corbis; Table 37:6: © Fancy Photography/Veer RF.

CHAPTER 38

Opener: © Science Photo Library RF/Getty Images RF; 38.3: © Barbara Nagle; 38.4: © Collection CNRI/Phototake; 38.5: © Dr. M.A. Ansary/Photo Researchers, Inc.; Table 38:2: © The McGraw-Hill Companies, Inc./Photo by JW Ramsey; 38.8a: © Michael Klein/Peter Arnold, Inc.; 38.8b: © Dr. P. Marazzi/Photo Researchers, Inc.; 38.8c: © Yoav Levy/Phototake.

CHAPTER 39

Opener: © The McGraw-Hill Companies, Inc./Jill Braaten, photographer; Table 39:1: © Purestock/Getty Images RF; 39.7a: © The McGraw-Hill Companies, Inc./Jill Braaten, photographer; 39.7b: © Lucy Nicholson/Reuters/Corbis; 39.7c: © The McGraw-Hill Companies, Inc./Jill Braaten, photographer; 39.8d: © Ian Hooton/SPL/Getty Images RF; 39.9a-b: © The McGraw-Hill Companies, Inc./Jill Braaten, photographer; 39.9c: © ELI LILLY AND COMPANY/PR NEWSWIRE/Newscom. HUMAPEN® MEMOIR™ is a trademark of Eli Lilly and Company; 39.9d: Courtesy Novo Nordisk; 39.9e: © Creatas/PunchStock RF; 39.9f: Courtesy Owen Mumford; Table 39:3: © Keith Brofsky/Getty Images RF; 39.11a: © Stockdisc/PunchStock RF; 39.11b: © Purestock/Getty Images RF.

CHAPTER 40

Opener: © Getty Images/Mark Thornton RF; 40.4: Courtesy American Regent, Inc.; 40.6: © Barbara Nagle.

Line Art and Text Credits

Note: Page numbers followed by f *indicate figures; those followed by* t *indicate tables.*

A